Charles Haddon Spurgeon was the greatest preacher of the nineteenth century in England and probably the whole world. The pungent and passionate sermons of the Baptist pastor brought home the gospel message to the hearts of his numerous hearers and more numerous readers. Tom Nettles has retold Spurgeon's life as a warm admirer, but he is careful to rest his judgements on detailed evidence. In particular *The Sword and the Trowel*, the magazine Spurgeon edited as pastor of the Metropolitan Tabernacle in London, is used as a quarry for an abundance of fresh material. Consequently this biography casts new light on Spurgeon's life, ministry and theology.

DAVID BEBBINGTON,
Professor of History, University of Stirling, Stirling

With the publication of *Living by Revealed Truth*, Tom Nettles has provided his readers with the premier interpretive account of Charles Haddon Spurgeon. Evidencing decades of serious engagement with this great Baptist leader of the nineteenth century, Nettles has given us an immense and monumental portrait of almost every aspect of the life of "the prince of preachers," including not only his numerous writings and multi-faceted ministry, but also his leadership practices and personal challenges. Educational, edifying, and enjoyable to read, this massive work is a masterful contribution to Baptist history and Christian biography.

DAVID S. DOCKERY,
President, Union University, Jackson, Tennessee

Charles Spurgeon is a mountain – a massive figure on the evangelical landscape. Tom Nettles now helps us to understand Charles Haddon Spurgeon as a man, a theologian, and one of the most influential pastors in church history. Nettles takes us into the heart of Charles Spurgeon's conviction and his pastoral theology. This is a book that will encourage, educate, and bless its readers.

R. ALBERT MOHLER JR.,
President, The Southern Baptist Theological Seminary, Louisville, Kentucky

Eschewing hagiography and dispelling the synergistic revision of some who are unhampered by information, Dr. Nettles provides the evangelical community with another edifying work on the life and ministry of the "Prince of Preachers." Readers are inspired to holiness of life, faithfulness in Christ's service, and perseverance in godliness by the moving account of this great Victorian evangelist who held and maintained through his preaching and pastoral ministry endeavors the great truths generally known as "the doctrines of grace."

C. BERRY DRIVER, JR.,
Professor of Systematic Theology, Senior Librarian, and Dean of Libraries,
Southwestern Baptist Theological Seminary, Fort Worth, Texas.

Fifteen years in the making, this is the first biography of Spurgeon to be written by a world-class historian who had access to the entirety of the *Sword & Trowel* magazine that Spurgeon edited monthly from 1865 to 1892. Because of the information and insights gleaned by Nettles from so much previously untapped and under-utilized material, *Living by Revealed Truth* is a massively important contribution to Spurgeon studies. Fresh and unique, this book will be enjoyable to laymen, profitable to pastors, and indispensable for scholars. Nettles' volume now takes an honored place among the most valuable of all resources pertaining to the Prince of Preachers.

DON WHITNEY,
Associate Professor of Biblical Spirituality, Senior Associate Dean for the School of Theology,
The Southern Baptist Theological Seminary, Louisville, Kentucky

A magisterial biography of England's greatest pastor! Tom Nettles has given the Church, like no biographer of Charles Haddon Spurgeon before him, a deep look into the mind of the most influential minister that Baptists have ever produced. Nettles presents Spurgeon in his own words, examining and ordering his thoughts as revealed in the massive sermon collection, his extant letters but especially in his editorials and essays in the pages of *The Sword and Trowel,* the monthly journal Spurgeon edited through much of his London ministry. Nettles gives the reader insights into Spurgeon's views on theology, the ministry, and church life that will pay rich dividends to any who will take the time to read this compelling story. If a minister reads only one biography of the great preacher, let it be this one!

JEFF STRAUB,
Professor of Historical Theology, Central Baptist Theological Seminary, Plymouth, Minnesota

Dr. Thomas Nettles is widely regarded as one of the foremost Baptist historians in our day, and rightfully so. His research is scholarly, his theology is lofty, and his heart for the church is clear. In his new book, *Living by Revealed Truth – The Life and Pastoral Theology of Charles Haddon Spurgeon*, Nettles presents the ministerial brilliance of the "Prince of Preachers," whose pastoral labors transcend generations down to this present hour. Revered by many as the greatest preacher since the apostle Paul, readers will be encouraged and edified by this engaging account of Spurgeon's life and ministry. Whether a pastor or layman, this narrative of Spurgeon's transcendent theology and enflamed passion for biblical truth will, most certainly, energize you in doing God's work, God's way, for God's glory.

STEVEN J. LAWSON,
Senior Pastor, Christ Fellowship Baptist Church, Mobile, Alabama

Living by Revealed Truth is one of those rare gems of Christian biography: it places in your hands the life a great man, written by an outstanding historical theologian. The combination brings Charles Spurgeon's life and thought to life. Tom Nettles's portrait of Spurgeon is eminently personal, historically vivid and theologically rich. I recommend it to anyone interested in seeing how theology and ministry, gospel and life, can unite in a single narrative of a life lived for the glory of God.

ROBERT CALDWELL,
Assistant Professor of Church History, Southwestern Baptist Theological Seminary, Forth Worth, Texas

Pastors and elders, especially those mentoring young men for gospel ministry, will find Tom Nettles' *Living By Revealed Truth* to be a treasure of pastoral theology. Written winsomely and comprehensively, the book presents a remarkable picture of how C. H. Spurgeon embraced the whole of pastoral ministry, and how he continues to influence yet another generation of gospel workers through his legacy. Much more than a biography or a pastor's manual, *Living By Revealed Truth* sets forth the details of a gospel-centered ministry in ways that give contemporary ministers motivation and direction for every stage of pastoral work.

PHILLIP NEWTON,
Senior Pastor, South Woods Baptist Church, Memphis, Tennessee

Charles Spurgeon was a once-a-century kind of preacher. He was a great gift to the church and through his writings and printed sermons, remains a great ally in the cause of Christ. That so many biographies about him have appeared since his death in 1892 is a testimony to his lasting influence. Like the other great Christian leaders in church history, Spurgeon was a pastor-theologian. As such, all of his ministry was shaped by biblical theology with pastoral sensitivity. Tom Nettles demonstrates how Spurgeon gave himself to the work of the ministry with this kind of self-conscious commitment to be a theologian of the Word. That commitment, Nettles shows, caused Spurgeon to preach, teach and minister with a confessional fidelity. He was not ashamed to embrace the evangelical, Christ-centered Calvinism of his Baptist and Puritan forebears. In fact, he regarded that system of truth to be imminently biblical and powerfully practical for all of his pastoral work. What Nettles makes plain is that for Spurgeon, all theology is pastoral theology. I cannot recommend this book highly enough. It should be widely distributed by all who love the gospel of God's grace that Spurgeon preached. Every pastor, ministerial student and those who work to train men for the ministry should carefully learn from the life and labors of Charles Haddon Spurgeon as Tom Nettles elucidates them. Nearly everyone who knows of Spurgeon admires him for his great accomplishments. Nettles helps us understand the theological underpinnings of those accomplishments. In doing so, the author, like his subject, has served the church well.

TOM ASCOL,
Pastor, Grace Baptist Church, Cape Coral, Florida

Despite his ongoing popularity, Charles Spurgeon has only recently begun to attract the serious attention he deserves. Tom Nettles' work now makes a major contribution to this growing appreciation of the man and his ministry. Mining neglected but important sources, he has given sharper definition to our picture of Spurgeon, and produced a highly stimulating and readable account.

MICHAEL REEVES,
Head of Theology, UCCF; author, *The Good God* and *The Unquenchable Flame*

Charles Spurgeon was the most influential preacher in the English-speaking world during the latter half of the nineteenth century. But he was also an influential Baptist pastor-theologian who saw himself as continuing the best of the older Puritan theological tradition. While numerous biographies of Spurgeon have been published over the decades, Spurgeon's thought normally receives short shrift from his biographers. This is why this new biography is so important. By focusing on Spurgeon's memoirs and published articles, Tom Nettles has filled an important gap in scholarship related to Spurgeon with this exhaustive intellectual biography of the Prince of Preachers. Many pastors and other casual readers will be encouraged by Spurgeon's commitment to a high view of Scripture and historic Baptist orthodoxy from a Reformed perspective. Scholars will be forced to reckon with Spurgeon the theologian as they pursue their own studies of the famed Victorian pastor. Nettles has spent his entire career promoting the recovery of a Spurgeonic theological vision among his fellow Baptists and other evangelicals. This fine biography will almost certainly contribute to that theological recovery.

NATHAN A. FINN,
Associate Professor of Historical Theology and Baptist Studies,
The Southeastern Baptist Theological Seminary, Wake Forest, North Carolina

It has long been my conviction that, despite the goodly number of Spurgeon biographies that have been written since the Baptist preacher's death in 1892, there really is lacking a definitive study that not only takes account of his remarkable ministry and the inspiring details of his life, but also adequately deals with the theology of the man. Finally, in this work by my dear colleague Tom Nettles, a sort of magnum opus upon which he has labored for many years, is justice done to not only Spurgeon the man and preacher, but also to Spurgeon the theologian. Here is an "all-round" study of Spurgeon that provides us with a fully reliable, substantial examination of an extremely important figure in the life of Victorian Evangelicalism and the world of that era. In the words of a command given to Augustine, whom Spurgeon rightly regarded as an ancient forebear of key aspects of his theology, Tolle lege ("Take it up and read!")—and you will be blessed.

MICHAEL A.G. HAYKIN,
Professor of Church History & Biblical Spirituality,
The Southern Baptist Theological Seminary, Louisville, Kentucky

Tom Nettles writes that his aim in compiling this biography of Charles Haddon Spurgeon was to probe deeply the great preacher's pastoral theology. However, may I may be so bold as to suggest that, as a result of his painstaking years of exhaustive research, Dr. Nettles has given the church a treasure even greater than that? This biography chronicles in well-documented detail Spurgeon's unwavering commitment to the authority and inerrancy of Scripture, his passionate exposition of the gospel doctrines of grace, his unquenchable zeal for the salvation of the lost, his undying desire to relieve the suffering of the poor, and his amazing perseverance through immense personal suffering of many kinds. While few figures in church history have enjoyed gracious spiritual gifts from the Lord in the same abounding measure as Spurgeon, Dr. Nettles reveals to us a man who nevertheless can be for all Christians – not just pastors – a marvellous example of Christian faithfulness we all might pray God would enable us to emulate. May it please the Lord, through the widespread reading of this biography, to inspire thousands of Christian men and women to seek from God's grace the sort of white-hot evangelistic zeal and unshakeable biblical commitments that were so characteristic of the pastoral ministry of Charles Haddon Spurgeon!

STEPHEN E. FARISH,
Pastor

LIVING BY REVEALED TRUTH

THE LIFE AND PASTORAL THEOLOGY OF CHARLES HADDON SPURGEON

TOM NETTLES

MENTOR

Scripture quotations taken from the King James Version of the Bible.

hardback ISBN 978-1-78191-122-8
epub ISBN 978-1-78191-273-4
mobi ISBN 978-1-78191-274-4

First Published in 2013
in the
Mentor Imprint
by
Christian Focus Publications
Geanies House, Fearn, Ross-shire
IV20 1TW, Scotland
www.christianfocus.com

Cover design by Daniel van Straaten
Printed in China

Contents

PREFACE

When volume XX of *The Sword and the Trowel* came from the binders, Spurgeon wrote, "We little thought when we commenced this serial that we should attain to Volume XX." It grew, however, in his mind to be not only a chronicle of the work of the Tabernacle but also "in some sense our autobiography."[1] This proved to be the case, because much of the material collected by his wife and his assistant J. W. Harrald for Spurgeon's posthumous *Autobiography* first appeared in this monthly pastoral missive. While mounds of valuable sermons and addresses from Spurgeon and others appear as the main body of the monthly fascicle, the sections of book reviews and monthly "notes" provide rich sources for understanding Spurgeon's life, opinions, theology, and view of pastoral ministry. It provides an ongoing commentary on the literature of the day, his views on the life of the church, reports on the multitudinous benevolences that he sponsored and supported directly as well as many others with which he had sympathy and sought to encourage others to support. Much of his personal life—joys, conflicts, and suffering—shows up in the notes included in a section noted as "personal." My focus, therefore, in seeking to understand his theology of pastoral ministry, has been on this large body of material, approximately fifty pages of material appearing every month from 1865 through 1892, always with Spurgeon as the editor.

Letters collected by his son Charles move through Spurgeon's life with the personal touch at which he was so transparent, playful, and adept. They are filled with his fears, his earnestness for Christlikeness, his love for family and friends, his intensity about gospel ministry, his candor about pain, and his perplexity with opposition. The soul of Spurgeon was spilled out into his letters.

Obviously Spurgeon's sermons published week by week from 1855 until far beyond his death provide not only insight into his homiletics, exegesis, and theological convictions, but also reflect his mind on the controversies, ecclesiastical relationships, and contemporary events. I confess that I have not read every sermon but have sought to delve into each volume, to some degree, of the *New Park Street Pulpit,* the *Metropolitan Tabernacle Pulpit,* a sizable number of sermon books that Spurgeon published on discreet subjects, *Spurgeon's Expository Encyclopedia,* a twenty-volume American edition of *Spurgeon's Sermons* (which contains many sermons that did not appear in either the *NPSP* or the *MTP*), based on sermons that were wired across the Atlantic and appeared in American newspapers.

From the biographies that appeared virtually immediately on the death of Spurgeon the one volume by G. Holden Pike, followed by his six-volume *The Life and Work of Charles Haddon Spurgeon,* is most important as it contains a large amount of primary sources to which only Pike, as a co-editor of *The Sword and the Trowel,* had access. Pike also wrote *From the Pulpit to the Palm Branch,* a narrative of the last eight months of Spurgeon's life and the many events and services surrounding his death and funeral.

Another valuable biography that appeared immediately (1892) was Robert Shindler's *From the Usher's Desk to the Tabernacle Pulpit,* which was a prequel to Pike's funeral volume. Shindler wrote frequently for *The Sword and the Trowel* and was, in fact, the author of the first series of

---

1. *Sword & Trowel,* January 1885, 25.

articles on the Downgrade, the controversy that so altered Spurgeon's final five years and changed the face of Baptist life in England. He spent much time with Spurgeon and had access to many events and personal conversations that help fill in personal details and make his narrative boil with life.

In 1920 W. Y. Fullerton, whose name will appear frequently in this volume, wrote a biography that is valuable. Fullerton, who was the most prominent evangelist sent out by Spurgeon himself, and a trusted friend during some very troubling years, provides some anecdotes that would otherwise have been lost and some personal insight and impressions that are valuable as the careful judgments of a close and admiring friend. Such judgments should not be dismissed as uncritical hagiography, for the evaluations of discerning men that have spent time in tense and distressing situations with prominent personalities should be taken seriously. They perhaps know more of what drives a person than others that are limited simply to written documents.

Russell Conwell, believed at the time to be the closest parallel to Spurgeon in America, wrote in 1892 a book called *Life of Charles Haddon Spurgeon: The World's Greatest Preacher*. It combines his personal contemplations on certain aspects of Spurgeon's ministry that had attained somewhat legendary status with a sane corrective to ideas that had grown out of proportion to reality. His personal acquaintance with Spurgeon again evoked descriptions of him and his ministry superlative in their tendency.

In 1933, J. C. Carlile, another of Spurgeon's students, wrote an intriguing volume with the title *C. H. Spurgeon: An Interpretative Biography*. Carlile never fails to surprise with his tremendous affection for Spurgeon on the one hand and his attempt to place him in a favorable light for a declining Baptist Union that still smarted from his resignation

and his torrent of doctrinal criticism. Spurgeon raged against what he perceived as the Union's toleration of an intrusive and parasitic, cankerous, heterodox modern thought. Carlile does not say it flatly, but he probably was dissatisfied with Fullerton's approach to Spurgeon. At virtually the same time as Carlile wrote and published, an American Richard Ellsworth Day published his biography of Spurgeon called *The Shadow of the Broad Brim*, and it was a citadel of admiration.

Books and chapters in books of reminiscences about Spurgeon offer valuable anecdotal information and often illustrate what was clearly a consistent aspect of Spurgeon's personality and spirituality. Peter Mordern, Arnold Dallimore, Lewis Drummond, and Patricia S. Kruppa have also written biographies of Spurgeon. Each of these was helpful in both factual content and historical perspective. Iain Murray has written insightfully on Spurgeon as a controversialist.

Archival sources at the Metropolitan Tabernacle and at Spurgeon's College I have not been able to access personally. Others that have written special pieces in a variety of journals from their knowledge of those sources have benefited me. While those sources would obviously provide an opportunity for valuable insight, the amount of primary source material available along with the ongoing labors of others have given me sufficient material for evaluation on the main object of my study—a presentation of the pastoral theology of Charles Haddon Spurgeon.

My special thanks to my publisher, Christian Focus Publications, for their patience of over a decade and a half in waiting for this manuscript. My wife, Margaret, also has proven her love through the patient endurance of those same years and has sacrificed thousands of hours that I might seek to present a fair and accurate picture of this strikingly human Baptist Demosthenes.

Soli Deo Gloria

INTRODUCTION

I would have every Christian wish to know all that he can know of revealed truth. Somebody whispers that the secret things belong not to us. You may be sure you will never know them if they are secret; but all that is revealed you ought to know, for these things belong to you and to your children. Take care you know what the Holy Ghost teaches. Do not give way to a faint-hearted ignorance, lest you be great losers thereby.[1]

On February 11, 1892, Charles Haddon Spurgeon was carried in a five-mile-long funeral procession. Bells rang from St. Mary's in Newington and St. Mark's in Kennington. Even public houses were closed and flags hung as half staff. Thousands of people in black lined the street and curved in a graceful line all the way to the grave site in Norwood Cemetery. Blue sky appeared above as the casket was lowered amidst palms and lilies, and a dove flew from the Metropolitan Tabernacle to Norwood and paused briefly over the crowd. A William Cowper hymn was sung, Archibald Brown spoke, A. T. Pierson prayed, and the Bishop of Rochester pronounced the benediction.

An open Bible pointing to his conversion text was removed before the burial, for the Word of God was not dead. The text read, "Look unto me, and be ye saved, all the ends of the earth: For I am God and there is none else" (Isa. 45:22).

At the same time, a memorial was held in Mentone[2] in France, where Spurgeon had died twelve days before. Austin Phelps related to those gathered at Mentone that he had been asked the previous day what he thought was the secret of Spurgeon's power. He answered: "Two things; first, he had one single object before him always, 'to win souls for God by preaching Christ, and Him crucified and risen'; second, his own personal faith in Christ was always feeding on Christ as revealed in Holy Scripture." Phelps continued to emphasize the centrality of Christ in Spurgeon's

1. MTP, 1891:318. This is from the *Metropolitan Tabernacle Pulpit*, sermons published by Spurgeon in yearly volumes from 1861 and continued year by year through 1917 by Passmore & Alabaster, Spurgeon's London publishers. The first six volumes of this series are entitled *The New Park Street Pulpit*. These will be referred to respectively as NPSP and MTP with the year and page number. The volumes used are those reprinted by Pilgrim Publications, in Pasadena, Texas from 1975 to 1980.

2. This is the English spelling of the town in Southern France that became the favorite respite of Spurgeon. The French spelling is Menton. The English spelling will be used except in direct quotations where the French spelling is used.

life and message but never disconnected from "As the Scripture speaks of Christ." Again he insisted, "His subject was always one—Christ; but it was Christ afresh from his view of him in God's written Word. Ever the same sun, but the sunshine is fresh every day."[3]

Phelps had caught the driving force of Spurgeon's life as succinctly as any. Spurgeon lived with all his might, while he did live, in the felt presence of the living Lord Jesus Christ, gaining each day and in each message fresh floods of spiritual nourishment as the Spirit witnessed to Christ's completed work, while, at the same time, none of his views of experience or his statements about Christ were other than that which is communicated in revealed truth, the written word of God. There have been others in the history of the church for whom the richness of relationship and the settledness of proposition meshed in perfect harmony to support a life of richly experiential and inviolably prescribed worship. One may find this beauty of Spirit and truth in Augustine, Anselm, Calvin, Bunyan, and Edwards; but I would not fear successful contradiction in saying that none of these surpassed Spurgeon in the pursuit and natural expression of that synthesis.

The approach here involves an effort to suggest that Spurgeon, in every aspect of his ministry, was driven by a well-developed, clearly artic-ulated systematic theology and by a commitment to a conversion ministry, both of which were conceived as consistent with revealed truth. A challenge to his viewpoint at the first dawning of the Downgrade Controversy elicited the response from Spurgeon that he only asked to be "clear of complicity in this boastful progress beyond what is plainly revealed." His theology was not regulated by the clock or calendar but "by eternal truth."[4] His preaching, the development of institutions and services, his publications, his perception of church life, his evangelism, his suffering, and the controversies in which he played a part all reflect a commitment to a system of truth developed from the Bible and expressed most clearly in Puritans and evangelicals such as Owen, Charnock, Bunyan, Newton, Whitfield, Romaine, Brooks, Manton, and Sibbes. Both denominationally and theologically Spurgeon saw himself as a devotee of the Particular Baptists as defined by the Confession of 1689. Every enterprise that claimed his energies emerged as a self-conscious commitment to a particular outworking of some part of this theology.

One sees it in the manner of his conversion and the way he related it throughout his life. One finds it again in the quiet conviction that he must be baptized as a believer though he had been sprinkled in his infancy. The immediate entrance into an evangelistic lay ministry blended the same rich ingredients of truth and life, while his call to preach embraced a desire to glorify the ever-present living Christ through the proclamation of the faith once delivered to the saints in the inspired Scriptures. In the founding of the orphanage and alms houses and other benevolent ministries his deep compassion was initiated and fueled by his thorough biblical knowledge and

---

3. S&T, April 1892, 154. Charles Spurgeon, *The Sword and the Trowel*, London: Passmore & Alabaster, 1865-1892. This monthly periodical edited by Spurgeon was bound yearly and continued its publication for years beyond Spurgeon's death. It contained sermons and expositions (often not found in the yearly bound volumes of Spurgeon's sermons), articles by other people, news about missions and evangelism, doctrinal articles and featured notices about monthly church life at the Metropolitan Tabernacle. Also the book review section contained around fifty reviews each month, most of these done by Spurgeon. This volume has used these bound volumes, heavily emphasizing the notices and reviews, for information about Spurgeon's life and ideas on a large variety of subjects. It will be noted as S&T with month, year, and page.

4. S&T, December 1883, 650.

complete commitment to the enactment of doctrinal principles. The Pastors' College developed from his loving concern about one individual combined with his theological commitment to the necessity for a thorough grounding in biblically based systematic theology, sound exegesis, expository preaching, and scripturally mandated pastoral theology. In reviewing *Systematic Theology* by A. H. Strong in 1886, Spurgeon gave vent to his weighty opinion on the value of theology when it is perceived as a tool serving the clarity of the Bible and produced in the confidence of the unerring coherence of revealed truth: "If our young ministers knew more of theology," Spurgeon urged, "that is to say of *the word of God*—they would not be so easily duped by pretenders to knowledge, who endeavour to protect their own ignorance by crying down a thorough and systematic study of revealed truth."[5]

The seamlessness of Spurgeon's mental movements within parameters that included both policy and ideal became more evident through his life. He did not fear to speak his mind on political issues and policies of the Prime Minister and Members of Parliament while relating his analysis to biblical issues and gospel issues that, to him, seemed self-evidently true and thus irrational, Byzantine, and counter-intuitive to deny. His exuberant enjoyment of nature, as well as his keen observation of human nature, provided an overflowing stream of theological, evangelistic, and moral application. He did not seem to mind at all, or feel it a burden or a curse, that his thoughts ran constantly in paths of theological reflection on every natural observation, human encounter, or personal conversation.

The God who created the world, cursed it at the fall, having already established the covenant of redemption in eternity, also revealed all this in increasingly clear increments in Holy Scripture until all was spoken at the close of the New Testament. The fullness of Scripture and the finality of redemption through Jesus Christ governed Spurgeon's understanding of all things and, in his view, should be the determining truth for all human thought and action. A challenge to Scripture or the gospel of sovereign grace made a crack in reality and introduced a magnetic pull into an abyss of unknowing, fragmentation, irrationality, self-destruction, death and, finally, the infinite horror of eternal divine wrath.

He expressed in many venues this ultimate confidence in Scripture as a superior form of knowledge. Frequently he was called upon to review books concerning the burgeoning scientific enterprise of the mid-to-late-nineteenth century. Upon examination of a book entitled *A Catechism of Geology and Sacred History for Young People*, Spurgeon reckoned the attempt to explain Scripture statements by the "infant science of geology" as "moderately successful." Yet, when science has done her fullest and best work, Spurgeon contended, "There will still be mysteries in the word of God that must be accepted as revelations rather than understood as the results of reasoning." Spurgeon was not afraid to exercise faith in "receiving the statements of the Scriptures." No independent confirmation of scriptural assertion was needed, for its authority was independent of human reason and research; its evidence was in itself and in its witness to the needs of the human soul, as interpreted through the entire fabric of redemptive truth, served as sufficient ground for receiving it as a revelation. "What we fear," Spurgeon observed, "is the attempt to reduce everything to the dead level of judgment by carnal reasoning." "Christian rationalism," he recognized, was very much the fashion, but also very

---

5. S&T, November 1886, 598.

dangerous to the doctrinal necessity of receiving the Bible on the basis of its own claims, its intrinsic excellence, and the witness of the Spirit to Christ.[6]

In his early ministry Spurgeon worked with virtually exhaustless energy. The schedule of speaking and writing occupied every waking hour. Mind and body aged exponentially after October 19, 1856, when the Surrey Music Hall disaster fixed a depression upon his spirit from which he never fully recovered. Derision, ridicule, and jealousy, from secular pundits and clergy alike, kept pace almost stride for stride with his rapidly increasing popularity. As the network of benevolent institutions developed, beginning with the Pastors' College, and the responsibility for the regular maintenance of them debt-free pressed on him, his physical and mental strength began to show signs of wear. He needed scheduled times to be away from the weekly pressures of the preparation and delivery of sermons, the oppressive weather and the thick floating muck called air in London, and the depressingly gray surroundings in earth and sky piled on top of the thick grime of the densely poor population of Southwark. Though some of his theologically offended contemporaries took advantage of Spurgeon's public admissions of physical malady and depression of spirit to dismiss the seriousness of his theological confrontations, there is no evidence that his mental acuteness or perfect sanity were ever threatened by his debilities. He had come to realize that he needed "Net Mending". "Our mind grows jaded, and our spirit depressed, our heart beats with diminished vigour, and our eyes lose their brightness, if we continue, month after month, and year after year, without a rest." Mental work, he believed, will as surely wear out

the brain "as friction will destroy the iron wheel." "It is bad policy to forego the regular vacation."[7] That was twenty-two years before he finally succumbed to the weakness of this present flesh.

Spurgeon loved and hated. Virtually without exception he loved people of all sorts. At the same time he truly hated the systems of religion and politics that blinded them to the clarity and purity and power of the gospel. "To hate error with perfect hatred, and yet to love the errorist, may seem a hard task; but the Holy Spirit can help us to perform it."[8] He felt no bitterness toward those that erred, for he knew that sovereign grace had opened his mind and heart to the light of truth. Bishops he loved, Episcopacy he hated; Arminians he embraced, while the peculiarities of Arminianism he found destructive; for Tories he had affection, but oppressive power and privilege gained by the mere fact of birth he not only opposed, but ridiculed; the poor he regarded highly, poverty and the indiscretions that created it he despised; those talented for business and thrift he celebrated, the quest for worldly splendor he resisted. The range of eleemosynary projects that he sponsored and supported could not have been sustained did he not have a marvelous capacity for love of all sorts of people and winsomeness with the rich that gained their full approval of his vision. The Earl of Shaftesbury expressed well the esteem won by Spurgeon for his benevolent ministries from many in places of influence. Shaftesbury expressed his regret that he could not attend at the Tabernacle a meeting of ragged school workers. "There is no man in the country, whose opinion and support in such matters I prize more highly than those of my friend, Mr. Spurgeon." He continued:

---

6. S&T, February 1881, 84.

7. S&T, August 1869, 358.

8. S&T, January 1883, 28.

It would give me singular pleasure after nearly forty years of work in the Ragged-school cause, to have the testimony and counsel of so valuable a man. Few men have preached so much, and so well; and few ever have combined so practically their words and their actions. I deeply admire and love him, because I do not believe that there lives anywhere a more sincere and simple servant of our blessed Lord. Great talents have been rightly used; and, under God's grace, have led to great issues.[9]

Even Spurgeon's wit went unwasted, for it found its expression in the teaching of scriptural truth. W. Williams attended Spurgeon's Friday lectures for fourteen years and often went to the Thursday evening services. He had a standing invitation to Spurgeon's home "of which privilege," Williams confessed, "I availed myself as often as conscience would allow." In harmony with thousands of other observers, Williams reported that "the wit of Mr. Spurgeon was proverbial." Referring to him as a "bubbling fountain of humour," Williams confessed to having laughed more in Spurgeon's company than in the entire rest of his life besides. Spurgeon believed that laughter in itself was a good thing and helped tone the mind for many of the charming incongruities slung into our experience by divine grace. "The religion of Jesus," he said, "puts no restraint upon innocent and healthy pleasure."[10] It is all the better if the quip or anecdote, or play on words becomes a barb by which an edifying point might remain lodged in the conscience. Browsing a bookshop brought an uninvited recommendation of a book on infant baptism with the cute remark, "Here, Mr. Spurgeon, is your thorn in the flesh." Undaunted, Spurgeon replied, "Finish the quotation,

brother—A messenger of Satan to buffet me."[11] Through several pseudonyms, the most famous of which was John Ploughman, Spurgeon made many a moral and theological point with a bit of humorous irony and honeyed vinegar. In a piece entitled "Great Thinkers Think Themselves Great Men," Spurgeon made many a pungent remark about feigned greatness and how little minds take little things to be marks of greatness. One such man thought he was great because he could stand on his head and drink a glass of beer and another because he knocked out a man's eye in a prize fight. The worst of the falsely great are those who deem themselves clever. At a distance they are swans but up close they are geese. And the worst of the clever are "those who know better than the Bible and are so learned that they believe that the world had no Maker, and that men are only monkeys with their tails rubbed off." Such talk one expects from Tom of Bedlam, but "now we get it from clever men. If things go on in this fashion a poor ploughman will not be able to tell which is the lunatic and which is the philosopher." Spurgeon went on to have John Ploughman bring the discussion of cleverness to a penetrating point:

> Many a drop of good broth is made in an old pot, and many a sweet comfort comes out of the old doctrine. Many a dog has died since I first opened my eyes, and every one of these dogs has had his day, but in all the days put together they have never hunted out a real fault in the Bible nor started anything better in its place. They may be very clever, but they will not find a surer truth than that which God teaches, nor a better salvation than that which Jesus brings, and so finding my very life in the gospel I mean to live in it, and so ends this chapter.[12]

---

9. S&T, December 1882, 632.

10. W. Williams, *Personal reminiscences of Charles Haddon Spurgeon* (London: the Religious Tract Society, 1895), 171.

11. Ibid, 162.

12. C. H. Spurgeon, *John Ploughman's Pictures* (Christian Focus Publications, 1989), 80-84.

Humor with no point, however, was indeed pointless. Ministers must not become "mere entertainers of the public, pouring out a number of stale jokes and idle tales." A scourge of small cords should be applied in some places that have become venues for entertainment assisted by ministers. "To make religious teaching interesting is one thing, but to make silly mirth, without aim or purpose, is quite another."[13]

Spurgeon interpreted his own ministry in terms of revealed truth. The content of Scripture's representation of human sin had been sealed in Spurgeon's own consciousness and the corresponding answer of the gospel satisfied his disturbed conscience. He found every proposition of Scripture surrounding him as a word of comfort, instruction, and conviction; divine truth "profitable for doctrine ... and instruction in righteousness." Consequently the veracity of Scripture had been confirmed in his experience and by its own internal consistency and he needed no external verification of its truth. He argued with no one about "problems" in the biblical text or in the Christian faith. No good could come of it. Those who raised such problems had not yet felt the weight of their sin or of their need for a Redeemer. Mere intellectual jousting would solve no issue in their minds, for the Scripture is not given in order that the vain philosophical cavils of resistant intellects might be satisfied, but that wounded consciences might be shown a perfect Redeemer. In that light, all he did in preaching, in controversy, and in benevolent ministries arose from his own perception of revealed truth. "We have received the certainties of revealed truth," he wrote, and "we do not bow to men's theories of truth." He did not argue, but declared that "there are certain verities—essential, abiding, eternal—

from which it is ruinous to swerve." The only thing new in theology is that which is false, and Spurgeon rejoiced that he was considered an echo of the past, the biblical past and the Puritan past, rather than a leading voice for error.[14] He did not regard modern thought or theology as Christianity at all, but a totally new cult.

In a benevolent way, Spurgeon considered himself as a universal filter for all human experience and its vicar for the sake of his people. Philosophers and sceptics could pose no question that had not rolled over him in the deep recesses of his own soul in his days of intellectual and spiritual turmoil before conversion. Compared to his struggles, the objections of current doubters were mere trifles and his people need not concern themselves with that which he already had answered. His opinion on books should serve as a shield for others; if he saw nothing edifying in it, then others merely would waste their time in investigating.

Spurgeon knew enough of suffering and mental distress to be a sure guide to fellow sufferers and to shield others from needing the experience for themselves. In explaining his suffering, he noted that "*The complete Pastor's* life will be an epitome of the lives of his people, and they will turn to his preaching as men do to David's Psalms, to see themselves and their own sorrows, as in a mirror. Their needs will be the reason for his griefs."[15]

The martyrdoms of the universal church recorded so poignantly by Fox found their way into his daily experience through the endlessly bothersome misrepresentations of the media and the mean-spirited opposition from many fellow-clergy. Lampooned and ridiculed with merciless

---

13. S&T, October 1879, 492-93.

14. Charles Spurgeon, *An All Round Ministry*, (Edinburgh: Banner of Truth Trust, 1978), 17.

15. S&T, May 1876 197.

glee by many whose fame was built on their ability to humiliate, he gathered these testimonies of opposition in large scrap-books as a memorial to his shouldering such humiliation for others as he patiently took his place with Christ outside the camp.

Biblical doctrine was verified for all his hearers because he knew it to be true; bibliology, Christology and soteriology, all flowed through his personal engagement to all that heard and read him. Their confidence in its power and sanctifying influences could be trusted largely on the credit of his thorough test of their genuineness. To an intellectually troubled inquirer he stated, "If you believe that I am a liar, you are free to think so if you like; but I testify what I do know, and state what I have seen, and tasted, and handled, and felt, and you ought to believe my testimony, for I have no possible object to serve in deceiving you."[16]

Not only did Spurgeon's conversion make him a conduit for all human experience, it gave him the key to all knowledge. Christ crucified trumped by infinite measure the most celebrated wisdom, polity, art, science, and philosophy of all peoples everywhere that did not come from the treasures of revealed truth. A true Christian in possession of God's wisdom in the cross is "in a right place to follow with advantage any other branch of science." It proved true for him. "I confess I have a shelf in my head for everything now. Whatever I read I know where to put it; whatever I learn I know where to stow it away." In former days all that he read and all that he observed just whirled together in mindless confusion, "but ever since I have known Christ, I have put Christ in the centre as my sun, and each science revolves round it like a planet, while minor sciences are

satellites to these planets." Since Christ had become the center of his personal universe, he declared with confidence, "I can learn everything now."[17]

Most prominently in his preaching ministry did Spurgeon show that his mind and heart formed a receptacle and a dispensary for the constant outgo and income of revealed truth. Week after week he poured forth what seemed to him the captivating, heart-forming, sinner-saving power entrenched in Scripture texts. The killing frequency of proclamation in Spurgeon's life compelled him toward such a death because he believed that relentless distribution was divinely ordained as the means by which revealed truth manifests its liveliness in breathing, under the blessing of the Spirit, spiritual, saving life into sinners. His mouth became a channel through which revealed truth flowed as a life-giving stream. He viewed texts not only as having their peculiarly appropriate interpretation, but embodying an entryway into the whole truth of Scripture. He paid attention to peculiar context but also brought his historic confessional commitment to bear in the sermonic presentation arising from the chosen text. The Bible could not be fragmented, in Spurgeon's view, to isolated pericopes or individualized developments of theology from book to book or era to era, but moved toward the fullest display possible in this life of the glory of God manifest in the Redeemer's redemption. Managing a biblical text without Christ and his saving work was a gross mismanagement, because the sum of all the truths revealed in Scripture finds expression in Christ.

This view of preaching expressed consistently his driving theological concern. The covenant of redemption, precious to Spurgeon from the ear-

---

16. Charles Spurgeon, *The Soul Winner* (Chicago: Fleming H. Revell, 1895), 110.

17. NPSP, 1855, 60.

liest days subsequent to his conversion until his dying moments, found its yea and amen in Christ and embodied all the "I wills" of God. Nothing partook more of the very nature of revelation and summarized the fullness of its intent than the covenantal transactions of eternity, and nothing seemed more certain in his own experience and ministry than the security brought by knowledge of that covenant. Because it was at the farthest limits of revealed truth, and went deeper into the eternal purpose and self-knowledge of the triune God than any other idea of Scripture, it was most foundational to our reception of every other item in that body of truth. It should be foundational to all theology and all confessional expressions of it. In his brief statement prior to his edition of the 1689 Baptist confession of faith Spurgeon wrote:

This ancient document is the most excellent epitome of the things most surely believed among us. It is not issued as an authoritative rule or code of faith, whereby you may be fettered, but as a means of edification in righteousness. It is an excellent, though not inspired, expression of the teaching of those Holy Scriptures by which all confessions are to be measured. We hold to the humbling truths of God's sovereign grace in the salvation of lost sinners. Salvation is through Christ alone and by faith alone.

That constitutes the abiding testimony of Charles Spurgeon. That, to him, was the message of Holy Scripture. It was nothing less than the sovereign work of the Redeemer explained for us in revealed truth.

1

BIRTH TO NEW BIRTH

Once I, like Mazeppa, bound on the wild horse of my lust, bound hand and foot, incapable of resistance, was galloping on with hell's wolves behind me, howling for my body and soul, as their just and lawful prey. There came a mighty hand which stopped that wild horse, cut my bands, set me down, and brought me into liberty. Is there power, sir? Aye, there is power; and he who has felt it must acknowledge it. There was a time when I lived in the strong old castle of my sins, and rested on my works. There came a trumpeter to the door, and bade me open it. I with anger chid him from the porch, and said he ne'er should enter. There came a goodly personage, with loving countenance; his hands were marked with scars, where nails were driven, and his feet had nail-prints too; he lifted up his cross, using it as a hammer; at the first blow the gate of my prejudice shook; at the second it trembled more, at the third down it fell, and in he came; and he said, "Arise, and stand upon thy feet, for I have loved thee with an everlasting love." A thing of power! Ah! It is a thing of power. I have felt it here, in this heart; I have the witness of the Spirit within, and know it is a thing of might because it has conquered me; it has bowed me down.[1]

Charles Haddon Spurgeon engaged the last half of the nineteenth century with the power of his personal experience of grace and the unshakeable convictions that the Bible was revealed, that Christ came, and that the Holy Spirit was sent to make sure that all of the Father's elect would have such an experience. If Spurgeon could not bend the rationalists, the latitudinarians, the modern-thought men, the purveyors of manners and virtue, and the Anglo-Catholics to his will in this matter, then he certainly would not conform a single degree toward them—and he would keep as many from their clutches as he could possibly reach. If he saw a human need that could be met and in so doing serve the cause of this gospel, he would meet it. If he saw a ministry needed to promote the clear proclamation and wide dissemination of this gospel, he would start it—and maintain it. If he could not keep his denomination resolutely faithful to the power of these truths, then he would die trying.

Spurgeon's Childhood

Born in the Essex village of Kelvedon on June 19, 1834, his parents were John and Eliza Jarvis Spurgeon. He was the first of seventeen children, only eight of whom survived infancy. Spurgeon's father would die at ninety-one years of age in 1902, having survived his eldest son by ten years. Spurgeon's family moved to Colchester before he was one year old. "Grace does not run in the blood," Spurgeon wrote in 1884 during his fiftieth year, "but it often runs side by side with it." He consid-

---

1. Charles Spurgeon, *Sermons of Rev. C. H. Spurgeon*, 20 volumes (New York: Funk & Wagnalls, 1857-1892) 1:104-05. This series contains some sermons that were not published in the *New Park Street Pulpit* and the *Metropolitan Tabernacle Pulpit*. It will be referred to as SS (for Spurgeon's Sermons), along with the volume number and page number. Sometimes titles of sermons will be included in the reference, sometimes in the text. For this same sermon, see NPSP 1855, 57, 58.

ered it a high honor to be descended from one that feared the Lord and particularly one from non-conformist stock.[2]

Such religious gumption, if not genetic, was certainly environmental, for the Spurgeons had first come to England from Holland near the close of the sixteenth century, refusing to submit their consciences to Philip II, the husband of Bloody Mary and king of Spain, who had sent the bloody Duke of Alva to force the sturdy Hollanders into the church of Rome. A subsequent ancestor, Job Spurgeon, suffered as a Puritan in England during the reign of Charles II, being imprisoned for the sake of conscience. He refused to be released on the promise of good behavior, that is to cease his non-conformity, and suffered as a sick man through an extreme winter.[3] When Spurgeon characterized his father in his seventies, he could have described these ancient forebears: "There is a strong fixedness of belief in our father's mind, and it would take an eternity of modern arguing to reason him out of his confidence."[4] He was not one to truckle with the inventions of the hour.

Spurgeon was named after two uncles, one maternal and one paternal, Charles Jarvis and Haddon Spurgeon. Four months after the parents moved to Colchester, his grandparents took him to live in Stambourne, in the country between Halstead and Haverhill. His grandfather had been pastor of the Independent congregation there since 1810, was a virtual oracle in the village, and stood in good graces with even the minister of the established church, James Hopkins. Spurgeon noted, "They preached the same gospel, and, without surrendering their principles, were great friends."[5] The tension that existed between Church and Chapel in many places in England was not a prominent factor in Stambourne.[6] The young Spurgeon remembered the "very brown" sugar along with the sugared bread and butter for Monday snack in fellowship with his grandfather, the Rev. Hopkins, and a resident who attended both church and chapel on any given Lord's Day.[7]

Spurgeon also recalled a great number of details about the house and its impressions on him, including its picture of David and Goliath, its plastered windows so darkened to avoid a window tax, and its rocking horse "on which even a member of Parliament might have retained his seat." The foxhunt fascinated him for its pageantry, its speed, and its mystery. Both hymn-memorizing and rat-killing earned him money, the latter more than the former, but Spurgeon knew, as did his hearers, "which employment has been the more permanently profitable." Every event, every item, every conversation, every relationship, every errand resulted eventually in spiritual and doctrinal lessons to Spurgeon. He learned to notice small but astounding elements

---

2. S&T, September 1884, 471.

3. Pike 1:1-5. G. Holden Pike, *The Life and Work of Charles Haddon Spurgeon*, 6 vols. London: Cassell and Company Limited, nd. Pike was a good friend of Spurgeon who wrote three biographies of the famous preacher. The last is the six-volume work cited here. One of the interesting and helpful parts of this work is its record of first hand experiences of acquaintances of Spurgeon throughout his life and even includes material observations from the Waterbeach friends who survived him. In addition many quotations from journals of the time, some of them obscure and difficult to find, add to the interest of Pike's account.

4. S&T, September 1881, 471.

5. Charles Spurgeon and Benjamin Beddow, *Memories of Stambourne* (London: Passmore and Alabaster, 1891), 10

6. This is an observation made by Benjamin Beddow, grandson of the minister that preceded James Spurgeon. *Memories of Stambourne*, 39.

7. C. H. Spurgeon, *Autobiography*, first published in 4 vols, 1897-1900, rev edition, 2 vols (Edinburgh: The Banner of Truth Trust, 1962 [vol 2, 1973]), 1:8. The next few un-noted quotations are taken from pages 3-13 of this volume. Interspersed quotes from other sources will be noted. This will be referred to as *Autobiography* in the two-volume Banner of Truth edition with volume and page numbers.

of nature and marveled in the fascinating wonders all around him. The apple in a bottle, the sparrows in the plaster wall just beside his bed, the kneading trough with a cabinet containing a pastry for "the child," the mangle used by many others in the town, all made pleasant memories for Spurgeon. He liked "all this rural life,"[8] and many of the spiritual and theological lessons he shared through his ministry came out of the way in which he developed analogies between nature and doctrinal truth.

Spurgeon loved to tell stories of the rural life of his grandfather and how God provided for them in, humanly speaking, straitened circumstances. In days prior to Spurgeon's sojourn with him, his main living came from the working of a farm. He had a cow that provided milk for his many children. One day the cow got the staggers and died, leaving them destitute of much of their sustenance. "God has the power to give us fifty cows if he so pleases," John told his distraught wife. On that day, the committee administering a fund for poor ministers met in London, and after distributing all the money to those that had requested it, they were left with £5. None knew him personally, but one knew of him and his integrity and his struggles and suggested that the £5 be sent to the Independent minister down in Stambourne in Essex. Another said that £5 would not do, and added another five; so two others did the same. The next morning, the Spurgeons received £20 in the post from the Lord in recompense for the departed cow. When he opened the note, and saw the money, he said to his wife, "Now, can't you trust God about an old cow?"[9]

The immediate dependence that rural village people had on the health of a cow, the balance of sun and rain, the sharpness of a plough, and daily health and pain, all produced a habit of proverbializing and a deep awareness of providence. Spurgeon's John Ploughman and some other pseudonymous characters arose from a combination of characters he met in rural Stambourne, not least of which was his beloved grandfather, and a farmer given to proverbial sayings called Will Richardson. Sometimes the young man would walk with Richardson when he was plowing. Richardson was well known for his "cramp" sayings which often would be repeated around the town, particularly his evaluation of a young preacher given to the novice himself, "Ah, young man, you have a good many stiles to get over before you get into Preaching Road."[10]

The love Spurgeon had for the common man, the confidence he had in good common sense, and the commitment he had for honest and long labor emerged from his observations of rural life and the work required to keep life merely above failure. In reviewing a book entitled *Plodding On; or, the Jog-trot to Fame and Fortune* by Henry Curwen, Spurgeon commended the book as likely to excite laudable ambition in youth by the narrative of victories of genius. All of the persons were plodders and all succeeded in life. "Working men will here see how they may climb if they will," Spurgeon remarked. With a bit of wise and sad observation in the background, he continued, "If the quart pot and an unwise marriage do not chain them to the lowest round of the ladder, they may mount if they will banish self-indulgence, and put forth their energies." Since the idea of successful plodders had been introduced, Spurgeon decided to add to the review his own concept of genius. "It would be a gross error," he urged, "if it were imagined that men of genius do

---

8. *Memories of Stambourne*, 98.

9. MTP, 1875, 657.

10. The anecdote is given by Mr. Houchin, the pastor that succeeded James Spurgeon at Stambourne. *Memories of Stambourne*, 141.

not work. To our mind, genius generally means that a man has a tendency and an aptitude for double toil in a certain direction, and hence he prospers in it." The genius for hard work was the only genius he believed in. A man that sought to succeed on supposed genius apart from diligent application had no place in Spurgeon's esteem.

His reminiscences of Stambourne came from a collection of them throughout early childhood and adolescence. He relished visits to his grandparents, especially on holidays, even after going back to Colchester to live at home. His father remarked about these times:

> It has been said that Charles was brought up by his grandfather and grandmother. The fact is, that my father and mother came to see us when Charles was a baby of fourteen months old. They took him to stay with them, and he remained with them until he was between four and five years of age. Then he came home to stay with us at Colchester. ... Afterwards he often went to spend his holidays with his grandparents, who were very fond of him. ... He was always reading books—never digging in the garden or keeping pigeons, like other boys. It was always books and books. If his mother wanted to take him for a ride she would be sure to find him in my study poring over a book.[11]

Breathing Puritan Air

Particularly beneficial to Spurgeon during these visits to Stambourne were the numerous opportunities for immediate and positive doctrinal impressions. Discussions at his grandfather's house, as well as among his father's friends, made Spurgeon pay close attention to the nature of theological argument. "I can bear witness that children can understand the Scriptures," Spurgeon insisted, "for I am sure that when but a child I could have discussed many a knotty point of contro-

versial theology, having heard both sides of the question freely stated among my father's circle of friends."[12] In addition, the love for books noted by John Spurgeon reflected an innate intellectual curiosity that Charles Spurgeon maintained all his days, but which was startled to life in his grandfather's room of books. One of the rooms behind a plastered window housed a true book lover's gold mine. Spurgeon met the martyrs of the English reformation and "Old Bonner," the bishop of London responsible under Bloody Mary for the burning of more than 200 of his parishioners. He also made a lifelong acquaintance with Bunyan and his Pilgrim which he read more than a hundred times throughout his life. Most memorably and reverentially did Spurgeon regard the "great masters of Scriptural theology, with whom no moderns are worthy to be named in the same day." He loved even the look of a genuine Puritan book with its margins, notes, type, and especially the "sheepskins and goatskins" in which they were forced to wander.

These volumes were left over from the very day of the Puritans and had been the possession of Henry Havers, a Puritan who left the parish church in 1662 when conscience would not permit him to comply with the Act of Uniformity. Three straight pastors by the same name, a grandson and then his nephew followed, served the church for its first eighty-six years. After the original Henry Havers vacated as rector of the parish, he continued to encourage the parishioners and teach them in other venues. The legislation of the Conventicle Act and the Five Mile Act brought renewed waves of persecution on his itinerant flock for ten years. Havers himself was once pursued by the authorities, hid himself in the kiln of a malt-house and eluded his pursuers when a spi-

---

11. Pike, 1:17.

12. SS, 2:347. "Teaching Children."

der wove a web over the door to the kiln, leading them to believe that he could not possibly be in there or he would have broken the web.

A long-time member of the congregation composed some loving lines of poetry about the three Havers and included the following verses about the ejected Puritan.

> *Havers the first* was rector here,
> His Zeal for God was warm;
> The living not to him so dear
> That he would e'er conform.
>
> He left his church and living too,
> To keep his conscience clear;
> His great concern was good to do,
> And much good did he here.
>
> He was far from being a Jude,
> He was a star of light;
> Yea one of the first magnitude,
> And always shined bright.
>
> Yea, he was like unto the sun
> In a bright summer day;
> Bright he begun and bright went on,
> And bright he went away.

The books that so enthralled Spurgeon were a gift to Havers from Thomas Green to be used by him and those that should follow him in the gospel ministry in that place.[13] The man that served as pastor of the congregation from 1776 to 1810, immediately prior to James Spurgeon (1810-64), was Benjamin Beddow, and he was grandfather to the man who aided Charles Spurgeon in the production of *Memories of Stambourne*.[14]

Spurgeon's commitment to exposition from early to late in his ministry showed the tenacity of his mental and spiritual attachment to this literary legacy and of his continued preference for it over the developing critical approach to scriptural scholarship and commentary. Preaching on "Faith" from Hebrews 11 in December 1856, Spurgeon set forth the outline using the divisions of the subject suggested to him by the Puritans. "The old writers, who are, by far, the most sensible—for you will notice that the books that were written about 200 years ago by the old Puritans have more sense in one line than there is in a page of our new books—and more in a page than there is in a whole volume of our modern divinity!" The subject he then divided into knowledge, assent. and affiance, "or the laying hold of the knowledge to which we give assent and making it our own by trusting in it."[15] Less meat and more pits became common fare from the modern handling of the text in Spurgeon's opinion. Twenty-seven years did not dampen his enthusiasm for the Puritans, for in 1883 he still protested, "If Puritanic preaching filled the pulpits, it would soon fill the pews." He asked for more "old-fashioned divines like Boston and the Erskines."[16] He found little in the theological productions of modern times to recommend to his students but was delighted when the Nichols Series of Puritans commentaries appeared. Though the modern critical approach encouraged some advances in understanding, the value of the Puritans was insuperable. "The Puritan age was one of great erudition, unwearied application, deep-felt experience, and unbounded veneration for the authority of the Divine Word." More breadth may come from the moderns, but not more depth. With the Puritans "we shall have both breadth and depth, and our theology, however, much extended, will still be the

---

13. Beddow *Memories of Stambourne*, 34-38.
14. Ibid., 40.

15. SS, 1:366.
16. S&T, June 1883, 303.

deep, deep sea."[17]

When examining a book on prayer in 1882, Spurgeon noted its thorough thinness and its "tameness of propriety as compared with the force and piquancy of the Puritans."[18] He did not want a book to "squeeze soft" but something "solid, substantial, and real." Modern theology was like whipped cream or the soufflé of the confectioner, very pretty but hardly anything at all. "In a cubic inch of Charnock, or Owen," he remarked in 1885, "there is enough matter to cover acres of the new school of writing."[19] George Rogers, the first tutor at the Pastors' College, speaking at the 1883 Conference, reflected Spurgeon's heart when he noted, "It is another distinguishing peculiarity of our College, and which accounts in a great measure for its spiritual results, that it adheres to the Puritanic in distinction from the Germanic theology."[20]

As for Spurgeon, he could quote from the Puritans at will, illustrate a point from a variety of Puritan authors, enter into discussion with each character of Pilgrim's Progress, analyze spiritual struggles from the narrative of *Grace Abounding to the Chief of Sinners*, and quickly compare the strengths, weaknesses, and local color of numerous Puritan authors. A sample of this brightens Spurgeon's comments on a newly published edition of the sermons of an otherwise unknown figure, Master Henry Smith, of the Puritan era, "the golden age of religion in England."

> He is not so apt in quoting ancient history as Master Brooks, neither is he so rich in figures culled from nature as Gurnal or Charnock, but

his baskets of silver, in which he places his apples of gold, are mainly of Scriptural workmanship. ... Perhaps no better instance can be given of his forcible way of impressing truth upon the memory and conscience than the famous extract from "The Dialogue between Paul and Agrippa." It is Smith at his best, simple as Bunyan, sound as Owen, interesting as Brooks, quaint as Adams, earnest as Baxter, but aptly scriptural in his illustrations as none but himself; in that one respect he appears as a bright particular star shining apart and alone.[21]

An American friend of Spurgeon's mature years, Wayland Hoyt, remembered this love for and inimitable knowledge of the Puritans. "He could repeat pages of them at will," Hoyt recalled, with no reason for extravagance in his recounting. "He knew precisely how this man and that man of them analyzed his text," Hoyt continued. Within the steady diet of Bunyan and scores of other Puritans, Hoyt located the foundation of Spurgeon's "nervous sinewy, plain, and yet picturesque Saxon."[22] A fellow-teacher at Newmarket, J. D. Everett, recalled walking on occasions with a fifteen-year-old Spurgeon giving long passages he had heard in open-air preaching and also recalled, "I have also heard him recite long passages from Bunyan's *Grace Abounding*."[23]

The suffering of the Puritans, the illustrations in Foxe's Book of Martyrs, the bloody strictures of Bonner and his crew, the Pope and his crew, the progress made for truth and the gospel through stocks, prison, burnings, and blood permeated Spurgeon's understanding of mission theology. That they did not count their lives dear to themselves in comparison to the great call-

---

17. S&T, February 1866, 94.

18. S&T, July 1882, 376.

19. S&T, June 1885, 269.

20. Comments by George Rogers in "Annual Report of the Pastors' College," S&T 1883, 281.

21. S&T May, 1867, 201, 204.

22. Wayland Hoyt, *Walk and Talks with Charles H. Spurgeon* (Philadelphia: American Baptist Publication Society, 1892), 21, 22.

23. J. H. Barnes and C. E. Brown, *Spurgeon, The People's Preacher* (London: Walter Scott, 1892), 20.

ing of working for the defense and propagation of the gospel—such scenes settled in Spurgeon's memory and molded his conscience. God's gospel would make progress when its propagators looked death in the face and did not relent. The issues of eternity overwhelm any temporal and, relatively speaking, momentary suffering that a gospel missionary might endure. When Baptist missionaries returned from Ireland because the Irish hooted them, and threw stones at them, Spurgeon snarled, "Now don't you think you see Paul taking a microscope out of his pocket, and looking at a little man who should say to him, 'I shall not go there to preach, because the Irish hooted me!'" What a small edition of a preacher such an intimidated creature must be. But they threw stones! Tell that to Paul with a face unashamed. But the police interfered, they might put us in stocks, and some might even die. "Our business is to preach the word," Spurgeon responded; "Where is that zeal which counted not its life dear, so that it might win Christ?" The killing of a few of our ministers would prosper Christianity, he preached; if men die by the hundreds and thousands in defense of hearth and home, so surely it is no great grief to lose a dozen to death in the cause of the gospel. "I would count my own blood most profitably shed in so holy a struggle," Spurgeon affirmed. When the gospel prospered aforetime, it did so because some laid down their lives for it and others walked "to victory over their slain bodies."[24]

In all his exuberance for the Puritans, however, Spurgeon was not ill-informed on the mistakes of church–state relationships in their manner of putting down heresy. Speaking of his detestation of Puseyism, that is, Anglican high church sacramentalism consistent with Roman Catholicism,

Spurgeon called for the "God of Gideon to be with the few whom he may make worthy to smite the great host who have covered the land!" He is quick to add, however, that "the Puritans erred in using carnal weapons, and hence their victory was shortlived."[25] That interpretation of Puritan greatness and weakness persisted throughout Spurgeon's years. Speaking to his College Conference in 1886 he said, "Our Puritan forefathers raised their walls, and laid their stones in fair colours, building well the city of God." Then came Oliver Cromwell, the "greatest of heroes" who handled the sword of steel as few have ever done. The carnal weapon, however, "agreed not with the temple of the Lord." The Lord seemed to say to him as to David, "Thou hast been a man of blood, and therefore thou shalt not build the house of the Lord." On that error, Puritanism faltered, and "all its exceeding stateliness of holiness, because its sons saw not that the kingdom of the Lord is not of Church and State, not of the law of nations, but purely of the Spirit of the Lord."[26]

Spurgeon would never be reconciled to any system of union of church and state, even a Puritan one; it was entirely antithetical to his understanding of the church as a holy disciplined congregation. That his godly grandfather and the wholesome citizens of Stambourne who were members of the "Dissenters" should be put at a disadvantage by the state for this matter of conscience, citizens that were a step above the common standard at that, never made sense to him and brought from his pen some of the most unvarnished sarcasm and rhetoric of incredulity in his entire corpus of writing.

Both the books and the ethos of Puritanism that permeated the atmosphere of Stambourne established a joyful sobriety in the spirit of the

24. SS, 1:328f. "Gospel Missions."

25. S&T, 1866, 340. "The Holy War of the Present Hour."
26. S&T, June 1886, 257.

young Spurgeon that kept England from forgetting them for the next fifty years. Specific instruction connected with all the meetings of the chapel imposed a pleasant spirituality and strong conviction on him. While his grandfather studied on Sunday morning for his message, "the child" sat in the room with his venerable grandfather. His silence was guaranteed by the prospect that if he talked, his grandfather might not make a point as clearly as he should for the sake of someone's eternal well-being.[27] That his silence was the fulcrum between heaven and hell, sobered the occasion for Spurgeon. He remembered how the people "heard a sermon" and how the gospel dispelled superstitions among those church members that "benumbed the brains of too many of the East Anglian peasantry." Prayer meetings and hymn-singing made indelible impressions on his young facile mind. Watts' hymns were valued above all almost to exclusivity. His grandfather, however, tried his hand at hymnody but "paid no attention to the mere triviality of rhyme."[28] Spurgeon concluded that he could be forgiven for the first volume of hymns only because he determined not to publish a second volume. If Watts' hymns provided a biblical aesthetic for spiritual worship, instruction in Watts' catechism gave a solid condensation of Scripture content for doctrinal reflection.[29]

Above all was the preaching of his grandfather. "The dew of the Spirit from on high never left the ministry," Spurgeon testified, and "wherever my grandfather went, souls were saved under his ministry." He died in February 1864, when Spurgeon was thirty and in his eleventh year in London; Spurgeon marked the occasion with a sermon on "He that endureth to the end shall be saved" (Matt. 10:22). Remarkably illustrative of the text in his mind, Spurgeon highlighted the faithfulness of his grandfather's life and the doctrinal consistency of his ministry. "In his early days, his sober earnestness and sound doctrine were owned of God in many conversions both at home and abroad." He lived down slander and abuse, lived beyond most of his friends, and multiplied his children and grandchildren in the spiritual realm through preaching not only at home but in many other churches. At his last conversation with his grandson Charles, the venerable James Spurgeon expressed an amazing consciousness: "I do not know that my testimony for God has ever altered, as to the fundamental doctrines; I have grown in experience, but from the first day until now, I have had no new doctrines to teach my hearers. I have had to make no confessions of error on vital points, but have been held fast to the doctrines of grace, and can now say that I love them better than ever." As he continued his words, he spoke, as summarized in Spurgeon's sermonic report, of the "preciousness of Christ, and chiefly of the security of the believer; the truthfulness of the promise; the immutability of the covenant; the faithfulness of God, and the infallibility of the divine decree." Christ's promise is as secure as his throne and "he must cease to be king before he can break his promise, or lose his people. Divine sovereignty makes us all secure." Spurgeon spoke gratefully, "I am thankful that I had such a grandsire."[30] Twenty years later, Charles Haddon Spurgeon could say of his grandfather that he "was a faithful minister

---

27. *Memories of Stambourne*, 91.

28. Ibid., 82

29. Ibid., 121, 122.

30. Charles Spurgeon, "Enduring to the End," in *Spurgeon's Expository Encyclopedia*, 15 vols (Grand Rapids: Baker Book House, 1977) 12:290-91. (This will be referred to as SEE followed by volume number and page number). Spurgeon says that his grandfather not only preached in his own pulpit, but made "very many journeys to other Churches." Drummond, however, makes the remark that "He rarely preached in any other church but his own." Lewis Drummond, *Spurgeon: Prince of Preachers* (Grand Rapids, MI: Kregel, 1992), 80.

of the New Covenant, whose memory is still fresh and fragrant in many parts of Essex."[31]

The Prophecy of Richard Knill

The famous prophecy of Richard Knill also had a formative impact on Spurgeon both in his quest for conversion and in his perception of Christian ministry. Richard Ellsworth Day minimized the importance of this event with the observation that "the importance of the prophecy we are inclined to dismiss with the remark of a contemporary biographer, 'Clergymen on a collecting tour are always much impressed by the high qualities of the children of the hosts.'"[32] Day's comment may reflect a realistic appraisal of the tendencies of common courtesy toward people upon whom one is dependent for success, but also tends to discredit the sincerity of Knill. All the historic testimony concerning this event should convince even the most skeptical historian that, at least, the milk of human kindness and the honey of human respect was neither soured nor adulterated by cupidity. Whatever the motivation of Knill, Spurgeon always admired him and felt that the words spoken were utterly sincere and savored of the reality of a rare glimpse of future events that God may at times give his saints.

Richard Knill, on deputation from the London Missionary Society, came into Essex in 1844.[33]

This corresponded with one of Spurgeon's visits to Stambourne. He heard Spurgeon's questions, listened to his comments, treated him kindly and lovingly and, waking "the boy" at 6:00 am, spent three mornings with him in prayer and earnest exhortation. Before he left he predicted that Spurgeon would preach one day in Rowland Hill's chapel as well as to great multitudes. Knill extracted a promise that Spurgeon would memorize the Cowper hymn, "God moves in a Mysterious Way," and have it sung when he preached in the chapel. The things came to pass precisely. Spurgeon viewed it as fulfilled in the combination of two events.

> After I had begun for some little time to preach in London, Dr. Alexander Fletcher was engaged to deliver the annual sermon to children in Surrey Chapel; but as he was taken ill, I was asked in a hurry to preach to the children in his stead. "Yes," I replied, "I will, if you will allow the children to sing, 'God moves in a mysterious way.' I have made a promise long ago that so that [*sic*] should be sung." And so it was: I preached in Rowland Hill's Chapel, and the hymn was sung. My emotions on that occasion I cannot describe, for the word of the Lord's servant was fulfilled. Still I fancy that the Surrey was not the chapel which Mr. Knill intended. How was I to go to the country chapel? All unsought by me, the minister at Wotton-under-Edge, which was Mr. Hill's summer residence, invited me to preach there. I went on the condition that the congregation should sing, "God moves

---

31. S&T, September 1884, 471.

32. Richard Ellsworth Day, *The Shadow of the Broad Brim* (Philadelphia: The Judson Press, 1934) 46.

33. Spurgeon gives the year (*Autobiography*, 1:27). In Spurgeon's letter to Knill (referred to later), written in 1853, he notes that Knill's visit was "eight or nine years ago." Why Pike dates it as 1848 [Pike, 1:24] is puzzling. Spurgeon was in Augustine's College in Maidstone that year, well into his education. His reading of Scripture would not have been nearly as impressive in one already involved in such a variety of subject matters as constituted his education by that time. In addition, the events of Knill's visit make much more sense for a ten-year-old than a fourteen-year-old. Even Pike's language doesn't seem consistent with his date of the event. "Mr. Knill had never before heard *a child of his little friend's*

---

years read the Scriptures at family prayer with such effect; and he had a presentiment for which he could not account, that the *little fellow* before him was destined to undertake distinguished service in the Church" [1:27]. Pike's knowledge of the details of the event must certainly mean that he had access to Spurgeon's account, but somehow he missed Spurgeon's dating, or perhaps it is merely a printing error. Henry Northrop, writing before Spurgeon's death, knew of Spurgeon's anecdote in its written form and knew that the date was 1844. Pike's discussion of Knill's childhood, his genial Christian spirit, his missionary labors, and his impact through preaching and the press enlightens and ingratiates the reader to the genuine self-effacing piety of Knill [also 2:257].

in a mysterious way"—which was also done. To me it was a very wonderful thing, and I no more understand to-day why the Lord should be so gracious to me.[34]

Spurgeon knew that many called this a legend, but he testified that "it was strictly true."[35] The exchange of correspondence on this prophecy and Spurgeon's recollection of it in public ways in subsequent decades should make any biographer pause before dispatching it from his considerations. In 1853, before Spurgeon was nineteen and while he preached at Waterbeach, he wrote Richard Knill to remind him of the words then spoken. Spurgeon's verbal demeanor brimmed with a grateful and deferential spirit. "That one interview," he said speaking of Knill's attempt to lead him to the Savior, "has made my heart yours." Spurgeon said that Knill's words, perhaps not meant so intensely by Knill himself, were now imperishable, had taken on the "reverence of prophecy," and to Spurgeon himself "a sort of stay to my existence." Though not directly responsible for his conversion, Spurgeon believed that Knill's words had helped work in him a "desire to gain true religion." Spurgeon had no penchant for superstition but that event held him fast and he looked forward to the time "when the whole shall come to pass."[36]

Two years later, after Spurgeon had moved to London and had begun at New Park Street, Knill wrote James Spurgeon with news of the positive edifying reports he had overheard on several occasions of the work of young Charles in London. Knill remembered well the visit to Stambourne and the conversations with Charles. "I have

prayed much *for* him and *about* him," Knill reported, "that God may keep him at the foot of the cross, that popularity may not puff him up."[37]

Spurgeon accepted Knill's words as a real specimen of divine interposition. He recounted the Knill incident and drew the conclusion that the words of Knill, in some sense, helped to bring about their own fulfillment. Beyond that, however, Spurgeon accepted more. "Our ordinary guides are right reason and the Word of God, and we may never act contrary to these," Spurgeon affirmed; "but still we accept it as a matter of faith and experience to us that on exceptional occasions, special interpositions do come to our aid, so that our steps are ordered of the Lord and made to subserve his glory."[38]

That this had been the case with him, Spurgeon freely admitted. His "personal pathway has been so frequently directed contrary to our own design and beyond our own conception by singularly powerful impulses, and irresistibly suggestive providences, that it were wanton wickedness for us to deride the doctrine that God occasionally grants to his servants a special and perceptible manifestation of his will for their guidance, over and above the strengthening energies of the Holy Spirit, and the sacred teaching of the inspired Word."[39] Sometimes, in Spurgeon's experience this happened at a time unknown to him. He periodically told anecdotes of speaking about specific things in sermons that turned out to be the exact case of someone listening to him. A merchant who made himself a thief by not giving proper change, a young man who came drunk to service immediately from a gin palace, and a husband whose cruelty had led to the death of one wife and now married to another—these sce-

---

34. *Memories of Stambourne*, 104.

35. *Autobiography*, 1:27. See also *Memories of Stambourne*, 101.

36. Spurgeon, *Letters of Charles Haddon Spurgeon*, selected with notes by Iain Murray (Edinburgh: The Banner of Truth Trust, 1992), 38-40. This will be referred to as Murray, *Letters*.

37. *Autobiography*, 1:29, 30.

38. S&T, September 1865, 426. "Two Episodes in my Life."

39. Ibid., 420

narios, and others, used as illustrations turned out to be exactly the case. "What an extraordinary thing it seems," Spurgeon commented, "yet, I can assure you that such extraordinary things are as commonplaces in my experience." He believed that not only in general way, but often in very specific ways, "God does help his servants rightly to divide the word, that is to say, to allot a special portion to each special case, so that it comes to pass upon the man as if everything about him was known."[40]

Spurgeon did not point to this phenomenon as a consciously received revelation from God. It was more like a providentially-designed distribution of rhetorical flourishes that Spurgeon often engaged in during a message. Often they were merely fanciful descriptions that Spurgeon inserted for the sake of a pungent illustration without any intention that an actual case of such sat before him. In 1890 he preached, "Over there is a man who has been in a half-a-dozen shipwrecks; and if he does not mind, he will be shipwrecked to all eternity! One here has had yellow fever. Ah sir, there is a worse fever than that on you now!" Others, he doubted not, had had cases of strange deliverances and had been between the jaws of death. They had "looked over the edge of that dread precipice, beneath which is the fathomless abyss," and vowed that if God spared their life, they would not be what they were before. And, indeed, they were not, for they were worse off than ever. "You are sinning now against light, and in shameful ingratitude. God have mercy upon you!" Some of his descriptions might have met precisely the case of a person, but Spurgeon did not intend them as an immediate revelation. He intended it as a pungent and graphic picture of the sinful tendency of delay and ingratitude

in the lives of all sinners when faced with the obvious merciful intervention of God in their lives. He used this device so often, and with a keen knowledge of the way that people live, sin, and die, that he was bound to have described someone's case from time to time. That it did not happen more often shows that it was not an absorption into the *paraklete*; that it occurred at all, tended to perpetuate an aura of the miraculous surrounding the life of Spurgeon.[41]

Just as surely, Spurgeon knew that such an idea was open to abundant abuse and Spurgeon spent a good bit of time tearing down idols of inflamed imaginations assumed to be the voice of God. "The most wonderfully well-attested narratives," Spurgeon observed, "seldom bear investigation, they are built up upon hearsay and tittle-tattle, and will not endure a strict examination; like most rumours, they fall like card-houses as soon as the hand of truth touches them." In a further comment about those who maintain adherence to these "ghost stories", Spurgeon wrote, "Half crazy people come to us in any quantity with such marvels, and we hope we have cured a good many by a little kindly raillery." Even with a withering blast against their unfounded conviction of a vision of divinity, "a considerable number leave us with the impression sadly confirmed in our minds that there are more lunatics abroad than there are in the asylums."[42] "But notwithstanding all the folly of hairbrained rant," he still averred, "we believe that the unseen hand may be at times assuredly felt by gracious souls, and the mysterious power which guided the minds of the seers of old may, even to this day, sensibly overshadow reverent spirits. We would speak discreetly,

41. For example see Russell H. Conwell, *Life of Charles Haddon Spurgeon* ([Philadelphia]: Edgewood Publishing Co., 1892), 68-88; 345-69.

42. S&T, 1874, 553 ff.

40. MTP, 1875, 94. "Rightly Dividing the Word of Truth."

but we dare say no less."[43] Early in his ministry in London, he believed that God might sometimes impress a spiritual action on the mind by some moral urge to do good, or consummate the thought that a Christian has to be a blessing to a person with the sense of the immediate appropriateness of action. "I am somewhat of a believer in the doctrine of the Quakers as to the impulses of the Spirit," he preached in 1855, "and I fear lest I should check one of them. If a thought crosses my mind, 'Go to such a person's house,' I always like to do it, because I do not know but what it may be from the Spirit."[44]

Yet in 1875 Spurgeon took a position on special revelation outside Scripture that is difficult to harmonize with his acceptance of the spiritual enlightenment of Knill or of others on occasion. "Do not tell me about the Spirit of God speaking to anybody more than is in the Bible," he taught as he spoke about revelations from God as the foundation of warranted faith. "What is in the Scripture the Spirit of God will apply to the heart, but if you want the Spirit of God to speak to you over and above that, you will never have it."[45] A harmonization is possible, but one must also realize that, in this matter, Spurgeon might have contradicted himself. To a Christian concerned about the progress of the gospel in the world, God might give intimations of his purpose in a specific case; to an unbeliever desiring a sign of God's salvific intent, he would receive none except the general but immutably true statements of salvation for believers. None can expect a revelation that he in particular is elect or reprobate, or may seek an actual assurance of God's merciful intention toward him apart from or prior to his obeying the commands and meeting the stated conditions of the gospel, repentance toward God and faith in Jesus Christ. None may expect the revelation, "Christ died for you," apart from believing that which is revealed in Scripture; in him alone, "We have redemption through his blood, the forgiveness of sin."

The Religious Tract Society published a biography of Richard Knill in 1879. Spurgeon noted that the reference to the famed prophecy was included and "the narrative is true." Beyond that he commented that Knill was "one of the most simple, earnest, straightforward soul-seekers that we ever knew." He never had to go out of his way to "lead a soul to repose itself on Christ." He came to such topics in his normal talk so naturally that it never seemed to be a special effort; he came to it as naturally as others come to meals. Though Spurgeon admired the "capital portrait" for the frontispiece, he would have liked it better had the inscription not been omitted: "Brethren, the heathen are perishing: will you let them perish?"[46]

An Exuberant Spirit, a Fertile Mind, and a Compromised Body

Spurgeon's years in Stambourne were lived in the presence of adults. He had no play with other children, though he was indulged child's play and secret hideaways, the favorite being an empty grave. Also, he remembered great tenderness and coddling and special treatment appropriate to such a formative age. The lack of other children combined with the pastime of sitting with adults to hear conversation meant, however, a very passive life physically for Spurgeon. Though his father noted that Spurgeon "was a healthy child and boy, having a good constitution," he also noted that he never played like other boys and always was studying and reading. J. D. Everett,

---

43. S&T, September 1865, 421.

44. SS, 1:140.

45. MTP, 1875, 47.

46. S&T, February 1879, 84.

his fellow tutor at Newmarket, described Spurgeon as "rather small and delicate, with pale but plump face, dark brown eyes and hair, and a bright lively manner, with a never-failing flow of conversation." Further refining the impression of his physical presence, Everett wrote: "He was rather deficient in muscle, did not care for cricket or other athletic games, and was timid at meeting cattle on the roads."[47]

One should not marvel that Spurgeon became chronically sick comparatively early in his ministry; rather, the marvel is that he was able to maintain such a trying and rigorous schedule of travel and preaching for so many years before it became impossible. The early onset of physical exhaustion perhaps made Spurgeon later intent on providing sufficient play space, opportunities, and encouragement for his orphans. At an outdoor meeting, preaching to over 12,000 at Hackney in 1855, at twenty-one years of age, Spurgeon, contemplating the rest of heaven, said: "Soon, this voice will never be strained again; soon, these lungs will never have to exert themselves beyond their power; soon, this brain shall not be racked for thought; but I shall sit at the banquet-table of God; yea, I shall recline on the bosom of Abraham, and be at ease forever."[48] Very early, he was yearning for rest.

On his return to Colchester in 1840, Spurgeon entered into a healthy family relationship with three siblings (two sisters and a brother), a deeply pious mother, and a preacher father who served as a clerk to support his family and preached on Sundays nine miles away. His siblings provided fodder for his leadership abilities, his father allowed him to read in the study and to be party to theological discussions that occurred frequently in the home, and his mother provided daily instruction in the way of salvation and earnest prayers for the salvation of all her children. Later, he could write with grateful memory: "I was brought up as a child with such care that I knew but very little of foul or profane language, having scarcely ever heard a man swear."[49] He did not need, however, to see the sins of others or hear the churlish conversation of the hardened to know that hardness of heart and rebelliousness of spirit came not by imitation, but by native propensity.

The Process of Conviction

Quite impressive and piercing to his conscience was his mother's apostrophe before God that she must bear swift witness against her children before his throne of judgment if they were not converted, for they knew the truth and had sincere admonitions from her to trust in Christ. "Certainly I have not the powers of speech," Spurgeon wrote as he reflected on the deep influence of his mother, "with which to set forth my valuation of the choice blessing which the Lord bestowed on me in making me the son of one who prayed for, and prayed with me."[50] His father recognized the massive weight that the mother's prayers exerted on Charles. During a ceremony in laying the first stone for the Metropolitan Tabernacle in 1859, John Spurgeon shared the story of the mother's earnest prayers. "I believe, under God's Grace, his mother has been the means of leading him to Christ," he said with disarming candor. "You are well aware that I go and talk in the best manner I can to a few poor people on the Sabbath-Day and God has blessed my labors. I thought, however, I ought not to go out on the Sabbath-Day, as God's people should train up their children in the best way they can." He believed that his absence was harming the children's religious training at

---

47. *The People's Preacher*, 19.

48. SS, 1:298.

49. S&T, February 1879, 60.

50. *Autobiography*, 1:44.

home until "I came home one evening about seven o'clock and went upstairs. I heard the voice of a mother pleading for her boy, Charles, and talking to him and the others and pouring her heart out in prayer in such a way as I never did in my life and as I never heard before."[51] After that he never felt that leaving the children in the hands of such a mother was at all neglectful.

Charles also began his formal education when he returned home and was put to school with Mrs. Cook until he was ten. He learned during this venture a lesson that marked him till his death. Having lost his pencils and wanting to avoid a scolding from both teacher and parents, Spurgeon entered into a debt with Mrs. Pearson, the shop owner, promising to pay when his Christmas money came to him. The farthing he now owed seemed like a life-forfeiture, for he was in debt. When his father learned of the transaction, probably from Mrs. Pearson, he gave Spurgeon a lecture on debts being like thievery that was sure to bring a boy to ruin and send him to prison and make his family a disgrace. Straight to the shop they went "like a deserter marched into the barracks, crying bitterly all down the street, and feeling dreadfully ashamed;" the farthing was paid and the debtor was set free. He vowed at that point that nothing would ever tempt him to debt again. He hated debt like Luther hated the Pope. He told this incident in the *Autobiography*, and also had John Ploughman do a plain-sense exposition of the experience.[52] "Some people appear to like owing money," Ploughman observed; "but I would as soon be a cat up a chimney with the fire going, or a fox with the hounds at my heels, or a hedgehog on a pitchfork, or a mouse

under an owl's claw."[53] These images surely communicate that Spurgeon could imagine no earthly condition more unpleasant and less desirable than the oppression of debt.

This incident of irresponsibility aside, Spurgeon was able to master whatever was set before him, and he transferred to Stockwell School in 1844. Again his mental alertness made him top of the class and gained for him, in the first year, a prize entitled "First Class English Prize" under the examination of T. W. Davids. This achievement gained for Spurgeon a book entitled *Natural History of Selbourne*. In 1848, Charles and his brother James Archer made the journey to Maidstone, southeast of London, to attend the St. Augustine's Agricultural College. Spurgeon was there for one year before he went to Newmarket in Cambridgeshire, where he also served in the capacity of usher, that is, a kind of assistant teacher or tutor. In August, 1850, he moved to another school, both to assist and to study in Cambridge, taught by a Mr. Leeding, a quite adept teacher Spurgeon had known as an usher in Colchester. Pike believes that Leeding, "next to Richard Knill, probably understood his young friend's bent of mind and developing genius better and anybody else."[54] This education came as a result of great sacrifice on the part of Spurgeon's parents who desired the best possible education non-conformity could offer in the England of their day.

At this distance, great difficulties attend any attempt to evaluate the quality of this hands-on education, either in content or pedagogical method. That his teachers felt he progressed well may be inferred from his value to them as an usher. That he felt quite confident in his progress, both in depth and in diversity, is clear from an advertisement he ran in a Cambridge newspaper near

---

51. NPSP, 1859, 362.

52. *Autobiography* 1:23, 24; Charles Spurgeon, *John Ploughman's Talk* (Ross-shire, Scotland: Christian Focus Publications, 1988), 56-63.

53. *Ploughman*, 58.

54. Pike, 1:45.

the end of 1853, while serving as pastor at Water-beach and just prior to his moving from the Park Street address in Cambridge to serve the New Park Street congregation in London.

> Number 60, Park Street Cambridge. Mr. C. H. Spurgeon begs to inform his numerous friends that after Christmas he intends on taking six or seven young gentlemen as day pupils. He will endeavor to the utmost to impart a good commercial education. The ordinary routine will include arithmetic, algebra, geometry, and Mensuration; grammar and composition; ancient and modern history; geography, natural history, astronomy, scripture and drawing; Latin and the elements of Greek and French if required.[55]

When in Maidstone, Spurgeon confronted a reasoned argument on baptism. The Anglican teacher sought to press him into an admission that the Congregational baptism of infants was invalid. The reasoning proved more ingenious than the teacher accounted for. The Bible records that only those who repent of sin and believe in Christ should be baptized. Infant baptism involves no repentance and belief; that practice, therefore, is not scriptural. The Anglican church, however, provides sponsors for the child to pledge repentance and faith in its stead. Anglican baptism conforms to Scripture, therefore, and demands the adherence of all non-conformists, so reasoned the clergyman. Spurgeon responded, "Oh no! I have been baptized once, before I ought; I will wait next time till I am fit for it." In later reflections Spurgeon wryly reported, "It is due

to the Church of England catechism that I am a Baptist."[56]

While at Newmarket, Spurgeon had confirmed for him the theology that he had imbibed from the books in his grandfather's and father's libraries as well as in their sermons. He befriended a cook, Mary King, who read the *Gospel Standard,* loved a strong Calvinist theology of experience, and attended the Bethesda Strict Baptist church. Robert Mattingly said she "was a staunch Calvinist, logical, clear-headed, and had a wonderful knowledge of the Bible."[57] Spurgeon often spoke with her of the doctrines of grace as distributed in the eternal covenant of grace and their impact on vital godliness. "I do believe," he said, "that I learnt more from her than I should have learned from any six doctors of divinity of the sort we have nowadays."[58] Some of these discussions took place in the fall of 1849 prior to his conversion "when under deep religious conviction,"[59] but those during the second half of the academic year, late winter and spring of 1850, were for mutual edification and spiritual and doctrinal instruction.

The "deep religious conviction" of which Everett spoke plagued Spurgeon for five years. Apparently, it began soon after his initial conversations with Richard Knill during one of Spurgeon's visits to his grandfather's home. The day of liberation for Spurgeon produced such joy that he could write that "one day of pardoned sin was

---

55. Drummond, 158 and Pike, 1:85. See also Spurgeon, *Autobiography,* 1:40, for an evaluation of the effectiveness of his education. J. D. Everett remembers him as a young man at fifteen whose grasp of a wide range of subjects was quite profound, accurate, and applicable. "He was a keen observer of men and manners," said Everett, "and very shrewd in his judgments." Also Pike, 1:39

56. *Autobiography,* 1:34-38.

57. Pike, 1:40.

58. *Autobiography,* 1:39.

59. Pike, 1:40. These are the words of Professor J. D. Everett who served with Spurgeon at Newmarket as an usher with him. He observed this relationship for himself. Spurgeon spoke with Everett and, in Everett's words, "told me in his own terse fashion that it was 'cook' who had taught him his theology. I hope I am not violating his confidence in mentioning this fact. It is no discredit to the memory of a great man that he was willing to learn from the humblest sources."

a sufficient recompense to the whole five years of conviction."[60] The *Autobiography* contains a twenty-three-page chapter entitled "Through Much Tribulation" in which Spurgeon chronicles his convictions and analyzes the progress and nature of such convictions for himself and for all who would be brought to Christ.

Various phrases and images used by Spurgeon to depict this work of God's Spirit are graphic and commanding. "Ten black horses were His team, and it was a sharp ploughshare that He used and the ploughers made deep furrows." "Our own vaunted strength has utterly failed us, and made us contemptible in our own eyes." "He who has stood before his God, convicted and condemned, with the rope about his neck, is the man to weep for joy when he is pardoned, to hate the evil which has been forgiven him, and to live to the honour of the Redeemer by whose blood he has been cleansed." "As soon as infancy gave way to childhood, the rod was exercised upon us. We can remember early convictions of sin, and apprehensions of the wrath of God on its account." "Who can tell how much each of these separate woundings contributed toward that killing by the law, which proved to be the effectual work of God?" "God's law was flogging me with its ten-thonged whip, and then rubbing me with brine afterwards, so that I did shake and quiver with pain and anguish, and my soul chose strangling rather than life, for I was exceeding sorrowful."[61] "Our heavenly Father does not usually cause us to seek the Saviour till He has whipped us clean out of all our confidence; He cannot make us in earnest after heaven till He has made us feel something of the intolerable tortures of an aching conscience, which is a foretaste of hell." "Was

there ever a bond-slave who had more bitterness of soul than I, five years a captive in the dungeons of the law, till my youth seemed as if it would turn into premature old age, and all the buoyancy of my spirit had vanished?" "Ah, me, how I seemed shut up then! I had offended against the justice of God; I was impure and polluted, and I used to say, 'If God does not send me to hell, He ought to do it.' I sat in judgment upon myself, and pronounced the sentence that I felt would be just." "Then I was brought down to see my corruption, my wickedness, my filthiness, for God always humbles the sinner whom He means to save."[62]

How the Spirit withers and blasts the hopes that a sinner has in his own power found expression in Spurgeon's experience. "When I was seeking the Lord, I not only believed that I could not pray without divine help, but I felt in my very soul that I could not." He could not even feel right, or moan or groan, as he wanted to, nor even long more after Christ as he knew he must. "This heart was then as hard as adamant, as dead as those that rot in their graves." He yearned for a tear, but had dry eyes, and wanted to repent, but could not, and sought belief, but found none. "I felt bound, hampered, and paralysed. This is a humbling revelation of God's Holy Spirit, but a needful one; for the faith of the flesh is not the faith of God's elect."[63] He illustrated this same truth over a decade earlier using a different image. His efforts at self-improvement only revealed a devil within him. His continued effort allowed the entrance of ten more devils. "Instead of becoming better I became worse; I had now got the devil of self-righteousness, of self-trust, and self-conceit, and many others had

---

60. *Autobiography*, 1:91.

61. "Strangling rather than life" is a phrase Spurgeon used several times when relating his personal experience to the nature of rebellion under the pressure of conviction. For example, see SEE, 12:146 and S&T, October 1871, 467.

62. Spurgeon, *Autobiography*, 1:53-72. Spurgeon uses all his powers of illustration and image to impress his readers, and hearers, of the depth of his own conviction. This was to encourage those who did feel so abandoned that hope for grace was plentiful. Those who remained casual about their sin, he hoped to arouse to conviction by these experiential expositions.

63. MTP, 1871, 380.

come and taken up their lodging-place." While he was busy sweeping and garnishing the place, the original he thought he had expelled brought with him seven others more wicked than he, and took up residence. "Ah, you may try and reform, dear friends," Spurgeon reminisced, "but you will find you can not do it, and remember even if you could, still it would not be the work which God requires." For God will not accept our self-righteous reformation, but "he will have renovation, he will have a new heart, and not a heart changed a little for the better."[64]

The word pictures that remain multiply with each sermon, each article, each lecture. Spurgeon taxed his own rich vocabulary and imagination to make his convictions and his real sinfulness clear. He even shared, using a vivid image of a rapid sea voyage, an attempt to cast himself into complete infidelity just when his convictions of his need for Christ were close to culmination. "Be thou my captain," he said to his reason as he thrust aside revelation along with any thoughts of God, Christ, heaven, and hell. "I went to the very bottom of the sea of infidelity," but the speed at which he doubted moved too rapidly until he doubted the existence of anything substantial, including himself. This shocked him back to reality and to see the necessity of God and revelation and heaven and hell. "Now, whenever I hear the sceptic's stale attacks upon the Word of God, I smile within myself, and think, 'Why, you simpleton! How can you urge such trifling objections?' I have felt, in the contentions of my own unbelief, ten times greater difficulties."[65]

Another image of the experiential history of Spurgeon's conversion he shared in a sermon entitled "The Sum and Substance of all Theology."

He supposed one of God's chosen so hardened and steeled against the wooing of God that there appeared no hope for him. Spurgeon proclaimed, "That man shall be arrested by God's grace, and that obdurate, hard-hearted one shall be made to see the mercy of God." He felt that he had been that man and if God could bend *his* will and bring *him* to Christ then none are beyond the effectual call of God. He quoted Josiah Conder's hymn.

> Why was *I* made to hear His voice,
> And enter while there's room;
> When thousands make a wretched choice,
> And rather starve than come?
>
> 'Twas the same love the spread the feast,
> That sweetly forced *me* in;
> Else *I* had still refused to taste,
> And perish'd in *my* sin.

The words, *sweetly forced me in*, were peculiarly relevant to his case, Spurgeon was convinced. "Oh, how long Jesus Christ stood at the door of my heart, and knocked, and knocked, and knocked in vain! I asked: 'Why should I leave the pleasures of this world?' Yet still He knocked, and there was music in every sound of His pleading voice." Spurgeon resisted further promptings of Christ through the Spirit, described in picturesque language, and set aside even the words of a pleading mother, "Let the Saviour in, Charlie." His actions replied, "Nay, I love thee, my mother; but I do not love Christ, thy Saviour." Black hours of sickness ensued but still he defied God with thoughts of alarming dimensions, "Nay, I fear not sickness, nor death itself; I will still defy my Maker." Then in images drawn from Solomon's Song, Spurgeon increased the drama of the conflict: "But it happened, one day, that He graciously put in His hand by the hole of the door, and I moved

---

64. SS, 5:88.

65. Spurgeon, *Autobiography*, 1:66, 67. Also see SS, 1:28. Spurgeon preached a sermon entitled "The Bible" when he gave this testimony of his brief flirtation with infidelity.

toward Him, and then I opened the door, and cried, 'Come in! Come in!'" He found, however with cutting despair, that Christ was gone. This led to search through the streets with weeping for "five long years." Christ could not be found and did not answer Spurgeon's weeping odyssey. "Oh, that I had never rejected Him? Oh, that He would but come again!" Spurgeon envisioned angels watching the mysterious change in his heart: "A great change has come over that youth; he would not let Christ in when He knocked, but now he wants Christ to come." Upon Christ's return with a desire to enter, would Spurgeon's soul again reject him? "Nay, nay; but I fell down at His feet, crying, 'Come in! Come in! thou Blessed Saviour. I have waited for Thy salvation, O my God!'" With such sweet necessity Spurgeon was "forced" and so would be all the elect. "There is no living soul beyond the reach of hope," he summarized, "no chosen one whom Christ cannot bring up even from the very gates of hell."[66]

In describing how Christ had divided the spoil with the strong, Spurgeon recounted the internal operations of Christ in his own conversion. "When the Lord Jesus Christ came into my hear—came to battle there—he did, indeed divide the spoil with the strong, for I was strong-willed, and desperately set on mischief, and for a while I was in the hand of a strong despair, out of which it seemed impossible that I should escape." Changing his images from the abstract to the concrete, Spurgeon depicted the bands that held him as "of iron, tough as steel, hardened in the fires of hell." But now Spurgeon was his, for Christ had won him, "and taken the prey from the mighty."[67]

The same struggle he described in illustrating the victorious nature of regenerating grace over the spiritual aversion of the natural man. In this short outburst of autobiography, Spurgeon combined both the inveterate resistance to spiritual things with the eventual relenting to efforts of self improvement and fleshly faith. "I must confess I never would have been saved, if I could have helped it," Spurgeon admitted. "As long as ever I could, I rebelled and revolted, and struggled against God." Every realization of spiritual duty met with stern resistance. "When he would have me pray, I would not pray: when he would have me listen to the sound of the ministry, I would not." Even moments when gospel truth softened his affections, Spurgeon mounted a counter-attack. When tears came to his eyes (something that eventually he sought according to another testimony) he wiped them away "and defied him to melt my heart." Upon the movement of his heart with the pathos of gospel truth, "I tried to divert it with sinful pleasures." As God's pursuit proved relentless, Spurgeon changed his tactic and opted for self-righteousness "and would not then have been saved, until I was hemmed in, and then he gave me that effectual blow of grace, and there was no resisting that irresistible effort of his grace." His depraved will succumbed, "and made me bow myself before the scepter of grace." Then he made universal application of his own experience of conquering grace: "Where God determines to save, save he will. God will have the sinner, if he designs to save him. God never was thwarted yet in any one of his purposes."[68]

A Memorable Conversion

An evangelical relic was bought and placed in the Stockwell Orphanage by its headmaster, V. J. Charlesworth. That relic was the elevated pulpit and staircase of the Artillery Street Primitive

---

66. S&T, April 1892. "The Sum and Substance of all Theology" preached in 1861.

67. S&T, February 1882, 53.

68. SS, 5:92.

Methodist Church from which an anonymous preacher spun the sermonic spell that lifted Spurgeon into heaven.[69] The events that led him to embrace Christ in the full pardon of sin, in Spurgeon's view of divine operations, were historical manifestations of a divine purpose irresistibly effected. His *Autobiography* expressed this in language strikingly reminiscent of sermonic accounts. "God gave me the effectual blow, and I was obliged to submit to that irresistible effort of His grace. It conquered my depraved will, and made me bow myself before His gracious sceptre."[70] In a communion sermon at Mentone, Spurgeon summarized the entire experience of conviction and conversion, telescoping it into a single mental and spiritual visit from a holy and offended, but yet gracious, Christ. The range of spiritual encounters in this visitation gave rise to a strikingly intense description of its impact. "The first discovery of his injured love was overpowering," Spurgeon recounted; "its very hopefulness increased my anguish; for then I saw that I had slain the Lord who had come to save me." He experienced the withering effect of the holy scrutiny to which Christ subjects his people.

> I do remember well when God first visited me; and assuredly it was the night of nature, of ignorance, of sin. His visit had the same effect upon me that it had upon Saul of Tarsus when the Lord spake to him out of heaven. He brought me down from the high horse and caused me to fall to the ground; by the brightness of the light of his Spirit he made me grope in conscious blindness; and in the brokenness of my heart I cried, "Lord, what wilt thou have me to do?" I felt that I had been rebelling against the

Lord, kicking against the pricks, and doing evil even as I could; and my soul was filled with anguish at the discovery. Very searching was the glance of the eye of Jesus, for it revealed my sin, and caused me to go out and weep bitterly. As when the Lord visited Adam and called him to stand naked before him, so was I stripped of all my righteousness before the face of the Most High. Yet the visit ended not there; for as the Lord God clothed our first parents in coats of skins, so did he cover me with the righteousness of the great sacrifice, and he gave me songs in the night. It was night, but the visit was no dream; in fact, I there and then ceased to dream, and began to deal with the reality of things.[71]

It happened on January 6, 1850.[72] School had dismissed early because of an outbreak of fever. Spurgeon's spiritual struggles were not left at Newmarket but clung to him as he made his journey home to Colchester. Unable to go with his father to his church in Tolesbury because of the snow, Spurgeon made his way to a Primitive Methodist Chapel on Artillery Street. According to his recollection the minister that day did not appear, and so an unlearned Methodist exhorter rose to give a brief message on Isaiah 45:22: "Look unto me and be ye saved, all the ends of the earth; for I am God and there is none else." The man recognized that a heavy-hearted visitor was among their small number and he expostulated with Spurgeon directly to look to Christ. He asked Spurgeon to obey his text. Christ has bled and died, risen from the dead and ascended to heaven, He alone can save. It is not a matter of

---

69. Bob L. Ross, *A Pictorial Biography of C. H. Spurgeon* (Pasadena, TX: Pilgrim Publications, 1974), 25; Also G. Holden Pike, *Charles Haddon Spurgeon* (New York: Funk & Wagnalls, 1892), 202.

70. Spurgeon, *Autobiography*, 1:71.

71. S&T, December 1886, 610.

72. Spurgeon, *Autobiography*, 1:125. Spurgeon wrote a diary of his spiritual contemplations from April 6, 1850 through June 20. The first entry says, "Born, January 6, 1850." Some controversy has ensued on the accuracy of Spurgeon's own recollection of this date, as well as who the preacher was when he was converted. Drummond discusses both these issues and their controversial points (Drummond, 114-31).

lifting a finger, or a foot, or going to college or being rich. Look, Look, Look, the man said, look to Christ and live. Spurgeon looked and "saw at once the way of salvation."[73]

References to this event are scattered throughout the entire corpus of Spurgeon's sermons. The snowy day itself provided reference for sermons. Preaching on the similitudes and parables of nature and providence, Spurgeon noted, "I remember well, how once God preached to me by a similitude in the depth of winter." Like his own soul in the midst of its struggle, the earth had been black, and there was scarcely a green thing or a flower to be seen. He could see over the landscape nothing but blackness, bareness, leaflessness—deadness wherever one looked. And then, that morning, "On a sudden God spake and unlocked the treasures of the snow, and white flakes descended until there was no blackness to be seen, and all was one sheet of dazzling whiteness." That was the time he was "seeking the Saviour, and it was then I found him." He remembered the sermon in the snow that said "Come now, and let us reason together; though your sins be as scarlet they shall be as snow, though they be red like crimson they shall be whiter than wool."[74] On that day his poor black soul was covered with the spotless purity of the Son of God.

The text used by the preacher seemed an inexhaustible gold mine of riches for gospel issues. The first Sabbath morning of 1856 fell on the day of Spurgeon's conversion six years before. Understandably, he preached on Isaiah 45:22 and entitled the sermon "Sovereignty and Salvation." He began, "Six years ago, today, as near as possible at this very hour of the day, I was 'in the gall of bitterness and in the bonds of iniquity,' but had yet, by divine grace, been led to feel the bitterness

of that bondage and to cry out by reason of the soreness of its slavery." In a fruitless quest for rest, Spurgeon "stepped within the house of God and sat there—afraid to look upward—lest I should be utterly cut off and lest His fierce wrath should consume me." The preacher for the day rose in his pulpit and read his text, "Look unto Me and be you saved, all the ends of the earth, for I am God and there is none else." Briefly, Spurgeon retold the event in a poignant sentence: "I looked that moment; the grace of faith was vouchsafed to me in the self-same instant." Spurgeon could "never forget that day while memory holds its place", nor could he help repeating the text that was the means of his saving knowledge of God. "How wonderfully and marvelously kind," he marveled, "that he who heard these words so little time ago for his own soul's profit, should now address you this morning, as his hearers, from the same text." He held a confident hope that "some poor sinner within these walls may hear the glad tidings of salvation for himself also and may today, on this 6th of January, be 'turned from darkness to light and from the power of Satan unto God.'"[75] As the twenty-two-year-old Spurgeon recounted the moment in which the preacher shouted for him to look, he stated, "I looked that moment; the grace was vouchsafed to me in the self-same instant; and now I think I can say with truth,

> Ere since by faith I saw the stream
> His flowing wounds supply,
> Redeeming love has been my theme,
> And shall be till I die.[76]

Later that year, in September, preaching out of doors before 12,000 people on the subject of "Heaven and Hell," Spurgeon closed with his per-

---

73. Spurgeon, *Autobiography*, 1:88.

74. NPSP, 1858, 333; SS, 5:120.

75. SS, 1:1, 2.

76. Ibid., 1.

sonal testimony as a compelling call to escape hell and be found in heaven. He began with a narrative of the severity of his conviction, "when my sins first stared me in the face. I thought myself the most accursed of all men." Though he had not committed great and open transgressions against God, he knew that he had sinned against much greater light than others and therefore "I thought my sins were thus greater than other people's." Cries for mercy were met with doubts of God's willingness to pardon him. "Month after month," he told, "I cried to God, but He did not hear me and I knew not what it was to be saved." He wished to die, but the remembrance of the worse world that awaited halted any action that would make him meet his Maker unprepared. God is a "most heartless tyrant," he thought, "because He did not answer my prayer." Then he would recall that hell he deserved and that to be sent there would be just. In this personal narrative, Spurgeon summarized the sermon's emphasis on the rightness of God's judgment in assigning hell as the destination of sinners. In that state of mind he "stepped into a place of worship and saw a tall thin man step into the pulpit—I have never seen him from that day and probably never shall, till we meet in Heaven." The man opened his Bible and "read with a feeble voice, 'Look unto Me and be you saved, all the ends of the earth. For I am God and beside Him there is none else.' Ah," Spurgeon continued, "I am one of the ends of the earth. And then, turning round and fixing his gaze on me, as if he knew me, the minister said, 'Look, look, look.' Why, I thought I had a great deal to *DO*, but I found it was only to *LOOK*. I thought I had a garment to spin out for myself—but I found that if I looked Christ would give me a garment." Then to those standing in the twilight hour of evening, having just moments prior endured Spurgeon's ferocious description of God's

vengeance standing over them with all of creation consenting to this glorious display of wrath, Spurgeon called, as he had heard his converting evangelist call, "Look, sinner—that is to be saved. Look unto Him all you ends of the earth and be saved."[77]

Speaking on justification in 1857, Spurgeon asked, "Oh! Have you ever seen the justified man when he is first justified?" He reminded them of how often he had spoken of his own first realization of pardon through the blood of Christ. "I had been sad and miserable for months, and even years; but when I once received the message, 'Look unto me and be ye saved, all ye ends of the earth,' verily, I could have leapt for joy of heart; I felt that I understood that text, 'The mountains and hills shall break forth before you into singing, and all the trees of the field shall clap their hands.'"[78]

When the Metropolitan Tabernacle first opened its doors for worship and its pulpit for preaching, Spurgeon again used his testimony to close a service. On Easter Sunday, at the end of the first week of inaugural services, Spurgeon preached on "Temple Glories," and closed the sermon with a simple gospel presentation, saying, "I do not think that on this first occasion I can do it better than by simply telling the story of how I was brought to Christ myself."[79] The basic outline as well as outcome is the same in each telling but each has emphases relevant to the context of preaching and each gives nuances of details that might be passed over in some other rendition. In this one Spurgeon included a memorable part of the preacher's exhortation, "Do not look to the Father to know whether you are elected or not, you shall find that out afterwards; look to

---

77. Ibid., 318, 319.

78. SS, 4:69.

79. MTP, 1861, 223.

me; look to Christ. Do not look to God the Holy Spirit to know whether he had called you or not; that you shall discover by-and-by. Look unto Jesus Christ; and then he went on in his own simple way to put it thus: – Look unto me; I am sweating great drops of blood for you; look unto me, I am scourged and spit upon; I am nailed to the cross, I die, I am buried, I rise and ascend, I am pleading before the Father's throne, and all this for you."[80] The man looked under the gallery and said, "Young man, you are very miserable." Spurgeon admitted that he was but that he was not accustomed to public remarks made about it. "Ah!, and you will always be miserable if you don't do as my text tells you; that is, look to Christ." Spurgeon, at that moment, stood in the newly finished, beautifully appointed, aesthetically enchanting Metropolitan Tabernacle "to preach in this great building the self-same gospel in the same simple tones. Sinners, look to Christ and be saved."[81]

Though much has been made of the intricate net of providence that brought about all the details of Spurgeon's moment of looking for life, and although efforts to specify the name of the preacher on that snowy day have met with frustration, and even doubt has been cast on the accuracy of Spurgeon's recollection of the date, he was abundantly clear in his immediate response that the work was the culmination of a lifetime of nurture in gospel-truth from his mother. On May 1, two days before his baptism, Spurgeon testified, "You, my Mother, have been the great means in God's hand of rendering me what I hope I am." He recalled the "kind, warning Sabbath-evening addresses" that were "too deeply settled on my heart to be forgotten." Her consistent admonitions "prepared the way for the preached Word,

and for that holy book, *The Rise and Progress*."[82] Through her influence he was ready to follow his Savior not only into the water but into the fire. "I love you as the preacher to my heart of such courage," he confided, and called her his "praying, watching Mother."[83]

The years did not diminish his conviction that "the solemn words of my good mother," the straightforward, earnest and specific application of biblical verses to his spiritual condition finally culminated in his conversion. After applying a verse-by-verse explanation of the Bible to each child, she would read from Alleine's *Alarm* or Baxter's *Call* and pry into the conscience of each with questions about how long they would linger in their unconverted state before seeking Christ. At her prayer she would plead for their souls; on one occasion she closed, "Now, Lord, if my children go on in their sins, it will not be from ignorance that they perish, and my soul must bear witness against them at the day of judgment if they lay not hold of Christ." Those words, that vision of a mother bearing witness against him, so Spurgeon testified, "pierced my conscience, and stirred my heart." [84]

The event laid the foundation for a story Spurgeon told very early in his ministry in a sermon entitled "Heaven and Hell", based on

80. Ibid., 224.
81. Ibid.

82. He refers to Philip Doddridge's book, *The Rise and Progress of Religion in the Soul*. Spurgeon kept up his regard for this work and for Doddridge as a biblical expositor and evangelist. Doddridge's academy, however, with its non-confessional open-endedness became a symbol to Spurgeon of how quickly decline could set in to an educational enterprise that was not clearly established on a confessional basis.

83. Written May 1, 1850, and contained in Charles Spurgeon, *The Letters of C. H. Spurgeon*, collected and collated by his son Charles Spurgeon, 1923, accessed on line at http://www.spurgeon.org/misc/letters.htm. This will be referred to as Spurgeon, *Letters*.

84. Spurgeon, *Autobiography*, 1:44. He records the memory in almost the same words in his sermon "Children Brought to Christ, not to the Font" (SS, 8:44).

Matthew 8:11-12. In the *Autobiography,* this anecdote focuses on a prayer at the end of an evening of family worship; in the sermon, it is told as a dream that a mother had and shared with her children. It would be quite easy for both accounts to be true and complementary, giving a more detailed picture of how that memorable evening unfolded that so framed Spurgeon's conscience about his culpability. "That was a dreadful dream," Spurgeon began the illustration, "which a pious mother once had, and told to her children."

> She thought the judgment day was come. The great books were opened. They all stood before God. And Jesus Christ said, "Separate the chaff from the wheat; put the goats on the left hand, and the sheep on the right." The mother dreamed that she and her children were standing just in the middle of the great assembly. And the angel came, and said, "I must take the mother, she is a sheep: she must go to the right hand. The children are goats: they must go on the left."

She thought as she went, her children clutched her, and said, "Mother, can we part? Must we be separated?" She then put her arms around them, and seemed to say, "My children, I would, if possible, take you with me." But in a moment the angel touched her; her cheeks were dried, and now, overcoming natural affection, being rendered supernatural and sublime, resigned to God's will, she said, "My children, I taught you well, I trained you up, and you forsook the ways of God; and now all I have to say is, Amen to your condemnation." Thereupon they were snatched away, and she saw them in perpetual torment, while she was in heaven. Young man, what will you think, when the last day comes, to hear Christ say, "Depart, ye cursed?" and there will be a voice just behind him, saying, Amen. And, as you inquire

whence comes the voice, you will find it was your mother.[85]

How could one so well schooled in the details of the gospel be so long in such turmoil over the way of salvation? Carlile remarked about this puzzling phenomenon: "Poor boy, brought up upon books of devotion: Dr. Doddridge's *Life and Progress of Religion in the Soul,* Baxter's *Call to the Unconverted,* and yet, not knowing the way. In truth the wind bloweth where it listeth."[86]

Spurgeon applied the doctrines of total depravity and effectual call to his own experience. In one of his earliest books, *The Saint and His Saviour,* the first chapter begins with an autobiographical recounting of the advantages of his childhood against which he sinned. "It would not be easy for some of us to recall the hour when we first heard the name of Jesus." He goes on, "In very infancy that sweet sound was a familiar to our ear as the hush of lullaby." He recalled the early impressions of church attendance, family worship, the Bible, hymn-singing, and fervent prayer. Visiting preachers often prayed invoking blessings on his young life, while at the end of such prayer he heard his mother's "Amen," thankful that her only "Amen" was not in confirmation of his condemnation. In spite of all this, being born in sin and shapen in iniquity, "These heavenly privileges did not of themselves avail to give us love to Jesus and pardon by his blood." Spurgeon concluded from his experience of privilege coupled with unbelief that he was a witness to the "fact of innate depravity, the birth-plague of man; and we can testify to the doctrine that grace, and grace alone, can change the heart."[87]

---

85. *SS,* 1:311, 312.

86. J. C. Carlile, *Charles H. Spurgeon: An Interpretative Biography* (London: The Religious Tract Society, 1933), 37, 38.

87. Spurgeon, *The Saint and His Saviour* (Ross-shire, Scotland: Christian Focus Publications, 1989) 1, 2.

The theology with which he interpreted his conversion, that is, the dependence on sovereign grace, was not the contrivance of years of reading and contemplation, but an immediate response to his early training as he reflected on the event. Three months after his conversion he told his father, "This faith is far more than any of us deserve; all beyond hell is mercy, but this is a mighty one. Were it not all of sovereign, electing, almighty grace, I, for one, could never hope to be saved. God says, 'You shall,' and not all the devils in hell, let loose upon a real Christian, can stop the workings of God's sovereign grace, for in due time the Christian cries, 'I will.'"[88] He had heard the gospel from his mother, his father, his grandfather, he had read the Bible and many good books; still, however, "when the Word of the Lord came to me with power, it was as new as if I had lived among the unvisited tribes of Central Africa, and had never heard the tidings of the cleansing fountain filled with blood, drawn from the Saviour's veins." Again he states, "It came to me as a new revelation, as fresh as if I had never read in Scripture that Jesus was declared to be the propitiation for sins that God might be just."[89]

A Paradigm of Grace

This experience remained fresh all of his ministry and gave an instant source for illustration or explanation of an experiential issue concerning a doctrine or text. Spurgeon was filled to the brim and overflowing with the divine reality of the work of the Trinity for a sinner's salvation, for he knew its truths from divine revelation in Scripture and personal regeneration. His unbearable rebellion and convictions ever loomed horrendously potent. In a message entitled "A Visit to Christ's Hospital," he recounted the pain of recalling

"when I was in this way myself; when I poor fool, because of my transgressions and my iniquities was sorely bowed in spirit. By day I thought of the punishment of my sin; by night I dreamed of it."[90] In "The Garment of Praise" Spurgeon described his own rebellion as defiance of the most irrational sort. How could he, he reasoned, "a creature that God has made, which he could crush as easily as a moth, have dared to live in enmity to him for many years"? When told of God's great love, Spurgeon "turned on [his] heel and rejected it."[91] He was able to describe in detail the mental anguish of an awakened mourner, for

> I have felt the same, that all hope that you shall be saved is taken away, and that you are utterly prostrate. ... I know what I am saying, that next to the torment of hell itself, there is but one sorrow which is more severe than that of a broken and a contrite spirit that trembles at God's word, but does not dare to suck comfort out of it. The bitterness of remorse and despair is worse; but yet it is unspeakable heart-breaking to bow at the mercy seat, and to fear that no answer will ever come; to lie at the feet of Jesus, but to be afraid to look up to him for salvation.[92]

He illustrated the desperate measures that a sinner in search of an eased conscience will take if hope may be found. He dashes pride to the ground, loses his sectarian spirit, and yearns for the place that he might find solace. "I know it was so with me," Spurgeon emphasized; "I never thought of going to the despised chapel where I was first brought to know the Lord, but it snowed so hard that I could not go to a more respectable place." Once in, Spurgeon related how the blessed message that his conscience craved reached him.

---

88. Murray, *Letters*, 24.

89. Spurgeon, *Autobiography*, 1:84, 80.

90. S&T, October 1871, 466.

91. SEE, 12:146.

92. Ibid., 144-45.

"When I got in, the preacher read his text—'Look unto me, and be ye saved, all the ends of the earth.' It was a blessed text and blessedly applied: but if there had been any stickling as to going into places, I should not have been there."[93]

Such distress on the part of a seeking sinner is itself an element of effectual calling. None would so earnestly grasp for forgiveness, in its real sense, but those in whom a divine work is proceeding. Again his experience illustrates the beautiful contours of the biblical doctrine.

> I believe God was at work with my heart for years before I knew anything about him. I knew there was a work; I knew I prayed, and cried, and groaned for mercy, but I did not know that was the Lord's work; I half thought it was my own. I did not know till afterwards, when I was led to know Christ as all my salvation, and all my desire, that *the Lord* had called the child, for this could not have been the result of nature, it must have been the effect of grace.[94]

Just as vivid in its presence, however, stood the reality of the moment of acceptance. It could be the same for any awakened sinner. "My soul melts in gratitude when I think of the infinite mercy of God to me in the hour when I came seeking mercy at his hands. Oh! Why will you not also come?"[95] That mourning can be turned to joy is proven in his experience of deliverance. "Some of us can never forget the hour of our great deliverance, it was the day of our espousals, the time of love, and it must for ever remain as the beginning of days unto us."[96]

That the years did not tend to exaggerate Spurgeon's interpretation of the clarity that comes to the mind about spiritual issues at conversion may be seen from a letter written to his father just three weeks after he looked to Jesus, and lived. Using the language of the senses, Spurgeon marveled that he "should have been so long time blind to those celestial wonders, which now I can in a measure behold!" He wanted to speak freely and unceasingly of the love of Jesus that "has opened mine eyes," and allowed him to say, "Now I see Him, I can firmly trust to Him for my eternal salvation." When he doubted, God renewed his faith and gave him confidence of his saving interest in Christ. He felt he could "give up everything for Christ," but even that would be nothing of a return in comparison to the love of Jesus. "How sweet is prayer!" he could say and lament any tendency to neglect it; "I would be always engaged in it." Moreover, "How beautiful is the Bible! I never loved it so before; it seems to me as necessary food." Such radical change in perception, such genuine knowledge, Spurgeon believed, could never have come without the Spirit's granting of life.[97]

A Baptist Baptism

One of the earliest fruits of his God-centered and Bible-centered transformation was a conscientious conviction about public profession of union with Christ. Spurgeon wrote his mother, "I should like to be always reading my Bible," which pleased her much, but the practice led him also to desire the kind of baptism pictured and practiced in the New Testament, a conclusion that confused her. His father and grandfather did not practice believers' baptism, why should he differ from them? The only thing that drove him to this divergence was the necessity of initiating his Christian life by punctilious obedience to re-

93. SS, 3:96.

94. NPSP, 1859, 132.

95. MTP, 1871, 392-93.

96. SEE, 12:148.

97. Murray, *Letters*, 19, 20.

vealed truth, as he saw it. "From the Scriptures," an auspicious assertion of foundation, "is it not apparent that, immediately upon receiving the Lord Jesus, it is a part of duty openly to profess Him?" Yes, and how? "I firmly believe and consider that baptism is the command of Christ, and shall not feel quite comfortable if I do not receive it."[98] Spurgeon had developed this conviction earlier, before his conversion, and now followed that early commitment to be baptized as a believer. At Maidstone, under the influence of his Anglican teacher, he had concluded that infant baptism had no support in the Bible. The Bible makes faith a prerequisite to baptism, so his teacher argued, but Independents baptize infants without faith. Anglicans, however, baptize infants with a sponsor that pledges faith for them. The young Spurgeon did not quite follow that logic and concluded that the Anglican was partially right and, therefore, wholly wrong. Should he ever be converted, he resolved, he would experience the ordinance in obedience to Scripture on the basis of his own faith, not that of another. In February he wrote his mother, "Conscience has convinced me that it is a duty to be buried with Christ in baptism, although I am sure it constitutes no part of salvation."[99]

In April, Spurgeon became a member of the Congregational church in Newmarket, writing his father with the news, "You will be pleased to hear that, last Thursday night, I was admitted as a member." This privilege came through some real determination on his part because the pastor had refused to meet with him and thus avoided the issue of membership until Spurgeon himself proposed that he be received at a church meeting. Even at that, he refused to participate in communion because he still was exercised in conscience about the issue of baptism, believing that he should not partake of the ordinance of union with the church until he had publicly submitted to the ordinance of union with Christ. He had come to believe that baptism must precede participation in the Lord's Supper: "I did not sit down at the Lord's table, and cannot in conscience do so until I am baptised." He allowed others freedom of conscience to do as they saw fit, but for him it would be "to tumble over the wall, since I feel persuaded it is Christ's appointed way of professing Him."[100]

Spurgeon had learned of a Baptist minister at Isleham named W. W. Cantlow. He had requested baptism from him, Cantlow had consented, but now Spurgeon awaited the permission of his parents. "As Mr Cantlow's baptising season will come round this month," he reminded his father, "I have humbly to beg your consent, as I will not act against your will." His father might have felt that Spurgeon's strong conviction on this point indicated too much trust in a form of baptism. Spurgeon assured him that he hated the idea of baptismal regeneration, did not entertain it for a moment concerning himself, but only wanted to follow his conscientious belief that the New Testament taught the immersion of believers only. His father's answer was slow in coming. As the date for communion got nearer, Charles wrote an urgent letter to his mother soliciting her intervention in case his father was hardening against his son's wishes. "I have every morning looked for a letter from Father," making no attempt to hide his anxiety over this; "I long for an answer; it is now a month since I have had one from him. Do, if you please, send me either permission or refusal to be baptized; I have been kept in painful suspense."[101]

---

98. Ibid., 20.

99. Ibid., 22.

100. Ibid., 23.

101. Spurgeon, *Letters*, April 20th, 1850.

This deference toward parents Spurgeon re-called in a sermon on baptism he preached in 1890. "I remember in my own case, my parents not believing in the baptism of believers, and I, being between fifteen and sixteen years of age, thought it my duty to consult my father and mother, and ask their counsel and advice." He felt that this was the right thing to do in his case, since he did not expect them "to see with me, but I did expect them to give me their loving concur-rence, which they did." He believed that in such a case other young people should do the same, though obedience to the Lord in this matter is always of urgent necessity.[102]

His father gave Charles permission to fol-low his own conscience on the matter, but could not embrace that conviction himself. When he served as honorary Chair of a meeting of the Metropolitan Tabernacle at the festivities open-ing the building in 1861, he said, "I rejoice there is so much harmony between us, even though we may differ, perhaps, in some points of view." By that he meant baptism for, pointing to the bap-tistery he continued, "I do not see clearly into this water before me, but if I did I would go down and be baptized at once." He then surveyed the crowd and urged them, "If there are any friends here tonight who have duly weighed this matter, and feel that Christ has commanded you to fol-low him there, it is your sin if you live another week without it."[103]

On May 3, 1850, his mother's birthday, Spur-geon walked eight miles with Mr. Cantlow to Isleham Ferry on the river Lark. The river divides

Suffolk from Cambridgeshire. There he was bap-tized along with two young ladies. The first bap-tism recorded at Isleham occurred in 1798 when Andrew Fuller baptized a father and his son and three others. The day of Spurgeon's baptism was cool and the gusty wind made the elements of baptism startling and bracing. One of the aides had started a peat fire for warmth and onlookers stood in boats and on the ferry and on the bank. Spurgeon describes the thoroughly solemn joy he experienced.

> The wind blew down the river with a cutting blast, as my turn came to wade into the flood, but after I had walked a few steps, and noted the people on the ferry-boats, and in boats, and on either shore, I felt as if Heaven, and earth, and hell, might all gaze upon me, for I was not ashamed, there and then, to own myself a follower of the Lamb. My timidity was washed away; it floated down the river into the sea, and must have been devoured by the fishes, for I have never felt anything of the kind since. Baptism also loosed my tongue, and from that day it has never been quiet. I lost a thousand fears in that River Lark, and found that "in keeping his commandments there is great reward."[104]

The story has been told often, and as true it bears repeating. Spurgeon's mother remarked that when she prayed the Lord would convert her eldest son, she did not request that he would become a Baptist. Young Spurgeon replied, "Ah, mother! The Lord has answered your prayer with His usual bounty, and given you exceeding abun-dantly above what you asked or thought."[105]

All of these events came back vividly to Spur-geon twenty-eight years later when he received a note from the vicar of Isleham that W. W. Cantlow had died. He reminisced, "We shall never forget

102. MTP, 1892, 461. Spurgeon had died on January 31 of this year and he had not preached in the Tabernacle since June 7 of the previous year. The 1892 volume, as those of all subsequent years, was filled with sermons preached on different occasions in earlier years, but not yet published. This sermon was preached on February 9, 1890.

103. MTP, 1861, 253.

104. Spurgeon, *Autobiography*, 1:149, 150.

105. *Autobiography*, 1:45.

rising early that morning at break of day for prayer, and then walking along the lonely country road in quiet meditation from Newmarket to Isleham to the house of Mr. Cantlow." Spurgeon recalled his kindly smile and the holy delight he exhibited when he welcomed the youth "who desired to confess his Lord in the Scriptural fashion." Cantlow encouraged him with many loving words. There in the vestry, for the first time, Spurgeon opened his mouth in prayer in a congregation of adults. "In the extremely gentle and cordial companionship of the pastor we spent a very happy evening, which we recollect was very cold, so that a peat fire, whose white appearance we still remember, was needed to warm the room."[106] Cantlow had been pastor of the congregation for thirty-two years when feebleness made him step down to be succeeded, in an unusual providence, by a student from Spurgeon's College, J. A. Wilson.[107]

This reminder of Cantlow also inflamed Spurgeon's resolute clarity on baptism. "We wish that all other believers were led to make a serious point of commencing their visible connection with the church by the ordinance which symbolizes death to the world, burial with Christ, and resurrection to newness of life." Reliving that experience, Spurgeon pictured the "open stream, the crowded banks, and the solemn plunge" which continued to operate as a "spur to duty and a seal of consecration." He wanted no controversy on that point for "he who first saved me, afterwards accepted me, spirit, soul, and body, as his servant, in token whereof this mortal frame was immersed beneath the wave." That outward sign continued to serve to "bring vividly before the mind and heart the spiritual meaning, and therefore is it dearly loved, for his sake who both ordained the ordinance and himself submitted to it."[108]

Christ's own submission to baptism prompted one of Spurgeon's special visits during his Roman holiday in 1871. Going to a catacomb outside the walls of Rome he descended deep into the ground where eight paths converged. Seven were closed but the one he came particularly to see held just what he had desired—a baptistery. He described it as "full of sweet, clear, running water and about four feet deep." A fresco was painted above it of Jesus standing up to his waist in the water with John the Baptist having placed his hand on Jesus' head. Spurgeon explained the posture as indicating that Christ was to be immersed. "He was not pouring the water on him. Here we stood, and prayed to the blessed one into whose Name we had been buried by baptism. It was a solemn moment."[109]

The spiritual power of obedience to the command and example of baptism had an immediate impact on Spurgeon. His *Autobiography,* under the oversight of Susannah, contains a diary that encircles his baptism, a three-month period of deep spiritual contemplation and comments on his daily activities. He gave it to Susannah soon after their marriage for her safe keeping; he never wanted to see it again.[110] Its dated entries run from April 6 through June 20, 1850. On the day of his baptism he wrote, "Blest pool! Sweet emblem of my death to all the world! May I, henceforward, live alone for Jesus!" Other words of devotion were followed with a vow: "I vow to glory alone in Jesus and His cross, and to spend my life in the extension of His cause, in whatsoever way He pleases. I desire to be sincere in this solemn profession, having but one object in view, and that to glorify God." Then, as an immediate recognition of the only power that could enable fidelity to such a vow, Spurgeon's white heat of excitement erupted in praise and prayer: "Blessing upon Thy

106. S&T, July 1878, 362.

107. Ibid.

108. Ibid.

109. *Autobiography,* 2:206.

110. *Autobiography,* 1:123.

name that Thou hast supported me through the day; it is Thy strength alone that could do this. Thou hast—Thou wilt. Thou hast enabled me to profess Thee, help me now to honour Thee, and carry out my profession, and live the life of Christ on earth!"[111]

Charles the Baptist

Spurgeon did not become a member of the church at Isleham, probably because of the difficulty of attending due to distance. He continued with the Independent congregation in Newmarket and partook of the Lord's Supper for the first time on May 5, "a royal feast for me, worthy of a King's son."[112] His days filled up tightly with class, study, and tract work and his diary filled up with rapidly maturing expressions of spiritual perception combined with theological application. One finds in these months the kinds of thought directed toward himself and his early Christian pilgrimage that colored his sermons for the next forty-two years. He confessed his own lukewarmness and lamented the "joking and levity" in a Sunday School teachers' meeting. After hearing a sermon on 1 Corinthians 4:7 he reflected, "Truly, I have nothing which I have not received; I can boast of no inherent righteousness. Had the Lord not chosen me, I should not have chosen Him." The whole transaction of divine initiative never lost its glow for Spurgeon. "Grace! Grace! Grace! 'Tis all of grace. I can do nothing, I am less than nothing, yet what a difference—once a slave of hell, now the son of the God of Heaven! Help me to walk worthy of my lofty and exalted vocation!"[113]

His abiding sense of divine sovereignty so engulfed his soul that he could not pass a day of

diary entry without an energetic burst of adoration of divine wisdom and mercy. His ability to apply these truths so gracefully and naturally in his preaching emerged out of the depth of his personal persuasion of their saving operation in his own case. "The Lord has visited me from on high. Rejoice, O my soul, leap for joy, renew thy strength; run, run, in the name of the Lord!" he wrote on May 19. "Free grace, sovereign love, eternal security are my safeguards; what shall keep me from consecrating all to Thee, even to the last drop of my blood?," he asked on May 25. He confided to his diary on May 29, "How happy am I to be one of His chosen, His elect, in whom His soul delighteth. ... Make me Thy faithful servant, O my God; may I honour Thee in my day and generation, and be consecrated for ever to Thy service!" The next to the last dated entry was on June 19, his birthday, when he noted that his true life began only at his conversion.

> My birthday. Sixteen years have I lived upon this earth, and yet I am only six months old! I am very young in grace. Yet how much time have I wasted, dead in trespasses and sins, without life, without God, in the world! What a mercy that I did not perish in my sin! How glorious is my calling, how exalted my election, born of the Lord—regenerate! Help me more than ever to walk worthily, as becomes a saint![114]

In an undated addition, near the end of the manuscript, Spurgeon penned a prayer that distilled the nature of his pastoral ministry, soon to be inaugurated. "May I know the joy and have the faith of God's elect; may I rejoice in free sovereign grace, saving me from the guilt and power of sin! Grace is a glorious theme, above the loftiest flights of the most soaring angel, or the most

---

111. Ibid., 131f.
112. Ibid., 132.
113. Ibid., 134.

114. Ibid., 142.

exalted conceptions of one of the joint-heirs with Jesus." He closed the paragraph with a statement of the confidence that sustained him in the fulfillment of his closing request. "All power is God's, and all is engaged to protect and preserve me. Let me have my daily grace, peace and comfort, zeal and love, give me some work, and give me strength to do it to Thy glory!"[115]

When Spurgeon went to Cambridge in the autumn, he joined the St. Andrew's Street Baptist Church there. Drummond states that Robert Hall served as pastor when Spurgeon joined,[116] but surely he meant to say that Spurgeon joined the church once served by Robert Hall. Hall served the church from 1791 to 1806 and died in 1831, three years before Spurgeon's birth. Another who served the church was Robert Robinson. Both Robinson and Hall were considered among the intelligentsia of English clergy. Robinson's reputation for orthodoxy declined in his last years and he died claimed by the Unitarians. Hall's theology started with a degree of suspicion and moved in a more orthodox direction. He was noted as one of the greatest orators of the English pulpit and among the most formidable advocates of civil liberty in the history of the English nation. When Spurgeon joined St. Andrew's Street Baptist Church he wrote his mother about the excellent preaching of Mr. Roffe.[117] In a letter to his father he remarked, "The Baptists are by far the most respectable denomination in Cambridge."[118] Early in October he wrote his mother about the fellowship at the church in Cambridge. "I have found a great many Christian friends; last Sunday

I had two invitations to tea. I went to the house of Mr. Watts, a coal merchant, and spent the time very happily. We read round with the children, and it seemed just like home-days."[119] This Mr. Watts probably was the person that Spurgeon hailed as brother after a communion service and received the response, "You have the advantage of me. ... I don't know what you mean." When Spurgeon reminded him that they had just taken communion together and he meant it, the man was rebuked gently and amused at the forthrightness of the sixteen-year-old Spurgeon. A friendly conversation resulted in an invitation to tea and eventually a standing invitation for every week.

Spurgeon had unshakeable Baptist convictions. He said, "I became a Baptist through reading the New Testament—especially in the Greek." Baptism was an ordinance of Christ, specifically commanded by him, a token to the believer of cleansing, "the emblem of his burial with his Lord, and the outward avowal of his new birth."[120] Though he refused to be rigidly sectarian in attitude, Spurgeon wanted to leave no doubt that he followed the Lord's command openly. He gloried in Anglicans such as Whitefield and Toplady, embraced certain aspects of the experiential religion of Methodist Wesley, highly respected the Congregational Independents and the old Puritans, found much to admire and emulate in the Scottish Presbyterians, read widely in both Luther and Calvin, and found the Dutch Orthodox very edifying in much of what they wrote. In 1853, in fact, he wrote a letter to his uncle encouraging him to be baptized at a baptism he was holding at Waterbeach on October 19. He said in his ingenuous style, "I should like to see my uncle following his Master in the water. I am almost afraid to mention the subject lest anyone should charge

---

115. Ibid.

116. Drummond, 158.

117. Spurgeon, *Letters*, to his mother, October, 1850.

118. Murray, *Letters*, 29. Spurgeon mentions three Baptist chapels: St. Andrew's Street, where he joined; Zion chapel, and Eden chapel. "Most respectable" includes the dissenting, or nonconformist, churches.

119. Spurgeon, *Letters*, October 3, 1850, to his mother.

120. *Autobiography*, 1:150-51.

me with giving it undue prominence." To put a punctuation mark on his wide affections he emphasized near the close, "I wish to live in unity with every believer, whether Calvinist, Arminian, Churchman, Independent, or Wesleyan; and though I firmly believe they are tottering, I do not like them well enough to prop them up by my wrangling at them."[121] Almost three decades later he still would testify after having been chastened for his "undenominational" remarks at a Ragged-school meeting consisting of Bible teachers from several church affiliations, "The whole truth is dear to us; bodies of men formed into denominations cannot enslave us so as to make us prefer them to the truth of God, or confine our Christian love within lines which are faint indeed compared with the life of the Spirit, whereby the saints are made one in Christ."[122] None of their doctrines or practices that he endorsed, however, contradicted the doctrinal foundation of Baptists. He agreed with the Particular Baptist confessional history and defended Baptist views of the church until his death. In his *Autobiography* he wrote very candidly.

> If I thought it wrong to be a Baptist, I should give it up, and become what I believed to be right. The particular doctrine adhered to by Baptists is that they acknowledge no authority unless it comes from the Word of God. They attach no importance to the authority of the Fathers—they care not for the authority of the mothers—if what they say does not agree with the teaching of the Evangelists, Apostles, and Prophets, and most of all, with the teaching of the Lord Himself. If we could find infant baptism in the Word of God, we should adopt it. It would help us out of a great difficulty, for it would take away from us that reproach which is attached to us—that we are odd, and do not as

other people do. But we have looked well through the Bible, and cannot find it, and do not believe that it is there; nor do we believe that others can find infant baptism in the Scriptures, unless they themselves first put it there.[123]

Spurgeon's commitment to baptism by immersion never wavered; every opportunity to espouse the view, he took. Book reviews, baptismal days in the Tabernacle, numerous articles against any aspect of ritualism—all these provided opportunities for defense of baptism of believers only by immersion. In a strongly positive review of *The Theology of Consolation; or, an account of many old writings and writers on that subject*, Spurgeon nevertheless took exception to some harsh treatment that the writer dealt to John Gill and himself on the issue of baptism. "We are sorry," Spurgeon began, "that the author should, in writing of Dr. Gill, have grown so angry about his distinctive Baptist principles as to go out of his way and make it the occasion of a savage attack upon the worthy doctor and ourselves." The writer, Rev. D. C. A. Agnew, was upset that Gill in the past, and Spurgeon in the present, included even in some otherwise helpful consolatory material "a vein of insinuation against all Christians who practice infant baptism." Spurgeon gave a gentle reminder that "in a commentary written by a member of the sect of the Baptists, it is quite seemly and honourable to bring forward before the eyes of hearers, not unprepared for the charge, and in connection with all relevant texts of Scripture, a full and reiterated detail of the commentator's baptismal theory, and its practical application." Agnew resented the unseemly and "unmanly style of warfare" that involved the insertion of "that ritualistic theory before the bewildered eye" of readers earnestly seeking devotional encouragement

---

121. Pike, 1:85.

122. S&T, December 1883, 650.

123. *Autobiography*, 1:152.

in eternal realities. Giving only a little slack to the tether on his amazing ability at ironic ridicule, Spurgeon responded, "Of course there is nothing unseemly and unmanly in thus dragging in an attack upon ourselves in a brief sketch of Dr. Gill and his work. Nothing unseemly and unmanly in calling what is to the Baptist a solemn spiritual ordinance a *'ritualistic theory.'* Why this sensitiveness to our speaking out our principles as he speaks out his? And if so confident of the truth of his own teaching on Baptism, why grow so wrathful about ours?"[124] To an extended defense of infant baptism filled with *ad hominem* ridicule of the Baptist defense of believers' baptism, Spurgeon concluded, "The Pedobaptists, we fear, will hardly thank Mr. Malcolm for really demonstrating that their cause is indefensible, and that our position is simply impregnable. The more the subject is agitated the better for us."[125]

Spurgeon, in fact, seemed to think that other evangelicals, particularly those of the paedobaptist type, needed the watchful eye of Baptists. "We fear," he stated, "that the tradition of infant sprinkling has a distinct tendency to foster sacramentarian views of an almost Popish character."[126] He stated this after pointing out a poem illustrating the purpose of infant sprinkling in a manual by Robert Steele expounding the Westminster Shorter Catechism. He asked his Presbyterian readers to assure him that they did not believe the following verses.

Sprinkle, sprinkle now,
Blessed Saviour thou!
From thy white hands sweetest water
On this little baby daughter;
On her fair brow Sprinkle, sprinkle thou!

Not by works of right
Sin-stained souls come white;
Not till thou from pit abysmal
Raise them, and with wave baptismal
Wash them clean and bright,
Sin-stained souls come white.[127]

Spurgeon did not want his love for evangelicals broadly and those that embraced the doctrines of grace particularly to be interpreted as a willingness to dissipate the strength of his conviction about baptism.

Wayland Hoyt presented Spurgeon as a true Baptist to the American audience hungry for any word about Spurgeon. "Mr. Spurgeon was a Baptist," he assured them. "He believed that the New Testament read toward the Baptist faith. He had little patience with the great irregularity and looseness which play such havoc amid too many churches called Baptist on the other side of the water." He admitted that Spurgeon was "not one with us in the practice of restricted communion," but took solace that "he was utterly one with us in a persistent demand for immersion as a prerequisite to church membership." Hoyt made the portrait even more pleasing by confiding to his readers, "Talking with him on, I think, the last day I ever saw him, he said to me that were he a pastor in this country, he should not clash with our practice of restricted communion."[128] What he evidently consented to in a private conversation, Spurgeon never indicated sympathy for in public. He started with a commitment to open communion and practiced it, no reservations evident throughout his ministry, and no hesitations to state publicly that he differed with his more strict Baptist brethren.

---

124. S&T, March 1882, 148.

125. S&T December 1882, 635. Mr. Malcolm was James Malcolm, author of *Infant Baptism Demonstrated to be Reasonable, Historical, and Scriptural.*

126. S&T, February 1885, 85.

127. Ibid.

128. Hoyt, 22f.

The spirit of Baptist independence governed only by Scripture and not subject to human regulations Spurgeon also protected and noted with pleasure. In a review of a book about the Methodist class system, Spurgeon expressed hope that such instruction would continue to be helpful to the "young and half-instructed." As a principle, however, "to make a cast-iron rule for all is a stretch of authority for which we can imagine no apology." Then with an undercurrent of denominational pride, Spurgeon remarked, "We are sure that no congregation of Baptists would ever submit to the class-system of Methodists; our people are both too good and too bad to be so readily controlled; they are too fond of freedom, and perhaps too little amenable to discipline." Then, as a commendation of a bit of this good freedom to the Methodists, Spurgeon issued a gentle admonition and word of counsel to his Methodist brethren: "calm consideration, candid judgment, deliberate action, and profound regard both for Scripture and the consciences of good men."[129] The Reformation was established on Scripture and conscience, and Baptists had constructed a theology and ecclesiology more radically consistent with both, in Spurgeon's way of looking at it, than any other Protestant group. He gloried in every gift given to the church catholic through all his beloved evangelical heirs of Reformation theology and Puritan devotion, but he could be nothing but a Baptist.

The Child is Father of the Man

Immediately upon his conversion Spurgeon began manifesting several characteristics that would be prominent throughout his entire Christian pilgrimage.

First, he interpreted his life and all its events, his emotions, and reactions in theological terms.

He saw everything in light of the divine purpose and measured his response externally and internally in light of biblical doctrine.

Second, his clear conviction concerning the doctrines of grace and God's covenantal pursuit of his people alone gave security to the tender Christian conscience and guaranteed a harvest of souls in evangelism.

Third, while yearning for edification from the pulpit he continually gave close and critical observation to every aspect of the art of preaching.

Fourth, he engaged in evangelism through any means that came to his hand.

Fifth, he showed his tendency to sickness and despondency.

Sixth, he had a propensity for self-analysis that resulted in universalizing his personal experience as a canon of judgment in a variety of situations.

Seventh, he committed himself to a position of no-compromise with the destructive influence of modern thought, nineteenth-century liberalism.

Finally, his commitment to Scripture remained the final touchstone in all of these other traits and created a habit of independence of judgment that was startling, refreshing, maddening, perplexing, and enraging to his contemporary churchmen and Christian thinkers.

Concerning the first trait, Spurgeon's letters during the twenty-two months between his conversion and his call to the church at Waterbeach consistently weave transcendent purpose into the fabric of his daily actions. He wrote his mother on May 3, 1851, one year after his baptism reminding her that we should be aware of the secret operations of providence every day. We should know that natural things do not control our lives; our position in the covenantal purpose

---

129. S&T, February 1874, 91.

of God does. His mother's year in "the vast howling wilderness" was lived leaning "on the arm of your Beloved." No step should she wish to retrace, for "Glorious, wondrous, has been the grace shown to all of us, as members of the mystical body of Christ, in preservation, restraint from sin, constraint to holiness, and perseverance in the Christian state." His blessings today are pledges of blessings tomorrow and forbid one to think that he shall ever leave them. "Mark the providences of this year; how clearly have you seen His hand in things which others esteem chance! God, who has moved the world, has exercised His own vast heart and thought for you. All your life, your spiritual life, all things have worked together for good; nothing has gone wrong, for God has directed, controlled all." He then quoted passages from Isaiah 40:27 proving that "we may have confidence that we, His own people, are secure."[130]

Second, Spurgeon's commitment to the comforts bound up in the doctrines of divine sovereignty never faltered during these months and established a pattern for his discussions in years to come. A sickness that normally would have been accompanied by despondency left him encouraged rather than distressed because he was able to draw on the security of doctrinal truth. "Since last Thursday, I have been unwell in body," he told his father, "but I may say that my soul has been almost in Heaven." He had seen his title clear and knew that "sooner than one of God's little ones shall perish, God Himself will cease to be, Satan will conquer the King of kings, and Jesus will no longer be the Savior of the elect." If his Father ordains doubts and fears, he will "not dread to meet them" since, even above the temporal doubts of his people, "the foundation of the Lord standeth sure, having this seal, the Lord knoweth them that are His."[131]

Third, Spurgeon could hardly conceal his passion for preaching and his frustration with bad preaching. Even before his baptism, he yearned for God to call him to preach. He loved his tract work, he coveted the times of spiritual conversation with his "tract people", and looked forward to greater usefulness. "How I long for the time when it may please God to make me, like you, my Father, a successful preacher of the gospel. I almost envy you your exalted privilege."[132] In April 1850 he wrote his mother about the man that she heard preach regularly, "I often think of you poor starving creatures, following for the bony rhetoric and oratory which he gives you. What a mercy that you are not dependent upon him for spiritual comfort! I hope you will soon give up following that empty cloud without rain, that type-and-shadow preacher, for I don't think there is much substance"[133] In 1875, Spurgeon recalled, "Before I had ever entered a pulpit, the thought had occurred to me that I should one day preach sermons which would be printed." He read the printed sermons of Joseph Irons and conceived that one day "I should have a penny pulpit of my own."[134] His growing awareness of the compulsion to preach heightened the pressure on his conscience about the necessity of making public his faith in Christ by a public baptism. He wrote his mother on May 1, two days before he went with Mr. Cantlow into the river Lark, before many witnesses, "I hope you may one day have cause to rejoice, should you see me, the unworthy instrument of God, preaching to others,—yet have I vowed in the strength of my only Strength, in the name of my Beloved, to devote myself for ever to His cause. Do you not think it would be a bad beginning were I, knowing it to be my duty to be baptized, to shrink from it?"[135]

130. Spurgeon, *Letters*, to his mother, May, 1851.
131. Ibid., To his father, April 6, 1850.
132. Ibid.
133. Ibid., To his mother, April, 1850.
134. S&T, January 1875, 3.
135. Spurgeon, *Letters*, to his mother, May, 1850.

Fourth, Spurgeon found his chief joy in the work of evangelism, the propagation of the gospel by tract or by word with the expectation that those words would become a link to eternal life for a perishing sinner. His younger brother, who would later become his assistant pastor, had made no profession of faith in Christ. Spurgeon sought to evangelize him through the mail. "Oh, that the God of mercy would incline Archer's heart to Him, and make him a partaker of His grace! Ask him if he will believe me when I say that one drop of the pleasure of religion is worth ten thousand oceans of the pleasures of the unconverted, and then ask him if he is not willing to prove the fact by experience."[136] "I think I never felt so much earnestness after the souls of my fellow-creatures as when I first loved the Saviour's name." He wrote texts of Scripture on slips of paper and dropped them anywhere. He carried tracts and handed them out on the street or dropped them from the window of a railway carriage. He confessed that some methods might have been imprudent but he wished always to have the zeal arising from a sense of pleasure in doing anything to serve God.[137]

Fifth, a tender conscience combined with heightened desires for holiness led to frequent journeys through the slough of despond. A delicate physical condition responded negatively to this consistent upturn of emotional pressure and in turn exacerbated his tendency to depression. Frequently one finds his physical and mental distress coinciding. He often gave words to the clarity and severity with which he judged his sinful residue: On February 19, 1850 he wrote his mother that he had "been in the miry Slough of Despond." He told her that his grandfather had sought to bolster his spirits, "but is that what I

want? Ought I not rather to be reproved for my deadness and coldness?" He prayed, heard and read, without doing any of them heartily but in "deadness and coldness." When he recovered from this bout with despondency, he described the extreme depth of it, as well as the remedy to escape it, a remedy that remained with him through his ministry, "In the blackest darkness I resolved that, if I never had another ray of comfort, and even if I was everlastingly lost, yet I would love Jesus, and endeavor to run in the way of His commandments: from the time that I was enabled thus to resolve, all these clouds have fled."[138] He always found action, filling his time with work for Jesus, to be the best remedy for despondency. Eventually, however, the load of work had the reverse effect and contributed to his sense of entrapment in the fog of an energy-less funk. Weeks, often months, of rest was the only thing that would do. Sometimes he begged his friends not to write him expecting a response or to ask him to speak. He had no energy for correspondence, nor enough spiritual reserve to go beyond that demanded by the immediate responsibilities of the Tabernacle.

Sixth, at times Spurgeon's focus on himself startled even him. Interpretations of this trait have run from heightened self-centeredness to self-forgetfulness, a willingness to be bared and humiliated for the sake of others. Both his view of the radical nature of grace and the overwhelming perversity of sin found expression in self-analysis. "But," (say you,) "he keeps talking all about himself," he acknowledged in a letter. "True, he does; he cannot help it," he continued. "Self is too much his master." Then with a startling image, the kind that filled his sermons and writings, he lamented, "I am proud of my own ignorance; and, like a toad, bloated with my own venomous pride, proud of

---

136. Ibid., to his father, April 6, 1850.

137. Spurgeon, *Autobiography*, 1:156.

138. Spurgeon, *Letters*, to his mother, February 19, 1850.

what I have not got, and boasting when I should be bemoaning." Whether sinful or mere spiritual transparency, one must become accustomed to Spurgeon on Spurgeon.

Seventh, Spurgeon's resolve against theological shift from the Puritan heritage, whom he considered the purest heirs of the Reformation, who were the purest heirs of Augustine, who was the purest [early] interpreter of Paul, never changed from the earliest days after his conversion. In November of 1850 he wrote his aunt and uncle, "Let the whole earth and even God's professing people, cast out my name as evil; my Lord and Master, He will not. I glory in the distinguishing grace of God, and will not, by the grace of God, step one inch from my principles, or think of adhering to the present fashionable sort of religion." He might be called a "tree-top antinomian" but he would endure the slander rather than endorse a covenant that was a mixture of works and grace, a strange combination something like linking a snail to an elephant, to use an image of Berridge. In his resolution never to be moved from truth, Spurgeon also recognized that a more desperate enemy still lurked in his heart. "May we be enabled to go on, brave as lions, and valiant for the truth and cause of King Jesus, and by the help of the Spirit, vow eternal warfare with every sin, and rest not until the sword of the Spirit has destroyed all the enemies in our hearts."[139]

Finally, Spurgeon would bow to no authority but Scripture, that sword of the Spirit by which he would wage warfare, not only against the enemies of his heart and mind, but against the enemies of truth. Modern critical attitudes toward the Bible, in Spurgeon's view, were attacks upon the majesty of God himself. If the gospel, that most mysteriously profound and exhaustively godlike of all

the works of the triune Jehovah, had commended itself by the work of the Spirit so perfectly to his deepest need and his most thorough knowledge of himself, then nothing in all of its pages could be untrue. Nothing in it could be unnecessary for communicating, and accomplishing, the full work of God for redemption. One that dared dismiss Scripture as erroneous in any part not only attacked the veracity and reign of God, but slit his own throat, leaving himself without light from above to guide into the treacherous shoals of death regnant with the wrath of God apart from the ransom to which Scripture alone bears witness. It is the book that God wrote and to deny it is to charge him with error. Spurgeon, therefore, felt fully warranted to proclaim, "This is the book untainted by any error!" but like its author was "pure unalloyed, perfect truth."[140] Thus his own judgment was freed from the oppressiveness of human opinion and the shifting theologies of modern thought or even the inherited traditional theologies of the past. Augustine was right on many things, but wrong on some important ideas. Calvin was unsurpassed as a theologian and expositor but transferred debilitating errors to his posterity. The Puritans were models as pastors and Christian thinkers, but held to some indefensible incongruities. Even his grandfather, his mother, and his father missed some of the plain truths of Scripture. Spurgeon loved them all, but departed from them all at points where Scripture set him free to do so. The Bible was his personal declaration of independence. The authority that pushed him beyond his parents in 1850 and that he preached in 1855, still ruled him on the day he died in January 1892.

There is nothing in God's Bible which is not great. Did any of you ever sit down to see which

---

139. Ibid., to his uncle and aunt, November, 1850.

140. SS, 1:31.

was the purest religion? "Oh," you say, "we never took the trouble. We went just where our father and mother went." Ah, that is a profound reason, indeed! You went where your father and mother did. I thought you were sensible people. I didn't think you went where other people pulled you, but went of your own selves. I love my parents above all that breathe and the very thought that they believed a thing to be true, helps me to think it is correct. But I have not followed them—I belong to a different denomination—and I thank God I do. I can receive them as Christian Brothers and Sisters, but I never thought that because they happened to be one thing, I was to be the same. No such thing.

God gave me brains and I will use them. And if you have any intellect, use it too. Never say it doesn't matter. It does matter. Whatever God has put here is of eminent importance—He would not have written a thing that was indifferent. Whatever is here is of some value, therefore search all questions, try all by the Word of God. I am not afraid to have what I preach tried by this Bible. Only give me a fair field and no favor and this Bible. If I say anything contrary to it, I will withdraw it the next Sunday. By this I stand, by this I fall. Search and see but don't say, "It does not matter." If God says a thing, it must always be of importance.[141]

---

141. SS, 1:37.

2

MADE FOR GOSPEL MINISTRY

I can say myself that I never did anything which was a blessing to my fellow creatures without feeling compelled to do it. I thought of going to a Sunday school to teach. On a certain day, someone called—asked me—begged me—prayed me to take his class. I could not refuse to go. And there I was held hand and foot by the superintendent and was compelled to go on. I was asked to address the children. I thought I could not, but no one else was there to do it, so I stood up and stammered out a few words. And I recollect the first occasion on which I attempted to preach to the people—I am sure I had no wish to do it—but there was no one else in the place. And should the congregation go away without a single word of warning or address? How could I allow it? I felt forced to address them. And so it has been with whatever I have laid my hand to. I have always felt a kind of impulse which I could not resist, but, moreover felt placed by Providence in such a position that I had no wish to avoid the duty and if I had desired it, could not have helped myself.[1]

Spurgeon entered enthusiastically into every opportunity for service to Christ that he could. He distributed tracts joyfully and consistently while still at Newmarket. He had seventy people that he regularly visited, taking his Saturdays for this visitation as well as tract distribution. He explained to his mother, "I do not give a tract, and go away; but I sit down, and endeavour to draw their attention to spiritual realities."[2]

He immediately became earnest about the salvation of his siblings. When Sarah expressed her faith in Christ, Spurgeon wrote, "I am so glad that Sarah, too, is called, that two of us in one household at one time should thus openly profess the Saviour's name." When he thought about the others, he considered what delight would accrue if "God should prove that they are redeemed ones included in the covenant of grace!" He closed his letter with greeting to all of them with the expressed hope, "May they become members of the church in our house!"[3]

Teaching Truth is the Fountain of Christian Life
Spurgeon's comments about calling and the covenant of grace remind us that his theology quickly fell into the lines of the Puritan divines that he had been reading. He knew that the saving gospel embodied the depths of the divine character and manifest the glory of the eternal purpose of God. Soon after his conversion he revisited the chapel where he heard the saving exhortation, "Look!" and sought comfort in his struggle with indwelling sin. The minister preached on a promising and suitable text from Romans 7, but, in Spurgeon's opinion, failed miserably. He took up his hat and left the chapel and concluded that Methodist theology was of "very little use for the children of

---

1. SS, 1:139. "The Church of Christ," delivered June 3, 1855.
2. Murray, *Letters*, 27.
3. Ibid., 28, 29.

God." It was like the parish pound, "a good place to put sheep in when they have strayed, but there is no food inside."[4]

His own sense of indebtedness to sovereign grace seemed to confirm the truthfulness of what he had read so often prior to the experience of God's call. At sixteen years of age he contemplated the trials of faith brought on by the subtle and destructive powers of indwelling sin. "I know that I am perfectly dead without Him," he observed; "it is His work; I am confident that He will accomplish it, and that I shall see the face of my Beloved in His own house in glory." Such preserving grace that supports faith "is far more than any of us deserve; all beyond hell is mercy, but this is a mighty one. Were it not all of sovereign, electing, almighty grace, I, for one, could never hope to be saved. God says, 'You shall,' and not all the devils in hell, let loose upon a real Christian, can stop the workings of God's sovereign grace, for in due time the Christian cries, 'I will.'"[5]

At Cambridge, Spurgeon involved himself in Sunday School work. He remarked that he had rather have the degree SST than BA or MA.[6] "I teach in the Sunday-school all the afternoon," he wrote his mother, adding, "Mr. Leeding takes the morning work." A couple of weeks later he wrote, "I have spoken twice to the Sunday-school, and am to read an Essay on some subject connected with Sunday-schools at the next meeting of the Teachers' Institute for the town." The boys he taught challenged him to greater certainty in the way he expressed himself in gospel truth and to be more catching in the way he produced an anecdote or illustration. His teaching soon attracted the other adult teachers and they requested that he give pointers on the lesson to them.

The superintendent encouraged him toward this; in fact, as Spurgeon later recounted, "I could not refuse to go; and there I was, held hand and foot by the superintendent, and was compelled to go on." But the compulsion was more than the pressure of human forces. "I have always felt a kind of impulse which I could not resist; but moreover, I have felt placed by Providence in such a position that I had no wish to avoid the duty, and if I had desired it, I could not have helped myself."

In spite, therefore, of his reluctance he taught, and soon this teachers' meeting had become like a small chapel. His preparations were done seriously and with fear and trembling, having little more than his Bible and serious reflection on his own experience under the searchlight of the Word. The urgency that characterized his preaching exhibited itself even then as he had an "intense desire to bring men to Christ." With death possible on any moment of any day, he looked upon all as "being foolish for attending to anything except their eternal business, and myself most of all foolish for not pointing dying sinners to a living Christ, and inviting them to trust in His precious blood."[7] He felt that urgency slip from him quickly and felt alarmed that something so real could become so remote under the power of one's native stupidity. He discovered that "unless I am baptized anew with the Spirit of God, and constantly stand at the foot of the cross, reading the curse of sin in the crimson hieroglyphics of my Saviour's dying agonies, I shall become as steeled and insensible as many professors already are."[8]

First Sermon and First Pastorate

Arising auspiciously from his success in Sunday School teaching was his participation in the Lay

---

4. *Autobiography*, 1:100.

5. Murray, *Letters*, 28, 24.

6. *Autobiography*, 1:157.

7. Ibid., 158-59.

8. Ibid., 160.

Preacher's Association. The "presiding genius," as Spurgeon called him, was James Vinter. Having observed the zeal and gifts of Spurgeon, Vinter, referred to by the young men of the Association as "Bishop Vinter," assigned him to go one Sunday evening in the autumn of 1850 to Teversham, three miles from Cambridge, "for a young man was to preach there who was not much used to services, and very likely would be glad of company."[9] This was an ingeniously worded sentence, for as it turned out Spurgeon was the young man to do the preaching. "A request to go and preach would have met with a decided negative, but merely to act as company to a good brother who did not like to be lonely, and perhaps ask us to give out a hymn or to pray, was not at all a difficult matter, and the request, understood in that fashion was cheerfully complied with."[10] He discovered this en route as his companion for the evening assured him that he had no intention of preaching and could not do so even if coerced. When Spurgeon discerned that he himself was the man, he protested that he was no minister and was quite unprepared. His companion stated even more emphatically that the same was true of him and that "there would be no sermon unless I gave them one."[11] Spurgeon's road-mate said that if Spurgeon would just repeat one of his Sunday School lessons it would be more fit and beneficial for these poor people than a studied sermon by a learned divine. Given the counter-resolve of his companion, and convinced that it would not do for no sermon at all to be given, he set his heart on a passage of Scripture that he had contemplated much in recent days, 1 Peter 2:7: "Unto you therefore, that believe He is precious." Surely, Spurgeon thought as he walked along, very surprised but seriously affected with the solemn responsibility, "I could tell a few poor cottagers of the sweetness and love of Jesus."[12]

On at least six other occasions Spurgeon preached on this text. In 1859, he recalled this event which he denominated, "the opening of my ministry." When he stood to preach for the first time in his life to the handful of poor people in the cottage, he remembered, "I felt my own inability to preach." The text, however, so elevated his mind that he could not have said "anything upon any other text." "Christ was precious to my soul,"—he relished the memory—"and I was in the flush of my youthful love, and I could not be silent when a precious Jesus was the subject." He remembered his Egyptian bondage, the gulf of flames which lapped around his tormented conscience ready to shroud him in everlasting burnings. With such vivid recollection he could speak of His preciousness who "had plucked me as a brand from the burning, and set me upon a rock, and put a new song in my mouth, and established my goings."[13]

In 1869, when in an "exceedingly depressed" state, Spurgeon again went to this text. He again reminded his hearers that this was the text "from which I first essayed to speak in public ... and I am sure it contains the marrow of what I have always taught in the pulpit from that day until now." He believed he could speak on it in his sleep and if he were dying he could "with my last expiring breath pour out a heart-full of utterance upon the delightful verse which I have selected."[14]

He visited it again in 1870 and in 1875. An 1890 sermon on this text will be discussed be-

---

9. Ibid., 1:182.

10. S&T, January 1880, 4.

11. Ibid.

12. *Autobiography*, 1:183. The story in the *Autobiography* is a slightly edited, mainly changes in pronouns from plural to singular, from S&T, January 1880. The Pilgrim Publications edition of NPSP includes it as the first entry for the 1855 volume.

13. NPSP, 1859, 137.

14. S&T, October 1869, 481. "A Sermon from a Sick Preacher."

low. Other sermons on the text were published in volumes of the *Metropolitan Tabernacle Pulpit* in 1906 and 1908. Obviously many of the ideas are repeated in these sermons. The intrinsic worth of Christ receives particular affection from Spurgeon's moving vocabulary while he also explores the experiential aspects of why Christ's worthiness in essence and in work is precious to the believer. Each sermon, however, added new insights and powerful applications unique to the setting in which it was preached.

His text for that virgin voyage into public proclamation had so intertwined itself into Spurgeon's heart that he spoke on it freely and passionately. Before the hymn could be sung one lady called out, "Bless your dear heart, how old are you?" Spurgeon refused to answer until the hymn was sung and then confessed only to being under sixty. And under sixteen, his inquisitress added.

After this, every weekend, and many week nights, saw the young Spurgeon going from village to village, and often in the village from door to door, come wind, come weather. Often a frightful sight in his protective clothes, Spurgeon's heart-searching, doctrinally-profound preaching more than compensated for his initial awkward appearance. He maintained a rigorous course of personal study in order to meet these regular obligations plus his Sunday School work, his tutoring, and his own guided program of study. "When I first began to preach," Spurgeon recounted, "this was my usual way of working. I was up in the morning early, praying and reading the Word; all the day, I was either teaching my scholars or studying theology as much as I could."[15] The evening then became his time for walking to one of the thirteen villages serviced by the Lay Preachers Association. The reading of the day found fertile soil in the meditations of Spurgeon on the journey and soon became the property of his congregation as he preached "simply and earnestly, what I had first received into my own mind and heart."[16]

Those evenings in barns and kitchens and cottages quickly honed the prodigious gifts of the "boy preacher of the fens" and made him a master of stating the profoundest truths in vivid images and plain language. The preparation for these meetings, combined with the impromptu necessity of communicating simply, clearly, and truthfully to congregations so unspoiled by education, formed in Spurgeon's mind a principle for ministerial qualification. Without such plain and mentally demanding labor, a minister could hardly rise beyond the conceit of professionalism in his calling. Spurgeon would require similar experience of all the men that later gained access to his college for preachers.

An assignment in October 1851 took Spurgeon to Waterbeach. The Baptist chapel had only twelve hearers that first Sunday. Spurgeon wrote his father the following week: "I have been busily employed every Lord's-day; not at home once yet, nor do I expect to be this year. Last Sunday, I went to a place called Waterbeach, where there is an old-established Church, but not able to support a minister. I have engaged to supply to the end of the month." Their former minister, for twenty years, came over from Cambridge as his father went to Tollesbury.[17]

Their appreciation for Spurgeon's preaching resulted in an invitation to preach for two more Sundays, then for six months and finally it expanded to more than two years. On December 31, 1851 Spurgeon wrote his father: "I preached twice

---

15. *Autobiography*, 1:185.

16. Ibid., 186.

17. Spurgeon, *Letters*, to his father, October 15, 1851.

on Christmas (day) to crammed congregations, and again on Sunday, quite as full. The Lord gives me favor in the eyes of the people; they come for miles, and are wondrously attentive. I am invited (to preach at Waterbeach) for six months. My reputation in Cambridge is rather great."[18] In January of 1852, he was asked to become pastor of the church. He consented. The yearly salary was only £45, but it enabled him to pay his rent in Cambridge since the people also gave Spurgeon gifts of food. He won a prize for an essay and with the prize money bought a Septuagint to assist him in studying the Bible. The number of invitations for hospitality he received while on the field testified to the affection the people felt toward him. He had a different home opened to him for food and rest every week. He felt himself cared for richly and abundantly and could not imagine how a people could love their pastor more.

Though now a pastor, Spurgeon had to continue his teaching for income supplement. This extra drain on his time served as no excuse, however, for diminishing his zeal for the gospel in his appointed sphere of labor. He actively engaged in personal soul-winning, going from house to house in Waterbeach, entering many places that would have shamed him had he been there for any other reason than that of giving the gospel to sinners. "I would sooner pluck one single brand from the burning than explain all mysteries," he explained as he reminisced about the first convert under his ministry at Waterbeach. "To win a soul from going down to the pit, is a more glorious achievement than to be crowned in the arena of theological controversy as *Dr. Sufficientissimus*."[19] In these days, the doctrine of election greatly consoled him. God's immutable decree guaranteed that a multitude no man can number is "ordained

to eternal life."[20] Also his itinerant preaching continued so that at the end of two years Spurgeon could assure his father, who was concerned about the need for formal preparation for ministry, that he had been for two years "as much a minister as any man in England; and probably very much more so, since in that time I have preached more than 600 times."[21]

Spurgeon was seventeen when he began preaching to this congregation of about forty people. After some months of preaching in the morning and again in the afternoon, the church requested that he preach in the evening also. He replied, "I can not always preach three times, for I am not so strong as a man."[22] At the end of two years, over 400 crowded in to hear the young preacher, with many standing outside. Conversions were many and the transformation of the entire town was remarkable. Swearing, illicit liquor stills, broken homes, public drunkenness, and general debauchery were replaced with industrious living, generosity, joy, and public and private worship. All of the 1,300 residents knew Spurgeon and many of the former leaders in crime had been converted, and others, yet unconverted, still attended chapel. "It was a pleasant thing," Spurgeon recalled, "to walk through that place, when drunkenness had almost ceased, when debauchery in the case of many was dead, when men and women went forth to labour with joyful hearts, singing the praises of the ever-living God; and when, at sunset, the humble cottager called his children together, read them some portion from the Book of Truth, and then together they bent their knees in prayer to God." He found

---

18. Ibid., to his father, December 31, 1851.

19. *Autobiography,* 1:197.

20. Ibid., 213.

21. Murray, *Letters,* 49.

22. *Sketch of the Life and Ministry of C. H. Spurgeon,* (New York: Sheldon & Blakeman, 1857), 52. This quote is a reminiscence from C. King, one of the deacons at Waterbeach during Spurgeon's time there.

real satisfaction in noting that throughout the village, "at the hour of eventide, one might have heard the voice of song coming from nearly every roof-tree, and echoing from almost every heart." So remarkable was the change, as Spurgeon observed and remembered it, that he felt with certainty "that it pleased the Lord to work wonders in our midst. He showed the power of Jesus's name, and made me a witness of that gospel which can win souls, draw reluctant hearts, and mould afresh the life and conduct of sinful men and women."[23]

The people at Waterbeach recognized that a pulpit genius was on their hands. Pike makes the studied judgment that "there was nothing of the mere flash-in-the-pan brilliance about his earliest sermons. Even among his rustic audience there were those who could readily enough distinguish between rhetorical fireworks and genuine sterling eloquence." More than this, however, noted particularly by the mature members of the congregation, was the "advanced Christian experience of the youth of seventeen who had accepted the pastoral charge."[24]

One of the deacons, Mr. C. King, gave a short narrative of the impact Spurgeon had on the church and the town:

> From Mr. Spurgeon's first coming to Waterbeach, he was generally well received, and soon became popular as a preacher. It was no unusual thing to see the labourers on the farms at a distance from the village literally running home when the duties of the day were over, that they might be in time to attend his ministry in the evening. At the early age of eighteen, he was unanimously chosen pastor of our little church. We have often sat under his ministry with a mixture of *pleasure, profit,* and

surprise, and have been ready to exclaim with the inquiring Jews named in the gospel, Whence hath this young man this wisdom and these mighty words? Our congregation soon rapidly increased. So that both the seats and the aisles were generally filled, and some could not obtain admission into the place. A reformation in the habits of the people soon appeared in the village; and about twenty persons were, in a short time, added to the church. Mr. Spurgeon's character and conduct were as amiable as his talents were attractive.[25]

Another experienced Christian, Potto Brown, the fabled Miller of Houghton, heard so much about the young Spurgeon that he invited him to preach at a private chapel that he maintained. The day was memorable for Spurgeon, for Brown essentially accused him of preaching someone else's sermons. No mere "prentice boy" could have stored such experience and theology into so small a time. Brown is described as "a man of imperious will, great determination, strong memory, yet at the same time with very marked eccentricities." All of these traits showed themselves when he, a close follower and friend of the American evangelist Charles Finney, attacked Spurgeon's clearly enunciated Calvinism. Spurgeon, though young and a guest in Brown's home, did not shrink from defending both his originality and his theology, characterizing Brown's Arminianism as "worthless theology." The afterlunch disputation, in which Spurgeon gave the imperious host "a Roland for his Oliver without compunction" in a "battle royal," sealed a mutual respect of the antagonists for each other and gave rise to Spurgeon's description of the experience as "felicitous misery." Brown was not accustomed to resistance in his critiques of the morning sermon but, as Spurgeon himself described it, "he had an

---

23. *Autobiography,* 1:193–94.
24. Pike, 1:64.

25. (Stevenson) *Sketch of the Life and Ministry of C. H. Spurgeon,* 52.

unpromising youth to deal with, who had no fear of Potto Brown, or Professor Finney, or any other Arminian before his eyes, but held his own opinions with a firmness which interested and did not displease the good but eccentric miller."[26]

While at Waterbeach, Spurgeon came to the attention of Joseph Angus, principal of Stepney College, a theological school supported by the Baptists. Angus believed that if the young phenomenon received some formal training, his usefulness could be multiplied. When the college principal went to preach at Cambridge, where he formerly had served, he did not see Spurgeon, for he was at Waterbeach, "four or five honest miles" away. Angus decided to contact Spurgeon on Monday asking for an interview. Spurgeon received the message on Monday, February 2, 1854, that Angus desired to see him, designating the home of Mr. MacMillan, the wealthy publisher, as the place. When Spurgeon arrived at the appointed time, he was shown to the drawing room. Angus, when he arrived, was placed in the parlor; neither was informed by the receiving maid of the other's presence. Angus had to leave to catch his train back to London and the interview never took place.

Angus, however, left a note for Mr. Watts, a mutual friend, expressing his hope that Spurgeon would apply for acceptance since the denomination needed men thoroughly prepared "so that they may occupy important posts, and wear well." "I should regret," Angus urged, "for your friend to settle without thorough preparation." Angus was sure that a prepared man would have greater usefulness and "fill a wider sphere, with preparation than without it."[27] While he contemplated these events on a walk to a preaching engagement, Spurgeon had the experience of divine leadership that settled the course of his life.

That afternoon having to preach at one of the village stations, I walked slowly in a meditating frame of mind over Midsummer Common to the little wooden bridge which leads to Chesterton, and in the midst of the common I was startled by what seemed a loud voice, but may have been a singular illusion, which ever it was the impression was most vivid; I seemed very distinctly to hear the words, "Seekest thou great things for thyself, seek them not!" This led me to look at my position from another point of view, and to challenge my motives and intentions; I remembered the poor but loving people to whom I ministered, and the souls which had been given me in my humble charge, and although at that time I anticipated obscurity and poverty as the result of the resolve, yet I did there and then solemnly renounce the offer of collegiate instruction, determining to abide for a season at least with my people, and to remain preaching the Word so long as I had strength to do it.[28]

Friends still encouraged Spurgeon to go to college but Spurgeon said, "I have no very great desire for it; in fact, none at all."[29] He knew that the idea of

26. S&T, April 1879, 158 "Potto Brown and the Browns of Houghton."

27. *Autobiography,* 1:209. Drummond tells the story, 171-72. The *Autobiography,* 1:207-17, includes Spurgeon's account plus the letters connected with the event. Spurgeon also gives the account in S&T, 1865, 424-25.

28. S&T, October 1865, 424-25. A most instructive note appears in S&T for January, 1877. "The men of the Pastors' College accepted the fraternal invitation of their brethren of Regent's Park College to spend the afternoon and evening with them. There was very hearty intercourse between the students and tutors of the two colleges, and much enjoyment in consequence. Mr. Spurgeon spoke upon *culture,* and Dr. Angus upon *go.* With prayers, hymns, addresses, and speeches the time passed away very pleasantly. ... [M]ay the men while in training, and when actually in the field, never forget that 'all we are brethren.'" S&T, January 1877, 45.

29. Murray, *Letters,* 36. Obviously Spurgeon was not opposed to training, for he would never have founded the Pastors' College had his own resistance to it been based on principled opposition. He felt that his training through reading and constant practice had carried him to a level of both knowledge and function in his field of calling that formal training, for him, would add little, if anything. When he presented to the deacons at New Park

his not pursuing recognized academic theological instruction disturbed his father. He wrote him to assure him that, should his father still think it best, he would do it; but he also gave several reasons why he felt it would not substantially benefit him in the task to which he was called. Formal study would benefit him more at a later date when he knew more; "when I know more I shall be more able to learn." He presently had a congregation of 450 that he was loathe to leave. Later, he would be more independent financially and less dependent on his father to provide anything. In addition, he did not consider himself uneducated nor void of opportunities for improvement.[30] He left the decision to his father. His father wisely left the matter to Spurgeon's own sense of calling.

Spurgeon decided to rest on his rapidly expanding experience, his personal drive in study, and the sanctifying effects of divine providence for his ongoing preparation for ministry. This decision soon would have all the marks of a special providence. He continued to teach at Cambridge while preaching at Waterbeach and in other villages nearby on week-nights. When possible he went to hear other preachers and benefited greatly from hearing William Jay preach on "Ever let your conversation be as becometh the Gospel of Christ." He heard John Angell James preach on "Ye are complete in Him."[31] Pike interviewed Edward Ingle, one of Spurgeon's former pupils, after Spurgeon's death, and, perhaps under the influence of his later fame and universal effectiveness, Ingle recalled a Spurgeon that created a "spell similar to what his students of later years have felt." He remembered that Spurgeon showed

him the book he wrote against the papacy, *Antichrist and Her Brood*, and that Spurgeon had told him he would "like to pull the old Pope from his throne." His engaging manner of creating interest in every subject he taught, the electric effect of his reading passages from history or literature, the way he pointed out analogies between the natural world and biblical truth, and the fervor and freshness with which he dealt with biblical passages seemed undiminished and compelling in the mind of Ingle even after a lapse of forty years.[32]

Spurgeon's final decision not to attend college disturbed his father slightly, thinking it could impede his son's future usefulness. Spurgeon wanted to give every assurance to him that he felt God's providence had ordered it so and that his decision not to go indicated no disrespect for his father's opinion. He wrote his father on April 6. "I have desired, all along, to act the part of a dutiful son to an affectionate parent," he assured John Spurgeon, "and if I fail, I feel sure that you and dear Mother will impute it rather to my weakness in act, than to a want of love." The matter simply came down to the fact that he considered it his duty to remain at Waterbeach, "for a short time at least." His friends had assured him "that never were more tears shed in Waterbeach, at any time, than when I only hinted at leaving. They could not give me stronger tokens of their affection than they did give." They prayed virtually in unison, "Lord, keep him here!" His popularity was so high in fact, that he felt he was in a dangerous place, perched on the pinnacle with the world before him. The anonymity of the vale would be much safer.[33] Though he had no confidence in himself and dreaded his tendency to pride, he had confidence in the divine purpose to save and

Street the theoretical objection that he had no college instruction, they responded, "That is to us a special recommendation, for you would not have much savour or unction if you came from college." *Autobiography* 1:249.

30. Spurgeon, *Letters*, to his father, February 24, 1852.

31. Pike, 1:75.

32. Ibid., 77-83.

33. Spurgeon, *Letters*, "To his father," April 6, 1852.

in the humbling tendency of the doctrine of election. Though he was no "Hyper-Calvinist," he believed that God's electing purpose guaranteed the success of gospel ministry. "Oh, if the clouds pass without rain, how sorrowful I shall feel." His passion for preaching was fueled by his confidence that a call to preach and the responsibility of a specific charge meant that God intended salvation through his ordained means. "When I have been thinking on the many difficulties in preaching the Word, the doctrine of election has been a great comfort to me. I do want men to be saved," he continued, "and it is my consolation that a multitude no man can number are by God's immutable decree ordained to eternal life. So we cannot labor in vain, we must have some; the covenant renders that secure."[34]

His decision concerning college and his convictions about usefulness seemed accurate, because blessings of friendship, fellowship, and conversion gave intensity to every moment in service of the church at Waterbeach. He wrote his mother in November 1852: "I am more and more glad that I never went to college. God sends such sunshine on my path, such smiles of grace, that I cannot regret if I have forfeited all my prospects for it." His decision was made because of love to God and his cause. Poverty in service to God was far superior to riches in service of self. His congregation increased both in size and love and hospitality. "During all the time that I have been at Waterbeach, I have had a different house for my home every Sabbath day. Fifty-two families have thus taken me in; and I have still six other invitations not yet accepted." Though the salary was small, their generosity to him personally was great. "Our anniversary passed off grandly," he effused, "six were baptized; crowds on crowds stood

by the river; the chapel was afterwards crammed, both to the tea and the sermon."[35]

A Radical Change Coming

In the autumn of 1853, Spurgeon's character and talents became known to William Olney, a lay leader of the New Park Street Chapel in London. Former pastors of this church included Benjamin Keach, John Gill, John Rippon, and Joseph Angus. Twenty-five years later, Spurgeon narrated the events of the few months in late 1853 and early 1854 that led to his settling as pastor in London. Spurgeon recounted his walk to Waterbeach and, as usual, his sitting at a table to select the hymns for the service. A letter from London was handed to him. "It was an unusual missive, and was opened with curiosity," Spurgeon noted. He had been invited to preach at New Park Street Chapel, Southwark, formerly the pulpit occupied by Dr. Rippon,—"the very Dr. Rippon whose hymn-book was then before us upon the table, the great Dr. Rippon, out of whose *Selection* we were about to choose hymns for our worship." Spurgeon quietly passed the letter across the table to the deacon who gave out the hymns, certain that "there was some mistake, and that the letter must have been intended for a Mr. Spurgeon who preached somewhere down in Norfolk." The deacon, however, knew that no mistake had been made. He knew Spurgeon could not long be confined to so narrow a venue, but was surprised that he so soon had been called to London. "He shook his head very gravely; but the time was come for us to look out the hymns, and therefore the letter was put away, and, as far as we can remember, was for the day quite forgotten."[36]

When Spurgeon was convinced that, for good faith and in deferential courtesy to his unexpected

34. Ibid., "To his father," April 6, 1852.

35. Ibid.,, "To His Mother," November 1852.

36. S&T, January 1879, 1, 2.

correspondent, he should respond to the inquiry, he wrote James Low on November 28. "My people at Waterbeach are hardly to be persuaded to let me come," he informed Low, "but I am prepared to serve you on the 11th December." After explaining his reason for suggesting that date, he felt he should probe Low's real knowledge of the situation and give him a chance to change lest Spurgeon come and "be out of my right place." He had served a church for more than two years, the membership had doubled, but "my last birthday was only my nineteenth." He admitted that he had never "known what the fear of man means, and have all but uniformly had large congregations, and frequently crowded ones." If his youth, however, would disqualify him, "by all means, I entreat you, do not let me come." In addition to regular preaching to his congregation, Spurgeon informed him that "almost every night, for two years, I have been aided to proclaim His truth." Unless informed otherwise, Spurgeon pledged to be there for December 11, arriving on Saturday afternoon, and returning on Monday.[37]

Soon another letter appeared assuring Spurgeon that everything in the first was true written in full knowledge of the preacher's age. Again his presence was requested, the date verified, and a place of lodging appointed.

Spurgeon lodged on that Saturday evening at a boarding-house in Queen Square, Bloomsbury. His dress, a "huge black satin stock," accompanied by a "blue handkerchief with white spots," set him apart in the eyes of his fellow boarders as a young man from the country "evidently in the condition known as verdant green." They told him stories of how great the London preachers were and how many thousands came to hear them preach. "One we remember had a thousand *city* men to hear

him, another had his church filled with *thoughtful* people, such as could hardly be matched all over England, while a third had an immense audience, almost entirely composed of the *young men* of London, who were spell-bound by his eloquence." Other magical feats of these preachers were hailed as astounding facts that hardly could be matched by such a novice. "We were not in an advantageous condition for pleasant dreams," Spurgeon admitted.

> On the narrow bed we tossed in solitary misery, and found no pity. Pitiless was the grind of the cabs in the street, pitiless the recollection of the young city clerks whose grim propriety had gazed upon our rusticity with such amusement, pitiless the spare room which scarce afforded space to kneel, pitiless even the gas-lamps which seemed to wink at us as they flickered amid the December darkness. We had no friend in all that city full of human beings, but we felt among strangers and foreigners, hoped to be helped through the scrape into which we had been brought, and to escape safely to the serene abodes of Cambridge and Waterbeach, which then seemed to be Eden itself.[38]

The experience of walking to the church the next day was no more encouraging than the evening's sleep. On a clear, cold morning, Spurgeon wended his way along Holborn Hill and certain tortuous lanes and alleys at the foot of Southwark Bridge. "Wondering, praying, fearing, hoping, believing,—we felt all alone and yet not alone." He expected divine help, and was "inwardly borne down by [his] sense of the need of it." Feeling the depth of his forlornness, when he first sighted the Park Street Chapel, he felt "for a moment amazed at our own temerity, for it seemed to our eyes to be a large, ornate, and imposing structure, suggesting an audience wealthy and critical, and far removed from the humble folk

---

37. Spurgeon, *Letters*, "To James Low."

38. S&T, January 1879, 2.

to whom our ministry had been sweetness and light."[39] There the intimidation ended. He could tell there would be a small crowd, the imposing nature of the building did not house an equally imposing auditory, and Spurgeon realized that he was not out of his depth.

The church had declined in recent decades so that a sanctuary built to accommodate 1,200 had only about 200 in attendance. Waterbeach had more than twice that many. Spurgeon's impression was that the congregation was a "mere handful." "The chapel seemed very large to the preacher, and very gloomy, but he stayed himself on the Lord, and delivered his message from James 1:17."[40] The effect on the congregation, if not electrifying, was much more than intriguing. T. H. Olney, present at that service and subsequently a faithful officer in the church, recalled at Spurgeon's funeral the significance of that service. "I had the honor of hearing his first sermon in London," Olney recounted, "and he then struck the keynote of his ministry." Upon remarking about the text Spurgeon chose from James, Olney continued: "It was a marvelous sight, that morning at New Park Street Chapel, when he came into the pulpit. He had the dew of youth upon him then. Few of you can remember him as the wonderful youthful preacher; but he spoke with the same confidence in the first sermon, and with the same eloquence, as in later years."[41]

That relatively modest congregation saw to it that a substantially larger number attended in the evening to hear this eccentric nineteen-year-old, "a gauche country youth of nineteen years,"

in the words of Charles Ray.[42] Susannah Thompson, a niece of the Olneys, had stayed home that morning but when her relatives returned to the house she found they were determined that the crowd would be more substantial in the evening. She went, other friends and acquaintances were contacted; other church families made the same effort and, as Spurgeon stated it, "There was an improvement even on the first evening, and the place looked more cheerful."[43] He preached with authority and clarity the serious truths of Scripture but he could also smile in the pulpit and coax a smile from his hearers. In the evening he preached from Revelation 14:5, "They are without fault before the throne of God."[44] Because of the quaintness of the expression, Susannah remembered verbatim one line in which Spurgeon spoke of the redeemed as "living stones in the Heavenly Temple perfectly joined together with the vermilion cement of Christ's blood."[45]

As he reflected on this twenty-five years later, Spurgeon recalled that he "had a happy Sabbath in the pulpit and spent the intervals with warm-hearted friends." When he trudged back that night to the Queen Square narrow lodging, he was not alone, and no longer viewed Londoners as flinty-hearted barbarians. "Our tone was altered," he wrote, "we wanted no pity of anyone, we did not care a penny for the young gentlemen lodgers and their miraculous ministers, nor for

---

39. Ibid., 3.

40. S&T, April 1876, 160.

41. *From the Pulpit to the Palm Branch* (London: Passmore & Alabaster, 1892), 118.

42. Charles Ray, *Life of Susannah Spurgeon* in *Morning Devotions by Susannah Spurgeon* (Edinburgh: The Banner of Truth Trust, 2006), 131.

43. S&T, April 1876, 160.

44. Pike 1:92-103. Pike, having at his disposal the account of eyewitnesses to events both at Waterbeach and in London, gives a charming account of Spurgeon's weekend there. Spurgeon says that the experience in the boarding house on Saturday evening was "about the most depressing agency that could have been brought to bear on my spirit. On the narrow bed I tossed in solitary misery, and found no pity." *Autobiography*, 1:248.

45. *Autobiography*, 1:281.

the grind of the cabs, nor for anything else under the sun."[46] He had bearded the lion in his den and found him not nearly as fearsome as he seemed from afar.

Spurgeon shared with his father the delicate movements of his mind concerning the opportunity before him. "I do not anticipate going there with much pleasure. I am contented where I am; but if God has more for me to do, then let me go and trust in Him." He surmised that the London congregation was "rather higher in Calvinism than I am." He had succeeded in bringing one church to his views, and believed "with Divine assistance" the same could happen there. "I am a Calvinist," he wrote, and "love what someone called 'glorious Calvinism,' but 'Hyper-ism' is too hot-spiced for my palate." That he was not a college graduate did not put them off, but rather pleased them. They had had enough of men seeking to air their education in the pulpit. Concerning his own people, he described them as "very sad." They wept bitterly at the sight of him, though in the pulpit he made no allusion to the subject of his leaving, and he believed it was too uncertain to speak of publicly. Still mulling over the theological issues, Spurgeon said, "It is Calvinism they want in London, and any Arminian preaching will not be endured." He had a high estimation of the theological acumen of the leading men, but they all "expressed their belief that my originality, or even eccentricity, was the very thing to draw a London audience." How such a view was consistent with any supposed "hyperism" is not clear, and Spurgeon never seemed to have difficulty from his own congregation on that issue, though he did from some of the other Baptist ministers. He thought the chapel "one of the finest in the denomination; somewhat in the style of our Cambridge Museum."[47]

Other preaching days, January 1 and 15, in London led the church to propose a six-month trial. Spurgeon agreed in principle, but felt another plan might succeed better. He approved of the prudence of the church in "wishing to have one so young as myself on an extended period of probation," and suggested that the probation be initiated at three months "and then, should the congregation fail, or the church disagree, I would reserve to myself liberty, without breach of engagement, to retire; and you could, on your part, have the right to dismiss me without seeming to treat me ill." If no reason to desist appeared at the end of three months they could engage for another three months under the same reasonable stipulations. After all, five persons had not seen fit to support the proposal. Spurgeon admired their "honesty and boldness," and desired that, if his trial proved unsatisfactory, the majority would follow their lead at the end.[48]

By April 19, however, the church in a special called meeting issued an invitation to Spurgeon to become pastor. Fifty male members of the church had met and petitioned the deacons to call the church meeting for April 19. On that day the church passed unanimously the resolution "that we tender our brother, the Rev. C. H . Spurgeon, a most cordial and affectionate invitation forthwith to become pastor of this church, and we pray that the result of his services may be owned of God with an outpouring of the Holy Spirit and a revival in our midst; that it may be fruitful in the conversion of sinners and in the edification of those that believe."[49] The five who had opposed the invitation to the trial period had evidently dropped their objections.

Spurgeon had come to a conclusion that, if nothing else, pecuniary matters must soon drive

---

46. S&T, January 1879, 3.

47. Murray, *Letters*, 41, 42.

48. Ibid., 46, 47.

49. S&T, April 1876, 160.

him from his little garden of Eden. In spite, therefore, of a struggle with the inevitable breaking of strong ties of mutual love and spiritual fellowship at Waterbeach, on April 28 he replied to the invitation: "No lengthened reply is required; there is but one answer to so loving and cordial an invitation. I ACCEPT IT. I have not been perplexed as to what my reply should be, for many things constrain me thus to answer." The call was providential, not of his solicitation, the place was honorable for its past and would support a youth with prayer, God who called would be faithful, and their kindness already had knit his heart to theirs. He laced his acceptance with reminders of covenant blessings, the biblical/theological construct from which radiated his entire understanding of divine revelation and redemption that included even this moment. "The first note of invitation from your deacons came quite unlooked-for," he reminded them, "and I trembled at the idea of preaching in London. I could not understand how it had come about, and even now I am in the hands of our covenant God, whose wisdom directs all things. He shall choose for me; and so far as I can judge, this is His choice." Spurgeon mentioned his profound awareness of the glorious names connected with that pulpit, names such as Benjamin Keach, John Gill, and John Rippon. He entreated them to remember both in private and corporate prayer that he would be faithful to the charge God placed on him and also asked that they remember his "youth and inexperience, and pray that these may not hinder my usefulness." In closing he set the context of his hopes for gospel success: "And now, commending you to our covenant God, the Triune Jehovah, I am, yours to serve in the gospel, C. H. Spurgeon."[50]

Soon after his acceptance of the invitation, the church began to make plans for an ordination service. Spurgeon believed ordination to be a hangover from Romish sacramentalism and complained against Protestants who maintained it. He responded quickly, therefore, to this proposed arrangement in a note that stated his position firmly in the context of a deferential spirit. On May 2, Spurgeon responded: "I have a decided objection to any public ordination or recognition. I have, scores of times, most warmly expressed from the pulpit my abhorrence of such things, and have been not a little notorious as the opponent of a custom which has become a kind of iron law in the country. I am willing to retrace my steps if in error; but if I have been right, it will be no very honorable thing to belie my former loud outcries by submitting to it myself." He did not believe that this formality would make him any more a minister than he already was and detested the dogma of apostolic succession and objected to its revival among Baptists "by delegating power from minister to minister." He believed in the glory of independency, that every church had the right, without assistance from others, of choosing its own ministers. "You, yourselves, have chosen me; and what matters it if the whole world dislikes the choice? They cannot invalidate it; nor can they give it more force." Other ministers had no more to do with him than the crown of France had to do with the crown of Britain. "Prelatic power is gone. All we are brethren." Spurgeon believed that the ceremony was meaningless and the charge received in public should be delivered only in private if a fellow minister believed it his brotherly duty to do so. "I do not know how I could sit in public to be told ... that I must not spend more than my income; and (if married), that I must be a good husband, and not let the wife say that being a minister had lessened

---

50. Spurgeon, *Letters*, April 28, 1854; Murray, *Letters*, 50, 51.

my affection, with all the absurd remarks on family and household matters. I do not know what sort of a homily I should get; but if I am to have it, let it be in my study; or if it be not a very good one, I cannot promise to sit and hear it." He was willing to endure such a thing as a penance for the sake of the congregation but he himself had a decided aversion to it.

Two weeks into the New Park Street pastorate, the noted actor who had just been converted and baptized, Sheridan Knowles, gave this admonition to his class in elocution at Stepney College:

> Go hear him at once if you want to know how to preach. His name is Charles Spurgeon. He is only a boy, but he is the most wonderful preacher in the world. He is absolutely perfect in his oratory; and, besides that, a master in the art of acting. He has nothing to learn from me, or anyone else. He is simply perfect. ... Why boys, he can do anything he pleases with his audience! He can make them laugh, and cry, and laugh again, in five minutes. His power was never equalled.[51]

He closed the evaluation with a remarkable judgment about his future usefulness and the worldwide influence of his sermons. The fulfillment of this prospective commendation began very soon.

A Famous London Pastorate

The New Park Street congregation had moved to that location in 1830 from Carter Lane. The unbroken connections of that congregation led back to 1652 when William Rider became pastor of a congregation that met in a private house in Southwark. Then, without a pastor for some years, the congregation called Benjamin Keach in 1668, who, in concert with his own theological change, led the congregation, at least in part, to move from a General Baptist theology to a Particular Baptist theology. He also led the congregation to build a house of worship in Horsleydown in 1672 during a brief interlude in the persecution of those times.[52] After Keach's death in 1704, Benjamin Stinton served for fourteen years, to be followed by John Gill from 1720 to 1771. John Rippon followed Gill and remained for sixty-three years, dying in 1836. Joseph Angus succeeded Rippon but remained only until 1840 when he accepted a position with the Baptist Missionary Society. Two pastors followed Angus; they were James Smith and William Walters. Susannah Spurgeon remembered him as a "quaint and rugged preacher, but one well-versed in the blessed art of bringing souls to Christ." She had seen him administering the ordinance of baptism and wondered "with a tearful longing whether I should ever be able thus to confess my faith in the Lord Jesus."[53]

During its history the church had enjoyed many years of flourishing but had had periodic declines in membership and fervency of spirit. In an auditorium that seated over 1,200, hardly more than 200 regularly attended.[54] Drummond claims that there could not have been more than eighty.[55] All of that changed very soon after Spurgeon's arrival.

Twenty-five years later, as Spurgeon reminisced about the early days as a means of showing the irresistible nature of divine providence, he recalled: "Twenty-five years ago we began this work for the Lord with a slender handful of friends, so slender, indeed, that it is easy enough to make a list of them." Just a "few poor, godly people were

51. *Autobiography,* 1:260-61.

52. For a helpful treatment of the life and thought of Benjamin Keach, see Austin Walker. *The Excellent Benjamin Keach.* Dundas, Ontario: Joshua Press, 2004.

53. *Autobiography,* 1:279.

54. *Autobiography,* 1:263, publishers note.

55. Drummond, 189.

the nucleus," and they were "as good as they were "as few." For years they had been discouraged and disappointed and were thus delivered from all "unpractical squeamishness"; he found them ready to join "with their young leader in an effort for restoring their church and increasing the kingdom of Christ." They prayed for prosperity and "prosperity came suddenly, like the bursting of a great rain cloud." Unlike the rain cloud, however, prosperity did not abate but continued with a downpour in abundance year after year.[56]

The London Pulpit

When Spurgeon arrived, the pulpiteers of London were mighty men of renown. That a nineteen-year-old, in less than half a decade, would rise to be the most prominent of all would have been unthinkable. An astute, but cynical, observer of *The London Pulpit*, who wrote a book by that name, mused: "I know not that there is a happier berth in the world than that of a fashionable Evangelical preacher in this enlightened city and enlightened age." The evangelical preacher was adored by the women, envied by the men, had his portrait in neighborhood shops, and received gifts of worsted wool slippers from the young women. His silver teapot was a gift of the congregation.[57] His slightly superior, worldly-wise comments usually framed a viewpoint 180 degrees removed from the studied opinion of Spurgeon. Ritchie celebrated the poetic thinker unbound by traditional creedal boundaries, the intellectual focused on subtle insights about current social and cultural trends, and suggested all the wrong criteria for the success, or lack of it, of the various London pulpits. On rare instances his opinion might intersect the plane of Spurgeon's

observations.

Anglicanism would survive because of the favored position it enjoyed and always there would be those that gravitated toward the predictable aesthetic pleasure of ritual. But for the success of dissent, the gravitational pull of the pulpit must be strong. That had been in decline. Ritchie claimed that two things contributed. One, "the pulpit is too much a repetition of creeds and theologies that are becoming extinct; and in the second place, there is a dead weight in the pews which masters the pulpit, and deadens its intellectual life." Ritchie was complaining, of course, but based on this observation he described dissenting ministers in a way that Spurgeon himself would affirm. They say things in private conversation that they dare not utter in the pulpit. When he seeks to give some vent to a repressed conscience, the vagueness of theological terms comes to his aid so that what he says in "one sense is understood by his hearers in another."[58] Ritchie concluded what Spurgeon would conclude, though with entirely different regrets, "No wonder then that the pulpit is so barren of power." Men with gifts generally chose the pen rather than the pulpit in a day of universal reading. In spite of such discouraging conditions, the "pulpit is not wholly deserted. It can still boast its consecrated talent."

Ritchie then surveyed the most popular pulpits in London within the first five years of Spurgeon's arrival. Though largely freed from "the buffooneries by which at one time it was disgraced", of the 1,200 clergy in London, one could hardly name a dozen "superior men."[59] Among Anglicans, Ritchie liked J. C. M. Bellew who ignored the ceremonial disputes in his own church for a Christianity that is "something proud, and majestic, and divine,—a universal remedy for a univer-

---

56. S&T, 1878, "Preface," iii.

57. J. Ewing Ritchie, *The London Pulpit*, Second edition. Revised, corrected, and enlarged (London: Willliam Tweedie, 1858), 69.

58. Ibid., 86.

59. Ibid., 21-23.

sal disease,—not a skeleton of dead doctrine, or a bone of contention, or an obsolete word, but a living, healthy, beneficent power."[60] Thomas Dale had a stylish congregation, whose young ladies had servants that carried the Book of Common Prayer. With a glare of silks and satins, feathers, and jewels they devoutly confessed themselves to be miserable sinners. "If the grace that is divine be as common there as the grace that is earthly, Mr. Dale's charge must be a happy flock indeed," and "one would hardly mind, in the midst of such rich city merchants and their charming daughters, being a miserable sinner himself. Such opulent misery and fashionable sin seem rather enviable than otherwise." His sermons, like his poetry, were highly polished but too invariably the same. Rev. R. Liddell was a Puseyite, whose intellectual and doctrinal commitments left him little to do but "expatiate on the sanctity of the priestly office, and the mysterious powers possessed by the Church." His was an educated congregation, but "in a wrong direction."

F. D. Maurice at Lincoln-Inn's Field was the quintessential intellectual, accused of heresy, but only because he resists the imposition of a human creed and "denies the doctrine of eternal damnation." He was a man of "study and thought" whose "voice is clear and agreeable." He differs from other clergymen "in his superior power of ratiocination and in the wider inductions on which he bases his doctrines."[61] According to Ritchie, though the more narrow religious journals loved to criticize Maurice, "No man has so earnestly laboured to Christianize—not the dark tribes of Polynesia, for then these journals would have been redolent with his praise—but the savages with white faces and dark hearts that we meet in our streets every day." Spurgeon would find Maurice the epitome of the liberal intellectual.

Rising high above all others in Ritchie's estimation was Herman Melville.[62] The magic of his voice had charmed every ear. He was tall and dark "with grey hair and blue eyes, with a face lit up with genius." Indeed, he was "the most brilliant preacher in the English Church." He begins with power and increases all the way through the sermon from text to conclusion, a phenomenon of magnetic passion and intellect, perfectly formed sentences and paragraphs, and breathtaking delivery "developing and illustrating his meaning with a brilliancy and rapidity unparalleled in the pulpit at the present day." His hell is a real place, "a bottomless pit where the smoke of their torment ever ascends—where the worm never dies—where the fire is not quenched." At the same time, none is more committed to the sanctity of the English Establishment "whose articles he has subscribed, and whose emoluments he pockets." He knows of no other church than that which the state supports. "Pulpits outside the Church are not only destitute of that power, but, alas! destitute also of all saving grace." Alas for Spurgeon, for none would be so like him and yet so far from him.

As for the Churchman Villiers, Ritchie considered him "a fine, well-made man" with a prepossessing figure, "a great thing in a public speaker." The pulpit is no place for "weak, stunted, deformed, wretched-looking men." Other desirable traits possessed by Villiers were a fine voice with excellent qualities in reading, a thing necessary to give any liveliness to the read part of the liturgy. His preaching was calculated to keep the attention of his hearers for "he is exceedingly active and energetic" in the pulpit, "his voice filling every part of the enormous church." Neither original nor intellectual, nor creative enough to reviv-

---

60. Ibid., 29.

61. Ibid., 55.

62. Ibid., 62.

ify old themes, he made "the common truths of orthodox Christianity" the staple of his discourse. "The theatre and the ballroom are the objects of his bitterest denunciations," a theme well-suited to enchant his congregation since "they frequent neither the one nor the other" and thus "care little what harsh things he says of those who do."[63]

Among the Independents, Thomas Binney of Weigh-House Chapel gained Ritchie's mature approval. He had been through the Slough of Despond and Doubting Castle, had struggled with Vanity Fair and had developed reasoned and tested answers to the destructive powers of each. "Such a man has a right to preach to me," Ritchie surmised; "If he has known, felt, thought, suffered, more than I, he is master, and I listen."[64] His prayers, not like the beautiful but cold and unchanging petitions of the Anglican liturgy, reach into the shifts of the human soul, make earth recede and heaven draw near. The preaching starts slowly but "at length you catch, like a gleam of sunshine in a November fog, a fine thought in fine language." Binney, so Ritchie judged, was a Christian Carlyle, with "the same faculty of realizing great and sterling thoughts; but with a light upon his way and in his heart which Carlyle has never known."[65] This commendation would be seconded by Spurgeon as he also found Binney one of the most thoughtful and earnest of the London preachers. Spurgeon reviewed books by and about Binney, and pointed out that while he had many imitators none of them had his gifts or the rarities of his imposing and sincere zeal.

Baldwin Brown of Clayland's Chapel, just above thirty, had great abilities and confidence and attainments commensurate with it. His main attraction is freshness, something of a code word for Ritchie. Brown's speech was "a living speech, not a monotonous repetition of old divinity. He has wandered out of the conventional circle. He has come in contact with great minds."[66] His view of things is broad and "manly" [meaning apparently original to him and not necessarily consistent with the doctrinal formula of the past]. His faith, therefore, "is a living one. His Christianity is practical—that by which men may shape their life as well as square their creed." He did not wander "weakly and sentimentally in other lands and in other ages," but brought his "mind and heart to bear upon the realities of the present day. The questions of our age, not of past ages, he discusses in his pulpit." To Spurgeon, this would seem like an inflated way of saying the man was tinged with modern thought of the most destructive kind, indeed what Spurgeon would publicly call "pernicious error."[67]

On the other hand, under the sneer of Ritchie, but soon a fast friend and supporter of Spurgeon, John Campbell ruled with a rod of iron over one section of the Congregational church. Some delight in such a rod and such a man, and they find it "a real blessing to get hold of a firm, dogmatic man, who knows his own mind, and who will kindly take care of theirs."[68] Campbell was "fluent in pen, meagre in attainment, seemingly master of no one subject, yet writing vehemently on all." Ritchie presented Campbell as a man that had "never said a word, or written a line, that is not narrow and sectarian and one-sided." Ritchie continued with line upon line of disgust and invective against Campbell. He considered Campbell "one of the failures of the age" for no man

---

63. Ibid., 73.

64. Ibid., 78.

65. Ibid., 79.

66. Ibid., 88.

67. This phrase was in a letter Spurgeon signed in conjunction with six other Baptist ministers including William Brock and Joseph Angus. *Autobiography* 1:485.

68. J. Ewing Ritchie, *The London Pulpit*, Second edition. Revised, corrected, and enlarged (London: Willliam Tweedie, 1858), 69.

had "talked more, or done less."[69] "Superficiality has ever been his bane. A fatal copiousness of words has ruined him." A failure in the pulpit, per Ritchie, he turned himself to the newspaper and thus hindered the men who would have done well what he did poorly.[70] With Ritchie's full rage intact, Campbell is just the kind of man who would come to the aid of an attacked and smeared Spurgeon.

Thomas T. Lynch would be given notoriety far beyond his true ability to provoke such because of a controversy that swirled over a book of poetry that he produced entitled *The Rivulet: Hymns for the Heart and Voice.* Spurgeon joined the list of commentators, slightly on the negative side, an event that will be discussed later. Ritchie, however, revealed the standard of his judgment by expressing his deep regret that Lynch had only a small congregation. That fact served as no indictment of the usefulness or talent of Lynch but as a reproach of the Christian church. "Not three hundred can be got to hear him; and yet I know no man better worth your hearing," Ritchie opined.[71] That allowed Lynch more time for the press, a fact that convinced many that their decision not to hear him was well-founded, although Ritchie was deeply impressed. "He is young yet. He is older in thoughts than in years," Ritchie believed, adding that "his inner life has been of richer growth than his outer one." Lynch would never be a popular preacher, "but to men of thought, especially to men of literature—to the school of Tennyson and Coleridge—his will always be a welcome name."[72] That which commended him to Ritchie would make him suspect to Spurgeon.

Conversely, Ritchie's expectations from a preacher at the intersection of authority and reason directly contradicted Spurgeon's deep-seated convictions. Ritchie described Martin of Westminster Chapel as "a man of one book," the Bible, and a man of one fact, "salvation by the cross," making him a man of one message and one mission,[73] "You are lucky if you get a seat, the chapel, which has recently been enlarged, being always full."[74] Ritchie put forth that description as a criticism and statement of his minimal worth as a preacher. Martin so focused his message because he so fully believed the biblical doctrine of total depravity—that fact in itself was enough to drive Ritchie to a philosophical excursus on the relation between set creeds, fixed doctrine, and the task of the Christian minister, as he saw it. "Is the language of the Psalmist, descriptive of himself, universally true?" Ritchie queried. "Is it true that man is born in sin, and shapen in iniquity; that he is depraved; that he hates what is good, and loves what is bad?" A positive commitment to that idea, so Ritchie surmised, "sufficiently accounts for the war ever carried on between faith and reason, the church and the world."[75] Ritchie thought it was a "terrible doctrine" and could not account for its popularity. Regrettably, those "who preach it are the most popular preachers." A gospel with that at the bottom tramples on the intellect and does, indeed, give the world to the weak and the despised and to the nothings. They are taught to feel themselves superior to "the science and literature and philosophy of man, which they hold but as dirt in comparison with the truths they teach and the discoveries they reveal. Their appeal is not to the intellect or the taste" since they care for neither.

69. Ibid., 96.
70. Ibid., 100.
71. Ibid., 103.
72. Ibid., 110.

73. Ibid., 116.
74. Ibid., 118.
75. Ibid., 111.

A man like A. J. Morris, however, says what is worth hearing. With him religion is a real thing He has fed his intellect on it, and squared his life by it. By its lamp "he is prepared to find his way when he comes to the valley of the shadow of death." The religion he preaches is as good for the counting-house as for the closet, and he "gives you something to think about as well." He has not taken up his own creed upon a trust; nor does he expect his hearers to do so; but he has a keen perception of spiritual realities and tries to give his people the same. Though Spurgeon loved, practiced, and promoted deep spirituality, he never encouraged its prosperity at the expense of definite truth.

Among the Baptists, Ritchie reluctantly liked William Brock, the pastor at Bedford Square attended by Sir Morton Peto. Brock was purely Saxon without the slightest pretension to elegance or grace. "Such men as he are not the men young ladies run after, fall in love with, get to write in their albums, buy engravings for their boudoirs; but, nevertheless, with their strong passionate speech, and indomitable pluck, they are the men who move the world."[76] But he moved a world that wanted quick pre-set answers, not refinement of philosophy—"It is in the Bible" satisfied him and pacified those that listened. "People want something positive and dogmatic" because they have little time for theology and even less to hear both sides of any issue. It must, therefore, be positive, plain, and settled, and Brock can give it to them that way.

As a distinct contrast among the Baptists, at Devonshire Square Chapel was the former great man among the Baptists, J. Howard Hinton. He had a small attendance for "Mr. Hinton has no clap-trap about him." He has long gone beyond the time that "young ladies take an interest in their darling minister", and with Hinton, "you must not merely listen to him, but must use your own intellectual powers as well." That exertion goes beyond the desires of most of the church and chapel goers of London. Those that do hear him are instructed by his sermons, have their views clarified and more enlarged, and gain a greater understanding of the Christian scheme. Hinton maintained an outline of Calvinism in his theology, while in essence, according to Ritchie's evaluation, he exploded it completely. For example, though he believed in human depravity, he preached that "no man is subject to the wrath of God, in any sense or degree, because of Adam's sin, but every man stands as free from the penal influences of his first parent's crime as though Adam had never existed, or as though he himself were the first of mankind." On the subject of the work of the Spirit, his emphasis on human responsibility so prevailed that he seemed on occasion almost to oppose the doctrine of regeneration. According to Ritchie, Hinton preached, "Without being moved thereto by the Spirit of God, and without any other influence than the blessing which God always gives to the use of means, you are competent to alter your mind towards God by obeying the dictates of your own conscience, and employing the faculties of your own being. Think on your ways, and you will turn your feet to God's testimonies. This is what God requires you to do in order to obtain deliverance from His wrath; and, except you do it without regard to any communication of His Spirit, he leaves you to perish."[77]

Ritchie possibly misunderstood the context of Hinton's declarations. Hinton, just two years after the publication of Ritchie's dubious com-

---

76. Ibid., 131.

77. Ibid., 139.

mendations, took a stand for theology that would certainly make Ritchie cringe. In the interests of "vital Evangelical truth—for the truth of God and the souls of men," Hinton wrote strictures against a book by Baldwin Brown because he detected a "theology fatally deficient in the truth and power of the gospel."[78] Spurgeon clearly supported J. H. Hinton's protest and entered the controversy in two tightly worded missives. Ritchie's approval, however, of Hinton's apparent slight defection from Calvinism, showed how he would evaluate Spurgeon's unabashed preaching of utter dependence on the divine Spirit at no cost to human responsibility. "At times," Ritchie admitted, "Mr. Hinton seems to contradict himself. But, after all, is not the theme one on which the human intellect can never be perfectly consistent and clear?"

For Sheridan Knowles, the former actor turned minister, Ritchie held little admiration. "Knowles does not shine in the pulpit as he did on the stage," but his sermons are "bundles of little bits of arguments tied up together as a heap of old sticks, and just as dry."[79] An honest and dogmatic man, he was but a "moderate preacher after all." It is not surprising that Ritchie would lampoon the rational powers of Knowles, for Knowles was an ardent and early supporter of Spurgeon.

The social plume for the Baptists was "THE HON. AND REV. BAPTIST NOEL." A convert from Anglicanism, and one of the royal chaplains at that, Noel was "of lordly origin" as the tenth son of a peeress whose sister was a lady in waiting to the Queen, and whose brother was an earl. No wonder that so many London shopkeepers and tradesmen resort to St. John's Chapel, Bedford Row, to hear him. "These good people felt that by going to hear him they were killing two birds with one stone—getting into the very best soci-

ety, and at the same time worshipping the God of heaven and of earth." As one of the plainest preachers of the metropolis, when he rises in the pulpit, "you feel that you have that undefinable mystery, a gentleman, before you," unsurpassed in "elegance of appearance, or urbanity of manner." His words are aimed at the heart, not the head; if he could not master the understanding, then he would go for the affections. "He may win you over by his gentleness, though he fail to convince you by his power." As we will see, Spurgeon's ilk found little place for approval in Ritchie.

John Cummings, among the Presbyterians, offended Ritchie's view of Christian ministry as deeply as any that he discussed. He was weary of Cummings' "Old Testament and his high-dried Scotch theology, and his Romanist antipathies, and his Millennial hopes." Instead of theories of grace, and other-worldly palaver, remember that men are finite and human. "Dr. Cummings preaches as if you had no father or mother, no sister or brother, no wife or child, no human struggles and hopes—as if the great object of preaching was to fill you with Biblical pedantry." Ritchie looked for a place that would make men "better, wiser, stronger than before." That Cummings' house of worship was so thronged spoke ill of the religious propensities of Londoners, in Ritchie's estimation.

Ritchie would much prefer, though not endorsing all that he stood for, a man like William Forster, a man of free inquiry, opposed to all creeds and fetters on the reason of man. When he left Calvinism, he also left any substantial orthodoxy. A new chapel was built for him, in Kentish Town, upon the agreement that "all definition of God, Christ, and the Holy Spirit, should be avoided, and that the clause, 'This place is erected for the worship of God, as the Father, through the Son, and by the Holy Spirit,' should be placed at

---

78. *Autobiography*, 1:482.

79. Ritchie, 145.

the head of the deed." Ritchie was willing to wait and see if Forster's approach to Christianity, unfettered by creed, would answer the ever-changing needs of the nineteenth century. Forster was so opposed to any authority outside the reason of man that he posited the query, "Have we not yet to learn that there is no *via media*—no middle way between Reason and Rome?" A man that grows and changes everyday cannot possibly give honest assent to an unchanging creed. "Wherever this tyranny is obeyed, there cannot be much depth of conviction, vitality of sentiment, growth of knowledge, and improvement of religious life."[80] Spurgeon could not even pause to consider the possibility of such a view being right, much less helpful. There was one unchanging gospel, the same in every age, sent forth for men who are one and all under the curse of imputed guilt and corruption of soul. None but Jesus in his redeeming work can do helpless sinners good.

The New Park Street Pulpit

The immediate success of Spurgeon so astounded London that periodicals vied for news about his services as energetically as people vied for places from which they could hear his sermons. Conveyance and pubs prospered as crowds moved across the Thames to "Charlie's." The New Park Street facilities, which had dwarfed the crowd on that first evening of Spurgeon's preaching, soon seemed small. Though he had wanted a wider sphere of service, the growth of the crowds overwhelmed Spurgeon with the sense of responsibility. Later he reflected: "When I first became a Pastor in London, my success appalled me, and the thought of the career which it seemed to open up, so far from elating me, cast me into the lowest depth, out of which I uttered my *Miserere*

and found no room for a *Gloria in excelsis*."[81] He wanted to return to obscurity or to emigrate to America where in the backwoods he might feel sufficient for the things demanded of him. Spurgeon learned to expect depression as a precursor to greater demands and larger blessing.

One of the first challenges of faith that he experienced came in a very physical form when, scarcely a year into his ministry there, a cholera epidemic struck London, most intensely in the neighborhood of New Park Street. Many church families lost members. Spurgeon was busy at funerals and at the bedside of many sick both in his church and in the homes of other persons who had visited the Chapel to hear him preach. A man who had scoffed at him in the first months of his ministry sent an urgent call to Spurgeon. He went and found the man dying and almost unconscious and unable even to respond to Spurgeon's attempt to present the gospel. Three years later Spurgeon referred to the panic that seized people during this time and the short-lived resolutions many made in the face of danger. "I remember, when last time the cholera swept through your streets, ye hurried to your churches, and ye prayed; terror sat upon your countenances, and many of you cried aloud for deliverance. It came. What did you do? Alas! for your piety! It was as the morning cloud, and as the early dew it passed away."[82]

Spurgeon's unrelenting efforts at ministry brought him to a point of exhaustion and he feared that he himself would succumb to the fatality that swirled all around him. On his way to a pastoral visit he passed the window of a shoemaker who had procured one of the signs that warned people against the entrance of certain streets in London and informed them where medical aid could be found. The lead word—the biggest and boldest

---

80. Ibid., 187–88.

81. *Autobiography*, 1:263.

82. NPSP, 1857, 386.

lettering—simply read "CHOLERA." In the middle of the sign a bold handwriting announced, "Because thou hast made the Lord, which is my refuge, even the Most High, thy habitation; there shall no evil befall thee, neither shall any plague come nigh thy dwelling." The reading of these words made Spurgeon personalize the promise and continued his visitation without fear of evil or harm, in his words, "girt with immortality."[83] Surely he referred to himself when, in a sermon in February 1855 on Christ crucified, he described a pastor in a series of illustrations of the power of Christ crucified. "What is it that empowers yonder minister, in the midst of the cholera, to climb up that creaking staircase and stand by the bed of some dying creature who has that dire disease? It must be a thing of power which leads him to risk his life. It is love of the Cross of Christ which bids him do it!"[84]

Meanwhile at New Park Street, as Spurgeon explained to a friend, "We are getting on too fast. Our harvest is too rich for the barn." Conversions were many and Spurgeon met with inquirers on Monday and Thursday evenings and had to send many away without seeing them. The conversion of T. W. Medhurst in this year led to the establishment of the Pastors' College, a story to be told later. The difficulty of helping all the inquirers led eventually to the election of elders in 1859 and Spurgeon's re-instituting the office of teacher in the church in 1862.[85] On Thursday evenings, people could scarcely find a seat for the week-night service. On Sundays the crowd was immense and the aisles became so full thirty minutes prior to the service that seat-holders could not get to their seats. "Many stand through the whole service, wedged in by their fellows, and prevented from escaping by the crowd outside, who seal up the doors and fill the yard in front, and stand in throngs as far as the sound can reach."[86]

Spurgeon likened the stuffiness of the place so filled, also lighted with gas lights, to the "black-hole of Calcutta."[87] He sought remedies for this in ways that startled his staid, traditional congregation. His suggestion that the unopenable permanent windows be removed was met with inaction. On one Sabbath the congregation arrived to find that some of the panes had been removed "as if they had been taken out by a glazier" and others in a less professional fashion. Spurgeon announced that a sum of £5 be set aside for finding the culprit and that, when found, he should receive the £5 as a reward. No one discovered or reported the perpetrator. "I have not felt it to be my duty to inform against the individual," Spurgeon wrote later, and "I trust none will suspect me, but if they do, I shall have to confess that I have walked with the stick which let the oxygen into that stifling structure."[88]

Something also would have to be done about space. At an evening service in 1854, Spurgeon called for a tearing down of the back wall just as the walls of Jericho had fallen by faith. "An aged and prudent deacon," so Spurgeon described him, approached Spurgeon at the end of the service and insisted, "Let us never hear of that again." Not to be intimidated or hindered in his view of the urgent need for more space, Spurgeon responded, "You will hear no more about it when it is done, and therefore the sooner you set about doing it the better."[89] Spurgeon had told the committee during the epistolary negotiations prior to

---

83. *Autobiography*, 1:272-73.
84. SS, 1:105.
85. *Autobiography*, 2:75, 77.
86. Murray, *Letters*, 52, 53.
87. S&T, April 1876, 160; *Autobiography*, 1:271.
88. *Autobiography*, 1:271.
89. S&T, "Our First Seven Years," April 1876, 161; Also, *Autobiography*, 1:271.

his call that he did not fear man and this deacon learned the truth of it. Though just beyond twenty years of age, his vision and resolution quickly established the grounding for his eventual nickname, "The Governor." The people could see that expansion was no mere headiness on the part of their pastor, but was a stewardship pressed upon them by the spiritual reality before them.

An Enforced Sojourn

A selected committee made a decision to expand the facilities. The plan seemed a bit awkward, but given the location and the limitations of the site and structure, it was a gallant effort to maximize their property. The vestries and school rooms were absorbed into the chapel, new school rooms were built with windows that would let down so that overflow crowds could be seated there and still hear the preacher.[90] This attempt at accommodation of the pressing crowds led eventually to the construction of the Metropolitan Tabernacle, but its present futility had to be demonstrated.

The renovation made the procurement of temporary accommodations necessary. Exeter Hall, a large public auditorium which held 5,000, was rented. It was north of the Thames, making it more accessible to the rest of London but more difficult for the New Park Street congregation. Not only did the members make their way there, but thousands of others came and the Hall was so bloated with people that thousands had to remain outside. Spurgeon gave a simple summary of the dynamic time: "The feeble folk at New Park-street soon felt strong enough to attempt an aggressive work by holding services at Exeter Hall, and, when this turned out to be more than a success, future progress was forced upon them rather than selected by them."[91] He wrote a friend: "It is strange that such

a power should be in one small body to crowd Exeter Hall to suffocation, and block up the Strand, so that pedestrians have to turn down by-ways, and all other traffic is at a standstill." [92]

As newspapers carried paragraphs reporting the stranglehold that Spurgeon's preaching was creating on the Strand, editors began to attack the cause of this strange phenomenon. So many coming to such a place to hear such a young and obscure preacher! Spurgeon recalled that the "most ridiculous stories were circulated" (probably the worsted slipper story by Mr. Ewing Ritchie himself, for he seemed fixated on such cartoonish presentations), "and the most cruel falsehoods invented, but all these things worked together for good."[93] Crowds did not diminish and Exeter Hall was overflowing throughout the time needed for the renovation.

Immediately prior to the move to Exeter Hall, Passmore and Alabaster had begun publishing the weekly sermons of Spurgeon in January. His sermon for January 7, 1855, was the first to appear. This contributed to the rush of people to hear Spurgeon. "Our place of meeting at New Park Street only sufficed us for six weeks after the publication of the 'Pulpit,' and the platform at Exeter Hall was occupied till June of the same year, when, the chapel having been enlarged, the congregation returned to its own abode, to be there crowded, inconvenienced, and almost suffocated for another twelve months."[94] Upon the return, hundreds that wanted to attend the services could not get in. Spurgeon was aware that many from other congregations attended and within the first month he began to chide them for taking up space that was needed by the derelict of their own neighborhood:

---

90. S&T, April 1876, 161.

91. S&T, 1878, Preface, iii.

92. Murray, *Letters*, 56.

93. S&T, April 1876, 161.

94. S&T, January 1875, 5.

This one thing I ask—never come here to gratify your curiosity. You that are members of other congregations, just consider it your duty to stay at home. There are many stray sheep about. I would rather have them than you. Keep to your own place. I do not want to rob other ministers. Do not come here from charity. We are much obliged to you for your kindly intentions. But we would rather have your seat than your company if you are members of other Churches. We want sinners to come—sinners of every sort. But do not let us have that sort of men whose ears are everlastingly itching for some new preacher—who are saying, "I need something else, I need something else."[95]

On another occasion, Spurgeon recounted the return to New Park Street with a vivid recollection of the glory as well as the difficulties of the inadequate renovation:

The return to New Park Street, enlarged though it was, resembled the attempt to put the sea into a teapot. We were more inconvenienced than ever. To turn many hundreds away was the general if not the universal necessity. And those who gained admission were but little better off, for the packing was dense in the extreme, and the heat something terrible even to remember. Our enemies continued to make our name more and more known by penny pamphlets and letters in the papers, which all tended to swell the crowd. More caricatures appeared, and among the rest [*sic*, best?] "Catch-'em-alive-O!"

Criticism and Praise

Life was happening fast for Spurgeon. The radical opposition of periodicals with such a wide circulation surely must have been a shock for one that had so recently been buried in anonymity in the rural village of Waterbeach. Though he took it as a blessing from the hand of God, it still gave him sleepless nights. He knew that this kind of treatment must surely disturb his parents also. He wrote his father in March 1855 asking him not to be "grieved at the slanderous libel in this week's *Express*. Of course, it is all a lie, without an atom of foundation; and while the whole of London is talking of me, and thousands are unable to get near the door, the opinion of a penny-a-liner is of little consequence." He assured his lifelong mentor that an answer would appear on all points soon. The "lie" claimed that Spurgeon in public had announced to the young ladies in the audience not to entertain hopes for him for he was already attached, and that they should not send him presents. The report was publicly exposed as a pure fabrication, a withdrawal and apology printed, in the context of an even more irascible spirit toward Spurgeon.[96]

In quick succession, correspondents and editors called his preaching a "prostitution of the pulpit," the "vulgar colloquial varied by rant" in which "the most solemn mysteries of our holy religion are by him rudely, roughly, and impiously handled," "blasphemy from a parson," "oratorical tricks, daring utterances, ... coarse sentiments, scholastic expressions, and a clap-trap style," "insolence so unblushing, intellect so feeble, flippancy so ostentatious, and manners so rude," "pulpit buffoonery" and alarmed readers with the complaint of the horrid reality that those who crowd so enthusiastically to hear this execrable display of pulpit Mountebankism "consists of people who are not in the habit of frequenting a place of worship."[97] For himself, though he could not fall asleep until morning light, he could say, "Hail reproach, and welcome shame." On top

95. SS, 1:146. This message was preached on June 3, 1855, upon the return of the congregation to the newly renovated chapel.

96. *Autobiography*, 1:313-16.

97. Ibid., 316-25.

of that, he could rejoice because "the devil is roused, the Church is awakening, and I am now counted worthy to suffer for Christ's sake." Suffering was good ballast to offset the giddy effect of the applause.[98]

Preaching on "A Lecture on Little Faith" in 1858, Spurgeon made an illustration of his experience on the necessity of laboring to "get as much as possible free from self."[99] For himself, he labored "to attain the position of perfect indifference of all men." He found that, when he heard praise and gave way to finding pleasure in it, censure and abuse would follow. He felt this even more keenly "for the very fact that I took the praise rendered me liable to lay hold upon the censure." He learned therefore to try, "especially of late," to regard both man's praise and censure as unworthy of notice, "but to fix my heart simply upon this—I know that I have a right motive in what I attempt to do, I am conscious that I endeavor to serve God with a single eye to his glory, and therefore it is not for me to take praise from man nor censure, but to stand independently upon the one rock of right doing."[100]

Spurgeon's conscious efforts to detach himself from both flattery and deflation allowed him to survey the benefits of this criticism. At the opening of the Metropolitan Tabernacle in 1861, he pointed to the power of the divine Spirit as the only source of effectuality in the ministry of any preacher and the sole explanation for any movement of revival. Criticism of him amounted to nothing in light of blessings from God:

> May the Lord here, while he uses human instrumentality, yet let you all see that "it is not by might, nor by power, but by my Spirit saith

the Lord." This has indeed been my mission, to shew the power of God in human weakness. I do acknowledge and confess what is so continually said of me. "The man is not educated." *Granted.* "His periods are unpolished." *Granted.* "His manner is rough." *Be it so, if you will.* "Himself a fool," *Aye, amen, and what else you choose.* Gather together all the epithets in the catalogue of abuse—come heap them here. But who hath done *this,* who hath saved souls, and called the people to his footstool? Why, if the instrument be mean, the more glory to him that used it. And if the man be nothing, "I glory in infirmity, that the power of God may rest upon me."[101]

To one that dared to write against the editorial orthodoxy on Spurgeon and speak of his great usefulness to the poor and irreligious of London, Spurgeon responded with humble, but eloquent, gratitude. "The head of the church," he affirmed, "has given me sympathy with the masses, love to the poor, and the means of winning the attention of the ignorant and unenlightened." He never sought popularity and cannot fathom how it has come, but should he change now to please the polite critic and leave the people that "require a simple and stirring style?" "I am, perhaps, *vulgar,*" he admitted, "but it is not intentional, save that I *must* and *will* make the people listen." The polite preachers and others may serve their class, but "God has owned me to the most degraded and off-cast;" Spurgeon's they were, and Spurgeon must have them. He thanked the editor for recognizing such was the case and for providing one favorable note within the "constant din of abuse."[102]

If some slandered, those that vied for space to hear him lifted him to the level of a force of nature. On a preaching tour in 1855 he reported to

98. Spurgeon, *Letters,* "To His Father," 4 March 1855.
99. SS, 5:139; NPSP, 1858, 321ff., Sermon 205.
100. SS, 5:139; NPSP, 1858.
101. MTP, 1861, 219, 220.
102. *Autobiography,* 1:318-19.

Susannah, his fiancée of a year, of extraordinary blessing and expressions of personal appreciation. On June 2, 1855, God gave him as he "preached like the chief of sinners, to those who, like me, were chief sinners, too." Souls were saved and "many were the tears, and not a few the smiles." Three weeks later he reported an outdoor service in which he "climbed to the summit of a minister's glory." He had preached to 10,000 in the field at Hackney, "twice as many as at Exeter Hall," he remarked. During the message profound silence descended on the massive crowd but afterwards "never did mortal man receive a more enthusiastic ovation! I wonder I am alive! After the service, five or six gentlemen endeavored to clear a passage, but I was borne along, amid cheers, and prayers, and shouts, for about a quarter of an hour," which to him seemed more like a week. "I was hurried round and round the field without hope of escape until, suddenly seeing a nice open carriage, with two occupants, standing near, I sprang in, and begged them to drive away." They did and he stood up as they drove off, waved his hat, pronounced a benediction toward the shouting crowd, and saw hats lifted from thousands of heads while cheer after cheer echoed through the fields. "Surely," he discerned carefully, "amid these plaudits, I can hear the low rumblings of an advancing storm of reproaches—but even this I can bear for the Master's sake."[103]

All of this convinced Spurgeon that New Park Street would become the center of a revival in London. He sought to lead his church to that conviction as they entered the newly renovated chapel. Based on God's promise to Jerusalem in Ezekiel 34, Spurgeon enlarged the sense of the text to apply it "to the church of Jesus Christ, and to this particular church with which you and I stand

connected."[104] If the lights of others only flickered, perhaps they can be set ablaze by the light that beamed from New Park Street. "If there is a flame here, let the flame spread, until all the neighborhood churches shall be lit up with the glory." In that way they would be a blessing and a rejoicing of the earth, for "there is never a revival in one spot, but it shall affect others." So exhilarated was Spurgeon by the relentless multiplication of conversions and pressing interest in the pure and simple message of the gospel he preached, that he crowned his sturdy pre-millennialism with an exuberant post-millennial hope.

> The little seed has grown to this—who knows what it shall be? Only let us strive together without variance! Let us labor for Jesus. Never did men have so fair an opportunity, for the last hundred years, "There is a tide that, taken at the flood, leads on to fortune." Shall you take it at the flood? Over the bar, at the harbor's mouth! O ship of Heaven, let your sails be out. Let not your canvass be furled. And the wind will blow us across the Sea of Difficulty that lies before us. Oh, that the latter day might have its dawning even in this despised habitation! O my God! From this place cause the first wave to spring which shall move another and then another, till the last great wave shall sweep over the sands of time and dash against the rocks of eternity, echoing as it falls, "Hallelujah! Hallelujah! Hallelujah! The Lord God Omnipotent reigns!"[105]

In addition, the foundation for Spurgeon's benevolent empire, "a city on a hill, which cannot be hid," was beginning to take shape. "I hope," he told his congregation on their return to the renovated chapel, "we shall never be satisfied, as members of Park Street, until we are a blessing, not only to ourselves, but to all the places round

---

103. Spurgeon, *Letters*, "To Susannah Thompson," June 2, 1855 and 23rd of the same month.

104. SS 1:136.

105. Ibid., 153.

about our hill."[106] Several agencies of work presently constituted their "hill." The Sabbath School that was growing and now called for more men. Next, the "Visiting and Christian Instruction Society" awaited ready workers with hearts for gospel saturation of Southwark. This was for visitation of the neighborhood, and Spurgeon already superintended a man "who labors zealously and earnestly in visiting the sick." Spurgeon felt very satisfied with the effectiveness of this man and called on others to join the work of this society in distributing tracts from door to door and to visit the numerous shops in the neighborhood of the church for a word of witness. Perhaps they would close shop on Sunday and attend chapel. Then with an auspicious, if also audacious, statement of vision, Spurgeon announced a general and a particular:

> Let me not forget any agency connected with this Church. There are several more which are places round about our hill—and the Lord has just put it into my heart to fashion other societies, which shall be made a blessing to this hill—and in a little while you shall hear of them. We have several Brothers in this congregation to whom God has given a mouth of utterance. These are about to form themselves into a society for proclaiming the Word of God. Where God has so blessed His Church and made us to be so noted and named among the people, why should we not keep on? We have been brought up to a great pitch of fervency and love. Now is the time for doing something. While the iron is hot, why not strike and fashion it? I believe we have the materials not only for making a Church, here, that shall be the glory of the Baptist churches in London, but for making churches everywhere throughout the metropolis! And we have more plans on hand, which matured by sober judgment and backed by prudence, shall

yet make this metropolis more honored than it has been by the sound of the pure Gospel and the proclamation of the pure Word of God. May God make all our Agencies—the places round about our hill—a blessing![107]

Brothers with mouths of utterance—material for a pastors' college. Materials for making a church, the glory of the Baptist churches of London, making churches throughout the metropolis—a big home base for founding other churches throughout the city and in other districts. More plans, matured by sober judgment, backed by prudence, the sound of a pure gospel, the proclamation of the pure Word of God—an open-ended consideration of anything to expand the impact of gospel ministry under the watchful eye of Spurgeon. When he later said that each enterprise was forced on him by providence, one can see clearly that providence found a man in search of a variety of ways to make known the gospel.

The vision was too big for the place. The place was constricted compared to the need for space for workers, and storage, and classes, and expanding fellowship, and places for earnest inquirers to hear the message. Spurgeon needed not only hundreds, even thousands, of workers to fulfill the calling worthy of his love of the gospel, but he needed one person exactly suited to him to receive expressions of personal love from his intense heart and to provide a haven of joy and support in his home life.

Oh, Susannah!

"Marriage and the Sabbath are the two choice boons of primeval love that have come down to us from Paradise, the one to bless our outer and the other our inner life."[108] Just as surely as Spur-

---

106. Ibid., 143.

107. Ibid., 144.
108. SS, 10:17.

geon kept the Sabbath, so did he look for the right wife. The need for a wife was met quickly. One of the hearers on the first evening that he preached for the church was a young lady named Susannah Thompson. She had been born on January 15, 1832, two and a half years the senior of Spurgeon. Though her parents attended New Park Street from time to time, Susannah's more regular attendance was influenced by the Olney family, her cousins by marriage. Her attendance on that first evening impressed her only with the irreverent quickness of his pulpit deportment, the quaintness of his speech, and the bucolic appearance of his clothes and hair—huge black satin stock, badly trimmed hair, and a blue handkerchief with white spots. By her own admission, Susannah possessed so little spiritual discernment that she could hear neither the profundity, nor the clarity, nor the earnestness of his gospel presentation so engaging and encouraging to others, but only felt regret at the ill-placed confidence of such a ridiculous figure in appearing before a sophisticated London congregation.

Evidently, Susannah had a mind filled with images and comparisons that at times could distract her and at other times, when harnessed by grace, provided a brilliant medium for communication. Her writings abound in apt and intriguing illustrations, analogies, and extended metaphors. One of her earliest memories at church was the "curious pulpit without any stairs" that looked like a "magnified swallow's nest," and a deacon dressed in silk stockings and knee breeches, a short, stout rotund man who, when viewed from the side perched on his undraped legs and wearing a long tailed coat, had an "unmistakable resemblance to a gigantic robin." His chirping out the verses of a hymn in a "piping, twittering voice" made the likeness complete. What images she envisioned as she watched the energetic young Demosthenes

went unexpressed except in the terse statement "some feelings of amusement."[109]

Susannah had been brought to faith only within the past year, late in 1852 or early 1853, under the ministry of S. B. Bergne of Poulty Chapel. When he preached on Romans 10:8 she said "that night witnessed my solemn resolution of entire surrender to Himself." She kept all this to herself, however, and the result was that a cold despondency crept over her spiritually, engendering the "sickly and sleepy condition" of her soul when she first encountered the preaching of Spurgeon. His friendship with the Olneys provided frequent opportunities for contact and she soon found a gift to her from her pastor of an illustrated copy of *Pilgrims' Progress* in which he had inscribed, "Miss Thompson with desires for her progress in the blessed pilgrimage."[110] This was dated on April 20, 1854, one day after the church had authorized a letter inviting Spurgeon to serve permanently as pastor. She gradually opened to him, as her pastor, her state before God and he gently guided her toward assurance that a work of grace indeed had been her experience at Poultry Chapel. During the next months their friendship grew, but in his mind it was more than friendship and he soon prompted her to see the same thing.

At the opening of the Crystal Palace on June 10, 1854, several friends had gathered and were having friendly banter occupying some raised seats waiting for a procession to pass. Spurgeon, typically, had a book with him, Martin Tupper's *Proverbial Philosophy*, that had a chapter on marriage contained this advice, "If thou art to have a wife of thy youth, she is now living on earth; Therefore, think of her, and pray for her weal." Spurgeon pointed to the words and whispered to Susannah, "Do you pray for him who is

---

109. *Autobiography* 1:279-80.

110. Ibid., 282.

to be your husband?" At that moment the counsel and concern and kindness of the last months coalesced into a realization of love that had not dared to come into her consciousness prior to that moment. After the procession, he asked her to walk with him on the grounds. "During that walk, on that memorable day in June," she wrote after the perspective of another forty years, "I believe God Himself united our hearts in indissoluble bonds of true affection, and, though we knew it not, gave us to each other for ever."[111]

What was sealed in their hearts, but yet unspoken, came into the open on August 2, 1854, when Spurgeon formally proposed to her in grandfather's "old fashioned garden" with high brick walls on three sides. She confided to her diary: "August 2, 1854—It is impossible to write down all that occurred this morning. I can only adore in silence the mercy of my God, and praise Him for all His benefits."[112]

Whenever possible, she attended service at New Park Street until eventually she was baptized there by her future husband on February 1, 1855. She had, like all others, to write out her personal experience of grace and the workings of God with her soul, and appear before the congregation to give a statement of faith and answer pertinent questions. "I happily passed through the somewhat severe ordeal," she later commented. Spurgeon found her letter to be far beyond what he anticipated in expression of faith and witness to the ongoing work of God in her. So much did the written testimony impress him that he wrote on January 11 an intensely energetic response showing much about his pastor's heart, his love for her, his gratitude to God, and the clear confidence he had in his spiritual judgments. Her testimony letters exceeded his expectations in verifying the

depth of her present religious experience. "I knew you were really a child of God," he assured her, "but I did not think you had been led in such a path." The Master had plowed deep and sown the seed of life equally deep, so that its struggles upwards "with the clods" are vigorous and its life deeply rooted.

Some of the deep struggles she manifested could find relief in "earnest labor for Christ." Though she had progressed much given her situation, she had little "actual contact either with the saints or with the sinful, sick, or miserable," whom he was convinced she could serve. This would bring spiritual warmth and remove doubting, "for our works thus become evidences of our calling and election."

Spurgeon had no desire to flatter her either as pastor or as one that loved her "with the deepest and purest affection." Therefore he would not trifle with her immortal interests. He was convinced that God had no intention of destroying her after having shown her the charnel house of her own corruption and enabled her "so unreservedly to cast [herself] upon His faithful promise." She was deeply schooled in the lessons of the heart; other lessons would come, but he exclaimed, "Oh! My dear one, how good to learn the first lesson well!" Then in an exhibition of strange confidence in God's opening to him something of his own eternal counsels, Spurgeon said, "I loved you once, but feared you might not be an heir of Heaven;—God in His mercy showed me that you were indeed *elect*." On that basis he felt liberated to reveal his love for her without sin, "but up to the time I saw your note," he continued with his revelry over her obvious Spirit-given discernment, "I could not imagine that you had seen such great sights, and were so thoroughly versed in soul-knowledge."

This revelation of the depth of her Christian experience made Spurgeon evaluate the gift of

---

111. Ibid., 282-83.
112. Ibid., 284.

her hand even more, knowing that God himself loves the gift and he may love it too. "Dear purchase of a Saviour's blood," he addressed Susannah, "you are to me a Savior's gift, and my heart is full to overflowing with the thought of such continued goodness." Spurgeon did not wonder at God's goodness, for it was consistent with even greater gifts; but he still could not contain his joy at these manifold mercies. They need fear no final separation, but for the present it was good that she was not there, for if she were, "I could only throw my arms around you and weep." He wanted for her the choicest favors, the companionship of the Angel of the Covenant, answered supplications, and conversation with Jesus in Heaven. He closed with a pledge of "pure and holy affection, as well as terrestrial love."[113]

Susannah had some hard lessons to learn about the absorbing demands of time made on her future husband. She sat quietly on their Monday evening dates as he edited sermons for publication that week; she found herself isolated in a crowd when he spoke and became so absorbed in his duties that he left her unaccompanied. Her angry return home without attending the service met with her mother's wise counsel that Spurgeon was no ordinary man, that God had an absolute claim on his life and gifts, and that she must never, never seek to gain preeminence in his heart. He discovered the difficulty soon after preaching, hurried to her home, where her mother helped negotiate the reconciliation. Susannah pictured the end result as "no patched-up peace between us, but a deepening of our confidence in each other, and an increase of that fervent love which can look a misunderstanding in the face till it melts away and vanishes, as a morning cloud before the ardent glances of the sun."[114]

Spurgeon's letters to "Susie" always exhibited an indivisible solution of ardent spirituality, intense love for her, deep desire for greater usefulness, unfettered love of God and the gospel along with a consciousness of the need for more purity and single-mindedness in his love for Christ. When she reported letters, she tried to edit the parts that were words of love toward her so that they would not seem like mere platitudes, but removal of them all was impossible. She explained:

> It is a difficult task, for little rills of tenderness run between all the sentences, like the singing, dancing waters among the boulders of a brook, and I cannot still the music altogether. To the end of his beautiful life it was the same, his letters were always those of a devoted lover, as well as of a tender husband; not only did the brook never dry up, but the stream grew deeper and broader, and the rhythm of its song waxed sweeter and stronger.[115]

A visit to Colchester in April 1855 gained enormous outpourings of love and approval from Spurgeon's parents and a feeling of pleasure, happiness, and acceptance on Miss Thompson's part. "I fear to pain you by thanks," she wrote him on the Saturday after returning, "for what I know was a pleasure to you," for his letter to her had said, "It seems almost impossible that I could have conferred or received so much happiness," and closed expressing as he often did their mutual affections, "I am your much-loved, and ardently-loving, C. H. S."[116]

Spurgeon was under a great strain preaching weekly at Exeter Hall. His voice still was maturing and his knowledge as to how to use it was not settled. Physically and vocally his body required recovery time after each Lord's Day. A variety of

---

113. Spurgeon, *Letters*, "To Susannah Thompson," January 11, 1855; Also Murray, *Letters*, 54, 55.

114. *Autobiography*, 1:290.

115. Ibid., 296.

116. Ibid., 291.

papers had found an opportunity for vivid caricature and harsh lampooning in the young energetic unsuspecting pastor of New Park Street. She ached to protect him from every point of tension and attack but had learned to commit to God's care both his preaching responsibility and the wrathful reaction of human enemies.

As often as possible they spent time together, more frequently the case after her parents moved to a house in Falcon Square in the City. She noted, perhaps strange to modern ears, "On Sunday mornings, I was nearly always allowed by my parents to enjoy his ministry."[117] For her spiritual benefit, to increase her awareness of the doctrinal foundations of his ministry and personal spirituality, and to involve her immediately in his multi-faceted zeal, he put into her hands an "ancient rusty-looking book" with instructions to read through it carefully and mark anything that was "particularly sweet, or quaint, or instructive." From her conscientious attention to the assignment, combined with his knowledge of the Puritan author Thomas Brooks, came the volume *Smooth Stones from Ancient Brooks*.

Through the year they exchanged Saturday letters. Often these were from remote places on Spurgeon's part because the number of his invitations outside London increased exponentially. An attempt at a vacation to Scotland in July was a disaster as far as that intent was concerned, although it increased his fame and popularity as a preacher. His letters, as indicated above, described the phenomenal and feverish popularity Spurgeon was gaining but included within them deeply contemplative examinations of the ways in which he missed her and the dimensions of his increasing love for her. "I knew I loved you very much before, but now I feel how necessary

you are to me, and you will not lose much by my absence, if you find me, on my return, more attentive to your feelings, as well as equally affectionate." So that she need not have any insecurity that his time away would induce diminished affection, he affirmed, "My darling, accept love of the deepest and purest kind from one who in not prone to exaggerate, but who feels that here there is no room for hyperbole."[118] Susie was not the only one to whom he expressed his deep longings for her. He wrote his father from the Highlands: "I am happy, but had rather be home again; you will guess the reason. I only want that one person to make the trip a very fine one;—but patience."[119]

During Christmas of 1855, they were apart but anticipating their wedding early the next month. He sent her a copy of the first published volume of his sermons, in a series entitled *The Pulpit Library*, inscribed with characteristic cleverness and affection: "In a few days it will be out of my power to present anything to *Miss Thompson*. Let this be a remembrance of our happy meetings and sweet conversations. Dec. 22/55. C. H. Spurgeon."

On January 8, 1856, after a time of prayer and contemplation at Falcon Square, a drive through London with her father to New Park Street Chapel, the exchange of vows and rings officiated by Alexander Fletcher of Finsbury Chapel,[120] she became the "loved, and loving wife of the best man on God's earth."[121] As at his preaching engagements, so his wedding saw a packed chapel with crowds lingering outside and many turned away. A ten-day honeymoon to Paris sealed their lives in the enjoyment of each other and seeing with united pleasure the many sites of the city

117. Ibid., 293.

118. Ibid., 297.

119. *Letters*, "To His Father," July 19, 1855.

120. Ray, 153.

121. *Autobiography*, 1:301.

and its treasures of art displays, museums, palaces, and breath-taking architecture in churches. They returned home to a modest house on New Kent Road. On September 20, twin sons, Charles and Thomas, were born to them. Years later he could say with unction: "What a near and loving relationship marriage has bestowed upon us! ... Oh the joy, the true, pure, elevated peace and joy which many of us have received through that divinely ordained relationship!" Not content with such acclamation, he crowned these exclamations with the observation: "We cannot but bless God every time we repeat the dear names of those who are now parts of ourselves."[122]

Increasing Demands

Between the return from the short honeymoon and the birth of the sons, life was more than hectic. He wrote to his friend, James Watts, on February 23, 1856, as a weary soldier writing a brother-in-arms: "Eleven times this week have I gone forth to battle, and at least thirteen services are announced for next week." Two-hundred eighty-two additions had been made the previous year to the church and in the first three months of 1856 more than eighty were added. Thirty already were proposed for the next month and "hundreds, who are equally sincere, are asking for admission; but time will not allow us to take in more." Visitors had included the Lord Mayor, though a Jew, who came up to the vestry to thank him; the Chief Commissioner of Police did the same. Better than that, however, there had been "some thieves, thimbleriggers, harlots," some of whom now were in the church, and also a "right honorable hot-potato man, who is prominently known as 'a hot Spurgeonite.'" Also concerning the recent important event Spurgeon added, "Wife,

first-rate; beloved by all my people, we have good reason mutually to rejoice."[123]

Undaunted by Spurgeon's perseverance through the earliest round of criticism, and unimpressed with the substantial growth of his congregation and the changing social condition of Southwark, some of the most prestigious London publications continued their effort to destroy this interloper and smother his influence with a blanket of snide condescension. Taking a volume of Spurgeon's 1855 sermons, the writer, Fitzjames Stephen, noted it as a most unwelcome fact that crowds were flocking to hear a man "who, though pious and able, seems quite unable to understand the commonest principles either of logic or of interpretation."[124] Spurgeon's less than submissive response to their judgments, his continued growth in popularity, and their deep loyalty to the Church of England created a recipe for mutual belligerence.

Spurgeon counted it a mark of true religion that the *Saturday Review* hated him. They objected to the use of the term and responded: "Hatred is not quite the feeling we entertain towards Mr. Spurgeon. Hatred selects objects worthy of an elevated sentiment. Nobody thinks of hating an absurdity or a public nuisance, a folly, a vanity, an emptiness, or a pretender; therefore we believe that Mr. Spurgeon has never secured the hatred of a single person in the world."[125] Spurgeon was the "Anabaptist Caliban" and an "ignorant conceited fanatic" from whom it was impossible to expect "either the information of a scholar or the manners of a gentleman, the language of refinement

---

122. SS, 10:17.

123. Murray, *Letters*, 61, 62.

124. Merle Mowbray Bevington, *The Saturday Review 1855-1868* (New York: AMS Press, Inc, 1966), 89; As per the title, Bevington reported on articles that appeared through 1868. All through those years this magazine was "acidly satirical" toward Spurgeon.

125. Ibid.

in controversy or the humanities of Christianity in personal intercourse." Any Anglican may be free to hold Spurgeon as a friend and yokefellow but not at the same time he serves as a bishop.[126]

Though the provocation was sufficient, Spurgeon could not find the kind of seething bitter invective that flowed so easily from the writers of *The Saturday Review*, but, aside from deflective comments about these attacks from time to time, he preferred to use his writing time for the edification of the scores of converts in his own church and for young Christians throughout England. In 1857 he published *The Saint and his Saviour*.[127] In this volume, Spurgeon gave free range to some of the most remarkable characteristics of these early years—in fact, traits that remained unaltered through the years although they were manifest with the maturity of one purified by fire. For one thing, Spurgeon showed how deeply impressed his own soul was with the doctrine of grace as spiritual sustenance and how seriously he expounded it as a means of evangelism and spiritual growth. For another, the freeness with which he criticized what he believed was an unfaithful pulpit in England was also abundantly evident. Each of the twelve chapters had a mingling of encouragement for believers and earnest warnings and evangelistic exhortations for the lost. Every chapter was followed by a two-to-three page message specifically to the unconverted.

Among his criticisms of a non-evangelical pulpit the following words manifest the urgency of his concern: "What are ye but polished bolts on the dungeon-door of the distressed, or well-dressed halberdiers, affrighting men from the palace of mercy? Ah! It will be well for some if they shall be able to wash their hands of the blood of souls, for verily in the cells of eternal condemnation there are heard no yells of horror more appalling than the shrieks of damned ministers."[128]

Spurgeon knew that his style and doctrine were an abomination to the "sneering critic" disdainful of Spurgeon's "sickly sentimentalism," the class of cleric that preferred a "cold, speculative, unfeeling divinity." Such opponents were "intellectual preachers" whose sermons, rather, "passionless essays," were sterile collections of "metaphysical quibbles and heretical doctrines." Such self-congratulatory divines were elated if only a small portion of their hearers could understand them. Their reputation as "intellectual" Spurgeon resented because it may be "settled as an axiom that falsehood is no intellectual feat, and that unintelligible jargon is no evidence of a cultured mind."[129]

Some of his contemporaries, even friends, believed that his criticism of his fellow clergy bordered on censoriousness and arose from pride. He knew the accusations well, had absorbed both the hostile and the friendly and wrote philosophically about it. "I have had knocking about enough to kill a dozen," he wrote a friend in 1855, "but the Lord has kept me." Somewhere among the clouds, he speculated, was a vast mass of nebulae made of advice about humility. "My pride is so infernal," he admitted, "that there is not a man on earth who can hold it in, and all their silly attempts are futile." His Master, however, had full power to do it, and often let him see his own insignificance so powerfully that he called himself "all the fools in the world for even letting pride pass my door without frowning at him."[130] Pulpit denizens void of gospel substance would never receive approbation from Spurgeon even to his latest days.

---

126. Ibid., 90.

127. Charles Spurgeon, *The Saint and His Saviour*. Tain, Ross-Shire, Scotland: Christian Focus Publications, 1989.

128. Ibid., 143-44.

129. Ibid., 338.

130. Murray, *Letters*, 57.

Time was too short and the message too urgent to dabble with lesser things.

For the doctrines of grace, however, Spurgeon found no way to exhaust either his vocabulary or his affection in advocacy. Even after his death, the one that knew him best and felt and saw his deepest convictions displayed in life and thought moment after moment, wrote: "Never to the last moment of his life, did he change one jot or tittle of his belief, or vary an iota of his whole-hearted testimony to the divinity of the doctrines of free grace."[131] God would have his way with his people and would do the same with unconverted sinners. In *The Saint and His Saviour*, Spurgeon saw the acceptance of divine sovereignty as essential to proper conviction of sin. "We are sure of this," he wrote, "that no convinced sinner, when under a sense of his ill-desert, will ever dispute the justice of God in damning him or quarrel with the distinguishing grace which Heaven giveth to one and not to another." Peace will not come to a person unable to subscribe to the "doctrine of sovereign, discriminating, electing grace." He must know that the bounties of Jesus are "in his own hand, and that none can lay any claim to them."[132]

Spurgeon's emphasis on these ideas was so clear that most of his critics seized on it as a major concern but one was particularly sparkling in his sarcasm about Spurgeon's message. "It is not Christian-like to say," so asserted the alarmed adjudicator of English orthodoxy, "'God must wash brains in the Hyper-Calvinism a Spurgeon teaches before man can enter Heaven.' It does not harmonize with the quiet majesty of the Nazarene."[133] Spurgeon himself would have a few things to say about the majesty of the Nazarene.

In discussing love for the Saviour, Spurgeon placed the doctrines of grace as the first stage in love. Apprehension of these in their personal application is not the highest element of love but certainly is foundational and necessary for a full-orbed manifestation of love to Christ. "If enabled to receive all the doctrines of the gospel, we bless the name of our Redeemer for his free grace manifested in our election to eternal life; for his efficacious grace exercised in calling us into his kingdom; for pardon and justification through his blood and merits, and for everlasting security by virtue of union with his divine person."[134] Even should one not come to see the more refined doctrines that matured and purified one's love for God such as the consideration of Christ in his offices of redemption, the manner in which he effects salvation, our experience of communion with Christ, a sense of the amiability of himself, his person, the relationship in which ongoing revelations of divine love to the heart are experienced, and a grasp of the blessings of union with Christ—even in the absence of contemplation of these—there is sufficient provocation in the sinner's realization that for him in particular grace has operated efficaciously and abundantly, to secure the most eminent virtues and the most ardent zeal.

The Royal Surrey Music Hall Disaster

Back at New Park Street, the exposure of Exeter Hall having made Spurgeon more intriguing than ever, even the expanded facility did not solve the problem of the crowds. Eventually it was seen that the only solution was a completely new structure. The proprietors at Exeter Hall decided that they could not rent the Hall for so long a time to one denomination; the church, therefore, agreed

---

131. *Autobiography*, 1:295.

132. Spurgeon, *The Saint and His Saviour*, 140.

133. *Autobiography*, 1:321.

134. *The Saint and His Saviour*, 298.

to the bold move to have services at the Music Hall of Royal Surrey Gardens. An entry into the minutes of the church narrated the catastrophic beginning of the adventure on October 19, 1856:

On the evening of this day, in accordance with the resolution passed at the Church meeting, Oct. 6th, the church and congregation assembled to hear our pastor, in the Music Hall of the Royal Surrey Gardens. A very large number of persons (about 7000) were assembled on that occasion, and the service was commenced in the usual way, by singing, reading the Scriptures, and prayer. Just, however, after our pastor had commenced his prayer, a disturbance was caused (as it is supposed, by some evil-disposed persons acting in concert), and the whole congregation were seized with a sudden panic. This caused a fearful rush to the doors, particularly from the galleries. Several persons, either in consequence of their heedless haste, or from the extreme pressure of the crowd behind, were thrown down on the stone steps of the north-west staircase, and were trampled on by the crowd pressing upon them. The lamentable result was that seven persons lost their lives, and twenty-eight were removed to the hospitals seriously bruised and injured. Our pastor not being aware that any loss of life had occurred, continued in the pulpit, endeavouring by every means in his power to alleviate the fear of the people, and was successful to a very considerable extent. In attempting to renew the service, it was found that the people were too excited to listen to him, and the service was closed, and the people who remained dispersed quietly.[135]

According to the observation of church leaders, this situation had a very serious affect on the "nervous system of our pastor." He and his wife had only a month before brought into the world twin sons, Charles and Thomas, and had for the

month felt that nothing could interrupt their happiness and joyful service together. Suzie was not, therefore, in the service and learned of the event only when a carriage arrived at the door, a solemn deacon entered and related to her the disturbing event. Immediately her husband arrived accompanied by concerned friends who left immediately; he spent the night weeping and tottering on the edge of a mental breakdown. He cancelled several preaching appointments, missed a Sunday in the pulpit, and spent time with his wife and new-borns at the home of a deacon friend in Croydon. After days of despair, he resolved, based on Philippians 2, that if abuse to him meant glory to Christ, then he gladly would endure all that came. The final days in retreat turned into a time of joy and spiritual resolution and a solemn dedication of the sons to the service of God.[136]

Spurgeon referred to this restoration in a sermon entitled "His Name—Wonderful." Without mentioning the specific event, Spurgeon, as he so often and effectively did, used the trauma of his own soul as a means of pointing to the power and absolute sufficiency of the gospel as it centers in the work of Christ:

I shall never forget the time when I first became restored to myself. It was in the garden of a friend. I was walking alone, musing upon my misery which was much cheered by the kindness of my loving friend, yet far too heavy for my soul to bear. All of a sudden the name of Jesus flashed through my mind. The Person of Christ seemed visible to me. I stood still. The burning lava of my soul was cooled. My agonies were hushed. I bowed myself there and the garden that had seemed a Gethsemane became to me a Paradise! And then it seemed so strange to me that nothing should have brought me back

---

135. S&T, April 1876, 163.

136. Charles Ray, *The Life of Susannah Spurgeon*, included in Susannah Spurgeon, *Free Grace and Dying Love* (Edinburgh: Banner of Truth Trust, 2006), 165-67.

but that name of Jesus. I thought, indeed, at that time that I would love Him better all the days of my life. But there were two things I wondered at. I wondered that He should be so good to me and I wondered more that I should have been so ungrateful to Him—but His name has been from that time, "Wonderful," to me and I must record what He has done for my soul![137]

Renewed Strength and Intensified Criticism

Spurgeon returned on October 31 to "occupy the pulpit in our own chapel".[138] A few more weeks brought him back to emotional evenness and readiness to resume his smothering schedule. He had to resume it, however, with a new awareness that strength was needed, not only for the demands of time and energy for ministry, but for sorting out the undreamt-of shock of the disaster, and dissipating the bile of criticism revived and invigorated by the event. How confident and aggressive his critics felt, how they justified themselves in firing their newly-forged flesh-devouring ammunition toward this threat to religious urbanity, this insult to propriety in religion! Spurgeon, some twenty years later, published one of the attacks on his ministry and person that came the week after the sorrow of the Surrey Music Hall. While he was enduring the "unutterable pain of the whole catastrophe," he had to cope with "the wicked accusations of the public press."

> Mr. Spurgeon is a preacher who hurls damnation at the heads of his sinful hearers. Some men there are who, taking their precepts from Holy Writ, would beckon erring souls to a rightful path with fair words and gentle admonition; Mr. Spurgeon would take them by the nose and bully them into religion. Let us set up a barrier to the encroachments and blasphemies of men like Spurgeon, saying to

them, "Thus far shalt thou come and no further;" let us devise some powerful means which shall tell to the thousands who now stand in need of enlightenment—this man, in his own opinion, is a righteous Christian, but in ours nothing more than a ranting charlatan. We are neither straightlaced nor Sabbatarian in our sentiments; but we would keep apart, widely apart, the theatre and the church—above all, would we place in the hand of every right-thinking man, a whip to scourge from society the authors of such vile blasphemies as on Sunday night, above the cries of the dead and the dying, and louder than the wails of misery from the maimed and suffering, resounded from the mouth of Mr. Spurgeon in the Music Hall of the Surrey Gardens.[139]

The undulations between adulation and sneering made Spurgeon keenly aware of the necessity of dependence on God both for humility and encouragement. "The Press has kicked me quite long enough," he observed to a friend, "now they are beginning to lick me; but one is as good as the other as long as it helps to fill our place of worship." Caricatures appeared, such as "Brimstone and Treacle", picturing a wild-eyed Spurgeon in a posture of energetic gesture standing beside an effeminate, well-coiffed and robed establishment minister with his hand resting on a velvet cushion on a draped pulpit. The cartoon clearly favored Spurgeon as a more desirable pulpit show than the sedate minister of ease. J. Ewing Ritchie referred to this caricature noting that, "Brimstone is supposed to represent the youthful hero of the Surrey Music Hall: the pulpit Adonis, curled and scented and lack-a-daisical, called Treacle, is supposed, though very wrongly ... to typify the subject of this sketch," J. C. M. Bellew. Ritchie remarked, "In spite of grey hair and sallow cheeks, Mr. Bellew has somewhat too much

137. SS, 5:26, 27. NPSP, 1858, 399.

138. S&T, April 1876, 163.

139. Ibid., 163.

the appearance of a lady's man, and his Christianity is evidently that which will do credit to the best society; nor is this to be wondered at. Has he not an uncle that is a Bishop, and has he not the *élite* of the *beau-monde* to hear him?"[140] The crowds that heard Spurgeon were not what Ritchie would consider the *beau-monde*, but they astonished Spurgeon and made him wonder what other preachers were up to "when with ten times the talent, they are snoring along with prosy sermons, and sending the world away?" He thought he knew the answer: "They do not know what *the gospel* is; they are afraid of *real gospel Calvinism* and therefore the Lord does not own them." The "man-made parsons" stayed angry and continued to revile Spurgeon as did some of the papers. But Spurgeon could see God's hand in it. "What a fool the devil is!" he exclaimed. "If he had not vilified me, I should not have had so many precious souls as my hearers."[141]

When Spurgeon introduced his sermons to the world as a written medium, he gave much the same testimony. "Little can be said in praise of these sermons, and nothing can be said against them more bitter than has been already spoken." The matter seemed to have run its course, though, and Spurgeon was at least glad that the opposition served a salvific purpose. Abuse exhausted itself and thoroughly spent its vocabulary in expectoration of its venom; "and yet, the printed discourses have for that very reason found a readier sale, and more have been led to peruse them with deep attention."[142]

Scarcely two months had passed since the emotional devastation of the fatal evening at Surrey when a second volume of sermons demanded another preface. In January 1857, he testified,

"Truly may the writer say 'Ebenezer,' for he marveled at the grace that made him able to write at all. Writing in the third person, he revealed that "Great and sore troubles have rolled over his head, he had been exceedingly cast down." He quoted a mournful song that ended with the verse, "The tumult of my thoughts doth but enlarge my woe: My spirit languishes, my heart is desolate and low." Yet he could say: "But now, by merciful restoration, he can again sing of the loving-kindness of the Lord, and make known his faithfulness unto all generations." His renewed health and vigor called for "new exertion and fresh gratitude."[143] Only God's upholding grace had allowed him to complete the second volume because such grace is necessary for preservation from year to year in light of exposure to "perils from friends and foes, from without and within, from success and from sadness."[144]

Spurgeon still could point to the divine blessing on his ministry as a verification of his doctrine. "Our ministry is a testimony that no new theology is needed to stir the masses and save souls; we defy all the negative theologians in England to give such proof of their ministry as we can." The old doctrines are victorious and raise people from the dunghill into the arms of Christ. Spurgeon averred that "best evidence of the truth of our holy religion" lay in the reclamation and regeneration of "drunkards, harlots, swearers, thieves, liars, and such like." He was willing to accept "all that is uttered to our disparagement, for therein we do but magnify the grace of God, who worketh by the least of instruments the greatest acts of his love."[145]

In 1857, when Spurgeon was twenty-three, several observers took it in hand to give an ac-

---

140. Ritchie, *The London Pulpit*, 31.
141. Murray, *Letters*, 56, 57.
142. NPSP, 1855, preface.

143. SS, 2:v.
144. Ibid., vi.
145. Ibid., vii.

count of his life and ministry. One was entitled, *Sketch of the Life and Ministry of the Rev. C. H. Spurgeon from Original Documents* written by "Stevenson," according to the *Critical Dictionary of English Literature.* This volume appeared in America published by Sheldon, Blakeman, & Co. as well as in England. J. Allen wrote *Life of the Rev. C. H. Spurgeon,* and a churchman published *Mr. Spurgeon's Critics Criticised.* In response to the severe criticisms of the Surrey Tabernacle pastor James Wells, Isaac McCarthy published, *What then Does Mr. Spurgeon Preach? Being an examination of Mr. James Wells's Review of Mr. Spurgeon's Ministry.* One who had misgivings about Spurgeon's use of the Puritans published *Contra and Pro: the Anti-Puritan Teachings of the Rev. C. Spurgeon on the Subject of Sanctification* exhibited by Pro-Puritan. The next year, 1858, saw the appearance of *A Review of Mr. Spurgeon's Discourses; or A New and Complete Refutation of Calvinism,* by the Rev. J. Hughes, February 1858.

Spurgeon clearly had the experience of a decade in mind when on February 14, 1864, he preached from "He that endureth to the end shall be saved." Autobiographical illustration flooded his mind as he contemplated the difficulties of endurance. "From the first moment of his call to the work, the preacher of the Word will be familiar with temptation," Spurgeon recalled. "While he is yet in his youth," he continued his musing, "there are multitudes of the softer temptations to turn the head and trip the feet of the youthful herald of the cross." Softer temptations soon must yield to the real venom that seeks an immediate overthrow of a gospel herald:

> And when the blandishments of early popularity have passed away, as soon they must, the harsh croak of slander, and the adder's tongue of ingratitude assail him, he finds himself stale and flat where once he was flattered and admired; nay the venom of malice succeeds to the honeyed morsels of adulation. Now, let him gird his loins and fight the good fight of faith. In his after days, to provide fresh matter Sabbath after Sabbath, to rule as in the sight of God, to watch over the souls of men, to weep with them who weep, to rejoice with those who do rejoice, to be a nursing father unto young converts, sternly to rebuke hypocrites, to deal faithfully with backsliders, to speak with solemn authority and paternal pathos to those who are in the first stages of spiritual decline, to carry about with him the care of the souls of hundreds, is enough to make him grow old while yet he is young, and to mar his visage with the lines of grief, till, like the Saviour, at the age of thirty years, men shall count him nearly fifty.[146]

Spurgeon at thirty described how the ten years of wild popularity and destructive opposition on top of the cares generated by the growth of the congregation affected the honest, earnest pastor. Gradually he earned the respect, and even well-tested praise, of the highest levels of English society and culture. Nevertheless, those who carped at him and his ways were never far away and constantly kept a refrain of hostility, giving dissonance to the air around Spurgeon's ears.

With hostility waning because of the sobering effect of an undiminished number of hearers, some disgruntled holdouts believed that, unlike the "excited thousands," the "thoughtful hearer" would learn nothing from Spurgeon's performances. After a Sunday at Surrey Gardens, our astute commentator on *The London Pulpit,* J. Ewing Ritchie, observed with disdain what Spurgeon observed with glory; "Nowhere more abound the vulgar, be they great or little, than at the Royal Music Hall on a Sunday morning." Spurgeon, the "youngest and the loudest and the most notorious

---

146. SEE 12:289-90.

preacher in London," brought his flock there to mingle with an unusual conglomerate. Ewing described Spurgeon's people, "the aborigines from Park Street Chapel," as "very plain, much given to the wearing of clothes of an ancient cut—and easy of recognition." He found the men narrow, hard, and griping to look at and the women worse, stern and unlovely. It should humor his readers that this group viewed themselves as sole strollers on the pearly streets of the New Jerusalem and as tea-mates at the marriage supper of the Lamb with martyrs and prophets and saints—with Abraham, and Isaac, and Jacob.[147]

But back to the "thoughtful hearer"—replacing a desired edification would be disgust—disgust with the noisy crowding, the commonplace prayer, the questionable style of oratory, the narrowness of the preacher's creed and its misrepresentation of the glorious gospel, and with "the stupidity that can take for a divine afflatus brazen impudence and leathern lungs." These are people that would not dare frequent the theatre but have an unquenchable thirst for the theatrical which they find slaked in Spurgeon.[148]

Among the most severe and sickening of the criticisms, that which came from the leading minister among the London Strict Baptists, James Wells, struck the deepest. Spurgeon did not reply in kind, but he cannot but have been shocked when Wells wrote in 1855: "I have—*most solemnly have*—my doubts as to the Divine reality of his conversion."[149] He recognized that Spurgeon was both affable and studious, in fact, more studious than many of the "slothful, negligent, emptyheaded" ministers of Wells' denomination. He was well-versed in Puritan literature and attractive to a massive variety of people, among whom

he listed free-willers, intellectual Calvinists, both high and low, along with the "philosophic and classic-taste Christian." Such wide appeal merely magnified the danger of the delusion. Wells put forth five closely reasoned arguments as to why Spurgeon's ministry was a fatal delusion. In summary, Wells believed that Spurgeon had massive popular appeal because he exhibited only the form of Christianity but none of the Holy Spirit power of it. Some of the truths he speaks will result in genuine conversion, but such will "after a time, leave his ministry, for a ministry that can accompany them in their rugged paths of wilderness experience."[150]

Spurgeon had written his father before he ever moved to London that he knew of the higher brand of Calvinism held by some of the London Baptists. "I am a Calvinist; I love what someone called 'glorious Calvinism,'" he told his father, "but 'Hyperism' is too hot-spiced for my palate."[151] That such a severe judgmentalism would accompany their hot spices must have surprised even Spurgeon. In principle, much of the analysis that Wells gave about "Intellectual Calvinism," the character of genuine conviction of sin, and false conversion, Spurgeon endorsed. He issued many warnings to his hearers on those matters. But that he, an acknowledged debtor to sovereign mercy alone, a refuser of human ordination, and an abstainer from formal school-centered education, would be accused of having a "secondhand ministry, deeply tainted with an Arminian spirit," must have amused Spurgeon as much as it bewildered him.[152] Being caught between two lines of fire left Spurgeon little place to stand among the religious pundits of the day. He used his own experience as a warning to those that sought to be faithful and preach the whole counsel of God:

---

147. Ritchie, 155.

148. Ibid., 157-59; also cited in Pike, 2:268-69.

149. Pike, 1:154.

150. *Autobiography*, 1:306-09.

151. Murray, *Letters*, 41.

152. Pike, 1:169.

Espouse but one phase of the truth, and you shall be cried up to the very heavens. Become such a Calvinist that you shut your eyes to one half the Bible, and cannot see the responsibility of the sinner, and men will clap their hands, and cry Hallelujah! And on the backs of many you shall be hoisted to a throne, and become a very prince in their Israel. On the other hand begin to preach mere morality, practice without doctrine, and you shall be elevated on other men's shoulders; you shall, if I may use such a figure, ride upon these asses into Jerusalem; and you shall hear them cry Hosanna! And see them wave their palm branches before you. But once preach the whole counsel of God, and you shall have both parties down upon you; one crying, "The man is too high," the other saying, "no, he is too low;" the one will say, "He's a rank Arminian," the other, He's a vile Hyper-Calvinist." Now a man does not like to stand between two fires.[153]

Spurgeon never retaliated directly to Wells, though in personal correspondence he referred to him as "King James" and thought his attack would shake his own throne, but he ever maintained that the hyper-Calvinists erred in their distinctive doctrinal stance on grace and human responsibility. Put plainly, Spurgeon believed that the preacher must emphasize duty as well as doctrine. Without calling his name, Spurgeon referred to Wells and his crowd as "a certain class of men of perverted intellect who will admire you [if you preach Calvinism], but once begin to reach responsibility" and their admiration ends and their carping criticism of "Inconsistency" falls in an ever-increasing crescendo around the head of the one who declares that if the sinner perish it is his own fault.[154] When preaching at

the Surrey Music Hall, Spurgeon preached a message entitled "Human Responsibility." Referring specifically to an idiosyncratic doctrine of the hyper-Calvinists, Spurgeon said, "I have often been rebuked by certain men who have erred from the truth, for preaching the doctrine that it is a sin in men, if they reject the gospel of Christ." He brushed aside the habit of this group to label him with opprobrious titles, and continued: "I am certain that I have the warrant of God's Word in so preaching, and I do not believe that any man can be faithful to men's souls and clear of their blood, unless he bears his frequent and solemn testimony upon this vital subject."[155]

The hyper-Calvinist did not believe that a minister had warrant to call on the unregenerate to believe. Belief came to elect sinners as an operation of the Holy Spirit on their souls and was thus a work of special grace not included in the duties of Adam in the unfallen state. Sins that brought condemnation were those of violation of the moral law written on the heart prior to the fall, but unbelief, that is, a failure to have faith in Christ as Redeemer, could not be a sin, and faith could not be a present duty, because no such action of the human soul was called for prior to the fall; no duty was required for something alien to the condition of innocent man. Spurgeon quoted a score of New Testament passages that denominated unbelief as the chief of sins, from which he drew the conclusion: "If they do not mean that unbelief is a sin, and *the* sin, which, above all others, damns men's souls, they do not mean any thing at all, but they are just a dead letter in the Word of God."[156] Very seldom did Spurgeon defend himself in this conflict, but he was not hesitant to take on the opposition on theological issues, and to seek to emerge triumphant when

---

153. Charles Spurgeon, *Revival Year Sermons*, (Edinburgh: The Banner of Truth Trust, 1959 [reprinted 1996]), 86, 87.

154. Ibid., 83.

155. SS, 5:426.

156. Ibid., 427.

he felt that concession of victory to them would compromise the pure faith and the consequent proclamation of a full gospel to sinners.

For Wells in particular, Spurgeon nursed an affection throughout his life and sought his good whenever possible. Spurgeon never met James Wells. Eventually Wells confessed to T. W. Medhurst: "I love Mr. Spurgeon, but I do not believe in his duty-faithism." When Wells lay in bed with his last and fatal sickness in 1871, Spurgeon wrote him a loving and consoling letter in which he stated, "Personally I own my great obligations to the furnace and the hammer; and I am sure that you also rejoice in the assurance that tribulation worketh patience, and brings, through the supply of the Spirit, a long train of blessings with it. ... May your sick chamber be the very gate of heaven to your soul."[157] Spurgeon expressed his genuine sympathy that his protracted confinement had kept him from the labor so dear to his heart. Calling to mind the many comforts of Scripture that God works joy and holiness in his people through suffering, Spurgeon noted: "Immutable purposes and infinite love have been themes of your constant ministry to others. May the Holy Ghost make these mighty floods of consolation to roll in upon your own soul, till all things else are swallowed up in your hearts holy joy!"[158]

If Spurgeon was unable to secure the blessings of the leading High Calvinist voice, or the approval of the dailies, weeklies, and monthlies, or the Christian wishes of the Church clergy, at least one self-professed high churchman pushed aside the prejudices by a cleverly conceived narrative of going to hear Spurgeon in the Music Hall on a Sunday morning. "Fancy a congregation consisting of 10,000 souls, streaming into the Hall, mounting the galleries, humming, buzzing, and swarming—a mighty hive of bees—eager to secure at first the best places, and, at last, any place at all. After waiting more than half an hour—for if you wish to have a seat you must be there at least that space of time in advance—Mr. Spurgeon ascended his tribune. To the hum, and rush, and trampling of men succeeded a low, concentrated thrill and murmur of devotion, which seemed to run at once, like an electric current, through the breast of every one present; and by this magnetic chain, the preacher held us fast bound for about two hours." This writer, calling himself *Habitans in Sicco*, finally issued an appeal to drop all prejudice against his Calvinism and his baptism and look at the stark reality that he was preaching to 10,000 people. He could fill the largest church in England with his voice, and more to the purpose, with people. Then with a sly flourish of irony he laid waste the starched proprietarians by a most unorthodox suggestion: "And may it please your grace, here are two churches in the metropolis, St. Paul's and Westminster Abbey. What does your grace think of inviting Mr. Spurgeon, this heretical Calvinist and Baptist, who is able to draw 10,000 souls after him, just to try his voice, some Sunday morning, in the nave of either of those churches?"[159]

The Fast Day Sermon

Ten thousand was dwarfed when the size of occupancy allowed attendance by all who wanted it. The opportunity came on October 7, 1857, when Spurgeon preached in the Crystal Palace. The Sepoy Mutiny in India had brought severe suffering and outrage to many and led to the necessity of a military execution of the mutineers. Spurgeon had preached on this event in September and, as a result, was invited by the directors of the Crys-

157. Pike, 5:35.

158. Murray, *Letters*, 73, 74.

159. S&T, April 1876, 164.

tal Palace to hold a service in the transept of the building on the day of fasting and prayer. He accepted. On the day before the service, as the pulpit was being secured, Spurgeon was testing the acoustics in order to decide the most advantageous placement. In order to hear the effects, he projected a loud and forceful sentence, "Behold the Lamb of God, which taketh away the sins of the world." Years later he learned that a workman in one of the galleries, heard the words, could not escape the power of such an admonition, and was converted.[160]

Beginning with a prayer Spurgeon asked for more than just an outward display of humility: "instead of sackcloth and ashes give us true repentance, and hearts meekly reverent; instead of the outward guise, to which some pay their only homage, give us the *inward spirit;* and may we really pray, really humiliate ourselves, and really tremble before the Most High God."[161] The hymn, "Before Jehovah's Awful Throne," Spurgeon read, and then asked the massive congregation to be "kind enough to sing it through." This was followed with an exposition of Daniel 9:1-19, another prayer, and another hymn, "O God Our Help in Ages Past," followed by the sermon, based on Micah 6:9: "Hear ye the rod, and who hath appointed it." In exposition and prayer and sermon Spurgeon evoked brilliant images of human filth and sin, the divine splendor manifest in judgment and grace, and claimed a status for Britain as the people of God in the manner of old covenant Israel. Reflecting on Daniel's solicitation for Israel because it was God's city, God's people, and called by God's name, Spurgeon commented:

And, my brethren, not Israel itself could boast a nobler history than we, measuring it by God's

bounties. We have not yet forgotten an armada scattered before the breath of heaven, scattered upon the angry deep as a trophy of what God can do to protect his favored Isle. We have not yet forgotten a fifth of November, wherein God discovered divers plots that were formed against our religion and our commonwealth. We have not yet lost the old men, whose tales of even the victories in war are still a frequent story. We remember how God swept before our armies the man who thought to make the world his dominion, who designed to cast his shoe over Britain, and make it a dependency of his kingdom. God wrought for us; he wrought with us; and he will continue to do so. He hath not left his people, and he will not leave us, but he will be with us even to the end. Cradle of liberty! Refuge of distress! Storms may rage around thee, but not upon thee, nor shall all the wrath and fury of men destroy thee, for God hath pitched his tabernacle in thy midst, and his saints are the salt in the midst of thee.

His prayer brought to mind the great atrocities of the rebellion and the necessity for the execution of justice on such violations of trust, citizenship, morals and humanity. "Thou didst rain hell out of heaven upon the cities of the plain. The cities of Inde are not less vile than they, for they have committed lust and cruelty, and have much sinned against the Lord. Remember this, O God of Heaven." He employed a forceful statement of the justice of military action against the bloody and outrageous rebellion by praying, "Bid them remember that they are not warriors merely, but executioners; and may they go with steady tramp to the battle, believing that God wills it that they should utterly destroy the enemy, who have not only defied Britain, but thus defiled themselves amongst men." He considered himself no apologist for the dominion of Britain in India, but the rebellion of the Sepoys was entirely another mat-

---

160. *Autobiography*, 1:534.
161. NPSP, 1857, 373.

ter. "With regard to the Sepoys, they are our voluntary subjects, they deserve the utmost rigour of the law. From their own oath they were our subjects; and if they have revolted let them suffer the punishment of their treason."

Moreover, the Indian government ought never to have tolerated Hinduism. A religion that consists of bestiality, infanticide, and murder, no one has a right to practice unless he is prepared to be hanged for it. Hinduism, Spurgeon preached, "is neither more nor less than a mass of the rankest filth that ever imagination could have conceived." Not only are their gods of despicable character, but "when their worship necessitates everything that is evil, not religion, but morality must put it down." A "religion that does not infringe upon morality is beyond the force of legislature," but the propagation and compulsion to immorality admits of no toleration. "If it be any man's religion to blow my brains out, I shall not tolerate it." And if under the embellishment of the name of religion one is encouraged to "commit bestial acts in public, I for one would touch his conscience" as well as hinder his act of worship.

England had sins aplenty also that had provoked God to make such executions necessary. Sins of the rich, sins of the merchant, sins of the poor, sins of the government, and sins of the church all had accumulated the increasing pressure of chastening justice on Britain. As for the church, not just that established by law, but all churches, "for many and many a year pulpits never condescended to men of low estate. Our ministers were great and haughty; they understood the polish of rhetoric, they had all the grandeur of logic; to the people they were blind guides and dumb dogs, for the people knew not what they said, neither did they regard them." The message was not intended to make men smile nor to give relief to any, but, in accord with the dictates of the government itself, intended for a serious call to repentance. Spurgeon urged in with all his might and all the power of his keen moral perception.

In the end, he could not close without a call to salvation. Urging on his audience repentance, not only for national sins but for personal sins against God, Spurgeon closed:

> Oh! if I might but have some souls won to Christ to-day, what would I give? What is all this great gathering to me? It is an extra labor, that is all. For this I do not labor. God is my witness, I sought you not; never once have I said a thing to court a smile from any man. When God first sent me to the ministry he bade me fear no man, and I have not yet met the man to whom I have feared to tell of God's truth. Nor you have I sought to please, nor you have I sought to gather here. I would preach the gospel; may God give me some souls as my reward! And if but one poor sinner shall look to Jesus, clap your wings, ye angels! enough is done, for God is honored.[162]

At the beginning of this service, Spurgeon requested one of his deacons to ask Susannah to move to a place where he could not see her, for her obvious intensity of concern for him made him nervous. That the entire affair produced an extraordinary drain on his mental and physical strength is also indicated from his sleep from Wednesday night, October 7, until Friday morning, October 9.[163]

One of Spurgeon's early defenders, Dr. Campbell, had positive comments about the service overall but clearly stated his difference with Spurgeon's prayer for vengeance, saying that "the idea of military butchery is most incongruous with the exercise of devotion."[164]

---

162. Ibid., 388.
163. *Autobiography*, 1:534.
164. Pike 2:279.

The Approaching Revival

In the context of that message, Spurgeon made reference to the spiritual stirring that he sensed, not only at New Park Street, but in many places around London. "I do hope that we have already seen the beginning of a revival. The last year has seen more preaching than any year since the days of the apostles. We are stirring in ragged schools, and in various efforts for doing good; but still the church is only half awake." A real revival Spurgeon hoped and worked for. He was seeing it all around him in his own ministry, but wanted others to partake of the glory of such a work.

Less than a year earlier, on Tuesday afternoon, November 11, 1856, he had preached at Whitefield's Tabernacle, Tottenham Court Road, at the 100-year celebration of the laying of the first stone for the building. He recalled the great movement of revival that had taken place during Whitefield's time and largely with Whitefield as the chief instrument. He had been in London long enough to read the city literature and see London as a paradigm of sin, the pulpit as stylish but dry and dead, church life a mere shell filled not with piety but with social status, theology as a mark of shifting human creativity and ingenuity rather than faithfulness to a historic standard of revealed truth, the church emerging as an honorable institution rather than a reproach to the world, worship-times as fodder for afternoon gossip and carping, and Christian life as formal rather than vital in its perception of the nearness and loveliness of Christ. Nothing less than a mighty work of God would do what London and the churches needed. He began the sermon, "Spiritual Revival the want of the Church," with an affirmation of absolute divine sovereignty in the granting of spiritual life:

> All true religion is the work of God: it is preeminently so. If he should select out of his works that which he esteems most of all, he would select true religion. He regards the work of grace as being even more glorious than the works of nature; and he is, therefore, especially careful that it shall always be known, so that if any one dare to deny it, they shall do so in the teeth of repeated testimonies to the contrary, that God is indeed the author of salvation in the world and in the hearts of men, and that religion is the effect of grace, and is the work of God. I believe the Eternal might sooner forgive the sin of ascribing the creation of the heavens and of the earth to an idol, than that of ascribing the works of grace to the efforts of the flesh, or to any thing else but God. It is a sin of the greatest magnitude to suppose that there is aught in the heart which can be acceptable unto God, save that which God himself has first created there.[165]

After treating all the areas that demonstrated the necessity of revival, he pleaded that men would cry mightily to God for such a reviving, for God alone can give it. There was no need of fresh machinery but true spiritual life. The train needs not a new engine but fire and steam in the one that is there. No new inventions will do, no contrivances will bring the life that is needed, but divine truth earnestly preached from a new heart under the power of the Divine Spirit. God already provided the means directly adapted to the great work of spiritual transformation, and substitution of a temporary manipulation may indeed accomplish what man can do, but will not be the channel for divine power. A Christian must cry, "Lord, revive thy work."

> The church wants fresh revivals. O! for the days of Cambuslang again, when Whitefield preached with power. O! for the days when in this place hundreds were converted sometimes under Whitefield's

---

165. SS, 3:74.

sermons. It has been known that two thousand credible cases of conversion have happened under one solitary discourse. O! for the age when eyes should be strained, and ears should be ready to receive the word of God, and when men should drink in the word of life, as it is indeed, the very water of life, which God gives to dying souls! O! for the age of deep feeling—the age of deep, thorough-going earnestness! Let us ask God for it; let us plead with him for it. Perhaps he has the man, or the men, somewhere, who will shake the world yet; perhaps even now he is about to pour forth a mighty influence upon men, which shall make the church as wonderful in this age, as it ever was in any age that has passed. God grant it, for Christ's sake! Amen.[166]

Less than three weeks after the Fast Day sermon, on October 25, 1857, Spurgeon dealt with the theme of revival again setting forth not only his hope for it, but his theory of its occurrence by divine decree. Based on Zechariah 14:7, "It shall come to pass that at evening time it shall be light," Spurgeon took the text, not in its immediate context but "as a rule of the kingdom, as one of the great laws of God's dispensation of grace."[167] In establishing general principle by mere human reason, Spurgeon knew that the collection of a large number of phenomena was essential. But this need not be done in matters of divine revelation. "Since God is immutable, one act of his grace is enough to teach us the rule of his conduct." God has set in general terms a principle that applied to a specific situation in Israel's history, and from that the Christian may deduce a generally applicable theory. God has said that at evening time it should be light. A merely human proposition would not justify any optimism concerning a

general principle, but when God has acted in a particular place based on this proposition, Spurgeon concluded, "I feel myself more than justified in deducing from it the rule, that always to his people at evening time there shall be light." His approach to this sermon therefore, expanded the doctrine, "There are different evening times that happen to the church and to God's people, and as a rule we may rest quite certain that at evening time there shall be light."[168]

For Spurgeon, evening meant that time from which one would expect the immediate onset of complete darkness. At that time, when darkness would seem the natural consequence, the light of revival comes. Marching on through daylight nothing it seems can conquer the light of the sun until the shadow of the earth gradually eclipses it. So the gospel seems to run with ever increasing power until it seems the world with all its black sludge of sin and bilious corruption appears to neutralize and then eliminate the power of grace. But, at that time, at evening, there shall be light. The early church, in its triumphs over a hostile, pagan, licentious and persecuting Rome, went from strength to strength and conquered. The darkness of sin and Satan under the guise of a Christian Rome seemed more impenetrable by grace and impervious to the truth than ever heathen Rome did, but God brought out his Luther and his Calvin. The Church of England fell into decay after the great far-advanced light of the Puritans—how could regression to putrefaction come after such a cleansing balm as Puritanism?—but arose the Bible moths so despised by the world, the Wesleys and Whitefield and their companions, and again light succeeded evening. "So has it always been—progressing, retrograding, standing still awhile, and then progressing

---

166. Ibid., 89.

167. SS, 4:275. This sermon, published in volume 4 of the Funk & Wagnall's American series of sermons, did not appear in the MTP until 1916, beginning on page 181.

---

168. SS, 2:275-76.

once more, and falling back again," Spurgeon theorized. "The whole history of the church has been a history of onward marches, and then of quick retreats." The overall impact, however, Spurgeon believed, was "a history of advance and growth, but which read chapter by chapter, is a mixture of success and repulse, conquest and discouragement. And so I think it will be even to the last."[169]

How extended through history that pattern should last, Spurgeon did not profess to know. He hoped for the inauguration of a time of "constant progress to the brightest day;" that but he did know. Perhaps English civilization would perish and another generation would sit under the ruined arches of London Bridge and wonder that so mighty a civilization had fallen so completely. If the final decline seemed utterly to obliterate the knowledge of God from the earth, it still would be succeeded by the day in which "this poor planet shall find herself unrobed of those swaddling bands of darkness that have kept her luster from breaking forth." And God "shall yet cause his name to be known from the rising of the sun to the going down thereof."[170]

Before any such final cultural and religious devastation, however, at least one more shining forth of light would be given, and Spurgeon was already a part of the first glimmers of it. Soon, England would participate in a revival that stirred America, Canada, and the British Isles. Spurgeon's preaching in Scotland, Ireland, Wales, and various places in England for the first five years of his New Park Street ministry clearly indicated a growing interest in the plain, uncompromised proclamation of Christ as the Mediator of the eternal covenant of grace. The observation of this awakening prompted J. Howard Hinton to take his stand against the vapid theology off Baldwin Brown. "The aspect of the times emboldens me," Hinton wrote. "It is not now dear brethren—above all times, it is not now—when 'the end' must be so near, and when so many cheering tokens of revival enkindle our hopes, that a perversion, or even a dilution, of the truth as it is in Jesus should find welcome or entrance among us." He hoped instead that such tokens of divine blessing on the preaching of the old gospel would encourage all to "contend earnestly for the faith which was once delivered unto the saints."[171]

Spurgeon would have thirty-plus years to observe the spiritual and theological dynamic subsequent to this brief but powerful visitation of the Spirit to the churches of England. The power of it would not subside in his congregation but he would see darkness settling around him, as forces already at work would be retarded but not extinguished by the temporary surge in God's gracious operations of gospel power.

An End and a Beginning

From November 23, 1856 through December 11, 1859, morning services were held at the Music Hall, Surrey Gardens. On May 16, 1858, essentially half way through this venture, Spurgeon preached on "Human Responsibility," having announced just two months earlier that he would preach more substantial and meaty doctrinal messages from that point forward. Earlier in this journey he had felt the raggedness of such an open situation and transient auditory. The months, however, had brought stability and familiarity with a massive number of faces, so that he considered the opportunity not only as evangelistic but as demanding meatier and more deeply doctrinal subjects. Like his New Park Street evening

---

169. SS, 4:277.
170. Ibid., 279.

171. J. Howard Hinton, "Strictures on some passages in the Rev. J. B. Brown's *Divine Life in Man*," in the *Baptist Magazine* March and April 1860, cited in *Autobiography*, 1:482.

crowd, this was a congregation and his duty to them was pastoral. Though many passages in different sermons could stand forth as representative of Spurgeon's earnest sense of responsibility to that mass of people from week to week, one passage in this sermon gives a succinct statement of Spurgeon's perception of his stewardship:

Oh to have such a message to deliver to you, to you I say, for if there is a people under Heaven to whom my text applies, it is you! If there is one race of men in the world who have more to account for than others, it is yourselves. There are doubtless others who are on an equality with you, who sit under a faithful and earnest ministry. But as God shall judge between you and me at the Great Day—to the utmost of my power I have been faithful to your souls! I have never in this pulpit sought by hard words, by technical language, to magnify my own wisdom. I have spoken to you plainly. And not a word, to the best of my knowledge, has escaped these lips which every one of you could not understand. You have had a simple Gospel. I have not stood here and preached coldly to you. I could say as I came up yon stairs, "The burden of the Lord was upon me." For my heart has come here heavy and my soul has been hot within me. And when I have preached feebly, my words may have been uncouth and my language far from proper, but my heart never has been wanting! This whole soul has spoken to you. And if I could have ransacked Heaven and earth to find language that might have won you to the Savior, I would have done so. I have not shunned to reprove you, I have never minced matters. I have spoken to this age of its iniquities and to you of your sins. I have not softened down the Bible to suit the carnal tastes of men. I have said damn, where God said damn—I have not sweetened it into, "condemn." I have not minced matters, nor endeavored to veil or conceal the Truth of God, but as to every man's conscience in the sight of God, I have endeavored to commend the Gospel earnestly

and with power and with a plain, outspoken, earnest and honest ministry! I have not kept back the glorious Doctrines of Grace, although by preaching them, the enemies of the Cross have called me an antinomian! Nor have I been afraid to preach man's solemn responsibility, although another tribe have slandered me as an Arminian! And in saying this, I say it not in a way of glorying. I say it for your rebuke—if you have rejected the Gospel—for you shall have sinned far above that of any other men in casting away Christ! A double measure of the fury of the wrath of God shall fall on you! Sin, then, is aggravated by the rejection of Christ.[172]

At the end of the three years of off-site ministry and pilgrim-worship for the congregation, the congregation returned to "the house which God has in so special a manner given to us."[173] On January 6, 1861 a written declaration was signed by Spurgeon and church leaders, "This church needs rather more than £4000 to enable it to open the New Tabernacle free of all debt. It humbly asks this temporal mercy of God, and believes that for Jesus' sake the prayer will be heard and the boon bestowed." On May 6 of that year another testimony was drawn up and signed: "We, the undersigned members of the church lately worshipping in New park Street Chapel, but now assembling in the Metropolitan Tabernacle, Newington, desire with overflowing hearts to make known and record the lovingkindness of our faithful God." The entire debt was paid and the document expressed shame at any doubt that might have lingered in their hearts about God's meeting the needs in a way that went beyond all that they had asked. As opening services at the Tabernacle were completed, the accounts showed that £31,332 4s, 10d had been received, and that amount spent. "Truly we serve a gracious God," wrote Spurgeon.[174]

172. SS, 5:428-29.
173. S&T, April 1876, 166.
174. Ibid.

3

THE METROPOLITAN TABERNACLE

Suppose the fire should come here, and the Master be seen more than the minister—what then? Why, this Church will become two, or three, or four thousand strong! It is easy enough in God to double our numbers, vast though they be. We shall have the lecture-hall beneath this platform crowded at each prayer-meeting, and we shall see in this place young men devoting themselves to God; we shall find young ministers raised up, and trained, and sent forth to carry the fire to other parts. ... If God shall bless us, he will make us a blessing unto all. Let but God send down the fire, and the biggest sinners in the neighbourhood will be converted.[1]

When the size of the congregation grew beyond the New Park Street facility, they decided that a new and much larger place of worship and church life was needed. During a nearly three-year stint at the Surrey Gardens Music Hall a location in Newington was procured, and the site was prepared. On Tuesday August 16, 1859 the first stone was laid. The ceremony included the reading of a brief history giving information about each of the pastors for the 207-year history of the church.

Faithfulness, Hiddenness, and Expansion

William Rider, Benjamin Keach, Benjamin Sinton, John Gill, John Rippon, Joseph Angus, James Smith, and William Walters all had served with distinction and had preached with faithfulness the doctrines of grace. Fresh venues of worship had often been called for through the years in light of a variety of circumstances. Beginning in a time of repression, "their meetings were held by stealth. Being unlawful for them to gather together for worship in a suitable edifice, they were compelled to go from house to house, observing the strictest secrecy."[2] During Keach's time, the church became numerous and constructed a large and commodious building in Goat's Yard Passage, Fair Street, Horseliedown. This facility was expanded during the time of Benjamin Stinton. A baptistery was constructed to avoid the difficulty of finding pools and rivers at appropriate times and seasons and "for the more decent administration of the ordinance." In 1718, at the cost of £160, the baptistery was enlarged, and renovation of the meeting house, including the addition of three vestries eleven feet square, was accomplished. Under John Gill, in October 1757, a new meeting house for the church and congre-

---

1. MTP, 1861, 223.

2. NPSP, 1859, 346

gation was built in Carter Lane, Tooley Street. During the closing years of Dr. Rippon's life, on February 7, 1830, the congregation worshipped for the last time at the old meeting house in Carter Lane. They surrendered it to the City for the approaches to the new London Bridge. For three years, the church assembled in different buildings through the kindness of other churches. Eventually, in answer to many prayers, they purchased a piece of freehold ground in New Park Street, where they erected a chapel which opened free from any debt or encumbrance on May 6, 1833. After Rippon's death three pastors came and went in less than twenty years, all of them still serving in ministry at different places.

The reciter of the history summarized the five years of Spurgeon's ministry with a sense of awe and blessing. Many saints, converted under the ministries of others, were wandering without a place to be fed. Spurgeon presented to them a lush pasture of nutritious food for sheep. "Many such were gathered into the fold of our fellowship," said B. W. Carr; "Here their souls have been restored, while they have found the Presence of the Good Shepherd, who makes us to lie down in green pastures and leads us beside the still waters." The work of conversion also was great as the Holy Spirit accompanied "the preaching of the Gospel with Divine Power, that almost every sermon proved the means of awakening and regeneration to some." The church thus became "an asylum for the aged, as well as a nursery for the babes of our Savior's family."[3] This continued blessing had made necessary this day of laying the first stone for a new place of ministry.

A Time to Gather Stones Together
The day's speakers included Spurgeon's father, his younger brother, James, Sir Morton Peto, the

Lord Mayor of London, pastors from the north and south and west of London and a peculiarly jocular Anglican that displayed an infectious evangelical ecumenicity, Joseph Payne. He had enjoyed, one occasion, being introduced as a person that "belongs to nobody because he belongs to everybody." A master of alliteration, rhyme, acrostics, and anecdotes, Payne used them all in regaling the crowd with his speech of admiration for Spurgeon. Spurgeon would not mumble, grumble, stumble, or crumble, but would pray and believe, persist and receive. He commented that he did not see the familiar initials CHS anywhere and wanted to make sure that their significance did not pass unnoticed. "Now, what does C.H.S. mean? Why, it means first, "Charles Haddon Spurgeon." But I do not mean that! C.H.S. means a Clear Headed Speaker, who is Clever at Handling Subjects in a Cheerful-Hearted Style. He is a Captain of the Hosts of Surrey. He is a Cold-Hating Spirit. He has Chapel-Heating Skill. He is a Catholic Humbug-Smasher; he is a Care-Hushing Soother. He is a Child-Helping Strengthener—he is a Christ-Honoring Soldier, and he is a Christ-Honored Servant. Those are all the C.H.S's and a very good set of C.H.S's they are!"[4] In a poem of nine stanzas that Payne wrote for this occasion, he sought to set forth both his gratitude and his hope embodied in the construction of the Tabernacle. The last two stanzas continued the demonstration of his love for Spurgeon.

Friend Spurgeon, the clearest of preachers I know,
Look on to the time when your language shall flow
Like a beautiful stream, without thickness or silt,
In the great Tabernacle that is to be built.

And thousands delivered from sin and from Hell,
In mansions of Glory forever shall dwell,

---

3. Ibid., 350.

4. Ibid., 365.

Who heard of the blood which for sinners was spilt,
In the great Tabernacle that is to be built.[5]

Another interesting adornment in this stone-laying ceremony was in the presence of Rev. J. Bloomfield, a man of the hyper-Calvinists. Bloomfield commended Spurgeon for his zeal and his clear affirmation of the atoning work of Christ. Though he had lost members to Spurgeon's congregation, he was glad that so good a man would be their teacher now and he prayed that both they and he would prosper in the gospel. When some of his friends denied that God could bless a ministry like Spurgeon's, Bloomfield responded, "I ask any man to look at the vast numbers that have testified before delighted audiences to the way in which the ministry of Mr. Spurgeon has been blessed to them—and I ask if God has not honored him?" In view of the seal of the Spirit on his ministry, "Where is the man who dares to speak against the success which he has realized so largely in his work?" Bloomfield loved his friends that had spoken harshly of Spurgeon, but had "always hated their harshness." So he had told them to their faces and "would tell them again." "I hate their bigotry," he confessed, "while I love the Truth of God they preach." He asked that divine blessing rest on the "ministrations of our excellent friend and honor him with increasing and abundant success, for His own sake. Amen."[6]

Money-raising efforts penetrated all the ceremonies with good-natured appeals, a large gift from an anonymous 83-year-old Anglican benefactor that included a £2,000 challenge grant. Any that so desired could lay a brick if they were willing to pay a shilling for the privilege of doing so. When the proceedings closed, a note was added to the transcript to be circulated as the weekly sermon concerning the continued need for financial help.

The Committee thinks it necessary to add, that notwithstanding the very great assistance afforded upon this occasion, their enterprise is very far from accomplishment. The freehold ground has been purchased and paid for; the excavation and throwing in of concrete for foundations have also been completed. And when this expense shall also have been fully defrayed, the Committee will find themselves with about 10,000 pounds in hand. The present contract for the erection of the building is 20,000 pounds, which does not include lighting, boundary walls and necessary furniture. The Committee therefore earnestly appeals to the Church of Christ for help in their arduous undertaking. Subscriptions will be joyfully received by the Rev. C. H. SPURGEON. Or by Mr. T. COOK, Hon. Sec., New Park Street Chapel, Southwark, S.E.

A Church for London

Ministry outside the walls of New Park Street had made Spurgeon's preaching an attraction, or a distraction, to all of London. The next two years would only serve to increase the truly metropolitan character of the congregation that would gather there and make the ministry more profoundly city-wide. The name itself, changing from a localized nomenclature like "New Park Street" to a pronouncement like "Metropolitan," showed Spurgeon's consciousness of the mission of the church and his intention to make a gospel siege upon the entire city.

From his first visit in December of 1853 Spurgeon had been a keen observer of London life. The city would be a mission field as well as a base for a mission to the world. It would be the rich, virtually exhaustless, source of listeners to a divinely

5. Ibid., 367.
6. Ibid., 270.

revealed gospel of salvation for sinners providing the constant proving of his divine call. It would be the bane of mental and physical health and the constant demonstration of the corrupting power of sin in concentration.

Spurgeon wrote to great heights of literary accomplishment when he sought to describe the most appalling features of the inclemency of London's atmosphere. As an opening illustration of the biblical position that life is a vapor, Spurgeon described a trip in a London fog at noonday as moving "through a mass of vapor looking almost as thick as melted butter." The "stinging savor of smoke made our eyes run with tears, and a most uncomfortable clinging cobwebby dampness surrounded us like a wet blanket." This sent a cold chill to the very marrow of his bones and produced a darkness that, "like a black pall, hung horribly over every street." Even the many lamps in the shops, burning as if night had set in, could not put cheer in the gloomy fog that "sensibly affected all the organs of our body." Other passengers were few, and those few "flitted before us like shadows, or passed shivering by us like wet sparrows looking out for shelter in a heavy rain."[7]

Twenty-six years later James Spurgeon would describe the setting of the Pastors' College in equally dismal terms. Noting that the health of the students during the year had not been worse than might be expected in the midst of such a severe and protracted winter, he reminded his readers of what they knew only too well: "Our College is not uplifted above the fog of London, but lies near the centre of the smoky metropolis—in the heart of England and the world." That location is good for many reasons, "but in the matter of health it is trying."[8]

Kruppa believed that Spurgeon idealized the country and saw the city as a place for the con-

centration of vice and filth.[9] Perhaps some of his evaluations arose from a tendency to epitomize into caricature the rural/urban conflict in values, style of life, healthy atmosphere, stress levels, and character development. Some of it, though, arose out of the sober observation that Spurgeon made about human nature in any situation. Lostness and spiritual disinterest, slovenly habits and personal apathy, were just as prominent in Waterbeach as in London, simply on a smaller scale. In London, however, the concentration of population led to an accumulation of social problems and the exacerbation of sinful activities when encouragement toward them found multiplication in groups of like-minded people, and the development of entrepreneurial ventures in vice. The quest for money combined with the corruption of leadership and talent created pockets of crime and vice that seemed impenetrable. This was a source of special distress for Spurgeon as he viewed the growth of corruption as rampant and massive compared to the growth of the power and fervent gospel ministry of the churches. In a soulful lamentation over London's desperate lostness, Spurgeon introduced a lengthy review of *The Seven Curses of London.*

> We wish every Christian man could be made aware of the vice, the destitution and the misery which surround him; it would make him a better servant of the Lord. We are a vast deal too comfortable. We simper with complacency at the good which we are doing, when, like Mrs. Partington's mop, we are scarcely pushing back one wave of the seething ocean of iniquity around us. At our pious gatherings we half persuade ourselves that the world is being converted, and that gross vice is a *rara avis* in the land, and all the while the devil, with almost undisputed sway, rules the masses,

---

7. S&T, February 1865, 85.

8. S&T, June 1891, 263.

9. Patricia Stallings Kruppa, Charles Haddon Spurgeon: A Preacher's Progress (Garland Pub., 1982), Chapter one.

and devours them at his will. Those lines of first-class residences, those long terraces of respectable houses, those miles of pretty villas, those leagues of busy shops—one rides along them by the hour, and feels that London is great, flourishing, wealthy, orderly; ay, but turn out of that broad thoroughfare, stop at Paradise Court or Rosemary Alley, take your walks abroad where many poor you see, note the ragged children, the filthy Irishwomen, the harlots, the drunkards, the swarms of villainous-looking big boys; and now, as you return, sick from the reek of gin and the mustiness of rags, you learn that London is poor, wretched, lawless, horrible.[10]

James Greenwood, the author of the book under review, stated that the first curse of London was neglected children. Three-hundred fifty thousand children under the age of sixteen were dependent on parish authorities for their maintenance. After the recitation of moving anecdotes designed to illustrate how desperate the situation was, Spurgeon remarked: "If these things be true of children left under the care of poor penniless widows, what a plea we have for our orphanage, and how grateful should we and our band of helpers be that we are allowed to do a little to prevent such misery."[11]

The second curse of London Greenwood listed as "Professional thieves," numbered at 20,000, "little short of the membership of all the Baptist churches in London." The difference, as Spurgeon observed, that among the number of thieves, "every individual member of this synagogue of Satan is an earnest, genuine, worker in the evil cause."

Professional beggars constituted the third curse, and Spurgeon felt that he could more than confirm Greenwood's statement. Spurgeon had seen enough of it to know that mendicancy was a profitable trade for the idle and vicious and supported an "army of the vilest loafers that ever disgraced a city."[12]

To alleviate the fourth curse, Greenwood advocated the licensing of "fallen women" and Spurgeon took time to register his disagreement. That policy in France had not improved the moral condition of the country or relieved the misery of its subjects. "May God avert from England," Spurgeon prayed, "the abiding pestilence of systematic debauchery, by which sin is made easy, and the path to hell more fascinating than ever."[13]

The fifth in this list of curses was drunkenness, related to all the others, "often their mother and always their nurse." Though Spurgeon opposed the prohibitionist, teetotal viewpoint, he had no sympathy for drunkenness and wanted every effort to diminish that curse to have its own measure of success.

Evidently, Greenwood made light humor at the expense of the strict prohibitionist group and Spurgeon took exception to his comments. "Their object is so praiseworthy," Spurgeon replied, "and the need of every well-intentioned effort so manifest, that it is a pity to throw cold water on any earnest temperance. If teetotalers are rather too prone to treat contemptuously the efforts of those who do not adopt their modes of operation, there is the more reason why the true temperance but non-teetotal man should behave with courtesy to his more irritable fellow worker, for whom he is bound to entertain a kindly esteem." The numbers of beer houses and gin palaces exceeded any estimation of what moderation might demand for the public good. The Bacchanalian missionary soon has his way and establishes an all-surrounding omnipresence of the stimulant that propagates the craving for

---

10. S&T, September 1869, 385f.

11. Ibid., 386.

12. Ibid., 389.

13. Ibid., 390.

more. "The accursed habit of intoxication lies at the root of the main part of London's poverty, misery, and crime."[14]

A sixth curse on London was the "betting gambler." So sly and deceitful was the promise of quick wealth for the price of a few postage stamps that the trade in betting had increased greatly in twenty years. A tribe of "blacklegs" and others feeds upon "this growing vice, swarming about it like flies around carrion." Spurgeon knew of the practice and had heard the voices of street urchins shouting the odds. Marvelous are the fortunes to be won but "more marvelous still is the senseless folly which can be duped by such manifest quackery."[15] He spent four more pages of text alternating between his and Greenwood's observations on the fever pitch enthusiasm reached on the days and hours of horse-races and the deceit used by certain "betting men" to take others for large sums of money.

For the seventh curse, the waste of charity, Spurgeon had little space and less heart to devote to its discussion. A hint of the nature of this problem appears in an article on "Theatre Preaching" in which the author Edward Leach made note of a "few men, calling themselves preachers and teachers, who actually live upon the money they obtain for charitable purposes, instead of devoting the whole to the object for which they professed to gain it."[16]

Spurgeon saw to it that *The Sword and the Trowel* published articles on work being done for the gospel in each of these levels of London perversity. But some remedy for all these rested in the power of his readers by devoting themselves to support "those efforts which we ourselves are making to educate the orphan, and to instruct a ministry capable, in God's strength, of dealing with these tremendous evils."[17]

If Spurgeon could have added another curse, he probably would have selected the theatre. The moral tone of the theatre was too bad for mending and the character of drama is such that the tendency always is toward quick corruption. While some advocated Christian attendance in order to raise the moral level, Spurgeon thought that was like advocating pouring a bottle of lavender water into the great sewer to improve its aroma. That which has such an attraction to the harlot and the debauchee should never be recommended as a school of virtue. Spurgeon claimed that he had never entered a theatre during the performance of a play, but when coming home from a distant engagement he had passed by and seen enough to "pray that our sons and daughters may never go within the doors." Should that practice ever become a habit among church members, Spurgeon believed it would prove the death of piety. "Who can suppose," he asked, "amusement surrounded with the seductions of vice to be fit recreation for a pure mind? Who could draw near to God after sitting to admire the performances of a wanton woman, and I am told that some who have dazzled London society are such."[18] London newspapers might belittle and lampoon Spurgeon, but London society would kill the soul.

The answer for "fallen women" was not licensing but redemption. Spurgeon carried an article by Edward Leach on "Homes with No Name," about houses that seek the restoration and reclamation of these girls that the city had crushed. He described how well-kept these houses were and how industriously occupied the young girls were that had been housed there. Writing about this, Leach confessed, almost forced one to go beyond

---

14. Ibid., 391.

15. Ibid.

16. Ibid., 401. Ibid., "Theatre Preaching," by Edward Leach.

17. Ibid., 396. "Seven Curses."

18. S&T, September 1879, 409.

the limits of propriety and modesty in language in addressing a subject matter that was so insidious. Ignoring the reality could have sad consequences, but "infinitely worse evils" could come from "exposing it in all its ghastly organizations to the innocent mind." Since the sin was increasing and its victims growing in numbers, and "since the exertions which Christian philanthropy should put forth are so imperatively necessary, and so inadequate" he took the challenge to deal with it "in terms as delicate as our vocabulary will allow."[19]

Leach went on to discuss how the problem was addressed by Christian philanthropists through the formation of homes, the tenderness and compassion of Mrs. Thomas, the woman most responsible for the organization and procedures used in the homes, and the love that the inmates of these houses had for her. Reclamation is difficult but many incidents of real conversion continued to encourage those involved in the work. No one should diminish the reality of sin in the choices made by the fallen women, but Leach also pointed to the reality that an abusive home life riddled with all the dissipation of poverty pressed many young girls to find both affection and support in the life of the streets. Leach asked, "Upon whom can the burden of their sin fall, but upon the parents who make these children domestic drudges, and buffet them about, and brutally and coarsely assail them?"[20]

Spurgeon recognized the poverty of the lower classes of London and sought to put it into theological context in his preaching. As a matter of covenant faithfulness Spurgeon believed that "God has never suffered his people to starve." The meeting of temporal needs as promised under the old covenant "is as true under the new covenant as under the old." The one that feeds insects as well as the prowling lion will not permit his "home-borne ones, those who are nearest his heart, to perish for lack of nutriment." As he surveyed the congregation he recognized that some "have been brought so low by poverty and affliction that you are qualified to speak." They had experienced "an empty cupboard with an empty stomach" and wondered where their supplies would come from. He knew that others compounded that difficulty with the reality that they were "houseless and homeless."[21] In ways almost miraculous, through a series of providences, God has provided for these so that they can say that his covenant never fails. God's faithfulness never diminished, however, the necessity for observation of need and compassionate action on the part of his people. London was a particularly ripe place for the exercise of such graces.

Systems that contributed to this grinding poverty must be challenged. Spurgeon made social comment on both the pollution and the repression of London and England generally through unconscionable industry. In 1856 Spurgeon spoke to the weavers of Spitalfields and used their plight to make a point in a sermon entitled "Songs in the Night." He looked to a time when "the sweet Sun of righteousness will arise with healing beneath his wings, that the oppressed shall be righted, that despotisms shall be cut down, that liberty shall be established, that peace shall be made lasting, and that the glorious liberty of the gospel of God shall be extended throughout the known world." One of the wrongs that would be righted and the oppressed that would be set free would be that group of weavers who "are generally ground down within an inch of their lives." Their masters, Spurgeon wryly surmised, must intend that their bread should be very sweet on the suppo-

---

19. S&T, October 1869, 446-47.

20. Ibid., 452.

21. SS, 6:232.

sition that "the nearer the ground the sweeter the grass," because none had to get their sustenance nearer the ground than those poor weavers. Spurgeon referred to a study from the House of Commons that reported the average wages of this group was seven to eight shillings a week. Their work, of course, was on "expensive articles, which my friends the ladies are wearing now, and which they buy as cheaply as possible." But surely, Spurgeon proposed, "they do not know that they are made with the blood and bones and marrow of the Spitalfields weavers, who, many of them, work for less than man ought to have to subsist upon."[22]

With the massive gathering at the Fast Day sermon in 1857, Spurgeon refused to miss the opportunity to talk about the "class sins" of England, particular the "sins of the rich." Workers' wages fall far below their value to their masters and cannot provide a living for the families dependent on them. The factory or the business is like a cauldron and every type of worker may be thrown in. "Put them in: heap the fire, boil the cauldron; stir them up; never mind their cries. The hire of the labourers kept back may go up to heaven: it does not matter, the millions of gold are safe. The law of demand and supply is with us, and who is he that would interfere." Would anyone step forward to dare prevent the grinding of the faces of the poor? The seamstress, the tailor, and the artisan all are owned by their lords and masters, are they not? But they shall get the ear of God and his rod shall certainly fall.[23]

Preaching in 1872, Spurgeon, speaking on the blessings of the covenant in changing the sinner's heart, illustrated with a statement of social ethics: "Look at our brooks and rivulets which have been, by a lax legislature, so long delivered over to

the tormentors to be blackened into pestiferous sewers—if we need to have them purged it is of no use to cast chloride of lime and other chemicals into the stream—the only remedy is to forbid the pollution, to demand that factories shall not poison us wholesale."[24] Spurgeon could see that sin destroyed not only the soul but would assault the very earth; and England, especially London, was reeling through blows of greed on its environment.

England was not immune to the scenes of riot and anarchy that followed the Franco-Prussian War. The damage wrought by the German army was nothing compared to that of republican upon republican. No building, no monument to patriotism or French heroism, was sacred but all experienced the fury of the opposing mobs. Homes were wrecked and devastation ruled. How happy that one may view this from afar, so an Englishman might muse, with the knowledge that unrest and civil war has long been unknown to the peaceful homes of England. At times Spurgeon wondered what France might have become had it embraced the Reformation, if an intolerant Catholicism had not remained in the ascendancy, had the Huguenots not been treated so mercilessly. Spurgeon warned, however, that "what has been done in Paris, may be done in London."[25]

The English character, that is the Anglo-Saxon blood, is not so superior to the French, the Gauls, that they are incapable of such bitter and severe reprisals for unjust treatment. One does not have to look too deeply into English history to find the sinister in the English character. Sir Walter Raleigh, for example, was "a brilliant courtier, a daring adventurer, an assiduous investigator in scientific discovery, the redoubtable annihilator of the navies of Spain, the munificent colonizer

22. SS, 2:178.

23. NPSP, 1857, 384.

24. MTP, 1872, 220.

25. S&T, January 1872, 6.

spending for his country £40,000 of his own fortune in endeavours to plant colonies across the Atlantic, a foremost literary genius in England's most splendid literary age." He managed to survive the dangers of the court of the "great penurious, capricious Queen Elizabeth" but ran afoul of her cousin James and "was unjustly beheaded in the reign of her poor, driveling successor, James I."[26] In the present, Spurgeon referred to the work of the Nine Elms Mission that did a "noble and extremely difficult work." He had learned of the "all but incurable deceit which characterizes many of the criminal class." If he had not learned it from Scripture, he certainly could have learned from London "the terrible needs of human nature."[27]

St. Giles had been a place especially known for its small pockets, and some large, of organized crime. The Christian mission superintended by George Hatton had transformed it so that it did not resemble the St. Giles of two decades previous. A visitor, however, who explored its rookeries might wonder if it could ever have been worse. "The grinding poverty from which so many suffer, the total neglect on the part of myriads of others of their best interests, and the neglected children who swarm on all sides, make up a picture well calculated to inspire us with despair were we not assured that even in St. Giles matters are on the mend, the present condition of the people being a marked contrast to the unrestrained savagery of former times."[28] After seventeen years of general work in the area, Hatton began to concentrate specifically on the question, "What shall be done with the criminal classes?" Thieves and their confederates headquartered in St. Giles began to draw special attention, so that some began to request help in leaving that manner of life. On other occasions, discharged prisoners gravitating toward their old element found both caution and help in escaping the sucking power of criminal activity and camaraderie. Some had breathed the air of criminality since childhood and the road to respectability was blocked with seemingly insuperable obstacles. Ease, of a sort, and immediate gain awaited them. Hatton sought to make first contact with released prisoners by setting up right outside the prison gates a breakfast for prisoners released on each day of the week. In one year, of 5,274 persons that were released from Coldbath Fields, 3,121 accepted the invitation to breakfast, and 1,125 signed the temperance pledge. He started with one, found it successful, and eventually spread it to three and would soon "cover the entire ground of the Metropolitan male local prisons." The work found such sympathy in many parts that many ways have been found to restore these men to respectable life and many "have experienced a saving change through grace." Hatton and his useful helper Mr. Wheatley were becoming recognized as "masters of the art of reclaiming criminals." Who can estimate the difference made in many lives when one person, formerly destructive, now contributes and is a force for right rather than one that preys upon society?[29]

J. Burnham, a Metropolitan Tabernacle evangelist, described the living conditions of the people that came out to the hop gardens to pick. Naming their residences as "London haunts," Burnham described their homes—"hardly worth the sacred name"—as "the abodes of wretchedness and filth; poverty, sin, and misery their constant companions." Besides such an unsavory home, they lived "shut in, for the greater part of the year, in dirty, narrow courts, where the sun scarcely ever finds its way," in conditions too crowded even to

26. S&T, November 1881, 578.

27. Ibid.

28. S&T, October 1883, 536.

29. Ibid., 538f.

be decent. Hop picking time, therefore, becomes a luxury. These oppressed humans "turn out for three or four weeks into the beautifully fresh and invigorating air of the hop gardens," where their humanity rises and they laugh and sing.[30]

One of Spurgeon's sons, Charles, pastor at Greenwich, proved to be as keen an observer of human nature and as profound a lover of sinners as his father. He specialized in making presentation of slices of life in a variety of places where he ministered and traveled. A visit to the United States resulted in a number of talks illustrated with pictures he arranged to have taken of places and people. He did the same for London society and entitled his presentation "Street Characters and Cries." Each of these characters allowed themselves to be photographed in action at their particular vocation. He began with the "sweep" whose early street cry did not quite suit everybody. Then would come the Muffin man with his muffled bell. He had an image and comment about the bare-footed gamin with his cigar-lights, the street musician blowing a popular air along with the "crossing-sweeper" and the milkman. The cat's meat man, the wild rabbit seller, and all the costers with vegetables and flowers made their appearance in Charles' presentation. Soon would come the coal man with his "'ere ye are, a shilling a hundred, best coal." Further musical productions came from "piano-organ grinders and the blind fiddlers and niggers." Mixed in with the colorful groups were vendors of hot pies and water cress, baked potatoes and shrimps, gingerbread, and herrings. Set up for business were the scissors-grinder and the chair mender and "boys of the black-shoe brigade," along with a variety of news-boys. Giving an additional splash of true urbanity were the cabmen, busmen, railway men

and the frequent interruptions of the fire-brigade, engine, horses, and all. Spurgeon of Greenwich included the open-air preacher as a participant in this city scene of "Street Characters and Cries." CHS hoped that the latter would never disappear from London life until every man woman and child was found in a regular place of worship, though he felt that drums and brass music that destroy the peace of our Sabbaths could be dispensed with.[31]

Much information about the economy, social status, moral tone, and living conditions of the various districts of London entered the pages of *The Sword and the Trowel* as the ministries of College men were discussed. G. Holden Pike, taking information from *The City Mission Magazine*, gave a description of an area behind Shoreditch Church, giving his article the title "A Picture of Shoreditch." Assuming that this district was Shoreditch, he described it as one of the most overcrowded and poverty-stricken areas of London. A man must have a constitution of steel and the heart of an angel to survive in ministry there, so the *Trowel* reported. One of the City Missionaries seeking to evangelize there was killed in a drunken brawl in one of its back streets. Its immediate appearance is one of flourishing gin palaces, narrow streets, and reeking courts. A closer examination shows that a number of skilled artisans, "workers in wood, leather, and iron," are there, whose workshops are numerous and have carved out a healthier region for sleeping and constitute "quite the upper classes in the back slums of a place like Shoreditch." Multitudes of others, however, are far below this group "whose work is as precarious as it is ill-paid, or who in an almost literal sense have to pick up their livelihood in the streets." In addition "there is the un-

---

30. S&T, December 1879, 576.

31. S&T, April 1885, 195.

numbered horde of the fallen and the criminals, thieves, cadgers, and nondescripts" of all sorts. The streets are filthy but the houses are filthier yet, and the "most common sanitary rules are ignored until an occasional epidemic sweeps the people into the grave as with the besom of destruction." Houses domicile multiple families, one family per room, making some houses the abode of twelve to sixteen families. The living quarter often has to double as a workshop. The normal outlets at the back of houses are no longer open space but are built upon by replacing small houses with large ones so that houses back upon each other with little space between. The hard living conditions are matched only by the ignorance of the population of genuine religion.[32]

Spurgeon received a letter of objection because the streets described were not really in Shoreditch. Spurgeon noted the legitimacy of the authorities' indignant reaction and pledged to investigate. He found that the only error was in the title and regretted any offense that had come as a result of that mistake. The mistake was natural, however, not unlike geographical mistakes made in other London periodicals when seeking to isolate the precise district in which certain neighborhoods lie. Spurgeon sent "an impartial gentleman to make diligent search" and the facts of the article concerning the conditions of the section under scrutiny were accurate. "What our commissioner saw and smelt with his own eyes and nose would be rather more startling than our constituents would care to read about." Spurgeon had a list of courts, places, and streets with an estimation of the number of families per dwelling and an eyewitness account of the sanitary conditions. "We are surprised that a pestilence is not created in such places." Designated the place as

Shoreditch was technically wrong, but giving the description of the place in question was accurate.[33] One of Spurgeon's students, Mr. Cuff, had begun work there and set up a chapel.[34]

By January 1880 Spurgeon was able to report that a Tabernacle, the Shoreditch Tabernacle, was completed and soon would be debt-free. Mr. Cuff had continued his ministry there and God had raised up a church. "The pastor's work in Shoreditch has attracted very general interest, and well it may, for if a strong and efficient Baptist church can be sustained amid the poverty of Shoreditch, it will be an encouragement to all who work for Christ in our great city." Archibald Brown had done a like work in Stepney, demonstrating "what earnest preaching of the simple gospel will do!"[35] Spurgeon issued a benediction on Cuff, his labors, and the church along with an emphasis on the character of the section of London in which the work was being done. "God bless you Brother Cuff, and God bless all those who help you. May you all go from strength to strength; and may the new Tabernacle be as a city of refuge to Shoreditch, and Bethnal Green, and all those swarming regions of poverty and sin." This kind of work expressed precisely the vision that Spurgeon had for the Metropolitan Tabernacle and its ministries in this complicated London where God had placed him to minister. As he continued his commendation of Cuff, he turned to the human source of Cuff's preparation and encouragement: "God bless also the College from which you sprang, and raise up friends who will see that the mother hive never lacks for money, and that as God sends new men there are all the supplies for their education and maintenance."[36]

---

32. S&T, April 1876, 199f.

33. S&T, June 1876, 286.

34. S&T, April 1876, 167.

35. S&T, January 1880, 34.

36. Ibid.

Spurgeon was always frank about the difficulties of London life and the various political and religious challenges of being an Englishman. No doubt, however, that he loved the country and the heritage of being a Protestant and a Dissenter, but an Englishman. When he saw an evaluation from an outside observer, Spurgeon found joy in sharing how the non-Englishman viewed the English character and contribution. Philip Schaff, the American biblical scholar who became one of the foremost historians of the church, visited the Bible lands, and, from letters written back to his friends and colleagues wrote a book entitled *Through Bible Lands: Notes of Travel in Egypt, the Desert, and Palestine*. He took advantage of his travels to make comparisons of the various people involved in what was called the "Eastern Question." He preferred the Czar, Alexander II, to the Sultan, but English rule to both of those. Spurgeon enjoyed Schaff's comments and shared them with the readers of *The Sword and the Trowel*:

> But I greatly prefer the constitutional scepter of England to the despotic government of Russia, which tolerates or persecutes Roman Catholics and Protestants as the interests of the State require. England is everywhere, at home and abroad, the friend and protector of civil and religious liberty, as well as of material progress, and allows fair play to missionary activities without distinction of sect. She has, moreover, shown a wonderful skill and success in planting colonies and ruling heathen and Mohammedan races. Her rule in India no matter how acquired, has been a blessing to the Hindoos, giving them peace and prosperity, and, without interfering with their religion, has opened the way for the orderly introduction of Christianity. Her motives, including the secret convention with Turkey, may have been purely selfish, but it is an undoubted fact that the interests of England are identical with the interests of constitutional freedom and an enlightened civilization. Wherever the British flag waves there is security of life and property and the rights of men; there is freedom of speech and of the press, there is vigorous and honest administration of justice, there is commercial prosperity, there is the literature of Shakespeare and Milton, there we find an open Bible and a free pulpit, the purity and dignity of woman, and the blessing of a Christian home. Viewed from this point of view, the English protectorate of Turkey, which may result sooner or later in annexation, promises to be in the end as great a benefit to the Turks and Arabs as England's reign in India has been to the Hindoos. She has, indeed, assumed an enormous responsibility and a most difficult task. It will tax all her capital and energy to lift Turkey out of the chaotic confusion and bankruptcy in which she is left after an exhaustive war. But she is better fitted for the task than any other government on earth, and she will have the hearty sympathy and co-operation of all true friends of those classic lands now fearfully prostrated, but destined to see a day of resurrection to new life. It may be doubted, indeed, whether the Turk can be truly reformed without ceasing to be a Mohammedan. In the transforming process he must become either an infidel or a Christian. We hope and pray that before long he will transfer his allegiance from the false prophet of Mecca to the true Prophet of Nazareth.[37]

Perhaps it was purely coincidental, but nevertheless ironical that Spurgeon included, one-half column removed, a review of a book entitled *The Young Rebels* which he described as an "amusing story" that occurred in America during "the war which liberated the colonists from the yoke of George the Third." Boys would be "pleased with the incidents and improved by the lessons."[38]

---

37. S&T, July 1879, 342f.
38. Ibid., 343.

Whatever difficulties George III might have created for England, Spurgeon had high esteem for the family of Victoria. "We rejoice," he said "in all the good which can be said of the royal family, and it is not a little." Victoria had nine children, forty-two grandchildren, and scores of great-grandchildren, most of whom were well-placed eventually among the royalty of Europe. Their second child, Edward, born in 1841, rebelled against the strict discipline imposed on him by Victoria and Albert, indulging freely in wine, women, and frivolity, a style of life that even marriage at the age of twenty-two did not impede. His wife, Princess Alexandra of Denmark, ignored his unfaithfulness though it caused divorces in other families. Spurgeon, who was well aware in 1879 of the reputation of this member of the royal family, acknowledged that "rumour continually babbles of one at least whose life casts a dark shade over the glory of the royal house." At that time he discreetly held judgment in abeyance, only commenting: "Whether those rumours speak truth or not we cannot tell; but if they do—shame on the profligate! Happy is the land which has virtue on its throne; but woe to the nation whose princes can justly be charged with licentious folly!" He earnestly hoped that such a calamity would "never overshadow our beloved country." Like a loyal Englishman, he wrote, "Long live the queen," and added, "and may all her sons be like their father, whose memory is still sweet and blossoms from the dust." While other nations were "darkened with the smoke of smouldering discontent," Spurgeon believed that it was good to "foster loyalty, and say the best that can be said of a beloved queen and her royal issue."[39]

No matter what the glory or the difficulties of the royal family, the possibility of "smouldering discontent" always roamed the streets of London. G. Holden Pike described the destitution of much of London society in an article entitled "The Bitter Cry of London." In the same context in which he wrote of the "horrible condition of our wretched City," and the "present condition of the miserable classes of the metropolis," he could picture a London that was "on the mend." Pike pointed to work by the London Congregational Union, the home mission work of the Baptists, the City Mission, and the Ragged School Crusade as having aided at different times to relieve pressures from a "volcano which was ready at any moment to burst into conflagration." Further relief of the great difficulties that still plagued the city must come from an accurate analysis of the situation. Not drink alone, but proper wages, housing, labor conditions, and job market combine with a spiritually destitute populace to make for a many-sided problem. Though the gospel is the cure for a wrong people, wrong circumstances still play a major role in perpetuating difficulties. "One room life in narrow, crowded streets, or still more foetid courts, would soon drive self-respect and energy out of the hearts of most of us."[40] The system of middlemen makes the wages of those near the bottom of labor hardly survivable, and an overcrowded labor market gives them little bargaining power. The answer for the jobless, so Pike suggested, would be "a system of emigration" to Canada where workers would be welcome and wages would be livable.[41]

Most of the destitute, however, were caught inextricably where they were, and the prospect of emigration to a better place was not even a dream. The mountain would not budge, so Spurgeon must go to the mountain. This new building, soon to be unveiled in 1861, would be the

39. Ibid., 344; review of *England's Royal House: The Home Life of the Prince Consort* by Rev. Charles Bullock [1829-1901].

40. S&T, January 1885, 20.

41. Ibid., 21.

launching place. It would be the center of consistent energetic efforts to place the gospel before every level of London society and provide an alternative life displacing every London vice. Its doors would be open from early morning until around 11:00 at night with the various activities on its campus and the numbers of groups assembling there and then dispersing into the city for a variety of evangelistic operations.

This constant activity, the hustling and bustling of group after group, the services on Sabbath and three times during the week, the meeting of the College and the night school, all challenged the upkeep of even such a sturdy and usable facility. By 1867 and 1883, the Tabernacle was in much need of cleaning. In 1867 they dismissed to the Agricultural Hall for five weeks, an event to be described below. For the month of August 1883, it dismissed its morning and evening service to the Exeter Hall. This was the fourth time that the congregation, now greatly altered and increased, had made this temporary transition. The expansion of New Park Street, the building of the Tabernacle, the first period of cleaning of repairs, and now its cleansing again had made pilgrims of the congregation. For those that could not make the trip, the lecture hall at the Tabernacle would be open for services, with John Spurgeon, Sr. filling the first spot. The Monday prayer meeting would also convene in the lecture hall, and the Thursday evening sermon would be in the chapel of Mr. Newman Hall. The proposal for Exeter was that the morning service would be for seat-holders but the evening service would be reserved solely for outsiders to be seated on a first come first serve basis. "Our hope," Spurgeon explained, "is that we shall gather a new contingent for our army." He wanted outsiders to hear the word and feel its power; the congregation prayed for an ingathering and returned to Exeter "with the joy-

ful expectation of a season of grace."[42] Spurgeon reported that conversions had been met with at each service and "hearts have been stirred up to seek the Lord with deeper earnestness." He expected more to follow.

The congregation would return to the Met on September 6 for the Thursday evening service to which nearly 4,000 persons came. The following Sunday, September 9 "every available inch of space" was occupied. For the evening of the ninth, "nearly as many people were shut out as were accommodated in the building."[43] The improvement of the surroundings confirmed his confidence that the amount spent in cleaning had been well invested. A balance of £1,100 still remained and Spurgeon insisted that givers come through, and come through quickly, for "We have never been in debt, and we do not intend to begin that system now." It could not be delayed, however, the "Central-house itself must not be neglected."[44] More than £1,200 was collected in that single effort providing complete satisfaction of the cost plus something for "other needful expenses." Happily he could report, "Thus, at one stroke, all shade of debt was averted."[45]

In October 1885, after more than thirty years of ministry in the city, Spurgeon preached in a prayer meeting about the need for revival. It is clear that he felt almost despair about the spiritual and moral and cultural condition of London. It was more than messy fog, and dampness, and frost, and filthy smoke and rivers that bothered him about the city. A breakdown in doctrine had led to a breakdown of discipline in the home and the children are as "dressy, as gay, as godless as the children of the non-

---

42. S&T, August 1883, 461.

43. Ibid., 562.

44. S&T, September 1883, 514.

45. S&T, October 1883, 562.

religious!" The reciprocal effects in society as a whole outraged Spurgeon. "This is a great difficulty to our poorer friends in this loathsome city, which is becoming as polluted as heathendom." A Christian mother had recently brought her child to the city for better opportunity and soon was horrified to hear him use profane language, being evidently unaware of its meaning. He learned it in the street close to his mother's door. If children cannot walk and run the streets without being morally polluted, where can the children of working people go? "All around us vice has become so daring," Spurgeon noted with distress and alarm, "that a blind man may almost be envied; but even he has ears, and will therefore, be vexed with the filthy conversation of the wicked." When asked how to avoid such degrading influences, given the virtually irreversible dynamic of city life, Spurgeon simply advised people to stay in the country. Those that presently live in the "breezy country village" should stay there, "and not come into our close streets, and lanes, and courts, which reek with blasphemy and dirty talk." Spurgeon, the natural rhetorician, master of simplicity in language, and punctilious watchman over his own lips, could not fathom why working men in their ordinary conversation would use "such abominable expressions, which have no useful meaning, and are simply disgusting?"[46] London not only had torn away the comeliness of the Tabernacle, it had smitten the spirit of Spurgeon.

In 1861, however, all the powers of nature, unceasing activity, and accumulating evil had not yet darkened his spirit, and a new building, symbolizing new possibilities and embodying an aggregate of past success, was ready to be put into service.

A Light Shining in a Dark Place

When the newly constructed Metropolitan Tabernacle opened in 1861, Spurgeon could not have anticipated the emotional weight that would press on him by 1885 with moral decline in the city and among the churches and theological decline as the accepted standard of modern Christian ministry. He believed that the completion of the construction of the Tabernacle signaled an advance for the gospel in the whole city. The building was baptized with a series of services involving every relevant sphere of interest in the progress of Spurgeon's ministry. Henry Vincent called the impressive building, "the noblest temple ever raised by Non-conformist zeal."[47] The two-week-long inaugural services showed it to be the concretion of the noblest vision for gospel proclamation ever conceived in the mind of one non-conformist minister. These services climaxed with a celebration of the exuberant grace of God toward sinners though a series of messages on the distinguishing doctrines of sovereign, effectual, irresistible grace. The *denoument* ensued with a proclamation that none of the elect shall be absent in the final census, that the whole world, therefore, is the field of legitimate labor for God-called, Spirit-gifted gospel teachers, and that an assurance of one's standing before God in salvation is not only possible and a great privilege of grace, but the duty of all to seek and not to rest content until it is attained.

A prayer meeting convened at 7 am March 18, 1861, was attended by 1,000 people. Spurgeon and several others prayed and a hymn was sung that narrated "that joyous gospel which we trust will long be proclaimed within our hallowed walls." The song of a present salvation founded upon an eternal covenant sung on this day would

---

46. S&T, October 1885, 516.

47. MTP, 1861, 331.

echo through the walls at Newington for the next thirty-one years of Spurgeon's ministry—and beyond.

> Saved from the damning power of sin,
> The law's tremendous curse,
> We'll now the sacred song begin
> Where God began with us.
>
> We'll sing the vast unmeasured grace
> Which, from the days of old,
> Did all his chosen sons embrace,
> As sheep within his fold.
>
> The basis of eternal love
> Shall mercy's frame sustain;
> Earth, hell, or sin, the same to move,
> Shall all conspire in vain.
>
> Sing, O ye sinners bought with blood,
> Hail the Great Three in One;
> Tell how secure the cov'nant stood
> Ere time its race begun.
>
> Ne'er had ye felt the guilt of sin
> Nor sweets of pard'ning love,
> Unless your worthless names had been
> Enroll'd to life above.
>
> O what a sweet exalted song
> Shall rend the vaulted skies,
> Then, shouting grace, the blood-wash'd throng
> Shall see the Top Stone rise.

One week later, another prayer meeting was held. That afternoon, March 25, Spurgeon preached the first sermon in the newly constructed Tabernacle. Spurgeon set forth an uncompromising Christocentric purpose in his preaching ministry at the Tabernacle. He pronounced the now famous words: "My venerable predecessor, Dr. Gill, has left a body of divinity, admirable and excel-

lent in its way; but the body of divinity to which I would pin and bind myself forever, God helping me, is not his system of divinity or any other human treatise, but Christ Jesus, who is the sum and substance of the gospel; who is in himself all theology, the incarnation of every precious truth, the all-glorious personal embodiment of the way, the truth, and the life."[48] One that preaches Christ must preach his full deity, his full humanity, that he is the only mediator between God and man, that he is the only lawgiver for the church, that he is the only king of the church. This Christ must be preached doctrinally, experimentally, and practically. He must be preached comprehensively—not just five strings, well-plucked till virtually worn out—but all the strings, the entire doctrine of Christ in all his beauty. This theme alone can reconcile the affections of the very diverse commitments that have existed among the great men of the various denominations. The theme of Christ unites them, though they might never have found fellowship in life, their unity since death has been founded solely on their common love for and trust in a perfect Savior.[49]

The Monday evening service, consisting of an "Evangelical Congratulation" delivered by W. Brock, seconded Spurgeon's emphasis on the preaching of Christ, propounded the renovating power of the gospel to fallen humanity, defended the holy tendency of preaching the doctrines of grace, and commended a full evangelical ministry brimming with intellectual and doctrinal integrity. "It is a vile and wicked calumny," Brock said with a peculiarly Spurgeonic emphasis, "that our doctrines of grace lead to licentiousness." "Never was there anything more palpably contrary to the truth." Interspersed were comments about the particular impact that the ministry in the Taber-

---

48. Ibid., 169.

49. Ibid., 172–76.

nacle would have. "We know that the place will be the birthplace of precious souls through successive generations; we know that the place will be like a great big human heart, throbbing, pulsating with beneficence and benevolence, obtained directly from the cross of Christ; and this great big human heart will be propelling far and near a thousand of influences, which shall be for 'glory to God in the highest, for peace on earth, and good will towards men.'"[50]

Brock viewed Spurgeon as competent naturally and as prepared by experience, education, intellect, and laborious personal study as the statesman in the senate house, the advocate at the bar, and the lecturer on the platform of an Athenaeum. He will be eloquent and mighty in the Scriptures, but preeminently he will "stand here a fellow-worker with God, so that the word will be in demonstration of the spirit and in power." The human would be confirmed by the superhuman, the natural accompanied by the preternatural, and the earthly given blessing by the heavenly. "With all that may be persuasive or argumentative or pathetic, with all that may be properly and intentionally adapted to commend the truth to every man's conscience in the sight of God, there will be the energy whereby God is able to subdue all things unto himself."[51]

At a special meeting of contributors on Tuesday evening, March 26, speakers gave many words of admiration for the structure and its capacious magnificence. Such grandeur of space seemed particularly appropriate for Spurgeon who could not be limited to a small number or a small space. Rejoicing in that increased exposure this new setting would give to the doctrines so faithfully preached by Spurgeon—election, effectual calling, justification by the righteousness

of Christ, all centering on the atoning sacrifice of Christ—one speaker said that it was no use trying to confine the eagle to a little cage for either he would break his wings or break the cage. He rejoiced that "it was not the wings of the eagle which had been broken, but the cage." Now the noble bird would have sufficient room to career through the firmament.

Spurgeon's immutable resistance to debt went on full display as he reiterated a vow never to enter the facility until debt free. Of a total needed of £4,200, including several superficial internal amenities, a collection of something more than £3,700 had been collected. This allowed the congregation to enter and complete the installation of carpet and some fittings as money became available. Upon this announcement the congregation rose to sing the doxology "with enthusiasm at the request of the rejoicing pastor."[52]

More important than this debt-free status, however, in Spurgeon's desires was an increase in prayer for his faithfulness in ministry. Interspersed with exclamations of confidence in God, Spurgeon laid his requests for prayer before the congregation of contributors. "What am I to do with such a work as this upon me? It is not the getting-up of this building; it is not the launching of the vessel—it is keeping her afloat." How could he as a young man, a feeble child, go in and out among such a people? "More than I have done to advance His Gospel, I cannot promise to do, for God knoweth I have preached beyond my strength, and worked and toiled as much as one frame could do; but I hope that in answer to your prayers I may become more prayerful, more faithful, and have more power to wrestle with God for man, and more energy to wrestle with man for God." He felt compelled to call upon all

---

50. Ibid., 183.

51. Ibid., 181.

52. Ibid., 190.

those that had benefited spiritually from his ministry to pray for him:

> If you have been edified, encouraged, or comforted through me, I beseech you carry me before God. And especially you that are my spiritual sons and daughters, begotten of me by the power of the Holy Ghost, you who have been reclaimed from sin, you who were wanderers in the wild waste until Jesus met with you in the Music Hall, in Exeter Hall, or in Park Street—you, above all— you *must* pray for me. Oh, God, we pray Thee, let multitudes of the vilest of the vile here be saved. I had rather die this night, on this spot, and end my career, than lose your prayers. My aged members, deacons, and elders, will not you be more earnest than ever? My younger brethren, my co-equals in age, comrades in battle; ye, young men, who are strong to overcome the wicked one, stand up with me, shoulder to shoulder, and give me your help. [53]

Mr. Moore, a churchman, spoke last in the meeting indicating that he had followed and marveled at Spurgeon even in the earlier days when he was not considered as sane as he was now. Had the responsibility of raising such a building debt-free fallen on the shoulders of a churchman, the process would have dragged on for ten years. Spurgeon, he believed, had done "the Church of England more good than any clergyman in it" and that neither St. Paul's, nor Westminster Abbey, nor the theatres, would be open for Sunday preaching without his influence.

The next evening, Wednesday March 27, representatives of the neighboring churches came together. More than 4,000 people from these churches assembled for this meeting chaired by Dr. Edward Steane. Steane had been active for years as a secretary in the Evangelical Alliance. In 1852 he edited a volume entitled *The Religious Condition of Christendom*.[54] He viewed Romanism and infidelity as the two great enemies of evangelical Christianity and would obviously be pleased that such a Hercules of evangelical truth, so fearless in confronting destructive error, was now situated with such abundant opportunity for influence in the city of London. He surveyed the structure with a sense of awe, wonder, and gratitude—"the largest sanctuary which had ever been reared by such churches as theirs to the service and glory of God."[55] Steane further indicated his pleasure by noting that "providence might have brought a brother who would have been an element of strife and discord, but God's grace had brought a brother among them, with whom they were one in feeling, one in doctrine, one in heart, one in sympathy, and one in Christ."

When Spurgeon responded to the celebrative introductory remarks of Steane that included a standing expression of love from both ministers and laity of the surrounding churches, he marked his experience as filled with grace and hope that such kindness had been his consistent experience from these neighbors. Spurgeon felt that it "was not easy for people to love him" since he often preached some "very strong things." The strength of his language, however, conformed to the needs of a shallow and careless age, and, by divine blessing, he found greater love and esteem from a variety of friends than if he attempted to speak smoothly. Spurgeon hoped for quarterly meetings of the various ministers that they might pray together and encourage each other in ministry to the glory of Christ. William Howieson offered Spurgeon "Godspeed" and multiplied blessings though, as the closest neighbor to the new Metropolitan Tabernacle, he stood to lose the most

---

53. Ibid., 192.

54. Edward Steane. *The Religious Condition of Christendom* (London: James Nisbet and Co., 1852).

55. MTP, 1861, 193.

members. He hoped that every pastor would now "horse the old coach better" to meet the new competition.[56] Howieson believed that the presence of Spurgeon in the Tabernacle would make all of his neighbors better preachers. Steane added that such an impetus to improvement, not only intellectually and functionally, but also spiritually, would serve the cause of the kingdom well. His tenure of forty years as a pastor taught him something of the unique challenges faced by a gospel preacher.

> He knew they were in danger of neglecting their own hearts, whilst they were professedly taking care of the souls of others; that they were tempted to substitute a critical study of the Scriptures as ministers for a devout and daily perusal of them as Christians; that they were apt to perform or discharge the duties of their office in a professional sort of way, instead of feeling themselves the power of those truths which they declare to others; that they were in danger of resting satisfied with a fervour and elevation of soul in public, instead of a calm and holy communion with God in private. If they were to give way to those things, then as the result of diminished spirituality, there would be a barren ministry.[57]

As more ministers in the surrounding area contemplated what it meant that Spurgeon, now outfitted with a facility of massive proportions, would have on their congregations, they emphasized their joint interest in the gospel success of all congregations. They had not come to place altar against altar but to publish the same God, the same gospel, the same Christ, the same atonement as an open fountain for the cleansing from sin. Punctuating these tributes were notices of Spurgeon's unusual natural gifts and acquired skills as well as the profound aptness of such a

structure as the Tabernacle for his use. Spurgeon had a "powerful and eloquent voice, and was well able to arouse the indifferent, and to make those who were careless and unconcerned thoughtful with regard to their souls."[58] The free-will gifts that purchased the Tabernacle came from those that recognized the "spiritual gifts with which God had endowed their friend, and were desirous that a building should be reared capable of holding as many thousands as could be conveniently reached by his diapason voice."[59]

Newman Hall, pastor at Surrey Tabernacle, indicated the impressiveness of Spurgeon and the new setting, as a rhetorical device in pointing beyond both to the preeminence of Christ:

> It is not the splendour of architecture, nor your glorious portico and majestic columns; not this graceful roof and these airy galleries, and these commodious seats so admirably arranged for worship and for hearing; it is not the towering dome, or the tapering spire emulating the skies; It is not clustering columns and intersecting arches through which a dim religious light may wander; it is not all these—though I do not despise the beauties of architecture—which is the glory of the church ... It is not the splendor of the pulpit—the eloquence that can wave its magic wand over a delighted audience till every eye glistens and every heart beats with emotion—the erudition that from varied stores of learning can cull its illustrations to adorn the theme—the novelty of thought, and sentence, and argument that can captivate the intellect and satisfy the reason—the fancy that can interweave with the discourse the fascinations of poetry and the beauties of style; no, it is not any one of these, nor all of these together. But it is Christ in his real and glorious divinity; Christ in his true and proper humanity; Christ in the all and

56. Ibid., 194.
57. Ibid., 195.
58. Ibid., 196.
59. Ibid., 198.

sole sufficiency of his atonement; Christ in His indwelling spirit and all prevailing intercession. This is the glory; and without this, though we had all other things, *Ichabod* must be written on the walls of any church.[60]

On Good Friday, March 29, Spurgeon preached on Romans 3:25 on *Christ Set Forth as a Propitiation*, to what he referred to as an "immense assembly."[61] On that evening he preached again out of Song of Solomon: "My beloved is mine, and I am his." Entitled *The Interest of Christ and His People in Each Other,* the sermon emphasized how Christ had made the church his own ("I am my Beloved's) and the embedded reality that such a claim makes the Beloved one ours ("And He is mine"). As he worked out the implications of this joint interest of Christ and his people, Spurgeon applied it to the opening opportunity for missionary labors in China. "Now, I do honestly avow," he stated in a moment of surprising revelation, "if this place had not been built, and I had had nothing beyond the narrow bounds of the place in which I have lately preached, I should have felt in my conscience bound to go to learn the language and preach the Word there." In God's providence, however, it had been built and he knew that "I *must* here abide, for this is *my* place." Others would not have such a gracious tie to keep them from answering to such an opportunity to show that indeed they do belong to Christ. A full persuasion of that reality would "make life cheap, and blood like water and heroism a common thing, and daring but an every-day duty, and self-sacrifice the very spirit of the Christian life."[62]

On Easter Sunday evening, March 31, on the first Sunday that the Tabernacle held the Sabbath service, Spurgeon preached from 2 Chronicles 5 and 7 on the dedication of the Temple during the reign of Solomon. The elaborately appointed Temple, constructed at immense expense, received the presence of God in the cloud and in the fire, the same presence that accompanied the people in the wilderness wanderings. Had that evidence of the divine presence not invaded and filled the temple, the entire ceremony and effort would have been in vain. So it must be with the Metropolitan Tabernacle. When the glory fell, the people fell to praise and said, "For his mercy endureth forever." "This is a grand old Calvinistic Psalm," Spurgeon commented and proceeded to drive the point home:

> What Arminian can sing that? Well, he will *sing* it, I dare say; but if he be a thoroughgoing Arminian he really cannot enjoy it and believe it. You can fall from grace, can you? Then how does his mercy endure for ever? Christ bought with his blood some that will be lost in hell, did he? Then how did her mercy endure for ever? There be some who resist the offers of Divine grace, and after all that the Spirit of God can do for them, yet disappoint the Spirit and defeat God! How then does his mercy endure for ever? No, no, this is no hymn for you, this is the Calvinists' hymn. [63]

On Tuesday, April 2, the London Baptist Brethren gathered for a celebration of this achievement, which, rightly so, they viewed as a significant accomplishment for the whole denomination. Spurgeon saw this meeting as an opportunity to promote "our success as a united body." The church belonged to "all the Baptist denomination," not to any one man or one church in particular, but first to God and next "to those who hold the pure primitive ancient Apostolic faith."[64] Spurgeon al-

60. Ibid., 200.
61. Ibid., 206.
62. Ibid., 214.
63. Ibid., 219.
64. Ibid., 225.

lied himself to the historic Baptist principle of liberty of conscience as well as the view of Baptist origins that saw Baptists, not as descending from Rome, but as existing in an independent and constant stream of witness in an "unbroken line up to the apostles themselves." Baptists were "persecuted alike by Romanists and Protestants of almost every sect," whereas Baptists had never been persecutors. They had never, nor do they now, "held it to be right to put the consciences of others under the control of man." Though willing to suffer, they desired no assistance from the state and consistently refused to "prostitute the purity of the Bride of Christ to any alliance with government, and we will never make the Church, although the Queen, the despot over the consciences of men."[65]

Sir Morton Peto, member of the House of Commons and a Baptist, chaired the meeting. He joined Spurgeon in celebrating the commitment that Baptists had fervently maintained to liberty of conscience and viewed the erection of the Tabernacle as a splendid monument to the voluntary principle—that Christ's people would love him and seek the proclamation of his name without the forceful exaction of monetary aid from an unwilling people. J. Howard Hinton spoke and, as others had done in other services, pointed to some of the unique gifts of Spurgeon. "Long may the life be spared which is so devotedly and laboriously spent; the intellectual powers which acquire and supply so large an amount of Evangelical truth; and the magnificent voice which, with so much facility, pours it into the ear of listening thousands."[66] His theme brought attention to the necessity of the work of the Spirit, "wherein lies the entire success of the Evangelical ministry." Present day conversion indicated that only small measures of the Spirit were being given but a time

would come in accordance with God's sovereign pleasure and power when the "whole world may be rapidly subdued to God."[67]

Alfred Thomas spoke about the necessity of maintaining the integrity of the Baptist ordinances, a Mr. Dickerson spoke of the differences that existed from the time of Benjamin Keach to the time of the building of the Metropolitan Tabernacle, and Jabez Burns reminded those gathered that the Baptist principle of personal responsibility had built not only the Tabernacle but provided the compulsion for a free church in a free society. Burns also reminded that the Baptist commitment had been tested when Roger Williams founded Rhode Island, "where he gave the utmost freedom of conscience, and did not demand from any of those who chose to dwell with him the least infringement of their Christian liberties."[68] Spurgeon commended a bill of Peto concerning the burial of unbaptized persons, encouraged the brethren to support efforts to provide good literature for preachers, and proposed an aggressive church-planting initiative among the Baptists. Baptists should not cower in shame before any Englishman because they possessed the poetry of Milton, the allegory of Bunyan, and the pastoral ministry of Robert Hall. He noted the distinctions that existed even among the group gathered as a show of strength. "Here am I a strict Baptist, and open communion in principle; some of our brethren are strict in communion, and strict in discipline; some are neither strict in discipline not in communion. I think I am nearest right of any, but you all think the same of yourselves, *and may God defend the right*."[69]

On April 3 representatives of the various denominations met for the purpose of celebrating

---

65. Ibid., 225.
66. Ibid., 227.

67. Ibid., 228.
68. Ibid., 234.
69. Ibid., 231-32.

Christian unity. The speakers kept to the subject of unity in diversity. The spirit of the meeting was established when the chairman, Edward Ball of Cambridgeshire, emphasized his desire that all Christians adopt the great maxim "that in essentials they should have unity; in non-essentials, liberty; and in everything they ought to have charity."[70] They should have "large eyes for each other's excellencies, and small vision for each other's defects." When praying and praising and distributing the Bible they put aside the points of division and labored together for the preeminence of Christ and his Word.

W. G. Lewis of Bayswater was bold enough to announce that he could have no unity with a man that did not hold to the inspiration of God's sacred Word. Nor did he find sufficient ground for unity with one that denied the "utter degeneracy of the entire human race in consequence of sin." The same held true for the necessity of deep conviction of sin in order to understand salvation, the atonement of Christ, the deity of Christ and the doctrine of the Trinity. While liberty in non-essentials should be observed, one must not forget that true unity cannot exist merely in such freedom as a passive requirement, but must actively embrace those truths that are considered essential.[71]

Octavius Winslow took the pulpit on the evening of April 4 and preached about "Christ's Finished Work", based on the words of Jesus recorded in John 19:30: "It is Finished." Winslow echoed Spurgeon's emphasis on the cross and forecast what Spurgeon's message would be for the next thirty years. Like Spurgeon, Winslow believed that the power of contending earnestly for the truth resided in the "simple, bold, uncompromising presentation of the Atoning and finished Sacrifice of Christ—the up-lifting, in its naked

simplicity and solitary, unapproachable grandeur, of the Cross of the Incarnate God, the instrument of the sinner's salvation, the foundation of the believer's hope, the symbol of pardon, reconciliation, and hope to the soul; in a word, the grand weapon by which error shall bow to truth, and sin give place to righteousness; and the kingdoms of this world long in rebellion against God, crushed and enthralled, shall yield to Messiah's scepter, spring from the dust, burst their bonds, and exult in the undisputed supremacy and benign reign of Jesus."[72] Christ's cry was the cry of a sufferer, the language of a Savior, and the shout of a conqueror. Nothing may be placed beside the completed work of Christ as an aid or supplement in his role of suffering and conquering Savior. Adding to the accumulating hopes and admonitions concerning the future occupation of the Tabernacle, Winslow concluded: "And now from my heart I ask the blessing of the triune God upon my beloved brother, the grand substance of whose ministry I believe from my very soul is to exalt the finished work of Jesus. And I pray that this noble edifice, reared in the name and consecrated to the glory of the triune God, may for many years echo and re-echo with his voice of melody and of power in expounding to you the glorious doctrines and precepts of Christ's one finished atonement."[73]

After services on Sunday, April 7, the congregation gathered on Monday evening to have their time of inaugurating their new place of worship. Spurgeon's father, John Spurgeon, served as chairman and conveyed regrets from his own father for not being there. The joy of the occasion might indeed be his death, and he wanted to die in his own church.

James Smith, a former pastor at New Park Street, reveled in the theological heritage of the

70. Ibid., 235.
71. Ibid., 241-42.
72. Ibid., 243.
73. Ibid., 248.

church and its perennial usefulness in the conversion of sinners. His prayer while he was pastor that God would "cram the place" had been fulfilled under Spurgeon; the blood-stained banner of the cross was continually unfurled in the preaching and the baptismal waters did not rest.

Spurgeon himself spoke about peculiarities of the church in its maintenance of an eldership as a separate office from the deacons, thus avoiding an unbiblical amalgamation found in many churches. This arrangement had made him "the happiest man on earth, and when he had any troubles, it was very seldom they came from the Church." In addition, he maintained a strict policy about baptism and church membership, opposite to many of the churches of the Baptist Union, but an open policy toward communion. This was just as it should be he believed—strict discipline and unlimited fellowship with all the church of God.[74] He illustrated both the strictness and the openness on the next two evenings. Stowell Brown preached a sermon on Christian Baptism on Tuesday. On Wednesday Spurgeon exemplified the "unlimited fellowship" by presiding with ministers of other churches in celebrating the Lord's Supper at the Tabernacle with believers from "all denominations."[75] He maintained this open communion view throughout his ministry.

As Spurgeon continued his analysis of the peculiarities of his congregation, he pointed to their advocacy of a specific confession of faith, as any lively church should. When life appears so does definite belief. "Creedless men were like dead limbs and would have to be cut off." In his congregation, Spurgeon proposed that it would be difficult for anyone to confute even the youngest member of the church "on any of the five points." They all loved the doctrines of grace. Even with

such a strong policy doctrinally, he had been accused by some of preaching Arminian sermons. Should it appear that way to some, he did not bother to correct the impression—Calvinism, Arminianism, Fullerism, or Mongrelism—none of the names were material to him in comparison with clarity, candor, and faithfulness in proclamation of the Bible. The Word of God defied all restricted systems and one day would appear thoroughly consistent and be displayed in beautiful harmony, although presently the narrow constriction of the human mind might not be able to discern it.

In addition to these happy conditions of the church, Spurgeon pointed to three strengths. Prayerfulness consistently bolstered all the work. Young converts were zealous for truth and action. Great unity characterized all that they did as a congregation. The danger, of which all were aware, was "that they might grow proud and be lifted up." Some, he indicated, were very anxious about him on that point, but he knew that divine grace, not advice from conceited individuals, would cure the evil.[76]

William Olney represented the deacons in giving a detailed catalogue of things for which to be thankful. Prominent among these blessings stood the "goodness of God in sparing to them the life of their beloved pastor, who had been engaged in very arduous and incessant labour for the last seven years, and yet was among them then in every respect a better and happier man for all his labour in the Master's cause."[77] The blessings he noted had prepared them for the reception of more and gave particular importance to the text, "Unto whomsoever much is given, of him shall be much required."[78]

---

74. Ibid., 261.

75. Ibid., 264.

76. Ibid., 261.

77. Ibid.

78. Ibid., 262.

Another of the former pastors, Joseph Angus, followed Olney with another load of advice, though "Mr. Spurgeon had told them they were overdone with advice." He would follow the deacon rather than the pastor on this occasion and continue with admonitions in light of the massive blessings and the golden future of opportunities. Spurgeon was doing a work that none of his predecessors from Gill on forward had been permitted to do. They should maintain their commitment to the old doctrines and a large-hearted catholic spirit. Such was the soundness of their creed and the scripturalness of their doctrines. "They held firmly to the views of John Calvin; they held the spirituality of the Christian church, and saw clearly into the meaning of the ordinances." This they should continue and "be always ready to give their hand and heart to all who loved the Lord Jesus Christ in sincerity and in truth."[79] Spurgeon then presented framed testimonials to two deacons that had been members of the church for more than fifty years and deacons for twenty-five and twenty-two years respectively, James Low and Thomas Olney.

In his sermon on Christian Baptism, Stowell Brown showed the prominence of believers' baptism in the Scripture and in early church history. He indicated that every attempt to support infant baptism biblically was remote and weakly inferential and employed a group of biblical references that had far more compelling applications and interpretations than their employment in defense of infant baptism. He acknowledged that their view of baptism made Baptists distinct from a large group of other denominations but that hardly justified the charge that Baptists made too much of baptism. The charge may be made with justice when Baptists say that baptism regenerates the soul, or that persons are made members of Christ, children of God, and heirs of the kingdom of heaven, by receiving it; when Baptists rush to baptize the sick and the dying while refusing a right to Christian burial to those that die unbaptized. When that happens, Baptists will deserve to be told that they "do most monstrously exaggerate the importance of this ordinance." Obedience to God and avoiding error justified the Baptist separation from Christian brethren on the grounds of differences on baptism. "A thing may not be essential, and yet it may be very far from unimportant." Brown emphasized that Baptists regarded infant baptism as the "main root of the superstitious and destructive dogma of baptismal regeneration." It stands as "the chief corner-stone of State Churchism," another error that Baptists oppose. They regard the practice unscriptural, "and to everything that is unscriptural we, as disciples of Jesus Christ, must be opposed; and we do trust that all who differ from us, and however widely they may differ, will still admit that we are only doing what is right in maintaining what we believe to be the truth of God with reference to this matter."[80]

The Doctrinal Matrix

Visible testimony to Spurgeon's recitation of the church's commitment to a confessional stance on the doctrines of grace came on the afternoon of April 11. Sermons on the five doctrines as represented by the acronym TULIP were preached. Before those messages, Spurgeon gave an impassioned defense of the system as a whole. Calvinists did not differ in essentials with evangelical Arminians such as Primitive Methodists and Wesleyans. Between Protestant and Papist, between Christian and Socinian, essential differences ex-

---

79. Ibid.

80. Ibid., 272.

isted that altered the very substance of the faith. Calvinists and Methodists, though disagreeing in the formal construction of their doctrine on certain issues, often expressed themselves on issues of prayer and salvation experience with harmonious sentiments. Spurgeon pointed to Wesleyan hymns that embodied Calvinist truth. Spurgeon found election, final perseverance, and effectual calling set forth in strong terms. Against Calvinism straw men abounded; and Spurgeon was not short of answers to these false representations. Addressing objections concerning the damnation of infants, fatalism, sovereign and unmerited reprobation, failure to preach the gospel to the unregenerate, and enmity to revivals, Spurgeon cleared away false allegations. He made it clear that hyper-Calvinism would not drive him away from true Calvinism. He spoke of it as he found it in Calvin's *Institutes* and in his expositions. "I have read them carefully," he informed his listeners. And his system was taken from the source and not from the common repute of Calvinism. Nor did he necessarily care for the name, Calvinism, but for the "glorious system which teaches that salvation is of grace from first to last." Spurgeon noted, for his own part, that he found that preaching these doctrines had not lulled his church to sleep, "but ever while they have loved to maintain these truths, they have agonized for the souls of men, and the 1600 or more whom I have myself baptized, upon profession of their faith, are living testimonies that these old truths in modern times have not lost their power to promote a revival of religion."[81]

Calvinism also has strengths of "little comparative importance" that nevertheless "ought not to be ignored." The system was "exceedingly simple" and thus easily accessible by unlettered minds. At the same time it "excites thought" and has been a challenge to the most active and far-reaching minds in intellectual history. Calvinism is "coherent in all its parts," and fits so well together that the more pressure that is applied "the more strenuously do they adhere." Spurgeon asserted that "You cannot receive one of these doctrines without believing all." Consent to any of these doctrines in its true form made the others follow of necessity. Though, as stated above, one might listen to his preaching on some occasions and think that he preached Arminianism, he did not accept the idea that any doctrinal contradictions existed in Scripture, and when considered in their most unadulterated form every point in the doctrines of grace arose from the biblical logic of human sin and salvation by pure grace. His emphasis on this was insistent:

> Some by putting the strain upon their judgments may manage to hold two or three points and not the rest, but sound logic I take it requires a man to hold the whole or reject the whole; the doctrines stand like soldiers in a square, presenting on every side a line of defence which it is hazardous to stack, but easy to maintain. And mark you, in these times when error is so rife and neology strives to be so rampant, it is no little thing to put into the hands of a young man a weapon which can slay his foe, which he can easily learn to handle, which he may grasp tenaciously, wield readily, and carry without fatigue; a weapon, I may add, which no rust can corrode and no blows can break, trenchant, and well-annealed, a true Jerusalem blade of a temper fit for deeds of renown.[82]

More important than these reasons, Spurgeon saw the doctrines as purely biblical and thoroughly consistent with Christian experience. These doctrines created neither sloth nor coldness nor

---

81. Ibid., 303.

82. Ibid., 304.

corrupt lives, but zeal for truth and holiness. After John Bloomfield preached on "Election" and Evan Probert preached on human depravity, the meeting adjourned until half past six. Spurgeon again took the floor to introduce the final three speakers and briefly introduced the sessions with another defense of the Calvinistic scheme of salvation. It is easy to raise objections against the system, Spurgeon conceded, as it is easy to raise objections against virtually anything, even one's own existence. But objections against Calvinism were not a tithe of the difficulties that might be pointed out in the opposite scheme. They do not unfold every aspect of the depth of divine wisdom or exhaust the fountains of God's purpose, but they do serve as a safe and consistent biblical guide that shall find every wave a friend to speed our ship on its journey toward the fullness of the divine glory.

J. A Spurgeon preached on particular redemption, James Smith on effectual calling, and William O'Neill on the final perseverance of believers. Prior to the final presentation by O'Neill, Spurgeon had a further comment to make on the purpose of the day's messages. He had observed that some seemed not to have sufficient patience to listen to a doctrine fully brought out. They wanted illustrations, anecdotes, and metaphors. John Newton spoke of these doctrines like lumps of sugar that could not well be given undiluted to the people but must be diffused throughout all the sermons. This day, however, was purposefully given over to the exposition of these doctrines in undiluted form so that the overall impact of their truth might be felt at once. That fact called for one final apology for the emphasis of the day:

> Has it never struck you that the scheme of doctrine which is called Calvinistic has much to say concerning God? It commences and ends with the Divine One. The angel of that system stands like Uriel in the sun; it dwells with God; he begins, he carries on, he perfects; it is for his glory and for his honour. Father, Son, and Spirit co-working, the whole Gospel scheme is carried out. Perhaps there may be this defect in our theology; we may perhaps too much forget man. I think that is a very small fault, compared with the fault of the opposite system, which begins with man, and all but ends with him. Man is a creature; how ought God to deal with him? That is the question some theologians seem to answer. The way we put it is— God is the Creator, he has a right to do as he will; he is Sovereign, there is no law above him, he has a right to make and to unmake, and when man hath sinned, he has a right to save or to destroy. If he can save, and yet not impair his justice, heaven shall ring with songs; if he destroy, and yet his goodness be not marred, then hell itself with its deep bass of misery, shall swell the mighty rollings of his glorious praise. We hold that God should be most prominent in all our teaching; and we hold this to be a guage [sic] by which to test the soundness of ministers. If they exalt God and sink the sinner to the very dust it is all well; but if they lower the prerogatives of Deity, if he be less sovereign, less just, less loving than the Scripture reveals him to be, and if man be puffed up with that fond notion that he is anything better than an unclean thing, then such theology is utterly unsound. Salvation is of the Lord, and let the Lord alone be glorified.[83]

On the Sunday subsequent to these Thursday expositions, Spurgeon preached a message that summarized the emphases of the day. In "The Last Census," based on Psalm 87:6, "The Lord shall count, when he writeth up the people, that this man was born there," Spurgeon focused on what is written, whose names will not be there, whose names will be there, who will do the writing, and for what purpose is the writing done. He empha-

---

83. Ibid., 322.

sized the individuality of the judgment, that fatal power of final impenitence, the certainty of salvation for all that flee to Christ, the perfect equity of God in determining the contents of the writing, and the truths demonstrated and mysteries solved when the writing is done. All God's jewels, all his sheep, and the names in the Lamb's book of life will be written. Satan will discover that he has gained not even one of them. Satan finally was overcome even in Job on the dunghill, David on the rooftop, and Peter in Pilate's Hall. The great Shepherd of the sheep preserved them in gentle proddings or startling reprimands but always in harmony with a subdued and humbly compliant will. The decree of God and the acts of man will be seen as in perfect consonance.

[A]nd how strange shall it seem as that great sealed book is now unclasped, it is found that all who were written there have come, nay come as they were written, come at the hour ordained, come in the place predestinated, come by the means foreknown, come as God would have them come, and thus free agency did not defeat predestination, and man's will did not thwart the eternal will. God is glorified and man free. Man—the man as he proudly calls himself—has obeyed God as truly as though he knew what was in God's book, and had studied to make the decree of God the very rule and method of his life. Glorious shall it be when thus that book shall prove the mystic energy which went out from between the folded leaves—the mysterious Spirit that emanated from the eternal throne—that unseen, unmanifested, sometimes unrecognized mysterious power, which bowed the will and led it in silken chains, which opened up the understanding and led it from darkness into light, and melted the heart and moved the Spirit, and won the entire man to the obedience of the truth as it was in Jesus.[84]

Having inundated the first weeks of Tabernacle meetings with strong affirmations of Calvinistic truth, "with shouts of sovereign grace,"[85] always with the evangelistic emphases that he felt were embraced within the system, Spurgeon followed on April 21 with a sermon on the Great Commission entitled "The Missionaries' Charge and Charta." Spurgeon admitted that he had seriously considered if it were his duty to leave England where so many churches and ministers existed to go to a land of pioneer labors. "I solemnly feel that my position in England will not permit my leaving the sphere in which I now am, or else tomorrow I would offer myself as a missionary." He indicated that one burden of his prayers was that many from that church would go as missionaries, a prayer fulfilled exponentially. In relating that prayer he again said: "I have questioned my own conscience, and I do not think I could be in the path of duty if I should go abroad to preach the Word, leaving this field of labour; but I think many of my brethren now labouring at home might with the greatest advantage surrender their charges, and leave a land where they would scarce be missed, to go where their presence would be as valuable as the presence of a thousand such as they are here."[86] In closing the message he made a similar statement as he called for others to feel a fire that could not be quenched to go where others had not gone. "Brethren, I envy any one among you—I say again with truth, I envy you— if it shall be your lot to go to China, the country so lately opened to us. I would gladly change places with you. I would renounce the partial ease of a settlement in this country, and renounce the responsibilities of so large a congregation as this with pleasure, if I might have your honours."[87] Be-

84. Ibid., 280.

85. Ibid.
86. Ibid., 287.
87. Ibid., 281, 288.

tween these bookends of missionary desire Spurgeon loaded a missionary theology. He showed that Jesus' command to teach all nations was a generous and gracious manifestation of love and divine condescension. The simple and singular method of teaching brought together the nature and needs of men with the message and prerogatives of God. As children we need to be dealt with gently and patiently and as ignorant and rebellious we need to have our lies replaced with truth and our recalcitrance replaced with child-like submission. If they will not be taught they will not enter the kingdom of heaven. In spite of all obstacles—ignorance and sophistication, barbarity and passivity, degradation and culture, literate and illiterate—teach them.

> The fact has been proved, brethren, that there are no nations incapable of being taught, nay, that there are no nations incapable afterwards of teaching others. The Negro slave has perished under the lash, rather than dishonour his Master. The Esquimaux has climbed his barren steeps, and borne his toil, while he has recollected the burden which Jesus bore. The Hindoo has patiently submitted to the loss of all things, because he loved Christ better than all. Feeble Malagasay women have been prepared to suffer and to die, and have taken joyfully suffering for Christ's sake. There has been heroism in every land for Christ; men of every colour and of every race have died for *him*; upon his altar has been found the blood of all kindreds that be upon the face of the earth. Oh! Tell me not they cannot be taught. Sirs, they can be taught to die for Christ; and this is more than some of you have learned. They can rehearse the very highest lesson of the Christian religion—that self-sacrifice which knows not itself but gives up all for him.[88]

Emphasizing the unique position of Baptists in fulfilling this commission purely and in the order given because of their enduring ecclesiological conviction that teaching always should precede baptism, he told his hearers "we ought to be first and foremost, and if we be not, shame shall cover us for our unfaithfulness." He held up the call insistently before his congregation: "I hear that voice ringing in the Baptist's ear, above that of any other, 'Go ye, therefore, and teach all nations, baptizing them in the name of the Father, and of the Son, and of the Holy Ghost.'"[89]

Christ's commission reflected the history of the church in its reflection of Christ's suffering. The church never could "plough a wave without a spray of gore." The church must suffer to reign, must die to live, must be stained in red to be clothed in purple, and must be buried and forgotten in order to be delivered of the man-child. It was by death that Christ became the mediator possessed of all power for the redemption of his people. Thus, the church has a right to all places; no place can take from it its right to teach. "Do ye pass decrees forbidding the gospel to be preached? We laugh at you!" Gospel heralds have rights without limits, and may not be forbidden by any earthly power to omit obedience to the risen Lord because his authority extends to all places throughout all times. The heralds of peace and salvation may not set their foot on any place to which Christ does not have the right. Resolutions against such are mockeries and waste-paper. "The church never was yet vassal to the state, or servile slave to principalities and powers, and she neither can nor will be." Because Christ not only has right, but he has might. He has might to change the hearts of princes and rule by Providence to open nations through revolution or through in-

---

88. Ibid., 283-84.

89. Ibid., 284.

crease of technology. In addition he has might in heaven. Cherubim and seraphim bow before him, he may grant the plentitude of the Spirit and clothe his ministers with power, and he has unrestrained warrant to intercede with the Father.

At the time of this message, 1,600 church members heard him while the entire congregation was 6,000. He pleaded with them all, member and listener alike, to consider the implications of there being none in such a congregation willing to go:

> Jesus! Is there not one? Must heathens perish? Must the gods of the heathen hold their thrones? Must thy kingdom fail? Are there none to own thee, none to maintain thy righteous cause? If there be none, let us weep, each one of us, because such a calamity has fallen on us. But if there be any who are willing to give all for Christ, let us who are compelled to stay at home do our best to help them. Let us see to it that they lack nothing; for we cannot send them out without purse or scrip. Let us fill the purse of the men whose hearts God has filled, and take care of them temporally, leaving it for God to preserve them spiritually.[90]

Spurgeon was determined that the Metropolitan Tabernacle would be home to a joyful, clear, and full presentation of the doctrines of grace. From there, the neighborhood, the city, the country, the kingdom and the world should hear the same message—the successful execution of an eternal purpose proposed by the Father to honor the Son with a people gained by dint of his own grace and perfect conformity to the wisdom, justice, and holy love of the Father. The opening of the Tabernacle served to announce that message as the foundation for all that would be done and preached there and culminated with an impas-

sioned proclamation of the certain success of the divine undertaking with a fervent plea for God's people to be the means of its world-wide advance.

Recess for a Needed Repair

The constant use of the Tabernacle from seven in the morning until eleven at night, sometimes with thousands of people present crammed into close quarters, being lighted by gas lamps, cooking being done in the kitchen for meals at all times of the day, and every inch having a virtually unending flow of traffic, after six years some thorough refurbishing was necessary. For five weeks, therefore, in 1867, March 24–April 21, Spurgeon held forth in the Agricultural Hall in Islington. This hall had not been built for oratory but for the display of farm implements and animals and for the showing of the garden products of English agriculture. For the sake of an opportunity to reach thousands that might never hear a gospel message outside this particular venue, Spurgeon decided to have 15,000 seats installed with standing room for about 3,000 more. So uncongenial were the facilities for oral address that many predicted an utter failure of this astonishing attempt. Only the Fast Day service in the Crystal Palace in 1857 exceeded the size of the crowds that pushed into the available space to hear Spurgeon for these five Sundays. None complained of not being able to hear. The handling of such a crowd—estimates from 15,000 to 25,000 have been given—did not get out of hand but proceeded with remarkable facility and cordiality.[91] In the American edition of *Spurgeon's Sermons*, the heading for the first of these sermons says, "The following five sermons ... were delivered in the Agricultural Hall, Islington, to an audience never numbering less than twenty

---

90. Ibid., 288.

91. For a brief summary of the five weeks see Pike, 4:200-08. The *Autobiography* tells about the event in volume 2:64-66.

thousand persons. It will be observed that they are very simple, and were intended to be."[92]

Often in the sermons Spurgeon referred to the size of the crowd and the unusual venue, using phrases like "the sight of this vast arena and of this crowded assembly," or "never before was such an audience gathered to hear one man." In reference to the normal use of the Agricultural Hall compared to the pool by the sheep market in Bethesda, Spurgeon noted, "If the physical infirmities of Jerusalem intruded into the sheep market, I shall ask no excuse if, on these Sabbath days, the spiritual sickness of London should demand that this spacious place, which has hitherto been given up to the lowing or cattle and to the bleating of sheep, should be consecrated to the preaching of the gospel, to the manifestation of the healing virtue of Christ Jesus among the spiritually sick."[93] For that reason he expressed a desire that "there should be more converted in this place than ever were converted at one time in any place since the world was."[94]

The messages even on paper express such a passion and energy that one need not wonder that Spurgeon required some days to recuperate from the energy extended, physical, intellectual, and spiritual, to such an enormous group after each of the five Sunday morning services. In an extended appeal to the unconverted to come to Jesus, Spurgeon exhibited the emptying effect that such a sight of massive numbers combined with his belief in their eternal destiny had on him. "Oh, if I could know how to preach the gospel so that you would feel it, I would go to any school to learn!" Even beyond submitting himself to the instruction of others, Spurgeon was willing to "consent to lose these eyes, to get greater power in my ministry; ay, and to lose arms, legs, and all my members." On he went, "I would be willing to die if I could but be honoured by the Holy Spirit to win this mass of souls to God."[95] This deep sense of responsibility led him also to punctuate his addresses with deeply emotional calls to prayer from those that were converted and especially from his own church members: "Brethren pray for us. If you, the members of the church, do not pray for me, I feel I shall have much to lay to your charge. Never was any one called to so great a work as this. I have this morning twenty thousand claims upon your prayers. I beseech you by the living God pray for me. It were better for me that I never were born to have this responsibility upon me if I have not your prayers."[96] In the fourth week again he urged, "I pause to ask, on my account, the prayers of God's people yet again, that the Holy Spirit may be my helper this morning. Oh deny not my earnest request!"[97]

The sermons were heavy with illustration and with very plain anecdotes and were all designed to bring the lost to evangelical repentance and an unadorned submission to Christ for pardon. This style, however, did not keep Spurgeon from his usual doctrinal themes. Total depravity, election, effectual calling, the perfection of Christ's person as a redeemer embodying in one person both eternal deity and true, though sinless, humanity, the eternal states of heaven and hell, the immediate moral responsibility of every person to turn from wickedness, profanity, drunkenness, pride, self-righteousness, and every other form of unbelief and to see in Christ the only perfection of righteousness that God can accept as consis-

---

92. SS, 9:186.

93. Ibid., 226.

94. Ibid., 186, 223.

95. Ibid., 243-44.

96. Ibid., 223-24.

97. Ibid., 247.

tent with his law and his holiness. He dealt with the events of death both for the saved and the unsaved, the nature of the disembodied condition of the Christian's spirit before the resurrection and the glorious character of eternal life after the resurrection. He talked about the obligations that were necessarily intrinsic to the pastor's calling, the travesty of those that would not preach the fullness of truth and work for the conversion of their hearers, and the urgency of zealous young men with gifts and zeal to make the ministry their aim.

The popular and accessible narrative style did not diminish Spurgeon's intent to set the gospel forth in all the splendor of its being the manifest wisdom of a sovereign and infinitely glorious God to save a people upon whom he himself had set his heart from before the foundation of the world. In the case of the lame man at the pool of Bethesda, "Our Lord acted according to his own eternal purpose, doing as he pleased with his own; he fixed the eye of his electing love upon that one man, and, going up to him, he gazed upon him." Jesus yearned for the healing and the salvation of that one out of all the sick that were gathered there because his bowels of compassion had been upon him from eternity past. "I know not whom Christ intends to save this morning by his effectual grace," Spurgeon remarked, but knew that his commission was to give the general call even though only God himself can bring that "irresistible grace" that distinguishes one from the other to bring salvation. He admonished his hearers not to "kick at this doctrine," for it was true, and their resistance to that gospel only showed their perversity and their unwillingness to be saved in God's way. They should not quarrel with God for "bestowing on others that which you do not care to receive." He went on to assure them that "if you desire his mercy, he will not deny it to you; if you

seek him he will be found of you; but if you will not seek mercy, rail not on the Lord if he bestows it upon others."[98]

On the first Sunday back in the Tabernacle Spurgeon preached from 2 Kings 3: "Make this Valley Full of Ditches." He spoke of the absolute necessity of the work of the Holy Spirit for the success of the church and that each person must not only work for the glory of Christ, but live in constant expectation that God would fill his church with converts. He referred to the just-completed services at the Agricultural Hall: "I have been greatly rejoiced at some of the conversions at the Agricultural Hall. I hoped to have heard of many who never went to a place of worship getting a blessing." He was confident that he would hear of them, but the remarkable phenomenon was that conversions came from "those who have been here before, or who have been regular attendants elsewhere for years." He did not go abroad to look for his own children but, "they say if you want to know something about your own house, you must go away from home." He wondered that, if to be the instrument of conversion for some of them, he must needs go afield. He referred again to the recent odyssey to the north, reflecting the added pressures to himself and his congregation, but all in the quest for expanded usefulness: "God knows with what earnest desires and endeavors I went to the Agricultural Hall to preach the Gospel, and with how simple and sincere a motive *you* went there, too! We certainly did not journey so far for our own comfort, but for the honor and glory of our Master. And God's Word must be followed with a blessing."

With all the anticipation of large numbers of conversions, it seems that Spurgeon had come to some point of a spiritual let-down and needed

---

98. Ibid., 236-37.

the assurance of a divine promise that indeed the ditches would be filled with water. Had not God led them there? Does God do such things without granting fruit? "But I cannot and *will not* harbor a mistrustful suspicion about the blessing of God resting upon that action," Spurgeon insisted with a spiritual fierceness and adamant refusal to be disturbed by immediate appearances of meager fruit. He knew that, along with him, "many of you are really solemnly in earnest with an Apostolic earnestness!" He protested not to prophesy, but to believe the divine providence and promise, that God will not withhold the evident work of his Spirit, for he would not have his people seek his face in vain. The church's earnest prayers and labors would neither be just air or a dream but the travail would bring forth children. God's own faithfulness was on the line. "The earnest agony of a living Church must bring forth fruit unto God, or else the Bible is no longer reliable, and the promise of God no longer sure. But He changes not, and therefore we will look for the blessing, knowing that it must come."[99]

Perhaps the journey had made him more cognizant of the urgency of concentrated ministry right there, right in the newly refurbished Metropolitan Tabernacle, for he insisted, "We *must* have the blessing in this particular Church! It were enough to break one's heart even to suppose it possible that we should not!" The following years would show that the blessing in that particular church would not diminish, but would only expand, and expand in such a way that Spurgeon would embrace death itself rather than shun the filling of the ditches.

---

99. MTP, 1867, April 28.

4

PREACHING THE WHOLE COUNSEL

We have known what it is to totter on the pulpit steps, under a sense that the chief of sinners should scarcely be allowed to preach to others.[1]

Preaching is a farce unless the minister hath fire within him; but when the fire is there, preaching is God's ordained and guaranteed way of bringing souls to himself.[2]

Gifts and Calling Requisite

Above all else, Spurgeon knew his gift and calling was in the proclamation of the gospel. When Spurgeon took application to the Pastors' College he advised, "Do not be a minister if you can help it."[3] Within that last phrase was the hinge of the matter. Some would be better to stay in their trade or other secular calling. He would thereby support his family, give valuable help in a church that needs lay ministers in evangelistic work, and not be a burden to a congregation where its needs go beyond his gifts and the support falls short of his needs.[4] He doubted not that there were "hundreds of men, half-starved, in the Christian ministry, who would act wisely if they could add a secular business to their sacred calling," and

relieve themselves from want and be set free. They would serve the Lord better if they "ploughed the field or opened shop" and it would not be disreputable to "do a little tailoring."[5] Spurgeon had sad experience confirmed year by year, that "many who think themselves called to preach are evidently under a delusion, for they have neither capacity for learning, nor ability for teaching."[6] He looked at the ministry of the gospel as a "high and honourable calling when a man is really fitted for it; but without the necessary qualifications it must be little better than sheer slavery with a fine name to it."[7]

On the other hand, none should stay out whom God has prepared and suited for the golden burden. He looked for five-talent men and some men of "the upper and middle classes

---

1. SS, 1:10.

  2. MTP, 1861, 221.

  3. S&T, March 1883, 110.

  4. See Spurgeon's discussion, "Leaving Secular Business," S&T, March 1883, 105-10.

---

  5. Ibid., 110.

  6. S&T, February 1875, 91.

  7. S&T, March 1883, 109.

that would consecrate themselves unto the Lord." Though their gifts might make them rich in business or famous in letters, Spurgeon coveted the "best men for Jesus," and, with sly irony, reminded Christians that the "noblest human mind is not too good raw material for the Lord to use in fashioning a minister of the gospel." The advantages of culture and education would give them a massive advantage for obtaining the necessary training in Bible and theology "and help them to take leading positions in the church." The poverty of the ministry makes parents discourage their young men from considering it. They should be willing to endure poverty, but, at the same time, "the cure for the poverty of our ministry lies in the increase of its mental and spiritual power." For those so suited, in Spurgeon's opinion and experience, "there is no more honourable, happy, and holy course open in this world than the ministry of a Baptist church."[8] Those that are gifted and have zeal for the gospel should see the ministry as God's intended purpose for them. "Aspire to this office, young men, whose souls are full of love to Jesus," Spurgeon told an enormous gathering of people in the Agricultural Hall in the north of London. "Fired with sacred enthusiasm, covet earnestly the best gifts, and out of love to Jesus try whether you cannot in your measure tell to your fellow-men the story of the cross." What could exceed in importance such a call and such a use of gifts, and what could more clearly express the supreme affection of a Christian! "Men of zeal and ability," he insisted, "if you love Jesus, make the ministry your aim; train your minds to it; exercise your soul toward it; and may God the Holy Spirit call you to it, that you also may preach the Word of reconciliation to the dying thousands." Not only gifts, love, zeal, knowledge, and excel-

lence issued the call but urgent need added her voice—"The laborers still are few: may the Lord of the harvest thrust you into his work."[9]

Many had mistaken their calling Spurgeon believed, and there would not be so much poor preaching and so many bogged down in the misery of non-success had a genuine compulsion from above been waited for. The man that cannot help it, however, will give himself, heart and soul, out of heavenly compulsion, and all manner of opposition and difficulty will yield to the "Woe unto me if I preach not the gospel." Without the impulse, however, where is the warrant? "That preaching which is inspired by vainglory must necessarily be in vain."[10]

Observers, Gawkers, Admirers, and Pundits

Though Spurgeon encountered much opposition in his ministry, none ever suspected that he lacked other-worldly compulsion or exquisite gifts of proclamation. An American observer noted in 1856, "The preaching of Mr. Spurgeon in London is one of the most remarkable phenomena of the present times."[11] Reducing the sermons to writing extended the effect of his proclamation, and he was exuberant about the opportunity to reach many times more through print than he did in the moment of delivery. His readers he called "the outer ring of my congregation" which he recognized as "far more numerous than those to whom I speak with my voice." He did not shy from asking those readers for "the great service of increasing my congregation by increasing the circulation of the sermons."[12]

The American observer found everything about Spurgeon impressive in the most edifying

---

8. S&T, February 1875, 91, 92.

9. SS, 9:246.

10. S&T, March 1883, 10.

11. ELM, "Introduction," SS, 1:v.

12. MTP, 1891, 588. "Letter from Mr. Spurgeon."

sense. Having remarked on his clear intelligence and the striking ways he used illustrations along with the amazing capacity for finding striking analogies between all that he observed in nature and the realm of spiritual relationships, he was particularly impressed with Spurgeon's conviction concerning the doctrine he preached and the absorbing manner of delivery. He recounted an event in which Spurgeon, while preaching in Exeter Hall, had a person, "a very kind friend," advise him that, though he was a Calvinist and a Baptist, he should recollect that, among his hearers, there was "a variety of creeds." Spurgeon responded, "Now, if I were to preach nothing but what would please the whole lot of you, what on earth should I do? I preach what I believe to be true; and, if the omission of a single truth that I believe would make me king of England throughout eternity, I would not leave it out. Those who do not like what I say, have the option of leaving it. They come here, I suppose, to please themselves; and, if the truth does not please them, they can leave it."[13] Preaching was not a technique to gather and please a crowd, but the manifestation of the voice as in instrument through which the entire soul and body dished out words of new creation and resurrection that reached the things that were not and made them be, and the things that were dead and made them live.

Natural elegance in body motion and clear articulation rose to the level of the content's sublimity. To illustrate the magnetism of his delivery, the writer quoted from *The Examiner* from Glasgow.

> Soon as he commences to speak, tones of richest melody are heard. A voice, full, sweet, and musical, falls on every ear, and awakens agreeable emotions in every soul in which there is a sympathy for sounds. That most excellent of voices is under perfect control, and can whisper or thunder at the wish of its possessor. And there is poetry in every feature and every movement, as well as music in the voice. The countenance speaks,—the entire form sympathizes. The action is in complete unison with the sentiments, and the eye listens scarcely less than the ear to the sweetly-flowing oratory.[14]

By 1857, the publishing of Spurgeon's sermons in America, combined with the reports of interested American visitors to England, led to the publishing of a book entitled *Sketch of the Life and Ministry of the Rev. C. H. Spurgeon*. His "life and ministry" already underwent scrutiny and analysis at twenty-three years of age. An Anglican minister was not even allowed to exercise his gifts publicly until he had completed his twenty-third year. Spurgeon, however, had already preached for years and was compared in this publication to William Jay, the Wesleys and Whitefield, both for his youth and his startling impact. When comparing him to Whitefield, the writer contended that Spurgeon was "not a whit" behind him in "graphic power, while he is vastly superior" in logic and illustration. "He grapples with the strongest truths, unfolds the profoundest doctrines, plies the lever with the stoutest arguments, and aims at convincing before he attempts to persuade."[15]

The writer inserted a long review of the Spurgeon phenomenon from the *Christian Review*.[16] G. N. Hervey, the writer of the review, analyzed Spurgeon's preaching and isolated several advantages that boldness gave to him. Spurgeon knew no master but God, no truth but Scripture, no power but the gospel, a combination that made him drive fearlessly to the conscience and affec-

---

13. SS, 1:ix.

14. Ibid., x.

15. *Sketch of the Life and Ministry of the Rev. C. H. Spurgeon* (New York: Sheldon & Blakeman, 1857), 88.

16. Ibid., 89-117.

tions of his hearers with a positiveness, and even dogmatism, about his task to see them saved. His boldness was joined to clarity. The reviewer pointed to this trait as quite remarkable in light of the overall mental and theological furniture of Spurgeon. "When we consider that Mr. Spurgeon's themes conduct him down into the deepest mysteries of Christian experience, and aloft away into the clouds and darkness of the divine purposes and providence—that he stops not on the confines of this world, but penetrates far into the unlimited light of heaven, and the smoke and glare of hell—when we consider these things, along with the fact that his mind is naturally of the poetic order, it is surprising that his ideas should be couched in language so luminous and distinct, that the most ignorant and feeble-minded of his flock could find no difficulty in comprehending them."[17]

The propensity to observe and assimilate all that came before him, his intimate and virtually infused knowledge of Puritan thought and doctrine melded so seamlessly with his own manner of expression, his ability to make pertinent, personal, and striking application, the abundance of allusions and metaphors that aided meditation, and the style that was so "simple, terse, idiomatic, and picturesque" all coalesced in a single sermon. The reviewer observed that Spurgeon's sentences were rather "laconic than periodic, and as he does not think in long, connected trains of argumentation, the successive sentences are separate dictates of the intellect, such as the generality can readily comprehend." In spite of hesitance to criticize a man so useful and obviously blessed of God to the conversion of hundreds, Hervey anticipated a time when Spurgeon would outgrow his tendency to "display an exuberance of fancy,"

to create distractions through the use of puns, to exercise a censorship over other ministers (a fault arising from an unmortified pride so surmised Hervey), and to denounce "the whole system of collegiate and theological education now in operation throughout the world."[18]

Hervey's hopes would never be entirely fulfilled. Spurgeon never felt it necessary to leave punning behind, he made it a practice to the end of his days to warn against ministers that shortchanged the gospel, and he established his own college to train ministers in a way that he thought fit for intensifying all the implications of revealed truth. In his college address in 1877, Spurgeon punned his point about piety by referring to some persons distinguished by what "might be called *mag*-piety" for they are happiest when they talk the most.[19] He could not resist a pun even in private correspondence and when his health was virtually an inch from death. From Mentone in 1890 he informed his brother that "My hand is not yet handy, but you see I can write handsomely;" and after a few more lines put humorously he closed, "I have to be penurious with my pen, for the hand soon aches."[20]

These touches of humor, as low as some might find them to be, Spurgeon defended, sprinkling his messages with humor as the use of "gathering bait" to make the fish come. Some of Spurgeon's contemporaries were "so dull, so monotonous, so long, and so sour," that he did not wonder that their pews were sparsely populated.[21] For Spurgeon the art of attraction included "a pleasant manner, an interesting style, and even a touch of wit."[22] He showed this even on an application for

---

17. Hervey in *Sketch,* 96, 97.

18. Ibid., 112-15.

19. S&T, May 1877, 199.

20. Spurgeon, *Letters,* To His Brother, May 1890.

21. S&T, September 1878, 422. "Fishing."

22. Ibid.

life insurance. When asked if he had ever had fits or convulsions, he responded, "No; unless convulsions of laughter are meant." When asked if he had any "Medical Gentlemen" besides the one listed (Dr. Palfrey, who had been his physician for twelve years by 1868), he responded, "Nobody, one doctor is quite enough for any man to survive."[23] Though he had been blamed for the "use of pleasantries," he continued to do so partly because he could not help it, but "chiefly because I have perceived that the interest is sustained and the attention excited by a dash of the familiar and the striking."[24] One observer of his preaching at the Music Hall in 1857, having heard that Spurgeon was outrageous in this tendency, commented that his command of language was considerable but did not lead to verbosity, his style unfettered, homely, and pointed; and that "there was a total absence of anything humorous or ludicrous, if it has been his habit to indulge in such things."[25] He apparently was more given to this in more comfortable and familiar surroundings where he knew his audience intimately. This penchant for humor was most amusingly displayed at his Friday lectures at the Pastors' College.

Since Spurgeon believed that humor was a vital weapon in the preacher's arsenal, he found particular happiness, as well as laughter, in a book by Charles Stanford, *The Wit and Humour of Life.*" Stanford protested against the superstition "which regards wit and humour as deadly sins." Finally, Spurgeon mused, an ally he embraced in his defense of humor and an "avenger of those fierce assaults which have been made on humour." Spurgeon hoped that the book would "shut the mouths of those melancholy critics who

think that everything solemn should be sad, and that anything approaching to pleasantry must be wicked." Stanford's defense of wit was as "wholesome and as holy as anything we have ever read." He hoped for a revolution in the ideas of many who "now blush when they smile, and put down an honest laugh in the category of things to be repented of."[26] This commendation was not written by a resentful and careless youth, but by an experienced and assaulted soldier only six years from his death.

Spurgeon also leveled criticism at "many preachers ... [who] do not treat the gospel as a practical thing, or as a matter of fact which immediately concerns the people before them." He wondered "what some sermons were preached for, what design the preacher had in concocting them," and lampooned preachers that had practiced for a very long while to "avoid troubling you in the least with the truth."[27] He had few kind words for the theological pabulum fed through the common ministerial education of the day.

Besides, we are invited to follow the guidance of men who are not qualified to be leaders. I have waited with a good deal of interest to see whether modern thought would be capable of producing *a man*, a man of mark, of profound mind, and philosophic genius; but where is he? Where is the man who will found a school and sway his fellows; a man for the orthodox to tremble at, a great Goliath, head and shoulders above his fellows. Truly there are some who think they have power, and so they have amongst those young gentlemen whose moustachios are on the point of developing, but they have no influence over those who read their Bibles, have had experience, and are accustomed to try the spirits.[28]

23. *Autobiography*, 2: between 178-79 in a section of photographs.

24. S&T, September 1878, 422. "Fishing."

25. Pike, 2:263.

26. S&T, March 1886, 140.

27. S&T, May 1877, 205, 206, 207.

28. Ibid., 197.

Those issues for which the critic hoped better things for Spurgeon never completely left. Their presence was not as abundant, they were tempered by maturity and more profound self-knowledge, but that which was fundamental to his perception of truth had not lost any of its luster. His wit was more selective, his perception of the transforming power of the living Christ more acute and tested, and his grasp of the transcendent and immutable character of revealed truth a fixed and sensibly perceived reality. In 1877 he wrote:

> Faith in the old orthodox creed is not a matter of choice with me now. I am frequently told that I ought to examine at length the various new views which are so continually presented. I decline the invitation: I can smell them, and that satisfies me. I perceive in them nothing which glorifies God or magnifies Christ, but much that puffs up human nature, and I protest that the smell is enough for me. ... I hope the truths of the gospel have become our life: experience has incorporated them with our being.[29]

John Campbell, forty years Spurgeon's senior, was one of Spurgeon's early supporters and was very favorably impressed with his preaching. He viewed Spurgeon as a force of nature, not of artifice, and therefore, genuine and truly powerful. He owed nothing to circumstance, to relation, to rank, or to the accidents of life. Externally, his voice, diction, and eloquence gave him advantage; internally, and primarily, his attraction lies in "the soul of the man—a soul large, liberal, and loving; a soul stamped by the characteristics of a little child, while putting forth the powers of one of David's 'mighties.'"[30] Campbell also early en-

dorsed Spurgeon's founding of the Pastors' College, calling it an "exceedingly interesting affair ... nothing to be compared with it in these islands." Spurgeon was "the very incarnation of the spirit of ecclesiastical revolution, ... A singular ecclesiastical originality." Heedless of antiquity or novelty, Spurgeon sought what was useful and found no rest until his object had been accomplished.[31]

Not as prone to effusive compliment and more direct in friendly warning, a fellow-Baptist writing in *The Freeman* found weaknesses in what others found to be strengths. Spurgeon at twenty-one years of age, if left uncorrected, exhibited traits, so warned the friendly critic, that had destructive tendencies. The critic may be forgiven for the embarrassing judgment that Spurgeon's sermons would "soon be forgotten forever." He commended Spurgeon for being able to reach the masses, for his lively imagination, his homely familiar figures of speech, his free colloquial manner of address, and enthusiastic ardor. His unquestionable sincerity and impassioned zeal make one pardon his follies and pray that God will be his protector from the dangers of having been placed in such a position of popularity. The commentator believed that Spurgeon's chief faults in preaching were not doctrinal, for his "doctrinal inconsistencies" can be corrected with mature study and reflection. The most sinister issue in Spurgeon's preaching is the "vice of vanity," the spring from which flows his "daring method of expounding Holy Writ, his intense egotism, and his habit of decrying his fellow-Christians and fellow-ministers." Out of this also arises his denunciation of Arminians, "(whose creed he evidently does not understand) in almost every sermon." The critic trembled because of the unstable precipice on which Spurgeon walked fearing that

---

29. Ibid., 211.

30. Pike, 2: 255.

31. S&T, 1882, Annual Report of the Pastors' College, 257.

the source of his current popularity might press him to the fatal side. "If, already, he can not only preach but print mere vulgar abuse of men who, in the sight of God, may be as sincere as he, and as holy, to what lengths of ribaldry may he not descend, when he finds that this knack of 'cordially-hating' brings around him a crowd of fulsome flatterers."[32] The critic had naught but good intentions, so he claimed, and pledged his prayer for Spurgeon that his strengths would be multiplied, and his usefulness commensurately extended and intensified and his weaknesses minimized or eradicated.

Spurgeon quickly learned that a preacher bent on pleasing all his critics would speedily leave the rank of the ministry. Using the third person, but reflecting on his own experience, Spurgeon made this observation: "At this time, when God raises up a man of original mind who strikes out a course for himself and follows it with success, it is usual to charge him with being eccentric. If his honesty may not be suspected, nor his zeal questioned, nor his power denied, sneer at him and call him eccentric, and it may be the arrow will wound." A man of decided worth, Spurgeon himself had experienced, will be surrounded with warm friends and red-hot foes. Men will cavil and object; it is their nature. Churchgoers in London hallowed the Sabbath rest with "pious gossip and sanctimonious slander." "Bring the walnuts, and let us crack the reputation of a preacher or two." By 1879 he was able to say, "So far as I am personally concerned, if the habit we are speaking of were not a sin, I do not know that I should care about it, for after having had more than my fair share of criticism and abuse, I am not one jot the worse for it in any respect; no bones broken, my position is not injured, and my mind is not soured."[33]

Nor did he want his young preachers to be soured. The accusation of eccentricity is a red herring, for everyone to some degree is eccentric, off center from a critic's perspective, that is, his own center and circumference. The modern thought of the day, nor the lover of amusements, nor the papist, nor the Puritan-hater provide any valid center of comparison. Eccentricity in such cases might be quite a good thing even as the sun's eccentricity to the earth's rotation and revolution is healthy and life-sustaining. Eccentrics have brilliant company by such a comparison.[34] Spurgeon described the purpose of his book, *Eccentric Preachers*, as a "plea for lenient criticism in reference to useful men,—an argument, not for license, but for liberty." He did not promote a single standard for mannerism, or condemnation because of their "individualities and originalities."[35]

The Purposeful Discipline of Pulpit Personality
Yet, Spurgeon did not want preachers to offend unnecessarily or create a grotesque figure in the pulpit, or affectations of voice, that would obscure the earnestness and importance of their message. Excellent content jumbled and mangled by a bumbling delivery shrouded a message. Needs and prejudices of the hearer must also be considered. In view of that, Spurgeon gave a substantial amount of formal instruction concerning delivery. He himself was master at both. Content and application met the auditors' ear in the purest, most engaging and pleasurable sensation of hearing available in any venue in the nineteenth-century English-speaking world. "I maintain," Spurgeon remarked, "that the best notes a man's voice is capable of should be given to the proclamation of the gospel, and these

32. J. H. Bains & C. E. Brown, *Spurgeon, The People's Preacher* (Philadelphia: American Baptist Publication Society, 1892), 52ff.

33. S&T, June 1879, 250f. "What is Eccentricity?"

34. Ibid.

35. S&T, August 1879, 389.

are such as nature teaches him to use in earnest conversation."[36]

Idiosyncrasies of speech should be corrected whenever possible. He recognized the variety of dialects that existed in the counties of London and pointed out the peculiarly distracting aspect of each, having something of their "rustic diet in their mouths." By this he referred to the "calves of Essex, the swine of Berkshire, or the runts of Suffolk" and added his opinion that the unmistakeable dialects of Yorkshire or Somersetshire were equally amusing. For one who defended naturalness and disliked affectation, Spurgeon was as relentless as he was merciless in hunting down unpleasant sounds that would dominate any message that came through the lips.

> It would be difficult to discover the cause, but the fact is clear enough, that in some counties of England men's throats seem to be furred up, like long-used teakettles, and in others, they ring like brass music, with a vicious metallic sound. Beautiful these variations of nature may be in their season and place, but my taste has never been able to appreciate them. A sharp discordant squeak, like a rusty pair of scissors, is to be got rid of at all hazards; so also is a thick, inarticulate utterance in which no word is complete, but nouns, adjectives, and verbs are made into a kind of hash. Equally objectionable is that ghostly speech in which a man talks without using his lips, ventriloquising most horribly: sepulchral tones may fit a man to be an undertaker, but Lazarus is not called out of his grave by hollow moans.[37]

He lectured, therefore, to his students at the College on methods of delivery and provided illustrations of gesture with purpose as well as illustrations of detracting gestures and voice production. Thinking too much of one's voice while being destitute of a well-informed head and an earnest heart would leave no edifying effect; conversely, thinking too little of the voice could result in the marring of "exceedingly precious truths" through monotonous tones that irritate like a bumble-bee in a pitcher. One should not speak in an affected way as if he had a wobbling dumpling in his mouth nor should he engage in a kind of enunciation that is "very lady-like, mincing, delicate, servant-girlified, dawdling." Spurgeon was sure that he could "whisper so as to be heard throughout every corner of our great Tabernacle, and I am equally certain that I could holla and shout so that nobody could understand me." Some of his students were "tearing themselves to pieces by needless bawling."[38]

Often neglected in other schools, Spurgeon gloried in the great attention given to the voice and appropriate delivery style at his College. "Care has been taken to inculcate proper pronunciation, delivery, and action." Perhaps more than any other vocation, preaching demanded the "perfection of ability in speech." He was intent, therefore, on removing "personal oratorical defects," and pursued the goal through discussion, impromptu speaking, sermonizing in class, and mutual criticism that produced a friction useful for "wearing off rough edges which else would have been in future years injurious to the preacher." None of this was done, of course without corresponding attention to the life of the spirit and complete submission to the preparatory operations of the Spirit of God. "Neither untutored confidence nor learned diffidence can take the place of the Spirit."

---

36. C. H. Spurgeon, "On the Voice", Lectures to My Students [First Series] (London: Passmore and Alabaster, 1881) 1:121. This work eventually became a four volume work and was reprinted in one volume by Pilgrim Publications n Pasadena, Texas, in 1990. When I quote I will refer to volume numbers in this order, Lectures (First Series), Lectures (Second Series), The Art of Illustration, and Commenting and Commentaries.

37. Ibid., 121.

38. Ibid., 120, 123, 125.

Nevertheless, Spurgeon continued to emphasize, "when a man has once submitted head and heart and tongue to the supremacy of the Holy Ghost, all other things may be added unto him without fear of injury."[39]

Supreme in preparation for pulpit power was a legitimate consciousness of weakness and dependence upon God for all. He saw enough of the finely-polished, pervasively prepared self-confidence to make him give severe warnings against it. He envisioned a newly minted college graduate who had read the journal reviews, and quarterlies, and a "little of the latest modern thought." When such take a text, they don't dare condescend to consult godly men of the past for its meaning and application, for such ancients dwelt in the dark ages, did they not. Not to them, but to the nineteenth century, that world of wonders that age of wisdom and learned critical studies—that will inform him. He strides from his chamber to the pulpit like a giant on new wine but no "dew of the Spirit of God is upon him," for he drinks from other fountains. "He speaks with astounding power, his diction is superb, his thought prodigious! But he is as weak as he is polished, as cold as he is pretentious: saints and sinners alike perceive his weakness, and by degrees the empty pews confirm it."[40] Such a man is too strong in himself to be strengthened with divine power; he is like painted fire that neither cheers nor warms anybody.

Such preachers are like ineffectual eye-glasses with gold rims, worn not for their usefulness but for the flash of the gilding. Polish, pompous manners and fine language mesmerize many, who like Caligula would feed their horses gilded oats, while the instructive preacher that has a less refined appearance will be passed by. "Manly Christians look more to the meat than the gar-

nishing," Spurgeon asserted, but he observed many in the church culture of Victorian England that ran "mad after flowers and finery." An appreciative congregation, filled with praise and laudations for the rhetorician, could be gathered by combining "scraps of Tennyson, obscure and suspicious, metaphysical jargon from the Germans, a spice of heresy from Maurice ... and a pinch of hair-splitting criticism" wrapped up in "poetical phrases and philosophical affectations." A focus on the "old-fashioned, unadulterated gospel, with plainness of speech" would only gain the condescending chuckle, even though such a ministry was the source of the conversion of hundreds and provided meat to "build up people in their most holy faith." Veneered spiritual simpletons prefer "Toplash with his scented pocket handkerchief and faultless cambric cravat," but true ministers must decide to be faithful and useful, providing milk for babes and meat for men, rather than vain flattery for vacuous heads and empty hearts.[41]

Use of education and refinement to achieve superficial power should not prejudice a called man against the legitimate discipline of learning and pulpit discipline. "Yet for all this," Spurgeon acknowledged, "the inference that ignorance is better than knowledge is a false one." In the absence of the Spirit, untutored confidence is no better than learned diffidence. Submission to the necessity of energy, strength and effectual blessing from the Holy Spirit, however, will only be enhanced into greater usefulness when one knows more of the Scriptures; "the better will he be able to bring forth things new and old out of his treasures."[42]

Truth in the head without a vocal apparatus to deliver it profits the work of the kingdom

---

39. S&T, 1882, Annual Report of the Pastors' College, 259.

40. S&T, August 1882, 405.

41. S&T, March 1872, 108.

42. S&T, June 1882, 259.

nothing. Care for the delivery package must not waver. Of remedies for bad throats Spurgeon had heard enough to drive him to sarcasm, but not too many to keep him from adding his own. Growing a beard might help protect the throat from colds, preaching more often would energize rather than harm the vocal apparatus, and taking as much cayenne pepper as the stomach can bear would strengthen the voice. Spurgeon kept a little glass of chili vinegar and water in front of him which he testified gave "fresh force to the throat whenever it grew weary and the voice appeared likely to break down."[43] He also advised parents to be attentive to the teeth of their children "since faulty teeth may cause serious damage to a speaker."[44] Spurgeon once bought a man a new set of teeth, thus saving both his articulation and his ministry, but expressed his thorough disgust with him, for in a time of crisis, he turned on him with them, and bit him.[45]

An effort to eliminate distractions should not create others by destruction of individual personality. In a short piece in *The Sword and the Trowel*, Spurgeon urged preachers to be natural in their style of delivery. Enclosed well-manicured gardens will please for a while, but the expansive uncultivated variety of the wild where sublime beauty is accentuated in its true nature by the simultaneous appearance of dried clumps of "coarse ungentlemanlike grass" along with gravel-pits, bumps, and irregularities. So it is in delivery. A "too elaborate style of preaching" might amaze and delight in the short term, but eventually "palls upon the mind, and even wearies the ear."[46]

The preaching that edifies year after year and maintains its hearers is "after the order of nature, original, unaffected, and full of spontaneous bursts which the laws of rhetoric would scarcely justify." Spurgeon advocated homely illustrations, quaintness, fullness of heart, thorough naturalness, and outspoken manliness as the qualities that would be as fresh after twenty years as at the first. The formality of a drawing room charms for an evening, but pity the man that endures it for a week. Spurgeon admired the Primitive Methodist preacher who, when asked to return thanks at a meal provided by the squire, expressed gratitude that he did not have such a good meal every day or he should soon be ill. "When we have occasionally listened to some great achievement of rhetoric," Spurgeon confessed for himself, "we have felt the same grateful sentiment rising to our lip."[47]

Although Spurgeon sought to keep himself clear of the "garnishing of eloquence or the trappings of oratory,"[48] he could hardly keep from it, so naturally did images and ideas flow from him. Elegance in rhetoric might be natural to some, as length of gait and length of neck is to a giraffe and a flamingo, but geese and sheep would look ridiculous in seeking to imitate such nature. From the sublime to the ridiculous is only a small step, and some that have sought to escape their native rusticity through artifice, have become feeble and should breathe again their native air and return "to that natural style from which they have so laboriously escaped."[49]

Surely Spurgeon must have been pleased at the description given of A. J. Clarke, the first evangelist sponsored by Spurgeon through the College. From the sophisticated and critical ven-

---

43. Spurgeon, *Lectures*, 1:134.

44. Ibid., 132.

45. William E. Hatcher, *Along the Trail of the Friendly Years* (New York, Chicago, Toronto: Fleming H. Revell Company, 1910), 243.

46. S&T, September 1871, 398. "Want of Naturalness in Preaching."

---

47. Ibid.

48. SS, 2:396.

49. S&T, September 1871, 398f.

ue of the Baptists of Bristol, a trustworthy and subdued observer described Clarke. "There is no attempt at the mere tricks of oratory, although he is an orator of no mean order—'a natural orator, with a number of very fine tones in his voice,' as a brother, whose critical opinion is worthy of respect, remarked to us." Further commendation noted that in the pulpit, as well as out of it, Clarke spoke "with an unstudied naturalness which makes men feel that his business is not self-display, but the exhibition of his Lord."[50] That was precisely the kind of impression Spurgeon taught for and hoped for in his students.

Reviewing a book of sermons by John Gregg, the Bishop of Cork, Spurgeon again emphasized the advantages of naturalness. "It is well with a Christian preacher," Spurgeon pointed out, "when his character and position supersede the necessity of studied eloquence and a display of learning, in order to gain the sympathy and confidence of his hearers." When such is the case a preacher is free to address his auditory in a "free and conversational manner." Gregg's sermons were a pattern of good preaching, "neither too intellectual nor too colloquial, too critical nor too diffuse, too emotional nor too inanimate." The sermons were instructional for the saints and reproving for those of a contrary spirit, a difficult combination. In addition, Spurgeon agreed with the writer of the preface that, in addition to "sound doctrinal teaching, and very able exposition of Holy Scripture, they will be found to contain all that force of language, heart-melting pathos, and irresistible power of appeal, for which, as a preacher, John Gregg was so remarkable."[51]

A compelling element of naturalness was "fire." Though Spurgeon was no fan of enthusiasm of a contrived sort, he greatly preferred fire and energy to the drone that produces an impression that the discourse is entirely inconsequential. "Fanaticism is to be preferred to indifference," he advised the College gathering, for "I had sooner risk the dangers of a tornado of religious excitement than see the air grow stagnant with a dead formality." Better to be too hot than to be lukewarm. When an ice-cold man is heard one does not doubt where he is and when a white hot man is heard one knows where he is; but a measuredly detached presentation soon gives one enough, or too much, of non-committal dullness. Better to be angered that to be lulled to sleep by a preacher that seems to attach no special importance to what he says. "A lukewarm sermon sickens every healthy mind."[52]

Spurgeon, therefore, in spite of all the instructions about voice, structure, pronunciation, theological clarity, and natural gesture could still say, "We prefer a sermon in which there may be no vast talent, and no great depth of thought, but what there is has come fresh from the crucible, and like molten metal burns its way."[53] A flame in the souls of the preacher, kindled from on high (not the strange fire of Nadab and Abihu), will heat the sermon red hot, and will be profitable to and remembered by all that come in contact with it.

As an example of a preacher that had natural eloquence but used it a way fully unconscious of his own verbal power, Spurgeon pointed to Robert Hall. In *Reminiscences of College Life in Bristol* Fred Trestrail focused on the ministry of Hall. Spurgeon gained more knowledge of Hall from these remarks than from any biography of him and saw Trestrail performing for Hall what Boswell did for Johnson, but without the mere trivialities so prevalent in Boswell. Though Hall was a seed-bed for much that Spurgeon scorned

---

50. S&T, December 1877, 560.

51. S&T, April 1879, 192.

52. S&T, July 1881, 313.

53. Ibid., 314.

in the development of nineteenth-century Baptist theology, when Hall's preaching skills were the subject of the discussion, Spurgeon commended Hall to his readers. "In these days of sensationalism and wild speculation, it is well to note how the great men of the past behaved themselves in the house of God." Trestrail pointed to "oblivion of self" as a prominent trait of Hall's pulpit style. Hall was absorbed in his subject and spoke eloquently as if unconscious of any superlative mental achievement. Completely absent was any sign of "betraying vanity, as to leave no doubt that reflection on himself, the tacit thought, 'It is I that am displaying this excellence of speech,' was the faintest action of his mind."[54]

Henry Ward Beecher cut quite a different figure. About the celebrated American preacher, Spurgeon said: "He is for versatility of genius and wealth of illustration altogether peerless; our regret is, that he is far from being as spiritual as he is spirited, and is more a model for an orator than for a divine."[55] But in the example of Hall, we find a servant of truth, wary of seeking to transcend the glory of this call, and refusing to seek to penetrate unrevealed mysteries. Any merely speculative idea, not susceptible of proof, held no attraction for him. He afforded himself no indulgence to move beyond the field of evidence into the unknown, to lead an invasion into the "majesty of darkness." Unlike other men of brilliance, therefore, Robert Hall "did not indulge visionary modes of thought, nor mere dreams of fancy."[56] Whether this was true of Hall throughout his ministry is a more complex question, but that Spurgeon commended this kind of chastened attitude toward speculation in a preacher is certain.

The Sermon in Execution

In reviewing a book on rhetoric by G. W. Hervey, Spurgeon viewed him as a man not very likely to influence his fellow men. Though his book was sufficiently comprehensive to be called a full system of rhetoric, he omitted those personal touches which impart warmth and interest to the matter and vivacity to the style. The index had such a conglomeration of special terms that Spurgeon found it ripe for suggestive jest. "The index of figures at the end of the volume contains a number of uncivilized words, such as Aganactesis, Amphidorthosis, Aloeosis, Epitrochasmus, Paradiegesis, and the like. It is really dangerous to have a book lying about which contains such a menagerie of untamable brute words; those given above are only a few little tame ones—think of a Proepixeusis or an Exouthenismus getting into one's library." Spurgeon advised against trying to pronounce such jargon until one had cut his wisdom teeth, and then he "had better have them soldered in before he begins."[57]

G. W. Hervey, however, should not be confused with G. N. Hervey. The latter Hervey was the cautious commender of the young Spurgeon. The former, however, wore well on Spurgeon during the subsequent years. In 1877, Spurgeon's ridicule of pulpits in *The Sword and the Trowel* that was included in volume 2 of *Lectures to My Students*, cited an insight from G. W. Hervey about Raphael's *Paul Preaching at Athens*. "By the way, it is interesting to note," Spurgeon added, "that Raphael in his representation of Paul at Athens evidently had in his mind the apostle's utterance, 'God dwelleth not in temples made with hands, neither is worshipped with man's hands': hence he delineates him as lifting his hands." Spurgeon expressed his indebtedness to G. W. Hervey's

---

54. S&T, November 1879, 538.

55. S&T, March 1871, 131.

56. S&T, November 1879, 538.

57. S&T, May 1874, 235.

"very able and comprehensive *System of Rhetoric*" for that insight.[58]

Equally, or more, important to comeliness of style and language is Christlikeness in spirit. *Preach Christ in a Christly Manner* was the title of an address delivered at the Pastors' College. On numerous occasions Spurgeon had shown Christ to be the true content of all sermons. "Whatever else you leave out, let Christ Jesus never be forgotten." "Preach all you know about Christ," Spurgeon continued. All that one has learned from the Scriptures, all that one has experienced at his hands, and all that the Spirit has enabled one to perceive and enjoy of Christ must be preached. All of Christ's doctrines, all that Christ set forth in life, all of his commandments, all of his sufferings, and all that he was. The job can never be completed if one preaches "his person, offices, relationships, works, and triumphs."[59]

This is the main glory of ministry, to preach Christ—his substitution, that he became a curse for us, dying the just for the unjust in the stead of his people. Christ must be preached in a lively, earnest, spiritual manner in order for him to be set forth plainly as crucified, even as Paul did before the Galatians. Spurgeon once heard a sermon that did not convey to him a single thought, for the speaker had been taking an "overdose of metaphysics."[60] To conceal the plain truth of salvation beneath a cloud of words, when God's honor and eternal human destiny are at stake, is treason to men's souls and diabolical cruelty. In these matters everything "should be as clear as the sun at noonday."[61] Like life-sustaining manna, so is the gift of the Father in his beloved Son to his people. "The gospel is manna, human speculations are but flying fowl, and often does it happen to those who feed thereon, that, while the meat is yet in their mouths, the wrath of God comes upon them."[62] We have no authority to give anything but the bread from heaven; nothing else will satisfy and prosper the soul in grace; nothing else will save souls. "Nothing else will bring you a soft pillow when you are nearing your last account."[63]

The manner of preaching Christ, however, is that manner that Christ himself would use. Spurgeon pointed out that Christ preached "most solemnly" but never "drearily." Rather he preached glad tidings, "joyfully." We should never enter the pulpit with the attitude, "What a weariness is this." Jesus also preached "meekly." He did not speak like a great man but like one of the poor to whom he spoke. He was meek and lowly of heart. "Scolding in the pulpit, bitterness in conversation, asperity of manner, and domineering over others are not for us, for they are not Christly things."[64]

At the same time we must preach Christ "courageously." Nothing cowardly or shirking characterized our Lord. Never go into the pulpit timidly, afraid of men's faces, but without "uttering or feeling defiance" confront the multitudes like an ambassador of God. Christ also used "simplicity of language." He had no preference for hard words. "Obscurity more befits the Delphic shrine than the oracles of God." Though it was simple, and clear, and filled with common everyday things, easily identified by the common people, it nevertheless was filled with "instruction." Do not preach a "simple gospel" for simpletons. Let there be real teaching in what you say, crystal clear but deep as the sea. Foundation truths are essential but building up the walls must necessarily follow.

58. *Lectures,* 2:102; S&T, August 1877, 356.

59. S&T, March 1881, 106.

60. S&T, June 1885, 263.

61. Ibid.

62. S&T, March 1881, 106.

63. Ibid.

64. Ibid., 107.

"The notion that we are only to cry, 'Believe in the Lord Jesus Christ, and thou shalt be saved,' and repeat for ever the same simplicities, will be fatal to a continuous ministry over one people if we attempt to carry it out." The pious platitudes repeated parrot-like by ministers of the evangelical wing of the established church had opened the door to the ostensibly more thoughtful productions of the high church ritualists. Jesus preached the gospel to the poor, but did not preach a poor gospel. His was "no shadow of empty oratory," but preached his pre-existence, his full deity and the mystery of his incarnation, his substitutionary death as a ransom, and his uniqueness as Saviour. "A fullness dwelt in him, and fullness therefore flowed from him." Jesus, in his proclamation, gave to men "the substance of eternal blessing. In simple language he proclaimed infinite mysteries, and none who heard him could say that he ever wasted time with barren words, or poured forth vain repetitions of worn-out phrases."[65]

Involved in Jesus' preaching was a wonderful mixture of devotion. He would intersperse his sermons with prayer. "You never find him for a single moment in a condition in which he was not fit to deal with men's souls, for you never find him out of communion with God." Pray the message in before you preach it out.[66]

Finally, Jesus had an intense affection for his hearers. He was filled with love and earnestly desired that they find in him alone their hope for eternal life. Some do not take Jesus, but Jonah, for their model, and they care more for their ministerial honor than they do for the destiny of men. "They have a sharp, short, spiritual bark about them, as if they suspected everybody, and most of all, those who came to confess their faith in Christ."[67]

Love for the hearer may be demonstrated by earnest efforts at achieving clarity and establishing a congeniality in the content that adheres to the mind. To accomplish this, Spurgeon believed in the power of chaste and clear illustration. He drew them from his own keen observations about nature and human nature, from his personal life and conversations, and from books. The Puritans provided a rich source of illustrative material and he published articles and books pointing to their illustrative powers. In reviewing an edition of *Plutarch's Lives,* Spurgeon noted that the "Puritans were wont to adorn and enrich their sermons with the incidents of antiquity stored up in Plutarch's Lives, and to this day there is no better storehouse of classic anecdote and illustration." The younger generation was too little acquainted with it. *Smooth Stones Taken from Ancient Brooks,* compiled with the help of Susannah prior to their marriage, was designed to illustrate the richness of Thomas Brooks in particular, but Puritanism in general, concerning the quotability and the aptness of illustrative material available in their sermons. Spurgeon's son, Charles, did the same for his father when he combed the books of sermons and published a volume entitled *Barbed Arrows,* a collection of illustrations, similes, and anecdotes used by Spurgeon in his preaching. The third series in Spurgeon's *Lectures to My Students* is devoted solely to "The art of Illustration." It consisted of seven lectures, four of which instructed as to sources from which illustrations and anecdotes arise.

Spurgeon saw illustrations as instruments, like windows, to let light in upon the subject of a sermon. They make a sermon pleasurable and interesting, they introduce ornament into the design, they enliven an audience and quicken attention. In one sense, Spurgeon saw anecdotes as condescension to weakness. Because the preacher

---

65. Ibid., 109, 110.

66. Ibid., 110.

67. Ibid.

often has the weak as his audience and often the most needy part of it, most sermons need illustrations and anecdotes.

Although a few have a natural demeanor and rhetorical style that makes an anecdote a disfigurement, in general sad is the man that will not make clear his meaning by a homely illustration. Spurgeon wanted to assail the stilted greatness of those that affected to be somewhat more than they are and sneered at anecdotes. "Affectation of intellectual superiority and love of rhetorical splendour have prevented many from setting forth gospel truth in the easiest imaginable manner."[68]

He also warned that illustrations can easily be abused. The sermon should not be all illustration, they must really cast light on the subject, they should not be too prominent, they should grow naturally out of the subject, and the illustration should have no need of elaboration. "He who condescends to use clap-trap of any kind deserves to be debarred the pulpit for the term of his natural life."[69] These figures must be in service of sound doctrine. The useful men of the past "were not story-tellers, but preachers of the gospel; they did not aim at the entertainment of the people, but at their conversion." They did not go out of their way to drag in anything for display. Spurgeon did not want to be the source of poor preaching by giving undue encouragement of illustrations and cause them to present "to the people strings of anecdotes instead of sound doctrines." That would be as evil as offering hungry men flowers in lieu of bread.

Older men, he observed used fewer illustrations, anecdotes and metaphors. This might be due to the decay of the imagination but is accompanied by the ripening of the understanding. Jesus used an abundance of illustration and did not speak to the masses without a parable. This was because they were not able to process didactic truth. From the apostles, subsequent to the coming of the Holy Spirit, we find theological discourses. "As Christian minds made progress," Spurgeon explained, "the style of their teachers became less figurative."[70] If illustrations are to be effective, they must be in service of truth.

Spurgeon pointed to the same reality at the close of his lecture on the "Uses of Anecdotes and Illustrations." He gave seven strong reasons for the use of anecdotes and reinforced his reasons with compelling anecdotes. His reasons were, they interest the mind and secure the attention of our hearers, they render the teaching vivid and life-like, they explain some difficult passages to dull understandings, they help the reasoning faculties of certain minds, they aid the memory, they arouse the feelings, and they catch the ear of the careless. At the end he issued the caveat that "we must take care that we do not let our anecdotes and illustrations be like empty casks that carry nothing." Every discourse must have some body, some suitable instruction, some really sound doctrine. The sermon is not a time to amuse with stories but to clinch solid truth in the heart. The truth is the master in a sermon and the anecdote its servant.

Spurgeon's illustrations were terse and simple stories, hardly ever expanding beyond one paragraph, and usually limited to one or two sentences. His most characteristic elucidating element was the vivid image couched within metaphors and similes. "Men hate election just as thieves hate Chubb's patent locks." The treasures of election are reserved for the elect and no oth-

---

68. *Lectures*, 3:15; see also Spurgeon's discussion of anecdotes in S&T, April 1883, 183-87 and May 1883, 217-24.

69. *Lectures*, 3:9.

70. *Lectures*, 3:7.

ers can enter into the riches of that grace. "When ye shall see dead men raising themselves from their graves, when ye shall see them unwinding their own sheets, opening their own coffin lids ... then perhaps ye may believe that souls that are dead in sin may turn to God." Spurgeon extended this metaphor even more in order to give visual and emotional strength to the biblical picture of the necessity of regeneration as a vivifying agent prior to any possibility of spiritual activity for sinners. "The covenant is, as it were, a lofty tree laden with fruit."[71] God has put all spiritual blessings into his covenantal arrangement and those blessings merely await the wind of the Spirit to make them fall into the experience of his chosen. "The ocean love of God, so broad that even the wing of imagination could not traverse it, sends forth its treasures of the rain of grace, which drop upon our hearts, which are as the pastures of the wilderness; they make our hearts to overflow, and in streams of gratitude the life imparted flows back again to God." The entire water cycle constituted an extended metaphor for the text, "We love him because he first loved us."[72] On the refusal of sinners to be persuaded by the loving call of the gospel he preached, "You are eating husks and missing the kernels. Your mirth is as the crackling of thorns under a pot: it flares, and blazes up, but there is no heart in it; it dies down in a moment, and leaves nothing but a few ashes."[73] "He that is shivering in his nakedness will rejoice to be clothed. A wretched sinner jumps at mercy like a hungry fish leaping at the bait," so he expressed how a man under deep conviction fled for refuge to the reality of substitute for righteousness and wrath.[74] He illustrated a refusal to learn anything

new by a simple image: "Others adhere to old teachings, like limpets stick to the rock; and yet these may only be ancient errors."[75] History, geology, literature, and common experience would provide material for these multitudinous pictures that often enlivened an abstract point.

Learning from his early childhood days, Spurgeon mastered the art of the quick and intense condensation of theological truth through the quotation of a couplet from a well-known hymn. Often, perhaps too many times, he used, "Nothing in my hands I bring, simply to thy cross I cling." For the glory of the moment of conversion he would quote, "E'er since by faith I saw the stream thy flowing wounds supply, Redeeming love has been my theme and shall be till I die." For the absolute sufficiency of Christ's death to bring the elect to a full salvation he quoted Toplady, "Payment God cannot twice demand, first at my bleeding Surety's hand, and then again at mine." Both negatively and positively he quoted from Newton's famous hymn, "'Tis a point I long to know, Oft it causes anxious thought, Do I love the Lord or no; am I his or am I not." Sometimes the middle lines of a verse would run seamlessly into a sentence: "Jesus Christ with 'the water and the blood from his riven side which flowed' has sprinkled not only many men but many nations, and the day will come when all nations shall feel the blessed drops which are scattered from his hands and know them to be 'of sin the double cure,' cleansing transgressors both from its guilt and power."[76] He could call lines from a wide variety of hymns and authors virtually at will and showed a massive and compendious knowledge of Christian hymnody from the Patristic period through the middle of the nineteenth century and

---

71. *Revival Year Sermons*, 78, 52, 57.

72. SS, 9:305.

73. SS, 18:206.

74. SS, 14:258-59.

75. Charles Spurgeon, *An All Round Ministry* (Edinburgh: The Banner of Truth Trust, 1978), 37.

76. MTP, 1875, 249.

they peppered his sermons in appropriate places to capture the poignancy of a biblical thought.

Drawing a lesson from his own experience, Spurgeon encouraged preachers to discover their gifts and their style that would be most useful by doing the hard labor of preaching in inconvenient places. Some who overestimate their gifts, or have not had them tried under fire, sleep in white neck-ties while "touching up certain superior manuscripts" that they hope ere long to "read from the pastor's pulpit." First, they must teach infants, give away tracts, and learn to preach on plain gospel themes in a farmer's kitchen. He must hold the interest of the carter's boy and the dairymaid, thus proving his ministry unctuous beyond any measure than that given by the "prim little man who talks for ever about being cultured, and means by that—being taught to use words which nobody can understand." To make the very poorest listen with pleasure and profit "is in itself an achievement, and beyond this it is the best possible promise and preparation for an influential ministry."[77]

To all of this the effective speaker must add brevity. "When a brother has all the virtues but brevity, might he not, by a little more study, add that also to his attainments?" Though a person cannot add one cubit to his stature, he might subtract one from his disquisitions. The everlasting gospel should not be preached everlastingly and though truth is eternal the sermon should not be. As the coster-monger said to the open-air preacher, "I say, old fellow, cut it short," he gave the same advice to preachers and promised to try "to practice our own precept."[78]

Preparation for sermons in Spurgeon's experience involved much more than the achievement of biblical force and appropriate brevity; it involved a wrenching of the whole soul. A describing Spurgeon's manner of preparation for the pulpit, Wayland Hoyt summarized his observations about the emotional aspect of Spurgeon's preparation for the pulpit. In Spurgeon's earlier years, after the formal preparation was complete, and "just as he was about to confront the throngs he knew were gathering to listen to him," he succumbed to a fearful, almost convulsive, nervous anxiety. For years, so he related to Hoyt, "in his earlier ministry he never preached but that he had beforehand a most straining time of vomiting. His stomach was able to retain absolutely nothing. In later years he vanquished this nervous tendency."[79] Corroboration for that report appeared in Spurgeon's description of his state of mind just prior to the Surrey Music Hall disaster. On his approach to the building, Spurgeon noticed that the private road that led to an entrance to the Music Hall "appeared to be filled up with a solid block of people, who were unable to get into the building. I felt overawed, and was taken with that faintness which was, in my youth, the usual forerunner of every sermon."[80]

Perhaps he overcame the wrenching physical difficulty connected with the anticipation of preaching, but it is doubtful that the emotional trauma ever ceased. In preaching at the College Conference in 1882, Spurgeon told his "boys": "For many, many years my own preaching was exceedingly painful because of the fears which beset me before entering the pulpit." As he continued, he changed his tense, confessing, "Often my dread of facing the people has been overwhelming. Even the physical feeling which came of the mental emotion has been painful; but this

---

77. S&T, January 1880, 5.

78. S&T, June 1885, 259.

79. Wayland Hoyt, *Walks and Talks with Charles H. Spurgeon* (Philadelphia: American Baptist Publication Society, 1892), 18-20.

80. *Autobiography*, 1:431.

weakness has been an education for me." He recounted having written about the terrible fears
and sickness to his grandfather, who responded,
"I have been preaching for sixty years, and I feel
still many tremblings. Be content to have it so; for
when your emotion goes away your strength will
be gone." If a man could preach and think nothing of it, Spurgeon taught, then the people also
think nothing and God does nothing.[81]

Much is made of Spurgeon's ability to compose his sermons mentally. Hoyt recorded his Saturday night ritual of hearing commentaries read
to him on the passage of Scripture selected, and
as he heard he composed. By 10:00 the sermon
was done. The next morning he went back over it,
uncovering and opening the mental baskets and
drawers in which he put his discreet points and
illustrations.[82] He assured G. N. Hervey, a writer
for the *Christian Review*, that "not one word of
his sermons is written before delivery" and his
only use of the pen was in correction of the errors
of stenographers. In the preface to his 1861 volume Spurgeon said, "These discourses are purely
extempore."[83] The texts of the sermons were "reported with singular accuracy" but since no manuscripts existed to which to compare the versions
of the amanuenses, "errors will creep in." The report was printed for his corrections and editions
the day after delivery and published the next.

According to his later descriptions, Spurgeon
did not entirely lay down the pen when getting his
sermon ready, but produced brief cryptic notes.
Often his only written help was on the front of an
ordinary envelope; later in life, needing to write
in a bolder hand, whether because of his eyes or
his hand he did not say, he used the half of a sheet
of note paper. "I sometimes wish that I had never

used even this," he wrote, "for the memory loves
to be trusted, and the more fully it is relied upon
the more does it respond to our confidence." Very
few ministers can entirely dispense with notes,
and some "go on crutches, and read almost all the
sermon." He considered that practice "lame business." Most of us carry a staff even if "we do not
often lean upon it." While a "perfectly able man"
required not even that much, Spurgeon was not
one of "these first-class brethren," and needed his
staff to cross Jordan.[84]

He also delighted in speaking about preaching
in special situations. Preaching out of doors, for
instance, demanded that the preacher say what he
had to say quickly and simply and be done with
it. If the message is diffuse, the street critics will
spot it and name it. Long-winded orations will either be punished with numerous witticisms or by
quietly walking away, leaving the true impression
that the speaker's ideas were as much dispersed as
his audience became.

The street preacher must use many illustrations and anecdotes and "sprinkle a quaint remark
here and there." Nothing labored or involved will
be tolerated or effective but the chain of thought
must be broken apart, "each link melted down
and turned into bullets." While thoughtful country crowds might enjoy purposeful silence as a
means of creating emphasis, the street crowd will
not stand for it, or stay for it. The delivery must be
snappy, short, and sharp. Intensity from beginning
to end most likely gains the hearing needed, and
the idea must be condensed and concentrated.

Sham, show, and chaff will be returned pressed
down, shaken together, and running over, but if
one has "something to say, look them in the face,
say what you mean, put it plainly, boldly, earnest-

---

81. S&T, August 1882, 406.

82. Hoyt, 20.

83. MTP, 1861, v.

84. C.H. Spurgeon, *My Sermon Notes*, A Selection of Outlines from Discourses Delivered at the Metropolitan Tabernacle
by C.H. Spurgeon (London: Passmore & Alabaster, 1884), vi.

ly, courteously, and they will hear you." Giving striking personification to his warnings about the crowd gathered to hear a street preacher, Spurgeon acted out the insulting powers of the crowd: "Crimey, wouldn't he do for an undertaker? He'd make 'em weep." So was the compliment paid to one solemn preacher. To another who took too long to say too little, the wits encouraged him to wet his whistle for he must be awful dry to have "jawed away at that rate about nothing at all."[85]

Spurgeon believed that even the best preacher must be prepared to take his share of street wit and, if need be, return in kind. "Primness, demureness, formality, sanctimonious long-windedness, and the affectation of superiority actually invite offensive pleasantries, and to a considerable extent deserve them."[86] If they ask for beer and bread instead of a tract, a sincere, manly, eye to eye assurance that the tract is given to do them good will usually silence the objection. Spurgeon advised against copying any local preacher, using wild gesticulations of arms and legs, or trusting any crowd to be honest. A ring of compatriots surrounding the preacher, especially ones that can sing, will be of great aid both for protection and for drawing a crowd. Speak so as to be heard, but do not bawl at the top of your voice for no one in earnest ever speaks that way.

> On, on with one monstrous shout,
> and you will weary everybody and wear
> yourself out.[87]

Spurgeon agreed with Edward Leach when he contended that street preachers must be men of "intellectual competency." If they are to deal judiciously and fearlessly with the evils confronted by young men in London life, many of whom have had to resort to the streets, they cannot be the type of "ignorant street preachers" that are mere bawlers of "fervent emptiness." These do immense mischief. Spurgeon added, "Harsh facts prove that illiterate street preachers have done irreparable mischief to open air missionary operations. It is only honesty and kindness to say as much." Leach contended that "we must employ those whose minds have been deeply imbued with the doctrines of divine truth, whose ordinary acquirements have been such as to warrant their teaching others—men of sterling, sound sense, shrewd in practical matters, and ready to meet the ungodly with heavenly wisdom."[88] Spurgeon agreed, and wanted the College to produce men that would qualify—good for the street as well as good for the church.

Not only on the street, but in the pulpit a man must be able to give his message in a great economy of words. "Certain brethren would preach better if they would not preach so long," he contended. Say what one has to say, and when done, quit. Do not ruin the good by following it with mind-benumbing banalities. Stop the wheel when the wheat is ground. Give people the truth, not all the means by which you arrived at the truth. "Our people do not want threshing-machines, and mills, and kneading-troughs, and ovens; they want bread."[89] Driving his point home clearly, Spurgeon illustrated with anecdotes of personal frustration.

> Once more let me hint to you that it is cruel to make your hearers hope that you are about to close, and then go on again, I have suffered this wrong from brethren at the prayer-meeting. I have felt sure that the friend meant to pull up, and he has

---

85. S&T, November 1876, 553.

86. Ibid.

87. Ibid., 554.

88. S&T, November, 1866, 535. "Young Men of London."

89. S&T February 1886, 51.

gone on again, without apology or reason. I am sure it must be dreadful when a preacher says, "To conclude," and then "finally," and then "lastly," and then, "finally and lastly." A certain divine, who is still in the body, is never very lively, but he has great gifts of holding on. When you think he has done, he issues a supplement, which is almost always headed, "Another blessed thought"! His hearers are apt to have thoughts which are not "blessed"; and would often agree with the American who said, "Oh, that the man would *quit!*"[90]

Preaching through a translator provided another context that tried the preacher's ability to condense thought to its mere pith. In summarizing his experience of this form of preaching Spurgeon stated, "It is always dull work to speak through an interpreter." He chafed under the reins of uttering a few sentences followed by a pause, only to begin again. "It is as murderous to all oratory as the old method of lining out the hymn was deadly to all music," Spurgeon judged, for one's "train of thought hardly starts, before it has to pull up." He could engender no "opportunity for warmth or vehemence." But, like street preaching, "by keeping to the marrow of the gospel, giving short sentences, and plentiful illustrations, attention can be gained and held." When he gave his best shot at this in Rome, he felt that "the best of feeling pervaded the meeting, and the truth was received with joy, though many there were strangers to it."[91]

The art of extemporaneity served not only on the street and in a stop-and-go translation mode, but gave opportunity to benefit greatly in emergencies. At a prayer meeting, one of his church members had a mental breakdown, or seizure, and had to be "carried out in a fit." Spurgeon showed his pastoral sympathy, his pulpit grace,

and his tenderness toward the human condition in his remarks on the occasion. "Possess your soul in quietness, beloved friends," he began, "When we are engaged in prayer, or in any other form of worship, interruptions may occur, especially in large assemblies. We cannot expect all nature to be hushed because we are bowing the knee." The "pitiful cry of our friend" reminded him that while they were in health, many even then were in distressing conditions and grievously tormented. This led to a consideration of both sympathy and gratitude. "Sympathy and gratitude are two choice emotions, and if both of these are aroused in the interruption we shall have gained more by it than we can possibly have lost." It is a great danger in a Christian to shield himself so from sickness and pain in an effort to maintain physical health that he becomes hardened to the misery around him. Christ did no such thing. Gratitude must also thrive, "Let the cry of pain remind us that we owe our Lord a song of thanksgiving for screening us from the greater ills of life,—consumption sapping the constitution, asthma, making it misery to breathe, epilepsy tearing us to pieces, or palsy causing every limb to lose its power."[92] A third application is more solemn. Though the friend was not dead, the suddenness of any affliction says "Prepare to meet thy God." He meant not only in confidence of having been washed in Christ's pardoning blood, but that the witness, and relationships, and details of life are such as at any moment are well-pleasing to God. "There should be no hurrying for a clergyman to administer the sacraments, or for a lawyer to write a hasty will, or for an estranged relative to make peace; but all should be arranged and ordered as if we kept our accounts closely balanced, expecting an immediate audit." After further ap-

---

90. Ibid., 54.

91. S&T, January 1872, 36. "A Sabbath in Rome."

92. S&T, September 1878, 403.

plication, Spurgeon closed, "Now that disturbing incident is over, and we shall settle down again all the more ready to unite in prayer and praise."[93]

Spurgeon the Expositor

Week by week disquisition to a congregation savored of different fare. In his regular pulpit ministry, was Spurgeon an expositor? If one were to judge the direction of his preaching only by a cursory understanding of what he announced in his first printed sermon, one might be suspicious of the expository nature of Spurgeon's ministry. Preaching with 1 Samuel 12:17, "Is it not wheat harvest today?" as a theme, he began with this declaration: "I shall not notice the connection; but I shall simply take these words as a motto; and my sermon will be founded upon a harvest field. I shall rather use the harvest for my text than any passage that I find here."[94]

A conclusion drawn from that one incident would be a significant misjudgment. Spurgeon would be surprised for anyone to accuse him of anything less than exposition. Often he did more, but, in his own perception, he never did less. On that day, the exposition, which always came earlier in the worship service than the sermon, was a running commentary on 1 Samuel 12. The verse, therefore, had already been set in context and the theme of a harvest time related to divine purpose was established in the minds of his auditory. "What are sermons but commentaries?" Spurgeon asked. "At least they ought to be." He advocated that the minister employ the best commentaries (Puritan!) along with his original study. The goal is a thorough understanding of the Bible through mastering it one book at a time. "The close, critical, exhaustive investigation of one

part best qualifies for a similar examination of another."[95]

For Spurgeon, true exposition meant, in Puritan fashion, using the whole Bible and all its doctrines in the unfolding of any one portion of Scripture. A typical way of sermon introduction for Spurgeon included his intent to explain the text. "Let us, then weigh the words of the text, for they are solemn words, they are well put together by that master of eloquence, Paul, and they were, moreover, dictated by the Holy Spirit, who telleth man how to speak aright. May he help us to expound, as he has given us the passage to explain."[96]

He did not avoid verse-by-verse exposition, but included it in every worship service as he did a running homily on a larger portion of Scripture from which was taken the verse that provided his text for the day. He disliked the plan of using short texts to the neglect of commenting publicly on larger passages. Preaching plus commenting required twice as much work for the minister but yet Spurgeon insisted, "Earnestly do I advocate commenting." The extra study will provide expanding and long-term benefits. "As a rule," he claimed, "I spend much more time over the exposition than over the discourse."

Spurgeon revealed his own manner of sermon preparation in describing the difference between the exposition and the discourse. "Once start a sermon with a great idea, and from that moment the discourse forms itself without much labour to the preacher, for truth naturally consolidates and crystallizes itself around the main subject like sweet crystals around a string hung up in syrup." Exposition, however, makes one stay with the narrative at hand, dealing with difficult ideas or knotty verses that require some hard work to

---

93. Ibid., 404.

94. MTP, 1904, 385.

95. S&T, February 1866, 94.

96. SS, 1:233.

crack. "You will soon reveal your ignorance as an expositor if you do not study."[97]

Some congregations ("What fools they must be") seemed to want a preacher that already knew everything so he would spend no time in the study. Spurgeon warned that one who "has ceased to learn has ceased to teach." For that reason, "He who no longer sows in the study will no more reap in the pulpit."[98] The preachers that "never hear the still small voice of their books will not be heard, bawl they never so lustily. Reading makes the full man, and it is the full man who alone can overflow for the profit of others."[99]

Spurgeon's conviction about the necessity of study for the exposition received unbiased accolades from a writer for the *Christian Review* in 1857. Having attended several services of different sorts governed by Spurgeon, he described the typical worship service. After indicating his thorough satisfaction with the hymn-reading and singing, the writer asserted that "his talent for exposition, which he regularly exercises, is truly extraordinary, and is no doubt enriched by considerable study." Spurgeon was not fastidious in his critical comments but was "discriminating, and at the same time pithy and practical." The observer believed that Spurgeon excelled in "spiritualization, and in happy turns of devout thought, and sidewise views of familiar passages." When joined with a voice that was "full, clear, and musical," usually managed around conversation level, but never given to "vociferous bursts and fulminations," these expositions formed gave a groundedness to the entire worship experience that embedded a persevering loyalty to Scripture in the soul of the believer and made the unbe-

liever know that there surely was a canon of truth by which he would be judged in the ultimate assize.[100]

One can be sure that the expository element of Spurgeon's preparation constantly fueled his discourses. For Spurgeon the bucket of syrup was oceanic indeed and the strings hung within it were as numerous as fishing lines in the Pacific. Large ideas implicit in Spurgeon's mind soon gathered an aggregate of supportive biblical truths that ordered themselves in the most attractive fashion for presentation. Logical or rhetorical ordering seemed naturally to flow as Spurgeon unfolded the great idea into its constituent parts—from a greater to a lesser, from a lesser to a greater, the investigation of equally important petals of a single flower, the argument from a major premise in syllogistic fashion, or several syllogisms, to a conclusion, the piling up of a variety of evidences to prove the point, the teasing out of a variety of implications that sealed the intrinsic importance of a foundational truth—the "sweet crystals" that clung to Spurgeon's submerged strings provided a virtually inexhaustible variety of shapes and forms that kept up interest both at home and abroad, both heart and head, for a full forty years of public ministry and in printed form for decades, now more than century-and-a-half, beyond. His regular expository ministry provided the fuel for the massive capacity he had for originality in sermonic presentation and for the concentrated biblical content even of his topical sermons.

Helmut Thielicke, a surprising admirer of Spurgeon, found Spurgeon's sermons to constitute a visit to the very ground of the historical setting of the Bible and a roaming through the spirits of those that lived in the biblical world—

---

97. Charles Spurgeon, *Commenting and Commentaries* (Edinburgh: Banner of Truth Trust, 1969), 24.

98. S&T, June 1886, 258.

99. S&T, March 1885, 105.

100. *Sketch*, 92, 93.

"actually bring that life into being by making the ubiquity of the Scriptures a real and living fact."

> When Spurgeon speaks, it is as if the figures of the patriarchs and prophets and apostles were in the auditorium—sitting upon a raised tribune!—looking down upon the listeners. You hear the rush of the Jordan and the murmuring of the brooks of Siloam; you see the cedars of Lebanon swaying in the wind, hear the clash and tumult of battle between the children of Israel and the Philistines, sense the safety and security of Noah's ark, suffer the agonies of soul endured by Job and Jeremiah, hear the creak of oars as the disciples strain against the contrary winds, and feel the dread of the terrors of the apocalypse. The Bible is so close that you not only hear its messages but breathe its very atmosphere. The heart is so full of Scripture that it leavens the consciousness, peoples the imagination with its images, and determines the landscape of the soul by its climate. And because it has what might be called a total presence, the Bible as the Word of God is really concentrated life that enters every pore and teaches us not only to see and hear but also to taste and smell the wealth of reality that is spread out before us here.[101]

At times, however, Spurgeon did feel the pinch of such constant production. "I suppose you do not think that I ever *get dried up* and find it difficult to say anything fresh in my sermons, and yet it is so." Whether the college men were glad to hear it or not, Spurgeon felt he must say that with more than twenty-seven volumes of sermons in print, "It grows harder to say anything new as those volumes increase." He often feared that he could not keep up the supply and felt consciously feeble, less than fit for holy work, feeling his last sermon to be his worst.[102]

It was such feeling that kept him consciously tied to Scripture. The ever-present hovering of biblical power in every part of his sermon was the natural outcome of his manner of perceiving the importance of the whole Bible. "I always find that I can preach best when I can manage to lie a-soak in my text. I like to get a text and know its meaning and bearings, and so on; and then, after I have bathed in it, I delight to lie down in it and let it soak into me." He not only knew the text but came under the intended influences of the text. His view of how a preacher should engage Scripture says much about the perennial transcendent ethos of even his printed sermons.

> Become saturated with spices and you will smell of them. You need not be very particular about the words and phrases if the spirit of the text has filled you. Thoughts will leap out and find raiment for themselves, a sweet perfume will distil from you and spread itself in every direction—we call it *unction*. Do you not love to hear a brother speak who abides in fellowship with Jesus? Even a few minutes with such a man is refreshing, for like his Master, his paths drop fatness. Dwell in the truth and let the truth dwell in you. Be baptized into its spirit and influence that you may impart thereof to others. If you do not believe the gospel do not preach it, for you lack an essential qualification; but even if you do believe it, do not preach it until you have taken it up into your self as the wick takes up the oil. ... Personally to me the gospel is something more than a matter of faith: it has so mingled with my being as to be a part of my consciousness, an integral part of my mind, never to be removed from me.[103]

The images in this quote point, however, to another source from which Spurgeon loved to draw, not only illustrations, but whole sermons

---

101. Helmut Thielicke, *Encounter With Spurgeon* (London: James Clarke & Co. Ltd, 1964), 9.

102. S&T, September 1882, 462.

103. S&T, May 1877, 210.

at times. His insatiable love of the created order, his near-delirious fascination with it and joy in it, in all its variety of shape, color, odor, delicacy, hardy durability, simplicity, complexity and pervasiveness constantly suggested to his mind lessons purified by biblical insight. The nature of God, the horror of sin, the character of assurance, the growth of genuine faith, the certainty of the revelation of lifeless shell, and the variety of human temperament in relation to spiritual experience all were suggested to him by nature. The washing of sheep, the dropping of moisture from a wall, the deadness of trees, a mouse in a field, the singing of birds at different times of the day, the organization of birds in flight, the activity of bees all provided theological reflection and fodder for sermons. When one wag observed that Spurgeon must encounter great difficulty in setting aside enough time for sermon preparation, Spurgeon said that there was never a moment in which he was not preparing a sermon. Invite me home to dinner, he suggested, and I'll even squeeze a sermon out of you. *Sweet Variety in the Garden* yielded to Spurgeon much information about the varying temperaments of God's people and the different circumstances under which they might flourish. The crocus, the *Cactus grandiflora,* the primrose, the tulip, roses, dahlias, the Star of Jerusalem, chicory, the buttercup, the water lily, the pink, daisies, and marguerites all show traits that encourage devotional and theological reflection. There is not a quarter of an hour in the day that does not produce the opening of a different flower. Linnaeus made a clock of flowers, so claimed Spurgeon, and a keen observer could tell time without a watch. In all this great variety the common denominator is response to the light all of which has its origin in the Sun. "Here then is a clear point of union for all believers of every shape and character," Spurgeon distilled; "we are

one in our need of Jesus, one in our joy in him, one in our growth beneath his heavenly influences." We turn to him like the heliotrope to the sun, and "towards him we are moving as truly, though as slowly, as the purple orchid moves towards the south, the land of the sun."[104] Nothing in all of God's creation could fail to speak a word about its maker, sustainer, and redeemer or fail to show the creature's dependence on its immutable and self-existent source.

Sermon Helps

Not all preachers, however, had the capacity for production that consistently flowed from Spurgeon. Some gifted preachers in England recognized that their brethren needed help and were eager to provide sermon outlines to ease the weekly tension. Jabez Burns was a prolific producer of sermon outlines for sale and from the constant flow of outline books evidently amassed quite a following, while royalties made the effort worthwhile. In 1875 when Burns produced *Two hundred Sketches and Outlines of Sermons,* Spurgeon took advantage of the occasion to comment on using other men's outlines. "We do not altogether deprecate the use of other men's outlines," Spurgeon began, "for every now and then a preacher may be hardly driven for time, or he may feel mentally incapable of new thought, or he may be a mere beginner and unable to arrange his matter." Yet constant recourse to such helps, that is, fully developed sermon outlines, Spurgeon bristled against, calling the habit "most pernicious" as well as "disreputable and dishonest." Donning the prophet's garb Spurgeon uttered a "Woe to those who speak in the name of the Lord, but only utter words which they have stolen, every man from his neighbor."[105]

---

104. S&T, November 1882, 558.

105. S&T, September 1875, 447.

During that same year, 1875, Mrs. Spurgeon took the first step toward establishing her book fund giving Spurgeon the opportunity to gain intimate acquaintance with the literary apparatus, or lack of it, of hundreds, perhaps thousands, of Baptist ministers. When she received responses to her first offer of books, Spurgeon, disturbed by what he learned, commented, "It is a sad fact that there should be so many needing such a present. Cannot something be done to provide ministers with books? ... Some of the applicants have not been able to buy a book for the last ten years! Does anybody wonder if preachers are sometimes dull?"[106]

By November, having had even deeper acquaintance with the bibliographical poverty of ministers, Spurgeon had changed his approach entirely. In recommending a book of Sunday School addresses by J. S. Fleet, Spurgeon gave a quite different type of counsel. "Though not believing in the plagiarism of a whole speech, we yet think that some who give addresses would be very wise if they were to borrow one of these, cut it into their own shape, and deliver it in their own style." He explained that there can be no monopoly on ideas, and when a man's own mind receives an idea, moulds it in his own style and utters it in his own language, "it is not dishonest for a man to deliver the substance of what he has read." Recalling that he had been quite intimidatingly judgmental toward the use of sermon outlines just two months earlier, Spurgeon closed, "We hope this sentence will be balm to those wounds which we inflicted in a former number when we denounced purloiners of other men's outlines."[107]

When he reviewed a bound volume of six months' publications in 1877 of *The Preachers Analyst*, including "copious sermonic references"

as an added tool to mine sermonic wealth from the sermons of others, Spurgeon was well-satisfied with its usefulness. "The work ought to be encouraged," he wrote, "and we hope it will be, by those whose time is limited, and who need trains of thought to be started for them." He added, "The references to works and sermons are a new feature in sermonic literature, and are exceedingly valuable." A more intimate and sympathetic understanding of the real world of poor, struggling Baptist preachers created an about-face in Spurgeon's view of sermon helps for a preacher.

Upon the publication of *Lectures to My Students* in 1881, Spurgeon continued what had become a constant refrain, that churches, "without diminishing the supplies of the minister's dinner-table, they give an eye to his study table, and keep it supplied with new works and standard books in fair abundance."[108] If they could get books, they should get only the best and most thoroughly proven, and make themselves master of those books. Otherwise they might borrow other's books judiciously (and always return them), master their Bibles, learn to think, observe all that is around them, study themselves, study others, study the saints, study inquirers, and be much at deathbeds. "I will part with all my books," Spurgeon claimed, "if I may see the Lord's Elijahs mount their chariots of fire."[109] Clearly, however, even though theoretically willing to part with his books, Spurgeon knew that books holding the mature thoughts of gifted men of God would serve as the means of producing equal energy and creativity of mind in those that would take advantage of the means.

Some had neither books nor time to grind fine flour from the field to the table, and Spurgeon made more progress in his compassion

---

106. S&T, August 1875, 402.

107. S&T, November 1875, 544.

108. Spurgeon, *Lectures to My Students*, 1:190.

109. Ibid., 1:200.

toward such and in pointing them to helpful volumes. In 1883, his reviews of *The Homiletical Library* stated, "We shall hope that many a hard-pressed preacher will get an idea out of this volume which will set his machinery going, and enable him to grind out his full measure of fine flour for his people."[110]

By 1884 Spurgeon had completely repented of his pronouncement of "woe" on connoisseurs of sermon outlines and felt more compassion than contempt for the struggling preacher. He began publishing sermon notes going through the entire Bible. The first volume presented sixty-four sermons from Genesis through Job entitled *My Sermon Notes: A selection of Outlines from Discourses Delivered at the Metropolitan Tabernacle by C. H. Spurgeon*. These notes consisted of a text, title or subject, introduction, a full outline with detailed subpoints in sentence outline form, and, for the last part, some suggestions for enlivening the presentation. In the preface to the first of the series, Spurgeon proposed "half-crown volumes, two upon the Old Testament and two upon the New" with the promise, "I shall see how far the first two are accepted by my brethren, and shall then, as health and time may permit me, proceed to the others."[111] A notice of them in *The Sword and the Trowel* specified them for "lay-preachers," but went on to consent "that ministers may get a lift from these sketches, when they are hard pressed; if so, they are heartily welcome."[112]

When the first edition of the first volume neared a sell-out, he promised the second volume soon, notes of sermons from Ecclesiastes to Malachi. He reiterated his purpose in helping the preacher whose business cares made his time for study at a premium. His work was not done "*in extenso* to suit the idler" but just detailed enough "to aid the embarrassed worker." By May 1886, when the third volume of *Sermon Notes* arrived, Spurgeon promised "to get on with the fourth portion, so as to complete this series of preachers' helps. We have abundant evidence of their value to overworked brethren."[113] He now gave a common-sense justification for the use of sermon notes prepared by others, particularly good ones like his.

His resort to this form of help developed not to "encourage indolence, but to help bewildered industry." He desired to help no man to "preach without thought" but he was not so hard as "to leave a weary mind without help." He wanted to "pour a little water down a pump to help it to draw up a stream from below" so as to set a jaded mind at work "to develop its own resources." Since he had already produced *Lectures to My Students* and *Commenting and Commentaries*, he felt that this step would be a logical and helpful extension of what he had already done in helping preachers build a small library of sermon water for priming the pump. None of the sermons, to his knowledge, had ever been in printer's hands, unless they had been reported by newspapers. As to method, Spurgeon expanded his "scanty" notes, which could be understood by none but himself, and added "certain pieces of my own, or extracts from the works of others, which are intended to brighten up the sermon." He realized that the "weary ones" for whom the book was intended would be as little able to take time and energy for anecdotes and illustrations as they were to divide the subject into a sermon.[114]

As hard pressed as some men were, Spurgeon still urged earnest preparation. "That which

---

110. S&T, March 1883, 141.

111. Spurgeon, *My Sermon Notes*, Preface.

112. S&T, November 1884, 598.

113. S&T, May 1886, 246.

114. Spurgeon, *My Sermon Notes*, v, vi.

comes from a man's mind without thought and research is comparable to that which comes of ground without ploughing or sowing. Words without thought are in no respect better than weeds."[115] Study and thought are essential to success in the pulpit and the Spirit does not minister to indolence and idleness. A man that is presumptuously lazy will find that he is left to "vent his nimble nonsense" with the embarrassing lesson that he will not reap where he has not sown. If a man has nothing to say, let him say it to himself and not force others to sit under a "barbarity which the Spanish Inquisition has scarcely ever excelled."[116] One may spend a short time in preparation for a sermon when he has several years or even decades of hard labor to reinforce and inform the brief minutes of specific study.

His own understanding of the relationship between the various sermonic styles and their relation to exposition he summarized in the preface to *Commenting and Commentaries*. Spurgeon placed himself as third person in the position of a "judicious critic" of contemporary preaching. Such a critic probably would "complain that many sermons are deficient in solid instruction, Biblical exposition, and Scriptural argument." Rather than fleshy, they are flashy; rather than solid, they are clever; and rather than impressive, they are entertaining. Doctrine is barely discernible and the brilliant harangues embody no soul-food. This critic, if forthright and honest, would "propose that homilies should flow out of texts, and should consist of a clear explanation, and an earnest enforcement of the truths which the texts distinctly teach." He would advocate expository preaching as the great need of the day and as most apt to protect against rising error while providing spiritual edification. The critic would not "unite in any indiscriminate censuring of hortatory addresses, or topical sermons, nor should we agree with the demand that every discourse should be limited to the range of its text, nor even that it should have a text at all." Nevertheless, he would continue to subscribe to the proposition "that more expository preaching is greatly needed, and that all preachers would be the better if they were more able expounders of the inspired Word."[117]

After careful attention is given to every aspect of theory and of practical preparation, both long term and short term, for the moment of preaching, still all is vain unless the competency experienced in the sermon is the competency of the Spirit and not of the human proclaimer. In a season when he felt acutely his own weakness, he delivered his soul to the College Fraternal.

> Look at the preacher who has no burdens. His sermon is in his pocket; there cannot happen any mischief to it unless a thief should steal it; he has rehearsed all his action, he is as safe as an automaton. He does need to pray for the Spirit of God to help him in his preaching, and though he uses the form one wonders what the prayer can mean. He surveys the congregation with the complacency of a gardener looking at a bed of flowers. He has something to say, and he knows what it is going to be, every word of it, and therefore he says it with ease, and comes down the stairs as pleased with himself as heart could desire: the notion of trembling is far from him, he is not so weak. Yonder is a poor brother who has been tugging away with his brains, wrestling on his knees, and bleeding at heart; he is half-afraid that he may break down in the sermon, and he is fearful that he will not reach the hearts of the people; but he means to try what can be done by the help of God. Be you sure that he will get at the people, and God will give him converts. He is looking up

---

115. S&T, August 1883, 373.

116. Ibid.

117. Spurgeon, *Commenting and Commentaries*, iii.

to God, for he feels feeble in himself. You know which of the two preachers you would sooner hear, and you know who is the really strong man of the two; the weak man is strong and the strong man is weak.[118]

Expository Preaching is Doctrinal Preaching

As one finds so abundantly clear in *Lectures to My Students* as well as his thousands of published sermons, Spurgeon looked to doctrinal content as primary and the *raison d'être* of preaching. Full submission to the authority of Scripture demanded that one be ready to embrace every doctrine of the Word of God. Preaching on election, early in his ministry in London, Spurgeon appealed to a wide audience to open their minds, remove their prejudices, dismiss preconceived objections and listen to the clear annunciation of the divine revelation on the subject. "Do not be ashamed to learn, and to cast aside your old doctrines and views, but to take up that which you may more plainly see to be in the Word of God," he urged. If it is not in the Bible, whatever he might say, or whatever any pretended earthly authority might say, reject it, for "the Bible must be the first, and God's minister must lie underneath it." The preacher does not stand on the Bible but preaches with the Bible above his head. "After all we have preached, we are well aware that the mountain of truth is higher than our eyes can discern;" The summit may be obscure and none is able to penetrate its topmost pinnacle, "yet we will try to preach it as well as we can."[119]

Systematization and coherence giving organization to mere human authority and eloquence in service of mere temporal matters might have their place in human society and might serve just causes, but the preacher had a higher call for the use of these gifts. Their utility found place before the immutably true word of God, the Bible. His preaching, virtually without fail, found a verse within its context that provided a window into the rich doctrinal content of the whole Bible. His message developed as an extended exposition of some aspect of theology hammered out for the benefit of saints and sinners in his congregation. He was not a theological taster nor did he pursue the discussion of mere theological abstractions to gain some intellectual and speculative satisfaction. Everything, however, that pertained to the gospel and had connections to the great truths of how God saves, sanctifies, and secures sinners Spurgeon claimed as sacred inviolable territory. "The sermons that are most likely to convert people," Spurgeon lectured, "are full of truth, truth about the fall, truth about the law, truth about human nature, and its alienation from God, truth about Jesus Christ, truth abut the Holy Spirit, truth about the Everlasting Father, truth about the new birth, truth about obedience to God, and how we learn it, and all such great verities."[120]

He insisted throughout his ministry, and in his teaching of other ministers, that "every preacher should labour to save his hearers. The truest reward of our life-work is to bring dead souls to life."[121] He did not see it as his duty to teach politics (though he was effective, because theological, in his political convictions),[122] or mere morals (though he had a greater impact for improvement of morals and the elevation of character than any man of his age); he did not relish in telling men what they ought to do but wanted

---

118. S&T, August 1882, 406. "Inaugural Address."

119. SS, 2:67.

120. Spurgeon, *The Soul Winner* (Chicago: Fleming H. Revell, 1895), 90f.

121. S&T, June 1886, 258.

122. Ibid., 294.

to "preach the good news of what God has done for them."[123]

Doctrine as doctrine, "apart from Christ," did not interest him. "We are only theologians as far as theology enshrines the gospel." In that, however, he found enough "to fill any one life, to absorb all our thought, emotion, desire, and energy, yea, infinitely more than the most experienced Christian and the most intelligent teacher will ever be able to bring forth." Should anyone accuse Spurgeon of narrowness in this view and "shut up to one set of truths," he would simply "rejoice to be shut up with Christ, and count it the truest enlargement of our minds."[124]

When he contemplated how he preached to thousands and thousands as year after year passed, he dismissed any suggestion that there was anything remarkable in his speech. The true answer, Spurgeon insisted, "is that I preach Jesus Christ to you." He desired no other theme and could dwell upon it for another 6,000 years and never grow weary of it. "You may preach what you will of your learning and your philosophy," he conceded, "and you may talk pretty things concerning God out of Christ." But even God-talk apart from Christ "will never stir the souls of men as the preaching of the Son of God has done and will do."[125]

This points to a Christocentric view of doctrine and gospel ministry. The Christocentric nature of both revelation and redemption convinced Spurgeon that a truly systematic theology must find its point of focus and its true coherence in Christ. His interaction with systematic theology he made obvious to his people so that they were not afraid of it; nor did they consider it irrelevant. But its service of genuine devotion

to Christ and conscious dependence on him appeared just as boldly.

An article for *The Sword and Trowel* entitled "Bands of Love: or, Union to Christ" began with the statement, "Systematic theologians have usually regarded union to Christ under three aspects, *natural, mystical, and federal,* and it may be that these three terms are comprehensive enough to embrace the whole subject, but as our aim in this article is simplicity, let us be pardoned if we appear diffuse when we follow a less concise method." He then proceeded to include those three divisions in his outline but added two at the beginning: *everlasting love* and *union of purpose.*[126] Those themes central to the covenant of grace dominated Spurgeon's plan for preaching and formed the center of gravity for his understanding of theology.

The very first entry in the first number of *The Sword and the Trowel* was entitled "What Shall be Done for Jesus." He speaks of the manifold ways in which the Eternal Father has honored Jesus. The decree of election as well as every other "after-manifestation of grace" has been brought to us through "the man Christ Jesus." He holds all the offices by which we know and are made right with God, that is, prophet, priest, and king. Spurgeon affirmed the orthodox view of Christ as God and man in one person, as he does literally thousands of times in his sermons and writings. "What can ye conceive of splendour blazing around the throne of the Most High, which will not also be seen gleaming with equal refulgence from the seat of him who is 'God over all blessed for ever?' It is with no trembling lip that we sing *his* praise." In summary Spurgeon stated it as a settled principle that "You cannot taste the sweetness of any *doctrine* till you have remembered

---

123. S&T, October 1877, 495.

124. Ibid.

125. MTP, 1870, 283.

126. S&T, August 1865, 373.

LIVING BY REVEALED TRUTH

Christ's connection with it."[127] Numberless times, early and late, he demonstrated this conviction in his preaching.

> Election is a good thing; to be chosen of God, and precious; but we are elect in Christ Jesus. Adoption is a good thing; ... ay, but we are adopted in Christ Jesus and made joint-heirs with him. Pardon is a good thing—who will not say so?—ay, but we are pardoned through the precious blood of Jesus. Justification— is not that a noble thing, to be robed about with a perfect righteousness?—ay, but we are justified in Jesus. To be preserved—is not that a precious thing?—ay; but we are preserved in Christ Jesus, and kept by his power even to the end. Perfection—who shall say that this is not precious? But he hath raised us up and made us sit together with him in heavenly places in Jesus Christ—so that Christ must be good positively, for he is all the best things in one.[128]

His focus on Christ, however, did not arise from immaturity of understanding or imbalance in his perception, but from a reasoned synthesis of biblical knowledge. For all of his emphasis on Christ he was nonetheless, and consequently, fully Trinitarian in all that he spoke and wrote. His preface to the first volume of the *New Park Street Pulpit* gave a forceful declaration of his Christ-centered intentions, while the first sermon of the series was entitled "The Immutability of God."

His preface stated, "He himself is Doctor and Doctrine, Revealer and Revelation, the Illuminator and the Light of Men. He is exalted in every word of truth, because he is its sum and substance." Spurgeon valued doctrine as "most precious when we see it distilling from his lips and embodied in his person." Sermons were not simply an art form to be admired for their symmetry or rhetoric but "are valuable in proportion as they speak *of* him and point *to* him. A Christless gospel is no gospel and a Christless discourse is the cause of merriment to devils." And if the reader has not yet understood Spurgeon's intentions, he says, "Jesus, Jesus, Jesus, only have we laboured to extol: may the Lord himself succeed our endeavours."[129]

The sermon, "The Immutability of God," based on Malachi 3:6, argued that God was immutable in his essence, in his attributes, in his promises, in his threatenings, and in his objects of love. He then gave four brief arguments supporting God's immutability from ontology, the necessity of perfection in God, God's infinity, and the fulfillment of prophecy. When some argued that Hezekiah's prayer changed an ostensibly immutable prophecy of his death, Spurgeon pointed out that the line of the Messiah would have been cut off had Hezekiah not recovered from the sickness. Prophecy of the Messiah had already determined the matter of recovery and shown the conditional and utilitarian nature of the prophet's message. "Sons of Jacob" who benefit from God's immutability are sons of election, persons of peculiar rights, peculiar manifestations, peculiar trials, and peculiar characters. Their chief benefit is that they are not consumed. They have been preserved from being consumed in hell and they have been preserved from being consumed in this world. "He loved them out of pure sovereign grace, and he will love them still. But we should have been consumed by the devil, and by our enemies—consumed by the world, consumed by our sins, by our trials, and in a hundred other ways, if God had ever changed."[130]

---

127. S&T, January 1865, 3.

128. NPSP, 1859, 141.

129. NPSP, 1855, preface.

130. Ibid., 8.

The sermon's introduction included a most expressive and powerful affirmation of the blessings of a knowledge of God as a triune God and the natural inherence of Christ-crucified in that doctrine.

> The most excellent study for expanding the soul, is the science of Christ, and him crucified, and the knowledge of the Godhead in the glorious Trinity. Nothing will so enlarge the intellect, nothing so magnify the whole soul of man, as a devout, earnest, continued investigation of the great subject of the Deity. And, whilst humbling and expanding, this subject is eminently *consolatory.* Oh, there is, in contemplating Christ, a balm for every wound, in musing on the Father there is a quietus for every grief; and in the influence of the Holy Ghost, there is a balsam for every sore. Would you lose your sorrows? Would you drown your cares? Then go, plunge yourself in the Godhead's deepest sea; be lost in his immensity; and you shall come forth as from a couch of rest, refreshed and invigorated. I know nothing which can so comfort the soul; so calm the swelling billows of grief and sorrow; so speak peace to the winds of trial, as a devout musing upon the subject of the Godhead. It is to that subject I invite you this morning.[131]

For this reason Spurgeon saw Christian growth as dependent on the attainment of doctrine distilled from Scripture into a system but embraced in the context of Christian experience. In a sermon on "Particular Election," Spurgeon exhorted his hearers that their faith be not merely a creed but genuine credence—"that it is not a mere belief of doctrine, but a reception of doctrine in your soul." But true credence will not grow apart from doctrine.

> A knowledge of doctrine will tend very much to confirm your faith. Try to understand God's Word, get a sensible, spiritual idea of it. Get, if you can, a system of divinity out of God's Bible. Put the doctrines together. Get real, theological knowledge, founded upon the infallible Word. Get a knowledge of that science which is most despised, but which is the most necessary of all, the science of Christ and of him crucified, and of the great doctrines of grace.[132]

Faith must embrace doctrinal truth. To the suggestion that the time would come when preaching the doctrines of grace would be passé, Spurgeon responded, "Out on ye, traitors, who tell us that we care to shape our gospel to suit this enlightened nineteenth century! Out on ye, falsehearts, who would have us tone down the everlasting truth that shall outlive the sun, and moon, and stars, to suit your boasted culture, which is but varnished ignorance!" No, still he would preach those truths that were mighty through God to the pulling down of strongholds, and he would maintain it to the death. "The church needs the doctrines of grace to-day as much as when Paul, or Augustine, or Calvin preached them; the Church needs justification by faith, the substitutionary atonement, and regeneration, and divine sovereignty to be preached from her pulpits as much as in days of yore, and by God's grace she shall have them, too."[133]

Without such knowledge and consent to specific truth, no faith is possible. A strong evidence of grace is the "*mind's perception of revealed truth and its obedience to it,*" Spurgeon argued.[134] Since God has lifted the veil through divine revelation, the true believer does not make or invent his own precepts, but he learns them from God.

---

131. Ibid., 1.

132. NPSP, 1857, 133.

133. SEE 10:315. "Christ and His Table Companions."

134. MTP, 1887, 558.

By this shalt thou know whether thou be a child of light, or a child of darkness. Are the doctrines of grace essential verities with thee? Whatever God has said about sin, righteousness, judgment to come, art thou ready to accept it at once? Whatever he has revealed concerning himself, his Son, his holy Spirit, the cross, life, death, hell, and the eternal future, dost thou believe it unfeignedly? This is to walk in the light. All other teaching is darkness.[135]

This constant effort to place Christ and the salvation that he brings at the center of his theology may be seen vividly in a development he gives to one of his favorite themes in two separate sermons. The theme of Christ's preciousness cheered and encouraged Spurgeon throughout his ministry and seemed to him the sum and substance of all true divinity. In 1869, he preached on this theme and warned his congregation not to reduce the knowledge of Christ to a mere creed, such as a state church might enforce, or insist on an orthodoxy that had no room for the true lover of Jesus that diverged on some point. Though he knew that pretensions to love covered many a heresy and he would be the "last person in the world to speak lightly of the value of sound doctrine" heartily wishing, as well as working, "that the doctrines of grace were more clear to our understanding, and more imprinted upon our hearts," he much more esteemed a true love of Jesus than all the heartless orthodoxy in the world. To integrate doctrine with true affection is the preacher's constant challenge; true affection has the ascendancy.

> I love Protestantism, but if there is anything in this world that I have a horror of, it is that political Protestantism which does nothing but sneer and snarl at its fellow citizens, but which is as ignorant as a cow about what Protestantism truly is. The great truths of Protestantism—not mere Protestant ascendancy—and the great secret power of those truths, far more than the mere letter of them, is the thing to be prized. You may get it into you head that you are a member of the one only true church; you may wrap yourself about with any quantity of self-conceit, but that does not at all prove you to be a possessor of grace. It is love to Christ that is the root of the matter. I am very sorry, my dear brother, if you should hold unsound views on some points; but I love you with all my heart if Jesus is precious to you. I cannot give up believers' baptism; it is none of mine, and, therefore, I cannot give up my Master's word. I am sure that it is Scriptural. I cannot give up the doctrine of election, it seems to me so plainly in the word; but over the head of all doctrine and ordinances, and over everything, my brother, I embrace thee in my heart if thou believest in Jesus, and if he be precious to thee, for that is the vital point.[136]

When he revisited his first preaching text, 1 Peter 2:7, on March 30, 1890, the Downgrade Controversy had pressed him down and made him appear reactionary and incompetent in the eyes of many contemporaries. The Baptist Union had treated Spurgeon as a false accuser of the brethren. Through all of this, however, he knew that his loyalties were generated by a view of the preciousness of Christ and his truth. For Christ to be precious means that he is our honor. This particular emphasis in the translation prompted new insights in Spurgeon. "Did you suffer reproach for Christ's truth?" he asks; "It is well: thus are you bound up in the bundle of life with him whom you love," he answers. "The day shall come when it shall be thought to be the highest honour that ever was to have been denounced as a bigot and cast out as a troubler, for the sake of Christ and

---

135. Ibid.

136. S&T, October 1869, 488.

his gospel." Strong on his mind is the recent flurry of ill-tempered publicity, but even stronger is the encouragement of this verse. "Some of us bless the Lord," Spurgeon insisted, "that we are associated with his old-fashioned cross, his time-worn truth, his despised atonement, his antiquated Bible." As for Spurgeon, embracing the marrow of this text, he bound the truths of Jesus as "a chaplet about my brow. Jesus, the Substitute, is my honor, and the doctrines of grace are my glory." [137]

The historical context made Spurgeon dwell more on the doctrinal issues as evidence of love to Christ. Christ is precious because as "God and man, he alone combines the two natures in one person." Remarkable and unparalleled is the simple fact "that while he is God over all, and has thus the fulness of the Godhead, he is also man, true man of the substance of his mother, and so has all the adaptation of perfect manhood." Spurgeon continued with his inimitable verbal display of the benefits that such a person brings to the people he redeems. His life gives life; his death rescues from hell; his resurrection justifies; his second coming gives us delight. He is prophet, priest, king, husband, brother, friend. In every type and office He "has a blessed use for the supply of some terrible need which afflicts his redeemed." Because of the power and perfection of his person and work Jesus is "set for the removal of your condemnation, the pardon of your sin, the justification of your person, the changing of your nature, the presentation of your offerings, the preservation of your graces, the perfecting of your holiness, and for all other good and necessary purposes."

In this sermon, Spurgeon not only proclaimed the doctrine in all its symmetry and fullness, he accented the reality that such straight adherence to lines of truth is a mark of loyalty to Christ.

A minister once said to me, "It must be very easy for you to preach." I said, "Do you think so? I do not look at it as a light affair." "Yes," he said; "it is easy because you hold a fixed and definite set of truths, upon which you dwell from year to year." I did not see how this made it easy to preach, but I did see how it made my heart easy, and I said, "Yes, that is true. I keep to one fixed line of truth." "That is not my case," said he; "I revise my creed from week to week. It is with me constant change and progress." I did not say much, but I thought the more. If the foundation is constantly being altered, the building will be rather shaky. ... It is an honour to be on the same lines of truth as the Holy Ghost. It is an honour to believe what the lips of Jesus taught. I had sooner be a fool with Christ than a wise man with the philosophers. The day shall come when he that cleaves most to the gospel of God shall be the most honoured man.[138]

Spurgeon was aware that his gift of spontaneous delivery and powerful oratory and imagination could not be duplicated, but he was utterly insistent that the same commitment to systematic presentation of doctrine from a Christ-centered standpoint be the method taught at his Pastors' College. Though a diversified course of study, including literature, science, and religion, formed the curriculum it was all pursued with a view to fitting the mind for its highest development in the truths of Scripture. "Let theology, in a word, be the principal study of the professed teacher of theology," Spurgeon argued, "and all other sources of information and mental improvement as may become subservient to this, placed within their reach." Now what kind of theology did he envision as central to the curriculum?

Calvinistic theology is dogmatically taught. We mean not dogmatic in the offensive sense of that

---

137. MTP, 1890, 90-91.

138. Ibid. 185, 186, 191.

term; but as the undoubted teaching of the Word of God. ... We hold to the Calvinism of the Bible. Extreme views on either side are repudiated by us. The cross is the centre of our system. ... This is our stand-point from which we judge all things. We have no sympathy with any modern concealment or perversion of great gospel truths. We prefer the Puritan to modern divinity. From our inmost souls we loathe all mystic and rationalistic obscurations of the plain and full-orbed doctrines of grace, and foremost of all of justification by the righteousness of Christ and atonement by his blood. ... We believe one of the secrets of the success that has hitherto attended the students from this College to be the doctrines they teach, and the manner in which they enunciate them, as though they believed what they say and wished others to believe them too.[139]

A steady feeding at Spurgeon's trough would make a sturdy theologian of any hearer. From the first sermon in the New Park Street Series to the last that he preached at the Metropolitan Tabernacle (June 7, 1891), a systematic theology of biblical teaching with the revelation and redemption of Christ at the center informed his every point. In this last sermon he spoke of saints who are true but nevertheless faint because "they have not yet come to fulness of growth in grace." Among that number are those who had no heart for controversy. Also among the faint are those who do not plunge into the deep of doctrinal truth.

> And some cannot advance any further with regard to knowledge; they know the fundamentals, and feel as if they could master nothing more. It is a great blessing that they know the gospel, and feel that it will save them; but the glorious mysteries of the everlasting covenant, of the sovereignty of God, of his eternal love and distinguishing grace, they cannot compass—these are a brook Besor

which as yet they cannot swim. It would do them a world of good if they could venture in; but still, they are not to be tempted into these blessed deeps. To hear of these things rather wearies them than instructs them: They have not strength enough of mind for the deep things of God. I would have every Christian wish to know all that he can know of revealed truth. Somebody whispers that the secret things belong not to us. You may be sure you will never know them if they are secret; but all that is revealed you ought to know, for these things belong to you and to your children. Take care you know what the Holy Ghost teaches. Do not give way to a faint-hearted ignorance, lest you be great losers thereby. That which is fit food for babes should not be enough for young men and fathers: we should eat strong meat, and leave milk to the little ones.[140]

Fit the Arrow to the String
In selecting a doctrinal theme, the minister must bear in mind the particular demands of the occasion. In a message on Paul's sermon before Felix, Spurgeon made the point that we must have an appropriate sermon. What the apostle did before Felix and Drusilla, "every minister ought to do." Given such an auspicious opportunity, however, many ministers "if they addressed kings and princes, would pour out before them the vilest adulation and flattery that ever came from mortal lips." The preacher must not trim his doctrine to flatter the audience. His goal must not be to attract a crowd by pleasing them in their sin. He must preach what is most needful for their eternal well-being. When addressing an antinomian audience some ministers might confine themselves strictly to predestination; others, addressing an audience of philosophers might "never mention such words as the covenant of grace and salvation by blood." The minister should shun ever preaching *before* a congregation and always endeavor to preach *to* them.

---

139. S&T, March 1866, 136

140. MTP, 1891, 317-18.

Neither powers of eloquence nor depth of learning are his goal but a message to prepare them for eternity. "It is not for me," he would say, "to be amusing you with some deep things that may instruct your intellect but do not enter your hearts; it is for me to fit the arrow to the string and send it home." In a change of metaphor, but still in the mode of drawing blood, he saw the task as "to unsheathe the sword—be the scabbard never so glittering, to cast it aside, and let the majesty of naked truth smite at your hearts." He proposed that personal preaching was precisely the business of the gospel minister. Knox did it before Mary, "flat to her face," and must we be personal and avoid generalities. Spurgeon was thankful that "from that fear I have been delivered long ago." No man that walked on earth was he afraid to reprove. "There are none of you," he stated plainly, "however connected with me by ties of profession or in any other respect, that I would blush to speak personally to, as to the things of the kingdom of God." Only by being bold and courageous and "sending home the truth" can the minister be free of the blood of his hearers.[141]

Spurgeon wanted to preach in such a way that if sinners "do not come to Jesus, their blood shall be upon their own heads, for the invitation is as free as the blessing is full." When some of his ardently Calvinistic hearers, whose ardency he shared, heard him issue urgent pleas for all sinners to come to Christ with full assurance that if they came he would receive them, and that the invitation to come flows from the lips of Christ himself, they felt, in the words of one such friend, "very uncomfortable when you are giving free invitations to sinners."[142] Spurgeon could not do otherwise, however, for he found such expressions of the openness of Christ's invitation to sinners in Scripture. "We know of no other limit to our invitation than this, 'Whosoever will, let him take the water of life freely.'" When he was preaching to sinners, he felt inclined to "beg everyone of them" to flee to Christ for "there is not a sinner in the world who is to be told that he may not come to Jesus and receive the whole of the blessings of the gospel." He would declare the "doctrine of God's sovereignty without toning it down, and electing love without any stuttering over it," but he would never give up "loving the souls of men, or cease from trying to bring in the lost from the highways and hedges." He had no delusions that he could make men come, for that was the work of the Holy Spirit; but he did seek to persuade them by the love of Jesus and the terrors of the Lord. "We can preach Christ to sinners if we cannot preach sinners to Christ." The Word of the Lord would not return void, but it must be preached as warranted—just as abundant in its freeness as it is powerful in its fullness.[143]

A sermon published in the November 1874 *Sword* embodies the combination of textuality, illustration, and theological exposition so pervasive in Spurgeon's proclamation. Ephesians 6:15 provided the text, "And your feet shod with the preparation of the gospel of peace." The title denoted that the sermon was built around an ongoing illustration about shoes: "Shoes for Pilgrims and Warriors." Each element of the sermon opened a different word or idea in the text and continued the development of the illustration. The sinews that gave bulk and strength ran along the doctrinal strands that penetrated the whole and constituted the true purpose of the discourse.

In our wrestling against the powers of darkness that will seek to bruise our heels, or trip us, or lame us altogether we find that infinite mercy has

141. SS, 4:197-99.

142. NPSP, 1859, 270.

143. S&T, October 1883, 546-48.

prepared gospel shoes for the feet. In structure, Spurgeon had only two major divisions. One, examine the shoes; two, try on these shoes. Under the first head he spoke of the "blessed maker" of the shoes and the material from which the shoes were made. Under the second head, we find that the shoes "fit perfectly," they give the wearer a "firm foothold," they have an apt "suitability for marching," they provide an effectual preservative from the "ordinary roughness of the road of life," they are good for climbing, they are good for running, and they are good for fighting. The sermon in its structure, thus, while not a metaphor, is nevertheless an extended illustration with memorable images exploring and taking advantage of the Pauline metaphor. Under each of the separate points, Spurgeon blends theological explanation with experiential application fixing in the mind the real biblical thrust of Ephesians 6:15.

The "blessed maker" is God himself and he has made a preparation "in which infinite skill has been displayed." The gospel of peace is his production and thus without a flaw. The material is the "peace which grows out of the gospel." This includes first "perfect peace with God." All other peace extends from this peace. "Let a man know that his sins are forgiven him for Christ's name's sake, that he is reconciled to God by the death of his Son, and that between him and God there is no ground of difference,—what a joyful pilgrim he becomes!" Given all that God has accomplished through the complete atonement of Christ we may march through life "booted and buskined for all the exigencies of the way, yea ready to plunge through fire and water, thorn and thistle, brake and briar, without fear." Spurgeon contrasted the judicial anger of God with the Father's care and asserted that one "sandled with reconciliation by atoning blood" will never faint but always be upheld.

A second part of peace with God, however, in addition to the "legal peace of justification," is a peaceful acquiescence to his ways with us. The well-shod pilgrim must have the "exceeding peace which springs from intimate, undisturbed communion with God." Beyond these aspects of peace with God, Spurgeon explored "peace towards ourselves," peace with our fellow men, peace with all mankind, showed how Jesus was shod with these same shoes, and affirmed that they would never wear out. Each part unfolded a biblical verse and included an experimental application of doctrine. Notice the freshness Spurgeon brings to the apparently rather hackneyed point of peace with all mankind.

> Be not easily provoked, bear and forbear, forgive and love on, return good for evil, seek to benefit even the most unthankful, and you will travel to heaven in the pleasantest possible manner. Hatred, and envy, and persecution may come, but a loving spirit materially blunts their edge, and oftentimes inherits the promise, "When a man's ways please the Lord, he maketh even his enemies to be at peace with him."[144]

In trying the shoes on, one finds that they are perfectly adapted to every demand of life, they never slip in the rough and dangerous places but always uphold him against every onslaught. For Spurgeon the image of the well-fitted, tenaciously sturdy shoe meant the thorough certainty with which Christian experience coincided with biblical truth.

> Tell him that the atonement is not true, preach up to him the bloodless neology of modern thought, and he ridicules the ineffectual attempt, because he knows whom he has believed, and feels a heavenly peace within flowing from the substitutionary

---

144. S&T, November 1874, 502.

sacrifice. Tell him that the doctrines of grace are a mistake, that salvation is all of free will and man's merit; and he says, "Nay but I know better. I know the doctrines of sovereign grace to be true by experience; I know I am God's chosen; I know that I am called, I know that I am justified, for I know that I have peace with God, as the result of all these." You cannot move him an inch, his creed is interwoven with his personal consciousness, and there is no arguing him out of it. In these days of skepticism, when no man seems to have any resting place, it is well to be so shod that you can and do stand on the truth, and cannot be blown about like thistledown in the breeze.[145]

Every element of trying on the shoes introduced a pertinent aspect of Christian experience culminating with one's finding that the shoes are good for fighting. In the hand to hand combat of Paul's day the feet served offensively, and men fought with their feet in conjunction with their hands. So it is with the Christian who will soon crush Satan under his feet. "What a tread we will give him when we once have the opportunity!" Spurgeon shouted. "We shall need to have our feet shod with the preparation of the gospel of peace to break that old dragon's head, and grind his snares to powder, and God helping us, we shall do it." In this we merely follow the lead already given: "Our covenant head has trampled on the old serpent, and so shall all his members."[146]

Because God intended sermons to bolster the tottering soul by means of confident and clear announcement of revealed truth, one cannot fathom the blasphemous incongruity of employing the pulpit for propagating error. The faithless do this purposefully, but the faithful may do it through poor strategy. Promoting unbelief, apart from willful infidelity, may arise two ways from

sermons. Ironically, these two ways stand in tension with each other. They are spoken of in the same article by Spurgeon and he gives no indication that his argument creates a dilemma. First, the minister should avoid the perpetual rehearsal of the theories of unbelief, even when he intends to give a correction. Such an approach, according to Spurgeon, has the tendency to stultify growth and risk some taking the poison but refusing the antidote. Some young men have had their first taste of infidelity from their well-intentioned ministers in such sermons.[147]

Some, therefore, do the devil's work unwittingly; others do it wittingly. Refusal to warn against the witting ones leaves the field open to them. One learns quickly in hearing some men preach that "nothing is certain with them but their own uncertainty." They make doctrines disappear like a conjuror makes animals disappear up a chain suspended on nothing. So-called, deep thinkers have the trick perfected. One end of their thought is suspended in the clouds and up this mental chain they send one doctrine after another to disappear in cloudland. "The doctrine of the substitution of Christ, the immortality of the soul, the plenary inspiration of Scripture, and other eternal verities" magically disappear. To refuse, therefore, to warn against such would be like admiring the rats for their ceaseless energy that undermine a Dutch dike or refusing to arrest a thief because he has such dexterity in his chosen profession. "Bah!" Spurgeon exclaimed.

> We execrate the thief, and with equal justice ought we to expose and to condemn the traitor who robs us of heavenly treasure, of truth vital to eternal life, truth which is absolutely needful to our soul's salvation. Pleas of charity to error are arguments

---

145. Ibid., 504.
146. Ibid., 505.

147. S&T, April 1879, 177. "Peril From the Pulpit."

for the murder of souls. Life and death hang upon the question of truth or falsehood; if lies be propagated, or truth be clouded, the watchmen of the Lord will have to give in their account for permitting it. For our part we shall not cease to warn till the occasion is removed, and at this present time that occasion is by no means gone.[148]

The advice, therefore, to avoid the introduction of heretical ideas in a sermon even to refute them was hard to follow even for Spurgeon himself. If no warnings are issued, infidelity will come full force unhindered; watch dogs must not be muzzled when thieves threaten the family. If warnings are issued, but the preacher offers no description of the error nor any analysis of its content and its consequent danger, he takes the part of a demagogue or a tantalizer. Preaching with both edification and warning is no easy task, but under Spurgeon's expertise, the Tabernacle had learned to appreciate the effort. During the 1879 evangelistic meetings at the Tabernacle, one of the evangelists, Mr. Clarke, was commended by the congregation in that he "smashed into those modern thought fellows."[149]

Preaching: An Extension of the Cross

Preaching garnered the best of Spurgeon's energy and served to deplete him of it more quickly than any other activity, for he embraced it wholeheartedly as the chief means ordained by God to hold forth his glory generation after generation in a fallen world. The greatest historical manifestation of divine glory, so Spurgeon intensely believed, occurred in the cross and resurrection. This redemptive event, however, by its very nature could not be repeated in every generation. "It is finished"—the phrase uttered by Christ that embodies the unique transaction of a satisfied justice—enunciated etymologically, soteriologically, and teleologically a finality, a consummation, to Christ's personal engagement to lose none of those the Father had given him.

The extension of the cross's saving power into succeeding generations and throughout the world sails on the wind and wings of the spoken word, a proclamation setting forth Christ crucified and risen as the object of faith. The preacher, in Pauline fashion, to the spiritual eyes of his auditory clearly portrays Christ as crucified. This proclamation, blessed by the Spirit of God, seals the message in saving power to all types of sinners in all types of places, making them justified citizens of heaven in possession of eternal life and useful agents of holiness and moral change on earth in this life.

Spurgeon, therefore, loved stories of transformation that came from the preaching of the Word. Some of these he heard immediately and some he heard years after the event. They fascinated him. They served as verification of God's call to him and equipping of him in spite of his having missed the academic training seen by many as essential for effective ministry. In addition, however, he believed these stories kept alive in his people a justified wonder at the wisdom of God in using proclamation to transform lives. A church member, on hearing Spurgeon preach on Psalm 57:4, "My soul is among the lions," wrote to Spurgeon and said that his own soul had been among the lions when he owned and operated a beerhouse. Hearing Spurgeon preach made him close the beerhouse on Sundays "in spite of great opposition, persecution, and personal loss." On one occasion the devil had tempted him to open again on Sunday, but "Christ gained the victory, and enabled me to close ever afterwards on

---

148. Ibid.
149. Ibid., 196.

the Sunday." His policy of closing began on the same Sunday that the Tabernacle opened.[150]

Sometimes, the effectiveness of Spurgeon's preaching was doubled by publicizing its effects in tract form. A tract entitled "The Fox Hunter" told of a young man that rode sixteen miles on horseback to hear Spurgeon preach. He had become burdened after reading a sign that quoted "Prepare to Meet Thy God." An advertisement of Spurgeon's appearance at a certain place prompted the journey; it was not disappointing. Spurgeon preached on the text, "Come unto me, all ye that labour and are heavy laden, and I will give you rest." At the close he said, "Doubtless, there are some young men before me who are weighed down with sin and misery, and wanting rest." While saying this Spurgeon pointed at one and then another in his audience, and began asking "Have you tried the blood, brother? Have your tried the blood? The blood of Jesus Christ which cleanseth us from all sin." The tract writer, Cheyne Brady, told that the "conscience-stricken sinner was melted under this appeal." Convinced of his status as a sinner, feeling that he deserved eternal death, he was enabled to see the remedy for his sin and uncleanness, the precious blood of Jesus Christ. He believed and left the chapel a new man in Christ. This report gave special pleasure to Spurgeon, for not only did it show that preaching was blessed with conversion, but the example of the conversion would now become a force in itself for the conviction of others. Preaching continued to preach through the literature it produced.

Stories of success showed the overall view that Spurgeon had of God's intent to use preaching as the primary means of calling his elect. He believed that ministers of the gospel should preach with expectation. He often would indicate in the body of a sermon that he expected salvation to come to some of his hearers in that very hour. This confidence lies behind the event frequently related in which T. W. Medhurst came to Spurgeon with distress over the fact that, at one point in his early ministry, little fruit seemed to come from his preaching. For three months he had labored without a conversion. As W. Y. Fullerton tells it, Spurgeon responded, "Why, you don't expect conversions every time you open your mouth, do you?" Medhurst responded, "Of course not." "Then that is just the reason you haven't had them," Spurgeon responded.[151]

G. Holden Pike, writing for *The Sword and the Trowel* gave a slightly different turn to the conversation. When Medhurst visited Spurgeon's home at 75 Dover Road, Spurgeon asked him how he was getting on, to which he answered, "Well, I don't know, sir, I'm afraid I have made a mistake." When Spurgeon asked his meaning, he responded, "Well, I've been preaching for six or seven months and have not heard of any conversions." "You don't expect conversions *every* time you preach, do you?" "No, I don't expect them every time." "Then be it to you according to your faith," answered Mr. Spurgeon. "If you expect great things from God you'll get them; if you don't, you won't." Pike then summarized the impact of the interview: "These words left an indelible impression on the mind of the student. He is able to say at the present time that he has never since that day preached without expecting a blessing; and the blessing has come according to his faith."[152]

Spurgeon did not always give such intimidating instruction, however, and perhaps as his

---

150. S&T, October 1879, 497.

151. W. Y. Fullerton, *C. H. Spurgeon: Biography* (London: Williams & Norgate, 1920), 232f.

152. G. Holden Pike, "The Work of the Pastors' College," S&T, January 1879, 12.

years passed he understood better the uniqueness of his personal experience of ministry. Revival fervor consistently surrounded his pulpit operation even when he was sick and distressed and undone, even when he personally could give no personal attention to those awakened under his public proclamation. "I have often been surprised at the mercy of God to myself. Poor sermons of mine, that I could cry over when I get home, have led scores to the cross," Spurgeon testified. Beyond that, "words that I have spoken in ordinary conversation, mere chance sentences, as men call them, have nevertheless been as winged arrows from God, and have pierced men's hearts, and laid them wounded at Jesus' feet." So remarkable had been the consistent success of Spurgeon that he stated, "I have often lifted up my hands in astonishment, and said, 'How can God bless such a feeble instrumentality?'"[153]

Spurgeon himself admitted, however, that he had gone from flying to running, and receded yet to a steadier pace. He did not strike fire with every sermon but saw the pace slacken. "We do not every day draw the net to land full of great fishes, but we experience dreary intervals of fruitless toil, and then it is no wonder that a man's spirit faints within him." So it will be with his college men, particularly those in much slimmer ponds than London. "In a small town or village, a man may soon have done all his direct converting work if the Lord greatly blesses him, and if, after a time, more souls are not saved, it may be because few unconverted persons attend his ministry." All this is under the direction of divine sovereignty for "God may have given the brother all those whom He intended to bless by him in that place."[154]

For others, such consistent blessing might not attend their ministry, but some encouragements would certainly come. To his prayer meeting in 1881 Spurgeon shared a story that he had just learned about Medhurst. He preached in the open air on one occasion in Glasgow. He saw no fruit from the preaching. One lady, however, just passing by heard a part of his message, came under conviction, was converted later, went to her dying sister and won her to Christ, and then herself became a Bible woman with a regular route of distribution where she led many to Christ. Spurgeon drew the conclusion, "Do not think when you preach at the street corners that you will at once see the harvest of your seed-sowing, although the Lord may so favour you." Quite a contrast to his earlier words to Medhurst, he continued, "If you see no immediate results your labour may, nevertheless, have been owned of God." He was quite sure that Medhurst had not heard of that remotely-wrought success, but perhaps now he would. His personal knowledge of it, however, is a small matter "for the deed is done, heaven is enriched, and God is glorified."[155]

Another more nuanced and patient understanding of success, without surrendering expectation, Spurgeon developed in a lecture on "The Soul Winner's Reward."[156] "I believe that most of you, who have really tried, in the power of the Holy Spirit, by Scriptural teaching and by prayer, to bring others to Jesus, have been successful." Conceding, however, that some present "have not succeeded" he had some patient and loving words for them.

I would recommend them to look steadily over their motive, their spirit, their work, and their

---

153. Charles Spurgeon, *The Soul Winner* (New York: Fleming H. Revell, 1895), 193.

154. *An All Round Ministry*, 132f.

155. S&T, March 1881, 121f. "Encouragement to Street Preachers."

156. *The Soul Winner*, 192f.

prayer, and then begin again. Perhaps they may get to work more wisely, more believingly, more humbly, and more in the power of the Holy Spirit. They just act as farmers do who, after a poor harvest, plough again in hope. They ought not to be dispirited, but they ought to be aroused. We should be anxious to find out the reason of failure, if there be any, and we should be ready to learn from all our fellow-labourers; but we must steadfastly set our faces, if by any means we may save some, resolving that whatever happens we will leave no stone unturned to effect the salvation of those around us. How can we bear to go out of the world without sheaves to bear with us rejoicingly?[157]

Spurgeon saw the situation with even greater gravity, and with a halt in his former confidence, as he surveyed the rapid and pervasive decline in doctrine and piety in the churches. "Compared with what it used to be," Spurgeon noted, "it is hard to win attention to the word of God." He explained further, "I used to think that we had only to preach the gospel, and the people would throng to hear it. I fear I must correct my belief under this head." He had no reason to doubt the attractiveness of the gospel, but he found that "a hardening process is going on among the masses." He did not doubt that "some of my brethren, who faithfully preach the gospel of Christ, do not find the people flocking about them." With this situation prevailing, Spurgeon refocused on the point that something more compelling than conversion drove the preaching task. "We do not regard it as our first business to convert sinners, nor to edify saints; but to glorify God." God Himself makes the preaching event an exercise in infinite satisfaction to Himself irrespective of the response of the hearer. "If we have preached God's truth, and on any one occasion no souls have been saved

thereby, we are still 'unto God a sweet savour of Christ' as well in those that perish as in those that are saved." Preach on, even in the absence of immediate visible response, Spurgeon would now advise, and find reason to rejoice in it for "the preaching of Jesus Christ is the burning of sweet odours before the throne of God, and to the Lord it is evermore an acceptable oblation."[158]

Even with the amended understanding that success sometimes will be secret, delayed, and not in the same proportion to one's work as that of another, Spurgeon remained convinced that a call to the ministry of preaching meant a call to see fruit. A call to be fishers of men is a promise that fish will be caught. Lack of success may point to a worldly life more intent on amusement and pleasure than on the riches of fellowship with Christ and the joy of being his disciples. It might point to faultiness in doctrine or lack of prayer. Repentance and amendments would be in order, yea essential, mandated by the disparity between the call and the fruit. So certain was he of eventual success that he was willing to state categorically, "He that never saved a sinner after years of work is not a minister of Christ." In Pauline fashion, again he said, "If the result of his life-work is nil, he made a mistake when he undertook it."[159]

But to resort to sensationalism to draw a crowd, or "attract a congregation," Spurgeon could not abide. Though early in his ministry in a hyperbolic moment he told a crowd in Scotland that he would stand on his head if it would help draw a sinner to Christ, he receded from that position. Though some might feel at ease in conscience about using brass bands and tambourines and all sort of noise to draw a crowd, such users should be prepared for the eventual failure of these methods and the necessity to become more

---

157. Ibid., 193.

158. *An All round Ministry*, 297, 299.

159. *The Soul Winner*, 293.

sensational. "What else is to be done?" he asked. "Will you stand on your head: Hornpipes have been tried; will you try the tight-rope? I cannot suggest to you a novelty—since we have already heard of Brummagem Bruisers, devil-dodgers, converted clog-dancers etc." Eventually such a method must decline to "those blasphemous insults in the eternal and incommunicable name which arise out of the desecration of the word 'hallelujah.'" Spurgeon suggested a true novelty—a meeting with no vulgarity and no slang. He also wearied of sensational advertising that led people on with the promise of greatness and rare opportunity. "Cheapjack advertising is altogether out of harmony with the grand truths and the glorious spirit of the gospel."[160]

The Sum of it All

Spurgeon by no means desired empty pews, but still held to the conviction that nothing was of greater interest than pure earnest gospel preaching. "I believe that the best, surest, and most permanent way to fill a place of worship is to preach the gospel, and to preach it in a natural, simple interesting, earnest way." The gospel possessed a singularly fascinating power and "unless impeded by an unworthy delivery or by some other great evil, it will win its own way."[161] Spurgeon then gave encouragement by a description of frequently-visited themes—the character of naturalness, simplicity, creation of interest, and, finally, downright earnestness. Resorting to his own experience as evidence, Spurgeon recommended the glorious themes of covenant theology as the true content that will never lose its appeal to fill the house.

Thirty years of crowded houses leave me confident of the attractions of divine truth; I see nothing as yet to make me doubt its sufficiency for its own propagation. Shorn of its graciousness, robbed of its certainty, spoiled of its peculiarities, the sacred word may become unattractive; but decked in the glories of free and sovereign grace, wearing the crown-royal of the covenant, and the purple of atonement, the gospel, like a queen, is still glorious for beauty, supreme over hearts and minds. Published in all its fullness, with a clear statement of its efficacy and immutability, it is still the most acceptable news that ever reached the ears of mortals. You shall not in my most despondent moments convince me that our Lord was mistaken when he said, "I, if I be lifted up, will draw all men unto me."[162]

To Spurgeon, naught else was preaching.

160. S&T, August 1883, 418-19.

161. Ibid., 421.
162. Ibid., 422.

5

THEOLOGICAL METHOD AND CONTENT

I would have every Christian wish to know all that he can know of revealed truth.[1]

The book is a divine production; it is perfect, and is the last court of appeal—"the judge which ends the strife." I would as soon dream of blaspheming my Maker as of questioning the infallibility of his word.[2]

Are the doctrines of grace essential verities with thee? Whatever God has said about sin, righteousness, judgment to come, art thou ready to accept it at once. Whatever he has revealed concerning himself, his Son, his holy Spirit, the cross, life, death, hell, and the eternal future, dost thou believe it unfeignedly: This is to walk in the light. All other teaching is darkness.[3]

Two traits of theological engagement that Spurgeon admired and sought to inculcate in his own extensive opportunities often seemed to conflict with each other. Both of these appear on the same page of book reviews in the April 1880 number of *The Sword and the Trowel*. One was kindness and the other was plainness. He commended Joseph Cook's discussion of transcendentalism with the words, "There is not trace of bitterness, however, in him, no mark of that savage Red Indian ferocity which is so usual in a theological debater."[4] One column later Spurgeon gave advice concerning "one of the most poetic, beautiful, pseudo-philosophical books on the Fatherhood of God which we ever read." Noting that it was altogether subversive of the truth of Man's ruin, redemption, and regeneration, he gave a recipe for its proper use. It is like preparing a cucumber: "Carefully peel and slice it, flavour with pepper, salt, and vinegar, and then—eat it?— oh no! *throw it on the dung hill.*"[5] Kindness can be interpreted as toleration, and plainness can be interpreted as unkindness, but they need not be antagonistic. In the execution of Christian theology, however, these boon companions must be kept aligned with arms locked together as they stride toward purity in thought and life. The Christian theologian must be clearly Christian and no less clear a theologian.

Whatever else he was, Spurgeon was a Christian theologian, and, preeminently as a "Pastor/ Theologian," he must covet the rightness of both the head and the heart of his people. For him the only true theology was a fully Christian theology and any attempt to gain a hearing by stopping short of a fully evangelical presentation of

---

1. MTP, 1891, 319
2. S&T, March 1874, 103.
3. MTP, 1887, 558.
4. S&T, April 1880, 187.
5. Ibid.

the gospel, even in apologetic situations, was a betrayal of the call of the Christian.

Going for the Jugular

"That department of polite literature called Natural Religion leads nowhere and profiteth nothing," Spurgeon maintained. An apologetic attempt by R. A. Redford in *The Christian's Pleas Against Modern Unbelief* failed in the lead task of making a truly Christian plea, Spurgeon pointed out. Redford made a noble attempt to create a neutral intellectual position by breaking down the citadel of objections in order to show that theism, the possibility of revelation, the existence of the miraculous, and other foundational issues were not irrational positions. "Our author imagines," Spurgeon observed, "that *simple theism* may become an adytum to the inner sanctuary of more select evidences." In his attempt to tear down the *negative* he has made a fundamental error by omitting an aggressive proposal of the *positive*. Spurgeon believed this approach mistakenly assumes that the philosophical argument for *possibilities* creates *receptivity*. Spurgeon was skeptical of the method and felt that best approach was always an insistence on the full package of the gospel. Bare theism and natural theology filled the air "with volatile sentiment, and expresses itself in lackadaisical phrases about 'the benevolence of the Creator,' 'the beauty of his works,' or 'the traces of design that are scattered through the universe.'" Such affirmations are a "paltry subterfuge" when what such poor souls need is saving faith; no good comes from dalliance with their prejudices.

Spurgeon, therefore, believing that it was preposterous for a Christian minister to plead with an infidel to become a theist, proposed a more robust and aggressive approach to dealing with "Modern Unbelief." His first postulate was, "He that cometh to God must believe that he is, and

that he is a rewarder of them that diligently seek him." The second was, "He that believeth in God must accept Christ as a mediator." The third continued, "He that accepteth the one mediator between God and men must receive the atonement." Any method that encourages less leaves a person with no reason to rejoice in God or sing praises to him with spirit and understanding. Apologetic methods that focused on creating neutrality and failed to embrace the full presentation of the gospel would be like trying to solve a crime problem by "intreating burglars not to carry fire-arms."[6]

Spurgeon wanted no theology or apologetic that was not fully Christian and eschewed any method of presentation intended to bring unbelievers only half way to truth. Such methods tended toward the opinion that openness to theism constituted right standing before God. The cure for limp and languid convictions on theology was a good soaking in the reality of one's own sin, a perception of the "sovereignty of divine grace, a participation in the renewing work of the Holy Ghost, and an abundant entrance into that life which deals with spiritual and eternal verities." Theology was not just a right head, much less a half-right head, but a healed heart. Without that, "savage orthodoxy usually begets a frivolous unbelief."[7]

A Fully and Exclusively Biblical Theology

Spurgeon was, nevertheless, fully in favor of apologetic works that aimed at disproving the validity of attacks, either direct or indirect, on the inspiration of Scripture. All parts of the Bible had been "vigourously assailed" at some time, but great powers of faith and ability had come to its defence and "left it more confirmed than before." Luthardt's defense of the Johannine authorship

---

6. S&T, November 1881, 582.

7. S&T, January 1883, 28.

of the fourth Gospel was worthy of the immense labor it involved in its establishment of the authenticity of the history of that book. All biblical students should be grateful to such defenders of the faith for "an attack upon the outworks of inspiration is aimed in reality at the citadel itself." Zeal for one must accompany zeal for the other.[8]

Spurgeon had a robust appreciation for the science of textual criticism. He knew that copyists of the various manuscripts had made several different types of errors—"minor errors of copyists"[9] —and investigated the work of such men as B. F. Westcott and F. J. A. Hort.[10] "It is of no small consequence for us to be as clear as possible," Spurgeon affirmed, "about the validity of the original tongue in which revelation was given."[11] Also, the work at recovering the original text, in light of the minor discrepancies between manuscripts, was welcome. "Provided we have an exact text," Spurgeon asserted, "we regard the words themselves as infallible."[12] Since Protestants have no magisterium standing between them and the text of Scripture, since "You and I find our anchorage in the infallibility of Scripture," and "we believe that every word of it is inspired," we have abundant confidence "that if we could get absolutely the exact words in which it was written at the first, we should have a book as perfect, certain, and immutable as God himself."[13] Textual criticism was moving close to that reality and had showed that the critical mass of Scripture was indisputably authentic textually.

Spurgeon advocated a pure Biblicism for theological construction. He loved the historic confessions and the pious and helpful writings of the Reformers and Puritans as well as selected numbers from the early Fathers and even some medieval writers, such as Bernard of Clairvaux, but all of these edified only to the degree that they opened to the mind that which already abided in scriptural revelation. Theology certainly is not new; nor has it been the product of tradition or development. One must "Ask for the Old Paths" for "the infallible Word of God is older than the supposed infallible pope." The priesthood of believers antedates the "priestcraft of the clergy," while "the epistles are older than the thirty-nine articles." God's true church is older "than any one of the sects." Lovers of antiquity must assure that their "antiquity is antiquity. Let the old be old enough."[14]

He believed, confirming the position of Robert Rainy, that the Scripture contained a perfect system "gradually developed in the Old Testament, and speedily completed in the New." When Rainy, however, filled out this biblical system with doctrinal developments in church history and the discoveries of modern times, and pointed to the "corporate teaching capacity" of the church, Spurgeon resisted. He knew of no corporate church and thus of no such teaching capacity. We may gain assistance through others that interpret Scripture doctrines, but no addition to the doctrines themselves may be allowed. "Development of Christian doctrine in the Scriptures is one thing, and the development of those doctrines after the completion of the Scriptures is another."[15]

These things should not be confounded. Christian doctrine, to the degree that God wants us to know, has mature development in Scripture. Neither individual theologian nor church corpo-

8. S&T, January 1876, 44.

9. S&T, April 1882, 162.

10. S&T, October 1882, 545.

11. S&T, September 1882, 494.

12. S&T, March 1874, 103.

13. S&T, April 1882, 162.

14. S&T, March 1879. "Incidents of Travel Clustering Around a Text," 107.

15. S&T, January 1876, 44.

rate may add to, diminish, amend, or dilute by false synthesis any assertion of the biblical text. We may find a way to give clear teaching on a variety of subjects and seek to show their mature biblical development and relations, and we may surely benefit from the way Christians through the ages have formulated these biblical truths and their practical applications; any effort, however, to go beyond the biblical text and its own internal development perverts the truth. "Fathers, schoolmen, reformers, Puritans, bishops, and even ecclesiastical courts are nothing in comparison with this oracle of God."[16]

For example, his treatment of indwelling sin and the enmity of the carnal mind against God focuses immediately on the text of Scripture. His knowledge of confessional statements and Puritan development of this idea was profound, but he wanted to draw his people into a square confrontation with the biblical text—"Let us, then weigh the words of the text, for they are solemn words, they are well put together by that master of eloquence, Paul, and they were moreover, dictated by the Holy Spirit, who telleth man how to speak aright. May he help us to expound, as he has given us the passage to explain."[17]

Likewise, in a sermon on the Lord's Supper, Spurgeon noted the changes made in it by Rome and said, "Let us be warned by these mistakes of others never either to add to or take from the Word of God so much as a single jot or title. Keep upon the foundation of the Scriptures, and you stand safely." An allowance of personal notions, whims, or fancies to determine "what is proper and right," instead of Scripture "and you have entered upon a dangerous course," that will result in mischief. "The Bible is our standard authority; none may turn from it."[18]

In the Inaugural Address at the Pastors' College Conference 1881, Spurgeon spoke of the necessity of fixity of belief. One's belief system must not look like an Italian peasant's garment, a marvel of patches pieced together in all kinds of patterns and colors accumulated from generation to generation. So are the creeds of some, "an agglomeration of philosophic rags, metaphysical tatters, theological remnants, and heretical cast-offs." But the preacher must believe that "when the Lord our God gave forth a revelation he knew his own mind, and that he expressed himself in the best and wisest manner, and in terms that can be understood by those who are teachable and truthful." God's revelation came with its own determined fullness and no new revelation is needed. An expectation of further revelation or inspired development is practical unbelief. Though sacrilegious hands twist and turn the Bible, "it is still the infallible revelation of God." Our religion is determined on the humble acceptance of what God has revealed with no additions or subtractions. Given all that is involved in human blindness to spiritual things, and our absolute dependence on divine grace for the content and grace of faith, Spurgeon proposed that "the highest form of adoration possible on this side the veil is the bowing of our entire mental and spiritual being before the revealed mind of God," that is, "the kneeling of the understanding in that sacred presence whose glory causes angels to veil their faces." Others may worship science, reason, and their own clear judgments, but the God we worship is the God of Scripture.[19]

As Spurgeon summarized the religious and philosophical commitments of cultures in the past and their virtual unintelligibility and complete obscurity today, he reflected that today's

16. S&T, April 1882, 163.

17. SS, 1:233

18. SEE, 10:307-08. "Christ and His Table Companions."

19. S&T, July 1881, 347.

systems that sought to render noxious any claim to supernatural revelation would likewise soon be mere curiosities. But the Bible, God's revelation, would still rule over minds and hearts as surely as Christ himself would rule. "For as surely as this book is the infallible word of God, so surely must Christ win the day."[20]

Human systems, no matter how aggressively they ridicule systems of revelation, especially the Bible, and no matter how tightly they argue their system or highly they value their insight, soon pass and are merely intellectual curiosities. "Systems of infidelity pass away like a dew-drop before the sun," Spurgeon reminded his simple hearers. But the Bible, the book that expresses the mind of the only and eternal God, "is the stone that shall break in powder philosophy; this is the mighty battering ram that shall dash all systems of philosophy in pieces; this is the stone that a woman may yet hurl upon the head of every Abimelech, and he shall utterly be destroyed."[21] Not only shall all false systems finally fail, and God's Word alone remain, yet even while they prevail temporarily, they destroy all that comes under their power. France in 1797 demonstrated the terror of living under a godless, Bible-less system. "The gospel of Pandemonium brought forth its Millennium, and anarchy created upon earth the express likeness of hell. If you would settle the pillars of order upon the basis of liberty, let the word of God be in the hands of all your citizens."[22]

Knowledge of God in its specific saving character so far exceeded the limits of human philosophy and reason that all systems must give way to the inexhaustible wonder of divine revelation. Nothing exceeded in importance the knowledge and nothing about the knowledge was more vital

than a vision of God's glory in the provisions of the gospel. "In vain dost thou jeer and mock, for eternal verities are mightier than thy sophistries, nor can thy smart saying alter the divine truth of a single word of this volume of Revelation."[23]

The way Spurgeon related ideas of biblical fullness and historical systematization served as a foundation for his criticism of R. W. Dale's *Laws of Christ for Common Life*. Spurgeon questioned, if not the candor, at least the relevancy of Dale's approach in his statement, "A man may believe in the Nicene Creed, and in the Creed attributed to Athanasius, or in the confession of Augsburgh, or the confession of the Westminster divines; but if he does not believe in the Sermon of the Mount—believe it seriously as containing the laws which must govern his own life—he has denied the faith, and is in revolt against Christ."[24] Spurgeon considered such paragraphs to assert a "vicious irrelevancy," of the nature of asking if a person preferred Jotham's parable in the book of Judges to Calvin's *Institutes*. The inference drawn from this contrived comparison amounts to a discrediting of the "choicest standards of orthodoxy." Spurgeon asked pointedly if Dale were revolting against all creeds including those "ancient Catholic Creeds, which sound Protestants, with one consent, were willing to accept."

As for his own part Spurgeon was jealous for such ancient landmarks, and believed that Dale's resistance to the imposition of any creed on the ministers or members of the Congregational churches could only lead to fragmentation and eventual decline as a force for truth and godliness. "What can you expect if you lack any element of cohesion"? How all of this confessional concern relates to biblical authority Spurgeon revealed when he put forward another inquiry that

---

20. S&T, February 1882, 50.

21. SS, 1:9, "Sovereignty and Salvation."

22. S&T, April 1882, 164–65.

23. SS, 1:42, "The Bible."

24. S&T, May 1885, 238.

he felt equally pertinent to Dale's strange proposition. "Why put forward an early discourse of our blessed Redeemer before he had set forth the full purpose of Redemption," Spurgeon queried, "or ever he said, 'The good Shepherd lays down his life for the sheep'—as if the Sermon on the Mount is to be accounted a complete body of divinity?"[25]

Dale's failure at the confessional level extended from an interpretive method that pushed him into misapplication and disfigurement of biblical truth. If one does not see the moral teaching of Christ in light of his redemptive work and his own humanity's dependence on divine grace, then Dale's supposed preference of the words of Christ to the words of a creed is not that at all—rather, it amounts to a preference of one's own narrow idiosyncratic creed to the confession of the church at large through the centuries. Which of these actually presents the greatest faithfulness to the Bible?

Loved With Everlasting Love

Spurgeon, therefore, looked at the meaning of all texts as expressive as one part of the larger biblical synthesis of meaning. The synthesis that satisfied Spurgeon's overall grasp of biblical teaching was covenant theology. "The subject is the basis of all theology, and ought to be a chief point of study among believers," he contended.[26] This idea he found perhaps the single most encouraging concept in the Bible. He began a sermon entitled "The Wondrous Covenant" with the words, "The doctrine of the divine covenant lies at the root of all true theology."[27] A preacher who grasps and maintains clarity on the distinctions within the covenant is a master of divinity. "I am persuaded," he affirmed, "that most of the mistakes which men make concerning the doctrines of Scripture are based upon fundamental errors with regard to the covenants of law and of grace."[28] Novelty in doctrine is not needful and may be fatal, he wrote to his American audience. "I have preached what I believed and delighted in," he told them, "and all my hopes for time and eternity rest in that everlasting covenant of grace which from my youth up has been my theme.

In "The Blood of the Everlasting Covenant," Spurgeon asserted that every relation we have with God has a covenant character and "that he will not deal with us except through a covenant, nor can we deal with him except in the same manner."[29] He described the covenant of grace as "made before the foundation of the world between God the Father and God the Son; or to put it in a yet more scriptural light, it was made mutually between the three divine persons of the adorable Trinity." In this covenant "Christ stood ... as man's representative." Though individual men would benefit personally from this arrangement, no individual man stood as a party to the arrangement. "It was a covenant between God with Christ, and through Christ indirectly with all the blood-bought seed who were loved of Christ from the foundation of the world."[30] The power of Spurgeon's theological conceptions and the joy of preaching consisted in grasping and conveying a clear vision of this divine initiative.

It is a noble and glorious thought, the very poetry of that old Calvinistic doctrine which we teach, that long ere the day-star knew its place, before God had spoken existence out of nothing, before angel's wing had stirred the unnavigated ether, before a solitary song had distributed the solemnity of the silence in which God reigned

---

25. Ibid.

26. S&T, June 1878, 312.

27. SEE, 5:449.

28. Ibid.

29. CHS, "The Blood of the Everlasting Covenant," in *Revival Year Sermons*, 36; SS, 6:212.

30. SS, 6:215.

supreme, he had entered into solemn council with himself, with his Son, and with his Spirit, and had in that council decreed, determined, proposed, and predestinated the salvation of his people. He had, moreover, in the covenant arranged the ways and means, and fixed and settled everything which should work together for the effecting of the purpose and the decree.[31]

Founded in the mysteries of eternal love, the perfect bond of unity within the triune God flung itself outward to bring in creatures for the enjoyment of that same love. Some among the sinful race of man, distinguished from others only by the words of Jehovah, "I have loved thee with an everlasting love," would have given to them every blessing that can flow from this infinite omnipotent love. That first blessing and the one that determined the necessary existence of all others flowed from the Father's selection in predestination.

> Long before those stars were kindled into flames— long before the sun begun his mighty course— long before the mountains lifted their hoary heads, or the deep clapped its hands in the tumultuous joy of tempest. Long before time began, or space was created, God had written upon His heart the names of His elect people. He had selected them, never to change His choice. He had united them unto the Person of His Son Jesus Christ by a Divine Decree never to be revoked. He had predestinated them to be conformed unto the image of His Son and had made them the heirs of all the fullness of His love, His Grace and His Glory.[32]

Within the framework of the covenant, originating in predestinating love, Spurgeon found his only source for the encouragement of Chris-

tians; his understanding of the gospel was built on covenant theology; all of God's actions toward creation, sin, redemption, providence, and final consummation were built on the covenant; his own exhilarating spiritual experiences flowed from lengthy meditation on the eternal and sure provisions of the covenant. "My soul flies back now, winged by imagination and by faith, and looks into that mysterious council-chamber, and by faith I behold the Father pledging himself to the Son, and the Son pledging himself to the Father, while the Spirit gives his pledge to both, and thus that divine compact, long to be hidden in darkness, is completed and settled—the covenant which in these latter days has been read in the light of heaven, and has become the joy, and hope, and boast of all the saints."[33] The sweetest consolation for the despondent saint comes in reflection on the everlasting covenant, an understanding of "what God did for us in past times." Nothing can give joy to the spirit and steel to the soul like a song of "electing love and covenanted mercies." When you are low, Spurgeon advised, it is well to sing of "the fountain-head of mercy," the "blessed decree wherein thou wast ordained to eternal life, and of that glorious Man who undertook thy redemption."[34] To see the "solemn covenant signed, and sealed, and ratified, in all things ordered well," reflecting that one is an object of eternal electing love, is a "charming means of giving thee songs in the night."[35]

For the sake of planting the reality of the covenant firmly in the minds of his people, Spurgeon loved to set it forth as a discussion between the persons of the triune God, though he knew clearly that he could not tell it "in the glorious celestial tongue in which it was written" but would "bring

---

31. Ibid.
32. SEE, 2:409; MTP, 1864, 207.

33. SS, 6:215.
34. SS, 2:173.
35. SS, 2:173-74.

it down to the speech which suiteth to the ear of flesh, and to the heart of a mortal."[36] The substance was the same in each successive libretto, though the exact words differed in accordance with context. In "The Gracious Lips of Jesus," a sermon preached around 1857, Spurgeon said, "When God the Father originally made the covenant, it stood somewhat in this form."

> My Son, thou desirest, and I agree with thee, to save a number, that no man can number, whom I have elected in thee. But in order to their salvation, that I may be just, and yet the justifier of the ungodly, it is necessary that some one should be their representative, to stand responsible for their obedience to my laws and their substitute to suffer whatever penalties they incur. If thou, my Son, wilt stipulate to bear their punishment, and endure the penalty of their crimes, I on my part will stipulate that thou shalt see thy seed, shalt prolong they days, and that the pleasure of the Lord shall prosper in thy hands. If thou to-day art prepared to promise that thou wilt bear the exact punishment of all the people whom thou wouldst save, I on my part am prepared to swear by myself, because I can swear by no greater, that all for whom thou shalt atone shall infallibly be delivered from death and hell, and that all for whom thou bearest the punishment shall hence go free, nor shall my wrath rise against them, however great may be their sins.[37]

The conversation continued with an appropriately worded response from the Son in scriptural language, "I delight to do thy will, O my God." On the basis of that covenantal arrangement all the saints were justified in the mind of God prior to the shedding of one drop of the Redeemer's blood. "The surety's oath was quite enough; in the Father's ears there needed no other confirmation," for by his Son's oath, the Father's heart was satisfied. His Son had sworn to his own hurt and would not change.[38]

Another of these dialogues constructed by Spurgeon included the stipulations made by the Spirit, as well as the agreement entered into by Father and Son. The Father and the Spirit carried one side of the covenant, and the Son the other. The Son carried the side that related to man while the Father and Spirit, in ways appropriate to each, pledged to honor the work of the Son on behalf of man. He imagined the Father speaking thus:

> I, the Most High Jehovah, do hereby give unto my only begotten and well-beloved Son, a people, countless beyond the number of stars, who shall be by him washed from sin, by him preserved, and kept, and led, and by him, at last, presented before my throne, without spot, or wrinkle, or any such thing. I covenant by oath, and swear by myself, because I can swear by no greater, that these whom I now give to Christ shall be for ever the objects of my eternal love. Them I will forgive through the merit of the blood. To these will I give a perfect righteousness; these will I adopt and make my sons and daughters, and these shall reign with me through Christ eternally.

In the same vein he envisions the Spirit, in viewing how the Father had given a people to the Son, joined in full harmony with these words:

> I hereby covenant that all whom the Father giveth to the Son, I will in due time quicken. I will show them their need of redemption; I will cut off from them all groundless hope, and destroy their refuges of lies. I will bring them to the blood of sprinkling; I will give them faith whereby this blood shall be applied to them, I will work in them every grace;

---

36. SS, 6:216.

37. SS, 4:97.

38. SS, 4:98.

I will keep their faith alive; I will cleanse them and drive out all depravity from them, and they shall be presented at last spotless and faultless.

That pledge in the covenant presently is operative, being scrupulously kept.

Christ himself then took the other side as the representative of the people, and covenanted with his Father:

> My Father, on my part I covenant that in the fullness of time I will become man. I will take upon myself the form and nature of the fallen race. I will live in their wretched world, and for my people I will keep the law perfectly. I will work out a spotless righteousness, which shall be acceptable to the demands of thy just and holy law. In due time I will bear the sins of all my people. Thou shalt exact their debts on me; the chastisement of their peace I will endure, and by my stripes they shall be healed. My Father, I covenant and promise that I will be obedient unto death, even the death of the cross. I will magnify thy law, and make it honourable. I will suffer all they ought to have suffered. I will endure the curse of thy law, and all the vials of thy wrath shall be emptied and spent upon my head. I will then rise again; I will ascend into heaven; I will intercede for them at thy right hand; and I will make myself responsible for every one of them, that not one of those whom thou hast given me shall ever be lost, but I will bring all my sheep of whom, by thy blood, thou hast constituted me the shepherd—I will bring every one safe to thee at last.[39]

On the side of the Son, the covenant is perfectly fulfilled. Only now he continues to intercede to bring all his blood-bought ones safely to glory.

Given the reality that all things are included in this covenant, should a sinner come to be sure of just one part of it, then he may assume that all

of it is his. All parts of it stand or fall together, for the one true God, the triune Jehovah has pledged as a manifestation of his own glory, faithfulness, and truth to accomplish every part of it—nothing of all events and things can be omitted from the provisions of this covenant because creation, providence, and redemption all serve its end. Thus if the most lowly and meek of sinners can be assured of forgiveness, he can be denied nothing from the eternal bounties of divine mercies or the temporal goodness of his providence. "When I know I am pardoned, then I can say all things are mine."[40] Spurgeon exuded an exhausting amount of spiritual energy on this point and stretched his gifts to the limit in emphasizing it.

> I can look back to the dark past—all things are mine there! I can look at the present—all things are mine here! I can look into the deep future—all things are mine there! Back in eternity, I see God unrolling the mighty volume, and lo! In that volume I read my name. It must be there, for I am pardoned; for whom he calls, he had first predestinated, and whom he pardons, he had first elected. When I see that covenant roll, I say, It is mine! And all the great books of eternal purposes and infinite decrees are mine! And what Christ did upon the cross is mine![41]

Spurgeon continued in an unrestrained accounting of all the things that the pardoned person could count as his on the basis of the unity and immutability of the covenant. On he went through the list, giving some indications as to the purpose of each gift contained in the covenant of grace. All the wheels and circumstances of providence, afflictions, prosperity, all the promises of the Bible, the future of the earth's dissolving in a great conflagration, the great judgment, the river

---

39. NPSP, 1859, 417ff. SS, 1:216-17.

40. SS, 4:65.

41. Ibid.

of death, the resurrection, and heaven—all belong to the pardoned sinner. "What though there be palaces there of crystal and of gold, that sparkle so as to dim mortal eyes; what though there be delights above even the dream of the voluptuary; what though there be pleasures which heart and flesh could not conceive, and which even spirit itself can not fully enjoy the very intoxication of bliss; what though there be sublimities unlawful for us to utter, and wonders which mortal men can not grasp; what though the Divinity hath spent itself in heaven, and doth unravel his glory to make his people blessed—all is mine!"[42] The covenant not only served as the basis for coherent theological construction, but embraced every point of the shield of faith wherewith one could quench all the fiery darts of the evil one.

In his devotional study *Morning and Evening* the covenantal arrangements of the triune God consistently make their way into the text. For example, on December 26 for the morning Spurgeon wrote:

Jesus is the federal head of his elect. As in Adam, every heir of flesh and blood has a personal interest, because he is the covenant head and representative of the race as considered under the law of works; so under the law of grace, every redeemed soul is one with the Lord from heaven, since he is the Second Adam, the Sponsor and Substitute of the elect in the new covenant of love. The apostle Paul declares that Levi was in the loins of Abraham when Melchizedek met him: it is a certain truth that the believer was in the loins of Jesus Christ, the Mediator, when in old eternity the covenant settlements of grace were decreed, ratified, and made sure forever. Thus, whatever Christ hath done, he hath wrought for the whole body of his Church. We were crucified in him and buried with him (read Col. 2:10-13) and to make

it still more wonderful, we are risen with him and even ascended with him to the seats on high (Eph. 2:6). It is thus that the Church has fulfilled the law, and is "accepted *in the beloved*." It is thus that she is regarded with complacency by the just Jehovah, for he views her in Jesus, and does not look upon her as separate from her covenant head. As the Anointed Redeemer of Israel, Christ Jesus has nothing distinct from his Church, but all that he has he holds for her. Adam's righteousness was ours so long as he maintained it, and his sin was ours the moment that he committed it; and in the same manner, all that the Second Adam is or does, is ours as well as his, seeing that he is our representative. Here is the foundation of the covenant of grace. This gracious system of representation and substitution, which moved Justin Martyr to cry out, "O blessed change, O sweet permutation!" this is the very groundwork of the gospel of our salvation, and is to be received with strong faith and rapturous joy.

The theme occupied Spurgeon's thoughts again on the morning of August 26, when he commented on Psalm 111:9, "He hath commanded his covenant forever."

The Lord's people delight in the covenant itself. It is an unfailing source of consolation to them so often as the Holy Spirit leads them into its banqueting house and waves its banner of love. They delight to contemplate *the antiquity* of that covenant, remembering that before the day-star knew its place, or planets ran their round, the interests of the saints were made secure in Christ Jesus. It is peculiarly pleasing to them to remember *the sureness* of the covenant, while meditating upon "the sure mercies of David." They delight to celebrate it as "signed, and sealed, and ratified, in all things ordered well." It often makes their hearts dilate with joy to think of its *immutability*, as a covenant which neither time nor eternity,

42. SS, 4:67.

life nor death, shall ever be able to violate—a covenant as old as eternity and as everlasting as the Rock of ages. They rejoice also to feast upon *the fulness* of this covenant, for they see in it all things provided for them. God is their portion, Christ their companion, the Spirit their Comforter, earth their lodge, and heaven their home. They see in it an inheritance reserved and entailed to every soul possessing an interest in its ancient and eternal deed of gift. Their eyes sparkled when they saw it as a treasure-trove in the Bible; but oh! how their souls were gladdened when they saw in the last will and testament of their divine kinsman, that it was bequeathed to them! More especially it is the pleasure of God's people to contemplate *the graciousness* of this covenant. They see that the law was made void because it was a covenant of works and depended upon merit, but this they perceive to be enduring because grace is the basis, grace the condition, grace the strain, grace the bulwark, grace the foundation, grace the top-stone. The covenant is a treasury of wealth, a granary of food, a fountain of life, a storehouse of salvation, a charter of peace, and a haven of joy.

During the year Spurgeon encouraged spiritual growth by meditation on the covenant in seventy-two different devotions. March contained only one that spoke of the covenant while December had nine. The least amount, other than March, was four in June and August.

Sermons regularly employed the covenantal arrangement of salvation as a vital part of his proclamation. The covenant of works made with all mankind through Adam posited life, corporate life, on the basis of obedience, but death for the whole on the occurrence of disobedience. When he fell, we all fell and became inheritors of sin and heirs of wrath, bound to sin and subject to misery.

Though the covenant of redemption was made before creation within the eternal will of God ap-

propriate to the distinct operations of each person of the Trinity, Spurgeon viewed its effectuality as dependent most significantly on the Son. In "Christ in the Covenant," he dealt with the place of Christ in the "covenant of eternal salvation" under the assumption that "Christ is the *Sum and substance* of the covenant."[43] He then summarized his attributes as eternal God and perfect man, his offices as prophet, priest, and king both in his humiliation and his exaltation, all the works of Christ that he did in our stead, all the fullness of the godhead in bodily form put in motion for empty sinners, the life of Christ in whom his people are hid, and the very person of Christ in his glorious, ravishing, delightful, endearing presence that contains all these other gifts and transcends them by taking us into the depths of pleasure that only may be found at his feet. Consistent with but beyond all the offices and descriptions of attributes, "the person of Christ is the covenant conveyed to you."[44] For Spurgeon, the Bible was a covenant book, and therefore, all its doctrines are particular distributions of the perfect covenantal provisions, both for the divine glory and human redemption.

Doing Theology Within the Bounds of Safety

Such a lofty center of theology some would convert into an excuse for passivity and pessimism. Not Spurgeon. He saw reason for action and great hope. Scripture was filled with ideas, doctrines and motives to drive us to make our calling, and thus, our election, sure. The covenant embodied all of divinity in its rich fullness and perfect symmetry—God and man, sin, judgment, and salvation, faith and action, heaven and hell. None need overstep the established boundaries of revelation or understate the things surely revealed. If we

---

43. SS, 2:395.
44. SS, 2:402.

know that where sin abounded, grace abounded all the more, we need not conclude that we magnify grace by pursuing sin. Spurgeon discovered as one of the treasures of divine revelation its power to halt the fallacious journeys of our sophomoric and sinful logic.

In a sermon on Deuteronomy 22:8, entitled "Battlements," Spurgeon expressed his view of the expositor's task in deriving theological ideas from Scripture. Battlements were placed around the roofs of houses to protect children, or inattentive adults, from falling off the roof to their death. While this implies, from the practical side, our obligation to do what we can for the temporal safety and well-being of our fellow man, its more profound application is that we not overstep designated boundaries for the spiritual and eternal safety of our own souls and the souls of others.[45]

Spurgeon affirmed that none need fear the "most high and sublime doctrines" of divine revelation, for God had "battlemented" it. No one need fear the doctrines of election, eternal and immutable love, or any point of revelation concerning the covenant of grace. It is a high and glorious truth, a truth of clear revelation, that "God hath from the beginning chosen his people unto salvation through sanctification of the Spirit and the belief of the truth." Many simpletons, however, have perverted this doctrine, perhaps some purposefully, into antinomianism, leaping over the battlements God has placed around it. Not only does God have a chosen people, but those will be known by the fruits of holiness, and their zeal for good works; not only will they be forgiven of sin, but purged from sin.[46] Spurgeon had already noticed, much earlier, that antinomianism prompted a reaction that led to others leaping over the battlements in the other direction. Be-

cause antinomianism, "through its perversions of truth," had made good men too wary of high doctrine, they had "run into the opposite extremes of error."[47] Thus ministers had begun to "prune the truth, and conceal the great distinguishing doctrines of grace, in a manner to be lamented." The result of this over-reaction was that "Arminianism lurks among us."[48]

The same divine cautions guard the doctrine of the perseverance of the saints—"A housetop doctrine indeed!"—in that while it holds great promise and comfort for the believer, yet battlements are in place to prevent its abuse. Spurgeon quoted Hebrews 6 and other warnings as applicable to Christians in order to show that "if the first salvation could have spent itself unavailingly, there would be no alternative, but a certain looking for of judgment and of fiery indignation."[49] Even so, in the doctrine of justification—the free, unmerited declaration of righteousness by which God pronounces the ungodly forgiven and esteemed as law-keepers—if no sanctification follows, then the presence of justifying faith is dubious. "Where faith is genuine, through the Holy Spirit's power, it works a cleansing from sin, a hatred of evil, an anxious desire after holiness, and it leads the soul to aspire after the image of God."[50] Paul and James cooperate in making sure both tower and battlement are in place. "Thus is each doctrine balanced, bulwarked, and guarded."[51]

On the matter of providence Spurgeon affirmed that "every particle of dust that dances in the sunbeam does not move an atom more or less than God wishes." All events of creation are so controlled by divine purpose; there is a mas-

---

45. S&T, August 1869, 349.
46. Ibid., 350-51.
47. SS, 3:vi.
48. Ibid.
49. S&T, August 1869, 351.
50. Ibid.
51. Ibid. 352.

sive difference between this and fate, however, for fate is blind but providence is full of eyes. Fate operates without any personal purpose of either mercy or justice, while providence arises from the wisdom of God who "never ordains anything without a purpose."[52] The Christian's involvement in ministry with reliance on the omnipotence and purposes of God, rightly seen, "never degenerates into fatalism." When one uses God's purposes as an excuse to do nothing, he has indulged a "terrible piece of mischief." Spurgeon would give way to no fatalist in his firm acceptance of "the fixity of God's decrees and the certainty of their fulfillment." But when one draws from that the inference, "therefore, I need not do anything towards the conversion of men, I do not tell him so, but I think that he is a fool." One might as well conclude that it is unnecessary to eat, drink, breathe, and work.[53]

Spurgeon explained the necessity of seeking such biblically integrated doctrinal fullness as a special stewardship for the preacher. Expounding the subject of faith and regeneration in 1871, Spurgeon gave insight into the dangers and difficulties involved in this pastoral delicacy. In making "full proof of his ministry" a pastor requires much divine teaching, not only in the manner and spirit of his ministry, but also much in the matter of his ministry. "One point of difficulty," Spurgeon advised, "will be to preach the whole truth in fair proportion, never exaggerating one doctrine, never enforcing one point, at the expense of another, never keeping back any part, nor yet allowing it undue prominence." Practical result depends on an equal balance, (symmetry and proportion as Jonathan Edwards would say), and a right dividing of the Word. One vital doctrinal area where much depends on such proper

relationship is in the positioning of the work of Christ for us, and outside of us, and the operations of the Spirit within us. "Justification by faith is a matter about which there must be no obscurity, much less equivocation; and at the same time we must distinctly and determinately insist upon it that regeneration is necessary to every soul that shall enter heaven," for Christ himself has made it essential. Spurgeon feared that "Some zealous brethren have preached the doctrine of justification by faith not only so boldly and so plainly, but also so baldly and so out of all connection with other truth, that they have led men into presumptuous confidences, and have appeared to lend their countenance to a species of antinomianism." A dead, inoperative faith should be dreaded and special attention must be given to avoiding it. To stand and proclaim, "Believe, believe, believe," without explanation as to the nature of faith, "to lay the whole stress of salvation upon faith without explaining what salvation is, and showing that it means deliverance from the power as well as from the guilt of sin, may seem to a fervent revivalist to be the proper thing for the occasion, but those who have watched the result of such teaching have had grave cause to question whether as much hurt may not be done by it as good."[54]

At the same time, Spurgeon saw an equal danger in the other extreme. While the emphasis on the new creature as necessary to salvation is clearly biblical, "some have seen so clearly the importance of this truth that they are for ever and always dwelling upon the great change of conversion, and its fruits, and its consequences, and they hardly appear to remember the glad tidings that whosoever believeth on Christ Jesus hath everlasting life."[55] Some have set so high a standard of experience and have been so "exacting as to the

52. SS, 2:201f.

53. *The Christian World*, June 8, 1878, 4.

54. MTP, 1871, 133f.

55. Ibid., 134.

marks and signs of a true born child of God, that they greatly discourage sincere seekers, and fall into a species of legality" that is just as necessary to be avoided as antinomian fideism. The sinner, deeply aware of his damnable failings, must never receive the impression that he is to look within for the ground of his acceptance before God, but must see clearly "the undoubted truth that true faith in Jesus Christ saves the soul, for if we do not we shall hold in legal bondage many who ought long ago to have enjoyed peace, and to have entered into the liberty of the children of God."[56]

Spurgeon proposed that the perfectly proportioned treatment in the connection of these doctrines appears in the third chapter of John's Gospel where both the necessity and secret sovereignty of the Spirit is taught along with the powers of simple faith in Christ. "So, too, in the chapter before us," Spurgeon said in calling his congregation's attention to John 3, "he insists upon a man's being born of God; he brings that up again and again, but evermore does he ascribe wondrous efficacy to faith; he mentions faith as the index of our being born again, faith as overcoming the world, faith as possessing the inward witness, faith as having eternal life—indeed, he seems as if he could not heap honour enough upon believing, while at the same time he insists upon the grave importance of the inward experience connected with the new birth."[57] As a true pastor/theologian, Spurgeon insisted, "I earnestly long that these two doctrines may be well balanced in your souls."[58]

The matter of hating the world and loving the world also called for deep theological understanding and refined powers of discrimination. Hearing the apostle say "Love not the world,"

resonates with the Christian love of holiness and the glory of Christ, and he feels it to be true that "if any man love the world, the love of the Father is not in him." One expected response, therefore, is a natural and visceral detestation of the world's putrid mass of evil. Nevertheless, Christ came to such a world and has said, "Ye are the salt of the earth." We are useless to God's glory if we refuse the preserve and do not give savouryness to the world even as a "nurse does to the little babe put into her arms."

> Unless you feed it, it will die; unless you clothe it, it will starve with cold; unless you bear it in your bosom, there is no shelter for it. The Lord has committed this poor world into the tender hand of His Church; and the very miseries of the world make us pity it; and love it in the next degree.[59]

By "next degree" Spurgeon meant that we could not love the world in its moral condition with a love of complacency but with a love of benevolence. The purposeful pursuit of such love constituted the imitation of Christ in his lamentations of concern for the hardness, blindness, and hostility of the response of Jerusalem to his works of mercy and teachings of true righteousness. "We shake our heads at the world, and as a sinful world we can only loathe it; but as a world of men with immortal souls, as a world of men that shall yet be washed cleansed, if God's Spirit go forth with us to the blessed work, we feel that we do not hate the world, after all, in that wrong sense." If indeed we are friends of God, we must be friends of man.[60]

Spurgeon's grasp of the entirety of the redemptive narrative in breadth and depth gave him an ever-present sensitivity to the necessity of a proper

---

56. Ibid.
57. Ibid.
58. Ibid., 135.

59. *The Christian World*, June 8, 1878, 4.
60. Ibid.

relation of the dizzying variety of truths that ever leapt forth from the pages of Scripture saying, "Do not forget me." He had no sympathy for those who would press this variety into an assertion of contradiction, nor did he look with approval on those that would harp on one without listening for the sympathetic vibrations of the strings of the other. Every part of biblical instruction exerted a defining discipline throughout the entire system, and made the conscientious doctrinal preacher work for precision in his explanation of each item of revealed truth. Spurgeon did not so much seek balance, as if all truths must be given equal weight, but he sought the right integration with each truth being given its due proportion.

The Problems and Strengths of Systems

When Spurgeon viewed the historic conflict between Wesleyans and Calvinists, Spurgeon saw many doctrinal points in common that would allow them to continue in friendly conversation with each other. When the two systems narrowed, however, in focus and the Calvinist discussion of depravity morphed into hyper-Calvinism and Wesleyan affirmation of human responsibility shriveled into self-righteous Pelagianism, he believed some merciless deconstruction was necessary. "It is time that we had done with the old and rusty systems that have so long curbed the freeness of religious speech." Systems that are doctrinally oppressive rather than freeing aids to biblical exposition should be "broken up" to allow "sufficient grace in all our hearts to believe everything taught in God's Word, whether it was taught by either of these men or not."[61]

By saying that all systems should be broken up, Spurgeon did not reject the systematization of doctrine as contained in Holy Scripture. He believed firmly in this approach and approved it frequently in his public statements. In a review of *The Age and the Gospel* Spurgeon pointed to the overconfidence that Wesleyans had in their own system. When Benjamin Frankland touted Wesleyanism as the balancing position between rationalism and ritualism on the one hand and Calvinism and Unitarianism on the other, Spurgeon felt that he had opened his mouth a little too wide. Wesleyanism had been very successful in its conversion work and had held its own against the destructive modernism of the day. But beyond those truths held in common by all evangelical Christians, Spurgeon saw "nothing in the distinguishing peculiarities of its doctrine or discipline from which we could gather any strong assurance of its ultimate predominance as the choicest form of Christianity."[62] His great admiration and encouragement toward Arminians focused, therefore, on truths held in common, not at all in the distinctions. On reading a biography of the Arminian apologist John Fletcher, Spurgeon remarked, "We do not sympathize with Fletcher's views in the great Calvinistic controversy, but none the less we reverence his holy character and admire his ardent zeal."[63] Wesleyanism, in Spurgeon's eyes, saw too little of "what Christ has done for us in comparison with what we are to do for him."[64] That did not indicate any slovenly spirit about work for Christ, but that Spurgeon clearly saw the necessity of an intense Godward focus in theology.

A review of a "holiness" book brought from Spurgeon comments on the need of theology for clarity. He mused concerning the doctrinal foundation of Pearsall Smith's new school of higher life teaching. "We begin to be utterly bewildered

---

61. NPSP, 1860, 133. "Election and Holiness."

62. S&T, December 1877, 575.

63. S&T, April 1883, 198.

64. S&T, December 1877, 575.

as to what Mr. Smith's disciples are publishing, since what they teach one day they appear to us to deny the next." Overall they are in a "mixed-up state." Though he commended their aim at a noble mark, Spurgeon recommended "some master mind to turn it over, arrange it, label it, and let the church know what is really meant by it." One should be able to tell whether it is fish, flesh, fowl, or "good red herring."[65]

The right integration of doctrines, "position and proportion in the faith," was essential as Spurgeon viewed the issue; the holiness and perfectionist schools muddled matters on that score. William Woods Smyth's *Life and Holiness* provided an aggravating example of how doctrines arranged with "unusual disproportion" profited little and confused much. "Holiness is in this author's work set forth in a manner disproportionate to faith; the love of God in the gift of his Son to the love of Christ in giving himself for us; the righteousness of sanctification to the righteousness of justification; the working out of our own salvation to the working of God in us to will and to do of his good pleasure." Without more proportion, clarity of expression, and logical arrangement it fell for short of its pious designs.[66]

Preaching in which no system could be discerned was unprofitable preaching. Rhetoric or eloquence without content amounted to a "finely, gloriously, polished nothing."[67] Saints, as well as sinners, must hear "about the Lord Jesus Christ ... my soul's welfare ... the heaven that is to come, or the hell that is to be shunned ... communion with Christ, ... the eternal covenant."[68] Many can preach without ever giving a hint as to any system

of divinity that they hold, so Spurgeon lamented. For they consider it the glory of the age that creeds have been cast to the wind. So it is with those that have nothing to say; but a preacher with principles soon will have a system. "It is impossible for a man to believe the things in God's Word without insensibly to himself forming a creed of some sort or other." Creeds, in Spurgeon's estimation, constituted an orderly way of laying out things more easily to communicate them to others. At least he was sure that one could hear him preach for a few times and "be pretty tolerably acquainted with our ideas of the truth of God."[69] So it was for sure, because Spurgeon's sermons were virtually an overflowing stream of systematic theology riveted to his soul and reaching out to his hearers with the earnest conviction that each one was responsible for a truthful and hearty response to each item of divine truth.

A marvelous example of the kind of theological arrangement he approved, Spurgeon found in Charles Hodge's *Systematic Theology*. In an 1872 review, he wrote that men like Hodge were valuable as well as rare. Spurgeon enjoyed seeing "the old theology rising in its wonted majesty, and clothed with its own verdure and fruitfulness into prominence in modern times." Both sides of the Atlantic would hail its publication as a token for good. Hodge refuted attempts to bring systematic theology "into disrepute, and to substitute a more unrestrained method of interpretation in its place." New approaches in both England and Germany were "carefully analyzed and weighed in the balances and found wanting." Men of "advanced thinking" would be compelled to see that they had no corner on intelligent reflection of the highest genius and scholarship.[70]

---

65. S&T, December 1875, 584.

66. S&T, March 1885, 144.

67. SS 6:234.

68. Ibid., 235.

69. Ibid.

70. S&T, March 1872, 141.

Spurgeon viewed the current outcry against creeds and confessions as coming "with an ill grace from those who profess to be governed by scientific principles and by a literary taste." If one viewed an account of great research from which a large number of truths had been distilled with no attempt at organization on the assumption that it is "impossible to systematize without weakening each separate truth, and frustrating the design of the whole," the observer would view this as a "serious reflection upon the author's wisdom and skill." How much greater an insult accrues to divine revelation to say it forbids any coherent organization. "Systematic theology is to the Bible what science is to nature. To suppose that all the other works of God are orderly and systematic, and the greater the work the more perfect the system; and that the greatest of all his works in which all his perfections are transcendently displayed, should have no plan or system, is altogether absurd." Faith in Scripture, if genuine and positive and abiding and consistent with itself, "must have a fixed and well-defined creed." Merely to assert that the Bible is one's creed and avoid expressing its many truths in one's own words is an empty and pointless boast. It is no better than infidelity. "Since we must have a system of truth, if our religion is in the Bible, the more perfect and enlarged that system is, the better." Hodge's work provided a good model of such a system.[71]

Fourteen years later, in 1886, Spurgeon called A. H. Strong's *Systematic Theology* "a remarkable body of divinity which may serve for Baptists as Hodge does for Presbyterians." He did not like it better than Hodge but found many similarities. He preferred the Princeton explanation of the atonement over the Rochester explanation, and would register a weighty exception to Strong's

view of the second advent. The work, nevertheless, is useful and will add genuine manliness to the doctrinal grasp of one that will study it. He used the occasion of this review to give strong objection to the anti-theological tendency he felt around him. "The silly outcry against 'theology,' which is so common nowadays, reminds us of the babble of illiterate bumpkins against all *larnin*." This was not spoken of the naïve but sincere believer but of the sophisticated rationalist that sought to debunk the historic faith by ridiculing the historic creeds and weighty theological discussions of vitally important doctrinal issues. "If our young ministers knew more of theology" Spurgeon urged, "that is to say of *the word of God*—they would not be so easily duped by pretenders to knowledge, who endeavour to protect their own ignorance by crying down a thorough and systematic study of revealed truth." Strong's work was an "invaluable Cyclopaedia."[72]

The inculcation of systematically arranged truth in the lives of children and young people could arm against the slide into heterodoxy observed in many denominations. He would have children "taught all the great doctrines of truth, without a solitary exception," so that in their later years they will be capable of holding them fast.[73] To facilitate this he proposed catechizing as the best method and promised to make available one "reprinted as cheaply as possible." His concern for this practice reached the level of absolute certainty as he instructed his congregation, "If we would maintain orthodoxy in our midst, and see good old Calvinistic doctrines handed down from father to son, I think we must use the method of catechizing, and endeavor with all our might to impregnate their minds with the things of God." The formal synthesis of scriptural categories in-

---

71. Ibid.

72. S&T, November 1886, 598.

73. SS, 2:346.

volved in "catechizing of the children in the essential doctrines of the gospel"[74] gave witness to Spurgeon's conviction that the Bible was learned best, not in an isolated verse by verse study, but by imbibing a coherent arrangement of doctrinal ideas related to the central importance of the covenant of grace. Verse by verse exposition would then yield exponentially greater understanding of the Bible when each text is related to its proper doctrinal context, and the whole is seen in the light of Christ as the covenant head.

Spurgeon's advocacy of breaking up the systems, therefore, did not involve a negation of systematic theology or of the intrinsic coherence of Scripture. He knew from his knowledge of historical theology that straightforward biblical exposition offered the only cure to doctrinal deformities caused by uninterrupted reasoning on pet ideas. Men of greatness all showed the weakness of their humanity in peculiar areas. Zwingli, Calvin, the Puritans, and Augustine all were "creatures full of incongruities and contradictions;" all made practical and doctrinal errors in pressing a system logically instead of allowing some of its edges to be contoured by closer submission to the biblical text.[75]

A striking example of this Spurgeon saw in Augustine. Augustine made serious errors on the "sacramentarian heresy" but is "most excellently inconsistent." He is "as clear on the doctrines of grace as if he had not been beclouded by mistaken views on baptism." On some points, Spurgeon wondered how Augustine could ever have been listed among the Romish saints; as he read the "utter rubbish" of Augustine's sacramentalism, "we equally marvel how he could have been so mighty a teacher of grace." These errors are allowed to become manifest that "no man may glory in men."[76]

74. SEE, 2:417; MTP, 1864 "A Promise for Us and our Children."
75. S&T, February 1876, 91.
76. Ibid.

Spurgeon also thought that it was possible to become so focused on the epitome of Calvinism as a system, that one might forget that some doctrines of genuine gospel power were not isolated to one of the five points of Calvinism. "I believe, most firmly, in the doctrines commonly called Calvinism," he affirmed, "and I hold them to be filled with comfort to God's people." Should one claim, however, that an isolation of those points is the "whole of the preaching of the Gospel, I am at issue with him." Some can preach those points without preaching the gospel, and some that do not preach those points, in fact, "to our great grief," deny those points, preach the gospel nonetheless, and "God has saved souls by their ministry." The doctrines of election, final perseverance, and so on, "go to make up a complete ministry, and are invaluable in their place," yet the "soul and marrow of the Gospel is not *there*," but is to be found in the great facts of the incarnation, substitutionary atonement, the operations of the Spirit, the resurrection and ascension of Christ. Paul gave the outline in 1 Corinthians 15 and 1 Timothy 3. "Facts about Christ Jesus, and the promise of life through Him—these are the faith of the Gospel!"[77]

A Historical Misrepresentation

Spurgeon's careful observations about systems, theologians, Arminianism, evangelism, and the bare-boned facts of the gospel, combined with his undeniably genuine fervor for the conversion of sinners, led Kruppa to judge that "He never escaped the rhetoric of Calvinism, but he managed to extricate himself from most of Calvinism's rigors." She puts herself in the camp of A. C. Underwood who believed that Spurgeon was caught in a "fundamental conflict between the theological demands of his Calvinism, and the emotional de-

77. SEE, 3:18.

mands of his evangelism."[78] She accepted Underwood's statement that "the old Calvinistic phrases were often on Spurgeon's lips, but the genuine Calvinistic meaning had gone out of them."[79]

An earlier biographer of Spurgeon, J. C. Carlile, sought to remodel Spurgeon along the same lines. In what can at best be viewed as a strange chapter, Carlile does all he can to blunt the perceived impact of Calvinism in Spurgeon's theology. While he views Calvin's doctrines of predestination and depravity ("one of the most terrible chapters in literature")[80] as dark and tragic, he sought to highlight Calvin's areas of Christology, skills in biblical interpretation, the authority of the Bible, and the church as a fellowship of holiness as rightly influential on the Baptists, especially Spurgeon. Though Spurgeon used Calvinistic terms, his real joy, Carlile was confident, lay in the freeness and universality of gospel truth. "Spurgeon made the centre and soul of his teaching the love of God, revealed in the mercy of Jesus Christ;" true enough but stated in a context in which he emphasized his judgment, "Theoretically there were limits to redemption, but practically the barriers were all taken down."[81]

Though Spurgeon preached eternal punishment, and brought it home clearly with his "vivid imagination and dramatic conception," Carlile focused on Spurgeon's tears and unceasing insistence "that there was no reason why any soul should be lost, that whosoever would trust Christ would find salvation."[82] Commensurate with that, Carlile observed that Spurgeon "loved to linger" over the tender aspects of the gospel, always emphasizing the invitation "whosoever will, let him come," focusing, not on the narrowness, but on the wideness of God's mercy. Carlile's presentation, the attempt of a former student that remained in the Baptist Union and served as an officer in it—his attempt, I say, to reconstruct Spurgeon, is not false as far as it goes, but de-emphasized ideas in which Spurgeon gloried, and made impotent and infertile doctrines that Spurgeon saw as vibrant and productive.

Carlile, Underwood, and Kruppa made their misjudgment that Spurgeon only reluctantly and superficially held to traditional Calvinist vocabulary at least partly because of Spurgeon's strategic resistance to his hyper-Calvinist brethren, his personal emphasis on evangelism, and his open-hearted spirit toward non-Calvinist evangelicals. He definitely parted company with the hyper-Calvinists, but doing so did not mean that "the Calvinistic meaning had gone out of" Spurgeon's theology. The points at which they resisted him, and that therefore led to his refusal to capitulate to their criticisms, were areas in which he believed he practiced true as opposed to false Calvinism. It was not a decline from, but a loyalty to, Calvinism that engendered this fissure.

The fact that Spurgeon was evangelistic, and fervently so, demonstrated clearly elsewhere in this book, only means that he did not see Calvinism as a muffling or suffocating theology, and did not see it as a theology that minimized either the warrant for or the usefulness of a universal proclamation of the gospel. Rather, he maximized it by seeing evangelistic proclamation as one fitting and pre-ordained element of the calling of the elect to salvation and as a presentation of the glory of God with such power that none should be exempt from approving, embracing, and finding delight in the God of the doctrines of grace. "If you come to Him, you need not trouble about

---

78. Patricia Stallings Kruppa, *Charles Haddon Spurgeon: A Preacher's Progress* (Garland Pub., 1982), 114.

79. Ibid. and A. C. Underwood, *A History of the English Baptists* (London: Carey Kingsgate Press, 1947, 203f.

80. J. C. Carlile, *Charles H. Spurgeon: An Interpretative Biography*, (London: Religious Tract Society, 1933), 143.

81. Ibid., 149.

82. Ibid., 147.

the secret decrees and purposes of God," Spurgeon emphasized. "There are such decrees and purposes, but they cannot, any one of them, be contrary to the Truth which Christ so explicitly declares here, 'Him that comes to Me, I will in no wise cast out.'" His declarations of sovereign purpose are true and his clearly stated promise of reception for all that come is equally true, and in the end both will all embrace the same people. But those that do not come, fail of the invitation out of their own stubborn refusal. "There is no secret purpose of God, nothing written in the great book of human destiny," Spurgeon clearly and insistently preached, "nothing in the mysteries of eternity which can ever make this declaration of Christ untrue to you, or anyone else!"[83]

Spurgeon had a real conviction that Reformation Calvinism filtered through Puritan pastoral theology manifests itself most purely in an evangelistic presentation of the gospel. "The doctrines of grace and Puritanic practice are not attractive to the flesh," Spurgeon reasoned, "but they are safe, they have been long tried, and their end is peace." These teachings constitute the "good way, made by a good God in infinite goodness to his creatures, paved by our Lord Jesus Christ with pains and labours immeasurable, and revealed by the good Spirit to those whose eternal good he seeks. It is the way of holiness, of peace, of safety, and it leads to heaven."[84] Spurgeon professed not to be ignorant of the novelties of modern thought and did not reverence mere antiquity, but he insisted that "the doctrines of grace are the marrow of the Gospel, and that the further men advance upon the teaching of Jonathan Edwards, Bunyan, Calvin, Augustine, and Paul, the further they go astray."[85]

Perhaps intensifying their misjudgment on this point is the manner of Spurgeon's practice of setting forth Christ as the only hope of all sinners in making an earnest and passionate plea for all his hearers to come to Christ with the personal assurance, biblically founded, that he will turn away none that come. On at least five separate occasions, Spurgeon preached on John 6:37 with the emphasis of Christ's willingness to save the worst of sinners, the utter dregs of mankind. He pledged to stop preaching if Christ would not receive them. "If it were ascertained that one soul came to Christ and yet He had cast him away, what would happen?" Spurgeon asked. "Why, there are thousands of us who would never preach again! For one, I would have done with the business." Should Christ refuse one he could not "with a clear conscience, go and preach from His Words, 'Him that comes to Me I will in no wise cast out.'"[86] If theology justifies the warrant to present Christ to all sinners with the assurance that if they repent and believe in Christ he will save them, the infinite and eternal issues at stake in this presentation warrant an insistent and passionate presentation. Christ's inexhaustible power and God's own character are on the line. In former days, even the devils might taunt, he saved harlots, and publicans and "sinners came and gathered about Him and He spoke to them in tones of love." But now one is come that is too vile for the Savior's grace! Jesus could not restore and cleanse him. Once he made a fine show but now but his power is exhausted. Spurgeon disclosed the horror of such a thought to him by exclaiming, "Oh, in the halls of Hell, what jests and ridicule would be poured upon that dear name and, I had almost said, *justly*, if Christ cast out one who came to Him!" But that can never be,

---

83. MTP, 1906, 390-91.

84. S&T, March 1879 108.

85. SS, 9:10.

---

86. MTP, 1894, 90.

for God's oath is as sure as his being.[87] Following an urgent argument that no filthy and begrimed sinner need consider himself outside the circle of those that Christ would receive, coming just as they are, Spurgeon placed his own eternal well-being alongside theirs, taking an anathema to himself if Jesus refused to receive them.

> Sinner, trust in Jesus: and if thou dost perish trusting in Jesus, I will perish with thee. I will make my bed in hell, side by side with thee, sinner, if thou canst perish trusting in Christ, and thou shalt lie there, and taunt me to all eternity for having taught thee falsely, if we perish. But that can never be; those who trust in Jesus shall never perish, neither shall any pluck them out of His hand. Come to Jesus, and He will in no wise cast thee out.[88]

On the third matter, Spurgeon's openness to non-Calvinist evangelicals, he felt true fellowship with these brethren, especially in light of so much ritualism and rationalism in other forms of Christian profession, and found no reason to provoke controversy with those that "equally hold by the atonement, the fall of man, regeneration by the Spirit of God, and justification by faith" and do not leave those doctrines as moot questions. Both Toplady and Wesley appealed to Spurgeon, though both showed great bitterness and denunciatory rhetoric toward each other. Both had equal "sweetness as to love to Jesus and devotion to the cause of the gospel." Spurgeon claimed to be "almost, if not altogether, of Toplady's mind in matters of doctrine," but nonetheless deprecated "the mode of warfare which led him to speak of

John Wesley as 'an old Fox tarr'd and feathered.'"[89] Rancor from the other side would be equally as verbose and energetic. Spurgeon worked to maintain both his distinctive theology as well as his friendship with believers that were zealous for souls and humbly and lovingly submissive to Christ. As shown elsewhere, he did not approve their distinctive theological ideas, but only those that were the shared commitments of all evangelicals.

His evangelical catholicity showed with particular strength in his relation with D. L. Moody. Here we can point to Spurgeon's focus on central evangelistic truth as sufficient for cooperation and encouragement of godly and zealous brethren. "Brother, do you desire God's Glory?" Spurgeon would ask. Hearing a positive note, he would respond, "So do I!" He continued, "Do you desire the salvation of souls? So do I!" And to clarify his concern that this salvation is seen through that central truth of the gospel, he asked, "Brother, do you preach salvation by the precious blood? So do I!" And still another important point of agreement, "Brother, do you believe in regeneration by the power of the Holy Spirit? So do I!" Once more, "Do you tell sinners to believe and live? That is exactly what I am telling them."[90] When Moody and his associates were criticized for the simplicity of their conversionist message, Spurgeon's ire soared against such impertinent objections: "So far as salvation through faith in the atoning blood is concerned, they preach nothing but what we have preached all our lives! They preach nothing but what has the general consent of Protestant Christendom."[91] The presence of saving truth in a sincere and zealous heart, free of corrupting error and heresy, would endear a man and his ministry

---

87. Ibid., 91.

88. *The Sum and Substance of all Theology* accessed at http://www.spurgeon.org/sermons/sum&sub.htm. This quotation is from the next to final paragraph of the sermon.

89. S&T, February 1874, 90.

90. MTP, 1875, 334.

91. Ibid., 337.

to Spurgeon even without the depth and beauty and power of a clear display of the doctrines of grace.

True Theology is Rightly Integrated Theology

In preaching on the Bible, Spurgeon mentioned that though all things in the Bible are important, there are epitomes of truth around which all other things revolve. One of the ways of presenting these summary truths was in the form of the three Rs—ruin, redemption, and regeneration. He told Sabbath School teachers, "Be sure whatever you leave out, that you tell them of the three Rs, Ruin, Regeneration, and Redemption." They are ruined by the fall, and if they are redeemed by Christ, Spurgeon put it, "they can never know until they are regenerated by the Spirit."[92] Beyond that, Spurgeon believed that "there is a better epitome in the five points of Calvinism;—Election according to the foreknowledge of God; the natural depravity and sinfulness of man; particular redemption by the blood of Christ; effectual calling by the power of the Spirit; and ultimate perseverance by the efforts of God's might." He followed that list with the statement, "I think that all those need to be believed, in order to salvation."[93]

In his sermon "The Sum and Substance of all Theology" Spurgeon argued that preachers should not avoid declaring the pre-mundane election of individuals to salvation while proclaiming, at the same time, the openness to all of the gospel call. His definition of election shows no halt in Spurgeon's step at all.

> The doctrine of Election is God's purposing in His heart that He would make some men better than other men; that He would give to some men

more grace than to other men; that some should come out and receive the mercy; that others, left to their own free will, should reject it; that some should gladly accept the invitations of mercy, while others, of their own accord, stubbornly refuse the mercy to which the whole world of mankind is invited. All men, by nature, refuse the invitations of the gospel. God, in the sovereignty of His grace, makes a difference by secretly inclining the hearts of some men, by the power of His Holy Spirit, to partake of His everlasting mercy in Christ Jesus. I am certain that, whether we are Calvinists or Arminians, if our hearts are right with God, we shall all adoringly testify: "We love Him, because He first loved us." If that be not Election, I know not what it is.[94]

Nor was Spurgeon hesitant about the obligation, and great privilege, of preaching this truth. Spurgeon knew of Baptists, excellent brethren, who never preached this "precious and glorious doctrine" and of others, excellent brethren, that dwelt solely on the five distinctive doctrines of Calvinism. "They have a kind of barrel-organ that only plays five tunes, and they are always repeating them." The former believe that these biblical ideas are not good for the pulpit, particularly in a mixed assembly. Spurgeon protested that this idea was "very wicked" and that there was no such thing as an unmixed assembly. The Bible was sent into a mixed world, and the gospel is to be preached everywhere to every creature. To a Welsh audience he proclaimed:

> "Yes," they say, "preach the gospel, but not these special truths of the gospel; because, if you preach these doctrines, the people will become antinomians and Hyper-Calvinists." Not so; the reason why people become Hyper-Calvinists and antinomians, is because some, who profess to

---

92. SS, 2:357.
93. SS, 1:37.

94. S&T, April 1892 , 149.

THEOLOGICAL METHOD AND CONTENT

be Calvinists, often keep back part of the truth, and do not, as Paul did, "declare all the counsel of God"; they select certain parts of Scripture, where their own particular views are taught, and pass by other aspects of God's truth. Such preachers as John Newton, and in later times, your own Christmas Evans, were men who preached the whole truth of God; they kept back nothing that God has revealed; and, as the result of their preaching, antinomianism could not find a foothold anywhere. We should have each doctrine of Scripture in its proper place, and preach it fully; and if we want to have a genuine revival of religion, we must preach these doctrines of Jehovah's sovereign grace again and again. Do not tell me they will not bring revivals. There was but one revival that I have ever heard of, apart from Calvinistic doctrine, and that was the one in which Wesley took so great a part; but then George Whitefield was there also to preach the whole Word of God. When people are getting sleepy, if you want to arouse and wake them up thoroughly, preach the doctrine of Divine Sovereignty to them; for that will do it right speedily.[95]

An American publisher of Spurgeon's sermons in introducing his sermon on the "Blood of the Everlasting Covenant", preached in 1859, noted that Spurgeon was a "sincere high Calvinist of the old puritanic school, holding the personal election of the saints by the sovereign good pleasure of God, wholly aside from the creature; and as sincere a hater of all free-will Arminianism, technically so called."[96] That Spurgeon was a "hater" of Arminianism at this point in his ministry might not be far from the truth. He loved Arminians as sincere persons and loved the emphasis on Christ that they shared in common with him, but he truly abominated the distinctive elements of their doc-

trine. "The Arminian holds the unnatural, cruel, barbarous idea, that a man may be God's child, and then God may unchild him because he does not behave himself." This was not the God of the covenant that Spurgeon saw in Scripture; it was another God. "I do not serve the God of the Arminians at all; I have nothing to do with him, and I do not bow down before the Baal they have set up; he is not my God, nor shall he ever be; I fear him not, nor tremble at his presence."[97] God never will cast away any of his elect; they are his by covenant with Christ himself as their representative and mediator. God cannot abrogate his covenant or break his promise. "If one of them for whom the Saviour died might be damned, then might the Saviour's blood be utterly void and vain."[98] The Arminian attempt to tame God, in Spurgeon's view, created an idol unworthy of respect and adoration.

Not only was theirs another God, their gospel was another gospel, at least in its peculiarities. "Good God!" Spurgeon exclaimed, "and do any persons teach that men can be quickened by the Spirit, and yet that quickening Spirit has not power enough to keep them? Do they teach that God forgives, and then condemns? Do they teach that Christ stands surety for a man, and yet that man is damned himself on his own responsibility?" Spurgeon had not learned Christ in that way and felt that such concepts were derogatory to divinity and dishonorable to the Savior. His substitution was an "actual, real, effectual deed." It produced positive deliverance, for Christ paid a penalty that God cannot exact twice. If Christ discharged the debt, the debt is discharged and cannot be revived. If sin was imputed to Christ,

---

95. Ibid., 152.

96. SS, 7:212.

97. SS, 6:241. This sermon, "Covenant Blessings" was preached around 1858 but was not published until 1900 in *The Metropolitan Tabernacle Pulpit.*

98. Ibid.

then did he suffer for it and "heaven itself can not accuse the sons of God any more of sin." Is this bold or presumptuous? Did not Paul himself say it, "Who shall lay anything to the charge of God's elect, if God hath justified and Christ hath died?"[99] To those that taught otherwise Spurgeon could only say, "Go, ye who believe in another gospel, and seek comfort. Yours is not the justification of the blessed God."[100]

If Spurgeon eventually became less exaggerated in his statement of disgust with the leading peculiarities of Arminiansim, he was no less convinced or less clear in his portrayal of Calvinism as truth, the only saving truth. Perplexity over Spurgeon's transparent, even aggressive, Calvinism alongside his fever-pitch evangelism ran high in virtually everyone but himself. Divine sovereignty did not seem a hindrance to him but an aperture to freedom and a sure promise of success in the most aggressive and innovative gospel preaching ventures in England. From the first to the last of his ministry Spurgeon never hesitated in affirming the complete consistency of these biblical truths, and if we might struggle with gaining clarity concerning their consistency, we could be convinced that no final contradiction in fact existed. Others noted Spurgeon's view, felt uncomfortable with it themselves, but knew that he had no difficulty. An early (1857) sympathizer with Spurgeon pointed out that "his success in winning souls to the cross," came precisely at the point of his "open and uncompromising declaration of the doctrines in question."[101] When the Scottish lawyer, political theorist, historian, and philosopher James Mackintosh observed that the more ardent Christianity became, the more closely it approached to the

Calvinistic form, Spurgeon's supporter, G. N. Hervey, explained the philosophical difficulty.

> To a mere philosopher, it might indeed seem strange, that a system which ascribes so much to the divine sovereignty and grace, and whose practical workings seem to him to be intended to waste the energies of the soul in the barren contemplation of what was in the Infinite mind before the world was, and to paralyze all its moral powers, by leading it to brood over its own helplessness—that such a system should, in its actual operation, rouse it to the most strenuous endeavors to obtain the free and unmerited gift of salvation.[102]

In Spurgeon's ministry and personal life, these doctrines produced all the positive benefits with none of the philosophically tortured difficulties. He felt that this should be so with everyone. In February 1874 Spurgeon published an article entitled "The Present Position of Calvinism in England." He was responding to an article by the Congregationalist Dale in which he stated that "Calvinism would be almost obsolete among Baptists were it not still maintained by the powerful influences of Mr. Spurgeon."[103] This was not an isolated judgment by Dale, because in 1881 he repeated the assertion, claiming "Mr. Spurgeon stands alone among the modern leaders of Evangelical Nonconformists in his fidelity to the older Calvinistic creed." On that occasion, in 1881, Spurgeon responded "If it be so, we are sorry to hear it, and we pray God that it may not long be true."[104]

In 1874, however, Spurgeon was more sure that Dale's observation was not true. While ad-

---

99. SS, 4:64, 65.

100. SS, 4:65.

101. *Sketch of the Life and Ministry of the Rev. C. H. Spurgeon* (New York: Sheldon & Blakeman, 1857), 104.

102. G. N. Hervey. "Spurgeon as a Preacher." *Christian Review* 22 (1857): 296-316, cited in *Sketch*, 104.

103. S&T, February 1874, 49.

104. S&T, February 1881, 85. Spurgeon was reviewing a book by Dale entitled *The Evangelical Revival and other Sermons* that included an address, "On the work of the Christian ministry in a period of theological decay and transition."

mittedly flattering to his vanity, Spurgeon did not believe it, and set out to demonstrate the healthy condition of Calvinism among the Baptists. He accepted without question the appellation, called it "eminently descriptive, though not perfectly so", for he was a good many things in addition to being a Calvinist. The Calvinism which it was Spurgeon's delight to preach was not obsolete but "growingly operative upon the minds of a large section of Christian people."[105] Spurgeon argued that the Calvinism of Owen, Charnock, Bunyan, Newton, Whitefield, Romaine, and "others of that class" was alive and well and provided the common matter for the sermons of men in the Baptist Union. Ironically, Spurgeon could attest that "Among the ministers of the Baptist denomination, there was never greater attachment to evangelical principles than at this moment, and those principles are more or less flavoured with the Calvinism now under discussion." Even among the General Baptists, Spurgeon contended that they "give more prominence to the grace of God, the work of the Holy Spirit, and the Godward side of salvation" and have among their membership "a considerable proportion of lovers of the doctrines of grace."[106]

Friendly bantering between the two camps of Baptists indicated to Spurgeon that both were more content to allow the text to speak rather than to contend for the peculiarities of the respective confessions and the confrontive doctrinal angularities that arose in a time of contention and dispute. Overall, Spurgeon summarized, "If the sermons now preached in Baptist pulpits could all be printed, they would be found to contain vastly more of what we call Calvinism than they did twenty years ago." Party names were less prominent, but "the essence and spirit of that

side of truth which has for brevity's sake been called Calvinistic, are more powerful among us now than they ever were at any previous part of the century." If Arminian Baptists had biblical emphases that were ignored by earlier Calvinists, then it is good that some movement in that direction has occurred; "We have certainly not thrown away the Five Points," Spurgeon assured the readers, "but we may have gained other five." Many readers of his sermons, all of which contain that "dreadful Calvinism," were found among the General Baptists as well as the Wesleyans, and some of the best preachers of grace are among the Wesleyans. The real despisers of Calvinism were not to be found among the solid earnest experiential Christians of any denomination but among the "superfine pens of literary men" who know "less of real religion than any other class in society."[107] Like Mackintosh, he observed that Calvinism and ardency in religion went hand in hand.

Spurgeon's celebration of real Christianity wherever he saw it, merely argues for the breadth of his affection for all the redeemed, for those whom Christ had claimed as his own, and not for any muting of his understanding of historical Calvinism or softening of his commitment to all of its leading distinctive doctrines. Just for good measure, he felt he should assure his readers of his clear commitment to the evangelical power of Calvinist doctrine.

> Those who labour to smother "Calvinism" will find that it dies hard, and, it may be, they will come, after many defeats, to perceive the certain fact that it will outlive its opponent. Its funeral oration has been pronounced many times before now, but the performance has been premature. It will live when the present phase of religious misbelief has gone

---

105. S&T, February 1874, 50.

106. Ibid., 51.

107. Ibid., 52.

down to eternal execration amid the groans of those whom it has undone. To-day it may be sneered at; nevertheless, it is but yesterday that it numbered among its adherents the ablest men of the age; and to-morrow, it may be, when once again there shall be giants in theology, it will come to the front, and ask in vain for its adversaries. Calvinism, pure, and simple, is but one form of Evangelism; it is not perfect, for it lacked some of the balancing truths of the system which arose as a remonstrance against its mistakes, but still it contains within it so large a measure of divinely immortal truth that it will never die. "Modern thought" is but the thistle-down upon the hill-side; the wind shall carry it away, but the primeval mount of "Calvinism," which is none other than Pauline or Christian doctrine, shall stand fast for aye.[108]

More than a decade later, 1885, Spurgeon reviewed *The Life of John Calvin* by W. Wileman, a friendly portrait of Calvin who had had his share of hostile presentations. For good measure, Spurgeon opined, "We do *not* believe that Calvinism is dead, but on the contrary we believe that its essential spirit permeates all Evangelical Christendom." It may seem out of style for a while, but within twenty years the tide of opinion will change. That is a small matter, however, for it is "far more to the point that the doctrine is true, and can never be crushed out while Holy Scripture remains."[109]

In a conscious demonstration of his catholicity of spirit as well as his unflinching commitment to Calvinism, Spurgeon reviewed *The Other Side of Things* by Wickham Tozer, a popular Congregationalist preacher and writer with a lively style and an imaginative approach to his subjects. In the preface to this work he had written, "Men differ in their *capacities* as widely as they do in their prejudices ... Calvin had a clear head and a cold

heart. John Wesley had a warm heart and an uncommon understanding. The former originated the system known as Calvinism, and the latter destroyed it—gave it its death blow."[110] Though impressed with the book overall, Spurgeon was amused, and amazed, at this particular claim, and countered, "Calvinism was never in better heart than now, and its power over human minds will increase as time rolls on, for although it does not comprehend all truth, it takes so clear a view of the Godward side of it, that it must abide." Spurgeon then invited Mr. Tozer to look at the "other side" of Calvinism.[111]

That which Spurgeon resisted was the epitomization of a singular idea from Scripture and using it to form a system unforgivingly consistent with that leading idea to the exclusion of other equally clear biblical propositions. This is what he meant when he viewed changes among the General Baptists and noted the possibility that he had gone down to them as much as they had come up to him. "If truth lies in the valley between the two camps, or if it comprehends both, it is well for us to follow it wherever it goes." He did not want a metaphysical system constructed from a narrow reading of the text, but a fully coherent system in which each biblical truth had its proper place, each portion of revelation feeding one's perception of the whole and unleashing the fullness of God's self-disclosure.

At the laying of the first stone of the Tabernacle in 1859, Spurgeon introduced one of the hyper-Calvinist brethren that had been friendly rather than ornery toward him. In his introduction he referred briefly to that conflict by saying, "I have been treated somewhat severely by that class of Brethren who are exceedingly strong in

---

108. Ibid.

109. S&T, March 1885, 141.

110. Wickham Tozer, *The Other Side of Things* (London: James Clarke & Co. 1874), x.

111. S&T, January 1875, 42.

their Calvinism." They suspected him of being a great heretic. He confessed it to be so "if it is heresy to judge of the Scriptures as God the Holy Spirit gives me ability and not to bend myself to the dictates of man!" His own experience of the depravity of the human heart had confirmed him as "a High Calvinist in the best sense of that term." He was not bitter towards others and loved "to preach the fullness of the decree of God." At the same time, he loved "so to preach it that I may combine it with practical exhortation and fullness of precept."[112]

If a person viewed total depravity in a way that diminished the true guilt and human responsibility for sin, his system opposed the Bible. If one constructed divine sovereignty in election in such a way as to render inoperable the appointed use of means and the legitimacy of calling on sinners to repent of sin, the Bible opposed him. If one viewed effectual calling as closing the mouth of a preacher in calling on sinners to trust in Christ with the promise that, if they would, he would receive them and save them, his doctrine sidestepped biblical practice. If one viewed God's preservation of his elect as indicative that the persevering quest for holiness on the part of the believer was presumptuous and mere legality, his system was a corpse. If one taught the doctrine of indwelling sin and consequently insisted that mortification of sin was futile and unnecessary for sanctification, he must be sure to correct the apostles in heaven. Spurgeon's Calvinism affirmed the first in each case and did not deny the second.

A robust view of divine providence secured this holistic and integrated approach to doctrine. He wanted his people to observe how the "hand of God's providence causes little things to lead on

to great matters." If Saul is to be led into the path of the prophet, beasts of burden must be lost and searched for in the ordinary way of duty. The wild will of asses brought Saul to Ramah and Samuel. "Hence it is most important for us to learn that the smallest trifles are as much arranged by the God of providence as the most startling events." God not only counts the stars, but the hairs of our head; not only are our lives and deaths predestinated, but our downsittings and uprisings. The events that shall be emblazoned on the eventual pages of history are not more providential that the fall of a grain of wheat, the leap of a fish, the trickle of a dew-drop, or the flight of a swallow.[113]

Everything moves in its proper sphere according to its own nature, including the will and interactions of man, but all respond to the decree of providence. God's hand is as much in "each stone of our pathway as in the revolutions of the earth." Often he saves in extraordinary ways just to show that all the power and the prerogative is his, and grace is utterly free. Often he saves those that have sought salvation for a long time, in order to encourage seekers by the truth that he may be found. It is foolish to believe that salvation will come without the use of means. Even in the most remarkable interventions of divine sovereignty in salvation, ordained means have been employed, and, so, "remarkable cases must never be used as a reason why we are not to do all that we can to bring sinners to Christ."[114] Instruments are channels for sovereign grace.

When Spurgeon could be of aid to a preacher of the gospel by influencing him to retain his hold on the doctrines of grace and preach them as truth, he saw it as a reason to be glad. He received a letter from an American reader in 1881 relating an incident in a pastor's life in which Spurgeon

---

112. NPSP, 1859, sermons 268-70.

113. S&T, March 1872, 109.
114. Ibid., 116.

had been the key stimulant. The pastor went to England with the purpose of attending services in many churches to hear all the "men of note" in London. Upon arriving he learned that Spurgeon was to speak one afternoon in a nearby hotel. The visiting pastor heard Spurgeon and suspended his plans to hear others, and for six weeks followed Spurgeon's trail of preaching wherever he went, both in the Tabernacle and at special meetings. "Your vindication of God's grace," the informant reported, "and advocacy of his sovereignty in salvation, and your clear presentation of faith and assurance so filled him, and confirmed his own views of divine truth that he returned to his own country strong in the Lord and in the power of his might." Like Spurgeon, the visitor was a champion of orthodoxy in his own American setting, "providing a striking contrast to the vapid utterances of the humanitarians and sentimentalists who abound in all our cities," and in being "truly a witness to the sufficiency of the Atonement, and a noble opposer of that science falsely so-called which belittles the word of Revelation." Though so like minded, he was too modest to introduce himself to Spurgeon.[115]

God's Truth is Our Truth

Given Spurgeon's commitment to proportion and symmetry as well as systematic arrangement in the preacher's doctrinal calling, one should not be surprised at his efforts to show the internal implicit nexus of relations in the doctrines of the Christian faith, and their particular coherence as manifestations of the covenant of grace. His sermons demonstrate his commitment to coherence and integration, indeed to the singularity of truth, in two ways. First he put every doctrine in its proper place and showed how each was related

to the others in a way consistent with the revealed character and purpose of God. Second, he consistently sought an infusion of these doctrines, so integrated, into the experience of God's people.

Preaching on "God in the Covenant," Spurgeon assured the listener that the coherence of both truth and experience found expression in the provisions of the new covenant. "And if any blessing is in the Covenant," he contended, "I am as certain to receive that blessing as if I already grasped it in my hands—for the promise of God is sure to be followed by fulfillment!"[116] Covenantal provision, manifest in revelation by promise, conveys the whole in any of its parts. It is made sure in the eternal purpose of God and secured in all secured in the covenantal promise, "I will be their God." The Christian must lay hold on this, for in that promise, that is, in God himself, all blessings reside, and he himself is their blessing. He has elected, justified, adopted, granted hope, and made himself the guarantee that all present needs shall be provided. His promise to be the God of his people is a "very sea of bliss, a very ocean of delight." In it the Christian may bathe his spirit, may swim to eternity and never find a shore, may dive "to the very infinite and never find a bottom." God's immutable promise purposes to make one's eyes sparkle, his foot dance, and his heart beat high with bliss. The objective certainty of these blessings comes into human experience in the effectual call of God. Though many of the aspects of God's activities are met with coldness and unbelief, his determination to bestow the blessings of the covenant cannot be resisted. "The effectual working of the Holy Ghost with the determination to save, could not be resisted, unless you suppose God overcome by his creatures, and the purpose of Deity frustrated by the will

---

115. S&T, June 1881, 294.

116. NPSP, 1856, 314.

of man, which were to suppose something akin to blasphemy." God has made a covenant within himself, and will not fail to bring it to effect.[117]

Most indicative of the immediate relation that the eternal covenant has to the experience of the elect is the doctrine of justification. Spurgeon linked its objective reality to Christian experience when he said, concerning faith, "Still to us personally one of the most wonderful of its effects is that it brings us justification and consequent peace."[118] Objective peace with God must precede peace of soul. Conscience could never rest as long as any well-founded fear existed that God might justly withdraw his favor. But according to Spurgeon's proclamation of the Reformed doctrine of justification, no fear need intrude, because nothing can remove from the elect the forgiveness procured by the blood of the God-man Jesus Christ. In the vindication of justice, we find the magnification of mercy, resulting in the strange combination of words, a just forgiveness. "Strange fusion of vehement Grace and vindictive wrath!" Spurgeon exclaimed, punctuating this point with a quick assertion of orthodox Christology, soteriology, and divine attributes in a call to the congregation to wonder: "Behold how Judgment and Mercy have linked hands together in the Person of the dying, bleeding, rising Son of God!"[119] More extended expositions of the doctrinal interweavings of justification bolstered these rapid volleys of admonition and amazement. "The point wherein faith comes into contact with pardon," Spurgeon explained, "is when faith believes that the Son of God did come and stand in the sinner's place." Accepting and resting in substitution as a divine gift allows the sinner to reason, as Spurgeon used the image of the dawning of truth on the conscience of a seeker: "Now I see how God is just, and smites Christ in my place. Seeing He condemned me before I had personally sinned, because of Adam's sin, I see how He can absolve me, though I have no righteousness, because of Christ's righteousness." By another he fell and by another he rises. "By one Adam I was destroyed: by another Adam am I restored! I see it! I leap for joy as I see it and I accept it as from the Lord."[120]

The same truth he put in more formal theological and confessional language in another sermon. "Notice," Spurgeon explained simply and concisely, "how this great work is done." The single word, substitution, suffices. "As the first Adam stood before God as the representative and federal head of the whole human race, and as it was by his sin that our whole race fell, it became possible for God to regard our race as a whole and to find for us another Adam who would come and stand in our place and represent us as the first Adam did." In the first Adam we fell, so in the second we are raised. "That second Adam is the Lord Jesus Christ, the Son of God and the Son of Mary, the Lord from Heaven," who upon earth "kept the Law of God in every jot and tittle and has woven a righteousness which covers the sinner from head to foot."[121]

Spurgeon needed to go further, however, to seal this truth to the experience of his needy sheep. When such a guilty one has acknowledged the justness of his condemnation, and also accepted it as put upon another, he may take his place as no longer liable to that sentence of death. "The penalty cannot be exacted twice. It were neither in accord with human or Divine righteousness that two individuals should be punished for the same offense unless both were guilty." The substitute of the guiltless Surety brought exemption

---

117. Ibid., 316-19.

118. SEE, 10:103.

119. Ibid., 107.

120. Ibid., 106.

121. Ibid., 96.

to the guilty sinners. With forceful rhetoric Spurgeon sealed the point with certitude: "That Jesus should suffer vicariously and yet those for whom He paid the quittance in drops of blood should obtain no acquittal could not be!" The eternal intent of such a substitution gave unending delight to Spurgeon and showed the inexhaustible storehouse of divine wisdom and loving-kindness in conjunction with immutable holiness and justice.

> When God laid sin upon Christ, it must have been in the intent of His heart that He would never lay it on those for whom Christ died. So then, there standeth the man who was once guilty, but he is no more condemned because another has taken upon Him the condemnation to which he was exposed. Still more, inasmuch as the Lord Jesus Christ came voluntarily under the Law, obeyed the Law, fulfilled the Law and made it honorable according to the Infinite purpose and will of God, the righteousness of Christ is *imputed* to the believer. While Christ stands in the sinner's place, the believing sinner stands in Christ's place. As the Lord looked upon Christ as though He had been a sinner, though He was no sinner, and dealt with Him as such, so now the Lord looks upon the believing sinner as though he were righteous, though, indeed, he has no righteousness of his own; and He loves him, and delights in his perfect comeliness, regarding him as covered with the mantle of his Redeemer's righteousness and as having neither spot nor wrinkle nor any such thing![122]

Only by this are sinners justified, and when so justified the soul may have a settled peace. "The Lord has not winked at sin. He has not treated sin as if it were a trifle. The Lord has punished transgression and iniquity. The rod has been made to fall and the blessed shoulders of our Lord have been made to smart under the infliction."[123] No flaw either in his suffering or his righteousness can be found. This massive operation of wise, just grace accrues to the sinner's account through faith. "God's plan, my Friend," Spurgeon explained, "is that you should hide yourself in Christ." As the Israelite laid his hands on the sacrificial animal under the Mosaic dispensation, so the sinner consents to Christ's bearing all and being all for him. He places his sin where God long ago laid it.[124] Unless the sinner comes with such unhalting reliance, the doctrine does him no good. To believe is not merely to receive a set of doctrines as true and "say that such and such a creed is yours, and then to put it on the shelf and forget it. To believe is to trust, to confide, to depend upon, to rely upon, to rest in."[125] All the effectuality of such belief rests, however, not in itself, but in the object of such trust.

Inextricably connected with justification other doctrines move in streams flowing in and out so that all the streams mix and none can be seen to flow without the influx of water from each of the others. No justification could be hoped for apart from One whose obedience and honor render God's mercy toward us consistent with his own immutable justice. Spurgeon viewed orthodox Christology as necessary to the doctrine of justification. He affirmed the deity of Christ as a manifestation of divine immutability. "When Christ in past years did gird Himself with mortal clay, the essence of His divinity was not changed—flesh did not become God, nor did God become flesh by a real actual change of nature." The orthodox language was employed to affirm the mystery of two natures in one person. "The two [that is, humanity and deity] were united in hypostatical union, but the Godhead was still the same." His deity in the manger was no less in essence or

---

122. Ibid., 106.
123. Ibid., 107.

124. Ibid., 97.
125. C. H. Spurgeon, *Christ's Glorious Achievements*, (Fearn, Ross-shire: Christian Focus Publications, nd), 20.

activity than it was "when He stretched the curtains of Heaven." When the blood of his humanity "flowed down in a purple river," he still was that "self-same God that holds the world upon His everlasting shoulders and bears in His hands the keys of death and Hell." The incarnation produced no change in his essence; "He remains everlastingly, eternally, the one unchanging God."[126]

Spurgeon looked at the union of the Eternal Son of God with genuine humanity as essential both for the ontological elevation of humanity and for redemption. For these results, the humanity must be real. "Our Lord's Manhood was no phantasm, no myth, no mere appearance in human shape."[127] Every aspect of his life showed the reality of his flesh, his human spirit, his human emotions, and his human dependence on the work of the Spirit and the will of his Father. Spurgeon's oratorical skills soared to their highest when he considered the purpose of the manhood of the Christ.

> O you whose loving eyes have looked upon the ensanguined rills which gush from the wounds of your bleeding Lord and have delighted to behold the Lily of the Valleys reddened into the Rose of Sharon with the crimson of His own blood—you can see God in Christ as you behold rocks rending, the sun darkened and the dead arising from their tombs at the moment of His departure from the earth! Behold in the writhing form of the Crucified Man the vengeance and the love of God, nor less behold Divine power sustaining the load of human guilt, and Divine compassion enduring such agonies for rebels so ill deserving. Truly this Son of Man was also the Son of God![128]

God's assuming human nature gave a true union of humanity with the Godhead and elevated it to a position beyond the intrinsically superior angelic beings. "What do you think of a Man who was in union with the God who is a consuming fire?" This truth indeed is great "if you consider the great honor which is thereby conferred upon manhood" by God's assuming "the nature of man into union with Himself." This gives humanity the preeminence among creatures, even above those angelic flames of fire that are ever before the throne of God. "Behold, and be astonished—a *worm* is preferred—a rebellious child of the earth is chosen! Human nature is espoused into oneness with the Divine! There is no gulf between God and redeemed man at this hour. God is first, over all, blessed forever, but next comes man in the Person of the Man Christ Jesus."[129]

Superior to ontological blessings, however, for fallen creatures is the divine purpose in redemption. Spurgeon called on hearers to wonder. "My Brothers and Sisters, the mystery appears greatest of all because it is so nearly connected with our eternal redemption." No putting away of sin by vicarious suffering would have been possible "if God had not become Incarnate." Sin is not removed except by atonement, and no atonement could be made except by One "of like nature to those who had offended." Death came by man and the resurrection must come by man. Jesus took human nature in order to take "the sins of His people upon Himself" and offer a propitiation for them.[130]

The dying Redeemer is the focus of all human history. All the ages meet in Calvary for in this event "Jesus is the central Sun of all events." One can never exhaust the wonder that "God should put Himself into the place of His offending creature, and in the Person of His dear Son should offer to eternal justice a compensation for the

---

126. NPSP, 1855, 2. "The Immutability of God."

127. SEE, 3:10.

128. Ibid., 10, 11.

129. Ibid., 11.

130. Ibid., 12.

insults which sin had cast upon law and rule!" When considered in the dimensions of wisdom, mercy, power, and purpose, "there is no greatness in Heaven or earth if it is not here in the bleeding flesh of Jesus, the Son of God!"[131]

More than obvious it is that a particular view of human sin is presupposed in the doctrines of atonement and justification. Adam as federal head of humanity has brought the entire race under condemnation. "The fall of Adam was our fall; we fell in him and with him," Spurgeon often repeated; "we were equal sufferers; it is the ruin of our own house that we lament, it is the destruction of our own city that we bemoan."[132] That federal standing, in Spurgeon's development of sin, more closely relates to justification than does our corruption. Corruption is an element of our punishment and relates more directly to regeneration in a comprehensive view of salvation. Flowing from the carnal mind, which is enmity against God, are sins that must be forgiven, sins that are damning and must be covered by the blood and righteousness of Christ; but the source of which is dealt with by an internal and effectual operation of the Spirit.

Spurgeon thus viewed human depravity as a fundamental biblical doctrine that, once apprehended, put in place all facets of redemptive truth. None could deny any other aspect of the doctrines of grace if human sinfulness was viewed in its proper weight. The Arminian, by leaving some remnant of free will by which a sinner may and must lift himself to faith, "diminishes the desperate character of the fall of man."[133] Should God provide all in salvation except the will to believe,

then all of what he has done might as well not have been done, for the sinner is just as impotent to do the step of faith as complete the righteousness of the law, or provide an atonement for himself. "And if God does require of the sinner—dead in sin," Spurgeon explained, "that he should take the first step, then he requireth just that which renders salvation as impossible under the gospel as ever it was under the law, seeing man is as unable to believe as he is to obey, and is just as much without power to come to Christ as he is without power to go to heaven without Christ."[134] The antinomian, who believes that man's inability renders his responsibility to believe null and void, also misstates the issue of depravity. "But once get the correct view," Spurgeon conceived, "that man is utterly fallen, powerless, guilty, defiled, lost condemned, and you must be sound on all points of the great gospel of Christ."[135] Depravity then becomes, in Spurgeon's perspective, a source of coherent development of doctrine.

That depravity involved utter dependence as well as utter guilt infused Spurgeon's preaching with an intensity of Edwardsean proportions in his utterances of the divine prerogative over depraved humanity. The curse is universal not only in its condemning verdict but in its corrupting power. "It is an awful thought," Spurgeon groaned, "that the trail of the serpent is on the whole earth; that the poison is in the fountain of every heart, that the stream of the blood in all our veins is corrupt; that we are all condemned."[136] And though universal in both these dimensions flowing from Adam as a covenant head, it is just—just with no exceptions, no mitigation of the sentence of condemnation for anyone. "But,

---

131. Ibid.

132. SS, 1:232.

133. Spurgeon, "The Necessity of the Spirit's work," *Revival Year Sermons* (Edinburgh: The Banner of Truth Trust, 1959, reprint 1996), 53.

134. SS, 3:197, "Salvation of the Lord."

135. "The Necessity of the Spirit's work," *Revival Year Sermons*, 53.

136. SS, 2:282, "The Curse Removed."

careless sinner," he addressed his audience, "learn that thy salvation now hangs in God's hand." His language in more than a few sermons indicates his familiarity with Jonathan Edwards. He continued, "Thou hast sinned against him, and if he wills to damn thee, damned thou art. Thou canst not resist his will or thwart his purpose." Human helplessness not only magnifies the dimensions of divine sovereignty and freedom but does nothing to diminish human responsibility and culpability. "Thou hast deserved his wrath, and if he chooses to pour the full shower of that wrath upon thy head, thou canst do nothing to avert it." That is, nothing that originates from the sinner himself either objectively or subjectively can suffice to assuage divine anger. But God, for his own purposes and glory, might show mercy. "If, on the other hand, he chooses to save thee, he is able to save thee to the uttermost." Salvation and damnation both are in the full power of an enraged deity. "But thou liest as much in his hand as the summer's moth beneath thine own finger. He is the God whom thou art grieving every day. Doth it not make thee tremble to think that thy eternal destiny now hangs upon the will of him whom thou has angered and incensed?"[137]

Salvation of Children

Native and total depravity did not exclude children. Adam stood for all his posterity, whether adult or infant, and when he fell he fell for them all.[138] Spurgeon could describe their natural condition in terms as graphic as those he would use with a vile voluptuary. Any qualification that a new-born had for heaven was not through its innocence, for it had none.[139] Taking David's lament as of universal application, Spurgeon pre-

sented the infant as "born in iniquity; in sin did his mother conceive him." Because of this, "He has an evil heart; he knows not God." Infants do not have good seed in them waiting to burst forth in works of benevolence and righteousness; nor are they merely neutral, spiritually susceptible to the earliest and most dominant religious influences, but "he hath evil seed within his heart."[140] His mind is a carnal mind, consisting of "enmity against God."[141] To those that claimed sin enters human experience by imitation, Spurgeon proposed a strikingly different reality. Suppose a child from its first day to live under carefully guarded pious influences, so that "the very air it breathes be purified by piety; let it constantly drink in draughts of holiness. Its ears hear nothing but "the voice of prayer and praise" and "notes of sacred song." That child, Spurgeon supposes, contrary to all its environmental influences, "may still become one of the grossest of transgressors" and "if not directed by divine grace, march downwards to the pit." Not by imitation, but by nature, the child is evil.[142] To parents with unconverted children Spurgeon assured them that "the wrath of God abideth on them. Die they must; and should they die now, to a certainty you are aware that the flames of hell must engulf them."[143]

Mitigating circumstances do exist, however, and parents may take action and hope accordingly. Though no predisposition to good exists, and though teaching in itself is ineffectual apart from the internal efficacy of divine grace, the child should be taught. The parent and other teachers may be used of God to place good seed, the good seed of the Word of God, in the child's mind. "Your child wants [lacks] teaching!" Though sin-

---

137. SS,4:426, "Human Inability."

138. MTP, 1861, 506.

139. Ibid.

140. SS, 2:352.

141. Ibid.

142. SS, 1:238.

143. *Revival Year Sermons*, "The Story of God's Mighty Acts," 32.

ful, parents may be "instruments to scatter seed upon that child's heart," and if it be not sown it is a certainty that "he will be lost forever, his life will be a life of alienation from God, and, at his death, everlasting fire must be his portion."[144]

Another mitigating influence was something like an age of accountability. Spurgeon believed that there was a particular point when a child became capable of sinning; at that point it was also a candidate for hell and susceptible to the saving influences of the Spirit of God. "As soon as a child can sin, that child can, if God's grace assist it, believe and receive the word of God." Though the heart itself is enmity against God, Spurgeon said that "it is not developed." At some point, therefore, the child "can learn evil," and thus "are competent, under the teaching of the Holy Ghost, to learn good."[145]

Until that point of learning evil, Spurgeon saw infants as under some gracious provision. When he spoke to mothers that he knew had lost children in infancy, he assured them that they would yet "know those dear Babes of yours." They had "marked their features when they lay panting and gasping for breath," and had "hung over their graves when the cold sod was sprinkled over them." They could be comforted with the thought, however, that "ye shall hear those loved voices again: ye shall hear those sweet voices once more; ye shall yet know that those whom ye loved have been loved by God."[146] Dying infants were a powerful means of evangelism in their deaths, for they provoked desires for heaven in the parents. "The darlings die, and in this they often do more than by their lives." How so one might ask, is a life cut so short better than a life that reaches full potential? "How many hard hearts have been bro-

ken, and stubborn wills subdued," Spurgeon answered, "by the deathbeds of infants!" He continued with the point, "How many a mother has had her first desires for heaven kindled by the flight of her little cherub up to the bosom of Christ!"[147]

Carlile recounted his knowledge of Spurgeon's view on this matter, when "It was represented that in the early days he taught that children dying in infancy who were not of the number of the elect, would be lost." Spurgeon responded in a letter to *The Baptist* averring that he had never, "at any time in my life, said, believed, or imagined that any infant under any circumstances would be cast into hell." He always had believed in the salvation of all infants, and intensely detested the opinions attributed to him. "I do not believe that on this earth there is a professing Christian holding the damnation of infants, or if there be, he must be insane or utterly ignorant of Christianity."[148] Claiming both Calvin and Gill for his contention, he insisted in unambiguously powerful terms that he "never dreamed of such a thing," nor had ever "imagined that infants dying as infants have perished."[149]

In his introductory address on the doctrines of grace at the opening of the Metropolitan Tabernacle, Spurgeon said that the accusation that Calvinists hold to the damnation of little infants is a "wicked calumny." The person that would dare say that an infant was in hell, Spurgeon labeled a "miscreant." All infants dying in infancy, Spurgeon opined, "are elect of God and are therefore saved." He saw this as one of the means (surely this shows that their salvation is an operation of grace and not of innocence) by which "Christ shall see of the travail of his soul to a great degree, and we do sometimes hope that thus the multitudes

---

144. SS, 2:352.

145. Ibid., 347.

146. SS, 1: 300. "Heaven and Hell."

147. SEE, 2:442.

148. Carlile, 237.

149. MTP, 1861, 506.

of the saved shall be made to exceed the multitude of the lost."[150] In a sermon preached later that year on "Infant Salvation" Spurgeon reaffirmed this by saying, "I do not see how it is possible that so vast a number should enter heaven, unless it be on the supposition that infant souls constitute the great majority." He considered a great relief to his mind that there would be more saved than lost, but did not have confidence that this majority would come from the present world of adults when in the present condition of the world, even the Christian world, so few were clearly Christian. "We must have the children saved, ... because we feel anyhow they must be numbered with the blessed, and dwell with Christ hereafter."[151]

Infant salvation, therefore, was indeed *salvation* and required operations of grace on their behalf both external to them and internal in them. Christ's death and the work of the Spirit wrought salvation. Infants dying in infancy were saved because they were elect; because elect they are redeemed by the "precious blood of Christ;" and because bought, they are regenerated. "No doubt, in some mysterious manner the Spirit of God regenerates the infant soul, and it enters into glory made meet to be a partaker of the inheritance of the saints in light."[152] The same provisions of salvation are made for all those that the Father gave to the Son, whether adult or infant. Spurgeon dismissed any idea that baptism bestowed a state of salvation, nor the faith of parents, nor a godly progeny. Salvation always and only arises from the sovereign gracious acts of the triune God. "All of them without exception," Spurgeon said speaking of infants dying in infancy, "from whosesoever loins they may have sprung, will, we believe, not by baptism, nor by their parents'

faith, but simply as we are all saved through the election of God, through the precious blood of Christ, through the regenerating influence of the Holy Ghost, attain to glory and immortality, and wear the image of the heavenly as they have worn the image of the earthy."[153]

Seemingly, the differences lay in two points. One, forgiveness did not relate to actual transgression (for infants were not held accountable), but only to original imputed guilt and to the root of enmity in the heart. Two, both their justification and regeneration came without hearing the word, for no true hearing is possible for those whose understanding is not formed for engaging a command, much less to follow discursive reasoning. When Spurgeon said, "I do hold that there is no doctrine of the word of God which a child, if he be capable of salvation, is not capable of receiving," he not only encouraged doctrinal teaching to children, but did so on the assumption that the need of salvation was concurrent with an age of discretionary thought.[154] Moreover, when he preached, "He who can change the course of a river when it has rolled onward and become a mighty flood, can control a newborn rivulet leaping from its cradle fountain, and make it run in the channel he desireth," he not only taught the possibility of childhood conversion but that infants also were susceptible to, and under the necessity of, the saving influence of the Holy Spirit.[155]

New Birth

Regeneration, therefore, for the most settled in their hostility, like Manasseh,[156] or the least practiced in rebellion is equally necessary. Regenera-

---

150. Ibid., 300.

151. Ibid., 509.

152. Ibid., 507.

153. Ibid., 510.

154. SS, 2:346.

155. Ibid., 347.

156. SS, 3:311ff.

tion, as a grace, gives spiritual life to the human spirit and makes it a willing recipient of all the blessings inherent in the atoning work of Christ. "Other parts of salvation are done gradually," Spurgeon observed, "but regeneration is the instantaneous work of God's sovereign, effectual, and irresistible grace."[157] So Spurgeon viewed the nature of the new birth. That work of the Spirit occurred in an instant and was fundamental to every other manifestation of spiritual life. Justification, of course, in Spurgeon's theology, was not a gradual process. The declaration of righteousness, proceeding from God as a judge watching over the just dispensation of his law, came also in an instant upon the first movement of genuine Spirit-wrought faith in the perfection of Christ's obedience. But for all the operations of God by his Spirit subsequent to regeneration and justification, a progressive realization of transforming influences and the chastened pursuit of freedom from corruption continued throughout this earthly life. Repentance, faith, mortification of sin, vivification of life and holiness, perseverance, all other sanctifying graces flowed into, and then from, the person that had been the subject of this sovereign operation of the new birth. God bestowed the source of spiritual life in an instant, and the rivers of living water gradually gave a sustained life to all spiritual fruit. "You shall never find simple faith in Jesus exercised by any life," Spurgeon instructed, "except the life that is born of divine seed in the new birth." In that way, "faith is as much the gift of God as Jesus Christ himself. Nature never did produce a grain of saving faith, and it never will."[158]

Spurgeon reminded his preaching students that no soul winning would ever be accomplished apart from the Holy Spirit's working of regeneration. Its "essence lies in the implantation and creation of a new principle with the man." Nursing something of a doctrinal idiosyncrasy, Spurgeon believed that in his fallen nature, prior to regeneration, man consists only of body and soul and "that when he is regenerated there is created in him a new and higher nature—the spirit which is a spark from the everlasting fire of God's life and love."[159] Thenceforward he may be said to consist of body, soul, and spirit. This is what Peter meant by "partakers of the divine nature," Spurgeon believed. Thus by regeneration, the formerly "soulish" man becomes a "spiritual man" capable of and naturally exhibiting the spiritual realities of repentance, toward God, faith in Jesus Christ, and increase of love for God and man. Because man's spiritual life is as dependent upon this divine creative act of regeneration as the world's existence was dependent upon God's power and prerogative, that work must precede all else.

Though Spurgeon used different images in explanations of this phenomenon from time to time, man's spiritual destitution and God's creative prerogative always sustained the substance of his teaching. Preaching on covenant blessings in 1872, Spurgeon, as he so often affirmed, said that God's "very first operation upon our nature is to pull down the old house and build Himself a new one that He may be able to inhabit us consistently with His holy spiritual Nature. A new heart is absolutely essential. We must be born-again or the Spirit of Truth cannot abide within us."[160] The same truth he asserted in a sermon *All of Grace*: "The man believes, but that belief is only one result among many of the implantation of divine life within the man's soul by God

---

157. SS, 5:93, "The New Heart."

158. MTP, 1875, 213. "Salvation by Faith and the Work of the Spirit."

159. S&T, December 1879, 558.

160. SEE, 5:475.

himself."[161] Again in preaching on "Human Inability," he taught that coming to Christ is "the first effect of regeneration. No sooner is the soul quickened than it at once discovers its lost estate, is horrified thereat, looks out for a refuge, and believing Christ to be a suitable one, flies to him and reposes in him." In a defense of justification by faith as a doctrine that does not induce moral frivolity, Spurgeon asserted, "When a man turns his eyes to Jesus and simply trusts Him—for we adhere to that as being the vital matter—there is accompanying that act—no, I must correct myself, there is as the *cause* of that act a miraculous, supernatural power which in an instant changes a man as completely as if it flung him back into nothingness and brought him forth into new life! If this is so, then believing in Christ is something very marvelous."[162] The grace of regeneration, stressed by Spurgeon's intended rhetorical emphasis of introducing self-correction, neither follows nor merely accompanies trust, but is the miraculous, God-driven cause of it. "The Spirit of God," Spurgeon reminded his congregation in 1888, "implants a love which is of heavenly origin, and renews the heart by a regeneration from above; and then we seek to be one with Jesus, but not till then."[163] A refusal to come to Christ is infallible evidence "that there is as yet no quickening; where there is no quickening, the soul is dead in trespasses and sins, and being dead it can not enter into the kingdom of heaven."[164]

In such a work of grace, the soul is necessarily passive. Arminianism falls to the ground in its explanation of this transaction and nothing will do but that "old-fashioned truth men call

Calvinism."[165] This portion of Calvinistic thought, "the immutable truth of the living God," gave all the glory to God and put man in his proper place as an absolute dependent in this matter because it is impossible for a man to make a new heart for himself. The heart, as the center of life, cannot create itself a new center. The exertions of the old heart cannot bring forth a new heart. A tree dead at its core cannot generate for itself a new core. Even so, "there never was a man yet, that did so much as the turn of a hair towards making himself a new heart. He must lie passive there—he shall become active afterwards—but in the moment when God puts a new life into the soul, the man is passive." Though he actively resists the early stages of God's call upon him, in the moment of regeneration all resistance falls and the positive infusion of new life is all of God; at that point, the recipient of this effectual call finds it indeed to be an "irresistible grace," does nothing, and must be described as passive as to any spiritual progress. "God, by overcoming, victorious grace, gets the mastery over man's will."[166]

In giving a more elaborate statement on the order of God's operations, Spurgeon explained in *Christ's Glorious Achievements*: "You were already from of old in the covenant of grace ordained to be the woman's seed, and now the decree began to discover itself in life bestowed upon you and working in you." Though the sinner might be unaware of its initial bestowment, "in infinite mercy" God dropped "divine life ... A spark of the celestial fire, the living and incorruptible seed which abideth for ever" into the soul of his elect. From this initiative of God, the elect person begins to hate and groan under the reality of personal sin as under a galling yoke to the point of its being unbearable. Such blessed persons be-

---

161. C. H. Spurgeon, "All of Grace," in *Memories of Stambourne* (London: Passmore and Alabaster, 1891), 137.

162. MTP, 1875, 347.

163. SS, 19:350.

164. SS, 4:411.

165. SS, 5:90.

166. SS, 5:90-91.

come the enemies of the serpent and of sin and are more and more the sworn enemies of evil.[167]

It is a work of omnipotence, a unilateral and irresistible action of God, one that he necessarily does without the aid of any creature, including the sinner who is the object of this action. It gives not only misery under sin and hatred of that misery-giving reality, but a heart, affection, for God. "So in the regeneration of our nature—in the changing the heart—the Lord alone is seen," Spurgeon proclaimed. "Who shall pretend to give another a new heart? Go, boaster, and suspend the laws of gravitation! Recall the thunderbolt! Reverse the chariot of the sun! Transform the Atlantic to a lake of fire and then attempt to change the nature of the heart of man!"[168]

As God alone created and sustains the natural order by his wisdom and omnipotence, so the time of regeneration is his alone. The voice of God in grace carries the same force as the voice of God in creation. "If God says: 'Let there be light,' the impenetrable darkness gives way to light; if he says: 'Let there be grace,' unutterable sin gives way, and the hardest-hearted sinner melts before the fire of effectual calling."[169] Creation exhibits the same power found in resurrection. The call, therefore, as well as consisting of a new creation, produces a resurrection from the dead. Effectual call "finds the sinner dead, it gives him life, and he obeys the call of life and lives."[170] Life precedes action and as surely as Adam could not resist being given life when God breathed into him the breath of life, neither can the sinner resist this life-giving call of God. "Every man that is saved," Spurgeon insisted, "is always saved by an overcoming call which he cannot withstand; he may resist it for a time, but he cannot resist so as to overcome it, he must give way, he must yield when God speaks."[171]

Spurgeon believed that the affections were the "most powerful part of our nature," so powerful, that "to a great extent", they "mold even the understanding itself." If the affections are defiled and fully corrupted by the fall, they prompt in every son of Adam a powerful disaffection toward God. The mental faculties, thus, "become disturbed in their balance." God, therefore, must commence his restoration of his elect at the heart. "Therein begins a work in which man cannot compete with Him, nor can he even help Him. God must do it."[172]

The same God, who made men, must, in dealing with the fountain of all affection and thus action (the heart), make them new. "And again, we repeat it," Spurgeon said at another place, "until these affections be renewed, and turned into a fresh channel by the gracious drawings of the Father, it is not possible for any man to love the Lord Jesus Christ."[173] If not, then it is also impossible for a person to have faith apart from this same renewal, for the assumption of faith is that a sinner has come to hate the life of sin and love righteousness as he sees it in its beauty in the obedience of Jesus Christ. "When the Spirit of God breathes on us, that which was sweet becomes bitter; that which was bright becomes dim. A man cannot love sin and yet possess the life of God."[174] When a Christian reflects on the reality of such a conversion, he cannot believe that he himself has effected it. "Men may hold free-will doctrine as a matter of theory, but you never find a believer hold it as a matter of experience."[175]

---

167. *Christ's Glorious Achievements*, 38.

168. SEE, 5:476, MTP, April 14, 1872. "Covenant Blessings."

169. *Revival Year Sermons*, "Predestination and Calling," 70f.

170. Ibid., 69.

171. Ibid., 70.

172. SEE, 5:476. "Covenant Blessings."

173. SS, 4:417.

174. MTP, 1871, 378.

175. SEE, 2:410.

Human Responsibility

Given this absolute dependence on God for the new birth, and therefore, all the consequent manifestations of spiritual life and blessings of salvation connected to it, one might legitimately wonder if Spurgeon held to any robust and realistic concept of human responsibility. In reading his sermons none can doubt that he called on sinners to come to faith in Christ while he maintained their dependence on the sovereign pleasure of God. He was able to embrace both of these ideas by holding resolutely to the distinction between natural inability and moral inability.

In his *Sermon Notes,* a text from Joshua, "Ye cannot serve the Lord," was treated under the title "Moral Inability." In his introduction, Spurgeon stated, "Man's inability lies in the want of moral power so to wish and will as actually to perform." Inability is not, therefore, "physical" inability but "moral inability." It does not come of man in the created nature but in the fallen nature. Since the inability is the result of sin, those that have it are culpable in the very possession of it, since it consists of a carnal mind, "self-will, self-seeking, lust, enmity, pride, and all other evils." None of these moral traits can be subject to the law of God and all are worthy of punishment. The doctrine discourages a sinner in the best possible way because it lets him know that nothing he does can save him, for it all is unrighteous. He must be given a new nature because "an impure fountain must pour out foul streams. The tree must be made good, or the fruit will not be good."[176]

Concerning the guilt of such an inability Spurgeon never wavered. If a man's heart is against God, then "we ought to tell him it is his sin; and if he cannot repent, we ought to show him that sin is the sole cause of his disability—

that all his alienation from God is sin—that as long as he keeps from God it is sin."[177]

Spurgeon made sport of any that would deny either the physical or mental abilities of any sinner to come to Christ. A sinner can walk to church and sit in a pew and listen to a sermon, and he can pray as easily as he can utter blasphemy. He can sing the hymns. "It is as easy for a man to sing one of the songs of Zion as to sing a profane and libidinous song."[178]

Nor is his inability mental. He can believe the testimony of a person about Christ as easily as he can believe a testimony about any earthly event; He can believe the Bible to be true or any of its individual statements to be true as easily as he can believe the statements of any other book presented with some plausibility. He can understand the guilt involved in sin as well as he can understand the guilt involved in assassination. "I have all the mental strength and power that can possibly be needed, so far as mental power is needed in salvation at all."[179]

There is, however, in the mind a certain kind of corruption, a vitiation that is "the very essence of Man's inability." Something deep in his nature constitutes his inability. Spurgeon used the illustration of a sheep and a wolf in their eating. The wolf would never respond to the voice of the shepherd nor would he eat the grass that the sheep eats. Though he has both mouth and stomach, he has no desire for such food. Can a mother stab her babe in arms through the heart with a knife? She can with physical strength but she cannot by disposition of love. Both the natural ability and moral inability are real and it is just to call them so.

Spurgeon explained moral inability by the confluence of four traits of the fallen human con-

---

176. Charles H. Spurgeon, *Spurgeon's Sermon Notes* (Peabody, MA: Hendrickson Publishers, 1997), 38.

177. SS, 1:244.

178. SS, 4:412. "Human Inability."

179. Ibid., 413.

dition. First, he spoke in terms of the "obstinacy of the human will"—built on Christ's affirmation that "you will not come to me that you might have life." Second, he observed that the "understanding is darkened." One may talk of all the glories of the most beautiful aspects of divine mercy and wisdom and the unregenerate understanding cannot perceive that beauty and sees nothing spiritually attractive in any of them. Third, Spurgeon pointed out that the affections are depraved. "We love that which we ought to hate, and we hate that which we ought to love" and until "these affections be renewed, and turned into a fresh channel by the gracious drawings of the Father, it is not possible for any man to love the Lord Jesus Christ."[180]

Conscience is the fourth human capacity that has been so perverted that man is rendered incapable of faith in Christ. A fallen conscience may discern a good many things because it has not been obliterated, but the evil conscience never did lead any man "to feel an abhorrence of sin as sin." It is not dead but it is "ruined, its power is impaired, it hath not that clearness of eye, and that strength, and that thunder of voice, which it had before the fall."

Spurgeon, however, wanted to go a step further than these four elements and say that the inability to come to Christ transcended the mere lack of a willingness to do so. "There is in man, not only unwillingness to be saved, but there is a spiritual powerlessness to come to Christ."[181] He appealed to the experience of Christians on the one hand, that willingness often led to a prayer for strength. If it is so in the Christian experience, how much more so in the unregenerate! "Do not all men see that there is a distinction between will and power?" A corpse not only is unwilling

but quite unable; what is lacking, therefore, is not only a will but actual power. The Holy Spirit enables, as two distinct realities, both the willing and the doing of God's good pleasure. Where he gives the will, he also grants the power and "to come to Christ truly is not in your power, until you are renewed by the Holy Ghost."[182]

When Spurgeon was accused of preaching that Christ grabbed people by the hair of the head to drag them to him, he responded that "I believe that he draws them by the heart quite as powerfully as your caricature would suggest."[183] This drawing, though infallibly irresistible, is not compulsion that violates a resisting will. "Christ never compelled any man to come to him against his will." The Spirit makes a man willing by going to "the secret fountain of the heart" and through a "mysterious operation" turns the will "in an opposite direction."[184]

In the interests of demonstrating this symmetrical and integrative approach at the core of Spurgeon's theology, we will come full circle to show briefly the relation between effectual calling and atonement. "All for whom Christ died shall be pardoned, all justified, all adopted. The Spirit shall quicken them all, shall give them all faith, shall bring them all to heaven, and they shall, every one of them, without let or hindrance, stand accepted in the Beloved."[185] The will of sinners shall not be done in the matter of salvation but rather the will of Christ in dying for those whom the Father gave him. Though one may say or feel that he doesn't want salvation, Spurgeon countered, "The gospel wants not your consent. It knocks the enmity out of your heart." The

---

180. Ibid., 417.
181. Ibid., 418.

182. Ibid., 421.
183. Ibid., 422.
184. Ibid., 423.
185. SS, 7:218. NPSP, 1859. "The Blood of the Everlasting Covenant," sermon 277.

hardness of sinners against Christ today is such that, should he appear, this generation would resist him again and put him to open shame, and execute him for "not one of you would consent if you were left to your will." But his death shall not be in vain and if some reject him others will not. "Christ *shall* see his seed, he *shall* prolong his days, and the pleasure of the Lord *shall* prosper in his hands." Some believe that many for whom Christ died will nevertheless be lost at last. "I never could understand that doctrine," Spurgeon replied; those for whom he died are as secure as the angels in heaven for "God cannot ask payment twice. If Christ paid my debt, shall I have to pay it again?" Certainly not; for those for whom he substituted himself certainly will come and "naught in heaven or on earth, nor in hell, can stop them from coming."[186] The success of this atonement is certain for the Spirit has pledged "I hereby covenant, that all whom the Father giveth to the Son, I will in due time quicken."[187] The Son's completion of his covenantal obedience brings about the gift of the Spirit for those for whom he died; and the Spirit induces the seeing, loving, trusting, and uniting of the elect person with Christ in the triumphs of his obedience.

This effectual call necessarily produces a change in perspective toward Christ and sin. Belief is "not merely to accept a set of doctrines and to say that such a creed is yours," but to feel one's personal need of each point of the creed. "To believe is, to trust, to confide, to depend upon, to rely upon, to rest in."[188] After a recitation of each point of Christ's work, Spurgeon asked, "Does thou therefore lay the whole weight and stress of the soul's salvation upon him, yea, upon him

alone?"[189] Faith also includes a clear perception of the evil of sin. Repentance as a clear constituent of faith means that the sinner and his sin must part. He must "forsake them, loathe them, abhor them, and ask the Lord to overcome them." The child of God cannot love sin but must hold it in contempt as long as he sees its presence anywhere. A desire for holiness grounds faith as a moral force in the true believer's life. While not saved by works, "the faith that saves us always produces works." Saving faith "renews the heart, changes the character, influences the motives, and is the means in the hand of God of making the man a new creature in Christ Jesus."[190]

Assurance

If saving faith may be analyzed as to its constituent parts, this leads naturally to the question as to how one may be assured that he has it. Spurgeon himself seldom experienced any lack of assurance that he was of the elect of God. The mental and spiritual change that happened at his conversion and the continual sensibleness of the glorious presence of Christ in his life left little room for him to have any insecurity of his gracious standing. He knew the same was not the experience of others, and so he gave constant attention to this issue.

Because of the ever-present oppressiveness of the state church and the nominalistic Christianity so rampant within it, Spurgeon often issued warnings about the danger of presumption. It was easy for the nominalistic mind-set to pervade all denominations and every Englishman, for after all, was not England a Christian nation? Because they had imbibed a presumptuous confidence of safety in Christ, Spurgeon observed many, "who, by hearing continually the most precious doc-

---

186. SS, 1:306-08.
187. SS, 7:216.
188. *Christ's Glorious Achievements*, 20.

189. Ibid.
190. MTP, 1875, 88, 89.

trine that belief in Jesus Christ is saving, have forgotten other truths, and have concluded that they were saved when they were not, have fancied they believed when as yet they were total strangers to the experience which always attends true faith." Their confidence was not grounded upon the divine word rightly understood, "nor proved by any facts in their own souls." They resented any suggestion of self examination by gospel tests as "an assault upon their assurance" and "defended their false peace by the notion that to raise a question about their certain salvation would be unbelief." Their ill-placed certainty has put them in a hopeless condition and they ignore biblical warnings and admonitions by "their fatal persuasion that it is needless to attend to them." Their historical knowledge of the work of Christ has settled them in a conviction "that godly fear and careful walking are superfluities, if not actually an offence against the gospel."[191]

On the other hand, both the witness of Scripture and his own experience led him to believe that some had so strong a sense of assurance combined with such a strong love of holiness as to make instruction in its elemental parts a superfluity. He believed that in some cases, the Spirit's witness prompted an infallible conviction of new birth, a knowledge beyond all question that one is a Christian. He wrote of Philip de Morny who stated "that the Holy Spirit had made his own salvation to him as clear a point as a problem demonstrated in Euclid." As clearly and as surely as the scholar of geometry solves or proves a proposition we may know that we have passed from death unto life. "The sun in the heavens is not more clear to the eye that his present salvation to an assured believer; such a man could as soon doubt his own existence as suspect his possession of eternal life."[192] This kind of experiential persuasion characterized Spurgeon's confidence.

Though Spurgeon found many reasons for full assurance to flourish in Christian experience, he was not naïve about the fluctuations in confidence even of the heartiest believer. Instead of unjustified over-confidence, these had unwarranted despair. "Can a man's faith grow so strong that he will never afterwards doubt at all. I reply, no."[193] He could see seasons in which even he had sung with Newton, "'Tis a point I long to know, oft it causes anxious thought. Do I love the Lord or no? Am I his or am I not?"[194] Though he had sung it, and others might sing it, it should be short meter, and not be sung too long.[195] Even the strongest faith will have periods of despondency and well may have "most painful doubts concerning his acceptance in the Beloved."[196] Some Christians, however, take on the character of Little-Faith and live their entire pilgrimage under a cloud. Such will get to heaven, because the blessings of the covenant extend alike in full and unchangeably to every true believer, but they very seldom think so.

If you meet him he is sometimes afraid of hell; very often afraid that the wrath of God abideth on him. He will tell you that the country on the other side the flood can never belong to a worm so base as he. Sometimes it is because he feels himself so unworthy, another time it is because the things of God are too good to be true, he says, or he can not think they can be true to such a one as he is. Sometimes he is afraid he is not elect; another time he fears that he has not been called aright, that he has not come to Christ aright. Another time his fears are that he will not hold on to the end, that

---

191. MTP, 171, 134. "Faith and Regeneration."

192. S&T, July 1882, 344.
193. SS, 5:143.
194. SS, 4:71.
195. SS, 6:327.
196. SS, 5:144.

he shall not be able to persevere; and if you kill a thousand of his fears he is sure to have another host by tomorrow.[197]

Assurance of pardon and thus of all the blessings of the new covenant, in Spurgeon's theology, should be a primary aim of those that hope in Christ. There is no reason that such confidence cannot be solid and a source of great joy for the true believer in Christ. It is an earnest of heaven itself and the source, not of presumption or arrogance, but of praise, worship, humility, and heavenly mindedness. "Out of heaven," Spurgeon taught, "there is no state so rapturous and blessed."[198]

The first grounds of assurance for Spurgeon came from the pure objective reality of the covenant of grace. For his own glory, God was determined, through his beloved Son, to save sinners. No sinner can ever have assurance apart from that reality of divine grace in which a number that no man can number will certainly be saved. Moving from that pervasive reality to the personal participation in it comes by way of knowledge of election. Spurgeon often dealt with the question concerning the personal knowledge of one's election. He did not believe that it was a moot point and that none should be concerned about it. One can know its reality, however, not by seeing into heaven and the eternal counsels, and deducing one's state from that, but by searching out the effects of election and concluding one's participation in eternal love by its present effects. "Have you and I been chosen?" he queried. Two other rhetorical questions followed—"Can we see the connection between the link of calling and the link of predestination? Have we made our calling sure?" If one has seen that his life—mind, heart, and body—

shows the evidences intrinsic to effectual calling, "we may infer most certainly that we must have been predestinated."[199] The short answer is, one may know that he is elect if he believes. It is not just any sort of belief, however, but a belief born out of a heaven-wrought fear of the Lord coupled with a desire to find him as shelter.

> Do you fear the Lord? Then so sure as you are a living man you are elect. You have the fear of the Lord before your eyes? Then you need have no doubt but that your names are in the covenant. None have feared the Lord who were not first loved by the Lord. Never one did come and cast himself at the feet of Jesus because he feared the penalty of sin, and none ever came to embrace the loving skirts of the Redeemer because he feared lest he should go astray, without having been first called and chosen and made faithful. No, the fear of God in the heart is the proof of being God's elect one.[200]

Enfolded in this fear of God were accompanying evidences. Have you cast aside your rags of self-righteousness for the seamless robe of the righteousness of Christ alone? Is your fear of hell a fear of sin and a fear of offending a loving and holy Father? Do you desire to be kept from disobedience to God's commands and to be consistently set free from both guilt and sin? Do you find Christ as the one in whom all these desires culminate, so that your life is surrendered to the Crucified? "Then you are elect; then you are justified; then you are accepted; and you have no more reason to doubt your acceptance and your election, than you will have when you stand before the throne of God amid the blazing lustres of eternal glory."[201] This great change from rebel to servant can be examined and internalized to such

---

197. Ibid., 133.
198. Ibid., 132.

199. SEE, 2:409.
200. SS, 6:242.
201. Ibid., 243.

a degree that it stands as a sure witness of one's call and thus of being eternally secured by divine choice. "It is so great a change, and so wonderful an effect of irresistible grace upon a man to transform him from an heir of wrath into a servant of the living God, that we have herein ground for comfort."[202]

The gaining of assurance honors Christ because it credits his work with success and fosters full submission to his lordship and sets him forth as the exclusive object of the penitent's affections. Neither the Arminian nor the hyper-Calvinist had grounds as secure for this blessing as the historic confessional Calvinist. He characterized the hyper-Calvinist, whom he called "the great *standard* men," as averse to Christian cheerfulness, habitually making declamation "against hopeful Christians, against people going to heaven who are not always grumbling, and murmuring, and doubting; fumbling for their evidences amid the exercises of their own hearts." These people rival Job and Jeremiah in grief and could themselves pen the distressful state of mind in Lamentations "vexing their poor hearts and smarting and crying, and wearying themselves with the perpetual habit of complaining against God, saying 'My stroke is heavier than my groaning.'"[203] The hyper-Calvinists feared presumption and found the sovereign purposes of God to be so shrouded in the mists of eternal purpose that none could be assured except those that received an infallible impression from the Spirit that they were among the chosen of God or that prior to belief they discerned that an internal prompting was, in fact, the effectual call of God.

On the other hand, the Arminian found assurance virtually impossible because of the synergistic nature of salvation, as Spurgeon saw it. Because every aspect of the work was universal, and many therefore, through failure on their part, would fail to procure a full salvation that was provided for all without exception, full assurance would always escape the seeker. "The Arminian says Christ died for him," Spurgeon noted, "and then, poor man, he has but small consolation therefrom, for he says, 'Ah! Christ died for me; that does not prove much. It only proves I may be saved if I mind what I am after. I may perhaps forget my self; I may run into sin and I may perish. Christ has done a good deal for me, but not quite enough, unless I do something.'"[204]

Universal atonement, universal call, and free will provided little, if any, ground for assurance of salvation. Solid ground for confidence, however, was found in the certainties of God's success in procuring salvation. "I may be called antinomian or Calvinist for preaching a limited atonement," Spurgeon countered, "but I had rather believe a limited atonement that is efficacious for all men for whom it was intended, than an universal atonement that is not efficacious for anybody, except the will of man be joined with it."[205]

Given all these qualifications, most Christians must seek assurance through the use of constituted means given by God to strengthen faith. Spurgeon suggested several. Faith may be strengthened, and along with it assurance, by meditation on the Word of God. One must be rigorous in this and not rest satisfied with just reading a passage "as long as your arm," but must take a smaller portion and demand that it yield its fruit and lay claim to any promise that may arise from it. When the promise arises, then prove it by thinking about its provisions and seeing that the experiences of your life show it to be so. Accumulate these promises through the years and the

---

202. SEE, 2:409.

203. SS, 4:84, 86.

204. Ibid., 219 "The Death of Christ."

205. Ibid.

instances of their proof—even mark them down as tested and proven—and see what abundant evidence is yielded and what a testimony may be given of divine mercy.

Associate with Christians of mature and deep experience and find how their struggles have issued in a confidence in the preserving power of God. God himself increases our faith by bringing trouble so that, by the secret workings of the Spirit, we will exercise that implanted faith and it becomes strong.

One must also endeavor to be as free of self as possible, giving in neither to spiritual pride nor to self-centered despondency. "Beloved," Spurgeon tenderly addressed his flock, "the only way in which you can maintain your faith is to live above the praise of self and the censure of self; to live simply upon the blood and merits of our Lord Jesus Christ."[206]

Most importantly, one must cultivate communion with Christ. "When you can not see him, then you doubt him; but if you live in fellowship with him, you are like to the ewe lambs of Nathan's parable. For you lie in his bosom, and eat from his table, and drink from his cup."[207]

Spurgeon cultivated this sense of the presence of Christ with unfailing consistency, even though his experiential level of assurance was virtually intuitive. He realized that, apart from conformity to special revelation, a person's highest and most exhilarating and ethereal connections with the divine were useless and filled with the danger of delusion. Scripture must define all and inform the Christian's mind in order to detect false spirits and recognize the true work of the Holy Spirit. In following this path, by diligent cultivation, a high level of assurance may be attained. "May a man so cultivate his faith that he may be infallibly

sure that his is a child of God—so sure that he has made no mistake—so sure that all the doubts and fears which may be thrust upon him may not be able at that time to get an advantage over him? I answer, yes, decidedly he may."[208] A man can be as sure of his acceptance in the Beloved as he is of his own existence.

Preaching about Hell

For those, however, that are not accepted in the Beloved in the eternal covenant, who do not have Christ as their substitute under the curse of the law, what then? What about those that receive exactly the treatment they desire in this life, that is, to be left to their own free will, what then? What about those that are left to do with the gospel as they determine in their own hearts, what then? And of those that have adopted the thought that there is no eternal danger to avoid, what then?

Hell and the task of the preacher created a massive burden for Spurgeon. He saw every sermon as an attempt to take sinners by the hand and lead them away from their determination to enter into eternity as enemies of God and, therefore, sure subjects of his wrath. "My hearer, give me thine hand," he pleaded. "Never did father plead with son with more impassioned earnestness than I would with thee." And then the ultimate question, "Why wouldst thou sit still, when hell is burning in thy face?"[209] And while his preaching had the potential to turn them, it also, if rejected, would "help to make their hell more intolerable." Their resistance to clearly stated truth would increase their responsibility and reveal more of their obstinacy and commensurately increase the intensity of their punishment. "O! ye that are left to your own free will, to choose the way to hell, as all men do when left alone—let these eyes run

206. SS, 5:140.
207. Ibid., 143.

208. Ibid., 144.
209. SS, 3:117.

down with tears for ye, because ye will not weep for yourselves."[210]

Hell manifested the glory of God. "God is so far sovereign, that he has a right, if he likes, to save any one in this chapel, or to crush all who are here. He has a right to take us all to heaven if he pleases, or to destroy us."[211] Death certainly must come. It rides on his horse and his hot breath blows on the neck of every man and "thou must die!" But for the wicked man, what then? Spurgeon asked, "Will it be heaven or hell?" If it is hell that rides along with death after you, where will you be when you are cast away from God? "Ah, I pray, God deliver you from hell," Spurgeon exclaimed, but then followed, "He is coming after you sure enough; and if you have no hiding place, woe unto you."[212]

God's coming after his enemies, Spurgeon taught, was necessary. One cannot suppose a God without justice so as to leave sin and wickedness and wrong unpunished. To suppose God as all love—love without justice, love without holiness, love without standards of right and wrong—would be to undeify God. If there is no punishment, there is no reward; evil receives the same as good and therefore its moral quality must be the same as good. "It were difficult to suppose him elevated high above his creatures," Spurgeon proposed, "beholding their disobedience, and yet looking with the same serenity upon the good and upon the evil; you can not suppose him awarding the same meed of praise to the wicked and to the righteous."[213]

Beyond such proper and compelling theological reflection, Spurgeon pointed to the Scripture as determinative of the reality of hell. Evidences of divine justice measured to the wicked appear sometime in this life, as Spurgeon illustrated by Scripture and anecdote, but the full display of wrath unmixed with any mercy would appear only in eternity. "Depart, ye cursed, into everlasting fire, prepared for the devil and his angels," summarized the fearsome reality indicated in many Scriptures and led to Spurgeon's expostulation with his congregation. "Do you feel that you are a fit subject for heaven now? Do you feel that God has changed your heart and renewed your nature? If not, I beseech you lay hold of this thought, that unless you be renewed all that can be dreadful in the torments of the future world must inevitably be yours."[214]

Danger accelerated with the attempts of some to eliminate fear by eliminating hell. Spurgeon knew that his view was considered as unphilosophical fear-mongering by a large number of nineteenth-century ministers. He preached about this tendency and the alarming result of it to his Surrey Music Hall congregation in 1856:

Indeed, because this age is wicked, we are told it is to have no Hell—and because it is hypocritical, it would have but feigned punishment! This doctrine is so prevalent as to make even the ministers of the Gospel flinch from their duty in declaring the Day of Wrath. How few there are who will solemnly tell us of the judgment to come! They preach of God's love and mercy as they ought to do and as God has commanded them—but of what use is it to preach mercy unless they also preach the doom of the wicked? And how shall we hope to effect the purpose of preaching unless we warn men that if they "turn not, He will whet His sword"? I fear that in too many places the Doctrine of future punishment is rejected and laughed at as a fancy

210. Ibid.
211. SS, 2:211.
212. Ibid., 216.
213. Ibid., 434.

214. Ibid., 439.

and a fantasy—but the day will come when it shall be known to be a reality![215]

Thirty-six years later, Edward White, a strong and able advocate of the doctrine of conditional immortality, admitted his deep admiration of Spurgeon but expressed his frustration at his uncompromising opposition to White's defining doctrine. He testified to the power of Spurgeon's influence when he wrote: "His refusal to listen to the doctrine of Life in Christ has formed a more serious obstacle to its popular diffusion than that of any other living man during the last twenty years." Spurgeon was not at all displeased with the complaint and hoped that he would have power "to be a more serious obstacle still." Spurgeon had tender regard for White but could express only regret that he had given himself to the propagation of "such mischievous doctrine, and that so many should follow him in it."[216]

Every single aspect of Spurgeon's theological method compelled him to a robust advocacy of the doctrine of hell. Biblical authority, distinguishing elements in the eternal covenant, an integration of all the doctrines of the faith left no alternative. Its reality left him no alternative but to see preaching as a continual burden that must be disposed of faithfully and earnestly week by week lest the gospel minister be reproached and hated more severely on the Day of Judgment for having failed to warn an endangered generation.

---

215. Ibid., 427.

216. S&T, July 1882, 377.

6

Spurgeon's Message of Christ's Atoning Sacrifice

I do believe that we slander Christ when we think that we are to draw the people by something else but the preaching of Christ crucified. We know that the greatest crowd in London has been held together these thirty years by nothing but the preaching of Christ crucified. Where is our music? Where is our oratory? Where is anything of attractive architecture, or beauty of ritual? "A bare service," they call it. Yes, but Christ makes up for all the deficiencies.[1]

The Lord Jesus Christ on his cross of redemption was the center, circumference, and summation of the preaching ministry of Charles Haddon Spurgeon. Its themes he repeated continuously and tirelessly but always with a freshness of power and passion that would startle his hearers and set them alongside the congregation at Galatia before whose eyes Christ was plainly portrayed as crucified. Spurgeon was a cataract, an avalanche, a flooding Mississippi in his unrelenting emphasis on the death by crucifixion of the Lord Jesus Christ. Redemption is the "heart of the gospel" and the "essence of redemption is the substitutionary atonement of Christ."[2] If in one analogy it is the heart, then in another it is "the cornerstone

of the gospel;" and when announcing it as his theme he, in some amazement, would ask himself before his congregation, "How many times will this make, I wonder? The doctrine of Christ crucified is always with me."[3]

Ironically, Spurgeon believed this truth to be so clearly delineated in Scripture that early in his ministry he doubted that it would ever be a point of controversy among Christians. "There are a few men who scoff at the statement and reject the thought of sacrifice," Spurgeon acknowledged in 1859, but these "never will be more than a few; they can never be many." The system which "denies the doctrine of atonement by the blood of Jesus ... can never succeed [and] they will never convince the masses." One should not argue against this tendency but rather destroy it "by our own personal determination to preach more earnestly and more consistently 'Jesus Christ, and

---

1. Charles Spurgeon, *The Passion and Death of Our Lord,* in *A Treasury of Spurgeon on the Life and Work of Our Lord,* 6 vv. (Grand Rapids: Baker Book House, 1979), 6:8. Hereafter this reference will be cited as P&D.

2. SEE, 8:97. "The Heart of the Gospel."

3. P&D, 34. "The Blood Shed for Many."

Him crucified."[4] Among the few that dared deny substitution, Spurgeon identified F. D. Maurice, McLeod Campbell, and "their great admirer, Mr. [Baldwin] Brown." They may go on with their preaching "but they will never make a convert of a man who knows what the vitality of religion is." Even with these easily identified few, Spurgeon vowed that "some of us must stand out against these attacks on truth, although we love not controversy." While he rejoiced in the liberty to dissent from these established and precious biblical truths, nevertheless, "that which infringes upon the precious doctrine of a covenant salvation, through the imputed righteousness of our Lord Jesus Christ, —against that we must, and will, enter our hearty and solemn protest."[5] The opportunities for such protest would become much more abundant.

By 1886 Spurgeon was troubled by the novel interpretations and philosophies of those who "deny the doctrines they profess to teach" and said that some who know what they believe "should just put our foot down and maintain our standing."[6] By April of 1887 Spurgeon, in the first months of the Downgrade Controversy, upgraded the potency of his language: "Our warfare is with men who are giving up the atoning sacrifice."[7] By October, Spurgeon wrote, "If we do believe in the inspiration of Scripture, the Fall, and the great sacrifice of Christ for sin, it behoves us to see that we do not become accomplices with those who teach another gospel."[8] In December, after he had resigned from the Baptist Union, he showed he felt obliged to "argue" right earnestly, to "come out in earnest protest," against those who "treat the Bible as waste paper, and regard the death of Christ as no substitution."[9]

Spurgeon knew nothing of a Christianity without the blood of Christ because Holy Scripture itself establishes the doctrine of the death of Christ as "the very core of Christianity." He contended that "a mistake on this point will inevitably lead to a mistake through the entire system of our belief."[10] "Christ's death for men is the great doctrine of the church" and so necessary to be dwelt upon continually that Spurgeon would "not feel satisfied without breaking bread on every Lord's-day"[11] and felt that it was impossible to think or preach on it too often. A man is never blamed in heaven for preaching Christ too much, and on earth among the sons of God the playing of that one string, a monotony to some, establishes such resonance and sympathetic vibrations that they could hear no more astounding harmony nor taste a greater and more delicious variety in all other doctrines put together than in the strumming of that one note or the slicing of that one fruit. "All good things lie within the compass of the cross," Spurgeon would say. It is in the cross that one can begin to grasp the whole of reality because "Its outstretched arms overshadow the whole world of thought" and indeed the death of Christ was the "hinge of the world's history."[12] "Its foot is planted deep in eternal mysteries and its top pierces all earth-born clouds, and rises to the throne of the most high."[13]

Centrality of Redemption

For a number of reasons Spurgeon insists on this centrality of the cross—that God himself intends

---

4. Spurgeon, "Our Suffering Substitute;" a Pamphlet printed by Chapel Library, Pensacola, FL, 2.

5. NPSP, 1860, 195, 196.

6. SEE, 8:97.

7. S&T, April 1887, 195.

8. Ibid., October 1887, 513.

9. Ibid., December 1887, 642.

10. NPSP, 1858, 130. "Particular Redemption."

11. P&D, 36.

12. P&D, 2.

13. P&D, 34-36.

it always to be fresh in our minds is seen in the establishment of two ordinances both of which are pictures of the death of Christ and its effects.

Central to Scripture

One reason for its centrality is that the entire corpus of Scripture finds its coherence on the assumption of the cross. Spurgeon's sermons on the Old Testament priesthood, sacrificial system, prophecy, prophets, kings, law, exodus, and many other themes all roll along on a majestic and clearly-lighted road to Calvary.

Spurgeon (for the most part) does not force the issue in these, it seems to me, but shows that he has clear warrant for such a procedure. Biblical theology, acknowledging that all of it is subdued to the glory of God, moves relentlessly from fall to redemption. The Bible cannot be understood apart from Christ and him crucified. Nor can the ministry and preaching of Spurgeon.

When Christ said, "It is finished," all the "types, promises, and prophecies were now fully accomplished in him." In fact, "the whole book, from the first to the last, in both the law and the prophets, was finished in him." From Eden to Malachi, from the red heifer to the turtle-dove, from a branch of hyssop to Solomon's temple, whether great or small all types were fulfilled in him. All prophecies, all apparent contradictions, all mysteries, the offices of prophet, priest and king as well as all of Israel's deliverers, to be worshipped and despised, to reign forever yet die and be buried—taken together they appear as indecipherable hieroglyphs till one comes forward and exclaims, "The cross of Christ and the Son of God incarnate."[14]

Speaking of the rending of the veil at Christ's death, Spurgeon inquires, "Does it not mean that *the death of Christ is the revelation and explanation of all secrets?*" "Vanish all types and shadows of the ceremonial law," Spurgeon continued, and explained further, "vanish because fulfilled and explained in the death of Christ." But even beyond its essential relevance to biblical understanding, Christ's death is the "key to all true philosophy." "God made flesh, dying for man—if that does not explain a mystery, it cannot be explained." And more, "If with this thread in your hand you cannot follow the labyrinth of human affairs, and learn the great purpose of God, then you cannot follow it at all."[15]

Central to Full Understanding of God and Man

Another reason for its centrality is that the cross is the epitomized display of the character of God and the depravity of man. His wisdom, power, justice, holiness, and love all are shown most clearly in the cross—more clearly even than in the law. Even so the cross shows the utter moral horror into which mankind has fallen. "You need not talk about the virtues of the world," Spurgeon would remind London; "It slew the Christ and that is enough to condemn it." And to make the point more pungently, he adds, "We want no other proof of its guilt; you cannot bring evidence more complete and overwhelming than this, they slew the Lord of life and glory."[16] And in another place, Spurgeon points his congregation toward the struggle of Christ with our sins: "See dear Friends, what an evil thing is sin, since the Sin-bearer suffers so bitterly to make atonement for it." Consider also the sobering implications of man's flippant treatment of the Lord: "Beloved, the treatment of our Lord Jesus Christ by men is the clearest proof of total depravity which can possibly be required or discovered. Those must

---

14. P & D, 581.

15. P&D, 646.

16. P&D, 3.

be stony hearts indeed which can laugh at a dying Saviour, and mock even at his faith in God!"[17] And one dare not pass over without great melancholy and dread the way that men today ignore such an infinite wonder as the cross. The devils themselves are incapable of a greater sin than this: "The incarnate God bleeds to death to save men, and men hate God so much that they will not even have him as he dies to save them." Though he stoops from his loftiness to their woe, they refuse to be reconciled to their Creator. "This is depravity indeed, and desperate rebellion."[18]

In an equally infallible and consummate way the character of God is displayed in the cross so that in contemplating it Spurgeon would say, "I have seen the foot of it go down deep as our helpless miseries are; and what a vision I have had of thy magnificence, O thou crucified One!" Truth, justice, holiness, wisdom, immutability, wrath, compassion, love, and grace all coalesce in the cross of Christ and dwell together without the slightest diminution of any attribute. "Learn ye my friends," Spurgeon called, "to look upon God as being as severe in his justice as if he were not loving, and yet as loving as if he were not severe. His love does not diminish his justice nor does his justice, in the least degree, make warfare upon his love. The two are sweetly linked together in the atonement of Christ."[19]

Central to Evangelistic Power

A third reason for the centrality of the cross is that by it sinners are drawn to salvation. Certainly sinners are drawn effectually by the Spirit of God who alone changes the affections and subdues the will. But the content of the truth to which one is drawn is that God has made the

One who knew no sin to be sin for us; and the manifest evidence of this effectual call is that one embraces Christ freely offered to us in the gospel. After an incomparable verbal barrage depicting the geographical and historical sweep of Christ's drawing power, Spurgeon said, "Christ's people shall be made willing in the day of his power; and the great attraction by which they will be drawn to him will be his death on the cross." In a discussion of the kingship of Jesus and how it applies to missionary endeavors he described the magnetic power of Christ being set forth as a king at the lowest part of his humiliation. "This it is that touches men's hearts," he said. "Christ crucified is the conqueror."

> Not in his robes of glory does he subdue the heart, but in his vestments of shame. Not as sitting upon the throne does he at first gain the faith and the affections of sinners, but as bleeding, suffering, and dying in their stead. ... and though every theme that is connected with the Saviour ought to play its part in our ministry, yet this is the master theme. The atoning work of Jesus is the great gun of our battery. The cross is the mighty battering-ram wherewith to break in pieces the brazen gates of human prejudices and the iron bars of obstinacy. Christ coming to be our judge alarms, but Christ the man of sorrows subdues. The crown of thorns has a royal power in it to compel a willing allegiance, the scepter of reed breaks hearts better than a rod of iron, and the robe of mockery commands more love than Caesar's imperial purple. There is nothing like it under heaven.[20]

Central to Doctrine

The cross is central also because it is the coherent factor in biblical doctrine. Often arguments are made that distinguish between preaching designed to edify the saints and preaching that

---

17. P&D, 511.
18. MTP, 20:504. "For Whom Did Christ Die?"
19. NPSP, 4:132. "Particular Redemption."

20. P&D, 365.

is strictly evangelistic. Spurgeon did not seek to make such a neat cut between the two. The sword of the Spirit, that sharp two-edged sword, itself could not cut so fine. Is the book of Hebrews for edification of believers or is it evangelistic? Is the emphasis on propitiation in 1 John not in the context of edifying and exhorting believers? May they not at the same time shed light on a path of hope for the unbeliever? Do those passages that edify believers not also show the way of salvation to unbelievers? Are not warnings designed at the same time to convict the ungodly and serve as a canon for examination for the saint and a means for his perseverance? And don't passages of comfort give pleasure to the children of God and, by God's grace, draw those blinded by this world by making them jealous for such pleasures as are at the right hand of God? Spurgeon preached many sermons that were specifically intended to call the unbeliever to repentance and faith; the universal response was that these brought the believers to exult in Christ in a more purified praise with a more refined grasp of the freeness of divine mercy.

Some may isolate passages from the whole biblical context so severely that they can give an outline, and word studies, and fairly acceptable advice without having any energy from the cross electrify its delivery. Spurgeon could not do this, and would not accept any attempt to do so as a biblical message. In a sermon on John 13:1, Spurgeon came to the close by summarizing his intent. "I have been preaching what I trust will comfort God's people;" he immediately added, "but I wish some poor soul would come to Christ through it." And, as if to establish the validity of his homiletical style and the unity of exhortation and evangelism, stated, "I believe that is the right way to preach the gospel." Referring briefly to the parable of the prodigal son, he began then to apply

the Father's words, "Let *us* eat." "So dear brothers and sisters in Christ, let us eat," Spurgeon encouraged, "and then sinners will begin to feel their mouths watering, and they will also want to eat, and to have a share of the feast." Pressing this point further and continuing to demonstrate the theory which supported his preaching, Spurgeon adds, "So if you and I enjoy the sweetness of the love of Christ, there may be some in the gallery, and some downstairs who will say, 'We wish that we knew it, too,' and they will be wanting it; that is the way to make them eat."[21]

The cross penetrated everywhere with Spurgeon because he believed it to be the defining factor of Scripture and, thus, of every aspect of the ways of God with men. This is particularly striking in the way Spurgeon developed its centrality to the doctrines of grace and the covenant of redemption. "Remember, dear friends," Spurgeon tenderly reminded his hearers, "that redemption is that which gives effect to all the other great blessings of God." All these "great blessings" need redemption to complete their design. Election, "the well-head of grace, needs the conduit pipe of redemption to bring its streams down to sinners." Our being chosen of God makes sure our obedience and makes necessary the sprinkling of the blood of Jesus. If the saints are chosen in *him*, of what avail would election be without *him*? Would calling be of any purpose without redemption? "Vain would it be to be called if there were no feast of dying love for us to be called to, and no fountain filled with blood to which we might come at the call." Christ's redeeming death "is the fulness of all the blessings of God," the "key of heaven, the channel of grace, the door of hope." It constitutes the substance of our worship, and thus the motivation for our perseverance, on

---

21. P&D, 19.

this earthly journey "and will be the theme of our eternal music above."[22]

The Person of The Redeemer

A key factor in Spurgeon's understanding of the atonement, and one to which he refers explicitly very often, and implicitly without fail, is the person of our Lord Jesus Christ in the orthodoxy given shape by Nicea and Chalcedon. Adhering to the mystery of godliness has been seen as essential to biblical soteriology ever since the church first engaged in literary interaction with the world. Irenaeus, Tertullian, and Athanasius all argued for the full deity and humanity of Christ, two natures in one person, as particularly necessary "for us men and for our salvation."

In "Our Suffering Substitute", Spurgeon says that "The Substitute was of complex nature [a favorite phrase with Spurgeon]. He was truly man, and yet He was truly God." In his manhood Christ shares the substance of his mother and all the natural creaturely weaknesses of humanity but without original depravity or imputed sin. Though hell's quiver of temptations was emptied upon him he stood invincible and invulnerable; indeed, "he *could not* be wounded by temptation." If he were to redeem man by paying man's debt for sin, and give man eternal life by conquering death then he himself must be man.

But let us also bear in mind that he was, in the Nicene phrase quoted frequently by Spurgeon, "very God of very God". His perfect humanity did not lower his perfect deity. Spurgeon declared, "We know nothing of a human atonement apart from the Deity of Christ Jesus. We dare not trust our souls upon a savior who is but a man." Neither all the men that have ever lived, nor all the angels that exist, nor all together, had they striven throughout eternity, could have wrought a sacrifice that should be a propitiation for the sins of a single man. They must utterly have failed. "None but the shoulders of the Incarnate God could bear the stupendous burden. No hand but that which set fast the spheres could shake the mountains of our guilt, and bear them away. We must have a Divine Sacrifice, and it is our joy to know that we have this in the person of our Lord Jesus Christ."[23]

Deity was required in the atonement because of the infinite and eternal issues involved in sin against God. "It is not possible to hold a proper substitutionary propitiation for sin unless you hold that Christ was God."[24] One of the classic developments of this idea is Anselm's discussion of the proposition, "You have not yet considered what a great thing sin is," in *Why God Became Man*. On occasion, Spurgeon combined the impact of this moral condescension on the part of our Lord with a contemplation of the metaphysical condescension. Not only did the Holy One come to dwell among sinners and bear their curse but the infinite, eternal, and unchangeable One put himself within the sphere and frame of the temporal and mutable to rescue them, from corruption yes, but from the mutability and declension of the temporal condition also.

> Who stooped to pick thee up, O insect of a day? Who stooped to save thee? Who but he who bears earth's huge pillars up and spreads the heavens abroad? The Son of God omnipotent, eternal, and infinite, has fallen in love with the fallen sons of men, and for them has donned the garment of human flesh, and in that flesh has suffered to the death, and died a most shameful death upon the gibbet of Calvary. Oh tell it everywhere that Jesus Christ, who is God over all, blessed for ever, has

---

22. MTP, 1874,159.

23. "Our Suffering Substitute," 6, 7. See also P&D, 232. "Majesty in Misery."

24. MTP, 1875, 159.

redeemed us! and after that, who will say that we do not belong to him?[25]

And in the sermon "Majesty in Misery" Spurgeon marveled that "the God, who had reigned in glory over myriads of holy angels, should be mocked by miscreants" who, in an infinite irony of the relation of the eternal to the temporal, "could not even have lived an instant longer in his presence if he had not permitted them to do so." The incongruity is unfathomable that "he who made the heavens and the earth, stood there to be despised and rejected of men, and to be treated with the utmost contumely and scorn."[26]

Substitutionary and Propitiatory

Absolutely essential for a proper biblical view of the atonement in Spurgeon's understanding is the affirmation that it is both substitutionary and propitiatory. He viewed these elements as inseparable and non-negotiable. In 1858 he preached, "Think how great must have been the substitution of Christ, when it satisfied God for all the sins of his people. ... think what must have been the greatness of the atonement which was the substitution for all this agony which God would have cast upon us, if he had not poured it upon Christ."[27] And thirty years later, "There is no way of salvation under heaven," he unfalteringly affirmed, "but by faith in the substitutionary sacrifice of Jesus Christ;" and, stirring in the ingredient of propitiation, he immediately continued: "and the way by which we are redeemed from eternal wrath is by Christ having stood as Substitute for us, and having died in our place."[28] And halfway between, in 1874, he preached, "Our Lord's death

was penal, inflicted upon him by divine justice; and rightly so, for on him lay our iniquities, and therefore on him must lay the suffering."[29]

Because of Christ's propitiatory substitution justice and mercy peacefully embrace and confer double honor upon each other. These two elements combine inextricably into one point as Spurgeon makes clear: "It was meet that the Substitute should bear a similar chastisement to that which should have fallen upon the sinner. ... he bore the pain the loss, the ruin, the separation, the overwhelming which is intended by death. He was even forsaken of God. ... The law demanded death, and death has fallen upon our great covenant head. ... Let us rejoice that the Lord Jesus Christ has evidently by his substitutionary sacrifice put away, not a part and a portion of our sin, but the whole of it. By bearing death itself he has removed all our legal obligations, and has placed us beyond the reach of further demands."[30]

Spurgeon often emphasized that Christ's position as covenantal head of the new race necessarily involved substitution. Jesus was not slain as a private individual, as Spurgeon developed this idea, but he was put to death as a representative man, and by that death sealed all the blessing of the covenant; all provisions of the eternal covenant were ratified. Spurgeon desired "more and more of this covenant doctrine" to be spread throughout England. A person who understands the "two covenants has found the marrow of all theology," according to Spurgeon, "but he who does not know the covenants knows next to nothing of the gospel of Christ."[31] The covenant of grace was well-ordered and made sure by the blood of Christ. "When the blood of Christ's heart bespattered the divine roll, then it could

---

25. MTP, 1874, 162.

26. P&D, 233.

27. NPSP, 1858, 132.

28. SEE, 1:366. "Blood Even on the Golden Altar."

29. MTP, 1874, 495. "For Whom Did Christ Die?"

30. SEE, 1:346. "Slaying the Sacrifice."

31. MTP, 1874, 444. "The Blood of the Covenant."

never be reversed, nor could one of its ordinances be broken, not one of its stipulations fail."[32] Among these was the determination to give new hearts and right spirits to the people for whom the surety of the covenant had died. While as covenant head his death produces forgiveness and justification, it also becomes the dynamic by which his people are made holy. "He forgives our sins with the design of curing our sinfulness. We are pardoned that we may become holy."[33] Spurgeon often pointed to the water and the blood from Christ's side and, in the tradition of Toplady, spoke of cleansing from both the guilt and power of sin.[34]

In a sermon on Zechariah 13:1 Spurgeon emphasized the double nature of the evil of sin. The fountain opened in the atonement removes "the offence rendered to God's honor and dignity." God has "punished that sin in the person of his own Son." The guilt, therefore, "of those for whom he was a substitute is put away consistently with the righteousness of the great Lawgiver." But, there is a second mischief, namely, "that our nature has become unclean" and "our mind is in itself biased towards evil and averse from good." God, therefore, does not grant a forgiveness that leaves "the sinner as he was in other respects." When forgiveness is granted, "a renewal of the nature is wrought; the fountain opened for pardon is also opened for purification." Not only is the offence removed, the love of offending is mortified.

> Herein is double joy, for does not every true penitent feel that mere pardon would be a poor

boon to him if it allowed him to continue in sin? My God, deliver me from sin itself, for this is the great burden of my soul. Oh could I have the past forgiven, and yet live an enemy to my God, enslaved by evil and a stranger to holiness—then were I still accursed! ... To love the wrong is the beginning of hell.[35]

Definite Atonement

In 1854, in Spurgeon's first full year as a pastor in London at the New Park Street pulpit, the American commentator Albert Barnes published an article in the *Church Advocate* entitled "A Limited Atonement Not to be Preached." Barnes claimed that "there is nothing that more cramps the powers, fetters the hands, and chills the heart of the preacher, than such a doctrine." The characterization he gave of the preacher who would dare do such is singularly unflattering: "one so clearly and thoroughly tainted in such a form of systematic theology, so fettered and bound by authority, and by the manacles of a creed so wholly under the influence of a theology derived from a past age," who himself is frozen by the doctrine he preaches. Barnes considered it so contradictory to every aspect of gospel ministry, so contrary to the purest feelings of a sanctified person, and so cold and withering in its influence on the heart that "men will not preach it." Should it be found to be an essential part of the gospel message, warm hearted ministers "would abandon preaching altogether, and engage in farming, or teaching, or the mechanic arts—anything; rather than have their better feelings subjected to constant torture." Barnes, moreover, found the doctrine so objectionable that he said not only that it should not be preached, but it could not be preached.

---

32. P&D, 583. "It Is Finished."

33. P&D, 41. "The Blood Shed."

34. For example, see "Ecce Rex," P&D, 359. "When the soldier with a spear pierced his side he had no idea that he was bringing forth before all eyes that blood and water which are to the whole church the emblems of the double cleansing which we find in Jesus, cleansing by atoning blood and sanctifying grace."

35. MTP, 1871, 39.

It is found in ancient books on divinity, written in a sterner age, and when the principles of interpretation were less understood, and the large and liberal nature of the gospel was less appreciated. It is petrified in certain creeds maintained by the church—made firm, like fossil remains in a transition state, when ancient opinions were passing to a more liberal form. It is taught in a few seminaries, where men feel themselves constrained to repress the warm emotions of their own minds to reach conclusions which they can scarcely avoid. But the doctrine is not preached, except when the heart is cold and dead. It is not preached when the soul is on fire with the love of men, and when the cross, in its true grandeur rises to view. It is never preached in a revival of religion—a proof, not feeble, that the doctrine is not true.[36]

Barnes could not have known that the warmest, most powerful preacher of the nineteenth century could and would preach the doctrine that Barnes found so unthinkable, and preach it without bringing a chill either to himself or his hearers. Spurgeon believed that the fountain of Christ's blood was open and would cleanse every sinner who came to it. He felt no more inhibition to invite sinners to the fountain of Christ's blood than he did to call on all sinners to repent and believe the gospel. Both effectual calling and effectual, or limited, atonement are doctrines of grace. Grace never serves as a barrier to anyone's coming to Christ, nor to the freedom with which ministers may, must, issue the gospel invitation.

Spurgeon labored to demonstrate the congruity between these two doctrines. The command to repent of sin and believe in Christ, Spurgeon said, is universal. He knew, however, that "there are some who will deny this, and deny it upon the ground that man has not the spiritual ability to believe in Jesus." His reply emphasized that "it is altogether an error to imagine that the measure of the sinner's moral ability is the measure of his duty." Universal responsibility merely accentuates the divine prerogative in grace for no one would ever "believe in Jesus with the faith here intended, except the Holy Spirit led him to do so." "Faith is too celestial a grace," Spurgeon continues, "to spring up in human nature till it is renewed." Christians must "rise above the babyhood" which truncates these doctrines and should "not find it difficult to believe faith to be at the same time the duty of man and the gift of God."[37]

Because of that, where belief exists, regeneration exists. "To believe in Jesus is a better indicator of regeneration than anything else, and in no case did it ever mislead." By the same token, to believe in Jesus is the sure indicator that Jesus has died for you. Faith does not consist in believing that Christ has died for me in particular but in coming empty-handed, and with a whole heart, to Christ himself who has died for sinners. And it is in trusting in him alone that one discovers that Christ has died for him in particular and with effect. Spurgeon says:

> I do not believe in Jesus because I am persuaded that his blood was shed for me, but rather I discover that his blood was shed especially for me from the fact that I have been led to believe in him. I fear me there are thousands of people who believe that Jesus died for them, who are not born of God, but rather hardened in their sin by their groundless hopes of mercy. There is no particular efficacy in a man's assuming that Christ has died for him; for it is a mere truism, if it be true as some teach, that Jesus died for everybody. On such a theory every believer in a universal atonement would necessarily be born of God, which is very far from being the case. When the Holy Spirit leads us to rely upon the Lord Jesus, then the truth that

---

36. Albert Barnes, *The Church Advocate*, 8.10.1854, 119.

37. MTP, 1871, 133-44. "Faith and Regeneration."

God gave his only begotten Son that whosoever believeth in him might be saved, is opened up to our souls, and we see that for us who are believers, Jesus died with the special intent that we should be saved. ... Merely to conclude that Jesus died for us on the notion that he died for everybody is as far as the east is from the west, from being real faith in Jesus Christ.[38]

Spurgeon pulled on this same cord of unity within the doctrines of grace in a "The Open Fountain." One will never participate in this fountain which eradicates sin and uncleanness unless one knows himself to be a sinner; but if there "be here one really guilty, one who feels his sin to be deserving the wrath of God;" one who mourns his sin, confesses his guilt, and feels himself undeserving and unworthy—"then you are the man to whom the mercy of heaven is this day freely proclaimed." In this context then it is no wonder that Spurgeon proclaimed the saving efficacy of the death of Christ with unbounded enthusiasm and generosity. Because the fountain is open "there is no barrier on account of uncircumcision or natural descent." We learn also that it is "personally approachable by us" and dependent on no mediator or intercessor other than the Lord Jesus himself. Also "the fountain is not barred by any amount of sin which we have already committed." No effectual barrier is created by the consideration of our inward sinfulness nor are there any "demands in the gospel requiring you to prepare yourself for it before you come." Spurgeon increased in boldness as he goes vowing to push any theologian into the fountain who would bar it from any sinner who is coming. "There cannot be anything in theology, nor in nature nor in heaven, nor earth, nor hell, which can shut what God declares to be open. If thou willest to be saved, if thou comest to

Christ, believing in him, there is nothing to shut up the fountain of life or prevent thee from being cleansed and healed. If there be any shutting and forbidding it is thy heart that is closed, and thy pride which forbids."[39]

It is clear that Spurgeon absorbed and implemented that line of thought developed and defended with such clarity and strength by Jonathan Edwards concerning the relation between natural abilities and moral abilities. The whole scheme of salvation springs from the holiness of God. Total depravity must be defined in terms of God's holiness and the sinner's antipathy toward that conglomerate attribute. "Your condition is not only your calamity, but your fault," Spurgeon insisted. The sinner must be not only pitied but blamed for he is without a *will* for what is good; "Your 'cannot' means 'will not,' your inability is not physical but moral, not that of the blind who cannot see for want of eyes, but of the willingly ignorant who refuse to look."[40] Election determines that we should be holy and without blame; effectual calling and the new birth produce the new creature who reflects true righteousness and holiness; perseverance implies that God's seed remains in us and we cannot continue in the direction of sin but must be holy; the cross draws sinners to it, if

---

38. Ibid., 139.

39. Ibid., 45. "The Open Fountain." If one examines the language of Spurgeon carefully and sets it in the context of the hyper-Calvinist conflict of the eighteenth and nineteenth centuries, from which Spurgeon himself received an abundance of criticism, Spurgeon's threat to push a theologian into the fountain makes perfect sense. Spurgeon appears to have in mind the kind of representation of the doctrines espoused by Lewis Wayman in 1738: "And last of all, only suppose the thing to be, that all who hear the Gospel should believe in Christ for life and salvation, according to what this author [Matthias Maurice] tells us is their duty; would there not, probably, be millions in the world believing in Christ for life and salvation, to whom God hath not given eternal life in Christ, and who shall never obtain salvation by him?" (*A Further Enquiry After Truth*, 19). In this context both the freeness of salvation and the unity of all aspects of the doctrines of grace become most relevant.

40. MTP, 1874, 493. "For Whom Did Christ Die?"

they are drawn savingly, because of its just verdict on their sin and its crushing display of the holiness of God. It is, therefore, the holiness of the cross that is a barrier to a sinner's embracing it, not the fact that in God's secret purpose he has determined that it shall certainly be saving in its effects for the people he has given to the Son.

Spurgeon was overwhelmed with the lavishness of God's grace in the atonement, and though he spoke clearly of its limited nature, it was always in the context of the certainty with which God carried out his purposes of grace. Infinite mercy that a holy God would condescend to save sinners, and do it in such a public promiscuous fashion so that none can complain that it was done in a corner! The certainty of the salvation that God accomplished gave endless material for Spurgeon's clear affirmations. "There is a fountain opened in the atonement, by which the offence rendered to God's honor and dignity is put away. What if we have sinned, yet the Lord has punished that sin in the person of his own Son, he has thus fulfilled his threatening, and proven the truth of his word. In Jesus Christ, therefore, the guilt of those for whom he was a substitute is put away consistently with the righteousness of the great Lawgiver."[41]

That "righteousness of the great Lawgiver," in conjunction with the substitutionary and propitiatory aspects of the atonement, was compelling to Spurgeon. They bore infinite comfort to Christ's people and Spurgeon would not have his listeners come short of any spiritual comfort legitimately theirs. Since Christ has suffered the penalty for sin and has made recompense to divine justice, if indeed the Lord Jesus has been condemned for us, then "While justice survives in heaven, and mercy reigns on earth, it is not possible that a soul condemned in Christ should also be condemned in itself. If the punishment has been meted out to its substitute, it is neither consistent with mercy nor justice that the penalty should a second time be executed."[42]

Clearly a favorite hymn of Spurgeon's was the Toplady number entitled "Whence This Fear and Unbelief?" He quoted it at length or in part on several occasions and was particularly attached to this verse.

If Thou has my discharge procured,
And freely in my room endured
The whole of wrath divine;
Payment God cannot twice demand,
First at my bleeding Surety's hand,
And then again at mine.[43]

He wanted no one to lose the ineffable mystery of the fact that God himself had died for man the creature's sin. And that this rendered such a certainty to its efficaciousness, and a limitlessness to its possibilities, that it would be impossible that it could not atone for any sin anywhere.

Never could justice be more gloriously exalted in the presence of intelligent beings than by the Lord of all submitting himself to its requirements. There must be an infinite merit about his death: a desert unutterable, immeasurable. Methinks if there had been a million worlds to redeem, their redemption could not have needed more than this "sacrifice of himself." If the whole universe, teeming with worlds as many as the sands on the seashore, had required to be ransomed, that one giving up of the ghost might have sufficed as a full price for them all. However gross the insults which sin may have rendered to the law, they must be all forgotten, since Jesus magnified the law so abundantly,

41. MTP, 1871, 39. "The Open Fountain."

42. MTP, 1875, 159.

43. P&D, 170, 477. "The Living Care of the Dying Christ," and "Christ's Plea for Ignorant Sinners;" also NPSP, 1858, 136. "Particular Redemption."

and made it so honourable by his death. I believe in the special design of our Lord's atoning death, but I will yield to no one in my belief in the absolutely infinite value of the offering which our Lord Jesus has presented; the glory of his person renders the idea of limitation an insult.[44]

For this reason Spurgeon used the nomenclature of limitation sparingly and with positive explanation in his exposition of the atonement. He preferred to speak of effectuality and certainty. But just as strongly, his consideration of "limitation" as an insult led him to reject the concept of universal atonement. In fact he was glad to use the term "limited" if one set the idea of "general" opposite it, for such a limitation was really no limitation at all.

> Now, beloved, when you hear any one laughing or jeering at a limited atonement, you may tell him this. General atonement is like a great wide bridge with only half an arch; it does not go across the stream: it only professes to go half way; it does not secure the salvation of anybody. Now, I had rather put my foot upon a bridge as narrow as Hungerford, which went all the way across, than on a bridge that was as wide as the world, if it did not go all the way across the stream.[45]

The infinite dignity of Christ's person demanded the utter success of his aim in giving himself up for the sake of sinners. Spurgeon's refusal to admit any limitation to Christ's death meant especially that its efficacy was not subject to man's will. If it were, then it falls short of its purpose in the punishment of every sinner who dies short of salvation, and the final arbiter of this infinite transaction set up in the decrees of eternity is the will of a mutable, temporal, fallen, rebellious

creature. The incongruity of it all should obliterate its feasibility.[46]

In addition to the dignity of the person who was substituted for us, two factors render this transaction certain and efficacious. First, it was the intent and purpose of God to save a people for himself by the sacrifice of his Son. "We declare that the measure of the effect of Christ's love, is the measure of the design of it. We cannot so belie our reason as to think that the intention of Almighty God could be frustrated, or that the design of so great a thing as the atonement, can by any way whatever be missed of."[47] Without blasphemy it is not possible to conceive that he has failed in his purpose. "It is quite certain, beloved," Spurgeon reasons, "that the death of Christ must have been effectual for the removal of those sins which were laid upon him." We cannot conceive that Christ has died in vain. "He was appointed of God to bear the sin of many," and it is "not possible that he should be defeated or disappointed of his purpose. Not in one jot or tittle will the intent of Christ's death be frustrated. Jesus shall see of the travail of his soul and be satisfied. That which he meant to do by dying shall be done, and he shall not pour his blood upon the ground in waste in any measure or sense."[48] If he has been condemned, those united to him in his death as indicated by their faith in him shall in no wise come into condemnation.

---

44. SEE, 1:348.

45. NPSP, 1858, 135, 136.

46. Spurgeon described the Arminian position this way: "The Arminian holds that Christ, when he died, did not die with an intent to save any particular person; and they teach that Christ's death does not in itself secure, beyond doubt, the salvation of any one man living. They believe that Christ died to make the salvation of all men possible, or that by the doing of something else, any man who pleases may attain unto eternal life; consequently, they are obliged to hold that if man's will would not give way and voluntarily surrender to grace, then Christ's atonement would be unavailing. They hold that there was no particularity and speciality in the death of Christ" ("Particular Redemption," NPSP, 1858, 130).

47. Ibid.

48. MTP, 1874, 160.

This statement of purpose leads to the consideration of the second point which contributes to the certain unfailing efficacy of Christ's death. That is, in some sense Christ's sufferings were quantitative. Spurgeon paints a vivid mental picture of the intensity and exact justice of Christ's substitutionary suffering for his people and suggests that his hearers suppose a man who has passed into hell. Then they suppose that his eternal torment should all be brought into one hour and multiplied by the number of the saved, a number past all human enumeration. Is it possible now to imagine what "a vast aggregate of misery there would have been in the sufferings of all God's people, if they had been punished through all eternity?" Then we should remember that "Christ had to suffer an equivalent for all the hells of all his redeemed." Christ gave God "the satisfaction for all the sins of all his people, and consequently gave him an equivalent for all their punishment."[49]

In speaking on "The Determination of Christ to Suffer for His People," Spurgeon considers why Christ refused the cup of wine mingled with myrrh. One of the reasons was that such a refusal was "necessary to make the atonement complete." If Christ had drunk from the cup, the atonement would not have been valid because he would not have suffered "to the extent that was absolutely necessary." Christ suffered "just enough, and not one particle more than was necessary for the redemption of his people." The ransom price would not have been paid had the wine cup taken away part of his sufferings. Had as much as a grain of his suffering been mitigated "the atonement would not have been sufficiently satisfactory." Insufficiency to any degree would have condemned his people to perpetual despair. The utmost far-

thing must be paid; inexorable justice cannot omit a fraction of its claim. Christ must go the whole length of suffering.[50]

Not only did Spurgeon see great comfort and assurance in the doctrine of limited atonement, he found the doctrine of universal atonement to be positively destructive of the moral attributes of God. His "Defence of Calvinism" includes a particularly striking presentation of limited atonement.

Some persons love the doctrine of universal atonement because they say, "It is so beautiful. It is a lovely idea that Christ should have died for all men; it commends itself," they say, "to the instincts of humanity; there is something in it full of joy and beauty." I admit there is, but beauty may be often associated with falsehood. There is much which I might admire in the theory of universal redemption, but I will just show what the supposition necessarily involves. If Christ on His cross intended to save every man, then He intended to save those who were lost before He died. If the doctrine be true, that He died for all men, then He died for some who were in hell before He came into this world, for doubtless there were even then myriads there who had been cast away because of their sins. Once again, if it was Christ's intention to save all men, how deplorably has He been disappointed, for we have His own testimony that there is a lake which burneth with fire and brimstone, and into that pit of woe have been cast some of the very persons who, according to the theory of universal redemption, were bought with His blood. That seems to me a conception a thousand times more repulsive than any of those consequences which are said to be associated with the calvinistic and Christian doctrine of special and particular redemption. To think that my saviour died for men who were or are in hell, seems

---

a supposition too horrible for me to entertain. To imagine for a moment that He was the substitute for all the sons of men, and that God, having first punished the Substitute, afterwards punished the sinners themselves, seems to conflict with all my ideas of Divine justice. That Christ should offer an atonement and satisfaction for the sins of all men, and that afterwards some of those very men should be punished for the sins for which Christ had already atoned, appears to me to be the most monstrous iniquity that could ever be imputed to Saturn, to Janus, to the goddess of the Thugs, or to the most diabolical heathen deities. God forbid that we should ever think thus of Jehovah, the just and wise and good![51]

This concept of a definite atonement encouraged Spurgeon in his evangelism also. When Jesus used the word "many" he indicated a certainty in the efficacy of his death. But just as surely he meant "many"—not just a few, but "many." "Let us expect to see large numbers brought within the sacred enclosure," Spurgeon encouraged his congregation. Because the blood is shed for many, the masses must be compelled to come in. While a group of half a dozen converts gives us joy why should we not expect half a dozen thousand at once! "Cast the great net into the sea," Spurgeon challenged and to his young men he urged, "Preach the gospel in the streets of this crowded city, for it is meant for many." And to personal workers he said, "You who go from door to door, do not think you can be too hopeful, since your Saviour's blood is shed for many, and Christ's 'many' is a very great many." No one shall ever trust Christ in vain or find the atonement insufficient for him. "O for a large hearted faith," he cried, "so that by holy effort we may lengthen our cords, and strengthen our stakes, expecting to see the household of our Lord become exceeding numerous." Isaiah 53, a crucial passage in Spurgeon's exposition of limited atonement, rivets fast the reality of "many." "He shall see of the travail of his soul, and shall be satisfied; by his righteousness shall he justify many, for he shall bear their iniquities." "Dwell on that word 'many,'" Spurgeon argued in his recapitulation, "and let it nerve you for far-reaching labours."[52]

Summary

Spurgeon's gift of oratory was exclusively his and one would be foolish to feel either capable or obliged to duplicate it. Giving adequate expression in human language to the glory and importance of Christ's substitutionary death taxed, even far surpassed, the massive talent of Spurgeon. His intense passion for Christ jumps off the pages of his published sermons and must have been mesmerizing and overwhelming in the spoken form. Even in reading his sermons one can feel his intensity about Christ's passion. It swallowed Spurgeon up. He exhausted himself verbally, emotionally, and physically seeking to transfer the mental and spiritual power which emanated to him from the cross and energized his ministry.

The unity of biblical theology, the eternal covenant, depended on the cross for its cohesion. For Spurgeon, it permeated the entire corpus of divine revelation and provided a touchpoint where the eternal and ineffable divine self-knowledge intersected with human observation. Even if occasionally he took disjointed verbal cues to engage in applicatory allegory, his overall vision was true and infused every sermon with the sweep of canonical theology flowing from every part of the Bible. In the cross one has a historic tangible presentation of the eternal purposes of God in the eternal covenant. Predestination, election, ef-

---

51. *Autobiography*, 1:172.

52. P&D, 43.

fectual calling—these are hidden from our view and are mysterious in their operation. The cross, though its power, wisdom, and dimensions are mysterious and unsoundable, nevertheless gives a location where all the metaphysical aspects of redemption become immanent. It is there that we can say, "These things were not done in a corner."

An atonement of certain and particular efficacy, far from increasing the distress of Christians short on assurance, should encourage them. Prior to any benefit gained by examination of personal experience for assurance of salvation, one must explore the historical reality and salvific certainty embedded in the cross. The death of the Word incarnate and the purpose of God to save sinners by that death, so Spurgeon surmised, should be immense encouragement to any person whose distress comes from a true picture of the lethal nature of his sin. Spurgeon would remonstrate endlessly and exhaust his creative and applicatory powers to show a downcast saint how firm and infallible his assurance might be once he grasps the reality that he who spared not his own Son will certainly give us all things.

Spurgeon proclaimed, and had palpable evidence for, the evangelistic power of definite atonement. His sermons surge and vibrate with the positive and optimistic application of the wondrous doctrine. Many who believed the doctrine seemed to operate as if it should be kept a secret. A minister should be forbidden to give public display of it. Spurgeon in contrast obviously meditated strongly on that biblical truth and found it to be a power with saints and sinners alike. It arms the evangelist with certainty and every sinner with hope. God saves sinners and will not bring this world to a close until the efficacy of Messiah's death has been fully satisfied. Every "coming sinner" may find real hope in the certainty of Christ's absolute victory on the cross.

For Spurgeon, the cross was both spiritual power and motivation to sanctification. The Christian is the purchased possession of Christ and his determination is that they shall be a peculiar people filled with zeal for good works. He shed his blood for this purpose, and, as surely as he will bring his blood and righteousness to them, so will he work in them holiness. Because by the cross we are bought with a price and are no longer our own, we may be sure that God will be glorified in the bodies of his people. He will transform their minds, recreate them in true righteousness and holiness, and mortify their flesh just as surely as he has rescued them from its dominance.

"God forbid that I should glory save in the cross of our Lord Jesus Christ, by whom the world is crucified unto me, and I unto the world" (Gal. 6:14).

7

THE CHALLENGE OF CHURCH LIFE
AND THE GOVERNANCE OF WORSHIP

Do all of you who are members of this church, know whether the Sunday-school is getting on well, or not? Now, speak the truth; do you? Did you ever make any enquiry about it? Then there are various societies for the spread of the gospel, connected with this church; do all of you know that there are such societies; and do you help them all that you can? Come, now put the matter to your own consciences.[1]

anagement of such a massive congregation as the church at the Tabernacle became was no easy matter for Spurgeon nor undertaken without a deep sense of inadequacy and desperate need. "I need your prayer for the work and ministry of this huge church," he told his congregation. "What a load rests upon me!" With over 5,500 for whom he was responsible, even with all the help given by elders and staff, including highly competent personal staff, "I have enough upon me," he admitted, "to crush me unless heaven sustains me."[2] He likened his brother, J. A. Spurgeon, and the elders to Moses' helpers in the wilderness, "else should I utterly faint." Beyond that, the general leadership required makes up a burden "which none can carry unless the Lord gives strength."

Before Spurgeon went to London, a "good old man" prayed for him that he "might always be delivered from the bleating of the sheep." Though he did not quite grasp its importance then, now that "hour by hour all sorts of petitions, complaints, bemoanings, and hard questions come to me," he fully understood it. Hearing such sounds is not helpful when he sought to "get the food ready for thousands here, there, and everywhere, who look for it to come to them regularly, week by week." He laid bare the depths to which his unrelenting responsibilities brought him when he confessed, "Sometimes I become so perplexed that I sink in heart, and dream that it were better for me never to have been born than to have been called to bear all this multitude upon my heart." Particularly difficult were those times he felt that he could not help and he was called on to do the impossible. Complicated matters called for great thought and careful deliberation and he

---

1. SEE, 5:30.

2. S&T, October 1881, 449.

would not proceed in any of these matters "without using my best judgment at all times." These recurrent issues took time, spiritual energy, mental strength and often brought complete fatigue because such "burdens are apt to press very hard on a sympathizing heart, and cause a wear and a tear which tell upon a man."[3] Spurgeon's great usefulness and inimitable gifts brought his early death. He could not have survived as well as he did without a sufficient number of devoted and efficient church officers and personal assistants.

Elders and Deacons

Without a clearly established procedure and a fully sympathetic group of elders and deacons even those recurrent matters, part of the life of any healthy church, could have been fragmenting. During the events surrounding the dedication of the Metropolitan Tabernacle, Spurgeon set out his understanding of the operations of a local church. He considered the church within itself a family, whole and entire, needing nothing outside itself to make it complete. They made no appeal to a synod or general assembly or looked to outside authorities such as bishops or archbishops. The church had its own bishop, that is, pastor, and its own presbytery or elders. It appointed its own deaconship and thus had no outside dependencies. "Should every other church become extinct its organization would not be marred." Spurgeon accepted a modified form of Episcopalian Presbyterian Independency as the scriptural method of church government, all of those words referring to functions within the local church family. One man had the oversight, the bishopric, of the church under God and gathered a presbytery around him, "that they may be with him the pastors of the flock." It maintained its congrega-

tional principles, and yet, for mutual assistance, not government, stood ready to enter into a kind of Presbyterian alliance with any other church.[4] Spurgeon went on the say that he knew of some churches that had amalgamated the elders and deacons. He did not know by what biblical warrant they did so, and he felt it to be a destructive mistake. It would have been impossible for his church to exist "except as a mere sham and huge pretence, if it had not been for the Scriptural and most expedient office of the eldership."[5] The deacons worked hard at the temporal interests of the church while the elders took the spiritual.

J. A. Spurgeon summarized the procedures concerning church membership and discipline practiced by the Metropolitan Tabernacle and the churches founded under the auspices of the church's societies. This presentation concerned the discipline as distinguished from the creeds and constitution. James Spurgeon made no claims that this procedure was perfect, but it was that which served this church best, the outgrowth of necessity, not of theory. While necessary diversity in churches due to the peculiar circumstances of pastor and people was recognized, the health of any cooperative union of churches depended on sustaining a sense of confidence in each other's discipline, including the method of receiving members and the causes and manner of dismissing them. "We have but small faith in ecclesiastical statistics, and what is worse, a limited confidence in letters of commendation from our churches," Spurgeon admitted, and he hoped for improvement as a result of laying out the practice of the Metropolitan Tabernacle.[6]

The Tabernacle had no written code of laws except the Bible and asserted that all "such printed rules as some have desired, and others adopt-

---

3. Ibid.

4. MTP, 1861, 257.

5. Ibid., 260.

6. J. A. Spurgeon, S&T, February 1869, 198-206.

ed, are only ferrets at the best of times, and snares and traps in periods of dispute and difficulty." Sanctified common sense, prayer, and knowledge of Scripture are unsurpassed in the stable governing of a congregation. If leaders acted in things temporal after a "truly business principle," and "in things spiritual as God's word and Spirit dictate," no formal statement of discipline and procedure would ever be required. In normal ongoing matters of business an undeviating practice would sustain the work in a healthy state and cooperative spirit, but emergencies called for special action "adopted to suit the exigencies of the case." No pre-established traditions should "forbid the course which wisdom suggests, even though it should be contrary to all the precedents of the previous history of the church." The presence of general principles, a toleration of an elastic interpretation of them as cases may require, combined with abounding confidence between pastors, officers, and members, will establish efficiency and harmony. Without the latter, in particular, no amount of rules can keep a church from lapsing into confusion and conflict.

First in importance in the orderly and spiritual governance of a church is its pastor. Though he is its servant, he also must "rule, guide, and discipline it as God shall help and direct by his Holy Spirit." The Tabernacle had two such officers laboring, but James Spurgeon recognized with all candor "that if two men ride a horse one must sit behind, and he who is in the front must hold the reins and drive." A co-pastorship will be a dismal failure should this understanding fail. In his particular case, he recognized that "one of the two brothers has been so instrumental in creating the necessity for additional help, from the very fullness of blessing resulting from his labors; and is, moreover, so superior in talent, influence, and power, it is a privilege to follow in the order of na-

ture and birth which God, from the first, had evidently designed." James Spurgeon was fully content to be known as his brother's helper. He had been asked to take the position in October 1867 for a three-month probationary period. After that, at a special church meeting in January 1868, James Archer Spurgeon came to be his brother's assistant pastor, with the clear understanding that he would not necessarily succeed his pastor to the pastorate should Charles die first, nor would he necessarily fill the pulpit in the absence of Charles. He was fully content with that clearly and cordially stated arrangement.[7] The pastor provided, therefore, the common center for all church life to avoid the unseemliness of having a "hydra-headed band of Christians."[8]

Charles Spurgeon seemed fully content with that arrangement also. During the inaugural ceremonies of the Tabernacle, with his father and his brother present, also in the presence of men that represented the last four pastorates prior to Spurgeon, even one that aided Dr. Rippon in his last years, Spurgeon indicated that he could envision no cessation of his ministry there prior to his death. "I do not think, that in the course of the next twenty years, you as a Church will have such a choice of pastors as you have had during the last twenty years. If I should die you can do so, I suppose, but I do not think that anything short of that, would get me to go away from this spot."[9]

He could not even envision any uprising in the congregation that would make him go. Spurgeon would never agree with a minister that gets in a conflict, shows the white feather, and resigns the charge. He was captain of the vessel, "and if there should be Jonah in the ship I shall as gently, and in as Christian a spirit as possible, pitch him out."

7. *Autobiography*, 2:79.
8. S&T, February 1869, 198-206.
9. MTP, 1861, 258.

A Jonah should not drive out the captain, but he must "stand by the ship in ill weather as well as in sunshine." Spurgeon knew that by God's grace he was called to serve that people in that place, "and if God's grace and providence shall move me, well and good, but nothing else whatever will."[10]

James Spurgeon envisioned the success of this central focus on the pastor as dependent on his "personal weight of piety and prudence, zeal, godliness, gentleness, and forbearance, as will inevitably place him in the front in course of time." No efforts to take advantage of the weight of the office "when sound judgment and weight of character are wanting, will ever result in anything short of failure and contempt." Pretensions to the office without its qualifications will inevitably devolve into disaster bringing shame to the man and an increasing burden on the people.[11]

Laboring beside the pastor are men qualified respectively for two different offices, deacons and elders. A man of judgment, prudent in counsel, and skilled in money matters gives evidence of such abilities as are required for the serving of tables, the disposing of finances, and the securing of needed funds for the church. These qualities combined with spiritual maturity qualify one for the office of deacon. Another might be gifted with speech so as to be apt to teach and exhort and lead devotional exercises in the church or prayer meeting, or give a word of comfort beside the bed of sickness, or in the house of mourning. These, again combined with spiritual maturity, constitute the qualifications of an elder.

The Tabernacle deacons, nine in number, were elected by the church, at the "suggestion of the pastor, after consultation with the previously elected deacons." Though in theory any member might nominate whom he pleased at such an election, there had never been a case of dissent from the recommendation of the pastor and deacons. They were chosen for life. Deacons were given the tasks of "care for the ministry" meaning the temporal well-being of the pastors, helping the poor of the church, regulating the finances, managing the church's property, and assuring for the order and comfort of all worshippers. To accomplish all this, all nine deacons had specific tasks assigned to them in managing the temporal and service affairs of the church. This prevented any uncertainty as to responsibility. One deacon served as general treasurer for many years, another managed all outdoor work, repairs of the exterior, keeping the gates, appointing doorkeepers, while another cared for all indoor repairs. More than one watched over the interests of the new churches established by Tabernacle evangelists, missionaries, and church planters, and another saw to the arrangement and provision of the weekly communion.[12]

Spurgeon loved his deacons and did all he could to encourage them and make their value known to the church at large through public commendation. Good relations with deacons meant longevity in ministry. When a former student, W. Williams, wrote Spurgeon seeking advice concerning a troubling deacon, Spurgeon responded in his patented laconic style, "Bear. Bear. Bear. Forbear. Forbear. Forbear. In yielding is victory. Fight the devil and love the deacon. Love him till he is loveable."[13] In a more obvious note of positive appreciation, Spurgeon wrote about the passing of "Our highly esteemed deacon, Mr. Thomas Cook." Spurgeon characterized him as a "spiritually minded, solid, and stable Christian" who exhibited a healthy fear of God. Severe illness did not embitter him but had a "ripening influence,"

---

10. Ibid.

11. S&T, February 1869, 49-57.

12. Ibid., 50.

13. William Williams, *Personal Reminiscences of Charles Haddon Spurgeon* (London: Religious Tract Society, 1895), 213.

making him rise from his bed "weak in body but strong in grace." He was among the rare kind that enjoyed "constant peace," in whose mind any rising doubts "were slain by full assurance." Spurgeon recalled younger days when Cook helped the pastor immensely by the major role he took in building the Tabernacle. He had a warm and gracious heart fully committed to the work. "We know well the spot," Spurgeon revealed, "where this devout Deacon knelt with his Pastor, all alone, amid the materials of the unfinished Tabernacle to implore a blessing upon those who should worship within those walls." The evening was dark, and only the angels and the Lord saw or heard the two brethren. "Who could desire a better consecration for any house of prayer than the secret pleadings of a godly man!" After a commendation of his wife and children, Spurgeon finished, "Farewell, brother beloved, the Lord fill up the gap thy departure has made."[14]

On January 3 and 12, 1883, Spurgeon lost two highly valued deacons. William Higgs was "our dear and valued friend and deacon, … A loving helper, … A valued counselor," and the treasurer and trustee of the orphanage. On the day of his burial William Mills also died. The church lost a "kind and careful guardian, and all of us a hearty friend." Other friends in the church also had died in recent days, so "these blows at the first staggered, not only the pastor, but all the circle of workers." Two days after the death of Mills, deacons, pastors, and elders met together for a meal and a time of prayer, self-examination, and communion. Spurgeon called it a "solemn, holy, hopeful gathering of men chastened in spirit."[15]

Less personal but equally to the point of what Spurgeon admired in a deacon was his parody on an article he read entitled, "The Hornless Dea-con." Since a horn is an offensive weapon, Spurgeon surmised, a "hornless deacon is one who cannot give offense, resent an injury, or inflict a wound. What a splendid acquisition to a quarrelsome church!" This hornless wonder would rule well and "reduce chaos to order by the mere force of Christian patience." Though few believed in the power of non-resistance, Spurgeon saw it as unbounded. He who yields will conquer and the one that suffers for love will manifest the greatest power in time. His harmlessness, however, should not extend to allowing people to forget their subscriptions, or indulge the minister "to draw twice the amount of his salary." "The kind gentle, but earnest deacon is invaluable. He is as an angel in the church, and does more than angel's service. Excellent man!" Suppose, however, that hornless meant failing to blow the ram's horn, but letting the minister do it all. Spurgeon did not commend such silence, but preferred a deacon like Stephen who could "both care for the widows and preach the gospel." Country churches would prosper more if deacons "would exercise their gifts, and keep the village stations supplied with sound doctrine." Spurgeon went on to investigate the possibility of the phrase meaning humility, not blowing his own horn, but at the same time faithful under discouragement and hopeful under difficulty. Or perhaps hornless meant that he is a teetotaller, not lifting his horn to be filled with wine. Good for him as long as he does not make the water-jug the symbol of his life, and "pour cold water over everything and everybody, in season and out of season."[16]

According to the article by James Spurgeon, the eldership at the Tabernacle was sustained by twenty-six brethren. At this time the church had 3,860 members. "Without the efficient and self-

14. S&T, September 1871, 430.

15. S&T, February 1883, 95, 96.

16. S&T, January, 1880, 9, 10.

denying labors of the elders," Spurgeon conveyed, "we should never be able to supervise our huge church." Unlike the deacons, the elders were re-elected annually, but usually continued for life in their office. If other elders were needed, names were proposed by the pastor to the already elect-ed elders, and after some time has been given for thought, the elders discussed the desirability of their election. If recommended "with general unanimity," the pastor put their names before the church, and, following the opportunity for dis-cussion, the vote of the church was taken. James Spurgeon believed that the heavy influence of the pastor in this process was entirely appropriate and any other plan would only produce weak-ness. The pastor had more at stake in the choice than any other single person. "No other plan," the loyal brother argued, "will enable him so faithful-ly to discharge his office of guide and shepherd. …Timidity here is a crime, and the affectation of modesty in not wishing to influence the church is to our mind a dereliction of duty." The impor-tance of this office made it necessary that a church that possessed unlimited liberty in its affairs see that its "junior and less instructed members" be directed in the choice of officers. The failure on the part of both a pastor and officers to do so be-cause of "fear of giving offense seems to us but the fear of man which bringeth a snare."[17]

He explained why this procedure was taken so seriously, involving so much meditation and such an active part of the pastor. To the elders is committed the spiritual oversight of the church, and such of its concerns as are not assigned to the deacons nor belong to the preacher. Interviewing inquirers, visiting candidates for church mem-bership, seeking out absentees, caring for the sick and troubled, and leading prayer meetings,

catechumen and Bible classes for the young men were all ministries discharged by the elders. One elder was supported by the church to visit the sick and destitute and to maintain currency with the church roll. Otherwise it would not receive regu-lar and efficient attention. Maintaining the dis-tinction in these offices, eldership and deacons, had served the church well and "is in a thousand ways a great assistance to good government."[18]

Essential for the health of any church is a well-ordered, biblically sound manner of receiv-ing church members. Those seeking membership by profession of conversion made application on Wednesday evening, between six and nine o'clock, to the elders. Two or more elders rotated each week for the purpose of seeing inquirers. When satisfied, the elder entered his observations in one of a set of books, called the Inquirers Books. For convenience in future interviews, a card was given the enquirer bearing a number cor-responding to the page where the elder recorded the candidate's experience. Arnold Dallimore's examination of this book showed that the entire interview process centered on the determination of three things. One, is there clear evidence of de-pendence on Christ for salvation? This involved a clear and felt knowledge of sin and a deep sense of the necessity of the cross. Two, does the candidate exhibit a noticeable change of character including a desire for pleasing God and a desire for others to believe the gospel? Three, is there some under-standing of, with a submission to, the doctrines of grace?[19] The only effective antithesis to merit salvation, in Spurgeon's view, was a knowledge of utter dependence on divine mercy.

Once a month, or oftener when required, James Spurgeon would see the persons approved

---

17. S&T, February 1869, 52, 53.

18. Ibid. 53.

19. Arnold Dallimore, *Spurgeon* (Edinburgh: Banner of Truth, 1995), 81.

by the elders. When he was satisfied, he nominated an elder or church member as visitor to be sent out by the church, at the next church meeting, to enquire as to the moral character and repute of the candidate. If the church appointee found the visit satisfactory, the candidate would come with him to the next convenient church meeting, and reply to questions put to him "from the chair."[20] These questions were designed "to elicit expressions of his trust in the Lord Jesus, and hope of salvation through his blood, and any such facts of his spiritual history as may convince the church of the genuineness of the case." This procedure proved to be "a means of grace and a rich blessing." Realizing that many would view this manner of receiving members as too rigorous and potentially discouraging to genuine but shy souls, James Spurgeon remarked, "None need apprehend that modesty is outraged, or timidity appalled by the test thus applied. We have never yet found it tend to keep members out of our midst, while we have known it of service in detecting a mistake or satisfying a doubt previously entertained."[21] He went on to point out the urgency of fidelity both in tending to souls and watching over the church:

> We deny that it keeps away any worth having. Surely if their Christianity cannot stand before a body of believers, and speak amongst loving sympathizing hearts, it is as well to ask if it be the cross-bearing public confessing faith of the Bible? This is no matter of flesh and blood, but of faith and grace, and we should be sorry to give place to the weakness and shrinking of the flesh, so as to insult the omnipotence of grace, by deeming it unable to endure so much as the telling in the gates of Zion what great things God has done for the soul. Of course, the system may be, and has been, abused, but we decline to recognize any argument

drawn from the abuse of what we use lawfully. It need not be an offense to any, and it will be an immense blessing to that church which watches for souls, and rejoices over one repenting sinner more than over ninety and nine just persons which need no repentance.[22]

After the testimony before the church, the candidate withdrew, and the appointed visitor gave his report. If the church voted to receive, the junior pastor baptized him or her after a week day service. The candidate was then received before the church at the first monthly communion, when the pastor extended the right hand of fellowship in the name of the church, and his name was entered on the roll of members.

At that point the baptized convert received a communion card (for some years the person was given twelve numbered tokens) divided by perforation into twelve numbered parts, one of which should be turned in each month at a communion service held every Lord's Day. If a member failed to commune for three months without any known cause, the elder responsible for his district would visit him, and send in a report on a printed form. A letter was written to those too distant to visit, a record of such visit or letter being retained. In a case of discipline, an elder, appointed by the body of elders, visited the person in question and reported his findings to the body. Should the matter demand action beyond caution and advice, the matter came to the church with a recommendation from the elders for censure or excommunication.[23]

This matter of discipline was taken seriously for the sake of the person, the church, and the other churches. By sad experience, the Tabernacle elders found that recommendations of mem-

---

20. S&T, February 1869, 53.
21. Ibid.

22. Ibid. 53, 54.
23. Ibid. 54.

bers of other churches were too often unreliable. Great caution was needed. Again the elders led the way in this matter. An elder visited the person requesting a transfer of membership and entered his observations in the transfer book. Any difficulty resulted in an arranged visit by one of the pastors. "Alas!" Spurgeon discovered, "membership with some churches is not always a guarantee even of morality."[24] Some churches retain a name upon their books for years after the person had ceased to commune. Even more sadly, they would grant a transfer of membership ignorant of the spiritual state of the person so retained, "as if all were satisfactory."[25]

Because of this experience the Tabernacle kept close knowledge of its members that had moved and granted them upon their moving a certificate for three, six, or twelve months, which had to be renewed at the end of that period with a report of the reason for renewal. Otherwise the membership would lapse. "We much prefer commending our brethren to the fellowship of other churches," Spurgeon informed, "where they may be of service, than to have them linger out a merely nominal connection with us."[26] Before granting that, however, the request was read to the church, accompanied by a statement of the person's reason for leaving and a history of their attendance while at the Tabernacle. If all proved satisfactory, the church authorized the usual letter of dismission to be sent.

The delicate nature of some of these matters prompted Spurgeon to offer an explanation of the rationale behind the process:

In all our business the aim is to have everything done openly and above-board, so that no one may complain of the existence of a clique, or the suppression of the true state of affairs. We occasionally ask the unquestioning confidence of the church in its officers in cases delicate and undesirable to be published, but otherwise we consult the church in everything, and report progress as often as possible in all matters still pending and unsettled. Nothing, we are persuaded, is so sure to create suspicion and destroy confidence as attempts at secret diplomacy, or mere official action.

When details of cases under discipline are kept from the church, the fact is openly stated, and leave asked for the maintenance of such public reticence; while any member is informed, that if dissatisfied, the pastor will give him the reasons why the elders have advised the removal of the offender, and their motive in not giving details of the sin. When it would be for the injury of good morals, or expose the pastor to a suit-at-law, the officers ask the confidence of the church, and request it to adopt their verdict in the case without hearing detailed information; this is cheerfully accorded in every case, and much evil thus averted.[27]

Church contributions of all sorts, particularly those given to the ongoing benevolent ministries of the church, were reported meticulously month by month. In addition, so that all would be set forth with integrity, all money matters underwent an annual audit by "unofficial brethren selected by the church." All accounts were read and record books produced at the annual church meeting, where all the members were urged to be present. Month by month meetings of deacons and elders were recorded and confirmed at the next meeting. Without previous notice no business would arise at the annual meeting except that introduced by the chair, or as sent up from an elders' or deacons' session. Exceptions to this could be

---

24. Ibid.
25. Ibid.
26. Ibid.

27. Ibid., 55.

considered unless the procedure was challenged as irregular.[28]

The Importance of Church Membership

Church membership, though clearly non-sacramental in itself, was seen as an important, perhaps essential, element of spiritual stewardship. In 1876 Spurgeon printed an article by Vernon Charlesworth answering objections to joining the church. Charlesworth recognized that many persons were resting on the completed work of Christ for salvation and cherished "a refreshing sense of God's pardoning love, manifested a genuine hope of having an inheritance in the skies," and yet were not identified with any assembly of God's people.

Charlesworth commended the faith and sincerity of these unattached Christians, but questioned their consistency. Some hesitated in church membership because "it was such a solemn thing to join a church." These fail to recognize that God already has made them members of the one body. "There is a wondrous inter-relation of being between the Lord Jesus Christ as Head, and all true believers who constitute his mystical body." No salvation exists apart from participation in this vital connection. Every visible church is a local expression of this unity. God already has joined every believer in this solemn union and the assembly on earth is a witness to the divine calling, whereas refusal to do so is a "contravention of Divine order, and is a guilty resistance to the Spirit of God."[29]

Others admit the duty but do not feel the necessity of immediate action. While ascertaining the genuineness of faith urges some caution and appropriate hesitation, this might turn into sinful procrastination. Nothing is more natural than an ardent desire in a new Christian to declare their "decision for Christ before the church and the world." Some could see no advantages in church membership that they already did not enjoy by their union with Christ. They still unite with the people of God in "social intercourse and public service" and have the advantage of being free of pew rents and regular contributions "to any enterprise to which the church is committed."

Rather than dwell on the negative implications of such cupidity, Charlesworth focused on advantages of organic membership. He pointed to "an immense satisfaction to one's own mind in the bond of fraternity to which we publicly subscribe," as well as an ever-present caution against the "spirit of worldliness into which all are so prone to fall." Visible connection in a covenanted body establishes a "blessed sympathy" by heightening concern for the welfare of one another. "Growth in grace is assisted" by mutual edification and a person's example of visible membership encourages others that could benefit by such a fraternal union as is found in church membership.

Others object because they see so much inconsistency in those that are church members. Charlesworth reminded the reader, without excusing the sinful frailty of church members, that none were without sin and all in need of greater sanctification. A mere observation of that reality should deter no one from doing their duty, joining in a body in which they could both admonish and receive admonition for greater purity of life. "I would ask," Charlesworth probed, "do those who demand the strictest consistency between the profession and lives of others detect no inconsistency in themselves? Are they without sin? Do they not judge others by a standard they dare not apply to themselves, demand more than they themselves are able to render, and withhold that

---

28. Ibid.

29. S&T, April 1876, 153.

charity from an erring brother which they feel they need?"[30]

Salvation is not gained by church membership some object. Charlesworth agreed, and warned against any that believed their church membership was a passport to heaven. But this objection is an idle plea and harmful to the development of piety. Others hesitate for they feel that they might fall away. Those that "withhold a profession and neglect a duty under the fear of falling and proving castaways, take the likeliest means of securing what they deprecate."

Others stay away from visible membership because they object to the ordinance of believers' baptism. Spirit baptism is enough and water baptism is unimportant. Charlesworth responded by asking if water baptism was a Christian ordinance and implied as an act of obedience in the apostolical commission? Does the uniform practice of the apostles indicate that they so understood it? To these objectors, and to those that pointed to their infant baptism as a reason to shrink from church membership based on believers' baptism, Charlesworth summarized: "Our present purpose is to show that the baptism of believers by immersion is an ordinance of divine appointment, and is commanded as a preliminary to the public recognition of believers as disciples of Christ."[31]

Others object that they have a fear of eating and drinking the Lord's Supper unworthily. If eating and drinking unworthily is a sin, refusal to eat and drink from a motive of fear is a more serious sin. If such a fear justified abstaining from participation, then none would partake, and the command of the Lord to "Do this" would be universally disobeyed. Charlesworth offered an encouragement that the danger implied in such a warning may be avoided through a right-minded approach to the Table:

But why should we eat and drink unworthily? Can we not come with our hearts rightly affected towards the Lord Jesus Christ, and discern in the bread and wine fit symbols of His broken body and shed blood? Can we not come mourning that so much evil lurks within us, and seek for grace to crucify the flesh with its affections and lusts? Can we not come in the spirit of reverent humility to worship the Father, and to hold communion with each other? Believe me, if we come thus, we shall not eat and drink unworthily, and to us the Saviour says, "Eat, O friends! Drink, yea, drink abundantly, O believer!"[32]

He warned against a spirit of self-righteousness in those that continued to profess their own unworthiness, as if they could ever rise to any condition of worthiness before a righteous and holy God. He closed his appeal by pointing to the conclusion of the matter:

In dealing with the above objections, we have endeavoured to reach the conclusion—that it is the imperative duty of all who are saved by virtue of their union with the Lord Jesus Christ, who "is the head of the body, the church," to avow the fact by an honest profession, and by obedience to his command to enter into sincere and hearty fellowship, that the unity of the Church may be apparent, and the worship and work of the Lord maintained in the world.[33]

Hale and Hardy

From the month by month reports of the church, very few of Spurgeon's hearers maintained serious doubts about the validity of church membership. *The Sword and the Trowel* contained the statistical information about the church's advance in baptisms each month. Yearly statistics were reported at the annual church meeting. In February

---

30. Ibid., 156.
31. Ibid., 158.

32. Ibid., 159.
33. Ibid.

1873, the report showed that 359 had been added to "the church in the Tabernacle" during 1872. Leaving to go "to other churches," presumably for reasons of proximity, were 131. Thirty-nine "died in the Lord." Other causes led to the dismissal of other persons leading to a net increase of 30; "but so long as souls are saved," reasoned Spurgeon, "we had sooner send them to other places that retain them, for our church is large enough already."[34]

In 1874, October, Spurgeon surveyed the ministry at the Tabernacle and felt overwhelmed with gratitude for the fullness of "spiritual blessing as well as other mercies." Many made public their confession of Christ, a spirit of prayer abounded, the attendance at prayer meetings and week-night services exceeded any numbers of the past, and, he continued, "the crowds on Lord's days eager to hear the word are greater than ever." He attributed all glory to the Lord, "who prospers his own truth." Spurgeon would not be surprised "if Satan should roar again." As in the past, mounting opposition "will be the decisive token that good is being done."[35]

At the prayer meeting on Monday, September 21, 1874, Spurgeon, who usually turned the baptizing duties over to his brother, or on some occasions to Vernon Charlesworth, took opportunity to baptize Charles and Thomas, his twin sons, "in the presence of an immense assembly." The attendance was a moving display of "hearty union with their pastor and his family in ways most touching to our heart." Mrs. Spurgeon was present for a few moments to see "her two boys yield themselves to be buried with Christ in baptism." The statistical report for that month read: "Baptisms at Metropolitan Tabernacle, by Mr. J. A. Spurgeon:– August 27th, twenty-three; September 3rd, twenty-one. September 21st, by C. H. Spurgeon, two."[36]

The strong spiritual condition of the church in 1874 made a report in the *Christian World* (perhaps this was the roaring lion he anticipated) all the more egregious. The magazine had reported that in Mr. Spurgeon's absence, many seat-holders left the worship service since the one they had come to worship was absent. Supposedly an American visitor upbraided the implicit idolatry soundly. Spurgeon was both grieved and outraged at the report and claimed that there was not a word of truth in it. All church officers reported that attendance was full and steady and every work carried on with excellence by the responsible parties. Prayer meetings, in fact, were better attended than usual and weekly offerings were increased over those of the past year. Inquirers continue to increase and many sheaves for harvest await the pastor's return. "The love, unity, zeal, and industry of the brotherhood have borne every strain without a sign of giving way; in fact, in nothing has there been any declension or failure, not any reason for issuing the unfortunate article to which we have alluded."[37]

Spurgeon explained this steadiness and the unflagging character of the work by referring to long-standing policies of receiving and retaining members. The work did not depend on "excitement" or "violent laboring to kindle fanaticism." The 4,880 on roll were *persons,* "living men and women who are really with us." Discipline was firm and "names are not allowed to remain year after year to swell a nominal force, and sustain a lie." The people know the gospel, are established in it, give to the causes the church sponsors, and "hence we are able to trust them in our absence." God's manifest grace through the years, Spurgeon

---

34. S&T, February 1873, 93.

35. S&T, October 1874, 491.

36. Ibid.

37. S&T, March 1875, 135.

pointed out, was not "so superficial and evanescent, that the Pastor's sickness can empty the pews and deaden the services." Because it is the work of God, "none shall depreciate it without protest."[38]

To reinforce this point, Spurgeon carried a report of the yearly evangelistic services held at the Tabernacle every February. His sickness caused his absence, and, at the end of William Olney's report about the "series of Special Services for the revival of religion," Spurgeon stated: "How all this ought to encourage *churches* to work, and not rest on the Pastor. Here we have a people deprived of their minister, and yet receiving a larger blessing, though no professional revivalist is called in to fill the preacher's place. God be thanked for our beloved co-pastor, deacons, and elders, and for a membership alive unto God by vital principles, and not dependent upon such a poor instrument as their so often afflicted preacher."[39]

When on November 7, 1875, sixty-nine persons were received for membership, in the context of praise for divine blessings, Spurgeon observed: "Our care is great, and our examination of candidates very rigid, but they come none the less, perhaps all the more."[40]

At the beginning of 1876 Spurgeon reported the basic numbers of 1875. In his absence the work had not flagged, for seventy converts awaited addition to the church when he returned from Mentone. These persons were not included in the report of 510 added to the church in 1875. Out from the Tabernacle went 208 to strengthen or form other churches and 66 "went home to glory." The clear increase was 136, leaving a membership of 4,813. Spurgeon observed, "We must win for our Lord at least one soul each Sabbath or our loss by death cannot be made up."[41] There must have been 100 dismissions for other reasons, or Spurgeon meant an increase of 236 instead of 136.

In February 1881 the report for 1880 ran thus: Increase by baptism, 314; by letter, 101; by profession, 38; total, 453. Decrease, by dismission, 147; by dismission to form a new church at Tooting, 5; by joining other churches with letters, 50; emigrated, 12; died, 74, excluded for non-attendance, 106; removed for other causes, 5; total, 399—leaving a net increase of 54, and making the number of members on the books 5,284. The notes said that "A happy meeting was held, and the reports showed that the hardness of the times and the illness of the pastor had not materially damaged the finances." As to spiritual progress, it was hoped that, in earnestness, unity, and prayerfulness, the Church was never in a healthier state.[42]

The church report for 1881 was presented on February 3, 1882. Spurgeon was happy to be well enough to attend and commented that "there was a thick fog outside, and some of it penetrated into the interior of the building; but the warmth of Christian affection and enthusiasm which prevailed throughout the whole meeting prevented anyone from feeling much of its influence." The huge, happy family gathered to tell what the Lord had done for them and by them during the year. Baptisms numbered 279, additions by letter 68 and by profession 35. Professions was explained as "those who have been previously baptized," making a total of 382 additions. The decrease totaled 315, giving a net increase of 67. Several categories again constituted the decrease: 144 dismissed by letter, 34 joining other churches without letter, 7 by emigration, 56 removed for non-attendance, 3 excluded [presumably for disciplinable offenses], 1 withdrawal, and 70 deaths.

38. Ibid.

39. S&T, April 1875, 189.

40. S&T, December 1875, 585.

41. S&T, February 1876, 92.

42. S&T, March 1881, 147.

Many of those, through the years, that removed by letter, were going to help start other congregations in different parts of the city to be served by students from the College. Those removed for non-attendance or joining churches without letter seemingly show that Spurgeon was unable to satisfy everyone and that a constant undercurrent, as in most churches, of discontent or disinterest continually brewed and produced a very consistent outflow from the Tabernacle. Those numbered as members of the congregation, however, were not misleading but constituted a disciplined, spiritually alert, and active body. The number of members was at 5,310.

For 1882, a net increase of 110 brought the total membership to 5,427. This included 65 deaths for the year, including two deacons and four elders. Spurgeon and the deacons made up a deficit of £150 for support of the poor and the almshouses so that the year could begin with a clean balance sheet. He explained something about the constituency of the church:

> The number of the poor of the church is very great, and quite out of proportion to the usual condition of churches. Hence the poor fund needs strengthening. The work carried on is great, and those who can afford to give largely are few in comparison with the needy who are in fellowship with us. It is our joy and honour to be a church in which the working class and poor abound; but this fact tries our finances sternly.[43]

He soon learned that William Higgs, one of the deceased deacons and a magnanimous supporter of all ministries of the church, had left in his will £500 to the orphanage, the same amount to the College, and an equal amount to the poor of the church. "This legacy will help us for some few years to meet the annual deficiency," Spurgeon explained, "and before it is all spent we hope some donor will more fully endow the Almshouses."[44]

Numbers for 1885 showed the difficulty of maintaining an increase each year in such a large congregation. The statistics read at the Church Meeting in February 1886 reported: Increase by baptism, 267; profession, 23; transfer, 62; restoration, 1: total 353; decrease, by dismission to other churches, 170; joining other churches without letters, 47; names removed for non-attendance, 129; emigration, 10; withdrawn from, for other reasons, 3; deaths, 73; total 432. The resultant number on the church-roll was 5,314. This represented a net loss of 79 members for 1885, and thus showed an increase in membership of four since 1881.[45]

Maintenance of such massive facilities and the support of so many works of outreach called for a home base that was increasing in number as well as in ability to give. The tension between spiritual blessings and the desire to see such blessing result in material increase was constantly on the mind of Spurgeon. He referred to this phenomenon in 1886. After noting the additions to the Tabernacle through the labors of church planting and other local missionary work, Spurgeon mentioned the attendance at the Tabernacle during the summer months. "The College is not in session for the men are having their vacation; the orphans are nearly all away; the seat-holders are most of them at the seaside." In spite of that, "crowds are even greater than usual, and many feel the power of the Word." Since most of these, however, "return to the country, we shall not have the home church thus increased." This should bring no regret, however, for "the Lord is with us and we magnify his name."[46]

---

43. S&T, March 1883, 148.

44. S&T, April 1883, 201.

45. S&T, April 1886, 195.

46. S&T, September 1888, 516.

Holy Living

Spurgeon, long before the Downgrade Controversy, saw society as a degrading influence on the spiritual lives of Christians. The church's witness for the gospel was directly proportioned to the holy lives of its members. Spurgeon, therefore, urged careful attention to circumspect living. Discipline of children was a first order issue. "A husband is king of his household," Spurgeon wrote, "and if he allows everything to be in a state of anarchy he must blame himself in some measure." Connected with proper discipline was the practice of family worship. This practice had declined sadly in recent years, and along with it pervasive family piety. "If there be no gathering for prayer in the morning," Spurgeon asked, "how can we expect to be prospered in the duties of the day? If there be no gathering for prayer at night how can we expect the Lord to guard the tents of Jacob through the night watches?"[47] Spurgeon's easily accessible devotional books were written with the hope of encouraging family worship. In the preface to *Morning by Morning,* Spurgeon expressed his hope that "our little volume may also aid the worship of families where God's altar is honoured in the morning." He had no desire to replace Mason, Hawker, Bogatsky, Smith, or Jay, but did aspire to a position among them. "Our happiness will overflow should we be made a blessing to Christian households," he continued. "Family worship is beyond measure important, both for the present and succeeding generations; and to be in part a chaplain in the houses of our friends, we shall esteem to be a very great honour."[48]

Christians also had begun to frequent worldly amusements. The theatre should hold no charm for a Christian because it does nothing to promote holiness. "Pass by it with averted gaze, the house of the strange woman is there." It can be no school of virtue that has such an attraction for the debauchee and the harlot. This practice of theatre-going will be the death of piety, Spurgeon believed. He made no compromise on that issue. He saw the approbation of theatre-going on the part of ministers as one of the most obvious signs of a loss of spiritual discernment and genuine piety. Society had become so accustomed to the low standard of morality, much of it prompted by the language and actions of the theatre, that "the very air is tainted with pollution and our streets ring with the newsboys' cries vending filthy papers and abominable prints." Christians must labor for purity, be earnest in prayer, make a covenant with their eyes, guard their lips, and avoid evil wherever it appears. Jesus will never chasten a Christian for not being worldly enough. The Christian's pleasure must reside in the glory of God, the beauty of Christ, for he has "tasted the high delights of fellowship with God."[49]

Many a promising young person has been lost to the work of the Lord by flirting with danger. A more libertarian view toward strictness in morality fosters looseness and paves a sure road to destruction. "God grant us grace," Spurgeon plead, "to keep in these peaceful paths, even though others should call us Puritans and ridicule our holy fear of sin."[50] To that end he recommended a newly published allegory that gave an engaging presentation of "the necessity and blessedness of Christian separation from the world and its pleasures." He recommended it as a gift to young people because it would soon "make the boundary between the church and the world more defined than it is today."[51]

---

47. S&T, September 1879, 408.

48. Charles H. Spurgeon, *Morning and Evening* (Geanies House, Fearn, Ross-Shire: Christian Focus Publications). This is located in the prefatory material under the title "Morning by Morning."

49. S&T, September 1879, 410.

50. Ibid., 411.

51. Ibid., 444.

Spurgeon insisted that a "revival" began and ended with the church. "Only in the river of gracious life can the pearl of revival be found." A church that needed revival was in a sad state, a sub-normal state, and came to that condition only by inattention, neglect of those unctuous gifts that are the privilege of each body of saints. Revival cannot come to the dead but to the living; to the living, that is, that have lost their light and strength. Revival would affect the world through the renewed holiness and gospel love that put the saints about their business, but revival cannot come to that which is not already alive. A revival brings the church to a condition in which they ought always to have been; "it quickens them, gives them new life, stirs the coals of the expiring fire, and puts heavenly breath into the languid lungs." This should be sought earnestly for all backsliders and at any time of declension in grace. Causes of decline include joining with worldly company and the stifling lack of life-giving atmosphere that accompanies such a life, the spiritual starvation that ensues upon failure to use means of grace such as prayer, feeding on Bible truth, conscious communion with God, earnest participation in the services of the Lord's Day, and cultivating a consciousness of the presence of the Spirit of God during personal and corporate prayer. Lack of these things brings about spiritual consumption—faintness after exertion, ebbing of vital energy, wheezing decaying lungs. "If they mourn for sin it is only with half-broken hearts, and their grief is shallow and unpractical."[52]

By what means is the church, or its individual members, in such spiritual coma to be revived? Vital godliness subsists on vital truth. This cannot be done by mere excitement, by crowded meetings, by stamping the foot, slamming the pulpit, and the "delirious bawlings of ignorant zeal." This might simulate revival in dead souls but for living saints other means are needed. Living truth nourishes the living heart by means of the Holy Ghost, but mere carnal excitement provides nothing substantial to sustain and enlarge life. If revival is to come "we must go directly to the Holy Ghost for it, and not resort to the machinery of the professional revival-maker." Ministers that are careless about the truths that cross their lips, church officers that are dead weight upon the Christian community, and members that do not relish the spiritual exhilaration of divine truth are all like smoke in the eyes and as agreeable to the lively saint as being bound to a dead body. They are sickening and make "the inmost spirit feel the horrors of mental nausea."[53]

Spurgeon did not want to need revival, but for those to whom it was necessary he urged earnest seeking in order that there might be abundant benediction. A four-verse hymn summarized his views. Verse three epitomizes the idea:

> Wake thy slumbering children, wake them,
> Bid them to thy harvest go;
> Blessings, O our Father, make them;
> Round their steps let blessing flow.[54]

Prayer Meetings

Vital to the maintenance of vibrant spiritual life in a church, and also to its revival, was the discipline of corporate prayer. Spurgeon made sure that each service of worship in the church was preceded by a prayer meeting. Often prayer continued by some individuals meeting in a special place, usually in a room under the auditorium, during the service. In September 1881 he mentioned that "The special prayer meetings before

---

52. S&T, December 1866, 531.

53. Ibid., 532, 533.

54. S&T, December 1878, 534.

our week-evening lecture have not only been well sustained all through the past month, but have increased in number and grown in fervency, and we are already reaping the firstfruits of what will, we trust, prove a good harvest of souls."[55] In 1886, an elder reported the blessings of having such a time of prayer before the week-day (Thursday) service, attended by around 2,000 people. "From this prayer meeting," elder G. E. Elvin wrote, "the Pastor ascends to the Tabernacle, evidently greatly refreshed, and as much in the Spirit as on the Lord's Day."[56]

Monday evening prayer meetings fueled all the ministries and other services of the church. Spurgeon described the atmosphere of this meeting in 1881 as "seasons of unusual power" and thus a precursor to "a blessing of an unusual extent."[57] From all over the world, requests had come to the Tabernacle for prayer, and were soon followed by statements of praise for answers. "These have tended to keep the meetings real and earnest, for there has been actual business to do with the Lord that heareth us." Each meeting had a distinct flavor, but "all are remarkable seasons of fervent devotion." Frequently over 1,500 people were in attendance. Spurgeon believed that the "key to the non-success of churches, and the small progress of individuals" was directly attributable to the lack of prayer.[58]

On an August Monday in 1881, Spurgeon spoke on the theme that permeated his view of biblical prayer, "Why We Have Not." Based on James' statement, "Ye have not because ye ask not," Spurgeon analyzed the lack of spiritual power, lack of conversion, and lack of additions to many churches, and concluded that the answer is found here—"Ye have not because ye ask not."[59] Churches prosper when many of its members know their way around the rooms and halls in the house of mercy. "If we are not at home in prayer everything is out of order" and one may easily get lost in the halls through lack of familiarity with the place of entrance to the mercy-seat. "Familiarity," therefore, "with the mercy-seat is a great point in the education of a child of God."[60]

Prayer is not a second-rate activity, but is a grand cement for unity of purpose, the proper discernment of gifts, and the submissive appeal of the children of God before the throne of his power for those ends that he judges most conducive to his glory. In prayer the child of God shoves aside self-confidence and absorption in worldly wisdom and finds greater conformity to the sovereign wisdom of his Redeemer. God intends to receive glory to himself through answered prayer and the urge to pray for the health of those that are sick, for the health of the church through the success of its various ministries, and for one's own spiritual advancement will receive answers from God according to his promise. It may seem a self-evident truth, and thus tautologous, but it opens clearly one of the central issues of Christian living to contemplate that prayerlessness finds no source from which to glorify God for answered prayer. Leaving oneself in the position of having little reason to glorify God for present care and present condescension to human need, leads to barrenness of spirit as well as fruitlessness in church life. They must pray, therefore, for the continued support of the ministry extensions of the church; "Commend them all to the Most High," he urged, "for whose glory they exist."

Spurgeon asked particularly for prayer for himself in the abundant opportunity to preach

---

55. S&T, September 1881, 486.

56. S&T, January 1886, 8, 10.

57. S&T, September 1881, 486.

58. Ibid.

59. S&T, October 1881, 493f.

60. Ibid. 498.

before so many on Sunday and on the weekday service because he trembled "lest the opportunity should be lost in any measure."[61] Proclamation without divine blessing would always be fruitless no matter how structurally sound and theologically straight the message appeared. "Do pray that I may preach with power," and for "the Holy Ghost to convert these eager thousands." Within reach of his voice were "persons of all nations, ranks, ages, and religions," increasing the stewardship of agony in prayer that they may be saved.

For his own strength in his heavy and distressing responsibilities he begged their prayer and for the sake of their own spiritual well-being he again asked their prayer for him:

> If I have been useful to you in any measure, pray for me; it is the greatest kindness you can do me. If the word as spoken by these lips has been a means of grace to your children, plead for me that others of the young may be brought to Jesus by my teaching. If you would find my ministry more profitable to your souls, pray for me still more, and let it not be said of your minister that you do not profit by his preaching, and that you have not because you ask not.[62]

A year later, Spurgeon described two prayer meetings on Monday evenings at the Tabernacle to demonstrate of how much variety they could consist. Hymns, including new hymn tunes, requests by letter for special prayer, verbal requests from the congregation, prayers by appointed individuals, brief hortatory comments from the pastor reflecting some element of a prayer request, involvement by the orphanage children's choir in one of the meetings including a new song from a Sankey song book ("Oh, What a Saviour that He

Died for Me") all made for real interest and genuine spiritual enjoyment. One man prayed that "the Lord would knock all the nonsense out of the pulpits." Spurgeon editorialized that he agreed, and that it seemed strange to him that men could preach entire sermons with no Christ in them. Crafty and clever though they be, they contained not enough gospel to save the soul of a mouse. Spurgeon commented that the woman who was so ignorant that she thought her minister was saying Jesus was our meat and physic when he actually spoke of a Christian metaphysic had far more sense than the minister. The record of these prayer meetings showed, according to Spurgeon, that a healthy variety in such meetings did not exclude there being an equality of power.[63]

The next month he included the record of two more prayer meetings. On October 9 Spurgeon set forth the cross as his theme throughout and summarized the evening with the observation, "Eight brothers had spoken with the Lord on our behalf, five hymns had been sung, and several short addresses given, and the hour and a-half was gone, all too quickly." For October 16 special attention was given to the Sunday School Union and other such organizations to encourage universal prayer for Sabbath-school work. Participating with Spurgeon in one season of prayer was Mr. Wigney, "the conductor of separate services for children on Sunday morning." In schools connected with the Tabernacle over 7,000 children were involved. The entire Ragged School movement had taken over 300,000 children off the streets of London. Spurgeon reminded the hundreds of workers gathered that the prevalence of irreligion, poverty, wretchedness, sin, superstition, and evil literature still present in many parts of London make this move-

---

61. Ibid.

62. Ibid., 499

63. S&T, November 1882, 588.

ment all the more necessary. The results for good should encourage all workers. The end of all their labors should be the salvation of the children. He related the story of the apple in the bottle to illustrate how important early formation was to the well-being and piety of the future adult population of London. The meeting closed with special prayer for all workers.[64]

Music and Worship

Anything that detracted from the fullest participation in the music by the entire congregation Spurgeon opposed. To the leader he warned, "The people come together not to see you as a songster, but to praise the Lord in the beauty of Holiness." He was not to sing for himself only, "but to be a leader of others, many of whom know nothing of music." Tunes should be easily learned by all so that none will be compelled to be silent when the "Lord is to be extolled in the assembly." None should be defrauded of their part in the worship because of the exclusive taste of the leader. "Simple airs are best," Spurgeon opined, and "very few of the more intricate tunes are really musical." Those whose concern is more for art than for corporate worship should meet at home for that purpose, but "the Sabbath and the church of God must not be desecrated to so poor an end. "Twists and fugues, and repetitions, and rattlings up and down the scale" amounts to noise-making more fit for Babel than for Bethel.[65]

He reminded musicians who might be enamored of the natural beauty of music when performed in technical purity, that "true praise is heart work." It is like "smoking incense that rises from the glowing coals of devout affection." While sound correctly executed brings delight of a sort, praise is not a thing of sound. Though,

in the congregation, inextricably connected with sound for most weighty reasons, the essence and life of praise still lies "not in the voice, but in the soul." The leader must tend the congregation to give to spiritual praise a suitable embodiment in harmonious notes. He must not employ means or music that destroys the spirit of corporate praise. "Take care that you do not depress what you should labour to express," he urged.

Carelessness can harm just as severely as fastidiousness. A leader must be discerning and understand both text and the impact of musical phrasing in selecting a tune that expresses the spirit of the psalm or hymn. Heedless repetition in time, tune, tone, and emphasis is an abomination. Selecting tunes at random is little less than criminal. "You mock God and injure the devotions of his people" by a careless offering of worship material that cost no thought or effort, no exercise of judgment. On the other hand, a well-selected harmony can help the pious heart to wing its way to heaven rather than "vex the godly ear by inappropriate or unmelodious airs, adapted rather to distract and dishearten, than to encourage intelligent praise."[66]

The "godly ear" Spurgeon referred to was perhaps his own. Spurgeon was indeed vexed at extremes. Slow and dull tempos with monotonous droning in large assemblies serves to swamp, drench, and drown the spirit of worship. On the other hand, he could not endure hearing hymns treated as jigs and dashed through at a gallop. One must be wise to find the fitting pace. Also one leads best who is noticed the least. A leader must have as his object "to induce all the congregation to join in the singing."[67]

The goal of truly corporate worship through singing meant that more in the congregation

---

64. Ibid., 631.

65. S&T, June 1870, 277. "How Shall We Sing?"

66. Ibid., 277-78.

67. Ibid., 278.

must not only have spiritual motives but some aptitude for the duty. He believed Psalm 33 called for this. In his exposition, Spurgeon contended that "He deserves the best that we have. Every Christian should endeavour to sing according to the rules of the art. So that he may keep time and tune with the congregation. The sweetest tunes and the sweetest voices, with the sweetest words, are all too little for the Lord our God; Let us not offer him limping rhymes, set to harsh tunes, and growled out by discordant voices."[68] A singing school using the sol-fa method Spurgeon had seen as a successful way to train many that know nothing of music the art of reading simple tunes. A few sessions employing such a method would expand the percentage of participation in the singing throughout the congregation as well as enhance its quality.[69]

At the same time, the pressure exerted by some to dominate this portion of worship must be systematically resisted. Professional singers as an element of worship Spurgeon detested. "The institution of singers, as a separate order is an evil," he bristled, "a growing evil, and ought to be abated and abolished."[70] He had in mind the practice when he commented on the phrase, "Praise is comely for the upright." He contended that "Praise is not comely from unpardoned professional singers." Rather, before God it is "a jewel of gold in a swine's snout. Crooked hearts make crooked music, but the upright are the Lord's delight."[71]

Sometimes self-appointed vocalists destroy the spirit of public worship by deploying themselves in such a way as to dominate the time of singing. "A band of godless men and women," he called them, "will often install themselves in a conspicuous part of the chapel, and monopolise the singing to the grief of the pastor, the injury of the church, and the scandal of public worship." At other times, a person with delusions about his own gifts, "with a miserable voice, will drag a miserable few after him in a successful attempt to make psalms and hymns hideous, or dolorous."[72] Yes, the obstacles to musical purity and simplicity were many.

Professional singers were no worse than organ players. Spurgeon found a book entitled *An Account of the Remarkable Musical Talents of Several Members of the Wesley Family* based on a great amount of diligent research that was worthy of a more profitable subject. "We are about as musical as we are Wesleyan," he remarked, but still he found some sentiments that he wanted to commend to "our organ-blowing brethren." The writer's observation that Wesley had a "great aversion to musical instruments being used in places of sacred worship" Spurgeon liked and, therefore reported an anecdote supporting the view. The Wesleyan commentator, Adam Clarke, that Spurgeon called the "Arminian perverter of Scripture,"[73] registered his own dissent from "all such corruption in the worship of the Author of Christianity." Clarke reported that when Wesley was asked if he objected to the presence of instruments in Wesleyan chapels, he responded tersely, "I have no objection to instruments of music in chapels, provided they are neither heard nor seen."[74] At least on that issue, Wesley expressed Spurgeon's sentiments exactly, but with exceptions for special cases as we shall see.

68. Charles Spurgeon, *Treasury of David 2 vols.* (Nashville, TN: Thomas Nelson, nd), 2:105.

69. S&T, June 1870, 278.

70. Ibid.

71. Charles Spurgeon, *Treasury of David*, 2:104.

72. S&T, June 1870, 278.

73. Handwritten in the front of an Adam Clarke commentary located in Spurgeon's Library at Midwestern Baptist Theological Seminary, Kansas City, Missouri.

74. S&T, September 1874, 438.

Spurgeon felt that the use of instruments in the normal corporate worship of the church increased the natural tendency toward externality, superficiality, and formalism in worship as well as in one's perception of the nature of Christian faith. "When the organ peals out its melodious tones, but the heart is not in the singing, dost thou think that God has ears like a man, that can be tickled with sweet sounds?" He asked. Don't think that God is as impressed with wordless sounds and mechanically produced tones and harmonies as we might be. "He is spiritual; the music that delights him is the love of a true heart, the prayer of an anxious spirit. He has better music than all your organs and drums can ever bring to him. If he wanted music, he would have not asked thee, for winds and wave make melodies transcendently superior to all your chief musicians can compose." Such music he compared to the unwarranted lighting of candles as an element of worship. "Does he want candles when his torch makes the mountains to be great altars, smoking with the incense of praise to the God of creation?" Spurgeon feared that ritualized, stylized, artificially produced attempts at worship would hide the true matters of heart worship from "many who externally appeared to be devout," about whom it could be said, "When they knew God, they glorified him not as God!"[75]

When confronted with the phrase, "Praise the Lord with harp," Spurgeon reduced this admonition to the necessity of external aids for the immaturity necessarily involved in old covenant worship. Israel still was in a state of training and "used childish things to help her to learn." Jesus, however, gives us "spiritual manhood" and we make melody without strings and pipes. Spurgeon did not believe instruments to be expedient but did not see them as "unlawful." Should those as mature as "George Herbert or Martin Luther ... worship God better by the aid of well-tuned instruments, who shall gainsay their right?" Neither he nor his people needed them and he felt that they would "hinder than help our praise." Others might choose differently, and they too live under gospel liberty. If they are used, however, it should only be as a help to the human voice, "for keys and strings do not praise the Lord."[76] When he reached Psalm 150, with its advocacy of trumpet, psaltery, harp, stringed instruments, organs, loud cymbals, and high-sounding cymbals, Spurgeon explained, though not too insistently and exclusively: "The gospel meaning is that all powers and faculties should praise the Lord—all sorts of persons, under all circumstances, and with differing constitutions, should do honour unto the Lord of all. If there be any talent, if there be any influence, let all be consecrated to the service of the universal Benefactor."[77]

Whatever he may have allowed in theory, Spurgeon had no fluctuation when it came to the regular worship times at the Metropolitan Tabernacle. At its opening in 1861 Spurgeon employed all the weapons in his arsenal in describing worship in that newly constructed building, consecrated fully to the glory of God in preaching and corporate worship. He insisted that a major part of the worship of the congregation would be found in their participation in the singing of hymns. Spurgeon delighted in the sound of voices lifted in praise to God. He wanted all to participate and that right heartily. The sounds of human voices should not be diminished or muted by lack of participation or by the dominance of instruments.

---

75. MTP, Intended for Reading on Lord's-Day, May 22, 1892, Delivered by C. H. Spurgeon, At the Metropolitan Tabernacle, Newington On Lord's-day Evening, July 13, 1890.

76. *Treasury of David*, 2:104.

77. Ibid., 4:464.

The stricture on congregational praise resulting from the use of several designated professionally trained voices simply does not meet the New Testament criteria for the singing part of worship. "What a joyous thing it is to hear the thousands praise God at once; every man contributing to the song." Variety would make the sound more glorious. "The poor coarse voice belonging to some of us, who never can learn music let us try as much as we well; the flute-like voices of our sisters, the deep resounding mellow bass of the full-developed man; all the different tones, and notes, and voices, perhaps expressive of our different degrees and growths in grace, of our different trials and or different temperaments, all join to swell one common hymn which rolls upward to the throne of God." Everyone that refuses to sing, every mute voice, and every dumb lip mars the song.[78]

He pictured the dissenting congregation with a choir composed of five or six to "sing to the praise and glory of themselves" while the congregation sits still not daring to "spoil music so magnificent." Some places designate the work that should be the glory of human tongues and lips and hearts to an instrument that makes sound without articulation of a message and with no heart feeling or rational involvement. "May that never be the case here," Spurgeon exclaimed, but "as often as we meet together here may the song roll up to heaven like the voice of many waters, and like great thunders."[79]

In order to minimize non-participation and increase rational involvement, Spurgeon lined out every hymn before it was sung. In 1881 he quoted a passage from the *Examiner and Chronicle* of New York. The writer urged that great care be given to the selection of hymns and not follow the "lazy and senseless example" of a minister that said, "I never give my self any trouble about the hymns." Singing, the writer claimed, constituted worship as much as praise and prayer and "the preacher who does not select his hymns with special reference to their appropriateness to the subject of his sermon, loses at least half of their effect upon the congregation." Spurgeon concurred and added that the "whole spirit of the service may turn upon the *reading* of a hymn, and therefore it is a matter to be done in the best style." The preacher may have little if any control over the singers but he certainly can "so read the hymns that the people shall be helped to praise God intelligently, and the sacred worship shall not be careless and slovenly."[80]

In a book on Psalmody, J. Spencer Curwen suggested that reading hymns verse by verse was unnecessary, Spurgeon objected and defended strongly his practice of reading before singing. No person should be made to listen to singing in which he cannot join. "It is wretched to go into chapels and tear through a hymn like mad, while you have no idea what the words may be which they are thus hurrying over." Everyone must be able to sing with the heart and join in the sense of the hymn, but if they have no books, or are blind, or cannot read, how can this be without giving it out verse by verse? "Those who believe in praising God by machinery may have no care about the words being known, but we do not believe in their praising bellows any more than in the praying windmills of the Kalmuck Tartars."[81]

---

78. MTP, 1861, 218.

79. Ibid.

80. S&T, April 1881, 179.

81. S&T, December 1877, 575. The Tartars of Kalmuck placed small windmills at the entrance to their dwellings as praying machines. The priest would write prayers on each wing of the wheel, and as the wind blew the prayers would ascend thus making petitions many times a day. "According to their doctrine, to render prayer efficacious, it is only requisite that it should consist of moving petitions; and, whether the motion be operated by the lips, a cylinder, or a windmill, is indifferent." Information taken from the *Imperial Magazine*, July 1830, 687.

Spurgeon commented on a variety of books used to aid worship, observing their strengths and weaknesses. When reviewing *A Complete Compend of Revival Music*, Spurgeon called some of the inclusions "execrable," but immediately recognized that some people "sing them with gusto, and get good out of them." Reluctantly he admitted that much about music in worship was a matter of taste, yielding to the old proverb "which bids us neither dispute with winds nor tastes." He nevertheless maintained his preferences while granting reasonable freedom to others. Ira Sankey published *Sacred Songs and Solos* in 1882. Spurgeon commended it highly within a certain context. "For our part," he reminded his readers, "we shall always adhere to our solid psalms and hymns, and the grave, sweet melodies of our well-worn tunes, when the people meet on the Sabbath." At other services, however, such as a revival service or week-day services a few of the Sankey type sprinkled in would "give pleasure to good people whose tastes differ from ours."[82] In a strange way of stating very strongly something of his personal taste he wrote, "We confess we prefer our old-fashioned psalms and hymns, and their solemn music, to all the new jigs in the world." And then adding for emphasis he noted, "We cannot yet 'jump Jim Crow' to the glory of God, nor yet tune the songs of Zion to nigger melodies."[83]

Spurgeon wanted the rhymes to be good, the syllables to have their proper length, for God "should always have the best of the best." Beyond all this, however, is the heart conviction of the singer and Spurgeon would rather have "the wild song of the revivalist with the homely street tune, sung from the very soul, than the noblest music that was ever penned, or ever flowed from human lips, if the heart be absent, and if the strain be not in accordance with God's Word."[84]

Spurgeon supported attempts to render the Psalms in New Testament content. Nothing could excel David's Psalms, he believed, and they should be used in an evangelical spirit, filled with "the gospel of Christ, of which they are, indeed, already full in prophecy." In this way the congregation would "sing the very words of the Spirit, and shall surely edify each other and glorify our God."[85] He cautioned, however, that great care and some sound common sense be used when adapting tunes to these renderings. In a review of *The Psalmist*, published under the supervision of Ebenezer Prout, Spurgeon noted: "In some instances there are two varieties of the same tune to different hymns—an experiment of very doubtful value. Some of the tunes rejected should, we think, have been retained, and if they have been sacrificed to modern taste, so much the worse for modern taste." Dominance of harmony over melody, Spurgeon felt strongly, was not conducive to effective congregational singing. Although harmony seemed to be the guiding principle of modern psalmody, Spurgeon, at the risk of seeming old-fashioned, had observed that "ordinary people must have a taking melody if they are to enter heartily into the Service of Song."[86]

A more extensive investigation of *The Psalmist* revealed "many excellent pieces adapted for organ and choir, but not so many good congregational tunes as we expected." It did not compare favorably with the Tabernacle's *Our Own Hymnbook*, in the tune selections and meters. Spurgeon employed 35 different meters while *The Psalmist* had 168. Most of the special tunes, therefore, with odd meters "must therefore be mere wastepaper."

82. S&T, September 1882, 495.

83. S&T, March 1876, 137.

84. Ibid.

85. MTP, 1861, 219.

86. S&T, April 1879, 193.

The needless alteration of established tunes only created confusion. He could not imagine the discontent and consternation caused by altering such well-known tunes as Spohr, Moscow, York, Stella, Wareham, Montgomery, or Huddersfield. "Part of the people would run one way and the rest another." Giving new names to old tunes also was useless, confusing, and gives a false impression. "A respectable melody does not need an alias."[87]

The resistance to that sort of innovation did not mean he was averse to the introduction of new hymns. He did not want the newness of a setting to befuddle the worshippers by their inability to participate. To alleviate this difficulty, a new tune to be sung in the worship of the Sabbath would be introduced into the Monday evening prayer meeting. Perhaps two hymns of that meter would be sung so that the "people caught the strain, and are now prepared to recognize it when the tune is used in the great congregation."[88]

The appearance of *The Congregational Psalmist Hymnal* gave Spurgeon an opportunity to give a disquisition on how tunes should be selected for a hymnal. He did not object to the inclusion of new hymns, for many were centered on the glory of Christ's person and work and on Christian experience. People can read words easily enough. The introduction of a new tune, however, called for more discreet and careful direction. People cannot readily adapt to another tune, and unless the entire congregation is able to sing it by the book the result is distressing. "In our judgment," Spurgeon opined, "too many of the tunes in the book require an instrument to render them, and when such is the case, they cease to be congregational." A hymnal compiled from the standpoint of the musical tastes of an organist, and not from

that of a precentor, "may contain very good music, but it will not, therefore, be a people's book."[89]

Selection of tunes formerly was made when they passed the test of a vocal quartet. Congregational singing requires such a standard. "Nowadays anything which can be played is foisted upon a congregation," Spurgeon complained, "with the result that many must remain silent during the service of praise." When editors are organists and not singers, worship-song declines. He knew he left himself open to the charge of being old-fashioned, but he loved tunes that people could sing and that would remain with them long after the time of worship was past. "Our modern musicians may affect a contempt for what they call the eccentricities of the old fugues and repeat tunes, but they must admit that they were musical, and that they did more to inflame the passion of devotion than those which can only be interpreted by a keyed-instrument." This led him to register his oft-repeated jeremiad against the gradual infusion of instruments in worship. He could hardly bear the loss of "glee singing" and with the piano and organ both deemed as a *sine qua non* of the sanctuary he felt that he witnessed the decline of congregational singing. The sophistication of tunes has meant that congregational participation has been late and intermittent in the normal worship service of the church. "Congregational music is music for the congregation to sing, not listen to; and the sooner this simple definition is regarded by our tune writers, the better." Spurgeon wanted worship to remain an expression of the people, not a special reservation for professionals.[90]

Though in the normal worship of the church, Spurgeon had no instruments and no choir, he was not averse to either in the service of special

87. S&T, January 1880, 33.

88. S&T, November 1882, 585.

89. S&T, November 1886, 597.

90. Ibid.

meetings. When his friend, Dr. Hillier, a Doctor of Music who "deserves the title" in that he himself is "a sort of condensed band of music," opened a new tabernacle in July 1871, he commented that the official opening on Sunday was "with sermons." On Monday, however, a public meeting was held. At that, the combination of a noble array of speakers, an earnest company, and "an effective choir made the public meeting a lively one."[91] It was Monday, not Sunday.

A choir might also serve well for evangelistic purposes. In commending those that operated so efficiently in the evangelistic services for the month of February 1879, Spurgeon wrote, "We have no wish to compare the style of the two chief speakers, or to contrast the methods of the sweet singers and players upon instruments, but we are delighted to hear that every address delivered by Messrs. Clarke and Fullerton has been felt to be 'in demonstration of the Spirit and of power,' while the lively strains from the voice and cornet of Mr. Smith, and the tender pathos in all Mr. Chamberlain's solos have had much to do with making the meetings a complete success." He also thanked heartily the members of the choir. Not only were they at all the services in the Tabernacle singing and making melody to the Lord under the leadership of Mr. Frisby, but many of them attended the Saturday night prayer meetings to help in the singing. At the College Conference in 1881, an evangelistic choir under the leadership of Mr. Frisby sang to crowded conditions. Their presentations consisted of "several old-fashioned tunes."[92]

Spurgeon's worship services were not only matters of concern for him but for all of London. His congregation contained editors from many periodicals in London and other publications sent reporters regularly to give to London and the world the news of what happened in a Spurgeon service. What did he say, how did he pray, how did he look, what did they sing? What was the effect of it all? *The Christian: A Weekly Record* gave a report of the New Year's Eve service for 1870, and included the words to a hymn Spurgeon composed for his congregation to sing.[93]

Many churches held these "watch night" meetings, but one of the largest was that held annually at the Metropolitan Tabernacle. In spite of wretched weather, and the "inconvenience to many of the anniversary coming on a Saturday night," between 2,000 and 3,000 people gathered at 11:00. The service began with prayer, a hymn, and reading of the twelfth chapter of Isaiah. Spurgeon observed that "the new year ... reminded them of their new birth, of the time when it was with them the beginning of days, and therefore it was fitting that they should come together and praise God for all his mercies." They had found God faithful in the past year and could continue forth with "with resolute purpose and holy calm, saying, 'the Lord Jehovah is my Strength and my Song.'" Another hymn was sung, "O God of Bethel, by whose hand, Thy people still are led," followed by a prayer of "very solemn and earnest thanksgiving" with supplication for "yet a more abundant outpouring of the Holy Spirit on individual believers, and upon the Church, and upon the work of the Lord in every place, that it may prosper and increase." Another hymn, "For Thy mercy and Thy grace, Constant through another year," was followed by Spurgeon's exposition of John 1:29, "Behold the Lamb of God." The reporter included a condensed version of Spurgeon's message:

---

91. S&T, September 1871, 431.

92. S&T, June 1881, 291.

93. *The Christian: A Weekly Record Of Christian Life, Christian Testimony, And Christian Work*, Volume for 1871, London, (January 5, 1871).

There was a great evil to be met—the sin of the world; there was a great remedy for this great evil—the Lamb of God; and there was a great duty enjoined—namely, to BEHOLD this Lamb of God. Sin was the source of all misery and woe, the true viper that poisons mankind, and puts everything out of joint, and this sin is only to be met and taken away by the substitutionary work of the Lord Jesus Christ. "He hath made Him to be sin for us who knew no sin." By beholding Him, looking, believing, trusting Him, this load of guilt and wretchedness would be forever taken away. We can see the sun and the moon, although millions of miles away, and so the look of faith will reach Christ, and bring Him close to us. It was not strength or wisdom that was required, there may be no knowledge of theology, but looking to Him and trusting Him would give life eternal.

Just before midnight the entire assembly knelt and spent the remaining minutes of the year in silent prayer. Then they sang the verses, "composed by Mr. Spurgeon just before coming to the meeting," and said good night with reciprocal wishes for a happy new year. In reporting the song, the writer changed the word "Nought" in verse three to "Nor."

> At midnight praise the Lord
> Ye who this temple throng;
> Lift up your hearts with one accord,
> And close the year with song.

> Light up the altar fire,
> Forget the chilly night;
> Let grateful love all hearts inspire
> Praise God with all your might.

> Into the coming year
> March ye with banners high;
> Nought in the future need ye fear,
> For Israel's God is nigh.

> But march with voice of praise,
> Let music lead your way;
> To God the Lord your voices raise,
> On this the new-year's day.

Spurgeon's intense convictions about music in worship made their way even to his graveside. Ira Sankey, at Spurgeon's funeral meetings, said: "I have held him up as an example to hundreds of congregations, as a man who could inspire his people to worship in hymns of praise, by devoting time to the reading of the hymn, and then himself standing and singing with the people. I hope this example may be largely followed by the ministers of the gospel. The praise of God is a part of the worship, and should not be slighted."[94]

Evangelism and Worship

Evangelism and worship could not be separated in Spurgeon's concept of church life. Though we have looked at evangelism separately, as well as the doctrinal controversy Spurgeon maintained against his peers, our subject calls for us to close the gap between these two to see how Spurgeon viewed the impact of worship on evangelism and at the same time how evangelism affected biblical faithfulness in worship. The itch for greater numbers, had, in Spurgeon's estimation of the times, reduced the spirit of holiness and separateness in worship. "The way of God with his church," Spurgeon contended in October 1888, "has been to sever a people from the world to be his elect—a people formed for himself, who shall show forth his praise."[95] Purity in the act of praise and worship was foremost in the predestining plan of God; the church ignores that at its peril. How foolish to think that "we can save men on a more wholesale scale by ignoring the

---

94. *From the Pulpit to the Palm Branch* (London: Passmore & Alabaster, 1892), 163.

95. SS, 19:360. "No Compromise."

distinction between the dead in sin and the living in Zion." If no separation of the church from the world, and no purity in praise were intended, then why did martyrs shed blood and confessors and polemicists contend to their hurt for a pure doctrine? There are two seeds, and "the difference will be maintained even to the end; neither must we ignore the distinction to please men."[96]

The threat of judgment hovered over an impure church that compromised its worship for the approval of the world. "We are of a distinct race: we are born with a new birth, live under different laws, and act from different motives." If the reputed sons of God marry again the daughters of men and embrace the world, thus violating the covenant, we will be swept away with "some overwhelming judgment, and, it may be, a deluge of devouring flame."[97] To gain converts by softening doctrine or holy practice will alter the question from "How can we get them" to "How can we get rid of them?" Eagerness for numbers and the inclusion of respectable people has "adulterated many churches" in doctrine and practice and made them "fond of silly amusements." These are the people that cannot abide a prayer meeting but rush to sensations, and our labor to get them has only served to "tarnish the spiritual glory of the church."[98]

Spurgeon enforced his concern with revealing questions: "Are you afraid that preaching the gospel will not win souls? Are you despondent to success in God's way? Is this why you pine for clever oratory? Is this why you must have music, and architecture, and flowers, and millinery? After all, is it by might and by power, and not by the Spirit of God? It is even so in the opinion of many."[99]

All of these concerns impinged on the time of corporate worship. "Brethren beloved, there are many things which I might allow to other worshippers which I have denied myself in conducting the worship of this congregation." He was committed to setting forth "the unaided attractiveness of the gospel of Jesus." He gloried in a "severely plain" service, free of the enticements of art and performed music, seeking to show his brethren "that there is no need to try doubtful expedients and questionable methods." His emphasis unceasingly had been Christ crucified, and the purity and simplicity of the gospel. Those thousands in the Metropolitan Tabernacle, a consistent reality for thirty-five years, had come to hear about the "cross without the blue lights of superstition or excitement, the cross without diamonds of ecclesiastical rank, the cross without the buttresses of a boastful science." Human contrivances and human art would only hide and cover the sharp edge of the gospel sword. "How is it that it does so little of its old conquering work?" Spurgeon asked. "Do you see this scabbard of artistic work, so wonderfully elaborated? Full many keep the sword in this scabbard, and therefore its edge never gets to its work. Pull off that scabbard. Fling that fine sheath to Hades, and then see how, in the Lord's hands, that glorious two-handed sword will mow down fields of men as mowers level the grass with their scythes." The church must not travel to Egypt for help or invite the devil to help Christ.[100]

The Lord's Supper

Though Spurgeon refused to take communion after his conversion until he was baptized, he would not make that which was a matter of conscience to him the same for other believers. He wrote

---

96. Ibid. 361.

97. Ibid. 362.

98. Ibid., 362, 363.

99. Ibid, 363.

---

100. Ibid. 363-65.

his mother soon after his baptism: "Grandfather has written to me; he does not blame me for being a Baptist, but hopes I shall not be one of the tight-laced, strict-communion sort. In that, we are agreed. I certainly think we ought to forget such things in others when we come to the Lord's table." For Spurgeon this was a matter of Christian charity.[101]

He maintained this conviction that the Lord's Table peculiarly showed the union of God's people in a way transcending all their other differences. He had little hope that Christians would ever agree on baptism, but, concerning our Lord's death, "all who really are his people are agreed." They did not come to the tables as Baptists, Methodists, Presbyterians, or Episcopalians, but "simply as those that form one body in Christ" who agree to show to all mankind the death of the adorable Lord.[102]

In 1861, when noting several peculiarities of the church, he separated himself from both the open membership churches as well as the strict communionists. He would rather give up his pastorate than give membership to a man that refused to follow his Lord in baptism. He believed that the mixed membership churches were "eating the very vitals of the denomination."[103] At the same time, Spurgeon disclaimed any right to refuse communion to any person professing faith in Christ that was in good standing in any Christian congregation. There was no reason he should not extend to him the fullest Christian fellowship.

Contrary to the anecdotal information relayed by some Baptists in the Southern United States, Spurgeon maintained the position to the end. When reviewing a compend of theology by J. M Pendleton, a strong closed-communion

American Baptist, Spurgeon commented on Pendleton's definition of the church. Pendleton wrote: "A church is a congregation of Christ's baptized disciples, acknowledging him as their Head, relying on his atoning sacrifice for justification before God, depending on the Holy Spirit for sanctification, united in the belief of the gospel, agreeing to maintain its ordinances and obey its precepts, meeting together for worship, and cooperating for the extension of Christ's kingdom in the world."[104] Spurgeon saw this definition as containing a hidden agendum: "This appears to be an innocently redundant definition, but when it is used as a means of refusing the ordinance of the Lord's Supper to any but baptized believers, as it is in the chapter on that ordinance, then we see the purpose for which it was inserted. There are other matters with which we do not agree."[105]

He thought a book on Baptist identity by W. B. Boggs was excellent except for the subject of "closed communion." Spurgeon was amused with the "question begging" approach Boggs took in saying that baptism should be before communion, "as if the question were one of time merely." For Boggs, it seems that point did not beg the question, other than assuming that believers' baptism was the only true baptism. Virtually all denominations agreed that none but the baptized should take communion. This presses the question of who is invited to communion into the realm of who is baptized in a scriptural manner. Spurgeon received criticism, challenges, and urging to a contrary by many American brethren. "Our American Baptist friends are continually challenging us to fight them upon the communion questions," he wrote in June 1874, "but really we feel so sure of our ground, and see so little

---

101. Spurgeon, *Letters*, Letter to Mother June 11, 1850.

102. SEE, 10:301. "The Object of the Lord's Supper."

103. S&T, May 1861, 260.

104. J. M. Pendleton, *Christian Doctrine* (Valley Forge: Judson Press. 1906), 330. The book was first published in 1878.

105. S&T, December 1878, 599.

force in their arguments, that we cannot feel any inducement to enter the conflict."[106] After a dozen more years, in 1886, Spurgeon looked at A. H. Strong's defense of strict communion and commented, "We feel so secure in our own view that we can afford to read all that can be said against it, and smile when we have done."[107]

He did not object to the taking of the Lord's Supper apart from the entire congregation with only a select group participating. At the death of two deacons early in 1883, a very large congregation met in the Monday prayer meeting on January 15 with "much solemn heartsearching, deep submission to our heavenly Father's will, and an earnest desire that his glory might be increased by the dark experience" of the loss of valuable members. Prior to the meeting of the whole congregation, however, the pastors, deacons, and elders met together for tea, prayer, and communion before the regular weekly prayer meeting. He called it a "solemn, holy, hopeful gathering of men chastened in spirit." At the breaking of the bread the Lord was "known among us."[108]

Without a thorough belief in the atoning death of Christ, no one can enter into the meaning or the spirit of the ordinance. The spiritual benefit derived from participating in it "does not come from itself, but from the help it gives to the exercise of faith in the realities brought to remembrance by its symbols."[109] This is in a review of *The Feast of Sacrifice; or, The Origin and Teaching of the Lord's Supper*. This book was published by the Church of England Book Society and surprised Spurgeon with its candor, its avoidance of discussions of Anglican ritualistic observance, and its high level of emphasis on the evangeli-

cal meaning and the experimental and practical design of the Supper. He clearly agreed with the major points made.

Spurgeon viewed the use of the elements of bread and wine as a purely symbolic way of pointing the recipient to a hearty remembrance of the historic once-for-all atoning work of Christ. The Supper helps the "exercise of faith" in the "realities," that is, the painful sacrificial, propitiatory, reconciling substitution accomplished by Christ's death and accepted by the Father.[110] The Supper is exalted, but not above measure, in that there may be an inward feeding on Christ without the external attendance on the Supper and there may be an external attendance on the Supper without an inward feeding on Christ. This should not encourage anyone to minimize the importance of partaking of the Supper, but to get greater advantage by partaking of it with accurate knowledge of the nature of its benefits, and to encourage those that are prevented from enjoying it by "needless doubts and fears."[111]

Spurgeon refused to consider using any substitute for fermented wine at communion. He reviewed *Yanim; or the Bible Wine Question* in which the authors concluded that "they have never met with unfermented wine in the East, nor are there any records, or traditions, that such wine was ever known there." Spurgeon concurred and said that there never was and never can be any such thing as unfermented wine though "it suits some men to call their messes by that name." There was much in England, however, called wine unworthy of the name, "and it is a shame to remember our Lord's death by drinking such vile concoctions." Spurgeon wanted that which was

---

106. S&T, June 1874, 290.

107. S&T, November 1886, 598.

108. S&T, February 1883, 96.

109. S&T, March 1885, 145.

110. MTP, 1905, 313-22. "The Object of the Lord's Death" SEE, 10:297-306. This was preached on September 2, 1877 at the Metropolitan Tabernacle.

111. S&T, March 1885, 145.

"as pure and good as can be had." No angry letters from pugilistic temperance people should be forthcoming, for his columns were not open to discussion and his own mind was made up. He was at one with those "temperate temperance friends who forbear to divide churches, and mar the unity of the saints upon this point."[112] The Supper was initiated with bread and wine and still there must be "nothing more than bread for food; wine still, nothing less than wine for drink."[113]

He did not specify as to how frequently the Supper should be taken, but he did feel that the words "as oft" indicated that it was to be very present in the minds of his people. "If there be any rule as to the time of the observance of this ordinance, it surely is every Lord's day." At any rate, it must not be infrequent, and "the oftener we meet for this purpose, the better it is for us."[114] Certainly the practice of once or twice a year was insufficient. Spurgeon practiced it every Sunday. "I thank God that, coming to this table every Sabbath-day, as some of us do, and have done for many years, we have yet for the most part enjoyed the nearest communion with Christ here that we have ever known, and have a thousand times blessed his name for this ordinance."[115]

This frequency of participation did not make the time of memorial any less impressive or beneficial. A communion service was held in the Tabernacle during the week following the death of Spurgeon. The writer said: "He who has missed seeing one of these services at the Tabernacle, has missed a sight unique in Christendom. The body of the building, and half the first gallery, filled with communicants, and the rest of the space occupied with interested spectators, is almost an overwhelming spectacle at any time." This observer reflected the viewpoint of Spurgeon and the congregation when he noted: "With few words, and quiet movement, the simple emblems of our Lord's death were taken in token of His body broken and His blood shed for His people." They recognized that Christ's death had "become the gate of life to us," and hoped also that in the removal of C. H. Spurgeon, their reflection on his absence from this earthly communion might become, "by the overruling grace of God, a deep and widespread benediction."[116]

Spurgeon did not believe that it was necessary for "an ordained or recognized minister" to preside at the Lord's Supper. He considered this a bit of "unmitigated popery." He saw no warrant for the limitation in Scripture and believed that stricture to be a manifestation of human tradition and superstition. "Stated minister" is little more than "priest writ large." "Even now we know of churches which have dispensed with the Lord's Supper week after week because the pastor was ill, there being, of course, no other brother in the whole community who had grace enough to preside at the table, or administer *the sacrament*, as some of the brotherhood call it. When matters have gone so far, it is surely time to speak out against such worship of men."[117]

Other aspects of corporate worship Spurgeon saw as having been infected by the priestism of Rome. The announcement of a benediction at the end of a service in itself savored of Rome, particularly when the function seemed reserved for a man of the cloth. Why could not any earnest brother ask for the blessing of God on the congregation? "Fiddle-de, dee is the only word which will enable us to vent our feelings," Spur-

---

112. S&T, January 1876, 45.

113. SEE, 10:315. "Christ and His Table Companions."

114. SEE, 10:297. "The Object of the Lord's Supper." Also see "Fencing the Table," SEE, 10:318.

115. SEE, 10:313.

116. S&T, March 1892, 137.

117. S&T, June 1874, 267.

geon commented, and so changed the subject to baptism. Spurgeon showed equal animosity to the popish fragments among non-conformists on this ordinance. The desire for the pastor to baptize was normal, Spurgeon conceded, "yet there is no reason he should do so on account of his office." Scripture does not represent it as an act peculiar to preachers and Paul did not seem to consider baptism as his official prerogative. Perhaps reflecting on his own physical condition, Spurgeon contended that "a vigorous Christian member of the church is far more in his place in the baptismal waters than his ailing, consumptive, or rheumatic pastor." The ordinance does not depend on the baptizer, so Spurgeon noted, but on the earnest and prayerful reception of the baptized. Faith in Christ, not faith in baptism nor the official standing of the baptizer, constituted the sole ground for the ordinance; its blessing came from the meditative spirit of the subject.[118]

Spurgeon's resistance to any kind of officialism in his position as pastor or in the administration of the ordinances made him feel deep sympathy for the witness of the Quakers. He maintained friendships among that group and sometimes spoke at assemblies of Friends. Their complete spiritualization of the ordinances, in Spurgeon's opinion, was no wonder because spiritual persons naturally revolt against the historic perversion, abuse and misinterpretation that they have undergone. Spurgeon retained the ordinances because he believed that the Lord Jesus himself had ordained them; he would, therefore, celebrate them "exactly as Christ ordained them."[119] When the Baptist Union met in Birmingham in 1876 a group of Baptist ministers ate with the mayor of Birmingham who happened to be a member of the Society of Friends. During the customary

speeches given by the ministers in appreciation for the hospitality of the city and the mayor himself, several mentioned that if they were not Baptist they would be Quaker. Spurgeon concurred with a strong affirmation: "We believe this to be the general feeling; certainly it is ours." Baptists and Quakers held a common "fear of priestcraft, sacramentarianism, and ecclesiastical domination over the conscience." Distinct from the Quakers, Spurgeon noted: "We maintain the two outward ordinances because they appear to us to be plainly taught in Scripture, and because when used only by believers they cannot be perverted into means of salvation." He understood, however, the fear of the Quakers, for "when we see them [the ordinances] regarded as saving ordinances, or as in any way contributing to salvation, we lament the perversion and marvel not that brethren are driven by honest, but erring impulses, to reject the outward symbol altogether."[120]

Sympathy for Quakers and practice of open communion did not mean that Spurgeon had weak convictions about being Baptist. When Dr. Landels, newly elected as president of the Baptist Union in 1876, challenged the Christian world in his inaugural address with the Baptist understanding of baptism, Spurgeon anointed him as Greatheart. He believed, in spite of criticism thrown at the good man, that Landels had entered the battle for a "good and great cause." "The Baptists have had enough of being patronized as a small sect, whose peculiarities were not offensively intruded." The spirit of indulgence shown by the "more respectable branch of the Congregational body" Spurgeon believed was "tinctured with contempt." Baptists had a "deposit of sacred truth to defend, and we shall not hesitate to battle for it." That Landels had put them into

---

118. Ibid.

119. SEE, 10:317.

120. S&T, November 1876, 529.

the necessity of doing so inspired Spurgeon to gratitude for "the bold man who is more eager to bear the responsibility of his office than to wear its honours."[121]

When Landels chaired the Baptist Union meeting, his presidential address provoked negative press from one paedobaptist press, calling him "the apostle of discord." Spurgeon rose to his defense and in doing so to the defense of Baptist distinctives as Landels defended them. "We have never heard a whisper or a complaint against him from any one of the thousands of Baptists among whom we move." Only cravens covetous of the favour of the wealthy would dissent from Landels' outspoken address. Spurgeon suspected that vilification of his character in calling him "the apostle of discord," constituted the only answer to his arguments. The cause which resorts to such weapons must sense its own weakness. Spurgeon had found that "the gentlemen who most loudly boast of their broadness and liberality of soul, are the first to wince when unpleasant truth is vigorously spoken." An honest opponent should be a delight to a true man, and no person living can doubt Landels' honesty. Landels, Spurgeon contended, was not one of those "who care not a penny for any doctrine whatever," but yielded himself to strongly held convictions. For that reason the word passed around, "Call him the Apostle of Discord, and say that the best of the Baptists are not with him; never mind the falsehood, it may serve for the occasion, and silence discussion, for if men once begin to think and search, much evil will come to our cause." Spurgeon, however, honored Landels as a Baptist champion, "brave as a lion and true as steel." The world must know that he does not stand alone.[122]

Nature of Church Life and Important Workers

Spurgeon's commitment to church planting generated a generosity on the part of his church members and encouraged other Christians and congregations to become involved. In 1874, the congregation at the Tabernacle opened a new Baptist chapel at Surbiton, near Kingswood. "The ground was given us by a generous friend," Spurgeon reported, "and the London Baptist Association gave £1000 towards the erection." Indicating high hopes for the new congregation he showed his commitment to continuance in this manner of evangelistic outreach from the church. "We are anxious to found Baptist churches, where there is need for them, and shall be always glad to hear of earnest friends who will co-operate with us in taking the gospel to destitute neighbourhoods."[123]

Spurgeon had a deep appreciation for those that joined him in his zeal for the Lord. He strongly believed that it was of utmost importance that Christians who attend classes should have work to do for their Lord. Without it, they miss the healthy exercise which is as necessary to the soul as spiritual food. The Olney family had been active before Spurgeon arrived and still were vital to the work subsequent to his death. In 1875 Spurgeon referred to William Olney as "our right-hand helper in spiritual things," and asked for ardent prayer from the church on his behalf as he suffered in a "continued illness."[124] Ten years later, Spurgeon presented William Olney as a "man immersed in business, who yet does the work of an evangelist, and fulfils the duties of pastor and leader to a large community of working people."[125] When Olney was restored to health from another serious illness in 1888, Spurgeon commented about the value of that family:

---

121. S&T, June 1876, 285.
122. S&T, November 1876, 529.

123. S&T, August 1874, 390.
124. S&T, September 1875, 449.
125. S&T, April 1885, 195.

"The prayers of the Lord's people at the Tabernacle have been graciously heard in the restoration to us of our beloved brother and deacon, William Olney, after long suffering, borne with a cheerful patience which has been a lesson to us all. Long may he now be spared to the Lord's work!" The next generation picked up the mantle without hesitation. Spurgeon rejoiced that Mr. William Olney, Jr., "continues, his laborious service at Haddon Hall, and week by week we see persons, some from the poorest and most degraded districts, brought to Jesus."[126] Spurgeon wished for many more such of Olney Jr.'s devotion and gifts.

Another worker of great faithfulness and effectiveness through the years saw powerful blessing in the ministry of Sunday School teaching. Mrs. Bartlett's Bible Class provided a reliable source of biblical instruction for young women and a steady stream of converts in the church. According to Edward Leach, Mrs. Bartlett was converted "with her whole heart to God" before her teen years. She immediately sought the "soul-good" of others and became a Sabbath-school teacher when she was twelve. According to Leach, "she was a spiritual mother even then; and many souls were brought by her to the Saviour."[127] This success made her desire wider usefulness, and she went to villages near her home to exhort "burly farmers and their still more boisterous sons to seek an emancipation from the tyranny of Satan." Her life had its share of affliction as she lost her husband to Asiatic cholera and she contracted a heart disease that made her health tentative.

In February 1856, Mrs. Bartlett moved from Dr. Steane's church to New Park Street, in order that she might be a member of the Christian community which her two sons were about to join. She did not for a time continue the active employment in which she had previously engaged as a worker for Christ; but her temporary retirement was only a preparation for future usefulness, and when, in the summer of 1859, at the invitation of Thomas Olney, she took for one afternoon the senior class in the Sunday School, which then comprised only three young women.[128] At the end of a month fourteen came. By 1861 at the opening of the Tabernacle the class numbered fifty.[129] Soon her class moved to the major lecture hall, room enough for 900 persons, where within three months the attendance increased to 300 and within a year 500. By 1866 the average attendance was 700.

This Sunday afternoon consisted of women exclusively, but not exclusively of members of the Tabernacle. Women from other congregations, both non-conformist and Episcopal, came. Now and then an elder would look in on the class and occasionally a man would visit, such as Edward Leach who commented: "On a recent visit to the class, it seemed to me that there was an undefined something in the prayer alone which robbed one of that calmness of mind so requisite in joining in a public supplication, but filled the soul at times with a holy exhilaration and devout expectation which fully compensated for loss of calm."[130] After describing the earnest and powerful way in which she addressed the class members, Leach asked: "If a woman can thus approach the Lord in supplication, how much do we not lose, my male friends, by not occasionally hearing her voice?"[131] Mrs. Bartlett made clear that she did not consider her talks and exhortations to be preaching. Leach gave a lengthy description of the impression it made on him:

---

126. S&T, September 1888, 516

127. S&T, March 1866, 113.

128. S&T, May 1879, 127.

129. S&T, March 1866, 114.

130. Ibid., 115.

131. Ibid.

It was an exhortation to press onward in the Divine life, in all works of womanly devotion to the Master's cause, and in the maintenance of a continual communication with Heaven. It was experimental—a woman's vivid fancy calling up scenes of spiritual conflict and cares, coloured with life and beauty. It was doctrinal—founded on the eternal verities of the great I AM. It was chiefly exhortative—recalling God's performances in bygone times of Christian experience, specifying the many sacred privileges of the present, painting bright pictures of coming joys and communions to be realized by faith in the far-stretched future. Better still—it was savoury, full of Jesus. Peculiarly tender and eloquent was her appeal to the unconverted. Convince a sinner of your real anxiety for his eternal welfare, and you have opened a channel in his heart for further communications. Few could resist admiring the exuberant and passionate utterances of this Bible-teacher.[132]

The activities of the class expanded to include a Tuesday evening time for prayer and exhortation and a Friday evening time for prayer only. Mrs. Bartlett's home was always open to the class, but for inquirers only. Spurgeon called her residence the "House of mercy." Scores of people were converted through this ministry and 100 were baptized at the Metropolitan Tabernacle in 1865 from her class and many others joined other congregations. Several developed teaching and evangelistic ministries of their own. Just one year before her death Spurgeon reported that "Mrs. Bartlett's class is carried on by her with as much vigour and success as ever." Of course her health was always feeble, but God provided strength as it was required. In spite of her frailty, "her words are so much attended with divine power that large numbers from her class are constantly added to the church."[133]

When she died in August 1875, the class asked her son to become teacher. He did. Spurgeon wrote that "the loss of our excellent Mrs. Bartlett" along with the illness of William Olney were subjects of "much earnest prayer." "We feel both these sorrows very greatly," he noted, but at the same time did not give the impression that the work of God was dependent on any particular gifted person. There was "sweet alleviation" to these sorrows and others made "zealous endeavours to supply every lack of service." In short, even with the interruption of the work of such pivotal laborers, "Nothing flags."[134]

When a special meeting, a "fete," was held in the orphanage in June of 1876, only 400 tickets had been taken by that morning of the event. The hosts planned for 2,000 and when 3,000 came they had to take quick action for provisions. Spurgeon was delighted with the thousands of handshakes and words of congratulations, overwhelmed with the contributions to the orphanage, and exuberant in his praise of the men in charge of the entire event. "Our best thanks are due and are hereby tendered to our friend Mr. Murrell and his staff for the tremendous exertions which they made on the day just past. They were at its close like men who had fought a great battle. The feeding of three thousand when the loaves and fishes grow by miracle does not involve the toil which has to be borne by those who on a sudden find that bread and butter and cake and hot tea are needed by a thousand more people than they expected, although they looked for two thousand. God bless the men who so cheerfully do the Church's hardest work." Spurgeon also urged the members to purchase tickets to an event in advance of the event itself so that proper preparations can be made.[135]

---

132. Ibid.
133. S&T, August 1874, 389.

134. S&T, September 1875, 449.
135. S&T, July 1876, 333.

Mr. Murrell was kept quite busy with this kind of event. When the "Butchers' Annual Festival" was held in the Tabernacle in March 1878, an event for which "a ton of meat" was prepared along with carrots, and bread and cake and tea, "the feeding of all this great multitude was accomplished by our marvelous deacon, Mr. Murrell, without a trace of disorder or a moment's delay." Spurgeon pushed the compliments steadily saying that Murrell could be the general of an army, so well does he organize.[136] And all of this is done merrily. Spurgeon was committed to the reality that a merry heart helps both body and soul in their daily travels, and saw these generously bestowed accolades as a part of pastoral oversight. Who would not be merry, and serve willingly, with such an encourager to lead by such sweet affirmation?

Mr. and Mrs. Pasfield served as general managers of the "tea department" of the Tabernacle. Spurgeon commented that they were "humble, laborious, useful and yet almost unseen servants of the church." While in the process of preparing for a large Sunday School tea, Mrs. Pasfield died on the spot. "Who could wish to die in a better case," observed Spurgeon, "in the full service of the church of God." She had to endure no "long illness, no enforced idleness, no sense of uselessness," but remained "active to the last." They did their work for the love of it and never felt imposed upon.[137]

When Spurgeon learned that a chapel on Highgate Road was seeking to raise money through a bazaar, he invited them to come to the Tabernacle to complete the effort and asked some of the leaders to aid Mrs. Coxeter and her friends bring the event to a successful end. They came up to the mark and were able to gain around £250.

Spurgeon believed that it was healthy for a church even when "loaded with home service, to lend a hand to brethren in whose enterprise we have no selfish interest." At such a time, pure Christian affection is displayed and exercised. He made sure to give public thanks "to the ladies who get up a Tabernacle Stall on the shortest possible notice." They "carried on its operations with so much vigour" that "the whole incident caused the Pastor great pleasure." This sort of work remarkably illustrated "the willingness of the people to aid in every good work."[138]

When Henry Hobson died, Spurgeon printed a personal eulogy displaying the values of personal character, strategic giving, and gospel labor that manifest a mature and comprehensive Christian character. Living in virtual anonymity, Hobson's careful use of his peculiar gifts, his way of making opportunities, his unselfish spirit, his love of souls, and his simple belief in the power of the gospel would be a credit to any local church and an example that could be emulated by any Christian:

A few weeks ago we suffered a great loss by the death of Mr. Henry Hobson, to whose memory we raised a verbal memorial at our Monday evening meeting, but we must also pour out a few elegiac sentences here. He was a quiet, unobtrusive member of the church; we suppose a butler who had saved enough money to purchase a comfortable annuity. Ever since we first knew him all his time has been spent in endeavouring to bring individuals to Christ, in his own way. He paid for a whole pew at the Tabernacle, and then went abroad into Hyde Park and other places, and invited young men to come and hear Mr. Spurgeon, promising them a seat. After service he entered into conversation, gave another invitation, and by other means sought to secure the person. Many has he in this

---

136. S&T, May, 1878, 225.

137. S&T, April 1877, 190.

138. S&T, July 1887, 334.

way led to the Saviour, and then to the church. His style of living was parsimonious that he might be able to give to the orphanage and the college, and especially that he might buy a weekly heap of sermons, which he distributed with great care in the parks. Although in advanced years, he walked erect, with somewhat stately tread and aristocratic air, and this no doubt enabled him to introduce his sermons and his seat-tickets where a less impressive physique might have failed. Scarcely known to anyone but to us, our comrade has our loving regrets until we meet again.[139]

All structure, all officers, all worship, all ordinances, all discipline were not merely perfunctory, but were employed for the purpose of producing such Christians. God gave them that the man of God would have a tested and tried maturity, fully equipped for every good work, and that the people of God would reach a unity in the faith and in the knowledge of the Son of God.

---

139. S&T, January 1879, 42

8

The Gospel is Evangelism

Do you ask me, What are you to do? Well, call for his help as loudly as you can. If you are like a lamb, bleat to him, and the bleatings of the lamb will attract the shepherd's ear. Cry mightily unto the Lord for salvation, and trust alone in the Lord Jesus. He will save you. If you were between the jaws of hell, yet, if you believed in him, he would surely pluck you out of destruction. God grant you may find it so, for Christ's sake.[1]

My poor faith is just as common as a bit of hyssop pulled up from the wall, but then I lay it asoak in the atonement; while I muse upon who Jesus was, and what he suffered, and for what purpose, till it is wet, saturated, and all becrimsoned with the vital flood. ... Thus you crimson the lintel and the door-posts. Let all men know that whatever you may have been, and whatever you now are, you do now believe in the substitutionary death of Jesus, oppose you who may. Witness, ye men and angels and devils, that Jesus' blood is our sole hope. He who thus believes is saved. Brother, go your way, and leap for joy. No man ever perished who from his heart rested in the atoning blood.[2]

Spurgeon's evangelistic ministry exhibited two characteristics fundamental to all that he did as a pastor. First, he reflected on his experience of conversion in at least a twofold manner. He unfurled it in length, breadth, and depth as a means of demonstrating the unassailable practicality of the great doctrines of the Bible. Biblical truths answer immediately the most pressing and lasting human needs. Also, he assumed a continuity between his struggles and questions and the manner in which God's Spirit dealt with him and the struggles of those to whom he preached. He recognized personality differences and the sovereign prerogatives of God in dealing with his sheep in ways peculiar to his purpose for them, but he also knew that large areas of analogy existed in the coming of any sinner to Christ.

The second fundamental issue of Spurgeon's evangelism is his theological commitment to the practice of evangelism. He would agree with the confessional commitment of Andrew Fuller who, in the straits of the hyper-Calvinist controversy a century earlier, said: "I believe it is the duty of every minister of Christ plainly and faithfully to preach the gospel to all who will hear it; and as I believe the inability of men to spiritual things to be wholly of the *moral*, and therefore of the *criminal* kind, and that it is their duty to love the Lord Jesus Christ and trust in him for salvation though they do not; I therefore believe free and solemn addresses, invitations, calls, and warnings to them to be not only *consistent*, but directly *adapted*, as means, in the hand of the Spirit of God, to bring them to Christ. I consider it as a part of my duty which I could not omit without being guilty of the blood of souls."[3] Spurgeon fully concurred

---

1. MTP, 1875, 516.

2. Ibid., 492.

3. John Ryland, *Life and Death of the Reverend Andrew Fuller* (London: Button & Son, 1816), 106.

and did not consider a man "faithful to his own conscience, who can preach simply the doctrine of sovereignty, and neglect to insist upon the doctrine of responsibility."[4]

The End Demands the Means

Spurgeon had no doubts that God alone saves and that he saves in accordance with a wise purpose eternally decreed from before the beginning of this present age. If the decree, however, did not operate on the basis of mere abstractions, but established the necessity of the incarnation, death, burial, resurrection, ascension, intercession, and glorious appearing of the Lord Jesus Christ—if the eternally begotten Son in conformity to the decree of God says, "Behold, I am come to do your will, O God"—then his servant must follow suit. If the atonement is necessary, so is its proclamation; if all who believe will be saved, they must be presented with the One in whom they are to believe; if belief involves the surrender of a sinner to the fullness of truths set forth in the gospel, then those things that fit the sinner for such surrender must be proclaimed and pressed hard into both mind and conscience. "We feel persuaded," Spurgeon told an audience at a meeting of the Baptist Missionary Society, "that all of you are on one mind in this matter; that it is the absolute duty, as well as the eminent privilege, of the church to proclaim the gospel to the world." God did not do his work of evangelism without instruments, but "has always employed means in the work of the regeneration of this world." The church must "do its utmost to spread the truth wherever it can reach the ear of man."[5]

The Pastors' College Conference of 1881 embodied Spurgeon's deep-seated earnestness for winning souls. Wednesday afternoon was given to prayer on "behalf of evangelistic effort" in anticipation of several addresses given on the subject, "How to Win Souls, and evangelize England." Graduates of the College spoke to the issue: A. G. Brown, E. B. Sawday, Vernon Chapel, H. E. Stone, and W. Y. Fullerton. Present and speaking also were members of the Baptist Union Evangelistic Committee: William Olney, W. Sampson, J. T. Wigner, and W. Penfold Cope. From Philadelphia in the United States came the son of Francis Wayland, H. L. Wayland, who spoke on the subject also. Spurgeon considered it a morning well spent and remarked, "No man could fail to be aroused to more earnest action."

> Much agony of heart was felt by some of the speakers as they described the sad condition of the masses, and expressed their fears that they were not even now reached in their lowest depths by any known agency. There was much good, practical talk, and we hope that something will come of it to the glory of God and the benefit of the people.[6]

Charles Spurgeon wanted evangelistic success. Whatever else might come as God expanded his ministry, he yearned for perishing souls, brands plucked from the burning. At least early in his ministry, before the debilitating effects of gout, nephritis, and periodic depression set in, he saw himself as an itinerant evangelist. "I protest," he preached, "if I could not itinerate this country of England, I could not bear to preach." Remaining set in one place would make the people gospel-hardened and the preacher indolent. "My highest ambition," he said, "that I may be found going through the entire land, as well as holding my head-quarters in one position." Itinerancy is God's great plan, for God's elect are scattered throughout; "God's elect are everywhere."[7]

---

4. *Revival Year Sermons, 1859*, "The Minister's Farewell," 84.

5. SS, 1:321.

6. S&T, June 1881, 290.

7. SS, 1:337.

Spurgeon wanted those that had "not been previously connected with any body of believers, or indeed, who have not attended any house of prayer." He valued "beyond all price the godless and the careless, who have been brought out from the world into communion with Christ." While he welcomed those from other communions that came for wise and providential reasons, he had no desire to obtain any "stealthily removed from friendly shores" but panted after those that were "captured at the edge of the sword from the enemy's dominions." Receiving members from other congregations did not strengthen the army, so he preferred, rather than cajoling unstable people from their present place of worship, to look after "perishing souls." He did not complain that he had been accused "of getting all the rabble of London around me. God bless the rabble! God save the rabble!" Suppose this derogatory term is even true, who needs the gospel more than the rabble? Many preach to refined ladies and gentlemen but "we want someone to preach to the rabble in these degenerate days." The most desperate, the most bloated whose brains have been drunk away, may yet shine like stars in the universe transformed by sovereign grace. "Fetch me out the worst," he yearned, "and still I would preach the gospel to them; fetch me out the vilest, still I would preach to them." This he would do in obedience to his Master who commanded that his audience be gathered from the highways and hedges.[8]

Searching for souls was not easy, especially in London, for the native depravity of man had been further degraded in hardness by the vicious life so easily followed and so oppressively dominant. "To seek for pearls at the bottom of the sea is child's play," Spurgeon told his congregation in 1888, "compared with seeking for souls in this wicked London." If God did not go with them and promise that he had a people, then their eyes would go blind and their tongues would wear thin before they would find any to grasp Christ as a Redeemer. Only by divine help would they bring with them the "chosen of the Lord." But as a church they were the Bridegroom's friends and they would "sigh and cry till we have found the chosen hearts in whom he will delight."[9]

Charles Spurgeon's first pastorate was at Waterbeach about six miles from Cambridge. The number of conversions that accompanied his preaching and his personal evangelism amounted to more than just numbers as the entire village was transformed, as noted in another chapter. He himself remarked about the Waterbeach ministry: "He showed the power of Jesu's name, and made me a witness of that gospel which can win souls, draw reluctant hearts, and mould afresh the life and conduct of sinful men and women."[10] Large crowds and numerous commendations of his preaching would not satisfy because Spurgeon longed to know that God had set his seal to his ministry through a conversion. One Sunday a deacon told him of the wife of a "poor laboring man" that had been convicted and found peace. She wanted to speak with Spurgeon. Early on a Monday morning Spurgeon's deacon drove him to the house to "see my first spiritual child." She was baptized, became a member of the church, bore a consistent witness and died within two years.

The thought of this particular seal brought from Spurgeon one of the most earnest and eloquent soliloquies on the grandeur of soul-winning in English literature. His adaptation of the messianic declaration of success to his own

---

8. SS, 1:304.

9. SS, 19:352.

10. *Autobiography*, 1:194.

case shows the continuity of means, in Spurgeon's view, from the completed work of Christ through the minister's proclamation of the gospel.

> Then could I have sung the song of the Virgin Mary, for my soul did magnify the Lord for remembering my low estate, and giving me the great honour to do a work for which all generations should call me blessed, for so I counted and still count the conversion of one soul. I would rather be the means of saving a soul from death than be the greatest orator on earth. I would rather bring the poorest woman in the world to the feet of Jesus than I would be made Archbishop of Canterbury. I would sooner pluck one single brand from the burning than explain all mysteries. To win a soul from going down into the pit, is a more glorious achievement than to be crowned in the arena of theological controversy as *Dr. Sufficientisimus;* to have faithfully unveiled the glory of God in the face of Jesus Christ will be, in the final judgment, accounted worthier service than to have solved the problems of the religious Sphinx, or to have cut the Gordian knot of Apocalyptic difficulty. One of my happiest thoughts is that, when I die, it shall be my privilege to enter into rest in the bosom of Christ, and I know that I shall not enjoy my heaven alone. Thousands are already there, who have been drawn to Christ under my ministry. Oh! What bliss it will be to fly to heaven, and to have a multitude of converts before and behind, and, on entering the glory, to be able to say, "Here am I, Father, and the children Thou hast given me."[11]

That reality was repeated year after year throughout Spurgeon's tenure in London. He himself could note truthfully, "He has given me a long period of happy and successful service, for which, with all my heart, I praise and magnify His holy Name. There has been a greater increase sometimes, of a little diminution now and then; but,

for the most part, the unbroken stream of blessing has run on at much the same rate all the while." That the ministry of the Metropolitan Tabernacle was truly powerful and effective in consistent evangelism is borne out by the numbers. In 1853 the New Park Street membership numbered 313. By the end of 1860 the membership had risen to 1,494. Though some came from other congregations, the bulk of these was converted and added to the church by baptism. For the next ten years the church added an average of 448 persons per year with a net increase of 267 each year. By 1870 the membership stood at 4,165. By 1882 the membership reached 5,472. The last ten years of his ministry continued to see hundreds of additions with an average of 269 baptisms each year. This includes the five years of the Downgrade Controversy. During some of these years there was a net loss in membership because, in addition to the normal attrition by death, discipline, and moving of residence, Spurgeon dismissed significant numbers to establish chapels in other parts of the city.

Did this consistent increase in numbers indicate that Spurgeon played fast and loose with the gospel? Did he manipulate his audiences and wring decisions out of them with no sensitivity to the necessity of the new birth? He certainly most ardently called for decision, and immediate decision. In 1874, he cautioned against lingering too long with enquirers, for they seemed to substitute the attention for their duty to believe. "Immediate trust in the Lord Jesus is the demand of the gospel, and it is dangerous to allow the anxious to look to meetings and conversations as a means of gainng what is even now to be had by an act of faith."[12] But did he ignore the nature of repentance and faith? Were these members taken in with little or

---

11.   Ibid., 1:199.

12.   S&T, April 1874, 191.

no concern to ascertain if a genuine work of grace had subdued them to Christ? Spurgeon's success and his exuberant use of all means legitimately at his disposal did not blur his sight of truth or dim the glory of God in his search for souls.

Manner of Accepting Members

In a speech to his students in 1888, Spurgeon reiterated a conviction that had governed his method throughout his ministry. The importance of the practice pressed more soberly on his awareness and conscience at that time because of the theological decline and worldliness he observed all around him. Though he still urged that the minister must labor for the immediate salvation of his hearers, he was equally clear that holiness must accompany profession. Good works are the necessary fruit of grace. For that reason he exhorted the men of his fellowship to "be careful about the admission of members into the church." Theological decline mixes well with increased worldliness and the churches now have far above their share of both. "Let the door of the church be open to all sincere souls," he urged, "but closed against all whose hearts are in the world. It is not even for the worldling's good that he should hold the form of godliness while he is a stranger to its power. As you love the Lord, and value men's souls, guard well the entrance of the church."[13]

Twenty-three years earlier, in 1865, *The Sword and Trowel* carried an article that described in detail about how inquirers were interviewed and how it was determined that they should be received into membership. After a summary of the growth of the church since 1854, George Rogers remarked, "This work has been not of man, but of God, and therefore it has not been overthrown."

At that time, there were ten deacons, chosen for life, and twenty-three elders elected annually who attended to the spiritual affairs of the church. The process for membership began with an interview with one of the elders, present at the Tabernacle on Wednesday night specifically for that purpose.

> A record is made by the Elder of the result of that interview in what is called the Inquirers' Book. If satisfied with the candidate, he gives a card, which qualifies for direct intercourse with Mr. Spurgeon, who devotes a fixed portion of his time to that office. If Mr. Spurgeon thinks favorably of the individual, the name is announced at a Church meeting, and visitors are appointed to make the most careful inquiries into the whole circumstances connected with the application. If this investigation is satisfactory, the candidate appears at a Church meeting where he is examined by the pastor, after which he retires, and the visitor gives his report upon the case. It is then proposed to the Church for its adoption, and if approved, the Pastor gives the right hand of fellowship. As soon after this as convenient, the candidate is baptized, and on the next Sabbath in the month ensuing, unites in the Communion Service, having first been recognized before the whole church by again receiving from the Pastor the right hand of fellowship.

Spurgeon spoke of the great joy that these lengthy interviews gave him. "Usually, so many came," he wrote, "that I was quite overwhelmed with gratitude and thanksgiving to God."[14] He commented on the character of these testimonies concerning their conviction of sin and their alteration of mind from an affection for the things of the world to a love of the gospel. Often, he would ask the enquirer to sit down while he related his experience of finding the Saviour. "Why sir," they would exclaim, "that is just how I have felt, but I did not

---

13. Charles Spurgeon, *An All Round Ministry* (Edinburgh: The Banner of Truth Trust, 1978), 311. Chapter entitled, "The Evils of the Present Time."

14. S&T, January 1865, 379.

think anyone else had ever gone over the same path that I have trodden."[15]

Spurgeon had reached a conviction early in his Christian life that the work of conversion was all of God. A journal of three months is larded with entries extolling the power and beauty of sovereign electing love.[16] He saw clearly his absolute dependence on and the inexhaustible necessity of gratitude for "the sparing mercies of the Lord, but especially for His great grace in electing me, by the sovereign counsels of His love, to be one of His redeemed ones."[17] "Truly I have nothing which I have not received; I can boast of no inherent righteousness. Had the Lord not chosen me, I should not have chosen Him. Grace! Grace! Grace! 'Tis all of grace."[18] These are the words of a sixteen-year-old.

When pastor at Waterbeach, Spurgeon was invited to preach at the dissenting chapel at Houghton, run largely by the eccentric but generous miller of Houghton, Potto Brown. Although the story has been related in another chapter, some of the implications are particularly relevant here. Brown had been host for Charles Finney in 1849 and had seen six foster children converted under his witness. His own background was Quaker and he was a devoted Arminian. After Spurgeon preached and returned to Brown's home, he found himself under assault not only for his theology but for what Brown suspected as plagiarism. One so young could not preach so astutely and passionately and give evidence of such mature experience unless he had stolen someone else's material. Brown soon learned that such was not the case and that his young guest was not a pushover. A battle royal progressed through the

afternoon in what Spurgeon later characterized as a "time of 'felicitous misery.'"[19]

This confrontive introduction to a Finneyite did little to endear the American evangelist to the young English Baptist Calvinist whose preaching on the doctrines of grace was as natural and unpostured as the beating of the heart. Drummond expressed perplexity at Spurgeon's lifelong resistance to Finney:

> It seems after this encounter in Houghton that Charles never had a profound appreciation for the ministry of Charles Finney. Perhaps Spurgeon was a bit too prejudiced toward Arminianism, so he failed to appreciate Finney's significant ministry. The American preacher made a tremendous impact not only in Houghton but later in London, preaching at Whitefield's Tabernacle. Whitefield had become Charles' idol. Still, scant references are made to Finney in the writings of Spurgeon, and when they do occur, they tend to be rather negative. This is unfortunate, because they shared much in common.[20]

They certainly shared the urgency of salvation as common beliefs and that the need for decision for Christ was immediate. Opposition to Unitarianism and universalism were also common commitments, but on virtually every evangelical doctrine Spurgeon differed strongly with Finney and found Finney's stance not only inadequate, but hostile to saving truth. Under Spurgeon's editorship, Vernon Charlesworth in 1876 reviewed the recently published autobiography of Finney. Significant differences emerge in the review. Spurgeon believed that intense preparation was needed for preaching and that the taking of a text must be done long before one appeared in the pulpit. Charlesworth highlighted Finney's prac-

---

15. Ibid.; See also *Autobiography*, 1:381.

16. *Autobiography*, 1:125-43.

17. Ibid., 1:141.

18. Ibid., 1:134.

19. G. Holden Pike, *The Life and Work of Charles Haddon Spurgeon*, 6 vols, (London: Cassell and Co., nd), 1:86.

20. Lewis Drummond, *Spurgeon: Prince of Preachers* (Grand Rapids, MI: Kregel, 1992), 168.

tice of not choosing a text until he arose to preach and then attributing both text and structure of the sermon to an immediate revelatory operation of the Spirit of God. Charlesworth remarked, "We have yet to learn that the promised aid of the Spirit justifies any minister's appearance before an audience, excepting under very special circumstance, without the most careful preparation." He went on severely to question Finney's claim of inspiration for his "every utterance" and pointed out that anyone who does such "absolves himself from the responsibility of any error into which he may unwittingly fall, and demands a divine sanction for any nonsense he may utter." Charlesworth had the conviction, doubtless shared by Spurgeon, that Finney must "have been mistaken as to the degree in which he preached under the Spirit's influence."[21] Finney reckoned his conversions by the hundreds of thousands, Charlesworth noted, but he failed to discover that there is a corresponding advantage in membership to the evangelical churches. "It seems," so Charlesworth wryly observed, "that Mr. Finney reckons every trembling Felix as a true convert."[22]

More severe, however, was Finney's presentation of the doctrine of evangelism. Spurgeon saw no contradiction between evangelism and the clearest and most forceful presentation of historic confessional Calvinism. The latter, he believed, was intrinsic to the purest evangelistic presentation of the gospel. "Again and again," Charlesworth pointed out, Finney heaps "ridicule upon the doctrine of substitution, as taught by Calvinistic theology." Not only so, he rejected the doctrine of total inability as an aspect of total depravity as "mere nonsense." If total inability were true, so Finney reasoned, then the atonement was not

grace but "a debt due to mankind on the part of God for having placed them in a condition so deplorable and so unfortunate." Charlesworth found it disturbing that this supposedly great evangelist denounced the doctrine of imputation as a "wonderful theological fiction." Instead of invoking the necessity of divine intervention by the new birth, Finney boasted that he told his hearers that it was their duty to make themselves a new heart and if they did their duty, they would be Christians. After posing some pertinent questions designed to uncover the weaknesses of the "Pelagian heresy" of Finney, Charlesworth dared to query if "the supposed benefit of Mr. Finney's labours has not been greatly overestimated." He did not wonder at the "evanescent character" of a large portion of the conversions for he did not believe "that the grievous errors which marred his testimony could have led up to conversions of the right kind, though they were evidently adapted to produce presumptuous confidence, and transitory excitement."[23]

With all his passion for souls, and his aggressive pursuit of their repentance, Spurgeon would not assume the place of the Holy Spirit or usurp the prerogatives of divine sovereignty. He seemed to have certain aspects of Finney's thought in mind when he lectured to his students that "we depend entirely upon the Spirit of God *to produce actual effect from the gospel,* and at this effect we must always aim." Notice the words, only the Spirit can produce the effect, but we aim at the effect. These two ideas are not antithetical but one is determinative of the other. The traits of the Spirit's work determine the manner and the content of the preacher's aim. Thus, he should "never aim at effect after the manner of the climax makers, poetry quoters, handkerchief manipulators,

---

21. Vernon Charlesworth, "Charles G. Finney, the American Evangelist." S&T, May 1876, 216.

22. Ibid., 217.

23. Ibid., 218.

and bombast blowers. Far better for a man that he had never been born than that he should degrade a pulpit into a show box to exhibit himself in." Rather they should aim at inspiring saints to nobler things, leading Christians close to their master, comforting doubters "till they rise out of their terrors, the repentance of sinners, and their exercise of immediate faith in Christ."[24]

But with the desire for immediate faith in Christ the preacher recognizes, as opposed precisely to the language of Finney, that "miracles of grace must be the seals of our ministry; who can bestow them but the Spirit of God? Convert a soul without the Spirit of God! Why, you cannot even make a fly, much less create a new heart and a right spirit. Lead the children of God to a higher life without the Holy Ghost! You are inexpressibly more likely to conduct them into carnal security, if you attempt their elevation by any method of your own."[25]

Spurgeon did, however, recognize the usefulness of Finney in certain contexts. When encouraging his students to learn to appeal to the understanding, he said, "I am not an admirer of the peculiar views of Mr. Finney, but I have no doubt that he was useful to many; and his power lay in his use of clear arguments." Spurgeon did insert in *The Sword and Trowel* a document from Finney entitled "How to Preach so as to convert Nobody."[26] Spurgeon agreed entirely with Finney's premise underlying the article, "It is generally conceded at the present day that the Holy Spirit converts souls to Christ by means of truth *adapted to that end*. It follows that a selfish preacher will not skillfully adapt means to convert souls to

Christ; for that is not his end." One of the pieces of advice concerning how not to convert sinners stated, "Do not make the impression that you expect your hearers to commit themselves upon the spot, and give their hearts to God."[27]

The Warrant and the Way

The practice of Spurgeon always reflected the theological realities of the warrant to faith, which is immediate, the command to repent and believe, which is immediate, and the way of faith, which often is greatly extended. If one focuses on any one of these to the exclusion of another, or fails to distinguish between them, he will present a contorted view of Spurgeon's evangelism. We will see that his sermons and writings are filled with both the warrant and the command. At the same time his instruction and method adheres to the reality of the way of faith.

What about the reality that some often arrive at a place of deep conviction and yet find no peace of forgiveness and no sense of Christ's acceptance? "It is one of the strange things in the dealings of Jesus," Spurgeon wrote, "that even when we arrive at this state of entire spiritual destitution, we do not always become *at once* the objects of his justifying grace. Long seasons frequently intervene between our knowledge of our ruin, our hearing of a deliverer, and the application of that deliverer's hand."[28] Though frequently conversion comes quickly on the heels of deep conviction it might not, and might not come at all. Spurgeon suggests that we remember that God is not our debtor. "Oh! Our hearts loathe the pride which bows not to Divine sovereignty, but arrogantly declares God to be under obligations to his creatures. Those who are full of this

---

24. Charles Spurgeon, *Lectures to My Students* (London: Passmore & Alabaster, 1881), 2:12. The lecture is entitled, "On Conversion as our Aim."

25. Ibid.

26. S&T, November 1875, 443-45.

27. Ibid.

28. Charles Spurgeon, *The Saint and his Saviour* (Ross-Shire, Scotland: Christian Focus Publications, 1989), 102.

satanic spirit will not assert this in plain language, but while they cavil at election, talking with impious breath about 'partiality,' 'injustice,' 'respect of person' and such like things, they too plainly show that their old nature is yet unhumbled by divine grace." Spurgeon goes on the say, "We are sure of this, that no convinced sinner, when under a sense of his ill-desert, will ever dispute the justice of God in damning him, or quarrel with the distinguishing grace which Heaven giveth to one and not to another." Jesus will have the sinner know that his gifts are in his own hand, totally within the pale of "sovereign discriminating, electing grace," are given freely, with the intention that the sinner will "know that his bounties are in his own hand," and none can lay claim to them as a right.[29]

Another reason for the delay in the way of faith has to do with the deeply Christocentric nature of conversion. Spurgeon, though modified in his preparationism, nevertheless believed that sinners at times had to be taught to use the means of obtaining peace. Go hear preaching that is being blessed of God for salvation, pray and call upon Christ, think of his promises, and meditate upon Christ. "Many souls mourn because they cannot make themselves believe; and the constant exhortations of ministers persuading them to faith, cause them to sink deeper in the mire, since all their attempts prove ineffectual." Not only are these exhortations useless, they are cruel. Faith must have an object, and the object must be perceived truthfully, and precisely in accord with the call to faith. Christ's work as the only acceptable atoner and atonement must capture the mind and heart. "Faith," Spurgeon argues, "is a result of previous states of the mind, and flows from those antecedent conditions, but is not a

position to which we can attain without passing through those other states."[30]

Faith consists of "knowledge, belief, and trust." We cannot stride to faith apart from knowing what to believe and why. "Some men endeavour to preach *sinners to Christ*; we prefer to preach *Christ to sinners*," he wrote, because he believed that a "faithful exhibition of Jesus crucified will, under the divine blessing, beget faith in hearts where fiery oratory and vehement declamation have failed. ... A true view of Calvary will smite unbelief with death, and put faith into its place."[31]

Paramount in his instructions to seekers was the words, "Know the gospel." Know how it "talks of free forgiveness, and of change of heart, of adoption into the family of God." One must know that those are the real needs they have. Then "know especially Christ Jesus the Son of God, the Saviour of men, united to us by his human nature, and yet one with God; and thus able to act as mediator between God and man." One must endeavor to know the doctrine of the sacrifice of Christ for "the point upon which saving faith mainly fixes is this." One must have clear ideas of the biblical presentation of substitutionary atonement, that Jesus was "made a curse for us," that is that God made him to "be sin for us that we might be made the righteousness of God in him."[32]

But with the fullness of Christ's saving work exhibited, with Christ crucified clearly set before the eyes of sinners, these truths must be believed, that is, the assent of credibility must be given to them as another element of the fitness of the human understanding previous to a call for trust. With this in place, however, there yet remains the gracious call of God to venture on Christ for full

---

29. Ibid., 140.

30. Ibid., 157.

31. Ibid., 57-59.

32. Charles Spurgeon, *All of Grace* (Chicago: Fleming H. Revel, nd), 44-46.

pardon and acceptance. This call to believe is not a human contrivance but intrinsically connected with the gospel. It is commanded: "Believe on the Lord Jesus Christ, and thou shalt be saved" (Acts 16:31). It is explicitly set forth as a condition on our part and everywhere implied by the very nature of the wholeness of salvation. "If we walk in the light as he is in the light, we have fellowship;" "If indeed you continue in the faith firmly established and steadfast, and not moved away from the hope of the gospel that you have heard." "We have become partakers of Christ, if we hold fast the beginning of our assurance firm until the end." It is a gift that is a constituent element of God's saving operation: "By grace are ye saved through faith, and that not of yourselves; it is the gift of God;" "He who began the good work in you will bring it to completion." "May your spirit and soul and body be preserved complete, without blame at the coming of our Lord Jesus Christ. Faithful is he who calls you, and He also will bring it to pass." "God has chosen you from the beginning [or, as the first fruits] for salvation through sanctification by the Spirit and faith in the truth. It was for this he called you through our gospel, that you may gain the glory of our Lord Jesus Christ."[33]

That faith is a gift, and that it arises only from the heart that has been the recipient of that mysterious working of the Holy Spirit should not for a moment hinder belief. "The Lord does, in fact, produce the new birth in all who believe in Jesus; and their believing is the surest evidence that they are born again."[34] He will not, however, believe for us, just as we cannot do the regenerating work for him. It is enough to "obey the gracious command; it is for the Lord to work the new birth in us." We sow seed with the firm confidence that the Lord causes the seed to grow, and we go about our business from day to day with a sense of obligation before us unhindered by the confidence that all works in accordance with God's providence. Even so, though God alone grants faith, we nevertheless venture and believe without a vision into the secret operations of God by which he grants the new birth. "We repent and believe," Spurgeon affirmed, "though we could do neither if the Lord did not enable us." Affirming the same idea in different terms, Spurgeon attested, "We forsake sin and trust in Jesus, and then we perceive that the Lord has wrought in us to will and to do of his own good pleasure." Should the reality that we can perform our responsibility only when God so wills and only if he empowers give perplexity? Spurgeon thought not. "It is idle to pretend that there is any real difficulty in the matter."[35]

We have taken a circuitous rout to say that the growth under Spurgeon's ministry did not come from manipulative methods. It came from God's blessing on an effort fully founded in a comprehensive grasp of the gospel and its effects. Spurgeon knew what God had done, and confessed his complete dependence on the work of the Spirit in accord with an eternally decreed sovereign purpose. He knew what God required of him and the manner in which that must be expressed.

Spurgeon as a Personal Evangelist
Spurgeon entered enthusiastically into every opportunity for service to Christ that he could. He distributed tracts joyfully and consistently while still at Newmarket. He had seventy people that he regularly visited, taking his Saturdays for this visitation as well as tract distribution. He explained to his mother, "I do not give a tract, and go away;

33. 1 John 1:7; Colossians 1:23; Hebrews 3:14; Ephesians 2:8; Philippians 1:6; 1 Thessalonians 5:23, 24; 2 Thessalonians 2:13, 14.

34. Charles Spurgeon, *All of Grace* (Chicago: Fleming H. Revel, nd), 87.

35. Ibid., 89.

but I sit down, and endeavour to draw their attention to spiritual realities."[36] He immediately became earnest about the salvation of his siblings. When Sarah expressed her faith in Christ, Spurgeon wrote, "I am so glad that Sarah, too, is called, that two of us in one household at one time should thus openly profess the Saviour's name." When he thought about the others, he considered what delight would accrue if "God should prove that they are redeemed ones included in the covenant of grace!" He closed his letter with greeting to all of them with the expressed hope, "May they become members of the church in our house!"[37]

Spurgeon's interactions with T. W. Medhurst provide an example of Spurgeon's personal evangelism that combined preaching, personal conversation, and letter. The various aspects of Medhurst's story are told in other places in this volume, but the entire relationship was begun in this episodic encounter. Because of fascination with the theatre and rhetoric, Medhurst, an apprentice rope-maker, had begun to attend the Surrey Chapel in 1854 to hear the hyper-Calvinist pulpiteer, James Wells. He also learned that Spurgeon was a rapidly rising star of the pulpit, recommendation sufficient to draw the young, and apparently vain, Medhurst. Over a course of weeks, Spurgeon learned Medhurst's name and frequently would ask him, "And how are you today Medhurst?" As conviction set in and increased, Medhurst would answer, "Oh, worse and worse." Spurgeon explained the gospel over and over, but Medhurst could not grasp that salvation, of necessity, was freely given. In despair, the frustrated seeker framed a letter to his persevering evangelist friend.

Dear Sir,—would you be kind enough candidly to inform me whether there is any hope that I belong to the elect family of God; whether Jesus Christ His Son has ever died for me, while my affections are in the world. I try to pray, but cannot. I make resolutions only to break them. I listen from time to time when you speak of the glory set apart for the saints, when you describe their feelings, their joys, but I have nothing to do with these things. Oh, sir, that Sunday morning you spoke of the hypocrite, I felt you were describing me. I go to chapel, hear the Word preached; go home, make resolutions, go to work, out in the world, and forget all, till the time of preaching comes again. I read the Bible, but with no interest; it seems no more to me than any other work that I have read before; it is to me dry and insipid. Christ has said that of all who come to Him He will send none away. How am I to come? I would if I could, but I cannot. At times I think I will give all up, and not go to chapel any more; but when the time comes I cannot stay away, but feel compelled to go once more. Do, dear sir, tell me how I am to find Jesus? How can know he died for me? And that I belong to his family? Dear sir, tell me, am I a hypocrite?[38]

He signed the letter, "I remain, yours in anxiety," followed by his full name Thomas William Medhurst. Spurgeon answered him with great clarity, pertinent interaction with the specific concerns of Medhurst, and with deep pastoral wisdom and affection. On July 14, 1854, he wrote:

DEAR SIR,—I am glad that you have been able to write to me and state your feelings. Though my hands are always full, it will ever give me joy to receive such notes as yours. You ask me a very important question, "Are you one of God's elect?" Now, this is a question neither you nor I can answer at present, and therefore let it drop. I will ask you an easier one, "Are you a sinner?" Can you say "YES"? All say, "YES"; but then they do not know what the word "sinner" means. A sinner is a

---

36. Murray, *Letters*, 27.

37. Ibid., 28, 29.

38. S&T, January 1877, 10, 11.

creature who has broken all his Maker's commands, despised His Name, and run into rebellion against the Most High. A sinner deserves hell, yea, the hottest place in hell; and if he be saved, it must be entirely by unmerited mercy. Now, if you are such a sinner, I am glad to be able to tell you the only way of salvation, "Believe on the Lord Jesus." I think you have not yet really understood what believing means. You are, I trust, really awakened, but you do not see the door yet. I advise you seriously to be much alone, I mean as much as you can; let your groans go up if you cannot pray, attend as many services as possible; and if you go with an earnest desire for a blessing, it will come very soon. But why not believe now? You have only to believe that Jesus is able and willing to save, and then trust yourself to Him. Harbour not that dark suggestion to forsake the house of God; remember you turn your back on Heaven, and your face to hell when you do that. I pray God that He will keep you from doing so. If the Lord had meant to destroy you, He would not have shown you such these things. If you are but a smoking flax, there is hope. Touch the hem of His garment; look to the brazen serpent.

My dear fellow-sinner, slight not this season of awakening. Up, and be in earnest. 'Tis your soul—your own soul—your eternal welfare—your heaven or your hell—which is at stake. There is the cross, and a bleeding God-man upon it—look to Him, and be saved. And there is the Holy Spirit, able to give you every grace. Look in prayer to the Sacred Three-one-God, and then you will be delivered.

I am, Your anxious friend,
C. H. SPURGEON.[39]

Medhurst remained unrelieved by the letter and his distressed condition enlarged to press him to the edge of dark despair. After other Sundays of continued darkness of soul, Medhurst resolved that *this* was to be his last. In looking at Scripture before the service he listlessly opened to

John 6:37 and read again, "Him that cometh to me I will in no wise cast out." G. Holden Pike recorded, "Quicker than lightning, almost before a word had left the preacher's lips the chain of bondage was broken, and the abiding peace of Christ flowed into the penitent's soul."[40]

The *Autobiography* includes a ten-page chapter entitled "Seeking the Souls of Men." Spurgeon begins it by saying, "I often envy those of my brethren who can go up to individuals and talk to them with freedom about their souls. I do not always find myself able to do so, though when I have been Divinely aided in such service, I have had a large reward. When a Christian can get of a man, and talk thus personally to him, it is like one of the old British men-of-war lying alongside a French ship, and giving her a broadside, making every timber shiver, and at last sending her to the bottom." He calls the practice of personal evangelism "a holy art."[41]

Spurgeon gave several examples of personal interviews. Crossing a river on a ferry Spurgeon spoke to the ferryman about the gospel. "I cannot say what was the final result of our conversation," Spurgeon remarked, "but I had the satisfaction of knowing that I had at least set before him God's way of salvation in language that he could easily understand." At the close of an interview with a lady steeped in what Spurgeon called "the sentiments of almost undiluted popery," Spurgeon surmised "I have reason to think that the little simple talk we had has not been forgotten, or unprofitable." One great advantage of dealing personally with souls, according to Spurgeon, is "that it is not so easy for them to turn aside the message as when they are spoken to in the mass."[42]

---

39. Ibid., 11.

40. G. Holden Pike, "The Work of the Pastors' College," S&T, January 1877, 12.

41. *Autobiography*, 1:373.

42. Ibid., 1:377.

In 1872, Spurgeon opened *The Sword and the Trowel* with a proposal about an evangelistic program to concentrate on those hearers at the Metropolitan Tabernacle that were as yet unconverted. "Some three months ago," he recounted, "having newly arisen from a sick bed, our heart felt heavy for the souls of dying men. Our ministry has never been without large results in conversion, but we were discontented and ill at ease because to such multitudes the Lord Jesus appeared to be without form or comeliness. Especially did it burden us to see so many of our regular hearers undecided."[43] In laying this issue before his congregation, he discovered that passion for the souls of the unconverted had been multiplying among many of his church members, including his deacons and elders. One brother asked pointedly in a thoughtful letter to Spurgeon, "Has he made our hearts to long and pant for the salvation of souls, without having some precious design?" Weeks of prayer and consideration followed, the idea of having evangelists or a special meeting was considered. These would not do. Finally, with the elders pledging their desire to follow with the prayer that he would not simply follow his own mind but "be led wholly of the Lord," Spurgeon responded:

> Impressed with a feeling of deep responsibility, we turned over plan after plan, and at last determined upon that which we thought would savour least of trusting in man, and show most that we believed the Lord had already heard prayer, and had made the preaching of his word effectual. We gave notice that the pastor would sit two whole days to see enquiring souls, and that each evening there would be a meeting at which he would speak upon the discouragement and encouragements of seekers, and any of the elders who felt moved to do so would exhort.[44]

When the day came, people were already waiting for personal counsel from Spurgeon and "streamed in all the day." Spurgeon looked particularly for "anxious" people, but found that most that came testified to their already having been converted in the former weeks of prayer. The number was too great for personal counsel for each one and "we had to appoint another season to see many of them. In the evening he spoke to more than 250 about discouragements; they listened for truth, life and death truth. "The Lord was there and we knew it." The next evening found still more, again many professing that already they had found salvation in Christ. "They told us that they had believed in Jesus," Spurgeon reported, "and we had but to question them as to their change of heart and life, and their renunciation of self and the world."[45] One inquirer left unconverted, but came back an hour afterwards reporting that he had found Jesus. That evening, between 400 and 500 persons were present in the lecture hall, "and the attention was almost oppressive to the pastor's soul." Spurgeon felt peculiarly interested in reporting the nature of the decorum at the meeting.

> There was not even the shadow of the excitement which reveals itself in noise and indecorum; all was as quiet as usual, more so indeed, and we were rejoiced to see it, for when intelligent people are on a life and death business, they are little inclined to bawl and shout. There is an emotion which blusters, but the deeper kind is too earnest to cause its voice to be heard in the streets. Eternity alone can know what the Lord wrought those two nights, and the secrets of how many hearts were then revealed.[46]

---

43. S&T, January 1872, 1.
44. Ibid., 3.

45. Ibid., 4.
46. S&T, January 1872, 5.

The Evangelistic Emphasis of his Preaching

Joel Beeke outlines the vitals of Puritan evangelistic preaching under five categories: Puritan preaching was thoroughly biblical, unashamedly doctrinal, experimentally practical, holistically evangelistic, and studiously symmetrical. Puritan preaching in general, Beeke points out, was plain, designed to reach everyone "that all might know the way of salvation." They addressed the mind with clarity, confronted the conscience pointedly, and wooed the heart passionately.[47]

That summary gives an accurate reflection of the preaching of C. H. Spurgeon. From his earliest days of consciousness until the end of his life, the Puritans instructed him. He could draw upon them at will and compare their strengths, note their differences, and recommend them for imitation in a variety of ministerial tasks. They were his tutors in Christ, theology, evangelism, counsel, and preaching. Though his sermons did not follow their form, he went after souls with the arsenal of truth, with the desire for the glory of God, and the same passion for sinners.

One would be hard pressed to find even one sermon in the entirety of the New Park Street Pulpit and the Metropolitan Tabernacle that did not include direct addresses to the unconverted. Doctrinal addresses, sermons for Christian comfort and edification, sermons on congregational issues, sermons on the ordinances—all these included potent appeals to the unconverted to flee to Christ and to do it "at once." No biblical subject could be considered unevangelistic, and that which blessed the saint was good as an appeal to provoke to spiritual jealousy the non-Christian. The message that was straightforward exposition of the gospel in an evangelistic way was seen as of great comfort and thrilling hope to the Christian.

Spurgeon preached specifically with the intent of seeing sinners converted. In the month after the Surrey Music Hall disaster, criticism came to Spurgeon for a number of reasons. All of these built on the premise that he was taking advantage of his popularity to collect more money to finance building a monstrous Tabernacle capable of holding 15,000 people. Spurgeon denied the accusations and explained, "I cannot bear to see, Sabbath after Sabbath, as many people go away as enter the chapel where we have been accustomed to assemble for worship." Under no provocation other than their desire to do so, people come in "large multitudes to listen to my feeble proclamation of the truths of the Gospel: … if it is a sin in me that they should do so, it is at least an uncommon sin, which many others would like to commit if they could." Though his present chapel was comfortable for his own people, and the move to the Music Hall was terribly inconvenient for them, "It is only with a view of winning souls to God that we have come to this larger place, and should we be accused of other objects the judgment-day will lay bare what our motives have truly been."[48]

A student and friend, William Williams, the author of *Personal Reminiscences of Charles Haddon Spurgeon*, heard Spurgeon say, "If you preach so as to convert souls, the Lord will not disappoint you."[49] Preaching to convert souls, for Spurgeon, meant laying out the full counsel of God to the sinner. He must know what sin is, what repentance is, what the marks of conversion are, what the atonement is in all its dimensions, that he is dependent on sovereign grace expressed experientially in regeneration, and other truths. All that the Master taught must be seen as efficient for evangelism. Nothing should be omitted, but everything given its proper place.

---

47. Joel Beeke, *Puritan Reformed Spirituality* (Grand Rapids: Reformation Heritage Books, 2004), 147-57.

48. Pike, 2:254

49. Williams, 171.

In *The Soul Winner* Spurgeon insisted on this in his first chapter.

> And, do not believe, dear friends, that when you go into revival meetings, or special evangelistic services, you are to leave out the doctrines of the gospel; for you ought then to proclaim the doctrines of grace rather more than less. Teach gospel doctrines clearly, affectionately, simply, and plainly, and especially those truths which have a present and practical bearing upon man's condition and God's grace. Some enthusiasts would seem to have imbibed the notion that, as soon as a minister addresses the unconverted, he should deliberately contradict his usual doctrinal discourse, because it is supposed that there will be no conversions if he preaches the whole counsel of God. It just comes to this, brethren, it is supposed that we are to conceal truth, and utter a half-falsehood, in order to save souls. We are to speak the truth to God's people because they will not hear anything else; but we are to wheedle sinners into faith by exaggerating one part of truth, and hiding the rest until a more convenient season. This is a strange theory, and yet many endorse it. According to them, we may preach the redemption of a chosen number of God's people, but universal redemption must be our doctrine when we speak with the outside world; we are to tell believers that salvation is all of grace, but sinners are to be spoken with as if they were to save themselves; we are to inform Christians that God the Holy Spirit alone can convert, but when we talk with the unsaved, the Holy Ghost is scarcely to be named. We have not so learned Christ. ... He who sent us to win souls neither permits us to invent falsehoods, nor to suppress truth. His work can be done without such suspicious methods.[50]

While no doctrine is to be hidden, Spurgeon recognized that a sermon intended for conver-

sion would naturally gravitate toward a particular cluster of biblical truths. In a lecture to his students entitled "On Conversion as Our Aim," Spurgeon pointed out, in 1881, that "the grand object of the Christian ministry is the glory of God." While the edification of the saints ranks very high as a means by which God is glorified, Spurgeon contended that "our great object of glorifying God is, however, to be mainly achieved by the winning of souls." As a reflection of the practice he unfailingly pursued, he urged his ministerial students to win sinners with the light and heat of doctrine. Any biblical doctrine has such potential but some, Spurgeon reminded them, are more clearly aligned with the purpose of conversion. Spurgeon pointed particularly to the person of Christ, the cross of Christ, sin in all its dimensions, the Law, justification by faith, the character of God, and substitutionary atonement; "all these truths and others which complete the evangelical system are calculated to lead men to faith." His short exposition of several doctrines includes the particular effect a doctrine might have on a lost person.[51]

For example, a preacher must "teach the depravity of human nature." A sinner must know his true culpability, his natural corruption and condemnation, and his inability to alter his own condition. If a preacher comes short on the full exposition of this doctrine, "you may expect few conversions." This leads naturally to his insistence on the "necessity of the Holy Ghost's divine operations." "Men must be told that they are dead," Spurgeon continued, "and that only the Holy Spirit can quicken them." The Spirit works according to his own good pleasure and none can "claim his visitations or deserve his aid." To the objection that this is very discouraging teaching

---

50. Charles Spurgeon, *The Soul Winner* (New York, Chicago, Toronto: Fleming H. Revell, 1895), 16f.

51. *Lectures*, 2:182-84.

he responded that it is good for one to be discouraged if he seeks "salvation in the wrong manner." Destroying confidence in their own abilities is a great help, Spurgeon contends, in driving them to Christ alone. "The doctrine of election and other great truths which declare salvation to be all of grace, and to be not the right of the creature, but the gift of the Sovereign Lord, are all calculated to hide pride from man, and so to prepare him to receive the mercy of God."[52]

What he called a "real bona fide substitutionary sacrifice" with the certainty of pardon is the "great net of gospel fishermen." It shows how God can be just and yet justify the one that believes. Justification by faith as well as the freeness, that is, sovereignty of God's mercy must be preached. God's love should be magnified but always in "connection with his justice." "Do not extol the single attribute of love in the method too generally followed," Spurgeon told his students, "but regard love in the high theological sense, in which, like a golden circle, it holds within itself all the divine attributes." If God were not just, he could not be love, for love as well as justice excludes every unholy thing as destructive of true beauty and selfless fellowship. For conversion, therefore, "Let boundless mercy be seen in calm consistency with stern justice and unlimited sovereignty. The true character of God is fitted to awe, impress, and humble the sinner: be careful not to misrepresent your Lord."[53]

Twenty-three years earlier [1858], and many times in between, Spurgeon had placed his finger on this need for fullness of truth as the best medicine at the minister's disposal. "We should not be selfish," Spurgeon emphasized, but should "always consider whether a thing will be beneficial to others." Truth always serves best in the case of needed conversion. Truth removes the scales from the eyes and brings in the heavenly light of comfort. No matter how perplexing a case may be, truth will provide the means to speak to it. "He who holds the truth, is usually the most useful man."[54]

One must not impute pragmatism to Spurgeon on this issue, as if he is merely seeking to use doctrine for a contrived purpose of his own. From the earliest days of his Christian life he held a mature grasp of the overall moral texture of biblical revelation. Divine immutability and divine sovereignty did not render God an amoral being. His unchangeable and infinitely perfect holiness does not render his moral actions void of true goodness and worthy of unending praise. God's sovereign decree not to save fallen angels but to leave them both under condemnation and in a state of utter averseness to holiness does not render their continued evil and increasingly hostile attacks on God's people and God's purpose less reprehensible. Human depravity and natural culpability as well as intrinsic susceptibility to wrath ["by nature children of wrath"] have no tendency to diminish the moral rightness of one's obligation to love and worship God and pursue all means by which his broken relation with his Creator might be healed. That a means of restoration for fallen humanity has been established makes that restoration a matter of ultimate moral concern for all the sons of Adam. "I have not kept back the glorious doctrines of grace, although by preaching them the enemies of the cross have called me an antinomian," Spurgeon noted, but with equal clarity he was sure he had not been afraid "to preach man's solemn responsibility, although another tribe have slandered me as an Arminian."[55] That the gospel's provisions

---

52. Ibid., 2:182.

53. Ibid., 183-84.

54. NPSP, 1855, 381.

55. NPSP, 1858, 237. The sermon "Human Responsibility,"

are designed exactly to coincide with the natural requirements of divine law means that a general proclamation of these provisions, even without an explicit accompanying command for repentance, should evoke moral desire for benefit from this revelation of a morally sustainable redemption. The hyper-Calvinist, by means of highly articulated theology of pre- and post-fall powers in humanity, does not assent to the seamlessness between human responsibility and the specific historical elements of the gospel. Spurgeon both intuitively and exegetically knew the difference between himself and them.

On the other hand, Arminianism could lay claim to no greater evangelical insight. Their resistance to the sovereignty of grace demanded that greater moral powers and prerogatives be either retained by fallen humanity or universally restored. Their gospel dilutes human sin and thus does not render one unreservedly dependent on the mercy of God for every part of his restoration to fellowship. Spurgeon believed that both the hyper-Calvinist and Arminian systems were unbiblical and did not consent to the ultimate consistency of revealed biblical truth.

Much less did he think that the truth resided within a bit of Calvinism and a bit of Arminianism, as if one dwelt on divine sovereignty and the other on human responsibility. Arminianism rightly affirmed human responsibility but drew wrong conclusions from it, so Spurgeon believed, and its faulty foundation created an error of the assertion. True Calvinism has within it a full accounting of human responsibility in the most robust way and does not cut the moral nerve between character and action in the way that Arminianism does. Arminianism assumes that each

man must have some confidence in himself before he can have hope for salvation; such an error many suppose to be a necessary compromise for usefulness to the lost. Spurgeon thought nothing was more ridiculous.

> Do not you think you need have errors in your doctrine to make you useful. We have some who preach Calvinism all the first part of the sermon, and finish up with Arminianism, because they think that will make them useful. Useful nonsense!—that is all it is. A man if he cannot be useful with the truth, cannot be useful with an error. There is enough in the pure doctrine of God, without introducing heresies to preach to sinners. As far as I know I never felt hampered or cramped in addressing the ungodly in my life. I can speak with as much fervency, and yet not in the same style as those who hold the contrary views of God's truth. Those who hold God's word, never need add something untrue in speaking to men. The sturdy truth of God touches every chord in every man's heart. If we can, by God's grace, put our hand inside man's heart, we want nothing but that whole truth to move him thoroughly, and to stir him up. There is nothing like the real truth and the whole truth, to make a man useful.[56]

Spurgeon's Calvinism, his systematic rejection of Arminianism, and his fervency in address to the ungodly constituted essential aspects of his view of evangelism and arose from his understanding of wholistic biblical truth. Both Arminians and hyper-Calvinists demanded that theology conform to a narrowly defined system more restricted than the biblical revelation allowed. Scripture conforms to a higher logic than human intellect and can penetrate and unveils mysteries beyond the scope of construction by mere human ratiocination. "The system of Truth is not one straight

---

demonstrates how every command and opportunity implied or specifically announced in the gospel is consistent with the moral nature of human responsibility.

56. NPSP, 1855, 381.

line, but two. No man will ever get a right view of the gospel until he knows how to look at the two lines at once, Spurgeon reasoned. "That God predestines and that man is responsible are two things that few can see. They are believed to be inconsistent and contradictory. But they are not!" Instead the apparent contradiction is upheld only by our weak judgment, and probably never will yield to present human contrivances to relieve the tension. "These two Truths, I do not believe, can ever be welded into one upon any human anvil," he insisted, "but one they shall be in eternity! They are two lines that are so nearly parallel that the mind that shall pursue them farthest will never discover that they converge—but they do converge and they will meet somewhere in eternity, close to the Throne of God from where all Truth springs!"[57] The truth, however, yet has a consistency and fullness of systematic expression more rich and satisfying than the logical circumference observable in either antinomianism, a virtual synonym for hyper-Calvinism in Spurgeon's parlance, or Arminianism. In his introduction to a sermon entitled "Election and Holiness," Spurgeon, once again, embraced a fuller truth than either of his opponents.

> He who preaches the whole truth as it is in Jesus will labour under continual disadvantages; albeit, that the grand advantage of having the presence and blessing of God will more than compensate the greatest loss. It has been my earnest endeavor ever since I have preached the Word, never to keep back a single doctrine which I believed to be taught of God. It is time that we had done with the old and rusty systems that have so long curbed the freeness of religious speech. The Arminian trembles to go an inch beyond Arminius or Wesley, and many a Calvinist refers to John Gill or John Calvin as an ultimate authority. It is time that the systems were broken up, and that there was sufficient grace

in all our hearts to believe everything taught in God's Word, whether it was taught by either of these men or not. I have frequently found when I have preached what is called high doctrine, because I found it in my text, that some people have been offended; they could not enjoy it, could not endure it, and went away. They were generally people who were best gone; I have never regretted their absence. On the other hand, when I have taken for my text some sweet invitation, and have preached the freeness of Christ's love to man; when I have warned sinners that they are responsible while they hear the gospel, and that if they reject Christ their blood will be upon their own heads, I find another class of doubtless excellent individuals who cannot see how these two things agree. And therefore, they also turn aside, and wade into the deceptive miry bogs of antinomianism. I can only say with regard to them, that I had rather also that they should go to their own sort, than that they should remain with my congregation. We seek to hold the truth. We know no difference between high doctrine and low doctrine. If God teaches it, it is enough. If it is not in the Word, away with it! Away with it! But if it be in the Word, agreeable or disagreeable, systematic or disorderly, I believe it. It may seem to us as if one truth stood in opposition to another, but we are fully convinced that it cannot be so, that it is a mistake in our judgment. That the two things do agree we are quite clear, though where they meet we do not know as yet, but hope to know hereafter. That God has a people whom he has chosen for himself, and who shall shew forth his praise, we do believe to be a doctrine legible in the Word of God to every man who cares to read that Book with an honest and candid judgment. That, at the same time, Christ is freely presented to every creature under heaven, and that the invitations and exhortations of the gospel are honest and true invitations—not fictions or myths, not tantalisations and mockeries, but realities and facts—we do also unfeignedly believe. We ascribe to both truths with our hearty assent and consent.[58]

---

57. NPSP, 1858, 337.

58. NPSP, 1860, 133.

Spurgeon's evangelism, therefore, comes not from a haphazard and uninformed zeal, but from the depths of theological conviction and conscientious obedience to Scripture. Sometimes Spurgeon might let loose with an infelicitous phrase, or raise a serious theological question with a manner of application, an appeal, or an interpretation, but his deeply inwrought system of thought and his constant practice at spoken communication makes him less prone to such inconsistencies than most of us. Both his zeal for souls and his conviction that only truth will convert may be seen in a sermon he preached at twenty-four years of age.

At the Royal Surrey Gardens Music Hall in December 1858, Spurgeon preached a sermon entitled "Compel Them to Come In."[59] In the introduction to the New Park Street volume in which the sermon is contained he remarked, "The sermon 'Compel Them to Come In' has been so signally owned of God, that scarcely a week occurs without some case of its usefulness coming to light. The violent, rigid school of Calvinists will, of course, abhor the sermon; but this is a very small matter when the Holy Ghost works by it in the salvation of men." In the sermon, given at a time when the opposition of London hyper-Calvinists was at a fever pitch, Spurgeon went hard after the sinner to seek his immediate repentance and remarked that "Some Hyper-Calvinist would tell me I am wrong in so doing." His insistence on the plainness and clarity of the doctrines of grace as an evangelistic tool presented no hindrance to Spurgeon in his insistent call to all sinners to repent of sin and turn even now to Christ.[60]

Spurgeon's extended and passionate appeal to the sinner matches the best in Baxter, Whitefield, and Edwards. His two purposes he stated as, "First, I must find you out; secondly, I will go to work to *compel you to come in.*" Layer upon layer of increasing earnestness and intensity of appeal bolstered with a stirring and gripping biblical foundation reveal the evangelistic convictions of Spurgeon. Depravity disables every man; every sinner is nevertheless responsible for his disbelief and must be called on to repent and believe; the means that fits the sinner to do this is the manifestation of the truth to his conscience; the preacher is responsible for genuine heart-wrenching passion for the soul of the lost person; the immediate power that effects the sinner's closing with Christ is the Holy Spirit.

In finding them out Spurgeon concludes that they are poor, maimed, halt, and blind. "You, blind souls that cannot see your lost estate, that do not believe that sin is so exceedingly sinful as it is, and who will not be persuaded that God is a just and righteous God, to you I am sent." The errand, according to Spurgeon, is more than any man can accomplish. "As well might a little child seek to compel a Samson, as I seek to lead a sinner to the cross of Christ." Though his commission is clear, and his work and words are fervent, he insists to the sinner that not only is he blind and lame and completely unfitted to do that which he is commanded to do, but the messenger also is unfit and powerless to do what he is called on to do. But for the sake of both sinner and the one seeking him, Spurgeon inserts the truth very

---

59. NPSP, 1859, 17-24.

60. Iain Murray has presented Spurgeon's controversy with the hyper-Calvinists with great clarity in its historical movement, its theological foundations, and its practical outworkings. *Spurgeon and Hyper-Calvinism* (Edinburgh: The Banner of Truth Trust, 1995). Also his *The Forgotten Spurgeon*, 45-52, dealt briefly

with this issue. Murray has overemphasized, however, the idea that Spurgeon focused preeminently on human responsibility in evangelistic situations. (*Hyper-Calvinism*, 112.) He has taken an emphasis that to me seems a minority emphasis for Spurgeon and has isolated it as Spurgeon's general operating principle. We have seen, however, that Spurgeon did not advocate any de-emphasis on the doctrines of grace as provocative of conviction and conversion.

early: "If God saith do it, if I attempt it in faith it shall be done; and if with a groaning, struggling and weeping heart, I so seek this day to compel sinners to come to Christ, the sweet compulsions of the Holy Spirit shall go with every word, and some indeed shall be compelled to come in."

Spurgeon then announces the gospel in its simple historical reality and the promises of eternal life endemic to it: "Believe on the Lord Jesus Christ and thou shalt be saved." But given the resistance of the sinner, Spurgeon tells him he will not be dismissed so easily for he has other commands from his Master. Spurgeon, with the unparalleled simplicity of his eloquence, leads the sinner to see his resistance through assuming the styles of command, then exhortation, appeal to self-interest, entreaty, and threatenings. "I must threaten you," he says. "You shall not always have such warnings as these. A day is coming, when hushed shall be the voice of every gospel minister, at least for you; for your ear shall be cold in death. It shall not be any more threatening; it shall be the fulfillment of the threatening. There shall be no promise, no proclamations of pardon and of mercy; no peace-speaking blood, but you shall be in the land where the Sabbath is all swallowed up in everlasting nights of misery, and where the preachings of the gospel are forbidden because they would be unavailing. I charge you then, listen to this voice that now addresses your conscience; for if not, God shall speak to you in his wrath, and say unto you in his hot displeasure, 'I called and ye refused.'" Spurgeon works to disenchant the sinner of the formidable fortress of a number of excuses and asks, "And now again, is it all in vain? Will you not now come to Christ? Then what more can I do?" All that is left is prayer and tears.

After all this, Spurgeon says that though the minister does not have the power of regenera-tion, he may still travail in labor until Christ is formed in them. God's promises are attached to these means and he says his Word will not return void. "What can we do then?" Spurgeon asks in closing. "We can now appeal to the Spirit."

> I challenge my master to keep his own promise. ... It is in his hand, not mine. I cannot compel you, but thou O Spirit of God who hast the key of the heart, thou canst compel. Did you ever notice in that chapter of the Revelation, where it says, "Behold, I stand at the door and knock," a few verses before, the same person is described, as he who hath the key of David. So that if knocking will not avail, he has the key and can and will come in. Now if the knocking of an earnest minister prevail not with you this morning, there remains still that secret opening of the heart by the Spirit, so that you shall be compelled. ... It is with him; he is master of the heart, and the day shall declare it, that some of you constrained by sovereign grace have become the willing captives of the all-conquering Jesus, and have bowed your hearts to him through the sermon of this morning.[61]

With the greatest of ease Spurgeon made his appeal to sinners in the context of his complete dependence on sovereign grace. The words uttered by Christ in the prophecy of Psalms, "Lo, I come," were words of hope and of sovereign grace. Spurgeon described persons at the end of themselves because of the full conviction of total depravity operating in their consciousness, to the "naked sinner, shivering in your own shame, blushing scarlet with conviction" but with "nothing left of your own," forbidden of conscience to "offer any plea by way of self-justification," to this one he comes "to be your robe of righteousness;" for this one the Lord will "put away his sin, through his own great sacrifice." In fact, Christ is the one

---

61. NPSP, 1860, 24.

"who draws your attention to himself." He comes unsought. "Herein is the glorious sovereignty of his love fully exercised, and grace reigns supreme. 'Lo, I come,' is the announcement of majestic grace which waiteth not for man, neither tarrieth for the sons of men."[62]

Every point of the sermon, in fact, pulsates with the marrow of sovereign grace reaching out in compelling love for sinners, sinners "for whom the eternal decree of God had designed the message."[63] Christ said, "Lo I come," according to "covenant purposes." He came because the "eternal counsel ran, Almighty grace, arrest that man." He comes because his heart is set on the ones that he loves; "Because he loved his redeemed from before the foundation of the world, therefore in due time he says, 'Lo I come.'" The sinner has need and nothing else, so Christ does come. If we had hope of our own, or a penny of our own, or rags of our own, or breath of our own, he would not come, but "now that you are naked, and poor, and miserable, and lost, and dead, Jesus reveals himself." His reason for doing so resides not in the sinner but in *His* grace. The sinner has no good in himself as to why the Lord should save him, but "because of his free, spontaneous, rich, sovereign, almighty grace, he leaps out of heaven, he descends to earth, he plunges into the grave to pluck his beloved from destruction."[64] His words "Lo, I come," mean that "without asking you, and without your asking him, he puts in an appearance in the sovereignty of his grace."[65] Spurgeon's closing moves naturally and with delicate grace to the free offer in light of absolute dependence.

Receive him: receive him at once. Dear children of God, and sinners that have begun to feel after him, say with one accord, "Even so, come quickly, Lord Jesus." If he says, "Lo, I come," and the Spirit and the bride say, Come; and he that heareth says, Come, and he that is athirst comes, and whosoever will is bidden to come and take the water of life freely; then let us join the chorus of comes, and come to Christ ourselves. "Behold the Bridegroom cometh; go ye out to meet him!" Ye who most of all need him, be among the first and gladdest, as you hear him say, "Lo, I come."

All that I have said will be good for nothing as to saving results unless the Holy Ghost shall apply it with power to your hearts. Join with me in prayer that many may see Jesus just now, and may at once behold and accept the present salvation which is in him.[66]

We find the same evangelistic urgency expressed in the absolute confidence in God's sovereign and particular pleasure in saving certain sinners in "An Urgent Request for an Immediate Answer." Taking his idea from Genesis 24, he likened Eliezer's urgency in seeking a wife for Isaac to the minister of Christ seeking souls for Jesus. Ministers of the gospel "are commissioned to search for those who shall be brought into the church, and at length as the bride of Christ, sit down at the marriage-feast in the glory-land above." As Eliezer prayed all along the way and put his success entirely in the hands of God, he knew that "it was the guidance of God, and not his own acuteness or wisdom, which led to such a favourable issue." So without earnest supplication for souls, preaching will be just so much hypocrisy. Again with earnest appeal and reasoning throughout, showing the greatness and loveliness of Christ, the infinite riches to be gained in trusting him, and the patent irrationality of refusing such ad-

62. MTP, 1891, 258, 261. "Lo I come."
63. Ibid., 251.
64. Ibid., 262f.
65. Ibid., 263.
66. Ibid., 264.

vantages Christ embodies in himself, Spurgeon stated frankly "I believe that I am sent to find out some appointed for Christ in the divine purpose and covenant, and I pray my Master that there may be many such."[67]

If Rebekah must leave her home and its familiar comforts to have Isaac, so Spurgeon called, "He wants those who will be willing to leave all, and be united to his Only-begotten Son, the Lord Jesus, who for our salvation came down from heaven, and took our nature, and lived in it; who took our sin, and died for us, that we might be pardoned and for ever saved." But for Spurgeon this open plea did not proceed on the grounds of a universal atonement, but on the certainty of an atonement impossible to fail of its end. "There must be souls that shall be eternally saved through believing on him," Spurgeon assured; "He cannot die in vain. He must have a people who shall be to him a bride, with whom he shall delight himself for ever and ever. And the question is, are there any such here?"[68] Such a vast crowd surely had many under divine appointment to salvation. "If he gives the hearing ear, will he not give the broken heart; and if he has led you to be anxious to listen to my message, are you not, many of you, the very persons whom he has appointed to be for ever united to his beloved Son?"[69]

Spurgeon had full realization that in the mystery of the divine–human interaction, that sinners, given over to themselves, resisted and refused certain spiritual operations, and as lost souls were, as it were, lost again. "I wonder," he said, "whether there are any marks in these pews where souls were lost, where some have parleyed with God, refused his grace, resisted his Spirit,

and gone thenceforth the downward road." Even with that reality working itself out in many hearts, Spurgeon still was assured that there would be "some mark where the grace of God has wrought effectual salvation." His hope was not in himself, in his pleading, or in their compliant spirit, but in the certainty that "some of you are now sitting in the very spot where you are predestinated to be born again unto everlasting life."[70]

While many would be lost, Spurgeon could not be satisfied if there were none who would be saved. If not, he felt he must give up preaching. "I cannot stand here beating the air. If my hearers are not converted, I have lost my time; I have lost the exercise of brain and heart. I feel as if I had lost my hope, and lost my life, unless I find for my Lord some of his blood-bought ones."[71] As Spurgeon continued to call for the well-considered but immediate decision of his hearers, and while he reminded them of the benefits to be gained in receiving him and the dangers of having him as judge instead of Savior, he did not fear that Christ would lose any for whom he had died. "Do not suppose," said Spurgeon, "that if you refuse Christ, he will lose the effect of his death." Isaiah 53 promised that the Messiah's travail of soul would surely bears its due fruit. "If you will not come to him," Spurgeon urged, "others will. If you reject him, he has a people who will accept him, by his almighty grace." God will send his messengers into the most unlikely places and gather together the most unlikely people, while others who now are invited will endure the eternal pains of outer darkness. "Oh," Spurgeon groaned, as if warning his audience that they had all to gain but that God would lose nothing by their negative response, "I charge you, think not that your refusal of the gospel invitation will leave any gaps

---

67. MTP, 1891, 589. "An Urgent Request for an Immediate Answer."

68. Ibid., 592.

69. Ibid., 592.

70. Ibid., 593.

71. Ibid., 593.

in the ranks of the redeemed!"[72] At the end of further earnest and unrelenting remonstrance with resistant sinners Spurgeon entreated, "God the Holy Ghost speaks by me now to souls whom God hath chosen from before the foundation of the world, and he says, 'Today, if ye will hear his voice, harden not your hearts.'"[73]

He closed the message by posing a question: "How is it to be done?" The plan is very simple, Spurgeon said. Its simplicity, however, is stated very carefully. "Jesus Christ took upon himself the sins of all who ever will trust him." This is substitution, and neither Calvinist nor Arminian could say the statement is untrue, but it is crafted in light of a conscience-driven commitment to particular redemption. "Come and rest upon his atoning sacrifice." This is a requirement from both the divine and the human standpoint, but establishes an open statement of the command and the promise for all willing to receive it. "Give yourself up to him wholly and unreservedly, and he will save you." Embedded within this statement the auditor hears the nature of true repentance and evangelical faith. The fact that such a response is possible only for those effectually called (as Spurgeon asserts in more ways than one in the message) does not render it less true or make its open-ended invitation built on the conditions morally consistent with the character of salvation less sincere. "Take him to be your Saviour by the simple act of faith. The pith of the matter is that I, being lost, give myself over to Christ to save me."[74]

In a sermon in February 1885 on Peter's blunder, his highly incongruous answer in Acts 10:14, "Not so, Lord," moved Spurgeon to discuss the power and deceitfulness of indwelling sin to produce a formalism, ceremonialism, and exclusivistic legalism that looks down on the "unclean" in worship. Suppose an evangelist "brings into the congregation all the poor people of the district and the very worst characters gather to hear him." The formalist does not rejoice, while true gospel fervor would shun partiality and "desire with equal earnestness the salvation of peer and pauper, of matron and harlot, of gentleman and vagabond." The condescending carriage of some toward their fellow man, "as if they were mere offal and rubbish, not worthy of the genteel notice," sickened Spurgeon.[75]

He noted a "minister in a certain neighborhood" that warned his church "against all such wicked persons as Moody and Sankey, and the like, because they were the means of saving the lower orders."[76] A battle governed by the same arrogance advances "when our old man fights against the gospel in its great principle of free, and sovereign grace." How can a saved sinner ever object to the grace of God to real sinners! Only a diseased man is a fit subject of healing, only a poor man is a fit subject for alms, only a drowning man is a fit subject of rescue, and only a sinful man is fit to be forgiven. None can come to Christ but those that come "all empty, and feeble, and sinful, and erring," suppliant for God's "free favor in Christ Jesus, spontaneously given on his part, without anything in us that can merit his esteem." To those that objected to his use of the term "Free Grace," as a redundancy, he replied, "We do not mind using a redundancy of expression when we are talking about it, ... for, as some people will not believe that grace is free, it is still necessary to make it very clear that it is so, and to say not only 'grace,' but '*free* grace.'"[77]

---

72. Ibid., 596.

73. Ibid., 599.

74. Ibid., 600.

75. MTP, 1885, 91.

76. Ibid.

77. Ibid., 92

For Spurgeon, evangelism was built on the premise that "Christ did not die for saints, but for sinners. He came not into the world because of our righteousness, but he died for our sins. The work of God is not to save men deserving salvation, but men who are altogether undeserving of it." A great flood of divine mercy rises fifty cubits above the tops of all our iniquities till they all are downed and covered "never to be seen again." He exclaimed, "What a grand article of the creed is that—'I believe in the forgiveness of sins!'"[78]

He pursued the same theme in "A Great Gospel for Great Sinners," a treatment of 1 Timothy 1:15-17. His assault upon sinners of all sorts allowed none to escape his probing language. None could rank themselves either outside the category of sinner or of eligibility for salvation. Even the theological infidel is a candidate. In Spurgeon's estimation, these were the worst kind of sinners, for they sinned against the greatest light.

> Especially must I rank him among the chief of sinners who has preached falsehood,—who has denied the deity of Christ—who has undermined the inspiration of Scripture—who has struggled against the faith, fought against the atonement, and done evil even as he could in the scattering of skepticism. He must take his place among the ringleaders in diabolical mischief; he is a master destroyer, a chosen apostle of the prince of darkness. Oh, that he might be brought by sovereign grace to be among the foremost teachers of that faith which hitherto he has destroyed! I think that we should do well as Christian people if we prayed more for any who make themselves notorious by their infidelity. If we talked less bitterly against them, and prayed more sweetly for them, good would come of it.

After an impressive display of the great sinners saved by Christ and from whom Christ according to the flesh descended, Spurgeon remonstrated, "Oh, dear friends, the Lord, who is rich in mercy, seeks a treasury in which to put his riches; he wants a casket for the sacred jewelry of his love; and these atrocious criminals, these great offenders, these who think themselves black as hell, these are the very men in whom there is space for his rare jewels of goodness." Abundant sin gives elbow-room for the infinite mercy of the living God. God's delight in saving sinners, in dealing patiently with sinners, should encourage great sinners to apply to him for mercy, to prostrate themselves "like the paper laid under the type to take the impression of almighty grace." His continual pleading with the great sinners before him led him to unfold repeatedly the theme of the text that Christ Jesus "came into the world to save sinners." Spurgeon had no desire to amuse them but to see them saved. His closing peroration reflected on Paul's exuberant benediction in verse 17 of the text:

> The saints shall never have done singing, for they remember they were sinners. Come, poor sinner, out of the depths extol him who descended into the depths for you! Chief of sinners, adore him who is to you the Chief among ten thousand, and the Altogether lovely! You black sinners, who have gone to the very brink of damnation by your abominable sins, rise to the utmost heights of enthusiastic joy in Jesus Christ, and all manner of sin and of blasphemy shall be forgiven you; and at the receipt of such a pardon you shall burst out into new-made doxologies to God your Saviour. ... O ye guiltiest of the guilty, the apostle Paul speaks to you, and stands before you as the bearer of God's white flag of mercy. Surrender to the King eternal, and there is a pardon for you, and deliverance from the wrath to come.[79]

---

78. Ibid.

79. SS, 16:220-21.

Evangelism Follows Theology

Spurgeon's evangelistic consistency and his passion for winning souls was so marked that some feared that his zeal for doctrine manifest in the Downgrade Controversy meant that he had forsaken the best for the good. Some devout persons, as well as some opponents, contended that his zeal would be better spent in the spread of the gospel than in doctrinal dispute. He consented that evangelistic work must continue, with full reliance on the Spirit of God. But one cannot go into such a battle unless he knows what weapons he must use for the "pulling down of strongholds." Going into gospel battle may be fruitless, or destructive, when enemies are in the camp. "How can those evangelize who have no evangel?" he asked, and "What fruit but evil can come of 'the new theology?'"[80]

This concern for theology as a necessary foundation to evangelism did not originate in the Downgrade but infused genuine zeal into his quest for souls from the first days of his ministry. At twenty-one, he warned against any attempt to make evangelism successful through the palatability of the doctrine. His concern at that time was the tendency of some to slide into something a bit more comfortable than their professed Calvinism when they felt it necessary to be a bit more human, and warm, and understanding and sympathetic. "How many there are who preach a gospel which they are afraid will not save souls," Spurgeon marveled; "and, therefore, they add little bits of their own to it in order, as they think to win men to Christ!" The bits of their own, whether of another confessional system or of the assured results of human criticism, created a fatal compromise in Spurgeon's view. "We have known men who believed Calvinistic doctrines, but who preached Calvinism in the morning and Arminianism in the evening." Why would any earnest man do such a thing? "Because," again Spurgeon pointed to the destructive element, "they were afraid God's gospel would not convert sinners, so they would manufacture one of their own."[81]

The compromise with Arminianism, so destructive to genuine gospel preaching in Spurgeon's perception, and among the greatest of offenses he could imagine early in his ministry, became no less dangerous in its tendency as years rolled on, but could not at all match the havoc wrought in the Christian ministry and in nominally Christian churches by the inventions of the Neologians. In the middle of his ministry the same conviction dominated his approach to evangelism when he stated, "It is ours to speak the truth boldly, and in every case we shall be a sweet savour unto God; but to temporize in the hope of making converts is to do evil that good may come, and this is never to be thought of for an instant."[82] What he said about the compromise with Arminianism early, about focus on truth in the middle, applied to modern thought with infinitely more dangerous implications. "I hold that a man who does not believe his gospel to be able to save men's souls, does not believe it at all. If God's truth will not save men's souls, man's lies cannot."[83] At least an Arminian believed that a soul needed saving. Men's lies had now permeated the entire body of doctrine.

Evangelistic Emphasis of His Writing

Spurgeon's many books had world-wide distribution. Many of the smaller ones were sold by colporteurs in the poorer and slum sections of

---

80. S&T, October 1887, 515. "The Case Proved."

81. SS, 1:326.
82. MTP, 1875, 639.
83. SS, 1:327.

London. Not only did he write tracts for mass distribution, but he wrote short but easily read books of theology with an evangelistic emphasis. Some were intended to edify the saints but always carried the message home to those yet without gospel faith. An advertisement for *Around the Wicket Gate* in 1889 stated, "We issue this book for one shilling, with no idea of remuneration, but simply that it may speak to lingering souls a word which shall lead them to decide for Jesus."[84]

Christ's Glorious Achievements consists of seven chapters of theological importance: "Christ the End of the Law;" "Christ the Conqueror of Satan;" "Christ the Overcomer of the World;" Christ the Maker of all Things new;" "Christ the Spoiler of Principalities and Powers;" Christ the Destroyer of Death;" "Christ the Seeker and Saviour of the Lost." Every chapter encourages the Christian in his love for Christ, his knowledge of Christ and thus his conformity to Christ. Each chapter also sets forth Christ as sovereign in his display of mercy and at the same time calls the sinner to go to him for mercy. Chapter one ends with the promise of a new heart contained in the new covenant as the only means by which the sinner will flee from sin to find in Christ the righteousness he needs. "This is one of the greatest covenant promises, and the Holy Ghost performs it in the chosen. Oh that the Lord would sweetly persuade you to believe in the Lord Jesus Christ, and that covenant promise shall be fulfilled to you. O Holy Spirit of God, send thy blessing on these poor words, for Jesus' sake."[85] The final chapter about "Jesus as Seeker and Saviour" ends with this:

I have been praying that he would bring this message under the notice of those whom he means to bless. I have asked him to let me sow in good soil. I hope that among those who read these pages there will be many whom the Lord Jesus has specially redeemed with his most precious blood, and I trust that he will appear at once to them, and say, "I have loved thee with an everlasting love, therefore with loving-kindness have I drawn thee." By grace omnipotent may you be made to yield to the Lord with the cheerful consent of your conquered wills, and accept that glorious grace which will bring you to praise the seeking and saving Saviour in heaven.[86]

All of Grace contains short expositions of the doctrine of grace. It begins with the words "The object of this book is the salvation of the reader. He who spoke and wrote it will be greatly disappointed if it does not lead many to the Lord Jesus. It is sent forth in childlike dependence upon the power of God the Holy Ghost, to use it in the conversion of millions, if so he pleases." The final chapter is a closing appeal of four deeply personal and winsome pages. The last paragraph catches the urgency.

Reader, meet me in heaven! Do not go down to hell. There is no coming back again from that abode of misery. Why do you wish to enter the way of death when heaven's gate is open before you? Do not refuse the free pardon, the full salvation which Jesus grants to all who trust him. Do not hesitate and delay. You have had enough of resolving, come to action. Believe in Jesus now, with full and immediate decision. Take with you words and come unto your Lord this day, even this day. Remember, O soul, it may be NOW OR NEVER with you. Let it be now: it would be horrible that it should be never. Farewell. Again I charge you, Meet me in heaven.

---

84. S&T, January 1889, 42.

85. Charles Spurgeon, *Christ's Glorious Achievements* (Ross-Shire, Scotland, Christian Focus Publications, nd), 25.

86. Ibid., 143.

In *The Kings' Highway*, written in his early twenties from sermons preached at New Park Street, Spurgeon wrote in the preface: "There is scarce a sermon here which has not been stamped by the hand of the Almighty, by the conversion of a soul. Some single sermons here have been, under God, the means of the salvation of not less than twenty souls." He tells those who will be distributing the books which sermons were "most signally owned in the salvation of the sinners." The sermon "None but Jesus" had been translated into the language of the aborigines of New Zealand and had been reported as leading to many conversions. The book begins with the simple but provocative sermon entitled "God's first words to the Sinner," based on Genesis 3:9. The first paragraph sets the tone, not only for the sermon but for the entire book.

> Adam ought to have sought out his Maker. He should have gone through the garden crying for his God, "My God, my God, I have sinned against Thee. Where art *Thou*? Low at thy feet Thy creature falls and asks mercy at Thy hands. I confess Thy justice and beseech Thy mercy, if mercy can be shown to such as one as I am."
>
> Instead thereof, Adam flies from God. The sinner comes not to God; God comes to him. It is not, My God, where art Thou? But the first cry is the voice of grace, "Sinner, where art *thou*?" God comes to man; man seeks not his God. There has never been found from Adam's day until now a single instance in which the sinner *first* sought his God. God must first seek him. The sheep strays of itself, but it never returns to its fold unless sought by the Great Shepherd. It is human to err, it is Divine to repent. Man can commit iniquity, but even to know that it is iniquity so as to feel the guilt of it, is the gift of the grace of God."[87]

Spurgeon discussed the question as intended to arouse Adam to see his state, to convince Adam of sin, to bemoan his loss, to show that God himself seeks his fallen creature to summon him to justice. The last section is a plain and chaste description, powerful in its impact, of the journey of the unrepentant sinner from health, to sickness, to unconsciousness, to death, to separation of soul and body, to resurrection with the rejoining of the "Ghastly spirit" with the resurrection body and "they twain, comrades in sin, are now companions in judgment." Then comes the display of the life worthy of damnation and the sentence to "everlasting punishment." Each part of the journey is punctuated with the recurrent theme, "Where art thou?" It closes with the pleading of the preacher, "I do beseech you by the blood of Him that died for sinners—and what stronger argument can I use?—think of the question, "Where art thou?" And then in phrases reminiscent of Jonathan Edwards' "Sinner in the Hands of an Angry God," he closed.

> Oh, that I could plead with you as a man pleadeth for his life! Would that these lips of clay were lips of fire, and this tongue no more of flesh, but a live coal taken with the tongs off the altar. Oh! For words that would burn their way into your souls! O sinner, sinner why wilt thou die? Why wilt thou perish? Man, eternity is an awful thing, and to meet an angry God is dreadful, and to be judged and condemned, what tongue can tell the horror. Escape for thy life; look not behind thee; stay not in all the plain; escape to Mount Calvary, lest thou be consumed. "Believe on the Lord Jesus Christ;" trust Him with thy soul; trust Him with it *now*, "and thou shalt be saved."[88]

---

87. Charles Spurgeon, *The King's Highway* (Ross-Shire, Scotland: Christian Focus Publications, 1989), 11, 12

88. Ibid., 24.

Spurgeon Provided His Congregation with Encouragement and Tools

Spurgeon *trained his congregation to think and order their lives with an evangelistic purpose.* He aimed at simplicity, the kind of simplicity that is in the gospel, but avoided superficial, minimalistic, misleading gospel-presentation programs that run rough-shod over the holy truths of the gospel. Nor did he promote "the raw, undigested harangues of revivalistic speakers whose heads are loosely put together." This should not prejudice a preacher from encouragement and instruction in how to participate in evangelism. In spite of many poor examples, Spurgeon made it his aim, and encouraged his students, to have "an army of enthusiasts" and "a church of soul-winners." If many are to be brought in, the whole church must be "aroused to sacred energy." A preacher should strive to have "every member energetic to the full, and the whole in incessant activity for the salvation of men."[89]

In October 1872, Spurgeon devoted a lengthy article to the instruction of ministers in how they were to energize the church for a harvest of souls during the autumn months. "We take it for granted," Spurgeon wrote, "that all are resolved that the season should be improved to the utmost, and all done that can be done to secure the blessing." The pastor is responsible to call the people to prayer and that he is so serious about the necessity of divine blessing on their efforts that none will doubt, but that all will join the effort in prayer. After such strenuous efforts in prayer, the church should each week "make some distinct inroad upon the territory of the arch-enemy." Something beyond the normal ongoing operation of gospel means is what Spurgeon had in mind—he suggested, as an example, the coverage of an entire area with a well-designed tract, by selected people.

Other means he also mentioned. In addition, the entire congregation should be plied hard with the gospel and "within her own suburbs the church should make it hard for sinners to be at ease. Appeals should not only come from the pastor, but from members." Everywhere a lost person turned he should be met with "expostulations, entreaties, invitations, and warnings." Frequent seasons should be made for preaching to and meeting with inquirers. The pastor and elders should lay themselves out to converse with all that indicate they are under concern of soul. "If the undecided will not come to us," Spurgeon urged, "we just go to them; the members of the church must individually see to them one by one." The bulk of seekers, however, will come to an interview if properly invited and will be willing to return if the first should prove profitable. Spurgeon was intense in his efforts to show ministers their duty in preparing their congregations for such evangelistic work and then in procuring the final effect themselves.

> What sweeter work is there than to speak to an audience gathered on purpose to learn the way of salvation? Sweet as it is, few find it easy to discharge the work aright. One goes away from such gatherings sighing and crying because one's heart is not more tender and one's mind more wise in soul-winning. No one can calculate the personal influence of a beloved minister when he comes side by side with a seeker and pleads with him alone. Under God it is like one of our old three-deckers lying side by side with an enemy's man-of-war and pouring in broadsides of red-hot shot; you may see the vessel under fire quiver from stem to stern, and its attempts at reply grow fainter and fainter at every round. Ministers who hold no such meetings, and give souls no opportunity for private discourse, are surely unaware of their duty or ignorant of their power.[90]

---

89. *Lectures*, "On Conversion as Our Aim," 191.

90. S&T, October 1872, 439.

That this was the case with Spurgeon resonated from many testimonies given at memorial services after his death. William Olney gave a sweeping example of the powerful impact Spurgeon had in encouraging his members to find a place of usefulness for evangelistic work.

Our dear Pastor ... had a remarkable power of infusing his own love for souls into the hearts of others. In response to his *Trumpet Calls to Christian Energy*, from this platform, men went out of this congregation in hundreds, to fling themselves into the slums of the South of London, and bring in members to this church out of some of the lowest parts of the neighborhood. As a consequence of this, there are, today, twenty-three missions stations, and twenty-six branch schools, and at these places there are every Sunday evening about one thousand of the members of this church working for the Lord Jesus Christ amongst the poor.[91]

The Sword and the Trowel regularly included suggestions as to how the members of the congregation, or ministers and laity among the readership anywhere, could redeem time and opportunities to introduce a word about the gospel. For years two tracts were published each month in the magazine to be used wisely in the introduction of conversation about the gospel. The tracts were produced with colorful fronts with an illustration depicting the subject from which Spurgeon would draw his evangelistic message. The point, though succinct, always included the reality of the danger of wrath and the freeness and abundant kindness of the gospel. "Cling to the Rock" pictured a river cascading though rough terrain with rocky cliffs on either side and begins with the words, "The craggy rocks frown upon the traveler, threaten-

ing to fall upon him as he journey sin [*sic*] their shade; and as he looks down from above upon their precipitous steps, his head whirls, and he shuns the brink, lest he be dashed to pieces by a fall; but the little trees and shrubs upon the sides of the precipice are safe from all fear of falling, because *they cling with all their might to the rock.*" After several lines reinforcing the idea involved in the image, he closed with this application:

The justice, greatness, truth, and perfection of God, which seem to frown upon others, are all our friends if we know how to cling to them, as they are set forth in the great atonement of our Lord Jesus Christ. If you can only cling to Jesus, poor sinner, you are safe. Neither your own weakness, not the storms of temptation, nor the hand of justice, can cast you to destruction while you cling to him. Learn from you heart to say, "Other trust away I fling, only to the rock I cling."

Spurgeon closed with two verses from "Rock of Ages."

"The Tempest" showed a fierce thunderstorm, black skies, lightning, and trees bending and broken alongside a river-bank with rocky crags highlighted by the flashes in the background. "How terribly Jehovah Thundereth!" the tract began. "He is not the soft, soulless, being that certain perverters of his Word would make him out to be. 'God is love,' yet is there also a terrible aspect to his nature." He wrote of the fierceness of his anger, and his fury as poured out like fire, and warned how vain and presumptuous was any attempt "to stand against such a Mighty One" because his eyes, like balls of fire, would see through you and find you out in any attempt at refuge from his wrath. Only one place was safe, so Spurgeon advised in his closing:

91. *From the Pulpit to the Palm Branch* (London: Passmore & Alabaster, 1892), 122f.

He makes the storm but he is himself our hiding place. The voice which breaks the cedars also speaks the promises, and so in the day of tempest we cower down beneath the wings of God, even as the little chickens hide under the hen. "The eternal God is our refuge, and underneath are the everlasting arms." Dear Reader, is he your God? Have you believed in his Son Jesus? If not, flee from the wrath to come! Flee at once!! Jesus will receive you, for he hath said, "Him that cometh to me I will in no wise cast out."

"The Hospice: Christ's Refuge" begins with the explanation, "Our engraving represents the Hospice of St. Bernard and the wild scenery surrounding it. The place is so cold that fish will not live in the lake, and we have seen the snow lying knee-deep at midsummer." This hospice is a refuge from the storm of certain death and receives pilgrims freely. Applying this to the reader of the tract, Spurgeon urged the following.

> Reader, whoever you may be, your soul is in danger unless you find rest for it in the atonement of Jesus Christ; we pray you trust in him, and enter into peace. He asks neither money, merit, nor preparation from you. Whosoever casts himself unreservedly upon the Mediator's merits is saved, even though he may not be able to see in himself so much as a single grain of merit. Jesus gives himself gratis to every willing soul. He will not refuse himself to you, dear reader. Try him at once! Let not your pride refuse his salvation because it is free, but the rather let your heart adore the generous grace of the Redeemer.

Just like St. Bernard's Hospice, no one coming to him has Jesus ever refused.

Spurgeon encouraged his people that in their evangelistic work they participated in Christ's victory over the devil in the crushing of his head. "I ought to add that every time any one of us is made useful in saving souls we do, as it were, repeat the bruising of the serpent's had." Women picking children from the gutters where they are Satan's prey to make them thieves and criminals do in their measure bruise the serpent's head. "I pray you do not spare him. When we by preaching the gospel turn sinners from the error of their ways, so that they escape from the power of darkness, again we bruise the serpent's head."[92]

Meetings at the Tabernacle

Special yearly meetings also trained the congregation to be always vigilant in their concerns for the souls of men. Spurgeon considered these special services, normally conducted in February, as a refreshing break from the normal routine by adding a certain intensity of effort that could not be maintained throughout the year. The sun is not always at noon, nor is the sea always at flood. Spurgeon placed no value on "spasms of effort and fits of excitement" but when the "Holy Ghost points thereto, they must rise to an intensity and vehemence which it would not be possible always to maintain." Spurgeon's description of this particular series of meetings provides intriguing insight into his approach to church evangelism. One sees how carefully Spurgeon sought to coordinate the vital elements of prayer, speaking, exhortation, counseling of inquirers, and preparation of helpers for evangelism.[93]

Preparation for the meeting began, as Spurgeon sought to follow a biblical principle, with a fellowship of the church leadership—"The bread with which the multitude was fed was first received from the Master's hands by the disciples, and then handed by them to the assembled crowd." Singing, fellowship, and prayer dominated the meeting, with the earnest desire for God's

---

92. Spurgeon, *Christ's Glorious Achievements*, 42.

93. S&T, March 1871, 136.

blessing on the special emphasis. All believed that it was needed, and none criticized the effort to obtain it. "Our brethren are not of the order of men that delight in inventing novel methods, criticising plans, and raising objections, but they have learned to prefer acting to caviling and practice to theory; hence the meeting was not marred by discussions or fault findings."[94]

The prayer time was fervent as "the holy light burned and glowed gloriously." On the Lord's Day, Spurgeon preached. Another prayer meeting was held in the afternoon and another in the evening service. Again on Monday, a threefold prayer meeting was held; at seven in the morning many gathered, at noon another group, and in the evening the entire Tabernacle was filled for prayer. In this evening gathering for prayer, "no excitement was manifest, but solemn earnestness revealed itself." On Wednesday, the church met so that "as a body, it might cry mightily unto God." Though the meeting was open both for prayer and speaking, "no unqualified brother wasted the time, as is so generally the case in such meetings." Only the fittest men spoke, and all were glad to hear them.[95] Friday was spent in prayer by the College students, joined by the ministers in London who were alumni. Spurgeon witnessed a "hearty agonizing petitioning, a general personal renewal of consecration to God, and a holy warmth of soul." Again, Monday was a day of prayer, all day long. It started before the sun had risen and continued without intermission for fourteen hours. Spurgeon himself was there at 10, at 12, at 3:30, and remained until 8:30. He called it a "season of importunate prayer, which can no more fail to be answered than the Lord himself can change." At the children's meeting on Tuesday, while Spurgeon spoke to the children, "their mothers were

upstairs holding a prayer-meeting that the Lord would help us." So through March 9 the meetings continued with prayer and preaching and counseling of enquirers. Spurgeon summarized, "Thus prayer and effort went hand-in-hand."

The pervasive emphasis on prayer arose from the firm conviction of Spurgeon that such evangelism really was the Lord's work. Prayer served with preaching as an ordained means of calling the elect. For Spurgeon, "Prayer is, under God, the great lever with which to uplift a church." He knew of no problem to be solved as to whether prayer is heard, for "we know it and have seen it." He believed that the "power of prayer is as much a fact, and as clearly to be seen as the influence of electricity, or the force of gravitation."[96] When prayer succeeded, it was because "the spirit of prayer was richly given." Spurgeon declared that the pastors "esteem the prayer-meetings to be the life of the church; they are never absent unless by the force of necessity." The people also, therefore, value the prayer meetings "and meet in such numbers as we fear are to be seldom found anywhere else engaged in intercession."[97]

The fruit of such labor in believing prayer could be seen in the earnest public seeking after salvation. On the first Lord's Day of the meeting, "After each service persons came forward who were pricked in the heart." On Monday evening Spurgeon reported that "enquirers were forthcoming, and some who had got beyond that stage pressed forward to avow themselves on the Lord's side."[98] On Thursday, at four in the afternoon, Spurgeon spoke at a meeting of young ladies "of an educated class just rising into womanhood." As a result, "anxious souls waited to have conversation with the elders and other friends." On the

---

94. Ibid..

95. Ibid., 137.

96. Ibid. 136.

97. Ibid.

98. Ibid.

second Lord's Day, February 19, elders visited the afternoon Bible classes, "to stir them up to seek the immediate conversion of the unsaved ones among them." The following day, while prayer was being held in other parts of the Tabernacle, "a church meeting was being held in another room, so that some of those who had come forward might confess Christ before his people." At the close of the day "many more seekers came forward, and male and female helpers were busy in conversation and prayer with person convicted and enquiring." On Tuesday evening, at a meeting of about 1,000 children, where there was "no tea, no music, no magic lantern to attract the boys and girls," gospel truth in all its fullness, both doctrinal and experiential, was presented and "an evident feeling of interest and awe rested on the assembly." For a young people's meeting scheduled for Thursday, a note was included, "Arrangements made that enquirers may meet with friends for direction and encouragement after the Lecture." Other meetings had similar arrangements and time announced for special appeals to the unconverted. In summary, Spurgeon observed that "a very general breaking down is taking place among the sinners of the congregation, and a great tenderness of heart is notably observable."[99]

The handling of these inquirers is a particularly interesting part of the task. On Tuesday, the pastors waited from eleven till one to see seekers. Many came. Spurgeon described the care essential for effective evangelism including both protection of the church and honest dealing with souls.

> The invitation to the wedding-feast of mercy brought in, as of old, both bad and good. Objectors came with their hard questions, the lovers of the loaves and fishes with their hypocrisies, the ignorant with their superstitious fears, the talkative with their presumptuous confidence; but there also drew near to the servants of God the broken-hearted, the desponding, the despairing, the believing, the rejoicing, the restored. It was a good day, and when the fishermen counted up the treasures of the net, after laying many aside, and assigning others to a course of further instruction, they found a residue of twenty-six whom they felt free to propose to the church for membership.

Spurgeon went on the give more details of the care involved in evangelistic counseling. No less that a quarter of an hour must be spent with each enquirer, but often twice to three times that much is required. This is necessary to form any estimate of the spiritual condition of the person and render efficient aid. In the evening more inquirers came and were faithfully dealt with by some of the elders and "other friends." These "other friends" were specially selected by the pastor for this purpose. He held prayer meetings with them and gave training for the most effective help throughout the time of meetings.

Counselors of inquirers looked for three pivotal evidences of true conversion. One focused on the nature of the individual's perception of his sin and dependence on the work of Christ. Did the inquirer seem to have a clear and distinct and abiding sense of the seriousness of his offense toward God, a healthy remorse for that sin, a desire to turn from it and cease such offensive behavior toward God; did he also recognize that God was willing to receive him through the atonement made by Christ and through that alone? Second, did the present determination of the person's soul indicate a clear intention to live for Christ and overcome the opposing forces of the world; did he feel the urgency of seeing others escape from

---

99. Ibid., 136-38.

the wrath to come? Three, with a full knowledge of his own unworthiness and his full dependence on God, did the person have some knowledge of the doctrines of grace and that mercy was the fountain from which his salvation flowed?[100] Spurgeon saw this as that natural result of the Spirit's work of regeneration and uplifting Christ. "I believe the man who is not willing to submit to the electing love and sovereign grace of God, has great reason to question whether he is a Christian at all," Spurgeon reasoned; "for the spirit that kicks against that is the spirit of the devil, and the spirit of the unhumbled, unrenewed heart."[101]

As a result of the conviction during the young ladies meeting, Spurgeon recounted that "that same night, in more than one house, friends were compelled to rise and administer comfort to young hearts in which the arrows of conviction had fixed." At the meeting, following the pastor's address, "beloved matrons in the church mingled with the youthful company and conversed with individuals concerning their souls." The evening service yielded more opportunity as "anxious souls waited to have conversation with the elders and other friends."[102]

Spurgeon's physical struggles kept him from participation in the special services of February 1875. William Olney sent him a summary of the events of the month. Among the highlights, Olney mentioned that "A very solemn feeling prevailed over all the meetings, and in the inquiry meetings, which were held afterwards on every occasion, very many persons were led to the Saviour and found joy and peace in him." At a final meeting, young converts were invited to meet with J. A. Spurgeon and the elders for a meeting of prayer and thanksgiving. Eighty-two persons stood in the meeting as "having sought and found the Saviour during the last three weeks." Between thirty and forty, according to Olney's reckoning, came to the platform and made a public profession of their trust in the Lord Jesus. "Conversion work has been very clear and genuine," Olney stated, and in recognition of the process established in this matter, continued, "and in many instance which will come before our beloved senior pastor's notice on his return among us again, the change was very striking and remarkable." Olney also noted that a weekly class for the new converts was arranged for under the instruction of "Elder Nesbitt" with Spurgeon's version of the Westminster catechism "being the class-book from which instruction is given." Evangelistic concern expanded throughout the congregation and into a variety of ministries. Members worked earnestly with the relatives and servants to attend the meetings and prayed "for their immediate decision for Christ." Classes taught by the elders, Mrs. Bartlett's class, the Sunday School at the Almshouses, and other classes reported increased interest and the continuation of conversion work. "It is the desire of the elders of the church that this good work should continue and increase," Olney stated, "and every means will be taken to foster it by special prayer and effort until far greater results are attained." His earnestness in this was intensified by the prospect that when Spurgeon returned "his heart may be greatly gladdened and a fresh impetus be given to the good work by his ministry. May he come among us in the power of the Holy Spirit, and enjoy a larger and richer blessing in the conversion of souls than has ever yet been given him."[103] Spurgeon's intensity for the

---

100. Arnold Dallimore, *Spurgeon* (Edinburgh: Banner of Truth, 1995), 81. Dallimore set forth these three ideas from an investigation of the "Record of Enquirers" book at the Metropolitan Tabernacle.

101. SS, 7:226.

102. Ibid., 137.

103. S&T, April 1875, 189.

souls of sinners had been embraced by his leadership and spilled over into the entire congregation.

In order to encourage zeal for souls and energetic methods of reaching the lost, Spurgeon put ideas before his people with which he did not entirely agree, but that had earnestness and some possible good in them. "How to lead the Young to decision for Christ" was such an article.[104] The article began by referring to the work of the energetic and well-known child evangelist Payson Hammond who by his successful evangelism of children had worked to dispel the idea that the cultivation of children proceeds on the basis of hopes of their conversion in later years. That was an egregious error according to Hammond. Pastor Malins of Newcastle agreed and stated, "We have never witnessed the union of these qualifications [traits for successful child evangelism] in the same degree in any man as in Payson Hammond, of America, and we have never heard of or seen more marked or abiding results than those of his works."[105] Malins recounted an occasion when he heard Hammond speak on sin and salvation in its relations to Jesus the Savior, particularly applied to a child's understanding "with the view of leading them to immediate decision for Christ." Not even Sabbath Schools had made much evangelistic impression on children "when compared with the labours of such men as Payson Hammond and Josiah Spiers," no, not even Moody and Sankey. Later the writer remarked, "When impression has been produced, it should be immediately followed up with the view of consummating it in decision for Christ."[106]

Malins pointed to the qualities requisite in one that would win children, what special truths should be made prominent, and what agencies should be used to give effect to the truth. Work-

ers should genuinely love children, be convinced that they can be led to conversion, and feel the urgency of "their decision for Christ in youth." The content must be precisely related to sin and salvation as both of these relate to Jesus Christ. Though they might be unsophisticated theologically and unable to embrace abstractions of doctrine, children can easily grasp the meaning of personal relations. Malins, following Hammond, believed that love and gratitude to parents serve as a perfect model for understanding both sin against and love for Christ. Parents are infinitely less worthy than Jesus and gratitude to them should be infinitely less than gratitude to Christ. The conclusion must be put forcefully, "What a wicked heart yours must be if it cannot and will not love and trust Jesus Christ!" Malins believed that this was the principal truth to which the Spirit bears witness, and "he will honour, as he has done, the longing, earnest believing efforts, to bring home to the hearts of the young."[107]

Malins' minimizing of theological content surely would cause hesitation in Spurgeon's desire to give full approval to Malins' argument. Malins wrote, "For just in proportion as the intellect is untrained, and the imagination and the affections are active, they are unfitted to grasp doctrinal statements, and so it is the more necessary, as far as human putting can do it, to present to them Jesus the loving one waiting to receive them in their sinfulness, and welcome and save them when they come."[108]

As for effectual agency, the author commended special services designed to meet the peculiar propensities of the young, "directed to produce conviction of sin, and immediate trust in Jesus." Inquiry meetings so that each child could be dealt with at a personal level were encouraged. Anec-

---

104. Ibid., 382-90.

105. Ibid., 385.

106. Ibid., 386, 389.

107. Ibid., 387.

108. Ibid.

dotes of personal experience in this type of evangelism with children, personal testimony, and heavy criticisms of older nay-sayers filled out the article. Much that Malins wrote would ring true to Spurgeon. In his final commendation of work for the conversion of children, Malins showed the options.

> Their conversion will obviate the necessity of seeking to save them from the firm grasp of the devil in older years; it will impart growing strength and earnestness to the church for the fulfillment of her mission to a lost world, and lessen the number of those who come into our church—able indeed to rejoice in the grace which snatched them as brands from the burning, but only able to lay the wrecks of wasted lives upon the altar of service.[109]

Agreements aside, much controversial material remained. Spurgeon footnoted the first page with a caveat and a statement of neutrality pregnant with caution. "The Editor is not to be supposed to agree with every opinion and statement contained in papers bearing their author's name. This excellent paper is printed by the desire of the Conference of the College, and it is hoped that it will draw forth other articles upon the same subject. The point on which all Christians are not agreed is the value of the labours of Mr. Hammond: we neither endorse nor criticize them."[110]

While he did not feel obliged to endorse the digest of Hammond, Spurgeon was none the less evangelistic. In February 1879, Spurgeon set aside the entire month, "as usual," for "special efforts to reach the unsaved." Again prayer was at the beginning and scattered throughout the special efforts. On February 3 a special prayer meeting was held in the Tabernacle followed two

days later by smaller meetings for prayer simultaneously in forty-eight different districts. Each Saturday evening a prayer meeting was held in several locations under the leadership of the elders. Accompanying Spurgeon with the preaching duties were several pastors, graduates of the College, as well as evangelists from the College Society of Evangelists (Clarke and Smith) and the Tabernacle Evangelists Association (Fullerton and Chamberlain).[111]

Spurgeon taught his church to see itself as an evangelistic organism with many members, each part doing that which it is gifted to do. No one does everything, no one does nothing, and everyone has a particular assignment from the Lord in the business of calling out his people. Each should consider his involvement as a privilege of infinite importance. "Those who are privileged to take part in holy efforts ought to think themselves highly favoured, for the day may come when, laid aside from actual service, they will envy those who keep the doors of the Lord's house. To wash the feet of the meanest servant of the great King is a high honour. And he may well congratulate himself who is permitted such an indulgence. To be present at the festival which greets returning prodigals is a still more joyous privilege, and those who are denied it have to be thankful when even the distant sounds of the music and dancing charm their ears."[112] He wrote those lines from France in the aftermath of the February evangelistic services and reflected his own feeling of sorrow at being so distant from the services in which the fruit of the month of evangelism became ripened for harvest.

In April, in narrating a more complete description of the events of the month, Spurgeon gave special attention to the number of workers from the congregation scattered throughout the

---

109. S&T, August 1875, 390.

110. Ibid., 382.

111. Ibid., 147.

112. Ibid.

building during preaching services. "At least 150 presented themselves as anxious to converse with enquirers, and night after night they were found scattered all over the building, watching for souls as those that must give account. They were all furnished with tickets on which were printed 'hints' as to the best methods of working, and twenty-three texts that were likely to be useful to them in their work, but they were all expected to be familiar with the Word of God, so as to give divine authority for their warnings, entreaties, instructions, or invitations."[113] The meetings were closed on March 1 with a meeting for prayer and testimony conducted by the elders. The following afternoon, Sunday, they visited the various Bible classes assembled for their regular study for the purpose of confirming those that had professed faith in Christ and "seeking to lead to the Saviour those who still remained undecided."[114]

According to the information given him, Spurgeon reported that prior to each service, prayer meetings were held, and after each service meetings for enquirers were necessary. "After the first few evenings the numbers remaining were so large that the young men's meeting had to be removed from the class room to the lecture-hall, and the meeting for females from the ladies' room to the one vacated by the young men." In his exile, Spurgeon was encouraged when the news arrived that some were saved in every service. As normal, Spurgeon carefully ascribed all glory to God.[115]

Another regular feature in which Spurgeon involved his congregation in personal evangelism was the surrender of their seats on a Sunday evening in order to allow "strangers" to occupy them. On August 10, 1879, he preached "The Plague of the Heart" to a capacity crowd. Prior to the meeting

at least three different prayer meetings for God's blessing on the effort occurred, one by a "meeting of chosen soul-winners" held in the afternoon and another by the pastor and deacons in their private vestry. "It was delightful," Spurgeon remarked, "to observe the discipline voluntarily kept up by the Tabernacle friends; for none of them were present, nor thought of being so." No crooked people or irregulars objected to the proceeding but all cheerfully complied and gave outsiders an opportunity to hear their pastor. The crowd that gathered had workmen in their "usual garb" and West End gentlemen at the height of fashion, higher and lower ranks equally represented. Men were in the majority, several clergy were present, and soldiers gave a dash of red throughout the crowd. Spurgeon described the atmosphere as "dense and drowsy" but the attention as "unbroken and the feeling deep." Scattered throughout, were the selected ones of his own people, the chosen soul-winners, that Spurgeon called "sharp shooters" who "gathered up each one his share of those wounded by the word." The aggressive and individualistic approach does not diminish the necessity of caution. Spurgeon explained:

> Results, however, are better seen after an interval than immediately after the service. So it has ever been with our ministry. The converts do not rush excitedly into an enquiry room, but they think over what they have heard, and where the arrows have entered the soul the convinced ones come forward in due time.[116]

When the "free service" met on June 12, 1881, Spurgeon felt it was "the most successful of our efforts in this direction to get those who are not in the habit of attending any place of worship." He suspected that on former occasions,

---

113. S&T, April 1879, 195.

114. Ibid., 196.

115. Ibid., 195.

116. S&T, September 1879, 446.

the crowd consisted mainly of those that had left their own places of worship to attend the Tabernacle. This time, however, "a large portion evidently belonged to the class that we have been most anxious to reach." How did he know? "The number who did not know the tunes was joyfully great; and the general aspect of the attendants was not of the usual religious order." His exclamation was that God would "capture these outsiders, and hold them fast by his grace!" The importance of prayer for Spurgeon's evangelism came before the public in his report as he wrote, "Importunate prayer was offered about this, and we expect answers from our God." Spurgeon felt unusual heaviness before he entered the pulpit, so "the deacons pleaded with God for him before he left the vestry." God granted utterance and after the service, "the same brethren lovingly gathered around their pastor and prayed a second time for the blessing. Surrounded by a body-guard of praying men the Lord's servant cannot fail."[117]

Spurgeon looked for places in London where he could plant churches and involve his people in the project. In 1881 he asked his friends around London to inform him of districts needing the gospel. "The thing to be desired," he wrote, "is a large hall or large room which we could hire, and a few true-hearted friends to form a nucleus." The city was growing faster than the churches and without strenuous efforts "London will become more and more heathen." He was more than willing to help provide preachers for such places and any other way in his power. He could not personally "tramp over this vast metropolis" making a personal survey, but he encouraged the brethren to "try to raise churches near their own abodes if there are none, or if those which exist are not really gospel-loving churches."[118]

The Needs of an Ever Present Harvest

Possibilities for evangelism in the city were endless; vast numbers of lost sinners, ever increasing, needed gospel witness. New churches were needed and present churches should strategize for the task. Beyond that, Spurgeon believed that evangelists with biblical qualifications and a clear call could increase the church's success in wielding the harvest sickle. One must be bold, but not careless; great blessing or great delusion would follow the wake of the evangelist.

---

117. S&T, July 1881, 355.

118. S&T, May 1881, 242.

9

USE OF EVANGELISTS

Vital godliness is not revived in Christians by mere excitement, by crowded meetings, by the stamping of the foot, or the knocking of the pulpit cushion, or the delirious bawlings of ignorant zeal; these are the stock in trade of revivals among dead souls, but to revive living saints other means are needed. … This, then leads us to the conclusion that if we are to obtain a revival, we must go directly to the Holy Ghost for it, and not resort to the machinery of the professional revival-maker.[1]

To call in another brother every now and then to take the lead in evangelistic services will be found very wise and useful; for there are some fish that never will be taken in your net, but will surely fall to the lot of another fisherman. … Sound and prudent evangelists may lend help even to the most efficient pastor; and gather fruit which he has failed to reach.[2]

Zeal for Souls and Zeal for Truth

As necessary concomitants to his love for the person and work of Christ, Spurgeon consistently worked to integrate the twin passions of love for truth and love for souls. The cold presentation of truth unaccompanied by a desire for the manifestation of its power under the Spirit of God in the capturing of souls made him nauseous. How could any so-called gospel minister preach without burning of heart for the universal acceptance of Christ in his perfect redemption? Surely a preacher would want all to submit to Christ as Lord. The Spirit, however, is still the Spirit of truth, and Christ is the truth, and only as such is he the way and the life. An effort, therefore, to pound out external response and decision by minimizing truth, par-

ticularly those hard truths of human depravity and absolute dependence on God's will and efficacious work, would do nothing to accomplish the actual work of conversion. Spurgeon loathed such chicanery and blasted forth against it, for it dishonored all the redemptive offices of each person of the triune God, corrupted the church, and deceived souls.

How, then, to effect an ongoing ministry of zeal for souls with an accompanying harvest without resorting to the manipulative technique that had flooded the ranks of the professional evangelist presented an ongoing dilemma for Spurgeon and often a case of conscience. While he longed for souls he would say quite frankly, "That experience which is feigned, and not really wrought in the soul, will prove to be nothing better than the painted pageantry of a dead soul—a disguise to go to hell in." While pressing for conversion, therefore, Spurgeon would say,

---

1. S&T, December 1866, 532. The article was entitled "What Is a Revival?"

2. C. H. Spurgeon, "On Conversion as our Aim," in *Lectures to My Students* (London: Passmore & Alabaster, 1881), 192.

317

"Pretend to no feeling which is not real. Profess no emotion which is not deeply and truly felt. In all things be sincere, and most of all be accurate when describing your inner condition before the heart-searching Jehovah."[3] In lamenting that many were church members and expressing pain for their perhaps fatal delusion, he would warn, "The fact of your being in the church may be very much to your spiritual injury; therefore do not confess with the mouth what you have not believed with the heart."[4] He committed himself to maintain the unity of zeal and truth, but where could he find others of like mind? He would have to train them, encourage them, caution them, and promote them. Even then, he would be on edge.

Train Them, Call Them, Send Them

The 1891 report for the Pastors' College included a report by W. Y. Fullerton from "The Pastors' College Society of Evangelists." Largely given over to his work throughout the country with a musician called Manton Smith, Fullerton reported on twenty-three places that had been visited. Though great variety in geography and social status characterized the number, "the gospel we have preached has varied not at all, and we have found, as of yore, that the old truth is suited to all men, whether they be subtle or simple."[5]

Fullerton presented an *apologia* for the effectiveness of itinerant evangelism and its usefulness for the church. The advance of the kingdom of God through conversion is the main goal, Fullerton insisted. While many attending the meeting probably already were converted and only needed assurance, and others already were under deep impressions of sin, "a considerable number of others have been drawn to the services, per-haps by curiosity, or by the extra effort put forth by some earnest friend, or to listen to Mr. Smith's singing or cornet, or even as during the past awful winter, to get shelter—who have been met with by the Spirit of God, and led to the feet of Jesus." Fullerton recognized that some disapproved of evangelism through protracted meetings. He was convinced, however, that such concentrated attention to salvation intensified the sense of the importance of an "instant decision and every excuse for importunate pleading with the unsaved." If brethren approve of preaching the gospel three times a week, how could they object to it being preached ten times a week.[6]

Following this article were lists of places visited by evangelists supported by a Tabernacle fund. In addition to Fullerton and Smith, this included a Mr. Burnham, about whom Spurgeon wrote, "We give in *The Sword and the Trowel* monthly testimonies to the success of this earnest brother's visitations." After Mr. Harmer's schedule, Spurgeon commented, "To all of these the Holy Spirit has set his seal by 'signs following.' Our magazine is made bright with records of revivals under Mr. Harmer." Though Mr. Harrison had been "invalided" for part of the year, he nevertheless had been able to make some missions. He is a true 'son of thunder,'" Spurgeon added, "and of consolation also." The year of intense evangelistic work done by Thomas Spurgeon in New Zealand was reported. "He continues his fruitful service, and is far on in his year of incessant labor. May the Spirit of God cause those broad fields to blossom as the rose!"[7]

That an 1891 report of the work of evangelists was included in *The Sword and the Trowel* is due to a carefully arranged beginning for the enterprise. First of all, undoubtedly due to the influ-

---

3. SEE, 5:370.

4. SEE, 5:166.

5. S&T, June 1891, 270.

6. Ibid., 272.

7. Ibid., 273.

ence of a friendship with D. L. Moody, Spurgeon had become persuaded "of the great value of the office and work of evangelists." Accordingly, he determined to sponsor evangelists through the College in 1877. He personally engaged to find them maintenance that "they may go through the length and breadth of the land and preach Christ."[8] Though he gladly took the responsibility and pledged cheerfully to "practice self-denial to pay the amount which is needed," at the same time he "would not deny any friend the pleasure of assisting."[9] The first two were A. J. Clarke and Manton Smith. He sent them on their first assignment in August of 1877.

Clarke displayed engaging natural gifts as well as those of a humble Christian. One observer described him as "every inch a man" with no "puerilities or babyisms about his style," who neither "whines nor bawls," and was by no means a dilettante.[10] Smith was the singer and also played a cornet, "by which means he not only fetches in the people to the service, but interests them when they are gathered together." Spurgeon had personally given him a "new silver trumpet, upon which is engraved a verse from the Psalms, "With trumpet and sound of cornet, make a joyful noise before the Lord and King." Both evangelists had been useful in conversion work and they were sent forth in the name of the Lord "with high hopes of blessing."[11]

The August *Sword and Trowel* carried a lengthy report of the evangelists' work in a squalid part of Dublin. Preaching and singing brought good crowds but also inflamed the Catholics and initiated a "tug of war" for the soul of the city.[12]

8. S&T, July 1877, 334.

9. S&T, December 1877, 560.

10. Ibid.

11. S&T, July 1877, 334.

12. S&T, August 1877, 394.

From Ireland to Bristol for meetings over the span of three weeks, the evangelists went. This would provide scrutiny under the eyes of seasoned and conservative Baptists extremely wary of the notorious tricks of the evangelists' trade. Spurgeon needed an evaluation from doctrinally minded, hard-to-please, Bible-centered advocates of the regulative principle for Christian worship and ministry. Should thumbs down be the judgment here, it would be difficult to make the effort successful. When G. D. Evans from Bristol wrote, the orientation of the article and his observations exactly suited Spurgeon's hope for the new ministry. Evans' first paragraph described well what was at stake.

Amongst the more staid and sober Christians of this ancient city there are many who have looked with some suspicion upon men who have assumed the name of Evangelists. Nor can this be wondered at, for our ears have been grossly offended and our hearts much saddened by the absurdities and vulgarities of some who, by their coarse manipulation of the gospel message, have spoiled its beauty and marred its glorious simplicity. It was therefore with considerable anxiety in the minds of many, and not without gloomy forebodings on the part of a few, that the visit of Messrs. Clarke and Smith to this city was anticipated. And even before the cornet was heard in our chapels, the thought of it was a source of disquietude. With well trained choirs and costly organs, what possible advantage could it be to introduce such an instrument into our midst? Besides, it was certainly a sensational means of reaching the people. And that word *sensational* is a dreadful one to ears polite. Well, the brethren have come and gone. They have preached and sung and played in several of our chapels. Crowds have gathered to listen to them. The services have been neither sensational nor vulgar. The prejudices of the most particular have not been offended. Hostile criticism has been disarmed. Our friends have left us with the goodwill of many hundreds of sincere, old-fashioned Christians, as well as with the blessing of many anxious souls, and the earnest prayers of our churches that they may have a long and useful career before them. Should they return to our midst at some future time, they will receive a hearty Bristol welcome.[13]

Clarke preached with great boldness without the offense of unwarranted dogmatism or insolent egotism but as a manifestation of intense faith in the verities of the gospel. The more he preached, the more favor he gained with the people. Suspicions against evangelists were ill-placed when viewing Clarke. Evans gave close observation to Smith and the effect of his trumpet. People, especially children, are naturally drawn to his genial manner. His singing, though not scientific, is of a popular character. His voice does not penetrate so far nor thrill so deeply as that of Sankey, but the rendering of some of the solos is deeply affecting and impressive. When not singing he used his cornet to lead both congregation and choir. The instrument, so suspect in principle, proved to be of immense usefulness in keeping the entire congregation on pitch and up to rhythm in the singing. He noticed this especially at George Muller's orphanage where the children lagged and became flat without the cornet but responded immediately and in a lively manner when it came to their aid. Evans saw particular advantage to the instrument in outdoor meetings in the summer, helping the farthest reaches of an outdoor crowd hear the music.[14]

The article closed with a strong affirmation of the office of evangelist as a biblical expedient for reaching "the untouched people who are in our congregations, and the vast multitudes outside who are not reached by our various ministries." Evans was convinced that the work must be en-larged and those adapted for evangelistic ministry must be sought out. The work is "as noble as the pastorate," Evans surmised, particularly when measuring "by the necessity that exists for it and the difficulties connected with it." This important note he added, a note for which Spurgeon specifically thanked Evans, for they "exactly state our feelings upon the matter." The italicized words emphasized: "*But it must be taken up as the business of the churches. It must not be left to unorganized Christianity*" He urged leading men in Baptist churches to become "its patrons and its helpers" if England is to be won for Christ.[15]

Early in 1878, as Spurgeon reported on the work of Clarke and Smith, he reiterated the need for evangelists *in connection with the churches* as the great need of the hour. It had been left to "unattached amateurs with serious results to church work." The slumbering churches and the frowns of officialism had hindered any innovation on this point. Spurgeon wanted "evangelists in full harmony with the churches" to "prevent the disorder which arises out of the present disorganized mode of doing or pretending to do the work."[16]

W. Y. Fullerton had received his initial encouragement as a full-time evangelist from Spurgeon. Recognizing his zeal and effectiveness, Spurgeon had asked Fullerton to preach the special February meetings at the Tabernacle in 1879, even when Spurgeon was away at Mentone. After Spurgeon returned from his health Sabbatical, he asked Fullerton to join Manton Smith at Bacup when the scheduled evangelist, A. J. Clarke, became ill. Spurgeon sent the note to Fullerton by the hand of Thomas. "Now I was to be launched on my life's work," Fullerton remarked in evaluating the significance of that invitation.[17]

---

13. S&T, December 1877, 560.
14. Ibid.
15. Ibid.
16. S&T, February 1878, 91.
17. W. Y. Fullerton, *Thomas Spurgeon: A Biography* (New York: Hodder and Stoughton, 1919), 86.

The life of the evangelist had been too intense for Clarke. In July 1879 Spurgeon reported, "During the past month a complete change has been made with respect to our esteemed evangelist, Mr. A. J. Clarke. We felt that the failure of his health indicated that for the present the Lord did not intend him longer to endure the excitement of evangelistic work." Under Spurgeon's guidance, Clarke accepted a pastorate in Australia at West Melbourne where Spurgeon prayed "this dear servant of the Lord may be the means of winning even more souls for Christ than he has won in the United Kingdom." He assured the Aussies that "a better man never visited your shores."[18]

Meanwhile Fullerton and Smith melded their evangelistic campaigns as an enduring duo moving from place to place seeming to thrive on the "excitement" that drove Clarke away. Spurgeon received the following correspondence from one of their earliest meetings together, in the West Ridings of Yorkshire. T. E. Cozens Cooke wrote from York.

Dear Mr. Spurgeon,
We have lately been favoured with the presence of your two excellent evangelists, "Smith and Fullerton." The moral atmosphere of an old cathedral city is anything but favourable to these special efforts, and we were not surprised that some of our "cultured" friends manifested their opposition by a warm newspaper correspondence. This, however, did us no harm, but almost daily advertised our services free of charge. Mr. Smith's attractive singing, and his colleague's heart-stirring addresses, were much appreciated, and the interest evidently increased. The meetings were largely attended every night, and considerably over one thousand copies of the hymn book were sold at the doors. Several persons professed to receive food, and we are trying to follow up the work. We parted

with our dear brethren with much regret, some of our friends gathering at the railway station, and singing their "Farewell" as the train glided away. Their affectionate, genial society, and above all, their unwearying devotion to the Master's work quite won our hearts, and we shall hope ere long to welcome them again. Our local expenses were heavy, but we are so glad to be able to send you (through Mr. Hillman) £10 for your "Society of Evangelists," with the earnest prayer that the richest blessing may continue to rest upon this and every other agency associated with your noble work at the Tabernacle.[19]

The evangelists moved on to Leeds for a protracted time of work from June 7 to June 25. There was a great stir, much good was sure to follow, and Spurgeon received a "glowing account" that he would share at a future date. Spurgeon also narrated a description of the work done by Mr. Burnham at Wooten, where great crowds came each evening and special liberty was experienced by the evangelist in giving attention to the children of ministers.[20]

The Leeds event of Fullerton and Smith received coverage in the August 1879 edition of *The Sword and the Trowel*. After the first week of services, the meeting moved to the center of town, giving a magnitude to the work that made "their visit an event long to be remembered by multitudes of our townsfolk." By Tuesday the South Parade Chapel was crowded and on Wednesday extra seats were provided. On Thursday the meeting adjourned to "the Circus," a large unoccupied building near the chapel and for a whole week "dense crowds, estimated at from three to five thousand, came together every night to listen to the preaching of the gospel." The evangelists stayed an extra three days, preaching

18. S&T, July 1879, 345.

19. Ibid.

20. Ibid.

to an overflow crowd each evening, and began holding noon-day prayer meetings at the Young Men's Christian Association and afternoon Bible-reading sessions led by Fullerton. Scores of enquirers were conversed with, "many of whom are now seeking admission to Christian churches; backsliders were reclaimed and the gospel was preached not only to regular church and chapel goers, but to a large number from the class of those who habitually neglect houses of prayer, and who, by the ordinary agencies on which we rely, are almost untouched." The writer regretted that the evangelists had to leave when the enthusiasm for the meeting was still at its height, and looked forward to seeing them return. He commended the evangelists themselves remarking of their apt gifts for the work to which they were devoted. He felt compelled to mention one other matter.

It seems almost incredible that the great hindrance in the way of carrying on and extending the work of the Society in connection with which Messrs. Smith and Fullerton labour is *want of funds*. I understand that Mr. Spurgeon has considerable difficulty in supporting the men already engaged while he is anxious to send forth other brethren whose gifts qualify them to render efficient service in this vast harvest field. Will not those who have it in their power to do so help a society which is in every way so worthy of confidence and sympathy, and give twice by giving quickly?[21]

Spurgeon never seemed hesitant to report the details of the work of Fullerton and Smith. In Halifax, in 1881, the church experienced a great blessing, took up a love offering that paid for the expenses of the entire week and £100 remaining to send to Mr. Spurgeon's Evangelistic Fund. The last evening of the meeting proved to be the crowning

of the work as many enquirers sought the aid of Christian workers at the close. The total number of inquirers that made a public attempt to speak with someone was 200, but "even this only represents a small portion of the good accomplished." The churches in the town would be numerically strengthened and many Christian revived. Spurgeon closed the report for May 1881 with enthusiasm for the prospects of another meeting with the same evangelists.

The evangelists have during the past month commenced at Sheffield a series of services which promise to be the most successful they have ever held. The town has been divided into five districts, in each of which a fortnight is to be spent, and the closing meetings are to be held in some large central spot. The ministers have heartily welcomed our brethren, who find that their visit has been preceded by a week of prayer all over the town, which has already witnessed the earnest of a great blessing.[22]

The July Issue carried a report of the Sheffield meeting by a "Visitor." The report noted the cooperative spirit in the churches, but also observed, "For ministers and representatives of existing churches to look askance at special services by well-chosen evangelists, is a policy difficult to explain, for they lose a splendid opportunity of quickening their own spiritual life, and of augmenting their usefulness." The writer, a bit nonplussed by the hesitance of some brethren, sought to present the evangelists as sterling church men that have "always desired and sought the earnest co-operation of their ministerial brethren, in order to consolidate their work, and to secure the pastoral oversight of those who are brought to a knowledge of the truth at their services." They are

21. S&T, August 1879, 389.

22. S&T, May 1881, 243.

auxiliaries of the churches, not rivals of honored brethren. The meetings seemed lively indeed, as the song service at the children meetings was "led and sustained by Mr. Smith's silver cornet." An evening song service included solos by Smith and Mr. Chamberlain from London and anthems and choruses by an "efficient choir." On top of that, Fullerton himself gave song services each Saturday night during the campaign in order to secure the attendance of the working men and keep them from the public houses and the street. The "Song Service" was a sermon broken up by songs that carried the theme of the message and illustrated its points. In addition, the addresses of Fullerton "were in the racy style which he has made his own, and which gives point to his appeals, and makes the truths he advances both strike and stick." Overall, so the writer observed, "as an entertainment it is sufficiently attractive to be popular, and we commend the expedient to those who are anxious to reach people."[23] At Abbey Road Chapel in November, the reporter narrated the gripping nature of the impact of the evangelistic duo by recording, "Once more the singer and the preacher were up to their work; the latter with power and skill wielding the two-edged sword of the truth right and left, unfalteringly and without pause, until women wept and strong men seemed spell-bound, and beyond a doubt the slain of the Lord were many."[24]

The zeal of Fullerton and Smith did not wane and Spurgeon's support of them and attraction to them did not wear thin. Smith had an exuberant personality and an ability to tell stories. He used this gift often with the children in a crusade and displayed it in a book of anecdotes about his own life. *Stray Leaves from my Life Story* contained a fascinating narrative about Cricksea Ferry that

Spurgeon considered "about as odd a narrative as will ever be likely to come under the observation of a student within fifty miles of London." Smith had the grace of being merry, even jolly, while being "earnest up to the eyes" and a picture of tenderness itself. In these stories, though, "from quite unexpected corners of his nature humour wells up, and floods the rest of his being." While the individual anecdotes were filled with fun, "the spirit and object are deeply serious."[25]

Spurgeon printed a letter from Fullerton as sufficiently indicative of the Spring work of the evangelists. He and Manton Smith distributed Spurgeon's sermons as a part of their evangelistic work and Fullerton narrated an unusual conversion connected with Spurgeon's written sermons. Fullerton had arranged with Passmore and Alabaster for 100,000 bound sermons to be laid aside for their use in evangelistic campaigns. In asking for Spurgeon's readers to contribute toward the ministry, he added, "No surer way could be conceived of sending a clear statement of the gospel into thousands of homes where it would otherwise be unknown."[26]

Spurgeon devoted hundreds of columns in *The Sword and the Trowel* to descriptions of the work of Fullerton and Smith, including letters from them and an abundance of letters from the churches in which they ministered. The depth of his trust in Fullerton may be seen from his reliance on him during the days of the Downgrade Controversy when he had him preach for him on several occasions when he was away. From Mentone he wrote, "I felt sure that the Lord would bless you at the Tabernacle, & now I feel grateful that he has done so." Though the weather was horrible all felt that "warmth and power were abundant in your testimony." Spurgeon told Ful-

---

23. S&T, August 1881, 409.

24. S&T, December 1881, 628.

25. S&T, February 1885, 82.

26. S&T, July 1882, 381.

lerton that to him it was "joy unspeakable to be associated with a brother so sound in the faith & earnest for souls. The blend is one only a divine hand can make." Spurgeon expressed hopes that the evangelists would have the best year ever but also warned Fullerton not to take too many meetings since his was "killing work." He advised him to "die at great length." Spurgeon also wanted Fullerton to provide some narratives for "S & Trowel" and gave an impetus beyond his personal invitation by saying, "This must be kept up or funds will go down."[27]

The positive reports that followed the evangelistic teams surely encouraged Spurgeon, for he believed that the gift of evangelist still operated in the church as one of the constituted means for the ingathering of the elect. One observer stated that Fullerton and Smith had the faculty for the "precipitation of decision." Spurgeon's interpretation was that "the Lord blessed them in bringing men to decision for Christ."[28] In early 1883 a pastor reported that Fullerton "preaches the gospel with a clearness and power I have never heard surpassed; and Mr. Smith has the happy gift of throwing over the audience such a mellowing influence that minds unconsciously open, like the flower to the sun, to receive without prejudice the solemn things they listen to." The services, night after night, were overflowing with "enquiring souls."[29]

Spurgeon knew that he must be careful in these reports, however, and worked hard to ascertain the truth of what was said, for Christians often feel that it is their duty and an evidence of true faith to use superlatives when speaking of the

effects of religious efforts. Though he maintained optimism about the success of gospel preaching in evangelistic settings, he did not like conflated reports or overzealous language. He likened it to sensationalist papers reporting of gooseberries "which are twice as large as possible." To speak of a "great work" where serious people have no knowledge of any "work" at all was "mischievous" and tended to damage the true work. "When Christian people," he observed, "find things overstated they lose confidence, and in the case of men of the world it is worse, for they use the exaggeration as material for jests." Better under the mark than over it, particularly when describing a work in which one is personally involved. "We must not put into print those sanguine ideas of things which our hopeful minds create in our excited brains. The cause of truth can never be aided by a deviation from truth." Exaggeration must be put aside and discouraging facts must not be suppressed. "Brethren who are apt to puff, let us whisper in your ears—leave the monstrous gooseberries to the newspapers, and speak every man truth with his neighbour."[30]

Zealous for Access

Though "puff" was forbidden, creativity in finding ways to get gospel proclamation to those untouched by the ordinary agencies on which the churches relied offended him in no way. "How to Get at Inquirers" by F. White proposed several ways, "in these days of revival and awakening," to get at inquirers and "drive men from one false refuge and another, until they are safely hidden in the cleft of the Rock of Ages."[31] Spurgeon would be offended by, and would oppose forcefully, any dilution of the gospel or of the distinguishing doctrines of grace, but unconventionality in get-

27. Spurgeon to Fullerton, handwritten copy on file in Archives at The Southern Baptist Theological Seminary. This letter is in "Charles Haddon Spurgeon correspondence with F. T. Snell," January 12, 1889. The letter begins, "Dear Friend."

28. Spurgeon, *Soul Winner*, 133.

29. S&T, February 1883, 97.

30. S&T, June 1881. 270f.

31. F. White, "How to Get at Inquirers," S&T, January 1865, 41.

ting to people posed no difficulty in his mind, but was the way of Christ himself.

In pursuit of that necessity, Spurgeon frequently included articles in *The Sword and the Trowel* concerning the work of full-time evangelists. Edward Leach contributed such titles as "Evangelistic work in London" in which he outlined several ideas about how to get a hearing from people on the street for the gospel. "The Earnest Evangelist" by Leach speaks of the spiritual qualifications for doing personal work in soul winning.[32] "William Carter and His Converts" talks about a man who had been able to get crowds of the lowest level of society to gather for gospel preaching. Though he endured much rowdiness, and had drunks and prostitutes, thieves and vagabonds all together, the interest level was high and remarkable conversions had occurred.[33] "Spurgeon Among the Costermongers" showed the consummate skill and passion of Spurgeon in his dealing with this element of English society and his personal desire to encourage those that had given themselves to full time evangelistic work.[34]

Spurgeon greatly encouraged his students to become church planters through evangelism in difficult places with the use of aggressive and creative means. Edward Leach recorded his observations about this. With some aggravating experience of the sorts of objections raised against innovative evangelism, Leach composed one side of an interaction with a staid and stolid opponent of daring attempts at gospel penetration. The characters generically were youth and old age, each with their doubts about the other. "Youth forms the occasion of many a solemn shake of the head: old age is the butt for the bitterest sarcasms

of youth." The aged accuse the young of "Inexperience" and the young look with disdain on the prudence of age as "old-fogyness." Prudence walks in silver slippers, fears the rough way, and indulges itself in "sugar-plums, compliments, card-baskets, ice-creams, tissue-like refinements, and lackadaisical joys of life." The heroism, a trait of youth, "walks trippingly over dangerous ruts, wears heavy buckram, cumbrous armour, and bears severe discipline." Prudence, friendly to sloth, has smothered many virtues at birth while so-called rashness has "nipped many vices in the bud." Other comparisons, to the detriment of the cautious aged, encouraged patience and tolerance for the rashness of youth, for it might repristinate an apostolic model and "plant it in the midst of opposition in a bolder, more chivalric manner, where you with timidity would fear to tread." So away with reticence that produces a nostalgia for "the return of gilt coat-buttons, knee-breeches, swallow-tails, and pigtails, … frill-shirts, and pleated tucks, and silk stockings (peach-coloured or otherwise)." Listen instead to a voice ready to risk all, not only the esteem of the aged but one's own life, that Christ may be heard where his voice has not come.[35]

Where does Spurgeon find examples of this exemplary apostolic boldness but in descriptions of what students from the Pastors' College were doing? A chapel in Wandsworth arose from the efforts of a young man who "had actually broken the rules of respectability and soberness by commencing to preach in the assembly rooms of a tavern, much to the disgust, doubtless, of my sage friend whom I had so weakly jostled with in argument." On another page we find the commodious chapel in Bromley necessitated by "out-door preaching of students," "Out-door preaching!" the

---

32. S&T, June 1867, 269.

33. S&T, January–February 1866, 12, 61.

34. S&T, April 1867, 176.

35. S&T, September 1867, 389-95. Article by Edward Leach entitled "Young Men and Evangelistic Work in London."

exuberant youth exclaimed. "What sayest thou to that, my old type-faced friend? But stop—do not smile, was not Christianity mainly propagated by out-door preaching?" Even as he launched into the defence of outdoor preaching he found another unorthodox example of gospel-success. A good-sized chapel grew from preaching in the "large room of an inn in Ealing," "I must have a little of Mr. Revivalist's disposition in my nature," Leach admitted, "for I involuntarily, yet I hope devoutly, ejaculated, 'Bless the Lord' for the chapel built by a congregation gathered together in an inn! Christ was born in an inn: why should not a church be born there likewise?" Pages that followed revealed many such examples to Leach, and led him to pray for "more young men of the same heroic temperament, for London sadly wants them." He did not disparage the old-fashioned ways of planting churches, but longed for the "old apostolic earnestness of purpose, the spirit of which it seemed to be had been caught by these evangelizing pastors."

Many more chapels, sixty needed immediately in East London, could not accommodate the number of people who have no means of attending public worship. "If prudence does not approve of every method of Christian service, necessity will do so. Respectability shirks what faith and works perform." The use, therefore, of "lodging-house preaching, open-air effort, and teaching in taverns and casinos may appear strange to the world," but God has blessed these "rash enterprises." When the god of the world stakes out a ground from which to extend his kingdom, there Christians must meet him. "All mutterings respecting the injudiciousness of men who evangelise among the masses is beside the mark: if it be not cowardly, it is unchristian." All Christians should rejoice wherever and by whomever "Christ crucified" is preached.

The steadiness of the attempts to penetrate London with established places for gospel preaching was in evidence at the yearly meeting of the "Metropolitan Tabernacle Evangelists' Association" on May 30, 1881. The members of the Association held over 3,650 meetings annually in which the direct object was "evangelizing some part of London."[36] They wanted more money and more men because recently they had had to turn down an opportunity to take charge of a mission hall in Brompton Hospital for lack of funds. On hearing the news several of the men began to pray in earnest for God's provision for this strategic opportunity and punctuated the prayers with short addresses "in such an excellent manner that we could see how well fitted they were for the work to which they had given themselves." The secretary of the Association, Mr. Elvin, required testimony to the usefulness of the evangelists sent out under his direction. One of these recommendations had come to Spurgeon's attention from a church where a week of services under their direction had been the means of the conversion of some twenty people. The letter shows how Spurgeon's sympathetic contemporaries viewed his efforts along this line.

> Would that other large and influential churches, besides that at the Metropolitan Tabernacle, would organize bands of evangelists to mission our great and sin-stricken cities. Are there not churches with many hundreds of members that are doing scarcely anything in this direction for the godless crowds among whom they are located? And are there not thousands of the Lord's people in those churches with gifts and leisure who might be induced to enter upon such a mission? We believe there are members, not only of young converts with their warm, fresh, yearning first-love, but of Christians

---

36. S&T, July 1881, 353.

of matured experience, whose talents now lie buried, who are ready to throw themselves into this work, if only the organizations existed. May God stir up his church to care more for the perishing; and may he lay upon his beloved believing ones the burden of souls so greatly that they shall be led to "travail" for them.[37]

Spurgeon felt deep satisfaction in the evangelistic success of the College graduates and shared with his readers, "who have helped us to train pastors and evangelists," the letters that described these efforts. A letter from John Downing in Australia, a graduate of the College is full of interest. The frequency of the meetings, the description of inquirers, the confidence exhibited in the operations of the Holy Spirit, and the pleasing references to Thomas Spurgeon would all be a sweet cordial to Spurgeon's mind.

Dear Mr. Spurgeon,

I feel impelled to let you know how the Lord has been working in Brisbane of late. In March last I had a run down to Tasmania, and came back to Victoria with Harrison, who was in College at the same time as myself, and who was then on the way to join Isaac for Evangelistic work. I asked Harrison to come on up to Queensland, and after working down south, i.e. in Victoria and N. S. Wales, he and Isaac arrived here in August. The first meetings were under severe disadvantage; the evangelists were unknown. It was the annual exhibition week, and people were mad after the young princes just arrived in the "*Bacchante*," but souls were saved, and the news spread so that at the next place between one hundred and fifty and two hundred went forward for personal conversation, and, as a consequence, the Christian enthusiasm steadily rose. The third church could not hold the throngs, and when anxious souls were asked to come into the vestries, they did at such a rate as to fill them

to overflowing, and this continued for nearly three months. Harrison's last meeting in any church was held in mine, and never before has such a crowd gathered there; every seat was more than full, every available inch of standing-room was occupied, and the overflow contented themselves with listening outside the open windows. When the preaching was over we could not get the people away, they wanted eternal life, and would not go without it. To my knowledge, there are scores upon scores professedly saved. Many have received assurance of faith; churches have been roused; pastors and other workers have been cheered, and the whole tone of religious life heightened. Harrison's Sunday-afternoon meetings in the Theatre Royal, too, were, numerically, a big success, though, through the lack of accommodation for personal dealing, very many slipped through our fingers. Except when your son Thomas was here, I have never seen such packed meetings. I might say that when *he* was here, fifteen months, ago, we took advantage of his presence and preaching to begin theatre-meetings in the only place we then could get, a little pokey, cockroachy hole, holding about four hundred. Through his instrumentality, and in the teeth of much prejudice, the place was filled, and from that has sprung a regular Sunday-evening theatre-service in a new theatre, holding over fifteen hundred, and which, when Harrison preached there last, was so packed that hundreds could not get in. Jesus of Nazareth has been passing by, and eyes once blind now see him, while the communion of souls granted to his people has been blessedly close and choice. The manifestations of the Spirit's power which have come under my own notice have been remarkable, this is one—We had finished a meeting, and the enquirers had gone into the vestries. I felt happy, and commenced to sing while the people were going away. Many stopped, and joined in the verse, "Glory, honour, etc." One fine-looking young fellow stood laughing while we were singing, but before we had finished, his stiff neck bent, and he broke down, fairly making

---

37. Ibid., 354.

a dash for the vestry in which were the anxious souls. At another meeting, several young Christians were in the church, praying for the anxious, who had filled the vestry. An ungodly young man did not want to leave his companion, and remained. While someone was praying, suddenly there burst over the solemnity of the meeting great sobs as if one were dying of grief. The Holy Spirit had come in convicting energy upon him; he has since shown by his consistent life that he is a new creature. He has applied for baptism; and there have been many cases somewhat similar. The work is still going on, and fresh cases of conversion are coming to light. … Wherever your son Thomas goes he carries a blessing, and is received very heartily, first for his father's sake, and then next time none the less so for his own. I wish he might be the flying angel of the everlasting gospel for the Colonies. Whichever way his Master will use him will be wisest and best.[38]

In October *The Sword and the Trowel* carried an appeal to its readers to contribute to the construction of the meeting house in Auckland for son Thomas' church. It also printed an extended letter of praise written by the church's secretary about the preaching and evangelistic work of Thomas. "The young man wears well," the secretary wrote; "The people like him for he is personal, spares not to tell of God's anger as well as his love; he does not mince matters, yet is so earnest in his appeals to heart and mind." He preached on strong texts and important themes with power, clarity, and passion, and the people crowded in to hear for they were not tired of hearing the gospel of Christ.[39] A son, so useful for gospel truth in such a distant part of the world, winning not only souls to Christ but respect and love from the people of God, certainly had a warming impact on Spurgeon's weary mind while he missed him the more.

Overcoming Complaint by Commendation

Other contemporaries complained, however, about Spurgeon's evangelists. When a Baptist newspaper was the source, Spurgeon could hardly believe it. That men of the world would have good reason to object to an effort to draw the masses to Christ Spurgeon could expect, but that brethren of the same denomination would carp seemed a betrayal of the most chilling kind. He found encouragement in this alone, that the gravamen of the criticism was that "their preaching has a decidedly Calvinistic tone." Evidently neither character nor zeal gave rise to the criticism but doctrine. Spurgeon hoped they would remain liable always to the same condemnation. He had not complained about brethren zealous for Arminianism, for he considered it a "frequent infirmity of noble minds."[40] The central truths held in common by Calvinists and Arminians composed the stuff of evangelism and Spurgeon found no reason to belittle those among the Arminians zealous for souls who preached about sin, condemnation, substitution, and faith alone.

Spurgeon sought to help his men by encouragement, personal appearances on their behalf, financial support, and personal recommendation, if he conscientiously could do so. The Tabernacle provided £100 per year for the Association and other expenses were met by the offerings taken in the churches where the men appeared and by donations from readers of *The Sword and the Trowel*. This organization produced "more preaching of the gospel than by any other means," Spurgeon believed. "*And it is the gospel;*" for him, "There's the joy of it."[41]

A commendation of the work from his own son Charles surely pleased Spurgeon. Fullerton and Smith had come to Greenwich on Janu-

---

38. S&T, March 1882, 151.

39. S&T, October 1882, 547.

40. S&T, January 1882, 43.

41. S&T, July 1881, 354.

ary 15 following a week of prayer, 500 attending the Thursday meeting, and distribution of 15,000 handbills. On Sunday afternoon, "Brother Smith, with his usual tact, held over 1,500 little ones, collected from four Sunday-schools, spellbound by song and speech." Not only children, but some "old boys and girls" were helped by these meetings and conversions already had occurred. Attendance increased each evening with the work "growing in interest and blessing." As he closed, "Charlie" thanked God for the arrival of the two brethren "especially as they are labouring at South Street as their head quarters." His report glowed with news of the children's meetings, meetings for women only and men only, "Song Services" on Saturdays, massive crowd on Sunday, and much converting work of the Spirit. He sent a "*bona fide* thankoffering of £55."[42]

One of his men, F. T. Snell, Spurgeon recommended in July 1887 to the "love and confidence of any Christian friends among whom he may sojourn." He recommended him as one who "by speaking and writing ... endeavors to evangelize." Snell supported Spurgeon and encouraged him during the Downgrade Controversy, for which Spurgeon expressed sincere appreciation. He requested that Snell pray for him "for I have need of guidance and help." In a series of letters, Spurgeon spoke of some of the financial difficulties that Snell encountered. Spurgeon had lent money, could not lend any more, but proposed to make a gift of the money that he already had lent Snell. Spurgeon made arrangements for Snell to establish a work on the Isle of Guernsey, with the aid of some contributors to his support. Spurgeon himself went to Guernsey, Snell arranged for the hotel and other accommodations, Spurgeon promised to preach

once a day, and made use of offerings given on the occasion for Snell's benefit. Snell's loan was thus repaid and Spurgeon remitted to Snell any excess "for work done." Snell soon fell into disfavor with the church, apparently, for Spurgeon wrote later that same year, "I do not see that you can do anything. You need bear what is in store for you with patience of soul. You can surely claim some sort of personal compensation for loss of prospective livelihood but perhaps they will meet that by offering you the place at [as?] a [illegible]. Your strength is to sit still." One year later, October 1890, Spurgeon wrote a recommendation for Snell to Baptists in America, where he eventually settled, apparently in Eau Claire, Wisconsin. "This is to certify that Mr. Snell has been an evangelist under my direction & has done good service as a Baptist Evangelist. He has founded and built up a church in the island of Guernsey, & has proved himself 'a workman that needeth not to be ashamed.' If a hard-working zealous minister is needed, who can initiate work, & carry it forward well, Mr. Snell is the man. I can recommend him without reserve. He is the man to succeed among a living enterprising people like our American brethren. The Lord be with him. C. H. Spurgeon."[43]

When Spurgeon was asked the difference between the Evangelists' Association and the Metropolitan Tabernacle Country Mission, he stated frankly, "We are not very clear about this; except that this Society sends the same men to fixed stations to raise churches, and the other is more of an evangelistic order, assisting churches already in existence. They are equally excellent, and might wisely be united."

42. S&T, March 1882, 152.

43. Handwritten letter in Archives at James P. Boyce Memorial Library at The Southern Baptist Theological Seminary, "Charles Haddon Spurgeon correspondence with F. T. Snell," October 2, 1890. All of the letters mentioned in this paragraph are in the same folder.

Spurgeon included the work of the colporteurs as straightforward evangelistic work. They could penetrate places that no other evangelical witness could go. In 1879 he reported that an army of colporteurs "covers our country." They went into dark hamlets and to the sick beds of neglected people bringing truth, light, and hope. Priestcraft was thus invaded in places formerly seen as impenetrable and where a non-conformist ministry could hardly be maintained. Through these book-spreaders, however, "a testimony has been kept alive which has sufficed to fetch out the chosen of the Lord from amid the gloom of superstition, and lead the Lord's elect away from priests and sacraments to Christ and the one great sacrifice for sin."[44] His commitment to evangelism soared on the wings of divine sovereignty and utter dependence on covenantal grace.

Moody and Sankey

During the 1873 Moody Crusade in Scotland, Spurgeon expressed his approval of the impact that Moody and Sankey had on congregations, writing, "It is delightful to hear of the Lord's work in Newcastle and in Edinburgh. May the Lord prosper our brethren Moody and Sankey more and more."[45]

In April 1874, Spurgeon gave eight full pages of *The Sword and the Trowel* to an eyewitness report of "Awakening in the North," the Moody–Sankey crusade in Scotland. The writer described the desire and expectation that permeated the Christian community prior to the arrival of the American evangelists. He repudiated the "irreverent fanaticism" of spasmodic and spurious concoctions of religious fervor, but pointed to the merging of a growing common desire for religious awakening with the spiritual gifts of the evangelists. The revival did not arise from the mere mesmerizing influence of the revival atmosphere, but the evidence pointed to a true working of the Spirit. The author formerly had little faith in revival work, but "with nets breaking and ships sinking from the freight of inquiring souls," he confessed to be in the presence of the Lord himself. This observer gave vivid illustrations of the unity of ministers of all denominations, their uncharacteristic humility before each other, the stirring of people from every level of society, the earnest and almost palpable sense of the presence of Christ in the meetings and continuing in the lives of the penitents, the salvation of entire families, the remolding of social circles. He witnessed a "divine blessing and leavening with grace of all classes and spheres of life and labour."[46]

But set aside the obvious operations of the divine hand, and look to the men through whom the blessing came. He judged Moody to be a good preacher with a masterly knowledge of human nature who possessed the precision and practical wisdom of a business man. He exhibited a father's affection, a scholarly grasp of Scripture truth, and had a burning zeal without being one-sided. The writer gave examples of Moody's massive appeal and attributed it to the highly developed polarities of his personality, his true tenderness and compassion on the one hand and his stern and uncompromising application of truth on the other. The attractiveness of the man was in some ways mysterious, the writer seemingly felt, and gave rise to an intricately conceived explanation of his appeal.

Taking a chief place in the Christian mission to the army during the American war, it was there that Mr. Moody acquired those rare gifts of sympathy, sagacity, and simplicity which characterise his

44. S&T, January 1879, 5.

45. S&T, February 1874, 93.

46. S&T, April 1874, 155.

preaching, and without which its style would be barely tolerable to correct ears. From want of grammar and for colloquial abruptness, as well as from its Americanisms, it is not in itself prepossessing; but it exercises the most perfect control over an audience, however great, and by means of an infinity of striking illustrations, it rises at times to heights of natural impassioned eloquence. Mr. Moody's *forte* confessedly consists in a certain kingly authority, by which every man about him is made to do his duty, and is set to work; a sovereignty which every one under its sway admits could only have been acquired by sitting long at the feet of divine wisdom.[47]

After pointing to the impact of the revival on the intellectual and educational centers of Scotland the writer observed, "It was a witness to the power of vital truth when so plain a man could command so learned an audience."[48] The article closed by narrating some details of conversions of a variety of persons from a school of blind children to a company of skeptics.

In April 1875, Spurgeon followed up by printing the opinion of a friend who was "one of the last men to be carried away by popular enthusiasm." Spurgeon had posed the oft-implied question about whether or not the "work of Messrs. Moody and Sankey would stand the test of time." This friend answered in a very positive way without endorsing every method or every convert. The churches were better and quicker and bolder to plan and execute programs of usefulness. The converts were as sound as those that would come in other times. "The men are worthy of all confidence and love," the trusted writer testified, "and their work leaves a real blessing behind, especially to those who go in for hearty co-operation with them."[49]

Spurgeon so thoroughly approved of the efforts of Moody and Sankey, "those two consecrated evangelists," with "revivals breaking out right and left," that he convinced Passmore and Alabaster to arrange for the rights of printing in Britain a book called *Handbook of Revivals* by Henry Clay Fish, published in Boston in 1874. "The book," Spurgeon related, "gives a great deal of information, meets many objections, and suggests many useful methods." Spurgeon personally supported an evangelist and commended the practice to wealthy Christians that they might "feel great joy in serving the Lord and his church by supporting a picked man." Due to the great success of Moody and Sankey he wanted "to bring both the book and the matter of evangelists under the notice of our readers."[50]

Later in 1875, Spurgeon preached at Bow Hall in London for Moody to an immense crowd and would have done so oftener had the effort not been so exhausting. He expressed his strong approval of the blessed work "which our American brethren have been privileged to carry on." He wished they would stay in one place, rather than trying to be two or three places at once, for he believed that the schedule would weary them and consequently they would lose power, and the schedule also would confuse the public.[51] He did not want to seem disapproving of them however, in any sense, and so again appeared with Moody in Camberwell Hall and testified publicly that "it has given us much pleasure to assist our brethren Messrs. Moody and Sankey at Camberwell Hall, and we would have done far more, only our own enterprises demand our constant attention." Spurgeon said that his heart was very warm toward them for their work's sake. He lamented, and was genuinely embarrassed by, the bigotry

---

47. Ibid., 156.
48. Ibid. 157.
49. S&T, April 1875, 190.

50. S&T, March 1875, 115.
51. S&T, June 1875, 283.

shown by the National Establishment in casting the indignity toward the true-hearted Americans of the epithets of schismatics and ranters. "Was there any need," he asked, "to grow [*sic*: throw] wrath at two Americans whose teachings are perfectly colourless as to any point in which mere Churchism is involved?" He was certain that true Christians in the establishment felt ashamed at this "wretched bigotry" of the worldlings of the Episcopal body.[52]

In June, Spurgeon, on the approach of the time when Moody and Sankey would come to London, encouraged his people to do all they could "to make this movement a success." They should pray, attend, take their friends, neighbors, and children, and do all they could to win souls "as the Holy Spirit shall enable you." Spurgeon recognized that some might have conscientious objections to aspects of the movement, and he would not ask a person to violate conscience, but he posed the question, "Do you not think that at the bottom of almost all objections raised against this work there is unbelief?" Excitement is present!—why not? The brothers have no remarkable talent! "I am sure," Spurgeon responded, "the Brothers do not pretend to have any talent whatever, for more unassuming men I never saw in my life, and that is one reason why God blesses them so much!" To the good people that maintained reservation and aloofness, Spurgeon pointed to the testimony of "well-instructed brethren" in Glasgow, Edinburgh, and Newcastle "that souls were saved in large numbers, that the Churches were edified and the tone of religious feeling improved." If we hold back, it will be because "we do not believe in God's working just now upon a large scale by simple instrumentality."[53] Spurgeon reinforced his views with stronger exhortations:

For my part, I would like to put it to myself thus—Could I justify myself in standing back when I come to my dying bed? Here are two men who have, for months, consecrated themselves to the preaching of the Gospel with no object in the world but the winning of souls for Christ. Baser calumny than to assert that they have a selfish motive never fell from the lip of Satan himself! They have no design nor object to gain but the sole Glory of God! They seek conversions, conversions to Christ, only! And, Brethren, if there were a thousand faults in them, who am I, or who are *you* to judge them and to say we will not help them in such a work and with such motives?[54]

Spurgeon's evangelical catholicity came to the front in pointing to his agreement with the evangelist in a desire for God's glory, the salvation of souls, a focus on the atoning blood, regeneration by the power of the Spirit, and the instrumentality of faith. "If we are agreed in this," he continued to ply his point, "for my part I cannot conceive any excuse for any man's holding back unless he has so much work of his own to do that he has no time to spare, in which case let him at least bid them God speed!" Failure to help now, could well result in a divinely imposed penalty for unbelief, a look at the Holy Land from afar with no taste of its fruit. Spurgeon did not want his people to think him superstitious, but experience and Scripture convinced him: "If you will not help and will hinder, you will be put aside and, perhaps, your own usefulness will be cut short" and you might live the rest of your life as a "doubting, miserable, carping, critical, faultfinding Christian."[55]

As the meetings progressed, some ministers raised protest against the possible damage that a simple belief in the message Moody preached

---

52. S&T, July 1875, 344.

53. MTP, 1875, 334-35.

54. Ibid.

55. Ibid.

would do to England. How would this gospel of faith and conversion affect the influence of Christianity for the higher virtues that it was the duty of the Christian minister to inculcate? Spurgeon was ready with an exposition of "Justification by Faith" and the power for holiness intrinsic to that doctrine. He did not forget to point out the incongruity of a Protestant objecting to the content of Moody's message. The criticisms implied that "it cannot really do any good to tell men that simply by believing in Jesus Christ they will be saved," and it may very easily do them serious injury "to imagine that they have undergone a process called *conversion* and are now safe for life."[56] In other words, so Spurgeon summarized the objections, "the doctrine of immediate salvation through faith in Christ Jesus is a very dangerous one" that will lead to the deterioration of public morality.

Spurgeon approached the defense from two fronts: first, the messengers that were under such an irrational attack and, second, the holy and virtuous tendency of the biblical doctrine of justification by faith. For the messengers, Spurgeon announced, "We are not so dastardly as to allow our friends to stand alone in the front of the battle, to be looked upon as peculiar persons holding strange notions from which the rest of us dissent."[57] Like Moody, Spurgeon preached the atoning blood, and had done so all his ministry and considered this as a teaching that had "the general consent of Protestant Christendom." This was an attack not only on Moody but on the Protestant faith and the Bible itself. "Deny inspiration," Spurgeon proposed, "and you have ground to stand on; but while you believe the Bible you must believe in justification by faith."[58] The objec-

tion to Moody and Sankey, in Spurgeon's mind, on these grounds amounted to a contest "between the Popish doctrine of *merit* and the Protestant doctrine of Grace!"[59]

Spurgeon did not, however, throw all caution to the winds on account of his affection for Moody. One of Spurgeon's hesitations about the Moody revival efforts was the evidence of genuine conversion through increase of church membership. In the beginning of 1876, Spurgeon was pensive about what seemed to be "a mere surface motion, and not a deep ground-swell of grace." Crowds were large, professed converts were many, but churches only slightly increased, and the tone of religious feeling had fallen rather than risen (seemingly confirming the demur of some). "The year which has just gone is disappointing: a year of revival which did not revive the churches, and of mass meetings which have left the masses very much as they were." If a hundredth of what was proclaimed "with a flourish of trumpets" had actually been accomplished, he would have begun the year in a far different frame of mind. Almost peevish, he complained about the great fanfare that had accompanied the revival effort [had he forgotten that he provided some of this fanfare and even some threatening to those that hesitated?] and he warned that "nations are not to be enlightened with a flash, nor cities sensationalized into religion in a month."[60]

Instead, Spurgeon reminded "those enthusiastic brethren who have had their gas pipes arranged for a general illumination to celebrate the instantaneous victory of the gospel," that they should regroup, rethink, defer the jubilation and "strip to their shirt-sleeves, and take their places among those who bear the burden and heat of the day." Their confidence, their condescending con-

---

56. MTP, 1875, 337.

57. Ibid., 338.

58. Ibid., 338, 339.

59. Ibid., 338.

60. S&T, January 1876, 2.

fidence, had made them ignore the men that labored from Sabbath to Sabbath casting often and just as often bringing back empty nets in preference for "a passing evangelist or two" quite sure that they could accomplish in a few days more than persevering laborers might ever hope for. Spurgeon warned that divine chastisement might follow this deprecation of "tearful sowers" by permitting a "large proportion of tares which certain reapers bring into the garner."[61]

Given a few more months to observe, Spurgeon's evaluation improved. In November 1876, Spurgeon mentioned that "during the last few months we have met with more converts from Messrs. Moody and Sankey's meetings than in all the time before." He concluded that many held back until they felt more secure in such a move, an idea Spurgeon commended. He had expressed disappointment with so few decided conversions at an earlier time and was now happy to be able to report otherwise. "We could not believe," Spurgeon indicated in defense of Moody, "that such earnest gospel preaching could be without saving result, but we feared that the converts would remain separate, and not unite with the churches."[62] Probably, this feared outcome prompted Spurgeon to carry the article by Vernon Charlesworth, "On Objections to Joining the Church," in April 1876.

Spurgeon did not turn sour toward Moody. During Spurgeon's trip to Mentone at the close of 1881, Moody and Sankey took the services at the Tabernacle for a Sunday. More than 12,000 people sought to gain entrance to a building whose maximum capacity was 6,000. Spurgeon's seat-holders left their tickets to others for the evening service, but that did nothing to relieve the pressure of people. "We see clear evidence," Spurgeon observed, "that if Messrs. Moody and Sankey again visit London no building will be sufficiently capacious to hold the crowds who will gather to hear them." Without regret or envy, he added, "May the Lord send a great blessing upon their efforts, and may London, on this occasion, have a double portion of the resulting benefit."[63]

Theological Reflection on the Necessity of Caution

Even when Spurgeon gave his most extended defense of Moody and his revival effort, he inserted cautions against the growing phenomenon of quickly transacted decisions apart from the rich matrix of gospel truth, spiritual conviction, repentance, and conscious dependence on divine grace. Spurgeon knew that "there has been a good deal of injudicious and misleading talk, at times, by uninstructed advocates of Free Grace." Some might have thought that they believed in Christ when they had done nothing of the sort. "I am afraid that some imagine," Spurgeon cautioned, "that they have only to believe something or other," or that "they have only to feel a certain singular emotion" and they will go to heaven when they die. Not every faith, however, is saving faith, but "only the faith of God's elect." Not every emotion denotes a changed heart, but only "the work of the Holy Spirit."[64]

One must be wary, therefore, of the possible ease with which deceit might infiltrate the inquiry room. "It is a small matter to go into an inquiry-room," Spurgeon warned, "and say, 'I believe.'" That avowal proves nothing, could easily be false, and will be demonstrated as true only if "you will become, from that time forward, a different man from what you were." A change in heart, soul, conduct, and conversation will provide that un-

---

61. Ibid.

62. S&T, November 1876, 530.

63. S&T, January 1882, 42.

64. S&T, July 1875, 339.

deniable foundation of fact when objectors look for evidence that justification by faith is a morally justifiable doctrine.

The Sword and the Trowel announced in October 1889 an evangelistic mission at the Tabernacle from Monday November 18 to Sunday November 24, conducted by Fullerton and Smith. It made special note of several special services and requested "the earnest help of all our friends in gathering in the non-church and chapel-goers, and in pointing souls to the Saviour."[65] The next few issues of the magazine contained ambivalent signals on the questions of the mass meeting and the employment of the inquiry room. The attendance, singing, kinds of addresses, and sermon texts for each evening were described along with the judgments of observers as to the spiritual impressions. One reported that "Some few held up their hands in token that they desired the prayers of God's people." Another spoke of a "flock of enquirers" and gave anecdotes of special impressions made on young children. A large inquirers' meeting saw many rise in different parts of the building to express a desire to be Christ's and "in response to the question, whether they would be Christ's, coupled with many admonitions to avoid rashness, saying, 'I will, I will.'" A reporter mentioned the special labors of several workers, but Spurgeon did not record his words explaining, "He is unaware of their modesty if he expects us to print what he has written." One earnest worker noted that many under deep impressions quietly slipped away rather than go into an enquiry room, shared many statements of conviction and hopeful conversion she heard from several that had attended the meetings, and, though she had few cards with specific information, was persuaded "that a genuine work of grace was done." Evidence of weeping on the part of many more convinced this sister, that this would "cheer the heart of our pastor and Mr. Fullerton."[66]

Other descriptions seem reluctant to highlight the inquiry room. "We are persuaded that only a small proportion of those who were impressed entered the enquiry rooms. Our Tabernacle enquirers have not the ways of others."[67] Some become deeply impressed after meditating upon what they have heard, rather than coming under the call to immediate decision. "Very few of them," Spurgeon noted, are "the hasty sort." Some who professed Christ had come to clear convictions as much as two years prior to the meeting, but "wished to test their conversion before avowing it." Spurgeon did not encourage this waiting; to some, such delay might seem wrong, but the overall effect is, Spurgeon observed, "Our members stand the trial of years." It is better to err on the side of purposeful delay than heedless profession. He knew that the quest for numbers as a standard of success could drive good people to covet a closed and energized environment to elicit apparent conversions. He therefore made it a point to emphasize, "Enquiry-rooms are not much used by us," but those instructed in the way of the gospel either find gracious friends to lead them to a fuller and purer state of mind or else they "come again to hear the gospel, and the Lord meets with them and removes their difficulties."[68]

Coincidentally perhaps, but most likely with direct purpose, Spurgeon published in the *Sword* a series of articles on successful evangelism that dwelt on a right combination of urgency and patience, duty and dependence. Robert Shindler, the author of the initial *Downgrade* articles, pub-

65. S&T, October 1889, 580.

66. S&T, January 1890, 44.
67. Ibid., 43.
68. Ibid., 45.

lished pointed discussions on Asahel Nettleton, his methods, impact, and the kind of evangelism he opposed. He contrasted Nettleton to Finney whom he characterized, like Charlesworth years earlier, as one that went "a long way in the direction of" Pelagianism.[69] Charlesworth's articles had appeared in 1876, the year after the Moody work in London. Shindler wrote, "The subject of revivals which we have so very briefly referred to, is one that demands consideration; and while we rejoice that in such preachers as Mr. D. L Moody, and others we could name, there is a more decided prominence given to the person and work of Christ than can be found in Dr. Nettleton's sermons, we are distinctly of opinion that certain other evangelists would be more useful, and their work more permanent, if they gave a due prominence to 'repentance towards God,' and more constantly and thoroughly laid the axe to the root of false hopes, and all those subterfuges which the deceitful heart of man is so full of ingenuity to invent, and so unwilling to renounce." Present work needs deeper foundations for more sure building.[70] Six other fascicles of *The Sword and the Trowel* carried anecdotes concerning Nettleton and his discussions of theological issues, including election, duty and special grace, universalism, the need for immediate repentance, the certainty of future punishment, the absolute dependence of sinful man on the mercy of God.

Jonathan Edwards, whom Spurgeon admired immensely, provided another example of doctrine and earnestness in the promotion of revival. Edwards was "the soundest of divines," Spurgeon averred, even "a standard of theology." At the same time no one ever sought to bring a congregation to higher intensity of feeling than did Edwards, without forsaking all he knew of the gospel. "Brethren," Spurgeon deduced, "we may not trifle with truth under any circumstances."[71]

Near the close of his ministry, Spurgeon saw this thoroughness of understanding, both the way and content of faith omnipresent in the ministries of Whitefield, Edwards, and Nettleton, slipping away in modern evangelistic techniques. The irony of this concern was its practical similarity with the rise of theological liberalism. The danger of these parallel phenomena resided in the converging of two apparently contrasting streams of thought. Infidelity—in its doctrinal criticism of depravity, effectual call, substitutionary atonement, imputation, and the necessity of Spirit-wrought repentance and faith—stood on one hand. On the other stood a reductionistic evangelism in which both techniques and message ignored the biblical content of *the* faith as a necessary precursor to a person's coming to personal faith in Christ. At his address in 1890 at the Annual Conference of the Pastors' College (reorganized in 1888 to exclude graduates that had compromised on issues of the Downgrade Controversy), Spurgeon addressed, in conjunction with other threats to genuine conversion, both these movements, a "wide range of matters" as he put it, in their destructive minimization of doctrine. The meetings at the Tabernacle that had employed the inquirer's room to such a large extent had recently ended, and he was still involved in the depressing struggle of the Downgrade. Spurgeon was obviously thinking through the totality of his lifetime of warfare for the truth, in light of his immediate experiences.

Theological latitudinarians deny the expiatory sacrifice of Christ and consider a substitutionary atonement "immoral." One cannot do this without at the same time murdering the doctrine of

---

69. Ibid., 24.

70. Ibid., 25.

71. S&T, July 1886, 401.

justification by faith. Spurgeon, therefore, insisted that evangelistic preaching must be filled with the theology of substitution. He could preach such an atonement *con amore* and did not feel constricted at all in his commitment to old Puritan thought and the powerful influence of John Calvin. Others that speak of "harsh dogmas" and seek to avoid the "tyranny of a certain iron system," see Spurgeon and his kind as "cribbed, cabined, and confined" by their theology—they suppose that John Calvin rides him "like a night-mare, and we lead dogs' lives under his lash." Such accusers know little of the joy that Spurgeon found in preaching such wonderful truths, and while regarding themselves as free, were true slaves and had never experienced the true joy and freedom of redemption. They also set aside the words of Christ as an infallible teacher. "I do not understand," Spurgeon confessed, "that loyalty to Christ which is accompanied by indifference to his words." One cannot respect Christ's person if he cares not for his words, nor can one have Christ's life without his truth. The source of modern thought, Spurgeon contended, is an unregenerate heart, and they are "downgrade" in doctrine because "they were never put on the up-grade by the renewal of their minds."[72]

The effects of true theology fail not only by the direct denial of its veracity, but may just as easily be harmed by substituting human contrivances for biblical truth in a misguided effort to do good. "Things are allowed to be said and done at revivals which nobody could defend," Spurgeon lamented. "Do you notice," apparently pointing to recent experience, "at the present moment the way the gospel is put?" While avoiding a criticism of anyone in particular, he characterized the method as employing the exhortation, "Give your

heart to Christ." While some good may reside in the exhortation, it should not substitute for the gospel admonition, "Believe on the Lord Jesus Christ, and thou shalt be saved."[73]

If we think that our substitutes do more good or reap larger results than the gospel way, we will create serious difficulties and engender a destructive enmity within the church. "I have known brethren tell sinners a great many falsehoods with the view of saving them."[74] He did not want one creed for the ministers' meeting and another for the enquiry room. Salvation is not promoted by the suppression of truth. "I can be a revivalist," Spurgeon affirmed, "and believe in election, the substitutionary sacrifice, and the work of the Holy Ghost." Spurgeon urged his preacher boys to let their zeal for conversions "be directed by a clear knowledge of the truth of God, for so it will work to the surest purpose."[75]

The same outlook rang through Spurgeon's admonitions in *The Soul Winner*. "I hold that I have no right to state false doctrines, even if I knew it would save a soul. The supposition is, of course, absurd; but it makes you see what I mean." His duty made him press truth, not falsehood, upon men, and he could not be excused, under any pretence, in palming a lie upon the people. To keep back any part of the gospel is neither right nor "the true method for saving men." All doctrine is saving truth. "If you hold Calvinistic doctrine, as I hope you do, do not stutter about it, nor stammer over it, but speak it out." The lack of a full-orbed gospel is behind the evanescence of many so-called revivals.[76]

Our tampering produces false theology, false ideas of Christianity, tolerates disobedience to

---

72. S&T, June 1890, 263.

73. Ibid., 263-64.

74. S&T, August 1886, 400. "Alexander and Bucephalus."

75. Ibid., 401.

76. *The Soul Winner*, 264.

the ordinances, and makes supposed believers impatient with calls to holiness. One may be sure, however, that Christ will not be trifled with, will not have "his words shuffled like a deck of cards," will be "Lord as well as Saviour" or will not be Savior. A supposed assurance of forensic justification "apart from a spiritual work within the soul—a change of heart, and a renewal of mind" does not yield a future of heaven.[77]

A Cautious Conclusion

The dangers he had always warned against in the resurgence of sacramentalism among Anglicans, as well as their ever-present doctrine of infant baptismal regeneration, were now complicated by insidious developments among evangelicals. His observations on modern revival technique hovered around a fear that the gospel might be in danger in the house of its ostensible friends from an incipient sacramentalism.

> Let me say very softly and whisperingly, that there are little things among ourselves which must be carefully looked after, or we shall have a leaven of ritualism and priesthood working in our measures of meal. In our revival services, it might be as well to vary our procedure. Sometimes shut up that inquiry room. I have my fears about that institution if it be used in permanence, and as an inevitable part of the procedure. It may be a very wise thing to invite persons who are under concern of soul to come apart from the rest, and have conversation with godly people; but if you should

ever see that a notion is fashioning itself that there is something to be got in the private room which is not to be had at once in the assembly, or that God is more at that penitent form than elsewhere, aim a blow at that notion at once. We must not come back by a rapid march to the old way of altars and confessionals, and have Romish trumpery restored in a coarser form. If we make men think that conversation with ourselves or with our helpers is essential to their faith in Christ, we are taking the direct line for priestcraft.[78]

Reflecting on the regularity of conversions in his preaching services, combined with the care to avoid such "priestcraft," Spurgeon observed with cautious satisfaction, "Those converted under our ministry are seldom of the 'after-meeting kind,' excited, and over-persuaded." Instead, they would go their way, think the matter over, and if the true work of the Spirit was present, profess their faith when "they have tried themselves, and tested their conversion."[79] Spurgeon's evangelism was a natural outgrowth of his biblical theology. His expressions of the freeness of salvation for all that desired it and would believe, his exhortations of the urgent and universal necessity of repentance toward God and faith in Christ, his enforcement of the full panel of his theological commitments in making these appeals, and his warnings against false doctrine, humanly-contrived faith, and potentially deceitful measures were all natural manifestations of a pastor committed to living by revealed truth.

---

77. S&T, June 1890, 265.

78. Ibid., 262.

79. S&T, October 1883, 562.

10

THEOLOGICAL FOUNDATIONS FOR A
BENEVOLENT MINISTRY

It seems to us that our Lord gave more prominence to cups of cold water, and garments made for the poor, and caring for little ones, than most people do nowadays. We would encourage our friends to attend to those humble, unobtrusive ministries which are seldom chronicled, and yet are essential to the success of the more manifest moral and spiritual work.[1]

Am I My Brother's Keeper?

The irrepressible aggressiveness and the ever-increasing scope of Spurgeon's ministries arose from his theology. Spurgeon uttered a very simple principle that constituted a major part of his feverish multiplication of societies at the Tabernacle. When he reported on the annual meeting of the "Ladies' Maternal Society," and mentioned that about 200 poor women had been helped in their time of need, and expressed a desire for the work to be carried on to a greater extent, "for there is great distress around us," he stated this principle that "Works of charity must keep pace with the preaching of faith, or the church will not be perfect in its development."[2]

This was during the same week that the annual butchers' festival at the Tabernacle had fed over 2,200 journeymen butchers. A truly gigantic undertaking, Spurgeon and the Butchers' Committee believed that it was not undertaken in vain, for "the men listen with great attention, and surely it cannot be that kindly reasoning with them upon temperance, kindness, and the fear of the Lord will all be lost."[3] His report on the 1881 Annual Butchers' Festival counted 200 men present with 300 to 400 master butchers and their wives. The layout of food for such an event was tremendous. The "provisions consumed" according to Spurgeon, were "nearly three-quarters of a ton of meat, seven and a half hundred weight of carrots, eight hundredweights of bread, more than a quarter of a ton of cake, a pailful of mustard, 40 lbs of tea, 200 lbs of sugar, 80 lbs of butter, and 130 quarts of milk." Several of the men of the church were involved in the planning and carrying through with the program including

---

1. S&T, August 1883, 425.

2. S&T, November 1879,544

3. Ibid.

"Mr. Frisby's choir [that] rendered good service by singing at intervals during the evening." Mr. Varley, the founder of this festival, was happy to see so many involved and so many butchers given this hospitality, but he expressed "his intense desire to see more fruit from it." Spurgeon asked the congregation to pray that God would "bless the addresses to the conversion of many of the butchers."[4] After another of these, the sixteenth annual event in 1883, Spurgeon observed, "The men are rough, but there is about them that honest heartiness which is characteristic of good soil." As usual, speeches mentioned vices endemic to the trade—drinking, gambling, swearing—but the burden of the message as always was Jesus as a Savior from sin. "Prayer is requested," Spurgeon again proposed, "that the testimony for Jesus thus given may be effectual for conversion."[5]

Spurgeon stated strongly that God was concerned about the temporal well-being of his creatures. Readers of *The Sword and the Trowel* complained when Spurgeon spoke strongly for the benefit of agricultural laborers. He did not apologize nor seek to diminish the urgency of seeking justice in these matters, but affirmed, "We shall, however, always have a tongue for the oppressed as long as we are able to speak." In many places relations and compensation were as they should be, but in others "the best workman earns barely enough to keep body and soul together." He did not blame men for complaining in such conditions and chastened ministers that would not speak out for the cause of the poor. If they refuse to do that, "What is the good of them?" He considered himself the "flatterer of no class," but the friend of all.[6]

Commending those who led the blind to church, showed strangers to seats, cut up bread and butter and tea meetings without fanfare or notice, or even caring for such, Spurgeon said, "We want more Christian ministries of the practical sort." Certainly he did not diminish the spoken word, but "the work of the hands is by no means a secondary result of divine grace upon the heart."[7] Benevolence was both good in itself, and good as a recommendation of the beauty of the gospel.

Though he would never have quoted "cleanliness is next to godliness" as a biblical verse, he did believe that godliness would make a person value cleanliness. It was simply a matter of loving one's neighbor as oneself and being aware that the corrupting effects of the fall extend to the propagation of disease and death through foul conditions. "No man has a right to be filthy in his person, or his house, or his trade, for even if he himself may flourish amid unhealthy accumulations of dirt, he has no right by his unclean habits to foster a deadly typhus, or afford a nest for cholera." Foul houses, unventilated rooms, and disgusting personal hygiene indicate a complete disregard for one's neighbor. Creators of such nuisances in crowded cities "are guilty of wholesale murder." Not only must a man avoid anything tending to the death or injury of those by whom he is surrounded, but he must do all he can to prevent the harm and promote the well-being of his fellowmen. According to Spurgeon, that was the moral teaching of the "ordinance of making battlements around the housetops—teaching, mark you, which I should like all housewives, working-men, manufacturers, and vestrymen, to take practical note of." The idea that one is "bound to do all in his power to prevent any harm coming to his fel-

---

4. S&T, May 1881, 242.

5. S&T, April 1883, 202.

6. S&T, May 1872, 240f.

---

7. S&T, August 1883, 425.

low men" supported Spurgeon's benevolent ministries.[8]

The Fast Day sermon in 1857 bought out the deep-seated conviction of Spurgeon concerning mutual obligations that employers and workers had toward each other, and that faithlessness in this area was a deep-dyed sin for which judgment would come.

The sinful rich oppressed the poor and trod upon the needy. Their average wage was "far below their value to their masters." They served as stepping stones to wealth. A man builds an industry as he would make a cauldron, a brew for his own wealth. "He is only a poor clerk, he can live on a hundred a year. *Put him in!* There is a poor time-keeper: he has a large family; it does not matter; a man can be had for less: *in with him!*" The tens, the hundreds, and the thousands that do the work are stirred into the cauldron wholesale. "Never mind their cries. The hire of the laborers kept back may go up to heaven: it does not matter, the millions of gold are safe. The law of demand and supply is with us, who is he that would interfere?" Do lords and masters not have the right to do with the people what they like? "Who shall dare to prevent the grinding of the faces of the poor?" But God executes righteousness and judgment for all who are oppressed; even the seamstress, the tailor, and the artisan in the crowded factory "who earn your wealth, who have to groan under your oppression, shall get the ear of God."[9]

He called on the poor to repent along with the rich, for their social sins were no less worthy of judgment. Multitudes deserved but little of their employers, for they worked only when watched and not with singleness of heart as to the Lord. "Were men better workmen, their masters would

be better," Spurgeon chastened. He pointed to hundreds that were excellent at propping up walls, who "ought to be busy at your own work—who, when your time is bought and paid for, steal it for something else."[10] No class in the society was exempt from the duty of acting justly.

When Spurgeon learned of possible fraud in a local hospital, he reported some of the details that he had learned from his source. One doctor saw and dismissed 120 patients in one hour and ten minutes, giving each an average of 35 seconds of time. Sometimes the rich take advantage of charity hospitals, posing as indigents, thereby avoiding fees and robbing both the poor for whom the hospitals were intended and the doctors that should receive a fee for their services. Spurgeon said that the abuses exposed were deploring, entailing misery on the poor and sometimes were the cause of death. People are crammed into room without care taken for the possibility of infectious disease, hurried appointments, called "knocking off," render poor treatment and many mistakes, some of them fatal. Spurgeon asked, "Why should such abuses, which, with our rapidly increasing population, are becoming simply intolerable, be allowed to remain for an hour?" He recommended that "on a subject so vital the Government should take prompt action. Certain hospitals in the Borough of Southwark will be all the better for a commission of investigation of the most searching kind."[11]

Adding more precision and unction to this commitment, however, were the peculiar duties that rested on a Christian minister. While benevolent work could be justified on the basis of the second great commandment alone, and should support all secular efforts at social betterment, the first great commandment combined with

---

8. S&T, August 1869, 349. "Battlements."

9. NPSP, 1857, 384.

10. Ibid., 385.

11. S&T, April 1881, 177.

gospel knowledge justifies the involvement of a minister and a church in these activities.

Spurgeon fleshed out the general principles for this in an article entitled "Offender for a Word." He had written an article expressing his disappointment that names of ministers appeared on the list as running for the London School Board. He believed that their time would be better spent ministering to their congregations, or if they served small congregations, they would have enough to do in seeking to make them larger. The response was that "vials of the hottest wrath" came pouring on his head from various quarters. He was taken to mean that no minister should ever do anything outside his local congregation, should never write a book, never found a school, or never give a lecture to a non-ecclesiastical society. According to those he offended, he wrote "dishonestly, inconsistently, and absurdly not to mention ever so many other adverbs." His own actions, so the criticism went, were most inconsistent with his teaching. "We wonder," Spurgeon pointed out, "it did not occur to our critics that we are not quite so far bereft of reasoning faculties as to commit such a gross self-stultification."[12]

With the desire not to be further misunderstood, Spurgeon explained: "All we meant was that in this case we do not think ministers are called to leave their spiritual work to become the directors of a movement which can just as well be managed by others." He undervalued neither national education nor the abilities of ministers in certain critical situations to lend their talents for such purposes, but normally the preacher of the gospel should not be needlessly entangled with the things of this life, but he should "make his ministry the one work of all his days." At times, the singularity of his focus on ministry

might move him into other things subservient to the accomplishment of that one great purpose. "When a missionary finds himself among uncivilized tribes he is in the pursuit of his one object, even when he makes bricks, delves the soil, or retails garments to the people." By the same token, a pastor in a rural district might have to keep a school to support himself in his ministry, or do other secular work. Any needful piece of "secular good-doing" is a proper province of action for a minister, but the more he can be set free from the necessity of such engagements the better. Had Paul received full support from the churches of Macedonia, he would not have established concurrently a tent-making business so that comfortable quarters might be maintained in military campaigns.[13]

Particularly in London, "with a teeming population perishing for want of the gospel, the winning of souls will not permit of the preacher's doing work which can be done by others." He took this position not because of any "squeamishness about the dignity of the cloth." He utterly rejected the distinction of lay and clerical. The particular gifts and calling of a minister of the gospel mean, however, that he must concentrate on that for which God had gifted him and to which God had called him. Every enterprise to which he gave his hand, heart, and head moved toward that single goal. Spurgeon viewed each benevolent activity in which he was involved in that light.[14]

That "teeming population" that was perishing not only hovered on the precipice of eternal judgments but on a razor's edge of life here and now. When Spurgeon gave caveats against political or commercial involvement, he certainly did not mean for any to keep their distance from compassionate involvement with the poor. Re-

---

12. S&T, December 1870, 570. "Offender for a Word."

13. Ibid.

14. Ibid.

lief of the body often was a necessary expedient for relief of the soul. The latter is superior, but the former is intrinsically an element of love for the whole man in all of his dimensions, eternal and temporal. The two are not unrelated even in physical proximity in Spurgeon's mind. He had often wondered at the "fewness of our deaths" at the Tabernacle; "far below the average of the life-tables." He noted that "godliness, bringing with it temperance, peace, and purity, has a tendency to produce long life."[15]

The clarity with which he maintained this view is seen in comments about a meeting of the "Metropolitan Tabernacle Ladies' Working Benevolent Society" in March 1881. After tea, Spurgeon and three others spoke and the receipts for the past year were reported. Spurgeon commented in his *Sword* report an increase in receipts would be welcome in that "these benevolent societies are among the best of our gospel agencies, following in their operations the line pointed out by our Lord when he fed the hungry people as well as taught them." Contact between these sisters and the poor is good for both parties, perhaps better for the ladies themselves. When the masses of the great cities shun places of worship, how is any hold to be taken on them? "Surely," Spurgeon contended, "it must largely be through the personal visitations of Christian people; and among the very poor this can only be done when we are prepared to relieve their necessities as well as to speak to them the word of life." He encouraged others that could not visit to send funds for the support of the visitors. "Send the shot if you cannot fire the gun."[16] Food transferred to evangelism, and evangelism often transferred to long-term health.

That Spurgeon's concern for the spread of the gospel quickly transferred into action and com-

ment for social and political justice was demonstrated throughout his ministry. The treatment of Jews in Russia provided a clear case in point. "All of our sympathies are aroused for the Jews who are being brutally treated in Russia." That the name of Christian became mixed with murder, plunder, ravishment, and a long catalogue of Russian atrocities would move a real Christian to mourn and break a heart of stone. That nominal followers of the Lord Jesus "should hound to the death the nation from which he sprang according to the flesh is a strange perversity of ignorant zeal, which all true believers should deplore day and night." Spurgeon assured the House of Israel that "all real followers of Jesus of Nazareth desire the good of their nation, and lament their persecutions." Christians must covet the souls of Israel for the Messiah who has come, but surely must realize that this will not be the case "while so much wrong-doing is perpetrated against them."[17]

All of his benevolences—and one must not doubt that in a real sense they were his—arose from the immediate indications of divine providence, survived on the basis of their justification from some element of immediate biblical authority, and subserved the ultimate goal of dispensing the gospel under the confidence that the perishing would be saved. When he reflected on the origin of the benevolences after twenty-five years of ministry, he said "these enterprises have succeeded each other by a natural rule and order of Providence as inevitably as the links of a chain follow each other." When others speak of his genius for organization, Spurgeon said "it would be far nearer the truth to say that he followed with implicit, and almost blind, confidence what he took to be the intimations of the divine will, and hitherto these intimations have proved to be what he thought them to be."

---

15. S&T, April 1881, 194.

16. Ibid., 195f.

17. S&T, February 1882, 97.

In pursuit of these "intimations" of providence, Spurgeon wanted to lay strong foundations in which this philosophy would permeate the ministry for generations to come. Evangelistic work and missionary labors he supported wholeheartedly, but perpetuity demanded deep roots in addition to the production of immediate fruit. Spurgeon told the story of Adoniram Judson, who told a friend that if he had 1,000 dollars to invest in the Lord's work, he would put it into planting colleges and "filling them with studious young men." That was like "planting seed corn for the world." Spurgeon enthusiastically agreed with this point, reminding his readers "to this we have laboured with all our heart, and soul, and strength to make the Pastors' College a seed-garden for the church and for the world." All such institutions Spurgeon congratulated and urged full support of them. Should the voices that denigrate the necessity of schools for training ministers ever be regarded "it will be a dark day for the churches and for the world." Spurgeon wanted the brethren to encourage and help the colleges more and more while assuring that their help was going to those that were "seminaries for the growth of unmistakeable gospel ministers."[18]

For Spurgeon, therefore, the establishment of a college was a "needful step in the spiritual training of the church under our care." Though the college was a spiritual enterprise, it called on Spurgeon to maintain among his people the knowledge of the financial needs. The response normally was so regular and abundant that the pecuniary demands of the college had distracted him no more than Paul was distracted in his instruction to Timothy. Spurgeon viewed that ministry as a "prominent part of our life-calling."[19] It also became an illustration of the College motto,

"Et teneo et teneor."[20] Spurgeon worked with a sense of mission to *hold*, and knew without doubt that he was *held*. By 1879, with the addition of other benevolent commitments, Spurgeon's view of the load incurred had changed. He wrote of "demands made upon head and heart" as pastor and administrator of "so many forms of Christian work." None can know the oppression but he who bears it, "and it is no wonder that sometimes the strain is too great, and mind and spirit sink into painful depression."[21] After twenty-five years of maintaining the College, Spurgeon noted that it was easy to plan, project, inaugurate, with a flourish of trumpets and to maintain an energetic devotion to a cause for a few years in a novel enterprise; but to spend half a life time in the same effort, "this is the work, this is the difficulty." To see it remain true to its noble original purpose and prosper in doing so, this surely shows the sustenance of grace. "We sought to promote the earnest preaching of the gospel of our fathers," he remarked, "and we have not failed."[22] In the meantime, however, "Old friends have fallen asleep, tutors have retired through very age, youths whom we called students are now in the prime of life as ministers, and the founder himself is weakened by repeated sickness till he feels but half his former self."[23]

His own sense of the oppressiveness of his work along with his love for gospel ministers, and his desire to see them well-equipped theologically and practically, was matched by his concern for their physical well-being. "We are very sorry that any minister should be poor," Spurgeon reminded his readers, "but glad that men can be found who are willing to preach the gospel in poverty."

---

18. S&T, April 1881, 175.

19. S&T, December 1870, 570.

20. S&T, June 1891, 337.

21. S&T, 1879, Preface.

22. S&T, 1882, "Annual Report of the Pastors' College," 257.

23. Ibid., 258.

Since such men should be helped, Spurgeon encouraged the giving friends to support the "Tabernacle Home and Foreign Working Society." Ladies made clothes for Christian workers at home and abroad who were poor enough to need such aid. "When we give alms to mendicants we frequently do more harm than good," he noted, "but to help a needy saint is altogether a good work, and to relieve a poor servant of God in the ministry is best of all."[24]

The Heavenly Use of Wicked Mammon

A constant theme of Spurgeon's toward the churches and prosperous Christians was the pecuniary condition of the ministry. "We glory in our brother ministers," he sang in a chorus repeated often, "for being willing to be poor," but the song turned to a growl when he continued, "we are vexed with the many of their hearers who thoughtlessly allow valuable servants of God to fret and pine in actual want." Do the people know that their minister cannot afford to eat meat, or buy clothes, or get common necessities while many church members "live at ease, and lay by considerable amounts"? He believed God's judgment rested on churches that allowed their ministers to struggle in poverty. Both physical and spiritual poverty clouded many congregations because they had not looked to the needs of their pastor. "The tears of ministers' wives are stopping the blessing; the shoeless feet of pastors' children are treading down all hope of spiritual prosperity." This occurs while many who profess to be too straitened in worldly things to give are actually storing up thousands to leave to children to make it easy for them to ruin themselves.[25]

This concern was expressed in another of the Tabernacle's societies, "The Poor Ministers'

Clothing Society." Acknowledgments of gifts received along with requests for help were regularly published in *The Sword and the Trowel*. "We looked in lately," Spurgeon wrote, "at one of the working meetings of this excellent society, and were delighted to see the number of willing helpers present, and the useful parcels about to be dispatched to the homes of some of our poor pastors."[26] The Metropolitan Tabernacle Maternal Society met on the second Tuesday after the first Sunday of each month. In November of 1882 the report indicated that 213 boxes of material had been "lent" to poor mothers during the year and 300 articles of clothing had been given. The report stated, as was so often the case, "After tea the chair was taken by C.H.S." His personal involvement in these societies involved giving, encouragement of others, and a large percentage of the time his own physical presence. "This society ought to do far more," the article urged, "and it is the Pastor's earnest hope that all the ladies of the Tabernacle will henceforth take a share in its work."[27]

The orphanage was forced on him by the clear indications of providence. Both the gift given for the purpose and the demands of poverty within his own congregation motivated Spurgeon to accept the work. In its ongoing operations, however, the trustees, the headmaster, and the regular contributors helped bear the burden and consequently eased him from concern of all the internal care. "The bounty of the Lord has not allowed even a feather-weight of financial anxiety to disturb us." While one could be justified in wondering if Spurgeon was aware of how he *seemed* to see the responsibilities of these works as a constant source of possible anxiety and even depression, he could still state with confidence,

---

24. S&T, July 1875, 344.

25. S&T, April 1881, 179.

26. Ibid., 197.

27. S&T, November 1882, 598.

"We do not feel that either of these institutions hinder our ministry, but are delightful fields for the fulfillment of it."

Spurgeon found George Muller's approach to supporting his Ashley Down Orphanage in Bristol as an independent and virtually irrefutable evidence for the truth of the gospel. Muller's approach, however, suited neither Spurgeon's personality nor his view of how he must employ the people in maintaining support for the benevolent institutions. Spurgeon regularly summarized Muller's yearly report of his Bristol work and added positive evaluations and encouragements to his readers to support it. In 1879 Vernon Charlesworth reviewed the yearly report from Muller. He stated Muller's purpose for founding the orphanage, in Muller's own words, not primarily for the safety and comfort of orphans, not for their education, nor even primarily for their salvation, but "that God might be glorified in its being seen, through this work, that he was as willing as ever to answer the prayers of his children, and how much, even now, can be accomplished through the instrumentality of prayer and faith." Charlesworth defended the integrity, spirituality, and wisdom of Muller, as well as his genuine Christian zeal for the salvation of souls. He failed to see, however, any moral difference between spoken appeals for funds and written statements as to the condition and necessities of the work. "There is a resistless plea," observed Charlesworth, "in the statement that in the homes at Ashley Down there are upwards of two thousand orphan children cast upon the tender Fatherhood of God." Charlesworth surely represented the view of Spurgeon when he said, "The principle of faith is not compromised in our judgment by the use of legitimate means to inform the Lord's stewards of opportunities for disbursing the bounty entrusted to them." George Muller certainly is

right in the uncompromising consistency with his principles, but "it does not follow that his fellow servants are wrong because they crown their faith with the diligent use of means to commend their work to the sympathies of the Lord's people."[28] Sometimes, in fact, Charlesworth believed, Muller's followers seem to "violate the principles of ordinary prudence, if not to border on fanaticism."[29]

These slight caveats from Charlesworth in no way reduced the deep respect that Spurgeon had for Muller and his child-like trust in divine provision. Muller came to worship at the Tabernacle on September 23, 1883, participated in the Lord's Supper with the congregation, and left immediately for India. Though he had been warned not to risk the ardors of the trip at his advanced age, he felt called to the task for the sake of the work that God had given him and "therefore his face is steadfastly set for Madras." Spurgeon could not help but express a deep feeling of love and admiration for an "honored friend [who] looks up for guidance with a childlike confidence seldom seen in these days of doubt."[30]

Precisely the absence of fanaticism while manifesting an unswerving trust in divine provision impressed Wayland Hoyt concerning Spurgeon's support of the enterprises. According to Hoyt, Spurgeon prayed steadily for God's prosperity upon all his enterprises, but "never sought in the least to cover the fact that as thoroughly and strenuously as possible he put his hand to plying second causes." He asked the people as often as he prayed to God with faith that God would "marshal and mass second causes for his help." Hoyt felt Spurgeon's practice worthy of explicit commendation and summarized Spurgeon's view by

28. S&T, November 1879, 513.

29. Ibid., 511.

30. S&T, October 1883, 562.

stating, "A Wild faith, which after all is nothing better than fanaticism, a contemptuous flinging aside of second causes, was at the farthest possible remove from both Mr. Spurgeon's mood and method." He commended Spurgeon's business habits, his "magnificent, shrewd English common sense," as well as his full trust in the "prayer-hearing and prayer answering God."[31]

More closely akin to his own style, and in Spurgeon's view a duplicate of his own personality, was the work of John Bost, founder and conductor of the Asylums of La Force. Eight institutions for invalids, the blind, idiots, and epileptics housing 366 inmates found their source of maintenance in the unresting exuberance of Bost. By his own description a very large man, Bost also, according to Spurgeon's estimation, was a very great man. Bost's father was an evangelist and pastor influenced by Robert Haldane. His opposition to the rationalism and Arianism of the Reformed churches and Bible Society representatives provoked significant opposition and at least one attempt to murder him. John was born in Berne as the second of ten sons of Ami. He was a gifted musician and studied with Franz Liszt in Paris. He underwent a deep conversion in 1840, studied theology and pastoral ministry under Adolphe Monod, was ordained in 1844 and began to serve a church that had dissented from the National Reformed Church. He soon developed a vision for caring for orphans and his congregation built the first building for them by their newly constructed chapel, completing the orphanage in 1848. In the face of opposition from local Catholic groups, an official inspection agency approved the project with enthusiasm. From this initial venture into benevolent work, the opportunities increased crowned with many striking incidents of success. Not only the orphans, but the emotionally and mentally challenged and the physically incapacitated began to find a place of love and nurture n the ministry of John Bost.

Filled with humor, emotion, and mental changes, Spurgeon found him "a man after our own heart, with a lot of human nature in him, a large-hearted, tempest-tossed mortal, who has done business on the great waters, and would long ago have been wrecked had it not been for his simple reliance upon God."[32] Bost was full of zeal and devotion, "brimming over with godly experience," and at the same time "abounding in mirth, racy remark, and mother wit." Bost was worn down with labor and troubled in spirit; he was full of tender sympathies and the cries and contortions of his epileptics, the sad state of his invalids and mentally challenged inmates would "often bring him very low" and cause great wear and tear on his heart. Spurgeon felt his own heart knit to that of Bost in brotherly affection for life. Bost not only believed God for the support of his work, but used ingenious methods to obtain it. While Muller's determination to use nothing but prayer might be the best method intrinsically, Bost's method and passionate involvement of others was admirable in every way and the "best which in his circumstances he could follow, and possibly in some aspects the best for the majority of workers."[33] When Bost died of a stroke in 1881, Spurgeon asked, "What will the epileptics do now?" He recalled this visit and commented, "Yet we are spared, and this riper brother has been taken. The Lord grant that it may be for the benefit of his church and the glory of his name."[34]

---

31. Wayland Hoyt, *Walks and Talks with Charles H. Spurgeon* (Philadelphia: American Baptist Publication Society, 1892), 16, 17.

32. S&T, May 1879, 231. "Interviews With Three of the King's Captains."

33. Ibid., 232.

34. S&T, January 1882, 42.

Spurgeon preached for money. Sanctification of the Christian demanded that he see his earthly wealth as a means of heavenly glory. To some that felt themselves perfectly sanctified and yet had fortunes in their possession of £200,000 to £300,000, he queried, if the could look on a world "living in vice and ignorance, out of which a chosen people are being saved by the gospel, without supporting those agents and agencies" that have evident divine blessing on them.[35] He did not believe that sanctification allowed a man to store up so much treasure on earth while so many works for the Lord Jesus needed help. He could never credit the sincerity of one that speaks of perfect consecration "till I see their gold, and their silver, dedicated to a larger, ay, even to a perfect degree." Men should not boast, but give. When the perfectly consecrated come to die, Spurgeon wanted to see how their last testament demonstrated the character of their will. "A man who is perfect before the Lord lays out his substance for God's cause, depend on that."[36]

Spurgeon found periodic reminders of the substantial and ceaseless needs endemic to each respective benevolence a workable system of support as well as a way to unleash the faith of Christians. A report of the "Work of Our Evangelists" ended with the lament that "the pecuniary support given to it is small." The writer was amazed that those that benefit from their work would not think to ask, "How do these men live?" Spurgeon had thought that the society would be supported by contributions from all the places that reaped benefit from their work, but found it seldom to be the case. Sometimes poverty explained the incongruity of having workers but giving no hire, but often simple negligence or thoughtlessness was to blame. The writer called for a "nobler or-

der who will count it a pleasure to share in this useful effort," and asked if a "soul-saving enterprise would be hampered" by lack of pecuniary support"? No, he did not believe that the "present straitness of funds" would long continue.[37] When funds became short at the end of 1883, Spurgeon printed, "Will friends be so good as to notice that our income for August and September for most of our Institutions has been far below the expenditure?" Holiday season regularly brought about a dip in the income but Spurgeon made sure that readers knew he was confident that "when good people get home from the sea-side they will think of us again."[38]

Spurgeon sought to make it so. He expressed the need quite pointedly in reporting the "commencement of a new era in our evangelistic efforts."[39] The church at Burnley had decided to place boxes at the doors of the chapel at every service marked for the reception of "Thankofferings." All local expenses were paid and the Tabernacle Evangelists Society received £100. If other places where services have been provided would follow suit then the burden of finances would be greatly lightened. "We are persuaded," Spurgeon remarked, "the bait of 'No collections' is needless and demoralizing. To teach men to give of their substance for the spread of the gospel is a part of the gospel, and tends greatly for their own benefit."[40]

Immediately putting into practice the stewardship of such teaching Spurgeon made a direct appeal in his preface to the 1879 volume of *The Sword and the Trowel*. "Old and faithful friends have gone home, and we need new helpers." Also a decrease in donors had only been made up by

---

35. SS, 13:340.

36. Ibid., 341.

37. S&T, September 1878, 431.

38. S&T, October 1883, 564.

39. S&T, November 1879, 545.

40. Ibid.

a few large gifts. "We do not like losing the love and the prayers of the small givers," he urged; "Where are they?" He then offered a straightforward opportunity for his readers to see the work of the Tabernacle as the call of God on their stewardship:

> Is this the work of the Lord? May he not, therefore, design that the reader whose eye now glances over the page should become a helper in our labour of love? It is a great enterprise—read our shilling "History of the Tabernacle" and see for yourself— and it needs many helpers. The Lord will direct them to us. Is he now directing you?[41]

He exhibited this zeal for direct appeal as a truly spiritual, biblically warranted procedure in his comments about the necessity of offerings for support of the Baptist Missionary Society. Williams Olney had been selected as the connecting link between the Society and the Tabernacle in collecting funds for that purpose. "He will doubtless take every opportunity of fulfilling his office of Missionary Remembrancer." Spurgeon knew that many churches had begun a more business-like manner of collecting funds for missions and urged all others to set aside immediately a brother, "and perhaps a sister also," to perform "the special work of ingathering the offerings made to this portion of the Lord's work." Calling to mind the efficiency of the Lord in gathering up the baskets full of food remnants following his miraculous feedings, he said, "Very much is lost for want of baskets in which to gather up the fragments. We are not doing all we ought to be doing for the perishing millions of heathen. Shall we always murder their souls by letting them die through our negligence? The very least we can do is to make arrangements for

the flow of the stream of liberality in the right direction."[42]

A reader of the *Sword* suggested that Spurgeon remember the missionaries as well as the heathen to whom they ministered. Both their own souls and their ministry in proclamation of gospel truth would find needed nourishment in the provision of sermon tracts sent directly to them on the field. The writer included a gift of £5 with the promise of regular contributions if this provision became an ongoing ministry. Spurgeon announced that the letter opened up "a new form of holy service," informed his readers that Mrs. Spurgeon had undertaken the task immediately by supplying 100 missionaries with the tracts, and would "increase the number as funds are forthcoming," and expressed his desire that a "few liberal friends" would supply the means, "so that nothing will be taken from poor ministers at home."[43]

His compassion for "poor ministers" young and old never waned and he did all he could without hesitation at every opportunity to garner support for their well-being. When W. Pool Balfern of Brighton had to give up his charge after thirty-five years of work because of sickness, Spurgeon made enquiry about his financial status. He found that Balfern had not been able to make adequate provision for himself and his wife; an effort, therefore, was underway "to increase the amount, so that in his old age and sickness he may not be reduced to want." Spurgeon himself had promised help and hoped, publicly and in print, "that the thousands who have profited by our worthy friend's preaching and publications will do the same."[44] Upon reviewing a book by Balfern, Spurgeon commented that "his pen is

---

41. S&T, 1879, Preface, 1879, iv.

42. S&T, August 1881, 418.

43. S&T, December 1883, 651.

44. Ibid.

never dipped in gall, but is always lovingly employed in the exaltation of Christ and him crucified." Because Balfern had had his full share of mental affliction and bodily suffering, his works bear the "aroma of the bruised spices."[45]

Spurgeon never indicated the slightest reticence to encourage the support of benevolences and missionary enterprises other than those immediately connected with the Tabernacle. Like George Muller, Hudson Taylor was a source of constant encouragement to Spurgeon. His zeal for the gospel and the lost of China deeply impressed him. Taylor often visited the Tabernacle and Spurgeon encouraged both prayer and giving for his work. On April 29, 1878, Taylor attended the prayer meeting at the Tabernacle and brought a "number of his friends of the China Inland Mission." The purpose was that eight new missionaries might receive the prayers of Spurgeon and his people as they were preparing to sail on Thursday. "It was a touching service," Spurgeon reported, "especially moving all hearts when one by one the missionaries stood up and special prayer was presented for each one." He called attention to the "heroic self-denial" of Taylor in sending back his wife to take charge of some orphans saved from famine in China, while he remained to conduct some necessary business in connection with the Mission. "Mr. Taylor gave some delightful instances of the way in which the Lord has heard his prayer in sending money and men, and also encouraged our hearts by proofs that the Holy Spirit is applying the gospel to Chinese hearts."[46]

As Spurgeon neared the time to open the Girls' Orphanage in 1881, he made an appeal to his readers that he now needed twice as much per month for maintenance of the children. "My trust is in the Lord alone," he affirmed, "for whose sake I bear this burden." God led him to establish the orphanage, his hand pointed to the necessity of an extension of its ministry, and he provided for its construction. He rested, therefore, in the providence of God, but was not expecting manna from heaven nor angels nor ravens to feed the children. Instead "it will be sent in a way which is more beneficial, for the graces of his children will be displayed in the liberality which will supply the needs of the orphans." That provision has been made for 250 boys for years, should not lead God's stewards to say that there is no need at Stockwell. The needs increase and press immediately, and friends must look to see if they can give much more aid than before. Spurgeon admitted that he had written his appeal with a measure of reluctance. "I hope it is not in unbelief," he added, "but as a reasonable service, that I have thus stated the case."[47]

Charles and Susannah were both deeply invested personally in each of the benevolences and he was not asking others to give in ways that he was unwilling. A ministry to the blind under Mr. Hampton "goes on admirably," Spurgeon reported in October 1875, "in all aspects but the pecuniary one." The work could not suffer interruption, however, and since the "funds have run out," Spurgeon, using the editorial *we*, noted "we have had to make him an advance." He also reminded his reading friends that "these poor blind people must have the gospel," and assured them that "it is the Lord's will, and we are confident he will send the means for getting them together to hear the word."[48]

Spurgeon spent not only himself but his in every effort that he felt produced fruit to the glory of God. On an October day in 1875 Spurgeon presided over a meeting to open a mission

---

45. S&T, July 1884, 383.

46. S&T, June 1878, 315.

47. S&T, September 1881, 479.

48. S&T, October 1875, 498.

in Walworth connected with the Tabernacle. Of £300 needed for accommodating "plain, well ventilated [of particular importance to Spurgeon], lofty, and moderately spacious rooms," £150 was collected. In the tea-time afterward a prayer meeting was held, full of pleading and prevailing. Spurgeon described what followed.

> At the close the pastor quietly said that some £150 more was required to open the new schools free of debt, that he would give £50 of it, and *that he did not mean to leave the Tabernacle till the other £100 was paid, for he could not endure to have the Lord's work in debt.* Amid a little joyous excitement friends came up to the table with offerings large and small; and though the monied friends were most of them absent the sum was soon made up, and with the singing of the doxology, the host of believers moved on, "a day's march nearer home," joyfully ready for the next enterprise which the Lord may lay upon them.[49]

For some time the financing of the College was his alone until the source of his financial liberality vanished as it were overnight. He explained that as he found young men ready to embrace "spheres of labour, and by their singular success in soul-winning, I enlarged the number but the whole means of sustaining them came from my own purse." Massive sales of his sermons in America combined with Susannah's economy, in his words, "enabled me to spend from £600 to £800 a year in my favourite work; but on a sudden—owing to my denunciations of the then existing slavery in the States,—my entire resources from that 'brook Cherith' were dried up." He still paid as large amounts as he could from his own income and "resolved to spend all I had, and then to take the cessation of my means as a voice from the Lord to stay the effort," for he was resolved

to incur no debt. "On one occasion," Spurgeon recorded, "I proposed the sale of my horse and carriage, although these were almost absolute necessaries to me on account of my continued journeys in preaching the Word."[50] At this point his advisors suggested that he make this a matter of a church, rather than a personal, ministry and take up periodic collections for the College.

Spurgeon, under the strong influence of church leaders ("over-persuaded by unwise friends" as Spurgeon called it), and risking the charge of "egotism," published a letter from a church where the orphan boys had sung. It was just the piece of appeal and testimony from an outside source that Spurgeon needed. "There is an idea in some quarters that Mr. Spurgeon is never in need of money to carry on his works, or if he is, he has only to mention the fact to his friends and admirers to provoke a golden shower." This impression is fine for those that give regularly, but a poor and erroneous perception for those that use it as an excuse not to give. The orphanage required £10 per day and the benevolences as a whole [in 1878] required more than £300 per week. Increasing the size of the constituency from which funds are drawn is necessary. "That the funds have always been forthcoming proves the confidence of the public in his wise administration. It is a fact which should be widely known that Mr. Spurgeon not only does not derive anything from the institutions he directs, but has for some years contributed to the Lord's work more than his official income as the pastor of the Metropolitan Tabernacle."[51] Spurgeon did not dispute this claim.

At his forty-eighth birthday, many people all over England, Scotland, Wales, and from other

---

49. S&T, December 1875, 585.

50. Robert Shindler, *From the Usher's Desk to the Tabernacle Pulpit* (London: Passmore and Alabaster, 1892), 136f.

51. S&T, September 1878, 417.

parts of the world desired to express their love for Spurgeon with gifts. This birthday recognition had been a yearly outpouring for some time. Spurgeon refused to receive personal benefit from this but channeled this generosity into the orphanage. "We are very grateful to all these thoughtful friends," Spurgeon acknowledged. "Some of them live hundreds of miles away, and yet never forget the Pastor's birthday." He explained his feelings about such exuberance toward him: "If this money were given to the Pastor for his own use he would feel humiliated by it; but now it comes with the blessing which maketh rich, and addeth no sorrow therewith. Poor orphans are helped, and we have the joy of it." On the *fête* this year, 1882, the orphanage benefitted to the tune of £1000. Two friends that contributed pounds commensurate with Spurgeon's age commented wittily that he grew "dearer" every year.[52]

For Spurgeon's fiftieth year in 1884, the congregation at the Tabernacle planned a Jubilee celebration on June 18-20. Spurgeon and his wife went through the week in good health and were joined during the week by his father, brother, four sisters, and his son Charles. Among the many that spoke over the three days were Canon Basil Wilberforce, Joseph Parker, Newman Hall, and W. Williams. D. L. Moody also spoke, giving a testimony of his indebtedness to the printed sermons and other works of Spurgeon. Greetings from scores of individuals, churches, and Baptist Institutions were noted or read. Upon the insistence of the givers, contrary to the twenty-fifth anniversary of his pastorate there, and despite Spurgeon's plea otherwise, gifts were given to Spurgeon himself and not to the various enterprises connected with the Tabernacle. When the money was in his hands, however, he immediately gave personally

£1000 to build and furnish the Jubilee House at the orphanage. He also gave specific amounts to the Almshouses, the Colportage Society, the Auckland Tabernacle in New Zealand under the oversight of his son Thomas, the deacons to be lent to the poor members of the church, the Baptist Fund, the Baptist Union Augmentation Fund, Mrs. Spurgeon's Book Fund and enough to St. Thomas's Hospital to make him a governor. He maintained a sufficient amount that he could immediately give to needs that arose without needing to explain to the public.[53]

J. W. Harrald read a list of the institutions connected with the Tabernacle: The Almshouse; the Pastors' College; the Pastors' College Society of Evangelists; the Stockwell Orphanage; the Colportage Association; Mrs Spurgeon's Book Fund, and Pastor's Aid Fund; the Pastors' College Evening classes; the Evangelists' Association; the Country Mission; the Ladies' Benevolent Society; the Ladies' Maternal Society; the Poor Ministers' Clothing Society; the Loan Tract Society; Spurgeon's Sermons' Tract Society; the Evangelists' Training Class; the Orphanage Working Meeting; the Colportage Working Meeting; the Flower Mission; the Gospel Temperance Society; the Band of Hope; the United Christian Brothers' Benefit Society; the Christian Sisters' Benefit Society; the Young Christians' Association; the Mission to Foreign Seaman; the Mission to Policemen; the Coffee-House Mission; the Metropolitan Tabernacle Sunday School; Mr. Wigney's Bible Class; Mr Hoyland's Bible Class; Miss Swain's Bible Class; Miss Hobbes's Bible Class; Miss Hooper's Bible Class; Mr. Bowler's Bible Class for Adults of both Sexes; Mr. Dunn's Bible Class for men; Mrs. Allison's Bible Class for young Women; Mr. Bartlett's Bible Class for young Women; Golden

---

52. S&T, July 1882, 379.

53. S&T, July 1884, 377.

Lane and Hoxton Mission (Mr. Orsman's); Ebury Mission and Schools, Pimlico; Green Walk Mission and Schools, Haddon Hall; Richmond Street Mission and Schools; Flint Street Mission and Schools; North Street, Kennington, Mission and Schools; Little George Street Mission, Bermondsey; Snow's Fields Mission, Bermondsey; the Almshouses Missions, The Almshouses Sunday Schools; the Almshouses Day Schools; the Townsend Street Mission; the Townley Street Mission; The Deacons Street Mission; the Blenheim Grove Mission, Peckham; the Surrey Gardens Mission; the Vinegar Yard Mission, Old Street; the Horse Shoe Wharf Mission and Schools; the upper Ground Street Mission; Thomas Street Mission, Horselydown; the Boundary Row Sunday School, Camberwell; the Great Hunter Street Sunday School, Dover Read; the Carter Street Sunday School, Walworth; the Pleasant Row Sunday Schools, Kennington; The Westmoreland Road Sunday Schools, Walworth; Lansdowne Place Sunday School; Miss Emery's Banner Class, Brandon Street; Miss Miller's Mothers' Meeting; Miss Ivimey's Mothers' Meeting; Miss Francies' Mothers' Meeting.[54]

In an address to Spurgeon from the deacons, B. W. Carr made the statement, "Your skilful generalship has laid ten thousand happy donors to your charities under lasting obligations to you for providing outlets for their benevolence." It allowed them to lay up treasures in heaven by paying "into the exchequer on earth of their substance."[55]

On the day of his Jubilee celebration the deacons greeted Spurgeon as "Pastor of this Ancient Church," and recognized that he had been "richly endowed by the Spirit of God with wisdom and discretion" whose conduct as "our ruling Elder has silenced contention and promoted harmony."

The original 300 had multiplied to nearly 6,000 and "under your watchful oversight the family group has increased without any breach of order." His natural abilities did not encourage indolent habits, his talents gave stimulus to diligence, prosperity did not elate him and success did not make him vainglorious but rather awed him into increased rigor of discipline. He had outlived the calumny that assaulted him in the early days, the "secularists who once denounced, now salute you." Where his theology had failed to convert them his philanthropy enchanted them. You are lifted in public esteem above suspicion, as a true man—no traitor or time-server." His very name was an emblem of purity and power and he was accounted "second to none among living Preachers."[56]

One may never be able to give an accurate count of the number of various benevolences and outreach ministers for which Spurgeon shouldered the burden of seeking financial support. It doubtless had a cumulative effect in the increase of stress on his life. He knew it, but the task of planting churches and rallying God's people to go beyond themselves in devotion to the cause of Christ were more needful than personal comfort. The phenomenon staggered Spurgeon himself, while he constantly affirmed that none of this was beyond the zeal of God for his own glory nor the power of God to raise up and sustain these ministries and more. Each gift was celebrated with a sense of gratitude. An anonymous gift of £350 from "a commercial traveler," a bequest of £900, the donation of silver plate worth £40, and the gift of 25 shillings generated by a lending library invented by children in Scotland all were received as manifestations of the glory of God in the generosity of his people.[57]

---

54. Ibid., 373.

55. Ibid., 375.

56. Ibid., 374-76.

57. S&T, June 1882, 317.

After giving a summary of a meeting of "The Green Walk Mission," conducted by William Olney and presided over by himself, and noting the multiplicity of services and activities engaged in by this mission, Spurgeon, apparently in a moment of amazement wrote, "It was a good meeting, and greatly cheered the Pastor's heart as he saw with what vigour the various branches of Tabernacle work are being carried on." He went on with a sense of privilege, "Here was a work large enough for a separate church, and yet only one of many boughs of the old tree."[58]

Amazingly, this report was followed by the report of a meeting of the "Metropolitan Tabernacle Loan Tract Society" the work of which had generated three other organizations, the sick Fund, the Maternal Society, and the Mothers' meeting, which Spurgeon characterized as "necessary adjuncts of the Tract work." In addition a mission in Bermondsey had been started through the tract work. William Olney, Jr. became the lead church planter at Bermondsey. In November 1882, Spurgeon announced that William Olney and friends had "secured a suitable site in the Bermondsey New-road for the erection of a missions-hall in which to continue the work of the last twelve years." The large hall should accommodate 700 persons, have a school room for 400 children, and rooms for Bible classes, mothers' meetings, and temperance work. At a cost of £5000, 2000 had been promised and Spurgeon insisted the "this business must be carried through with spirit: done at once, and well done, and no debt." Every true friend should take his share of giving.[59]

The money did not come in as quickly as desired, and when Spurgeon returned from a period of rest, he made a strong appeal for the "thousands upon thousands of the working-classes" in the Bermondsey area without God. With real intensity of purpose, Spurgeon asked what should be done with so few churches and chapels there with little ability even to touch the hem of the evil. Though he had "no desire to try brass bands and tambourines" even that would be better than *status quo*. God had given an excellent leader for the work and a band of choice and holy men and women ready for the work. They did not need grandiose and elegant architecture but room and shelter were not superfluities. Those who could not go into the streets to preach, or go from door to door among the poor, as these would, ought at least to be the Master's stewards to build a hall for them. "We shall not beg," he wrote with some obvious irony, "for the building is for our saviour Jesus." Those that love him will prove their love in "substantially aiding in a work which is for his honour, and for the good of souls whom he loves." Ongoing needs of college, orphanage, colportage demanded the regular help of friends, so this matter must be settled quickly and not be allowed "to encumber the march of the army."[60]

A bazaar garnered most of the remaining money needed for construction and encouraged Spurgeon to say, "This great enterprise will be inaugurated most hopefully; by the help of a few more givers the matter will be put out of hand. Another well opened in the wilderness!"[61] The work grew and in 1884 Haddon Hall was built and occupied as the center from which evangelistic and social efforts were promoted with great effectiveness.[62]

Viewing all of this as the pastor of this highly driven, keenly spiritual, and practical-minded group of Christian workers, Spurgeon could only

---

58. S&T, December 1881, 626.

59. S&T, November 1882, 598.

60. S&T, January, 1883, 43

61. S&T, February 1883, 96.

62. S&T, May 1886, 221-23. "Two Years at Haddon Hall."

rejoice and wonder at the relentless growth of these gospel-promoting services.

> The proceedings throughout were of a most enthusiastic character, and all who were present must have felt that they had come into contact with Christian workers who were all alive, and seeking by every means within their reach to bring others to the Saviour. This is another hive of Tabernacle bees, and we bless the Lord that they work together without using their stings, and the result brings glory to God and benefit to all concerned. When will all churches be alive, and work, not by some stereotyped rule, but just as the free Spirit prompts one and another to engage in this service or that? Our army forms itself into regiments by a natural process, and these attack the enemy with weapons off all kinds, advancing to the war from all points of the compass.[63]

These efforts and the continued multiplication of monetary needs for Spurgeon's "friends" constituted a large part of his efforts to prompt God's people to attempt great things for God's glory and the good of souls. In August 1881 Spurgeon made appeals for four different mission stations in districts in London. He gave generously to each cause himself but could not shoulder the entire burden. He would welcome with gratitude any friends that would help shoulder the work. Three other chapels were being erected and more urban places need to be occupied speedily for Christ, "unless they are to be left as strongholds of priestcraft or indifference." The people on the spot, in Spurgeon's observation, cared little about the work, but Spurgeon wanted to arouse them to care about their souls. Few care about the truth at first, and unless helped from the outside no place to meet would be provided. "We are at this moment treasurer for four rising places," Spurgeon explained and listed the places as Cheam, New Brompton, Gipsy Road in Lower Norwood, and the village of Hornchurch in Essex. For each of these he mentioned how much was needed to finance suitable places in which to meet. Cares both monetary and spiritual spiraled and circled in and out of each other's sphere in Spurgeon's mind. They often seemed to be united but then would slip through what appeared to be a common plane without connecting. He needed money to do the spiritual work. God needed nothing and the work of the Spirit could not be made more effectual by the medium of exchange that circulated in human society but Christ himself had encouraged the wise and aggressive use of wicked Mammon for heavenly purposes. God had made it so, and Surgeon wanted God's people to make the best use of a finally perishable treasure.

No one knows the many cares which come upon us in connection with the work of extending our churches in needy districts. Large sums could be advantageously used, but they do not come. Our own purse is not spared, but the work is great and demands large, and yet not so large but that a few wealthy persons could make it easy. We sometimes sink in spirit as we see how little the souls of men are cared for by those who call themselves the Lord's. If growing London is not provided with the means of grace coming generations will blame us. As the Lord enables us our utmost shall be done.[64]

Spurgeon's College

The greatest influence for good or evil in the world, and peculiarly in the church, Spurgeon believed, consists of those that purport to be ministers of the gospel. And yet preachers of power

---

63. S&T, December 1881, 627.

64. S&T, September 1881, 487.

are "few and far between."[65] It is but justice, Spurgeon believed, that ministers be withheld from the church if the churches do not learn how to value such gifts. True ministers are of the Lord's choosing, endowing, and qualifying. An effort to supply the churches by eliciting services of the unconverted is foolish and destructive and an intrusion into the office of the Holy Spirit. Wolves are set over the sheep and the evil one is allowed to sow seed in the field of the kingdom. Neither universities nor Episcopal hands can supply a divine call and endowment.

The depth of his conviction that no human agency can call, set aside, and endow a minister of the gospel overflowed in one intense and extended sentence. "Both those who usurp the Spirit's office and send, and those who admit to the imposture and are sent, may think themselves mercifully favoured that they escape the immediate judgment of God; but they may be assured, beyond all hope, that no power of a divine kind ever will or can rest upon the ministrations thus inaugurated, for God will not own the messenger of men, nor set his seal to a commission which did not originally emanate from his throne."[66] The surplice may fall on uncalled shoulders, but not the prophetic mantle.

Those men, however, whom God has converted and commissioned must receive instruction—neither the eloquence of Apollos nor the humility of Timothy will alone suffice, but Aquila and Paul must come alongside. Pure churches have not only prayed the Lord of the harvest to send forth laborers, but always found ways to give instruction to a called ministry without fear of intrusion on the work of the Spirit. Some of delusive conviction have feared this, but "their own decline both in numbers and ability will ere long

either convince them of their error or cause their extinction." The Spirit will not do by supernatural means what he has already provided for by natural means. "He has given us an inspired book, but he does not enable human beings to read it without having learned their letters, neither does he miraculously endow men with a knowledge of the original tongues."[67] Since men in their pursuit of the divine will are not to be as passive recipients like Belshazzar's wall or Balaam's donkey, "preachers must be instructed in some measure, and the only rational questions which can be raised relate to the measure, the manner, and the subjects of the instruction."[68]

Spurgeon fervently hoped that the church had gone beyond the day "in which we need seriously to argue for the utility of mental and spiritual culture." He resisted and resented that "conceited ignorance which is infallible in its own assertions, and therefore refuses further light." God needs not our education but even less our ignorance, and does not isolate himself to the "uncouth and boorish" but may use a man intent on learning. As conversion makes thrifty, honest stewards, so illumination of the inner life makes men prize intelligence and knowledge with the pursuit of further opportunities to dispel the darkness and walk in the light. After further striking biblical illustrations of this idea, Spurgeon came to the point, "Our assured conviction is that there is no better, holier, more useful or more necessary Christian service than assisting to educate young ministers."[69] This conviction was only intensified with the years as he reflected in the Annual Report of 1882: "When we think of the value of a well-instructed minister of the gospel, and of all the beneficent institutions which are sure to

---

65. S&T, June 1875, 249.

66. Ibid., 250.

67. Ibid., 250-51.

68. Ibid, 251.

69. Ibid., 252.

spring up around him, we sometimes think the work of training ministers to be superior to all other services done to the Lord and his church."[70]

In the light of that conviction, Spurgeon developed the Pastors' College. The opportunity to prompt a student toward the expansion of natural gifts and knowledge of literature, science, and culture had no intrinsic merit apart from the growth of the student in spiritual fervor and effectiveness. Spurgeon showed the depth of his conviction and the raciness of his style by reinforcing this conviction in a series of sentences each bearing the power of a proverb.

> They are not to be warped into philosophers, polished into debaters, carved into metaphysicians, fashioned into literati, or even sharpened into critics, they are to be "thoroughly furnished unto every good work." The Scriptures must be their chief class-book, theology their main science, the art of teaching their practical study, and the proclamation and exposition of the gospel their first business. With all knowledge they may intermeddle; but upon the knowledge of Christ crucified they must dwell. Books and parchments should be prized, but prayer and meditation should be supreme. The head should be stored, but the heart also should be fed with heavenly food. The tutors should be men of equal learning and grace, sound scholars, but much more sound divines, men of culture, but even more decidedly men of God.[71]

Ten years later in 1885, as Spurgeon reflected on the development of the Pastors' College, he remained unchanged in his overall perspective. He wanted to "maintain and spread the gospel of the grace of God" by educating men called of God to witness for Christ. More particularly, he aimed to "explain and expound the doctrines of grace so that they might be clearly understood and firmly held by our rising ministry."[72] His mark would be missed completely if the institution merely gave knowledge without inculcating a "holy enthusiasm for the doctrines of grace and their publication in the name of the Lord."[73]

The scholars are thrown together in an atmosphere of mutual edification, sharpening one another by critical engagement without fault-finding. Learning skills and truth without losing zeal or spirituality should be the aim of the school. Its connection with "the largest church in Christendom" gave many advantages. The students were members of the church at the Tabernacle and expected to unite in its meetings for prayer and participate in its ministries. Church government, revivals, Christian fellowship, homiletics, pastoral oversight, dealing with men's souls—all were displayed in practical outworking before them and enforced by classroom discussion. "An observant young man cannot fail to carry away with him ideas, plans, methods, and stimulating influences which will perhaps unconsciously affect his whole future career."[74] The prosperity of the college in 1882 allowed the institution to support several men that had gone out from it to destitute areas and gather congregations. "Thus it continues to be," Spurgeon reminded his supporters, "what it was designed for at the beginning,—a home mission, attending to the necessities of the people to the utmost of its power."[75]

Spurgeon's view embraced not only a church-centered education but a family-centered living situation. He did not enter into controversy with other arrangements, but believed that students

---

70. S&T, 1882, "Annual Report," 260.

71. S&T, June 1875, 252. "A Plea for the Pastors' College."

72. S&T, 1885, "Annual Report," 307.

73. Ibid., 308.

74. S&T, June 1875, 253. "A Plea for the Pastors' College."

75. S&T, Preface, 1882.

living in families of the church minimized the temptation to levity, maximized the experience of family worship, sobriety, and economy, and maintained them in normal life. In addition they would never have either too little or too much living space for the students and would avoid embarrassment on both counts.

Spurgeon never rejected a student on account of meagerness in education or culture as long as he was convinced that the student's call was from God and his zeal deeply ingrained. Some knew only that the Bible was true and Christ was a precious Saviour, but all had demonstrated tenacity in that they had preached for two years, sometimes in spite of ridicule and opposition. Nor did their complete inability to finance their way hinder his accepting them. The crudeness and ignorance of some reflected poorly on the college, but Spurgeon would not muzzle them, for their failures would teach them. As Spurgeon analyzed this, he showed his determination not to be dissuaded from his purpose by the loud critics, ever-ready to pounce on a Spurgeonic enterprise. "It is, of course, harder work for them," Spurgeon acknowledged, "and their mistakes and early failures have been quoted against the College; but," Spurgeon countered, "if they can bear the labour, we can endure the discredit, knowing that the pleasure of seeing their future usefulness will abundantly repay us for the occasional pain of being taunted with their inefficiencies and crudities."[76] If God sent them 500 such men, he would accept them all and God would prompt his stewards to pay up commensurate with the opportunity before them.

Spurgeon had emphasized the necessity of hard work from the beginning of the enterprise and often returned to that theme. In July 1871 Spurgeon advertised for more students: "We have need of more students at the College. Many have gone to pastorates. Several have been removed by sickness." He looked for the Lord's provision of really gracious earnest young men, no matter how poor, nor how many. Approving the fitness of the applicants took some weeks, and in order to make the August start date, the applications needed to be prompt. "Only devout, hardworking, studious, holy men need apply. A life of toil and probable poverty lies before them; and if they are not called of God to the work, woe to them. Whosoever is truly called, we shall be glad to take as Aquila did Apollos, and show him the way of God more perfectly."[77]

The first student, and for some time the only student, in the college was T. W. Medhurst.[78] Only four months younger than his mentor, Medhurst was born on October 31, 1834. From the time of his birth his religious training was among the dissenters. In his youth he was apprenticed to a rope-maker in London and soon began to attend Surrey Tabernacle where James Wells was pastor. The thought and fascinating rhetoric of Wells attracted Medhurst and he became a devoted attender of not only Sunday but also week-night services. Soon he heard of an unusual service, a missions' service, to be held at Maze Pond Chapel. He was struck with the preaching of a very young man newly arrived in London as pastor of New Park Street. He resolved to go to hear him preach in his own pulpit. Overcoming a great trauma of conscience (for after all, the new minister was reputed to be an Arminian), Medhurst went and heard Spurgeon preach on Hosea 6:3: "Then shall we know *if* we follow on to know the Lord." Spurgeon substituted "as" for "if", replac-

---

76. S&T, June 1875, 254.

77. S&T, July 1871, 333.

78. See S&T, January 1877, 9-15.

ing the translators' supplementary particle. This led to regular attendance and a growing conviction of sin interspersed with short interviews with Spurgeon. Medhurst was led to a Christian profession under the influence of Spurgeon in 1854. Through a series of letters, in which Spurgeon answered Medhurst's question, "Am I one of God's elect," Spurgeon led him to focus on the elements of calling that were consequent to election. Spurgeon finally interviewed Medhurst, was convinced that he had been converted, and baptized him in the New Park Street Chapel on September 28, 1854.

Medhurst's zeal for Christian work—distributing tracts, visiting the sick, teaching Sunday School, preaching outdoors from which conversions resulted—led to the discovery of gifts for Christian ministry. He had just finished his apprenticeship and was ready to enter into a trade with the promise of good success. Spurgeon called him into his vestry and suggested that he leave his trade to concentrate on study for the pastoral ministry. Medhurst took two weeks to deliberate and took Spurgeon's suggestion as the will of God for him. Spurgeon arranged the financing for his livelihood and, after trying for a time to provide personal tutoring in a theological course, Spurgeon sent him to study under C. H. Hosken at Mill Road Boarding School in Kent in July 1856. He returned to study under George Rogers at the Independent church in Albany Road, Camberwell, a district of Southwark, London.

Spurgeon created the contact between Medhurst and his first church at Kingston-on-Thames. He performed the marriage ceremony of Medhurst to his first wife and advised him to accept a call to the Baptist church in Coleraine in Northern Ireland as his second pastorate. "Go and the Lord be with thee!" he advised, expressing an intense interest in Medhurst's usefulness;

"I shall have as much joy in your prosperity as in my own." "What will poor Kingston do?" Spurgeon asked. "I will help them as aforetime." Spurgeon wrote Medhurst frequently, particularly at times of trial for his "first student." A severe "personal and domestic trial" brought solace from Spurgeon as did the death of a daughter in May 1884. "May you be sustained under your heavy trial! Now that you and your dear companion are most fully realizing the void which is made in your household, may you find living consolations flowing into your hearts!" During the time of this difficulty, Medhurst collected £100 to give to the orphanage. "Many sons have done gloriously," Spurgeon commented, "but Brother Medhurst has excelled them all, notwithstanding many afflictions and heavy trials."[79]

Another trial in December 1885, some malady or depression concerning his wife, brought Spurgeon's empathetic lines: "The Lord help you! You are indeed tried. I wonder whether there is some special need in your case and mine for these continual cuts of the knife. It is assuredly according to wisdom and love, and there we must leave it." His wife's death in February 1886 brought Spurgeon's words: "The Lord sustain thee! It is well that your trial should end, even though it be in this crushing loss. ... I pray the Lord to reveal his love in this dark hour." In 1888 Spurgeon signed a copy of volume five of the *Treasury of David* to Medhurst: "To my always loving and ever-faithful friend, and brother, and son, T. W. Medhurst, to whom I am most tenderly attached, in whose usefulness I heartily rejoice, and by whose loving acts I am often solaced in my affliction—a small token of my love."[80]

---

79. S&T, January 1885, 44.

80. All the above taken from G. Holden Pike, "The Work of the Pastors' College," S&T, January 1877, 12 and T. W. Medhurst, "The First Student's 'Wreath'", S&T, May 1892, 210.

Medhurst wrote a pamphlet entitled "Is Romanism Christianity?" while he served as pastor in Glasgow, an article that was republished in "The Fundamentals" in America. Ernest W. Bacon in his biography made the erroneous claim that Medhurst "crossed over to America and became head of some strange sect, and appeared arrayed in gorgeous robes, a sad anticlimax for Spurgeon's first student."[81] This error was followed by Patricia Kruppa in her study of Spurgeon. In fact, Medhurst remained faithful to his Christian calling until his retirement in 1910. He died at eighty-three years of age on February 18, 1917. His first-born son, however, named after Charles Spurgeon, Charles Spurgeon Medhurst, ended a twenty-year missionary career in China in 1904, the Baptist Missionary Society requesting his resignation because of his connections with the Theosophical Society. He lived his last six years, dying in 1927 in Sydney in Australia as a minister in the Liberal Catholic Church, an ecclesiastical organization founded in order to accommodate those that wanted to express their theosophical worldview in the context of Christian ideas.[82] C. S. Medhurst translated the *Tao-te-Ching* of Lao-tzu into English comparing its text with passages from the New Testament, Christian spiritual and pietistic writings, philosophical writings, and other eastern metaphysical writings. He closed his introductory analysis with the words, "May this renewed effort to increase the range of the Old Chinese Mystic's influence, distribute to others some of the quiet peace which the study of his work has brought to the translator."[83]

As Spurgeon gave thought to how Medhurst and others could best be educated, he knew that the monetary barrier would be a virtually insuperable hindrance to their education. Spurgeon wanted to provide for education, books, clothes if necessary, and even incidental expenses. No man of discernible gifts and compelling call should lack a requisite education for lack of money. In addition, Spurgeon's views of the gospel and of the content of training were distinct from the prevailing opportunities in the dissenting academies of the day. "I may have been uncharitable in my judgment, but I thought the Calvinism of the theology then taught to be very doubtful," Spurgeon recounted in 1870, "and the fervour of the generality of students to be far behind their literary attainments." He went on to explain the accumulating concerns that culminated in his decision to establish the College:

> At the time it seemed to me that preachers of the grand old truths of the gospel, ministers suitable for the masses were more likely to be found in an institution where preaching and divinity would be the main objects, and not degrees, and other insignia of human learning. Mine was a peculiar work, and I felt that without interfering with the laudable objects of other colleges, I could do good in my own way. By these and other considerations I felt led to take a few tried young men, and to put them under some able minister that he might train them in the Scriptures, and in all other knowledge helpful to the understanding and proclamation of the truth.

His quest for a person with a common heart and with qualifications for the task ended on George Rogers, Pastor of the Independent Church, Albany Road, Camberwell. He was born at Ardleight Hall in Essex, historic Puritan country. Rogers

81. Ernest W. Bacon, *Spurgeon, Heir of the Puritans* (Grand Rapids: William B. Eerdmans Publishing Company, 1968), 91.

82. See Judith C. Powles, "Misguided or Misunderstood? The Case of Charles Spurgeon Medhurst (1860-1927), Baptist missionary to China," *The Baptist Quarterly* (April 2010), 347-64.

83. C. Spurgeon Medhurst *The Tao Teh King: A Short Study in Comparative Religion* (Chicago: Theosophical Book Concern, 1905), xix. Reprint by Forgotten Books.

was converted and given desires for Christian ministry at an early age. His parents, without compromise of conviction, saw to it that he received an education "in harmony with that design." As staunch independents, they would receive nothing from the established church, but put him for two years under private tutorship "of a minister of considerable classical attainments in Northamptonshire." After that he entered a college at Rotherham in Yorkshire. Prior to his settlement in Camberwell, Rogers had served two different congregations. He was founding pastor of that Albany Road congregation and labored there for thirty-six years, when, at almost sixty, he came to Spurgeon's notice. Particularly attractive to Spurgeon was this: "Amidst all the changes that have been going on in theological views during his lifetime, and particularly in his own denomination, Mr. Rogers has faithfully adhered to the old evangelical truth; he has been a Puritan from his childhood, and is a Puritan still. He has a well-defined creed, and is not ashamed to own it." Earlier Spurgeon described Rogers in similar terms and with equal affection. "This gentleman is a man of Puritanic stamp," Spurgeon approvingly noted, "deeply learned, orthodox in doctrine, judicious, witty, devout, earnest, liberal in spirit, and withal juvenile in heart to an extent most remarkable in one of his years." Spurgeon described their relationship as one of "uninterrupted comfort and delight" and "in spirit and temper he is a man with whom our communion is perfect." Except on the point of baptism, they were of one mind and heart, and equally intense in their desire to work and in their love for the task. "Into this beloved minister's house the first students were introduced, and for a considerable period they were domiciled as members of his family." Though he turned seventy-five in 1874, "his eyes are not dim, nor his natural force abat-

ed. He preserves the joyousness and geniality of his youth, and exhibits a measure of dry wit and sanctified humor sufficient to make the severest study a pleasure to his young disciples."[84]

In August 1869 Spurgeon printed an article on the College from *The Examiner* published in New York. The article was largely descriptive, made some points of evaluation, but spoke positively of its suitableness for the purpose of providing an adequate ministry for "a particular sphere of society, in a land where society is cast in inflexible moulds."[85] The student population arose largely from the Tabernacle evening classes, composed of large numbers of the lower middle class population so abundant in the Tabernacle. Some also came from the Bible class for young men and the Evangelists Association. It was supported at the rate of £5,000 per year by offerings from the Tabernacle and special gifts from donors. The students learn from tutors "under the direction and with the stated teaching of Mr. Spurgeon himself," along with George Rogers, and James Spurgeon. The subjects included English language, Mathematics, Logic and Natural Philosophy, Intellectual and Moral Philosophy, Latin, Greek and Hebrew, Biblical Literature, Systematic Theology and Homiletics. The article emphasized, twice, that the theology taught was Calvinistic. The normal course was for two years duration, though abbreviated at times in order to supply preachers for much needed mission work. At that point 186 students had gone from the college, of which 177 still served in ministry. They had begun forty-four new churches and erected thirty new chapels. Eleven church starts were being contemplated in destitute districts of London. The writer sought independent evaluations from

---

84. S&T, April 1870, 146, "Concerning the College"; S&T, April 1874, 151ff; Shindler, 136.

85. S&T, August 1869, 382.

brethren not connected with the Tabernacle of the effectiveness of the ministers sent from the college. Obviously, it had Spurgeon's full support, and "He is not the man to spend his strength on unavailing labours." Other opinions, from a variety of backgrounds, were "not widely apart." The reporter revealed that "The evangelical spirit, the godly, earnestness of the young men, and the great usefulness of their labours of winning souls to Christ and gathering churches, were fully recognized and applauded." He found also that the *esprit de corps* of Spurgeon's young men sometimes took forms "which are not agreeable to outside brethren." Coincident with confidence in the immediate evangelistic usefulness of the college men was some hesitation as to whether they had the "intellectual discipline and culture necessary for sustained and permanent usefulness on the same fields."[86]

Spurgeon was unapologetic about the theological stance of the college as well as the kind of person that might apply. Any that did not share his theological views should not apply, for their sure refusal would only cause consternation, both for the student and the president. Advertising for the Michaelmas term in 1874, Spurgeon said, "Applicants must be preachers of some experience and ability, sound in the faith, and earnest in soul, or we cannot receive them." Such as these should certainly apply, however, for "of such brethren we cannot have too many." He also made it clear that "no consideration of poverty or backwardness in education need prevent earnest and efficient speakers from applying to us."[87]

In deflecting criticism, Spurgeon sought to be magnanimous. "To single out an instance of failure, and to measure all by that standard, would be so unfair that we do not suspect any "Christian of such injustice," he wrote in 1874; "to expect that all should be as distinguished as some have been, would be unreasonable, but without vaunting, we can claim that as winners of souls, as founders of churches, and as workers in the ministry, the men from the Pastors' College occupy, by God's grace, no dishonourable position."[88] When they came, they must have gifts and experience that no education could provide; their first study would be in Bible, doctrine and homiletics that would help them sustain a lifelong ministry of the Word; if they could stay longer they would receive instruction that would help them adjust more readily to a wider variety of cultural settings for effective ministry.

Celebrating twenty-five years of ministry in London in 1879, Spurgeon called the Pastors' College Conference in May a "joyous occasion" in which the "presence and power of God were manifestly felt." He gave a brief resume of the college's accomplishments and a defense of its relevance. The number of men that passed through the college was 548, of whom 432 remained in the field and in the Baptist ministry. He explained that a slight shift in approach had occurred.

From the first we have given as good an education as the exigencies of the times allowed, but as the demand for ministers is not now so pressing, and the supply of students is also larger, we have been able to allow our young brethren a longer term of study, and the majority of them now remain for three years instead of two. We have never deserved the reproach of lowering the standard of ministerial education, for we laid out our life to raise it. We hope soon to sweep away the last rag of reason for the charge. The gospel and the Holy Spirit are with us far before human culture,

---

86. Ibid., 381-82.

87. S&T, August 1874, 390.

88. S&T, June 1874, 255.

but, when we have these, the more a man knows the better.[89]

In the first series of *Lectures to My Students* published by Spurgeon, he explained that "in the Pastors' College definite doctrines are held and taught." These were summarized as the "doctrines of grace and the old orthodox faith." They held no "sympathy with the countless theological novelties of the present day, which are novelties only in outward form." Their stance on doctrine was well-known and they made no profession of latitudinarian charity. In the second series of *Lectures* Spurgeon gave another advertisement for the College and expanded the doctrinal explanation a bit:

> As it would be quite unwarrantable for us to interfere with the arrangements of other bodies of Christians, who have their own methods of training their ministers, and as it is obvious that we could not find spheres for men in denominations with which we have no ecclesiastical connection, we confine our College to Baptists; and, in order not to be harassed with endless controversies, we invite those only who hold those views of divine truth which are popularly known as *Calvinistic*,—not that we care for names and phrases; but, as we wish to be understood, we use a term which conveys our meaning as nearly as any descriptive word can do. Believing the grand doctrines of grace to be the natural accompaniments of the fundamental evangelical truth of redemption by the blood of Jesus, we hold and teach them, not only in our ministry to the masses, but in the more select instruction of the class room. Latitudinarianism with its infidelity, and unsectarianism with its intolerance, are neither of them friends of ours; we delight in the man who believes, and therefore speaks. Our Lord has given us no permission to

be liberal with what is none of ours. We are to give an account of every truth with which we are put in trust.[90]

The same year as the publication of the Second part of *Lectures to My Students*, Spurgeon included in the Annual Report of the Pastors' College another strong affirmation about the theological commitment of the college to a uniform and clearly articulated Reformed orthodoxy. No compromises were allowed but all was to be held clearly and without equivocation. In 1881 he wrote:

> The College started with a definite doctrinal basis. I never affected to leave great questions as moot points to be discussed in the Hall, and believed or not believed, as might be the fashion of the hour. The creed of the College is well known, and we invite none to enter who do not accept it. The doctrines of grace, coupled with a firm belief in human responsibility, are held with intense conviction, and those who do not receive them would not find themselves at home within our walls. The Lord has sent us tutors who are lovers of sound doctrine, and zealous for the truth. No uncertain sound has been given forth at any time, and we would sooner close the house than have it so. Heresy in colleges means false doctrines throughout the churches; to defile the fountain is to pollute the stream. Hesitancy which might be tolerated in an ordinary minister would utterly disqualify a teacher of teachers. The experiment of Doddridge ought to satisfy all godly men, that colleges without dogmatic evangelical teaching are more likely to be seminaries of Socinianism than schools of the prophets. Old puritanic theology has been heartily accepted by those received into our college, and on leaving it they have almost with

---

89. S&T, 1879, Preface.

90. Charles Spurgeon, *Lectures to My Students* (London: Passmore & Alabaster, 1881), vi.

one consent remained faithful to that which they have received.[91]

Not only was Spurgeon unashamed of the "creed," he was unashamed of the caliber of student and the product of the education. His aim was to help men that had no funds for education. Had they been required to pay "they must have remained illiterate preachers to this day." Spurgeon, therefore, often provided not only tuition and books, but frequently board and lodging and in some cases clothes and pocket money.[92] These disadvantages prompted some critics to accuse the college of doing slipshod work. Spurgeon resented the criticism as "based upon falsehood and created by jealousy"; and while in its twenty-five years the school "never deserved to be charged with giving a mere apology for an education," if the reproach was ever in any sense warranted, "it is utterly undeserved now that the time of study has become more extended, and a fuller course of training has thus become possible."[93] Spurgeon was not interested in scholarship for its own sake, but provision of learning experiences to make more efficient and prepared ministers of the gospel. To increase prestige by refusing the poor man or the "zealous young Christian whose early education has been neglected" would mean missing many eminent and useful men from all ranks, neglecting many a diamond in the rough whose polishing would involve pains that would, nevertheless, be rewarded a thousandfold. Spurgeon wanted to see the ploughmen, the fisherman, and the mechanic taught the ways of God more perfectly and enabled to proclaim "in the language of the people the salvation of our God."[94]

Spurgeon's delight in the acceptance of his college men by the churches and their prosperity in their work appeared in virtually every edition of *The Sword and the Trowel*. F. J. Ward had settled at the Baptist church on Mermaid Street in Rye, Sussex, had been given an excellent formal welcome by the churches there and ministers of the surrounding area, and "the church and congregation have been much revived since Mr. Ward's brief labours among them."[95] Mr. Layzell had a similarly impressive welcome at the Baptist church in Ashdon near Walden, Essex.[96] He was "pleased to see how much Mr. Crabb is beloved by the church in Rothesay, who have given him a handsome testimonial in token of their respect for him, and of thankfulness at his election to remain with them rather than remove to a more remunerative sphere of labor." Other men from the college had been called to spheres of labor in the churches. "Mr. Jeffrey, a much beloved student, has settled over the church in St. Paul's Square, Southsea. May the richest prosperity attend him. Our dear brother Mr. Mayers will, we trust, strengthen the hands of the brethren in Bristol; his place in Battersea is ably supplied by Mr. Bax, of Favesham. Mr. Davidson has removed to Chipping Sodbury. Mr. Williams has finished his studies with us and commenced at Clay Cross; Mr. Rotham has settled over the church at Stourbridge; Mr. W. Townsend at Enfield Highway; Mr Soames at Crook, and Mr. Kitchener at Walsingham, both in Durham; and Mr. Askew at Burton-on Trent." After twenty-six years he could say: "Among the many good men and true, there are certain names which are known throughout our whole denomination as men of power and influence." London would not soon forget Archibald Brown, Cuff, Sawday, Bax, Williams, Frank White, while

91. S&T, 1881, Annual Report, 301, 310.

92. Ibid., 302.

93. Ibid.

94. Ibid., 302f.

95. S&T, September 1871, 431.

96. Ibid.

Bristol rejoiced in Gange, Reading in Anderson, Cambridge in Tarn, Bradford in Davis, Leeds in Hill and others, just as valuable if virtually anonymous who for "Christ's sake and the love of the church, bear the thousand ills of penury without a murmur, and labour in the midst of their poor congregations, having no reward but the smile of the Great Father in heaven."[97] Calling these names and places and contemplating the ministries improved and strengthened through the instruction received at the college drove Spurgeon to great sacrifices to maintain the stability, and improve the facility, of the college.

Whereas in 1882, Spurgeon had reported that he had "diminished the number of students" in light of a glut of ministers for the number of positions available in the denomination, an urgency for the continuation of the college and not stinting its enrolment was increased by 1884 when Spurgeon began to see palpable evidence of theological decay in some of the churches of the Baptist Union, and a spirit of fear of confrontation hovering over the corporate meetings of the Union. The peril of diminishing the output of the Pastors' College lay in the fact that "there is an orthodox and a heterodox party in almost all the churches," and he foresaw lines of division drawn soon. "We must be ready with good, well-educated men, to teach the old faith, and to teach it intelligently, and with fullness of instruction." Those willing to open their eyes will see that "alarming alterations are coming on faster and faster, and the old landmark men must fix their positions, and maintain them as for dear life." The facts made it all the more necessary for his friends to help with the college that it might "raise up many a true defender of the faith once delivered to the saints."[98]

Even when compared with the highly visible

and necessary work of mercy at the orphanage, Spurgeon preferred that support of the college be maintained. He seemed to fret a bit that the college, his "first and chief institution," took second place in affection to the orphanage, for "common humanity pleads for orphans," while "there must be a love of the gospel to make a man care for students."[99] As for himself, Spurgeon testified in the third person: "Even his love for the orphanage cannot make him place the college in the second rank. No amount of sympathy for the widow and the fatherless will ever make him forget the important work of training men to preach 'the glorious gospel of the blessed God.'"[100] At the prayer meeting on December 28, 1881, an offering was taken to make the total for the college £1881 for the year. "Most people," Spurgeon winced, "forget the old love—the college, to help the new one,— namely the orphanage." Supporters should do the one and not leave the other undone. "Is it not as good a work to train a minister as to educate an orphan?"[101]

Spurgeon received many letters from former students. At the end of a compilation of achievements of the college students in a variety of venues in England, one of the reports contained a letter that could not but encourage Spurgeon to continue the work with all the zeal he could muster. The letter was intended to give joy and encouragement to the "President" for to him "I owe my conversion, college training, and those undefinable blessings which come from knowing him, and being brought under the spell of his influence." The student prayed that the Lord would preserve Spurgeon's life, promote his health, and increase his happiness.[102]

---

97. S&T, 1882, "Annual Report," 262.

98. S&T, Preface, 1884.

99. S&T, October 1882, 546.

100. S&T, January 1882, 43.

101. S&T, February 1882, 97.

102. S&T, June 1884, 328.

When the Australian alumni met in conference they took the opportunity to express their "unabated love" for Spurgeon and the "continued, nay, growing sense of obligation to the Institution where we received so much invaluable preparation for our life work." They never failed to give exuberant expression of love for Mrs. Spurgeon, "that tried and true friend of all the students." They reported on the moves and ministries of their fellows in Australia and expressed admiration for the courageous work of other college graduates in missionary labors in difficult places. The words of exhortation and gratitude from these students must surely have overcome the carping of the educational pundits of England. "May you, beloved President, be greatly strengthened and encouraged in your heavy charge," they wished for him personally, while for the college they desired a "constant succession of men in training whose 'all is on the altar,' and may we all be steadfastly expecting to share the joy of Christ's coming day that's coming by-and-by." Spurgeon responded: "Very heartily do we reciprocate the sentiments of our Victorian brethren; and over land and sea, we send to them, and to every member of the Conference, our Christian love and good wishes; and for each one we pray that 1886 may be the holiest and happiest year we have ever known, and the most richly blessed in the work of winning souls."[103]

When he could, Spurgeon extended the time of study for the students. Some always had to leave early, perhaps earlier than they should. But he had no power to retain them. Eager churches assaulted their consciences with visions of souls perishing for their negligence in going to the ministry sooner. When he did succeed in keeping some in school in spite of the entreaty of a church,

"the good deacons of the eager churches thought me a sort of harsh jailer, who locked up his prisoners, and would not give them up at the entreaty of their friends." On one occasion a deacon wrote Spurgeon and admonished him to loose the student for the Lord had need of him; Spurgeon wryly remarked that "I would have let the young man go if I had thought that he was one of the donkeys to whom the passage referred." Spurgeon was persuaded that "it is good to give the brethren a longer space for preparatory study."[104]

To Spurgeon, as president, fell the uncongenial task of dismissing a student that could not perform well enough to benefit from the training provided. "Young men who come to us loaded with testimonials, are occasionally found after a while to be lacking in application, or in spiritual power." After admonishment and trial with no improvement, "they have to be sent back to the place from whence they came." Others, however, Spurgeon called as "good as gold" but their "heads ache and their health fails under hard study." Sometimes from lack of mental capacity "they cannot master the subjects placed before them." They must kindly, but firmly, be set aside.[105] This condition pointed to the difficulty of selecting the right students for training. He used 2 Timothy 2 as a guide; they must take faithful men that would be able to teach others also. In looking at the combination, Spurgeon recognized that finding both in one person was rare indeed. Faithful included both doctrine and experience. He did not look for feverish enthusiasm without a grounding in truth; nor did he seek a formal rigidity of orthodoxy that exuded no warmth of love for God, the gospel of Christ, and fellow sinners. He explained:

---

103. S&T, February 1886, 93.

104. S&T, June 1881, 303.

105. Ibid.

Men who have a deep experience of the things of God, and a grip of truth which they cannot relax, are likely to remain faithful to it, and are to be preferred. Faithfulness is better than scholarship, the two combined are best; but we can give the second, the first must come from God alone: therefore, to begin with, we must mainly keep our eye on the spiritual jewel of faithfulness. Alas, we are frequently deceived, and even the letters of pastors and the judgments of churches cannot save us from this calamity.[106]

Aptness to teach, however, even more remote from the possibility of early judgment, made the predictability of success more complicated. One might be faithful, eager to learn, submissive to authority, and a marvelous student of the classroom and colleague of fellow disciples. But the lack of ability to teach often proved an embarrassment to these other fine qualities. Spurgeon had observed the sad event and had lamented the loss in the investment of time and energy on the part of tutor and student.

The truth is in them, but they cannot either get it out of themselves or get it into others. In all probability the persons to be taught could give no reason for their aversion; but the aversion is plain enough; the brother has no winsome ways, he has something forbidding in his countenance, or his tones, or his general style; one could hardly light on the exact point of disqualification; but the fact is clear, the man cannot teach, for nobody will learn of him. Matters of temper, heart, and spirit, and even of mannerism, in some secret manner impress common folk for or against a person who aims to be their teacher; and it is of no use arguing against that impression, for it will not be removed by argument.[107]

This gift, at least in matters of doctrine and spiritual application, came by sovereign bestowal of the Holy Spirit, a "nameless endowment, a mystic anointing, a sacred unction from the Holy One by which the man is qualified as he never could otherwise have been by all the teaching which his fellow Christians may bring to bear upon him."[108] The college always walked carefully with great circumspection, for its task was holy and the tendency to human corruption either in content, method, or attitude was great. The impossibility of absolute uniformity on these matters would emerge soon enough.

Although in 1881 Spurgeon observed a remarkable unanimity in theological and spiritual commitment among the college men and could write "they have almost with one consent remained faithful to that which they have received,"[109] four years into the Downgrade Controversy, Spurgeon had painfully seen "the torrent of error so strong, that certain of them have been carried off their feet, and stand no more with us." For the others, however, he remained thankful and saw in them "the firmness and growing graces ... against whom the floods cannot prevail." He would have counted the labor well repaid, had the few that departed also remained true, but as it stood "there were with us many men valiant for the truth, and loyal to their heavenly King" that would light up a candle in dark places never to be blown out. David Gracey added that "Peace and brotherly harmony have dwelt among us," as well as a "sincere and hearty love of the Saviour, his truth, and the souls of men." Many went beyond their strength in pursuit of evangelistic work.[110]

Though the largest amount of work extending from the college focused on those that toiled in

---

106. S&T, 1883, 264. "Concerning College Work as we see it."
107. Ibid., 265.
108. Ibid., 266.
109. S&T, 1881, Annual Report, 301, 310.
110. S&T, June 1891, 264.

connection with the churches, others labored as missionaries and evangelists at home and abroad. Both church planting and itinerant evangelism had become vital through the college ministry, so that connections were maintained with the North Africa Mission and other places throughout the world. Their labors were often in the hard places, and at times when churches had been gathered, others would come and reap the benefits. Spurgeon viewed this dynamic with an element of lingering despondency concerning his relations with the Baptist Union, but sought to place it in the more comprehensive context of labor for eternity, not present applause. "Churches have been founded by us in numbers never before approached by any school of the prophets," Spurgeon reported, but noted that "others have not been slow to appropriate the churches we have gathered, when the rough work has been done." They had made no complaint, and did not intend to. "That we increased a denomination which cares not for us, is a fact which will be better understood in a coming age than just now. If God is glorified, and souls are saved, it is enough."[111] The denomination sought to discredit the college by calling its men "uneducated" but Spurgeon insisted that the charge was untrue and would not be made if such accusers were more educated themselves. College graduates were simply swelling the ranks of the "unemployed" among ministers according to other accusers. Ministers of the gospel are not members of a trade union, Spurgeon countered, and his intention has always been to pray that the Lord of the harvest would not diminish, but send forth more laborers into the harvest, and his intent was to act in accordance with his prayers. "Among the novelties of the present age is the crime of helping too many

men to get instruction in the things of God, too many men to be soul-winners. We wonder what next!"[112]

James Spurgeon, vice-president, looked upon the completed year in 1891 as confirmation of "our faith in the necessity for, and the efficiency of, our system of preparation for the ministry of the gospel in this age of doubts, lukewarmness, and growing conformity to the world." Undiminished was the need for a "definite proclamation of the leading doctrines of the old Puritanic creed."

David Gracey, principal of the Pastors' College in June 1892, giving the first report for the college after the death of Spurgeon, reminded the readers of *The Sword and the Trowel* that "the Pastor's College was the first of [Spurgeon's] philanthropic institutions."[113] Not only so, it was the "dearest to his heart." The power of Spurgeon's vision and the clarity with which he communicated it became clear in Gracey's articulation of his understanding of the purpose of the Pastors' College. Spurgeon was convinced that the time was ripe for men who, like Rowland Hill would proclaim the simple gospel in homely language to the common people, and that providence had given this time for such a harvest. He knew how the South London folks had responded to his straightforward gospel preaching. He did not disparage the abundance of gifts that were being provided in other areas of Christian work—historians, learned commentators, polemical and critical divines, philosophical apologists, ecclesiastical politicians, and organizers of religious work in various sectors of the population—but in his view the country was destitute of men prepared for, fit for, and committed to the "simple preaching of the gospel." When preaching should be the primary aim of the church, men rushed

---

111. Ibid., 262.

112. Ibid., 260.

113. S&T, June 1892, 277.

for other honors and preaching was absent in the places in which it should be conspicuous; indeed "the poverty of the distinct and direct means for supplying 'the simple gospel' ... appeared great on all hands, but greatest where the population was poorest and most dense."[114]

This concern for "the masses" put Spurgeon far ahead of politicians and social reformers in their efforts to deal with the difficulties brought on by poverty, dense population, and unhealthy living conditions. Because of his purpose, Spurgeon looked at qualifications in a somewhat different way than the Baptist colleges. "No consideration of social superiority, means, or even educational attainments only, has ever weighed in favor of a candidate; and no early drawbacks of poverty, lowly station, or educational defects have ever of themselves closed the door against an applicant." The one demand of every candidate for acceptance is clear evidence that "he has been called of Christ, and endowed by Him with natural and spiritual gifts for effectively preaching the Word, as pastor, or evangelist, or missionary." Encourage these gifts and the gospel flourishes. If difficulties arose, students were encouraged to ask their questions without fear of being held up to ridicule or contempt. Honest wrestling with personal difficulties was considered a valuable part of the training, for such head-on confrontation was needed in the day by day practical problems future ministry would throw before them.

The educational methods used varied widely because of the multi-faceted, and often bewildering, character of the gifts and backgrounds possessed by the students. Subjects taught included a number of fundamental and elementary courses, courses in general knowledge, classics, and language, as well as divinity and homiletics. Spurgeon liked to include a course in basic science because of the expansive impact it had on the minds of the students and the interesting source of illustrations it provided. Spurgeon included a lecture in *Lectures to My Students* entitled "The Sciences as Sources of Illustration." He even provided a scientific apparatus that they might engage in elementary scientific experiments. David Gracey explained his part of the curriculum in 1891. He used Hodge's Handbook for one course in theology and gave his own lectures in systematic theology in the other. At various times, given the preparation and propensities of students, he led students in a study of Lucretius, *De Rerum Natura*, the first book of Livy, or the First Oration of Cicero. In classical Greek he had taught the First Book of Homer, the Sixth Book of Herodotus, and Plato's *Apologia* of Socrates. In New Testament Greek, he had guided students in reading through Acts, Ephesians, Philippians, Colossians, and Romans. He had drilled several students carefully in Hebrew grammar and, at the junior level, read through Genesis. Those at the senior level had read portions of Psalms, Hosea, Isaiah, Job, Exodus, and Deuteronomy.[115]

Mr. Fergusson taught philosophy, ethics, and communications. He felt that the spirit of independent enquiry had been excellent during the year and would contribute to each preacher's usefulness in the field of labor for which God had especially gifted him, that "he would give *himself* to the church and to the work of God—himself and not another." Aiding in this object were studies in Wayland's Ethics, Butler's Analogy, Trench's English Language, past and present, Bain's English Composition, and Fowler's Logic.

Mr. Marchant, a tutor specifically devoted to language studies, reported concerning the con-

114. Ibid., 278.

115. S&T, June 1891, 264.

tinued and growing need for men from the college in the fields of labor, contending that the increase of the number of good men in the field would only expand, rather than diminish, the need for more. In preaching, the supply creates the demand. Seed sown frequently, with harvests following, establishes and expands the need for more such preaching and harvesting. The world given such seed and harvest, will cry for more. Language courses, Marchant reported, had been accomplished with usual success and "quite up to the average attainment."

Mr. Cheshire, the teacher of science, expressed his intent that far beyond the exact knowledge of science he wanted to inculcate, his work would be a failure unless with it, "there came deeper reverence and a fuller appreciation, that all ever-present forces are but evidences of the Eternal mind, upon which they rest. And whence they come." He also had provided some demonstrations of the practical uses of science in debunking immediate difficulties created by the deceits of spiritual mediums.[116]

Thomas Bowers also reported on the variety of theological, language, and Bible courses had been offered in the evening to men coming from places of work and labor he had seen in their knowledge and their work ethic. Haydn Pinkess gave a brief report on a shorthand class, attended by thirty students, and its success in teaching this very useful skill employing a system developed in "Manual of Phonography" by Isaac Pitman.[117]

With the sting of criticism concerning the nature of the education provided at the College, Spurgeon affirmed those that labored so diligently taking the greater part of the burden. The course was "not an easy one," Spurgeon remarked, as the variety of Gracey's labors along with the comprehensive offerings throughout the curriculum should demonstrate, "and a lover of ease, after carrying it on so long, would feel inclined to drop it." As for him, though others shouldered the academic load, "to one who has so much to do, the one day in the week which is given to the College is by no means a small addition to our own toil."[118] His brother added: "The President's health has been so good throughout the greater part of the year, that the students have greatly enjoyed, and been much benefitted by the increased instruction afforded by his Lectures on Friday afternoons."[119]

With all this variety in approach, one goal was aimed at—each student would avoid cowardice and take distinct and decided positions for truth and doctrine, "discarding all dissembling and trimming and masterly neutrality." Should they pay a price by enduring the scorn of those that catered to the last new thing in theology, they would buy also spiritual and moral fiber along with "pluck, industry, and faithfulness in the work of Christ." Pastors' College men often were those called as a last resort to places abandoned by all others, places that were almost dead and despairing of any future. Such a position they embraced gladly, leading to the reviving of causes virtually lost to gospel witness. To be used "as the forlorn hope of the churches" was not an insult but a crown to be worn gladly. The doctrine was that of Spurgeon, also considered that which dominated in times of spiritual awakening and evangelistic harvest. It was espoused by the Puritans, the Re-

---

116. S&T, June 1891, 268.

117. A representation of sounds by distinctive characters; commonly, a system of shorthand writing invented by Isaac Pitman, or a modification of his system, much used by reporters. The consonants are represented by straight lines and curves; the vowels by dots and short dashes; but by skilled phonographers, in rapid work, most vowel marks are omitted, and brief symbols for common words and combinations of words are extensively employed.

118. S&T, June 1891, 262.

119. Ibid., 263.

formers, and Augustine, and arose biblically from the Pauline epistles and the discourses of Christ. These truths contain the "vital essence of the gospel" and express the "eternal verities of Christ's salvation" and thus are the most "potent and persuasive," though not the most pleasing, ever addressed to the hearts of men. They are the "clearest mirror of the grace of our Lord Jesus Christ, and the chosen channels through which the Holy Spirit pours his renewing light and life and love upon mankind."[120]

Spurgeon wanted the college to be a perpetual testimony to the recovery of true doctrine at the Reformation and its students to demonstrate the same courage that the Reformers did in the face of dangerous hostility. During 1883, at the 400th anniversary of the birth of Luther, Spurgeon made special efforts to insure a visible witness to that desire for future generations. Spurgeon had collected a large number of pictures that presented the Protestant Reformation and had them mounted in displayable form for showing in a variety of venues. During 1883, he put them on display at the orphanage in order to draw visitors and several churches made arrangements to display them. After making appearances in Southend and Kilburn, the pictures came back to the Pastors' College for November 5-8. After that they would be at Exeter Hall under the auspices of the Luther Commemoration Committee. On November 11 Spurgeon took his part in the Luther Celebration by preaching in Exeter Hall in a special service for young men. His own son, Charles, pastor at Greenwich, would fill his pulpit at the Tabernacle.[121] Spurgeon reported that at the close of his sermon at Exeter Hall, some twelve young men "came forward spontaneously, and avowed their faith in the Lord Jesus Christ." The

sermon was published under the title "A Luther Sermon at Exeter Hall."[122] On November 28 he lectured at the college on Luther using a method of projecting pictures called "lantern views." The final residence of the collection was the college.

Pastors' College men speckled the country "from Wick to Redruth, from Norfolk to Wales." They had the largest Baptist congregations in London, almost every Baptist pulpit on the Isle of Wight, and served in Jersey, Guernsey, and Isle of Man. Baptist work revived in Ireland through their labors. Spain, Turin, Naples, and "the fierce Mohammedans of North Africa" were engaged by Spurgeon's men. The Congo felt their witness and almost every important town of South Africa had a Pastors' College trainee. New Zealand, Tasmania, Australia as well as the Falklands, Bahamas, and Jamaica had gospel witness through their zeal. In South America as well as Canada, and in the United States from New England to the western frontier, they had found places for service of Christ and the gospel.[123] *The Sword and the Trowel* carried notes virtually every month of Pastors' College men being settled in some place of service.

In 1891, neither Spurgeon's perspective nor his public defense had changed. In what would be his last report on the college, he emphasized: "We have no occasions to be ashamed of our students, nor of the marked advance which they have made in preparation for their life work." Though all could have done better, he felt obliged to "praise the grace which has enabled us to do as well as we have." Within that accounting of accomplishment Spurgeon included 845 men that had studied for sacred ministry. Virtually all had been preachers for at least two years before they applied to the institution. The college,

---

120. S&T, June 1892, 280,

121. S&T, November 1883, 609.

122. S&T, December 1883, 652.

123. S&T, June 1892, 280, "Mr. Spurgeon's First Institution."

therefore, had not essentially increased the number of preachers but hopefully had improved the quality of the preaching and their understanding of pastoral duties. They came, for the most part, with no, or very deficient, learning. The College was established for that sort, that is, "men of good natural parts, who had not been able to acquire a sufficient education in their earlier days." Spurgeon had opened a door of hope "for those who could not pass an examination in the standards of scholarship, but yet had been used of the Lord in the winning of souls." Indeed, the education had not quenched their zeal, but in God's grace he had "made them to be successful winners of souls."[124]

Buildings

In 1871, Spurgeon began to call for a separate building for the college, and hoped, in print, "that the means will be sent in due time."[125] He soon received a £500 gift in celebration of his 1,000th published sermon "toward our College buildings."[126] The rooms they occupied under the Tabernacle were very dark, and they had to burn gas nearly all the year round, all day long. This made the rooms unhealthy. He also anticipated an increase in numbers and the space was limited. The construction of a separate building was not needless but absolutely necessary. He looked to God and to his stewards for help. At the rear of the Tabernacle, freehold land was purchased from the Ecclesiastical Commissioners. It had once been the rectory garden. Carlile wrote that Spurgeon "declared that he intended to grow dissenters in it instead of cabbages." He laid the foundation stone on October 14, 1873. The college was opened by a series of special-invitation

meetings during September 1874, finally costing, including furnishings, over £15,000. The buildings also served the Sunday School.[127]

"The College Buildings are promising well," Spurgeon wrote early in 1873. "They are massive and commodious. A considerable sum of money will yet be needed to completely pay for them, and we dare not and will not incur a debt."[128] In the late summer of 1874 Spurgeon noted that a large legacy soon would be paid to the college, but it could not be used for the college buildings. Much remained to be done as soon as funds were available, for he would not go in debt. In the meantime, "while this hay is being made the flocks continue to eat, and cannot live on provender to come, so friends must remember their stewardship."[129] On August 28, Friday afternoon at the normal time of the lecture to students, Spurgeon gathered all the students round him in the lecture room, and "after praising God for finding the means for the building, he gave an address, and then the brethren united in pleading that the instructions given and received in that room might be attended by the divine blessing, so that able ministers of the New Testament might be there equipped for service." From there the group went to the room set apart for "Prayer and the Communion" and prayed again asking that they would always be fervent in prayer. To the large hall they went next where college public meetings would be held and prayer was offered again for "friends and helpers, that they might be blest in return for their kindness" and in order that they might continue to help still. From there to the common room the group moved, a place where the men would meet between classes in

---

124. S&T, June 1891, 259. "A Brief Review of College History."

125. S&T, July 1871, 333.

126. S&T, August 1871, 382.

127. J. C. Carlile, *Charles H. Spurgeon: An Interpretative Biography* (London: Religious Tract society, 1933), 232.

128. S&T, February 1873, 93.

129. S&T, September 1874, 438.

free conversation. Appropriately, they prayed that leisure moments would yield nothing that would grieve the Spirit of God in their times of lighter communications. "Thus," Spurgeon summarized, "with prayer and song four important parts of the house were set apart for their holy uses." In the evening Mrs. Bartlett's class came to tea, toured the new building for the college, and each one brought a gift. "No one held back, and no one needed the slightest approach to pressing"[130]

At the end of the festivities, Spurgeon still needed £2,000 to complete the work. When some of the papers reported that the money was needed to "remove the debt," he recoiled against the very use of the word. Perhaps it was a debt, for Spurgeon had committed to the construction and completion of the facilities before money was in hand; but he insisted, "We have never had a debt or thought of such a thing; we have paid all demands on the spot, and shall be able to do so to the last penny; for if anything cannot be paid for, it cannot be had." No debt exists until the time to pay an instalment arrives, "and down on the nail we have paid each portion hitherto, and have no fear as to the rest." The Lord's stewards would yet be moved to send help, and the ending will be provided just as surely as the beginning. To make up the £2,000 Spurgeon wrote to all the seat-holders and church members to attend a tea, four groups meeting on September 8, 11, 15, and 16. All received tickets for the tea and were encouraged to bring a gift when they came. Spurgeon heaped words of praise on each group as he reported the meetings: "What loving words they gave their pastor! Their grips of the hand he will never forget." The groups differed in size but the spirit of hearty love was the same as each group gave according to its ability. "If any-

thing in this world could afford perfect content it might be found in a pastor's heart when he found himself so generously supported in a work most dear to him," Spurgeon reported, for "never was greater enthusiasm or warmer zeal expressed in any cause." The four evenings, with subsequent in gatherings, supplied the £1,000 anticipated in these meetings. Spurgeon proposed that a "good bazaar" should be arranged for the other £1,000. He announced that the bazaar for the "last stone of the College would be held immediately after Christmas."[131] The bazaar was not needed as a matured legacy more than completed the amount needed.

Book Fund as a Means of Benevolence to the College Pastors

Though the book fund was designed to put godly and sound theological literature into the hands of pastors of all denominations, at times it served as a means of benevolence for destitute pastors' families. Susannah Spurgeon related an incident of "one of our own men" whose health had severely declined and whose church was "unable to keep their pastor in the common necessaries of life." The doctors insisted that Australia, "the Utopia of feeble folk," held the key to his survival. He must go alone, leave his wife and three mites of children in England to live by the needle of the struggling wife. Susannah, upon hearing the story, believed that all of them must go together, but the Pastors' Aid Fund was never designed to sustain such heavy expenses. Soon, however, a sum came into the hand that encouraged her. Only £16 short she was. The family agreed to undertake the voyage together, exuberantly, and the next morning a £15 gift to Mr. Spurgeon arrived from an "unknown correspondent." He viewed

---

130. S&T, October 1874, 589-90.

131. Ibid., 491.

this as divine provision for the struggling family and promptly applied it to the cost of fare, supposedly with Spurgeon providing the other pound, though the report does not say so. God's provision did not stop with the fare that allowed the family to stay together, but also sent clothes from the hands of his stewards to provide for "the outfit of the husband" and "all that was requisite for the comfort of mother and children." In her report of this Mrs. Spurgeon asked, "Can eyes which have seen so clearly the goodness and lovingkindness of our God ever be obscured by the wicked mists of distrust and doubt?" So it was in all the benevolent activities of Spurgeon and the Tabernacle; "The Lord will provide," he believed, and thus when needs were met he believed that it was in direct honor to his promises given in his word. "Believers in the living God shall not fail nor be discouraged, but they shall see and admire the wonderful faithfulness of the Lord their God."[132]

The provision of books themselves, moreover, was considered one of the most necessary works of charity for the good of the church of God. "There is an absolute famine of books among poor Baptist ministers, and the work of supplying them is one of the most needful which Christian charity can undertake." When the mind of the pastor is fed, the entire church of God is fed with spiritual bread.[133]

Spurgeon was concerned about the physical well-being of pastors and their families as they reached the age at which they could no longer preach and earn income. Upon returning from the Baptist Union meeting in 1875 Spurgeon urged, through *The Sword and the Trowel* adoption of the proposed Annuity Fund for Aged Ministers and their Widows. He believed that the

absence of such a fund, and certainly delay in effecting it now, was sinful. Spurgeon proposed that wealthy Baptists immediately pledge £100 a year each for five years so as to raise a fund of £20,000 to £50,000, and that churches strain themselves, make a "desperate effort," to put their minister on the fund "with all the premiums paid up for life." Insuring each minister for life for an amount that he will receive as a right is one of the "grandest causes conceivable." Baptists must see to it that the reproach on them for negligence in this area is rolled away, and soon. "Infirm ministers and widows of the Lord's servants have a claim upon us, and our Baptist friends must not allow the present project to end in talking and planning." Spurgeon called for a secretary and a liberal public.[134]

Carlile records an event in which Spurgeon preached to a crowded church meeting hall in Hertfordshire, where William Skelton was pastor. Noticing that Skelton's suit was on the verge of self-destruction, he commented after the sermon that he expected the congregation to gather nothing on Spurgeon's account. He did, however, think that the pastor might not object to a new suit of clothes. He volunteered, therefore, for his faithful deacon William Olney to give half a sovereign promising that he would do the same. The people must come up with the rest that was needed. Carlile commented the "the sum was given and more than one suit was provided."[135]

Orphanages
Boys' Orphanage
Spurgeon consistently maintained that the Stockwell Orphanage is "the second work."[136] He looked on it as a "Great work" and certainly one

---

132. S&T, March 1881, 130f.

133. S&T, November 1875, 545.

134. S&T, November 1875, 545.

135. Carlile, 127.

136. S&T, March 1881, 133.

that thrilled him, gave him great satisfaction in its display of pure benevolence. "The God who answers by orphanages, let him be Lord," Spurgeon paraphrased Elijah.[137] His personal child-likeness emerged during seasons when he was to be at some function with the orphans, particularly Christmas. Conversions also were aplenty at Stockwell, and that, after all, was the primary intention of the institutions. If it eventually served as a feeder for the Pastors' College, it would enhance its usefulness all the more and tend to make it a subsidiary to his main goal of training defenders of truth and winners of souls.

Spurgeon began the orphanage, as he noted on many occasions, "by a direct providential indication, which he could not mistake nor resist." In 1866, he received a letter from an unknown correspondent, Mrs. Hillyard, offering £20,000 to establish an orphanage for fatherless boys. He learned that she was a devout Christian lady, at that time in fellowship with the "Brethren," who had determined to devote her substance to the Lord's work. Her generosity was prompted by a note in *The Sword and the Trowel* stating the necessity of a school for the poor where "all that we believe and hold dear shall be taught to the children of our poorer adherents."[138] Nothing could dissuade her from the resolution to make Spurgeon the agent of effecting her life purpose. When he visited her he suggested that she might have a relative that could use the money or she might give it to the orphanages run by George Muller. No, Spurgeon was the man for the task she envisioned, for it was, after all, his vision. Having enough to occupy his energies with the work of the Metropolitan Tabernacle and the Pastors' College, Spurgeon, nevertheless, consented to the

new undertaking, convinced that it was of the Lord. Increased burdens would be compensated by increased strength, so he concluded. When it was discovered that Mrs. Hillyard's gift was presently tied up in legal matters which would be too expensive to unravel, others, having caught the vision of this new ministry, began to give. The £20,000 was put into the beginning of an endowment fund. Voluntary gifts brought in £3,000 to purchase a site for the buildings.[139]

Contributions came in rapidly. Mr. and Mrs. Tyson, in commemoration of their twenty-fifth wedding anniversary, gave enough money to erect the first house, named the "Silver Wedding House." The Tysons continued to give "very largely since then." The second was presented by a city merchant only revealed as J. H., the house bearing the name "The Merchant's House." Mr. William Higgs and his employees built the next, designated as the "Workman's House." The Family Thomas Olney presented "Unity House" in memory of Mrs. Unity Olney, the wife of the recently deceased senior deacon of the Tabernacle. The sum of £1,400, raised by the Baptist churches of Great Britain, as a testimony to Mr. Spurgeon, secured the erection of the next two houses. Students of the Pastors' College and graduates serving as ministers contributed funds to erect the seventh house, called the "Students' House. The eighth came from the generosity of the Sunday Schools of the country and so named "The Sunday School House."

In addition to the various homes for the children, a large dining-hall and kitchen, a laundry, a commodious school-room, and a covered playground were added. The whole of these buildings cost £10,200, and were completed entirely free from debt. Each house accommodated about thir-

---

137. W. Y. Fullerton, *C. H. Spurgeon: Biography* (London: Williams & Norgate, 1920), 241.

138. S&T, August 1866; Fullerton, 242.

139. S&T, August 1870, 385ff., and S&T, 1880, 367ff.

ty boys, governed by a godly matron. This arrangement was designed to compensate for the loss of
the parental home and secure the best influences
for the children in the formation of Christian character. The children were taught a "sound English
education, under the British School system."[140]

Selection of children was completely apart
from monetary considerations so that the needi-
est were the surest to gain admission. Each case
was considered on its own merits; orphans and
fatherless children between ages six and ten were
selected. Spurgeon believed that "The plan of
electing the cases by merit without canvassing
and polling deprives the Institution of the aid obtained by the purchase of votes, and so renders
the obtaining of funds a greater difficulty, but the
saving to the poor widows, and the certainty that
the most needy cases obtain the benefits of the
Institution, are two beneficial results worth far
more than the trouble they involve."[141] Widows
would be out only the expense of procuring a few
necessary certificates and of travel to the institution, a few shillings at most. "An honourable body
of Christian Men," as Spurgeon called his committee, saw the necessity of this arrangement and
were pledged to the proper execution of the trust
deed.

Inmates also had no need to meet a sectarian
test. They were selected "irrespective of denominational association." In 1880 the largest number
of students was from the Church of England and
the third largest designation was entitled "not
specified." Spurgeon pointed to the conversion
of the children as "our absorbing aim." More important than the "peculiarities of any denomination," the children were taught "the truths of our
common Christianity," surrounded by a gracious
atmosphere, and instructed in "the knowledge

of Christ."[142] He added in considering this trait:
"This is as it should be, for it would be a calamity to be deplored were theological differences
allowed to mar so beneficent a work as that of assisting the widow and the fatherless."[143]

In addition, the institution was open to all
classes in the community. "When a family is bereft of their bread-winner," Spurgeon reminded
his readers, "the poverty involved may differ in
degree, but in every case the widow is an object
of pity, and the fatherless children claim compassionate regard."[144] Spurgeon had to consider the
English prejudice against mixing various classes
of children all together, but he pointed to the example of American schools that "embrace scholars from every section of the community, to the
mutual advantage of all concerned."[145] He listed
the different "classes" from which students had
come. The largest number, 142 came from a class
known as "mechanics," the second largest, 104,
was denominated "labourers and others." Other
categories included "shopkeepers and salesmen"
(91), "manufacturers and tradesmen" (72), "law,
bank, and commercial clerks" (59), "minister and
missionaries" (21), policemen, postmen, firemen,
shopmen, soldiers, mariners and watermen, so-
licitor (1), cab proprieters, journalists, railway officials, physicians and surgeons, accountants, and
gentlemen.

No geographical prejudice governed the acceptance either. Children came from 66 districts
of London and from 106 towns representing 32
counties. Wales sent six and Ireland sent two.
Spurgeon did not like the idea of uniforms for the
children because it "marks them out as charity
children, and condemns them to a monotonous

140. Ibid., 385ff.
141. S&T, 1870, 387.

142. S&T, 1880, 369.
143. S&T, 1881, "Annual Report, 435.
144. S&T, 1880, 370.
145. Ibid.

sameness in appearance." He advocated "the best broadcloth which money can buy" as the most economical and durable for a boy that, as well, provides sufficient variety to assure that their "individuality is not sacrificed to a common type, and that they are free from what has been aptly called 'a workhouse appearance.'"[146]

Spurgeon encouraged help of all kinds from all places. When he received the gift of a pig, some fowls, and a truck of coals, he improved the situation to call on other "farmers, coal owners, gentlemen, and ladies" to follow such an example. "Gifts in kind are very gratefully received at the orphanage," he acknowledged, "and when they are articles of food they pleasantly vary the diet."[147]

From August 1867 until March 1870, the boys' orphanage admitted 154 residents and had removed only 6. By March of 1880, there had been 568 total admissions with 324 removals for a total in residence of 244.

Spurgeon saw the needs of childhood not only in terms of food, shelter, and clothing, but in terms of family relationships, maternal care, and pure childish delight. His vision for the orphanage included all of these, as well as provisions for health care. Spurgeon bore in mind that children needed some constant inflow of hope, both short term and long term in the temporal sphere, and a clear vision and grasp of eternal hope through the gospel of Jesus Christ. For long-term temporal hope, the orphanage provided education and eventually job placement; for short-term hope, Spurgeon kept up a daily rhythm of meals, conversation, play, friendship, nurture, and discipline, a rhythm through the year of events filled with fun and delight for the children. He himself seemed to thrive on these events, particularly the

special celebration of Christmas. Several guiding principles consistent with Spurgeon's view of the central place of the home in a biblical understanding of human growth governed the orphanage from the beginning. Spurgeon believed these proved wise and in no need of major amendment. Arranging the accommodations on the model of a home, "The Cottage Home System" as Spurgeon denominated it, gave the children more than four walls and a roof by providing a home atmosphere where "the virtues of Christian character shall be fostered and developed."[148]

Spurgeon took many measures, in a purposely ostentatious way, to ensure the health of the inmates of the orphanage. Not only did the facilities include an infirmary, bathing facilities, a laundry, and sufficient space for exercise, even in messy weather, but physicians were also on call. In the report for 1879-80, the title page lists not only all the officers of the orphanage, and the trustees, but also the medical team ready to be of service (the Honorable Consulting Physician, Henry Gervis, the Honorable Consulting Surgeon, J. Cooper Fourster, the Honorable Consulting Ophthalmic Surgeon, J. C. Wordsworth, the Honorable Dentist, W. O. Hinchcliff, the Medical Officer, William Soper), and to handle the medical procedures involved in the acceptance of a child to the orphanage. The children were investigated carefully for any danger of infectious diseases, and the status of their vaccinations was ascertained, with vaccinations given if they were not up to date. They were all examined before leaving for any holiday and upon returning. Soper also noted that "Special precautions are taken to prevent the admission of dirty heads, as, in my experience, they are a sure forerunner of the bugbear of institutions, viz., sore heads, which, for months, baffle

---

146. Ibid., 373.

147. S&T., October 1874, 491.

148. S&T, 1880, Annual Report, 368.

the skill of nurses and doctors." He also ruled out epilepsy, ruptures, and visual defects so that "no child is admitted unless in a condition physically to face the battle of the little world upon which he enters." Aunts and mothers visited the orphanage on the first Wednesday of the month, but not during February. They sought to prevent epidemics being brought into the house. In 1881, Spurgeon gave additional information that "during their term of residence in the Institution all the boys are total abstainers, no alcoholic liquors being allowed except by order of the doctor, but most of them are pledged abstainers with the approval of their friends."[149]

Even with the strictness of Soper, however, sometimes the compassion of Spurgeon and the trustees overruled his exclusions. He seemed to complain, but was letting the reader know that something other than cold hard science ruled the final decisions of care for children. "It must be allowed," he inserted, "that some few delicate and undesirable cases are admitted, but beyond my province; and this can only be explained by the President and Trustees being blessed with large hearts and *liberal* ideas, so that a case of true merit is rarely cast adrift." This did not mean that they were willing to put the rest of the community at risk, for "a house has, when necessary, been taken at the seaside during the summer, where delicate cases have been sent, and with very great benefit to the children."[150] A passing note concerning the orphanage in 1871, showed the constant vigilance in health issues upon which Spurgeon and his medical team were insistent: "In the orphanage we are greatly favoured by God in the matter of health. Only one child has had the small pox, and from other epidemics we have been free."[151]

---

149. S&T, 1881, Annual Report, 435.

150. S&T, 1880, 376.

151. S&T, September 1871, 430.

Both caution and compassion contributed to the overall well-being of the entire institution. The inspection of 1877 produced the kind of report that Spurgeon felt gratified in sharing with his supporters. F. J. Mouat wrote on March 16, 1877:

I have today visited for the second time the Stockwell Orphanage, and examined into the system of training and education pursued in it, with special reference to an inquiry in which I am now engaged, regarding the pauper schools throughout the country. In many important particulars this institution is well in advance of most kindred establishments which I have yet seen. The plan of feeding and clothing in particular is excellent, and the instruction of the class rooms is conducted with intelligence and life. The boys look healthy and happy, and I shall only be too glad if I succeeded in transplanting some of the advantages of this place to the pauper schools, in which they are much needed. I have seldom enjoyed a visit to any school more thoroughly than that of which I am now leaving the most imperfect record.[152]

Spurgeon, in typical holistic fashion, looked to physical well-being, emotional stability, and joyful relationships as well as the preeminent concern of salvation. Another desirable outcome for Spurgeon would be the increase of the ranks of God-called men to the ministry. He set forth a hopeful scenario:

Many of the boys give promise of early piety, and of future usefulness. Our main end is to accomplish this by God's grace. The hope is cherished that from time to time some of the elder boys will be set apart as monitors in the school for several years, thus securing a good teaching staff; and, if really converted to God, and displaying ability

---

152. S&T, April 1877, 190.

and a call to preach the gospel, it is a cherished belief that some of them will be ultimately drafted off to the Pastors' College, to be educated for the ministry. In this way a return will be made to the church for valuable help rendered in support of the orphanage, and the glory of God will be promoted by a succession of faithful pastors.[153]

Using the warranted means to help bring about such a spiritual harvest, not only were the orphans involved regularly in Lord's Day worship, but family worship was also conducted twice daily, before the morning and evening meals. Normally the headmaster conducted this but at times Spurgeon himself was present for the exercise, and at times a visitor was asked to speak. As a means of service and acquaintance with the broader dimensions of church life, an orphanage choir was formed that went to churches to perform. They were warmly received; the entire process seemed to intrigue Spurgeon. For example, from December 2 to 6, 1878, the choir of thirty boys went to Southampton, Portsmouth, and Isle of Wight. Spurgeon reported: "Friends everywhere vied with one another in the heartiness of the reception which they gave to Mr. Charlesworth and his choir of thirty boys. Large crowds gathered in each place to listen to their singing, and liberal help was given to the institution." Spurgeon estimated that the orphanage would benefit from the tour by over £100. While the monetary gain encouraged both the headmaster and the president, the goodwill of the churches meant as much and the opportunity to develop excellence in the use of gifts for God's glory pushed forward the ultimate goal of the institution. Spurgeon, with obvious pleasure, reported how Mr. Mackey of Southampton described the excitement and positive response of his church in

lining up bed and breakfast for the boys as well as a tea in the afternoon before singing. He also gave his judgment of the quality of their concert: "The capital precision and tunefulness of the several pieces delighted the listeners."[154]

Spurgeon knew that anticipation of happy moments served as a buoy to the spirit. He worked to gives seasons of such anticipation for the orphans. Christmas provided a natural opportunity and Spurgeon did not let it pass without intense promotion beforehand and jovial reporting afterwards. In *The Sword and the Trowel* for December 1870, he gave a playful resume of a discussion held at the orphanage about the celebration of Christmas: "C. H. S. had promised that he and Mrs. Spurgeon would spend Christmas-day with the boys, and have a grand holiday. Dreadful discovery—Christmas day falls on a Sunday! Then C. H. S. must be preaching, and the day is sacred, and so there can be no holiday. Suggested that we had better keep it on Monday. C. H. S. proposes Tuesday. Proposal unanimously rejected on the ground that it is so late." He pointed to the difficulty of Monday because there would be "no time to make the plum-puddings on the day, and as the day before is Sunday, we must give up pudding." An alternative was suggested: "Case met by the proposal that the aforesaid pudding could be made on Saturday. Cook to be consulted." Another suggestion arose. "If any person has a box or two of oranges to spare, there are friends at the orphanage who will guarantee that they are not spoiled if forwarded on the 22nd or 23rd December. Some youngsters ready to guarantee it with personal responsibility to see the matter attended to." Though modesty would not permit the "juvenile debaters" to ask for a Christmas tree, Spurgeon took it on himself to make the sugges-

---

153. S&T, August 1870, 385ff.

154. S&T, January 1879, 42-43.

tion because "even orphan boys are fond of nuts, cakes, raisins, etc." So, he did and the suggestion carried without a dissentient. "Great question awaiting resolution! Will any good angels be found to leave any of these dainties at Stockwell! General unanimous and hearty expression of 'We hope so.' C. H. S. also hopes so. Means to see about it. A Merry Christmas and a happy new year to all friends."[155]

As Spurgeon reported about the events of the day, he presented it as a joyful day from morning till night and a memorable time for the orphan boys. One regular donor, Mr. Bath, gave six dozen bunches of turnips with the hope that some one else would provide the mutton. It happened, as Mr. Priest, from Morden, sent a whole sheep, "and so the mutton and the turnips were both on the spot." One lady had the young ladies in her school make shirts for the boys, the number totaling 700. Many persons helped by giving pocket money to the boys.[156]

As he prepared for the next year's event, December 1871, Spurgeon called the 1870 Christmas "a day indeed. A day of feasting, and romping, and general glee." Both gifts and food were plenty, nothing was wasted, and everything was enjoyed. Now, as Christmas approached again, the chairman (CHS) looked for provisions for the boys. He was particularly solicitous for the provision of a rocking-horse for sick boys in the infirmary. He had asked for it publicly earlier and surprised that he did not already have enough to make up a virtual Croydon fair, but, alas, "Not one horse, bay or grey, black or chestnut, had come to the orphanage door. Wonder whether it will come at Christmas with a load of Christmas-tree ornaments on its back; perhaps it has been waiting to have the pack packed and strapped on."[157]

In 1877 he mentioned special injunctions, ostensibly from the orphans themselves, that he not forget to mention to the friends to provide "the roast beef and plum pudding, oranges, and so on, so that the orphans may have a high day at Christmas." Spurgeon agreed with the doctrine systematized by "the boys" that Christmas should never be forgot. Since the president was to dine with all the matrons and master, as well as the boys, "shall the cupboard be bare?" He also reminded givers that as he was soon to be away on the Continent, he would have much less care if the general funds were replenished. Otherwise, he would be like the old lady in the shoe, "feeling that he has so many children he does not know what to do."[158]

Spurgeon, though he had to miss the celebration during some of his latter years (1884 being the last time that he attended the Christmas celebration at the orphanage), never was disappointed at the response of the church at the Tabernacle in caring for the orphanage residents. In 1887, the year in which the Downgrade Controversy broke and just a bit over a month after he had taken the distressing step of resigning from the Baptist Union, Spurgeon nevertheless strapped on his exuberant spirit for the sake of the children. "The very first thing must be to speak up for our orphans concerning their treat for Christmas," Spurgeon reminded his readers again, as he wrote from Mentone. "Just before leaving England we had boys and girls together, such a company, and we had a little treat; but we promised that, whether C.H.S. could be with them on Christmas-day or not, we would try and make it a glorious day for them." In his persistent, insistent, but inimitably gracious style, Spurgeon opened the larders of his Tabernacle congregation with the appeal,

---

155. S&T, December 1870, 574.

156. S&T, February, 1871.

157. S&T, December 1871, 571.

158. S&T, December 1877, 577.

"Will our friends again bedeck the tables of the fatherless on the day of universal joy? The friend who used to give a new shilling to every orphan is not now able to do it; for which we are truly sorry. Is there no other large heart endowed with a large purse?" It would take £25 to give a shilling to each child, girls and boys, "but it is such a help for pocket-money for quite a time after, that we would like to keep it up." "Ladies and gentlemen, between the ages of 90 and 4," in imitation of a call from the children, Spurgeon spoke, "we, the Stockwell five-hundred, both lads and lasses, will thank you if, by gifts of money, or goods, you will help us to a happy Christmas-day in 1887. Thank you five hundred times over for having done so in years gone by." Then in an unintentional but poignant reminder of the sickness and distress that so often separated Charles and Susannah Spurgeon at this time of the year, he added, "Mrs. Spurgeon will be glad to receive the Christmas money-gifts, and to reply for us. Presents in kind should be directed to Mr. Charlesworth, at The Orphanage, Stockwell."[159]

This constant attention to the children reaped great benefits for them in immediate joy and long-term memories. The first orphan, John Maynard, who spent sixteen years at Stockwell, wrote to the children as an adult: "Tomorrow is Christmas, and as I think of the many enjoyments you will have, your many presents of shillings, fruits, &c, your dinner of roast-beef and plum pudding, and then your hearty cheers, which will make the older people press their hands to their ears; I am reminded of days gone by, and of sixteen merry Christmases spent at the Stockwell Orphanage. To-morrow I shall think more of you while I am trying to make my fifteen little black boys as happy as I can. They will not have shillings, oranges,

roast-beef, or three cheers, and three cheers repeated; but we will kill a pig for them, and make a plum-pudding as best we can."[160]

Spurgeon could not have asked for a more fit and consistent headmaster for the orphanage than Vernon Charlesworth. Like Spurgeon, born in Essex, he served as assistant to one of Spurgeon's close friends in ministry, Newman Hall, at Surrey Chapel. He was a man of the kind of theological commitments, evangelistic intentions, personal refinement, and steady devotion that Spurgeon needed for the position. Fullerton summarized: "His influence on the boys, his advocacy of the orphanage, and his guidance of affairs were a great asset for many years, until in 1914 he finished his course."[161] He served as an elder at the Tabernacle. Charlesworth wrote several hymns including "A Shelter in the Time of Storm." The following poem appeared in *The Sword and the Trowel.*

As you gather around the family board
With its costly dainties piled;
In a cottage near, there is scanty cheer
For the helpless Orphan child.
In the mildly glow of Christmas fire,
While the wind blows cold and wild,
And the blinding sleet drives down the street,
O! think of the Orphan child.

When you rest in your soft and cozy bed,
Ere sleep has your eyes beguiled,
One moment spare, and breathe a prayer
For the comfortless Orphan child.

He once was happy as you are now,
When fortune on him smiled;
Now of parents bereft—in the world he is left
A desolate Orphan child.

---

159. S&T, December 1887, 641.

160. S&T, April 1886, 178; from a letter written on December 24, 1885, by John Maynard at Underhill, Congo River.

161. Fullerton, 244.

And shall he be left in the streets to roam,
As outcast, lone and wild?
"God forbid!" you say; then help, I pray,
To provide for the Orphan child.[162]

On rare occasions a child died. When it happened the usual cause was some debility already present when he, or she, arrived at the orphanage. A young boy named Phillips died on February 2, 1881. Charlesworth wrote for the April *Sword and Trowel* an article entitled "Gone Home" telling the story of Phillips, his sickness, conversion, early piety, and death. Though it was common to use such incidents to enforce spiritual truth and particularly to investigate the spiritual anatomy of child conversion and celebrate the triumph of grace over weakness, and the superiority of eternal life over temporal vigor and strength, its predictability did not diminish its sincerity nor its importance. Life was precarious for the first ten years on average. At birth, the average life for males was thirty-nine years. If a child made it to ten years of age, however, a female would average another sixty years and a male another forty-nine. At forty, a female could on average look toward another thirty-four years and a male to another twenty-six. These statistics show that the first ten years were critical and issues of eternity loomed large for all ministers of the gospel, particularly views of the spiritual state of infants and young children.

Young Phillips' death had been expected. Charlesworth explained, "The little fellow ... had been an inmate of the infirmary upwards of twelve months, and though the object of loving ministries, the disease, which had carried off his parents and four of their children, had taken too firm a hold of his constitution to yield to the skill of either doctors or nurses."[163] One sibling remained, a sister, who was also sick, and came to the infirmary in her last days from an aunt's home to see her brother one last time. She died in the infirmary, and within forty-eight hours so did Phillips. "While there is something inexpressibly sad in recording this closing chapter in the history of a family, the sadness only chastens the joy which the hope inspires that they have all 'gone home.'" Charlesworth wrote of some of the peculiar blessings of heaven and then pointed to the reasons for the specific hope that the dead child was there. After a brief anecdote of the child's expression of love for Jesus, Charlesworth wrote: "He was conscious he loved the Saviour, and he added, 'I do not think I should ever have sought the Saviour, as I have, if it had not been for my illness and pains.' We may not be able to solve the deep mystery of pain," Charlesworth continued, "but we need not entertain a doubt as to its designed ministry." For such scenes and outcomes as this the orphanage was committed. "It must ever be a sacred joy to the subscribers and managers when, in the exercise of their trust, they are able to provide the shelter of a fold for these tender lambs of the flock. We never look upon these little one without regarding the Saviour's command to Peter as intended for the disciples through all time—'Feed my lambs': and we rejoice that we are permitted to hold and exercise the commission it implies."[164]

In 1886, Spurgeon received word that John Maynard (who wrote the Christmas letter), "our first child in the orphanage," was "smitten down with fever on the Congo."[165] This caused "sorrow of no common kind" for all that were involved with the orphanage. He had sailed in August and

---

162. S&T, October 1871, 482.

163. S&T, April 1881, 162.

164. Ibid., 167.

165. S&T, April 1886, 177.

had been there only a few months when he wrote to Vernon Charlesworth and included a letter to the children of the orphanage. Ironically he had included in the letter to Charlesworth the prophetic observation, "You will be glad to know that thus far I have enjoyed excellent health on the Congo, though I am for the present settled at not the healthiest station; for it is here that most of our men have died, within a month or six weeks after arrival. ... I have attended several cases of fever with our boys and workmen on the station, and also the traders down river." After having been at the orphanage for sixteen years, "Sixteen Merry Christmases," he became a chemist and dispenser and moved to Africa to work in one of the English towns, and to learn the language of the area in order to work with the native population. His success at this in Port Elizabeth moved him to try to do more and he soon was preaching with great favor with the "Kaffirs, Fingoes, and Hottentots" as well as the English at Graaf Reinet. Desiring more training for this newly discerned call, he went back to England and became Spurgeon's son a second time by his entrance into the college.[166] Spurgeon described him as "diligent and fervent, active and consecrated, decided and humble." He volunteered for the Congo. "He seemed just the man," Spurgeon observed, "partially acclimatized by having been in a semi-tropical climate, and doubly equipped by a knowledge of medicine as well as divinity." Maynard sailed for the Congo with the Baptist Mission soon to be joined by his chosen wife. At the time Spurgeon received the news of his death, he had no way to give solace to the young lady, and could only write the tragic lines, "She has gone, but when she arrives she will be a widow without ever having been a bride."[167] To Spurgeon, the taking away of the firstfruits of

the orphanage so soon in death posed a peculiar difficulty. He asked for the Lord to comfort the begrieved betrothed and "work a lasting blessing to her in some unforeseen way." For himself, "Bowing our head in silent grief, we can only feel that the ways of the Lord must be right, and therefore his name must be praised."[168]

An important milestone of provision was reached on July 25, 1871 when the first boy left the orphanage to be settled in life set out for Redditch. "May he turn out well," the report stated, "and be the pioneer of many more." The lady who arranged for the opening was thanked, and notice was given that "We shall need more openings for the lads."[169] In the years to come Spurgeon regularly included letters from former residents that were now profitable to the world and to the kingdom. He worked with purpose to "make the boys happy as well as orderly" and believed that "nowhere in the world are there more open countenances, joyful faces, or more obedient children than at the Stockwell Orphanage." In the wake of such care, Spurgeon felt it important to encourage donors with the success of those that spent their time there and then succeeded. "The success in life," Spurgeon emphasized, "of many who have gone out from the institution causes us unfeigned delight: the young men cling to their orphan home in a right loyal manner, and already donations from them are coming in."[170] From New Zealand, one wrote in 1881: "I should like to know how the orphanage is going on now. I expect there are none of the boys whom I knew so well now left there, I often think of the time when I was there too, and feel grateful to God for the way he has led me, for it was owing to the religious instruction I got there that I was led to

---

166. S&T, September 1883, 516.

167. S&T, April 1866, 177.

168. Ibid.

169. S&T, August 1871, 382.

170. S&T, February 1878, 92.

believe on the Lord Jesus Christ." He taught a boys class in a local Wesleyan congregation as he waited for a Baptist church to be founded. He had finished an apprenticeship in a painting and sign-writing business and sent £1 for "the institution which in his hour of need befriended him."[171]

A high moment in the relation between the orphanage and the college came in April 1878 at the college conference when the first graduate from the college that had entered from the orphanage accepted a pastoral calling in Willingham. Mr. Latimer received £10 worth of books subscribed by the trustees, masters, teachers, matrons, nurses, and every body in the orphanage. At this meeting Spurgeon said that he did not believe that the day was too distant when "he should begin to strike out for the Girls' Orphanage." He had waited for some providential indication that it was right and he felt, through several events, "certain premonitions that the Lord meant him to take up the work." He now only waited for the signal.[172]

Girls' Orphanage

In his editorial for the *Sword* for 1871, Spurgeon began preparing his readers for the support of an addition to the orphanage. "A Girl's Orphanage would be of the utmost value," Spurgeon contended, "for now we can only help poor widows who have boys." Besides," he added. "our gallantry sometimes blushes when we are accused of caring only for the male sex." Already with enough to do, Spurgeon believed that this was right and in due time the steward would come to light to provide the "large sum to build the girls' houses." His work would be intensified, "but he who sends the work will give the strength. Our sole aim is to glorify God, and serve his poor peo-ple." He made it clear that his constant requests for money to support new projects did not enrich him one farthing, "but the reverse; nevertheless, those that insinuate that we are well paid for all we do are quite correct, only they mistake the sort of coin."[173]

After a delay of some years, in 1879 Spurgeon's work on the girls' orphanage began. With an initial £50 given by Mrs. Hillyard, another £50 by himself, three other friends followed suit and a fourth gave £100. In 1879, at his anniversary of twenty-five years in London, Spurgeon stated: "On June 19, we were able to make a fair start with the *Girls' Orphanage*, and this to us is the second great advance of 1879." In spite of depression and disaster in almost every quarter, and in contrast to many charitable institutions advertising their abject poverty, Spurgeon reported that "to the honour of our gracious Lord, we wish to bear witness that never have our college and orphanage been so well supported as during this trying season." By September Spurgeon was able to write: "Once more we have to adore the loving-kindness of our faithful and blessed God for having marvelously supplied the wants of the work to which he has called us. Our friends know that we bought a house and grounds called the 'Hawthornes' for £4000." On the very morning that the purchase was to be finalized, July 30, Spurgeon received a letter informing him that a legacy of £1,500 for the Girls' Orphanage had been secured. Soon the entire amount of £4,000 was gathered, the purchase completed, and put in "the hands of the whitewashers and painters." An intervening meadow between the Hawthornes and the boys' orphanage, again by providential intervention, was purchased completing the entire tract of land. The Hawthornes included one house on the

---

171. S&T, August 1881, 419.

172. S&T, May 1878, 226.

173. S&T, 1871, iv.

property, while supporters had promised seven more houses, along with other helps, including "a freight of bricks from Sittingbourne, and some gas fittings from Cheltenham."[174]

In the Annual Report for 1880 Spurgeon retold the story and added the information about what still needed to be done:

> [A]s there are school-rooms also, the contract amounts to £11,100, which is more than we expected; and, as we cannot go into debt, we have decided to leave the two end houses for the present. Then we must provide for roads and drainage, also Bath, Play-hall, Infirmary, Dining Hall, and Furniture and School Apparatus, before the scheme is sufficiently complete to admit the 250 girls contemplated. Here is a grand opportunity for Christian friends to come forward and assist in making the Stockwell Orphanage a complete Institution for 250 fatherless boys and 250 fatherless girls. We believe the money will come as the necessity arises. Past mercy forbids a single doubt. Our treasury is the bounty of God, and therefore our motto is, "The Lord will provide."[175]

Foundation stones for the first four girls' houses were laid on June 22, 1880, at the celebration of Spurgeon's forty-sixth birthday. One was called "The Sermon House" and was given by C. H. Spurgeon and his publishers, Passmore and Alabaster. Other houses were "The Limes" given by Mr. Rickett in memory of five children; "The Olives," the foundation stone laid by Mrs. Samuel Barrow in memory of her husband who had given and collected the amount for the building; and a fourth was erected by gifts from the trustees of the orphanage "to express their joy in this service of love."[176]

Funds for the remaining two proposed houses were not sufficient; memorial stones for the Reading House and the Liverpool House were laid on October 4, in conjunction with the annual meeting of the Baptist Union held that year in London. Spurgeon was unable to attend because of sickness, so he wrote a note to be read by his brother. In light of the prospect of 500 inhabiting the houses in the near future, Spurgeon asked rhetorically where bread would be found for such a crowd. He answered, "Faith sees a sure supply when she knows that thousands will be praying for it." He assured the gathered Baptists that he would rather have their prayers than a gift of £20,000, "for something more than money is needed—health for the children, wisdom for the managers, patience for the teachers, grace for us all."[177] Whether to build a chapel for worship, or convert the dining hall into the worship facility and build a new dining hall, perplexed the leadership at the moment but either would involve a substantial outlay of cash. The report concluded, "We would not spend a sixpence needlessly. No money has been wasted in lavish ornament, or in hideous ugliness." The buildings did not resemble a workhouse or a county jail but "a pleasant residence for those children of whom God declares himself to be the Father." Additional buildings provided no luxury but the fulfillment of necessity. "As we endeavour to lay out money with judicious economy," The report closed, "we feel sure that we shall be trusted in the future as in the past."[178]

Following the close of the report, Spurgeon announced a bazaar to be held at Christmas in the "schoolroom of the Metropolitan Tabernacle" to raise funds, hopefully "Ten Thousand Pounds at the Least," to build an infirmary, a dining hall,

---

174. S&T, 1879, preface, iv. S&T, August 1879, 397; S&T September 1879, 448.

175. S&T, 1880, Annual Report, 378.

176. S&T, 1881, Annual Report, 441.

177. G. Holden Pike, *The Life and Work of Charles Haddon Spurgeon*, 6 vols (London: Cassell & Co., nd) 6:246-47.

178. S&T, 1881, Annual Report, 441.

a large bath, and a play hall, as well as to make necessary roads, and lay out the grounds. The last word was with Spurgeon: "Friends, help us to complete this blessed work!"[179]

In 1881, he included an artist's rendition of the buildings and ground and gave a brief statement of the challenges of the present and his vision for the future:

> The entrance and dining hall for the boys, on the left, are familiar objects to our readers. Something similar will be required on the right hand for the girls, with a chapel or large hall for our great public meetings, to be placed where the artist has sketched a thicket of trees. For this expense we have not even made an estimate at present, but will be met, we hope, by *the Bazaar next Christmas*. The left-hand range of houses is all occupied by our two hundred and fifty boys, and the handsomer pile on the right, with covered way in front of the lower windows, contains the houses and schools for two hundred fifty girls. We do not wish to see the orphanage increase beyond this size; for this number of children the ground-space is admirably adapted, and we may say of it, "there is room enough and to spare." The number of children is quite enough for one management, if we only consider the domestic arrangements, while financially the burden is quite sufficient, and we shall need extra-ordinary help to carry the work to completion. So much, however, has been done that no excuse for unbelief remains; ... Friends will scarcely need to be told that the great square which makes the orphanage is not surrounded by fields, as our woodcut would imply; that is a freak of the draughtsman's imagination; yet the site is open, airy, and healthy; and being under the eye of the people and friends at the Tabernacle, it is more likely to be cared for than if it stood shivering alone upon some bleak hillside. The advantages of a country site are very great, but for convenience of oversight, for securing

sympathy, and for command of the markets our position could not be excelled.[180]

As supporters of the orphanage prepared for the bazaar in 1881, Spurgeon gave encouragement through the pages of the magazine. He had used his sword to stir up the readers to give him mortar for his trowel. In his spirited appeals for financial support, Spurgeon knew that he was writing to many supporters that he had never seen, "but to whom he speaks week by week and month by month through the printed page." They had helped him carry on all his institutions up till then and he had "no fear that they will desert him now." Mr. Charlesworth had stated that between £10,000 and £12,000 would be needed for the completion of the girls' portion of the orphanage. Spurgeon hoped that "by the beginning of next year, by the Bazaar and other means, a good portion of this sum will be in hand." They should write at once to let him know what they were willing to do and by this means "gladden his heart."[181] A celebration of Spurgeon's forty-seventh birthday brought an offering of £1,500 to the general fund, both for boys and girls, but the completion of funding for the soon-to-be-completed girls' house was needed. He was pleased to announce a legacy left by Mr. Vickery provided all the fittings for the school rooms at a cost of about £300. The traveling of the orphanage choir always brought money as well as new donors, so Spurgeon, finding the idea of a choir quite useful for this purpose, asked that their schedule be filled up— "We shall be very grateful to all who by helping this work will bring grist to the orphanage mill, which is for ever grinding."[182]

179. Ibid., 444.

180. S&T, March 1881, 133.

181. S&T, July 1881, 354.

182. S&T, October 1883, 564.

In August of 1882, he announced through the *Sword* that he had decided to "proceed at once with the erection of the next portion of the Girls' Orphanage buildings."[183] Spurgeon had invited friends to attend a *fête* in celebration of his forty-eighth birthday "by liberal contributions for the maintenance of this holy work of caring for the widow and the fatherless."[184] That plus a legacy of £900 plus some silver plate and a £1,000 contribution from "a friend" brought the building fund to around £4,000, encouraging Spurgeon to proceed with the laundry, leaving the dining hall, kitchen, and master's house until later. In February 1883, he thanked his generous donors for the liberal help they gave in supporting all the institutions. "The addition of girls to the orphanage has much increased the need," Spurgeon commented, and added, "but we joyfully believe that the Lord is in proportion multiplying the number of our helping friends."[185] Fullerton gives the girls' wing very short comment: "Though the extension was undertaken with some hesitance, similar experiences of God's goodness attended this enterprise, the necessary funds were forthcoming, the quadrangle was completed, with Infirmary, Gymnasium and Dining Hall, and there it stands to-day [1920], a monument of philanthropy and faith."[186]

Colportage

Robert Shindler, pastor at Eythorn, had become an advocate of the colportage work and made several observations in its favor after its second year of operations. The Second Annual Report of 1869 contained remarks from Shindler in addition to the statistical report, comments from the committee, and the testimonies of the men themselves. Shindler had seen its advantages in "country districts," especially where basic evangelical truth was not widely disseminated, "a description which will apply with alarming truthfulness to thousands of parishes in Great Britain." He saw it as a valuable means of evangelization through the sale of good books. It served as a pioneer to more established evangelistic work. Again, it would be a valuable auxiliary to "existing churches and missionary operations."[187]

The colporteurs themselves found their work very difficult, but the difficulty bears direct proportion to its necessity and its fulfilling character. They spoke of "timidity" and "backwardness" in spiritual matters, and saw others as "very dark and unlearned" and with such a strong love of sin "that the name of a religious book makes them at once" refuse a purchase. Similarly another reported that "the noes were unanimous." Often they had to contend with opposition from "bigoted Papists," one, a woman that stood before the colporteur "with the poker, and her other fist clenched, like a lion" as he spoke to her about Jesus. Gradually, however, they saw an openness develop with their persevering labor through their appointed district where many had come to look upon them "as real messengers of mercy." These contacts eventually resulted in many opportunities for evangelistic work. Phrases that indicate the workers' confidence in the effectiveness of their work deal with the internal power of truth, if not the certain conversion of souls: "What a blessing that book was to his soul," "becoming anxious about her soul," "some passage of God's truth brought her everlasting peace." Though discreet in their conclusions, sometimes the book-men would find a case they looked upon as genuine conversion:

183. S&T, August 1882, 447.

184. S&T, June 1882, 316.

185. S&T, February 1883, 95.

186. Fullerton, 244.

187. S&T, March 1869, 135.

I learned on visiting S------, that the words "Shew us they mercy, O Lord," which were on the cover of a "Friendly Visitor," had taken such effect on the heart of a woman that she went from neighbour to neighbour, entreating them to show her "what she was to do to be saved," and pray for her. All refused, then she thought God told her within that there was mercy still which she believed in, and obtained, for she said to me when I again entered her house, "since you were here, Christ has saved my soul and forgiven all my sins;" we prayed together, and her breathings were fervent. I believe this is a genuine case.[188]

The committee looked at the overall experience, work already done, possible impact for the gospel and were convinced that this was a "suitable and practicable method of meeting the necessities of our rural districts." All over England, no organization met the people on their own level, and in their own homes, or offered an opportunity for a regular supply of religious literature. Plenty of novels and trashy periodicals circulate in increasing numbers. Were it not for the colporteur, in many locations, that would be the only class of reading procurable. The knowledge that a healthy alternative, that is, the glad tidings of salvation, cold supplant these injurious works through the colporteurs encouraged the committee. The accounts testified of an increase in interest, not from a mere love of novelty, but from the substance of the contents. In an optimistic query, the committee encouraged the project—"May we not believe that the 48,000 publications supplied by this association during the past year, will, with God's blessing, in many instances tell upon the minds of the purchasers, and lead them to think seriously of the concerns of their soul?"[189]

Selling books was not the colporteurs' only labor. Many of the men had assisted in the revival of evangelistic work among the churches in their districts. This labour did not foster a sectarian spirit, for their intent was to assist any denomination "for the one object of spreading the fame of Jesus, and the glad tidings of his salvation." The committee did not express surprise that large numbers attended these meetings. Proclamation of the simple gospel of our Lord with a warm heart was calculated to bring earnest seekers. This extension of the colporteurs' usefulness prompted a desire to extend the work to every village. "England is *our* field," they emphasized, "and though many parts are doubtless supplied with colporteurs by private individuals, and therefore to a great extent unknown, yet there is no lack of room." If many churches and private individuals would contribute "the small amount of £30 per annum," it would enable the committee "to carry the work into every county." General subscriptions remained of equal importance to sustain the work already under way. In words that readers had grown to anticipate, Spurgeon added, "In this matter each of our friends may help."[190]

The very next year Spurgeon urged the work on his readers with the observation, "The Colportage Association deserves a hundred times the support it now has. We wish some person, less loaded than we are, would take up the enterprise." He was suggesting that someone with sufficient zeal and savvy undertake the enlargement of the public's participation in this work, because "There ought to be a society for it as large as the Religious Tract Society. If it is worth while to print books, it must surely be equally important to sell them."[191]

---

188. Ibid., 136.

189. Ibid., 137 .

190. Ibid.

191. S&T, December 1870, 574.

In 1874, after the fifth year of operations for the Colportage Society, Spurgeon confessed his initial fears that "this society would turn out to be one child too many." His love for it increased through the years and its work was always a source of both fascination and satisfaction, but the support for it always lagged just a bit behind comfort and thus kept a constant pressure on Spurgeon's mind and taxed his creativity in finding ways to plead for funds. He had observed an increasing stability, however, and felt optimistic about the colportage work and reported that it moved at a "healthy pace", with new ministries opened in Worcester, Studley, and Croydon. Other places would open up speedily and some stability and identification would be given to the society by its being housed in the new facilities of the college. He saw it soon emerging as one of the largest societies in England, having thirty-five workers then deployed. "Priest-ridden" England needed the work of spreading Bibles and evangelical literature.[192]

The pace remained slow; Spurgeon was a bit frustrated as to how something so word-centered, so evangelistic, and so capable of penetrating the dark places of England did not catch the spiritual imagination of his readership. At first Spurgeon was able to point to the economic climate as sufficient reason for the lagging of funds in 1879. "Some few matters of income are in arrears," he informed the people, "especially the fund of the Colportage." Neither the Pastor's absence nor any failure of generosity on the part of friends at home explained the fact. He looked instead to "the general depression of trade throughout the country, which has diminished the sales of the colporteurs and also made it difficult for the local committees to keep up their guarantees." A gift of £160

preserved the colportage work for a time, but £1,000 was needed "to put the work into a sound condition." For the moment, it was kept from absolute bankruptcy and his faith and expectation received new life. "We do not abate our assurance that God will send means for his own work. Will our friends kindly read the article upon Colportage in this number of the magazine?"[193] This was in May.

In August, a deeper perplexity and distress seemed evident in his pleadings. "It becomes increasingly evident that the objects and value of the Colportage Association are not known as they should be, beyond a very limited circle of friends who have watched its operations, and appreciated its value in spreading evangelical truth among people." Spurgeon hoped to increase interest and commitment by sharing reports of some of the county associations connected with the Tabernacle ministry. The costly but profitable labors of these unsung gospel purveyors, as well as the poignancy and drama of some cases, could help arrest serious attention. One local association employed six colporteurs who mainly visited villages, hamlets, and isolated houses, in order to sell copies of God's word, and books and periodicals of a healthy moral character. They frequently occupied, with great acceptability, the pulpits of some of the village chapels and stations and worked in the Sunday School and in week-night Bible classes. Another association reported an increase of sales of nearly 50 percent on last year's report in spite of unusual interruptions to the work of the agent. One interruption came as a result of seven weeks' severe illness, brought on by overwork. A second came "through injuries received in an attack made upon him by three drunken men, and by whom he was left uncon-

---

192. S&T, October 1874, 491.

193. S&T, May 1879, 242.

scious on the road during one of the most severe nights in the past winter."[194] Surely an example of suffering for the gospel, and right there in Christian England, would spark the zeal of Gospel-loving Christians.

A September 1879 word from Spurgeon continued the appeal: "Will all our readers examine carefully the annual report of this society, and give it all the help they can? No more needful or efficient agency exists, and yet we have to live from hand to mouth in reference to it from lack of capital and shortness of funds." But, merely daily bread might be what God had ordained for this work, for the "good Lord does not leave the work actually to fail, but finds us just enough in the hour of emergency to prevent the machinery from actually standing still." As a matter of conscious and responsible stewardship, however, for those that see and sympathize with such a spiritually profitable effort, and understand its needs, a faithful engagement would mean that the month-by-month financial straits would soon cease.[195] By the time the year was closing, and Spurgeon composed his preface to *The Sword and the Trowel,* he lamented, "O that we could do more for Jesus! Our Colportage, which is a great blessing to thousands, does not yet increase to dimensions worthy of its value. It is no small thing to have seventy or eighty workers diligently engaged in spreading healthy literature and visiting the poor; but we ought to have four times as many, and would have them if the funds were forthcoming."[196]

The next year, Spurgeon used the decrease in the number of colporteurs as a positive enforcement of the continued pressing need for them. In what would surely be seen in contemporary political rhetoric as a masterful spin, Spurgeon reported, "things are looking more hopeful for the Colportage Association, one feature of the outlook being that friends who had been compelled to suspend the work in some districts for lack of funds again apply for a colporteur, which shows that were the agency has been fairly tried, its great value was appreciated, though local circumstances compelled a temporary suspension of the work."[197] Spurgeon told how one book, passed around from the original to other persons, resulted in the conversion of several individuals, and an entire family in America was converted through a tract that had been left in Shropshire and sent by post to them from relatives. A couple in an isolated part of New Forest was converted through the visit of a colporteur. The one reporting this conversion argued: "Indeed, five or six thousand magazines and books cannot go into the homes of these people every year, replacing bad literature or none at all, without, through the divine blessing, gradually but surely elevating, refining, and Christianizing them." Those that would ponder the benefits of this work would soon enable the committee to increase the staff from sixty-four, up to the number of eighty that had been employed the year before. Some could provide the yearly stipend of £40 to support a local agent, but others, unable to do so, could contribute to the general fund, "which continually needs help."[198]

The reports each month always showed advance in the distribution of literature but often included other benefits that accompanied the work of these men. A report in 1882 mentioned the blessings of God on the Gospel Temperance Movement in one of the "darkest villages" on this workers' territory. One hundred, he claimed,

194. S&T, August 1879, 398.

195. S&T, September 1879, 448.

196. S&T, 1879, Preface, iv.

197. S&T, March 1880, 142.

198. Ibid., 142-43.

had "signed the pledge, and donned the blue ribbon. Praise the Lord!" This had happened in a five-month period; they remained staunch and true, were anxious about their soul's salvation, and "now instead of being found in the alehouse singing the devil's songs, they are to be heard singing the songs of Zion." Notorious drunkards had been saved, and now they "are respectably clothed, and in their right mind, and as the result we have been enabled to sell books to them, and others who before spent the greater part of their wares in strong drink and tobacco." Sobriety was good for the colporteurs' business. Another individual had thrown his pipe into the canal, given up beer, signed the pledge, and with the money he saved ordered from the colporteur *The Life of Christ* and other books as well.[199]

Spurgeon continued to emphasize the pure nectar of the work of colportage and the ongoing need for some financial breakthrough to put it on solid ground financially. "The colporteur is the bearer of light amid the darkness of ignorance, of truth where the errors of sacerdotalism and skepticism prevail, of medicine to counteract the unhealthy production of the press, and of the tidings of salvation to a lost and guilty world."[200] At the same time he kept pointing to the need for some to sponsor this ministry and increase the number. After reporting the way that some had taken up the task and used ingenious methods and consistent zeal to support the work, Spurgeon said: "We marvel every day that this holy service is not taken up on all hands. We will not weary our readers and ourselves by arguing the matter attain."[201] Spurgeon had resigned himself to the cycle, and there it stood, either limping along with unsure support,

or soaring with the glory of setting forth gospel truth.

Anxiety for Their Support

Wayland Hoyt joined with others in celebrating Spurgeon's perfect mixture of trust and energetic genius. Earlier in his ministry, Spurgeon thought that he might seek to emulate George Muller in promoting a "Believe and See" method of raising funds, but he came eventually to differ with Muller.[202] Hoyt reported that Spurgeon prayed steadily for God's prosperity upon all his enterprises but "never sought in the least to cover the fact that as thoroughly and strenuously as possible he put his hand to plying second causes." As Hoyt observed, and as this chapter has shown, "He asked for contributions and various support as often as he prayed." He expected great things of God, but "none the less did he himself attempt, and urge others to attempt, great things for God." Hoyt spoke of Spurgeon's "business habits" and "his magnificent, shrewd, English common sense" as the rallying point for divine provision and human effort. While he labored, "he depended more trustfully than any man I ever knew upon the prayer-hearing and prayer-answering God."[203]

While close examination of Spurgeon's life confirms the impression of his reliance upon and trust in a God that hears prayer, as well as his personal labors for the maintenance of every endeavor, he nevertheless proved to be so radical in both directions that it created a mental and spiritual tension difficult to manage. On the one hand, he minimized the personal dimension of the success of the work. While "kind friends" spoke of his "genius for organization" and his "great practical common sense" he rested everything on divine

---

199. S&T, August 1882, 447.

200. S&T, February 1883, 97.

201. S&T, April 1883, 204.

202. Lewis Drummond, *Spurgeon: Prince of Preachers* (Grand Rapids, MI: Kregel, 1992), 420.

203. Hoyt, 16, 17.

providence. With sincere placidity and resignation he could write: "At the close of twenty-five years we see a vast machinery in vigorous operation, in better working condition than ever it was; and, as to means and funds, perfectly equipped, although it has no other resources than, 'My God shall supply all your need, according to his riches in glory in Christ Jesus.' Gratitude bows her head, and sings her own song to her Well-beloved, to whom it belongs."[204] In 1882, before leaving for a time of rest on the Continent, he noted that "six hundred persons are dependent upon our incomings, and it would be a serious thing to contemplate a time of distress; but we do not contemplate it. On the contrary, we believe that our God will fill up all our need, and the more needs we have, the more room there will be to contain the fullness of his liberality."[205] Upon his return from this respite, however, he was forced to comment, "Note the smallness of all contributions during our absence. We must coal the ship again."[206]

With this reality looking him dead in the face, Spurgeon labored with his tendency to despondency and the sheer magnitude of what he had undertaken in adding so many other institutions that cried for his personal attention in the matter of generating support in addition to a mammoth congregation and the day-by-day needs endemic to maintaining such a flock. When the college expanded in 1875 to ninety-two men Spurgeon announced "our weekly payments cause our cash in hand to melt like snow in the sun." The output

of ministers demanded by the needs of the times brought even a large sum given "very nearly to the end of our tether." He asked for constant prayer, for the "work is a very responsible and anxious one. Who is sufficient for these things?"[207] The weight of this responsibility and its impact on Spurgeon's mental state will be extended in the chapter on sickness and depression. One example of the combination of trust, anxiety, his plying second causes, and his magnificent, shrewd English common sense is seen in a paragraph about the orphanage.

> The orphanage funds are reduced so low that at the time of writing this paragraph we have nothing in hand to go on with: nevertheless we are not afraid that want will happen to us, for the Lord never has failed us and never will. We have a daily demand for £10, and sometimes, when pain makes us low in spirit, the arch-enemy suggests that we shall run aground, but we have not listened to his suggestion for a moment; we believe and are sure that the Lord will provide, and we are looking for abundant supplies with as much confidence as we look for the rising sun. We cannot, however, forbear the remark that those of God's servants who have wealth, and believe that we are faithfully and efficiently conducting the orphanage, ought not to allow these trials of our faith to happen to us, or to be so frequent. If it be a work laid on the hearts of believers, let them see to it.[208]

---

204. S&T, Preface, 1878, iii, iv.

205. S&T, October 1882, 546.

206. S&T, January 1883, 43.

207. S&T, October 1875, 498.

208. S&T, November 1874, 542.

11

Personal Theory and Preferences in the Production of Godly Literature

The power to read is a peril rather than a benefit, unless it can be exercised upon right material.[1]

And now, reader, if thou art a renewed soul, may our covenant God feed thee, keep thee, and perfect thee; and may the words of thy brother in Christ be the means of some little comfort and edification to thee.[2]

Spurgeon scoffed at publishers that offered rough and destructive material to children. The mental hunger incurred through learning to read must be met with good food, the right nutriment, and every author and publisher who attempts it deserves encouragement. Regretting the "fearful amount of scandalous literature" sold to boys in little newspaper shops, stories about "rawhead and bloody-bones tales, lives of burglars and highwaymen, and even worse stories," Spurgeon was determined that he would do all he could to encourage and produce godly literature for all ages.[3] He would warn against the useless, the heretical, and damaging, and recommend the edifying and positively interesting.

Books, Books Everywhere, Nor Anything to Read
This ideal he contemplated after years of pursuing the goal in his own writing and in the distribution of literature through Mrs. Spurgeon's Book Fund. He wanted her work, inaugurated in 1875, "to be sustained and increased till no needy preacher of the gospel should find himself destitute of daily food for his mind."[4] He pointed to this effort, not a soured dream, but as a hope to some degree fulfilled with promise of more godly effect still. He entreated the "good Lord [to] send his Spirit with the books given, and make them to be a testimony to the gospel of grace, a comfort to the servants of the Lord, and a means of revival to the churches among which they labour." The books went to every part of the church of God, even to men of doubtful orthodoxy. This door for distribution of such literature, now open and effectual, presented vast opportunities for good. "It may be

1. S&T, October 1874, 489.
2. SS, 2:vii.
3. S&T, October 1874, 489.
4. S&T, 1875, "Preface," iv.

that the truth may influence the preacher, and through him may spread to his congregation." A candle lit in dark days shed precious and necessary light, and to "put sound doctrine in the way of ministers is to cast salt into the fountain, and should the Lord use it to the healing of the spring the streams will be sweet."[5]

Spurgeon knew as well as any that nineteenth-century England, the Victorian Age, produced a massive amount of literature and was celebrated world-wide for its output by such notable figures as the Brownings, Alfred Tennyson, Charles Dickens, Thomas Carlyle, George Eliot, and others. One could not ignore a compelling literary style and powerful thought simply by marking it off as unorthodox. When George M'Cree analyzed both the literary style and the theological viewpoint of these writers, Spurgeon applauded the attempt of someone to take "in hand the mystic, pretentious skepticism of the period, a fashionable vanity whose day has been too long already." Particularly helpful was the author's exposure of the subtleties of the alliance of poetry and deep thought with error. "Few could so well have distinguished between talent and its perversion, genius and its aberrations." In reprobating heresy, which Spurgeon often did, one must not fail to give sincere admiration to the talent and ability of an author, which he also did. Conversely, in admiration of originality, one must not wink at deadly error. M'Cree admitted the beauty of the cup, but all the more vehemently warned against the "poisonous draught which it conveys to us."[6] We find Spurgeon always seeking to bring these two together, edifying, God glorifying content and engaging magnetic style.

Spurgeon wanted his literary productions to provide "entertainment and edification."[7] He looked at nature and saw that the first was normally bound to the second, for God had joined them together. Note the beauty and usefulness of fruit, the flight of a painted butterfly among herbs of the garden, and how the "cerulean blue of the cornflower smiles forth from amid the stalks of the wheat." The High Priest's robes had exuberant beauty mixed with highly typological redemptive themes, and the sacred candlesticks provided not only light but had "knops and flowers upon the branches." Even so, Christian magazines must not be relegated to "pious platitudes, heavy discourses, and dreary biographies of nobodies." He wanted the literature to be "as vivacious and attractive as the best of amusing serials, and yet as deeply earnest and profitable as the soundest of divines would desire."[8]

About a chronicler of British non-conformity Spurgeon made the comment: "If the writer had possessed genius and literary ability, this might have been a highly interesting work; but as the writer's sole qualification is his honesty of purpose, the work is most reliable and dull." Had the writer used a bit of the wit that he condemned because of his lack of it, he might have secured both the reading of his book and remuneration commensurate with his labor.[9] Spurgeon tried, therefore, month by month through the pages of *The Sword and the Trowel* to pour out edifying and educating material in an attractive and earnest, and at times witty, way.

Both by example and encouragement we find this combination in an 1871 article entitled "Use the Pen." Spurgeon stated his view of the importance of literature in the spread of the gospel. He reminded young pastors (he viewed the field as a thirty-seven-year-old) that "two fields of usefulness" were open to them. They should regard the

---

5. S&T, March 1885, 107.

6. S&T, April 1876, 184.

7. S&T, Preface 1875.

8. Ibid.

9. S&T, November 1882, 591.

utterance of truth with the living voice as their main work calling for their chief attention, but "the publishing of the same truth by means of the press is barely second in importance, and should be used to the full measure of each man's ability."[10]

Spurgeon frequently reminded readers of his books and *The Sword and The Trowel* that by a little effort on their part to expand the subscription base or recommend and give his books they could greatly expand his usefulness, and share in it themselves, without increasing his labor. Even so he told these young ministers that "it is a surprising thought that what is written to-day in our study may in a few weeks be read beyond the Alleghanies [*sic*], and before long may lift up its voice at the Antipodes." So marvelous was the enduring nature of the press that a well-crafted sentence might still be forming a mind 500 years hence. "The possibility of doing good to the souls of men is a grand incentive which needs no other to supplement it, and such a possibility beyond all question exists when warm-hearted thought is expressed in telling language, and scattered broadcast in type among the masses."[11]

They should look to their goosequills, "your Gillets, or your Waverleys, and see if you cannot write for Jesus." Spurgeon had seen his share of poor aggravating literature, as will be noted later, and would not mind if a great fire were loosed in London that consumed ninety-nine of a hundred books—a fine purification. As well, he would on bended knee beg most preachers to avoid the temptation to put their thoughts in print. But for the man who begins to burn with something to say, let him practice composition until he can express himself plainly and interestingly and write for readers. Take advantage of periodicals, let them serve the cause of true religion, and

dare to be a moulder of the public mind. Though young men should be determined to write, they also should be content to write through serious labor on style and interesting content. Do not print that which cost the writer nothing. "Read good authors, that you may know what English is," Spurgeon advised; "you will find it to be a language very rarely written nowadays, and yet the grandest of all human tongues."[12]

His frustration with poor writing often appears in his book reviews, a section that became one of the most popular and influential features of the magazine. A kind spirit and orthodox intentions did not justify insipid prose or soporific style. The beauty of the language and the clarity and interest of the style should not suffer in service of truth, but should be employed as the most fitting display of the love of truth. God is a God of beauty and proportion and symmetry and he comes to us as the Word, both in flesh and in Scripture. As guardians of the Word, Christians must not be slipshod in the use of words. At the same time, Spurgeon would not suffer fools easily in their folly. Arrogance of language and prideful singularity and boastful ambience of style and content would cause Spurgeon to engage all the talent he had for destruction by ridicule. He did not pledge an easy time for anyone that wanted him to say something about the communicative power of a literary production.

One of the most unvarnished examples of this kind of critical response came when Spurgeon reviewed *The Interpreter: Some Selected Interpretations of Scripture* by S. R. Bosanquet. It was assured of a speedy sale, Spurgeon quipped, "if readers will only recommend this book as much as the author admires it." Spurgeon illustrated the "modesty" of the writer by quoting his dismissive

---

10. S&T, August 1871, 355.

11. Ibid.

12. Ibid., 355-57.

attitude toward the entire history of interpretation on the author's selected passages, and closed with his own dismissal, "Dry, dull, dogmatic is our humble estimation of this interpretation."[13] Another embarrassment for a totally different style of book carried the brief notice: "Five sentimental love stories written in the gushing style so dear to the soul of boarding-school young ladies. What more can we say to recommend the non-purchase of this volume?"[14]

Remarking on a book, the content of which would certainly please Spurgeon as it showed the evils of "State-Churchism," he admitted that he did not "possess fortitude sufficient to read it through." The author possessed the stuff of martyrs not only in opposing the system of church and state union, should persecuting times return, but "he is so thoroughly dry that we are sure he would burn gloriously."[15] Spurgeon exemplified his advice to write "transparent words, such as bear your meaning upon their forefront." Writers should aim to excel, never to rest content, produce good copy that will only be the step to something better. "This is a great work," were the first words by which he recommended *The History of Protestantism* by Wylie, but he feared that "before the work is all complete a good many readers will be weary of it." Not because of its content, for on that account he wanted to see it in the hands of every Englishman, but because "we find it rather prosy." Though he disliked the genre of fiction, he recognized that the writers employed a style that was attractive. "Only now and then do we meet with an historian whose style is as charming as that of the writer of fiction," and Mr. Wylie certainly did not match that mark.[16]

The purpose, however, of excellent composition is that it might carry with power the message of truth. Manner is important, but matter is more so. "It is folly," Spurgeon aphorized, "to open your mouth merely to show your teeth." Have something to say or leave the ink in the bottle. But try. Burn half a ton of paper in the trying and when a page is produced that is not more fit for the fire than for reading, print it. "To be a soul winner by your books when your bones have mouldered is an ambition worthy of the noblest genius, and even to have brought hearts to Jesus by an ephemeral paper in a halfpenny periodical is an honour which a cherub might envy."[17] He warned against any attempt at poetry. "Write reason before you write rhyme," he admonished with all the earnest frustration he could muster, for throughout his life he increased in his amazement at the vain attempts at poetry he received for review. They should subject their writing to criticism, not be thin-skinned, focus on fact, not sentiment, and resist worrying readers with "ill-timed moralisings and forced reflections." Never pen a sentence that on death-bed reflections you would want to blot. Should these encouragements be attended well, Spurgeon would have no cause to repent of his advice to "use the pen."[18]

To make one's writing worth reading, a few simple rules would help. Virtue embraces brevity. "Be Short," Spurgeon admonished. Aches and ills may be borne if we know they are over soon. Even pleasures become insipid if they are protracted beyond the limits of reason and convenience. "Long visits, long stories, long essays, long exhortations, and long prayers" seldom profit those who have to endure them. Tell your message when you speak, and hold your peace. "If you write, boil down two sentences into one,

---

13. S&T, October 1878, 506.

14. Ibid., 507.

15. S&T, February 1874, 92.

16. S&T, February 1876, 89.

17. S&T, August 1871, 358.

18. Ibid., 359.

and three words into two."[19] A translation of a manuscript of lecture notes by Franz Delitzsch, *Old Testament History of Redemption,* modeled the combination of profundity and brevity in its style. Full of "verve, suggestiveness, and fullness of thought," Spurgeon looked upon the volume's style as "gold in the nugget, a forest in an acorn, and a sermon in a sentence." Several examples from the translated manuscript elicited Spurgeon's observation, "Such specimens as these will show the kind of writing which Delitzsch indulges in, and the sort of sentences that Mr. Curtiss [the translator] would not willingly let die."[20] Learn to be short, and increase the value.

Spurgeon also would admonish, "Be clear." For Spurgeon, clarity meant that every level of society could benefit. If they could read, they could understand; if they could not read but could hear, they still could understand. Spurgeon did not aim for a reputation of erudition in his writing but for plainness and clarity. This goal combined with his powers of imagination, his massive vocabulary, his wit, his penetration into human nature, and intense desire to attract readers of all strata of society, made for some amazingly attractive literary passages. Given the occasional flourish of style, his greatest pleasure lay in the desire of the common and uneducated to find and read, or hear others read, Spurgeon. When he learned that the boys of the orphanage liked to read *The Sword and the Trowel,* he wrote a short article for them. In explaining his pleasure in their interest, he told them about a man that, because he did not like Spurgeon's plain way of speaking, "took the trouble to write and tell me he had met with some poor negroes who were reading my sermons with great delight." His correspondent was not surprised because his evaluation of Spurgeon's material was

that it was "just such as ignorant black people would be sure to relish." While the letter-writer thought that he would send Spurgeon into "a fit of the blues after that slap in the face," Spurgeon told the boys, "I was as jubilant as I knew how to be, and praised God with my whole heart, because even an enemy admitted that the Lord had taught me how to reach the hearts of the poor."[21] From this incident Spurgeon gathered that his sermons in print "were clear enough to be understood by anybody who was not so conceited as to darken his own mind with pride." And certainly, Spurgeon added, if the boys read the magazine it can be neither over people's head nor "can it be said to be very dull and dreary."[22]

His Own Writing as a Ministry

One of his deacon's Joseph Passmore, who owned, along with his partner, James Alabaster, a publishing house, saw massive potential in putting Spurgeon in print. Spurgeon had no aversion to this at all, but had conceived publishing as an extension of his calling even earlier. "Before I ever entered a pulpit," so he reported, "the thought had occurred to me that I should one day preach sermons which would be printed." This vision emerged from his regular reading of the penny sermons of Joseph Irons.[23] From Spurgeon's pen had come, in 1853, the first number of a short series entitled *Waterbeach Tracts* and, in the *Baptist Reporter,* his testimony of his resolution to be baptized in a scriptural way due to the conversation with a clergyman in Maidstone. After his move to London in 1854, two brief expositions from Psalm 84 appeared in *The Baptist Messenger.* Also in 1854 the first of his sermons to be printed appeared in the long-established *Penny Pulpit* published by James Paul.

---

19. S&T, September 1871, 408.

20. S&T, April 1882, 193.

21. S&T, November 1874, 506.

22. Ibid.

23. *Autobiography,* 1:393.

When Passmore suggested in 1854 the publication of the sermon on a weekly basis, Spurgeon accepted the proposal. Passmore had been kind to Spurgeon from the beginning of his ministry at New Park Street, and, in response to a present from Passmore, Spurgeon wrote: "I trust the harmony between us may never receive the slightest jar, but continue even in Heaven. We have, I trust, just commenced a new era; and, by God's blessing, we will strive to make it a glorious one to our Church."[24] How much of a new era they had begun would rapidly be known. They began with the first sermon of 1855 on the immutability of God based on Malachi 3:6,[25] and continued printing without intermission for thirty-six years during Spurgeon's life. Until May 10, 1917, when the paper shortages of World War I made the cessation necessary, unpublished sermons continued to appear on a weekly schedule, bound yearly as part of the *Metropolitan Tabernacle Pulpit* series. James Alabaster died in 1892 several months after Spurgeon, but Passmore lived until August 1895 and continued printing and publishing all of Spurgeon's works until his death. When James Alabaster died, *The Sword and the Trowel* carried this note:

> On Saturday, November 19, just as these "Notes" were being printed, Mr. James Alabaster was "called home," after being laid aside less than a week. His loss is most keenly felt by his family and partners in business, especially by the head of the firm, Mr. Joseph Passmore, with whom Mr. Alabaster had been in close personal friendship for nearly forty years. We have tried to picture the meeting [in heaven] between the beloved Pastor and his esteemed publisher; for, although Mr. Alabaster was a staunch adherent of the Church of England, he loved the same Lord whom Mr. Spurgeon served,

and was an equally devout believer in the faith once for all delivered to the saints.[26]

Not only did Passmore and Alabaster contribute to the massive impact of Spurgeon's ministry world-wide, they made it possible for him to be one of the main contributors to the various benevolences that he began from the Tabernacle. In an undated letter, but clearly sometime after the sale of Spurgeon material had begun to grow exponentially, Spurgeon noted with sincere gratitude to Passmore this unexpected by-product of publishing: "As you have to-day paid to me the largest amount I have ever received from your firm at one time, I seize the opportunity of saying, what I am sure you know already, that I am most sincerely thankful to God for putting me into your hands in my publishing matters." The liberality of Passmore and his partner had "been as great as it has been spontaneous." Even beyond, or without, personal benefit, Spurgeon delighted to help his friends prosper. They had been kind and generous as his "share of profits has always exceeded my expectations, and the way it has been given has been ever more valuable than the money itself." Spurgeon assured him, "Your growing welfare lies very near my heart, and nothing gives me more pleasure than to see you advance in prosperity."[27]

Financial matters in the business of publishing were not merely serendipitous to Spurgeon, however, for he quickly learned that business is business. Apparently, despite massive sales for thirty years of *The Saint and His Saviour*, published in 1855 before he had decided to do all through Passmore and Alabaster, Spurgeon received only the initial £50 contract price from James S. Virtue. The amount was virtually nothing in comparison with the profit that accrued to the publisher from its sale, but Virtue

---

24. Spurgeon, *Letters*, To Mr. Passmore, May 17, 1854.

25. *Autobiography* 1:394.

26. S&T, December 1892.

27. Spurgeon, *Letters*, Letters to Mr. Joseph Passmore (undated).

"never deemed it wise to add anything to it." Virtue also sold the sheets to Appleton & Co. in America who turned around and sold them to Sheldon, Blakeman & Co. Spurgeon said that he never repeated that mistake and never put another work into the hands of James Virtue. Spreading the gospel through literature is a good thing, but who gains earthly prosperity through the labors involved is not unimportant. Fairness in that matter meant that no cooling of affection marred the relationship with Passmore and partner through the years. Spurgeon felt perfectly free with his publishers and prodded them to excellence in a most curiously humorous way. During the publishing process for *Morning by Morning*, Spurgeon reminded his publishers that timeliness was absolutely essential because of the press of his own schedule. He did it in such a charming way that none could be offended but only endeared by the reprimand:

> Dear Mr. Passmore,—Have you retired from business? For, if not, I should be glad of proofs for the month of November of a book entitled *Morning by Morning* which, unless my memory fails me, you began to print. I was to have had some matter on Monday; and it is now Wednesday. Please jog the friend who has taken your business, and tell him that YOU always were the very soul of punctuality, and that he must imitate you.
>
> I send a piece for October 31, for I can't find any proof for that date.
>
> Please let the gentleman who has taken your business have it soon.
>
> Yours ever truly,
>
> C. H. SPURGEON.

P.S. Has Mr. Alabaster retired, too? I congratulate you both, and hope the new firm will do as well. What is the name? I'll make a guess,—MESSRS. QUICK AND SPEEDY.[28]

Overseas publications formed a major part of Spurgeon's ministry. When his first sermons began to be sent by wire across the Atlantic to appear in American papers, Spurgeon was not entirely satisfied. Some objected that their quick appearance meant that someone was using the Sabbath to reproduce and send the sermon. That was not received well. Quick delivery also meant that the sermons "were so battered and disfigured that we would not have owned them." The eggs were cracked in the transmission and the life crushed out of them. In light of that disappointment Spurgeon wrote, "We much prefer to revise and publish for ourselves, and as these forms of publications are permanent, their usefulness becomes in the long run greater than would come of a wide scattering of faulty reports."[29] If matter was published anywhere under the name of Spurgeon, he wanted to make sure that it was Spurgeon indeed.

Perhaps even more than the weekly sermon, Spurgeon's chief means of contact with his people, and many other friends of the Tabernacle, came through *The Sword and the Trowel*. Even when he was laid aside for months in a row on occasion, he hardly ever failed to produce his copy for the monthly magazine. Spurgeon began publishing *The Sword and the Trowel* in January 1865. "We feel the want of some organ of communication in which our many plans for God's glory may be brought before believers, and commended to their aid," Spurgeon explained. "Our friends are so numerous as to be able to maintain a Magazine, and so earnest as to require one." He intended for that monthly contact, including messages that he preached in other venues, or material written particularly for the magazine, supplement the weekly sermon. He could say many things there that would be out of place in a public discourse.

---

28. Spurgeon, *Letters*, Letters to Mr. Joseph Passmore.

29. S&T, August 1883, 461.

In addition the general Christian reader could learn first hand, rather than through rumor or the press, what happened at the Tabernacle. After a decade of less than satisfactory experience with reports from other sources of news and information, and just plain nastiness, Spurgeon had a clear path to the public mind.

Some friendly reader suggested twenty years later that a particularly lively magazine had maintained this quality "notwithstanding the absence of the Editor." Spurgeon gave a concise and potent explanation of his ongoing and unfailing ownership of all that went into the magazine. "The Editor is never absent from the Magazine," he insisted, "but personally reads every line of each number." No one should blame a supposed subordinate for any article that appears for "the Editor hides behind nobody." He personally shoulders the blame for all. He denigrates the ability of none of his writers nor assumes that they are unable to fight their own battles, but "the Editor never wishes it to be imagined that he merely puts his name on the cover of the magazine, and leaves it to be produced by other people." His continual endeavor was to make the Magazine "as good as we can make it, and we would do better if we could." Absences from home, however, never meant a delegation of editing or writing duties to others; on the contrary, when debarred from other labors, he gave more time to making his magazine an instrument for good.[30]

The first monthly appearance of *The Sword and the Trowel* contained Spurgeon's exposition of Psalm 1. Each month thereafter he composed an exposition with few intermissions, so that by September 1868 he included his exposition of Psalm 34. Meanwhile he had collected his expositions of the first twenty-six Psalms, added "Ex-

planatory Notes and Quaint Sayings" plus "Hints to Preachers" and put them before the public in a volume entitled *The Treasury of David*. The November 1869 *Sword* contained a notice from Spurgeon:

Owing to our inability to do so much as usual in public preaching, we have given our energies to the pen. We hope to issue in December our first volume on the Psalms. The comment has appeared in "The Sword and Trowel," but the vast mass of illustrative matter which we have collected from all quarters has not appeared before. We hope that we have done service to our brethren in the ministry by this labor of love, and if the Christian public appreciate our work, we shall (D.V.) persevere till we have completed the Psalms. The volume is printed on large and thick paper, and contains more than five hundred pages. Such a work is usually issued at ten shillings and sixpence, but we have resolved to keep the price down to eight shillings, at which rate we do not expect to be adequately remunerated pecuniarily, but shall have none the less satisfaction if the wages of hearing that we have done good shall fall to us.[31]

In the Memoranda for January 1870, Spurgeon, still convalescing from an attack of gout, wrote, "Many of our hours of pain and weakness have been lightened by preparing the first volume of our book on the Psalms for the press. If we could not preach we could write, and we pray that this form of service may be accepted of the Lord."[32] In the preface he reiterated this theme by describing his situation, "It may be added, that although the comments were the work of my health, the rest of the volume is the product of my sickness."[33] He

---

30. S&T, April 1885, 194.

31. S&T, November 1869, 524.

32. S&T, January 1870, 47.

33. Charles Spurgeon, *Treasury of David,* 2 vols (Nashville, TN: Thomas Nelson, nd), 1:vi.

promised to have it reviewed by a "candid friend" by the next month. The friend, a "venerable minister, told Spurgeon that what "he had conscientiously written we might conscientiously print." Among the many substantial observations on the form and content of the volume, the reviewer stated: "We shall be much mistaken if this book does not secure for the author a far higher position among biblical interpreters and thoughtful students of theology, than has hitherto been awarded him. It cannot fail, too, to increase the confidence reposed in the theological teaching of the author in whatever way it may be communicated, since it must ever be regarded as the result of the same reverence for the authority of the Scriptures, and sincere and careful enunciation of its truths."[34]

By November 1870, Spurgeon gladly reported: "Friends will be glad to know that the edition of our first volume on the Psalms is rapidly disappearing from the publishers' stores, and Vol II is almost ready to take its place. Vol II will be published in December."[35] He had promoted the sales just a bit out of some frustration. He had learned that he was deprived of some of the sales because the word was out that "It is all in the 'Sword and Trowel.'" He decided, therefore, not to put the Psalms regularly in the magazine, and then would issue volume one in parts that people could purchase for eight shillings and thus purchase the work by degrees. This concession, however, Spurgeon called a "bad plan" and contended that "they had better buy it bound."[36]

His desire to hear that he had done not only well, but good, was fulfilled. Spurgeon enjoyed employing the positive reviews of others in order to promote the usefulness of

his labors in writing and commenting. When William Taylor, a homiletician from New York, commended Spurgeon's *Treasury of David* in his Lyman Beecher lectures, Spurgeon quickly took advantage of the high estimation and cited Taylor's evaluation. "To comment well you must make as careful preparation for it as for a more formal exposition; studying attentively not only the original Scriptures, but also everything that the best expositors at your command have said upon the section," Taylor opined. In illustration of his contention, he pointed to "Mr. Spurgeon's 'Treasury of David,' which, over and above its value, from its references to the works of others, is beyond all price for the illustrations which it gives of the best mode of turning the utterances of David to practical and devotional account."[37]

When Volume 5 appeared in 1878, Spurgeon farmed it out for review with instructions to be just as candid and critical as he himself would be with the work of another. The reviewer stated, "We are not surprised to learn that he broods long over each Psalm before he attempts to commit his thought to writing, and waits for those seasons of intenser feeling when a kind of inspiration prompts him, refraining at other times with a salutary fear, lest any of his meditations should 'exhibit signs of fatigue and decline.'" Giving a brief summary of the importance of the section of Psalms covered by the volume, the reviewer drew attention to the phenomenon that "our author's increasing acquaintance with the Scriptures strengthens his conviction that *their inspiration is verbal as well as plenary*. Of course! Philology and exegesis are as important branches of science as geology or Genesis. In any case,

---

34. S&T, January 1870, 44; February 1870, 89-91.

35. S&T, November 1870, 531.

36. Ibid., 532.

37. S&T, November 1876, 527. William M. Taylor, *The Ministry of the Word* (New York: Anson D.F. Randolph and Co., 1876), 225. Taylor quoted Spurgeon about seven times in the course of these lectures. Spurgeon reviewed and quoted from the book as published by T. Nelson and Sons (London) in 1876.

the minuter the examination the more satisfactory will be the consequence of research."[38] As Spurgeon was nearing completion of Volume 6, he noted that an America publisher, "Messrs. Funk," was being "abundantly rewarded" by publishing the existing volumes in America. "May a blessing rest on our work," he wrote, "as it will now be read by thousands of American pastors."[39]

In the Preface to *Commenting and Commentaries*, Spurgeon informed his literary audience that the first volume of *Lectures to my Students* was to be followed by another volume including two lectures on commenting. Instead he decided that a better plan was to introduce the topic of commenting in two lectures and then give a catalogue of commentaries that "might help the student to carry the advice into practice." Spurgeon pointed out that this would be "no small labor," but would be of service to many. He passed through between 3,000 and 4,000 books in producing this selection of works. He condensed, and re-condensed, gave evaluations of each book listed, told what each could expect to pay for it as a used book. "We are very mistaken," Spurgeon commented, "if our work does not prove to be of the utmost value to purchasers of books." He was aware, through his work with Mrs. Spurgeon's Book Fund, of the dismal pecuniary condition of most ministers and so realized that many of them were not among these purchasers. He labored, nevertheless, with "no object in view but the benefit of our brethren." Any reasonable expectation of sales would hardly repay Spurgeon's bare expenses, but "it will be remuneration enough to have aided the ministers of God in the study of his word."[40]

The power, usefulness, atemporality, and spiritual life that press through every pore of the pages of this work captured the mind of so formidable a twentieth-century theologian as Helmut Thielicke. In his condensed edition of this work, Thielicke called it "an inexhaustible store of stimulating material," and proceeded to provide a cultural, theological, and methodological critique of contemporary Christianity and preaching using Spurgeon as the foil and instructor of all.[41]

In November 1877 Spurgeon led off his section of book notices with three of his recently published works. Two almanacs for 1878 were ready: *John Ploughman's Sheet Almanack* and *Spurgeon's Illustrated Almanack*. For the fifth consecutive year, Spurgeon had come up with 365 fresh proverbs. Spurgeon designed it for the cottage, the kitchen, and the workshop. If his readers would put it up, their visitors would read it. The second almanac was textually based and was intended for daily counsel and comfort. The third book was the second series of *Lectures to My Students*. He included woodcuts illustrating pulpit posture and gestures. He asked readers to buy it and give it to a young minister in which they had particular interest.[42] When Thielicke studied these he saw something deep and worldly in the most profound incarnational sense. "Spurgeon is well aware that many preachers stand in their own way because uncontrolled mannerisms—some defect of speech, a monotonous delivery, a repulsive facial expression, a constantly clenched fist or a continually pointed finger—curb the congregation's willingness to listen, or produce a deadly—and spiritually deadening!—boredom." Spurgeon, according to Thielicke's observation, could warn against boredom in speech and man-

---

38. S&T, October 1878, 506.

39. S&T, May 1882, 249.

40. S&T, March 1876, 137.

41. Helmut Thielicke, *Encounter With Spurgeon* (Cambridge: James Clarke & Co. Ltd, 1964), 7 and 1-45.

42. S&T, November 1877, 534.

ner while avoiding the error against which he declaimed. He lampooned boredom in a "sprightly and amusing fashion," doing it so well and with such appropriate caricature and humor, that these comic pulpit figures he paraded before their eyes in both word and picture, made the young preachers "vow spontaneously never to become such a dreadful preacher as that."[43]

Again in November 1886, three of his volumes headed the book notices. A second edition of 10,000 of *All of Grace* was ready. A fellow minister wrote Spurgeon, "It will prove a swift torpedo boat among the enemies of our King, and a lifeboat to many shipwrecked souls." Again, *Spurgeon's Illustrated Almanack* was ready; Mrs. Spurgeon had selected the text for each day. "It brings us thousands of friends," Spurgeon remarked, "and enables us to exchange kindly greetings." *John Ploughman's Almanack* was ready and, according to Spurgeon, "John has by no means fallen off in the quality of his annual broadside." Some editors had called this production the "King of Sheet Almanacks" and Spurgeon seemed to agree, thinking the sale should be ten times what it was because it is "as lively as a cricket, and as fresh as new milk." Even folks who will read nothing else will read this, Spurgeon believed, for "there is a spice of fun in it, and the fun catches them like salt on the little birds' tails."[44]

When he published *Be of Good Cheer: The Saviour's Comforting Exhortation enlarged upon* he wrote, "We hope the reader will be as pleased with the spiritual as we are with the material part of the book." It was designed for those who like the writer had been under the distress of a long illness. "Comfort is to be found even in this troubled world," Spurgeon reminded the reader.

"Floods do not cover all the high hills, the waters are assuaging, hope rules the hour."[45]

During 1882 Spurgeon published his immensely popular *Farm Sermons*. Though it was "kindly handled by critics" one reviewer thought the woodcuts should have been English scenes rather than eastern husbandry. Spurgeon responded by asking, "How could we have illustrated the text about threshing the wheat with horses, and the cumin with rods, if we had kept to English scenes." Volume 6 of *Treasury of David* met with a large demand in America. In addition, as had been the yearly task since 1855, he published the *Metropolitan Tabernacle Pulpit* Volume 27 and had nearly brought to ripeness for publication the *Metropolitan Tabernacle Pulpit*, this time Volume 28, bringing the total number of sermons to 1,696. He wrote that he had "only coasted around the marvelous subjects which fill the Scriptures" and was only now at the beginning of the divine theme.[46] The annually-bound edition of *The Sword and the Trowel*, now numbering Volume 17, reached the public. Spurgeon was pleased that "it fetches good prices at second-hand," an evidence of one of the desires he had in producing such a massive amount of literature, adding "and this is about as good a test of literary value as we can give." Its readership also served to show that the days of irrational reaction against his ministry had virtually ceased leading him to comment happily, "We are often surprised to meet with approving readers, not only as we naturally expected among our own denomination of Christians, but among the clergy of other churches and residents in foreign lands."[47]

He described his book *The Clue of the Maze* as the "author's personal testimony as to the way

---

43. Thielicke, 8.

44. S&T, November 1886, 594.

45. S&T, May 1881 233.

46. S&T, 1882, Preface and January, 33; July, 373.

47. S&T, January 1882, 33.

in which he gained sure foothold, and escaped the slippery and dangerous ice of scepticism."[48] In the same year, 1886, *All of Grace* was written for the unconverted. He had put his whole heart into it and "fertilized every page with prayer." He believed that God would bless it to the conversion of many.[49]

In May 1869, Spurgeon's gentleman farmer persona, *John Ploughman's Talk*, had sold nearly 30,000 in just a few weeks.[50] By November it continued "to sell with great rapidity. We have now reached the seventieth thousand."[51] He had begun the series of homely moral proverbs, punctuated with evangelical truth, in *The Sword and the Trowel* in 1868. He introduced other pseudonyms such as William Ploughman, cousin to John, Nathanael Plainspeech, and Searchwell but found John to be the perfect combination of all the wise plain people that he had known from his grandfather to Will Richardson. By 1881 sales had risen above 300,000 and another printing was made. Some complained that it consisted simply of a number of proverbs strung together. Spurgeon agreed and admitted that the book contained no original genius at all and yet there were now 310,000 in print with a clamor for still more. It is simple, but no one else had ever done it. He added some engraving to this edition and hoped that the sales would run to over half a million. "Its strength," Spurgeon noted, "lies in the wholesome proverbs which are floating about everywhere, but have here been diligently collected, and congenially dovetailed, so as to make up lively continuous reading, intended to convey good morals to the myriads of working men who will never read that which is dull and dreary,

however profound may be the instruction contained therein."[52]

In publishing a Scripture commentary for families, *The Interpreter*, Spurgeon aimed at giving both variety and ease for leaders of family worship. He committed the review of this new work to his college principal, George Rogers. Rogers set this work in the context of Spurgeon's other publications designed to give opportunities for spiritual edification to readers. "Among the many thousands who have Mr. Spurgeon on the Sabbath in his preached or printed sermons, and in the closet in his *Morning by Morning*, and *Evening by Evening*, and in the study in his *Treasury of David*, there are few, we presume, who will not welcome him in *The Interpreter* into their families. It will also be an excellent companion to *John Ploughman* in many a home." Rogers believed that Spurgeon was no less noted as an interpreter than as a preacher and that his public expositions were as valued as his sermons. Since the recording and publishing of all those seemed impracticable, this book would meet the need in part for such pithy exposition. The compass of all Scripture could be brought into focus within a couple of years and "by pertinent observations to enliven and fix the meaning and design of each portion in the mind and in the heart."

A Significant Investment of Time and Labor

Spurgeon seemed to have a deep investment in informing his wide readership how much labor his literary accomplishments cost him. Several reasons might come to mind. He wanted to demonstrate that a lack of formal education did not inhibit a critical and insightful investigation of a massive amount of scholarship. He wanted his church to know that his hours in the study or his

48. S&T, March 1886, 138.

49. S&T, June 1886, 288.

50. S&T, May 1869, 236.

51. S&T, November 1869, 524.

52. S&T, December 1881, 622.

weeks of convalescing were not hours of freedom from work, but involved the most oppressive kind of labor. He wanted those that read books to know that books did not pop into existence fully-formed as Minerva did from Jupiter's head, but grew and came together slowly by an arduous process of their birth-, and then nurturing-, parent. They should appreciate the process of reading and find some point at which they could thank God for faithful stewards. He wanted them to know that their souls' best interest was at his heart and he would not offer to God, or them, that which cost him nothing. Perhaps his motive was a mingling of all of these, but it is clear that their knowledge of his labor was important to him.

As he described the process through which he labored in bringing Volume 1 of *The Treasury of David* to publication, he commended the work of his friend and amanuensis John L. Keys for his labors at the British Museum and Dr. Williams' library. Spurgeon himself, moreover, had "ransacked books by the hundred, often without finding a memorable line as a reward." The beneficiaries of such fruitless search "little know how great labour the finding of but one pertinent extract may involve; labour certainly I have not spared."[53]

In January 1874 in his brief preface to the book review section, Spurgeon acknowledged that a larger number of book reviews than normal appeared. That was because so many books came from publishers but also because "we have tried to make the brief reviews as interesting as any other matter is likely to have been. Amid many engagements, it is not without hard labour that we have been able to examine with care so many works."[54]

By September 1874 Spurgeon had finished some years of labor on a book for family worship, mentioned above, entitled *The Interpreter*. It had been published in installments initially but finally was bound in one volume. In describing his "heavy toil" he said that the few remarks made on the selected texts of Scripture "have cost us much more thought than if we could have written at length." Far more trouble was expended in the tedious process to "cull and select matter to occupy a few lines" than if he had liberty to write unbound by space. He emphasized that his comments had "cost us much care", for in each case he "consulted the best expositors, and studied the word laboriously."[55] Soon Spurgeon was receiving letters of commendation for the book and he published some in the *The Sword and the Trowel*. One aged minister, C. J. Donald, wrote, "My people have often thanked me for placing 'The Interpreter' before them; by it their faith in the truth as it is in Jesus has been greatly confirmed, their views of Christian privilege and duty enlarged, and their personal piety promoted."[56] Could Spurgeon want more from any labor of mind and hand?

In celebrating twenty years of published sermons, Spurgeon described the labor of producing one sermon per week for publication as "far greater than some suppose," usually occupying "the best hours on Monday, and involved the burning of no inconsiderable portion of midnight oil." Because his constituency deserved the effort he "never grudged the hours, though often the brain has been wearied and the pleasure has hardened into a task."[57]

When he produced *Commenting and Commentaries*, after he spoke of the massive amount of literature that he had read, and sifted through

---

53. *Treasury of David*, 7:v.

54. S&T, January 1874, 35.

55. S&T, September 1874, 432.

56. S&T, January 1875, 44.

57. Ibid., 5.

for the benefit of his readers, he remarked, "Probably not one reader in a hundred will have any idea of the expense, labour, and research which this catalogue has involved."[58] In a different genre, the research involved in his almanacs also took much time and careful labor. The appearance of *John Ploughman's Sheet Almanack for 1876* was inaugurated in the *Sword* with Spurgeon's admission, "This penny sheet costs us more pains than anything else which we do in the course of the year; for, after four or five years of publishing, the proverbs become scanty, and we have to labour hard to escape repetition.[59] Perpetuating the labors beyond the interests of a mere year was the intent of *The Salt Cellars, being a Collection of Proverbs, together with Homely Notes thereon.* Those *Almanack* proverbs were gathered and rearranged into quaint words and those more spiritual, enhanced then by some "homely" remarks by Spurgeon. He wrote a series of thematic books that he called shilling series. When the fourth volume, *The Mourner's Comforter* appeared, he wrote, "These small books cost us considerable pains, but we shall be more than recompensed if we hear of good arising from their perusal."[60] His goal was to prepare twelve such volumes. These included *Christ's Glorious Achievements, The Bible and The Newspaper, Seven Wonders of Grace, The Spare Half Hour, The Mourners Comforter, Eccentric Preachers, Good Cheer,* and *Gleanings Among the Sheaves.* Apparently these are the only eight that were printed in this series, for, in an advertisement for the series in 1895 put at the end of Mrs. Spurgeon's *Ten Years After,* they are the only ones listed.[61] Other

volumes that sold for a shilling in one of their bound forms were *All of Grace, The Metropolitan Tabernacle: Its History and Work,* the *Memorial Volume* of sermons preached during the celebration of Spurgeon's twenty-fifth anniversary in his London ministry and others. Even *The Christian World* noted that Spurgeon provided a vast body of excellent religious literature for the common man at a cost he could afford. The catalogue of books still published by Passmore and Alabaster in 1895 by Spurgeon himself included eighty-one separate titles, including several of the massive and popular multivolume works.

Depression, rejection, pain, and rain could not damp Spurgeon's sense of redeeming the time. In the winter of his retirement to Mentone after his resignation from the Baptist Union and the flurry of controversy and accusation (1887-88), a rainy day allowed contiguous hours of quiet meditation accompanied by a ceaseless flurry of putting his devotional thoughts to paper. At the end of the day, he had produced thirty-one single page devotions as the first month's installment on *The Cheque Book of the Bank of Faith.* He handed the pages to Joseph Alabaster to be sent to London to begin the process of setting the type. The completion of the work engendered in Spurgeon a greater wonder at the depth and power of biblical truth and the surety of its promises than he had up to that time perceived, for he had now gone "outside the camp" bearing the reproach of Christ and had found ever renewed strength in the sustaining power of God. He explained the context that produced these encouragements to take God's promises as personal blessings to be drawn from his eternal covenant provisions for his people:

I commenced these daily portions when I was wading in the surf of controversy. Since then I have been cast into "waters to swim in", which

---

58. S&T, March 1876, 137.

59. S&T, December 1875, 583.

60. S&T, July 1878, 356.

61. Susannah Spurgeon, *Ten Years After* (London, Passmore & Alabaster, 1895), page 5 of eight pages at the end of the volume advertising works by C. H. Spurgeon.

but for God's upholding hand, would have proved waters to drown in. I have endured tribulation from many flails. Sharp bodily pain succeeded mental depression, and this was accompanied both by bereavement, and affliction in the person of one dear as life. The waters rolled in continually, wave upon wave. I do not mention this to exact sympathy, but simply to let the reader see that I am no dry-land sailor. I have traversed those oceans which are not pacific, full many a time: I know the roll of the billows, and the rush of the winds. Never were the promises of Jehovah so precious to me as at this hour. Some of them I never understood till now; I had not reached the date at which they matured, for I was not myself mature enough to perceive their meaning.[62]

Mrs. Spurgeon's Minister's Library Fund

This ministry started in 1875. In the July issue of *The Sword and the Trowel* Spurgeon announced as the last of his "Notes," "Mrs. Spurgeon, our beloved and afflicted wife, begs us to say that she has been so much interested in reading the book entitled 'Lectures to my Students, by C. H. Spurgeon,' that she would like to bear the cost of giving a copy to each of a hundred poor Baptist ministers who would accept it of her." This initial effort was limited only to Baptist ministers.[63] When she gave her own rendition of the beginning in her book *Ten Years of My Life in the Service of the Book Fund*, she reported that, in response to her exuberant expression of a desire to see every minister in England possess a copy of *Lectures*, Spurgeon asked her, "Then why not do so: how much will you give?" That question prompted her to locate a nest of "crowns" she had saved through the years, enough to purchase 100 copies to give.[64]

Mrs. Spurgeon speedily distributed the 100 copies of *Lectures to My Students*, and had so many requests still unfulfilled that she gave a second hundred. They disappeared just as quickly. Spurgeon seemed to think that the effort was over but the experiment had proven that someone needed to give attention to this crying need of books for desperate ministers. "Mrs. Spurgeon has done her fair share in this matter," Spurgeon announced, "and leaves the further supplying of poor ministers and students to the generosity of some of the friends, with whom our publishers would make generous terms." No other applications could be fulfilled; the short ministry to ministers had been pleasurable, "but it is a sad fact that there should be so many needing such a present." Genuinely puzzled at the condition he had rapidly been made aware of, Spurgeon asked, "Cannot something be done to provide ministers with books? If they cannot be made rich in money they ought not, for the people's sake, to be starved in soul." He was astounded that "some of the applicants have not been able to buy a book for the last ten years! Does anybody wonder if preachers are sometimes dull?"[65] The query, just like the earlier suggestion to Susannah, found a home quickly.

In his preface to the 1875 *Sword and Trowel*, Spurgeon announced, "Two fresh trees of smaller growth have been planted, namely the Missions among the poor blind people of London, which deserves to be well watered; and last, but not least, *Mrs. Spurgeon's fund for supplying poor ministers with books*, which has made many hearts leap for joy, and must, under the divine blessing, be a fruitful source of benefit to the churches. This work ought to be sustained and increased till no needy preacher of the gospel should find himself

---

62. Charles Spurgeon, *The Cheque Book of the Bank of Faith* (Ross-shire, Scotland: Christian Focus Publications, 1996), iv, v.

63. S&T, July 1875, 344.

64. S&T, April 1886, 156.

65. S&T, August 1875, 402. "Notes."

destitute of daily food for his mind."[66] Spurgeon saw a famine in the land on this account of sufficient literature for ministers, especially in their ability to purchase it, and wanted his friends to join him and Susannah in providing literature essential to the ministerial life of a gospel preacher. He was reiterating what he had rapidly discovered in this ministry of distributing books. In November he told his readers that he had met with preachers who had only four books, some that had a few more, but all of "worthless character." Such a destitution of essential tools existed that Spurgeon called it "an absolute famine of books among poor Baptist ministers." Inflamed with a new outlet for Christian service, Spurgeon now pronounced that this effort was "one of the most needful which Christian charity can undertake." Feed the minister's mind, and feed the church. Spurgeon did not run thin on his commitment to the necessity of the Spirit's work for any spiritual profit, "but by supplying instructive books we have at least used the means."[67]

In June 1876, she reported a great blessing with both contributions of funds and requests for books steadily arriving. Spurgeon felt deep gratitude that a work so helpful had been placed in the hands of his "beloved one," also called "our beloved sufferer." One generous supporter placed in her hands the means to supply all the Calvinistic Methodist preachers in North Wales with a copy of *Lectures to My Students*. Another did the same for South Wales. "It is no small work for an invalid, and a daily sufferer, to send out many hundreds of these, besides parcels of books to applicants."[68]

The overwhelming response taxed both the funds and the energy of Mrs. Spurgeon as demand far exceeded the books available through contributions. Spurgeon requested, therefore, as a kind "hint" that "when perfect strangers of various denominations apply to her they should mention the names of some well-known individuals who could recommend them. Our beloved wife is anxious to do her work well and judiciously, and it would grieve her very much if she found that unworthy persons perverted this good work to their own undue advantage. It is needful, therefore, that she be enabled to judge each application."[69] When Mrs. Spurgeon wrote to the "Editor" of the *The Sword and the Trowel* and proposed that she be allowed to make public the contributions and expenditures of the book fund for those that had so generously contributed during the past months, he of course consented to the space and proposed some "impartial person to act as auditor." His sympathies were so intense in the work that he could not possibly provide an audit satisfactory for the public. "Perhaps this work will become a permanent institution," he suggested, "and therefore its auditing must be done in the most orthodox and public fashion by some public business man." He hoped before the year was out there would be more to audit.[70]

Testimonials provided impetus for persevering in the demanding task of superintending this expanding ministry. A provision of six books of sermons from Spurgeon had a threefold impact on the life of one poor minister. His own spiritual state was so low that he first perused the volumes for the sake of his own vexed and desperate soul and found renewed zeal and a strengthened arm for the fight. In addition to that, they gave him more profound insight into the gospel, imparting an intense earnestness to his preaching and making him more importunate in his pleadings with

---

66. S&T, 1875, Preface, iv.

67. S&T, November 1875, 545.

68. S&T, June 1876, 285.

69. S&T, September 1876, 434.

70. S&T, December 1876, 569.

sinners to receive Jesus. Beyond, that, his people noticed the change and thanked him for such searching sermons and such strong presentations of the gospel. They began to join him in earnest prayer for the conversion of souls. "I have thus, my dear Mrs. Spurgeon, told you briefly and very poorly the good I have received from the volumes you sent me. … Should you be able to send me some more, I can promise you a very attentive and an ardent study."[71]

At four years old, the book fund entered on a time of a still more useful existence. Spurgeon's compassion for poor ministers grew commensurate with his increasing awareness of their desperate need. Until they are "sufficiently paid to be able to buy books for themselves" someone must "work to find them brain food." God had blessed Mrs. Spurgeon's distribution of books, "for the recipients have written again and again to acknowledge the invigoration and the reviving received through the volumes." Others had been stirred by this avalanche of need to consider the great evil of ministerial poverty, and books have been spontaneously given which otherwise would not have filled the pastors' shelves." Increased funds and increased demand had tested Mrs. Spurgeon, but "the poor suffering worker had yet strength sufficient, as she hopes to have for another year." It would grieve her if friends of the ministry slacked in giving on account of her illness.[72]

Again, Spurgeon promoted the book fund report in 1882, reiterating his observation of the vast need that ministers had of literature to feed the flock under their charge. Reading and meditation, hours of study were essential for the preparation of a sermon. Many had barely enough change to buy bread and the pennies set aside for monthly pulpit help were gone to physical suste-

nance for the family rather than spiritual invigoration for the one that now must lead sheep to a desert. Baxter, Doddridge, and Henry had now left the library for table food, and food for thought escaped an already withered brain. "It is therefore one of the delights of our life," Spurgeon continued, "that our beloved wife has made ministers' libraries her great concern." She had over 6,000 names on her list and knew every book that had been received by each one of them. "The work is not muddled but is done as if by clockwork." With all the blessing attending the work and all the progress that had been made, Mrs. Spurgeon informed her contributors that "there are still hundreds of men in the ministry whose stock of books is totally inadequate to their needs, and who though painfully conscious of their famishing condition, are unable to procure the aliment which would nourish their souls, and promote their spiritual and mental growth." She continued therefore to "deal forth our treasure lovingly and gladly till they be exhausted."[73]

Spurgeon appealed both to the warranted self-respect of a minster and the personal soul-interest of those that must hear them. "When poverty displays itself in a man's sermons, it is more grievous to him than when it is seen in his clothes," Spurgeon told his readers. "No man ought to be kept short of books; as well deprive a workman of his tools." If a common craftsman worked under the weight of such destitution of tools, what would the outcome be for his clients? "These men are to produce fresh interesting living, stimulating thought: the task is in itself no easy one; in the name of common-sense supply them with every known help for the cultivation of their minds." If preachers in the pulpit remain thus poverty stricken, think also of the poor pew-sitter. "If

71. S&T, February 1878, 79.

72. S&T, January 1879, 41.

73. S&T, May 1882, 220.

we are to endure two addresses from them every Sunday, let us be merciful to ourselves by giving the good men something to think about, that they may not bore us with inane repetitions, nor send us to sleep with dull platitudes."[74]

The *Annual Book Fund Report* allowed Spurgeon to keep his message of ministerial need before his public. The Report, written by Mrs. Spurgeon, reminded readers of both the good that the fund did and the needs of those whom it served. "We want poor ministers to have more sympathizers," Spurgeon pressed, and nothing in print had greater power to induce that than his wife's narrative. "Read," he insisted, "and let your hearts break, if you will, for the sorrows of those who feed the flock of God, and are in return but scantily fed themselves." Brethren from all denominations had drunk from this fountain and "many more are pressing forward to be refreshed."[75] By the end of 1885 some 80,000 books had been given to over 12,000 ministers of all denominations. Other ministries had been added, such as the inclusion of printed single sermons to missionaries and other Christian workers. Monthly issues of *The Sword and the Trowel* had been given to many a poor minister and a "Pastors' Aid Fund" had distributed £330 to £400 yearly as well as large gifts of clothing to destitute minister and their families.[76]

There appeared in 1886 Susannah Spurgeon's personal history of the book fund, *Ten Years of my Life in the Service of the Book Fund.* The first printing had 2,000 in it and they were all gone in a short time. The idea had been to tell the story and then gradually phase out the high demand on Susannah's time and depleted energy. "Unfortunately," Spurgeon noted, "it tends to increase a work which we proposed to diminish; let us hope that fresh strength will be given." Its sales, nevertheless, pleased him, and he promoted it by saying that "the volume is tasteful without, and delightful within" for it contained "a wealth of real poetry written as prose."[77]

As Spurgeon intimated, Susannah initially felt that the record of ten years would bring to culmination her intention in having established the fund. Her report for 1886 acknowledged how short-sighted such a conclusion was. "When *Ten Years of my Life* was published, I did not intend to issue any further account of my work." She wiped her pen, shut up the inkstand, closed her eyes, and dropped into a comfortable doze! Soon she realized that she must be up and doing for her "clamorous letters could not be instantly silenced; the wheels of my work went on revolving with their usual quick precision of movement, and I had to follow them, or be caught in the entanglements of neglected duties, and crushed by the weight of a reproachful conscience." The addition of a year of life, the faithfulness of friends in their contributions, and abundance of money, and strength for the task took her through another year of the book fund.[78] She would continue to issue yearly reports, with rare exceptions, until 1902.[79]

One occasion of a missed report was the winter that she accompanied her husband to Mentone for his last winter of life. In February 1892, the magazine notified the contributors: "Mrs. Spurgeon desires us to say that it will not be possible for her to prepare any Report of the book Funds work this year. If spared she hopes to be able to give an account of her stewardship early in 1893;

---

74. S&T, March 1885, 106.

75. S&T, March 1881, 130.

76. S&T, April 1886, 157.

77. S&T, May 1886, 246.

78. Mrs. C. H. Spurgeon *Ten Years After* (London: Passmore & Alabaster, 1895), 11.

79. Charles Ray, *Life of Susannah Spurgeon* (Edinburgh: Banner of Truth, 2006), 220.

and she will then send to her subscribers a balance-sheet for the two years during which her work has been necessarily so much in abeyance in consequence of her husband's long and serious illness." Even after his death she was able to fulfill her stated hope that she could resume her much-loved labours. When she returned home she would be "glad then to receive applications for grants, and also contributions to enable her to continue her book-distribution. While she is at Menton, the Fund must be regarded as closed."[80]

After twenty years of the book fund and several other benevolent initiatives that flowed from it, Mrs. Spurgeon described her perception of its usefulness employing her oft-used analogy of the lemon tree in her house. "As I lovingly look upon my symbolic tree, every branch and twig and leaf seem emblematic of the various departments of Book Fund service." She wrote of the Fund itself as the "great central stem." From that springs the largest limb almost rivaling the Fund itself in strength and usefulness, the Pastors' Aid Fund. A widely-spreading branch from that limb was the Westwood Clothing Society to help clothe the families of poor pastors. A sturdy bough bore the inscription, Home Distribution of Sermons, and "an equally-vigorous offshoot dedicated to the *Circulation of the Sermons Abroad.*" Another twig supported the fruit entitled Foreign Translations of Sermons, the Auxiliary Book Fund and the *Sword and Trowel* distribution formed separate branches, "while the many thousands of *tracts and pamphlets* which are circulated by the Fund are well represented by the twigs and leaves which spring from the larger stems." When blossoms appeared but only withered she felt the imperfection of all things on earth. Some hopes never bore fruit and the best of intentions often

withered. "Our best services are too often marred by the unfruitfulness of unbelief. The emblem tree fails here because it is of earthly growth; but the God-given work, of which it has for twenty years been the imperfect symbol, has borne much fruit to the glory of the Master, and to the exceeding comfort of His poor servants."[81]

Spurgeon's Reviews

Spurgeon wanted publishers to know that he did not write every review that appeared on the pages of *The Sword and the Trowel*. "Publishers are rather too much in the habit of quoting remarks made in our Review Department as if they must necessarily be every one the personal production of the editor. Now, we beg to give notice that to quote us from *The Sword and the Trowel* is fair and right, but to begin with 'Mr. Spurgeon says' is not always truthful. We do write the major part of these notices, and we are responsible for them all, but we could not *in propria persona* get through so many books, and therefore many of the reviews are by other hands."[82] Sometimes initials mark those by other persons, at other times the style may seem to be distinct from Spurgeon's, and on occasions the nature of the material was such that Spurgeon preferred others to comment on it. "Let it be understood," he explained, "that after making a large reserve for our own perusal, we parcel out the manifold miscellaneous books sent us to specialists, each man an expert, according to our judgment, in his own department of literature."[83] Frequently he would intersperse his own remarks in a review that was largely done by another. His sense of stewardship, however, for recommending helpful literature, and warning against destructive ideas, meant that whether the content

---

80. S&T, February 1892, 92.

81. Susannah Spurgeon, *Ten Years After*, 391-92.

82. S&T, December 1879, 593.

83. S&T, March 1886, 137.

is his first hand or someone else's, he stood by the analysis and recommendation.

Spurgeon observed the difference between quality of literary style and orthodoxy of content. The later always was preferable but a noble blending of the two always was desirable. He himself sought to recognize elegance and genius in style and composition even when he felt compelled to warn against content. The point was made clearly in a book Spurgeon reviewed entitled *The Religion of Our Literature*, which we mentioned earlier in this chapter. The writer, George M'Cree, examined the theology of several well-known literary figures of England and evaluated the way in which their attractive style could mask their alliance with error. "Few could so well have distinguished between talent and its perversion, genius and its aberrations." Many that lack discernment have, "in reprobating heresy" denied the "ability of its defender" and on the other hand some, in "admiration of originality ... have winked at the deadly error which it propagated." M'Cree admired the beauty of the cup but also exposed with vehemence "the poisonous draught which it conveys to us."[84]

Just such a contrast Spurgeon saw in the life and convictions of Edward Pusey. In an address entitled *To Whom Shall We Go?*, a reviewer marked the great ability and the strong religious tone of the address while demolishing the "Babel tower of priesthood." In his reflections on the man and his position, Spurgeon confessed that Pusey was "one of the greatest of puzzles, — an eminently devout, humble, Christian man, supporting a claim to priesthood which is in itself unholy, arrogant, and antichristian! Lord what is man!"[85]

Never a flatterer, Spurgeon's honesty about books often led to a brutality that caused him

to issue a warning to publishers against sending him books. He promised to give his honest judgment upon them, but could not enter into a controversy over what he said in a review or even respond to protests. Frankly but courteously he warned, "Those who do not relish our notices of their books should be careful not to send us any more, but we earnestly urge them not to write to us to complain, for it will only be a loss of their time and postage." He did not ask for books; publishers, editors, and authors had their liberty about that. Nor did he promise to review all books sent to him; he used discretion and claimed the "liberty of silence." Often he chose silence over criticism, for criticism would publicize views that he felt were so harmful, or disgusting, that they should not be given even the courtesy of comment. He would tear such books into small shreds or commit them to the fire, or both.[86] Upon taking time and trouble to criticize a book, he had no intention to justify his criticisms to the author in private. No one likes his writing severely handled, he knew, and "each author believes his own publications to be faultless." He could not please all and was sorry to displease anyone. He was well aware that "there are editors who butter and sugar their clients all round, and we recommend thin-skinned writers to send on their compositions to those amiable gentlemen." He had avoided membership of the *Mutual Admiration Society* and had instead "a very unpleasant way of saying what we think, whether we offend or please." His favorable evaluation had sold whole editions "because the public believe our reviews are honest and discriminating." He did not intend to change, "and therefore, take notice, ye who want nothing but approbation."[87]

One publisher certainly regretted the day he sent Spurgeon its prize product for review. He

---

84. S&T, April 1876, 184.

85. Ibid.

86. *Autobiography*, 2:420.

87. S&T, May 1875, 233.

could express a withering kind of outrage when he felt injustice was done in a publication. In reviewing *The Heart and its Inmates*, Spurgeon pointed out that the engravings, without due acknowledgment, were taken from an old work that originated in Germany and was available in almost any print shop. "We feel bound to denounce such literary larceny as unworthy of a professing Christian." He went on to declare his astonishment that "anyone should copy parts of the engraving, alter them to their disadvantage, and then palm them off as his own. It is as barefaced a proceeding as if a man should deliver portions of Bunyan's Pilgrim as his own original conception."[88]

One critic of Spurgeon took the view that he was too kindly disposed toward books that ought to be criticized severely. Spurgeon viewed this as a novel complaint against his work and assured the critic that many an author thought otherwise. "If the writer we have referred to," Spurgeon proposed, "will only put a volume through the press we will gratify him if we can; if he thinks our knife is blunt we will borrow a lancet for the occasion."[89] Perhaps he would even consent to bring the one word verdict he brought to an author's assertion in *The Problem of Evil*, speculating that "it has never actually existed," concisely evaluated by Spurgeon, "Rubbish!"[90]

Novels and Poetry

Spurgeon did not hide his peevishness about certain issues in literature. Misleading titles vexed him. A promising title by a promising author, *Shall We Know One Another?* by J. C. Ryle, produced only a short paper on the subject along with a variety of other short essays. Spurgeon had been drawn in looking for a book on such

a pleasing subject. Disappointed, he generalized, "We wish this foolish and deceptive way of giving titles would go out of fashion; it is not truthful."[91] Spurgeon's titles normally were straightforward, but on occasions he was capable of an intriguing cleverness such as "He who would Please all Will Lose His Donkey and Be Laughed at for His Pains."[92]

Also, he disliked novels. Only rarely did he say anything positive about a novel that was submitted to him for review, and then it was loaded with caveats. "The common novels of the day are sorry teachers of morality; they teach a great deal more of immorality. The religious fiction of the day is little better: it is either goody-goody, teaching men and women how to be babies, or else it is suggestive of doubts which minister weakness to the soul."[93] He felt particular disgust with the attempt to use fiction as a vehicle of Christian truth. He did not object to the sentiments expressed in religious fiction if those sentiments were indeed true, but "to the form in which they appear. Religion needs not the dress of fiction. Christianity always looks best in her own sweet simplicity, and certainly does not need borrowed plumes."[94]

In commending a series of biographies, Spurgeon gave a discussion of the disadvantages of novels compared to such edifying truth. "Life under the influence of fiction is becoming more and more untruthful and frivolous," Spurgeon contended. While he had no desire to forbid fiction-writing he would keep it "in due subordination to history and fact." Pepper, salt, and mustard have their place on the table but not as the main

---

88. S&T, May 1880, 242.

89. S&T, July 1883, 392.

90. S&T, August 1871, 379.

91. S&T, June 1871, 286.

92. Charles Spurgeon, *John Ploughman's Pictures* (Christian Focus Publications, Ltd, 1989), 28.

93. S&T, April 1882, 164.

94. S&T, April 1877, 189.

course. Just as condiments should not substitute for the substantial part of the meal, so much novel and little solid literature dwarfs the mind and soul. "Character built up on the dreams of novelists cannot be substantial; but minds nourished on the records of noble lives are far more likely to be made sublime."[95]

Through the years he made mention of several novels by Emma Jane Worboise, a writer of "multitudinous novels." Emma Jane Worboise served as first editor of *The Christian World Magazine*, a venture of James Clarke, the entrepreneurial publisher of Spurgeon's nemesis, *The Christian World*. She was the daughter of an Anglican clergyman, and, though some called her "the novelist of Evangelical Dissent," Julie Melnyk indicates that her "Evangelicalism was tempered by Broad-Church tolerance."[96] Spurgeon was familiar with the novels written by Worboise, and, though he did not approve of the genre of novels, reported positively of her work. In 1866, he gave a brief notice to a book entitled *Lost and Found*, a "Temperance Tale by the Author of *Jane Grey's Resolution*." Though no author is given and catalogues have not turned up an attribution, the style of writing, the content, the nature of the characters, and some autobiographical material that forms part of the setting for the book all point to Worboise as the author. Spurgeon, giving vent to his persistent frustration with the medium, wrote, "It may be some organic defect in our mental structure, or it may be our love of reality, but for some reason or another, we had almost as soon be flogged as read a story of this sort." He admitted that it may be the most popular "ever written" but he had "no stomach for the fight; that is to say,

we have neither the leisure nor the taste to read works of fiction, however excellent their drift or admirable their style."[97]

In 1870 he wrote, "Anything that this talented authoress may write is sure to find a host of readers; we on principle object to all religious novels, though we believe that those penned by the writer of this book are intended to be beneficial to their readers, and they are certainly as little objectionable as any we meet with."[98] Later, in 1873, he gave a notice of her novel *Canonbury Holt: A Life's Problem Solved*. He wrote simply, "Another religious novel, by a lady eminently gifted in that direction."[99] Spurgeon disliked religious novels with greater zeal than just plain meaningless novels, but was informed that Worboise was one of the best at her craft and that *Emilia's Inheritance* was one of her best. The best Spurgeon can do under the circumstance is to issue another warning against spending any time with a novel, but if they cannot be content without reading fiction, Worboise might "give them better pabulum than most writers."[100]

Poetry rarely made the list of commendation for Spurgeon. "The cross and burden of our reviewing lies in the poetical department," he confessed. "We can never please the authors, and the authors do not often please us." When he pondered why they persisted, and determined that it could not be for profit, he thought that it must be because they thought that they bestow pleasure; Spurgeon wanted to relieve them of that misperception. "If we never saw another fresh book of verse while dwelling in this 'vale of tears,' we could manage to subsist upon the old ones, and should not 'bedew our pillow with the briny

---

95. S&T, April 1881, 193.

96. Julie Melnyk, "Emma Jane Worboise and *The Christian World Magazine*: Christian Publishing and Women's Empowerment," *Victorian Periodicals Review*, No. 2 (Summer, 1996) 29:131-45.

97. S&T, June 1866, 286.

98. S&T, May 1870, 236.

99. S&T, March 1873, 140.

100. S&T, March 1875, 137.

drops,' as one of our friends would put it, though salt in dew would be a remarkable novelty."[101]

Spurgeon told the anecdote about the historian Lord Macaulay who supposedly said that prize sheep were good for nothing but to make tallow candles, and prize poems were only fit to light them with. Though he promised not to light candles with them, Spurgeon sighed that "we are weary of verse both rhymed and blank, and cannot read more that a few pages of any form of poem."[102] He received books of poems and most often rued the experience and warned his poetry writers to throw them in the trash before they sent them to him because it would save him the trouble of doing it. The effort to write poetry is "a weakness of many noble minds, and of a few ignoble ones also. Our soul is burdened with the *poor try* that is daily sent to us."[103]

The principle of poetry Spurgeon adored and viewed it as one of the most sublime, and rarest, gifts of God; the delusion of so many, that they above others were favored with this rare jewel ("the weakness of many noble minds"), evoked in him an incredulous aggravation. As the nomenclature of "Word" points to Jesus Himself, Spurgeon knew that communication could move from the lowest and most humble contexts to the infinitely glorious. Each person must discover with a sense of humility and reverence the most appropriate sphere for the use of his normal talents of word. Each person also had a range of communication and must with wisdom explore and exploit its usefulness in appropriate contexts. Only rarely did Spurgeon aspire to poetry and normally that was in private correspondence with his wife or on special occasions in hymns for his church. The full range of language was legitimate, but each

person's gift must be guarded and not trampled upon by those that want it but don't have it. The common people of broad experience were excellent at proverbs, and Spurgeon collected, enjoyed, and commented on thousands of them. Though he mourned over most attempts at poetry, puns, like proverbs, could flow with ease from the common folk. They probed some interesting characteristics of language in manifesting a kind of internal rhythm and allowed the poetic propensity of Everyman a legitimate outlet—at least he loved to make them. He was criticized early in his ministry for the habit of making puns in the pulpit, even at serious moments in the sermon. He introduced a review written from the standpoint of a family cat with a clever play on the word. "'Only a Cat,' but a wonderfully clever cat to write a catalogue of the catastrophe which happened unto it. We understand cats far better than we did before Tom Blackman catered for us. Having a catarrh, though not a cata-baptist, we have so well studied this amusing book that we are almost ready to be catechized upon, and to give categorical replies."[104] When asked to make a comment on a particular kind of stationery, Spurgeon objected that he did not judge articles "other than literary; but as these are letter-ary, we will for once give an opinion."[105] In concluding the review of a book by J. Tongue, Spurgeon commented, "Our author is not a 'tongue of fire.'"[106] Spurgeon could do even worse than that, and have fun doing it.

But to ask people to pay for such trivialitites under the guise of supporting an artist presented a moral dilemma. After a mild commendation of some verse, Spurgeon added, "Whether they are worth the price charged for them we hesitate to say; but they are much better than some costlier

101. S&T, December 1874, 578.

102. S&T, May 1881, 233.

103. S&T, April 1876, 185.

104. S&T, March 1877, 138.

105. S&T, October 1886, 545.

106. S&T, April 1882, 194.

and more pretentious volumes it has been our sad penance to review."[107] Spurgeon found himself in an awkward position with one book of poetry and demonstrated graceful discretion in his note: "These poems are sent us for review; but we have no heart for such cruel work when we find that the writer is a blind man, and that friends have written out his verses, and aided him in preparing them for the press." Spurgeon recommended that the same kind friends should, for love's sake, sell the books among their own acquaintances.[108]

Another anecdote designed to discourage poetry-senders referenced an Assyrian archaeological dig that uncovered a poem written on tile, and adjacent was a club and part of a human skull. Spurgeon promised not to keep clubs around so as to spare his skull when sent books of poetry but said, "We are tried up to the boiling point by the poetic coals which are heaped upon us." If poets did not find their poetry reviewed they should send him thanks rather than complaints for avoiding what certainly would have been a painful experience had he chosen to expose their "precious compositions." They should expect no more because Spurgeon never would "wittingly entice our readers into the purchase of a book which is not worth buying." Spurgeon's table groaned with Tennysons and Cowpers in an embryonic condition, and if "they would be so good as to take offence, and never send us another specimen of their wares, we would bless them in our heart of hearts."[109]

Only his love for Christ-centered gospel orthodoxy transcended his disdain for lame attempts at poetry. It would have been better, in his opinion if Trissine, the inventor of blank verse, had "never lived at all." To the pretenders at po-

etry he warned against their stringing "long lines of nonsense, with such an absence of all thought, that you are altogether unbearable." Write if they must and as much as they can, for it is good for the paper trade, and might be good for them, but "with the utmost vehemence of our outraged nature, we entreat him not to send his manuscripts to us," for thieves might inadvertently steal such precious treasures, or rats might eat them, or the immoderate cleaning habits of Mary might whisk them away, or the fireplace might need fuel, a picture of which he included using this phrase as a circumlocution, "or they might even drop into THE RECEPTACLE BELOW."[110]

To maintain his principle of general hostility toward contemporary efforts at poetry, Spurgeon often introduced a positive review with a sober warning. When digging into *The Poetical Works of Thomas Cooper*, Spurgeon told the story of Cardinal de Retz who requested Menage to give him a few lessons on poetry in order that he might be a better judge of the mass of verses brought to him every day. Menage responded that it would be impossible to lead him to master the rudiments of criticism without occupying too much of his time, so he shared a virtually fail-proof technique. He advised him to "look over the first page or two, and then to exclaim, 'Sad stuff! Wretched poetaster!! Miserable verses!!!' and ninety-nine times in a hundred you will be sure you are right."[111]

Spurgeon went on to give more than three full columns to Cooper largely because of his overall reputation as standing very high in "the hierarchy of intellect" and because the "grace of God has softened the stern man, and made him gentle as a child." Even the earlier days of steely protest and stirring public speaking as a chartist and honest

---

107. S&T, November 1883, 602.

108. Ibid.

109. S&T, January 1882, 37.

110. S&T, July 1884, 351.

111. S&T, September 1878, 410.

and yearning skepticism Spurgeon viewed him as far superior to the contemporary expressions of worker discontent and religious doubt. When Cooper reluctantly allowed an earlier poem, "The Purgatory of Suicides," to be reprinted, a poem Spurgeon described as "an interesting history of a soul in the dark pining for the light," Cooper insisted on a preface to set the production in context: "I earnestly beg to have it remembered that he who so irreverently expressed his skeptical thoughts and feelings in the gaol more than thirty years ago, has, for the last twenty years, been traversing the entire length and breadth of Great Britain, devoting his whole life to preaching, lecturing, and writing, in explication and defence of the Evidences of Christianity, and purposes, by divine help, to continue his labour of duty to the end of his earthly life." Both his skepticism and his Chartism were handled nobly in poetry, Spurgeon argued, and the latter has been vindicated and the former cured. In the right places he struck his blows, always yielding a two-edged sword. He would do more good at lecturing than writing poetry, Spurgeon advised, though he did well at both. Some of his poetry fell rather flat, but verses dispersed throughout the whole were "of the finest order." "Still we do not think," Spurgeon contextualized, "it will ever be widely popular, nor that Cooper will outshine Cowper."[112]

In the hands of William Cowper, however, even the commonplace took on transcendent qualities. "The most trifling event becomes charming, and the smallest gossip blossoms into something fascinating." Perhaps the talent and religious fervor of Cowper made any competition fade and seem even unworthy of the effort in Spurgeon's mind, for even in his correspondence, "The simplest letter in the whole selection bears the mark of poetic genius; the language and style are so vivacious and pleasing that you feel that no ordinary pen has been at work for you." It was not only the poetic quality that drew Spurgeon to Cowper, but the point of view from which Cowper viewed all things. More than books on religious topics, Spurgeon asked for books on common subjects viewed by a mind saturated with the religious perspective. "A leisure hour cannot be more interestingly spent than in seeing the manners and customs of a hundred years ago displayed to the life by one who saw them from the standpoint of a poet and a Christian."[113]

When presented, however, with something that sustained both poetic quality and good instruction, Spurgeon would recommend it. "Amid mountains of rubbish," he confessed, "we now and then find a jewel." Dr. Macduff wrote a poem that Spurgeon liked, earning a mild accolade as a "pleasing versifier, and though he is by no means a great poet, he puts the grandest truths into striking words, and frequently lets fall an expression worthy to live."[114] Ray Palmer had the fortune to catch Spurgeon on a good day with his *Voices of Hope and Gladness*. The writer of "My Faith Looks up to Thee," Palmer tapped into Spurgeon's reservoir of hope. "We reckoned not merely upon poetical beauty, but spiritual quickening therein," Spurgeon noted, "nor have we been disappointed." The poems "throb with spiritual life," put in language that is "forceful and chaste." The style and diction "make their power and beauty felt." The binding, paper, printing, and illustrations ("charming woodcuts"), always important for Spurgeon, were excellent, and should command for the book a large sale.[115] On the other hand, when he reviewed Lyman Abbott's comments on

---

112. Ibid., 411.

113. S&T, January 1878, 41.

114. S&T, April 1876, 185.

115. S&T, June 1881, 287.

Matthew and Mark, he led off the review with "We do not admire the American style of this book. The frontispiece is abominable, and the letterpress ugly." Abbott's comments themselves, according to Spurgeon, were only mediocre.

Also Elizabeth Prentiss gained a reluctant positive word from Spurgeon. Prentiss was the daughter of Edward Payson, a noted New England minister. Her name was not noted, only that she was the author of *Stepping Heavenward*. She also had written some charming children's works and the hymn "More Love to Thee." Her husband also was a minister of the gospel and their lives had had the steady hand of purifying providence on them. Spurgeon could not have been familiar with these facts or he would not have been quite so reluctant to investigate the book. When her volume, *Religious Poems*, first arrived he exclaimed, "Poetry again!" He continued that this "grunt" rose as naturally as that of a working man that says, "Cold mutton again!" and was provoked into a lengthy discourse about the ills of poetry and the dangers of reviewing works of any sort that he did not like. Many books he simply laid aside and then would receive other copies. To review them would only invoke rage from the authors; and Spurgeon had no wish to hurt anyone, nor to be hurt, and, therefore, he quietly forgot to review such works. Having vented himself thus, he was ready to consider the *Religious Poems* in an unbiased frame and found that they were "not so very bad after all." They were, in fact, "endurable" and could be read with a "degree of pleasure." "We are thawing," he recognized, and went so far as to say that "we have read many verses which are a great deal worse than these." Another elevation of tone brought him to say that "some of them are really good." Gradually shedding his visceral distaste for new efforts at poesy, he now admitted, "The spirit and the doctrine are all we

could desire, and the versification is correct and pleasing." Then in an effort to curb his growing enthusiasm, Spurgeon slowed down gently with the appeal, "That is no more than we are bound to say, and considering our state of mind, it is a good deal." Then in a further *apologia* for his blunt dislike for being imposed upon by another book of poetry he stated, "Cover a man with rhyme ants and see if they do not make him rather irritable." He condescended to include one of Prentiss' hymns, calling it a "very pretty bit," at the end of the review but not before playing the martyr for his efforts. "We are all right again after reading it, but we hope our readers will be grateful to us for undergoing such toils and dangers among the poets, and will appreciate any spoils with which we can enrich them."[116]

Another lament about poetry followed by a positive review came when he received *The Morning Song, a Ninefold Praise of Love*. Normally he found books of poetry requiring him to "traverse morasses of poetry, as flat as pancakes, and as monotonous as desert sands." This work, however, put him in a "land full of beauty, a land of hills, and valleys, and brooks of water." The verse "refreshed and exhilarated" him and he predicted that the writer, John Watkins Pitchford, would provide a minstrelsy yet to be heard in the world. Particularly important to Spurgeon was the combination, necessary in a good poet, of an observant naturalist and a devout heart.[117] Pitchford published several other books on themes of redemption and gained a moderately enthusiastic following for his work. Lines from the book reviewed by Spurgeon include these concerning Christ's suffering in book seven, "The Song of Love's Triumph." Pitchford, in one stanza pictured Christ's contemplation of his death in Gethsemane, and included these lines:

---

116. S&T, December 1874, 578.

117. S&T, October 1886, 549.

And all were His. For in that awful hour
He bore the heavy load of human grief,
And all the guilt of man, sin's bitter pangs,
Rebukes of conscience, stern remorse, whose fang
Gnaws out the heart of life; the wrestlings, doubts,
And haunting fears that dog the sinner's steps,
And on the threshold of eternity
Hold him in grip; ...

The blood piacular from every pore,
As by ten thousand agonies drawn forth,
Rushed as anticipating the rude nails,
And vengeful spear; and the Redeemer rose
Clothed in the vesture of His sacred blood.
Alone the wine-press of God's wrath He trod,
Disputing to the utterance with these,
Our bitter foes. Yet would I sing, O Christ,
Thy love triumphant over every pang;
Most glorious theme to chant the praises high
Of the victorious love that trod on death.[118]

He wanted to return to the volume when he could "set apart an hour or two for deliberate reading."[119]

Spurgeon revealed his true heart toward the poetic spirit in his comments on *Ingleside and Wayside Musings* by I. R. Vernon. Though not rhyme, the prose was so elegant that it embodied the spirit that Spurgeon looked for in poetry. "Truest poetry is often found where no rhymes jingle, and no measured feet restrain the flow of thought." Though Vernon's book was written in prose fashion, Spurgeon found it to be "pure unalloyed poetry." The author had a "quick, but far seeing eye, and a mind which muses deeply and expresses itself by the use of a facile pen." His admiration of Vernon is significant because of the power of his literary treatment of "There shall be no more Sea." Spurgeon adopted Vernon's poetic interpretation. Vernon lamented the prospect of losing the ocean with its "semi-transparent curves, crisping into silver-white" and its "crash of billows, and heave of swells," its "delicious murmur" as well as its "shrill roar of shallow waters searching every pebble as they leave the rattling beach." He took it as a figure meaning "no hindrance any more between the intercommunion of nations, that there shall be no separation of peoples any more. Ay, further, that the reserve which impassably parts here mind from mind, and soul from soul, shall then flee away, and the isolation which now in kindling moments we deplore and strive against, may then be forever past."[120]

In Spurgeon's evening comments for December 19, he took that text as his theme. He began with the same lamentation that Vernon had: "Scarcely could we rejoice at the thought of losing the glorious old ocean: the new heavens and the new earth are none the fairer to our imagination, if, indeed, literally there is to be no great and wide sea, with its gleaming waves and shelly shores." He also used language very similar to Vernon's when he called to mind its "glassy smoothness and its mountainous billows, its gentle murmurs and its tumultuous roarings." "A real physical world," which he believed the new heavens and the new earth to be, "without a sea it is mournful to imagine." It would be a bare iron ring "without the sapphire which made it precious." No, he believed it to be a metaphor, holding the spiritual meaning of "no *division*—the sea separates nations and sunders peoples from each other." The world to come shall have no barriers but only "unbroken fellowship for all the redeemed family." In this sense there shall be no more sea. Vernon wrote of the "isolation which now in kindling moments we deplore and strive against" as for ever in the

---

118. John Watkins Pitchford, *The Morning Song, a Ninefold Praise of Love.*(London: Elliot Stock, 1883) 228-30.

119. S&T, October 1886, 549.

120. S&T, June 1878, 313.

past. Spurgeon concurred that the image of the sea referred to the constant inconstancy of the earthly state that would give way to the "heavenly state [where] all mournful change shall be unknown, and with it all fear of *storm* to wreck our hopes and drown our joys." Poetic prose that had the power to lift the mind to a new literary consideration of divine revelation pleased Spurgeon and brought him not only aesthetic joy but interpretive insight into the nature of revealed truth.

The fact that he relented from time to time and gave commendations must not mislead the reader, however, for Spurgeon kept up his promises to dump poetry in the waste basket. "Poetical effusions are for the most part prosy delusions," he maintained, hoping that his whining about the burden of reading such trash would serve as sufficient warning to wean the "minor poet from rhyming, and inspire him with love to his drapery, grocery, carpentry, or bakery!" The retail trade, Spurgeon advised, is far more useful than wholesale poetizing. Guessing at dates of prophecy and writing verse were as unprofitable as getting blood out of gate-posts. "Trespassers beware," he chided; "A waste basket is kept on the premises."[121]

Books of General Interest

Spurgeon sought constantly to expand his own appreciation of all that God's world held as a testimony to the manifestation of his glory in his creation and in the propensity of those made in God's image to match that creative drive. He demonstrated, therefore, a breadth of appreciation for books that expanded the mind with the beauty as well as the objective data uncovered through science, exploration, and art. He recommended these kinds of books to his readers with

less frequency than books on theology, biblical studies, spirituality, and Christian biography, but some time given to this genre would be well spent and beneficial to the soul. A book on *Recent Polar Voyages* kept Spurgeon up into the "small hours" investigating all the vivid and numerous illustrations to find out what the pictures meant. "We can scarcely remember to have seen a book so interesting in itself, and so lavishly embellished with first-class engravings."[122]

Spurgeon said that the *Home Naturalist* was "worthy of all praise." It was not for youths that longed for anecdotes and adventure stories but for those interested in some earnest and energetic work. One of the lessons gave plans for building a terrarium along with suggestions for populating it with lizards, newt, frogs, and snakes. Spotted salamanders seemed just right also and Spurgeon was sure that they would make delightful pets. The snakes, however, were a bit bold and Spurgeon did not think that he would set up a terrarium.[123]

A book about dogs caught his attention as being worthy of a late Christmas present, but said that "It will be in season even as late as the dog-days." Dogs, he knew, and he saw confirmed in this book, are "no more perfect than men are, and they are often very like their masters in their vices." They deserve to be treated kindly, tenderly, and all that their "best friends can say of them."[124]

He recommended a book on coal as instructive upon the "fuel which the Lord has stored away in the cellars of the earth for his favoured creature man." It told the history of coal formation, coal extraction, horrendous explosions, and mines flooding with water. The collier had a hard and dangerous life and this book consisted of the "best coals only." He recommended it strongly

---

121. S&T, August 1882, 413.

122. S&T, April 1877, 187.

123. S&T, November 1877, 534.

124. S&T, February 1882, 92.

to young people, not only for education, but to make them grateful that they were not diggers of black diamonds.[125]

He commended a guide book to museums and galleries of Rome to aid visitors to that city. Far different than a mere guide book developed by the trade for quick sale, this was a "chatty, masterly production of a writer of ability and taste." A book of solid instruction that possessed all the charm of the best fiction told the stories of famous explorers like Marco Polo, Vasco de Gama, Columbus, and others. These stories "stir the blood, stiffen the upper lip, and give force to character." He promoted it as "invaluable for young people."[126]

Spurgeon had a compelling interest in the subject of slavery and was naturally drawn, therefore, to *The Life and Times of Frederick Douglas from 1817 to 1882*. Written by Douglas himself, who at twenty-one, had managed to escape to the free states and had become a lecturer on slavery advocating abolition, the book gave a "vivid picture of slavery ... free from that questionable sensationalism in which American fiction-writers have indulged when treating of this subject." Spurgeon considered the book a "triumphant vindication of the cause of the slave" and a corrective to the manifesto of Jefferson Davis that attempted a vindication of "himself and of his fellow conspirators against freedom and right." The work by Davis "deservedly lies unread on the booksellers' shelves" while Douglas' will never suffer that fate.[127]

Reviewing Children's Literature

Remembering the fascination of books, pictures, adventures, and people that waited for "the child" at Stambourne to peer into Fox's *Book of Martyrs*

and Bunyan's *Pilgrim's Progress*, Spurgeon was eager to evaluate and recommend to parents, or to the children themselves, books that would inflame their imagination with the wonder of adventure, the fascination of the world of nature, and the commendation of virtuous heroism. Books! Children must have books that would entice them with learning, and with the power of words, and would give them desires to know all that God had made and that would make them willing to risk all for a good cause, that is, the glory of God and the sake of truth.

He felt rage at the "vile literature which certain wretched publishers prepare for boys." His desire was to produce as well as promote books that "catch the eye of youth, in order to inculcate good morals." Were it within his power he would have the "concoctors and vendors of poisonous trash for children treated as felons." The "wholesome cat" would suit them, in his opinion, for they are "more wicked than those who commit assaults upon the highway; garrotters only inflict bodily injury, but these harpies poison the soul." The best way to strike them a blow, given their legal status, was to "print cheaper and better things, and cut them out in their own market."[128]

He exulted in a book, *Facts and Phases of Animal Life, and the Claims of Animals to Humane Treatment*, that brought instruction and helped build up the mind with knowledge. Mere stories "puff up the soul ... and teach it nothing." Spurgeon considered this book as wheat among the chaff, the kind of which "there cannot be too many." He himself had derived great pleasure in going through it page by page "for our own personal delectation." It cannot detract from its worth that it teaches "humanity to animals while it amuses the youthful reader."[129]

125. S&T, August 1882, 439.

126. S&T, May 1882, 245.

127. S&T, August 1882, 438.

128. S&T, December 1875, 585.

129. S&T, January 1883, 38.

Perhaps not with equal vehemence, but with sincere distaste, Spurgeon disliked stories of unrealistic goodness. Stories about "miraculously good boys without shoes and stockings", who talk better than saints or angels, were far too many. However touching a dozen or so of such impossible narratives might be, he was "growing hardened by the repetition of them for the hundredth time."[130] He had seen too much of the stultifying effects of poverty and sin on real boys to be impressed with indefensible fantasy posing as encouragement. Quite another matter were the stories printed in *Kind Words*, which had the right tone and moral, but were almost as "sensational as those of the 'The Bloody Hand' or 'Jack Sheppard' type." Boys like to read them and let a boy get into one of the stories "and he will never be content till he has got through it." Spurgeon had frank cautions about sensational literature for the young, "but since the boys of England will read sensational stories, it is a good and lawful thing to provide them with such as are morally wholesome, so that they may not be ruined by the abominations of the sensual press." It is not a matter of what we prefer, Spurgeon admitted, but of what the boys prefer and "how far we can gratify their tastes, and at the same time guard their morals."[131]

In late 1870 he reviewed a series of six volumes, that he recommended as "quite a little library for Tom and Maggie, and so beautifully bound, too." The whole six would be a "glorious Christmas-box." Giving one "would be sure to make eyes flitter, and little hearts rejoice." He supposed the child might ask, "Mr. Editor, have you honestly read all these six books through?" He would answer, "No, Maggie, I have not, but I feel sure you will, if papa buys them for you." How

did he know that they would be good all the way through? "When I get a little taste of a cheese I know whether my friends will like it, and having poked my book-taster into these, I think they will suit you and Tom."[132]

In January 1874 he recommended several children's books, one of which had seven morals "all connected with total abstinence." He was sure it would find interested readers "though it certainly does not fascinate us." Morgan and Scott published *Frank, the Record of a Happy Life* that Spurgeon found to be "more spiritual than the preceding books" and like to be very useful, "if boys can be induced to read it." Concerning *Florrie Ross, or the Voice of the Snowdrops* Spurgeon had a decided opinion about the artwork at the front, that he called a "hideous scratch for a frontispiece." A little girl says, "Look Murphy, are not these pretty?' Spurgeon replied on behalf of Murphy, "No, they are dreadfully ugly, and so are you, and so am I." Pull out the frontispiece, Spurgeon snarled, and the book is commendable.[133]

Special attention must be given to boys, Spurgeon consistently argued, and literature must mix real adventure, courage, valor, mental challenge, and solid instruction. *The Boy's Own Annual* exceeded his expectations. Far superior to other boys' magazines it "contains a wealth of interesting stories tales, incidents, pictures, riddles, jokes, and all else which can delight the soul of a boy. If our young Englanders do not prefer this paper to the penny dreadful they are downright dolts, and deserve to be trounced." The *Annual* outparleyed Peter Parley, and all the other "Boys' Own Books" are "thrown into the cold shade."[134]

He loved *Once Upon a Time, or, the Boy's Book of Adventures.* These surely reminded him of the

---

130. S&T, March 1878, 140.

131. S&T, January 1879, 37.

132. S&T, December 1870 573.

133. S&T, January 1874, 37.

134. S&T, January, 1880, 32.

days of free roaming and the thrill of observation that made his childhood a constant adventure. "Adventures indeed, and plenty of them," he exulted—"lost on the Alps, captures by brigands, attacks of robbers, and perils of Indians, in a French prison, on a rock:—we have, in fact, such a choice of adventures that every youth's heart should be more than satisfied." If getting a boy to read was a worthy goal of a book then he scarcely knew of one more likely to succeed. Another book for boys not only had great adventure but would etch geography indelibly on the boy's mind. *Frank Powderhorn* was a book about Indians and Spaniards in South America and the challenges of the terrain, animals, plants, and bugs that made everyday life a challenge. A boy will pick up geography and never forget it. Spurgeon confessed that that book did not tempt him to emigrate to Argentina:

> In insect life this land is rife,
> With bugs the fields are swarming;
> Big spiders run beneath the sun,
> Whose bite is most alarming!

> We've large supplies of blist'ring flies,
> In this delightful region;
> Locusts and ants devour our plants,
> For here their name is legion.

> Of scorpions, too, we have a few,
> Black venomous, and glistening;
> I might say more upon this score
> If you had the time for listening.[135]

Sermons for children, an essential but special art in Spurgeon's opinion, were more difficult to produce. When a heterodox magazine disliked *Sermons to Children* by John Gregg, Bishop of Dublin, Spurgeon expected himself to find real interest in reading them. They were not pleasant

reading, however, for a certain roughness pervaded them. That style may be "especially attractive to Irish children," Spurgeon surmised, "but we scarcely think that English ones would be fascinated thereby." He was not.[136]

Good Biography

Spurgeon called Boswell's *Life of Johnson* "a stupid book and yet the very model for a biographer."[137] He disliked biographies that were just collected incidents with no interpretation. Such a writer did not know the difference between a pile of bricks and a mansion. In reviewing a biography of Philip P. Bliss, Spurgeon found nothing striking either in the matter or the style of the memoir giving rise to his comment, "Writers of readable biographies would appear to be more scarce than the materials to work upon."[138] When Thomas Binney died, Spurgeon remarked: "Fortunately for his own fame, Mr. Binney has not fallen into the hands of a regular biography writer, or he would have been buried in a huge mound of his own letters badly arranged, huge lumbering sentences of bombast, and a vast aggregation of the opinions of nobodies about him."[139] A biography of William Huntington, however, that was little more than that, gained his attention. "A chatty, gossipy book upon one who had, and still has, both ardent friends and fierce detractors," he called it. Though the author filled it with incidents of the most common place order, it still was worthy of a full reading because of the prominence of the subject and the first nature of the compilation of original anecdotes, letters, and remarks. Overall, Huntington's reputation suffered with Spurgeon as he read this "impartial compilation."[140]

---

135. S&T, May 1880, 242.

136. S&T, September 1880, 486.
137. S&T, November 1871, 530.
138. S&T, July 1877, 332.
139. S&T, June 1874, 286.
140. S&T, November 1871, 530.

He was glad that a readable biography of William Carey had been written that was "solid, accurate, and profound," as well as "gracious, appreciative and clear." Such a book George Smith had provided to help overcome the book on Carey by Eustace Carey. Spurgeon erroneously called the nephew Carey's son. About that work he fumed, "William Carey has at last arisen from the grave into which his son Eustace cast his memory. That many-adjectived worthy piled a vast heap of letters over his father's coffin, and called it a 'biography.' Never was so deadly a 'life' ever presented to the public." Smith's volume, however, made one warm to the greatness of Carey while setting some of the conflicts of his life in an understandable context.[141]

John Treadwell's biography of Luther prompted Spurgeon to admit, "We could read fifty lives of him without feeling that the subject had been compassed, much less exhausted." Such abundant material could only arise from a never-resting man—a "great, earnest, forceful man, who never wasted five minutes in trying to stop mouse-holes with cheese." The publishers had done their task admirably to give "in change for half a crown this elegant, well-printed essay upon one of the greatest of men."[142] The 400th anniversary of Luther's birth in 1483 brought about several treatments of different aspects of Luther's life, theology, and contribution. For its popular appeal, Spurgeon liked *Luther Anecdotes: Memorable Sayings and Doings of Martin Luther.* The anecdotes were "most useful and seasonable at this moment" and would find many readers "who would never wade through a biography."[143] He also commended his friend G. H. Pike for his selection of "many interesting anecdotes, facts, and remarks concerning

Luther and the Reformation" and several other books giving attention to the pivotal influence of Luther in the recovery of the gospel. After gaining latitude for judgment through engaging such a large number of Luther books, he confirmed Treadwell's as "perhaps superior to any of the Luther books. It is worthy of a careful reading."[144]

The 400th anniversary of the death of Wycliffe brought about several biographies. One by Emily Holt he called, "The best popular life of Wycliffe which has yet come under our eye." He particularly commended her flowing style and her gracious spirit, adding: "It is a great pleasure to read anything which she writes, and this is one of the very best of her productions. Long may it be ere her inkstand is dry and her pen ceases to move at her will."[145] All reminders, especially those well-written and beautifully bound, of thoughtful, doctrinally-sound resistance to the tyranny of Rome were sure to receive commendation from Spurgeon.

A good reminder of the stately heroism of John Knox, "the greatest of Scotchmen," would inevitably draw a positive pronouncement from Spurgeon. Mary Queen of Scots was an "ill-mannered" queen, playing "the vixen as best her furious feebleness permitted her," whereas the hero Knox conducted himself as a "calm father with a peevish, passionate child." Knox was no "trimmer" but rather a "god-like hero." Scotland, indeed any country, could benefit from such a man.[146]

Another Scot, Robert Murray McCheyne, had been printed in Spurgeon's magazine through his sermon abstracts on more than a dozen occasions. When an abridgement of his *Memoir and Remains* was published Spurgeon welcomed it

---

141. S&T, March 1886, 139.

142. S&T, May 1882, 243.

143. S&T, November 1883, 602.

144. S&T, December 1883, 649.

145. S&T, July 1884, 382.

146. S&T, March 1885, 140.

heartily, but inserted an immediate caveat that should it keep anyone from the full work, the event should be regretted: "We found it not only a means of grace many years ago to read Mc-Cheyne's life, but a whole host of means of grace in one." He could remember no other book that was "so refreshing and sanctifying to our soul." He trusted readers of the abridged version would not have an abridgement of the blessing.[147]

His propensity against both poetry and the romantics found some balancing ballast in a biography of William Wordsworth by A. J. Symington. As far as Wordsworth was concerned, Spurgeon concluded from the read that Wordsworth's strength was "in his having sympathy with the spirit which is embodied in visible things, and in his perception of the moral teaching of all things that are." Spurgeon's own love for nature and his commitment to see sermons in virtually every natural phenomenon[148] made him more friendly toward and grateful for this insight than Wordsworth's mystical intuitism could have prompted in itself. Spurgeon's admiration for Symington probably helped Wordsworth's cause for Spurgeon commented: "It is not easy to conceive how Mr. Symington can know so much about so many people, but he writes as one who understands his subject, and is no mere sketcher whose hurried outline is as likely to be a caricature as a portrait."[149]

George Needham, an American evangelist, wrote a biography of Spurgeon in 1882. Spurgeon could not have been happy with it as a true biography, for it proceeded precisely along lines that Spurgeon detested in biographical writing. It seems, however, Spurgeon decided to be gentle with one that had showed him such "loving esteem." He did comment that nothing original had been done. It was made up of Spurgeon's sermons, books, speeches, and magazines, mainly his own words cleverly arranged and made into a consecutive narrative. "We are amazed," he confessed, "that so great a tome can be compiled from our sayings and doings." If the effect should be helpful, then he could not regret having been so "bigly biographed during life."[150]

In 1870 Luke Tyerman released his three volume biography of John Wesley, entitled *The Life and Times of John Wesley*. Spurgeon was in a dilemma. The volume was much too important to be dismissed with a brief notice, or to be delayed a month for a longer review. Spurgeon believed that it would "become the standard book on the subject." He considered it "real history," for, *"mirabile dictum* for a Wesleyan," Tyerman wrote impartially and did not hesitate "to censure and even to condemn where truth demands it." Spurgeon called Tyerman's work a "worthy commencement." Spurgeon could not hide his personal admiration for Wesley, believing that few men excelled him. His contributions would not fade but even coming generations would call him blessed. "But he was mortal, and therefore erring; full of heavenly treasure, and therefore earthen, for such vessels doth the Lord make the depositories of his wealth of grace to the sons on men."[151]

When a more reverential treatment of Wesley appeared Spurgeon remarked, "It was not to

---

147. For sermons see S&T, 1866, 241, 345, 504; 1867, 5, 114, 153, 193, 260, 294, 385, 442; 1868, 5, 55, 207, 307, 354, 392, 518; 1869, 127, 170, 513; 1870, 252. See also November 1867, 494-98, "The Sainted McCheyne." This is from the review section of *The Sword and the Trowel*, but through a failure accurately to notate, the exact location has escaped this author.

148. As an example of Spurgeon's use of nature for substantial sermonic material see his *Teachings of Nature in the Kingdom of Grace* (London: Passmore & Alabaster, 1896). This book, containing 56 selections of articles, sermons, and brief essays, does not move from nature to sermon but from a biblical text that has some reference to a natural phenomenon into an exposition of how the gospel employs that natural phenomenon as an apt illustration of spiritual truth.

149. S&T, August 1881, 417.

150. S&T, November 1882, 596.

151. S&T, November 1870, 531.

be expected that our Methodist friends would rest content with Mr. Tyerman's sternly faithful, and unceremoniously severe, life of their leader." Spurgeon admitted that Tyerman's "fidelity was a bit overdone," but reiterated that "Tyerman's volumes will long remain a singular monument of his industry and rigid honesty; and whatever emendations are proposed in them had need be well substantiated, for Tyerman is a masterly dealer in facts."[152]

J. B. Wakely compiled two books by accumulating anecdotes of Whitefield on the one hand and the Wesleys on the other. Spurgeon was surprisingly positive. He normally made short work of piles of anecdotes posing as a biography but these he found instructive, particularly in light of the edifying character of all the lives involved. About Wesley, Spurgeon exclaimed, "What a miracle of consecrated ministry was this man!" He kept not only a diary but an horary, living not merely by the day but "by the quarter of an hour." "In the mere matter of time," Spurgeon noted with a degree of irony, "he lived twice as much as most men, and *though he had the gout*, no man ever did so much as he did in the same space of time."[153] Spurgeon loved Christian workers that crammed their lives full of activity for God's glory.

A book on Whitefield consisted of twice-told tales but Spurgeon still found them challenging and spiritually invigorating, having "heard the trumpet peal, and felt the strong desire to rush into the battle." "Our model," Spurgeon confessed, "if we may have such a thing in due subordination to our Lord, is George Whitefield, but with unequal footsteps must we follow in his glorious path."[154] The republication of J. R. Andrews

biography of Whitefield he was "right glad to see that what cost us five shillings can now be had for sixpence." If every minister in the three kingdoms had the biography, "It would set the church ablaze." Some wealthy man, Spurgeon suggested, should see to it that every manse in the United Kingdom possessed a copy.[155]

Edward Leach contributed scores of articles to *The Sword and the Trowel*, and had the loyalty of Spurgeon. When Leach simulated a biography of a colorful and well-known London evangelist, Spurgeon found the tension between friendship and honest evaluation of literary worth a test of his skills. *Incidents in the Life of Edward Wright* gave Spurgeon the opportunity to commend two worthy servants of the gospel and promote a standard of credibility in literature at the same time. One line in the review shows Spurgeon's ability to warn while at the same time commend where appropriate. "If we did not know Mr. Wright, far better recognized as Ned Wright, we should doubt the actuality of many of the marvels of wickedness here detailed." He would not be surprised "if some of the statements should be challenged, for we, with all but unbounded faith in author and hero, are compelled here and there to question their literal accuracy." At the same time Spurgeon called Wright a "wonder of grace" and "one of the most powerful instrumentalities now employed by God on the south side of the Thames." Spurgeon had for him the "deepest regard and the highest admiration" and was sure that the book would command a large sale.[156]

Spurgeon never advocated the sacrifice of style for the sake of an excellent subject. He would be predisposed to love any information about the famous Irish evangelist, Thomas Toye, a "famous winner of souls," known in his day for

---

152. S&T, January 1876, 89; review of *The Living Wesley as he was in his Youth and in his Prime* by James Rigg.

153. S&T, October 1879, 489.

154. Ibid.

155. S&T, October 1883, 559.

156. S&T, December 1870 572.

"holy ardour, mixed with a dash of eccentricity," a man "widely known and heartily beloved." The author of the book *Brief Memorials of the late Rev. Thomas Toye, Belfast* was his widow. Spurgeon acknowledged that it was "lovingly done" but she was "evidently a novice at book-writing." Toye deserved a "biographer of the most skilful and accomplished character." He hoped that Mrs. Toye's "affectionate tribute" would be but the precursor of a fuller memoir. "There must have been enough of incident and of racy speech in connection with Mr. Toye to have made him a choice subject for the pen of a ready writer." Obviously, Spurgeon encountered a disappointing work about a compelling subject.

He had an insurmountable resistance to mere "tale-books." Though he glanced over some he did not peruse any of them, and confessed frankly that "we would sooner break stones." But folks loved religious fictions and he did his best to let them know which of them were well-intentioned. He did not advise reading them to any great extent. "A little pastry may be all very well (our slow digestion suggests that the less the better), but to live upon it would be to generate dyspepsia and all sorts of ills; even so, an interesting story now-and-again may be a relief and a pleasure, but a constant course of such reading must injure both mind and heart." From the quantity of fiction that he received he felt that perusal needed no encouraging, but "a little repression might be healthy."[157]

Spurgeon's hatred of sacramentalism, formalism, and officialism made him look upon Quaker life in positive ways. A book about Stephen Grellet, the French Quaker, allowed him to make a point about the strength of Quaker life. He liked the book thoroughly, both from the standpoint of subject and author. "With much spiritual edification we have studied Mr. Guest's version of this saintly man's story." He called on readers to buy and read it "through and through." The theological point driven home is "that the work of conversion and sanctification is the standing proof of the gospel, and that holy lives are the best answers to infidel objections."[158]

In 1879, Spurgeon recommended the *History of the Reformation in Germany and Switzerland* by K. R. Hagenbach with the personal note, "We have been greatly charmed with it." It had all the interest of "light reading" and yet was "solidly instructive." He inserted a section from Hagenbach illustrating the heights of Luther's courage. Hagenbach was not half so cloudy as most of his brethren and "infinitely more interesting."[159]

Spurgeon's friend Paxton Hood published a biography of Oliver Cromwell that Spurgeon liked very much. Cromwell was not handled gently, but honestly, and the result was one in which the true praiseworthiness of Cromwell emerged. Spurgeon did not commend war but did commend genuine heroism and wished that the present age might see Cromwell's type of religion and manliness once again that "we might see its power under more genial circumstances than those of civil war." Many that boast in Cromwell nevertheless deride his Calvinistic faith, but Spurgeon asserted that they would never produce such heroes with their modern notions. "God and his sovereignty, the covenant and its certainty, grace and its glory, predestination and its infallibility, the word of God and its authority—these must come back if England is to see Cromwellians among her sons."[160]

---

157. S&T, December 1879, 593.

158. S&T, May 1881, 233.

159. S&T, January 1879, 39.

160. S&T, January 1883, 37.

12

LITERATURE ABOUT RIGHT, WRONG, AND TRUTH

If a man can purchase but very few books, my first advice to him would be, let him purchase the very best. If he cannot spend much, let him spend well. The best will always be the cheapest. Leave mere dilutions and attenuations to those who can afford such luxuries. Do not buy milk and water, but get condensed milk, and put what water you like to it yourself. This age is full of word-spinners—professional book-makers, who hammer a grain of matter so thin that it will cover a five-acre sheet of paper; these men have their uses, as gold-beaters have, but they are of no use to you.[1]

Congregations must be the better for their ministers having a fresh store of mental food[,] ... for if preachers are supplied with sound literature, which they value, their ministry must be influenced for good.[2]

All literature has the natural tendency to influence the mind. From the most trivial poetry and banal novel to the most thoughtful biography or provocative essay, time and intellectual energy consumed in reading will create impressions of some sort, for good or ill, for increasing serious maturity or justifying flippant and selfish immaturity. Spurgeon, on that account, often ignored and sought by pure silence to minimize the impact of some, sought to ridicule the point of others, and sought to encourage the public knowledge of those worthy of such important mental stewardship. Another kind of literature, and that upon which he spent the largest portion of his time, was designed by its very nature to form one's views of right and wrong and truth and falsehood. For that reason, CHS gave himself to a rigorous perusal of multi-

tudes of volumes of this genre. His own soul was in the balance and the spiritual well-being of his readers could often flourish or wane through a word of his fitly, or unfitly, written.

He Advocated Literature that Argued for Elevated Morality

Spurgeon felt so strongly about the level of morality in society and appreciated company in this crusade so much that he even found a comrade in a man that had ridiculed him early in his ministry, Canon Wilberforce. The book was *The Trinity of Evil*. Indulging his love of punning, his ability to extend an image, and his talent for alliteration Spurgeon welcomed a "canon in cannonading against such gigantic foes as infidelity, impurity, and intemperance. The shot seem to have been made white-hot in the heart-fires of the author, and then fearlessly and forcefully hurled with

---

1. Charles Spurgeon, *Lectures to My Students*, (London: Passmore and Alabaster, 1881), 192.

2. S&T, 1880, "Preface," iv.

powerful precision at each pernicious practice."[3] He went on to evoke churches to erect such batteries until these monster evils were all destroyed.

At the same time Spurgeon demurred at the genre's tendency to meddlesome faddishness. He found much good and some silliness in a book entitled, rather ostentatiously, *The Practical Moral Lesson Book*. The book claimed to embrace "the Principles which, as derived from the Teaching of Scripture and the Writings of the most eminent Authors, should regulate Human Conduct." Spurgeon was specifically solicitous that fathers have their sons read a chapter concerning masturbation, couched of course in proper Victorian circumlocutions: "Fathers would do well to make their boys read the chapter concerning chastity, where in a very delicate, veiled manner a certain secret sin and all other uncleanness is solemnly spoken of." Spurgeon also found good advice in chapters on food, pure air, light, clothing, exercise, opium, alcohol, and mental excitement. When it came to experimentation on tea and coffee, however, Spurgeon had had enough. Running experiments involving the distillation of certain constituent elements of tea, an American scientist found that in certain proportions it would kill rabbits and cats. Spurgeon concluded that it was more "calculated to alarm rabbits and cats than to influence anybody else," and issued the warning with obvious decrepitation, "There you tea-drinking reader, tremble for yourself and your rabbits, and your tabbies!" He also advised the editor to "let our tea-tables alone, or if he must assail them, to do so without the help of this American doctor and his 10,860 cats."[4]

In crusading against wrong, one must not misrepresent one's perceived opponents. Tapley Ward wrote a book on *Temperance Tales*, and after his name placed the initials I.O.G.T. Spurgeon asked, "What, in the name of Alpha, Beta, Gamma, Delta, and all the rest of them, is the meaning of I.O.G.T? Does it mean, "I object to Grog in toto?" Spurgeon confessed that he had no admiration for sensational stories at any time, and even less for these. "Why did not Mr. Tapley keep to his tap?" Spurgeon was all in favor of the vindication of "teetotalism" but it did not have to involve the abuse of the hyper-Calvinists. Among them dwelt some of the most ardent teetotalers in England. Though he had issues with those brethren, he was sorry to see them misrepresented. In a subtle vein of facetious humor, he criticized Tapley for being so little acquainted with the "Hypers", not only on their habits of abstinence, but to fault them for "preaching too arousingly to sinners." Spurgeon quipped, "We thought that Satan himself would never have accused Hyper preachers of this."[5]

In his notice of *Cruel Wrong*, Spurgeon blasted the double standard often involved in the devastation left in the wake of fornication. "Where the sins of young 'gentlemen' are winked at, and poor women alone are made to suffer the shame of sin, incalculable misery must follow." Amusement at the sowing of "wild oats" on the part of men, as if fornication were a natural and pardonable folly necessary to developing maturity, must be stopped, and the "age must be made to see unchastity on the part of men in the fair, truthful light, as being in every way as evil, and in some respects more evil, than the same offence in women." Merely waging war against the foul practice, however, and exposing the sorrow and cruelty it generates, will do little good unless the brightness and beauty of holy purity be cherished. Nevertheless, books that "reveal the hidden things of darkness, have their appropriate ministry."[6]

---

3. S&T, July 1886, 371.

4. S&T, May 1871, 236.

5. Ibid., 234.

6. S&T, April 1886, 187.

Sometimes Spurgeon indicated his irritation at the zeal some demonstrated against the consumption of anything alcoholic. "No man has a right to deny another his Christian liberty in this matter," he contended, "but," he added, "it is safest to feel quite free to do without." A majority of his own students, as well as students in other denominational colleges, had pledged to be total abstainers. This was not true of those in Wales. Though not a crusader, at this time, on the radical side of this issue, Spurgeon reminded his readers that "we never hear of characters being ruined, and dishonour being brought upon the cause of Christ, through a man's drinking water."[7]

A writer from America chronicled briefly Spurgeon's personal bout with the issue of alcohol consumption. "By a strange providence I was permitted to see him in 1868." At thirty-four Spurgeon had once taken the pledge of abstinence, according to the writer Fulton, but had "gone back to his wine and beer, and smoked to an alarming extent." Men wept over this and pleaded with him, and according to this American teetotaler, "the battle was fought and the victory was won" and Spurgeon "became a total abstinence champion."[8]

Though Spurgeon became a clear advocate of abstinence from alcohol, he maintained some ambivalence on how aggressively one should impose that view on others. The pressure brought to bear on him from many quarters was never far from his mind when this subject arose, and the freedom, circumspectly claimed by some, to partake discreetly he could not condemn. As an example of this personal tension, he commended *Fireside Homilies* by Henry Alford as "full of good wholesome teaching" that must have made the good man's household "a little heaven." Spurgeon won-

dered, however, how the "total abstaining friends" would respond to the Dean's remarks on Christ's turning water into wine. Spurgeon quoted a long paragraph of Alford's words to his daughters. God has given a lavish and abundant creation to be enjoyed upon which his creatures may exercise much discretion by divine grace, and find it a source of joy, or "which man's evil way may turn into mischief." Had some of "our present philanthropists been guests at that wedding we should have had them beseeching the Lord of bounty and grace not to create wine that might inebriate, as we have them now trying to fain credence for the fiction, that what he did create was not wine at all." Then in a tender irony to his daughters he advised, "Well, darlings, let us be thankful in our bodies and our souls that God knows better, and that we are in his hands." Spurgeon gives this particular comment of Alford not to refute him, but to allow the word to be said without it coming from him. Peculiarly sensitive to how the public regarded words from himself, Spurgeon wrote, "If *we* had been guilty of such an utterance we should have had half the Templars in England writing to us, and as we are already the best advised, instructed, lectured, bullied, persuaded, threatened, warned, denounced, be-rated, and scolded man in England, we are happy that it is Dean Alford, and not C. H. S. who has committed himself in this way."[9] It was too late, however for the Dean to take on himself some of the attention with which Spurgeon had been favored, for the book was by the "late" Henry Alford.

In August 1880 Spurgeon announced that the companion volume to *John Ploughman's Talk* was about to be published. He believed that *John Ploughman's Pictures* would "amuse and interest our friends." Its publication would be accompanied by a new edition of *Talk* which would bring the

---

7. S&T, June 1878, 316.

8. Justin D. Fulton, *Charles H. Spurgeon, Our Ally* (Chicago: H. J. Smith & Co., 1892), vii.

9. S&T, March 1885, 137.

number in print to 300,000. Though some thought such books were of small utility he had "received continual evidence to the contrary." "Persons who read the quaint proverbs of John Ploughman are induced to read Spurgeon's sermons, and by this means are led to Christ, while others are helped on in the paths of temperance and thrift."[10]

Though he chafed under the pretensions and absolutistic claims of the "teetotalers" for some years of his ministry, Spurgeon overall was their friend and advocated a lifestyle of sobriety and thrift realizing that intemperance was the ruin of many a household. In 1865 he spoke at the organizational meeting for the "United Kingdom Bank of Hope" and saw W. R. Selway, a member of the executive committee of the National Temperance League, place medals around the necks of his twin sons and heard them pledge in their first public utterances, "I hope to be a teetotaler all of my life."[11] The object of the League was the "promotion of temperance by the practice and advocacy of total abstinence from intoxicating beverages."[12] The specimen, therefore, that he gave of the new *Ploughman* was entitled "He had a hole under his nose and his money runs into it." Among its choice and pithy sayings of wit, stated in the style of proverbs: "If a pot of beer is a yard of land, he must have swallowed more acres than a ploughman could get over for many a day, and still he goes on swallowing until he takes to wallowing." In fact, if the convictions of John Ploughman are identical with those of Spurgeon, in this article he sided with the teetotalers when he lamented, "Certain neighbors of mine laugh at me for being a teetotaler, and I might well laugh at them for being drunk, only I feel more inclined

to cry that they should be such fools. O that we could get them sober, and then perhaps we might make men of them."[13] Spurgeon indicated that he had received some harsh treatment for efforts to reduce the opportunity for drunkenness that he saw so frequently in the Southwark district.

> Now, if we try to do anything to shut up a boozing house, or shorten the hours for guzzling, we are called all sorts of bad names, and the wind-up of it all is—"*What, Rob a poor man of his beer?*" The fact is that they rob the poor man *by* his beer. The ale-jug robs the cupboard and the table, starves the wife and strips the children; it is a great thief, housebreaker, and heartbreaker, and the best possible thing is to break it to pieces, or keep it on the shelf bottom upwards.[14]

Spurgeon's language is reminiscent of the claims of the temperance movement when it pictures a man that has signed the pledge. "In a short time a decided improvement takes place in their circumstances; they, with their wives and families, are soon better clothed and better fed, and needed articles of furniture are brought to their dwellings; the children are sent to school; attendance is given to the house of God, and teetotalism is praised to the skies."[15]

No later than 1882, Spurgeon had become convinced that "teetotalism" should be "praised to the skies." He reviewed *The Drink Problem and its Solution* and approved its suggestions that "the only true solution of the drink problem is to be found in the total *legislative prohibition of the manufacture, importation, and sale of intoxicating liquors as beverages, or articles for dietetic use.*" Spurgeon did not condemn this as an impractical suggestion; moreover, when he looked at the

---

10. S&T, August 1880, 401.

11. W. Y. Fullerton, *C. H. Spurgeon: Biography* (London: Williams & Norgate, 1920), 38.

12. *The Temperance Record* (January 8, 1870), 18.

13. S&T, August 1880, 401f.

14. Ibid., 403.

15. *The Temperance Record* (January 8, 1870), 20.

possibility of legal means being taken to curb the insane abuse of alcohol he solemnly stated, "Most devoutly do we hope such a measure will soon be upon the statute-book; together with a Sunday-closing bill for England; and act for the abolition of grocers' licenses, which have been the means of a frightful increase of drunkenness, especially among women; and any other legislation which will prepare the way for the final overthrow of the power of alcohol in these realms."[16]

This strong language coincided with Spurgeon's election as president of the "Metropolitan Tabernacle Total Abstinence Society." Due to sickness, he was unable to preside at this first meeting, and his General Baptist friend John Clifford performed that duty. He did, however, manage to send a letter espousing unequivocally the goal of the total abstinence movement. After apologies for his absence due to sickness, Spurgeon expressed his conviction that "next to the preaching of the gospel, the most necessary thing to be done in England is to induce our people to become total abstainers." They should not strut with peacock feathers or putty medals and assault the moderate drinkers but go after the real drunkards in order to bring "the poor enslaved creatures to the feet of Jesus, who can give them liberty."[17] He was glad that, at the Tabernacle, the temperance work was in the hands of men that loved Jesus and would not be satisfied with sobriety alone but looked also for the initiation of genuine piety. They saw anything "short of the new birth as short of that for which they live and labour." For himself, Spurgeon would help in the movement where he could, but "our own work lies in the preaching of the gospel, and by that work all our energies are absorbed."[18]

16. S&T, April 1882, 199.

17. Ibid., 201.

18. S&T, October 1882, 547.

At a prayer meeting in September 1882, the congregation prayed for a woman's husband, addicted to drink now but formerly a gospel proclaimer. Spurgeon commented, "It is a dreadful thing that so many hopeful spirits, bright spirits, loving spirits, who were beloved by all who knew them, should fall by little and little through the insidious habit of drunkenness." Determined not to take too much, but lured on by appetite, they destroy themselves and those dearest to them. "This withering sin touches the character as with a hot iron, and all the beauty and the joy of life fade away." Elevating the intensity of his rhetoric with a question, "How can this plague be stayed?" he lamented the possibility that "those who have preached to others should themselves fall short of the kingdom." Drink, in slaying its millions, "has dragged down men who stood like angels in their brightness, and quenched them into degradation and misery till they were like to devils in wickedness and fury." The doing and undoings of drunkenness made one despair, for, though all sins are deadly "this is a sword with which men play till it cuts them to the heart." Spurgeon wanted to blunt the sword and pray for the wounded.[19]

Baptists developed an aggressive approach to the temperance cause and Spurgeon fully approved of it. Spurgeon reviewed Volume 1 of its periodical *The Bond of Union: the Organ of the Baptist Total Abstinence Association* in March 1885. After congratulating the workers on their vigorous labors, he urged all Baptist ministers to "fight the demon of our country with all their might." Such almighty work could not fail to drive them to "total abstinence." From personal experience he could say, "Whatever a man's views to begin with, he is not long in personal contact with the evils of drink before he resolves to be quit of

19. S&T, November 1882, 586.

the vile thing, root and branch." He likened it to the embrace of an octopus. None would be satisfied that a few of its arms and suckers should remain, but "he tugs and tears, right and left, to be rid of every particle of the loathsome thing." Once free from it, no one desires to return for "the rest and refreshment which come of being free from alcohol far exceed any which its presence can bestow." He included himself among the number of those that had been "on the teetotal spree for years" and would be sorry to have to fall back to "the terrible self-denial of habitual imbibing."[20] Spurgeon had become a full convert to the principle of total abstinence.

Though not as visible and destructive in England itself as drunkenness, no less devastating to human life in general and no less severe an evil was the Indo-British opium trade. It brought millions into the budget of the British government of India, but was done so at the cost of myriads of Chinese. "If war is slaying its thousands, the opium trade is slaying its ten thousands." Abolition of this, in Spurgeon's estimation, was as essential as the abolition of slavery in the first part of the nineteenth century and just as urgent a moral issue. "Well would it have been if the virtuous and tender-hearted Queen of these realms had refused the title of Empress of the Indian Empire so long as this self-inflicted curse upon itself and other nations remained." One could not look, however, to the government for the initiative in getting rid of this curse. Like all great measures for public welfare, this must come from the people. "General sympathy must be awakened, and agitation upon the subject must be continued and increased until some Wilberforce or Clarkson shall force it upon the attention of the Government." He advocated participation

in the Anti-Opium Society until such agitation of the subject can make this outrage a matter of national conscience. The loss of £5-6 million in revenue would be more than compensated for by the moral gain "to the honour of the English nation," and the credibility of the witness of Christian missionaries.[21]

In light of the implications of such issues as drunkenness, illicit trade, and slavery for human life and especially the integrity of gospel witness, Spurgeon felt that awareness of political issues was especially incumbent upon Dissenters. Not only did these social/moral issues demand some immediate solution by legal means, but the massive struggles Dissenters had endured to attain religious freedom and political equality demanded knowledge, so that Englishmen might know how to execute both their duties and their freedoms. He recommended that fathers see to it that their boys were aware of the facts contained in *The Roll Call* which condensed the political record for the years 1775 through 1880. "The record is well written," Spurgeon commented, and is calculated to feed the minds and rouse the spirits of young Liberals. Conservative youth will not be pleased with the unwelcome truths here set in order; but it might do them good to see history as others see it."[22]

Theology and Apologetics Designed to Aid the Minister and the Believer

Spurgeon looked for works of scholarship that defended the faith once for all delivered to the saints and aided believers in giving a solid defense of Bible truth. He had little confidence, however, in the true efficiency of such apologetics to make a dent in the fabric of unbelief. In a brief commendation of a book that displayed in forensic form

---

20. S&T, March 1885, 141.

21. S&T, January 1880, 38.

22. S&T, May 1881, 233.

the evidences for the resurrection, Spurgeon consented that "we should like to see this pamphlet in the hands of our young men of to-day, that they may not be seduced by the demon of 'modern thought.'"[23] At the most emotionally transparent level, however, he wished that "these defences were no longer needed," for theologically he had "no great faith in their efficacy, good as they are."[24] The source of unbelief lay more profoundly in the heart, though confusion of mind could serve as a source for the heart's resistance. "The blindness," he said, contemplating this issue in 1878, "is upon the heart as well as upon the mind, and men grope at noonday as the blind feel for the wall."[25] He held the same position in 1886 but had even greater skepticism about intellectual honesty in an unbeliever. A discussion of *Doctrine and Doubt* Spurgeon found convincing, but only "convincing to the candid." Who can turn from their doubts those that resolve to disbelieve? Aids in seeking to do such are welcomed, but "chiefly we look up to the Holy Spirit, and beseech him to create saving faith in men; for there is not upon the earth one grain of it which is not of his working and there never will be." He was more and more of the conviction that "all who accept the truth are under a divine anointing, and that while men remain in their natural blindness the clearest reasoning will never make them see."[26]

A solid defense of revelation, if it did not indulge too much in advertisement of the arguments of infidels, but proposed a "discreet advocacy of the claims of Christ" and positive exposition of the "bulwarks of our holy faith", was always welcome.[27] Such a book was *The Truth of Scripture in Connection with Revelation, Inspiration, and the Canon* by James Given. He called in an "armoury of weapons of defence against skeptical objections—weapons which intelligent men may handle to purpose." The writer furnished not only the right kind of ammunition but guided to other sources from which appropriate weapons could be gathered. Given did this with boldness, assuring his readers that the loud voices of infidelity had no stronger arguments than had already been put forth and put down, and would not be a whit more successful than in the past. It was a "masterly piece of apologetics, and we have had the utmost pleasure in its perusal." Spurgeon planned to spend more time with it "for it is plainly worthy of no ordinary reading." The way in which the author removed apparent discrepancies and difficulties makes "faith to laugh at her assailants, and grow rich on their spoils."[28]

A cohort of three apologetic works he reviewed in April 1882: *The Logic of Christian Evidences* by G. F. Wright, *The Great Problem* by "a student of science," and *The Resurrection of Jesus Christ* by John Kennedy. Each of these volumes showed the "reasonableness of Christianity in reply to those who affect to regard it as a phenomenon of human fabrication" and ignore its own claim to be a system of divine revelation. If answering unbelief could be condensed to a pure matter of sound argument, then all caviling against the gospel soon would cease, Spurgeon reaffirmed, and the deference shown infidelity by Christian apologists should "rebuke the defiance of those who persist in treating the gospel as a fable." These three works will help believers to admire the beauty of Christianity from every perspective and will strengthen them in many ways against all attempts to discredit that which has

---

23. S&T, December 1883, 644.

24. S&T, April 1886, 188.

25. S&T, June 1878, 314.

26. S&T, April 1886, 188.

27. S&T, June 1878, 314.

---

28. S&T, March 1881, 146.

been implanted in their hearts. Christian teachers have urgent need for Christian knowledge so that they can form a true "salvation army" made up, rank and file, of "something better than raw recruits who rely on anecdotes to attract attention." So impressive, in fact, is the evidence of Jesus' resurrection from the dead, "to doubt it were to discredit all the classic literature which has fostered the civilization of the human race." But for those whose hearts are as yet unchanged and who revile Scripture as pious legend, who think miracles are a mirage of the mind, "ascribe doctrines to pious dotage, and resent precepts as puerile" no amount of logic [or alliteration!] will reach them, and such books as these are "not very likely to be the means of converting many infidels." That thought, however, should not disconcert believers, for the savants "fight with feathers against the citadel of our faith." In a sentence that captures Spurgeon's confidence in the self-authenticating power of the gospel as clearly as any, he contended, "The living power of the gospel of the grace of God gives us such lively satisfaction every day that if the evidences of the past could be effaced, our experience of the present would amply suffice to confirm us in their credibility." The evidences are useful and encouraging to minds that love the beauty of divine truth, to those to whom the word has been the means of the new birth, and will help equip them for faithful and effective service; but the converting power still is God's alone. In these matters, the mind will be convinced only of what the heart has seen, heard, and tasted.[29]

He did appreciate *A Popular Handbook of Christian Evidences*, Part II. "Amid the scoffs and sneers of *savans* and simpletons, it is well for our young men to know how compact the historical proofs of the gospel really are." Though evidences do not convince the unbeliever, such books still perform no small service in the light, strength, confidence, and intellectual certainty they set before the saints. Spurgeon, in fact, thought the evidences so coherent that he used Job's description of the scales of Leviathan metaphorically for the compelling nature of whole field of proofs. "They are shut up together as with a close seal. One is so near to another that no air can come between them. They are joined one to another, they stick together, that they cannot be sundered."[30] Even though an unbeliever cannot be brought to believe by Christian evidences, he certainly should be.

A review of *The Mosaic Origin of the Pentateuchal Codes* by Geerhardus Vos, a fellow at Princeton, carried the dual theme of appreciation and regret combined with his own pride of detachment from some of the modern fights over the biblical text. Carting away rubbish was a good exercise for schoolboys, Spurgeon reflected, and added that "training in metaphysics is about the best qualification for a Reviewer of the new theology." He did appreciate the contribution of his transatlantic brethren for their "scathing criticism of modern Teutonic literature." For himself, however, often he only learned of the existence of a new theory when someone declared it exploded. Perhaps he was behind the age and his library similar to an old directory, but his books nevertheless were the "survival of the fittest." He confessed never to have read a line of those renowned scholars Graf, Kuenen, and Wellhausen "who affect to find traces of forgery in the Books of Moses." He never intended to read a line of them "and we smile as we are informed that they have been duly refuted and disposed of."[31] Had he been able to see the future, Spurgeon probably would have regretted having the edge of conde-

---

29. S&T, April 1882, 197.

30. S&T, March 1883, 140.

31. S&T, July 1886, 371.

scension in his pen as he dismissed Geerhardus Vos as a "schoolboy."

A similar admission comes in a review of *A Critical History of Philosophy* by Asa Mahan. The book was a "popular survey ... readable and refreshing all the way through." He confessed that he was "out of court" as a critic, for "the Vedas or the Shasters we have never read. Neither Kant nor Comte are on the shelves of our library." He noted that all his knowledge of these subjects and writers was second-hand.[32]

Second-hand knowledge, however, in his case was quite profound as he had traversed the territory a number of times from the perspective of many expert writers. His own schedule of reading, preparation for sermons and lectures, editing, writing, and speaking made it necessary for him to trust others to do the original work in these areas remote to his own primary calling. He was always happy to have access to essays that would keep him abreast of the times, to have the suggestion of ideas upon which he could expand by his own fertile imagination and critical faculties, to get a supply of arrows for his armory, and to continue to develop arguments against the modern infidelity growing like weeds on this philosophical soil.

Not only was it impractical and impossible for everyone to have a firsthand knowledge of the vast array of philosophical and critical literature produced since the seventeenth century, for the clear approval of truth and assurance of a genuine knowledge of God it was unnecessary. Spurgeon believed that Christian experience itself served as a credible apologetic for the truth of Christianity. In a review of a book by R. W. Dale, Spurgeon commended his appeal to the power of true religion and added, "we feel sure that the effect of the gospel is its best evidence, and the phenomenon of conversions its surest proof." Scientists arrayed their supposed facts against the gospel, but Christians have "personal contact with God" which puts an end to the superstition of priestism and "the unbelief which rejects the Scriptures."[33] Years of reading apologetic literature only confirmed his basic conviction that "experimental proof of our holy religion is the best and most readily available" evidence. This he had sought to develop briefly in *Clue of the Maze* and he welcomed its further investigation in *Doctrine and Doubt; or, Christ the Centre of Christianity.*

When books took positions that Spurgeon strongly affirmed but did it without sufficient coherence or credibility, he had to be careful not to dissociate himself from the true assertion or approve an insufficient foundation for its defense. Such was the case with a new translation of the New Testament (*The New Testament Translated from the Purest Greek*) that used the words "immerse" and "immerser" instead of the foreign word "Baptist." Spurgeon admired the translator's honesty in using the true translation instead of the circumlocution involved in transliteration. He hoped that the present revisers of the Authorized Version would have as much honesty. Either they should translate it fairly, or "confess inability for the work at hand." Nonetheless, he felt compelled to question the overall scholarship and judgment manifest in the present translation of John Bowes. "The task undertaken in this book is evidently a delicate and difficult one, demanding much learning and great discretion: we cannot, however, find these manifest here, and therefore, while admiring the translator's honesty, we think he has failed in his attempt."[34]

Occasionally books appeared that had such a straightforward purpose and executed it so

---

32. S&T, December 1883, 646-47.

33. S&T, October 1874, 488.

34. S&T, December 1870, 573.

clearly and well that Spurgeon felt no need to provide a caveat. Writing on the Trinity, George Paterson in *Scripture proof for the glorious doctrine of the Trinity* handled the subject so impressively that Spurgeon said it was "fitted to be a class-book on the subject for students, and a standard book of reference for ministers."[35] He commended the Meyer Commentary series on the New Testament as "scholarship of the highest class" and by "universal consent" the most dependable for "accuracy of criticism and exegesis."[36]

Normally Spurgeon did not like books of comparative religion, for they implied too much compromise and at times sought to show that people all over the world were searching for God. He eschewed the term "comparative theology" as misleading and did not "believe in the theory that fallen men are seeking after God and truth."[37] George Rawlinson's *Religions of the Ancient World* was quite to his taste because Rawlinson vindicated the orthodox position that "there is one true revelation, and that other religions are the result of the depravity of man's nature."[38] Moreover, he found one by James Wells, not the hyper-Calvinist, to be quite helpful and relating the right tone about comparison of other religious teachers to Jesus. Wells milked all he could out of the heathen religious thinkers in order to compare their insights to the revealed truth of Christianity. As he wrote in the last chapter, "We can thus hope to read off the highest water-mark which unaided human speculation and virtue have reached, and we may then compare it with the Christian standard."[39]

In his preface, Wells told why he decided to publish such a book, the study for which had been a mere curiosity and avocation in earlier days. "He is naturally disposed to think that others, especially young men, may be helped by a study which broke for him the spell of non-Christian thought, and which has strengthened his own Christian convictions and desire for Christian Service."[40] Nearing the end of his discussion of Aeschylus, Wells observed, "Like all heathen writers, our poet does not clearly distinguish between sin and crime, nor has he any conception of the spirituality and universality of moral law. He does not brand with guilt the evil motives and wishes which do not proceed to action. It has been truly said that crime and criminal belong to every language; but that sin and sinner belong to the Christian vocabulary only. Aeschylus does not hold, as some of our scientific men do, that sin cannot be forgiven and that the past is irreparable. Even in his gloomy theology he finds place for pardon"[41] Spurgeon certainly liked the subtle subversion of modern theology by Wells' preference for Greek heathenism over them. Following an astute, and at times moving, account of how Dionysius the Areopagite might have heard the preaching of the Apostle on Mars Hill informed by the haunting natural theology of Aeschylus, Wells closed with an intriguing, if not compelling, proposition.

Aeschylus, unconsciously and in ignorance, reveals the profound affinities between Christ and the natural conscience. He proves, to borrow a phrase from the Church Fathers, that the divine book and the human breast agree. We point to him as a proof that there abides in the inmost soul of man an indestructible Christ-need, which asserts

35. S&T, September 1870, 437.

36. S&T, March 1881, 146.

37. S&T, March 1883, 145, review of *The Faiths of the World*.

38. S&T, May 1883, 240.

39. James Wells, *Christ and the Heroes of Heathendom* (London: The Religious Tract Society, 1886), 131.

40. Ibid., 4.

41. Ibid., 28.

itself to a thoughtful pagan, even when entangled with a contradictory theology, and belonging to an age and race intoxicated with materialism and sensuality. The pacification of the conscience and the purification of the soul which Aeschylus sought, and in the reality of which he firmly believed, the Gospel offers to every man under heaven. What was but a dim and fleeting shadow to the great Greek is an historical reality to the Christian. The fancies of the Greek tragedian, corresponding in some respects so strangely in general outline with the faith of the Christian, may help us to believe that the Maker of our hearts is also the Author of the Gospel, and that in Christ Jesus He has made exquisitely complete provision for all the needs of sinning and perishing men.[42]

After similarly insightful discussions of Socrates and Plato, Wells discussed Epictetus and Stoicism. Stoicism challenged the cruel and unbridled immorality of Rome, made adamantine men, and riveted specific virtues in the souls of its followers. Epictetus emerged as the saint of heathenism. Its weaknesses, however, were found in its immutable pretensions to strength. Wells quoted Cicero the Stoic saying, "We boast justly of our own virtue, which we could not do if we derived it from the Deity, and not from ourselves." Stoicism would view a religion of grace as a contradiction in terms, for "the essence of virtue lay in its being an unaided achievement, and grace thus spoiled all goodness." Living in light of forgiveness of sin merely insulted the Stoic, who would have to "renounce every virtue he prized before he could receive the Gospel." Wells argued that stoicism robs men of necessary solace from without and drives the soul in upon itself. When sorrowful, the Stoic points to the resources in our own heart, forgetting that "it is the heart which is overwhelmed and most needs succour." The

soul must be *invictus* within and without, exterminating God-given emotions and creating of its devotee, not more of a man but less of a man, and in the process destroying the feminine in woman. Spurgeon would gravitate toward Wells' discussion of grace and suffering emotion. Even in these two points, Wells had shown the religious superiority of Christianity to Stoicism, and thus the highest of heathendom.

His carefully crafted language finally led him to a strong affirmation of the necessity of divine revelation as present in the Bible and the superiority, and peerlessness, of Christ. "They who say that we owe more to modern culture than to the Bible, are like the countryman who maintained that we are more indebted to the moon than to the sun, because the sun shines by day, when we don't need its light; or like the boy who, surveying himself in the looking-glass, declared that his father took after him. The Gospel has greatly lessened its own evidences by having lessened the surrounding darkness." Because of the improvement in culture in every aspect due to the influence of the Bible, Wells claimed, "It may thus easily happen that some modern sages light their taper at a torch which they scorn, drink of a stream whose source they ignore, and feed on the fruits of the tree they would fain cut down; they would rob the mother of her own children, and preserve the sunbeams while destroying the parent sun."[43]

With Christ, moreover, Wells saw no possible comparison in the heathen world. The gap is so wide as to challenge even the idea of comparison. "I contrast Christendom with Heathendom, and Christ with the sages," he reminded the reader, "and I discover that He is utterly beyond all competition or comparison, and that as there is a heavenwide difference between Him and the

42. Ibid., 38.

43. Ibid., 131.

foremost of them, the phrase, 'comparative religion,' is scarcely correct. Thus I am able to give to the unbeliever a reason for the faith that is in me."[44] When Christians are challenged by the spirit of modern culture to make concessions on the absolute and exclusive worthiness of Christ in his teaching and in his work of reconciliation, Wells urged one to maintain the confidence implicit in the evidence—"When we place Christ and the sages side by side we shall feel more than ever that the Christian thinker is not required to make concessions, for by the aid of the law of contrast we shall gain the fullest persuasion of the peerless excellences of Christ as the Light and Life of men."[45]

In one section, however, Wells discussed the idea of knowledge of God by an operation of the Spirit outside the parameters of a proclaimed gospel or a read Bible. He firmly consented to the Bible's teaching that "all who are saved are saved by Christ only, and that men who know the Gospel are saved through the Gospel only." At the same time he did not think that the Bible taught "that the merit of Christ cannot overflow the ordinary means of grace, or that there can be no salvation outside the visible Church." In our just certainty that Christ is the only way, "We must have a care not to narrow the area of the Spirit's power, for He is ubiquitous as the wind, and 'worketh when, and where, and how He pleaseth.'"[46] He believed that the apostle worked toward leaving this door open in Romans 1 where "his words certainly seem to imply that some of the sages walked with God according to their light, and that they were accepted of Him."[47] The confidence in reason that had gradually inundated Anglicanism through the seven-

teenth century influence of Archbishop Tillotson found fresh expression in Wells' confidence in the congeniality, though rarely acquiring a positive response, between reason and revelation.

Spurgeon said that Wells displayed great skill in "charming minds into attention, and then instructing them most solidly." The readers acquainted with the heathen thinkers would "peruse these pages with satisfaction." For once, Spurgeon acknowledged, he had become tolerant of the science of comparative religion for Wells' use of it was most admirable. "Those who talk of our divine Lord as one among many teachers may here learn how far the best of those many are removed from him." They are like glow worms, and he is the Sun. Spurgeon did not mention his reaction to the concept of the believing God-fearer among the heathen.[48]

The strange omission of any comment about this matter might have two or three explanations. One, Spurgeon relied too much on another reviewer before he made his own comments and his helper did not see Wells' hesitance to "narrow the area of the Spirit's power." The beauty of Wells' discussion in every place else in the book and the clear affirmation of the absoluteness and revelatory foundation of Christianity in comparison to all other religions and philosophies might have created such a disposition in favor of the book that it was not read critically enough. Second, if Spurgeon did all the work on this book and merely sampled pivotal places he himself might have missed the opportunity for his usual caveat on problem passages.

Third, Spurgeon himself might have been open to such a possibility. In an exposition of Romans 1:1-25, commenting on verses 19 and 20, Spurgeon said, "Men who never heard the gospel

---

44. Ibid., 151.
45. Ibid., 156.
46. Ibid., 152.
47. Ibid., 154.

48. S&T, November 1886, 595.

can see God in his works if they open their eyes. There is written upon the face of nature enough to condemn men if they do not turn to God. There is a gospel of the sea, and of the heavens, of the stars, and of the sun; and if men will not read it, they are guilty, for they are wilfully ignorant of what they might know, and ought to know."[49] Did he hold the possibility that, by the aid of the Spirit, some men might read the gospel of the sea, the heavens, and the stars rightly? This seems unlikely for Spurgeon is clear in an exposition of John 1 that "There is no way of knowing God, and being reconciled to God, except as we receive Jesus Christ, his Son, into our hearts, and learn of him, through the Holy Spirit's teaching, all that he delights to reveal to us concerning his Father."[50] In an exposition of Romans 10 he clearly stated that the word of faith that is to be believed for salvation is "wherever Christ is preached, and wherever his Word is read."[51] In a sermon on "Gospel Missions," Spurgeon urged zeal in the enterprise by presenting a scene of "tens of thousands of spirits who are now walking in outer darkness; could I take you to the gloomy chambers of hell, and show you myriads upon myriads of heathen souls in unutterable torture, not having heard the Word, but being justly condemned for their sins."[52] There does not appear to be any facet of Spurgeon's theology that would support option three. His understanding of human depravity, the bondage of the will, the relationship of regeneration to the means of preaching the word—all these do not give room for some one apart from the gospel to read the "gospel of the sea" rightly. Instead, either he let down his guard or he felt that the loophole was inconsequential.

Books of Sound Theology combined with Spiritual and Experimental Power

"From a dry unspiritual scholarship may the Lord deliver us! It is as destructive as the heat of Nebuchadnezzar's furnace," Spurgeon wrote in his review of J. Hawker's *Unpolished Gems of Scripture.* Spurgeon found wonderful entertainment in the "deep spirituality of his tone, the graciousness of his doctrine, and the freshness of his thought."[53] Each of these three things attracted Spurgeon, and their intertwined presence in one volume obviously gave him lasting pleasure. He labored for those traits in his own work. In his extensive labors, including his writing, editing, and publishing, he kept pressing for fresh gospel application to the spiritual life of the Christian and the conversion of the sinner. He did not write secular works, and did not even advocate the reading of novels. Most attempts at poetry were worse than vain, in his opinion, and wasteful of energy. He did "not feel the influence of poetic zephyrs" but stood in need of "at least a Miltonic hurricane to make us sensitive to the power of poesy." He delighted in trying his hand at hymns, for one could express Christian experience, doctrinal truth, and urge sinners to believe, but his attempts were comparatively few and prompted by special occasions or urgent situations. In his reviews, he gave himself to "the piety, the doctrine and the experience" of the volumes sent him, "for these we may aspire to know something of."[54]

He felt no compunction, however, in reviling, sometimes with great subtlety, books that trifled with devotion, that offered pious titles with little substance. His comments on *Quiet Words for Quiet Moments* simply stated, "Very quiet, qui-

---

49. MTP, 1892, 252.

50. SEE, 12:493.

51. Ibid., 480.

52. SS, 1:340.

---

53. S&T, July 1866, 371.

54. S&T, December 1870, 571. "A Winding Rill of Thought in relation to Nature, Providence, and Grace."

etude itself."[55] In reading *William Louge of Wyke-ham* he admitted that he "dozed off sweetly while trying to read it, and therefore we can strongly recommend it as restful." He wandered among monks and other medieval personages until he "dropped off into dreamland," but still could not discover why the story was written. "Never mind," he closed, "it did us good. We are the better for the nap."[56] His one object in his own pen-work was to spread the gospel as clearly with the quill as with his pulpit.

Spurgeon often showed a playfulness in dealing with a book that he intended to recommend with gusto for its fiery and contagious spirituality and religious fervor. In a book of Welsh preachers, he wrote, "Moreover, as their language is according to their own judgment—and they ought to know—so heavenly, so divine, it is no great marvel that those who use it are able to produce extraordinary results. As we see it in print, we feel that our friends are right; it is an unearthly language, and to us unutterable. Ll and a w, double l again and a y, and then the rest of the alphabet shot down like a load of coals. What can this muddle mean? The man who can pronounce these jumbles of consonants must be a born orator." With all mirth aside, Spurgeon, recommended the volume as one that would make the reader "fall in love with Welsh piety, and to long for its like in our English villages."[57]

Throughout his ministry, from the first days of preaching as a teenager, Spurgeon had placed great value on works that combined doctrine and experience. Doctrine, well blended into human experience and expressed plainly in literature, formed the surest path to true spirituality for the reader. A person could absorb the doctrinal truth and contemplate its spiritual application and power, its provocations for conviction and assurance, and by such mental work and spiritual meditation eventually make those experiences his own. This healthy blending of truth and experience that constituted true spirituality were formed into the soul by the work of the Spirit in a multitude of ways throughout the life of the Christian pilgrim. Carlile commented on the usefulness of Spurgeon's early acquaintance with this kind of godly literature:

> The rustic congregations knew the ring of sincerity. They might gape at displays of rhetorical fireworks, but they were not moved by them. As they listened to the youth of seventeen they were amazed at the depth of his experience. Many of his utterances bore indications of his industrious reading of the Puritan Fathers. But Spurgeon made the experience his own; in truth, it was amazing how deep and varied his spiritual experience appeared to all who knew him. It was not simply that he read experimental theology with unflagging interest and profit, but that he himself was so sensitized in spirit that he took on the experiences of others and lived them until they became his own.[58]

Spurgeon, on the basis of that sort of deep personal benefit, enjoyed and had the highest recommendation for books that showed the "anointing with fresh oil" in which "life, fervour, and joy" would gleam on each page.[59] He showed his lifelong commitment to the true integration of revealed truth, its systematic arrangement into comprehensively developed doctrines, and the consequent life altering, life building, spirit enriching, God-honoring power in such arrangements. He never found any books that rivaled the Puritans for their combination of biblical

---

55. S&T, February 1874, 90.

56. S&T, May 1883, 239.

57. S&T, November 1883, 558.

58. J. C. Carlile, *Charles H. Spurgeon: An Interpretative Biography* (London: Religious Tract Society, 1933), 85.

59. S&T, December 1870, 571.

doctrine and spiritual health. In reviewing a volume by F. Godet, *Studies on the New Testament*, after some mild commendation of it, he stated the standard by which he judged all spiritual literature: "In truth, good as this volume is, it is nothing comparable in weight of thought and depth of instruction to the grand old Puritan writings, which, to us at least, are ever new and full of suggestiveness."[60]

At the top of the Puritan standard for spirituality, creativity, and practical theology—the book that rendered all mere novelists as pretenders to literary art—was *Pilgrim's Progress* by the tinker from Bedford, John Bunyan. An allegory entitled *The Voyage of Life* by "a Sea Captain" conveyed good gospel truths for sailors, but the lengthened allegory "would have required the genius of a Bunyan to have sustained with unfailing interest to its close."[61] The library at his grandfather's house had introduced him to the adventure of *Pilgrim's Progress*, a story he never outlived. "We cannot have too many editions of this work," he commented on reviewing an inexpensive but nicely produced edition of "the incomparable dreamer's great work."[62] He sought to review every edition of the dreamer's *Pilgrim* and, if possible, commended it for a particular audience appropriate to the binding, type-press, and price. He thought that a polyglot version was a brilliant idea; when English and French were printed side by side, it would greatly benefit those "learners of the French tongue." The version he reviewed, however, was "worse than useless for such a purpose." Though well-presented and nicely illustrated, "the French does not tally with the English, and is misleading." He refused to call it a translation but a "mere bash with the force and beauty of the

original altogether cut away." Bunyan's poetical expression, pithy phrases, and even the form of the dream are either left out, mauled, or travestied to such a degree that Spurgeon concluded "We never knew a good idea so badly realized."[63] An edition that appeared in 1885 with large print, notes by Robert Maguire, and illustrations by H. C. Selous and M. Paolo Priolo, captured Spurgeon's fancy. "We shall lay this volume by," he began rather inauspiciously, "till our eyes force us a second time to the spectacle-maker." Then the large letter volume would be a precious pearl. "Father Honest himself could not have found fault with it, and Christiana would have danced for joy if she had possessed it." He advised Harry and Alice to get their shillings "and buy one for dear old Grandpapa."[64]

A book by A. Tholuck translated from German by Robert Menzies pleased Spurgeon greatly, both for its robust and sincere spiritual power and for its provenance. Evidently Spurgeon considered Tholuck in the same spiritual category as E. Lehmann about whom he wrote, "Written with that child-like faith which we see to perfection in Germans when the Lord sweetly leads their subtle intellects to the Redeemer's feet."[65] Tholuck met Spurgeon's most important standard. "To us," the plural for *me*, "estimating books by the standard of the heart, this is the book of the season," he judged, for the portion that he read was "marrow and fatness." Tholuck entertained no "dry theorizing or dead philosophizing" but went straight toward "vital truth glowing with every charm of grace. The pages are rich, pre-eminently rich with unction, and full of experimental truth." This was not a book to be done with quickly, but contained sustaining spiritual power for the believer, "if

---

60. S&T, April 1877, 185.

61. Ibid., 187.

62. S&T, June 1871, 285.

63. S&T, April 1877, 188.

64. S&T, January 1886, 34.

65. S&T, July 1886, 370.

he be of our mind," the standard of measure to which Spurgeon often referred. And it arose from Germany, an opportunity for "rebuilding what it once laboured to destroy." Spurgeon did not like the chapter on baptism, and certain other blurs. Perfection characterizes only those things that are altogether of the Lord.[66]

A book by James Paton containing twelve meditations on the twenty-third Psalm, Spurgeon recommended as "fraught with experimental matter" and "rich with the Erskine and Rutherford vein of spirituality. Full-grown believers will delight in the deep doctrines and high experience of the author." Rev. H. Tarrant's book *Times of Refreshing* chronicling the history of revivals, "some real and some questionable," was "earnest" but incomplete, yet breathed "a gracious fervent spirit."[67]

His friend, James Grant, produced one that could be the title for a Spurgeon biography, *Sources of Joy in Seasons of Sorrow; with other help on the Homeward way.* Aptly titled, this book had matter "so rich and choice that sad hearts must be encouraged." From his own experience Spurgeon knew that nights of grief needed reminders of the divine purpose in suffering as well as the genuine sympathy of Christ in such. Out of Grant's fifty volumes, none excelled this, according to Spurgeon. "The more spiritual the reader," Spurgeon wrote, in the kind of intimidating judgment to which he gave himself on occasion, "the higher will be his estimate of the mighty truths compressed into this volume."[68]

The spiritual ecstasy that Spurgeon seems most often to have been conveyed by a deep contemplation on the personal nature of the doctrines of grace—that special regard that the Father has for all those given to the Son in the covenant of grace. In the circumference of that circle of special, immutable, eternal redemptive blessings Spurgeon found himself enrapt in amazement and lost in wonder. "The antiquity of the covenant of grace demands our grateful attention," he encouraged his hearers; "it is a truth which tends to elevate the mind." He continued by expanding the intensity of his recommendation: "I know of no doctrine more grand than this." His own experience in giving attention confirmed his recommendation affirming, "It is the very soul and essence of all poetry, and in sitting down and meditating upon it, I do confess my spirit has sometimes been ravished with delight."[69] He knew that this meditation was too high for many, but, nevertheless, he recommended it as the most profound and direct cure to spiritual darkness when it descends on the saint. Only God can give a "song in the night" to the deeply distressed Christian. God himself must speak to his soul: "But let God come to his child in the night, let him whisper in his ear as he lies on his bed, and how you see his eyes flash in the night!" No human can do such a thing but "it is marvelous, brethren, how one sweet word of God will make whole songs for Christians. One word of God is like a piece of gold, and the Christian is the gold-beater, and he can hammer that promise out for whole weeks." Spurgeon, at twenty-three, claimed that he "lived on one promise for weeks" and hammered it so finely that he plated his "whole existence with joy from it." The matter for contemplation in its purest proof went back behind time to the reality of "electing love and covenanted mercies." What beyond this could be filled with more sublimity and a more profound

---

66. S&T, December 1870, 573.

67. Ibid., 530.

68. S&T, February 1871, 92.

69. Charles H. Spurgeon, "The Blood of the Everlasting Covenant," in *Revival Year Sermons* (Edinburgh: Banner of Truth Trust, 1996), 43.

source for undying and ever-increasing fullness of joy. Spurgeon teased out this matter of contemplation before he surrendered to other truths fit for giving song for those that could not maintain so high and intense a vision.

> When though thyself art low, it is well to sing of the fountain-head of mercy; of that blessed decree wherein thou wast ordained to eternal life, and of that glorious Man who undertook thy redemption; of that solemn covenant signed, and sealed, and ratified, in all things ordered well; of that everlasting love which, ere the hoary mountains were begotten, or ere the aged hills were children, chose thee, loved thee firmly, loved thee fast, love thee well, loved thee eternally. I tell thee, believer, if thou canst go back to the years of eternity; if thou canst in thy mind run back to that period, or ere the everlasting hills were fashioned, or the fountains of the great deep scooped out, and if thou canst see thy God inscribing thy name in his eternal book; if thou canst see in his loving heart eternal thoughts of love to thee, thou wilt find this a charming means of giving thee songs in the night. No songs like those which come from electing love; no sonnets like those that are dictated by meditations on discriminating mercy. … In our darker hours it is our joy to sing;

> > Sons we are through God's election,
> > Who in Jesus Christ believe;
> > By eternal destination,
> > Sovereign grace we now receive.
> > Lord, thy favor,
> > Shall both grace and glory give.[70]

In April, 1871, Spurgeon discovered a work by Maritius Bohemus, written in 1654. It was entitled, *A Christian's Delight; or, Morning Meditations upon One Hundred Choice Texts of Scripture.* Spurgeon included a selection from this book to encourage Sabbath reading for his congregation. He found these meditations "instructive and suggestive." These texts are precisely the kind that Spurgeon loved and that he himself produced in articles of spiritual comfort. Lines from one entitled "Christ's Power in our Weakness" demonstrates the deep Reformed spirituality so enthralling to Spurgeon. "When we are most sensible of our own impotency, then we must infallibly look for his omnipotency … Christ's sufficiency will supply all thy deficiency; Christ's blood is valid enough to satisfy for thy sinful defects, and his *power* strong enough to rescue thee out of all thy infirmities. If thou art *insufficient,* Christ is *all-sufficient.*" Christ is neither a baby, unable to do anything for us, nor a bungler, incapacitated by lack of wisdom to use the material he has chosen, but "Christ's *power* is the *power of God*, and thy weakest weakness is not too weak to be strengthened by him."[71] The deepest spirituality lay within the depths of a profound abandonment to the sovereignty of God.

Among his contemporaries Spurgeon commended F. B. Meyer to his readers. He saw Meyer's "earnest, faithful, evangelical ministry" as a "fitting protest against the error which abounds around him." His voice was "clear for the gospel" and his people heard him with gladness. *From the Pit to the Throne* by Meyer showed the parallels between Joseph and Jesus, a highly attractive and much discussed theme, but one whose treasure has not been exhausted. "Our friend," Spurgeon called Meyer, "still brings forth from the old mine many nuggets of new gold."[72]

Spurgeon greeted the Hodder and Stoughton reprint of William Jay's eight volumes with enthusiastic approval. Printed from old plates that were "a good deal battered" the publisher kept

---

70. SS, 2:173-74.

71. S&T, April 1871, 199.

72. S&T, March 1886, 139.

down the price and sold each volume separately if procurers so desired. All the better in Spurgeon's opinion, for then one could pick the "Morning and Evening Exercises," an incomparable guide to prayer, "so clear, so pithy, so rich, so evangelical, they must ever retain a firm hold upon the hearts of Christians." Spurgeon longed for more Jays. "We would give some two or three dozen of the general run of doctors of divinity for one such a Master in Israel as William Jay of Bath."[73]

Spurgeon liked Octavius Winslow as "good, sound, and spiritual," but believed that his book on the130th Psalm missed an opportunity to be much better. Showing his own massive acquaintance with bibliography, Spurgeon commented, "We wish our excellent author had appreciated John Owen more fully, and if he had also studied Andrew Rivet's Meditationes, Sibbes' *Saints' Comforts, being divers sermons on Psalm 130,* George Hutchinson's forty-five sermons on the same theme, and Archbishop Leighton's Meditations, he might have put himself into a position to have achieved the work which his title set before him."[74] In spite of Winslow's lack of literary breadth, Spurgeon was sure that the work was good for edification, and that was the true aim of the author.

Strength Perfected in Weakness, a memorial of Mary Richard, gave Spurgeon opportunity to reflect on the spiritual power of suffering. He recommended that it be put into the hands of a suffering Christian to "show the peerless value of the school of affliction, and the high degree to which the apt scholar in that college may attain." Mrs. Richard, for twenty-six years in bodily anguish, became one of the "ripest of believers." Spurgeon included a few choice quotations from her experience, such as, "It is no matter to me what comes, so long as it comes through my Saviour's fingers,

and all is mixed with heaven." Other theologically grounded observations from the sufferer prompted her fellow sufferer, Spurgeon, to note, "In the school of affliction the Master gives the lessons practically. The learner is carried beyond the sphere of oral explanation, and compelled to exercise himself at his task; and his proficiency becomes proportionately great."[75]

This deeply experimental element of Spurgeon has been misinterpreted. Carlile included a chapter entitled "Spurgeon the Mystic." He rightly defined Spurgeon's spirituality as fully harmonious with his activism in benevolence, evangelism, and earthy personality, his times of deep distress, and his endless stream of personal contacts each week. True mystics, Carlile rightly contended, dare greater deeds than most normally healthy people ever would attempt. He included appropriate quotations from Spurgeon's sermons about the exhilaration of the presence of Christ and the ecstasy of intimate communion with Christ. He showed convincingly that Spurgeon had an emotional and mental openness to powerful experiences of the felt presence of Christ. That which contorts his description of Spurgeon as a mystic is his abstraction of Spurgeon's spiritual profile from his doctrinal commitment. Carlile presented Spurgeon as a mystic in harmony with those great spirits through the ages that not only did heroic deeds but in whose "contemplation of the vision beautiful" they maintained the "unspeakable preciousness of the Presence." He presented Spurgeon as one that "proclaimed Christ the Son of God, the historical and spiritual reality, the abiding Presence made known to all who tread the mystic path."[76] This message, Carlile claims, was born in "Spurgeon's own experience."[77]

---

73. S&T, April 1887, 188.

74. S&T, February 1875, 88.

75. S&T, July 1881, 349.

76. Carlile, 279.

77. Ibid., 278.

That in itself is true enough, but from that intensity of personal presence advocated by Spurgeon, Carlile deduced that a commitment to inspiration was non-essential to the "mysticism" he described. While Spurgeon found "solemn delight in the consciousness that he walked with the Lord in the light of His Word," and would "appeal without hesitation to the very words of Scripture, taking the promises at their face value," Carlile could conceive of such delight accompanying any view of inspiration as long as there is solid confidence in the presence of Christ. "Whatever views may be held concerning inspiration," he reasoned, "it will be admitted that it is no small gain to the man who faces ridicule or is received with raptures of applause," both true in Spurgeon's experience, "to realize that he is not only doing the will of his Lord but that his Lord is really present with him."[78] In the same vein he could quote Canon C. E. Raven, "The grandeur of the Epistle to the Romans lies not in its formulae, which like all metaphors are often inadequate, but in its passionate testimony to the reality of Jesus and to the power of His love."[79] Spurgeon's spirituality would never tolerate an exaltation of experience at the expense of the adequacy of the inspired metaphors of Pauline theology. Carlile judged that Spurgeon's mysticism infused his soul with a catholicity born of experience. "He knew there was a unity of substance in Christian experience," Carlile reasoned, and though a variety of theological systems and ecclesiastical paths mark their external ways, "they tread the same mystic road."

One writer, William Herbert Crook, was thoroughly convinced by Carlile's presentation of Spurgeon as a mystic. In a seminary dissertation on Spurgeon, Crook began his development of this subject with the sentence, "Spurgeon was a mystic." He pointed to Carlile alone as the biographer of Spurgeon to have given the idea "respectable consideration," and viewed Carlile as "his most discerning biographer."[80]

Many have missed this side of Spurgeon, so Crook claimed, because they were more impressed with his frank and often rude roughness of exterior in speech and his life of feverish action. Crook pointed to the diary, the *Autobiography*, hymns and sermons, and the evidence provided by Carlile, to show that mysticism did not characterize only a phase of Spurgeon's life, but pervaded it from youth to death, formed the most intense and enduring aspects of his life as a Christian and a minister, and "mellowed stern Calvinism and transcended narrow concepts which would otherwise have greatly limited his influence."[81] Spurgeon's "desire for intimate communion with God," his yearning for "personal sanctification," and his desire "to be chosen as an effective servant of God," fueled his mysticism and led to an ongoing series of ecstatic religious experiences. Once Spurgeon's intimacy with Christ was established, "he was not dependent upon the revelation of Scripture alone."[82]

Carlile, preceding Crook in rendering neutral the revelatory and regulatory status of Holy Scripture in mystical experience, pointed to each mystic's awareness of the *Presence* and called that *Presence*, Christ. Spurgeon would never have diminished his expectations of the doctrine of Christ for a testimony of an awareness of the *Presence*. But Carlile in 1933 was interested in rehabilitating Spurgeon for acceptance by the

78. Ibid., 277.
79. Ibid., 280.

80. William Herbert Crook, *The Contributive Factors in the Life and Preaching of Charles Haddon Spurgeon*: A Thesis submitted to the faculty of the School of Theology, Southwestern Baptist Theological Seminary, July 1956, 110-11.
81. Ibid., 124.
82. Ibid., 117.

increasingly liberal Baptist Union. Many things about Spurgeon were controversial and puzzling and only of passing value, so he noted. Much was of eternal good. "The passing must not be allowed to obscure the abiding," Carlile asserted, but there still is something that "rings true across the years." Spurgeon's most important contribution may be "the spiritual enrichment of the life of the time and all time, found in the eternal truth of the Divine Presence." Carlile found little to recommend to his age of Spurgeon's doctrine, but believed he was valuable for his honesty, his work ethic, his sense of individual worth, his tenacity of purpose and his serenity of spirit. He could celebrate a Spurgeon that "kept close to the centre in spite of a theology that was somewhat the worse for wear."[83] The kind of spirituality that Carlile, and Crook, distilled from Spurgeon was not the kind that Spurgeon advocated in his sermons, his reviews, or endorsed in any form. Spurgeon's spirituality was inseparable from his confessional orthodoxy and Calvinist soteriology.

One illustration of Spurgeon's doctrinally grounded discernment of spirituality undergirds his critique of Phoebe Palmer. For her school of "Perfect Holiness" Spurgeon could only generate warning. He found little in it to attract him or to make him recommend it to others. "The higher life spoken of here seems so near akin to self-righteousness and spiritual pride that we look on it with fear and suspicion." The holy persons that he knew mourned their imperfections while those of the Palmer version "who have spoken in raptures about their full consecration have hardly attained to common morality." David and Paul hardly would have recognized this new order of spiritual paragons and "yet, who knows? These older saints may not have been so very inferior—eh?"[84]

Carlile's desire to rehabilitate Spurgeon for his generation skewed his judgment of particular themes in Spurgeon's writing and preaching. Detached from their rigorous doctrinal and biblical framework, certain discussions in the Spurgeonic corpus could well have provoked Carlile's categorization of Spurgeon. He was not therefore, completely baseless in characterizing Spurgeon's view of spirituality. Spurgeon often indicated that some aspects of experience were so intense and beyond the normal that only a graced few could know them. A book by "F. M." spoke to Spurgeon so deeply that he shared it with friends at his Mentone retreat. Pastors would find suggestions for sermons, devout laity would find sweet simplicity, the heart-felt experience, and benefit from the holy tone of the writer. All would benefit from the female author's depiction of the "fullness of Christ, and of his supreme love." But it is not a book for everyone, not even for every Christian, "but for those who dwell in the inner circle, and know the marrow and fatness of secret spiritual meat."[85]

In a rare recommendation of poetry, Spurgeon called *The Lost Blessing,* a book of sonnets by Anna Shipton, a "precious gain to the church of God." He surmised, because of the genuine intimacy of dialogue that served as the poetic vehicle, that the "authoress lives at the feet of Jesus, or rather in his bosom, and she receives intimations of guidance which none but such can know." The sonnets were "mines of richest experience." Such a book must be fenced from most Christians, however, for there is "too much of the fanciful and impulsive in some of the chapters." If nine out of ten readers followed her lead in trusting their impressions to be true spiritual guidance, they would "go wrong, perhaps very wrong, for they would mistake their own day-dreams for the

---

83. Carlile, 296.

84. S&T, March 1885, 144.

85. Ibid., 139.

voice of the Holy Spirit." Babes in grace, therefore, would not find the book a safe guide. But for those that "really dwell in the inner circle it will be very dear." Some, Spurgeon surmised, fancy that they live close to God, but "it is quite another thing actually to do so." "The secret of the Lord is with them that fear him," Spurgeon quoted, but immediately warned strangers "not to intermeddle." In spite of this warning, he included fifty-six lines of her poetry including the following:

> Lord, I would be nigh thee,
> Looking in thy face,
> Listening for thy whisper,
> Feeling thy embrace.
> From all other refuge
> To thine arms I flee:
> Spirit, soul, and body,
> Consecrate to thee. [86]

This was not the only time that he encountered Shipton in his reviews or in recommending her lines as useful poetic literature, or in issuing gentle caveats about the experiential orientation of her content. Five years earlier, in 1866, Spurgeon reviewed a book of her poetry entitled *Whispers in the Psalms, Hymns, and Meditations*. He called them "charming in style, spiritual in matter, heavenly in tone."[87] In 1882, in reviewing *River Among the Rocks*, he gave a mild warning that "this may lead to a mysticism that is misleading."[88] Shipton, Spurgeon opined in reviewing *The Upper Springs and the Nether Springs; or Life Hid with Christ in God,* "has a very sweet, tender vision of truth, and abounds in love for a personal Christ." Since she had proved to be useful to the "weak and suffering ones," he hoped for a large sale for the vol-

ume.[89] In January 1884 he reviewed *God With Us; or The Believer's Portion* by Shipton. He noted that those who knew her style would find "all the tender, personal love for Jesus, and the power to interpret his truth that springs therefrom." "Afflicted Christians" would particularly find "sympathy and understanding of their needs."[90]

Spurgeon's spirituality savored of an Edwardsean aroma. Mere speculative or notional understanding did not bear the same weight as a sensible knowledge of Christ's presence. One cannot embrace a true sense of this kind of truth through a bare grammatical and syntactical understanding of the words alone, though it does not rise above or come apart from the actual content of Scripture. Words give true cognitive communication of the reality but only the Spirit infuses the spirit with the experience. One cannot describe the sweetness of honey so as to give genuine knowledge of that reality. It will not be known in truth if one has never tasted its sweetness. So it is with the genuine presence of Christ. It is beyond the assurance of salvation, and beyond a fertile contemplation of Christ as exceedingly fair and majestic. We desire the actual, though spiritual, coming of Christ to visit us and inflame our souls with the rapture of his presence.

> If now, with eyes defiled and dim,
> We see the signs, but see not Him,
> Oh may His love the scales displace,
> And bid us see Him face to face![91]

Doctrines of real presence in the Eucharist, whether Catholic or Lutheran, are not helpful for they miss the point that the real physical pres-

---

86. S&T, June 1871, 284.

87. S&T, March 1866, 187.

88. S&T, November 1882, 594-95.

89. S&T, October 1883, 543.

90. S&T, Jan 1884, 41.

91. Crook, 115, citing Conwell, *Life of Charles Haddon Spurgeon*. (Edgewood Publishing Company, 1892), 483.

ence is currently only in heaven; but his spiritual presence is not less real. "I believe," Spurgeon affirmed, "in the real presence of Jesus with his people; such presence has been real to my spirit." Just as surely as he came physically to Bethlehem and Calvary, so surely does he come by his Spirit to his people in their times of communion with him. Spurgeon was as sure of "that presence as of our own existence." He contemplated no "emotional excitement rising into fanatical rapture," but of sober fact when the "Lord's great heart touches ours." Spurgeon described it as a "delightful sense of rest" invaded by no "thought of foes, or fears, or afflictions or doubts." Such a presence induced a "laying aside of our own will" for a state in which "we are nothing, and we *will* nothing." In the throes of this Presence "Christ is everything, and his will is the pulse of our soul. We are perfectly content either to be ill or to be well, to be rich or to be poor, to be slandered or to be honoured, so that we may but abide in the love of Christ. Jesus fills the horizon of our being."[92]

Covenant blessings come sometimes "even when we have not got the Bible with us," Spurgeon preached. Immediately following a strong defense of meditation on Scripture as a mean feeding the soul "with choice morsels of royal dainties" he spoke about bringing Jesus Christ to one "without the use of the word; simply in meditation and communion." He does not mean to propose an isolated experience ungoverned by biblical truth, but a time of communion separate from the time of preaching or the time of actual Bible reading and contemplation of a particular passage. The soul does not feed on externals or emblems or propositions, but on Christ himself. We do not eat doctrine, but Christ. All that the Christian loves in the faith—truth, the word, preaching, ordi-

nances—he loves for the sake of Christ. Our food is not the implements of the tabernacle but the paschal lamb. "And are these not most sweet and happy moments, when the spirit is carried aloft in blessed communion, when Jesus Christ seems very pleasant and very precious, when we place our head on his bosom, when we seem to feel his heart and know his love for us, when we lose ourselves in him and almost forget that we have a separate existence, being 'Plunged in his Godhead's deepest sea, And lost in his immensity.'"[93]

But such communion in the reality of Christ was, for Spurgeon, to be separated from all fanciful notions and ungrounded perceptions. True, the person of Christ himself constituted the joy and exhilaration of the experience, but only when the Christ enjoyed was the Christ that was God and man in one person, the righteous man and holy God conjoined to view sinners through that one face and that singular act of obedience, the propitiatory substitute for his elect, and their present advocate and mediator. Without these attributes and actions he is not the Christ that may be enjoyed in a consuming experience of love, and the consuming experience may be enjoyed only because all these historical, legal, and moral requirements have been answered fully and once for all; but the exalting delight itself comes from being enwrapt in the warmth of Jesus as the one through whom we may enjoy an immediate fellowship in the glory of the triune God now made sweeter by our having been brought there at such infinite cost. Carlile grasped the intensity of Spurgeon's spirituality, but mistakenly abstracted it from Spurgeon's doctrinal and biblical roots.

While Spurgeon called for an elevated morality, separation from worldliness as an element of true holiness, and an intense intimacy with the

---

92. S&T, December 1886, 613.

93. SS, 6:231.

triune God, he looked askance at claims to perfection. Spurgeon approved a Methodist preacher's observation that "there is nobody who can stir up so many church rows, and keep them boiling so long, as your brother or sister who has received the 'second blessing' and is living the 'higher life.'" Spurgeon added his own comment to this brother's note, that "the most unsatisfactory members we have ever had have been those who were most satisfied with themselves."[94] One man became so sanctified that he could no longer live with his wife, and another member had "so clean escaped from sin" that he left the church in disgust. Observing an even more radical bent, Spurgeon detested the claims of some that they participated in attributes of the deity and were "no longer sinners or liable to sin." The error, in some an "amiable delusion," could rapidly progress to a blasphemous imposition. It is an ill day when Christians "take to bragging and boasting, and call it 'testimony to the higher life.'" He loved, promoted, and zealously sought true holiness and a right perception of union with Christ, but eschewed that "boastful holiness which had deluded some of the excellent of the earth into vain-glory."[95]

He commended a book entitled *Scriptural Holiness: not sinless perfection* by Charles Graham. If the "holiness" people meant no more by their views than Graham explained, Spurgeon did not know why so much noise had been made over the matter. Graham's explanation "wheeled away much fanatical rubbish" and affirmed the "commonplaces of experimental divinity." Spurgeon gave his whole heart to anything that would promote true holiness, but when he heard boasts of sinless perfection "we get out of their company as quietly and quickly as we can, making double

haste if the moon happens to be near the full."[96] Sinless perfection not only insulted his theological integrity but appeared just a bit loony.

A biography of Asa Mahan prompted the remark, "He differs as much from our theology as if he were a Pelagian, and meanwhile he is a strong perfectionist." The eighty-two-year-old Mahan described how wars were won, as well he should, and though Spurgeon did not "accept much of his testimony," he was glad to admire the "good man's frankness, courage, and directness, and we think none the less of him because his mind and ours would never run in harness together."[97] Courage and real spirituality Spurgeon could commend, but he deeply regretted their connection to a misleading doctrinal matrix.

Spurgeon had a personal appreciation for careful scholarship and its usefulness to the church. He always longed, however, that scholarship and orthodoxy be suffused with the pulsation of spiritual life. In a new translation of the last German edition of Hagenbach's *History of Christian Doctrine*, Spurgeon endorsed the flowing style of the translation and the usefulness of its material to "metaphysical thinkers" as well as a "select circle of scholars." The vast work done by Hagenbach opened up the massive history of many theologies from the patristic era to the present and "may sometimes prove useful for reference." There is, however, an intelligent constituency that finds this kind of subtle enquiry and expression "very repulsive" and looks elsewhere for instruction. The doctrinal developments through the ages weary them and seem to produce an endless variety of competing systems. Technical knowledge of this dizzying variety of competitive systems may aid spiritual growth for some, but "Pastors and teachers who aim at the perfecting

---

94. S&T, May 1883, 212.

95. S&T, January 1876, 3.

96. S&T, September 1881, 486.

97. S&T, January 1883, 39.

of the saints, the work of the ministry, and the building up of the body of Christ, generally prefer to get their cisterns replenished higher up the river, above the bridges, and nearer the springs."[98] The Bible must be the purest source from which one studies the works of God in redemption and from which one finds the power for spiritual growth. Historical theology aids when it leads to clearer views of Scripture, but deceives when one seeks in it a substitute for direct knowledge of the mind of God through Scripture.

Commentaries

While Spurgeon had reservations about some of the subtleties of historical theology, he knew that it could help if it led to positive insight into the history of interpretation of Scripture. Commentaries, especially the old ones, were simply slices of historical theology concentrated into the biblical text. Chrysostom, Luther, Calvin, Gill, and Clarke all made commentary directly on the text, but reflected some of the peculiarities of the historical conflicts and developments of their age. In his *Commenting and Commentaries* Spurgeon gave immense help to the contemporary minister through recommending a vast variety of types of helps in books new and old. "You are not such wiseacres," he told his students, "as to think or say that you can expound Scripture without assistance from the works of divines and learned men who have labored before you in the field of exposition." He had no wish to bother with those that thought otherwise because he had no hope of shaking them from their pretension to infallibility.[99] Spurgeon knew the historical and theological provenance of the hundreds of commentaries he annotated and could give the most engaging and

informative of comments in the greatest economy of language.

Universally and perennially helpful were Matthew Henry, Matthew Poole, John Calvin, John Gill, Adam Clarke, and a host of commentators on single books. He could not hide his deep admiration for Calvin as a man ("that prince among men") or as a commentator ("Of all commentators I believe John Calvin to be the most candid."). Calvin pushed forward the light in every text "with fairness and integrity", given its words and context, and has less tendency of any commentator to press texts to fit a doctrinal system "which he feels to be important, or some theory which he is anxious to uphold." This was one of Calvin's prime excellences.[100]

Though Spurgeon greatly respected Gill, a former pastor of his congregation, as a Hebraist and a master "cinder-sifter" able to find the few nuggets of gold in the midst of "perfect dunghills and dustheaps" of rabbinical learning, he was too addicted to Arminian hunting, and in giving too many options as to what a text did not mean, when no man of sense ever thought of such. When free of this overly sensitive polemicism, he was full of "good, sound, massive, sober sense in commenting," but on some passages "not congenial with his creed," he could be found hacking and hewing in order to bring the word into a more systematic shape.[101]

A new edition of Adam Clarke's commentary on the whole Bible received a notice with a caveat, "We greatly appreciate the exposition for its learning, though we do not accept all its theology."[102] No Methodist should be without his Adam Clarke, for, as Spurgeon had observed in *Commenting and Commentaries,* "Adam Clarke is

---

98. S&T, November 1881, 579.

99. Charles Spurgeon, *Commenting and Commentaries* (Edinburgh: Banner of Truth Trust, 1969), 1.

100. Ibid., 4, 5.

101. Ibid., 9.

102. S&T, November 1883, 603.

the great annotator of our Wesleyan friends; and they have no reason to be ashamed of him, for he takes rank among the chief of expositors."[103] Just to maintain peace in his library, however, he made sure that he inserted Doddridge between Clarke and Gill. Spurgeon showed his remarkable capacity for gleaning what was good and leaving what was unhelpful in recommending Clarke for certain advantages peculiar to him while also maintaining, "I do not find him so helpful as Gill, but still from his side of the question, with which I have personally no sympathy, he is an important writer, and deserves to be studied by every reader of the Scriptures."[104] He issued a personal perspective less larded with encomiums, but more discreetly, by writing on the title page of his own copy under the name of Clarke, "Arminian Perverter of Scripture."[105]

As the market continued to grow, however, Spurgeon sought to keep up himself as well as aid his pastor readers in knowing how to invest their meagre incomes or encourage more wealthy members to treat their ministers to books that would help their preaching and thus the whole church. Spurgeon gave the highest marks to the *Pulpit Commentary*. "In our judgment their value to the preacher far exceeds that of any other modern commentary." As he commented on the Old Testament, he looked forward to the New, for "if all the books of the Bible are treated in the same manner with equal devoutness and freshness, the Pulpit Commentary will become the standard book for ministers." He judged it as far superior to Lange, and he was very positive toward Lange. He never used the *Pulpit Commentary* without receiving great benefit and his

praise of it was hearty and conscientious, not cold and formal.[106]

The errors of D. Whedon in his *Popular Commentary on the New Testament* were so abundant that Spurgeon began the review, "One of the weakest commentaries ever issued. It is from our point of view, unsound in doctrine, and the author seems to us to have an utterly confused mind upon everything he touches." Among his errors were his attempt to prove that "new wine" was the unfermented juice of the grape, and that infants were baptized as "virtual" as opposed to "actual" believers. The man, so Spurgeon surmised, "had been riding on a whirligig and had unsettled his brains." Such a confused head dealing with the Word of God is a tragedy for, since his gross misjudgments have actually made their way into a book, "many will follow blindly these hare-brained interpretations." Whedon "runs against the doctrines of grace like a bull at a red flag," an egregious example of which is his erroneous declaration in dealing with Romans 8:8 that "faith is the precedent condition in order to regeneration."[107] For Spurgeon, obviously, the carnal mind was such that apart from a sovereign action of regeneration, no faith could arise for "if we have not been regenerated ... our carnal mind is still at enmity against God."[108]

Spurgeon appreciated etymological and syntactical work in a commentary, but if all that labor produced a theologically defective view of the message of the Bible, he saw little ultimate value in the work.

Theological Observation with Warning

Second only to Spurgeon's desire to give hearty and positive encouragement to readers to take advantage of books that had the beautiful com-

---

103. *Commenting*, 10.

104. Ibid.

105. Copy in Spurgeon's Library in the possession of Midwestern Baptist Theological Seminary, Kansas City, Missouri.

106. S&T, August 1882, 437.

107. S&T, April 1876, 140f.

108. SS, 1:240.

bination of theological soundness and spiritual meatiness was his calling as a watchman wielding the sword of the Spirit to ward off unedifying theological ideas. He did this in two ways. First he gave clear warnings against books that contained or led to theological error. Second, he advocated books that exposed theological error; sometimes he advocated them without reservation, but often with a caveat.

Of the second sort Spurgeon found *Bible Truth and Broad Church Error* much to his liking. His wielding of the sword necessitated the laying bare of the ideas and the holders of those ideas that were dangerous to the people of God. While this book is discussed in the chapter on controversy, here the point is Spurgeon's advocating the literature that would expose damaging error. "The opposing theories investigated and refuted are those of Colenso, Bushnell, Maurice, Robertson of Brighton, Ward Beecher, and Dr. Young. We would advise all those, and their name is legion, who have been captivated with the aberrations of these writers to give ear to the instructions of this book, and give glory to the Lord their God before they cause darkness, and before their feet stumble upon the dark mountain." He commended the book as "an uplifted standard against a flood of error." He particularly noted that those troubled with doubts "upon the eternity of future punishment" will here find such plain teaching of Scripture upon the subject as leaves nothing further to be desired."[109] But just in case some needed more than that one book, Spurgeon also advocated William Reed's book *Everlasting Punishment and Modern Speculation*. It included the whole Scripture proof of the eternity of future punishment, refuted all the arguments that could be adduced against it.[110]

Completely distasteful to Spurgeon was the task of giving even negative notice to works of infidelity. He knew that they were false and would, therefore, in due time fall apart of themselves if they were not helped along by some adventuresome dragon-slayer. F. L. Steinmeyer took up the sword to do the nasty task in *The Miracles of our Lord in relation to Modern Criticism*. Spurgeon pointed to it as a work that demonstrated "how the infidel observations of Strauss and others of that school can be met by a man of equal thought and learning." Steinmeyer had also the "faculty of suggesting trains of thought, and hence he will be of use even to those who take no interest in what Strauss may have said or not said." Though Spurgeon admired Steinmeyer for jumping to the fray, such an engagement would never interest Spurgeon, so he claimed. He preferred instead the "marrow of the gospel" but had little appetite to compete with "the snarling of dogs over the bones, or even in the whips of those who lash the dogs away." A critic like Strauss and those of his school that are so brazen as to "rob us of the miracles of our Lord our only relation towards him is that of an intercessor, praying the great Lord to open the blind man's eyes, or cast the devil out of him."[111]

Matthew Henry Habershon ventured into the wasteland of skepticism to search out a few dragons also. He displayed an impressive bit of erudition in his *The Wave of Scepticism and the Rock of Truth*, lectures delivered to the young men of Highbury Park Church. Spurgeon expected great things from them if they could "listen to such lectures as this and enjoy the argument." Habershon's design was "to show how the influence of German anti-Christian literature can be withstood and neutralized" by supplying an antidote to the German poison. Spurgeon viewed it as a

---

109. S&T, May 1874, 237.

110. Ibid., 236.

111. S&T, May 1875, 236

noble design, but advised that those of his readers who were unacquainted with the skeptical work "need not take the poison for the sake of appreciating the antidote." The evil in all these replies resides in the necessity of bringing "bad books and their blasphemies under the notice of many who otherwise would never be defiled thereby." The consequence cannot be avoided when the reply is urgent, but Spurgeon suspected that "nine times out of ten all skeptical books had better be allowed to rot of themselves." Without the replies, they would starve for publicity.[112]

An excellent example of the absurdity, according to Spurgeon, of publicizing infidelity through seeking to answer it came in Joseph Parker's interaction with the American skeptic Robert Ingersoll. Spurgeon shoved aside Parker's *Ingersoll Answered* with a gruffness that showed Spurgeon's utter disdain for the supposed intellectual respectability of Ingersoll as well as his suspicion of the trustworthiness of Parker's orthodoxy. He was amazingly short in his one-sentence dismissal of Parker: "We neither care for Ingersoll nor the answer to him." Spurgeon found "enough to do in England with cutting up our own brambles; nine out of ten of our people know nothing of this American briar, and there is no need they should." End of review. Spurgeon grudgingly gave approval even to the most orthodox answers to infidels and critics, but he felt no obligation to give encouragement to what he thought was a compromising approach to apologetics.

Spurgeon's befuddlement with Parker went along the lines of his evaluation of Henry Ward Beecher. Doing as well as he could to respect and honor the great God-given gifts so obvious in many of his contemporaries, and yet coveting their talents for a more steady and trustworthy

defense of received confessional Protestant orthodoxy, Spurgeon seemed verbally to throw up his hands in bewilderment. Beecher, Spurgeon admitted, was "for versatility of genius and wealth of illustration altogether peerless; our regret is," he continued," that he is far from being as spiritual as he is spirited, and is more a model for an orator than for a divine."[113] Later he gave the same kind of accolade followed by his serious reservation. "We consider Mr. Beecher to be the greatest genius of the age," Spurgeon wrote, "and we only wish we were quite sure as to where he is, or will be, in theology."[114]

So it was with the dazzling Joseph Parker. Parker's published lecture clearly showed that he grasped every issue introduced by Ingersoll with a philosophical profundity and seriousness of purpose not even dreamed of by Ingersoll.[115] Spurgeon was bound to have appreciated a certain element of every opposing argument presented by Ingersoll and would have entered wholeheartedly into the experiential aspect of Parker's refutation. At one point on Scripture, Parker testified, "The mystery that is in the Bible corresponds precisely with the mystery I have found in my own heart. It searches me as no other book does, and puts into language the thoughts for which I find no other speech."

Spurgeon might have wondered when Parker mentioned others that "basely abused" the Bible, for he did not think that Parker would have meant by *abuse* the same thing that Spurgeon meant. That which would have made him see Parker's answer as incomplete, and finally inadequate, was the reticence of Parker to press his advantage to

---

113. S&T, March 1871, 131.

114. S&T, January 1872, 41.

115. Joseph Parker, D.D. *Ingersoll Answered. An Examination of His Discourse Entitled "What Must I Do to be Saved?"* London: Bordon Hunt, Richard Clarke, 1881.

112. Ibid.

a full blown proclamation of orthodoxy and the gospel. Parker's stinted approach coincided with his truncated view of the gospel, in Spurgeon's outlook. Spurgeon would have approved the earnestness that made Parker blast the uproarious laughter that punctuated Ingersoll's speech. "Clowns and mockers are never consulted on great occasions," Parker affirmed, and "any man who answers the gravest questions of my heart with gibes and sneers, with puns and quirks, and seeks to turn my agony into an hypocrisy, and my sin into an occasion of displaying his own powers of ridicule," he would resolutely refuse to take as a counselor. He gave good advice when he said, "Believe me, young men, he is not necessarily your wisest guide who can make you laugh most uproariously, and find fun for you amid the most strenuous inquiries of the mind."

But, when Parker had gained the advantage in showing Ingersoll's lack of seriousness and puerile misunderstanding of historic Christianity, he used this ascendancy for his own idiosyncratic faith, and not for historic orthodoxy. "I have nothing to do with what the lecturer vaguely calls 'orthodox religion,'" Parker boasted. He did not undertake to defend any particular sect and asserted that "creeds of human making ... have done more harm to Christianity than has ever been done by any form of speculative infidelity. No theological creed has ever received my signature." He considered his theology "too sublime to be fastened to any form of unchangeable terms, and my faith too transcendent to be chained by propositions which value their form rather than their inspiration."

Spurgeon, satisfied with the faith once delivered to the saints and condensed in the historic creeds, had no difficulty in affirming their theology, and suspected foul play where anyone considered himself above them. Parker, like Spurgeon, eschewed priestcraft and sacerdotal magic, but

found Christ's deity in the character of his teaching and vital goodness, a man who introduces us to the knowledge of God. Spurgeon could not help but be suspicious when Parker's exalted celebrative language insisted on stopping short of the language of the creeds. Parker found in Jesus "security in His almighty strength" and regarded "Him as the Son of Man, the Son of God—God 'the Son,' above all others in intellectual force, in moral heroism, in personal righteousness, and in every attribute of mind and heart." None else could be "the Priest of humanity, the SAVIOUR of the world."[116] Again Parker's language seemed exalted but suspiciously consistent with the liberal Christ. "I call you to Christ," Parker proclaimed. "The more deeply I study His character the more do I see that He is the only Saviour of the world." In Parker's mind this "working Peasant, a carpenter's Son, a root out of a dry ground," stood "above all other men in the clearness of His insight, the range of His outlook, the heroism of His courage, and the splendour of His sacrifice." To Parker, Jesus was "none other than Emmanuel—'God with us,'" for "when I want Him most He is most to me; when the wind is coldest His touch is warmest; when heart and flesh do fail He is the strength of my heart and my portion for ever."[117]

Parker would call the Athanasian creed "venerable" without any specific affirmation of its contents, but rather warned against ridiculing the "*truth* that may be overlaid by error."[118] And though Parker again gained the advantage over Ingersoll in disposing of the infidel's pointless shallowness on issues of sin and the present moral propensities of humanity, he fell far short of Spurgeon's views of the need for radical and effectual intervention by God for the redemp-

116. Parker, 36.
117. Ibid., 61.
118. Ibid. 50.

tion of humanity. Ignoring his historic confessional position, Parker stated the case solemnly; Christianity utters no weak whine about "circumstances" nor treats life as a series of clever or clumsy tricks but is full of original vitality. Made in God's image, man was "endowed with freedom of will" with the "terrible power of disobeying his Creator." "In the exercise of the functions which made him a man, he lost his first integrity, and his heart went astray from God." God went after him, loved him, "called him home, offered him forgiveness and restoration, redeemed him with unspeakable price, and now surrounds him with all helpful and restorative influences." In this quest, however, "even God cannot interfere with the moral independence of manhood. The human (such is the mystery) must always have the power of rejecting the divine. In the end every man will be judged according to his works, whether they be good, or whether they be bad."

Parker's insightful remonstrance against Ingersoll falls short. His defense of Christ's deity is more alarming than reassuring. He tackled Ingersoll's jokes about the new birth, faith, and damnation with a withering reprimand, but his did not follow with a biblical presentation of the new birth, the relations between faith and the substitutionary death of Christ, and the sobering reality of eternal punishment. As an unusual piece of irony, Spurgeon gave greater commendation to an answer to Ingersoll by a Roman Catholic priest than he did to Parker's interaction. Father Lambert "hugged him to death with arguments from which there is no escape." In the Roman Catholic priest "the champion of atheism has found his match."[119]

The next month Spurgeon reviewed Parker's three volume work on *The Inner Life of Christ as revealed in the Gospel of Matthew.* Spurgeon re-

minded his readers that he differed from Parker but also admitted that he felt the "great value of thoughts so fresh and original." He described Parker as "a man by himself, after no class, and belonging to no school." Probably for that very reason Spurgeon went on to say, "he is not all we could wish, but he is a man, a man of genius, and a man of power."[120] Spurgeon could admire the strengths of an individual but had no truck for a prideful isolation from the historic witness of the church.

A book by Samuel Ives Curtiss about the Levitical priesthood interacted with [sigh!] German higher critics. Spurgeon recommended it for those who "are at all troubled upon the subject whereof it treats." For himself, however, he again reiterated that too much attention to skeptics and infidels is not a good or necessary thing. "We confess," he wrote, "that we are not so constituted as to have patience with the nonsense which breeds in the minds of German dreamers, nor do we personally value the learned works which are meant to counteract their maunderings." A dose of Kant, Schleiermacher, or Hegel made him "more ready to laugh than to reason" because he found their wonderful philosophies like "wretched cobwebs that the practical mind walks through" without knowing they are there. Sadly, these nightmares influence unstable minds and it is well to have them chased away. "Follies of the learned may thus be fairly overturned by the wisdom of the learned."[121]

J. C. Ryle stood tall in Spurgeon's estimation as a thinker and trustworthy theologian, except when he defended the peculiarities of Anglicanism. *Old Paths* was sound and orthodox throughout and even bold enough to affirm election and the perseverance of the saints. The writing indulges in no obscure, high-

---

119. S&T, February 1885, 89.

120. S&T, February 1882, 91.

121. S&T, July 1878, 357.

flown language soaring into "sublime nonsense," but is simple and plain so that even the poorest may understand. Spurgeon hoped that Ryle would live long and continue to point to the old paths, and that at the next Church Congress would be a "little less tolerant of those new roads which he very well knows lead down to death."[122]

Spurgeon's personal warnings against destructive publications abounded both in number and variety. He cared not for books that were thin in instruction, and could be frank and candid in his lack of appreciation for their imposition on the public. "I have seen enough of the writings of one or two evangelical bishops not long deceased to wonder how they came to be printed," Spurgeon protested, "even much less sold; for there is really nothing in them." He supposed that printing them was proper and their appearance on the shelves naturally resulted in some sales. "But what an imposition on the public!" He asked his college men to tell him "why Archbishop Sumner's comments were ever submitted to the press. Did weakness of thought ever reach a deeper degree of imbecility?" Such production, mere pap and milk and water, made the evangelicals lose ground to the ritualists in the established church.[123]

Mere displays of learning, although containing no theological danger held little fascination for Spurgeon. Henry Julius Martyn's book *The Christ of the Gospels* dealt with the incarnation, miracles, teachings, and resurrection of our Lord, gave evidence of wide reading and impressive knowledge of heathen mythologies, philosophical writers, and the classics but little else. "One can scarce see 'the apple tree' for the overshadowing 'trees of the wood.'" A certain order of readers

might find great value in it, "but to that order we do not belong."[124]

A treatment of the kingdom of God by James S. Candlish also had little value in Spurgeon's estimation. Candlish minimized issues such as incarnation, atonement, and church in his discussion. For Spurgeon, the idea of kingdom in its relationship to sacrifice dominated the prophetic materials, and both the beginning and ending of the "gospel." The four Evangelists entertained incarnation at the beginning, two of them with specific birth narratives, and sacrifice and resurrection at the end. Does it not seem that these would be the leading indicators of the kingdom in the Baptist's proclamation of repentance in light of the inaugurated presence of the kingdom, and then that which Christ himself continued: "Jesus came into Galilee, preaching the gospel of the kingdom of God, and saying: The time is fulfilled, and the kingdom of God is at hand; repent ye, and believe the gospel." Spurgeon saw the kingdom as unfolding in three scenes: the revelation of the righteousness of God in the incarnation and passion of Christ; second, as a growth like a seed planted or a tree growing; and third, "as a predicted manifestation of unrivalled sovereignty that puts down all other rule and authority, when the Son of God shall reign in our nature, King of kings, and Lord of lords; of whose kingdom there shall be no end." Imagine his regret, therefore, when Candlish, after giving some hope that his insights could prove beneficial, unfolded his driving concern by pressing the kingdom into a form of social idealism as presented by such thinkers as Leibniz and Kant. This concluding lecture Spurgeon considered a "disastrous failure" which Candlish sought to salvage by the brilliant move of adopting a German word "Aufklarung" to ex-

---

122. S&T, November 1877, 535.

123. S&T, March 1881, 110. "Preach Christ in a Christly Manner."

124. S&T, November 1870, 529. This author is not, of course, the Henry Martyn (1781-1812) that was the justly famous Anglican missionary and linguist.

press it. Those who seek an ideal social condition are workers with God, so Candlish claimed, and soon such an ideal social state would be reached in which we glorify God by developing a perfect human society. Spurgeon's understanding, though, focused on a kingdom that cannot be shaken, not an ideal to work for, but one that would be given that is eternal in the heavens. "Probably our author does not see where he is going, but we have seen these speculations about a mythical kingdom of God used by others to conceal determined attacks upon the cross of Christ." Even though the honored Free Church of Scotland had given its *imprimatur*, Spurgeon felt no motivation on that account to give it the least countenance.[125]

Candlish was shocked. He wrote Spurgeon about the review, the substance of which was written by another but edited, approved, and endorsed by some personal contribution of Spurgeon. Spurgeon saw no reason to alter the judgment upon the book itself, but was glad to have Candlish's response, which he printed. Candlish recognized that there would be differences between evangelicals on any number of issues, but he could not understand "how anyone who has read it with any care could fail to see that I maintain the kingdom of God to be a supernatural divine institution, founded on the great facts of the Incarnation and Atonement of Christ, and the regenerating work of the Holy Spirit, and that my references to philosophical systems are designed to prove that none of them can secure the realization of that perfect state of society which is made possible and certain by the kingdom of God proclaimed and established by Christ." If the book were injurious to any great Scripture truths, Candlish regretted it and would reconsider. He wanted Spurgeon to know, however, that the re-

view presented its design and meaning "the very reverse of what they really are."[126] Spurgeon saw no reason to alter his published understanding of the book itself, but was glad to have and to share Candlish's explanation of his meaning.

The Expositor, a periodical edited by Samuel Cox, did not rank well with Spurgeon. When the editor called the story of the long day of Joshua a "childish blunder," Spurgeon did not "believe him one bit" and proclaimed himself as "among the simple people who believe that when Joshua bade the sun stand still there was a real prolongation of the day." The new periodical contained "substantial and scholarly articles" but he did not believe it would live; it had taken on a task that was self-defeating. The presentation of weighty biblical subjects in piecemeal fashion was sure to gain scant readership, but longer articles would soon send a periodical to its long home.[127]

The collected fascicles appeared as Volume 1 and Spurgeon reviewed it in September 1875. No one can read *The Expositor* without gaining instruction and finding his mind awakened to thought, but he had need be on the alert against a "tendency to new senses, by which miracle is frittered down." He hoped that his service to his brethren in ministry would make Cox "more attracted to those old-fashioned views of things which are not less reasonable than the new." Spurgeon did not think *The Expositor* the kind of literature that could be used profitably by revival preachers, but a "more quiet, educated order of ministers will read with interest; and, if these brethren add discretion to their interest, they will, upon the whole, read with profit."[128]

The next time Spurgeon examined the publication he reiterated that "the serial is sometimes

---

125. S&T, February 1886, 90.

126. S&T, March 1886, 137-38.

127. S&T, February 1875, 89.

128. S&T, September 1875, 448.

a little too broad to be quite to our mind," but, remembering his prediction of a short life, Spurgeon expressed his pleasure to know that "Mr. Cox is encouraged to continue it." "Our fear," he reminded the reader, "was that it would shoot over the heads of the bulk of our ministers, and so would fail to find a constituency, and we are delighted to have been mistaken."[129] When Spurgeon reviewed Volume 4 in 1877, he called it "fresh and full of interest" and though he often differed totally with the opinions of the writers, he was glad to see their opinions clearly stated for "they are thoughtful and weighty." The work would be useful to men "whose discriminating faculties are in healthy exercise."[130]

In reviewing Volume 8 of *The Expositor*, Spurgeon, continuing the same ambivalence toward the monthly publication, remarked that much that was admirable was mixed with a subtle unbelief. In the exposition on Balaam's ass, the writer introduced a defence of the "plain statement of Scripture" that brought forth a principle that "virtually deprives us of every revelation worthy of God, for it leaves us no perfect and infallible declaration of the divine mind." There is no such thing with God as an imperfect revelation, but the same light that shines in John also shone in Genesis, though in "another manner." "How greatly we wish," Spurgeon sighed, "that men would not try to rob us of the infallibility of Scripture, for it is the anchorage of Protestant and Christian faith!"[131] Spurgeon's opinion that the periodical would be short-lived was wrong for it was published from 1875 through 1884 with Cox as the editor. The publishers, Hodder and Stoughton, continued with W. Robertson Nicoll for the years 1885-1923. James Moffatt became editor in 1924.

Spurgeon's instincts about its tricky theology however, were right. Its editor, Samuel Cox (1826-93) was a Stepney graduate in 1851, and in 1877 published a book affirming universalism, *Salvator Mundi: Or, Is Christ the Saviour of All Men?*[132] Cox was not at all bashful in setting out what he thought was a helpful position for the advancement of Christian truth. He began his preface, "The main object of this book is to encourage those who 'faintly trust the larger hope' to commit themselves to it wholly and fearlessly by showing them that they have ample warrant for it in the Scriptures of the New Testament." He believed that the more serious, intellectual, and spiritual part of each congregation would respond with relief and joy to hear their minister state plainly this case. This is a truth that makes God "a just God and a Saviour to us and the gospel veritable good news."[133] In Cox's large circle of acquaintance he knew of none of the more "thoughtful and cultivated preachers of the gospel" that held the "dogma of everlasting torment." Cox closed his preface with an earnest invitation to preachers:

> Of those teachers and preachers who honestly retain the dogma which attaches an endless torment to the sins of time no man can ask more than that, while they preach it with sincerity, they also keep their minds open to any more light which may break out upon them from God's holy Word; but of those who have seen that light and yet will not suffer it to shine through their teaching, what can one say but that they are less worthy of their high calling than those that still walk in darkness.[134]

Now that Spurgeon knew that he walked in darkness and was only marginally worthy of his call-

---

129. S&T, February 1876, 90.

130. S&T, January 1877, 43.

131. S&T, February 1879, 84.

132. Samuel Cox, *Salvator Mundi: Or, Is Christ the Saviour of All Men?* London: Henry S. King, 1877.

133. Ibid., vii, xi.

134. Ibid., xi.

ing, he felt justified in informing his readers, "We cannot write in unqualified commendation of the later writings of Mr. Cox." Though much of their popularity was due to the literary talent and taste displayed in them, Spurgeon submitted that still more interest arose from "their adaptation to the sceptical tendencies of modern times." Puritan theology had been gradually put aside with its robust grasp of human sin and the commensurate answer given in the atonement of Christ. Cox demonstrated personal evangelical feeling but had a lofty view of human nature "irreconcilable, without much hypercriticism and forced interpretation, with the inspired record." Cox accepted the premise that every person had some earnest desire for the Lord God of Israel, even the prophets of Baal. By such an assumption, a "roseate hue is thrown over the worst of men," minimizing the vast morass of evil resident within each human and humanity as a whole, and brings into question that God made so vast a provision for its cure. "From the author of *Salvator Mundi* we differ widely, but our esteem for him renders it painful in the highest degree to do so."[135] Nor until six years had passed was Cox removed from his editorship of *The Expositor* as a result of the position taken in *Salvator Mundi*. Almost five years after the publication of *Salvator Mundi*, Spurgeon reviewed a book that provided a trenchant critique of the "larger hope," including a few blows at *Salvator Mundi*. "Surely it is time to leave it alone now," Spurgeon opined, "and it will die out of its own weakness."[136]

Spurgeon found Marcus Dods' "rational principle of interpretation" productive of some very dry and unspiritual fare in his interpretation of the Judges in *Israel's Iron Age*. The authors that Dods commended ran a bit too close to the bor-

der of heathenism. When Dods compared them to the seamen that "must lift the misty veil of the horizon and penetrate its mystery," Spurgeon proposed agreement if he would change the metaphor to pirates.[137]

In *The Gospel for the Nineteenth Century* Spurgeon found no gospel such as was proclaimed in the first century and hoped earnestly that no other century would be contaminated by that propounded in this book. The example theory was set forth as the "remedy for all human woes," while the "life giving doctrine of an atoning sacrifice is left out." What is implied in the book *Ecce Homo* and in Dr. Farrar's *Life of Christ* is explicitly and unhesitatingly argued. Justification means God receives us for our approval of Christ's blessed life; our desire to be like him is sufficient for God's receiving us as such. When this is received, so the book argued, none need ever talk again about substitution, or a wrathful punishment of Christ on our behalf, for these two views cannot co-exist. Christ's deity is maintained, so the author argued, for if the perfect example is to be effective it must be adored. None but the Son of God should be adored. Spurgeon believed the reasoning to be fallacious, for Adam was a sinless man and would have been justified by keeping the Law simply for righteousness' sake. So if Christ were a perfect man that inspired us to righteousness simply for the beauty of that righteousness, would not this suffice without pushing us into idolatry. "It is marvelous to us," Spurgeon remarked, "that any one can so thoroughly admire and endeavour to imitate the moral beauties in the life of Christ and suppose this to be all that is meant by 'the glorious gospel of the blessed God.'" Deity and blood atonement cannot be sundered in the biblical gospel.[138]

---

135. S&T, September 1878, 413.

136. S&T, March 1883, 147.

137. S&T, March 1875, 135.

138. S&T April 1880, 189-90. *The Gospel for the Nineteenth*

Some writers might be helpful in one area but dubious in another. Each should stick to his strengths and not write under the delusion of omnicompetence. He had commended a book by James Frame as a delightful exposition of Psalms. When he put his hand to straightforward theology, however, Spurgeon felt compelled to warn his readers that Frame's book on original sin contained views "generally known as Morrisonian, or Ultra-Arminianism."[139]

A book entitled *The Four Gospels and the One Christ* gave Spurgeon the opportunity to insist that only one gospel existed because there indeed was only one Christ. "The title is an impossibility," he reminded the readers, though he knew very well that no argument for a multiplicity of gospels ever entered the mind of the author. Spurgeon, encouraging care and doctrinal concepts as wedded inextricably to the words employed to convey them, spoke of the "fourfold narrative of the life of the One Christ" and credited the author with demonstrating the value accrued to our understanding through the four accounts. Unique themes characteristic of each gospel establish a better authentication than could have been achieved with a single narrative, "however complete that one narrative might be." The book contained a harmony, a study of Old Testament quotations in the New and other pleasing features, but "we should have liked the book more if the one great design of the life of Christ, as preparative to his death, had been kept more in view. The one Christ lived that he might die for our sins, according to the Scriptures."[140]

For no theme did Spurgeon express more urgency than that of the sacrifice of Christ. He took advantage of the publication of Alfred Cave's *The*

Scripture Doctrine of Sacrifice to drive home the importance of defending that doctrine in light of the theological proclivities of the nineteenth century. "That the scriptural doctrine of sacrifice should need to be elaborately stated and defended in the nineteenth century, and in our own favoured land, and that it should be needed in the upper sphere of the theological literature of the present age, is a lamentation, and shall be for a lamentation."[141] The Spurgeonic lamentation would be extended both in volume and mournfulness in the years to come. A teacher wrong on this doctrine could not be right on anything else because it stood in the front rank of the "first principles of the oracles of God." Cane traced the doctrine through the whole of Scripture showing its truly substitutionary and expiatory character. He then compared the biblical doctrine to those modern views showing them to be "erroneous in proportion as they have departed from the old evangelical faith." R. W. Dale was commended for many of his fundamental principles in his lectures on the atonement, but criticized for not carrying them out to the legitimate consequences. "He has seemed to us," Spurgeon joined in, "at the close of the Lectures as though half afraid of having gone too far in the right path."[142]

The elegantly worded Dale made a strong case for developing a theory of the atonement, in spite of many hesitations due to the mysteries of the connections of law, punishment, righteousness and the inter-trinitarian connections with the doctrine—deep and infinite mysteries in one way of reckoning them. He wrote, "It is hardly possible for us to escape a conception of the sacrifice of Christ which will amount to a theory of the

Century was written by Thomas Gribble. *Ecce Homo* was written by Sir John Richard Seeley.

139. S&T, May 1871, 236.

140. S&T, February 1874, 92.

141. S&T, January 1878, 44.

142. Ibid. This refers to the Congregational Union Lecture for 1875 entitled *Atonement* by R. W. Dale. London: Hodder & Stoughton, 1875.

atonement."[143] Though many may refuse to speculate on the mysteries involved, "if there is habitual trust in the Lord Jesus, as the propitiation for the sins of the world, we shall have a theory, spite of ourselves."[144] He also proposed to show that "there is a direct relation between the death of Christ and the remission of sins, and to investigate the principles and grounds of the relation."[145]

Rightly, in opposition to some of the dilutions of Frederick Robertson, Dale contended, "The real truth is that while He [Jesus] came to preach the gospel, His chief object in coming was that there might be a gospel to preach."[146] Spurgeon also would have complete sympathy with Dale's judgment that, "But for the transcendent work of mercy consummated by Christ on Calvary, God would be not only hostile to sin, but hostile to those who take sides with sin, from the first moment of their revolt against the eternal law of righteousness. For sin is a personal act, it has not existence apart from the sinner."[147] Though advocating an orthodox Christology and a real and true connection between the death of Christ and forgiveness, and in some sense explaining it as a vicarious death by which God was enabled both to inflict and endure the penalty of sin so as to justify his not inflicting it on the actual sinner, "the grandest moment in the moral history of God,"[148]

Spurgeon, along with Cane, still felt that Dale withheld affirming the full implications of all that his argument had gained. Not imputation but union with Christ in his original relation to God as our representative constituted the ground of forgiveness. Spurgeon was as strong on union with Christ as Dale, but he saw imputation as fundamental to both atonement and justification and as necessary to our legal union with him in his saving work. It is at this point that Dale seemed to fail. Dale said, "Our own relation to the Father is determined by the relation of Christ to the Father. By no fictitious imputation or technical transfer, but by virtue of a real union between the life of Christ and our own life, His relation to the Father becomes ours. It is ours with the same qualifications with which His life is ours. In Him both the life and the relation exist in a transcendent form."[149] Again he emphasized this in asserting, "This supreme act becomes ours—not by formal imputation—but through the law which constitutes His life the original spring of our own. His eternal trust in the Father, His eternal joy in the Father, His eternal love for the Father, are the root of the trust and joy and love of which we are conscious in the Divine presence."[150] Though Dale spoke freely of the infliction of penalty he avoided the idea of an infliction of wrath. Spurgeon appreciated what Dale had done, but hoped for more, and was glad that Cane had raised the issue.

Dale's *Lectures on Ephesians* provided the same experience of interrupted hope for Spurgeon. They were "worthy of thoughtful and candid consideration," but also provided the inevitable conflict with Calvinism. Spurgeon affirmed clearly his endorsement of a positive Calvinism and found Dale, "though assuming at times a defiant attitude," more "in accordance with us than his words might seem to imply." Dale avoided systematic theology wherever possible in order to give "full scope and play" to his own rich imagination and reason. This propensity led him

---

143. Dale, *Atonement*, 11.
144. Ibid., 12.
145. Ibid., 19.
146. Ibid., 46.
147. Ibid., 345.
148. Ibid., 393.
149. Ibid., 420.
150. Ibid., 422.

to unconscious internal conflict in his position. Though all men are elected and predestinated to adoption as sons, this appointment of God is effectual only in some. Original sin *per se* is denied while its universal effects are admitted. The death of Christ is indispensable for the forgiveness of sins, but the relationship is obscure. Substitution is discarded, but Dale dances so close to it that his resistance to it seems absurd. He provided an onslaught of nuanced verbosity in order to affirm while denying the necessity of real substitution. Spurgeon quoted Dale: "Unless by a supreme act of humiliation, and sacrifice, and love, Christ descends from his glory, and stands by our side; unless the dark and awful shadow of our sin falls upon him; unless he freely consents to have brought home to his very heart the guilt of the race; unless he submits to some experience of the woe and loss by which the guilt of the race is punished; his moral relations to the Father will not be the perfect expression of the relations which must exist between us and God if we are to receive the pardon of sin."[151]

Surely this was a strenuous task for Dale to labor so much to create a real reason that the sufferings of Christ identified with our guilt and became the reason for our forgiveness, and at the same time avoiding an out-and-out assertion of substitution. Dale seemed to espouse a type of moral government view in saying that "We find in Christ the ideal submission of the race to the justice of the divine vengeance against sin." Spurgeon commented, "We do not see how an ideal submission to the justice of the divine vengeance against sin could avert the reality either from Christ or from us."[152] Imputation, so Dale declared, is an intolerable fiction, that is, of our sin to Christ and his righteousness to us. Transfer of both righteousness and sin, however, in the sense of an "ideal" are admitted. Spurgeon thought that it was strange that Dale would admit effects without out a cause and expressed his objection cogently: "The predestination of all men to an ideal righteousness in Christ, which is obtained by some only, and the attainment of that righteousness by submitting to its ideal manifestation in the person of Christ, is surely not less fictitious than the so-called intolerable fiction of imputation."[153] Spurgeon commended the practical part of the exposition as a profit to all classes of hearers.

This same ambivalence toward Dale showed up in his review of Dale's Yale Lectures on preaching. The Lectures themselves were "well worth reading" for they said a "thousand good things." Spurgeon found himself agreeing with most of what Dale said and wondered that it should be so for Dale himself was a "man of original and independent mind, and in some of his teachings he has embraced modern error." Spurgeon felt that his soul's leaning and convictions "bind him to the great evangelical doctrines of the gospel" or he would roam "we know not whither." Dale embodied both evangelical conservatism and spiritual radicalism, but his lectures were "fresh without being wild" and "careful without being servile."[154]

Horace Bushnell's observations on the pulpit also provided something commendable, but to be searched out with caution. Though hidden in the midst of much that was rubbish there was a "fund of fresh, bright, powerful truth that compels our admiration and respect." His views of qualifications for preaching were "about as fresh and suggestive as anything that could be said on such a well-worn theme; and the student or preacher should be dull indeed who is not quickened

---

151. S&T, December 1883, 643.
152. Ibid.
153. Ibid., 644.
154. S&T, January 1878, 41.

thereby." Bushnell's words would do good when taken in by careful and discriminating reading.[155]

Newman Smith's attempt at defense by retreat Spurgeon found positively distasteful. *The Orthodox Theology of Today* smelled like an attempt to sell a bit of truth for some honor among men. "The fewer of such defences of orthodoxy, the better," Spurgeon fumed, for "orthodoxy is quite able to take care of itself" if it can just be saved from its feigned friends. "Apparent vindications," so Spurgeon judged Newman Smith's doctrinal explanations, "accompanied with gentle hints of improvement are the sappers and miners which do the preparatory work of the enemy." Distress at being thought old-fashioned has been the ruin of some well-intentioned, but intimidated, men. Finally, Spurgeon had to say, "We know nothing of Mr. Newman Smith, but we do not care for his book."[156]

Smith had served both Presbyterian and Congregational churches in America throughout the New England area, was a graduate of Bowdoin College and Andover Theological Seminary, and had imbibed the New Theology influenced by Schleiermacher' romanticism. He also had published *The Religious Feeling, a Study for Faith* and *Old Faith in New Lights*. Spurgeon would encounter another production by Smith in 1885 and found it even more distasteful than *The Orthodox of Today*. In *The Reality of Faith* there was no reality and no faith. Enough of this stuff already glutted English life and Spurgeon saw no need to go to America "for more of the rubbish." Smith's work would suit the "modern school of doubt" for it was pretentious, talked about faith without any and nothing for it to rest upon. The 300 pages of "sublime balderdash" could just as easily have been 3,000, for "you have nothing to do but muddle your brain, and set your tongue going, and the result is unbounded nothing in big words."[157] As Spurgeon moved closer to the Downgrade the borders within which he tolerated theological nonsense narrowed into a much more straitened path.

A recommendation without reservation Spurgeon gladly accorded to Horatius Bonar. He met perfectly Spurgeon's ideal for theological instruction as "sound, forcible, and free from crotchets." His book *The Rent Veil* met the criterion of being a "corrective" to false ideas and, at the same time, "a mean of comfort and instruction." The issue of "Perfection" was peculiarly onerous to Spurgeon, and Bonar provided the right touch on that teaching in declaring "there is no day nor hour in which evil is not coming forth from us, and in which the great bloodshedding is not needed to wash it away." Spurgeon proclaimed this is certainly true and then continued with his own comment. "Through the veil, which is the Redeemer's flesh, is our one access to God; not merely when first we believe, but throughout all our Christian experience. No instantaneous faith will bear us beyond the necessity of daily cleansing with the blood." Even more important than that theological idea, though certainly connected with it, Spurgeon admired Bonar's defense of *substitution*. "Substitution is righteousness," Bonar commented, as he showed the intensity of the attack on substitution through the years. Had the idea not been so inextricably founded on Scripture images, explanations, and types it could not have survived the poisonous darts cast at it through the centuries. "The Bible and truth of substitution cannot be sundered," Bonar insisted, for the Bible makes no attempt to accommodate objections on this point or to "smooth angularities and make

---

155. S&T, May 1882, 249.

156. S&T, September 1882, 495.

157. S&T, February 1885, 89.

the doctrine less philosophically objectionable." The mercantile nature of the Bible's presentation of substitution hardly yields to any other interpretation, so the method of the objector must be, not to "reinterpret" them, but to eliminate them. "Why are they there," Bonar asked, "if substitution and transference be not true?" Spurgeon could not have found a writer more to his own taste and expression than Bonar when he wrote, "Substitution may be philosophical or unphilosophical, defensible or indefensible; still it is imbedded in the Bible; specially in the sacrificial books and sacerdotal ordinances. Its writers may be credited or discredited; but no one can deny that substitution was an article of their creed, and that they meant to teach this doctrine if they meant anything at all."[158]

Giving notice of a book entitled *A New Basis for Belief in Immortality,* Spurgeon scoffed at the gullibility of intellectuals that fell for the phenomenon of spiritualism. Skeptics of the present day, Spurgeon believed, are often "grievously afflicted with unrest." This book suggests a remedy quite as bad as the disease. "With a delicate pathos, such as we meet with in advertisements that describe the symptoms of sufferers, and prescribe patent medicines warranted to effect an immediate cure, Spiritualism is propounded in this treatise as a sure relief and a safe remedy for this soul sickness that is prevalent among agnostics." The phenomena of automatic writing, clairvoyance, and trance speaking initiated by Kate Fox in Hydersville, New York, in 1848 has had an attraction among educated people. A strange world indeed. When the Bible is made to support this lying wonder, Spurgeon went from sorrow to horror. "In the hands of some interpreters the Bible is made to teach anything they like to impute to it." [159]

Though generally impressed positively with A. B. Bruce, Spurgeon found it necessary to warn his readers against Bruce's approach in *The Chief End of Revelation.* He envisioned such a gradual unfolding of revelation "as to rob the earlier books of the Bible of their force and power, and indeed to reduce the value of the Old Testament generally to a very low point." Bruce does not see in the faith of Abraham the profundity of gospel truth upon which Paul insists, and he seems more intent on pleasing the cynical Matthew Arnold in his view of prophecy than in understanding the true soul of the Old Testament. Spurgeon viewed his work as a compromise with German theology. "To us," Spurgeon lamented, "it is a great ability misdirected, and we feel sure it will produce just the opposite effect intended; compromises do not generally end in the conviction of doubters."[160]

Spurgeon never appreciated softness on issues of inspiration and revelation. He resented and opposed as much as possible the liberal pressure brought to bear by German critical studies. For the most part he viewed their work as detrimental to evangelical truth. For the writings of Frederick Godet, however, he made an exception. He considered him "always thoughtfully evangelical" and believed that he consecrated his learning "not to the bewilderment, but to the enlightenment of his readers."[161]

Rev. W. Taylor in his book *Freedom of the Will* failed to attract Spurgeon's admiration, not only for his avowed purpose of showing that "the distinctive doctrines of Calvinism are opposed to the freedom of the will," but for his failure to interact with pivotal evidence. He simply asserted that "human volitions are independent of divine decrees." He failed, in addition, to investigate the distinction between natural ability and moral

---

158. S&T, April 1875, 188.

159. S&T, July 1881, 352.

160. S&T, August 1881, 416.

161. Ibid., 417.

ability but simply uttered a decree denying that any distinction exists. The evidence for the discussion that would be forthcoming by looking at the delivering up of Christ at one and the same time by the Jews and by the counsel of God is ignored. Nor does the reader learn "how prophecies, depending upon the free agency of thousands and in different ages, could have been fulfilled." Taylor admits the agency of the Holy Spirit in conversion, but not beyond that exerted on those who finally resist his operations. Equally, and perhaps more, disturbing is Taylor's affirmation that "there is no natural or moral inability to sin either on earth or in heaven." This position challenges the doctrine of divine immutability. Spurgeon was willing to remain content with the assurance that "he who made the human will knows how to influence it, without destroying its freedom" and how to "make it willing in the day of his power here, and how to secure its voluntary and yet eternal enjoyment of him hereafter."[162] Spurgeon's vocabulary showed his awareness of the work of Edwards and the Reformers on these issues.

Distribution of Sermons

A friend with the initials "J. B. U." wrote Spurgeon: "I believe you have little knowledge of the extent to which our Sovereign God and Father, in his infinite grace, has used and owned your sermons in blessing, where the means of grace were but scant, or entirely wanting."[163] He said this in conclusion to a story about the conversion of a man on board a schooner where, each Lord's Day morning, the captain read one of Spurgeon's sermons to the "assembled ship's company." The man in question testified that "his spiritual birth was the fruit of one of those sermons." The mo-

ment of new birth came during the reading of the sermon from the text, "Against thee, thee only, have I sinned, and done this evil in thy sight." The converted man freely acknowledged "the arm of the Lord and his sovereign grace in his repeated interference with man's purpose, and the saving efficacy of God's truth to his soul's salvation." He had become one of the "most earnest and devoted of the Christian brotherhood at Dover."[164] This testimony, plus scores like them, convinced Spurgeon that perhaps even more fruitful than the oral proclamation of the word from Sunday to Sunday was the distribution of those same messages through the press. He followed the advice that he gave his students, "The publishing of the same truth by means of the press is barely second in importance, and should be used to the full measure of each man's ability."[165]

In 1854, several of Spurgeon's sermons appeared in the *Penny Pulpit* series by Mr. James Paul. Spurgeon had printed a number of specially written tracts in 1853 called "Waterbeach Tracts" but not until August of 1854 did his first sermon appear in print as number 2234 in Paul's series. Eventually it was printed in volume 50 of the *Metropolitan Tabernacle Pulpit*. Spurgeon noted that others had been printed in a small magazine called the *Baptist Messenger*, the first of which appeared in September 1854 entitled "The Valley of Weeping."[166] They were not "regularly reported" but there was "so good a demand for them, that the notion of occasional publication was indulged, but with no idea of continuance week by week for a lengthened period."[167] When the effort

---

162. S&T, November 1881, 579.

163. S&T, November 1870, 533.

164. Ibid.

165. S&T, August 1871, 355.

166. Charles Ray. *A Marvelous Ministry: The Story of C. H. Spurgeon's Sermons, 1855-1905* (London: Passmore & Alabaster, 1905); S&T January 1875, 4.

167. S&T, January 1875, 4.

resulted in the weekly publication of sermons followed by their being bound annually, while the efforts of others sputtered and halted, Spurgeon could only rejoice, and ask others to rejoice, at the gracious providence that had allowed him to sustain such a ministry for so long. The best explanation he could give was—"The sermons contain the gospel, preached in plain language, and this is precisely what multitudes need beyond anything else. The gospel, ever fresh and ever new, has held my vast congregation together these many long years, and the same power has kept around me a host of readers."[168]

These readers could be found in the most obscure places giving vibrant fellowship to some otherwise lonely and isolated people. A Wesleyan minister wrote Spurgeon from Natal on his way to join soldiers on the Zulu border saying that he had found in "a small wayside hotel in a wild, lonely part of this colony" some copies of his sermons and a copy of *The Sword and the Trowel*. When he asked the landlady how they got there, she said that she received them every month and added, "They are my best friends in the world." The Wesleyan found her to be a bright, happy Christian that never had an opportunity to attend public means of grace and seldom had anyone with whom she could talk about the Savior. In spite of such isolation, "she maintains a quiet, settled peace." It would have done Spurgeon good, the correspondent was sure, to hear her say, "The good I get out of those sermons is more than I can tell, and, although I have never seen dear Mr. Spurgeon, yet he preaches to me every Sunday, and I love him very, very much." She sent along her sermons to a Christian man in another lonely place, where he read them to his friends and neighbors. Some of them had been soundly

converted. The Wesleyan himself read Spurgeon sermons and periodical regularly.[169]

In September 1879, Spurgeon shared in his "Personal Notes" letters from several individuals that had benefitted from the world-wide distribution of his sermons. A friend in Jersey sent a donation for the Girls' Orphanage with the news that "God has been graciously pleased to bless them to the salvation of my soul." This friend had been able to collect about 600 of the sermons and prized them "above every other means of grace save *the book*." Another from Glasgow signed himself as "Your living son in Jesus," who explained how he had been led to a deep experience of conversion through reading the sermon "The Search Warrant." He first came to grasp the simplicity of faith and then to see the "beautiful, glorious, altogether lovely form of our wounded Emmanuel." He testified that "Christ was everywhere, and even myself had vanished, for I was a new creature." Another wrote from Manchester to report that her father, a drunkard, had been converted through reading Spurgeon's sermon, "Seven Wonders of Grace." From a missionary with the China Inland Mission a report came that he had translated Spurgeon's sermon, "The Hiding of Moses by Faith," for a native pastor. Together they prayed that Spurgeon might be spared to the church for years to come. An English emigrant to South Africa wrote to say that he first encountered a Spurgeon sermon in 1860 when the Presbyterians' service on board ship read them each Lord's Day. Now he gathered some twenty-five people together each Sunday evening to "read one of your loved and highly appreciated sermons, and we seem to be as familiar with your name as if we met every Sabbath at the Tabernacle." Such reports constantly cheered Spurgeon, made him determined to keep up the

---

168. Ibid.

169. S&T, August 1879, 399. Letter from Dundee, Natal, May 26, 1879.

barrage of gospel literature and removed any reticence to recommend to others the distribution of his sermons.

Spurgeon heard of a young man that felt called into missions and applied through the China Inland Mission. This call came through reading Spurgeon's sermon entitled "The Divine call for Missionaries." When asked what his motive was for entering into missionary service the candidate replied "The glory of God in the salvation of the heathen." In what context did this call with such a motive come? "A sermon by Mr. Spurgeon on 'the Divine Call for Missionaries.'"[170]

The Seventy-Third Regiment in India received, through one of its bandsmen, a Spurgeon sermon each week. They would read nothing else of a religion character but fifty or sixty would pass around the sermon and all read it with profit. A young man from Germany was asked to translate Spurgeon's sermon, "The Seven Sneezes," into German. During the translation, his father noted, "I could plainly see that what I had hoped was taking place, the Lord was touching his heart and showing him his position. When he finished the translation I asked him whether he too felt any signs of life, and he acknowledged he desired from his whole heart to become a Christian." The young German did not yet have full assurance of faith, but his father believed that a work of grace had begun and would be brought to completion. He was very grateful for the gift of "these splendid sermons, from which I have derived much blessing."[171] Spurgeon probably was delighted to be able to send back to Germany a good dose of pure gospel in exchange for so much German skepticism skipping into England.

A man from Scotland wrote Spurgeon sending a "thankoffering" for the benefit received from printed sermons. For two years before she died, his wife was unable to attend church and the man himself was "so deaf that he cannot hear his own minister's voice." He and his wife read the sermons, passed them on to friends who then passed them on to others. He suggested that Spurgeon might propose to the sermon-readers to "seek out some invalid person who is not able to go to church, and make a present of the sermon instead of allowing it to lie idle on the shelf." Absence from church and scarcity of pastoral attention made the Scots couple consider themselves "one of Mr. Spurgeon's people."[172]

In April 1881, Spurgeon reported on the positive effect that several printed sermons had. In France, a woman was converted through reading "Compel Them to Come In." A female member of the church started a ministry in another town and committed it to others. Several sermons had been useful in both conversion of unbelievers and restoration of backsliders. The woman wrote, "I wish those who have any of these precious messengers of mercy lying idle in their cupboards would lend them themselves, or give them to those who would circulate them among those who need the glorious truth that they contain." Spurgeon nudged his readers, "Will someone take the hint?"[173]

James Culross wrote from Glasgow that 70 young people distributed sermons of Spurgeon to 1,000 homes per week, rotating four sermons between the homes on a monthly basis. He held a *soiree* at his church for all that received these sermons each week. Over 600 persons came to the social event, gave testimony to the good that the sermons did them, and sent a letter of gratitude to Spurgeon for his labors with prayer that "you may long be continued in health and strength to

---

170. S&T, October 1879, 496.

171. Ibid.

172. Ibid.

173. S&T, April 1881, 197.

carry on the various departments of your noble work."[174]

Even the most apparently fortuitous and accidental contact with Spurgeon's sermons bore fruit. These remarkable stories Spurgeon loved to share, for, to his mind, they demonstrated that the breath of God would blow in accordance with his own sovereign purpose quite independent either of the intentional or the careless distribution of his simple gospel preaching. The publication *Joyful News* carried the following correspondence about an event in Nottingham:

> I was asked to go to a public-house, and see a woman who was dying. I found her rejoicing in the Saviour. I asked her how she had found the Lord. "Reading that," she replied, handing me a torn piece of newspaper. I looked at it, and found that it was part of an American paper, containing an extract from one of "Spurgeon's Sermons," which extract had been the means of her conversion. "Where did you get this newspaper from?" I said. She answered, "It was wrapped round a parcel which was sent me from Australia." Talk about the hidden life of the good seed! Thank of that. Sermon preached in London, conveyed to America, an extract reprinted in a newspaper there, that paper sent to Australia, part then torn off (as we should say, accidentally) for the parcel, despatched [*sic*] to England, and, after all its wanderings, conveys the message of salvation to the woman's soul. God's word shall not return to him void.[175]

That was Spurgeon's point.

---

174. S&T February 1882, 98.

175. S&T, March 1883, 205.

13

Theology and Controversy

I have received a measure of pity because I am in opposition to so many; but the pity may be spared, or handed over to those on the other side. Years ago, when I preached a sermon upon Baptismal Regeneration, my venerable friend, Dr. Steane, said to me, "You have got into hot water." I replied, "No; I do not feel the water to be hot. The truth is far otherwise. I am cool enough; I am only the stoker, and other folks are in the hot water, which I am doing my best to make so hot that they will be glad to get out of it." We do not wish to fight; but if we do, we hope that the pity will be needed by those with whom we contend.[1]

"Ahab's quenchless feud seemed mine," so Ishmael confessed in the quest for Moby Dick. Spurgeon clearly saw the white whale of destructive error tear the spiritual limbs from many a seeker and dare an assault on the integrity and rule of God himself. No area of Christian truth had been without its detractors and all revolt and rebellion seemed renewed in his lifetime. It was his thorough satisfaction with the living waters of revealed truth that made his feud with error quenchless indeed.

Apt and Ready for Convictional Controversy

Though Spurgeon's most intense concentration of mental energy and spiritual devotion was expressed in his commitment to preaching the gospel for the salvation of sinners, his lengthy and complex involvement in theological controversy was not far behind and was vitally connected to his first love of gospel preaching. Given the situation of truth unchallenged, Spurgeon could say, "To win a soul from going down into the pit is a more glorious achievement than to be crowned in the arena of theological controversy as *Doctor Sufficientissimus*."[2] And though one should not go around with his fist doubled up and with a theological revolver in the leg of his trousers, he must nevertheless "be prepared to fight, and always have your sword buckled on your thigh, but wear a scabbard."[3] Sometimes, as he later admonished, the scabbard must be thrown away.

If men preached ever so powerfully with natural gifts and yet had no saving message what good was any pretended kind of evangelism or how would they ever "win a soul from going down into the pit?" Christ invested churches with

---

1. Charles H. Spurgeon, *An All Round Ministry* (Edinburgh: The Banner of Truth Trust, 1960 [1978 paperback reprint]), 395.

2. Charles H. Spurgeon, *Lectures to My Students*, 4 volumes in one (Pasadena, TX: Pilgrim Publications, 1990) 1:83.

3. Ibid. 2:43f.

a saving gospel message and commissioned them to preach it with no warrant to alter that message. Its ministers were ambassadors, not legislators. The only lawgiver and king is Christ and his mandate is in Scripture alone. The minister is a man under authority and has no right to compromise either message or practice by introducing ideas from his own brain or from another source of religious tradition. Every system, therefore, that altered the shape of the gospel or that questioned the utter veracity of Scripture as divinely revealed truth was an enemy to the souls of men, to the glory of God, and to Spurgeon.

One cannot be true, Spurgeon believed, unless one were willing to make controversy on every challenge to true religion. "When the gage of battle is thrown down," he told the Baptist Missionary Society, "I am not the man to refuse to take it up."[4] The unsheathed sword gleamed and the scabbard posed no temptation when vital truth suffered assault. He was not willing to do this for any kind of trouble at all, however, and preferred peace and would seek a high degree of toleration within the clearly marked sphere of central gospel verities. He wrote, "I had rather run a mile any day than quarrel, and that is saying a good deal, for miles are long to legs which have the rheumatism."[5]

Though W. Y. Fullerton judged that "Mr. Spurgeon was too earnest, too intent on the eternal meaning of things, too sure of his own standing to be a good controversialist,"[6] one must take seriously that Spurgeon purposefully named his monthly magazine, not *The Trowel*, but, *The Sword and the Trowel*. His intent was to do battle. His earnestness, rather than weakening, intensified his quali-

fications. He was after something beyond himself, beyond the mere appearance of vanquishing a foe, and beyond the awe of men; he was after the glory of God in the defense of his truth. If this were not his intent, he chose very poor words for his preface to the first volume of the monthly magazine when he wrote, "Foes have felt the sword far more than they would care to confess, and friends have seen the work of the trowel on the walls of Zion to their joy and rejoicing."[7]

For his 1880 Almanack, Spurgeon wrote a piece bristling with a theological militancy indicative of deep-seated concerns. "When invasion threatened in olden times, they beat the drums and summoned all good citizens to the defence of their country." Only the feeble and cowardly held back. Hearths and homes are dear and "rouse the patriot's fighting spirit." No less should be expected when the war is spiritual and we "know that truth is assailed, [and] the glory of God is the object of attack." Using the weapons of the word and all-prayer, no enemy shall pass unchallenged. "Ritualism and Rationalism, a double enemy, have come in upon us," and not only fight from without but now infiltrate the churches. Sensationalism and prideful academics join forces to impugn the old fashioned gospel as stale. "Let us, therefore, set our faces like flints against all adulteration of the pure word, [and] all bedizenment of simple worship. If we give them an inch they will take an ell." Prefer the charge of bigotry than the reality of guilt before God for giving way to Popery and infidelity. "It is as much our duty, under God," Spurgeon acknowledged in a familiar and oft-repeated refrain, "to conserve the truth as to convert sinners." He reinforced the conviction with the stinging comment, "It is idle to talk about missions to this and that while the eternal

---

4. W. Y. Fullerton, *C. H. Spurgeon: Biography* (London: Williams & Norgate, 1920), 303.

5. S&T, April 1881, 160.

6. Fullerton, 303.

7. S&T, 1865, Preface.

truth is disregarded, [and] the essential doctrines are frittered away." Generosity cannot be set in opposition to that which is just and the circumference cannot expand if the center disintegrates. "The Lord make his people more zealous for the faith once delivered to the saints."[8]

In spite of what some resisted admitting and others viewed as regrettable, at least one American friend saw Spurgeon's courage in controversy as a compelling quality. Rejecting the picture of Spurgeon as the "goody goody sort of man," J. D. Fulton, a Brooklyn pastor, viewed Spurgeon as his "ally in proclaiming Christ as the Saviour of the lost, in fighting Romanism, in defending the Bible as essential to the life of liberty, in lifting the warning signal of danger concerning 'The Downgrade' and the so-called 'New Theology,' and in defending at every cost what he thought truth."[9]

Iain Murray made a virtually identical observation in his *The Forgotten Spurgeon*. Noting the variety of ways in which Spurgeon's biography had been handled, Murray summarized, "Controversy and theological debate, it is said, were not Spurgeon's roles and in so far as he engaged in them he was out of his true calling." From such an opinion he entirely dissented. He concentrated on the controversy that arose early in Spurgeon's ministry over his clear proclamation of Calvinist doctrine in an unambiguously evangelistic context. Neither Arminian nor hyper-Calvinist quite saw the rationale for such unadorned boldness and freedom. Murray discussed also the controversy over the sermon on baptismal regeneration and evangelical Anglicans and, third, the Downgrade Controversy. He correctly pointed to controversial interaction, as highlighted in these

three, as extremely important in Spurgeon's outlook on his own stewardship of truth.[10]

Spurgeon's controversies fall into three major types. Controversy at the first level came at the point of immediate conflict over scriptural teaching. This involved a clash of messages and a clash of confessions. Spurgeon had much to say in this area and spread his remarks over a wide field including persons, denominations, and movements. The second level of conflict emerged with those that held a confessional position ostensibly, but felt themselves justified in functioning in opposition to it. Sometimes this was because their theology was better than the confession, and led Spurgeon to admonish them to leave their church and place themselves at the behest of divine provision. Others ministered outside the parameters of, or in opposition to, their confessions because they believed less and worse that the confession proclaimed. For these he felt special alarm and was particularly disdainful of their hypocrisy. A third type of controversy focused on the theological differences that he had with other publications, including periodicals and books. For the most part this type involved a single interaction but on occasions resulted in prolonged, and sometimes bitter, insulting exchanges.

Controversies of the first sort always focused on conscientiously held theological divergence. Often these were short lived and established a standing relationship on confessional differences. At their best, when doctrinal differences were small, these brief battles brought mutual respect for faithfulness while contending for the truth in its purity. Shots across the bow on particular doctrinal points would punctuate Spurgeon's writings and preaching when he felt that reiteration of a theological idea in opposition to error

---

8. From a handwritten document in Archives at the Southern Baptist Theological Seminary.

9. Justin D. Fulton, *Charles H. Spurgeon, Our Ally* (Chicago, Philadelphia: H. J. Smith & Co., 1892), ix.

10. Iain Murray, *The Forgotten Spurgeon* (Edinburgh, The Banner of Truth Trust, 1978 reprint), 10-13 and *passim*.

was necessary. When these differences concerned matters that did not attack the doctrines of Scripture, God, Christ, or salvation, Spurgeon sought ways in which to express his unity on these most central issues.

For example, Bishop Ryle was always good on experimental Christianity, the importance and craft of preaching, and the central issues of the gospel though he functioned under a cloud, in Spurgeon's view, of Episcopacy. When he preached the gospel, Ryle was right; when he played the bishop, Ryle could expect Spurgeonic lampoons. His book *Simplicity in Preaching* "out-Ryles anything we have ever read for raciness and direct home-thrusting power." Spurgeon saw so much power and wisdom in it that he recommended that every student of preaching should memorize it. "Dr. Ryle," Spurgeon admitted, at least on this point, "has not been spoiled even by being made a bishop!"[11] Even beyond Ryle's gifts in preaching, Spurgeon would acknowledge, "While with all her faults he loves the Church of England still, he loves the souls of men much more, and most of all the gospel of their salvation." Ryle's experience of the gospel had made him great by its gentleness and earnest by its threats and promises. Spurgeon commended his intensity in appeal to sinners and denoted his evangelicalism even apart from a statement of the leading doctrines. "The practical claims of the gospel upon true believers are here most scripturally and lovingly enforced," Spurgeon wrote of Ryle's book *Practical Religion*, "and at the same time the self-deceived and unconcerned are called upon to see how much they also need the atoning blood."[12]

Spurgeon could have been describing his own message. Concerning a cordial meeting of devotees of different denominations in South-ampton on October 27, 1881, after Spurgeon had preached, he reported, "It was a singular sight to see at these services men of all grades and creeds, and even more remarkable to observe with what kindliness they received the preacher of the Word." He observed softening candor towards long-despised truth, friendly discussion, and, more important, "spiritual communion both in conversation and prayer." In a statement of great ecumenical breadth, Spurgeon proclaimed, "The life of God in the souls of believers triumphs over even important difference of ceremonial and doctrine. In honestly dealing with each other in the spirit of love to Christ we shall, by the Holy Ghost's guidance, find the way to mutual edification and enlightenment, and so to real unity."[13] Societies formed for the purpose of achieving unity will do less than "congresses, and conferences, and meetings" in which opportunity is given for genuine spiritual fellowship built on shared experience and commonly held truth. Such meetings, Spurgeon believed, would increase knowledge and common regard for those differing in less central matters. Pointing out differences among such brethren was not unnecessary and had its appropriate place, but the large field of genuine camaraderie in revealed truth far transcended the stubborn differences.

Controversies that involved major confessional differences in vital areas evoked ongoing resistance on the part of Spurgeon and prompted his most exquisite displays of sarcasm and close analysis. Roman Catholicism and certain aspects of Anglicanism were major opponents in this type of conventional controversial engagement. Arminianism provided another chief position to which Spurgeon took explicit exception in its distinctive theological ideas. With many Armin-

---

11. S&T, November 1883, 604.

12. S&T, August 1879, 393.

13. S&T, December 1881, 626.

ians he managed warm and mutually respectful relationships, but he consistently resisted their defining peculiarities as erroneous while he commended them for their defense of biblical inspiration, their true zeal for souls, their urgency for conversion, and their proclamation of forgiveness on the basis of nothing less that the cross of Christ. Hyper-Calvinists he often scolded for their development of leading doctrines into an oppressive metaphysical system that produced serious omissions in their practice. Frequently, Spurgeon gave passing rhetorical references to the theological misperceptions behind those practical idiosyncrasies. In reviewing a work on the tabernacle by Robert Sears, Spurgeon called Sears "one of those thoroughly sound Suffolk Baptists, of the old school, of whom we should wish to see many more." Sears was a "staunch old Calvinist, firm in the faith, but without the gall which generally goes with high doctrine."[14]

For those, however, that were untrue to their public confessional commitments he reserved a peculiarly tragic outlook. These were "Ministers Sailing Under False Colours."[15] Spurgeon knew ministers in the Reformed churches on the Continent who had endeavored to retain their "offices and their emoluments" while blaspheming the atonement and denying the deity of Christ. They deny the inspiration of Scripture "yet remain in churches whose professed basis is the inspiration of the Bible."[16]

Much of his scorn on this issue fell, not on heretical divergence from an orthodox confession, but on orthodox evangelicals that functioned under the authority of a sacramental ritual. Ministers well-entrenched in the Reformation doctrine of justification by faith put into the mouths of babes, in accordance with the required rites of the church, a profession of their faith in Christ and their union with the church when those ministers knew that no such thing existed. He found the same thing true with evangelical Anglicans, an issue to be developed below.

These latter violated conscience, while the former violated justice. Spurgeon argued strongly for the civil right of every person to hold whatever theology he felt correct and to use all his energies to propagate it. Repression of conscience in these matters is an opprobrious and disgraceful business. At the same time, however, for a man to maintain his office who has denied a confession he has pledged to uphold has "all the elements of the lowest kind of knavery." To claim such as a legitimate spiritual liberty reeks of reverse oppression, violation of conscience, and persecution; Spurgeon indicated nothing but the sternest abhorrence for the "license which like a parasite feeds thereon." So obvious was the unreasonableness and absurdity of one's claiming this as his right, that Spurgeon barely had patience to expose it. "The whine concerning persecution is effeminate cant," he responded.[17] "Treachery," Spurgeon boiled, "is never more treacherous than when it leads a man to stab at a doctrine which he has solemnly engaged to uphold, and for the maintenance of which he receives a livelihood."[18] One who has made such a change must offer a resignation from the body whose faith he can no longer maintain nor nourish.

The question arises as to whether a standard of doctrine should be required at all. Preaching on the Bible at Exeter Hall in March of 1855, Spurgeon had affirmed the centrality of the doctrines of grace as standards of theological truth that should be believed if one were to believe the

---

14. S&T, December 1875, 583.

15. S&T, February 1870, 69.

16. Ibid., 70.

17. Ibid., 72.

18. Ibid., 70.

Gospel, when he began considering the wording at the beginning of the Athanasian Creed. He halted from such a start as this—"Whoever should be saved, before all things it is necessary that he should hold the Catholic faith, which faith is this." Then Spurgeon stopped and said, "When I got so far, I should stop, because I should not know what to write." He professed to believe "the Catholic faith of the Bible, the whole Bible and nothing but the Bible." As far as making any other determination beyond that, Spurgeon asserted, "It is not for me to draw up creeds. But I ask you to search the Scriptures, for this is the Word of Life."[19] He demurred at the ostentation of placing an ecumenical creed at the level of absolute authority on a par with Scripture, but he did not resist the necessity of making clear condensations of biblical truth as a confession of what one believed and as a guideline for loyal ministry. Only a race of triflers would agree to have a minister unbound by any set of standards. Should churches throw away all creeds, Spurgeon's argument would have no relevance, he admitted, "for where there is no compact there can be no breach of it."[20] This situation would have immediate and painful relevance seventeen years subsequent to the writing of this article, as it would be at the heart of the Downgrade Controversy. For the moment, however, Spurgeon only pointed out that churches do have creeds and doctrinal expectations. "Protest by all means against creeds and catechisms," Spurgeon urged the conscientious non-subscriber, "but if you sign them, or gain or preserve a position by appearing to uphold them, wonder not if your morality be regarded as questionable."[21]

If a minister is found to be inconsistent with the standards, what should be done? Spurgeon had a succinct and reasonable approach to the problem:

> They should have a patient hearing that they may have opportunity to explain, and if it be possible to their consciences, may sincerely conform; but if the divergence be proven, they must with all the courtesy consistent with decision be made to know that their resignation is expected, or their expulsion must follow. The church which does not do this has only one course before it consistent with righteousness; if it be convinced that the standards are in error and the preacher right, it ought at all hazards to amend its standards, and if necessary to erase every letter of its creed, so as to form itself on a model consistent with the public teaching which it elects, or with the latitude which it prefers. However much of evil might come of it, such a course, would be unimpeachably consistent, so consistent indeed that we fear few ordinary mortals will be able to pursue it; but the alternative of maintaining a hollow compact, based on a lie, is as degrading to manliness as to Christianity.[22]

Within this same category, Spurgeon placed those that he denominated "Advanced Thinkers." These lurked within all denominations during the latter half of the nineteenth century, according to Spurgeon, and every Christian in all denominations must be wary of them. Spurgeon had nothing but disdain for such puff-up creatures. He hated their arrogance, their dishonesty, and their destructiveness. Their arrogance made them look upon themselves as the cultured intellectuals of the day. "Let half a word of protest be uttered by a man who believes firmly in something, and holds by a defined doctrine, and the thunders of liberality bellow forth against the bigot."[23] Some have given an honest look at the supposed fresh air of

---

19. SS, 1:37.
20. Ibid., 71.
21. Ibid., 72.

22. Ibid., 73.
23. S&T, November 1871, 495.

nineteenth century intellectual superiority and have found it a mere revamping of "old, worn-out heresies" passed off as deep thinking. The avant-garde, nevertheless, look with arrogant pity on those that still adhere to benighted creeds of the past. They consider themselves manly and coura- geous to be willing to preach their creedless mes- sage in churches founded on the doctrines that they assail. Spurgeon did not find this a point of manliness; if they would put themselves out and refuse to eat the bread of the orthodox they might be entitled to a verdict of manly honesty, but their retention of privilege shows that they fight, "not with the broad sword of honest men, but with the cloak and dagger of assassins."[24]

Spurgeon gave positive marks to James White who delivered a series of nine lectures that surely helped settle their listeners in the faith. White's presentation stood in contrast to the many Con- gregational churches where orthodoxy would be a novelty and emptiness a sparkling fascina- tion. Spurgeon, relieving the sober tension with a playful representation, had heard recently of "Rev. Empty Brainbox" who had resigned his Independent church in Sleepyton. The newly at- large minister reasoned that he had "outgrown the creed of the Congregational body, and felt the necessity of greater liberty than he could obtain among the Independents." Spurgeon was incredulous at the covetous grasp for more free- dom. "What on earth could he want?" The creed had long been meaningless for he knew Congre- gationalists who believed anything and "some who believe nothing." The limits of creed "would seem to have vanished into thin air." In truth, Mr. Empty Brainbox simply had nothing to say; the cupboard was bare. "Doth the wild ass bray when he hath grass?"[25]

This aggressive assertion of the right of free- dom is vicious and aims at total annihilation of Christian truth. True liberality, they contend, means that one should be sure of nothing. Opin- ions, not truths, we utter, and "therefore, culti- vated ministers should be left free to trample on the most cherished beliefs, to insult conviction" and to teach anything as directed by their own cultured and enlightened thought. No more sa- cred duty for the enlightened minister may be conceived than that of sneering at the man of a creed. Spurgeon cynically observed the sense of duty exhibited in their imperative of entering the synagogue of confessional bigots under cover of adherence to outmoded doctrines in order to inveigh against them in the very midst of the darkened foes of enlightenment. These arrogant, dishonest men make it their duty to destroy the faith of others from the very pulpits consecrated to defend what they assail. If anyone bothers to object to this intrusion and oust the intruder, the charges of illiberality begin to fly and the ejected infidel becomes the object of sympathy and de- fense by the secular press. "Our pity," Spurgeon protested, "is reserved to the honest people who have the pain and trouble of ejecting the disturb- er: with the ejected one, we have no sympathy; he had no business there, and, had he been a true man, he would not have desired to remain, nor would he even have submitted to do so had he been solicited."[26]

Spurgeon objected to the charge from such broad-minded spirits that he and others of his confessional ilk were lacking in liberality. Their accusation would be true, Spurgeon admitted, if the matter between them was one of mere opinion. But Spurgeon had invented none of his doctrine; he received it from the witness of the

---

24. Ibid., 496.

25. S&T, May 1874, 235.

26. S&T, November 1871, 498.

church to the truth as contained in the historic creeds which were but witnesses to the deposit of truth given in Scripture. While he did not consider himself a believer in "stereotyped phraseology" nor a promoter of "stagnant uniformity," he found removing the landmarks and throwing down the ramparts a sure method to produce doctrinal chaos. In short, he was a steward and a steward must be found faithful, not innovative or filled with liberality in the matter. A liberal spirit toward the matter of stewardship is nothing short of infidelity, even treason, to the master whose charge we keep. One may not negotiate with any of the truths given to us as a matter of trust; "it is rebellion, black as the sin of witchcraft, for a man to know the law, and talk of conceding the point."[27] To give a man poison under the guise of being liberal minded about chemistry or anatomy is still murder. "No fiction do we write," Spurgeon testified, "as we bear record of those we have known, who first forsook the good old paths of doctrine, then the ways of evangelic usefulness, and then the enclosures of morality."[28]

Spurgeon had advice and an observation for the proponents of the "Advanced Thought" that unshackled the intellect and gave such liberality of spirit:

Let our opponents cease, if they can, to sneer at Puritans whose learning and piety were incomparably superior to their own; and, let them remember that the names, which have adorned the school of orthodoxy, are illustrious enough to render scorn of their opinions, rather a mark of imbecility than of intellect. To differ is one thing, but to despise is another. If they will not be right, at least, let them be civil: if they prefer to be neither, let them not imagine that the whole world is gone

after them. Their forces are not so potent as they dream, the old faith is rooted deep in the minds of tens of thousands, and it will renew its youth, when the present phase of error shall be only a memory, and barely that.[29]

In the Preface to the 1871 *Sword*, contextualizing his confidence that the old faith is rooted deep in the minds of tens of thousands, Spurgeon summarized his concerns for the theological direction of the churches which caused him "alarm and much distress." He pointed to a "craving for novelty, a weariness of the once honored truth." Sickened by the churches' coquetting with Infidelity and toying with ritualism, Spurgeon confessed that he did know which of the two lovers to despise the more. "They are both arrant knaves and seducers, and those whose hearts are true to the Lord Jesus will utterly detest them." But such warnings, and such detestation, gained for the one that resisted their enchantment the epithets of "unenlightened, bigoted, and out of date." That did not bother Spurgeon, and he would not be slow to warn for he was convinced that there was nothing new in theology but that which was false, and even that was as old as the serpent himself. "Our sword will never rust for lack of enemies to smite; they multiply like the race which sprang of the dragon's teeth." Should the time come, and he believed it would soon, restating his optimism of the month before, when a recoil from advanced thought would ensue, and the faithful would be "pestered with hypocrites as now we are with heresies."[30]

Two decades would prove that Spurgeon's confidence in how deeply rooted the old faith was in the churches was ill placed. The influence of the liberal spirits would increase in both con-

27. Ibid., 498.
28. Ibid., 499.

29. Ibid., 500.
30. S&T, 1871, Preface.

tent and spirit of toleration within his own Baptist denomination so that he, rather than they, would be severed, if not in fact ejected, from the fellowship of those whose heritage he defended. He would not pretend fellowship with those with whom he disagreed upon vital points of truth. If they would not leave, or could not be dismissed, he would sever from them by dismissing himself. When his act of personal dissociation from the unholy alliance replaced the act of disfellowshipping, the theological progressives, even though they could not stomach his theology, found his action insulting. He responded that "to separate ourselves from those who separate themselves from the truth of God is not alone our liberty, but our duty." Having done so, he wished to be left free. "Those who are so exceedingly liberal, large-hearted, and broad might be so good as to allow us to forego the charms of their society without coming under the full violence of their wrath."[31]

Spurgeon's response to the surprisingly relentless advance of "advanced thought" in his own denomination led Kruppa to observe, "It was Spurgeon's tragedy that he lived long enough to witness the comfortable intellectual assumptions of evangelicalism disrupted by the twin challenges of science and higher criticism. He saw his task as one of resistance rather than reconciliation, and he devoted his last energies to a fruitless crusade against modernism."[32] While it is true that he devoted his last energies to this crusade, one can see clearly that he devoted not only his last energies but his early energies. And he would never have admitted that his fight was fruitless; he maintained his own witness and faithfulness unimpaired and that, combined with his confidence that truth would descend from the scaffold to live, was fruit enough for him.

The decision to fight, however, according to Kruppa, "has impaired his reputation with posterity, for the future belonged to his opponents. He failed to stem the tide against the future, and his life ended on a note of defeat," but nevertheless, a defeat without surrender. One could not have expected him to make any other decision or to care about his reputation with a posterity committed to heresy. He did not change his theological persuasion nor his posture toward theological modernists. Spurgeon knew, and so practiced, that constant vigilance was as much a necessity as a virtue in protecting the purity of the faith once for all delivered to the saints.

Not Easily Offended

The open profession of such determination against doctrinal unfaithfulness must not make one think that Spurgeon was unreasonable in his consideration of the dynamics of controversy. Spurgeon did not react negatively to a theological idea simply because others may have thought it unsound. He judged for himself. He did not shift into his controversial mode over matters that were light. Some departures he would ignore believing they would pass away from the deadness within them; some differences he bore in good spirit realizing that orthodox men had taken different views through the ages; some idiosyncrasies he tolerated well enough because of how encouraging and healthy to Christians the overall impact of one's ministry.

As much as he suffered at the hand of hyper-Calvinists, he much preferred them and their influence to the supposed liberal-mindedness of the liberals. In a discussion of Calvinism among the Baptists of England, Spurgeon indulged in an entertaining aside contrasting the hyper-Calvinists with the modernists:

---

31. S&T, December 1888, 620, "Attempts at the Impossible."

32. Patricia Stallings Kruppa, *Charles Haddon Spurgeon: A Preacher's Progress* (Garland Pub., 1982), 478.

We believe that these brethren, whatever their failings may have been, have done good service in keeping much precious truth stirring among the churches; and we should therefore rejoice to see them renew their youth, with more loving hearts and candid minds. They have been far too much despised and slighted. They ought not to be driven into isolation, but their alliance should be sought by their Baptist brethren, and Christian intercourse would lead to mutual advantage. As far as we have had an opportunity of judging, the bands of exclusiveness are not so strong as they once were, and a more liberal spirit is asserting itself among them. It was not, however, to this ultra kind of Calvinism that Mr. Dale referred, for it has never been maintained by us, though we would ten thousand times rather embrace it in its most rigourous form, than fall into the any-thing-arianism of modern thought. Even the stern spirit of our high doctrine friends we would prefer to that of the new theology. We used to think that Hyper-Calvinists were sometimes rather acid, but since we have met with religious liberalism we count all things sweet in comparison with the proud, contemptuous airs of large hearted bigots for liberality. Some articles of a certain free-thinking *Christian* paper, in their supreme contempt for "the simple gospel," exceed anything ever before manifested in that line; the art of sneering could no further go; they display a scorn which would be less intolerable if it could be regarded as the fruit of strong convictions. A strong, hard-shelled Calvinist holds his own tenaciously, because he believes that there are truths in the world worth holding, but your "cultured thinker" abhors in his magnificent soul all who will not make ducks and drakes of gospel doctrine after his own fashion.[33]

John Gadsby, the son of William Gadsby, the doyen of hyper-Calvinism in the early nineteenth century, published a book of sermons, sermon fragments, and letters of his father. Spurgeon said, "Though shrinking from certain of his extreme opinions, we venerate Gadsby's memory, and wish that there were many like him." He said that he was interested in anything about Gadsby and particularly found charming and refreshing that "old-fashioned savoury talk, which was the staple of the discourse of our High-Calvinistic brethren of the past generation."[34]

When Charles Waters Banks died in 1886, Spurgeon seemed melancholy at the idea of the passing of this generation of men. Banks, as much as his position and context would allow, sought to befriend Spurgeon when others criticized him and James Wells even questioned his conversion. "He loved the doctrines of grace," Spurgeon remarked about Banks, "but he did not like to smear them over with wormwood, as some of his comrades thought it wise to do," He went on to note that the "old-fashioned high Calvinists are passing away, and we are among those who miss them." They were not all that they should have been but "they were good men and true, and believed firmly what the Lord had taught them." They were not quick to learn more, but were "faithful to the light received." Better men have not taken their place. Cleverness and pretended liberality has replaced "positive and fixed belief." Spurgeon preferred "the narrowness of those who have gone than the emptiness of those who ridicule them."[35]

He even sought to protect Wells from a second-hand misrepresentation passed on by Paxton Hood. He did not agree with Hood's estimation of Wells as a preacher and informed his readers that "some of the stories to the detriment of these good men are mere distortions of fact."[36]

---

33. S&T, February 1874, 50.

34. S&T, March 1885, 144.

35. S&T, May 1886, 246.

36. S&T, October 1886, 546.

He knew that some of the stories were inaccurate when Hood heard them and others older than the men themselves. Spurgeon had had many an age-less anecdote applied to him also.

He was also surprised at the dismissive atti-tude Hood took toward William Huntington, the "coal-heaver," calling his ministry "spiritual rib-aldry" and his book on answered prayer "as de-testable as it is queer and curious." Spurgeon took exception to these judgments, somewhat amazed that a man of Hood's Christian experience and biblical knowledge would deprecate a Christian's testimony to the divine mercy and condescen-sion in answering the prayers of a simple needy child. Spurgeon could write a larger book than Huntington's of like answers but had decided not to do so for they would not be believed and it "might be casting pearls before swine." The com-monplace character of Huntington's requests and the corresponding answers seemed to offend "su-perfine critics" but Spurgeon believed the stories and had himself experienced the detailed provi-dences to which Huntington testified. Hunting-ton had been treated with harshness in the Bap-tist literature of the early nineteenth century as a notorious antinomian and scurrilous critic of any that dared question any of his opinions. Spurgeon showed his remarkable frankness, balance, and tender appreciation for the evidence of divine power and grace in the ministry of Huntington:

> We are not going to extol "the Bank of Faith" as altogether unexceptionable, for we greatly regret the stern way in which its author sees the judgments of God falling on all who disagree with him; but even in this we had rather a man should see too much than too little of the hand of God in terrible events. Of course the times were rougher and more plain-spoken than ours, and many expressions are used by Huntington which are not melodious to ears polite; but then he did not conceal the fact that he was a coal-heaver, and he never aspired to a higher degree than S.S., a sinner saved. When it is remembered that he knew the Bible by heart, and was accustomed to quote texts, and give chapter and verse many times in a sermon; and that, too, of passages almost unknown to common readers—it will never do to sneer at his preaching. One aged man told a friend of ours that he heard W. Huntington preach for two full hours, and nobody in the place seemed to have noticed the lapse of time. Many of his people were deeply experienced Christians, and it has been my privilege to have known their descendants, and to have heard loving testimonies to the piety of their forefathers. Singular, eccentric, and faulty as Huntington may have been, he might have met his critics in almost any field but that of science, and have disdained to set them among the dogs of his flock.[37]

In reviewing a book entitled *Boston Monday Lectures* by Joseph Cook, though some repre-sented him as unsound in some areas, Spurgeon remarked, "So often are such attainments set in array against religion, that we were charmed in this case to find them zealously engaged in be-half of the truth."[38] Spurgeon felt the urge to shout when he saw the champion "smiting the Philistines hip and thigh." Cook, a graduate of both Harvard (1865) and Andover (1868), was a prolific lecturer throughout the world and stood for orthodoxy against materialistic evolution, criticized transcendentalism, and questioned the orthodoxy of Theodore Parker. He did not stand in opposition to theistic evolution but was very careful in his language on the issue. Spurgeon evidently read Cook carefully and was willing to bend to his method of engagement because of the

---

37. S&T, November 1886, 584-85.
38. S&T, June 1881, 282.

arena in which he chose to defend the faith. "Mr. Cook's lectures are answers to infidels," Spurgeon explained, "and the tendency of fair controversy is to concede too much, or to fashion definitions with such extreme care that the thing defined is missed by the original believer though fully present in the intent of the controversialist." Those ambiguities certainly were true of Cook, but "his heart and soul are with the orthodox, and he never differs essentially from Calvinistic teaching; indeed he goes farther than half the Calvinists of modern times." Careful study of Cook's language would often lead Spurgeon from an initial shock to a pause and consideration with the result that he might consider the argument "awkwardly put" but accurate, "liable to misconstruction," but true. Spurgeon assured his reader that he was as "anxious for the maintenance of sound doctrine as any man living," but he was unwilling to impute to a man serious departures from the faith, denounce and ostracize him for his willingness to defend evangelical truth in a way designed to engage the infidelity of the day. He would never make him an offender for a word. "If anything could shake our faith in the grand old cause of evangelical doctrine," Spurgeon argued, "it would be the bitterness and narrowness of certain of its upholders." Concerning Cook, "we again express our confidence in the man and his communications."[39]

It is probable that he had read Cook in preparation for his appearance in London on a lecture tour of Europe. So positively impressed was Spurgeon that he had Cook in the Tabernacle three times during May 1881. All who heard him testified to Cook's orthodoxy. Spurgeon trusted those that recommended Cook and though not endorsing "every expression used by Mr. Cook," he found every reason to approve his "intense earnestness for the old-fashioned gospel" as well as "his ability to defend against philosophical skeptics." Spurgeon also confirmed Cook's adherence to that form of the gospel "which is known as thoroughly Calvinistic."[40]

Convinced Minds and Changed Lives

Ability in polemics, must, in a defense of Christian truth, be supported by earnestness. Controversy was a necessary evil in Spurgeon's view. He did not like to give any time publicizing errant and destructive views. The option, however, was to let them go unchallenged, and this was neither safe for the sheep nor consistent with the example of the apostles. His preferred method of refutation, however, was to point to certainty of knowledge gained from his own experience and the experience of Christians as verification of the biblical gospel, the deity of Christ, the reality of substitutionary atonement. An ounce of truth will remain when a pound of error seeps away.

Not only did he point to the life-saving power of the old gospel for common sinners, and often notorious sinners, but to the self-effacing God-centered labors of prominent Christian leaders. Among his most endeared fellow laborers were Hudson Taylor and George Muller. The character of both as well as the demonstrable soul-altering, life-saving results of their extensive toils for the glory of Christ held its own refutation of all the objections of skeptics. "Mr. Taylor," Spurgeon informed his readers, "is not a man of commanding presence or of striking modes of speech." Little about him would be impressive as a leader as he is "lame in gait, and little in stature." His spiritual manhood, however, manifested noble proportions; there is no self-assertion but only an unshakeable confidence in his call to carry the

---

39. Ibid.

40. Ibid., 294.

gospel to China. "He is hampered by no doubts as to the inspiration of the Scriptures, or the truth of Christianity, or the ultimate conquest of China for the Lord Jesus." He is too "conscious of consecration to the living God, and too certain of his presence and help to turn aside to answer the useless quibbles of the hour."[41]

Likewise, George Muller "believes God with great reality, and practically takes him at his word, and hence his peace is as a river." By faith Muller had great sense of purpose and moved beyond mere submission to the divine will into a sheer delight in every demonstration of divine glory and faithfulness through provision in the context of trial. Spurgeon himself responded, "O that we could all learn this lesson and put it into practice." Spurgeon reveled in the gracious, joyful exuberance about life and friendship and God that covered every word and action of Muller and commented energetically on his humility and beauty of character. Muller's preaching and life abounded in a simple testimony "to facts by which he has for himself proved the love and truth of God." The daily provision for 2,050 orphan children confirms every promise of Scripture for Muller; "with speculations he does not intermeddle, but the eternal verities he handles with practical, homely, realizing faith." Because of such evident demonstrations that Scripture is true, "modern thought and the higher criticism never trouble this happy man." He lives far above the fray and soars aloft. Those more bound to earth and less conscious of the presence of heaven "are distracted and tormented by the discordant voices of error." Muller, however, "hears the voice of the great Father in heaven, and is deaf to all besides. In his old age, still hale and strong, he ministers the word with

ceaseless diligence, journeying from place to place as the Lord opens the doors and prepares his way."[42]

Equally necessary as an accompaniment to the irrefutable life was the careful and extended expose of error. William Ritchie provided a model for controversial interaction in his *Bible Truth and Broad Church Error*. The term "broad" referred to the broad way that leads to destruction rather than the ecclesiological nomenclature of one part of the established church. The book should "make us blush for the age in which we live" Spurgeon wrote. But he welcomed this book as an antidote to the errors it deplored. First, the author established clearly the biblical truth on a number of doctrines, then exposed the deviations from each, and pointed out the source of the error, and the road for a return to health. "The principal subjects which are thus treated," Spurgeon summarized, "are the inspiration of the Scriptures, the incarnation, atonement, and justifying righteousness of Christ, the fatherhood of God, the duration of future punishment, the extent of redemption, and the restitution of all things." Spurgeon advised all who had been "captivated with the aberrations of these writers to give ear to the instructions of this book, and give glory to the Lord their God before they cause darkness, and before their feet stumble upon the dark mountains." The book was an "uplifted standard against a flood of error."[43] That was a flood that would never nourish but only parch the barren ground. Spurgeon's fight against that flood would never be satisfied until the day he died. Life and light are the unopposable answers to the absolute claims of death and darkness.

---

41. S&T, May 1879, 228-30.

42. Ibid.

43. S&T, May 1874, 237.

Some Minor but Revealing Skirmishes
The Rivulet

Spurgeon's participation in the Rivulet controversy early in his ministry came from his conviction that inculcating definite truth in a plain, forthright, and aggressive biblical manner was essential in Christian worship. Fullerton surmised, "In retrospect it seems much hubbub about very little."[44] Fullerton, however, surely must be wrong if the theological issues were quite what its main participants say they were. Since, however, it was over a book of poetry and both perceived denials and affirmations are quite open to dispute and other interpretations, the controversy did not amount to such a critical importance as later conflicts would. Given that, as to its representation of the earnest commitment of Spurgeon to clarity in the expression of biblical orthodoxy, his fairness in presentation, the brief and sometimes humorous interaction is paradigmatic.

One friendly commentator, J. Ewing Ritchie, gave his opinion on this supposed tempest in a teapot. In November 1855, Thomas T. Lynch published *The Rivulet*, a volume of religious poems for both private perusal and public worship. *The Eclectic Review* gave it favorable marks and *The Morning Advertiser* countered with its concerns that "the Rivulet was deeply tainted with deadly heresy." When ministers of his denomination came to Lynch's defense, *The Morning Advertiser* made those ministers the subjects of its censure. More publicity and controversy as well as confusion followed, and, in the words of Ritchie, "Reverend gentlemen and Christian laymen quarreled with all that bitterness which usually distinguishes the divine—pamphlets and letters were plentiful as blackberries."[45]

The Congregational Union postponed their meeting on account of the strife thus generated.

Ritchie summarized the results: "The publicans complained, and the *Advertiser* for a time directed its attention to more congenial subjects than those connected with theology. Moreover, the connection of John Campbell, Spurgeon's friend, with the *British Banner* was terminated, and Mr. Lynch "had a much speedier sale for his poems" than otherwise he would have had. Externally, according to Ritchie, Lynch was a failure. He was "a small spare man" whose "bodily presence is contemptible" and whose voice was so weak that one could scarcely hear him. In addition, his appearance was "so homely that you would never think that in such a casket a soul of any greatness could be enshrined." He was, nevertheless, so Ritchie assured his readers, one of the few men in London worth hearing.[46]

G. Holden Pike gave a less sarcastically inclined description. When James Grant, editor of *The Morning Advertiser*, reviewed *Hymns for Heart and Voice, The Rivulet*, he commended its literary and intellectual merits.[47] Its verses were specimens of poetic celebration of the beauty of and beneficence of nature, or how certain aspects of nature show us something of nature's Creator. This content, however, hardly qualifies it as Christian poetry. "There is not, from beginning to end, one particle of vital religion or evangelical piety in it." The name of Jesus only occasionally enters the verses but "there is not one solitary recognition of His divinity, of His atoning sacrifice, or of His mediatorial office." Such vital doctrines as "the inherent depravity of man" and the necessary agency of the Holy Spirit in conversion and sanctification find no voice; in short, the whole could easily have been written by a Deist.[48]

---

44. Fullerton, 291.

45. J. E. Ritchie, *The London Pulpit*, second edition, revised, corrected, and enlarged (London: William Tweedle, 1858), 109.

46. Ibid., 105.

47. G. H. Pike, *The Life and Work of Charles Haddon Spurgeon*, 6 vols (London: Cassell & Co., nd), 2:208, citing *The Morning Advertiser*, February 7, 1856.

48. Pike, 2:209.

Grant's review, so both Ritchie and Pike observed, was severely reprimanded in the cultured press of the day and many ministers entered the fray on either side of the issue. *The Eclectic*, under a new editor, made its mark in the controversy by challenging Grant's presentation of theological concerns, which in turn provoked a response by Grant, and then a counter-comment by *The Eclectic* endorsed by fifteen non-conformist ministers. *The Baptist Messenger* now engaged the issue with a piece expressing regret that the fifteen had intervened especially since, "we greatly fear it betokens on their part an evident leaning towards a transcendental theology—the blighting influences of which have proved most fatal to many once flourishing churches."[49] Grant himself again pressed the issue home in a most practical manner to these protesters by quoting a number of hymns and asking which of them would dare to line-out such non-descript religiosities in his pulpit. John Campbell analyzed the poetry and sent a series of open letters through his paper, *The British Banner*, to professors and principals of Baptist and Independent colleges in England pointing out how these presentations of supposedly Christian truth had no more distinctive Christian theology than the hymns used by Unitarians.

As some of the wrath began to subside, Spurgeon himself wrote a review, "Mine Opinion," that criticized mainly the murkiness of the views of truth hidden within the poetry. In *The Christian Cabinet* for May 23, 1856, Spurgeon, calling the controversy a "fierce affray" and aligning himself wholly "with the men who have censured the theology of the writer of the hymns," spoofed the book's mystical spirituality by recommending it for possible suitable venues. "If I should ever be on amicable terms with the chief of the Ojibe-

was," Spurgeon mused, "I might suggest several verses from Mr. Lynch as a portion of a liturgy to be used on the next occasion when he bows before the Great Spirit of the West Wind." Spurgeon called on the Delawares, Mohawks, Choctaws, Chickasaws, Blackfeet, Pawnees, Shawnees, and Cherokees (showing an impressive display of knowledge of native Americans, with whom he had sincere sympathy) to find in Lynch's collection their "primitive faith most sweetly rehearsed."[50] Like others he found no way to recommend its contents for Christian worship. If there had been no controversy over the book, none should have felt compelled to join sides and either approve the whole or censure the whole, for it clearly was written for a select group who are free to enjoy it without the opprobrium of others. The orthodox that came to his defense, in Spurgeon's opinion, did so more in sympathy "with the *man censured* than with the *man singing*,"[51] Should such sentiments pass as sufficient for Christian affirmation, then the battle is the Lord's, and "We shall soon have to handle truth not with kid gloves, but with gauntlets—the gauntlets of holy courage and integrity."[52]

Lynch agreed but indicated that Spurgeon was too young "in the experience of the world's sorrows and strifes to know what the old faith really is."[53] Spurgeon knew precisely what the old faith was and soon would know enough of the world's sorrows and strifes. In 1872, after sixteen years advancement in the world's sorrows and strifes, Spurgeon reviewed a publication by Lynch after his death. "Too much noise was made concerning this author while alive," Spurgeon clearly recalled. "He became notorious by accident, and was

---

49. Pike, 2:210 citing *The Baptist Messenger*, iv. 116.

50. *Autobiography*, 1:478
51. Ibid., 1:479.
52. Ibid., 1:481.
53. Pike, 2:212.

forced by opposition into a prominence which neither his merits nor his demerits deserved." Perhaps the memory of this first venture into public controversy was a bit stinging still, and Spurgeon confessed that he did not have enough patience to read through the volume but what he had read had "just enough 'tincture of error' in it to give it an ill odour."[54]

Lynch's staying power proved amazing to Spurgeon, for in 1885 a series of Thursday evening lectures by Lynch was published. Spurgeon could ask, "Who remembers the great splash called 'The Rivulet Controversy?'" Few earned honor and most showed weakness in that controversy, according to Spurgeon, for Lynch was lynched by Dr. Campbell and he in turn kicked out very vigorously. The colors of the advanced school presently made Lynch's advanced views seem altogether pale. "He wrote some real poetry as well as some heterodox couplets; and we doubt not that he held much precious truth, though in solution with his own imaginings." Now at this distance, Spurgeon found him interesting, a man of wide reading, and one that must have been a lovable person. He did not wonder that friends that might not have agreed with his eccentricities nevertheless took his part in the controversy.[55]

Joseph Parker

Charles Spurgeon marked Joseph Parker's recent coming to London by reviewing a book of his sermons. Perusing *The City Temple: Sermons preached in the Poultry Chapel, London 1869-70* gave opportunity for Spurgeon to remark, "Although we are far from endorsing all Dr. Parker's doctrinal teaching, we hail his advent to the City as a great gain to the Evangelical church at large, and to Dissent in particular." When Parker sets

his heart upon preaching gospel truth, Spurgeon called his words "weighty and powerful." Parker's so-called parables and addresses had a different flavor and the reader would not be poorer without them. Spurgeon wished he had filled the volume with discourses as valuable as those on the Holy Spirit. "Every man has his way," Spurgeon conceded, "and the Poultry preacher has a very distinct one of his own." Even with this distraction, Spurgeon saw "no pandering to the latitudinarianism which so largely leavens the Congregational body." Spurgeon hoped that Parker's "intense energy and remarkable powers of eloquence" would influence others under the anointing of the Spirit to set up a bulwark of defense of the cross of Christ among the Congregationalists.[56]

Spurgeon regularly reviewed Parker's new works when they appeared, often finding something to commend, and almost as often issued a caveat concerning his theology. He reviewed Parker's *Ad Clerum* with the recommendation, "Young men must be great dolts if they can read his advice and derive no profit from it." He added, "Our grief that Dr. Parker should have gone aside to certain modern heresies is intense, and we pray that he may soon see his way out of them." He made sure the reader knew that "none of that mischief" marred the volume before him.[57]

Parker's restatement of *The Priesthood of Christ* had nothing in it that Spurgeon could make himself commend. He hoped that some in Parker's own denomination would have enough courage to expose the "mischievous tendencies of this book." The chapter on "Ultimate Aspects of Christ's Priesthood" Spurgeon gave the ultimate denunciation in calling it "the most evil piece of writing it was ever our misery to read." Parker wrote in such a way as to avoid being blamed specifically

---

54. S&T, September 1872, 433.

55. S&T, October 1885, 546.

56. S&T, September 1870, 427.

57. S&T, December 1870, 573.

for positions explored in the book, all of which Spurgeon pronounced as "unutterably bad." Even an honest infidel should dislike Parker's slipperiness and lack of resolve to shoulder the burden of his doctrinal proposals. "The underlying idea of preaching one thing when you mean another, disguise it how you please, and justify it how you may," Spurgeon fired, "is simply detestable."[58]

In December 1879 in a purely spontaneous gesture of brotherly unity in a singular cause, Parker urged his congregation to give an offering for the Stockwell Orphanage. Spurgeon remarked, "Our intercourse with him has been but slender, hence the utter spontaneousness of his kindly deed was the more striking and refreshing to our heart." Parker sent a letter include a check for £20 explaining how it came about and included a very careful sentence of restricted encouragement to Spurgeon, "Use it for the boys or girls just as you like, and always remember that the City Temple is open when you care to occupy it in the interests of your orphanage."[59]

On February 15, 1883, Spurgeon preached, at the invitation of Parker, at the City Temple. "Never was a reception more hearty than that accorded to us by Dr. Parker," Spurgeon exclaimed, "who has on many other occasion displayed a kindness towards us for which we are at a loss to account, except by the largeness of his own heart."[60] Parker's treatment of the book of Acts brought Spurgeon to say that Parker is "a man of genius, and whenever he speaks he has something to say, and says it in his own striking manner." Parker always was original, his thoughts were his own and the jewels he spread along the way were "from his own caskets and not others."[61]

Spurgeon clearly found Parker intriguing and he had an irresistible attraction to Parker's native genius. Always original, Parker could not but entertain even if one must always be on guard against being led astray. Spurgeon had to fence each compliment with a caveat, but was far from dismissing Parker as unworthy of attention. His sermons on Genesis were "bright and original, and altogether Parkerine." He was startling as well as edifying and practical even if many passages needed to be "interpreted into the commoner forms of thought." His comments would not quite be to the mind of the readers of Gill and Henry, but to Lange and other moderns he was second to none. Parker did things his own way and filled up the thoughtful reader with an abundance of stimulating manners of expression, and "whether you endorse it or not, you are struck with the singular ability and special originality of the preacher."[62]

Certainly Spurgeon's ambivalence toward Parker through the years could have soured Parker's disposition. Parker returned the ambivalence, however, and fluctuated between the polarities of great admiration and condescending snobbishness. It seems that resentment was gradually building and would press itself out during Spurgeon's most vulnerable time.

One of the harshest and most unfair, as well as irrelevant, caricatures of Spurgeon and his position came from Parker when the Downgrade Controversy provided opportunity to pounce on Spurgeon's adamantine stance for doctrinal orthodoxy. He wrapped an insult around a compliment, but gave a good summary of his rocky relationship with Spurgeon:

> When people ask me what I think of Spurgeon, I always ask which Spurgeon—the head or the

---

58. S&T, January 1877, 42.

59. S&T, January 1880, 45.

60. S&T March 1883, 149.

61. S&T, February 1885, 86.

62. S&T, June 1885, 290.

heart—the Spurgeon of the Tabernacle or the Spurgeon of the Orphanage? The kind of Calvinism which the one occasionally represents I simply hate, as I hate selfishness and blasphemy. It is that leering, slavering, sly-winking Calvinism that says, "Bless the Lord we are all right, booked straight through to heaven first-class" ... But when I turn to the orphanage all is changed. All is beauty. All is love ...[63]

Spurgeon on Science

A Christian's ambivalence toward science is rooted in the proneness of many scientists to use their success in mastering the scientific method of research, and the many advances in medicine, technology, mechanics, and numerous other areas to justify their assumption of authority as metaphysicians. Spurgeon observed this tendency; while, therefore, he nurtured a healthy respect for science and scientists, his acceptance of their philosophical ontology was far from impressive. "The most absurd theories will have their admirers," Spurgeon noted, "if they come from men of great scientific attainments." Their actual discoveries will fuel admiration for their speculation. The dynamic in the scientific world, Spurgeon noticed is the same as in the world of finance. Just as thrift and sound investment policy leads to real wealth and then fuels "ruinous speculation," so "real scientific knowledge often leads to more than ordinary folly." The ones to whom we should be able to look for "real acquisitions and clear reasonings in natural science are the first to overleap its boundaries and to substitute their own reveries for established facts."[64]

They may reason themselves into the descendants of "apes, lobsters, and material molecules," but they have no warrant to do so for others.

Charles Elam, an M.D., in *Winds of Doctrine* reasoned that if the prevailing evolutionary thought afforded the only plausible "solution of the various problems of ontology, then it follows naturally and of necessity that matter is all-sufficient, and that man is an automaton without spirit or spontaneity." Were it so, immortality is a dream, volition and responsibility mere delusions, virtue, vice, right, and wrong merely words without meaning, and "education, government, rewards, and punishments are illogical and mischievous absurdities." Spurgeon appreciated Elam's scientific refutation of the errors involved in evolutionary metaphysics but was more thankful that "our own common sense upon these subjects still remains."[65]

Spurgeon found himself utterly opposed to the flood of evolutionary literature following the publication of Darwin's *The Origin of Species*. The theory in Spurgeon's view was atheistic, illogical, and those who believed and defended it were gullible. At times, however, he indicated openness to the question of the age of the earth and at others he welcomed refutations of a supposed ancient origin of humanity. His response to a book entitled *Echoes From Distant Footfalls; or the Origin and unity of the Human Race* included the concession, "Nine very sensible lectures upon the antiquities of our race, dealing most wisely with the supposed geological proofs of its extremely remote origin. Here we have much learning, and an equal measure of piety. The little book will be useful."[66]

In reviewing a book entitled *Darwinism and Design; or, Creation by Evolution* by George St. Clair. Spurgeon contended that to argue for design from Darwinism was irrational. "If greater beings are evolved from less, the power must be

---

63. Murray, *Forgotten Spurgeon*, 181.

64. S&T, May 1877, 233.

65. Ibid.

66. S&T, May 1874, 235.

in them or given to them; and if in them we have a chain of effects producing causes more powerful than themselves; we cannot accept, therefore, the apology here made for Darwinism in reference to design." The very places, Spurgeon contended, where the greatest strength of argument and evidence was needed were the weakest and most absent of demonstration. Critical differences call for compelling evidence. How something moves from inorganic to organic, from vegetative to instinctual, from instinctual to rational has no demonstration in St. Clair's evidence; he "fails to show the transition from one to the other, and to produce examples in which that process is still going on." We know seeds become plants, and boys become men, and eggs become chickens; we see it regularly displayed all around us and from the presence of these phenomena we learn to explain them and make scientific observations about them. Nothing about the critical leaps in evolution has ever been observed, and therefore, is incapable of description. The attempt to affirm design in Darwinism demonstrates its absurdity.[67]

To theories that seek to discover six periods of millions of years in the geological record as indicated by the six days of Genesis, Spurgeon objected that the intent of the biblical record was not to teach geology. "This supposition is absurd," Spurgeon contended, "and has so far failed that it may be safely affirmed that the theory of six definite periods could not have been suggested by the facts themselves." He also dismissed any attempts to allegorize "what is narrated as literally true" in favor of the most recent scientific assertions, as calculated "to weaken our faith at the commencement of our Bibles in all that is to follow." Men try various procedures to steady the ark of God, "but it needs not their help."[68] He dealt with another

attempt to lengthen the days of creation into "six long divisions of time." Spurgeon acknowledged some of the reasons brought forth by geology for lengthening the days and at times even making them overlap. The value of this study he saw as preventing "others from wasting their energies in the same direction." The institution of a literal Sabbath in the moral law based on the other six days of labor "compels us, against all criticism and reasoning, to conclude that the six days were literal as well as the seventh." If the seventh is a literal day, then it is not a day in the same sense that the other six are days and would constitute no reason for its observance as such.[69]

Scientific theories passed away quickly from one generation to the next. "The march of science, falsely so called, through the world may be traced by exploded fallacies and abandoned theories." Continual wreckings of false hypotheses have scattered debris and left in ruins the once proud outposts of scientific thinkers from generation to generation. "As the quacks which ruled the world of medicine in one age are the scorn of the next, so has it been, and so will it be, with your atheistical savans and pretenders to science." The vaunted *facts* derived from naturalistic assumptions that are supposed to drive the believer from the words that God has penned, are like bubbles to be burst when pricked by the sharp edges of honest investigation. More are being blown, however, and "we are expected to believe in whatever comes, and wait with open mouth to see what comes next." Science is often just an excuse to hide, or justify, unbelief. "Show us a man of science worthy of the name, and then we will not follow him if he dares to oppose revealed truth." But those that would do their work with open minds, not as a cloak for destruction of faith, but, like Newton, "reverent

---

67. S&T, July 1874, 337.

68. S&T, January 1876, 43f.

---

69. S&T, April 1878, 185.

toward the Scriptures," and they will be followed not only by their own generation but by those of the future.[70]

Though he was hostile to Darwininan theory as a system, he did not approve of a method of argument that merely insulted the opposition. A book by Robert Payterson entitled *The Errors of Evolution* did not make his list of desirable books. "This book cannot be accepted as a contribution to our sacred literature," he wrote; the approach was disrespectful. "The weapons of our warfare would indeed be carnal if we lent ourselves to offensive personalities in contending for the faith." He objected to the coarseness of Payterson's presentation citing in particular some chapter titles such as "On Geological Evolution—'Why did not Moses make a fool of himself like the Chinese, Hindoos, and Evolutionists?'"[71] Spurgeon had his own way of ridiculing the ridiculous and casting sarcasm on some theological and cultural icons, but he did not warm to mere declamation.

He was willing, moreover, to concede a measure of autonomy to science and then to work to maintain biblical truth in its context. A striking example of this is found in his sermon on Christ as the "Destroyer of Death." "Geology tells us that there was death among the various forms of life from the first ages of the globe's history, even when as yet the world was not fitted up as the dwelling of man." Spurgeon could accept this and still regard death as the result of sin. Acceptance of the idea that animal death depended on the entrance of sin meant that "those deaths before Adam [were] the antecedent consequences of a sin which was then uncommitted." He justified this by establishing an analogous relation between salvation before propitiation and death before the commission of sin. "If by the merits of

Jesus there was salvation before he had offered his atoning sacrifice, I do not find it hard to conceive that the foreseen demerits of sin may have cast the shadow of death over the ages which preceded man's transgressions."[72]

While Spurgeon severely doubted, and at times scoffed, at the conclusions of some scientists derived from speculative hypotheses, he considered science the friend of divine revelation. "For our own part," he affirmed, "we hail the light that streams upward from the dark places of the earth." He welcomed archaeology, geology, and physical geography as "the very sciences that God has ordained to be his witnesses, to frustrate the tokens of liars, to make diviners mad, and to confirm the word of his servants the prophets."[73] "We have no fear," he commented, "for the result of the conflict between science and religion: the God of Nature is the God of the Bible, and when we read both aright we shall not see conflict, but deep unity and harmony."[74]

He admitted a review into *The Sword and the Trowel,* probably written by another, but approved at least in part by him, in which this summary is stated: "The Darwin theory of evolution, as it is commonly called, does not appear to him [that is, the author of *The Day-Dawn of the Past*] subsversive of the inspired narrative of *Genesis.* Only he stipulates that, if satisfactorily demonstrated, it must be accepted as a discovery of the way that God took to work out his own purposes, and not as an alternative method of accounting for things that are, without the intervention of a Creator, by whose will they were made and by whose will they consist."[75] He does not fully ap-

---

70. S&T, May 1877, 199.

71. S&T, April 1886, 189.

72. Charles Spurgeon, *Christ's Glorious Achievements*, (Ross-Shire, Scotland: Christian Focus Publications, nd), 106-07.

73. S&T, June 1881, 286.

74. S&T, February 1882, 88.

75. S&T, June 1882, 308.

prove of that slight capitulation to Darwinism, but he seeks to disarm the concession in a rather mild way by pointing out that Darwin took an existing evolutionary theory and added the idea of "natural selection" as its *modus operandi*. That in itself indicates that evolution is a disconnected theory looking for a way to survive. Whether the theory is fit or not, only a long future will tell for, he noted, "To our feeble apprehension, modern philosophy is just now in the primitive stage of protoplasm—a mass of jelly; and its loose ideas will probably take as many aeons to develop into solid facts as the interval they compute between chaos and cosmos."[76]

An attempt to show that "both scientifically and theologically the first two chapters of Genesis are true," received the sincere appreciation of Spurgeon, but also elicited the frustrated remark, "We are getting weary of this constant defence of the Pentateuch."[77] A Christian minister should know that it is true, preach it as truth, and expect the God of truth to bless its preaching for the edification of saints and the conversion of sinners.

Spurgeon saw the prejudices of the guild operating in the reaction against James Southall's work *The Epoch of the Mammoth, and the Apparition of Man on the Earth*. Spurgeon noted that Southall "gets the cold shoulder in scientific circles." This is because he martials scientific facts "to refute certain scientific hypotheses that have too easily become popular in this age of pyrrhonism." Southall's intent was to "reconcile the results of scientific research with the received interpretation of Scripture." He summed up the evidence to show that "the Scriptures have not been broken." Spurgeon knew that that enterprise was not in fashion, for scientific circles were exclusive and their development of hypotheses was uncongenial to the

certainty of Scripture on certain issues. The "bias from which they vaunt themselves to be pure betrays itself too palpably." They are not pleased with the confirmation of ancient truth but delight in detecting a semblance of discrepancy "between sacred testimony and modern discovery." He had little confidence in the assumptions that governed the reasoning from research to hypothesis. "After pursuing their enquiry into the operations of nature with commendable patience, they perplex themselves with endless conjectures as to the explanation of the conflicting phenomena which they have observed." When poised on the edge of the facts, verdict is delayed, for new discoveries are constantly before them and the cultivation of an attitude of entire disinterestedness is necessary for the success of their craft. They cultivate therefore, on the one hand, a bias toward naturalistic answers and, consequently, on the other, a sense of condescension toward the finality espoused by theologians on ultimate questions. Science does not pose a problem; hesitance toward the supernatural does.[78]

This tension that scientific assumptions produced in the Christian doctrine of particular providence generated a bit of ridicule toward Spurgeon. Spurgeon had referred to the cold winds that he experienced in Marseilles as sent of God to produce a particularly sanctifying affliction.[79] Writing in the pages of the *Christian World* periodical a medical doctor with the pseudonym "Adelphos" rejected Spurgeon's assumption of God's particular personal providence in this matter, saying that God designed the winds for the benefit of a certain kind of vegetation. Spurgeon just happened to be in the way and his assumption that God designed the resulting malady for him was to make God vindictive. The error, both

---

76. Ibid.

77. S&T, July 1882, 375.

78. S&T, June 1881, 286.

79. S&T, March 1877, 139-40.

in science and theology, lies at the door of the M.D., according to Spurgeon. Should the doctor be correct about the vegetation (Spurgeon was dubious about this), that purpose did not inhibit an all-wise God from using the wind for other particular purposes. "A particular providence, even in the lighting of sparrows, and in the number of the hairs of our head, is the doctrine of the Bible, and it is also matter of fact." This does not have to be a matter of sight, demonstrably true scientifically for Spurgeon, for it is a matter of belief, a submission to Scripture truth. "The fact that wind and weather can be scientifically predicted, and that they are produced by fixed laws we know quite as well as M.D.; we are quite scientific enough for that: but this by no means opposes the grand doctrine that the hand of the Lord ordereth all things." Fixed laws do not operate apart from divine power or purpose, and his hand is present in the ordinary course of things as much as in those events we call miracles. Spurgeon did not consider himself either irreverent or irrelevant to believe that God is in all things, not only here and there. "When we testify to our faith in God's love it is hard to be accused of representing God as a capricious and vindictive ruler." True science would recognize that God can accomplish more than one thing by his determinations and the "unscientific inferences belong to M.D. and not to us."[80]

Ongoing Strife with Periodicals

The numbers of periodicals that Spurgeon read was massive, and that he took issue from time to time with their viewpoints, politically, theologically, socially, or personally should come as no surprise. It was all in the interest of clarifying truth, or making those that gained the public's attention more careful in their presentation. He had suffered much at the hands of pundits and cartoonists, and at times had benefitted from them, but he always shuddered at misrepresentation whether to his denigration or his advantage, whether a deflation or a puff. The intense interest in everything Spurgeon made it impossible for him to respond to everything, but certain types called for rapid and unwavering confrontation.

When the *Westminster Review* reported, "among other falsehoods and misrepresentations," that some of his own deacons described him as "a regular pope," Spurgeon called it "an unmitigated lie, for which there has never existed a shadow of foundation." He challenged the paper to produce a single name and address and he would respond with all the names and addresses of the deacons so that the reporter could either verify the statement or "admit himself to have uttered a gratuitous falsehood."[81] When his friends Arthur Mursell and William Landels lectured before his college men, Spurgeon wryly observed, "It is most remarkable that, while the *Westminster Review* was announcing these brethren as our opponent, they were actually of their own free will serving us as friends." Mursell's lecture, in fact, took a particularly Spurgeonic texture as he laid "such scathing sarcasm upon the modern schools of thought, and such a defence of the old orthodox faith, as we have seldom, if ever, heard" and he hoped that they would never forget it.[82] In reviewing a book of interesting incidents in Baptist history by J. J. Goadby, Spurgeon remarked, "If this book does not interest a reader, we give him up; he must surely be as ignorant as the writer in the last *Westminster Review*, who evidently knew more about pewter pots that Baptists."[83]

---

80. S&T, April 1877, 189.

81. S&T, January 1872, 46.

82. S&T, December 1871, 571.

83. S&T, November 1871, 531.

The *Daily News* described the watchnight service held at the Tabernacle on December 31, 1873. "The account was more interesting than true," Spurgeon reported, "for the remark as to the devil's causing the people to drag the tune, and sing slowly, was an interpolation by the reporter." Spurgeon himself may have made a similar remark at some time, but certainly not that evening, he claimed, but "the temptation to be smart is very powerful with reporters when Spurgeon is the subject." He would not have minded the reporter commenting on the "melodious singing of hundreds of our people in the area fronting the Tabernacle" after midnight. The music had a charming effect, held hundreds spell-bound. Spurgeon had never heard anything more sweet, but the reporter did not find it to his purpose to give any such positive message.[84]

When Spurgeon preached at the London Tavern on January 6, 1874, both the *Daily Telegraph* and *The Christian World* reported on the message. Though the *Telegraph* normally achieved accuracy and some degree of sympathy with Spurgeon, on this occasion the accuracy lay with *The Christian World*. Supposedly, according to the report given to the *Daily Telegraph* and transferred from it uncorrected to the *Freeman*, Spurgeon commended devotees of Rome for their zeal and praised the Crusades. His words actually encouraged the believers of truth to excel the servants of Romish superstition in zeal and diligence as he himself planned to continue a spiritual crusade upon heathenism and sin. "Our rule has been not to correct reports or answer charges made in newspapers," Spurgeon noted, "since we should have nothing else to do." He made an exception in this case because two usually friendly papers had printed errors peculiarly misleading.[85]

The open-air preachers of London came to the Tabernacle in January 1876 and Spurgeon preached to them, giving them some practical advice about style and content in the art of open-air preaching. By the time his remarks were reported in the weekly and daily periodicals, he wondered if he had been at the same meeting they reported. "The method adopted," as Spurgeon observed it, "seems to be to pick out every sentence in which there appears to be a funny observation, and leave out all the rest." This method rendered the speech an absurdity and turned what should have been an honest report into a slander. One of his friends, who had not been there but read the reports, wrote upbraiding him for having ridiculed the preachers. Spurgeon found it discouraging to find himself caricatured by those that should be giving a report. Though some of the older religious papers were managed as well as the daily secular papers, "certain of the newer issues are scandalously managed in the matter of reporting." These penny ventures insert reports from men that can hardly spell, and "whose ignorance is so great that they mistake the most common theological terms and names."[86]

One publication with which Spurgeon had an ongoing battle for more than two decades was *The Christian World*, the product of an entrepreneurial publisher named James Clarke. He had begun this paper in 1857 as an unsectarian and evangelical newspaper, a "general intelligencer" for broadly evangelical thinkers in England. Spurgeon seems first to have paid close attention to *The Christian World* in 1866. The lead review for that year in *The Sword and the Trowel* gave a sterling recommendation from Spurgeon. He said that the editor "is manly in his utterances, and decided in his teachings, keeping back no

---

84. S&T, February 1874, 93.

85. Ibid.

86. S&T, April 1876, 141.

truth because of its angularity or unpopularity." This newly minted periodical avoided the malady of non-denominational publications in becoming "namby-pamby, truckling, timorous, and any-thing-arian." He continued the recommendation of the editor by saying, "His leading articles are admirable, his selection judicious, and his news fresh and varied." He recommended everything except "the religious novels, and if we should ever be able to screw up our grim judgment round to allow us to recommend works of fiction, we should most certainly put the tales in the *Christian World* in a very high place." He urged his friends to seek the extension of the influence of a "paper so excellent" for it certainly commanded his "constant and increasing confidence."[87]

Within six months, Spurgeon's confidence began to decrease. By June, Spurgeon's correspondents had disturbed his mind about the theological ambience of the religious periodical. He felt embarrassed that he had not noticed certain theological leanings and had given such an enthusiastic welcome. The mitigating circumstance featured the editor as "a gentleman whom we highly esteem, a man of great ability and generous spirit." In addition, "his paper, for its freshness of news, and its power of writing, deserves every encomium, while its aid to all sorts of practical work, in the cause of religion and education, commands our gratitude." Lately he had noticed, however, "from numerous letters and personal remarks ... there is a growing want of confidence in the theology of the paper in certain directions." He concurred. "Theologically," he judged, "it does seem to us that of late the articles in the paper are generally loose and frequently dangerous." He gave such a notice, not to interfere with the perfect freedom of the editor in the conscientious prom-

ulgation of his own views, but to dissociate his influence from the "promulgation and palliation of what we feel to be very serious error."[88] When his correspondents began to write to him complaining about the "the heterodoxy of the *Christian World* newspaper," he responded that "no one is more grieved at the fact than we are, but we have not even the remotest share in the conduct of the paper, or any sort of connection with it." Though he had always wished the paper well, he was "sorry that it takes the course it has."[89] Future days would prove the instincts of Spurgeon true. An obituary of the publisher, James Clarke, described him in terms exactly suited to irritate and alarm Spurgeon. "His breadth and boldness continually caused the weaker brethren to tremble. To admit into 'News of the Churches' the headings 'Unitarian' and 'New-Church,' was sure proof that he was on the 'down-grade.' Many were scandalized at the latitude afforded alike to Annihilationists and Universalists to advocate their heterodox views."[90] This reference is a scarcely subtle poke at Spurgeon as one of the "weaker brethren."

Frequently, *The Christian World* had correspondents in Spurgeon's services to report on the sermon or other events that might happen. The memorable defense of smoking given in the Tabernacle was reported in *The Christian World* on the occasion of George Pentecost's visit in September 1874. When Pentecost, asked to give some personal reflections on Spurgeon's call to holiness in his sermon, revealed that God had led him to relinquish his indulgence in "the best cigar which could be bought." After Pentecost explained what led him to that conviction and encouraged others to find a similar point of scrupu-

---

87. S&T, January 1866, 43.

88. S&T, June 1866, 286.

89. S&T, October 1871, 478.

90. *Typo*, 26 May 1888, 37. This was a religious magazine published in New Zealand.

losity for the sake of holiness, Spurgeon rose with the task of saving himself, his guest, and making clear the point of his sermon. "Well, dear friends," he began, according to the newspaper report, "you know that some men can do to the Glory of God what to other men would be a sin." Notwithstanding Pentecost's personal conviction, Spurgeon declared, "I intend to smoke a good cigar to the Glory of God, before I go to bed tonight." He saw no commandment in Scripture, "Thou shalt not smoke," and he had no intention of introducing the eleventh or the twelfth commandment. Some may have developed a conscience against it, just as another may believe he should not get his boots blacked; if so, the one must not smoke and the other must refrain from boot-blackening, for whatever is not of faith is sin. The fact is, Spurgeon emphasized, "I have been speaking to you about real sin, and not about listening to mere quibbles and scruples." Spurgeon was not ashamed of his smoking and, therefore, "I mean to smoke to the glory of God."[91]

A firestorm arose around these impromptu remarks reported in *The Christian World*, so Spurgeon responded with a longer defense of his smoking policy by writing a letter to the editor of the *Daily Telegraph*. Spurgeon regretted the occasion that prompted the "unpremeditated remarks" and regretted as well the tone of the newspaper article that reported it. He observed the arising of a "Pharasaic system which adds to the commands of God the precepts of men." He did not intend for their sneers to interrupt either his liberty or his serenity. To the degree that the expression "smoking to the glory of God" had an ill sound, Spurgeon did not justify it; but its intent was not abstract but specific and contextualized:

When I have found intense pain relieved, a weary brain soothed and calm, refreshing sleep obtained by a cigar I have felt grateful to God, and have blessed His name; that is what I meant and by no means did I use sacred words triflingly. If through smoking, I had wasted an hour of my time—if I had stinted my gifts to the poor—if I had rendered my mind less vigorous—I trust I should see my fault and turn from it; but he who charges me with these things shall have no answer but my forgiveness.[92]

W. M. Hutchins responded with a lengthy investigation of Spurgeon's accusations of Pharasaism, and, pointing to his universal and unprecedented influence, all the bad that would accrue to families as a result of his strong endorsement of cigar-smoking. Sadly, others already had fallen into the errors that Spurgeon had managed to avoid and did not have the salutary reasons for smoking claimed by him. Did Spurgeon believe that those involved in temperance organizations from his own Tabernacle were Pharisees? Had he forgotten that the Apostle Paul himself would refuse to embrace his freedom of eating meat should such eating harm his brother? Spurgeon's principle can be distilled to this—"that a Christ man is at liberty to exercise self-indulgence in all matters against which there is not direct and express command in Scripture."[93]

Hutchins insisted that his chief concern in addressing Spurgeon was to point out the "essential viciousness of the principle" he had adopted and its inapplicability to myriads of circumstances. Taking up one's cross and following Christ demanded a sacrifice of self-indulgence for the good of one's neighbor and, thus, the glory of Christ.

It does not appear that Spurgeon relinquished smoking, for even during the Downgrade, an

---

91. Fulton, 345.

92. Ibid., 347.
93. Ibid., 353.

American visitor, William E. Hatcher, tells an amusing anecdote in which he joined Spurgeon in a post-dinner cigar after midnight. Hatcher had given up the habit for ten years but felt he could not deny to Spurgeon a moment of fellowship in the relaxed atmosphere of cigar smoke.[94]

When a biography of George Pentecost appeared in 1882, Spurgeon reviewed it in a lukewarm manner. He appreciated the fact that he was one of the few American Baptists that did not embrace closed communion. "Whether he is always wise we should not care to say," Spurgeon commented, "but he always desires to be right, and his heart is warm and true." Pentecost wanted to be useful in the work of God and for the good of men, but hardly enough of remarkable incident characterized his life to make a very readable biography.[95] At that time he was in England to aid in a Moody crusade. Perhaps his moment of highest notoriety came with his innocent remark that stirred the controversy about Spurgeon's smoking.

Plymouth Brethrenism

Spurgeon strongly supported and encouraged Bible believers wherever he found them. The doctrine they derived from the Bible was fair game for his analysis and criticism. The Plymouth Brethren, however, in Spurgeon's view had an irritating combination of idiosyncratic theology, a sense of condescension, a divisive spirit, and a disintegrative ecclesiology that drove him to sound the alarm against them. In reviewing one writer's analysis of Brethren by question and answer, *A Catechism of the Doctrines of the Plymouth Brethren*, Spurgeon stated, "Nearly all the errors of Plymouth Brethrenism are here adduced

and ably refuted." He believed that the method of questions and answers made the points plain to a broad spectrum of readers. The reasoning was scriptural and the feeling was generous innocent of any consciousness of superiority in debate. Spurgeon would like "to have seen the perversion of the great doctrine of imputed righteousness more prominently dealt with."[96]

The turn that the Brethren took under the influence of J. N. Darby, moreover, irritated him even more. In reviewing *A Caution Against the Darbyites* by J. E. Howard, Spurgeon commented, "We are delighted to see that certain of the original Brethren are protesting against the Darbyites." He recommended the pamphlet for it revealed "how tyranny may hide itself under proud assumptions of non-sectarianism."[97] He referred to the experience of Lord Congleton, because "he knows them better than we wish to do." Under interrogation Lord Congleton provided a witness that Spurgeon saw as informative and valuable for his readers. When asked if he tried the Darbyites, Congleton replied: "I have tried them ('try the spirits whether they are of God') and found them false prophets, in every sense of the word *false*. They are *false* in what they say of their brethren, they are *false in doctrine*, they are *false* in their work."[98]

While Spurgeon wanted to do all he could to expose the errors of the Brethren, especially of the Darbyite injection, he resisted making *The Sword and the Trowel* a forum for this controversy. When some of the Brethren requested that he print their response to a bit of strong criticism from the pen of his friend James Grant, he refused to publish either their response or Grant's reply. "We do not intend to enter into a contro-

---

94. William E. Hatcher, *Along the Trail of the Friendly Years* (New York: Fleming H. Revell Company, 1910), 247-48.

95. S&T, November 1882, 591.

96. S&T, January 1866, 45.

97. S&T, June 1866, 285.

98. Ibid.

versy upon the matter of Brethrenism," Spurgeon clarified, for "dissentients have the same power to use the press as we have; and they have their own magazines in which to defend their creed and character." As far as the Grant material was concerned, he believed most of Grant's charges and his detailed defense of them to be correct. "We do not mean to insert it," he maintained, "as we have excluded, and probably shall exclude, the criticisms of his opponents."[99]

That choice, however, did not keep Spurgeon from publishing a more amicable investigation of the Brethren. Arthur Augustus Rees wrote *A Second Friendly Letter to the Christians called Brethren, on the Subject of Worship and Ministry*, a pamphlet that achieved the delicate balance of "*suaviter in modo,* and the *fortiter in re.*" Rees, so Spurgeon judged, "having known the mysteries of Brethrenism," exposed them thoroughly. "He takes the bull by the horns, and attacks their favourite claim to be under the Spirit's guidance in all their spontaneous and often absurd effusions."[100] Believing the Bible is one thing; believing oneself to be an oracle is quite another.

In 1870 Spurgeon still felt the need for warnings against the tendency of Brethren, particularly Darbyite, influence. When Edward Dennett published a lecture on *The Plymouth Brethren: their Rise, Divisions, Practice, and Doctrines*, Spurgeon used the occasion to vent some of his personal objections to the fallout of Brethren influence. "This admirable concise, and able lecture should be read and circulated by every minister—and these are legion—who is worried by the Plymouth unbrotherly confraternity." Dennett presented facts that would seal a "richly-merited condemnation" on the Darbyite system. Though some churches benefitted from the good in the early Plymouth movements "the cloven hoof soon appeared, and the good was speedily overbalanced by the evil." He did not know of any age or place in which "more glaring inconsistencies [had] been perpetrated in the name of Christianity, or more sectarian principles been promulgated under the pretence of unity." His esteem for men as Christians did not mitigate the harm of "the system, or rather chaos which they have created." From his observation, he felt that their conduct towards other believers deserved the most severe censure, while "Mr. Dennett deserves universal thanks for his trouble and fidelity in exploring their depths of error."[101]

Spurgeon did not merely leave it up to others to describe the net effect of Plymouth Brethren claims to its non-sectarian, non-denominational only-people-of-God status. Unchanged in his opinion as late as 1886, Spurgeon repeated his approval of the Christian character of the many individuals that he knew among this group, but their corporate posture provided a virtually irresistible opportunity for schism and sectarian pride. They were the wheat, all others were chaff. "After creating no end of heart-burning in churches, and unnatural hatred in families; after warring among themselves, and splitting and splitting again, these brethren have left us as the net result of their exertions a sect which exceeds all others in party spirit and bitter exclusiveness."[102]

Connected with this kind of claim to be the only church of Christ, Spurgeon also inserted a critique of the Transatlantic group, the "Campbellites." "If the Campbellites wish us to believe that they are *the church of Christ*, they should also let us know what they are as to their distinctive views." He was willing to accept their claim to be Christians, and he welcomed any brothers

---

99. S&T, August 1869, 381.

100. Ibid., 380.

101. S&T August, 1870, 382.

102. S&T, October 1886, 516.

that would join in the fight against evil and for the gospel, but the "invidious claim to the title" of Christian did not impress Spurgeon but rather put him on guard to see if they would prove it by a greater "likeness to their Lord, and their clearer manifestation of the spirit which vaunteth not itself."[103] Since the late 1820s Alexander Campbell and his followers had caused controversy within Baptist churches and associations in the Southern United States, and as a result Baptist churches had lost thousands of members. Among their distinctive beliefs were the rejection of all creeds, the justifying effect of baptism as the biblical expression of faith, and exclusive claim to be the *Church of Christ*. In Spurgeon's mind this sort of sacramental ecclesiology fostered division and bitterness and was a sure way to avoid true unity. Pointing to all others as sectaries was "to cement our walls with dynamite, and lay the foundations of peace upon barrels of gunpowder."[104]

Interpretations of Prophetic Material
Without doubt Spurgeon believed in the inspiration of the entire Bible and believed that every part played its own role in opening a more complete revelation of the gospel and its implications. Apocalyptic literature, therefore, carried fascinating if mysterious baggage for Spurgeon's inspection. He personally looked for the literal fulfillment of the restoration of the Jews to the land prior to the coming of Christ and his earthly rule:

> I think we do not attach sufficient importance to the restoration of the Jews. We do not think enough of it. But certainly, if there is anything promised in the Bible, it is this. I imagine that you cannot read the Bible without seeing clearly that there is to be an actual restoration of the children

of Israel. "There they shall go up. They shall come with weeping unto Zion and with supplications unto Jerusalem." May that happy day soon come! For when the Jews are restored, then the fullness of the Gentiles shall be gathered in. And as soon as they return, then Jesus will come upon Mount Zion to reign with His ancients gloriously and the halcyon days of the Millennium shall then dawn. We shall then know every man to be a brother and a friend. Christ shall rule with universal sway![105]

While his own views were premillennial, he cautioned against too much detail in treating apocalyptic material. "Of expositions of this mysterious Book there are swarms, *and yet not one*," Spurgeon judged in reviewing yet another attempt at giving a credible treatment of Revelation. He left the reader to judge what he meant by "*yet not one*." This particular book was "more rational in its interpretations, and more sensible in its speculations" than most books on the Revelation tended to be. Spurgeon observed that "A sort of fascination draws minds of all sorts towards the insufferable light of the Apocalypse, and around it they flit and dart like birds aroused at midnight by the introduction of a torch."[106]

The Franco-Prussian War brought about the musings of many enthusiastic apocalypticists, and Spurgeon found it his best part to warn against such misplaced fervor. S. A. Blackwood's *The Last Trump* saw in the war signs of the speedy sounding of the last trump. Spurgeon said that these same prognostications "were equally clear to the vision of interpreters 300 years ago, and yet their lucubrations were disproved by time, as we venture to believe the intimations of our modern seers will be."[107] Finding the precise

---

103. Ibid., 517.
104. Ibid., 518.

105. SS, 1:136.
106. S&T, April 1876, 140.
107. S&T August 1870, 382.

prophetic meaning of the drying up of the Euphrates, Louis Napoleon, the Emperor Phocas, the year 1873, and other matters was fitter entertainment "for spiritual children than for men in Christ Jesus."[108]

Prophetic quacks played on the credulity of the less informed members of the churches. "Pretenders to prophecy have risen in all times, and have all been equally unworthy of trust," Spurgeon lamented. With the numbers of these he was surprised, given the law of probabilities, that not more had conjectured correctly. He would not concede that these were serious attempts at biblical interpretation, for he found "no interpretation, but only theories tacked on to texts, and Scriptures twisted to support imaginings." He would be more likely to be "instructed by the cackling of geese, or the flight of vultures, as by the maunderings of men who are crazed with Daniel-on-the-brain." The favorite antichrist was Louis Napoleon who surely would wonder how his English friends would be so keen to see in him a dragon and a beast.[109]

The next year, 1871, Spurgeon learned that the recent ecumenical council, Vatican I, was Armageddon, and that the drying up of the Euphrates referred to the overthrow of the Spanish monarchy. "That is quite enough for us," he wrote in disgust. Should he give himself such exegetical latitude he was sure he could find the answer to the "Eltham murder, the Tichborne case," and even find the last Derby winner.[110] "We cannot help observing that the more of these prophetical books we are doomed to review, the more sick are we of the entire business." Spurgeon advised men to "leave the mysterious oracles of God to be interpreted by providence." All of these fanciful schemes, outlines, and prognostications "dishonour the sacred word from which they profess to draw them." He advised the Author, Mr. Wylie, to turn his pen to something useful.[111]

Nathaniel Starkey entitled a book *Things which must shortly come to pass; for the time is at hand.* As an attempt at comedy it would have had more merit. Spurgeon found the contents "about as grotesque as its title." The rapture was a favorite theme of the author and of "those who are left behind he draws several fantastic sketches." Even funnier reveries appeared as the author surveyed the political and social landscape "with some fine touches of fancy." The history of predictions of the antichrist should be a severe warning against any attempt to make another but Starkey was undeterred in his "strange mingle-mangle of serious things with comical thoughts." It was a pity that some flashes of pure gospel were "overshadowed with paltry gossip."[112] At another book's suggestion that the British were Israelites, as well as the Turks and the Germans, he responded "There is not an argument in the book worth the trouble of demolishing."[113]

Spurgeon believed unequivocally in the return of the Lord in glory to establish his rule in the earth, but the eschatological mania that sought to find current concrete matches for the apocalyptic symbols of Scripture were not only doomed to failure, but were distractions from pure gospel preaching and the demanding call of day-by-day Christian discipleship.

---

108. Ibid.

109. S&T, September, 1870, 432.

110. S&T, July 1871, 332. The murder of 17-year-old Jane Maria Clousen in May 1871 in Kidbrooke Lane, in Southeast London ended with the accused Edmund Pook being acquitted. In the Tichborne case, which began in 1871 and lasted for years, Arthur Orton claimed to be Roger Tichborne in order to receive a sizable inheritance.

111. Ibid.

112. S&T, January 1880, 33.

113. S&T, September 1872, 432.

Spurgeon and War

Spurgeon's view on war could be summarized in a sentence he wrote in reviewing *The Mad War-Planet*. Not a fan of poetry normally, the content of this poem so distilled Spurgeon's hatred of war, that he wrote, "The poem pleads vehemently, eloquently for peace. Would to God its voice could be heard. It ought to call the Christian Church to do her duty as to war, and that duty plainly is to denounce it utterly and without reserve."[114] He followed his own advice, denouncing it by every means he could muster. Though he defended the British army in its vigorous quelling of the Sepoy Rebellion in India, he viewed that, not as war, but as the legitimate execution of domestic justice for crimes against civil society. In May 1855, preaching "Thoughts on the Last Battle" in Exeter Hall, one of the word pictures that he displayed was of a war-mad tyrant gasping the last breaths of life and envisioning the sins that lingered to his account immediately before standing in the gaze of the Lord of Life:

> Imagine a conqueror's deathbed. He has been a man of blood from his youth up. Bred in the camp, his lips were early set to the bugle, and his hand, even in infancy, struck the drum. He had a martial spirit; he delighted in the fame and applause of men; he loved the dust of battle and the garment rolled in blood. He has lived a life of what men call glory. He has stormed cities, conquered countries, ravaged continents, overrun the world. See his banners hanging in the hall, and the marks of glory on his escutcheon. He is one of earth's proudest warriors. But now he comes to die, and when he lies down to expire, what shall invest his death with horror?[115]

The sin of war. The spirit of a widowed mother passed by and reviled him saying, "Monster! my husband was slain in battle through thy ambition." The husband then appeared, and revealing his gaping wounds cried, "Once I called thee monarch; but, by thy vile covetousness thou didst provoke an unjust war. See here these wounds—I gained them in the siege. For thy sake I mounted first the scaling ladder; this foot stood upon the top of the wall, and I waved my sword in triumph, but in hell I lifted up my eyes in torment. Base wretch, thine ambition hurried me thither!" Pomp and splendor might accompany the man of war in this life, but the prospect of eternity foreshadows unbearable dread. This had been a bloody man and "his hands were red with wholesale murder."[116]

In 1878 Spurgeon analyzed the periodical war interest that seemed to assault the English spirit. Even after all the lessons, disappointments, and outrages of the past, "We are still pugnacious, still believers in brute force, still ready to shed blood, still able to contemplate ravaged lands and murdered thousands without horror, still eager to test our ability to kill our fellow men." Mythical "British interests" were the foundation of much of this, but the fact is, the national bull-dog wants to "fix his teeth into somebody's leg, and growls because he does not quite see how to do it."[117]

The warrior must learn the tenets of peace. Spurgeon was vivid in his depiction of all the demonic traits of war and the necessity of exorcizing them from the country. "The fight-spirit must be battled with in all its forms, and the genius of gentleness must be cultivated. Cruelty to animals, the lust for destroying living things, the desire for revenge, the indulgence of anger—all these we must war against by manifesting and inculcating pity, compassion, forgiveness, kindness, and goodness in the fear of the Lord." Spurgeon in-

---

114. S&T, May 1871, 235.

115. SS, 1:278.

116. SS, 1:279.

117. S&T, March 1878, 146.

sisted that the truth about war be put plainly as loss of time, labor, treasure, and life, and its tendency to satanic crimes must be laid bare. "It is the sum of all villainies, and ought to be stripped of its flaunting colours, and to have its bloody horrors revealed; its music should be hushed, that men may hear the moans and groans, the cries and shrieks of dying men and ravished women. War brings out the devil in man, wakes up the hellish legion within his fallen nature, and binds his better faculties hand and foot."[118] It hurls nations back to barbarism and retards the growth of everything good and holy.

Only as a dire necessity as the last resource of an oppressed people can it be considered. At that point it might be heroic and the lasting results might compensate for the immediate evils. The remedy for war, peace teaching, is but the practical side of gospel preaching. Loving one another and loving one's neighbor is set in the context of "Love is of God." The evangelistic task of the Christian church has nothing in common with the waging of war, Spurgeon argued. "Above all we must evangelize the masses, carry the truth of the loving God to their homes, preach Jesus and his dying love in their streets, and gather men to his fold." The work of soul-saving aims a blow at the root of the war-spirit. Conversion to Christ makes a man a lover of his race and fosters repentance from blows and battles. Sanctification recreates a hater into an embodiment of love. Spurgeon looked for such a powerful and extensive work of the Holy Ghost that "we shall see their outbursts of rage become less frequent and less violent, for there will be a strong counteracting influence to keep down the evil, and to restrain it when in a measure it breaks loose."[119]

Spurgeon even employed the philosopher Immanuel Kant as an advocate of peace. A 1795 treatise by Kant, *A Philosophical Treatise on Perpetual Peace*, had been republished in which he argued against mere political artifices in a treaty that would only prepare the way for future war. Spurgeon derided the "bluster of the daily press" provoking "endless national jealousies" from which no good could come. The chivalry of peace, Spurgeon believed, was far better than the chivalry of war, and the heroism that would protect and save life more valuable than that which imperils and destroys it. "Let the Peace Society continue to put forth such pamphlets as this," Spurgeon advocated, "in the interest of pure goodness and moral greatness, and its protests will yet fall upon worthy ears."[120]

No respecter of persons, Spurgeon went from Kant to John Ploughman in the campaign against war. In a letter addressed to Napoleon, Emperor of the French and William King of Prussia, Ploughman began, "I beg to send my most disrespectful compliments." If someone accused him of violation of the scriptural principle "Honour to whom honour is due," Ploughman responded, "Kings who go to war about nothing at all have no honour due to them. So I don't send you so much as would lay on your thumb nails."[121]

Ploughman had a good bit of advice for the two with his usual series of proverbial aphorisms, but loaded with a deadly, but befitting, seriousness cloudy with the gray, dismal consequences of the business of war. Do they have too much money and need to burn it in powder? Do they have too many people and need to make murderers and murdered of many of them. They are like boys with new knives who must cut at something. "One of you has the gout," Spurgeon said, a subject he knew a good bit about, "and that does not

---

118. Ibid., 148.
119. Ibid., 149.

120. S&T, April 1885, 192.
121. S&T, August 1870, 352ff.

sugar the temper much, and the other is proud about having beaten his neighbour; and so you must needs let off your steam by beginning a murderous war." Ploughman believed nothing good would come of it and told them so. "You are as daft as you are days old if you think any good can come of it. If you think you will get ribands and flags by fighting, you had better buy them at first hand of the drapers; they will come a deal cheaper, and there will be no ugly blood stains on them."[122]

With clear message that wars were often the results of personal grudges with little or nothing to do with national honor or justice, Spurgeon advised the two national leaders to "strip and go at it yourselves as our Tom Rowdy and Big Ben did on the green." To have others fight their battles showed the epitome of cowardice. Though opposed to fighting in any case, Ploughman offered, "if it would save the lives of the millions," to mind their jackets while the two of them "had a set-to with fisticuffs." In light of the cause, he would even "encourage you both to hit his hardest at the gentleman opposite." Ploughman invited them to Surrey for the battle, and the police would accommodate them with protection while they went at it. If they bloodied their shirts some ploughman would lend them the smock frocks if they would promise to return them. He would even arrange for Madam Rachel to be released from jail to enamel their eyes if they get a little blackened. In fact, Ploughman suggested, the keepers of Agricultural Hall would probably gladly arrange for them to be a main event wrestling spectacle. "So you could get glory and ready money too, and nobody would be killed." As he thought about that proposal more, it appealed to Ploughman for he could wash his hands of the

entire matter. He held little desire to be near two such kicking horses.[123]

It seems that Ploughman's grandfather was right about the tendency of the "Bonyparts," for though the nephew seemed a quieter sort than the famed uncle, "as the old cock crows the young cock learns." The German king's consent to go into butchering seemed a strange occupation, but he must be a very bad disposed man or he would be ashamed of killing his fellow creatures. "When war begins hell opens, and it is a bad office for either of you to be gate-opener to the devil; yet that's what one of you is, if not both."

Spurgeon then put some powerfully graphic language and images in the mouth of his friend John Ploughman. He had no stomach to see a kitten drown or a rat suffer, but a man! "Where's your hearts if you can think of broken legs, splintered bones, heads smashed in, brains blown out, bowels torn, hearts gushing with gore, ditches full of blood, and heaps of limbs and carcasses of mangled men?" If they considered the language disgusting, they must concede how much worse the thing itself is. "How would you like to let a man into your palace-garden, and run a carving knife into his bowels, or cut his throat? If you did that you would deserve to be hanged; but it would not be half so bad as killing tens of thousands, and you know very well that this is just what you are going to do."[124]

They were no better than cut-throats condemned by law, except they were worse. "Is there so little want in the world that you must go trampling on the harvest with your horses and your men? Is there so little sorrow that you must make widows by the thousand! Is death so old and feeble that you must hunt his game for him, as jackals do for the lion? Do you imagine that God

---

122. Ibid.

123. Ibid.
124. Ibid.

made men for you to play soldiers with? Are they only meant for toys for you to break?" He questioned their genuine humanity with mothers, sisters, homes, perhaps creatures "who were never suckled at a woman's breast, and therefore have no human feeling." The blood they have shed will choke them when they die, but harder still will it be to "bear the heavy hand of God when he shall cast all murderers into hell." Whoever has caused the war should be more hated than the common hangman and "instead of being called 'his majesty' you ought to be hooted as a demon."

For Ploughman, the great speeches made by the respective kings merely showed the leanness of their cause and the scantiness of their justice; the worst cause usually gets the best pleading for "men who cannot walk take to horseback." He pleaded with them not to cut their fellowmen with swords, "tear them with bayonets, blow them to pieces with cannon, and riddle them with shots." While they fancy that the end of their quest is glory, Ploughman told that the plain English word for such glory was damnation, which would be their lot if they went on cutting and hacking their fellow man. They must stop the war. "Before the deep curses of widows and orphans fall on you from the throne of God, put up your butcher knives and patent men-killers, and repent." The closing identified John Ploughman as "one who is no servant of yours, but a Fighter for Peace."[125]

Ploughman was forced to produce a follow up in September due to the vitality of the response to his first bits of advice. From the Emerald Isle he received a hostile note that promised him that if he were not quiet about the issue, the French emperor would blow down the English Protestant places of worship and he had some friends that had designed a bullet for his head. "I suppose I ought to choose a spot for a grave, and order a coffin at once," Ploughman pondered, "but I have done nothing of the sort. Threatened folks live long, and though the shooting season is near, I am not a partridge, though this fiery gentleman tries to make game of me."[126] Ploughman seemed a bit bewildered about the response of an Irishman to his letter, but perhaps a Fenian, as he assumed his disturbed opponent was, is not at peace unless he is at war and "they think themselves Frenchmen born out of their native country." The Fenian movement had been actively seeking independence from British rule for decades, had organized secret pockets of resistance to the English government, and had recently, 1867, plotted an uprising which eventuated in the killing of a police officer and the arrest and hanging of three Fenians. Spurgeon's hard stance toward the "Fenians" was intermingled with his strong denunciation of "Home Rule" for Ireland. He had Ploughman remark, "Sure I am the cause of the Fenians and the welfare of Ireland are two things quite as different as the appetite of a cat and the life of a mouse."[127]

After answering the misgivings of a German reader and a Quaker, Ploughman reminded his readers that he was "on the side of peace." "With all this soldiering about, one is apt to get in a fighting humour, and forget that war is a great crime—murder on a huge scale—and little less than hell let loose among men. 'Thou shalt not kill,' is as much a divine command as 'Thou shalt not commit adultery.' No one supposes that adultery of a great scale would be right; then why should killing be? War pays the papers well, no doubt, but it is a wretched business, and may God soon send an end of it. Some men seem ready to cry, 'Fight dog, fight bear;' but such fellows ought

---

125. S&T, August 1870, 354.

126. S&T, September 1870, 432. "A Letter about his other Letter."
127. Ibid.

to be put down between the two, to let them have a taste of it."[128] When some people complained that his style was too rough and uncouth, Plough-man promised to "take as much notice of what they say as the mastiff did of the gentleman in the yard at night, when he told him to lie still, for his voice was not musical, and his teeth were ugly." Spurgeon, through Ploughman, told the readers, probably in defense of his style in general, "Some improvement in style can be improvement for the worse, as the fox said when his tail was cut off in a trap. You may pay much for your schooling and be all the worse for your learning."[129]

In 1871 he recommended a book entitled *The German Drummer Boy; or, The Horrors of War.* "God speed the pens which write for peace," he began, "and dry up the quills which in glowing terms write up the pageantry of war." After encouraging the publishers to do all they could to spread abroad that book he reiterated, "Our heart chides us if we have failed to urge upon our readers and hearers the absolute sin of every kind of war. 'Thou shalt not kill,' is a command, the breadth of which is not excused but aggravated by the largeness of the scale on which the killing is conducted."[130]

In 1876 Spurgeon published his prayer that the Lord would preserve peace and remove from office any rulers that would not learn wisdom on this matter. Disraeli had come out in support of a Turkish policy that had resulted in atrocities of the government against Turkish Christians. Supporters of Disraeli were vexed with Spurgeon's public stance on the issue presented in the form of prayer. Even Gladstone had come out of retirement to oppose the policy of Disraeli. When Spurgeon's prayer prompted answers from the

earth, many of them were not sympathetic with the petition. "To us," he responded, "mere party politics are nothing; but when we see war threatened on behalf of a detestable tyranny, contrary to the dictates of humanity and religion, we cannot do otherwise than implore the Judge of all the earth to save us from such an astounding wickedness, and to remove from office the man whose rash bravados give rise to our fears." Many abusive letters to him bore no name, for which Spurgeon expressed thanks in hope that their omission meant that they still had some feelings of shame. His prayer made the papers and was translated into German and Serbian and was read by a relief worker among fugitives from Bosnia. He felt gratitude for a merciful expression and wrote, "While to the persecuted Christians of Turkey ... the attitude of the English government is so incomprehensibly hostile, a token of sympathy and pity, and the evidence that they are not forgotten by the English people, is doubly precious." Spurgeon's words opposing the policy of Disraeli in his pugilistic posturing against Russia's intervention and his pro-Turkey policy had "cheered and comforted many sorrowful hearts." The correspondent continued, "Oh, may they but be heard! And the thousands now groaning in slavery and exile, the victims of Turkish barbarism, be delivered from the hand and power of the wicked."[131]

One important case in which Spurgeon justified war came as he contemplated the presence of slavery in America and particularly among his fellow Baptists. On an evening week-night service in 1860 an escaped slave, John Andrew Jackson, spoke for an hour of his experiences as a slave and of his escape. Greatly moved, and reflecting the mood of the entire congregation

---

128. Ibid., 433.

129. Ibid.

130. S&T, March 1871, 131.

131. S&T, January 1877, 45.

Spurgeon called slavery, "the foulest blot that ever stained a national escutcheon, and may have to be washed out with blood." Though he considered America a glorious country in many ways, he believed that it might have to learn its lesson about slavery "at the point of a bayonet" or have true freedom carved into her with a bowie knife or sent "home to her heart with revolvers." "Better far should it come to this issue," he advocated, "that North and South should be rent asunder, and the States of the Union shivered into a thousand fragments, than that slavery should be suffered to continue."[132]

When his references to slavery were omitted in their American printing, Spurgeon learned of it and responded in heated terms in a letter to be published in an "influential paper in America." He wrote "I believe slavery to be a crime of crimes, a soul-destroying sin, and an iniquity which cries for vengeance." When asked to write an article on the Christian view of slavery, Spurgeon declined in light of pressing engagements and pressures involved in the building of the Metropolitan Tabernacle, but he did manage a substantial letter to the *Watchman and Reflector* in which he reiterated, "I do from my inmost soul detest slavery anywhere and everywhere, and although I commune at the Lord's Table with men of all creeds, yet with a slave-holder I have no fellowship of any kind or sort." This plain speech about a deeply divisive topic brought severe consequences for Spurgeon's popularity and pocketbook in America. The sale of his sermons, which was massive, was virtually ended for the years 1860-65. He knew this would happen, but as he interpreted man-stealing as

inextricably identified with slavery and mentioned as a particular violation of the ten commandments, the principle was so clear that no amount of political or pragmatic concerns could sway him in a different direction. His bound volumes of books were committed to the fire in public ceremonies in several places in the South.[133]

Interlude

Each of these controversies marked Spurgeon in particular ways and demonstrated his tenacity about truth and gospel clarity in a diversity of contexts. In Spurgeon's view of the comprehensive nature of divine revelation, any expression of theology, worship, or moral outlook could not be isolated entirely from impact on the gospel. These called for earnest, though often brief, warnings and a perpetual circumspection but not a consuming visceral warfare. They inflicted damage of light and momentary consequence capable of repair by some doctrinal darning in particular spots. Though war was of severe consequence, its moral lineaments were so distinct that no extended doctrinal analysis was called for, as Spurgeon saw it. Other conflicts, however, so thoroughly disemboweled the body of gospel truth that they called for unreserved and relentless doctrinal opposition with a purpose, if possible, to destroy them. Any pretensions to biblical fidelity these systems asserted were so fundamentally compromised by their errors, that there was too little baby left to maintain any of the bathwater. To these we now turn.

---

132. J. C. Carlile, *Charles H. Spurgeon: an Interpretative Biography* (London: Religious Tract Society, 1933), 159.

133. Ibid., 160f.

14

Destroy or be Destroyed

One who is very valiant for the truth said to us, "This must be a soldiers' battle." In that utterance we heartily concur. … The ministers also cry "Peace, peace, where there is no peace." If sturdy individuality took up the matter, and godly men were determined not to remain in league with those who depart from the truth, the issues would be speedy. … Every man who keeps aloof from the struggle for the sake of peace, will have the blood of souls upon his head. … The crisis becomes every day more acute: delays are dangerous; hesitation is ruinous. Whosoever is on the Lord's side must show it at once, and without fail.[1]

Spurgeon viewed truth strictly in terms of divine revelation. He was neither conservative nor liberal. Roman Catholicism and Anglicanism both were conservative, holding to a long pattern of tradition that sought to conserve liturgical and doctrinal developments in the church. Both of these bodies saw these as defensible on the basis of a priesthood that had been granted divine guidance beyond the pages of Holy Scripture, but justified on the basis of centuries of accumulated consent to certain ideas and practices.

Protestantism had brought in a resistance, no, a rebellion against, the power-maintained privilege of tradition for a return to the Bible alone and a confidence in Christ's distribution of gifts to all members of his elect body, not just the ordained few. Protestantism, however, throughout the nineteenth century had moved its locus of au-

thority from the Bible alone with a confidence in its clarity, to a confidence in the intellectual progress of human learning. This was accompanied by a growing hegemony of naturalism; it de-objectified and internalized Christian truth to conform to modern patterns of thought, and constituted liberalism.

Spurgeon looked to be a plague on both these houses. The conservatism of Roman Catholicism and Anglicanism either destroyed or tamed the gospel to fit their respective cherished traditions. The liberalism of modern-thought Protestantism massacred the gospel with a smile as if it were an act of benevolence. Spurgeon could make no treaties of peace with either option. True biblical Christianity would not vanish from the earth, for God would never fail to build his church and call his elect. But if its present adherents failed to wage war against the foe, they would be disloyal to their Master and deserved to be destroyed and

---

1. S&T, December 1889. 632-35.

have the mantle of stewardship passed to another generation. He was determined not to fail his.

Roman Catholicism

Spurgeon considered both Roman Catholicism and High Church Anglican claims as the true church and thus the only center of Christian union as utterly absurd. The true church of Christ was older than either. Roman Catholicism had the oldest institutional claim to such but no amount of time can make its distinctive errors into truth; Anglicanism arose out of the Reformation rendering demonstrably vain their claim to antiquity. "Taking Holy Scripture as our guide," Spurgeon proposed, "we are amused at the effrontery which is shown by those two bodies of ecclesiastics when they boast of being *the church of Christ*; they might as well profess to be a company of angels, or a herd of buffaloes."[2] He often employed such amusing metaphors and felt no inclination to be less aggressive in his ridicule. He felt sure that "the powers of sarcasm, ridicule, and contempt are never more fittingly exercised than upon the fallacies and blasphemies of idolatry."[3] By this he did not refer to the Old Testament Canaanites but to nineteenth-century Roman Catholicism.

When one journalist accused Spurgeon, because of his denunciation of priests, of having less Christianity than the monk that brought Christianity to England, Spurgeon responded, "It would have been a great blessing if that monk had never touched these shores, and it will be a day of jubilee when the last monk, friar, nun, and priest shall die out from among them." Showing charity to priests is like showing charity to tigers and rattlesnakes.[4]

Throughout his ministry, Spurgeon never was reconciled to the universal pretensions and the implied sacramental implications of these two establishment bodies. He resented the nomenclature of "sect" placed on those orthodox evangelical Christians that resisted conformity to those power-vested ecclesiastical institutions. Instead, that kind of failed exclusivism was the "essence of schism" and the "soul of sectarianism."[5]

In January 1872, he recounted his experience of a Sabbath in Rome, "where Satan's seat now is." Though Spurgeon sought a place of pure worship, he still found sufficient provocation for being appalled at the superstition and idolatry which "defiles St. Peter's." Paul would be puzzled at the credentials of Pius IX in his claim to apostolic succession, when "his palaces, and his teachings, and his pretensions are things unknown in the word of God."[6] Spurgeon considered Pius IX, Pio Nino, the "most blundering of living men," no less than "the most incomprehensible enthusiast in existence."[7] The dogma of the Immaculate Conception, the decree of Papal infallibility of Vatican I, and the Syllabus of Errors have marked that Pope as the "assailant of all the best hopes and aspirations of the human race." Having risen to the position in 1846, each succeeding stage of his reign has marked him as an enemy of "moral progress and evangelical religion" as well as the "bitter enemy" of all attempts to distribute the Bible to all people. He is the leader of a conspiracy in Rome to re-impose on the world the "pre-Reformation thralldom" during which time the Pope's law could blight a nation. Patriots as well as Christians must take note.

Though Spurgeon supported liberty of conscience and was a firm advocate of disestablish-

---

2. S&T, October 1886, 515.

3. S&T, October 1866, 497.

4. S&T, July 1874, 341.

5. S&T, October 1886, 515.

6. S&T, January 1872, 34, 35.

7. S&T, February 1878, 68, 69.

ing the Anglican Church, he found the deceit of Rome and its historical brutality toward dissent sufficient reason for warnings against Rome not only as a soul-destroying religion but a nation-threatening political force. Gaspard de Coligny, the "gallant defender of the Huguenots," had a "great and candid mind" and threw off the yoke of priests in exchange for submission to the word of God. He labored hard to form colonies to which French Protestants might flee from Catholic persecution, hoping for a state in which "Catholic and Calvinist might dwell together without cutting each other's throats." Coligny's candour and his generous, conciliatory, and trustful spirit, admirable in every way in itself, gained for his efforts the Massacre of St. Bartholomew's day. "Rome," Spurgeon reminded England, "does not understand the milder qualities of good men," for the scarlet woman always scoffs at truth and righteousness. She always deserves suspicion and "by energy she ever needs to be held in check." The murdered body of Coligny should send fair warning to all that wariness of Rome must be a constant principle, and "when she speaks like an angel, believe her not."[8]

In an article entitled "The Religion of Rome" describing a variety of pious frauds invented by Rome to astonish and overwhelm the gullible, Spurgeon closed with a species of the contempt he felt Rome deserved for such deceit. "Our ancient enemies have small belief in our common sense if they imagine that we shall ever be able to trust them, after having so often beheld the depths of Jesuitical cunning and duplicity." English Protestants must give no uncertain sound in informing archbishops and cardinals that "we are aware of their designs" and will cooperate with them in nothing. Spurgeon knew that such an immutable stance would be ridiculed itself as bigoted. The accusation would only bring a smile, for it comes from the "church that invented the Inquisition." Spurgeon's stance toward Rome was summed up in the words, "No peace with Rome."[9] He commended, in fact, a historical novel, a rare bit of condescension for Spurgeon, based on the English Reformation, for he believed it would "inspire a wholesome hate of the machinations of the Papacy, love for the word of God, and faith in the God of the word." Because of these effects Spurgeon, called the book "charmingly entertaining and instructive" and worth a "cart-load of the so-called religious novels now so plentiful."[10]

Spurgeon posted a review of *A Glimpse of the Great Secret Society* by William Macintosh, "a clear orderly statement of facts" about the Jesuits. Spurgeon believed that "of all the mysteries of iniquity to be laid bare when 'there is nothing secret that shall not be made manifest,' this must surely have the pre-eminence." The Jesuits were wickedness clothed as piety, more infernal that human, and thus necessarily hidden. Their machinations had been responsible for some of the most tragic events in European history since the sixteenth century and were largely responsible for the outrageous developments of the recent ecumenical council at the Vatican in Rome.

The Vatican Council prompted Spurgeon to propose that "there is need that a new and deeper anti-papal feeling be produced, which, being sustained by knowledge, shall abide upon the public mind." The mere nominalism and tradition-based religion of most of Anglicanism had created a condition in which there was "a great falling-off in the old Protestant feeling of the country." He had hope that a book by John Kennedy would help accomplish a truly evangelical anti-papal-

8. S&T, September 1882, 497.

9. S&T, January 1873, 23.

10. S&T, June 1881, 286.

ism. Kennedy's *Four Lectures on the Claims and Worship of Rome* discussed the "infallibility of the Pope, the false basis of the papacy, Mariolatry, and the characters of the popes," in a masterly way. Though it might not convert Papists "it is at least laudable to instruct our own people, lest they fall into the same delusions." Kennedy's lectures should "go far to foster a healthy abomination of the superstitions and blasphemies of the Papacy; therefore, let them fly abroad in thousands."[11]

The "superstitions and blasphemies" continued by the Pope's Council, had deep historical roots as Spurgeon observed in January 1874. The Scala Sancta in Rome had long been a major stop along the tour of pilgrims looking for places to achieve remission from penalty in Purgatory. Luther himself had made this stop. Reflecting in the pious legend of the removal of the Scala from Jerusalem to Rome, Spurgeon quipped that it must have "required a considerable amount of angelic engineering to remove them to their present site" from Jerusalem. In years past, doubters of the veracity of the incredible legend of their removal to Rome "have been judged to be rank infidels, and have been considered worthy of the direst pains of perdition." Crawlers up the sacred staircase looked absorbed in their prayers and genuflections while the priests looking on seemed contemptuous of the crawling devotees, a pastoral transgression that made Spurgeon's blood boil. Spurgeon uttered words from some of David's fiercer Psalms excusing himself by contending that "a man must be even more perfect than John Wesley or Pearsall Smith, if he can look upon such a scene without righteous indignation, intensified by a little mixture of human nature." After observing that the Church of England soon would be on the same road, Spurgeon summa-

rized his reaction by assuring the reader, "Our abhorrence of Popery and everything verging upon it rose to a white heat as we saw how it can lower an intelligent nation to the level of fetich [*sic*] worship, and associate the name of the ever-blessed Jesus with a groveling idolatry."[12]

Historical reminders of Rome's oppressiveness and superstition were diminished in no degree by a trip to Southern France in January 1877. "We were in the country of the Camisards and other heroic strugglers for our holy faith against the outrageous tyranny and sevenfold persecutions of Popish monarchs," he reported to his people. Valence, still the headquarters of the Reformed Church in the South, was there. Orange had provided safety as a city of refuge for the persecuted Huguenot. "The blood of saints has bedewed all that fruitful region, and watered the neighbouring desert with its priceless drops," Spurgeon recalled, while pointing to a more ominous historical reminder, "the monstrous dungeon-like pile of Avignon." Those sad walls were etched with the perpetual refutation of Rome's lying claim to apostolical succession, and perpetual unity and catholicity. Within them reigned the popes of the Babylonian Captivity and several successive Antipopes, "making the Papal church a two-headed giant, each head cursing the other with equal vehemence and infallibility." Dining within the shadow of those walls now provided no terror from the cave where, using Bunyan's figure from *Pilgrim's Progress*, "Giant Pope has gone to bite his nails, and grin at Pilgrims whom he is not longer able to devour."[13]

Anglicans and Roman Catholics argued as to which of their respective successionist theories constituted them as the true church. Spurgeon responded with entire candor: "A plague on

---

11. S&T, January, 1872, 41

12. S&T, January 1874, 3-7.

13. S&T, March 1877, 139.

both your houses." Correspondence between the Most Rev. Dr. Henry Edward Cardinal Manning, Lord Archbishop of Westminster, and Rev. C. Bullock gave Spurgeon an opportunity for reflection. Bullock was a strong churchman but, according to Spurgeon "thoroughly evangelical and far more a Christian than a churchman."[14] Bullock had vaunted himself over Spurgeon in the past "as if he had won a great victory" while Spurgeon thought "he had made a great stupid of himself, and proved nothing."[15] On this occasion Bullock sought to put Rome to flight in its exclusivistic claims. While he admired the effort, Spurgeon again thought that Bullock fell short. "If Romanism were capable of refutation and conviction by argument, this pamphlet would surely reveal to it its errors and follies; but when a system relies on its traditions and prejudices rather than upon Scriptural authority or common-sense arguments for its existence, what can be done to overthrow it?" Bullock did not argue from a position of strength in Spurgeon's mind, for Anglicanism also perpetuated itself in the same manner—tradition, prejudice, and secular power. He expressed his resolute conviction, unshared by Bullock, that "the best testimony against Romanism and Anglicanism is a sturdy Nonconformity that knows nothing of priests, or liturgies, or saving ceremonies, and believes in deed, not merely in word, in the headship of Christ over his church."[16] Though Anglicanism, through it confessional assertions, could produce robust evangelicals, many of the criticisms to which papal Rome was subject could just as easily fall on the shoulders of the power-maintained privilege and sacramentally disposed defenders of the Tudor-created Church of England.

14. S&T, February 1876, 90.
15. Ibid.
16. S&T, February 1881, 85.

Church of England

In the heat of his spiritual resentment toward the pretensions of Anglicanism as an "established" church, Spurgeon said, "I remember reading about a three-headed dog which kept the gates of hell, but I never dreamed of a two-headed church till I heard of the Anglican Establishment."[17] Though he had, and openly professed, nothing but the greatest respect for Victoria as a person and honorable monarch for England, her "royal will and pleasure" had nothing to do with the church of the Lord Jesus Christ. No head or governor can share the authority with Jesus over his church, its truths, its prayers, its worship, or its members. The Church of England has bowed before the kingdoms of this world, but, as for Spurgeon, "We have another king,—one Jesus." None can rule in the church beside him; moreover, the queen, "honored and beloved as she is, she is by her sex incapacitated for ruling in the church." Paul, as an inspired apostle, forbad it when he said, "I suffer not a woman to teach, nor to usurp authority over the man, but to be in silence." A church that bows to the authority of any mortal, man or woman, "commits fornication with the kings of the earth, and virtually renounces her allegiance to Christ to gain the filthy lucre of state endowments."[18] Where it was Protestant in its true doctrinal sense, Spurgeon looked on the Church's witness with gratitude and a sense of unity; where it was jealous for its political ascendancy and its liturgical longevity, Spurgeon found it distasteful and bordering on apostasy.

The consistent tension between Spurgeon and the Church of England arose from his theological convictions on several fronts. In its basic evangelical exposition of the gospel in the Thirty-nine Articles, Spurgeon found strong consent. At Ex-

17. SS, 8:74.
18. SS, 9:75.

eter Hall in 1855, he told the large crowd, many of whom probably were members of the Church of England, "Now, my hearers, 'the Bible alone is the religion of Protestants;' but whenever I find a certain book much held in reverence by our Episcopalian brethren, entirely on my side, I always feel the greatest delight in quoting from it." He sought their incredulity when he asked, "Do you know I am one of the best churchmen in the world; the very best," and went on the explain, "if you will judge me by the articles, and the very worst, if you measure me in any other way." Measured by the Thirty-Nine Articles, Spurgeon professed to stand second to no man in preaching the gospel contained in them. He found those articles to be "an excellent epitome of the gospel." In particular, on this occasion he quoted at length the article on original sin, concluding, "I want nothing more. Will any one who believes in the Prayer Book dissent from the doctrine that 'the carnal mind is enmity against God'?"[19]

The Trinity, the Person of Christ, the inspiration and sole authority of Scripture, justification, indwelling sin, sanctification, election, and other teachings Spurgeon approved and found reason for deep appreciation for this heritage in England. In preaching on election, Spurgeon set in context the things that he appreciated and those that he abominated concerning Anglicanism. "There are some of you who belong to the Church of England," he noted, "and I am happy to see so many of you here." He acknowledged that "now and then I certainly say some very hard things about Church and State," yet acknowledged that he loved the church for its "many godly ministers and eminent saints." Assuming that they were "great believers in what the Articles declare to be sound doctrine," he quoted article 17 on predes-

tination and election. Any churchman, Spurgeon concluded, "if he be a sincere and honest believer in Mother Church, must be a thorough believer in election." Other portions of the Prayer Book contained practices and teachings "contrary to the doctrines of free-grace, and altogether apart from scriptural teaching." But by staying close to the Articles, one would find the biblical doctrine of election of a specific people to eternal life. While admitting that he himself was "not so desperately enamoured" of that book as they, he pointed again to the article to prove "that if you belong to the Establishment of England you should at least offer no objection to this doctrine of predestination."[20]

Power-maintained privilege, however, offended his understanding of the gospel and assaulted his sense of the rights of Englishmen. The church's status as state-supported incorporated all the badness and poison that seeped into Episcopalianism and had a tendency to corrupt even the best of its "godly ministers and eminent saints." It flew in the face of true gospel ministry. "The establishment is, as we believe, itself an error; and it works for error rather than for truth."[21] "The days of establishment are numbered," he believed, even as he talked about the Church of Scotland. "A State Church is to us a gross injustice, and a terrible blunder, and so we war against it."

State support engendered a host of evils including the sale and exchange of "livings." Spurgeon pointed out that they were advertised in "The Church and School Gazette" where "by the dozen these sons of Simon Magus advertize their wares." Guilt for this abomination is widespread in Spurgeon's opinion, for "every churchman is morally responsible for all this iniquity, for by his connection and support he countenances the

---

19. SS,1:243-44.

20. SS, 2:68, 69.

21. S&T, January 1886, 42.

system under which such things are tolerated." Further than that, however, "since the Anglican Establishment is a National Church, we are all guilty of its iniquities unless to our utmost we express our dissent and discharge ourselves from the responsibility."[22]

In Spurgeon's exposition of Isaiah 49:20-23, he rejected the ancient contention that it gave any support to a state church with monarchs as nursing fathers or mothers. The passage teaches no headship, but humble submission to the truth expressed most appropriately when the state gives "full liberty to the preaching of the gospel. This is all that the true Church asks, and all she can ever fairly take if she is loyal to her Lord."[23] This unfettered, as well as unaided, freedom Spurgeon admired in the American experience. "Brethren in the land of the West," he addressed them in 1857, "I am linked to your great republic by ties which daily multiply." Among the advantages he noticed was this: "Ye are unfettered; no State Church spreads its upas shade over your churches, and no reverence for antiquated errors checks your progress."[24] Six volumes of American sermons later, in the year following the publication of his "Baptismal Regeneration" sermon, Spurgeon wrote his American brethren again with a familiar theme: "Your ever growing nation is the hope of the world. Untrammelled by a State-church, free from a thousand traditional bondages, you occupy a vantage-ground denied to us." He went on with what he felt were by-products of a country unshackled by the flaccid Christianity of a state church:

Much then is expected of you; and your brethren in England confidently look for great things at your hand. May you be rich in grace at home and abundant in labors abroad. May the millions who fly to you from every shore, never lower your moral and spiritual tone, but rather may they be drawn upward by your elevated godliness, and become "holiness unto the Lord." Across the ocean, my brethren, I salute you.—"The Lord lift up His countenance upon you, and give you peace!"[25]

What was true in America was not true in Ireland. In August 1869, Spurgeon denounced the House of Lords for a "tyrannical action" that made him query "how long these titled defenders of injustice are to rule a free people and forbid the nation to fulfill its will." He believed that the bishops should be removed from the Upper House, sent to their flock where they should have enough to do of true gospel labor. They are always the friends of "everything oppressive" and continue the "monstrous injustice of compelling the Dissenters to support a church with which they have no sympathy." Spurgeon even sought sympathy for the Catholic population of Ireland. "How men calling themselves Christians, much less Christian bishops, can have voted for the gross wickedness of compelling a Romish population to support a church which they abhor, utterly staggers us," Spurgeon wrote. He believed that the actions of the Lords stamped "the whole party consenting to such a scheme with the black brand of hypocrisy and covetousness."[26]

The Prayer Book's teaching of baptismal regeneration set the evangelicals in the church in a severely compromised position, Spurgeon believed. The rise of Puseyism convinced Spurgeon that the real tendencies of Anglicanism were toward Rome. "Witness the Rome-ward tendency of many officials, and the sacramentarian-

---

22. S&T, November 1865, 540.

23. SEE, 12:288.

24. SS, 3: vi.

25. SS, 9:10.

26. S&T, August 1869, 381.

ism preached from so many pulpits, and judge whether a Protestant Dissenter can think the Anglican Establishment a bulwark for the faith."[27] The "Baptismal Regeneration Controversy" was provoked by a sermon on the subject on June 5, 1864. Spurgeon said it was delivered with the full expectation that the "sale of the sermons would receive very serious injury."[28] Spurgeon told his publishers that he was about to destroy their market for sermons in one single blow. He counted on losing friends and receiving many a blow from angry foes. The latter he received, but the sermon sold in massive numbers and gave a rousing call to evangelicals in the Church of England to live consistently with the truth.

While they believed in the doctrine of salvation by faith their church catechism taught that infants experienced regeneration at their baptism. Spurgeon knew that a considerable number of faithful hearers and readers would not only censure but condemn him for this intrusion into the conscience of Anglican evangelicals. "If I forfeit your love for truth's sake, I am grieved for you," Spurgeon implored, "but I cannot, I dare not, do otherwise."[29]

After a demonstration that the Catechism indeed taught that baptized infants were regenerated by the Holy Spirit, made members of Christ, children of God, and inheritors of the kingdom, he lamented the case of evangelicals bound up in a scene of contradiction. He then congratulated those for their honesty who believed it and taught it openly. "Let us oppose their teaching by all scriptural and intelligent means, but let us respect their courage in plainly giving us their views." The case differs entirely for those, however, who believe otherwise, yet gain the livings by subscribing to words they repudiate in their preaching. How can anyone stand up in his pulpit and say, "Ye must be born again," when he has already assured them by his "'unfeigned assent and consent' to it, that they are themselves, every one of them, born again in baptism." The rapid advance of "popery" can only be increased by such want of straightforwardness in evangelical ministers. Worldly people cannot be impressed when a minister preaches a doctrine opposite to what his Prayer Book teaches.[30]

For the bulk of the sermon, he sought to prove, and passionately so, that it was a false doctrine calculated to damn sinners through false assurance. The dogma has no support from the facts. Moreover, promises are made in the first person on behalf of the child that the most godly person on earth knows cannot be kept in this life; only true belief and a work of the Spirit of God can give any desire for the realization of such promises.[31] Many godparents themselves are ungodly and make promises for the child that they themselves have no intention of fulfilling. "I do beseech you to remember," Spurgeon urgently reminded, "that you must have a new heart and a right spirit, and baptism cannot give you these." "You must run from your sins," he continued, "and follow Christ; you must have such a faith as shall make your life holy and your speech devout, or else you have not the faith of God's elect, and into God's kingdom you shall never come." He called baptismal regeneration a "wretched and

---

27. S&T, January 1886, 42.

28. S&T, January 1875, 5.

29. SS, 8:13.

30. Ibid. 16–18.

31. The Prayer Book says. "Ye have heard also that our Lord Jesus Christ hath promised in his gospel to grant all these things that ye have prayed for: which promise he, for his part will most surely keep and perform. Wherefore, after this promise made by Christ, this infant must also faithfully, for his part, promise by you that are his sureties (until he come of age to take it upon himself) that he will renounce the devil and all his works, and constantly believe God's holy Word, and obediently keep his commandments."

rotten foundation" and a "deceitful invention of antichrist." Whether a man call himself Baptist, Presbyterian, Dissenter, or Churchman, if he states that baptism saves the soul then "he states what God never taught, what the Bible never laid down, and what ought never to be maintained by men who profess that the Bible, and the whole Bible, is the religion of Protestants."[32]

Spurgeon then explained why faith and faith alone saves followed by an exposition of how faith is connected to baptism. How dear the theological truth was to Spurgeon and how deeply he felt its importance may be seen in how severely he was willing to characterize the Anglican ministry, both sacramentalists and evangelicals. "We have been cultivating friendship with those who are either unscriptural in creed or else dishonest; who either believe baptismal regeneration, or profess that they do, and swear before God that they do when they do not. The time is come when there shall be no more truce or parley between God's servants and time-servers."[33] Friendship and fellowship must never be bought with the blood of souls or gained at the forfeit of truth.

The turmoil and personal criticism brought on Spurgeon by his public accusations of theological inconsistency did not make him shy of the subject. On July 24, in light of a text that had often been quoted against him, Mark 10:13-16, he preached "Children Brought to Christ, Not to the Font." He set the sermon in context. "Replies they certainly are *not*, except to one another," Spurgeon remarked. "I marvel that a Church so learned as the Anglican cannot produce something a little more worthy of the point in hand." They may have read the discourse but "by reason

of mental absorption in other meditations, or perhaps through the natural disturbance of mind caused by guilty consciences, they have talked with confusion of words and have only been successful in refuting themselves and answering one another." He called them "the worst shots that ever practiced polemical artillery."[34]

The text they marshaled to the defense of infant baptism, in Spurgeon's words "has not the shadow of the shade of the ghost of a connection with baptism." As Spurgeon developed the theme as to the necessity of bringing little ones to Jesus, and excoriating every device used to keep them back, he declared, "Faith is the way to Jesus, baptism is not. … Coming to Jesus Christ is quite a different thing from coming to a font."[35] He reinforced his denunciation of the font ritual by emphasizing, that "the font is a mockery and an imposition if it is put before Christ." To be baptized after coming to Christ is well and good. "But to point you to it either as being Christ, or as being inevitably connected with Christ, or as being the place to find Christ is nothing better than to go back to the beggarly elements of the old Romish harlot instead of standing in the "liberty wherewith Christ has made us free," and bidding the sinner to come as a sinner to Christ Jesus and to Christ Jesus alone."[36]

He went deeper and preached an all-out attack on the Book of Common Prayer. One evangelical in the church sought to dismiss his views through accusing him of ignorance and a simplistic approach to complicated theological issues. Spurgeon, therefore, in light of such profound ignorance asked for help from the "fathers in the faith" who are "expressly ordained to instruct the ignorant." The Rev. W. Goode, the Dean of Ripon,

32. Ibid. 20-27.

33. This sermon may be found in Lewis Drummond, *Spurgeon: Prince of Preachers* (Grand Rapids, MI: Kregel, 1992), 787-802; MTP, 1864: June 5; Baptist Doctrines, ed. Jenkens, Charles A. (St. Louis: Chancy R. Barnes, 1882) 114-50. SS, 8:11-35.

34. SS, 8:36.

35. Ibid., 46.

36. Ibid., 49.

had written, "As to that young minister who is now raving against the Evangelical clergy on this point, it is to be regretted that so much notice has been taken of his railings." Spurgeon was to be pitied "because his entire want of acquaintance with theological literature" left him "utterly unfit for the determination of such a question, which is a question, not of mere doctrine, but of what may be called historical theology."[37] Were Spurgeon wiser, he would realize how little were his qualifications for passing judgment on such a point and how groundless, based on court decisions, were his charges against the evangelical clergy. He is free of course to hold what theology pleases him but "when he undertakes to determine what is the exclusive meaning of the *Book of Common Prayer* and brings a charge of dishonesty against those who take a different view of that meaning from what he does, he only shows the presumptuous self-confidence with which he is prepared to pronounce judgment upon matters of which he is profoundly ignorant." So incapable was Spurgeon of rational discourse that "to hold a controversy with him upon the subject would be to as little purpose as to attempt to hold a logically-constructed argument with a child unacquainted with logical terms."[38]

Since he was so simple, Spurgeon asked for only one answer to his many inquiries. For all that the Prayer Book requires, where is the "Thus saith the Lord?" Where is that authority for the clearly-stated assertion of regeneration for the baptized infant? Indeed where is it for confirmation and for its special details. Wherein lies the authority for the power of absolution of sins for a dying man. "You evangelical clergy," he queried, "dare you claim to be successors of the apostles, and to have power to forgive sins?" Where is the word in Scripture that warrants a burial to every baptized "thief, harlot, rogue, drunkard, and liar who may die in the parish 'in sure and certain hope of the blessed resurrection?'"[39] Spurgeon would not be intimidated; he must drive the point home. He pictured a solemn scene in hell when the falsely assured communicant confronts his equally deceived priest: "And what think you, sirs, must be the curse that fills the mouth of damned souls, when in another world they meet the priest who absolved them with this sham absolution!" What kind of reproaches will fill the ears of the priest that sent his parishioners to perdition with a lie in their right hands?

> I have been severe, it is said, and spoken harshly. I do not believe it possible to be too severe in this matter! But, Sirs, if I have been so, let that be set down as my sin if you will, but is there any comparison between my sin and that of men who know this to be contrary to the Word of God and yet give it their unfeigned assent and consent? Or between the sin of those who can lie unto the Holy Spirit by pretending to confer Him, who goes where He wills, upon men who as likely as not are as graceless as the very heathen?[40]

Spurgeon continued his criticism of Anglicanism in general, as an established church, its contradictory confession that endorsed justification by faith and practiced sacramentalism in baptism, and the inconsistency of the evangelical within its borders. In 1870 Spurgeon, writing in general about theological inconsistency, pointed out that "Ministers are to be found who deny baptismal regeneration, and yet put into the mouths of children such words as these, 'In my baptism, wherein I was made a member of Christ, the child of God,

---

37. Ibid., 63, 64.
38. Ibid., 64.

39. Ibid., 71.
40. Ibid., 72.

and an inheritor of the kingdom of heaven."[41] He wondered how the Christian conscience could give such language to a moral being unaware of a commitment to status made by another for him, especially when its substance was denied by the very instigator of the pledge.

With the smile of vindication moving his pen, Spurgeon printed and made brief comments on an article that appeared in *The Irish Church Advocate*. Footnoting the article as his own introductory comment, Spurgeon recounted, "When we preached our well-known sermon upon Baptismal Regeneration we were favoured with so abundant a measure of abuse that the charge of slander and *vituperative declamation* brought against us in this article sounds very mildly in our ears." The article was "thoroughly Irish" and Spurgeon reprinted it without alteration, as a complete vindication of his sermon.[42] The writer quoted Spurgeon's sermon as an example of how the disputed paragraphs on baptism "afford slanderous tongues strong ground for misrepresenting the true doctrine of our church, and impugning the morality of the whole body of our evangelical ministers." Spurgeon, in his "vituperative declamation," provided a "painful illustration of this evil." When the writer suggested that Spurgeon assumed that "baptismal regeneration is the doctrine of the Church of England," Spurgeon noted, "And very naturally too, since the writer admits under the head of *secondly* that 'the paragraphs alluded to in their plain grammatical meaning teach the doctrine of baptismal regeneration.'" The writer reminded his readers that the "highest ecclesiastical tribunal" in England (Parliament) had ruled "baptismal regeneration is not a doc-

trine which every man who has honestly accepted the Prayer Book is bound to teach," and that he is "as free to denounce the figment of baptismal regeneration as [Spurgeon] is." Spurgeon wryly continued, "Yes, and then they go on teaching it all the same." An Act of Parliament can not make right what is wrong or make it seemly for one to denounce a doctrine in one form and inculcate it in another. If the Romanist may be condemned by evangelicals in the Church of England as being out of accord with the Prayer Book, Spurgeon wondered, by what reason may an Evangelical, equally out of accord, be found excusable? The writer asked, "Why retain in our baptismal service these objectionable paragraphs, which not only give a plausible ground of accusation to the enemies of our church, but which sorely wound the consciences of many of its best friends."

The writer objected to the verbal subterfuge exercised in seeking to circumvent the apparent meaning of the paragraphs. In addition he regretted the thoroughly sacramental tone of preaching it engenders in those that actually do believe in baptismal regeneration, when they announce to their audiences that in baptism they have been born again. Retaining the "more than ambiguities" of the Prayer Book would, according to the Anglican author, make the minister instrumental in the "positive inculcation of one of the most radical and dangerous errors of the apostate church of Rome." Spurgeon wondered what the phrase "more than ambiguities" meant if it did not mean precisely what he had said eleven years earlier without any ambiguity. Spurgeon closed his interaction with a note of irony:

We hope the writer will continue to dilate upon the same subject. He is a very helpful fellow-worker, and he is welcome to abuse us to any extent. An abler advocate we could hardly wish

---

41. S&T, February 1, 1870, 69.

42. S&T, September 1875, 413. The article was entitled, "The Baptismal Service Practically Considered," extracted from "The Irish Church Advocate" of July 1, 1875.

for; he not only proves our point, but in his own way honours us with his commendation, for although "vituperative declamation" in the plain, grammatical sense means something rather objectionable, we have no doubt that the writer, by "a laboured explanation" could show that he intended—"honest outspoken rebuke." We thank him heartily.[43]

Puseyism, the name given to the strong high church sacramentalist movement in the Anglican Church led by Edward Pusey, embodied in Spurgeon's opinion everything he loathed in the theology of Rome and the dissolute tendencies of a state church. As to Pusey himself, to Spurgeon he remained "one of the greatest puzzles,—an eminently devout, humble Christian man, supporting a claim to priesthood which is in itself unholy, arrogant, and antichristian!" Spurgeon could only exclaim when he considered the contrast between his person and the office to which he laid claim, "Lord, what is man!"[44]

Foundationally, every objection to Roman Catholicism applied to Puseyism. "Popery, with its secret confessional and priestly interference at dying beds, is essentially a fox. Puseyism, pretending to be Protestant, and gradually bringing in all the foolery of Rome, is a deep fox indeed."[45] Some called it a fungus on the church, but Spurgeon argued that it was "the legitimate form of that community, sanctioned by its past history, and prescribed by its liturgy and catechism."[46] Though modest in its early pretensions and heavily disguised, Spurgeon saw it now (1866) as "openly and avowedly what it has always been—ritualism, sacramentarianism, priestcraft, An-

tichrist." It has clothed itself piece by piece with the garments of Rome cast on the dunghill in the Reformation until "at last her likeness to the Apocalyptic sketch of the woman on the scarlet-coloured beast is as clear as noonday."[47]

Spurgeon did not diminish his outrage that, under the guise of Anglicanism, Rome had weasled its way back into Protestantism. In 1875 on reviewing *The Mother of Jesus not the Papal Mary*, he listed some of the prayers to Mary currently lifted in High Church Anglican worship and demonstrated the deep-seated perplexity at the historical and theological irony. "Is it not time that these abominations came to an end?" he queried. Then he answered by query, "How can they end while the motley crew who man our Established Church find themselves able to eat the bread of a Protestant nation and teach as much of Popish idolatry as they please?" If they have to have their Maries, they should pay for them with their own money, Spurgeon fumed, and then, announced, in another obvious irony, "but to tax us for this abomination is tyranny."[48] This assertion 100 years earlier had bolstered a revolution.

Spurgeon called for a doctrinal crusade against Puseyism for the "gospel of Jesus is assailed by its ancient enemies." Who will stand? Someone must have courage instead of prudence, faith instead of policy and be "simple-minded, outspoken, bold and fearless of consequences." As a minister of Christ, Spurgeon with transparent forthrightness answered his own call: "We are willing so to act as the Lord may enable us, for such is well becoming in a soldier of Jesus Christ. A constant, unmistakeable, and uncompromising testimony against Puseyite idolatry we desire to bear; let every one of the pastors of our churches

43. Ibid., 417.

44. S&T, April 1876, 184.

45. S&T, October 1865, 499.

46. S&T, July 1866, 339.

47. Ibid., 340.

48. S&T, November 1875, 544.

be of the same mind."[49] Characteristically, this crusade must be waged with doctrine.

> Personal effort must also be used to propagate the truth upon the matters now assailed. … Not alone the first rudimentary truths of the gospel must be taught, but the whole circle of revelation; we must conceal no distinctive doctrine, and withhold no unpalatable dogma. In the parlour and the kitchen, in the shop and in the field, we must lift up the cross and abase the crucifix, magnify the gospel and ridicule superstition, glorify the Lord Jesus and expose priestcraft.[50]

The impact of this movement merely demonstrated the reality of what Spurgeon contended about the Anglican state church. A loyal layman in the Church wrote an expose of Puseyism entitled *Puseyism the School of the Infidels, or "Broad Church" the offspring of "High Church" with a few Words to the Evangelicals.* Spurgeon reviewed the book with a note of joy that honest Protestantism might still survive in England. "Our battle," Spurgeon explained, "is not against, but *for* all true Evangelicals in the Church." He sought to prompt one of two responses in his severe dealing with their inconsistent position. One, that they "may be nerved to leave it." Two, that they may be "roused to demand alterations, which will make it honestly tenable."

Though Spurgeon had clear views on Puseyism and the dangers of its road to Rome, and he was clear about calling for disestablishment of Anglicanism, he was ambivalent about a clear break between government and religion. When he looked at the reality that only an act of the divine Spirit could ever make a man a Christian or build the House of God as a true spiritual habi-

tation, he wanted no favors from Parliament for any aspect of religious conviction. Government could only produce hypocrisy from a religious standpoint, for the gospel alone by the Spirit's power produced true worship of God. The only good Parliament could ever do religion was "by mistake." Proposing laws of the land to touch religion brought from Spurgeon the protest, "Hands off! Leave us alone!" He wanted no "Sunday bills and all other forms of acts-of-Parliament religion," but only a "fair field and no favor." Faith had nothing to fear and "Christ wants no help from Caesar!" Rather than dabble in formalizing religion, Members of Parliament should "repent of the bribery and corruption so rife in their own midst before they set up to be protectors of the religion of our Lord Jesus!" He feared the result of borrowing help for religion from government for it looked as "if I rested on an arm of flesh instead of depending on the living God." Even Sabbath enforcement was no place for government to meddle. Certainly the Lord's Day must be respected, "and may the day soon come when every shop shall be closed on Sunday—but let it be by the force of *conviction* and not by force of the policeman."[51]

Spurgeon had the old Puritan/Baptist zeal against all unbiblical, gospel-compromising forms, teachings, and practices. He constantly was on the look out for opportunities to lampoon Anglican theology and ritual as well as the pretensions involved in its establishment as the state church. He asked for people to distribute his articles against Anglicanism. "A crusade upon the doctrines of the Anglicans is needed." He would support political action toward disestablishment, but "the religion question is the more important." "If the Church of England were disestablished to-

---

49. S&T, July 1866, 342.

50. Ibid., 343.

51. MTP, 1867, 239-40.

morrow," he could affirm without hesitation, "it would be equally needful to protest her deadly errors."[52]

In 1869 Peter Bayne wrote an article for *The Christian World* that most certainly would please Spurgeon. An address to Lord Shaftesbury entitled "The New Alliance between Church and State" called on Shaftesbury to seek a disestablishment of the church by throwing the evangelicals on the good will of Christian people rather than seeking by political means an overthrow of the ritualists and the latitudinarians. Bayne had some analyses that sounded Spurgeonic in theology and power of conviction. In fact, he referred to Spurgeon's answer to an evangelical clergy that wrote him complaining of Spurgeon's contention that Anglicanism had been given over to the ritualists, that he considered "the right of the ritualists to remain in the Church to be exactly as good as that of the Evangelicals."[53] Bayne clearly agreed, and asked, "Has not the ambiguous position of the Church breathed a subtle poison into the moral life of the nation? Has it not promoted a slippery prudence, a judicious meanness, a sanctity, sly and sleek, a sordid contentment with half-truths and half-falsehoods, a tolerance, nay, an admiration, for 'the glistening and softly spoken lie?' Can the conscience of England be as noontide clear if the Church of England is an organized equivocation?"[54]

More severe and dangerous than this callousness to moral clarity, Bayne spoke of the theological compromises necessarily involved in such a union between church and state, the gravitational pull of which would end in Romanism on the one hand and universalism on the other. Bayne call on Lord Shaftesbury, therefore, to lead in the formation of a Protestant church in England [mentioning only the Episcopalians, Presbyterians, and Congregationalists], free of state control and state support, and thus free for missionary, benevolent, evangelistic, and philanthropic work of the sort that arises from "spontaneous, personal, present, giving of intelligent, active-minded men." He argued that "to hand back her emoluments to the nation and to go free would be to get rid of all that is anomalous, depressing, shameful in her position, and to give new power to all that has secured her the respect of Christendom and the affection of her children."[55]

Spurgeon would be sympathetic with much of Bayne's proposal, even though his perceived union was of paedobaptists only, because of its call for a "free church in a free state" and the complete equality of all dissenters. Spurgeon hated the union of church and state. His sermon on the Prayer Book in 1864 rose to a height of indignation on this issue that must have been withering to any Anglicans that visited the Tabernacle on that day. He described the charade of creating a newly-minted priest as "fresh from the dissipations of college life, the sinner bows before the man and rises a full blown priest—fully able to remit or retain sins! After this, how can the priests of the Church of England denounce the Roman Catholics?" How convenient to have the Puseyites and Papists to fume against, but when the admonition begins "at *home* and we give our Evangelical Brethren the same benefit which they confer upon the open Romanists, they are incensed beyond measure!" Spurgeon would not spare them, for they, "despite their fair speeches, are as guilty as those whom they denounce" He exclaimed with a deep-seated conviction, "Protestant Eng-

---

52. S&T, November 1870, 532.

53. Peter Bayne, "The New Alliance between Church and State" in *The Christian World*, January 1869, 6.

54. Ibid., 7.

55. Ibid., 14f.

land! Will you long tolerate this blasphemy? Land of Wickliffe, birthplace of the martyrs of Smithfield—how long is this to be borne with?" If one contradicted his concern by saying it was none of his concern, he asked pertinently, "Is it not the National Church?—does not its sin rest, therefore, upon every man and woman in the nation—Dissenter and Churchman—who does not shake himself from it by open disavowal?" The church claimed him as a parishioner and if it could to pay its church rates and did indeed "take from me my share of tithe every year." In light of such abominations, Spurgeon called, "Arise, Britannia, nation of the free, and shake your garments from the dust of this hoary superstition!"[56] In 1871, in fact, he led his congregation, "the church at the Tabernacle," to petition Parliament for the disestablishment and disendowment of the Church of England. It was more and more a feeder to the church of Rome. Its position as a "government-favored sect, is an insult and a wrong to all other churches."[57]

His apparent call for a secular Parliament combined with his strong convictions that the church should be disestablished does not tell the full story about Spurgeon. His involvement in the Liberation Society and his call that "perfect religious equality be found everywhere"[58] confronted the inevitable test of context. When faced with all the implications of an a-religious government, he modified the nature of his argument. If one wanted a purely spiritual church, and wanted religious persuasions of the people to arise from the power of the Spirit of Truth and that only, then one way of thinking was in order; if one wanted justice

and public morality built on revealed principles of equity and human dignity then he looked to a general Christian consensus. It was, after all, on the basis of Protestantism, the blood of English martyrs, and the nature of English freedom that he warned against the danger of Rome. This was Protestant England.

The radical stance of some of his Liberation Society cooperants, therefore, he could not bring himself fully to support. In 1870 he posed "A Few Questions for Present Consideration." Though he consistently contended that the state, as such, "ought neither to patronize nor persecute religion," he firmly dissented from the idea that "the State has nothing to do with religion."[59] In a series of well-formed queries, Spurgeon outlined several spheres in which he believed it impossible for religion, specifically, Christianity, and the State to go separate directions. Jesus has not relinquished his Lordship over the earth, and he does not intend for his people to act as if the earth were not the Lord's. On matters of policy where people cast their vote, Christians must vote according to the Word rather than in line with infidelity. Sabbath rest is instituted both for church and government and may not be cast aside without a violation of God's law. Spurgeon had a strong aversion against the repeal of any laws that honored the day as a day of rest for all. It already provided chaplains for the armed forces, allowed Bible studies in jail, dismissed Parliament on Sunday, closed public houses for part of the Sabbath, as well it should. Should a government disregard the claims of God in these matters, it would still be religious, but religious in the lowest sense and "to all intents and purposes atheistic." Spurgeon believed that a minority of the nation were in a position of non-faith and proposed that the government

---

56. SS, 8:73.

57. S&T, March 1871, 139.

58. See Drummond, *Spurgeon*, 529. Drummond's chapter on "Spurgeon the Politician" gives a summary of his involvement in the Liberation Society and other political issues, 509-48.

59. S&T, July 1870, 330. "A Few Questions for Present Consideration."

should not be controlled by the "negative faith or non-faith of the minority." In questions regarding religion, "must not the government decide for respect to God and his Word?"[60] He challenged the "believers in the non-religious principle" to carry the logical inferences of their scheme to its end and see the devastation. He hoped they would never succeed. He worked, in fact, to extend the prohibition of mail delivery on Sunday by supporting a motion by Charles Reed in the House of Commons to do away with postal service on the Lord's Day throughout England. It was not done in London and the rest of the country would not suffer for its loss. Sunday deliveries involved 20,000 postal employees "needlessly." "A letter-carrier's life must be sheer slavery," Spurgeon noted, "when he has to work seven days in the week, *and rest never.*" He urged the churches to take up the cause for "It amounts to a national sin."[61] By ignoring the Sabbath, Spurgeon argued, the government would become a persecuting government.[62] In questions that necessarily regard religion the government must "decide for respect to God and his Word."[63] Suppose all religion must be removed from the classroom; how could any desire teachers of such colorless character? How could non-conformists look with pleasure upon the country when praying for it? He strongly supported the teaching of biblical knowledge and ethics in the school system as long as it was not the catechizing of students into Anglicanism. Spurgeon posed another question that showed his commitment to religious instruction in schools as a means of building character needed by all levels of society. "Is it really believed by Christian men that mere reading, writing, and arith-

metic, without religious instruction, will elevate our street Arabs, and train the waifs and strays of London to be honest men and good citizens?"[64] Did Englishmen bleed and die to gain a liberty that would deny permission for children to read the Bible in school? Christian men must not join with the pagan nations of Psalm 2 that conjoin in the chant, "Let us break his bands asunder, and cast his cords from us."[65]

Even as he revolted against state-churchism, he confessed, "all the instincts of our soul revolt against the unreligious teaching which certain Nonconformists would impose upon this nation." He acknowledged that a strict logician might make him appear inconsistent, even as a man that felt logic demanded that the straightest and quickest route to a destination should always be taken would break his neck through consistency by jumping off a cliff rather than take a zig-zag route down. He knew that the mass of his brethren were convinced by the radically secular non-conformist argument. On his opponent's premises, Spurgeon could argue that Parliament should sit on Sundays in order to avoid all religious favoritism and the Civil Service should be compelled to work seven days a week "because any preference shown to the Christian religion by the State would clash with the *Nonconformist principles.*" Thus, try as he might, his heart recoiled against the so-called Manchester solution, an attempt to eliminate Bible instruction in the day schools.[66]

Though he shrank from pure secularism as a governing principle of the nation, he had nothing but pure disdain for the arrogance generated by the privileged position of Anglicanism. In an article entitled "Our Own Dear Popish Church,"

---

60. Ibid., 330.

61. S&T, March 1871. 139.

62. S&T, July 1870, 330.

63. Ibid., 330.

64. Ibid., 331.

65. Ibid.

66. S&T, September 1872, 432.

Spurgeon applauded Rev. Fredrick Aubert Gage, Vicar of Great Barling, Essex, for his pristine clarity in stating his theological views and his corresponding hatred of Dissent. Gage was not guilty of using words of worldly charity to gloss over the differences between his Anglicanism and the doctrines of evangelical Dissenters. By the same token, "Towards the church of England as a State church, and as maintaining many Popish doctrines, Nonconformists only stand in truth and sincerity when they avow themselves decidedly hostile." Man to man and Christian to Christian, charity must prevail, but "charity toward a corrupt system is falsehood to truth, danger to ourselves, injury to our fellow men, and dishonour to God." The differences between non-conformity and Anglicanism are not trivial, but clearly distinct on matters that corrupt the gospel. A façade of worldly charity toward such a system is a pious fraud and a traitorous desertion of "Christ's truth for the sake of pleasing men."[67] The Vicar could not have made the options more clear.

Gage's catechism did not mince words in declaring that infant baptism was the means of regeneration, sanctification, and indeed, justification. Gage also lacked no clarity in declaring dissenters as engaged in idolatrous worship, heretics indeed that are protected unnaturally by the laws of the state so that the "wholesome law of the Church" cannot be acted upon. "Bravo!" wrote Spurgeon with the wish that Gage's brother priests would be as honest "and then the land would the sooner be rid of you." Spurgeon saw in such speech the "lion's claw to which soft words about charity act as a pad." He thought he could smell "roast man somewhere, and hear the chains of the Lollard's Tower rattling anew." Those dissenters that had parted least from the form and

order of Anglicanism were most dangerous because most likely to mislead. Spurgeon agreed entirely, and hoped that the Great Barling Elijah would "end their halting between two opinions, and make them good, sound Dissenters." Even to enter a dissenting meeting house, according to Gage, would produce spiritual havoc in the life of the Anglican faithful, but the same was not true of Romish chapels. Spurgeon urged all fellow dissenters to enter their protest against the downright idolatry, the full acceptance of Roman Catholic superstitions, that prevailed in the State church. "It is true," he conceded, "that there are good men, yes, very good men in the Establishment, but this is no reason why we should deal leniently with a system which allows and supports deadly error."[68] Nothing but clear and relentless opposition would help the good men in the establishment to come out; false charity would serve no good and be infidelity to truth and unloving to fellow men. Dissenters must be as vigilant against Anglicanism and Romanism as Rome was against Carthage.

> No peace, no truce, must there be between the champions of a spiritual faith, and the devotees of Sacramentarianism. We must teach our children the protests for which our fathers died; we must expose to their detestation the fopperies and elegancies which cover up the enormities of priestcraft; we must break up the inclined plane down which weakly Nonconformists descend, by the halfway house of Evangelicalism, into the abyss of Tractarianism. An end to all truckling and coquetting; we are the determined foes of the system which is now styled our National Religion, and can never cease to oppose it while we reverence the Bible, while we love the souls of men, while we obey Christ, and believe in God.[69]

---

67. S&T, October 1870, 463.

68. Ibid., 467.

69. Ibid.

By 1877 Spurgeon believed Anglicanism's complete capitulation to Rome was entirely possible. The ritualists, these "double-faced gentlemen," gained ground steadily and had virtually succeeded in mesmerizing the evangelicals. Staunch Anglicans at first disliked the Popish revival, and progressed to toleration, excuse, and admiration. Spurgeon found it amazing that in so short a space of time, daring men "should have set up the old idols, and brought back the entire Romish paraphernalia,"[70] Reunification within ten years would not astonish Spurgeon. Only secular interests and the dread of disestablishment prevented it. The National Church was "drunk with the wine of Rome's abominations."[71]

In a time of acute despondency about the religious state of England, Spurgeon listed superstition as one of the evidences of "sad times." He called the Anglican church a "popish joss-house" in which "self-styled priests entice silly women to the confessional, and amuse them with masses and processions." He could not restrain himself: "Vile imposters!" he named them—the clergy of an "avowedly Protestant church, and supported by this nation, they are yet ravenous to eat out the very vitals of Protestantism" through their superstitious crucifixes and stations of the cross before which they can find fools enough to bow. The leaven makes its way in the meal.

Year by year Spurgeon warned against the dangers to men's souls implicit in the state-church system. "This is the delusion of England," he contended. "We have not half so much to dread Popery as we have that nominal Christianity, fostered by a national Church." He believed that millions of Englishmen think they are Christians because "they were sprinkled in infancy with holy drops, and because they have come to the Lord's Table."

Miserably unaware they were that in so doing they ate and drank damnation to themselves, not discerning the Lord's body. So much profession and so little possession was the "curse and plague of England," a condition perpetuated by slumbering people listening to sleepy ministers that would not tell the truth for fear of hurting feelings. Spurgeon was determined, however, to be clear of their blood should they go on and perish in this fatal delusion. He would thrust his hand into their soul to make them tremble with the thought whether they be right with God or no.[72]

When Alfred Potter, Rector of Ashton, produced a pamphlet in defense of Confirmation using an imaginary conversation with a cottager named John Blake as the vehicle, Spurgeon jumped on the opportunity to expose the fallacy of the Rector's argument. Continuing the literary convention, Spurgeon constructed an interview between *John Blake* and *The Rector of Ashton*. Blake had gone to another minister, Mr. Waterton who was "an Anabaptist and a Calvinist," to help clarify some things that had been confusing in the initial interview. Among the issues set straight was the appropriation of a quotation from Calvin about laying on of hands. The Rector had suggested that Calvin affirmed the sacrament of Confirmation on the strength of that quotation, and Blake had learned from the minister Waterton the full context. In fact, so Spurgeon presented the industrious Blake, he had even copied that larger context from book four of the *Institutes* demonstrating that Calvin had not said at all what the Rector asserted. Blake did not take kindly to the attempt "to make a poor man out to be a Simple Simon" and, therefore, he had taken liberties "to put matters on the square a little." Having finished reading the revealing quotation,

---

70. S&T, 1877, Preface, iii.

71. Ibid.

72. MTP, 1861, 295.

cottager Blake said, "I feel awfully sorry for you, you had better have done without Calvin." Even if one could construe that Calvin made room for some kind of laying on of hands, "what he would have meant by it was as wide as the poles asunder from what you mean by Confirmation, for you told me that in Confirmation 'the Holy Spirit supplies grace for growth in holiness.'" The Rector, offended that a simple cottager had dared question his presentation, had "insulted him to [his] face," asked the cottager to leave at once. He did but, having foreseen that the Rector would so excuse himself of the expose, Waterton had written a letter for Blake to leave with him. "I meant no offense," said John, "but if truth offends, so must it be."

Spurgeon did the reader of the *Sword and the Trowel* the favor of printing the letter for the benefit of all. In this letter, the Calvinistic Anabaptist Waterton undertook to show how every attempt to support Confirmation with Scripture was as ill-fated as the Rector's attempt to cite Calvin in its defense. "I say that the bishop cannot give the Holy Ghost, and you know he cannot," so wrote Waterton. No Scripture supports such a fable, and the effort to lead people to think so is not only an untruth, it is positively harmful. It promotes presumption of forgiveness and the graces of salvation where none exists, demeans holiness, operates under the trappings of superstition, fosters self-deception, and treats with unaccountable solemnity a practice that reduces reverence for God and endangers the souls of men.[73]

In another piece of literary irony, Spurgeon considered, through the means of John Ploughman's cousin, William, the possibility of a country with a Baptist establishment. The dissenting Episcopalians would justly howl at the imposition

of taxes for the support of a clergy for which they had no sympathy. The Baptists, taking warrant from their conviction that the original churches consisted of persons immersed upon profession of faith, had engineered an ecclesio-political relation that required the entire nation to support their church. Others were schismatics. Cousin Ploughman sympathized with the Anglicans, that is, Episcopalians, and pointed out the injustice of the Baptists in betraying their own commitment to a free gospel and a regenerate church in pursuing their ill-gotten power. They taxed the Episcopalians, as well as the Presbyterians and Methodists, for their baptismal robes, their water, and reserved for their cousins and nephews certain church positions that they blatantly call "livings." The means of education serve their own ascendancy and leave others, that they so unlovingly and in such an unbrotherly manner label as schismatics, to manage for themselves at great expense and sure disadvantage. They profess to believe the Baptist Confession of Faith but are divided into three distinct theological parties, but still all claim to be of the same communion. They refuse proper ground for burial to Episcopalians, Methodists, and Independents, isolate them to unsanctified ground as if an unimmersed person even in death could contaminate the orthodox with the heresy of sprinkling. Ploughman rises to a state of heightened incredulity in expressing his sympathy for the repressed Anglicans:

Sir, ought these things so to be? Why should a Baptist oppress an Episcopalian? Why should the Episcopalian be blamed if he feels the oppression keenly and struggles to escape from it: Is there any justice in the state of things which I have represented to you? The gospel rule that we should do to others as we would that they should do to us appears to have been entirely ignored.

---

73. S&T, November 1870, 497-505. "Confirmation."

Episcopalians in that country have to support their own ministers, and do so with no little difficulty, because few of the great and noble cast in their lot with them; why should they be called upon to sustain those of a body with which they do not agree, which enjoys, moreover, the patronage of the highest in the land? They ought in the eyes of the law to be equal to Baptists or any other religionists. I feel ashamed of Baptists who can occupy such a position of unrighteous vantage. Ask the Baptist Union if they are not also ashamed? Ask the Episcopalians of England if they are not indignant that such gross injustice should be endured by brethren of their own faith and order?[74]

Sometimes, seeing things in reverse reveals the grotesqueness of reality.

Equally as grotesque was the proposal of the vicar of the parish of Elstow to build and repair his church and install a stained-glass window, gaining his contributions by making it a memorial to John Bunyan. "Why not repair a Catholic chapel as a memorial to Martin Luther?" Spurgeon queried, or make the Baptist chapel at Elstow as a memorial to Charles II? Bunyan needed no memorial to hold his place among the men of England. Should the vicar succeed in his project, Spurgeon was sure that the ghost of John Bunyan would haunt the church until the stained glass window was removed.[75]

Not only did an Anglican try to rob the grave of Bunyan to find funds for Episcopalianism, the Rector of Newington thought that he could rob the sheepfold of Spurgeon for new life for his parish. In a celebratory mood for his thought that he had found new blood for the parish and the Anglican establishment, Mr. Maclagan "loudly crowed at the Church Congress, because he had done this under the very eaves of Mr. Spurgeon's Tabernacle." Spurgeon had received scores of Anglicans into the Tabernacle but had never made it a matter of boasting at denominational meetings. Unaware of a single name that had gone from the Tabernacle to the parish, Spurgeon warned Maclagan, in a rural proverbial fashion, not to count unhatched chickens, or even worse, unlaid eggs. On an evening when Spurgeon had 1,200 at a prayer meeting, he sent a friend to find out how many had "responded to the tinkling bell of our parish church," and found, including priests and officials, twenty-two persons present. "Great boast, little roast," Spurgeon concluded. He was not above pointing to numerical success as an indicator of spiritual power, especially when it came to Establishment vis-à-vis non-conformist.

The status of a state church, in Spurgeon's opinion, had the tendency to corrupt even so sound a man as J. C. Ryle. Spurgeon loved Ryle and commended his writings and ministry consistently, but felt that it was edifying in spite of his position in the state church and in spite of the titles he was forced to bear in that position. In a review of Ryle's addresses to children, Spurgeon publicly opined that "the esteemed author cannot be otherwise than soundly evangelical and gracious," although he exhorted children in a "manner which he would hardly use towards adults." Ryle simply manifested what Spurgeon considered "a common fault with many who talk to the young." But this manner gave comfort to Spurgeon for it showed that "our friend retains his simplicity though he bears the title of 'Right Reverend' and 'Lord Bishop.' It must need a great deal of grace," Spurgeon remarked, "to wear such dignities and retain one's naturalness." In spite of such titles Spurgeon viewed Ryle as a "Dissenter inside the church."[76]

---

74. S&T, November 1872, 495.

75. S&T, June 1874, 286.

76. S&T, June 1881, 286.

This observed persona, however, drove Ryle from time to time to justify himself to his fellow churchmen by showing his zeal for the establishment. Ryle had sought to do just that in a tract entitled *Dissent and the Church* and had been answered in a "very sensible reply" by a John Browne. Like others of the evangelicals, he can "put on priestly airs" when he pleases. "Strip a Russian," Spurgeon proverbialized, "and you find a Tartar." By the same token, "set certain Evangelicals agoing against Dissenters and you see a Pope." Spurgeon called Ryle himself, "good, very good," but at the same time his "churchianity is bad, very bad." Had he never heard of a *mouton enrage,* Ryle's threats and indignations would have caused Spurgeon to hold up his hands and cry "Amazing!"[77]

Similar ambivalence met Spurgeon's readers when he noted that Ryle's *Thoughts on Baptism* "is certainly the poorest defence of Paedo-baptism which has yet appeared, poor as most of these have been." Ryle's zeal for his church had outrun his discretion and would do no good to strengthen that position. At the same time Ryle's *Thoughts on Sickness* was "wise and helpful" and evidence that the Liverpudlian was "thoroughly at home in this kind of practical teaching."[78]

Newman Hall came in for equal if not greater laudations from Spurgeon as a useful Anglican. Hall, in fact, avoided the ire of Spurgeon on two unusual accounts. One, he wrote a book of poetry, a pet peeve of Spurgeon, that Spurgeon described as "good and better." Second, in the heat of the Downgrade Controversy, "when all around, modern thought is poisoning the air, he remains true to the doctrine of the cross, and declares the gospel more boldly than ever." Spurgeon could not let the fact that he was Anglican go entirely

without chastening, so he wrapped his resistance to Anglicanism in the soft cloth of a true fondness for Hall and appreciation for his influence for the gospel. "He is fonder of a liturgical service than we shall ever be; but we have no quarrel with him on that account, for he loves the gospel," Spurgeon emphasized, "and therefore we can forget his gown and prayer book."[79]

By 1874, Spurgeon had hope that the system of establishment was falling apart and attempts to salvage it would only bring about its downfall. The government had made two attempts to "patch up the old house of Establishment, but the concern is too rickety to bear any extensive repairs." Debate over the Patronage Bill and the Public Worship Bill, Spurgeon referred to as "pieces of new cloth pieced into old garments;" Disraeli, unintentionally, had "commenced the separation of church and state."[80] When the *Church Times* reported a letter by Archdeacon Denison that asserted, "Divorce between Church and State is become not right only, but necessary to the keeping of true religion," Spurgeon hoped that the Archdeacon "is evidently having his eyes opened to some things."[81]

A perambulator through the city churches on a Sunday in 1883 noted the sparseness of the congregations, the incomprehensibility of services read from the Prayer Book, the museum-like quality of many of the city churches, the architecture (restorations by Sir Christopher Wren subsequent to the great London fire) and historic interest of some (e.g. the parish of Miles Coverdale along with the plaque erected to his memory, as well as another commemorating John Newton), and the genuine difficulty of serving such parishes when the masses of the population had gradu-

---

77. S&T, November 1870, 529.

78. S&T, February 1885, 86.

79. S&T, March 1888, 141.

80. S&T, August 1874, 390.

81. S&T, September 1874, 438.

ally moved to the suburbs away from the grime and crime of the city itself. Many of the ministers, some poorly remunerated and some exorbitantly beneficed, were feeding stalls without flocks, receiving pay for virtually no service to the cause of religion. Most remarkable, however, was the nature of the preaching, which the observer assumed would be similar in most of the remaining city parishes.

> This kind of gospel, which we take to be mere legalism is common enough in the Church of England; at all events, it is the pabulum which is chiefly offered to seeking souls in the City pulpits, though, or course there are exceptions now, as there were in the days of Newton and Romaine. This gospel consists in leaving off sin, in being good, and in attending church.[82]

The church could be greatly purified, the leaven removed, so Spurgeon believed, if the small band of hyper-Calvinists in its borders were given their way. Commenting about *Memorials of the Rev. Charles Rolfe,* Spurgeon noted that Rolfe "belonged to the small but intense company who within the Anglican pale hold to Calvinistic doctrine in its severest form." Rolfe was a holy man, whose spirituality coincided with that of many that would not adopt the severities of his system, a demonstration as to "how the life of God in one man is to the same vital principle in another." To Rolfe, "Arminianism in any form was his abhorrence, and Ritualism his detestation." Though Rolfe would not have owned the language, Spurgeon viewed him as a "Dissenter within the Church." "He was a Particular Baptist who had lost his way, and stumbled into a rectory." Though Rolfe despised Arminianism, he loved genuine spirituality more and had high esteem for Jim-

my Lee, a local preacher among the Wesleyans. Though in itself unbiblically constricted, Rolfe's theology was built for strength, and strength is needed now. Spurgeon proposed an experiment. "A few hundred Hyper-Calvinists in the Church of England, whatever they might be deficient in, would, at least, make short work of its Popery, and call the people back to the essence of Protestantism. We devoutly wish the experiment could be tried."[83]

The Growth of Rationalism in Theology

Spurgeon was seen as such a distinctive influence among evangelicals that some thought he was fully capable of founding a new denomination. The observation arose from America and was based on Spurgeon's minimal activity in the Baptist Union and his fervid activity from the base of his ministry at the Metropolitan Tabernacle. Spurgeonism, similar to Wesleyanism, would gain its peculiarities by the influence of its own college, its missionary agencies, and its ministers "trained in Spurgeon's college, imbued with Spurgeon's intense spirit, copying with an unconscious but ludicrous fidelity even the minutiae of Spurgeon's manner of speech, proud of their connection with Spurgeon's name, and in constant communication with the 'Head Centre' in London."[84] Spurgeon reprobated any such attempt to do this and expressed his opinion on this matter in strong terms. That he had any desire to start a new sect or separate from the Baptist denomination was an "unfounded libel." "We preach no new gospel, we desire no new objects, and follow them in no novel spirit." He loved Christ more than any sect, truth more than any party, and, though he was not exclusively denominational, at the same time was in open union with the Baptists for the sim-

---

82. S&T, April 1883, 166.

83. S&T, October 1879, 491.

84. S&T, April 1866, 138.

ple reason that he could not endure isolation.[85] He would have to endure that soon enough.

The charge of "Spurgeonism" re-emerged just a bit later, this time from a disgruntled, somewhat latitudinarian Baptist dissatisfied with the influence of Spurgeon within the Baptist Union. Amused and a bit bewildered by the same nomenclature used for two such radically different complaints, Spurgeon responded "now we find ourselves in hot water in precisely the opposite direction, having in the eyes of some been guilty of exercising too preponderating an influence upon the Baptist body."[86] He had picked up his participation in the Baptist Union, and had found it congenial and encouraging. "If our brethren feel that during the few months that we have been seen more manifestly among them we have been burdensome, we have been very much misled by their hearty manner toward us." He had no intention to surpass any other person in influence but was happy to contribute to the prosperity of the whole in maintaining the "purity of the gospel of Jesus, and a hallowed practical zeal for the Master's glory." Edward White, a Baptist minister in Camden Town, seceded from the Baptist Union because Spurgeon did not "bend the knee to the modern liberalism which is just now so popular" and represented the "orthodoxy which it is fashionable to depreciate." White found the atmosphere Spurgeon created repressive and therefore left for a more suitable theological climate. Spurgeon found it strange that "one of the freest of all denominations has not room enough in it to hold us both." If others of the same doctrinal ilk, influenced by an "abundant portion of the vagaries of modern thought," were influenced to leave, and then received by the Congregationalists, it would indicate that more than friendly discussions

about ordinances separated them—the issues would be truth and vital godliness. In light of the developments over the next two decades, Spurgeon's analysis of this phenomenon is worthy of note. "We are suspected of bigotry," he observed, "but we do not leave a denomination because all do not swear by our Shibboleth." Nor did he want another denomination to become the receptacle for malcontents who were offended simply by another man's influence, especially when those denominational migrants were leaving a "free community which has never tried to fetter them." If the presence of one of the preachers of orthodoxy rendered the denomination an unsavory home for the broad school, Spurgeon observed, "the old faith is evidently safe without the safeguard of tests."[87] Within two decades Spurgeon would call for the necessity of a doctrinal test for membership in the Baptist Union. Mere influence was no longer sufficient to preserve purity.

In 1877 Spurgeon wrote of "spots of rationalism" that should cause concern among the Dissenters. He knew of a denomination in England "which is sadly gangrened with a pseudo-intellectualism which counts it manly to doubt." The orthodox believer they considered weak-minded, only worthy of their sublime pity. This kind of thought Spurgeon argued would alienate people from churches that espoused it, wither all that was worth preserving. Even the superstitions of Rome would appear more lively than the "cold negations and the chill of perpetual questioning" generated by modern thought.[88]

The desire to be held in honor among one's peers often pushed students and tutors into the stream of the avant-garde thought of the day. An affectation of liberalism, to be regarded as original and possessed of a breadth of mind and

---

85. Ibid.

86. S&T, June 1866, 281.

87. Ibid., 283.

88. S&T, 1877, Preface, iv.

candor of judgment that rescued one from the mere parroting of outworn dogmas and repeating another age's thought, soon became the new manliness. "To be mere old-fashioned teachers of a time-worn faith is not a tempting object for ordinary carnal ambition," Spurgeon warned and further observed that "everywhere the noxious endeavor to do something more than rehearse the teaching of revelation and obey the rules of King Jesus is working evil." He and his colleagues believed the "doctrines of the gospel to have been settled when the Spirit first inspired the Bible."[89]

Among the most susceptible of the formerly received doctrines of revelation to the ravages of the newly enlightened age was the doctrine of eternal punishment. The rational elite proposed several options to the teachings of a strict and eternal manifestation of retributive justice— anything but hell!

Spurgeon carried a series of articles by his friend, and the principal of the college, George Rogers, on the subject of annihilationism. In 1871, Rogers responded to the arguments of Edward White that the Scripture was not clear enough on the subject of eternal punishment to declare it a truly biblical teaching. Dr. Leask, the editor of a periodical named *The Rainbow* sought to put an end to the controversy by the bald assertion "Eternal suffering is not the doctrine of Scripture." He refused to insert a letter from Rogers in his paper, so Spurgeon printed the exchange of correspondence in *The Sword and the Trowel*. Though Rogers dealt with other interpretive issues, all hinged, in his opinion, on the answer to the proposal, "Whether there are not instances in the New Testament in which the doctrine of eternal punishment is affirmed as decisively and fully as it could have been affirmed in the Greek

language? Whether in fact the eternal happiness of the righteous, or the eternity of God, is expressed in stronger terms?" White maligned him in a brace of exquisite sarcasms as a "gentlemen who always writes in the tone of a tutor, and one possessing the rare power of assertion requisite for converting untrained youths, from town and country, in little more than two years into expositors of God's word, and pastors of Baptist congregations." Rogers' response was measured and to the point, dealing in no *ad hominem* thrusts but only with the specific questions at hand. He closed his letter with the observation: "His allusions to myself personally, and to the College with which I am connected, are wholly irrelevant to the occasion; and in my opinion would have been better omitted for his sake rather than my own. I trust I have had no other aim that to defend what I hold to be the teaching of the word of God; nor am I conscious of having transgressed the rules of fair controversy in so doing."[90]

Spurgeon traced the development of anti-hell theory through its appearances in numerous books through the years. He found that restorationism was vying with annihilationism as the alternative to hell. Jacob Blain in his book *Hope for Our Race, or God's Government Vindicated* moved from a former defense of annihilationism for a more optimistic restorationism. He was as "sure about it as he was about his former error." Spurgeon found the penchant for novelty a childish trait and biblical interpretation the mere servant of such novelties. "When men wish to defend a theory, with what ease can they wrest Scripture, and argue so as to convince themselves and bewilder others!" He had observed a "mob of reasonings, fancies, whimsies, heresies, crazinesses, imaginations, and wickednesses," vying to devour

---

89. S&T, 1883, 261, 262. "Concerning College Work as I see it."

90. S&T, February 1871, 88. 89.

one another as they seek to be the victor over "the old doctrine of eternal punishment." Spurgeon was "content to abide quiet, for they will surely eat up one another." The opposition was divided even against itself "and will come to nought." The devil of unbelief was tearing those whom it has possessed. Spurgeon hoped it would come out of them.[91]

Spurgeon gave much more thorough and serious attention to this in 1874, in a review of *Everlasting Punishment and Modern Speculation.* Spurgeon commended this as a balanced and thorough treatment of the subject from the standpoint of the whole Bible. "No such thoroughness of statement and Biblical research has appeared on the other side," Spurgeon commented, but instead, the "wonderful discoveries of modern thought upon the subject" had to be gathered from "pamphlets, periodicals, and religious newspapers." Partial views and isolated criticisms prevailed but none afforded "a fair and full investigation."[92]

Spurgeon still held that the variety and contrariety within the opposition favored the truthfulness of the belief in the eternity of future punishment, belief in which to that point had been virtually universal. New views included immediate annihilation at death, temporary punishment to be followed by annihilation, temporary punishment to be followed by a new probation, or by restoration to innocence and bliss. Each of these propounded insuperable difficulties in the others while agreeing that punishment cannot be eternal. This cacophony favored a presumptive argument "that the old doctrine is not false, because no opposite can be found that is agreed upon to be true."[93]

Spurgeon believed that the resistance to eternal punishment lay not so much in any truly doctrinal or exegetical difficulty as in the personal dispositions of the objectors. "Some few who are in all other matters sound in the faith," Spurgeon admitted, "may have been troubled in mind upon this subject." In general, however, it was in company with a falling away from other vital evangelical truth. "Its effect, in fact," Spurgeon explained, "upon all our ideas of sin and holiness, and consequently of the remedial scheme of redemption, is one of the strongest objections against it."[94]

In the final analysis, the effect of all these schemes was to render impertinent the distinguishing doctrine of historical orthodox Christianity. For example, universalism, a very popular option, supposedly presented a system full of mercy, but is "subversive of all the first principles both of law and gospel." Universalism eventually resolves all things into one and supposes no qualitative difference between good and evil, atheism and the worship of the true God, the utmost degree of profanity and the highest degree of piety, rejection of and the reception of Christ, and Nero and the Christians he burned. Only time distinguishes them. "Wait a while. All in the end will be equally holy and happy." Evil will become good, impiety will grow into piety, "the germ of heaven is in hell." Give enough time and "it will burst as from a bitter bud into all the blessedness of heaven." Against all scriptural principles, these schemes dissolve any essential difference between sin and holiness, or the standing of being under the law and under grace? "They are the same species, only one is of longer growth than the other."

This calling evil good shows clearly the origin of such a contrivance. Revolting to human reason as it may be, the eternity of future punishment

---

91. S&T, January 1872, 41.

92. S&T, May 1874, 236.

93. Ibid.

94. Ibid.

is in harmony "with all the principles of the divine government, and as such is clearly revealed in the Scriptures." Two questions related to the Bible have been unanswered by the opponents to the doctrine of hell. First, should God intend to teach his creatures that there is an eternity of punishment for unforgiven, unredeemed sinners, could he have chosen more explicit language and more clear discourse than that found presently in Scripture? Second, "supposing eternal punishment to be derogatory to the divine character," why does Scripture not give cautions against entertaining such an idea.[95]

By 1878 Spurgeon said the "new doctrines have certainly gone tolerable lengths now, and from annihilationism to restoration has been a mere foot-race." Soon he expected the ungodly to be exalted at once, with no stop in between, to heaven and the righteous sent to outer darkness. The sympathies of modern preachers were toward the unbelieving, doubt was celebrated and viewed as a sign of salvation. "We may naturally look for a heaven prepared for loose thinkers, who are so brave as to despise all creeds and believe in nothing whatever." Those deserving of being cast aside were believers in plenary inspiration, who view sin as a terrible evil and therefore affirm the justness of eternal punishment. Liberal modern thinkers see such folks as narrow-minded bigots. "Everybody is received as a Christian nowadays by the Broad School except those who are so indeed."[96]

Though Spurgeon had great distaste for argument by mere assertion, he found apologetic assurance in the reality that pamphlets degenerated into such on this subject. It cemented his cynicism toward the viability of the opposition. Robert Reynoldson's book *Everlasting Punishment not Everlasting Pain* was materialism under the guise of annihilation. The publication was as feeble as it was fallacious for it substituted assumption for argument, and dogmatism for demonstration, thus, instead of seeking to prove the truth of his position, engaged only in dogmatic assumption. "Instead of the infallible standard of Scripture," Spurgeon noted with a weariness of such frustrating contrivances, "we are constantly referred to the 'instincts of humanity.'" This amounted to a "kind of religious rationalism" as a usurper to "devout faith in the Bible and its declarations." At this point, Spurgeon did not see religious rationalism as capable of wooing to itself many converts. It was not manly enough. Only the most feeble would embrace it.[97] Feeble or not, manly or not, Spurgeon was at the front edge of finding such rationalism to be more of a threat than he originally discerned.

In the 1877 Inaugural Address at the College Conference, Spurgeon produced a lengthy admonition to the attendees to preach in such a way as to put to flight all the uncertainties and doctrinal dissipations engendered by the sophistical pretensions of modern thought. Their idea of progress is progress from the truth; they are "progressing backwards." Their ideas of reaching new heights in intellectual development is an "ascending downwards." Spurgeon had seen too much of chapels that formerly were places of conversion power now shut up to green grass in the front and spiders inside. A *Unitarian Baptist Chapel* promotes a frost-bound religion because Christ is not lifted up and thus none are drawn to him. "Where are your converts? Where are your hearers? Where will your churches soon be found?" These are questions that must be asked.[98]

The answer already existed in the generation

---

95. Ibid.

96. S&T, February 1878, 88.

97. S&T, November 1879. 539.

98. S&T, May 1877, 196.

of Socinian Dissenters who graduated from dissenting academies like that of Dr. Doddridge. "That worthy man did not dogmatize to the 'dear young men' who came to his college, but adopted a plan of letting them hear the argument upon each side that they might select for themselves." The method brought as much destruction as if error had been firmly promoted, for "nothing is worse than lukewarmness to truth." Should his alumni have time to read some of what the modern-thought men produce, "you will not be long before you are weary of their word-spinning, their tinkering of old heresies into original thought, and their general mystifying of plain things." Until they produce a man worth following, Spurgeon advised against their answering the call of these progressives, "At the present we are not likely to leave Calvin and Paul and Augustine to follow you."[99]

Spurgeon, in fact, believed that the preaching of Calvinism left very little room for one's falling off into modern thought. One of his brother ministers was not surprised that Spurgeon had little trouble with his church members being lured away, for Calvinism "does not allow them enough scope." His advice, therefore, was "Preach the doctrines of grace, dear brethren, and those who like not your Lord will either be changed themselves or change their minister."[100]

Spurgeon grew weary of the ever-renewed challenges to the "old faith" that animated the creeds of the Puritan tradition, and felt, therefore, a particular blessing in being without religious periodicals for brief periods. They were among the "heaviest affliction of the church of God." The consistent recycling of infidelity under the guise of "modern thought" ("too cowardly to wear its proper name") brought ever-increasing compro-

mise to the biblical certainty of eternal punishment until Spurgeon would not be surprised to see the opinion that "the devil himself is God." He felt happy relief in getting "away from the continual smother of their deceitful teachings." He read the Bible "by sunlight" and the more he turned to that volume the more he was confirmed in the old creed, and the more certain he was that "the modern spirit is deadly to grace, fatal to zeal, and hostile to the truth of God."[101]

When a man bears testimony to conversion, one finds the same words and feelings that would have been expressed 500 years ago—the same loathing of sin, the same fear of wrath, the same sense of utter dependence on a perfect redeemer. He found that predestination and election still stirred up consciences, even though these old-fashioned truths by 1886 had long ago been ignored by the mass of public teachers.[102] Despite opposition and derision, these doctrines stirred up the nests of many and drove them out of themselves to Jesus. The Holy Spirit "has not changed his view of things, nor has he set his seal to modern thought, nor withdrawn it from the cross." Saving faith in Christ still fastens itself "upon the atoning blood and the substitutionary sacrifice, just as it used to do a hundred years ago." In 1886, John Newton could still have found "gracious hearts feeding on the self-same verities as in his own day, and their voices of need or of satisfaction would be precisely the same."[103]

When Spurgeon began to notice the decline of old-fashioned doctrinal piety much closer to home, that is, within his own Baptist Union, the crisis began to transform his world from cosmos to chaos. As late as 1878, in spite of the increasing pressure to capitulate to modern thought, Spurgeon still

99. Ibid., 197.
100. Ibid., 202.
101. S&T, March 1878, 99, 141.
102. S&T, April 1886, 155.
103. Ibid.

viewed the Baptist Union as a place of genuine fellowship and joy, referring to a meeting at the Tabernacle as a "true love feast" of about 450 ministers.
After-dinner addresses by a number of the preachers were "thoroughly hearty and fraternal."[104]

By 1883, however, he saw a division coming
soon as he observed that the darkness of heterodoxy stood out more boldly in silhouette against
the brightness of orthodoxy. "There is sad need to
keep the Sword out of its scabbard," Spurgeon announced, for he saw doctrinal decline all around —
decline of the most egregious and killing sort. No
doctrine was left unassailed or holy thing regarded
as sacred. "Truths once regarded as fundamental,
are either denied, or else turned inside out till nothing of their essence remains. Holy Scripture is no
longer admitted to be the infallible record of revelation; but is made to be a door-mat for 'thought'
to wipe its shoes upon." [105] The first *Sword* entry of
1883, "A Languid and Limp Young Man," denoted
certain elements of the days of overwrought conviction and heretic-hunting bigotry that Spurgeon
was not sad to see go, but the loss of men of met-
tle and truth was not healthy. Now he found that
men were "disloyal to God in order to be charitable to men" and propounded a Christianity "from
which the Fall and the Atonement have both been
eliminated."[106] While he attributed this increasing
laxity and modernization, a degeneration from the
oak to the willow, to the "various denominations,"
he saw Dissent in general as highly susceptible to
this decline. He still maintained the consolation
that "brave spirits can afford to bear the present
phase of the world's madness, confident that, when
the Lord gives sanity, men will return to the primitive truth, and cast their idols away."[107]

As the autumn meeting of the Baptist Union
approached for 1883, Spurgeon informed his
readers that his absence should not be misinterpreted. Though he had been pressed to preach, he
had successfully declined because of "conscious
physical weakness." Younger brethren must be
asked and they should not fail to appear through
an excess of modesty. Though he laid no claim to
modesty, his numerous appearances at the autumn meetings, under the insistence of valued
brethren, made him choose now to "shrink from
being too conspicuous."[108]

Perhaps he wished that he had been more
conspicuous, for when friends reported what
they viewed at the meeting, Spurgeon was sobered. Though Union officials declared that the
event had nothing to do with an official invitation
or even approval of the Union, a "denier of our
Lord's Godhead" was given a welcome by some
and the "loudness of loose thinkers," though disproportionate to their number, disturbed some
deeply concerned brethren. Vital truths held by
a group are not to be trifled with, Spurgeon pronounced, and, as a mater of personal conviction,
"I for one, have not Christian fellowship with
those who reject the gospel of our Lord Jesus
Christ, neither will I pretend to have any."[109] Then
in giving a preview to a refrain that would be
heard more frequently and insistently four years
hence, he warned:

This much is very clear to me,—there is a point
beyond which association may not be carried, lest
it becomes a confederacy in disloyalty. This point
can be speedily reached, if it be not felt by all that
the unwritten law of the Baptist Union takes it for
granted that its members adhere to those grand
evangelical truths which are the common heritage

104. S&T, June 1878, 315.

105. S&T, 1883, Preface.

106. S&T, January 1883, 26, 27.

107. Ibid., 27.

108. S&T, October 1883, 562.

109. S&T, November 1883, 607.

of the Church. We cannot remain in union on any other basis. Creeds are of little use as bonds; for men have learned to subscribe to words and to interpret them in their own sense; but there can be no real union among Baptists unless in heart and soul we all cling to the Lord Jesus as our God, our Sacrifice, and our Exemplar. We must be one in hearty love to the gospel of his grace, or our unity will be of little worth.[110]

Spurgeon would give a greater importance to unity in a creed as the infant controversy developed, but for the mean time he wanted to assure his brethren in the Union of his confidence in their soundness and of his love for them. "No number of men under heaven are heartier in love to Christ crucified, and to one another, than the great majority of our Brethren in the Union." He affirmed that he was at one with them, and that he intended no pain by his writing, but "I can say no less if I am to bear a conscience void of offence towards God."[111]

Some of the brethren did take offense, however, and sought an audience with Spurgeon to set him straight on the facts of the Union meeting in order to give him a chance to "modify his harsh judgments." He had not sought carefully enough to ascertain the facts and thus postured himself in a contemptuous and cruel way toward those "who are as faithful to the Master, and as anxious to know and teach the truth, as himself." The letter calling Spurgeon to account appeared in *The Baptist* for November 9, 1883, and was written by J. G. Greenough and James Thew.[112]

Responding in a way that would become more common in months to come, *The Christian World* published letters critical of Spurgeon's confronta-

tional stance and dated theological propensities. "The pretended advance is evil, and only evil," he responded, and he only asked to be "clear of complicity in this boastful progress beyond what is plainly revealed." He had no time to "pretend to a fellowship which we do not feel." His theology was not regulated by the clock or calendar but "by eternal truth."

In late 1884, when one of Spurgeon's correspondents accused him of "having fellowship with all the heresies of the Baptist Union," he denied to be a party to any such thing. His connection continued only through contribution to the fund for helping poor and aged ministers and the support of home-mission work. "For what may be done at the debating meetings we have no sort of responsibility, for we have ceased to attend them." He did not plead consciousness of physical weakness this time but stated plainly, "It would pain us greatly to be supposed to have any fellowship with modern doubt." His fellowship was not with the Baptist Union *per se* but only with the "great mass of our brethren" that still were "quite free from loose views." With those that love the gospel he felt "fellowship of the heartiest kind."[113]

In January 1885, he printed an article showing the moral weakness of universalism from the *Millennial Harbinger,* an American publication, and commented, "As Universalism is appearing in England, and is even to be found in Baptist pulpits, it is well to have a good look at the intruder." He wanted to bring universalism to light and expose it as unscriptural, immoral, and heretical. His observation concerning the growth of false theology, his warnings against its dangers produced a resurgence of criticism from the press. A periodical entitled *The Preacher's Analyst* devoted some space to Spurgeon in 1884, to which

---

110. Ibid.

111. S&T, November 1883, 608.

112. G.H. Pike, *The Life and Work of Charles Haddon Spurgeon,* 6 vols (London: Cassell & Co., nd), 6:269.

113. S&T, December 1883, 650.

Spurgeon responded in February 1885. "One of the numbers of this periodical contains a most amusing denunciation of that dreadfully bitter bigot, C. H. Spurgeon." What a charming display of literature, and such edifying insight to "see him castigated for his well-known uncharitableness," He noted how easily the editor could move from one piece in which he would "rave and foam at the mouth" into another that displayed a temper "quite kind, and good, and rational." Spurgeon was happy for the remarks upon himself because it helped him to give a more objective evaluation of the rest of the volume.[114]

When he wrote the Preface to the 1885 volume of *The Sword and the Trowel*, Spurgeon summarized his concern, "For the moment, the main battle is with Rationalism." He observed little overt atheism, deism, or honest infidelity but saw plenty of examples of "men who subscribe our creeds and hate them, employ our terms and attach false meanings to them, and even use our pulpits as places of vantage from which to assail the vital verities of our faith." His previous efforts to warn were greeted with censure in the periodicals and he was resistant to being pushed into a position of crying "Peace, peace," where there is no peace. For him it became increasingly needful to "strive against a love of quiet than against its opposite." Trimmers drone on about union, but "peace with deadly error is falsehood to souls, and treason to God."[115]

At every opportunity Spurgeon sought to expose the presumptuousness and arrogant claims to priority that the modernists assumed as they intruded into traditional conservative places of preaching and witness. Professedly Christian ministers "entered by stealth into pulpits once occupied by good men and true." They inserted into the ministries and messages "universalism of the most pernicious kind," defended Socinianism, scoffed at the inspiration of Scripture while hiding behind the motto that the Bible alone is the religion of the Protestants. A convenient motto when needed to escape the supposed oppression of a creed. Add to that mere professional preaching and *ex officio* creed-repeating and one has a combination of wretchedness and despicable ministerial posturing that is the "devil's most effectual method of propagating falsehood and defeating truth."[116] In 1884, Samuel Cox, a Baptist, was dismissed as editor of *The Expositor* because of his increasingly liberal viewpoints that began to color the magazine more boldly in that direction. "No amount of ability on the part of a writer can make him less dangerous if his views are unsound," and none that teach unscriptural doctrine should be continued in employment "merely because they make a magazine pay." Each man must spread truth as far as he knows and must not be a party to the circulation of error. The publishers settled with Cox on generously fair terms but that did not stop the liberals from lifting a shriek of "persecution." Spurgeon was not surprised at this for the advanced school had no true idea of mental liberty. With a keen sense of irony, Spurgeon personified what he felt was the real arrogance of the proponents of modern thought:

> Superciliously they reckon that they do us honour by allowing us the privilege of being snubbed. Know ye not that the orthodox fools are bound to let their enlightened opponents say whatever they please, and to thank them and pay them for saying it? The orthodox have, in fact, no right but that of being exterminated. The men of advanced views have a right to take their pulpits, edit their periodicals, and in general play all the tricks they

114. S&T, February 1885, 82.

115. S&T, 1885, Preface, iv.

116. S&T, February 1884, 51.

please; and if this be in the least objected to, the protester is a persecutor! Bah![117]

Contributing to the sick spell he experienced in the winter of 1885 was the mental burden of considering that the "times are dark, false doctrine abounds, and a doubting spirit is in the air." He hoped for a Pentecostal visitation, a heavenly fire that would descend on the annual Conference of Pastors' College graduates and students.[118] Sick and distressed, and so tired that the "bow was ready to snap," but nevertheless determined, Spurgeon preached at the conference on Isaiah 50:7, "Therefore have I set my face like flint."[119]

He told his congregation in the autumn of 1885 that in this day of "declension and vanity" they needed a revival of "old-fashioned doctrine." At first, so the critics harped, Calvinism was too harsh, then evangelical doctrines were antiquated, and now the Scriptures themselves must be altered and improved. Neither total depravity nor the atonement are preached—punishment for sin has obediently stayed hidden from view—and though the deity of Christ is not assailed, the gospel he gave is questioned, criticized, and set aside. Missionaries are sent, not to deliver the nations from the wrath to come but to prepare them for the new and higher realm into which they will enter at death. "I confess," Spurgeon snorted, "I have better hopes for the future of the heathen than for the state of those who thus write concerning them."[120] A revival of preaching that had the infallible standard of the Bible at its foundation, and ruin, redemption, and regeneration as a summary of its content, was the immediate need of the hour. "Beware of those who say that there

is no hell," Spurgeon warned, "and who declare new ways to heaven. May the Lord have mercy upon them."[121]

By March of 1886, Spurgeon had had enough of the apparent policy of gradualism tolerated by the Baptist Union in allowing the infidelity of modern thought to infiltrate the fellowship. He had given much, preached at the meetings, defended the theological integrity of the Union, engaged in and complimented the fellowship but now believed a dangerous spirit of toleration had become a destructive principle. Correction was needed. "Who Are the Persecuted?" he asked in an article. The days of narrowness and bigotry clearly are gone, and good riddance said Spurgeon. But firm adherence to principle has been thrown out with it, and now, any that desire doctrinal guidelines and clear exclusive statements of truth are viewed as uncooperative, intolerant persecutors. Bur liberalism, Spurgeon contended, is "more bitter than the old bigotry, more intolerant than the old sectarianism. It will not allow orthodoxy to call anything its own; it would filch from it every house it has built, every pulpit it has raised."[122]

They clamor for charity while giving none, ask for a generous spirit while robbing the treasury of truth, and assault the consciences of believers and complain of being persecuted. They claim a right to pulpits whose creed they detest and of whose worship they do not approve. "Until it can be proven," Spurgeon boiled, "that it is the natural right of hogs to root up our flower-gardens, it will never be proved that it is the right of rationalists to destroy our churches."[123] Their ideal of freedom would eliminate any rights of worship and theological discretion of a local congregation:

---

117. S&T, February 1885, 83.

118. S&T, April 1885, 194.

119. S&T, June, 1885, 296.

120. S&T, October 1885, 515.

121. Ibid.

122. S&T, March 1886, 106.

123. Ibid., 107.

Let him take his opinions anywhere he likes in the open market; nobody denies his liberty of speech; the world is large enough. But if Christian people are so simple as to say that they do not desire to hear him blaspheme their God and his gospel, in the name of justice what right has he to force himself upon them? What right have newspapers to denounce those who will not receive him? What justification is there for his outcry that he is persecuted? Forsooth, he is persecuted by not being allowed to persecute other people![124]

Spurgeon had taken strong positions through the years on modern thought, its sinister destructive influence, its arrogance and haughty claims to superiority, and its grasping for ecclesiastical prerogative, but had focused his attention mostly on other denominations. That Spurgeon had in mind activities within his denomination became clear in the final two paragraphs of this broadside. "We have desired peace, and therefore have been quiet," he noted; "we have hoped for the best, and have waited in patience." He had believed in the brethren and expected to see them return to a better mind. His patient endurance and hope for change had been met only with effrontery and greater boldness in proclamation of error. He lamented division of the past and foresaw that more would be calamitous without bringing relief. Plain, honest witness-bearing was always a biblical action, however, "and if it be coupled with a decided withdrawal from fellowship with error, it may in due time work for good." None could expect him to "meet in professed communion with those who insult our religion," nor to supply pecuniary aid for the advancement of error. He would not erect a platform and furnish an audience for adversaries of the faith. "When the interests of our Lord clash with those of de-

nominations and societies, we need no time for deliberation. The ties of friendship, and the bonds of ecclesiastical union, are as rotten threads compared with the bands of love which unite us to Christ and to his holy gospel."[125]

In April, Spurgeon commented, "Denominational papers are silent upon the solemn matters upon which we wrote in our first article last month. No doubt they have their reasons." He quoted with approval the comment made in the *Word and Work* when it reprinted Spurgeon's article fully. "Surely the time is not distant when those who are in agreement upon fundamental truths must take some definite action towards a firm and united testimony."[126]

When he spoke about these sobering realities to his Pastors' Conference in May, Spurgeon's tone was different. He thought he saw the energy waning in the camp of infidelity; if so, he was wrong. Perhaps he simply took a look at it in the light of eternity and saw it as a mere speck to be wiped away in accordance with divine decree. On closer inspection, the "modern thought" that had looked very much like a terrible lion, now appeared like a fox, or even a wild cat. The mountain had brought forth its mouse and soon "advanced thought" would be mentioned only by "servant girls and young Independent ministers." The purveyors of modern thought had seen their congregations dwindle away beneath its withering power and "they are, therefore, not quite so enamoured of it as they were." Looseness in doctrine usually was of a piece with general looseness of religion. "Want of soundness in the faith is usually occasioned by want of conversion" and the people to whom these speak have observed that they have not been "remarkable for abundant grace." More than the changing tide of theological

---

124. Ibid., 108.

125. Ibid.

126. S&T, April 1886, 194.

opinion, however, Spurgeon trusted in the eternal truth of divine revelation and the certainty that those who fear the name of the Lord shall "pass on to possess the promised inheritance."[127]

Spurgeon also had come to think that great crusades for radical change were doomed to failure. He admired the valor and conviction of those who believed they could halt the decline of the denomination, but Spurgeon advised his men, "Even our own denomination must go its own way." They should use their powers for work well within their reach, and realize that they could not remove the earth of the curse of thorns but should make a few blades of grass grow in their own little plot. They must learn to do more by doing less.[128] The man who previously could not be restrained within the bounds of a single congregation, but must itinerate throughout the land, now only prayed for sufficient strength to be faithful to the charge immediately before him.

Spurgeon could not rest in good conscience, however, until he had given one last shot at calling his brethren back from the edge of a theological death-plummet.

---

127. S&T, June 1886, 255.

128. Ibid., 255, 257.

15

The Downgrade Conflict

It is my highest ambition to be clear of the blood of all men. I have preached God's truth, so far as I know it, and I have not been ashamed of its peculiarities. That I might not stultify my testimony I have cut myself clear of those who err from the faith, and even from those who associate with them.[1]

Spurgeon was not in the business of creating a stir over minor issues. He despised wrangling over minutiae, splitting over whims, and arguing over issues that could be reduced to merely personal differences. In an 1879 woodcut article entitled "Much Ado about Nothing" he pictured a ploughman, a young boy, four horses, and a plough all stopped in a field with the cause being the capture of a small field mouse. Such was typical of much religious squabbling that arose over a "point of order," "merely personal differences," a "personal feud," or an "infinitesimal point of opinion." These things went on while "the masses are perishing for want of the gospel." Good men are willing to spend time and money in "inventing and publishing mere speculations, while the great field of the world lies unploughed and the hemlock of vice is running to seed all over it." Away with small matters that divide and

sap spiritual strength for truly mammoth challenges that demand legitimately all the Christian's energy and wit. "O that love to God and a concern for the salvation of men would lead good men to use their brains and their hearts, and leave little things alone while eternal matters call for their attention." A particularly onerous violation of Spurgeon's perception of Christian calling occurred when "a whole denomination of Christians will debate and dispute over merely personal differences which only in the smallest degree affect the grand enterprise in which heaven and earth are concerned."[2]

A denominational dispute over style, merely personal preferences, or even new ideas that were harmless in consequence but thieves of precious energy and time did not attract Spurgeon at all. He would never have involved a denomination in battle over mere personality. Truth was too dear,

---

1. SS, 19:399. "No Compromise."

2. S&T, October 1879, 488.

souls were too precious, and the glory of Christ of too much consequence to detract from them for lesser things. Only when those very things were the issues would a confrontation be commensurate with the cost of it.

Spurgeon Reveals an Impasse

In addition to his reticence to promote division over a field mouse, he had enjoyed great popularity in the Baptist Union and frequently was asked to occupy the prime place of preaching at Union meetings. In 1875 he wrote, after having returned from the Baptist Union meeting in Plymouth, "We felt ashamed to be so very prominent, for it is the last thing in our thoughts to wish to be placed in the front; but friends would have it so, and we yielded." He wanted other and younger men to be brought forward and the preachers and speakers to be selected from "as wide a range as possible."[3]

It was not, therefore, in the interest of a petty personal concern, unless Spurgeon's sense of proportion completely vanished, that he led a charge beginning in 1887 that threatened the existence of the Baptist Union. More than mouse-catching was at stake. The historic Christian faith was receiving scourging and beating in the house of supposed friends. As Spurgeon put it, "The case is mournful. Certain ministers are making infidels. Avowed atheists are not a tenth as dangerous as those preachers who scatter doubt and stab at faith."[4]

When Spurgeon began publishing articles in his monthly magazine, *The Sword and the Trowel*, in which he lamented the theological direction of his denomination and of non-conformity in general, he had little comprehension of the widespread nature of the movement he characterized as the "downgrade." The preface to *The Sword and Trowel* that year remarked:

We have had enough of "The Down-Grade" for ourselves when we have looked down upon it. What havoc false doctrine is making, no tongue can tell. Assuredly the New Theology can do no good towards God or man; it has no adaptation for it. If it were preached for a thousand years by all the most earnest men of the school, it would never renew a soul, nor overcome pride in a single human heart ...

The sword and trowel have both been used this year with all our might. We have built up the wall of the city, and have tried to smite the king's enemies. How could we help it? No loyal soldier could endure to see his Lord's cause so grievously wronged by traitors. Something will come of the struggle over the Down-Grade.[5]

This preface was written after the events of 1887 and, therefore, after Spurgeon's withdrawal from the Baptist Union. Even with his jeremiad concerning the Down-Grade, Spurgeon indicated a greater optimism than, as later events proved, he had any evidence for exhibiting. That he really expected something to come of the struggle is indicated by a letter he wrote from France to his wife. Some of his brethren had accused him of unscriptural conduct by leaving the Union after making only general accusations concerning the theological integrity of his brethren. Spurgeon courteously but soundly denied their accusations and claimed that he had laid his specific complaints before the leaders of the Union on various occasions in private. He contemplated the hope that his leaving might provoke some progress. "Now, something will be done. Not until I took the decided step could I effect anything."[6]

In March of 1887, an article entitled *The Down-Grade* appeared in *The Sword and the*

---

3. S&T, November 1875, 545.

4. S&T, August 1887, 399.

5. S&T, 1887, Preface.

6. C.H. Spurgeon, *Autobiography*. Comp. Susannah Spurgeon and Joseph Harrold first published in 4 volumes, 1897-1900; rev. ed. 2 vols. (Edinburgh: Banner of Truth Trust, 1973) 2:471.

Trowel. The author, Robert Shindler, traced the historical development of several non-conformist denominations from soundness of doctrine into various hues of heresy. Spurgeon attached a footnote to this first article in which he requested "earnest attention" to the warning implied by Shindler. He continued, "We are going down hill at break-neck speed."[7]

Article two, appearing in April, continued the historical study of languishing denominations and sought to pinpoint the "causes of the sad decay in piety and principle."

> In the case of every errant course there is always a first wrong step. ... Is it doubting their doctrine, or questioning that sentiment, or being skeptical as to the other article of orthodox belief? We think not. ... The first step astray is a want of adequate faith in the divine inspiration of the sacred Scriptures. All the while a man bows to the authority of God's Word, he will not entertain any sentiment contrary to its teaching ... But let a man question or entertain low views of the inspiration and authority of the Bible, and he is without anchor to hold him ... If this be a fact—and who can disprove it? —then we live in dangerous times, and there is great peril very near all those, whoever they may be, who call in question the inspiration—the divine inspiration—of the Word of God.[8]

Shindler, though personally devoted to Calvinism as an overall theological system, was clear in highlighting the problem as directly linked to one's view of the authority of Scripture rather than any disagreement between Calvinists and Arminians. Spurgeon agreed. He had pleasure in his fellowship with evangelical Methodists, though he would wish them Calvinists, and stated "we care far more for the central evangelical truths than we do for Calvinism as a system." Those who agreed in affirming the eternal verities of salvation, even though they would sidestep Spurgeon's Calvinism, were "by no means the object of (Spurgeon's) opposition."[9] In 1877 Spurgeon pointed out that the Wesleyan Methodists "have adhered to their own distinctive creed while nearly all other denominations have been unfaithful to theirs." If they have changed, he said then, it has been for the better, for neither the favor of the wealthy classes nor the pressure for "freedom on inquiry" had moved them from their first principles. Spurgeon counted them as "fellow witnesses for Christ: witnesses to his atoning death and justifying righteousness, though not to the same extent to the glorious privileges derived from them."[10] When Spurgeon reviewed *Record of Events in Primitive Methodism*, written by a Primitive Methodist minister Thomas Russell, he noted that "There is more similarity between this humble Methodist and the apostles than could be found in all the bishops of the United Kingdom, even if their cathedrals and palaces were searched with candles."[11]

> Our warfare is with men who are giving up the atoning sacrifice, denying the inspiration of Holy Scripture, and casting slurs upon justification by faith. The present struggle is not a debate upon the question of Calvinism or Arminianism, but of the truth of God versus the inventions of men.[12]

Even though this position was taken early in Spurgeon's presentation of the issues, some continued to pass it off as his desire to stir the coals of the feud between Calvinists and Arminians.

---

7. S&T, March 1887, 122.

8. S&T, April 1887, 170.

9. Ibid., 195.

10. S&T, March 1877, 138.

11. S&T, November 1869, 524.

12. S&T, April 1887, 195, 196.

On the contrary, he insisted many Arminians are "earnestly on our side," he wrote in December. He made no effort to conceal his Calvinism but this battle was for foundation truths that do not belong to one party or another. Don't drag that red herring across our path, Spurgeon, chided, for Calvinists and Arminians can argue other points and "maintain Christian harmony at the same time." The relationship is quite different, however, with those that "treat the Bible as waste paper, and regard the death of Christ as no substitution." "We have come out in earnest protest" against this clear infidelity "and feel great content of conscience in having done so."[13]

Robert Shindler, in June of 1887, continued focusing his attention on the issue of biblical inspiration. He wrote an article highlighting the trial of five professors at Andover Theological Seminary in Andover, Massachusetts. It served as a case in point providing evidence that the first step "in departure from orthodox belief" was variance with the creed of the seminary "and the general belief of orthodox Christians" on the subject of inspiration. The trial showed that they held the Bible to be fallible "not only in matters of science and chronology, but in some of its religious teachings also."[14] Scripture, according to these Andover professors, did not arise from revelation but rather from the inner consciousness of the religious writers and must be interpreted by the present-day reader's inner consciousness. Therefore, the words of Scripture are not infallible but serve only as vehicles of inspiration. In light of this tendency, these professors taught that the humanity of Christ limited his faculties to the point that he was fallible; the atonement consisted merely of his assumption of human nature, adopting all humanity into himself ren-

dering them salvable and giving them power to repent, and had nothing to do with a vicarious death fulfilling the just demands of the law. Other doctrines suffered a similar fate under the guidance of a so-called Christian consciousness. In fact, the Christ of the Gospels and the Epistles is gone and the whole church might well weep with Mary, "They have taken away my Lord, and I know not where they have laid him."

Only firm conviction in the full inspiration of Scripture will save the church from such a plight according to Shindler:

> Look at the work of Luther and others in Germany, at the work of Zwingle in Switzerland, at the work of Calvin in France, and at the work of the Puritans in England. Mark the career of President Edwards, of George Whitefield, of the founders of Welsh Methodism, of the Haldanes in Scotland, of Robert Haldane at Geneva, of the late Dr. Malan in Geneva, … and the most successful soul-winners in England, and you will find them to a man sound on the inspiration of Holy Scripture. The Wesleyan Methodists of all parties are sound on that question. And whatever "down-grade" tendency there may be in their Arminian theology, faith in the inspiration of the Word of God and in the atoning work of the Lamb checks all downward progress.[15]

Spurgeon himself entered his protests to the Downgrade in August of 1887 in an article entitled *Another Word Concerning the Downgrade*. He showed as much concern for the evidence of spiritual decline as for theological decline. "At the back of doctrinal falsehood," Spurgeon opined, "comes a natural decline of spiritual life." To discern which of these comes first poses a difficulty, but Spurgeon later reiterated, "It is clear to every one who is willing to see it that laxity of doctrine

---

13. S&T, December 1887, 642.

14. S&T, June 1887, 275.

15. Ibid., 279-80.

is either the parent of worldliness, or is in some other way very near akin to it." The connection is indissoluble and the "men who give up the old faith are the same persons who plead for latitude as to general conduct."[16] In fact, as the controversy unfolded, some were more eager to question Spurgeon's theological critique than his analysis of the spiritual life of the churches. "Doctrine has been the ground of battle in the Down-Grade struggle which has been chosen by our opponents," Spurgeon revealed, "but on the matter of prayer-meetings and worldliness, they have been prudently silent."[17]

Since the counter-attackers chose doctrine as the place most likely to discredit the alarmist, Spurgeon, while not ignoring the distressing spiritual decline, went from sermon to sermon and journal to journal pointing out what he considered obviously fatal doctrinal errors. Primary sources for illustrating his point throughout the controversy came from his perennial nemesis, *The Christian World* magazine. Spurgeon described his relation to this magazine when he wrote, "We view matters from a point of view which is precisely the opposite of *The Christian World*." As mentioned earlier, he formed a principled objection to their theological agenda shortly after having given a positive mark to them for the theological candor of the editor. When he quoted it, as he did frequently, in confirmation of his own observations, he referred to the paper as "our antagonistic cotemporary."[18] In exposing the doctrinal slide among so-called evangelicals, Spurgeon pointed to *The Christian World* as the periodical to which was "largely due the prevalence of this mischief." By 1887, the publisher claimed a weekly readership of 500,000. Spurgeon was happy

that they did not hide their hand but manifested their faith, or lack of it, in bold contours for all to see. He looked to the following paragraph as peculiarly symptomatic of the downgrade slide of theology:

> We are now at the parting of the ways, and the younger ministers especially must decide whether or not they will embrace and undisguisedly proclaim that "modern thought" which in Mr. Spurgeon's eyes is a "deadly cobra," while in ours it is the glory of the century. It discards many of the doctrines dear to Mr. Spurgeon and his school, not only as untrue and unscriptural, but as in the strictest sense immoral; for it cannot recognize the moral possibility of imputing either guilt or goodness, or the justice of inflicting everlasting punishment for temporary sin. It is not so irrational as to pin its faith to verbal inspiration, or so idolatrous as to make its acceptance of a true Trinity of divine manifestations cover polytheism.[19]

That magazine's admission of the facts, including the cavalier dismissal of the importance of Trinitarian theology, justified, in Spurgeon's view, his earlier attacks upon the tenets of modern thought, which was "no more Christianity than chalk is cheese." Destitute of "moral honesty" and posing as the old faith with needed improvements, in the new theology "the atonement is scouted, the inspiration of Scripture is derided, the Holy Spirit is degraded into an influence, the punishment of sin is turned into fiction, and the resurrection into a myth."[20] This skepticism which "has flashed from the pulpit and spread among the people" has emptied, and kept empty, places which the preaching of the gospel had filled. As they ply destructive ware, these "destroyers of our churches appear to be as content with their work as monkeys with

---

16. S&T, December 1887, 606.
17. Ibid.
18. S&T, January 1889, 40.

19. S&T, October 1887, 513.
20. S&T, August 1887, 397.

their mischief." Spurgeon expressed his conviction that "a little plain-speaking would do a world of good just now." In the same way that thieves hate watch-dogs and love darkness, so the downgraders want no noise raised and desire to be left alone. He warned believers to buy new latches for the door, keep the chain up because some under the pretense of begging for the friendship of the servant really aim to rob the Master.[21]

Spurgeon found 1887 to be a year, similar to that of Zephaniah's time, when many were "sorrowful for the solemn assembly" and "to whom the reproach of it was a burden," when "in our solemn assemblies *the brilliance of the gospel light is dimmed by error.*" Spurgeon pointed to doubtful voices among the people that spoiled the clarity of gospel testimony. Truth has been replaced by the imaginations of men and the ephemeral assertions of recent thought. Philosophy replaced revelation, the "larger hope" replaced the infallible pronouncement and judgments of God; "The gospel of Jesus Christ, which is the same yesterday, today, and for ever, is taught as the production of progress, a growth, a thing to be amended and corrected year by year."[22] Such a situation brought about personal remorse because "the house of the Lord is to many of us, our own house, his family is our family." If Christ be not praised and honored and his gospel thus lose its luster, "we feel that our own personal interests are blighted, and we ourselves are in disgrace." This is no small thing, Spurgeon contended, for "it is our life."[23]

Infinitely great is the matter of doctrinal dilution and divergence. Trivialities do not exist on the issue of the comfort of God's people in his truth and their increasing joy in him, increase of holiness, and reliance on his daily grace. "When the pure gospel is not preached, God's people are robbed of the strength which they need in their life-journey." Poison and barrenness replace bread and luxuriant pastures. They become wearied and despondent when instead of true spiritual food "they are worried and wearied with novelties which neither glorify God nor benefit the souls of men."

> When the doctrines of grace and the glorious atoning sacrifice are not set clearly before men's minds, so that they may feel their power, all sorts of evils follow. It is terrible to me that this dreadful blight should come upon our churches; for the hesitating are driven to destruction, the weak are staggered, and even the strong are perplexed. The false teachers of these days would, if it were possible, deceive the every elect. This makes our hearts very sorrowful. How can we help it?[24]

In agreement with a correspondent who commended Spurgeon and pointed to the dismal state of theological instruction in an unnamed theological college, Spurgeon queried "Is there no doctrine left which is to be maintained: Is there no revelation? Or is that revelation a nose of wax to be shaped by the finger of fashion? Are the sceptics so much to the fore that no man will open his mouth against them?" Spurgeon contended that one could find no common ground between inspiration and speculation, between an affirmation and a denial of the atonement, between a doctrine of the fall and "the evolution of spiritual life from human nature," and between the punishment of the impenitent and the indulgence in a "larger hope." But that is precisely what many were willing to do and what they believed he should consent to do. "As a matter of fact,"

---

21. Ibid., 399f.

22. MTP, 1887, 602.

23. Ibid., 604.

24. Ibid., 605.

Spurgeon noted, "believers in Christ's atonement are now in declared religious union with those who make light of it; believers in holy Scripture are in confederacy with those who deny plenary inspiration; those who hold evangelical doctrine are in open alliance with those who call the fall a fable, who deny the personality of the Holy Ghost, who call justification by faith immoral, and hold that there is another probation after death, and a future reconciliation for the lost."[25]

Close at hand, again, to confirm Spurgeon's analysis of the present state of doctrine among dissenters, *The Christian World* in December 1888 pronounced Mr. Spurgeon "well within the mark" in pointing to a "marked defection from the doctrinal standards maintained by their fathers, and still upheld by him." The defection became more visible every day, so they said. They were not congratulating Spurgeon on his rock-solid antiquarianism in theology, but did, for his purposes, serve as a convenient verification of his contention.

Spurgeon quite agreed and only two months before had written, "Every day affords more and more evidence that while many are true to their Lord, unbelief has sadly eaten into Congregational and Baptist churches." Throughout the controversy, Spurgeon did not swerve from his central argument that the issue was neither denominational nor sectarian, but Christianity or infidelity. While he did call for a confessional basis for unity, that basis did not go beyond an affirmation of Protestant evangelicalism as opposed to infidelity. "We are represented as wishing to force upon the churches a narrow creed. Nothing was further from our mind," Spurgeon argued, and pointed out that he had been represented as a "sectarian bigot" because of his "demand for agreement

to vital truths common to all Christians." There he stood as a Calvinist, not demanding that the Union espouse a Calvinistic creed but embrace "one which will let the whole world know that brethren are associated as Christians, and that those who do not agree to the first principles of our faith will be intruders."[26]

Doctrine alone was not the problem, but its fragmentation led to other difficulties. "At the back of doctrinal falsehood comes a natural decline of spiritual life, evidenced by a taste for questionable amusements, and a weariness of devotional meetings."[27] When pastors of repute defend the playhouse because they have been there, at the same time they diminish the spiritual meetings in their churches, so is there any wonder that "members forget their vows of consecration, and run with the unholy in the ways of frivolity?" Spurgeon was sure he would be accused of prudery, bigotry, and joylessness, but he was just as sure that these epithets would demonstrate the low state of spirituality in the churches. When the narrow way and the shouldering of the cross become bigotry and worldly joy is seen to trump "joy unspeakable and full of glory," the church has lost its light and salt. Decline in doctrine and decline in spiritual life go hand in hand. "The doctrinal soon affects the practical," he emphasized.[28] "When the old faith is gone, and enthusiasm for the gospel is extinct, it is no wonder that people seek something else in the way of delight. Lacking bread, they feed on ashes; rejecting the way of the Lord, they run greedily in the path of folly."[29]

As he waited for demonstration that the case was far otherwise than he had stated, Spurgeon found that no one "has shown that prayer meet-

---

26. S&T, October 1888, 562.

27. S&T, August, 1887, 397.

28. MTP, October 1887, 604.

29. S&T, August 1887, 398.

25. S&T, November 1887, 558.

ings are valued, and are largely attended; no one has denied that certain ministers frequent theatres."[30] Rather, in this Laodicean syndrome, prayer is neglected, vain amusements of the world take the luster of holy zeal off the saints, and when Christ by his atoning sacrifice would give them "gold tried in the furnace, and white raiment," they learn to be content with "education, oratory, science, and a thousand other baubles."[31] Spurgeon was convinced that "even irreligious men, who themselves enjoy the amusements of the theatre," realize that ministers that attend the playhouses are "unfit to be their guides in spiritual things." When Spurgeon saw that *The Nonconformist*, a "fit companion for *The Christian World*," argued, "If the conventional prayer-meetings are not largely attended, why should the Christian community be judged by its greater or less use of one particular religious expedient?" and at the same time was unwilling to see a "great branch of art [the theatre] placed under a ban, as if it were no more than an agency of evil," he concluded that "the fact that it is debated is to us sufficient evidence that spiritual religion is at a low ebb in such quarters."[32] Prayer a mere "religious expedient?" Absurd!

Given this state of affairs, Spurgeon did not wonder that many serious-minded persons among the Dissenters were moving back to the ritualism of the established church while others went to the "Brethren," the Darbyites, and still others opted for complete detachment from any identifiable denominational connection. Dissent for the mere sake of dissent is the "bitter fruit of a willful mind," a "degradation," mere "political partisanship," and a "travesty of religion" thus not worthy of maintenance. Some unspiritual

men care nothing for truth and grace but pursue finances, numbers, and respectability. Doctrine does not matter as long as "the political aims of Dissenters are progressing, and there is an advance in social position."[33] When the gospel is fully preached, however, with the Holy Spirit's blessings and the churches consequently thrive in conformity with the New Testament pattern as a vital spiritual force, non-conformity may justify its existence. But when "the gospel is concealed, and the life of prayer is slighted," the entire enterprise "becomes a mere form and fiction."[34]

During these months Spurgeon engaged S. H. Booth, Secretary of the Baptist Union, in private conferences concerning the new theology and even infidelity of many members of the Baptist Union. Readers of *The Sword and the Trowel* frequently sent Spurgeon reports of issues in their own churches or in other churches that they knew in some firsthand way that verified the substance of the theological and spiritual alarm bell he was ringing. He solemnly laid specific evidence before Booth while he continued in *The Sword and the Trowel* to write about theological problems without connecting them with persons in the Baptist Union. Booth reciprocated with some tales of his own. Spurgeon's hesitation to call specific names in his publication, though he continued his theological lamentation, was fueled, in part, by a hope that the situation could be set aright without name-calling, and perhaps he hoped that Booth would support his revelations to such a degree that the weight of their joint testimony would bring about some positive action. In fact some of Spurgeon's information had come from S. H. Booth himself.[35]

---

30. S&T, September 1887, 461.

31. MTP, 1887, 603.

32. S&T, October 1887, 514.

33. MTP, October 1887, 604.

34. S&T, August 1887, 399.

35. W. Y. Fullerton, *C.H. Spurgeon* (London: Williams and Norgate, 1920), 315.

Spurgeon never retreated from maintaining that he had sufficient facts, and could give a precise list of names, with clear and indisputable supporting evidence, to assure the veracity of his claims. "Never let anyone suppose," he wrote, "that we build up our statements upon a few isolated facts, and bring to the front certain regrettable incidents which might as well have been forgotten." He then committed to God alone the prerogative to "reveal the wretched facts which have come under our notice." As far as he was concerned in the matter, "their memory will, we trust, die and be buried with the man who has borne their burden, and held his peace because he had no wish to create disunion."[36]

A flurry of letters and analyses concerning the theological tone of British Christianity in denominational papers including *The Baptist* gave the impression that, overall, all was well and very little departure from accepted theological positions could be detected. Spurgeon read the letters differently and what others regarded as "mere changes of expressions" he saw as "novelties which we judge to be fatal errors from the truth." He observed a "careful balancing of sentences, and a guardedness of statement" which, knowing what he did privately, enabled him "to read a good deal between the lines." The confidence that he shared with S. H. Booth was beginning to aggravate the theological convictions of Spurgeon and make the possibility of continued fraternity in the Baptist Union seem even more remote. "To break the seal of confidential correspondence or to reveal private conversations would not occur to us," he insisted; "but we feel compelled to say that, in one or two cases, the writers have not put in print what we have personally gathered from them on other occasions." In an effort to allay the

fears of others, Spurgeon suspected that they had forgotten their own.[37]

With these facts before him, and the expected support exponentially receding from view, Spurgeon wrote more desperately of the situation than he had in any previous time. He despaired of help among the Baptists. Spurgeon pointed to reports that appeared in other religious monthlies of decline from orthodoxy and spirituality among the ministers and in the churches, and inferred that "There is no use in mincing matters: there are thousands of us in all denominations who believe that many ministers have seriously departed from the truths of the gospel, and that a sad decline of spiritual life is manifest in many churches."[38]

At the beginning of Spurgeon's protests he was challenged by a "friendly critic" to produce the "names of those who had quitted the old faith." Had he done so, Spurgeon surmised, the critic would have been "among the first to lament the introduction of personalities." Now, however, Spurgeon believed that the papers, both liberal and evangelical, had proved his case in their introduction of letters from Baptist ministers that constituted "an ingenuous avowal of the most thorough-going advance from the things which have been assuredly believed among us."[39] In this way, Spurgeon "unwillingly … fulfilled our unhappy task of justifying a warning." If what he had provided in this article did not give "overwhelming evidence, it is from want of space, and want of will, and not from want of power." Sadly, however, "those who have made up their minds to ignore the gravity of the crisis, would not be aroused from their composure though we told our tale in miles of mournful detail."[40]

---

36. S&T, September 1887, 463.

37. S&T, October 1887, 510.

38. Ibid., 511.

39. S&T, October 1887, 513.

40. Ibid., 514.

Spurgeon's Decision to Withdraw

In a clear indication of an announcement he soon would make, Spurgeon justified his absenting himself from the upcoming meeting of the Baptist Union. He posed the question to his readers, "Are brethren who remain orthodox prepared to endorse such sentiments by remaining in union with those who hold and teach them?" After several paragraphs of laying out more of the disgusting phenomena of spiritual and doctrinal downgrade, he answered, "We cannot be expected to meet in any Union which comprehends those whose teaching is upon fundamental points exactly the reverse of that which we hold dear. … With deep regret we abstain from assembling with those whom we dearly love and heartily respect, since it would involve us in a confederacy with those with whom we can have no communion in the Lord."[41] In this action, however, he maintained the hope that "those who banish us may yet be of another mind, and enable us to return." There was a very small window of opportunity, however, for the possibility of Spurgeon's "return" to his rightful place of fellowship among his beloved Baptists. His words had made it clear, that, contrary to later interpretations, he had great respect for the many that held firm to the faith, did not condemn them either for their views or their conscience, but that the few that did not hold firm and yet were received as fully in accord with the purposes of the Union caused a stumbling-block to his conscience that he could not overleap.

The autumn meeting of the Baptist Union failed to mention the Downgrade. Spurgeon concluded that he had no hope of changing the structure from within. This was a matter of deep disappointment to him, for he felt that those that did not belong were being successful in ousting one that did belong. They may maintain their liberty, but "that liberty cannot demand our cooperation." From others, the liberals received both cooperation and liberty, and Spurgeon felt invaded. "If these men believe such things, let them teach them, and construct churches, unions and brotherhoods for themselves!" but, for the honor of honesty, "Why must they come among us?" But they had come, and were determined to stay, and the body turned its head away from dealing with it. Even so, one thing was sure: "In no case will we give them fellowship, or profess to do so." He resigned, therefore, from the Union in October of 1887 and announced his action in the November *Sword and Trowel*: "We retire at once and distinctly from the Baptist Union."[42]

On October 28, 1887, he wrote to Booth, "I beg to intimate to you, as the secretary of the Baptist Union, that I must withdraw from that society." He regretted but had no choice and would give his reasons in *The Sword and the Trowel* for November. "I beg you not to send anyone to me to ask for reconsideration" because he had delayed too long already and each day proved that he had taken his action none too soon. He professed that no "personal pique or ill-will has in the least degree operated upon me" but he took the step only on the highest grounds. Booth responded with a "sense of pain," felt this put some uncertainty in the future, let Spurgeon know that he had "wounded the hearts of some—of many —who honour and love you more than you have any idea of, and whose counsel would have led to a far different result."[43] That Booth felt a different result could have come from counsel demonstrates how far less he was disturbed about their common knowledge than was Spurgeon. Car-

---

41. S&T, October 1887, 515.

42. S&T, November 1887, 560.

43. G. H. Pike, *The Life and Work of Charles Haddon Spurgeon*, 6 vols (London: Cassell & Co., nd), 6:287.

lile, in his striking and contemplative biography of Spurgeon, noted that "Dr. Booth believed that agreement would be reached by conference and compromise, he was 'a born amalgam'; his policy was to keep silent in order not to widen the dispute."[44]

The deacons and elders of the Metropolitan Tabernacle wasted no time in giving their pastor assurance that they united with him in his stand of conscience. On October 27, 1887, the day before Spurgeon actually penned his letter to Booth, they wrote succinctly;

> Resolved, That we, the deacons and elders of the church, worshipping in the Metropolitan Tabernacle, hereby tender to our beloved Pastor, C. H. Spurgeon, our deep sympathy with him in the circumstances that have led to his withdrawal from the Baptist Union. And we heartily concur in our sincere appreciation of the steadfast zeal with which he maintains the doctrines of the gospel of our Lord Jesus Christ in their inspired and apostolic simplicity.

Spurgeon had convinced the officers to say no more and omit several paragraphs that went into great detail as to their high esteem for him and his ministry. Later the burden of opinion, in light of the momentous issues and the part their pastor had played in clarifying what was at stake, they insisted on the publication of a larger statement.

> Our former resolution was passed with unanimous and unhesitating concurrence. But, touching only on one point, it was generally thought inadequate to convey to you, our dear Pastor, a full sense of the affection, the confidence, and the esteem in which you are held by us all. Of this, however, we can offer you no more fitting exposition than the readiness

of each and every one to approve ourselves as "Helps" in the diversified gifts, administrations, and operation of the Holy Spirit with which you have, after the divine order, been so largely entrusted.

And it may not be altogether inappropriate, or inopportune, to record our conviction that you have done good service, on a wide and constantly-widening scale, by affirming the inspiration of the Holy Scriptures of the Old and New Testament; by inculcating the doctrines of grace, as taught by the apostles of our Lord Jesus Christ, under the immediate guidance of the Spirit of God; and by preserving in our midst the uncorrupted simplicity of public worship.

Permit us to add our fervent hope, and our devout prayer, that your vigorous protests against the innovations of "modern thought" in pulpits supposed to be orthodox, will eventually largely promote the unity of the churches of Christ throughout the world.[45]

From the beginning of his actions in this controversy, Spurgeon had recognized that loss of fellowship would be the natural outcome. The extent to which he would be isolated in that eventuality, he did not understand. In his first personal interaction in April 1887, Spurgeon knew that the call for unity and peace would be strong. If not based on the truth of God, however, no real unity existed, though external harmony may persist. A confederacy without truth was a conspiracy rather than a communion. "It is exceedingly difficult in these times," Spurgeon remarked, "to preserve one's fidelity before God and one's fraternity among men."[46] The former must be preferred to the latter. He sang the same tune in August by stating, "It now becomes a serious question how far those who abide by the faith once delivered to the saints should fraternize with those who have

---

44. J. C. Carlile, *C. H. Spurgeon: An Interpretative Biography* (London: The Religious Tract Society, 1933), 249.

45. S&T, December 1887, 641f.

46. S&T, April 1887, 195.

turned aside to another gospel." While love and unity have their legitimate claims, one cannot lend support to betrayers of the Lord. One might have to "overleap all boundaries of denominational restriction for truth's sake," even against the protest of those that argue instead for "denominational prosperity and unity."[47] It is certainly as irrational as it is unbiblical for the "enemies of our faith" to expect Spurgeon to call them brethren and "maintain a confederacy with them."[48]

In September, Spurgeon proclaimed that a chasm had opened between orthodoxy and heterodoxy and no man could go both ways. "Neither when we have chosen our way can we keep company with those who go the other way." He urged every person to use caution, each to take his place conscientiously, not in the spirit of "suspicion or division, but in watchfulness and resolve." On such consideration, "Let us not pretend to a fellowship which we do not feel," Spurgeon went on, "nor hide convictions which are burning in our hearts."[49]

When the October meeting failed to produce any action, Spurgeon was bewildered, but not entirely surprised. He knew how deeply the desire for unity ran and he was "far from undervaluing it." He also knew how often and shrewdly the argument for liberty resounded among his fellow Baptists, and to him "the mercy is that we do not know of any man who desires" the submission of one man's conscience to another. But surrender of truth under the guise of these things is "treason to the Lord Jesus." The refusal of the Union to consider the problems Spurgeon pointed out caused him to make the observation that "they begin to look like Confederacies in Evil." He explained:

Believers in Holy Scripture are in confederacy with those who deny plenary inspiration; those who hold evangelical doctrine are in open alliance with those who call the fall a fable, who deny the personality of the Holy Ghost, who call justification by faith immoral, and hold that there is another probation after death, and a future restitution for the lost.[50]

In view of this situation, Spurgeon concluded that he had no choice but to separate. His solemn conviction taught him that where "there can be no real spiritual communion there should be no pretense of fellowship." To seek to maintain such where "known and vital error" dominates "is participation in sin." Those who accept "Holy Scripture to be the inspired truth of God cannot have fellowship with those who deny the authority from which we derive all our teaching."[51]

After Spurgeon's resignation, S. H. Booth denied having received any critical information from Spurgeon "such as would have justified them in laying it before the council of the Assembly."[52] When Spurgeon, now in Mentone, France, heard of Booth's claim he was perplexed to bewilderment: "For Dr. Booth to say I never complained is dismaying. God knows all about it and will see me righted."[53] On December 30, 1887, he wrote to Mr. C. M. Longhurst: "When centered upon my painful task, I did not expect that so many whom I esteem would deny the existence of the evil. It would be far easier to deal with the erring than with those worthy brethren who protect them."[54] It was probably faint comfort to Spurgeon when, on November 3, *The Christian World* confirmed

---

47. S&T, August 1887, 400.

48. Ibid., 397.

49. S&T, September 1887, 465.

50. S&T, November 1887, 558.

51. Ibid., 559.

52. Pike, 6:292.

53. *Autobiography*, 2:472.

54. Pike., 6:293.

his complaint while criticizing him by certifying, "It is a plain and literal fact that those who share the opinions he condemns constitute a very large majority of all thinking Christian people."[55]

Spurgeon spoke sincerely and with some sympathy of the "paternal partiality" of a denomination's leadership that made them turn a blind eye to evil and influenced, not their truthfulness, but their judgment. It gave them a guardedness of statement natural to an administrator determined to preserve the prestige of a body. This was "so natural, and so sacred" that Spurgeon did not have the heart to censure it. But also, the protective instinct he recognized as so powerful that "quite unconsciously and innocently, they grow oblivious of evils which, to the unofficial mind, are as manifest as the sun in the heavens." Concerning the power of this protective attitude Spurgeon wrote:

> If we were not extremely anxious to avoid personalities, we could point to other utterances of some of these esteemed writers which, if they did not contradict what they have now written, would be such a supplement to it that their entire mind would be better known. To break the seal of confidential correspondence, or to reveal private conversations, would not occur to us; but we feel compelled to say that, in one or two cases, the writers have not put in print what we have personally gathered from them on other occasions. Their evident desire to allay the apprehensions of others may have helped them to forget their own fears. We say no more.[56]

While Booth and Spurgeon were mutually aware of difficulties and had common knowledge of the specific views of several individuals, the denials of others made Spurgeon say in some amaze-

ment, "their *not* seeing cannot alter the conviction of a man in his senses who has seen it, has seen it for years, and is seeing it now. The witness rubs his eyes to see whether he is awake."[57] As for Booth, he simply did not consider the nature of the problem worthy of reprimand, or loss of unity a fair exchange for theological confrontation. Giving some direct thought to this phenomenon after forty-six years of mulling it over, Carlile, in 1933, made the striking observation: "Spurgeon never was righted. The impression in many quarters still remains that he made charges which could not be substantiated, and when properly called upon to produce his evidence he resigned and ran away. Nothing is further from the truth. Spurgeon might have produced Dr. Booth's letters; I think he should have done so."[58]

Spurgeon found this politicizing of theological truth that led to the coddling of heresy as alarming, saddening, and infuriating. "My blood boils that so many men should dare to assail that which the Lord Jehovah has appointed," Spurgeon preached in the month following his resignation from the Baptist Union. He viewed the atoning work of Christ as elemental, as constituent, to Christian faith and he "would not speak sweetly of those who deal scurvily with Christ. If they be enemies of Christ, our Sacrifice, they cannot be friends of ours. We shake the dust off our feet against those who reject the doctrine of a crucified Saviour, slain in the sinner's stead." The intellectual commitment to the doctrine so inhered in his affections that his whole being revulsed at any tampering with this God-given remedy for sin. "Oh it brings the tears into our eyes, and the blood into our cheeks, that any should trample on the precious blood, and speak ill of the vicarious sufferings of Christ!" The glory of God, the grace

---

55. Cited in Carlile, 252.
56. S&T, October 1887, "The Case Proved," 510.
57. Ibid.
58. Carlile, 248-49.

of God, the covenantal arrangement of salvation, and thus the sinner's hope all are bound up in the substitutionary death of Christ and, therefore, Spurgeon said, "As we love the souls of men, we will spend our last breath in the defence of our Lord's substitution."[59]

For the modern reinterpretations of Christ's atonement that marginalized substitution as out of keeping with an enlightened ethical sense, Spurgeon felt an alarm in his soul:

> We cannot help regarding those as worse than carrion crows who would desire to touch this sublimest though simplest of all doctrines, that Jesus Christ bore our sins in his own body on the tree. They dare to say that it is immoral to suppose that our sin could be transferred to Christ, or his righteousness to us. Thus, to charge the essential act of grace with immorality, is to profane the sacrifice of God, and count the blood of Jesus an unholy thing.[60]

Thus, Spurgeon saw the Downgrade not only as an assault upon any number of verities of the Christian faith, but as an *attitude* toward doctrine. He said he had been "slenderly cheered lately by a large number of brethren who have greatly sympathized with me, and helped me to fight the Lord's battles by bravely looking on." Spurgeon found lack of theological nerve quite a bother. He also found theological indifference quite opposed to the spirit of the gospel. His desire was faithfulness to "the doctrine of truth" as well as the "spirit of love." While seeking to avoid personal bitterness, the Christian nevertheless must "spare none of the errors which insult the sacrifice of our Lord, destroy the way of salvation in this life, and then seek to delude men with the

dream of salvation after death." These errors are complicated by the fact that many who know better "closed their eyes to serious divergencies from truth." Perhaps they felt that these errors would simply go away as those who held them passed from the scene or reformed under the influence of advancing knowledge. Spurgeon had no such confidence but contended that the "new views are not the old truth in a better dress, but deadly errors with which we can have no fellowship." Spurgeon regarded the so-called modern thought as "a totally new cult, having no more relation to Christianity than the mist of the evening to the everlasting hills."[61]

Response of the Baptist Union Council

Spurgeon's persistence in withholding specific information of the sort that the council would consider "proof" of heresy, was due in part to the presence of John Clifford on the council. Clifford's personal admiration for Spurgeon's spiritual qualities is a fact well-attested as is the fact that Spurgeon was personally fond of Clifford. Spurgeon had preached at the opening of the new facility at Westbourne Park. Spurgeon published an article by Clifford in the first year of *The Sword and the Trowel*, July 1865, entitled "The Utilization of Church Power." Clifford asked a very Spurgeonic question as the basis for the article, "In what way may the entire spiritual force of each redeemed man and woman be brought into the most efficient activity of the well-being of men and the glory of Christ." What could Spurgeon possibly have been suspicious of in Clifford's very practical and spiritual word of admonition to ministers in this context:

> Let me speak freely unto you brethren. Do you think that we, as ministers, have sought sufficiently

---

59. MTP, 1887, 639-41.

60. Ibid., 640.

61. Pike, 6:291.

for the means of quickening and encouraging our own spiritual life, our own religious fervor, our devout aspirations for deepened holiness and zeal? We have meetings for the discussions of doctrines; they are good. Not a word will I say against them. We have attended to organizations which sharpen the intellect, please the fancy, and extend the range of scriptural knowledge; these are good. Not a word will I say against them. But when I remember that the apostles gave themselves to prayer, as well as the ministry of the Word, and further that the efficiency of Church-work hinges in so large a measure upon the character and spirit of the overseer, I am impelled to the conclusion that more attention ought to be paid by ministers of the gospel to those means which may issue in the quickening of their religious life and the increase of their spiritual fervour.[62]

His practical suggestions harmonized perfectly with Spurgeon's view of seeking to implement every gift of every member and every opportunity for gospel influence. Every addition to the church should not be the mere addition of a name but of a life fully intent on practical work for the advance of the gospel, holiness, and the glory of Christ. The talents and peculiar gifts of women should be fully utilized, with the exception of teaching in the assembly. Christian businessmen can elevate the moral influence of a neighborhood by investing in strategic places and being successful at helpful constructive enterprises. Conversation meetings in church on Sunday evenings can bring sinners to a knowledge of Christ and engage church members "possessed of special aptitudes for such work." Clifford also found useful the practice of inquiring into the spiritual condition of the relatives of church members "followed up by advice concerning the unconverted, as to the means most likely, speaking after the manner

of men, to bring about their conversion to God."[63] Spurgeon did all of these things and the advice for such relevant and spiritual means of making the gospel known he was happy to give wide distribution through his monthly paper.

Fullerton reported the incident in which Spurgeon said to Clifford, "I cannot imagine Clifford, why you do not come to my way of thinking," referring to Calvinism. Clifford responded, "You see, Mr. Spurgeon, I only see you about once a month, but I read my Bible every day." Fullerton, who knew them both well, listed Clifford as "one of Mr. Spurgeon's most ardent admirers."[64] A review of the *General Baptist Magazine*, bound volume for 1871, began with the commendation, "Our General Baptist friends were wise in their generation when they obtained the able services of Mr. Clifford. He has made their magazine worthy of them."[65] Seven years only increased Spurgeon's estimation of Clifford's ability. "*The General Baptist Magazine* is edited with marvelous vigour," Spurgeon wrote in 1879, "and in every page reveals a masterly hand. Mr. Clifford is eye and soul to the General Baptist body: long may he be preserved to fill his place among the brethren."[66] When Clifford edited a book of eight lectures given by General Baptist ministers, Spurgeon commended the book, though "all the world knows that C. H. S. is not a General Baptist," as an important and well-executed undertaking by the General Baptists. He commented, "Our friend, Dr. Clifford, speaks too generously of C. H. Spurgeon, otherwise we have no fault to find."[67] Early in 1882 Spurgeon gave a notice to the *General Baptist Magazine*, particularly the editor "whose

---

62. S&T, July 1865, 307, 309, 310.

63. Ibid., 310, 311.

64. Fullerton, 255.

65. S&T, February 1872, 92.

66. S&T, January 1879, 37.

67. S&T, August 1881, 416.

vigorous intellect has made their magazine a power."[68] This conflict had the potential to diminish the luster of that admiration in both parties.

Spurgeon may have hoped that Clifford would resign from the Union and encourage those of his mentality to do likewise. Perhaps he was one that Spurgeon described when he wrote, "Numbers of easy-minded people wink at error so long as it is committed by a clever man and a good-natured brother, who has so many fine points about him."[69] When it became evident that Clifford was firmly entrenched in Baptist Union life and had no intention of leaving and even failed to see any degree of equivocation in his own position, Spurgeon abandoned all hope of reversing the direction of "downgrade" theology.

Drs. Culross, McLaren, Clifford, and Booth wired Spurgeon that they were coming to visit him in France to deliberate how the unity of the denomination might be maintained. Spurgeon discouraged their coming and asked that they await his return. He had no desire to be put at a disadvantage by being the cause of such great expense, especially when he suspected that they only intended to fix on him "the odium of being implacable."[70] From Mentone, he wrote to an American pastor and newspaper editor, T. T. Eaton, in Louisville, Kentucky, explaining his actions, since some aspects of his resignation from the Baptist Union were not quite clear. He told Eaton:

> I do not wish friends in America to judge the matter hastily. They cannot know the ins and outs of the case. But I would have them believe that I would not have quitted our Baptist Union if I had not felt driven to do so.

It has never comprehended the more strongly Calvinistic brethren; but that is not my complaint. It has in it a few very pronounced "modern thought" men. These are by no means to be charged with reticence, they have had sufficient opportunities to inflict their novelties upon us. I have protested and protested but in vain.

Many do not believe that this "new theology"exists to any degree worthy of notice. I know that it does and cannot but wonder that any should question it. Of course those who think all is well think one a needless alarmist.

Another section is first of all for peace and unity and hopes that the erring ones will come right, and therefore they are grieved to see the matter ventilated.

Others hope to purge and save the Union. All my best desires go with these; but I have no hope of it. Essentially, there is no doctrinal basis to begin with and many believe this to be a great beauty. "Down with all creeds" seems to be the watchword.

Protests failing, I left; and this has caused more enquiry than a thousand papers would have done. I do not see that I could have done else. Others might not be under such a compulsion till they have tried to mend matters and have failed as I have done. With no confession of faith, or avowal of principles, there's nothing to work upon; and I do not see the use of repairing a house that is built on the air.[71]

Spurgeon summarized themes that would be visited many times in the coming months, and particularly with the conciliation group appointed by the Council. Spurgeon met with this group, minus Dr. McLaren, in January of 1888 and their subsequent, if not consequent, action confirmed Spurgeon's suspicions and justified his confession that he had "no hope" of a doctrinal purging. One week after that meeting, the council of the Union met

---

68. S&T, February 1882, 87.

69. S&T, August 1887, 400.

70. *Autobiography*, 4:257.

71. Handwritten letter in Eaton file, The Southern Baptist Theological Seminary Archives.

and voted a virtual "censure" of Spurgeon because he had not supported his charges of doctrinal laxity by naming the offending parties. Again, Spurgeon could not bring himself to name individuals but was content with describing the problems in general, being fully convinced that everyone could plainly see that his concerns had abundant substance and that he had made his case by necessary inference in his October article. Such charges, according to the council, ought not to have been made. The resolution of the Union was as follows:

> That the council recognizes the gravity of the charges which Mr. Spurgeon has brought against the Union previous to and since his withdrawal. It considers that the public and general manner in which they have been made reflects on the whole body, and exposes to suspicion brethren who love the truth as dearly as he does. And as Mr. Spurgeon declines to give the names of those to whom he intended them to apply, and the evidence supporting them, those charges, in the judgment of the Council, ought not to have been made.[72]

Spurgeon responded quickly to this action in an article entitled "The Baptist Union Censure." Technically, this was not the action of the Baptist Union nor did the Council indicate their action was a "censure." Spurgeon, however, took advantage of the action to make clear his stance toward this reprimand. In addition to his confidential arrangement with Booth and his personal deference toward Clifford, Spurgeon revealed another reason that he felt the revelation of names would be useless. It was a major theme of his letter to Eaton. "I brought up no charges before the

members of the Council," Spurgeon explained, "because they could only judge by their constitution." The constitution, however, had only one proposition for a doctrinal basis for the Union, the belief that "the immersion of believers is the only Christian baptism." Only if one foreswore his baptism would he be in default of the doctrinal basis of the Baptist Union. If he had brought charges the Council could do nothing. Should he expose himself to the threat of a lawsuit and gain nothing by it? The Union, as it stood, was incompetent for doctrinal judgment.[73] As he had suggested earlier, it seemed that the Union was not "an assemblage of evangelical churches," but "an indiscriminate collection of communities practicing immersion."[74]

Spurgeon felt the council had betrayed him by sending the four men to "deliberate" with him on the best means of preserving the unity of the denomination in "truth, and love, and good works." Though such was the stated intent of their attempt to "deliberate," their real intent was to provoke a recantation from Spurgeon, the failure of which would produce a censure. "It is quite as well," Spurgeon philosophized, "that their resolutions should be as incomprehensible as their doctrinal position is undefinable." That, in fact, was the particular issue that he initiated as a valid point of "deliberation" in the meeting. He spoke to the men about the necessity of a more substantial doctrinal basis for the Union, that is, "that it be formed on a Scriptural basis."

One of the saddest aspects of this episodic meeting was the inevitable break of relationship with these four men for whom Spurgeon had had deep respect. Booth had been an intimate friend and confided much in Spurgeon, but his capitulation to denominational policy could do nothing

---

72. Sir James Marchant, *Dr. John Clifford* (London et al.: Cassell and Company Ltd., 1924), p. 160. Also see Carlile, 251, on this event. He sees Booth as the least admirable character in this entire affray; he could have put it right at any moment by revealing that Spurgeon's claim about the correspondence and the reporting of names was true.

73. S&T, February 1888, 81.

74. Letter to C. M. Longhurst in Pike, 6:294.

but sever that trust. He used Spurgeon's honor as a means to keep him from exposing the information that was common to Booth and Spurgeon. Alexander MacLaren was a great preacher whose books Spurgeon had often reviewed and given superlative marks. In 1875 the Baptist Union met in the lecture hall at the Tabernacle and MacLaren chaired the meeting. Spurgeon called him a "noble example of the cultured master and the simple believer united in one. The influence of his inaugural address must be salutary to an immeasurable degree."[75] Spurgeon welcomed the weekly publication of Maclaren's sermons with a sincere bravo for messages "so full of grace and truth." Maclaren—so Spurgeon wrote in 1885—was a "man of no ordinary stature." He was "eloquent, thoughtful, masterly, and for this reason, and because of the divine life which is in him, he does not pander to the age, but abides by the gospel of all ages." Spurgeon could think of no other sermons that he would more heartily commend to the younger brethren.[76]

Clifford, a General Baptist had been an object of Spurgeon's affections and admiration for decades. He viewed the gifts of Culross as superlative and his potential for good unlimited. Spurgeon's review of Culross' book on the church at Laodicea made the point emphatically. "Above all living teachers," Spurgeon affirmed, "we prefer Dr. Culross. He ought to preach to all the ministers in London at least once a week." It was neither Culross' voice nor eloquence that so commended him to Spurgeon, but his "ripeness of thought and beauty of expression which in our judgment are scarcely equaled, and not in one instance surpassed, by those of any other living teacher known to us." Spurgeon saw the world as richer for every book he published and prayed

that his life would be long and that he would send forth a large number.[77] When he reviewed his book *The House at Bethany*, Spurgeon gushed, "In him we find depth without obscurity, breadth without laxity, unction without affectation, and orthodoxy without bigotry."[78] If any could have persuaded Spurgeon to stay, these were the fellows. But they all knew too much to make an appeal other than that of peace and unity; for Spurgeon, purity preceded both.

The Hardening of the Positions

Soon after that meeting, on February 5, Spurgeon preached a message on Jesus' words to the church at Pergamos, "Thou holdest fast my name, and hast not denied my faith." The meeting and the censure were fresh on Spurgeon's mind. His refusal to be swayed by the reasoning of the subcommittee meshed with certain points of the sermon. Eternal punishment, in the theological discussions of the day, often came up as a shocking and, therefore, incredible concept. "Horrible doctrine! cried one the other day." That it is horrible does not mean that it is untrue. "It is not ours to judge of our Lord's teaching by our sentiment, we are to receive it by faith," Spurgeon countered; "He speaks terribly of the doom of the wicked, and he is not capable of exaggeration." In light of attack on him because of his belief of Jesus' words, Spurgeon asked aloud for "grace to persevere to the end! Oh for fidelity and constancy, so that neither gain nor loss, exaltation nor depression, may induce us to quit our Saviour!"[79]

Spurgeon's stirring the coals of this doctrinal fire revealed several that professed to believe as he believed but had no heart for pursuing a conflict over doctrine. Spurgeon reminded his lis-

---

75. S&T, June 1875, 283.

76. S&T. February 1885, 84.

77. S&T, November 1874, 540.

78. S&T, January 1877, 42.

79. SS, 19:42f. "Holding Fast the Faith."

teners that in a day of battle, "Those who sneak into the rear, that they may be comfortable, are not worthy of the kingdom." He felt keenly the insults heaped on him by many whose general disdain for Spurgeon's doctrine made them take advantage of his having provoked this conflict. He knew that he must "bear ridicule for Christ's sake, even that peculiarly venomed ridicule which 'the cultured' are so apt to pour upon us." Though he sought to keep the conflict at the level of principle and not resort to a defense of his person, sometimes the arrogance set against him made him grab for self-respect. While being willing to be "thought great fools for Jesus' sake," he also maintained that "some of us have forgotten more than many of our opponents ever knew, and yet they style us ignorant." Faithful soldiers bear shame for the courage of their convictions, yet "they call us cowards." "For my part," Spurgeon continued, "I am willing to be ten thousand fools in one for my dear Lord and Master, and count it to be the highest honor that can be put upon me to be stripped of every honor, and loaded with every censure for the sake of the grand old truth which is written on my very heart."[80]

For Spurgeon, doctrinal divergence meant that the gospel he preached was seen as unnecessary, the Christ he preached did not exist, and the souls saved under his ministry he had labored over uselessly. When he surveyed these implications, modern redefinition looked absurd. "When I remember my dear brethren and sisters in Christ who have fallen asleep, whom I saw die with triumph lighting up their faces, I feel quite content with the salvation which saved them, and I am not going to try experiments or speculations." He held that confidence because of the perfection of the Saviour. "To talk of improving upon our perfect Saviour is to insult him. He is God's propitiation; what would you more?" To change such perfect good news as the gospel set forth made no sense and reached the depths of Spurgeon's disgust. "My blood boils with indignation at the idea of improving the gospel. There is but one Saviour, and that one Saviour is the same for ever. His doctrine is the same in every age, and is not yea and nay." If modern proposal for theological change were authentic, what an absurd scene would eternity hold forth. "What a strange result we should obtain in the general assembly of heaven," Spurgeon envisioned, "if some were saved by the gospel of the first century, and others by the gospel of the second, and others by the gospel of the seventeenth, and others by the gospel of the nineteenth century!" Imagine the scene. "We should need a different song of praise for the clients of these various periods, and the mingled chorus would be rather to the glory of man's culture than to the praise of the one Lord. No such mottled heaven, and no such discordant song, shall ever be produced." The scene presents too ridiculous a vision to justify the movement of one inch. "To eternal glory there is but one way; to walk therein we must hold fast one truth, and be quickened by one life. We stand fast by the unaltered, unalterable, eternal name of Jesus Christ our Lord."[81]

Virtually at the same time that Spurgeon was delivering his soul in that message, John Clifford delivered a public statement defending the Council's action and warning against any reversal of its reprimand at the Union in April. Voices to "reverse the vote of censure" were being heard. Clifford said that a reversal would be tantamount to the Union's absorbing into itself all the worst and most unfounded accusations made by the

---

80. Ibid., 44.

81. Ibid., 49.

pastor at the Metropolitan Tabernacle. Do Union ministers really "make infidels" and "scout the atonement, deride the inspiration of the Scriptures, degrade the Holy Spirit into an influence, turn the punishment of sin into a fiction and the resurrection into a myth?" Should those men that will meet to discuss the work of the Baptist denomination say to the world, "We turn the Bible into wastepaper?" Surely, Clifford argued, it is not right that Spurgeon be allowed to say anything that he likes and none may whisper a word of objection. Spurgeon's energies, gifts, and influence should be put to better use than causing baseless suspicion and quarrels:

> Is it too late to ask Mr. Spurgeon to pause and consider whether this is the best work to which the Baptists of Great Britain and Ireland can be put? Is not the fateful crop of disturbing suspicions, broken purposes, imperiled churches, and wounded but faithful workers, already in sight enough? Oh! It pains me unspeakable to see this eminent "winner of souls" rousing the energies of thousands of Christians to engage in personal wrangling and strife, instead of inspiring them, as he might, to sustained and heroic effort to carry the good news of God's Gospel to our fellow-countrymen! Would it were possible even now to reverse the direction of those newly quickened forces and guide them into the application of Christianity to the lessening of the sin and misery of our race![82]

Spurgeon felt heartsick. On February 17 he wrote to a "venerable friend" saying, "My heart has been ready to sink within me. The subtlety of those who defend union with the errorists is amazing, and come upon me every now & then as if a sheet of fire flashes in my face. Friends have forsaken me, & foes wrest my words." Though he

acknowledged a bright side to the entire conflict, he felt that at times "the dark side is most present." Both foes and friends, as he mentioned, gave his emotions such a work-out that "sometimes a fit of weeping & sobbing comes over me." He felt that he might die under the strain, and would willingly do so, but "the feeble would draw ill inferences from it."[83] Fresh on his mind at the writing of the letter was a brewing conflict with some few of his "own men."

Even with the growing and more determined tide of criticism arising from within Baptist ranks, among the most difficult developments Spurgeon faced in this turmoil was the defection of men that had graduated from the Pastors' College. "The evil leaven," he wrote "has affected some few of them who were educated in our College."[84] The attempt to remove them from the association uncovered other sympathizers, a group of one hundred that signed "a mild protest" against Spurgeon's attempt at creating clarity and certainty of the theological basis for the conference. Up to this time Spurgeon believed they had a unanimously held consensus. The Downgrade spirit in the midst of his own men was a fact that Spurgeon described as "the sorest wound of all."

C. A. Davis, a leader of the opposition party, had frequently contributed articles to *The Sword and the Trowel*, and had been active in the college conference. Davis contributed "How we get Peace by the Substitute" in September 1870, writing as a man after Spurgeon's own heart. "Christ is all in all to the believer," he began. "Not only at conversion, but all through life the doctrine of the cross is the life and soul of his peace. In proportion as he retains a clear view of Christ *as his Substitute,* he enjoys peace with God."[85] In April 1878

---

82. Pike, 6:297 citing Clifford in *The Pall Mall Gazette,* February 8, 1888.

83. Handwritten letter from the private collection of Gary Long.

84. S&T, March 1888, 148.

85. S&T, September 1870, 418.

Davis, a pastor in Manchester, had presented an "extraordinary paper" on "Jesus, the Preacher's Model."[86] A decade later, Davis received an imploring letter from Spurgeon on February 18, 1888 explaining that his attempt at protest would be a "purposeless conflict" and that Spurgeon had had "all I can bear of bitterness." Ironically, at this very time, Davis sent a letter to *The Sword and the Trowel* giving a positive report of the work of Fullerton and Smith, Spurgeon's evangelists, in Reading. as "solid and helpful."[87] Approval of evangelism, however, did not substitute for faithfulness to the revealed truth of God. Spurgeon wanted a clear understanding of the "basis," that is the theological commitments, on which the college conference proceeded and wanted no one in the conference that did not agree wholeheartedly. He proposed, therefore, and told Davis his proposal, "I propose to resign my office, and I shall hope that those who vote 'Yes' will support me in forming a new Conference." The "Yes" vote would be an approval of the interpretation given by some of the London alumni of the "basis" for the conference and strictly enforced in forming the new conference. Davis' procedure opposing this, "which I will not describe," Spurgeon wrote, "has caused me the utmost grief, and forced me to this decision."[88] He did not wonder that some might suspect his motives as well as his procedure because so much dust had been thrown in the air that even the eyes of an archangel would be blearied. Nevertheless, he had hopes for clearing the air:

> It is no small solace that nearly four hundred have voted yes right straight; and it will be a still greater

joy, if, after the explanation given, many of you will do the like. By your love to me, I beseech you do nothing which would be half-hearted. We can do each other more good apart in open-hearted honesty than together with suppressed ill-will. It has been my joy to serve you, and I hope it will still be my privilege; but we can only work together on the lines of the old Gospel, and if any of you are in love with "advanced thought," why do you wish to stay with such an old fogey as I am? Go your way and leave me an immovable old man, possibly the proper object of your pity, but assuredly not of your enmity, for I have striven to benefit you all according to my light and capacity. May the grace of our Lord be with the faithful among you, leading you to be wholly and boldly on the Lord's side in this day when men cannot endure sound doctrine! Yours heartily, but in much sorrow, mingled with hopeful love, C. H. Spurgeon

When the votes on the "Basis" were given, 432 of 496 voted for the procedure recommended by Spurgeon. During the process of receiving votes Spurgeon, having extended the time of voting to February 23, wrote in the March *Sword*, "We cannot, therefore, announce the final result here, but after the scrutineers have presented their report, we shall have an important communication to make direct to all our faithful brethren." "All that we can do now is to indicate that an overwhelming majority has voted in favour of the explanation of the basis of agreement on which the Association was formed." The others gave different levels of objection to it. As Spurgeon explained it, at least in part, "Some protest against our method of procedure, and others threaten to force themselves into our assembly, though they have departed from the faith that we hold."[89]

A light in a dark place a letter from his students in New Zealand must have been. They ex-

---

86. S&T, May 1878, 227; See also S&T, May 1886, "The Rainbow About the Throne," 230-33.

87. S&T, March 1888, 151.

88. Pike, 6:298.

89. S&T, March 1888, 149, 150.

pressed their admiration for "the loyalty towards the claims of conscience and the convictions of duty that has led you to withdraw from the Baptist Union of Great Britain and Ireland." Their memories of the college were delightful and refreshing and they still sought to maintain the truths that he had propagated with valor and faithfulness. As they mentioned the names of former students that were now men at work for the gospel in this remote corner, it could not have hurt Spurgeon's spirit that the letter included the information, "It is your son's privilege to preside over the largest church in the Colony, and to be the preacher of the Union sermon at this Conference."[90] Much closer to home, however, former students moved Spurgeon to a distasteful, perhaps even bitter, procedure.

According to his previous plan, Spurgeon dissolved the conference. Ian Randall has investigated the letters received by Spurgeon during this crisis and has summarized the variety of responses that the college men had to Spurgeon's attempts at a clearer theological basis for the conference. The flexibility they desired on the meaning of the term "doctrines of grace" and their desire for maintenance in membership of those that held sympathy for the "larger hope" shows why Spurgeon was driven to such distress during this critical moment of the controversy, and explains his desire for starting over.[91] Should any object that his power to do so was unwarrantable, then he would merely state that "I personally retire from my office as president." He asked others not to seek to convoke the old conference; it would only bring about "an unpleasant collision." At the same time he invited all that voted "Yes" to unite

with him in forming the conference anew. They had given him great encouragement by their enthusiastic love for him and for the old faith. To those who had not treated him kindly, he hoped "to erase from my memory the whole of the unhappy past, and to begin a new Conference without an atom of resentment towards those who will not be with us in it."[92]

The conflict, though uncovering another point of division among Spurgeon's connections, proved the making of greater unity and of greater theological resolve for many others. While the "evil leaven" had affected many, the "great bulk of the host" he found to be lovingly enthusiastic for his stance and to be "faithful and thorough brethren." Spurgeon believed, "as a band of men we shall march on with all the greater and clearer confidence in God." He wanted the college and its men to provide a "great breakwater, firmly resisting the incoming flood of falsehood."[93]

This February 1888 affair of dissolution and reconstitution must have been one of the most distasteful and trying, not only to Spurgeon, but to those graduates that dissented from the president in some way, and to his wife who was aware of the constant stress on her husband's mind because of such a surprising and counter-intuitive aspect of the doctrinal dispute. Even after his death this conflict within the fraternity of college men weighed heavily on the mind of Mrs. Spurgeon. She wrote a letter of gratitude to them for their genuine expression of grief in the death of her husband and their devoted mentor. She mentioned their "responsibility" as his students. After a series of statements about his courage and consecration and unique gifts, she brought them to think candidly about "the faith he loved so well, and fought for so valiantly (even unto death); the

---

90. Ibid., 150.

91. Ian Randall, "Charles Haddon Spurgeon, The Pastors' College and the Downgrade Controversy," in *Discipline and Diversity*, ed. Kate Cooper and Jeremy Gregory (Woodbridge, UK: Boydell Press, 2007), 366-76.

92. Pike, 6:298f.

93. S&T, March 1888, 148.

gospel of the grace of God which he preached so fully and faithfully; the 'sound doctrine' which was at the foundation of his power and success." Turning from him to them, she wrote, "These are yours still, and are left for you to defend and proclaim in the stormy days to come." As her husband would have done, she urged all to be faithful to their charge and not "depart from the faith" or "turn aside unto vain jangling." This straying age will focus its eyes on "Spurgeon's men" and will exult when any depart from the old paths or fail to keep the up-grade. "*Never* let them be successful in your case, dear brethren! Better never to have been connected with the 'Pastors' College' at all, than to be one of 'our own men', and afterwards dishonour the Lord."[94]

Having cleared the air for the college conference on the confessional basis for their union, Spurgeon now looked for the Baptist Union to do the same. In earlier times, before the intrusion of advanced thought and the consequent manipulation of language, members in the Union had clear knowledge of what their brethren meant by their use of historically confessional words such as deity, incarnation, atonement, inspiration, justification, and final judgment. He told the reorganized meeting of the conference, "The Pastors' College Evangelical Association," on April 16, that when men differ on some issues yet hold in common fundamental truth, a confession is not needed; but "when men come in who count the blood of the Covenant an unholy thing," the time for plain speaking has come. Spurgeon, increasingly savvy about the inner workings of the process and distrustful of the great latitude offered in mere assertions, looked for a substantial and clearly evangelical document. Inclusivism would not meet the demands of the moment but would

be treasonous. When he used terms, he did not claim to have an idiosyncratic definition to which all must heel, but he wanted them understood "in the common and usual sense attached to them by the general usage of Christendom." At all costs, and the costs would be dire, he believed, policy should not dictate the outcome, but plain truth. "Let it above all things avoid the use of language which could have two meanings contrary to each other. ... Right is safe, and compromise by the use of double meanings can never in the long run be wise."[95]

Once Spurgeon grabbed the principle that fellowship depended on the willingness to declare with no uncertainty the truth as the basis of union, he carried it through every organization of which he was a part. He had participated for years in the London Association and was instrumental in giving it new life when an organizational meeting convened at the Metropolitan Tabernacle on November 10, 1865. He sent the invitations that brought about the new organization and presided at the first meeting. The purpose was described as "the co-operation of the Associated Churches in efforts to advance the kingdom of Christ in connection with the Baptist denomination in London and its suburbs." This included the erection of at least one chapel per year. The only doctrinal statement in the founding document was article one of the rules that described the Association as "The London Association of Baptist Ministers holding Evangelical Sentiments, and the Churches under their care."[96] When, twenty-two years later, a resolution calling on the executive of the Association to "prepare a sound evangelical basis" for its membership was moved but not passed, Spurgeon resigned from the Association. After his resignation the Association continued

---

94. S&T, April 1892, 206.

95. S&T, March 1888, 148.

96. S&T, January 1866, 37.

its talks about a "creedal basis," some saying that Spurgeon was at the bottom of that continued struggle. Spurgeon flatly denied it, and never held over the Association's head "the arrogant bribe of personal return if a creed should be adopted." His course was simple and final. "As soon as I saw, or thought I saw, that error had become firmly established, I did not deliberate, but quitted the body at once. Since then my counsel has been, 'Come ye out from among them.'"[97]

By 1891, this conviction reached even into Spurgeon's political connections with the Liberation Society. Though it always had included theological liberals, it seemed, with an exception here and there, that the intent was political and religious equality for all denominations. The theological issue became so overwhelming in Spurgeon's mind during these years, that he could not risk fraternity at any level with those that held diminutive views of Christ, the cross, justification and the Bible. He was in league with too many of them in the Liberation Society. If he had broken union with Baptists over these issues, how could political goals have a greater claim on his loyalty? Now he saw that their influence was just as much toward the liberalization of theology as it was toward the liberalization of English politics, society, and ecclesiastical relations. Hoping for their success in achieving religious liberty, Spurgeon, in 1891, pointed to the spiritual issues of "these days" as prompting his words, "We will not by this question be brought into a parent union with those from whom we differ in the very core of our souls upon matters vital to Christianity."[98]

This theme of confessional clarity he repeated with resolute consistency, and he reported that

he knew number of others that would "never discontinue their request until they obtain it." The strangest phenomenon of all would be that the majority would have to recede before the minority. An inclusive document, so he believed, would bring the entire Baptist Union to a great crisis, a "parting of the ways, and the old school and the new cannot go much further in company; nor ought they to do so." He had written for the April edition of *The Sword and the Trowel*, "The Baptist Union meets in full assembly on April 23, and the great question before it will be — 'Is this Union to have an Evangelical basis or not?'" He hoped the question would be discussed "with good temper, and that the decision will be of the right kind."[99]

As Spurgeon learned more of exactly what the Council would propose for acceptance as a confessional statement, his spirits sank again. Rumors spread that he requested a "narrow sectarian form of teaching," or a "personal peculiarity of persuasion;" he wanted only the "faith once for all delivered to the saints," a clear agreement on "the central teaching of revelation" and that the "grosser forms of error should not be tolerated within the bounds of the Christian body to which we belonged." He had proposed a "form of sound words" to the Council as a basis for union, but feared that "a strenuous endeavour will be made to get the scanty and objectionable historical statement of the Council carried through as a substitute for that which is requested." Though his lament appeared in the May number of *The Sword and the Trowel*, he wrote in anticipation of the annual meeting of April 23, and confessed, "We write hopelessly."[100]

When the Baptist Union meeting in April of 1888 finally did vote a confessional stance as a basis for union, the wording was purposely am-

---

97. S&T, December 1888, 617. "Attempts at the Impossible."

98. Lewis Drummond, *Spurgeon: Prince of Preachers* (Grand Rapids, MI: Kregel, 1992), 530. It is cited this way in Drummond. It would seem that the word should be "apparent" rather than "a parent."

99. S&T, April 1888, 197-98.

100. S&T, May 1888, 249.

biguous and, according to Spurgeon, "could legitimately have two meanings contrary to each other." This type of confession appeared designed for the lack of decisiveness characteristic of the Union as Spurgeon perceived it:

> After next Monday's Union Meeting, several brethren may have made up their minds; but until then, they will sit uneasily upon the fence. I have, with commendable forethought, endeavoured to drive a number of tenterhooks and other useful nails into the top of that fence, to assist them in retaining their hold; but I fear they are not deeply grateful to me. Theirs is a position which I never was able to occupy myself, and therefore I have no very profound sympathy with them. One or two learned divines are trying their utmost to get down on both sides of the fence; but it as a perilous experiment. Some are trying to get down on the winning side, and others would prefer to keep their judicious position world without end. Neutrals, in the end, have the respect of neither party; and, assuredly, they are *the difficulty* in every controversy.[101]

Giving opportunity to assuage the conscience, no matter which way one voted, was the intention of the document, largely the work of John Clifford, the Baptist Union president for that year. Clifford wanted all members of the Union to be able to sign the document in good conscience and set the stage for broad acceptance of the ambiguous confession by an equally ambiguous but exceedingly powerful presidential address. The Spring Assembly of 1888 was ready to explode and Clifford was intent on defusing the situation. Sir James Marchant describes Clifford's address:

> The task was threefold. The message must express convictions held strongly by the speaker, or it

could not honorably be given; it must encourage the more liberal thinkers among the delegates, and those who cared most for freedom of thought and speech, for they were entitled to this support from a man like Dr. Clifford, substantially of their own school; it must reassure the more conservative and, if possible, the most conservative, who feared that the fundamentals of Bible truth and evangelical faith were in peril. Not only were these things essential at any time, because right: they were specially so now, because the situation was strained and irritated and near disaster. The address deserved to succeed.[102]

Succeed it did—at least as far as Clifford's intentions were concerned. Spurgeon, who had looked forward to this vote with vital interest, had written, "It will be wise to see what the respective numbers are."[103] If winners and losers were to be pointed out, Clifford won and Spurgeon lost. The confession was adopted by a majority of 2,000 to 7, including the affirmative votes of many of Spurgeon's most ardent followers. Given the overwhelming affirmation of such a noncommittal confession, Iain Murray expressed the puzzling nature of the event by speculating that "a number of evangelicals voting could not have understood what they were voting about."[104] Rather, they thought it was a great victory and to the advantage of orthodoxy. Spurgeon's own brother, James, seconded the motion and considered that Charles Spurgeon was vindicated. Other Spurgeon supporters cheered and felt his point was gained. "My brother," Spurgeon wrote to a friend, "thinks he has gained a great victory, but I believe we are hopelessly sold. I feel heartbroken. Certainly he has done the very opposite

---

101. Charles Spurgeon, *An All Round Ministry*, 290f.

102. Marchant, 164.

103. S&T, April 1888, 198.

104. Iain Murray, *The Forgotten Spurgeon* (Edinburgh: The Banner of Truth Trust, 1973), 148.

of what I should have done." Even with that disappointment, Spurgeon believed that James had "followed his best judgment."[105]

What was so ominous in all of this to Spurgeon was the manner in which it all came about in the rush of the moment. Charles Williams of Accrington moved the acceptance of the resolution along with a footnote acknowledging that some brethren differed on the interpretation of Matthew 25:46 on the point of "everlasting punishment." He made a speech defending the intent of the footnote to tolerate that difference. When James seconded the resolution of the council, he did not intend to second Williams' defense of the footnote. Spurgeon received a full account of the entire affair and viewed it as exactly consistent with the tottering theological condition of the Union. He had hoped, if with only scant reason, that something positive might be done. "But what was done?" he asked. "The resolution, with its footnote, with the interpretation of its mover, and the re-election of the old council, fairly represent the utmost that would be done when everybody was in his best humour." Was the adopted confession satisfactory? Did any two parties share the same sense of its meaning? Does not the whole virtue of the thing, in fact, lie in its pleasing both sides a little? And at the same time is this not the "vice and the condemnation of it?" How strange that James Spurgeon would think that such a hybrid would vindicate his brother, or answer his deepest concerns. On the contrary, however, the vote merely confirmed the Council's previous censure of Spurgeon and unquestionably solidified him in his conviction that he could never recall his resignation. "I was afraid from the beginning that the reform of the Baptist Union was hopeless, and therefore I resigned. I am far more

sure of it now, and should never under any probable circumstances dream of returning."[106]

Attempts to give Meaning to the Conflict

The drama of this conflict over creeds continued to haunt the historiography of Spurgeon. J. C. Carlile in 1933 commented, "Among Baptists there has been age-long hostility to authoritative creeds. Baptists stand for liberty, the right of each individual to receive the truth from his Lord." Using language of E. Y. Mullins, Carlile called creeds "barriers to the free development of personality," causes of division and hypocrisy, and "instrument[s] of persecution." Carlile believed that Spurgeon's desire for a definite theological basis for union meant that "he had gone back upon the traditional position of Baptists."[107] Carlile's own misperceptions of the use of confessions in Baptist life made him misjudge the concern of Spurgeon in matters related to a union of churches as opposed to the necessity of perfect religious liberty in civil society.

One week before the April meeting, Spurgeon preached to the alumni of his Pastors' College on the subject "The Evils of the Present Time, and Our Object, Necessities, and Encouragements." Spurgeon clearly outlined the issues at stake in the Downgrade controversy. Again he pointed to the inspiration of Scripture as the main issue. Other doctrines mattered, but without a divine revelation, conceded to be such, the construction of doctrine with hopes of unity was a moot point. Second to that, Spurgeon mentioned vicarious atonement.

> Brethren have always differed on minor points, and it has not been unusual for us to meet each other, and discuss matters of doctrine upon the

---

105. Fullerton, 313f.

106. S&T, July 1888, 339.

107. Carlile, 255-56.

basis of Holy Scripture. All were agreed that, whatever Scripture said, should be decisive; and we only wished to ascertain what the Lord had revealed. But another form of discussion has now arisen: men question the Scriptures themselves.

We used to debate upon particular and general redemption, but now men question whether there is any redemption at all worthy of the name. We used to converse upon which aspect of the atonement should be made most prominent, but in the vicarious sacrifice we all believed. Alas! We have doctrine of the putting-away of sin by the blood of our Lord Jesus is spoken of in opprobrious terms.[108]

Without affirmation of the full inspiration and infallibility of Scripture, preachers are like weather-cocks spinning in a different direction with every wind that blows. For any doctrine to have certitude and permanent meaning it must proceed upon an unerring basis:

Unless we have infallibility somewhere, faith is impossible. The true faith teaches us facts which cannot be questioned. Where is faith to build if there be no rock, and nothing left us but shifting sand? As for us, we find infallibility in the Scriptures of the Old and New Testament, and our one desire is to have them opened up to our minds by the holy Spirit.[109]

In spite of Spurgeon's specific and clear references to this paramount issue and his explicit disavowals that his conflict arose from narrowly Calvinistic sympathies, his contemporaries virtually unanimously failed to see the theological concerns he so ardently and energetically expounded. There were four basic reactions to Spurgeon's

claims. Many claimed that he was merely trying to bind the Union to the back of John Calvin. A second group lamented that he had forgotten his natural gift of soul-winning and succumbed to being a mere controversialist. A third judgment concluded that Spurgeon's sickness and age (though he was but fifty-two when the controversy began) had caused him to be irrational and reactionary. A fourth reaction, which served to confirm Spurgeon's claims concerning the entire situation, stated that Spurgeon's theology was out of date and harmful to the progress of the modern mentality.

Though outbursts against Spurgeon's supposed intention to commit the Baptist Union to the "hateful doctrines of Geneva" were widespread, two illustrations of this will suffice. George Hill, a Baptist minister, insisted that Spurgeon would exclude all from the Union who had "learned anything about the ways of God with Men" since their college days and could not agree with Hodge's *Outlines of Theology* or Cole's *On Divine Sovereignty.*

One of the harshest and most unfair, as well as irrelevant, caricatures of Spurgeon and his position came from the famous Joseph Parker. Spurgeon had regularly reviewed Parker's new works when they appeared, found something to commend in each one, but always issued a caveat concerning his theology. In December 1870 Spurgeon had reviewed Parker's *Ad Clerum* with the recommendation, "Young men must be great dolts if they can read his advice and derive no profit from it." He added, "Our grief that Dr. Parker should have gone aside to certain modern heresies is intense, and we pray that he may soon see his way out of them."[110] He made sure the reader knew that "none of that mischief" marred

108. C. H. Spurgeon, *An All Round Ministry*, 285-86.
109. Ibid., 287.
110. S&T, December 1870, 573.

the volume before him. Parker took advantage of the Downgrade stir to issue an insult around a compliment:

> When people ask me what I think of Spurgeon, I always ask which Spurgeon—the head or the heart—the Spurgeon of the Tabernacle or the Spurgeon of the Orphanage? The kind of Calvinism which the one occasionally represents I simply hate, as I hate selfishness and blasphemy. It is that leering, slavering, sly-winking Calvinism that says, "Bless the Lord we are all right, booked straight through to heaven first-class". ... But when I turn to the Orphanage all is changed. All is beauty. All is love ...[111]

By September 1888 Spurgeon could say, "The Pastor and Church at the Tabernacle are now free from all hampering connections with Unions and Association but by no means without communion of the warmest kind with the Lord's faithful people." He declared his patience on this matter, asked the people to believe nothing that the newspapers wrote about his intentions because his only intent was to wait and see what God would do.[112]

His desire for fellowship with "the Lord's faithful people" found an outlet in an informal fraternal that he and several like-minded friends began. Having learned his lesson well about religious affiliation that had no clearly stated, conscientiously subscribed doctrinal basis, the brethren convened their fraternal on the basis of a confession of faith. This confession expressed the beliefs of the "fraternal" begun by seven men and gradually endorsed by others. The original seven were C. H Spurgeon, A. G. Brown, J. Douglas, W. Fuller Gooch, G. D. Hooper, J. Stephens, and Frank

White. Spurgeon's son, Charles, was one of the signers. The articles were brief. After a statement of their belief in Scripture in light of the contemporary challenges to its authority, they lined out an abstract pointing to doctrines clearly defined in the long history of Reformed Protestantism concluded by an affirmation of the premillennial return of Christ.

> We, the undersigned, banded together in Fraternal Union, observing with growing pain and sorrow the loosening hold of many upon the Truths of Revelation, are constrained to avow our firmest belief in the Verbal Inspiration of all Holy Scripture as originally given. To us, the Bible does not merely contain the Word of God, but *is* the Word of God. From beginning to end, we accept it, believe it, and continue to preach it. To us, the Old Testament is no less inspired than the New. The Book is an organic whole. Reverence for the New Testament accompanied by skepticism as to the OLD appears to us absurd. The two must stand or fall together. We accept Christ's own verdict concerning "Moses and all the prophets" in preference to any of the supposed discoveries of so-called higher criticism.
>
> We hold and maintain the truths generally known as "the doctrines of grace." The Electing Love of God the Father, the Propitiatory and Substitutionary Sacrifice of his Son, Jesus Christ, Regeneration by the Holy Ghost, the imputation of Christ's Righteousness, the Justification of the sinner (once for all) by faith, his walk in newness of life and growth in grace by the active indwelling of the Holy Ghost, and the Priestly Intercession of our Lord Jesus, as also the hopeless perdition of all who reject the Saviour, according to the words of the Lord in Matt. xxv. 46, "These shall go away into eternal punishment"—are, in our judgment, revealed and fundamental truths.
>
> Our hope is the Personal Pre-millenial Return of the Lord Jesus in glory.[113]

---

111. Murray, *The Forgotten Spurgeon*, 181.

112. S&T, September 1888, 515.

113. S&T, September 1891, 446.

The word was about that Spurgeon wanted to force this creed "down the unwilling throat of the Baptist Union." Spurgeon pitied the "poor souls" that felt so intimidated and quickly sought to dispel their fears of his intention. He did agree with Joseph Parker on at least one point of his protest, the orphanage stood as a testimony to his true faith, a translation of creed that "even men of the world can understand, … where living faith shows itself in works of mercy for the widow and the fatherless (James ii. 14-18)."[114]

An abundance of religious pundits seemed more than willing to give Spurgeon as much verification as he needed that his representations about the religious climate, including that of the Baptist Union, were not bugbears of his imagination but real. *The Christian World* more than obliged him in their sarcastic description of the signers of the confession as "a little band of faithful adherents to the truth amidst a faithless church." He and his friends were among those little-minded people to whom "the profoundest thought, the highest learning, the devoutest inquiry, are by implication branded as treason to the truth, if they have reached conclusions different from those propounded in this manifesto." The idea of infallibility is "the reward of the resolute refusal to allow the light of science and scholarship to fall upon the divine Word. All must be wrong except the few who can pronounce this Shibboleth." Spurgeon considered their resistance a compliment. Another paper, *The Echo*, called the Manifesto "a voice from the Dark Ages." A paper that he identified simply as "a northern newspaper," wrote

> No one who does not possess the power to an alarming extent of persuading himself anything, can possibly, if he have any real acquaintance with the controversy, hold the views as to the sense

in which the Bible is divine revelation which prevailed in almost all the churches fifty years ago, it is not that theories have been formed; but facts have been brought to light which must modify old-fashioned opinions, and have already modified them to a considerable extent. It did not, however, require any new discoveries of criticism to disprove the dogmas of verbal inspiration upon which Mr. Spurgeon and his friends insist as one of the prime essentials of Christianity. If it be an essential, then Christianity is not better than a myth. And these men, with all their boasted loyalty to religion, ought surely to see that in associating the Christian belief with unnecessary, unprovable, and directly disprovable dogma, they are doing the work of the atheist and unbeliever, who stand by smiling to see the process of destruction going on from within. If religion and verbal inspiration must stand or fall together, then it is the latter alternative which will happen— assuredly they will fall.[115]

This continual misrepresentation on the part of many of Spurgeon's contemporaries indicated one of three things: they refused to believe he spoke the truth about his real concerns; or they really did not understand what he was trying so desperately to point out; or they deliberately misrepresented him in order to cloud the issue so as not to be found out themselves. Spurgeon knew this was the case and in May 1891, some four years after the first Downgrade article appeared, wrote, "We spoke not without knowing what we were about." For reasons we have listed above, he said, "It was not possible for us to give up all our authorities, nor would it have served any useful purpose to have published names," but he spoke the truth without exaggeration. "Matters were even worse than we knew of," he continued, for he dealt "not only with the lion of open unbelief, but with the foxes of craft, who profess to love the

---

114. Ibid., 447.

---

115. Ibid., 448.

gospel which they labour hard to undermine." He would not soften one syllable of his witness against the doctrinal and spiritual deception of the age, but would add emphasis to it.[116]

The second reaction was characterized by the creation of a dichotomy between theology and missions. These decriers claimed that theological controversy would destroy evangelism. The natural implication is that toleration of all kinds of theology would enhance evangelism. John Clifford lamented that Spurgeon, that eminent winner of souls, insisted on "rousing the energies of thousands of Christians to engage in personal wrangling and strife, instead of inspiring them, as he might, to sustained and heroic effort to carry the good news of God's Gospel to our fellow countrymen."[117]

Spurgeon decided that he no longer needed to protect the name of Clifford since he was so bold in his public opposition to Spurgeon's stance on the Baptist Union and so careless in his doctrinal associations otherwise. He feigned evangelistic concern as a façade of Christian spirituality but had no clear view of the uniqueness of Christ or the absoluteness of the Christian gospel. In May of 1889, Spurgeon noted Clifford's presentation of an address at South Place, Finsbury, a chapel consisting of auditors more radical than the Unitarians. He appeared there, not just as John Clifford the local church pastor, but as John Clifford the president of the Baptist Union. The chapel had a series of plaques around the wall commemorating Moses, Voltaire, Jesus, Thomas Paine, Zoroaster, and others. Spurgeon was unable to contain himself:

The blasphemous association of our Lord with Thomas Paine and Voltaire creates an indescribable feeling in a Christian mind, and makes us wonder how a man, professing to be a servant of the Lord Jesus, could associate himself with such a place. Well might the Union resent our complaints against its more obscure wanderers, when its President, before he closed his year of office, would thus publicly associate himself with the deniers of our Lord's divinity. Has the body of Baptists over which this gentleman presides become so easy-going and docile that it will by its silence endorse the action of its President? Is it really so, that to preserve their confederacy any amount of looseness will be tolerated? We do not see that anything worse can be invented than that which the governing party either condones or admires. On the "Down-Grade" the train travels very fast: another station has been passed. What next? And what next?[118]

It was precisely in service of evangelism that Spurgeon so insisted on a common doctrinal stance— a stance that would have been recognized as the same gospel preached 50 years before, 100 years before, 300 years before, and preached by Christ and the apostles. For Spurgeon, there could be no evangelism without a clear knowledge of the gospel and he would not be tempted by empty rhetoric. "When we lie a-dying," Spurgeon mused, "if we have faithfully preached the gospel, our conscience will not accuse us for having kept closely to it." He would have no sorrows that he did not turn fool or politician to increase the congregation. If one would refuse to be saved by the substitution of Christ, no other hope could be proffered and Spurgeon knew that he would be cleared at the great white throne "of all complicity with the novel inventions of deluded men." All the evangelism that he knew was to set before the eyes of sinners "the unaided attractiveness of the gospel of Jesus," to give with earnest entreaty the "mes-

---

116. S&T, May 1891, 249.

117. Murray, *The Forgotten Spurgeon*, 167.

118. S&T, May 1889, 244.

sage of free grace and dying love." Only in doing this would he be clear of the blood of all men.[119]

The evangelistic power of the immutability of the "old gospel" as opposed to "progressive theology," a new establishment of purgatorial hope by way infidelity instead of pious superstition, grounded his thought in his aggressive expose of the destructiveness of "Anythingarianism" and "Pan-indifferentism."

> Do men really believe that there is a gospel for each century? Or a religion for each fifty years? Will there be in heaven saints saved according to a score sorts of gospel? Will these agree together to sing the same song? And what will the song be? Saved on different footings, and believing different doctrines, will they enjoy eternal concord, or will heaven itself be only a new arena for disputation between varieties of faiths?[120]

The destructiveness of the new theology to true evangelism surely was on his mind when he included in his volume *The Soul Winner* a chapter entitled "Encouragement to Soul-Winners," based on James 5:19f: "Brethren, if any of you do err from the truth, and one convert him; let him know, that he which converteth the sinner from the error of his way shall save a soul from death, and shall hide a multitude of sins." The verse teaches, so Spurgeon believed, that the error was a doctrinal error, "some truths which must be believed ... essential to salvation." Neologians, while feigning concern for warmhearted evangelism, really do not believe in such a thing as conversion or any untruth, if there be such, worthy of condemnation. They utter wicked nonsense about "more faith in honest doubt than in half the creeds." Firmness they re-

gard as bigotry, and, unlike the apostles, they do not seek the conversion, but the congratulation, of a man in doctrinal error. Men of "modern thought" have learned that "the Deity of Christ may be denied, the work of the Holy Spirit ignored, the inspiration of Scripture rejected, the atonement disbelieved, and regeneration dispensed with, and yet the man who does all this may be as good a Christian as the most devout believer!" What fools the martyrs were to suffer flames here to avoid flames hereafter. "O God, deliver us from this deceitful infidelity," Spurgeon prayed. He added two reasons as benefits of this deliverance. Doctrinal infidelity "does damage to the erring man, and often prevents his being reclaimed" and at the same time "does mischief to our own hearts by teaching us that truth is unimportant, and falsehood a trifle, and so destroys our allegiance to the God of truth, and makes us traitors instead of loyal subjects to the King of kings."[121]

The third attitude expressed relative to Spurgeon's concerns sought to make him an object of ridicule and pity. *The Sword and the Trowel* in February of 1890 reported that one newspaper attempted to comfort Spurgeon at his "worst stage of depression concerning the doubts of the day" by the assurance that religion can never pass away. Other English Baptists informed some American inquirers that Spurgeon conducted himself in such a manner because "sickness and age had weakened his intellect."[122] A twentieth-century historian of English Baptists, A. C. Underwood, continued that ridicule of Spurgeon by stating "A sick man, he viewed with deepest concern all departure from the theology of the Puritans." Underwood added to the insult by implying that Spurgeon was simply intellec-

119. SS, 19:364-66.
120. S&T, April 1888, 158f.
121. *The Soul Winner*, 300-01.
122. S&T, February 1890, 93.

tually incapable of appreciating the advances of modern thought.[123]

When one critic suggested that Spurgeon's accusations came from his sickness, not his theological acumen, Spurgeon showed his entire disgust with this dodging of theological issues. "Our opponents," he says, "have set to work to make sneering allusions to our sickness." His solemn observations about theology are suggested by his pain, according to the critic, not his brain. This lack of Christian courtesy showed, in Spurgeon's judgment, that the new theology had introduced a new tone and spirit. Adherence to old-fashioned faith determines that a man must be an idiot and should be treated "with that contemptuous pity which is the quintessence of hate." If a theological watch-dog is known also to be ill, "impute their faith to their disease, and pretend that their earnestness is nothing but petulance arising from their pain."[124]

The fourth reaction to Spurgeon was the most straightforward and honest of all and came in the form of an emboldened rejection of the theology and bibliology espoused by Spurgeon. The most popular, politically astute, and outspoken representative of this school of thought was John Clifford. Clifford published a book after Spurgeon's death entitled *The Inspiration and Authority of the Bible*. Clifford's forthrightness certainly vindicated Spurgeon, for Clifford affirmed in unambiguous terms that he definitely rejected the inerrancy and infallibility of Scripture. In fact, Clifford believed that "we seriously imperil the authority and limit the service of Scripture every time we

advocate its absolute inerrancy.[125] In a chapter entitled "Three Defences of an Inerrant Bible" Clifford makes a determined effort to dismantle the major defenses presented in favor of an inerrant Bible. First, the autograph theory is indefensible since it can be neither proven nor disproven in the absence of the autographs and assumes God was careless in not preserving them. It is "as unwarranted as it is useless, and as mischievous as it is unwarranted." Second, Clifford denied that the Bible claims infallibility for itself. Neither Jesus nor the apostles should be quoted in favor of inerrancy; in fact, it is more consistent with all we know to believe that men moved by the Holy Ghost should not be error-free. Third, to use inerrancy as a doctrinal safeguard was useless and unnecessary according to Clifford. Most people are saved simply upon hearing a simple testimony from a preacher of the cross and have no concept of inerrancy one way or the other. Furthermore, the dogmatism demanded by the inerrancy doctrine is out of harmony with the actual facts of Scripture. True doctrine can only be harmed by such close identification with this untimely doctrine. Given the spirit of the modern world, the teaching of inerrancy is one of the surest ways of frustrating the redeeming purpose for which the Revelation of the Christ is given.[126]

The authority of Scripture for Clifford lay in the believer's encounter with the living Christ. Under the guidance of the Holy Spirit, who will guide us into all truth, the simple Christian can discern the true Christ from the false or embellished Christ in Scripture. One can discern the Christ of faith from the Christ of history simply by reading the text and bearing in mind the tendencies of admirers to exaggerate and embellish

---

123. A. C. Underwood, *a History of the English Baptists*, (London: The Baptist Union of Great Britain and Ireland, 1947) 231.

124. Drummond, 824. Drummond includes several articles on the Downgrade that appeared in *Sword and Trowel*, March-October, as appendices to his biography of Spurgeon, 802-34. This is from S&T, September 1887, 462.

---

125. John Clifford, *Inspiration and Authority of the Bible*, third edition (London: James Clark and Company, 1899), 63.

126. Ibid., 78.

by manufacturing deeds and words Jesus never did or said. The pious, like Clifford, will have no trouble discerning where he hears the true Christ and where he hears the echo of the community.[127]

Clifford's criticisms and reconstructions, however, are both inadequate and pointless. His rejection of the autograph theory because it is hypothetical shows that he never grasped the principle that a stream is never purer than its source. A corrupt source can never produce a pure stream. A stream that can be identified with its pure source is itself pure. Any downstream corruptions that can be isolated and corrected make the stream again as pure as its source. Also, his arguing against the autograph theory was irrelevant since Clifford rejected the authority of many textually certain passages. Parts of the Old Testament teach a mechanical deism, a low morality is justified by attributing actions to God's command, and the imprecatory Psalms advocate unrestrained hate towards one's enemies, according to Clifford. The finding of the autographs would neither change those passages nor Clifford's rejection of them. Clifford well recognized that fact.

His treatment of Christ's view of Scripture is shallow and reveals his epistemological inconsistency and subjectivity. He claimed that Jesus "distinctly and with repeated emphasis, sets his authority against, and over, that of the legislative records of the Old Testament."[128] He also denied that Jesus ever had any intention of defending the verbal truth of Scripture, but was here in person to "bring the Divine ideal into the actual experiences of the hour of men".[129]

His exegesis of the Scriptures with which he dealt is faulty, and reflects prior adherence to the results of the burgeoning historical-critical method. He also omitted the preponderance of Scriptures relevant to that subject and dismissed the apostolic witness to the inspiration of Scripture with incredibly insufficient investigation. His mishandling of 2 Timothy 3:16 is so pathetic as to be almost comical:

> Is there no "breath of God" in Eccesiasticus? Are not the books of the Maccabees profitable for instructions in righteousness? ... Was the New Testament in existence as a whole before the middle of the Second Century? Surely these and similar considerations ought to make us pause before we take the sayings of Paul about his own Inspiration, and of Peter about the Inspiration of the Prophets and use them as if they had in their minds at the time every chapter and verse of either the Protestant or the Roman Catholic Bible.[130]

Paul, as indicated above, was not the only apostle to suffer at the hands of Clifford. Peter's statement in 2 Peter 3:16 concerning Paul's writing is not mentioned and his affirmation concerning the Spirit's activity in inspiration is managed in an equally irresponsible manner:

> Inspiration is not always Revelation. It is a movement of God within the soul. It is essentially subjective; it is human and it is perfectly consistent with all we know of God's action ... that men moved by the Holy Ghost ... should not be error-proof. The Bible ... is a collection of fragments, of quotations, of comments upon quotations, ... of genealogies and laws, written by men, and in parts edited and re-edited by men, and it is not fair to contend that Peter's statement includes every line within the Testaments, and is applicable to each part in the same sense.[131]

---

127. John Clifford, *Ultimate Problems of Christianity* (London: The Kingsgate Press and James Clark and Co., 1906), 58.

128. Ibid., 65.

129. Ibid., 67.

130. Ibid., 73, 74.

131. Ibid., 72, 73.

In rejecting the necessity of inerrancy as a doctrinal safeguard, Clifford severely begs the question. He begins by assuming that any doctrine affected by his "experiential" method of interpretation is certainly not essential to the Christian faith. If a doctrine falls it is not essential, ergo, the loss of inerrancy affects no essential doctrine. A thorough reading of Clifford's works, however, show that he had in fact compromised some basic evangelical truths that Spurgeon considered essentially and broadly Christian.

For example, Clifford's highly rhetorical messages on evangelism fail to escape an implicit if not an explicit universalism. In 1920, Clifford delivered the first series of "The John Clifford Lectureship" established by the National Council of British Brotherhood. The lectures were published as a book under the title *The Gospel of World Brotherhood According to Jesus*. Chapter 3, "Is man as man a son of God?" Reveals these tendencies quite clearly:

> Jesus never treats the fact of sin as breaking off or hiding the filial relation of the offender to God ... As sin does not destroy God's relation to us as Father, so it cannot prevent or end our relation to Him as sons. ... As the holiness of the new redeemed and regenerated soul does not create the relation, so sin does not extinguish it. It is eternal. It is fundamental. The prodigal son is still a son, and it is not likely the fatherly heart will forget him, or that he will find rest till he sees him seated at the family table. ... According to Jesus, then, man's sonship to God is an indefensible fact, a glorious gospel, Sin does not destroy it, ... Thus the truth that we are the children of God, and that he is our Father, embraces, completes and harmonizes all other truths we possess regarding Him, ourselves and our world.[132]

---

132. John Clifford, *The Gospel of World Brotherhood According to Jesus* (London: Hodder and Stoughton, 1920), 28, 29, 46.

Consistent with his universalism, Clifford rejected eternal punishment and interpreted those biblical passages which seem to indicate such as judgments upon world civilizations. Empires which failed in incorporating adequately the concept of the brotherhood of man into their culture would perish never to rise again. These judgments, however, according to Clifford, were not brought against individual people. The "post-mortem" salvation against which Spurgeon warned found a warm advocate in the enlightened, modern thought of John Clifford.

Clifford had certainly denied a penal substitutionary view of the atonement, another touchstone of orthodoxy in Spurgeon's view. He sought to maintain the word "vicarious" but so interpreted it as to render it senseless as far as any historic understanding of the word is concerned. Clifford had no patience with "the 'appeasing' content of the symbol of propitiation" and claimed that the "paying a debt" metaphor is "so seriously charged with error as to make it more mischievous than useful." He reduced the rich storehouse of New Testament allusions to sacrifice and death to an ambiguous affirmation that these simply refer to, in the words of Livingstone, "the inherent and everlasting mercy of God made apparent to human eyes and ears. ... It (the death of Christ) showed that God forgives because he loves to forgive." He rejected the ransom and satisfaction theories. The concept of imputation central to substitutionary atonement and justification by faith were appallingly unethical. His caricature is so common as to defy comment but certainly clear enough to justify the suspicions of Spurgeon.

> Add to this the non-ethical doctrine of the external transfer of guilt, and merit; the acceptance of the processes of courts of law with all their glaring faults and inevitable imperfections as adequate

representations of God, though always obscuring and often omitting the very heart of God; and it becomes clear that the whole forensic theory bases the redemption of man not on the fact of the Divine Fatherhood revealed in it, but on the arbitrary and cruel despotisms of the Imperial Court of Rome.[133]

Clifford believed he had escaped the cultural aberrations that made the old encasements of theology disposable. Now the contents could be enjoyed in purity. Spurgeon believed this attempt to separate form from matter ill-conceived in theory and absolutely devastating in practice. The virgin-conception is not a form that embodies another and more timeless truth; it is the truth. Substitution is not a mere vehicle for another way of viewing Christ's death; it is the truth. Imputation is not a simple accident of culture within which the essence of justification is hidden; it is the essence, the real truth. The deity of Christ is not simply a gaudy verbal dress intended to protect the lasting reality of another view of Christ's person and his unique power and holiness; it is form and substance in one and cannot be altered without the absolute loss of all that Jesus brings to us. Rather than seeing himself as helplessly bogged down in a number of socially constructed forms irrelevant to the modern age, Spurgeon looked at the self-proclaimed rescuers of Christianity and saw them, not as robed in the righteousness of Christ, but as smothered by the swaddling of cultural anti-supernaturalism. They had lost their lives without knowing it, and felt themselves more fit for the age. Perhaps so, but unfit for eternity. Perhaps he had them in mind when he preached about the wedding garment in May 1888. Who is the man that appears without the garment?

He says that he is loyal to Christ, and he expects all his fellow guests to be firm friends with him, for is he not in the banquet as much as they are? But he does not mean by loyalty what they mean by it. He is among believers, but he is not truly of them. He talks about atonement; he does not mean substitution. He talks about the divinity of Christ; he does not mean the Godhead of Christ. He talks about justification by faith; but he does not mean the old-fashioned doctrine. He speaks of regeneration, but means evolution. He girds himself with the garment of philosophy, but he refuses the robe of revelation, for the cut of it is too old-fashioned for him. He is no more a wedding guest than he is a merry-andrew; perhaps, not so much so. He wears raiment in which the robe of righteousness and the garments of gladness are not to be seen. The looms of free grace and dying love have never woven him a wedding dress. His robe is not of God's provision; it is from his own wardrobe. He glories in his own culture, and not in the revelation of God, nor yet in the work of divine grace upon the heart. He is in the church, but he is not in Christ. He has a name to live, but he is dead.[134]

The Tension between Time and Eternity

From the perspective of more than a century and a quarter, one must now vindicate Spurgeon's representation as true and unembellished when he warned, "But how are we to act towards those who deny his vicarious sacrifice, and ridicule the great truth of justification by his righteousness?" He contended that these are not just "mistaken friends, but enemies of the cross of Christ." Circumlocutions and polite turns of phrase are inappropriate to characterize such ideas for "where Christ is not received as to the cleansing power of his blood and the justifying merit of his righteousness, he is not received at all."[135]

---

133. John Clifford, *The Secret of Jesus* (Manchester; James Robinson, 1908), 105.

134. SS, 19:204-05.

135. S&T, November 1887, 559. "A Fragment Upon the Down-Grade Controversy."

Another doctrine Spurgeon saw as essential which Clifford minimized was the historic space-time fall of man. Spurgeon had warned that "those who hold evangelical doctrine are in open alliance with those who call the fall a fable."[136] Clifford accepted the judgment of biological evolution concerning the ascent of man and transferred that into the spiritual sphere. Just as evolution experienced many deviations and degradations along the way, so has man's spiritual progress seen intermittent periods of decline, though, in both cases the predominant trend is upwards. "In short, not one 'fall of man,' but a succession of falls."[137]

Clifford's method of interpretation leaves many questions unanswered and provides no criteria by which to judge the claim to credibility of any doctrine. Disagreement over which words and actions are really those of Jesus can be resolved by no court of appeals, outside of the "spirit-led consciousness" of a third party. Clifford was quite confident that Jesus' promise of the Spirit to "guide you into all truth" was given to all the generations of Christians as well as the apostles. Through much painstaking, proper application of reason, and scientific interpretation of Scripture, the Spirit guides us into the truth. "It is not that truth itself is given us, as you may give a book to a reader, ... but we ourselves are taken where the truth is." In the final analysis, one can only be sure of the voice of God, when his consciousness assures him that he has properly read the universal Christian consciousness and he speaks the mind of the Spirit.

Clifford's universalism rescued him from the dilemma proposed by the possibility that one's reason might fail to assure him of truth. Even in those cases where the searcher is beset by confu-sion, Clifford assures him that since he is God's workmanship, God can never leave him or forsake him. "He will not leave man to perish."[138] Furthermore, if the community in writing the Gospels tended to embellish or exaggerate, as Clifford was quite willing to admit, one could only conclude that the most exalted and extreme claims of Jesus were those produced by the community. "The disciple ... surrounds his master with a spectacular magnificence on external and meretricious glory, a flimsy and gaudy covering that the original would despise."[139] The supernatural events of his life as well as his radical claims to deity must certainly, therefore, arise from the community. The theologians can hardly defend the deity of Christ in its traditional orthodoxy upon that basis. Yet, the Baptist Union was much more accepting of Clifford and his mentality than of Spurgeon.

Three decades after Spurgeon's death, *A History of British Baptists* by W. T. Whitley could explain the Downgrade Controversy in half a paragraph and never mention the name of Spurgeon. In an amazing display of grammatical passivity, Whitley narrated:

> Here and there the experiments were widened so as to provide amusements on church premises on many evenings, hoping thus to prevent a drift to the theatre, the dance-hall, the billiard-room, the public-house. But these churches seemed to some onlookers [Spurgeon?] to be not inoculating against these places, rather training for them; at last there came a trumpet-blast against the Devil's Mission of Amusement. While this did much to steady and rally, ... A fresh turn was given by a series of articles which traced the harm back from outward amusement to doctrinal declension, and

---

136. Ibid., 558.

137. John Clifford, *Ultimate Problems*, 269.

138. John Clifford, *The Christian Certainties* (London: Ibister and Company Limited, 1894), 80–85.

139. John Clifford, *Ultimate Problems*, 58.

which presently threw out vague charges against denominational leaders. When these were not formulated, nor any definite men were named, the Council of the Union sought explanations unavailingly, and at last had to say mildly that a charge ought either to be substantiated or withdrawn. The incident led to a painful severance of friendly relations, in some measure compensated by a happy emulation in various forms of Christian service. The check was soon balanced by the eager union of the New Connexion with the main body of Baptists.[140]

In view of these positions assumed by Clifford, vice-president and president of the Baptist Union in the initial years of the Downgrade, it is no wonder that Spurgeon considered the case hopeless and proved hesitant to reveal the names of those he opposed. What Spurgeon had feared and ridiculed in "Modern Thought" in general for decades had now become painfully concentrated in the people that he had viewed as the future hope for a pure and powerful expression of biblical Christianity free from all the emoluments and corruptions of a state church.

Now the Baptists were on a road to something even worse. Baptists, unlike former days, were unwilling to set forth precise doctrinal definition and tended to reduce Christianity to an amorphous evangelical "experience" or "spirit" rather than evangelical doctrine. Sir James Marchant in speaking of Clifford's strategic address before the Spring assembly of 1888 said "it gave the central position to the cross—and that is the gist of 'evangelicalism.'" However, merely a central position to the cross does not mean that one has a historically evangelical interpretation of the cross. Clifford obviously did not. The word evangelical became so debased that A. C. Underwood could apply it

to T. R. Glover (as well as call Glover "Christocentric") who expended great amounts of intellectual energy seeking to undercut the supports of historic Christianity. Underwood also calls Clifford "an ardent evangelical" and betrays the present stance of the Baptist Union by commending Clifford for not confusing "the permanent element in Christianity with its theological expression."[141]

The Downgrade movement revealed that many Baptists had joined the spirit of modern skepticism by giving up any confidence that in Scripture one had before him the infallible rule of faith and practice. For the Baptist Union, believer's baptism by immersion was the only basis for union, but, unsurprisingly, several churches in good standing did not even require that. Clifford's church left the whole question of baptism to the individual conscience. Also, the leaders became much more jealous of a humanistic view of liberty of conscience than for the Lord God of hosts. Even the six-point statement of 1888 was worded in such a way that men of opposite opinions could agree with it. The Union had been formed for the practical benefits a closer association of individual churches would give and few safeguards were taken to protect their doctrinal integrity, probably because they never fathomed that such safeguard would be needed. When trouble came, the vast majority preferred unity at any cost rather than obedience to Scripture.

The Downgrade controversy became a classic display of the dynamics of controversy. Alternate pressures play upon the conscience and reveal the location of the most potent affections. Love of truth, fear of disapproval, care to maintain existing relationships, awareness of public impression—all of these converge, clash, amalgamate, and synthesize to form a complex variety of

---

140. W. T. Whitley, *A History of British Baptists* (London: Charles Griffin & Company, Limited, 1923), 326f.

141. Underwood, 232.

responses when a clear cause of division moves from the horizon toward the center of our being. This conflict showed that many ministers were either unwilling to come to a full understanding of issues at stake or were willing to compromise truth for the sake of unity. Disunity will hurt the spread of the gospel was the cry which Spurgeon often heard. He was urged to stay within the Union and resist the drift from the inside. Spurgeon was willing rather to lose his position as a leader, which he did, than to compromise his stance for God's truth by showing external unity with those who denied that truth. In a sermon preached in 1891, "Three Names High on the Muster Roll," based on Daniel 3:16-18, Spurgeon wondered at what the outcome would have been had the three Hebrew children taken the course of saying, "We can do more good by living, dying would cut short our opportunity of usefulness." Spurgeon applied the answer to himself in bold strokes:

> If an act of sin would increase my usefulness tenfold, I have no right to do it; and if an act of righteousness would appear likely to destroy all my apparent usefulness, I am yet to do it. It is yours and mine to do the right though the heavens fall, and follow the command of Christ whatever the consequences may be.[142]

---

142. Cited by Murray, *The Forgotten Spurgeon*, 162. MTP, 1891, 426.

16

SPURGEON AND BAPTISTS IN AMERICA

Much then is expected of you; and your brethren in England confidently look for great things at your hand. May you be rich in grace at home and abundant in labors abroad. May the millions who fly to you from every shore, never lower your moral and spiritual tone, but rather may they be drawn upward by your elevated godliness, and become "holiness unto the Lord." Across the ocean, my brethren, I salute you,—"The Lord lift up His countenance upon you, and give you peace!"[1]

On January 31, 1892, the Baptist world lost two of its most eminent and useful servants. Basil Manly, Jr., of The Southern Baptist Theological Seminary in Louisville, Kentucky, died there of pneumonia, a complication of being struck on the head by a thief in the fall of 1887. Charles Haddon Spurgeon, English Baptist preacher, died that same day in the south of France at Mentone, just a month more than three years after J. P. Boyce had died in Pau, France. C. H. Hudson wrote to John Broadus on February 2:

The daily papers of this morning announce the death of two eminently godly and useful men— Rev. Charles H. Spurgeon, of London, and Dr. Basil Manly, of Kentucky. The Baptist world mourns their loss. Their voices are now hushed in the sleep of death. Their words live on, and will continue to live, till they themselves shall awake to newness of life.[2]

In the summer of 1888, Boyce, for the sake of his health, managed a trip to Europe. His daughter, Lizzie, accompanied him and narrated the events of the trip. One Sunday they were able to attend the Metropolitan Tabernacle in order to hear Spurgeon. He was suffering one of his frequent gout attacks, a malady held in common with Boyce, and preached while seated. Boyce and his daughter noticed the great physical likeness between the two men and Boyce commented, "I wish I were as much like him in preaching power." Afterwards in Spurgeon's greeting room Boyce and Spurgeon spoke about the Pastors' College and gout remedies and doctors. Boyce's emotions began to create physical difficulties for him. His daughter remarks, "Father was so much

---

1. SS, 9:10.

2. A. T. Robertson, ed., *Life and Letters of John A. Broadus* (Philadelphia: American Baptist Publication Society, 1909), 400.

excited by this interview with the great preacher that he became pale and exhausted, and began to pant for breath; so we had to cut short our stay, and leave for the hotel." As he went away, Boyce's eyes filled with tears as he observed, "How little I have accomplished, compared with that man! If I can only get well and live a few years longer, I'll make greater efforts."[3]

Boyce's admiration for Spurgeon was shared by his co-worker John A. Broadus. In 1870 Broadus commented upon visiting the Tabernacle and said that he was "greatly delighted with Spurgeon, especially with his conduct of public worship." He was "an excellent reader of Scripture, and remarkably impressive in reading hymns." In addition the prayers "were quite what they ought to have been." The congregational singing, to Broadus' discriminating ear, was as good as can be conceived. Broadus felt that the sermon fell short of Spurgeon's average in freshness but was "exceedingly well delivered, without affectation or apparent effort, but with singular earnestness, and directness." All in all the entire worship experience was as close to his ideal as he ever expected to see in this life. Though he acknowledged that Spurgeon had faults and deficiencies, he affirmed, nevertheless, "Spurgeon is a wonderful man." Paramount in this judgment is Broadus' conviction that "He preaches the real gospel, and God blesses him." At a quarterly meeting of the London Baptist Association Broadus heard Spurgeon speak again, "a capital address." Broadus himself was invited to speak; in his own opinion, Broadus "succeeded pretty well."[4]

These visits from the two great theological educators in early Southern Baptist life fit within the pattern of appreciation and fascination that Southern Baptists had with Spurgeon since news of his ministry first began to tantalize the public interest. George W. Truett gave personal testimony to this pervasive influence in a sermon preached in London at the centenary celebration of Spurgeon's birth. He reminisced that "From my earliest recollections, my sense of gratitude to Charles Haddon Spurgeon has been a living thing in my life." Truett traced Spurgeon's printed sermons across the ocean and into the homes of America "until they came to a little mountain home in the remote country." The pastor of First Baptist Church in Dallas said, "Week by week, I read those sermons, often reading them over and over again, until they became a part of my inmost life."[5]

The sermons mentioned by Truett first began to be published in the autumn of 1854 when about a dozen were printed. At the beginning of 1855, Spurgeon made arrangements with a printer in London to print one sermon each week. Eventually finding their way into the southern United States, Spurgeon's lines provoked comments and analysis from leading Baptists of the South. E. B. Teague, pastor at that time of La Grange, Georgia, wrote an article entitled "Rev. C. H. Spurgeon and his Theology" for the *The Christian Index*.[6]

---

3. John A. Broadus, *Memoir of J. P. Boyce* (New York: A. C. Armstrong and Son, 1893), 334. This visit occurred after Spurgeon had resigned from the Baptist Union and rejected the sufficiency of a declaration of doctrine adopted subsequent to Mr. Spurgeon's resignation.

4. *Life and Letters of John A. Broadus*, 244, 247.

5. George W. Truett, *The Inspiration of Ideals*, comp. & ed. Powhatan W. James (Grand Rapids: Wm. B. Eerdmans Publishing Company, 1950), 149.

6. E. B. Teague, "Rev. C. H. Spurgeon and his Theology," in *The Christian Index* (October 9, 1856), 162. Teague was a highly respected pastor and educator of Alabama and Georgia who graduated from the University of Alabama when Basil Manly, Sr., was president. He was fully conversant with the details of Calvinistic thought and considered himself a high Calvinist who considered Andrew Fuller's approach to "be the scheme of the Bible." Teague also opposed manipulated "excitements" in matters of church life. "To excitements got up *anyhow* and *by all means*—to revival *machinery*, put in requisition to compensate for a year's indifference and worldly—he hopes ever to except," Teague remarked about himself. But to Spurgeon's impact for revival he took no exception: "To New Market Street Revivals [he means New Park Street],

Teague sought to trace the theological lineage of Spurgeon as well as that of his "ministerial and personal peculiarities." Teague's reading impressed him with "the immeasurable distance, in point of holy zeal, between most of us and such men." Time with a Spurgeon sermon would stimulate one "to more prayer, more exertion, more simplicity and directness. God grant it!"

According to Teague's analysis, Spurgeon adopted "the entire theological system" of John Gill "except his limited invitation to sinners." Though "it has often been believed that high Calvinism is incompatible with burning fervor and melting pathos," the reader should know that "Spurgeon is a high Calvinist, but pre-eminently fervid and touching, and genial and healthy." And though some suppose that high Calvinism has not been a prominent characteristic of successful evangelists, "Mr. Spurgeon appears to be winning very many to Christ."

Within four months of Teague's article a major editorial on Spurgeon by Joseph Walker appeared. Accepting Spurgeon, still only twenty-two years old, as ushered in by divine providence, Walker recognized that the "spontaneous verdict of extolling assemblies" would overwhelm any attempt at philosophical explanation of Spurgeon's appeal. "The magic touch of genius, especially when felt through the medium of eloquent oratory, is irresistible."[7] Apart, however, from any inexplicable elements, Walker commented: "We

have read some six or seven of these sermons with profit and delight. They are vastly superior to the printed sermons of Whitfield [sic], and appeared to us to be just such discourses as the churches of the nineteenth century need." Walker reported that the sermons were Calvinistic in doctrine, "unmixed with even a shadow of heterodoxy." He challenged his readers to read them, investigate them thoroughly, and "if he himself is sound in the faith which was once delivered unto the saints, he will find nothing of which he may reasonably complain." Spurgeon's unique method of presentation and illustration "sends pure Gospel truth right to the sinner's heart. This we call *preaching*." In short, the sermons are sound in doctrine, popular in capacity, and urgent in application. "We like such sermons," Walker persisted, "and wish that the churches could have them more frequently."

The Texas Baptist in January of 1857 carried a vivid description of this peculiarly Spurgeonic preaching when Spurgeon was twenty-three years old and in the flower of his New Park Street years. The writer said Spurgeon was "of the middle size —thick set in figure, with a deep, capacious chest, and a throat, and tongue, and lip, all formed for vehement oratory." This writer said that Spurgeon read the Psalm "abruptly" and prayed with "startling rapidity." Spurgeon's pre-sermon exposition, when done well, was admired as "the perfection of an expository reading before, and as preparatory to the sermon." It was a "rapid running commentary" filled with a "torrent of words" and" striking remarks, quaint and pithy."[8] When C. H. Toy in 1866 observed this part of the service he called the exposition "one of the most interesting parts of the service—a practice which might be with profit introduced into our churches, where

in December and January as well as July and August, he certainly makes no objection." Cathcart's *Baptist Encyclopedia* described Teague in enviable terms: "Superior in scholarship, profound in theological research, eloquent in the presentation of thought, he stands second to no man in the State as instructive preacher. Gifted beyond measure in conversation, thoroughly read in classic and historical literature, and possessed of a devout Christian spirit, combined with a rich flow of agreeable anecdotes, he is one of the most companionable men."

7. Joseph Walker, "Spurgeon of England," in *The Christian Index* (February 4, 1857), 18.

8. "Spurgeon in the Pulpit," *The Texas Baptist*, ed. George W. Baines (vol 3, no. 1, January 7, 1857),1.

instruction is greatly needed."[9] The Texas correspondent, noting an essential ingredient for successful expositions of this sort, also exclaimed, "And how well he knows his Bible!"

Spurgeon's language was such as made "the common people hear him gladly." It was "thoroughly English, vernacular: scarce a Latinized or Greek borrowed term." Within these verbal swaddling clothes thrived "the rich, full, old doctrine of the Puritan age—election defended, asserted, sovereign grace vindicated and glorified; Christ set forth as crucified and slain."[10] E. B. Teague said, "Mr. Spurgeon makes the way of salvation so plain, in the people's own language and by the people's own illustrations, that nobody can misunderstand him."[11]

The Texas paper continued its remarks on the manner and matter of the sermon. Spurgeon took as a text four words from a passion narrative, "There they crucified him." The divisions of the sermon were four. "1st The Place:"—Mt. Calvary, Golgotha its present horror, its ominous symbolism, its providential place in the history of redemption; 2nd The Victim: —Who endured such shame and was the object of such a plot? the Lord of Glory, the author of life; 3rd The executioners —who plotted and who carried out the exquisitely horrid event?; 4th The punishment—the shedding of blood in sacrifice in the most humiliating, defenseless manner; "How natural the divisions!" exclaimed the correspondent. "What vivid clearness of illustration and force of application on each head!" But look at him as he prepares to describe the crucifixion. "Hear him lower his voice and say, 'If you have tears, prepare to shed them now!' Ah you say, that is Shakespeare, and you are shocked. So was I; but then I said, half or three-

fourths of this crowd don't know it, and it is all natural to them." In a moment, however, with all the intensity of Spurgeon's presence and all the possible vehemence of his oratorical gifts, "in a voice of thunder and with flashing eye," Spurgeon turned on the backslider, almost an apostate, crying "You crucify him afresh!" Then placing a hand on a thick nail in the back of the pulpit and with the motion of pounding nails with the other as a hammer he charged on the sinner and backslider an awful guilt. According to the correspondent the assembly was thrilled.

Spurgeon seemed to communicate intuitively that integration of biblical truth, the sovereignty of divine mercy consistent with undiminished human responsibility. The writer of the article observed that he "preaches the doctrine of grace with great courage and fullness: and like Paul, like Whitefield, like Berridge, and Romaine, he freely invites all to our saviour." James Perryman, commenting on Teague's earlier article about Spurgeon and taking exception to Teague's negative insinuations about the practical history of High Calvinism (mild though his insinuations were), pointed to Jesse Mercer as a Georgia Baptist who was doctrinally, experientially, and practically sound and consistent. Spurgeon, according to Perryman, only did what Mercer had done before him: He "comprehended the whole truth and believed, as all true ministers of the gospel do, that the gospel could not be preached as it is in Jesus, unless the whole system be taken in fundamentally and practically" with both the obligation and accountability of the sinner "clearly set forth and urged."

Occasionally, the popular character of Spurgeon's preaching led to negative impressions from some observers. As a matter of fact, C. H. Toy's 1866 visit to the Metropolitan Tabernacle left him surprised, pleasantly, by the reserve of Spurgeon,

9. *Religious Herald*, August 16, 1866.
10. *The Texas Baptist*, "Pulpit."
11. Teague, "Spurgeon," 162.

for Toy had heard that Spurgeon "had a sensual look, and that he was deficient in modesty and dignity."[12] Toy's own opinion changed, as will be noted later. Perhaps, especially in the early years, Spurgeon's remarkable language and voice created such emotion that a variety of interpretations was inevitable. The correspondent for the *Texas Baptist* in 1857 noted with admiration the verbal images and anecdotes Spurgeon used, but also conceded that there were "extravagances and much of self," that he took "liberties with his audience" and dealt "too much in stimulants." Those idiosyncrasies, however, were far better than "these myriads of London allowed to perish unwarned" and markedly superior to "that miserable negation of truth, which our younger preachers are setting forth as a new and better gospel."

Francis Wayland, president of Brown University, noted author of ethics, mental philosophy, and theoretician and practitioner of preaching, did not see within Spurgeon "extravagance" and "much of self." He interpreted his mannerism in the opposite way. "While he is accused of egotism," observes Wayland, "he seems to me to forget himself and his reputation more than any man I know of." Wayland saw Spurgeon functioning in the manner of Paul doing all things for the sake of the gospel: "He seems not to care what people say of him or do to him, if he can only convert them."[13]

Wayland's remarks came after having read a volume of sermons that appeared in 1858, when Spurgeon was twenty-four years old, one year after the Texas report. Wayland was a lifetime observer of Baptist life, theological development, and preaching style. In his *Notes on the Principles and Practices of Baptist Churches* he offered pages upon pages of interesting and helpful insight on preaching, how to prepare for it, of what it should consist, what to avoid, and how to do it. He was insistent upon both earnestness and urgency in preaching, couched in the plain talk of ordinary people. The preacher should "urge every motive, … press home every consideration, that can be derived from heaven and hell, from time and eternity" and "never close a sermon until conscious of having done [his] duty." He should preach in the language of "popular address, plain, simple, and easy to be understood. Vocabulary should approach as nearly as possible to that which the hearers use in thinking, and ordinary conversation, purified, of course, from vulgarity and provincialisms, from cant, slang and technicality." Wayland seemed disturbed that an atmosphere of formality and professionalism might sap the strength from the pulpit, that vivacity would be sacrificed to a vague pedantic notion of what was *proper* for the pulpit "as though a preacher of the gospel were lecturing to a class on the proprieties of rhetoric." He pressed his readers with urgency to consider whether it was time for a "change to come over us", and that a preacher aim "more at interesting and converting men, and less at the reputation of refinement of style, and exquisiteness of propriety."[14]

The articles for Wayland's book were finished in 1856, published in 1857. The next year he read Spurgeon's sermon book and found in him a representative of the ideal Baptist preacher. Several traits encouraged Wayland. Wayland wrote:

> First, the manifest truthfulness of the man, arising from his perfect belief in all that he says. The

---

12. C. H. Toy, *Religious Herald*, August 2, 1866.

13. Francis Wayland and H. L. Wayland, *Life and Labors of Francis Wayland*, 2 vols. (New York: Sheldon and Company, 1867) 2:231-32.

14. Francis Wayland, *Notes on the Principles and Practices of Baptist Churches* (New York: Sheldon, Blakeman, & Co. 1856), 322, 323.

truths of religion are as much a verity to him as his own existence. Second, his intimate acquaintance with the whole Bible. It bubbles up everywhere as soon as he begins to speak. He uses it with great power to express his own ideas. Third, as a result of this, is his manner of making a sermon. He does not draw an abstract truth out of the text, but expands and illustrates the very text itself. It opens to him a train, or several trains of thought, which he illustrates from everything around him. It is owing to this that he has so great variety. Were he to deduce abstract propositions, he would of necessity often repeat himself. Fourth, he takes the very range of the thoughts of his hearers. They therefore, all follow him.[15]

During the American Civil War, Baptist papers in the South picked up on every thread of evidence that Spurgeon supported their cause. One minister reported that Spurgeon declared himself a "thorough Confederate." When introduced to a preacher from North Carolina, Spurgeon is reported to have grasped his hand very cordially and said, "I am pleased to see you; May God establish you and your people! They deserve their independence." One may honestly wonder how the report of such an event could possibly be accurate. The Southern papers also carried snippets from Spurgeon's sermons. Though they had been offended at his remarks on slavery, and had ceased buying his books, and had even burned them earlier, they still desired some food from his table and some sense of his approval.

In March of 1866, the *Religious Herald* published an article taken from the *Watchman and Reflector*, a Baptist magazine from Massachusetts, a paper Spurgeon had used some years before to make clear his reprobation of slavery. Entitled "Analysis of Spurgeon's Power," the article listed doctrinal, experiential, and functional aspects

of Spurgeon which combined to make him effective. This effectiveness may be measured in terms of the ministries and men coming from his influence which are "Divine testimonies to his Christian fidelity and skill." The integration of his views of God and man, law and gospel, and his deep and vivid Christian experience give vitality to "the truths which he sees so clearly and which he has power to tell as few men have been able to do." The writer also writes in rapt admiration of Spurgeon's use of language and his voice. "His mastery of plain direct, vigorous English is wonderful" and he had no equal in this respect in the world at that time. He uses no redundant words but each sentence is the exact measure of his thought. He employs ornament but never reaches after it; it "leaps forth and light[s] up the course of his thought, as sunbursts glorify the road of the traveler." All this restrained and balanced beauty is spoken "with a voice whose volume, compass, flexibility and musical clearness permits no sentence to fail of reaching the most distant hearer." Even though it has such richness and power, it "creates no unpleasant sensation in those nearest the platform,—a voice, too, as fully mastered as was the violin in the hands of Paganini."

C. H. Toy, who in 1866 was an up and coming linguistic expert, analyzed Spurgeon's speech as "racy vigorous English." It was "largely monosyllabic, direct, and with a sometimes Shakespearean fervor and poetry", spoken in a voice which "easily filled the house," in Toy's opinion.

May of 1866 saw another series of Spurgeon articles in the *Religious Herald*. Written by an R.H.S. from Culpeper Court House in April, the articles describe a visit in March of 1863 to "Spurgeon's far-famed 'Tabernacle'." His impressions at the size of the crowd soon gave way to the marvelous decorum in seating such a large and crowded group. When Spurgeon entered all was

---

15. *Life and Labors*, 231, 232.

quiet and attention given to the leader of the worship. Spurgeon announced the hymn "All Hail the Power of Jesus name" and read the entire hymn "with great beauty and emphasis" and selected as the setting "that magnificent old tune ... 'Coronation.'" R.H.S. was particularly impressed with the beauty of the unrivaled human voices as "tongues flamed, and souls soared aloft on wings of melody." Similarly impressed was C. H. Toy who reported that the congregational singing was "very grand and inspiring." The congregation followed the leader with "astonishing facility of movement, there being less dragging than is commonly heard in our comparatively small congregations." R.H.S. expressed particular delight that "no huge organ drowned the sentiment of the hymn with alternate shrieks and groans." The doctrinal foundation of the writer's evaluation of organ accompaniment is not quite clear when he points out that Mr. Spurgeon and his church reject the "*symbol* of the old for the *reality* of the new dispensation, and 'make melody in their hearts to the Lord,' not in *brazen pipes*."

Spurgeon's sermon that day was on "The Joys of Jesus" and had two divisions: (1) The joy of doing good; (2) the joy of being good. The day before had produced a scene of earthly pomp and splendor with the arrival of Princess Alexandria, the bride elect of the future king. The whole city had been enveloped in a luminous wreath of gas light. Spurgeon compared this with the more glorious scene when "the Lord would ride triumphant through the exultant hosts of the redeemed at the great nuptial day of the Lamb and church triumphant."

Then pausing for an instant, as if to view the glorious scene his faith-illumined imagination had drawn, he exclaimed with a thrillingly exultant voice, "Ye kings, ye are crownless! Cast your crown at His feet." By this masterly stroke the audience seemed to be easily let down from the fearful height to which they had been carried, and a glance at the solemn faces of some near me, told me how deeply they were impressed with a sense of the superiority of heavenly over earthly things—of the glory that is yet to be revealed to the glory which attends the riches and power of this world.

In a subsequent article the same writer described the effect of Spurgeon's preaching from the standpoint of method of argument, voice, and gesture of body. His argument he characterized as *luminous* rather than *logical*. He does not seek to crush error by building up layers of logic and proofs until the opposition is crushed with the weight of the case; instead he seeks to dispel darkness by the light he sheds in the simple exposition of truth. His language "remains deeply impressed upon the memory through its extraordinary force and simplicity, and continues to burn there with increasing rather than diminishing light, when fanned into flame by reflection." Toy observed this same impression in Spurgeon's speech, a "faculty of exciting and sustaining enthusiasm—of making his impress upon his hearers—of arousing and carrying on thought."[16] The simplicity, originality, and truth of Spurgeon's divisions and illustrations filled with "natural and life-like pathos" and maintained within the bounds of revealed truth stirred the very depths of the heart. R.H.S. joined with virtually all other observers in commenting on the extraordinary qualities of Spurgeon's voice. It was a voice "remarkably loud, clear, well-modulated, soft and thrilling, especially in emotional passages."

Also noted as worthy of remark was the manner of Spurgeon's gestures. In his lectures to his students, some of the most entertaining and hu-

---

16. C. H. Toy in *Religious Herald*, August 16, 1866, 1.

morous moments came when Spurgeon enlarged upon posture, action, and the art of gesture in preaching. Perhaps it was in this vein that he was observed by the Boston Baptist pastor, George Pentecost, when he reported, "He had the college boys, or men, some eighty in all, at his house, entertaining them before they began their full term of study. He was bubbling over with humour and wisdom all the time. I never saw such a combination of genius in one man."[17] He often made his wisdom ride the wings of humor as he described, or imitated, uncomely habits and physical trappings in preaching. Spurgeon felt that pulpits were an abomination. "What horrible inventions they are!" he exclaimed. "No barrister would ever enter a pulpit to plead a case at the bar. How could he hope to succeed while buried alive almost up to his shoulders?" Some pulpits would remind a minister of his mortality for they were nothing but coffins set on end. "But on what rational grounds do we bury our pastors alive?" he asked. He felt that they should be destroyed like the walls of Jericho and Joshua's curse upon their rebuilding should be uttered over the old fashioned pulpit.

In the Tabernacle, his pulpit was designed for his style of preaching. R.H.S. noticed that Spurgeon generally walked "quietly to and fro in the pulpit, with his arms suspended at his side or folded on his breast; then having one hand in his bosom, while the other was raised." In gesture, therefore, Spurgeon practiced what he taught. He emphasized that "Unstudied gestures, to which you never turned your thoughts for a moment, are the very best, and the highest result of art is to banish art, and leave the man as free to be graceful as the gazelle among the mountains." Gestures should be understated, not repetitious

or monotonous, should not create a ridiculous situation for the preacher, should be in harmony with the unfolding of the message and should not draw attention to themselves. "Absolute inaction is better than overwrought posturing" and appropriate actions overdone "had better have been left undone."[18]

> The risks of too little action are by no means great, but you can plainly see that there are great perils in the other direction. Therefore, do not carry action too far, and if you feel that you are naturally very energetic in your delivery, repress your energies a little. Wave your hands a little less, smite the Bible somewhat more mercifully, and in general take matters rather more calmly.[19]

Though Spurgeon's first rule is that an action "should never be excessive,"[20] he made wonderful allowance for personality and nationality in the naturalness of gestures. In addition, at times gestures must be sufficiently strong when the poignancy of an idea would be betrayed by a feeble or even moderate gesture. R.H.S. noticed that Spurgeon's manner of address conformed entirely to the principle of simplicity in primitive Christianity, being "very humble, devout, quiet, and almost entirely free from gesticulation." C. H. Toy remarked that "his bearing throughout was exceedingly modest and quiet, and his manner, while it exhibited firmness and decision, had nothing unduly bold or unreverential in it."[21] R.H.S. made the observation that Spurgeon employed only one violent gesture when preaching from the text, "I have a message from God for Thee." In that sermon he imitated the "violent manner

---

17. Justin Fulton, *Charles H. Spurgeon, Our Ally* (Chicago, Philadelphia: H. J. Smith & Co., 1892), 342.

18. C. H. Spurgeon, *Lectures to My Students*, 4 vols in 1 (Pasadena, TX: Pilgrim Press, 1990) 2:110, 111.

19. Ibid., 111.

20. Ibid., 108.

21. C. H. Toy in *Religious Herald*, August 2, 1866, 1.

of the assassin to illustrate the suddenness with which death—the last messenger—sometimes attacks the impenitent and hardened sinner." This moderation combined with the dead earnestness of his address "gives the audience the entire possession of their faculties, and the attention is at once drawn from the speaker to his remarks."

The sermon Toy heard, in his opinion, "had in it nothing remarkable in thought, expression or manner;" but he still felt the readers might be interested in how Spurgeon developed his text. Preaching from Matthew 16:15, Spurgeon spoke of how we should think of Christ, and divided the sermon into six parts. First, he is God; secondly, he is man; third he is creator and upholder of all things; fourth, he is ruler of men, setting up and casting down; fifth, he is mediator; sixth, he is redeemer. Toy gave brief elaboration of Spurgeon's exposition on each point. For example, if Jesus is not God "What becomes of the doctrine of election? If he is not eternal, what becomes of the Eternal covenant with the Father; what of Perseverance of the Saints?" or the value of redemption. His humanity elevates all humanity and demonstrates the purity and patience that should characterize our walk in this world. "He was misunderstood, but He sublimely maintained His purpose and His self-respect."

Toy may indicate more about his own values and tendencies than Spurgeon's when he observes: "Without being learned or profound, he instructs by his spirituality and directness, and the cogency of his appeals to Christian experiences is especially remarkable." Toy was also impressed with the consistency of the large and attentive crowds that attended Spurgeon's ministry as well as the "vigorous life that he has infused into his church."

The young Virginia scholar extended his remarks to acquaint the reader with Spurgeon's generosity (out of a large income he lived on £200 per annum, devoting the rest to his benevolent enterprises, so Toy reported), his humble public demeanor (to intended insults he responded with a gentle smile and a bow), his church planting (he called on a large number to cease attending the Tabernacle in order to form a church in another part of the city to which a student from the college would be sent, "who would no doubt carry with him Spurgeon's Calvinistic boldness and directness" adds Toy), and the spirit of evangelism and revival that permeated the atmosphere of the Tabernacle. The membership at that time was increasing at the rate of seventy a month "keeping the baptistery in almost constant requisition." "It was one incessant revival," R.H.S. remarked, "and these baptizing occasions added, as they generally do, much to the interest among the people."

Among the several interesting observations C. H. Toy made in his two articles about churches in London in general, and Spurgeon in particular, concerned Spurgeon's brother, James. Having mentioned the "Calvinistic boldness and directness" of the young ministers sent out by Spurgeon, he included parenthetically "His brother, James Spurgeon, is a young man of pleasing and forcible address." Earlier, the Texas correspondent in 1857 had referred to James with an optimistic prophecy: "He [Spurgeon] has a younger brother studying in the Baptist college at Stepney, who they say will be superior to himself." How we misjudge the future may be observed by the title to an article by J. B. Gambrell some fifty-plus years later, "First and second Fiddles." The introduction included observations about Charles and his brother James Spurgeon. Gambrell and Broadus had been discussing the ministry of the Metropolitan Tabernacle and the vital part of James in the ministry. Broadus suggested the article to Gambrell. He wrote:

It is certain that Charles could never have done even approximately the work he did if his quiet, methodical, but very forceful brother had not supported him in his multitudinous labors. It was James who managed things. It was James who constructed and kept in repair the vast framework which supported the activities of his illustrious brother. Charles Spurgeon was a genius of the highest order, and James Spurgeon was a genius, but of a different order. They supplemented each other, but in such way that James was never much known. They worked together very much as the engineer and the pilot in carrying a ship across the great waters.[22]

R.H.S. referred to and expressed his doubts about an accusation that Spurgeon's pupils were said to "copy him with ludicrous exactness." Gambrell had heard the same reports and knowing that "the imitative faculty is very strong in the human make-up" gave an amusing spin to the stories about imitation. Gambrell not only loved stories about Spurgeon, he was one of the greatest spin doctors Southern Baptists have ever produced. Introducing an article on "Theology and clothes" he wrote:

It is said that Spurgeon once went out with one of his students to preach for him. A very sincere sister said to the great preacher, "Brother Spurgeon, I liked your sermon, except one thing: I did not like your imitating our pastor so much."[23]

None can copy Spurgeon, R.H.S. reminded his readers, and it would be foolish to seek to imitate him especially in the length of his sermons since he himself reminded his people that he did not engage the Tabernacle to sleep in. "He is alto-gether unique, and I for one am willing to let him remain so." In closing with an observation which may still be pertinent R.H.S. spoke of Spurgeon as the "Modern Luther."

I have no doubt but that the reader thanks God with me, that he has raised him up to contend for "the faith once delivered to the saints," and hopes, with me, that his life may be prolonged, until he shall see that gigantic and venerable stronghold of Popish superstition and error, which is now tottering beneath his powerful and well-aimed blows, tumbling in ruins around him, like the ancient Babylon, never again to be raised.

R.H.S. did not share that opinion alone, for in B. H. Carroll's impassioned, if somewhat disjointed, sermon on the death of Spurgeon he said, "With whom among men can you compare him? He combined the preaching power of Jonathan Edwards and Whitefield with the organizing power of Wesley, and the energy fire and courage of Luther. In many respects he was most like Luther."[24]

Carroll admired Spurgeon for a variety of reasons. He loved his preaching and pulpit power, his appeal to the common man, his zeal for benevolence and philanthropy, his utter sincerity, his plan to educate ministers with spiritual power being central to the process, his ministerial labors, his sanctified use of money, and his doctrine set forth in word and life without fear. Carroll reminded his Nashville audience that day that nearly all of Spurgeon's sermons "are upon the fundamental doctrines of grace." He reminded them that Spurgeon's life and ministry "have demonstrated that the doctrine of a free salvation, none of works but all of grace, promotes the highest form of practical piety." Spurgeon's "ministry

---

22. J. B. Gambrell, *Parable and Precept* (New York: Fleming H. Revell, 1917), 55.

23. Ibid., 70.

24. B. H. Carroll, *Baptists and their Doctrines*, ed. Timothy and Denise George (Nashville: Broadman-Holman, 1996), 61.

and its results prove that not Arminianism but *The grace of God that bringeth salvation … teaches us, that denying ungodliness and worldly lusts, we should live soberly, righteously, and godly in this present world.*" His ministry also "demonstrated that while salvation is free, none of works but all of grace, yet the sinner must seek the Lord." Spurgeon's ministry, according to Carroll, "has demonstrated the power of a gospel which insists on man's depravity, the necessity of regeneration, the plenary inspiration of the Scriptures, and the undiluted doctrine of substitutionary, vicarious expiation."[25]

George W. Truett said that Spurgeon "had no sort of fellowship with the nerveless, hazy, intellectual libertinism that plays fast and loose with the eternal verities of Christ's gospel." Instead he held fast by the "great themes of divine revelation: the sovereignty of God; the holiness of God; the love of God; the grace of our Lord Jesus Christ; the solemn wonders of the cross; the divine forgiveness of sins; the fellowship of Christ's sufferings; the power of his resurrection …" Giving coherence to all was the fact that Spurgeon "avowed himself a Calvinist." Truett then spoke of the great strengths of Calvinism in the social and political spheres, warning any that they should not "jocosely sneer at Calvinism." It is a theology that "laid hold of man and lifted him above the heads of priest and bishop and archbishop and cardinal and pope and king and president and potentate and told him that he must answer directly to God."[26]

Another prominent Southern Baptist of the nineteenth century, William E. Hatcher, spent a considerable amount of time with Spurgeon during the height of the Downgrade Controversy. Hatcher had admired Spurgeon for a third of a century and his time with Spurgeon was the fulfillment of a dream. He engaged with a New York Baptist paper, *The Examiner*, to write a series of articles on the Downgrade Controversy and went to London for that purpose.[27] American Baptist knowledge of the issues was partial, but largely reflected a trust of Spurgeon's analysis and actions. For example, James Lawton of *The Christian Index* had reported on Spurgeon's withdrawal from the Baptist Union, squelching rumors that Spurgeon had ceased being a Baptist. He explained that the action was precipitated because "the Union itself had become unsound in doctrine and practice." It maintained fellowship with some who were "grossly heretical, and this, too, against Mr. Spurgeon's earnest remonstrance." Mr. Spurgeon withdrew "not because he was *not* a Baptist, but because he *was*." Lawton then added, with astounding confidence both in the universal approbation of Spurgeon and the undiluted confessional orthodoxy of Baptists north and south: "Every Baptist church in the United States would have done the same thing."[28]

Spurgeon spoke freely with Hatcher of the Controversy revealing that he "felt keenly the strain of it." Yet "his bearing was lofty and magnanimous to a degree." Spurgeon said that "he honored a candid opponent and found unspeakable support in friends who were decided and trustworthy, but that to him the heaviest strain of his life was to endure those who were on both sides of the conflict." Spurgeon approximated bitterness only once when uttering a philippic

---

25. Ibid., 55-78.

26. Truett, 160, 161.

27. Hatcher's summary of his "Downgrade" analysis appeared as "Spurgeon and the Baptist Union" in *The Examiner*, November 29, 1888. His autobiographical book of anecdotes, *Along the Trail of the Friendly Years* (New York: Fleming H. Revell Company, 1910) contained a chapter entitled, "Glad Days with Spurgeon." The biography, Eldridge B. Hatcher, *William E. Hatcher: A Biography* (Richmond: W.C. Hill Printing Co. 1912), contains other reminiscences of this visit.

28. James Lawton, *The Christian Index*, November 3, 1887, 2.

against ingratitude. "Why, a preacher lost all of his teeth and with it his power of articulation, and in my sympathy I gave him a full set of artificial teeth and he turned around and bit me with them." Hatcher said there was "something admirable in the high note of indignation and resentment with which he uttered his contempt for the ingrate."[29] In his article in *The Examiner* Hatcher worked diligently to write in a balanced fashion; in spite of, or perhaps because of, that, his words are turgid with admiration for Spurgeon:

> His temper is beautiful. He is not angry at anybody on the earth. There is a resistless charm in his cool and imperturbable humor. He is as amiable as if all England were resounding his praises. Upon the heads of the false teachers he strikes tremendous blows, but there is no wicked heat in his blood. He is fighting as he believes for the truth, and not to get the better of an antagonist. But let this be said: For an honest opponent Spurgeon has respect, but for a false or trimming friend he feels a contempt which not even his royal and lovely nature can conceal. He does not mind the man on the other side, but he needs grace in double measure to bear with the man who is on both sides. His behavior in the strife has not been perfect. But it has been notably lofty and magnanimous. He does not praise men insincerely, or for partisan purposes, and it may be added that he is far too noble to inflict intentional injury on those who are against him.[30]

Hatcher interviewed opponents of Spurgeon who presented a "commendable spirit" and, while condemning the course of Spurgeon, were, nevertheless, "courteous in the tones and terms of their criticism." Others, however, had words that were not so fitly chosen and "who painted their opin-

ions with their passions." Hatcher acknowledged no benefit from them or admiration for them:

> When a man told me in noisy terms that Spurgeon "did not know what he was doing, and there wasn't a word of truth in what he said," or when another said with an air diplomatic, and tone sympathetic, "Mr. Spurgeon, you see, is very sick, and we feel uneasy about him"; or when another with a crafty smile, "Well, Spurgeon is vastly personal—essentially Spurgeonic, and cannot work anywhere unless he is allowed to lead," I counted it a waste of time to make notes; I simply left and went to see some other man.[31]

Hatcher oozes admiration for Spurgeon and exudes wonder and bliss in being able to write of his personal conversations and experiences with him. He traveled with Spurgeon, ate with him in fine homes, heard him preach, assisted him in services at the Tabernacle, accompanied him on ministeri-

---

29. William E. Hatcher, *Along the Trail of the Friendly Years*, 242, 243.

30. Hatcher, *The Examiner*, November 29, 1888., 1.

31. In his analysis of the justness of Spurgeon's accusations and withdrawal, Hatcher found no cause to question Spurgeon's actions. Spurgeon believed sincerely that doctrinal error existed and was tolerated within the Baptist Union "and it became with him a matter of conscience to utter his protest and back that protest by his own action." Hatcher's own investigation uncovered doctrinal compromise on the issue of eternal punishment and he therefore found no reason to doubt Spurgeon's perceptions of the condition of the Union and certainly his own actions. "If Mr. Spurgeon felt that he could not trust the church to work out the aforesaid problem, or if he felt that it was not a problem but a doctrine, it is not remarkable that he asked that he might withdraw." Again, after further careful discussion Hatcher stated, "Mr. Spurgeon felt that he had to choose between staying in an organization which allowed if it did not foster false doctrine, and that of going out, in token of his respect for scriptural truth." Hatcher hoped that Spurgeon's action would have the effect of calling "back the liberal element to conservative ground, and it surely ought to cause the great body of good men who constitute the Union to be more watchful against the incoming of error." Hatcher knew that the separation was final and irreversible, that the Baptist Union would continue even though suffering some loss, Spurgeon's work would continue to prosper, no new denomination or association would emerge from so called "Spurgeonism", and that perhaps God intended to work good in the Baptist Union from the conflict. "Let it be so, and we shall yet rejoice that the Down Grade, has become the Up Grade, along which many shall rise to loftier achievements."

al trips, shared stories with him, and, in deference to his greatness, smoked a cigar with him. In social situations he noted that "Spurgeon bore himself superbly, mingling with the people, joining in cordial fashion in the chat, and now and then, with an admiring group around him, he talked gloriously, mixing seriousness and humor, telling a story, cracking a jest, stirring everybody to joyous laughter and filling his listeners with admiration and delight."[32] A day at the orphanage Hatcher called "one of the memorable days of my life" and of an afternoon with his ministerial students he said, "truly I never had a happier time with a body of students than was mine that afternoon." In addition to the "almost adoring reverence with which everybody treated him,"[33] Hatcher learned to feel what a "simple, transparent, pure-hearted man he was." Such extended and intimate knowledge of Spurgeon gave Hatcher imperturbable confidence in writing, "It was not pique, nor gout, nor baulked ambition, nor the desire to start a new sect which moved him."[34]

Having spent an afternoon with Spurgeon in the company of two other Southerners, Rev. Henry McDonald of Georgia and Rev. L. R. Thornhill of Virginia, the three walked away late in the afternoon under "the spell of the most unique personality of the nineteenth century." Finally McDonald broke the silence: "What do you think about it?" One of the other two answered, "We have seen a man of God."[35] Hatcher duplicates the emotions of Boyce when Hatcher wrote in his notebook: "Sunday August 12th; heard Spurgeon. Sat on the pulpit and made the prayer. I felt myself unfit to pray for him, – so exalted is he in my eyes."[36]

When recrimination of Spurgeon for his Downgrade action crossed the Atlantic and went into Baptist lecture halls in the person of Joseph Parker, it received even less cordial a greeting than Hatcher had given it. In Milwaukee, Parker spoke and issued an "uncalled for, ungenerous, and unjust characterization of Mr. Spurgeon" which did not "catch the popular breeze it sought." The Examiner's Milwaukee correspondent noted that "Every body knows Mr. Spurgeon is Dr. Parker's peer in every respect and his superior in most respects." The writer observed further that "American Christians are not so far forgetful as to applaud an abuse of Mr. Spurgeon even by so conspicuous a personage as Dr. Parker." Parker, it seems, had a crusade against Spurgeon[37] and took his tirade on the road, hoping to stir up American support for anti-Spurgeon latitudinarianism, for the Milwaukee report was followed by a Minneapolis report which wryly commented, "Mr. Parker vanished from our sight—and $500 at the same instant, the price of one evening's scintillations." Parker, so the report says, "gushed and gyrated, and made a cruel, sickening, thrust at the greatest of living preachers." Then to drive home his point, the reporter addressed the absent Parker: "This comparison thou didst institute for thyself, Mr. Parker. The field was thine. No man acted in thy stead."[38]

Spurgeon's unblemished character and consistent godly zeal in ministry had sculpted a full-life figure of trustworthiness. The only proper response to Spurgeon was imitation, not criticism. The only effect of a criticism launched at Spurgeon was scorn for the perpetrator. Every aspect of his

---

32. Hatcher, *Along the Trail*, 245.

33. Ibid., 249.

34. Hatcher, *The Examiner*, November 29, 1888.

35. Eldridge B. Hatcher, *A Biography*, 283.

36. Ibid.

37. Even in Hatcher's article he recorded, "The ever notorious Dr. Joseph Parker, whose highest genius appears in finding texts for his sermons outside of the Bible, took Spurgeon as his text and preached on him, and at him, and against him."

38. Both reports appear in *The Examiner*, December 15, 1887, 4.

person, his deportment, his preaching, his theology, his activities, his sociability, his spirituality, his ministry, his writing, and his temperament had been scrutinized for more than thirty-seven years by the time of his death. Baptists in America could not be persuaded to believe any ill report. Both pulpit and print were filled with lament at his death and gave full testimony to the fullness of his salutary and beneficent influence. *The Examiner* for February 4, 1892, carried an article on his death. After mourning the loss, not just for Baptists, but for the world and chronicling the massive and magnificent accomplishments of his ministry the writer showed how closely tested and thoroughly approved was Spurgeon's Christian witness:

> In person Mr. Spurgeon was of medium height and stout build. He had a massive head and large features of the heavy English type. In repose his face, while strong, might have been called phlegmatic if not dull in expression. But when he spoke it glowed with animation of thought, quick flashes of humor, benignity, and earnestness and every phase of the emotion that stirred within him. He had many elements of power as a preacher. His voice was of marvelous sonority and sweetness. His language with all its simplicity, was marked by faultless correctness and inexhaustible wealth of diction. He was as far as possible from being a rough or coarse speaker although he had at ready command a vast vocabulary of homely Saxon words. No one from merely reading his sermons, can form any idea of their effect when delivered. The immense Tabernacle, with its two galleria thronged with eager listeners, became a true temple of God's Spirit. The plain sturdy man, standing on his bare platform almost in the midst of the mighty congregation, was a real apostle. In listening to Mr. Spurgeon, one recognized that the chief element of his commanding force in the pulpit was his profound and burning conviction. The message he gave had for him supreme importance. All his

soul went with its utterance. The fire of his zeal was consuming, intense, resistless. When that fire went out on earth a potent spiritual impulse was withdrawn, the absence of which will long be felt.[39]

The strength of support for Spurgeon evident in these reports reflects a studied and conscientious admiration that had begun with a sensation and had grown and solidified so as to be virtually unchangeable. Both the depth and breadth of this is clear in the fiftieth birthday greetings written to Spurgeon in 1884 by the faculty at The Southern Baptist Theological Seminary:

> Louisville KY, June 27, 1884: The undersigned professors in the Southern Baptist Theological Seminary, beg leave to offer respectful and hearty congratulations on your fiftieth birthday. We thank God for all that he made you and has by his grace enabled you to become and achieve. We rejoice in your great and wonderful work as preacher and pastor, and through your orphanage and your Pastor's College; as also your numerous writings, so sparkling with genius, so filled with the spirit of the gospel. Especially we delight to think how nobly you have defended and diffused the doctrines of grace; how in an age so eager for novelty and marked by such loosening of belief you have through long years kept the English-speaking

---

39. *The Examiner*, February 4, 1892, 5. Not everyone handled Spurgeon's death quite so tastefully. One advertiser sought to make merchandise of the event by claiming to have "Unquestionable evidence that he might be alive and well today had he followed his own wishes." Supposedly Spurgeon pleaded with his doctors to administer Warner's Safe Cure. "The doctors refused and threatened to abandon the case." After several testimonials about its miracle working power, the advertisement closed: "The sad hearts who mourn to-day the untimely death of Mr. Spurgeon may cherish his teachings, but cannot recall his life. He has gone, and his death is both a lesson and a warning. Had he followed his own judgment in his physical life as he did his conscience in his spiritual affairs, he would probably be alive to-day to bless the world with his teachings and inspire by presence? [*sic*] May this not be a lesson to you? May you not also require shelter from the great bodily dangers which surround you? Can you afford to neglect the warning? *The Christian Index*, March 3, 1892.

world for your audience while never turning aside from the old-fashioned gospel.

And now, honored brother, we invoke upon you the continued blessing of our covenant God, May your life and health be long spared, if it be his will; may Providence still smile on your varied work, and the Holy Spirit richly bless your spoken and written messages to mankind.[40]

Only on one issue have I discovered Southern Baptists to disagree with Spurgeon—his practice of open communion. When reports first began to come to America about Spurgeon, it was assumed that his practice was closed communion. The final paragraph of Joseph Walker's 1857 analysis lauded Spurgeon for his purity in maintaining a thoroughly baptistic view. As more knowledge of his actual practice emerged, most Baptists in the South felt he was inconsistent. Toy called his allowance of communion to non-members a "deplorable error." In 1887, an editor of the *Christian Index*, James S. Lawton, said that Spurgeon "is not, and never was, a thorough-bred Baptist. He is what is known in this country as an Open Communion Baptist." Justin Fulton, a minister in Brooklyn, an admirer of Spurgeon in every matter except this one, said, "There seemed to be no poorer use to which the Metropolitan Tabernacle could be put than to hitch it on to the waning fortunes of Open Communion."[41] Hatcher reported that he allowed occasional communion to visitors coming through but would refuse communion to those who lived nearby, came frequently to service, but refused to join the church. Walker said that Spurgeon's "tendencies seem to be in the right direction." According to Hatcher, Spurgeon told him, "If I lived in America and in the South where the Baptists practice strict communion, I should

practice it also." [42] Concurring with Hatcher's report, Walker wrote, "It would not astonish us if he should finally come to adopt the views of the American Baptists."[43] This, Spurgeon did not do.

Other than that, Southern Baptists not only agreed with Spurgeon on virtually every theological point upon which he took a stand, but admired him in gargantuan proportions. They encouraged him not only in his benevolent, educational, and publishing, and preaching ministries, but in his conflicts also. Carroll probably spoke for them all when he said:

Yes, Spurgeon is dead. The tallest and broadest oak in the forest of time is fallen. The sweetest, most silvery and far-reaching voice that published the glad tidings since apostolic times is hushed. The hand whose sickle cut the widest swath in the ripened grainfields of redemption lies folded and nerveless on a pulseless breast, whose heart when beating kept time with every human joy and woe. But he was ready to be offered. He fought a good fight. He kept the faith, and while we weep, he wears the triple crown of life and joy and glory, which God the righteous judge has conferred upon him.[44]

---

40. A. T. Robertson, *Life and Letters of John A. Broadus*, 341, 342

41. Fulton, *Charles H. Spurgeon, Our Ally*, 342.

42. Eldridge B. Hatcher, *Hatcher*, 285.

43. *Christian Index*, November 3, 1887, "Spurgeon." In March, 1892, after Spurgeon's death this same paper carried an article on his view of communion written by W. A. Perrin of Spurgeon's College, and delivered before the Cleveland Baptist ministers' conference. "Wrong impressions have gone abroad in regard to his position in respect to the communion question. This has led some other denominations to claim him as their own. But he was Baptist to the backbone and at heart a close communionist. My last interview with him, a few days previous to my leaving for this country, proves this. After a very lengthy conversation on the subjects relative to American theology, he said: 'Have you made up your mind on the communion question? You are going to a country where the majority of Baptists are close communionist. Really, if I had to begin my ministry again, I should certainly commence with a close-communion church. I am led to believe the American Baptists are right, but I cannot alter the usages of my church, which have been of so long standing'" (*The Christian Index*, 3.24. 1892, 1). This anecdote finds no support in the consistent witness of Spurgeon even to his latest years. He remained satisfied that his open communion views were right.

44. Carroll, 59.

17

SICKNESS, SUFFERING, DEPRESSION

I know you will tell me that the gold must be thrust into the fire, that believers must pass through much tribulation. I answer, Truly it must be so, but when the gold knows why and wherefore it is in the fire, when it understands who placed it there, who watches it while amid the coals, who is sworn to bring it out unhurt, and in what matchless purity it will soon appear, the gold, if it be gold indeed, will thank the Refiner for putting it into the crucible, and will find a sweet satisfaction even in the flames.[1]

On one occasion, in the midst of a severe time of sickness and mental distress, Spurgeon commented on eleven deaths that had occurred among the Tabernacle membership in one month. "We have often wondered," he mused, "at the fewness of our deaths, far below the average of the life-tables." He followed with the observation that "Godliness, bringing with it temperance, peace, and purity, has a tendency to produce long life." Sometimes, however, a combination of other situations serves to make miserable and cut short the life of even the godly. Spurgeon came into a series of circumstances from which there was no escape; each contributed its own part to the never-ceasing tension that challenged his faith and his health for more than thirty-five years. Sickness and distress of a palpable sort recurred frequently during the last twenty-two years of his life. His loyal "Armour-bearer," J.

W. Harrald, estimated that from the age of thirty-five Spurgeon was out of his pulpit for one-third of the time either in pain, sickness, or convalescing.[2]

A Living Theology of Suffering

He knew something of this, however, by the time he was twenty-two, for in January 1856 he preached, apparently with more than theoretical speculation, "God teaches his people every day, by sickness, by affliction, by depression of spirits, by the forsakings of God, by the loss of the Spirit for a season, by the lackings of the joys of his countenance, that he is God, and that beside him there is one else."[3] However real these experiences were to Spurgeon at twenty-two, by and by they would be as real and as constant as life itself.

Twenty-five years later he still held to divine purpose in suffering. In The "Sitting of the Re-

---

1. S&T, March 1866, 100. "Bells for Horses."

2. *Autobiography*, 2:194

3. SS, 1:10.

595

finer," Spurgeon pointed to the Word, fellowship with Christ, and the presence of the Holy Spirit as means of purification. God is determined to purify his people for he has elected them to holiness. None need complain against election if they have no desire for holiness. "Sirs," he chided, "if you do not wish for purification and holiness, why should you quarrel with God because He doesn't give it to you?" He also looked to a variety of providential interventions as God's way of sitting to refine his sons of Levi. "Such is the stubbornness of our flesh, that the Lord uses for fuel in His furnace sharp and heavy trials of different kinds," Spurgeon emphasized, with no change of perception over the quarter of a century. "Adversity assumes many forms and in each and all of its shapes the Lord knows how to use it for His people's benefit." He continued:

> Christ sits as a Refiner when He takes away prosperity and brings the wealthy down to poverty. He often refines men by the losses which they sustain of beloved friends. Bereavement burns like a furnace blast and, oh, how much of carnal love has been consumed by it! We have known persons greatly purified by the Holy Spirit by passing through depression of spirit, inward grief and soul sorrow. Spiritual pain has been blessed to some and physical pain to more.[4]

Spurgeon never doubted that his exquisite pain, frequent sicknesses, and even despondency were given to him by God for his sanctification in a wise and holy purpose. After six years, to be followed by sixteen more, of such suffering Spurgeon gave his pastoral thought on the issue in an article entitled "Laid Aside. Why?" We may ask God questions, Spurgeon believed, if we do so without murmuring. Should a commander of

soldiers, of his own will, render his most zealous fighters incapable of entering the fray, would we not be at a loss to discern his motives? "Happily for us," Spurgeon responded, "our happiness does not depend upon our understanding the providence of God." The Christian is able to believe even when he is not able to explain and is content to leave all to the wisdom and goodness of his heavenly Father. "The painful malady which puts the Christian minister *hors de combat* when he is most needed in the conflict is a kind messenger from the God of Love, and is to be entertained as such." It puzzled Spurgeon, nevertheless, and led him to assert, "but how it can be so we cannot precisely tell." He sought, however, both by experience and by biblical example to shed some light on the subject. Every paragraph is evidence in itself that Spurgeon wrote in the throes of a bout with severe pain and mental distress. At the close of the article he confessed, "Just now, when anguish fills the heart, and the spirits are bruised with sore pain and travail, it is not the best season for forming a candid judgment of our own condition, or of anything else."[5]

Filled with sentences that were self-contained units of axiomatic significance, Spurgeon built a case for the instrumentality of suffering in increasing one's faith, encouraging humility, developing patience alongside effectiveness in service, deeper imitation of Christ by participation in his sufferings, the benefits of a change of spiritual atmosphere in which to grow fragrant spiritual fruit, true sympathy and fellowship in binding up the hurts of the broken-hearted, and fatherly chastening for more unadulterated devotion to the glory of God and his cause in the world. He was careful on this last point to avoid the syndrome of Job's friends. "Yet it is not good,"

---

4. MTP, 1881, 4.

5. S&T, May 1876, 198.

he warned, "to attribute each sickness and trial to some actual fault, as though we were under the laws, or could be punished again for those sins which Jesus bore in his own body on the tree." How uncomely would it be to judge the greatest sufferer as the greatest sinner; equally unwise would it be to apply "so erroneous a rule to ourselves, and morbidly condemn ourselves when God condemns not."[6]

A very striking image with riveting barbs illustrated Spurgeon's understanding of the Lord's detestation of conceit and his use of suffering to obliterate it. "Consciousness of self-importance is a hateful delusion, but one into which we fall as naturally as weeds grow on a dunghill." His discussion of suffering as an opportunity for increased faith provides an example of the sweetness and condensed power of Spurgeon's treatment of the issue:

> Let us consider awhile. Is it not good for us to be nonplussed and puzzled, and so forced to exercise faith? Would it be well for us to have all things so ordered that we ourselves could see the reason for every dispensation? Could the scheme of divine love be indeed supremely, infinitely, wise if we could measure it with our short line of reason? Should we not ourselves remain as foolish and conceited as spoiled and petted children, if all things were arranged according to our judgment of what would be fit and proper? Ah, it is well to be cast out of our depth, and made to swim in the sweet waters of mighty love! We know that it is supremely blessed to be compelled to cease from self, to surrender both wish and judgment, and to lie passive in the hands of God.[7]

This theology had been verified, purified, and annealed to his heart by 1890. In preaching on Christ

as "Our Compassionate High Priest," Spurgeon mused, "I could not get on without those sick beds and those bitter pains, and those weary sleepless nights." Blessedness comes through smarting, if we would be helper of the people of God. The Christian must glory in his infirmities and sicknesses for they will be made useful "for the comfort of God's sick people." Not less so did Spurgeon glory in his depression, for here he felt very close to Christ because in all our affliction he himself also was afflicted. So will it be with the minister:

> Our depressions may also tend to our fruitfulness. A heart bowed down with despair is a dreadful thing. "A wounded spirit who can bear?" But if you have never had such an experience, my dear brother, you will not be worth a pin as a preacher. You cannot help others who are depressed unless you have been down in the depths yourself. You cannot lift others out of despondency and depression, unless you yourself have sometimes need to be lifted out of such experiences. You must be compassed with this infirmity, too, at times, in order to have compassion on those in a similar case.[8]

Surrey Music Hall Disaster

Due to the great growth of the congregation at New Park Street, the congregation decided that it would hold its morning services at the Chapel and the evening services at Exeter Hall, in order more easily to accommodate the great crowds that desired to hear Spurgeon. From June 8 through August 24 in 1856 the congregation met at Exeter Hall, but found the arrangement very inconvenient and the proprietors of the Hall came to believe that its dominance by one denomination was not appropriate. Spurgeon agreed.[9]

---

6. Ibid.

7. Ibid., 196.

8. MTP, 1892, 180. This was a Thursday evening sermon on April 3, 1890, and was prepared for reading on the Lord's Day, April 10, 1892.

9. *Autobiography*, 1:428.

Still in need of a large space to meet the demand of the public and to fulfill an evangelistic mandate and opportunity, the church, after free discussion and objections from some who called it the "Devil's House," decided to rent the Music Hall of the Royal Surrey Gardens for one month, beginning on the third Sunday of October, showing a willingness to go even to the Devil's house to win souls for Christ. The facility, known widely for the amusements and pageantry regularly sponsored there, would serve for just over three years as the preaching venue for the most popular preacher in England. On the morning before that first evening service, hopes and fears ran high. Spurgeon asked the congregation to "Prove the Lord" by their courage and commitment to such a bold, foolish as many insisted, venture in trust of a God whose power is shown in their weakness, whose wisdom overcomes their foolishness, and whose purpose overcomes their vacillations. Even if he, so Spurgeon preached, should have to stand where "thunder-clouds brew, where lightnings play, and where tempestuous winds are howling" he was, nevertheless, born to prove the power and majesty of God. The events of that evening caused him "to pass through the greatest ordeal of [his] life."[10]

One of Spurgeon's students, William Williams, recalled the visceral reaction that Spurgeon had when any event or conversation reminded him in a graphic way of that terrible event. Spurgeon asked Williams about his text for a sermon and Williams responded, "The curse of the Lord is in the house of the wicked, but he blesseth the habitation of the just." Spurgeon gave a deep sigh, his countenance dropped and he moaned, "Ah me!" When asked what vexed him he responded, "Don't you know? That is the text I had on that terrible night of the accident at the Surrey Music Hall." Williams did not know it and resolved never to mention either the text or the event to him again. "I cannot but think," he wrote, "from what I saw, that his comparatively early death might be in some measure due to the furnace of mental suffering he endured on and after that fearful night."[11]

After twenty years of printed sermons, Spurgeon recalled many of the pivotal events by which the circulation of his sermons increased to wider and wider audiences. Among those factors he mentioned the move to the great hall in Surrey Gardens where he preached for more than three years. This hall, Spurgeon believed, had been prepared by a marvelous providence for just such a time, "for its main use and benefit to any one in any sense, until it was turned into a hospital, was connected with our occupation of it." The great providence included, however, this event. Though he dared to mention it, he demurred "even at this distance of time" to trust himself "to write upon the deadly horror which passed over my soul during the calamitous panic which brought to a speedy end the first service in that place." He recognized, nevertheless, that "God marvelously overruled the sad event for his own glory, leading vast numbers of all ranks to besiege the edifice, and crowd it continually." For the printed sermons these events "opened a far wider door than before."[12]

Robert Shindler, who knew Spurgeon from 1855 after his settlement in London, and wrote often for *The Sword and the Trowel*, recalled the effect that the Surrey Music Hall calamity had on Spurgeon. At the Baptist Union meeting in 1881, twenty-five years after the event, Spurgeon was

---

10. Ibid., 1:431.

11. William Williams, *Personal Reminiscences of Charles Haddon Spurgeon* (London: The Religious Tract Society, 1895), 46.

12. S&T, January 1875, 5.

announced to preach at Portsmouth. Long before the time for service, the room was packed and hundreds of others were pressing to get in. This created some confusion just as Spurgeon moved to the platform to take his seat. The confusion so disturbed him that "he seemed entirely unmanned, and stood in the passage leaning on his hand." He told Shindler that the scene's likeness to that at the Music Hall was so vivid that he felt entirely unable to preach. He did preach, and, according to Shindler, preached well. Spurgeon himself referred to this event in *The Sword and the Trowel*. He believed that the "vast audience had a remarkable escape from an imminent peril." A newspaper had remarked that Spurgeon appeared nervous, and he responded, "Who could avoid it amid that dense throng, in a frail building, with constant interruptions?" His public reminiscence of the scenes that caused his propensity toward fright was stated in strong language: "The horror of great darkness which passed over the preacher's soul, few can understand but those who have once seen a multitude flying in panic, and people trodden to death in the crush."[13]

The Pressure of Ceaseless Labor

During an episode of particularly acute pain in the fall of 1869, Spurgeon had to explain why his contribution to the *Sword* was beneath its usual volume. "The Editor's painful indisposition compels him to forego his usual monthly notes, and also the Exposition of the Psalm." Then he noted with an honest self-perception that suffused all his communication: "Too great pressure of work has produced a disorder whose root is more mental than physical." To him, the combination of "wearisome pain, added to relative affliction and ever increasing responsibility," constituted

"a burden under the weight of which unaided mortal strength must sink." Since nothing in his temporal situation brought relief or the prospect of pleasure, he confessed, "An all-sufficient God is our joy and rejoicing."[14] Spurgeon sometimes seemed to know better how to handle pain, adversity, and opposition than friendship and commendation. When a small book appeared in 1869 with high commendation of his "*Labour, and Success*," Spurgeon wrote, "When Christian friends write in our honour we feel great shame that we so little deserve their praise, and painful prostration of spirit that we should have had a word said in our favour." Surely the writer's views were due more to "grateful affection than to calm judgment."[15] Public approval pained him, for each accolade seemed to produce the greater stress of exalted expectation. The increasing responsibilities of which he spoke, including the demands of the benevolent ministries, flew upon him relentlessly and in ever-more strident insistence. The ministry of preaching and publishing made a part of this increase.

Spurgeon gave several names to his distress through the years—gout, rheumatism, neuritis—combined with overwork, depression, and constant stress, and guilt over feeling stress. He seemed instinctively to know that gout was not the simple answer to all that surged through his body and mind. Hannah Wycoll has made the point, that his "condition was diagnosed as Bright's Disease, or chronic nephritis, a disease of the kidneys, causing severe pain and swelling due to accumulation of fluid which can distend the whole body, and severely restrict breathing."[16] The history of gout in his family makes it possible

---

13. S&T, December 1881, 626.

14. S&T, October 1869, 479.

15. Ibid., 477.

16. Hannah Wyncoll, ed. *The Suffering Letters of C. H. Spurgeon* (London: Wakeman Trust, 2007), 10.

that at times his bodily complaint arose from that source, but probably the severity of it is explained in terms of the severe aggravation of joint pain by the peculiar symptoms of Bright's Disease. Spurgeon's terms and perception will rule the narrative, but we will understand that he probably had more reason for pain than even he knew.

Even as he celebrated a twenty-year ministry of publishing sermons in 1875, Spurgeon printed a candid caveat to the sense of exhilaration that such success brought him. He reviewed the twenty-year history of consecutively published sermons and admitted the "mental wear and tear involved in printing one sermon a week," and, though Scripture is an inexhaustible quarry, "the selection of the next block, and the consideration as to how to work it into form, are matters not so easy as some think." Month after month pulpit preparations are not slight matters especially when one considers how heavily one feels what is at stake.[17]

Relentless labor had a twofold effect, the result of which was an insoluble dilemma. It tended to increase the work load exponentially and it ruined the physical condition so that labor became impossible. Reflecting clearly on his personal experience Spurgeon told his students and graduates from the college: "The consecrated flame will, perhaps, consume *you*, burning up the bodily health with too great ardour of soul, even as a sharp sword wears away the scabbard, but what of that? The zeal of God's house ate up our Master, and it is but a small matter if it consume his servants. If by excessive labour we die before reaching the average age of man, worn out in the Master's service, then, glory be to God. We shall have so much less of earth and so much more of heaven."[18]

Late in 1869, in the middle of November, Spurgeon was suddenly laid aside by an attack of the smallpox, which he called "that dreadful disease." It struck him just as he had so filled his schedule that he needed to be "in a thousand places." He prayed fervently that none of the work would suffer, and especially the orphanage and college. Spurgeon noted that in just a few hours, without knowledge of Spurgeon's indisposition, a friend called and left £500 for the orphanage. "How condescendingly did the Lord thus ease his poor servant's mind! We felt a sweet peace and holy joy in leaving all the rest of our work in the same hands." In just a few days another gift arrived of £1000. Again Spurgeon acknowledged that all provision was from God and he gladly "set to our seal that God is true." We have many other sources of anxiety, as flesh would call them, but the gracious dealings of our God compel us to call them founts of joy, since they give us excuse for appealing to his bounty." He printed the letter and let the donor know that his donation encouraged the trustees to take 50 more boys in the orphanage and to complete the number of 200 as soon as possible.[19]

By the middle of 1871, Spurgeon's pains and distress returned with power and with a more extended attack than hitherto experienced. Acknowledging that he had been relatively free from difficulty since Christmas of 1869, he wrote, "On the last day of the annual Conference we were laid prostrate by an attack of our very painful malady. It will, we fear, be our cross till death." The attack came upon him "as an armed man, and great has been our bodily anguish beneath its strokes." He had to suspend his personal work and thus wrote few notes for the monthly *Sword*. He gave thanks to his brother and others for their faithfulness

17. S&T, January 1875, 7.
18. S&T, May 1877, 211.

19. S&T, December 1869, 566.

and ability to "conduct affairs so well in our absence. The Lord's name be praised."[20]

The next month carried an article entitled "The Pastor's Illness" written by George Rogers. The debilitating nature of Spurgeon's 1871 bout with his perennial afflictive encounter was accentuated when Rogers explained with candor its thoroughness. Spurgeon could not rise to write words of "counsel and encouragement" because of the "restlessness and pain of his bodily affliction." Though so low in health, Rogers said he was "sustained and cheered" by reports of the good attendance at the Tabernacle, the reception given to the preachers, and the offerings made to sustain the college and the "several agencies, instituted by him as auxiliaries to his ministrations." The obvious concern and prayers of his people greatly encouraged him. None should think it strange, Rogers wrote, that ministers are laid aside just when it seems that their presence is most needed. They too are subject to the sovereign providence of God and must say, "If the Lord will." Scripture and history confirm this reality and it should bring no surprise nor discouragement when it occurs. The cancellation of speaking engagements must evoke prayer and understanding from those so disappointed, and curtailment of any invitations for the future must surely be seen as necessary.[21]

Rogers had his own explanation of what brought about this crisis in strength and health. He believed that the excitement of the recent college conference exacerbated the difficulties of an already nearly exhausted state in need of vacation. The intense excitement of so many bright, youthful, useful and "valiant soldiers of the cross, who had imbibed his spirit, and had been trained through his instrumentality" put his strong sen-

sibilities to the severest test. The intelligence and devotion and the manifold gifts and operations of mind evident in the presentation of papers intensified the effect of this highly emotional week and, whereas, in normal circumstances such operations would strengthen and encourage, an already depleted body and mind were pushed to a crisis point by the his overcharged emotions.[22]

Spurgeon intended to take his trip to the Continent for rest but was unable even to travel. Three months of pain and weakness was made more unbearable by a thirteen-week absence from the Tabernacle pulpit. He hoped to resume his ministry in July. In spite of the great difficulties encountered, Spurgeon reported, as a duty as well as a pleasure, God's goodness in the event. "My beloved people have overflowed with love to me. Everybody has been kind. Prayer has been fervent. Our various works for the Lord have been well sustained. The congregations have been excellent, and the prayer meetings especially large." He informed all his readers that they should not ask him to preach for them in the next few months, "for I cannot comply with their requests without incurring fresh sickness." When a friend suggested that he evangelize a few months in every year and edit a weekly paper, he acknowledged the kindness of the confidence but sighed, "Why not expect me to become rival to Atlas and carry the world, or the successor of Hercules with twice his labours? A five-pound note for the orphanage is of more value than the wisest inventions of new tasks for an over-wrought man."[23]

A Chronic Experience of Varying Degrees

Any gain of strength encouraged Spurgeon. Friends began to suggest all sorts of remedies for his recurrent difficulties. He told them that

---

20. S&T, May 1871, 237.

21. S&T, June 1871, 282.

22. Ibid.

23. S&T, July 1871, 333.

he was indeed better, though still feeble. He had taken one service for each Sunday for a month. "Though greatly pressed to rest, to travel, to take a voyage to Australia, to go to Hydropathic Institution, to make a trip to America, to visit Switzerland, to stay in Scotland, to try Buxton, Bournemouth, Scarborough, etc. etc. we feel it our duty to begin work gently and prudently, little by little, but still to begin." He gave thanks to all those friends so concerned as to suggest ways of improvement but, though he knew he was "overwrought", he found no way to escape the pressures his own zeal had created, and he declined to pursue anything but duty.[24]

By September he described himself as "quite recovered" but "still weak and not able to work up to his usual point." Again he requested that no invitations to preach be given for he would merely have to refuse. Taking note, therefore, "will spare both them and us the time occupied in writing needless letters."[25] In December, he finally relented and informed his church and friends, "We have been enabled to continue our ministry and other labours under very considerable difficulty from feeble health, and now, in order to gain rest and escape the fogs which close the year, we have felt bound to make a short sojourn in the warmer climate of the south of France."[26]

Spurgeon recounted the experience with pain that so dominated 1871 in the preface to that year's bound volume of *The Sword and the Trowel*. In spite of the aggravating to debilitating difficulties, he assured his readers that "unmingled mercy" suffused the entire experience. The struggle taught him "to count his sore sicknesses as his choicest blessings." Though he did not deny others the right, he could not "sing of mercy *and of judgments*," for his music was of love alone. Spurgeon never liked pure sentiment and unrealistic cant spirituality, but he would not let his readers think that this language was merely "superfine sentiment, or high-raised enthusiasm." No, he wrote "soberly and in quiet earnest." He had found "affliction sweet, and the cross so richly profitable, that it is by bare justice to regard it as a richly paternal blessing." Always ready with analogies from his observations of nature he likened the painful assault on his health to a spade that loosens the earth around a tree and "sets the roots at liberty to suck the fatness of the soil." If he could complain, then well might "the mown grass murmur at the clouds which renew its verdure." He had no inclination to let his "heart speak one injurious word of pain and depression, which work in us the comfortable fruits of righteousness." He went so far, in fact, as to "wish our readers no richer benediction that the sanctification of every providence to their soul's highest good."[27]

In 1874 Spurgeon endured the same undulations of pain and greater pain. In March he began his "notes" with a confession of having a "jaded mind" brought on by "rheumatic pains."[28] He wrote his report of the college conference from a "desert place" where he had "fled to recover from the wear of this exciting week."[29] In July, an Anglican clergyman wrote to him and said that his gout was sent to him as a judgment of God because of his opposition to the Church of England. Spurgeon wondered, in light of that theology, what the death of the Bishop of Oxford from a broken neck meant.[30] In November he informed his readers that most of October saw him unable to function because the change of season "brought on a rheu-

---

24. S&T, August 1871, 382.

25. S&T, September 1871, 430.

26. S&T, December 1871, 570.

27. S&T, 1871, Preface.

28. S&T, March 1874, 142.

29. S&T, May 1874, 241.

30. S&T, July 1874, 341.

matic affection, which was very painful, but far less severe than on any former occasion." Perhaps remembering his former invincible exuberance he mused, "It must be a high privilege to be always able to work for the Master with vigour."[31]

Again in 1875, Spurgeon found himself waylaid by pain and distress. So indisposed was he that he could not even take his planned trip to Mentone but made him a prisoner at home. Pain had seized him like an armed man making his hands and feet good for nothing but suffering. "We had much to do,—too much," he complained, "and to our grief we could not even so much as think of all the good things we had planned." Both his surgeon and his physician, based on years of observing Spurgeon, advised him that the "disease springs from mental causes, and can be as fairly reckoned upon, when an extra pressure of care or labour occurs, as the tides may be calculated by the moon." He would have to rest, and when reinvigorated, would be at work again. "It is very sad to be pulled up thus in full course," he lamented, "when good is to be done and so much of it lies before us."[32]

When Spurgeon returned to health, he felt that he needed to reserve his strength for the requirements of tending the ministries of the Tabernacle. Throughout April and May of 1876 he stayed in his chamber, and, when finally able to preach on "the Lord's Day", he informed his readers that it would be that way for some months to come. "All engagements to preach abroad must stand postponed or cancelled, and no new work of any sort can be undertaken."[33]

This plea seemed not to have universal effect for in the next month he begged friends "not to press him so importunately to preach every day and every where." To the "eager pleaders" who asked for "just one day at our anniversary!" he called to "have some mercy." If they replied to his "no" answer with another invitation explaining why their invitation should be an exception, he requested that they enclose a stamp so that he would not be out a penny as well as the time to say no again. "Could any one of our readers guess what a public man's correspondence costs him? Make it a penny less," he reconfirmed, "by not asking him to preach when he is not well."[34]

Early in 1877, Spurgeon again got away to Mentone but encountered a cold wind in Marseilles that prompted an attack of rheumatism and "caused us intense pain and weakness." His friends sent him freely their fail-proof remedies for which Spurgeon thanked them profusely and asked that they be kind enough "not to send us any more remedies: we know of at least 50 infallible cures, and are embarrassed with medical riches which, like the miser, we hoard up for the benefit of others."[35] He admitted that one of the most extraordinary, even if equally useless, was the recommendation that he keep a pair of turtle-doves or two young pigeons in the room. In south Germany the doves were called "gout pigeons." The only relation Spurgeon could see between the birds and rheumatism was that the noise they made would end the short periods of respite that he had and so hasten the final end of all anguish.

Concern for Thomas

Given Spurgeon's chronic pain and illness, the frailty of his son Tom must have been a constant concern for the Spurgeons. Both Charles and Tom were baptized on September 20, 1874, at eighteen years of age by their father. They soon became involved in preaching at Bolingbroke in

---

31. S&T, November 1874, 542.

32. S&T, February 1875, 92.

33. S&T, June 1876, 284.

34. S&T, July 1876, 333.

35. S&T, April 1877, 189.

a private home. The crowds grew and led to the building of Bolingbroke Chapel in 1877. When it became clear that Thomas was ill-affected by English weather, his mother advised a voyage. His father concurred and wrote him, "You will preach, I am sure, but without good training you cannot take the position which I want you to occupy." Doubtless, the father had in mind a position at the Metropolitan Tabernacle. "Theology is not to be learned in its amplitude and accuracy by one destined to be a public instructor without going thoroughly into it, and mastering its terms and details." Spurgeon, again even in this incidental way, revealed how central theology was to his entire understanding of pastoral ministry. "Perhaps a voyage may give tone to your system," that is, might strengthen him physically so that he could stand the rigors of "two years of steady application."[36] Thomas left for Australia on June 15, 1877. Spurgeon announced it briefly in the *Sword*, writing, "Here, perhaps we may be allowed to notify our Australian friends that our son, Thomas Spurgeon, left us for Melbourne, on June 15, taking a voyage in the *Lady Jocelyn* for his health. We shall be grateful to any friends who will extend kindness to him. He will be willing to preach as opportunity may occur."[37]

The voyage proved to be a stimulant to his health. He landed in Australia on August 28. Soon after Thomas landed, Christopher Bunning made contact with him and saw to it that he was most heartily welcomed by everybody. Thomas spoke to a crowd of more than 4,000 at the Melbourne Town Hall "with much profit to his hearers and credit to himself."[38] Bunning described a journey he took with Thomas through the bush country

on which they managed several times of preaching. After a day of wandering through miles of trackless shrub, they held a service in a woodshed where Thomas, "with divinely imparted skill, combated excuses of all kinds" while Bunning preached on the Lord's opening the hearts of the first converts of Europe. Other preaching engagements, social events, and witnessing opportunities sanctified this tour of the bush of several weeks. It could not have but helped immensely the spirit of CHS when Bunning closed the letter with a high commendation of both his sons:

> God has made him the instrument of much blessing to many, but most of all, I think, to me and mine. I believe that the foregoing and other work Thomas may do in the Colonies, if the Lord will, may prove no mean help towards preparing him for what I pray may be a gloriously useful life. I must rejoice with you, beloved sir, in the fact that both your sons are called so unmistakably to the ministry of the gospel. Though perhaps not remembered by Charles, now in college, I desire to send affectionate Christian salutation to him. To you, honoured President, I must ever remain, Your very grateful ex-student, Wm. Christopher Bunning.[39]

While Thomas found time to mend, he admired the tireless zeal of a friend, Mr. Varley, who preached every day. Thomas found some opportunities to preach in Australia, but accepted the time of rest as preparation for greater usefulness later. His mother digested his letters home for publication in *The Sword and the Trowel* and his father wrote him with the compactness demanded by his schedule, but with expressions of hope for the future. "When I have you and Char at my side to preach the same great truths we shall by God's grace make England know more

---

36. W. Y. Fullerton, *Thomas Spurgeon: A Biography* (London: Hodder & Stoughton, 1919), 49, 50.

37. S&T, July 1877, 334.

38. S&T, January 1878, 31.

39. Ibid., 40.

of the Gospel's power." These words encouraged Thomas to pray for "full consecration and that consuming zeal which God has helped you to."[40] Charles was "working well at College and will, I trust, come forth thoroughly furnished," his father wrote. "When you come home I hope that your practice in Australia will lessen your need of college training so that one year may suffice. Still every man regrets when in the field that he did not prepare better before he entered it. We shall see."[41]

On August 26, 1878, Thomas received the cable, "Mother's worse, return." He was able to leave by September 12 and arrived home toward the last of October. By November his father was sick and Thomas was called on to preach five times at the Tabernacle. These messages were published under the title, *The Gospel of the Grace of God.* His father said they were "full of the truth of the gospel, and of living earnestness. The style is all aglow, sparkling with metaphor, warm with affection, burning with zeal." He also admitted that probably he was prejudiced in the young man's favor.[42]

In the middle of January, Thomas accompanied his father to Mentone, where he had a regimen of study under the guidance of CHS. By April 13 they were home again. Thomas entered the Pastors' College but "ill health often interrupted his attendance."[43] He left again in October 1879 for New Zealand. This was a sad event for the elder Spurgeon and he preached that evening at the week-night service, "No, my Lord, I am a woman of a sorrowful spirit." Until his father's death, Thomas remained in New Zealand and Tasmania with the exception of five months on

a fundraising tour of England. *The Sword and the Trowel,* however, ever kept the name of Thomas Spurgeon before its readers, in humorous articles, travelogues, sermons, and reports of full-time evangelistic success. His father worked with zeal among the supporting friends of the chapels and missionary labors, to raise funds for the building of Thomas' Tabernacle in Auckland, New Zealand. An effusive thank you letter in the *Sword* from Thomas was followed by his father's remark, "We have no doubt that when we receive a picture of the proposed chapel, and the work has commenced, friends will give ample help to our son."[44]

Another letter and report from Auckland brought Spurgeon to express something of his fears for his over-stretched son. Thomas had a "heavy task before him," and Spurgeon prayed that in his efforts to collect funds "he may not break down under the pressure which this must bring upon him." The cities of Australia were wide apart and thus the "toil and weariness of a collecting-tour to a young man who is not strong."[45] The loss of the adult companionship of Thomas, even with the knowledge of his gospel faithfulness down under, placed an atmosphere of melancholy on the spirit of C. H. Spurgeon, as he feared that overwork might produce a like chronic struggle with depression and fatigue.

Depression and Candor
In July 1877 Spurgeon had to cancel appearances at Liverpool, Norwich, and Maze Pond because of pain and sickness. He kept up a schedule at home but asked friends not to ask him to come and speak. If he exerted himself to do more than that, he knew he would be "laid aside pretty frequently with depression of spirit and pain of body;" he preferred therefore the relative seclu-

---

40. Fullerton, *Thomas Spurgeon,* 71.

41. Ibid.

42. S&T, November 1884, 598.

43. Fullerton *Thomas Spurgeon,* 87.

44. S&T, February 1883, 96.

45. S&T, March 1883, 149.

sion of keeping steadily on with home duties for the comparative quiet might renew strength for future endeavors.[46] Early in 1881, he had been ill for five weeks and "during that time I have been brought into deep waters of mental depression," but at the same time had had more "quiet of heart than aforetime."[47]

Elizabeth Skoglund has pointed to Spurgeon as a master for understanding the inner-workings of depression on God's faithful servants. He also had keen insight into its origins mentally and physically, and gave profound theological interpretations of it. He did not analyze depression as having unexceptionally its roots in sin. That origin was possible and sometimes was the clearest explanation, but frequently the explanation for its assault on the spirit was far removed from a sinful disposition, and its remedy was often something other than repentance. "Spurgeon was far ahead of his time in perceiving this important relationship between emotions and the body," Skoglund observed, an insight he gained because of the connection he consistently experienced between his chronic ailments and his ever recurring depression.[48] In sharing his pain, of body and of spirit, openly, Spurgeon became a great source of comfort and counsel to others. His own vulnerability to this condition and the criticism he received for it, made him acutely sensitive to the experience of others and allowed him to find scriptural and theological examples to explain this very common, but nonetheless distressing, human condition. Skoglund accurately noted that "the black clouds of depression never permanently left Spurgeon's life until he went to be with his Saviour."[49]

Skoglund also drew from some of Spurgeon's sermons to show that Christ himself felt depression, obviously not sinfully so, but as a result of the impact of his knowledge that formerly sustaining mercies were now being withdrawn. He began to be very heavy, so the Evangelists tell us, and if we would have some kind of sympathy with him in his sorrow "sometimes even to us the grasshoppers must be a burden, that we may in all things be like our head."[50] Her survey of Spurgeon's progress from his early ministry to his death convinced Skoglund that "In spite of, and very likely because of, the depression in Spurgeon's life, he became a spiritual giant for God." Skoglund found in Spurgeon's experience and his ability to analyze it carefully a profound help in counseling Christians walking under the shadows of a cloudy pilgrimage.

Spurgeon's student and biographer, J. C. Carlile, saw in Spurgeon this same element of edification through the way in which he bore with constant pain. Carlile observed that the greater part of Spurgeon's career "was lived in fellowship with physical pain." In bearing it himself with buoyant resignation, suffering contributed "to the comfort and the strengthening of others." In later years as he sat uneasily and ponderously in the chair in his private room, talk was difficult as breath came only through pain, and, even in sitting, he leaned hard on his walking stick. "The enemy has me today," he once said, "in both knees. I am afraid I cannot walk to the platform." He began the arduous stroll by straightening himself up, tightening his lips, he stood with the aid of his cane on one side and a helping arm on the other. Along the corridor he would struggle, and then into the College room where, as Carlile recalled, "the rafters rang with the welcome of one hundred

---

46. S&T, July 1877, 333.

47. S&T, February 1881, 92.

48. Elizabeth Skoglund, *Found Faithful* (Grand Rapids: Discovery House Publishers, 2003), 143.

49. Ibid., 150.

50. Ibid., she quoted *The Saint and His Saviour*, 135.

and twenty men." He straightened himself more, reached the platform and sat down. "Then the enemy gave him another twinge; his face was drawn for a moment but when he looked up with a new light in his eye, he said, 'God gives to some a talent for suffering.'" Reflecting his own judgment and conversations that he had with the men present, Carlile noted, "That afternoon many men felt ashamed that they had ever spoken of their paltry little aches and pains. They had seen a great soul in physical agony."[51]

The Hard Years of 1878 and 1879

As the time came for finishing the editorial work for *The Sword and the Trowel* in December of 1877 for the January magazine 1878, the first entry in the notes stated, "Mr. Spurgeon is completely laid aside and in a condition of pain which prevents his doing anything."[52] In January, "worn out with weariness of brain" Spurgeon left for a period of rest. Each year certain symptoms appeared with "painful force" and indicated that "the strain upon the mind must be loosened or the periods of rest lengthened." The strain of ministry of such a large congregation combined with the growing responsibilities of the benevolent enterprises made it necessary to take steps to "remove some of the burden to other shoulders."[53]

As far as the congregation itself was concerned, Spurgeon felt an increasing burden over the statistics of increase and decrease. When 1877 produced a gross increase of 437, dismissals of various sorts of 337, giving a net increase of 100, Spurgeon sighed, "It is remarkable how large a gross increase is needed to make any clear increase. As a church grows older this difficulty increases, and

great work must be done for but little statistical result." The important issue, however, was that "souls are saved and whether other churches on earth or the hosts triumphant above are the gainers, it is equally a matter for rejoicing."[54]

Deacons suggested that he take some extra weeks away. One in fact suggested twelve, for sometimes even seven or eight weeks is not sufficient for a thorough recovery. The deacon had a horse that was as "good a bit of stuff as ever lived, but too free (very like yourself), would overdo himself if he had the chance, and at last got queer in the legs and giddy in the head." The horse needed three months on good soil to regain strength and perspective and "being sold he fetched the original price."[55] Spurgeon had no desire to be sold at any price but smiled at the congenial comparison. He seemed to get better "every five minutes" he said and looked upon Mentone as a "charming retreat, unsurpassed for its warmth, sunshine, and scenery."[56] Not only was the weather and scenery a tonic for Spurgeon, but he found the fellowship remarkably encouraging, as ministers from both Church and Dissent formed a "practical Evangelical Alliance." The minister and evangelist of the French Church were very attentive both to visitors and to Mentonese.

In July 1878, Spurgeon was unable to keep an appointment to preach at Witney "for the severe weather confined us to our bed." Spurgeon's father went instead and filled the place well. Spurgeon made it clear that he feared to make engagements "since we are so often laid aside in the most painful manner, and disappointment is the result." When it became known that he was going to Scotland for rest, requests for sermons along the way began to mount. Spurgeon was perplexed

51. J. C. Carlile, Charles H. Spurgeon: An Interpretative Biography (London: Religious Tract Society, 1933), 130f.

52. S&T, January 1878, 45.

53. S&T, February 1878, 91.

54. Ibid.

55. S&T, March 1878, 142.

56. Ibid.

about this, not knowing quite how to process such severe kindness. He did not lose his sense of humor and irony in describing his perplexity. Invitations came from a "large number of Scotch towns, and from places on each of the three lines of railway, but we were entreated just to make a few hours stay and preach in North Wales, as also on the Cumberland coast, which as everybody knows are both on the road to Scotland if you choose to make them so." He could not calculate how many pence he had been fined in the form of postage for providing "no" answers to all these requests. Just a two hour stop and take the next train multiplied by twelve made it dubious that he ever would reach Scotland. "This, too, when a man is out for a holiday!" The matter to Spurgeon was not as easy as simply saying, "No," for he had rather be flogged than refuse a preaching invitation. As it turned out, Spurgeon's health, or lack of it, caused a postponement of the holiday.[57] None need be offended, therefore, for Spurgeon did not come near the towns of invitation, but found his respite on a painful bed.

Soon he was able to travel and to Scotland he went. A friend, Mr. Duncan, had a yacht and days were spent "cruising in sunny seas, and usually anchoring at night in lonely bays." There distractions came not from the rumble of traffic nor ceaseless noise of city life, but from the "scream of sea-birds, the cry of the seal, and the splash of leaping fish." There he experienced a bath of rest, intense enjoyment and repose, for which he expressed gratitude, that no "exhibitions, artificial recreations, or medical preparations can afford."[58] He did not observe only, however, but fished and found the time exhilarating. In using his fishing trip as an illustration for evangelism, he described what must have been a vivid experi-

ence on board the yacht. "It is very encouraging to feel that a large creature of some sort is tugging away at the other end of your line. Up with him at once! It is better still to have two hooks and to pull up two fish at a time, as one of our friends did. To do this twice every minute, or as fast as ever you can throw the line is best of all. What an excitement! Nobody grows tired, and the day is hardly long enough. Up with them in with the lines! What, another bite? Quick! Quick! … This is good fishing."[59]

On November 10, 1878, Spurgeon became sick and called on his sons to preach for him. "Son Tom," stepped into the breach taking the evening service that had been specially designed for "outsiders," the quarterly occasion when Spurgeon's regular hearers stayed home to allow others to attend. Tom preached five times and Charles once. Spurgeon wrote, "It has been a delight of no ordinary kind for both of the sick parents to hear on all hands the highly favourable judgments of God's people as to the present usefulness and ultimate eminence of their sons."[60]

Spurgeon preached once in December and by the middle of January went to his retreat in France at Mentone. According to Fullerton, this location, "of all the places in the French Riviera was the chosen retreat during the last quarter of the nineteenth century of those who sought winter sunshine apart from the gaieties of fashion."[61] Thomas Spurgeon accompanied him on this trip. Spurgeon wanted to give some special attention to the reading of his son and assigned him Carlyle's *French Revolution* and A. A. Hodge's *Outlines of Theology*. During this visit the younger Spurgeon met George Muller, Hudson Taylor, and John Bost.

57. S&T, August, 1878, 416.
58. S&T, September 1878, 421.
59. Ibid., 424. "Fishing."
60. Fullerton, *Thomas Spurgeon*, 82.
61. Ibid., 83.

During the stay in Mentone he wrote his congregation.

To hearers at Tabernacle and elsewhere

Beloved Friends

By the tender kindness of God the journey hither was made without excessive fatigue, and now I trust that genial weather will bring with it rapid restoration. This place has participated in the severe weather. It has swept over the continent so that I miss just now the bright sunshine to which I have been formerly accustomed, yet it is comparatively warm and so far is beneficial to an invalid. Rest is the main thing, and I hope to find that I may come back to you strengthened for sacred service.

It is at the request of many that I write these few lines, otherwise I should be better content to say nothing about myself. Tottering on my staff today in weakness I look forward hopefully to the time when I shall stand among you in fulness of vigour. God grant that mental, and above all spiritual strength may be given me for the preaching of the word in your midst, that my long bodily affliction may assist to that end. I trust I shall not be forgotten in your prayers when it is well with you, I hope also that the various enterprises, such as the College and Orphanage will not be allowed to languish because the President is ill. Peace be to you all.

Your very heartily,
C. H. Spurgeon

In the Preface to 1879 volume of *The Sword and the Trowel* (written probably in December or late November 1879) Spurgeon summarized the painful struggle with sickness and depression experienced during the year. "Its earliest hours saw the Pastor a prisoner, unable to rise from the bed of pain." This caused him to take a "furlough of three months, during which his pain of body ceased, his spirits revived, and his mind recovered from a pressure which had somewhat overpowered it." Demands on both head and heart generated by ministering to such a large congregation as well as superintending so many forms of Christian work Spurgeon found impossible to describe to any but those that had felt such themselves. "It is no wonder that sometimes the strain is too great, and mind and spirit sink into painful depression," Spurgeon confessed, "from which there is no recovery but by rest."[62] This three-month furlough, was preceded by two months of such debility that Spurgeon had to ask others to fill his pulpit from November 10 until he left in January. During this time he wrote that he wished "zeal and fervor were not restrained and hampered by being yoked to painful infirmities of the flesh." He wanted his people and all his friends to know that he certainly would do more "if we were not laid prostrate at the very moment when our work requires our presence." He pledged that every interval of relief would be "laid out in his service." As mentioned above, his sons were among those that supplied, Thomas filling five of the services.[63]

In the throes of this onslaught, Spurgeon tried to respond to the need for writing some memorial piece relative to the celebration of twenty-five years at the church. Spurgeon wrote, "Our ill health at this moment scarcely permits us either to hold a pen or to dictate words to another; we must therefore leave till another season such utterances of gratitude as the fullness of our heart may permit us." He had experienced many common blessings for which he was grateful, but the abundant and extraordinary favors given him in the relationship with his people throughout this semi-jubilee could not be "acknowledged fitly

---

62. S&T, 1879, "Preface," iii.

63. S&T, December 1878, 600.

with the tongues of men or of angels, unless a happy inspiration should bear the thankful one beyond himself."[64]

As he wrote the "Notes" for January, again his debilitating illness rose to the fore. "Should there be errors in the notes, or in acknowledgment of goods, or in aught besides, it is hoped and believed that the editor's ill-health will be a sufficient apology. We have done our best; but with a pained and wearied brain, which is the root of our malady, we cannot but fail in many ways." Though the celebration of the month was about his ministry, he kept as much aloof as he could from the excitement. He asked that friends understand and excuse him if he continued to do so, "for our head will not bear it." At the same time that he was pressed to the limit in pain and distress, he reported that "Mrs. Spurgeon has been passing through a very grievous time of pain and weakness." She felt unequal to the task of writing a report on the book fund. Her husband would have helped, but he had been laid aside also "tossing to and fro in pain."[65]

In the next month this supine state continued, with a matching sense of mercy. "During the past few weeks, long weeks indeed, we have been laid aside by illness. There have been intervals of ability to write, as our readers will see by articles in this and last month's magazine, but for the most part we have been a prisoner, under bonds to cease from work." Spurgeon represented his case as one of happiness and favor, filled with mercy, but with necessary sharp pains and excessive labors in order for the joy not to get out of bounds. These contrasting phenomena of life were meant to balance each other. In the midst of all, Spurgeon said, "We are now recovering strength, and before this sheet meets the reader's eye, we hope to be out of the colds and damps in the south of France." He was surrounded with close friends and "love floats in the atmosphere we breathe." Again, Susannah would be unable to accompany him. He commended her to his friends that they would not forget her in his absence. The church officers had made an earnest appeal that he take sufficient time to rest for the longer good of his ministry among them. "We print it," Spurgeon noted "because it will interest some of our friends."[66]

Dear Pastor,

It is with much earnestness and love that we, your church-officers, wish to lay before you this, our united appeal.

We consider it to be the path of wisdom for you to lay on one side for three months your public duties in our midst, so as to obtain the complete rest you so much require. Your many labours, in season and out of season, in which we heartily rejoice, have led us to the conclusion that, unless you renew your power by a long cessation from active work, you will be prevented from the continuance of it in the future. Our hearts have sorely grieved over the suffering and weakness which have seized you so often of late, and we, therefore, deem it imperative that you should try the effect of an entire change of scene for three months. We will make any arrangements you may desire for the carrying on of your work while you are away, but most affectionately yet firmly we press our unanimous judgment upon you for your consideration. We shall miss you sadly, and shall hail with joy your return to your loved and prosperous labours; still, we cannot but see that you are wearing yourself away at your post, and must spare yourself for the future welfare and service, not only of our own beloved church, but of the whole Christian world.

---

64. S&T, January 1879, 3.

65. Ibid., 41.

66. S&T, February 1879, 86.

The officers not only sent this letter, but arranged that everything should be provided for in the pastor's absence. When it came to care for their pastor, they would do nothing by halves.

By the middle of March, in company with many friends, Spurgeon could say that he was better, "though weak in the knees, and liable to sharp rheumatic pains at every change of weather." He hoped to return to preach by the second Sabbath of April. The conditions at Mentone always helped him. The air of Mentone was dry, the weather is usually fine, and the Hotel de la Paix, well-ordered in every respect, provided him every conceivable comfort and hospitality. He was surrounded by "friends of the choicest kind, who seem to come and go in succession, as if by arrangement." Dr. Bennet, his physician, as usual, "exercised his best skill for our recovery."[67]

He saw Hudson Taylor as well as George Muller. Both of them were friends of Spurgeon and he admired them greatly. On this occasion, about Muller he wrote "We count it a surpassing joy to have been indulged with this man of God. His preaching is most spiritual and strengthening; but in private he impresses us even more. His evident happiness and holy peacefulness read a blessed lesson to one who is far too apt to be cast down." He promised to write a bit about some of his visitors "if our mind be in fit order." He followed through with this promise for the May issue. Meanwhile, he went on to say, "We are revived in spirit, and strengthened in nerve, though a little perplexed by the report of the Colportage Society, which we desire to bring before the Lord in prayer, at the same time that we use the means by informing the people." Spurgeon confessed to the need for a large measure of faith, and, with his usual idoneous simplicity, felt confident that the Lord would supply the needs of his own work. "We cannot afford to be anxious, for this would neither honour the Lord nor benefit our mental or physical health." Later he described the immediate need the colportage ministry had of an infusion of £1,000.[68]

Pain and Benevolence

That note concerning the colportage ministry pointed to the reality that the benevolences that flourished under his superintendency also wore away his emotional reserves. His relationship to these generated an increasing manifestation of trust as well as a deepening source of distress. This process had begun years earlier.

Urgency saturated his words in 1870 when he wrote, "Will friends forgive us for reminding them that the greatest kindness they can do us is to prevent all temptation to anxiety of mind on our part by supplying with regularity of liberality the needs of the College, Orphanage, and Colportage."[69] Two years later he continued expressing this urgency through his commendation of the creative ways that givers of small gifts sought to expand their impact for good. Spurgeon took special note of "several small sums from working men who have been led to help the orphanage through reading *John Ploughman's Almanack*," commending their suggestions for increasing the revenues. One such reader "wants us to urge some hundreds of workers to send 2s. 6d. each, as he has done, and so increase the income." Spurgeon thanked him for his spontaneous liberality, hoped others would imitate it for the sake of the orphans, and commended such giving by exclaiming, "The more the merrier." When another reader sent half-a-crown, acknowledging that the Almanack was worth it, "John Ploughman lifts

---

67. S&T, April 1879, 193.

68. Ibid., 193–94.

69. S&T Jan 1870, 47. "Memoranda."

his hat to that friend." Another reader of John Ploughman predicted a great sale for the book, and enclosed four guineas, as "an equivalent for 1,000 copies, towards the Stockwell Orphanage Funds, trusting that many of your readers may follow the example."[70]

The combination of "shrewd English common sense" and prayer was exhibited fully in a prayer meeting talk in August 1881. Summer travel often made people forgetful of the consistent needs back in London and, so Spurgeon confessed, caused "trial of my faith." "I see the waters ebbing out, and at times the tops of the rocks are left bare, and I can see the weeds and the mud, and I do not enjoy the sight at all." He had rather see plenty of sailing water "for the fleet of charity." While thankful that they had never been in actual debt, he also hoped for more regularity in giving. With the recent addition of the girls' orphanage he confessed to a trial of mind: "I say to myself, 'I do not see any more people taking a share in the work,' and the question arises, 'However will you keep them?'" His answer was that he did not know, but that God did, and he could find the means. He will not cast away a "good work that is undertaken for his sake." So, he urged the 1,500 present for the prayer meeting, "pray about it lest it be true that we have not because we ask not." He spoke with urgency, begging prayer for all the equally useful agencies, not because "I have any unbelieving anxiety, but because the Lord has said, 'For this will I be enquired of by the house of Israel to do it for them.'"[71] Every new benevolence, each new society, every founding of a church in a needy area added to the mental burden of Spurgeon, increased the urgency of his appeal to his giving friends, and gave new impetus for importunate prayer before the throne of grace.

Sometimes Spurgeon seemed to use his health as leverage for gaining financial support. In 1871 he asked his hearers, "if they are profited by the word I preach, and desire to show their thankfulness," to do a personal kindness to him by contributing to the Stockwell Orphanage. "I am not well enough to bear anxiety," he informed them, "and I hope those I have laboured for will keep me from it by the constancy of their support of this and my other Institutions." Should the support be steady and sufficient it would guard him against "depression of spirit, and gladden me in the service of my Lord."[72]

Before going away in 1874 he informed his people that he had prayed for "some little store in hand to last while we were away." Such provision would keep him from "temptation to worry about finances while seeking rest." His prayer had been heard "in some measure," and funds increased. "Never had we so many tokens of love from our friends as just now. We thank them all, and take courage."[73]

One year later, upon a painful seizure in January, Spurgeon playfully mentioned all the prescriptions friends had given him to cure gout which would surely have killed him if he had taken them. Early in his life, before his own affliction was evident, Spurgeon himself had been humorous in suggesting a cure for gout for his grandfather, assuming he must have gout in the hand since he had not returned answer to his letters. "If he is alive," Spurgeon quipped, "and not gone beyond the seas, please to give him my kind love the first time you meet him, and tell him I suppose he must have gout in his hands, so that he cannot write." Should that be so, Spurgeon suggested, "keep all wines and spirits from him, as they are bad things for gouty folk; and be so good as to fo-

---

70. S&T, December 1871, 570.

71. S&T, October 1881, 498.

72. S&T, 1881, 485. Stockwell Orphanage Report.

73. S&T, February 1874, 92.

ment his hands with warm water boiled with the heads of poppies. By this treatment, the swelling will subside." At that point Spurgeon suggested that the fictitious friend to whom he composed this missal, place his grandfather at a table, put a pen in his hand, make him write his name and put it in the post. "Ah, 'tis a sad thing," observed the healthy nineteen-year-old Spurgeon, "people will get gouty!"[74]

Spurgeon had gotten gouty and now had no remedies to suggest but one. The best remedy for him, if friends really were concerned that he improve, would be "freedom from any anxiety about either College, Orphanage, or Colportage while we are away. If the funds keep up, and the works are carried on by those engaged in them, and especially if the Lord will bless the enterprises, it will be better to us than all the lotions, liniments, specifics, and elixirs put together, with twenty sorts of magnetisms thrown in."[75]

Again in 1879 we find how closely Spurgeon believed his health was connected to levels of anxiety prompted by assurance or insecurity of financial support for the benevolences. As he readied himself to leave England in November and December to escape the fogs in order to avoid the sickness that regularly attacked him during those months, with the hope of improved health and strength for the rest of the winter, he immediately thought of the financial state of the charity work. "Our only difficulty is that during our absence funds fall off," Spurgeon reminded the reading friends, "and, therefore, it would be a very great relief if the stores were well replenished before we went from home. This would make our holiday doubly restful."[76]

His readers became accustomed to these appeals for funds to insure his health and would respond immediately upon hearing of his plans to go to the Continent. This became a bit of leverage in his hands also. When he left in November of 1881, he managed his appeal along those lines. "Friends who take an interest in our work will greatly ease our mind if they will send in specially abundant help for all the institutions while we are away," he reminded his readers and then added, "We once had watchful friends who promptly sent in generous aid whenever they saw that the pastor was ill, for they thought it would be ministering to his health if they kept every work in going order." Then the gentle application for such continued sensitivity, "Some of these friends still survive, and the Lord is preparing more, for his work must not falter."[77]

The support of these benevolences was constantly on his mind. The prospect of worrying, worried him. The specter of fear stared at him so that he needed evidence of blessing to take courage. With the increase of responsibility in the coming years, the emotional and mental toll exacted on the health of Spurgeon would multiply. Before the bazaar in January 1882 for completion of the funding for the girls' orphanage, Spurgeon felt one of his old enemies creeping into his body. Massive mobilization of friends all over England was underway garnering sufficient goods and people for an extraordinary amassing of income. "It would be a great comfort," he told his readers, "to have just a line assuring us that our confidence is well-founded." Then he told the reader that "the fogs are coming over us, and the Pastor stands in daily fear of a return of rheumatism; in which case he will have to leave this land of damps at once." But how could he go with such pressure for his presence at this critical stage of development of plans and publicity? "It would tend to health,"

---

74. Spurgeon, Letters, "To His Aunt," 1853.

75. S&T, February 1875, 92.

76. S&T, October 1879, 497.

---

77. S&T, November 1881, 583.

he informed, "to see the good work going on with vigour."[78] Bazaar preparation must go on in his absence and will surely succeed if "every member of the church, every sermon-reader, and every magazine subscriber" would send in something. "Remember," he urged, "this is for the *girls* and the little ones plead for themselves."[79]

The heights of joy generated by the brilliant successes of each respective charitable inflow, demanded a corresponding outflow of mind and heart from Spurgeon in a way that no other mortal could understand, and no other mortal could bear. Though he surrounded himself with capable administrators of like mind in doctrine and concern, none could take his place in the public appeal generated by every enterprise. It was Spurgeon's Tabernacle, Spurgeon's College, Spurgeon's Orphanage, Spurgeon's preachers, Spurgeon's colporteurs, Spurgeon's almshouses, and Spurgeon's fatherless children. He could not shove any of it off his shoulders; he knew that his urging, his presence, his reporting, his special ambience of justification for each ministry carried the day. No minute of any day was free from an ever-increasing demand on his skills of appeal, his facility of explanation, his face as the monument of trustworthiness and his ministry as the source of "thankofferings" for the people's investment. Where could he go, that this responsibility did not follow; what could he do ever to absent himself one moment from the care of so many people, the payment of so many salaries, and the maintenance of so much property? It demanded, moreover, not just administrative genius and never-ceasing investment of wise and experienced judgment, but the assumption of continued spiritual blessing on his life and ministry. What if that ceased?

Spurgeon made sure that none could doubt his commitment to the funding of the agencies and that he personally sacrificed for their well-being. The beginning of the twenty-five-year celebration saw the leadership of the Tabernacle propose that a gift, a testimonial be given to the pastor. Spurgeon approved the taking of the testimonial offering but stoutly refused to receive any of it as a personal gift. Though a gift to a pastor for lengthy service was a worthy gesture and in many other cases would be right for pastors so honored to receive the offering gladly to lay aside for their families, "in our own case it did not seem to us at all fitting that the offering should come into our own purse." Though it would not be sinful to receive it, his conscience and heart revolted against the idea. He did not want to monopolize an honor that in reality belonged to the whole church. He proposed that the offering come but that it be set to the aid of the poor in the church. "To aid the church in its holy duty of remembering the poor, which is the nearest approach to remembering Christ himself, seemed to us to be the highest use of money."[80]

He had begun to prepare for this a year earlier as he approached the end of twenty-five years of ministry in the congregation. In January 1878, he told the deacons that the "heaviest burden was the Almshouses." They had a scantily endowed fund sufficient for six widows but now supported seventeen. That, added to the gifts to the poor, including poor members, exceeded £1,000 in expense each year. He requested, therefore, that an effort be made to raise a £5,000 endowment and "this part of the church work would be put into proper shape." He would regard this as a proper way of celebrating his silver anniversary of ministry. Though he himself could bear the

---

78. S&T, October 1881, 535.

79. S&T, November 1881, 583.

80. S&T, January 1879, 6.

burden, he would not like to leave such a load for his successor should he be called away soon. His administration would be no blessing should the church find that they had facilities for widows to starve in, but no provision for their daily bread. When the occasion arrived, therefore, the care for the widows was increased and the bed of pain he occupied was assuaged. "All the while that we have been tossing to and fro in pain," Spurgeon set the personal context, "the money for the various objects has flowed in at a rate seldom experienced before. It seems as if the Lord had bidden his stewards take double care of our work while we were suffering. To God be the first praise, and then to every donor our personal gratitude."[81]

As proceeds for the Memorial continued to come, Spurgeon again commented on the relation between their generosity and his health. Contemplating a trip to Mentone, he remarked, "This rest is rendered the more truly restful by the fact that our subscribers have been doubly generous to the various funds, and thus make us feel that no work will suffer while we are away." Even with the possibility of such an increase in endowment, Spurgeon could not afford to let anyone forget that "the outlay for the various enterprises goes on." He felt relief, however, in the present security, both earthly and heavenly, of "a fair balance in hand on all accounts, and the assurance that kindly hearts will not forget to keep all needs supplied, and yet above that the confidence that our God will supply all our needs."[82] Donations had reached £2,300 with the promise of another £1,000. He continued his determination, in spite of efforts to convince him otherwise, that no portion would be kept for himself, but that he would divide the amount among the various institutions. The committee insisted, however, on marking the

event with a tablet in the Almshouse schoolroom and giving some memento of the occasion to the Spurgeon household—"some substantial bronze, or piece of furniture, with a suitable inscription"[83] At the end of year, as Spurgeon wrote the preface for the 1879 *Trowel*, he reported a final total of the Memorial testimony gift, given by "our beloved people," of £6,223 10s 5d. Spurgeon had the pleasure of handing it all over to trustees for the Lord's work. He felt great relief knowing that "our *Almshouses* are now endowed, so that the support of the aged sisters will never become a burden to the church."[84] By 1882 Spurgeon had found that "the amount provided by the Pastor's endowment" was not sufficient for the old ladies to live upon. "A few more hundreds," he reported, "would put this institution beyond want."[85]

When he returned from Mentone in 1879, after the refreshment of rest and the great victory of the Memorial, he reported, "We are revived in spirit, and strengthened in nerve, though a little perplexed by the report of the Colportage Society." As usual, he wanted to bring the need before the Lord in prayer, "at the same time that we use the means by informing the people." He needed faith that sufficient provision would come to meet the requirements for the Society and to maintain equilibrium in his own health. "We cannot afford to be anxious, for this would neither honour the Lord nor benefit our mental or physical health."[86] He went on to describe a situation in which the funds for the Colportage Society were cripplingly low and he called for an inflow of £1,000. "Now there are 82 colporteurs and the stock is too low to go on with, paying cash. Any other way of acting is difficult in practice and unsound in prin-

---

81. Ibid., 41.

82. S&T, February 1879, 87.

83. Ibid.

84. S&T, 1879, Preface, iii.

85. S&T, March 1882, 150.

86. S&T, April 1879, 193.

ciple." For the sake of Kingdom work, the labor of the colporteurs in gospel preaching, temperance, lecturing, tract distributing, and sick visiting must be continued. No fewer than 75,000 families were being visited monthly. All of this, from a human standpoint, stood in peril, and Spurgeon looked "up to God for immediate help." He could not think that God willed to "for us to stay this holy service, which he is so greatly blessing." All silver and the gold belonged to the Lord, and he could provide it through a single donor or raise up many friends to make up the amount.[87]

Having told the "brothers and sisters in Christ" of the pressing need, he assured his readers that he would make no abject appeal, or put advertisements in the paper about our distress." The trial had come when he had no personal reserve to bear it, "judging according to the weakness of our flesh." He resolved, nevertheless, to "rejoice in it in spirit, and bless the Lord, who will supply the need as surely as he lays the burden upon us." Just to press a bit more purposefully on the regular donors, Spurgeon wanted them to understand that colportage was not of secondary importance to the college and orphanage. Though Spurgeon could not hide from anyone his instinctual delight in the college, his commitment to the ongoing immediacy of the practical work of the colportage must be embraced by his supporters. "It is doing a grand work for the Lord in benighted districts, and we love it by no means less than any other of our institutions." He recognized that he failed to interest others in it with sufficient urgency, but now "seeing that we are powerless in the matter, and straitly shut up by urgent necessity, we cast the whole business upon the Lord, expecting to see his delivering hand." Spurgeon felt the awkwardness of the timing—

just after such large giving to the Testimonial, and just before the annual college meeting—and realized that a bare appeal to the Christian public was not likely to prevail. An appeal, however, "to the Lord is never unseasonable, neither is he straitened. The confidence of the psalmist must be his: "My soul, wait thou only upon God; for my expectation is from him."[88]

Needs were never-ending, and pressure unremitting, so Spurgeon must find ways to continue the appeals. Success continued to turn the handle on the vise that enclosed his mind and conscience. Upon completion of the purchase of the ground for the Girls' Orphanage in 1879, Spurgeon publicized a method of gaining regular contributions for the maintenance of the orphanages. First, the furnishing of the house would call for donations and then "increased help to feed all the boys and girls." Special friends could help us much if they would allow Spurgeon to send them collecting books. He wanted to get a "little band of helpers who would correspond with us personally, and help us regularly by collecting in different towns and villages among their friends."[89] Spurgeon needed no more mouths to feed and no more property to maintain, and his friends did not need another source of constant appeals. His own health could not endure the pressure of the increased responsibility, but neither could he turn his back on the providence that made the new mercy possible or the obvious need for a care facility where destitute girls might thrive.

In 1881 when he reminded his supporters that the college educated 100 men in training for ministry and also taught 200 men at night to improve their "out-door preaching, Sunday-school teaching, and other gracious work," he also informed them that expenditures exceeded donations by

---

87. Ibid.

88. Ibid., 194.

89. S&T, September 1879, 448.

£1,500 per annum. Considerable legacies had enabled the work to proceed without hindrance. Whether support in this way could be continued in the future, Spurgeon confessed not to know, but he was convinced that God would do what is right. At that time more than 500 ministers of the gospel had been trained. Though he loved the orphanage and rejoiced in the enthusiastic response of all to the needs of that work, he pointed out that "many will give to an orphanage out of natural compassion, who will not contribute to a college out of zeal for the truth." All the needs had been supplied, "nor shall we ever find ourselves forsaken, for the work is the Lord's." Donors must be aware, however, that long-term continuance of all work depended on the maintenance of the college. "While departures from orthodoxy startle us on all sides, it would ill become the lovers of the old-fashioned gospel to withdraw their aid from an institution which keeps to the Puritanic lines of doctrine, and has no ambition to be held in repute for 'progressive ideas,' and 'advanced thought.'"[90]

Wayland Hoyt found Spurgeon to be placid under the weight of so many responsibilities. Hoyt looked at Spurgeon's ministries and calculated what it must take to sustain them. "I was thinking of the orphans he must feed, the old Christian women he must care for, the professors' salaries in his Pastors' College he must pay, the students he must supply with teaching, many of them with bread and clothing, since they were too poor to buy these for themselves." Lost in the seeming impossibility of it all, Hoyt asked, "How can you be so easy minded? Do not these responsibilities come upon you sometimes with a kind of crushing weight?" Spurgeon looked at Hoyt "with a sort of holy amazement, and answered,

'No; the Lord is a good banker, I trust him. He has never failed me. Why should I be anxious?'"[91]

Spurgeon did indeed feel the ponderous immensity of the human situation and stated his susceptibility to physical and spiritual weakness with candor; never far behind, however, was the conscious testimony of reliance on God to care for his own work in the world. The delicate intersection, so ever-present in Spurgeon's theology, of human responsibility being merely one element of God's sovereign management of the world, made him never lose perspective even when under the most oppressive pressure. When in 1880 he reported that for six months the Lord had tried him "with sharp pains," he also stated that the Lord had removed "all cause for serious care as to the financial needs of my many institutions." We see here not only the candid recognition that the institutions were his, he felt the responsibility more than any single person on earth, but that the "trial of straitened supplies" had been kept from the suffering servant. God provided even though sickness weakened not only the physical efforts but the fervency of prayer. "I do but feebly trust and pray," Spurgeon complained, but as a matter of pure grace, "God most richly answers; and when in hours of crushing agony both supplication and confidence seem to need an effort beyond the strength of the tortured mind, the Lord deals with me after his own gracious fashion, 'exceeding abundantly above all that we ask, or even think.'"[92]

Receipts were reported each month in *The Sword and the Trowel* for all the benevolences, each contributor being listed by name. Weekly offerings at the Tabernacle were taken for the college. The Evangelists' Association received funds

---

90. S&T, March 1881, 133.

91. Wayland Hoyt, *Walks and Talks with Charles H. Spurgeon* (Philadelphia: American Baptist Publication Society, 1892), 10.

92. S&T, April 1881, 161.

from donors as well as from the churches served by the evangelists. Spurgeon expressed at least mild concern in 1881 when he had not "received any amounts lately from the places visited by the evangelists" though he was sure that the spiritual results of the work of Fullerton and Smith at Sheffield would be "followed by a corresponding thankoffering." In addition the Yorkshire Association was "waiting until the close of Mr. Burnham's engagements to pay over in one sum the amounts received from the churches which he has helped." Given the slowness of the thankofferings, Spurgeon noted that "general subscriptions will be heartily welcomed for this work, which the Lord has so signally owned to the salvation of souls, and the edification and comfort of believers." In the same way, though the Colportage Society flourished in the spiritual benefit it encouraged, "the general fund is very low, and help has been received to a very limited extent during the past six months." On that account Spurgeon would look "prayerfully to the Lord, through his people, to supply our need."[93]

Spurgeon never panicked, never indicated anything less than full confidence in God's provision, but felt keenly the personal responsibility for reminding the people that they are stewards. He did so with gentleness and gratitude in most cases. Late in 1884 his fight with pain cost him dearly but he was able to say, "During our extreme weakness we have been kept from all anxiety as to funds for the Lord's work by the continual thoughtfulness of friends." The Lord would reward those that ministered to the needs of students, orphans, and evangelists. "Surely we are favoured above most others of our Master's servants by living in the hearts of so many gracious persons." His gratitude was "deep and inexpressible."[94]

To the end Spurgeon saw sickness, debt, and donation as inextricably reciprocal in power. Before the opening of the Surrey Gardens Memorial, Spurgeon found the fund £272 short. "We have never opened any of our home buildings with a debt," he reminded the people. "Are we to do so now?" Should we at this hour come down to the common level and depart from our former most honorable course. Absolutely not. Well, shall the place be shut up for lack of funds? "Dear brethren," Spurgeon pleaded, "your old friend is not well, and the doctor says he must not be worried; so please clear off this evil thing." Eliminate the strain and never allow the word "debt" to mar a memorial of gratitude. Then with a marked sense of both urgency and authority he closed the appeal, "Let the whole amount be at 'Westwood' before the sun has risen on the 2nd of June."[95]

Spurgeon's illness delayed the opening of the new building for the Carter Street Schools from June 2 until June 23, but "the balance of the money required for the purchase of the land and the erection of the buildings" had been contributed so that they took possession of the premises "without a shadow of debt hanging over them."[96]

Public Interest in Personal Pain

Spurgeon, due to popular interest, informed the readership that in the future his notes would include a section of "personal" notes. These personal notes would consist mainly of letters that he had received about the impact of his published sermons for the salvation of their readers. Upon his return from France in the spring of 1879, accompanied by Tom, he was encouraged by being "heartily welcomed at the Tabernacle on April 13."[97] Fullerton added details: "When father and

93. S&T, July 1881 357.

94. S&T, January 1885, 42.

95. S&T, June 1891, 348.

96. S&T, July 1891, 417-18.

97. S&T, May 1879, 242.

son appeared together in the Tabernacle pulpit on the thirteenth of that month, the congregation glad to greet them both, spontaneously rose and sang the doxology."[98] Spurgeon was concerned about the low state of funds for the benevolences but was convinced that by "divine blessing" soon all would be "in good sailing order." He thanked those friends that had urged him to take a longer time of rest. It could not be done however, as several things needed his personal attention. He reminded the readers that "the Pastor is not able to take any work beyond that which is due at home, and it will be in vain to press him to do so."[99]

By October of 1879, Spurgeon again saw the need for rest and escaping the English winter with its fog and dampness. "At this time, or a little later," Spurgeon reminded his readers, "we have been ill for several successive years, and we are advised to go away before the illness comes, in the hope of getting strength to go through the rest of the winter." He intended to follow his physicians' advice but felt the difficulty this presented to the benevolences. "Our funds fall off," he lamented, "and therefore it would be a very great relief if the stores were well replenished before we went from home. This would make our holiday doubly restful."[100]

The year 1880 did not provide Spurgeon respite from sickness or absences or dependence on the grace and continued provision of a loyal and devoted congregation. He sent a word of deep gratitude to his congregation through the preface of the 1880 *Sword and Trowel* for their constancy even with a "crippled minister, who has been away from his pulpit more than three months out of the twelve."[101] This painful admission reflected

the sad reality that his recent move of house had not materially benefitted his health. In August of 1880 he and Susannah moved to "Westwood" on Beulah Hill in Upper Norwood. The ground had springs on it that were supposed to be healthy and the higher ground was calculated to diminish the effects of fog and cold in the winter. "On the top of the Delectable Hill we trust that the fresh breezes may tend to give health and prolong life."[102] How could one know if it did or not?

Spurgeon addressed the subject of suffering in 1881 through the medium of a book review. Sir Emilius Bayley provided the occasion in a book entitled *Deep Unto Deep: An Enquiry into some of the deeper experiences of the Christian Life,* Spurgeon identified several factors of suffering to which a minister of the gospel must be sensitive. He recommended the book to young ministers, "for we are persuaded that there is far more need to study the pathology of the Christian soul than many of them wot of." Sore straits and depths of anguish constitute the experience of many saints and have legitimate claim on the "sympathy and the knowledge of every faithful minister of the gospel." Speaking obviously from his experience as a pastor but as truly from his own struggles, Spurgeon observed, "Physical infirmities and social bereavements, for example, may appear very common afflictions, though they plunge the soul into deep grief, but the influence they produce on sensitive minds is often so peculiar that each case requires specific attention." Old sins rise up to torture and haunt the memory of the saints even after the deep experience of forgiveness, and the temptations of Satan assault others with spiritual horrors—these are "not to be lightly thought of by those to whom Christ has committed the oversight of any church or congregation." In ad-

---

98. Fullerton, *Thomas Spurgeon*, 85f.

99. S&T, May 1879, 242.

100. S&T, October 1879, 497.

101. S&T, 1880, Preface.

102. S&T, August 1880, 421.

dition to Bayley, Spurgeon pointed to other and older authors that were "much tossed about on the stormy main" and thus knew "how to tend sea-sick souls in every stage of their sad complaints, whether staggering to and fro, or brought to their wits' end." Such men were Augustine, Luther, Bunyan, Gilpin, Brainerd, Edwards, and he even added "William Huntingdon." Spurgeon would doubtless have listed himself as among these suffering healers, for he had experienced first hand the "pathology of the Christian soul" as prompted by physical distress, emotional crushing, and social bereavement. Finally, however, it was not an issue that was strictly at the mercy of human experience. Any help from other quarters was welcomed, and Spurgeon believed that Bayley's "acquaintance with modern discovery has helped him to find illustrations of a problem that is started and solved in the sacred Scriptures."[103]

In March of 1881, Spurgeon provided few notes for the magazine because of the incapacitating sickness of late winter. "More wearisome days have been appointed us, but yet the Lord has been very gracious, and we have good hope of permanent recovery when frosts and damps become fewer." The church members had urged him to go away for a month's rest. He felt overflowing gratitude for their kindness and wanted to give the greatest deference to their judgment, but he felt no release from his post. Where can he find meaningful respite in "this land of damp," while the charge that constituted the burden still rested upon him? "We should only lose our home comforts," Spurgeon surmised, "and like a snail carry our load on our back wherever we might crawl." Work would only accumulate and "while it is undone, where could we rest?" Should he find the Garden of Eden, the "Serpent would

be at us till our arrears are pulled up, and till we see the Lord's work going on again with its usual vigor."[104] When the Annual Church Meeting was held, Spurgeon was "disabled in both arms." He remarked that the "warm love of his attached people cheered his heart, and though another season of suffering awaited him, it was a sunny oasis in the desert of pain."[105]

Undiminished difficulties plagued him throughout March so that his note in the April *Sword* repeated a familiar refrain. "Personal affliction has continued through the month of March, and it has been with difficulty that the weekly sermons and the monthly magazine have been prepared." He recognized divine providence in giving him "intervals of possible effort" when "all sail has been crowded on, so that we are not compelled to lie high and dry on shore." An earnest prayer of exclamation expressed both his frustration and his hope, "O for health and strength!" He felt that if he had those, he could do a great deal of work. He refused to allow a questioning and disgruntled spirit to leave the last impression, so added, "yet it may be a greater and a better thing to bow the head in silence and say, 'It is the Lord, let him do as seemeth him good.'"[106]

Spurgeon was able to be present for the entire college conference in May 1881 but "on Saturday was overtaken by a rheumatic affection of the heel, which prevented his being able to stand." Because of the pain, he missed preaching that Sunday. That year in fact he stated in the "Annual Report of the Pastors' College" that he had been "very ill through the greater part of the past year [1880-81], and have therefore been unable to give much personal service to the College." It was a sore trial and the slack created by his illness has

---

103. S&T, February 1881, 84.

104. S&T, March 1881, 147.

105. Ibid.

106. S&T, April 1881. 194.

been taken up by his brother J. A. Spurgeon. He also mentioned that he was pleased that few had to be dismissed from the school for "frequent depression of spirit has made it undesirable to have much trying work to do."[107]

Though some pressed him to take some time off at the end of the summer in 1881, Spurgeon insisted that it would not help and that his obligations in ministry simply prohibited it. "Many Sundays spent in the sick room forbid any further absence from home." He was, in fact, happy to report improved health and an ability to prepare the weekly sermons, edit the magazine, write books, and speak in public. As a specimen of the work that was normal per week, Spurgeon sought to encourage his readers that his strength at present was sufficient for a consistent outlay of work. He had preached five sermons, superintended three prayer meetings contributing his normal brief extemporaneous homilies, chaired two public meetings, made a speech at a third, officiated one communion, and been able to do one college afternoon of two hours' lecturing. Some of these occupied far more time in preparation than in execution. He was thankful to be able to work and wished for strength to do more.[108]

By October, however, he felt rheumatism approaching and, in spite of much work to do for the girls' orphanage, he turned the tasks over to others and made way for France in the first week of November. On the evening before he left he presided at the annual meeting of the Pastors' College. He bade the group gathered good bye for a few weeks and then gave a reading in the character of John Ploughman supported by a display of engravings from *John Ploughman's Pictures*. J. A. Spurgeon expressed the wish of all present that his brother would greatly benefit by his holiday.

Spurgeon had lined up preachers for the times of his absence, including his brother, his son Charles, and a Sunday given over to the evangelists D. L. Moody and Ira Sankey.[109]

On Saturday November 5 he sailed for Mentone and arrived safely at the Grand Hotel. "The warmth of the air, the brilliance of the light, and the dryness of everything" greatly enhanced his chances of a quick recovery. "If rheumatism does not depart in such balmy weather," Spurgeon lilted, "it must indeed be hard to dislodge." He arrived with great lumbago pains but they were gone in a night. Such relief did Mentone provide that he urged those of his readers that were "not tied to the land of fog and frost" to try the hospitality of his host, M. Georgi, "who has for years laid himself out to make me comfortable."[110]

Near the end of this visit Spurgeon wrote, "We have been in a land where the sun's first beams call you to open the window and let in the balmy air; where in midwinter the flowers which exist in our conservatories are flourishing and flowering in the open garden." Added to that joy was the pleasantry that the people speak no English, did not know him by reputation, and he could walk the streets without the hindrance of every third person's either begging or proposing questions. Though he sounded quite eremitic, he still had enough callers "to keep the day from stagnation." Even at that, one must not underestimate the value of the time alone for Spurgeon. He considered it "no mean blessing." In the absence of people—blessed absence for his purpose—there were "olive gardens and the woods, and here one can be lost to every human eye." This combination of virtual anonymity, a limited number of courteous and respectful visitors, engaging soirees with nature, and judiciously attentive hosts made this

---

107. S&T, 1881, 304.

108. S&T, August 1881, 418.

109. S&T, December 1881, 626.

110. Ibid.

as perfect a repose that could be had on earth. He had five weeks of it, and was thankful.[111]

Mentone provided not only a salubrious atmosphere in which Spurgeon felt that he could heal and thrive, but a close evangelical community for encouragement, worship, edification, and warm fellowship. Beyond that the very geography of the place invited one to contemplate the presence of Christ. The seashore, the vines of grapes, the olive trees, and palms made Spurgeon exclaim, "Thy land, O Immanuel!" "While in this Mentone I often fancy that I am looking out upon the lake of Gennesaret, or walking at the foot of the Mount of Olives, or peering into the mysterious gloom of the Garden of Gethsemane." The narrow streets of the old town were such as Jesus traveled in Galilean villages. This location invited Spurgeon to expect the presence of Christ and turn all his days into Sabbaths, his meals into sacraments, and earth into heaven.[112] Spurgeon returned to preach on Christmas day and on the following day had the pleasure of attending Christmas at the orphanage where "all went merry as a marriage-bell."[113]

Full recovery still eluded him. By the final days of March 1882 when it was time to produce the *Sword*, Spurgeon wrote, "The magazine is demanded, and the Editor can scarcely think two consecutive thoughts." If an idea occurred it soon flew out of reach like the boy's butterfly, or if captured soon became so mangled that it was not worth the having. Readers must forgive and put extra effort into getting something good from the magazine thus compensating for the editor's malady of both hand and head. "We could not postpone the affliction, or we would have had the magazine first, and the gout afterwards; but

the sickness waylaid us, and stopped us just when the hour for labour had arrived." If only legs and arms were affected, he would bear the pain manfully and proceed; "but the essence of our mischief is the brain, and, with the foe penetrating head-quarters, it is not easy to carry on the war." He hoped the readers would be as kind as his Master and not expect more than he could give. He reminded them that God fed them from his little wallet when he was but a child, and now that he is older with hardly strength enough to lift the breakfast-basket of younger days, "you will pray that the Master will not stint the feast because he weakens the servitor."[114]

He renewed his oft-published request that all invitations for outside engagements cease. He could barely keep up with the demands of work at home. Nothing additional could be attempted unless he wanted to come to a condition where he could "do nothing but lie and suffer excessive pain, with its consequent weakness of body and depression of spirit." In spite of his insistence to the contrary, he sill received requests by mail and sometimes deputations, forcing an interview in person, to issue the urgent need that some venues had of him. He was waylaid at odd corners and inconvenient times by those "who bored us with twenty requests to do the same thing, when we told them that it was not possible." Nevertheless he issued to them the "richest blessing for the chastisement which they alone have brought upon us."[115]

By April, he plodded on through debilitating pain and appeared to make his annual inaugural address at the conference of the Pastors' College Association. He told the loving group that had gathered, "After my severe illness I am trembling like a child who is only commencing to use his

111. S&T, January 1882, 42.

112. S&T,. December 1886, 613.

113. S&T, February 1882, 97.

114. S&T, April 1882, 1.

115. Ibid., 200.

feet." Barely could he keep himself up and he wondered aloud what a group could expect from a man that could hardly stand. For six weeks as he had considered what to say, he found his mind out of gear and his memory like the leaking buckets of the daughters of Danaus and his labors as vain as the stone-rolling feat of Sisyphus. His brain had been so occupied with "sympathy for the poor body that it has not been able to mount aloft with the eagle, nor even to plume its wings for the lower flight" that was his task for the morning. Appropriately, he preached on the text, "When I am weak, then am I strong" and prayed that he would be able to give some encouragement that had come to him, as the old saints used to say, "experimentally."[116] He still urged his men to feel earnestly the full weight of the responsibility put on them by virtue of their position as heralds of the gospel.

His contemplation of weakness, however, brought him to a reverie seldom indulged by Spurgeon, He looked at weakness brought on by *"An oppressive sense of responsibility."* One should not carry his sense of responsibility too far so as to be unable to sustain it; "it may cripple our joy and make slaves of us." One should not push himself beyond his physical and mental strength. Faithfulness does not always equal visible success. You can teach but you can not make people learn; make things plain, but you can not make the carnal man have spiritual interest. "We are not the Father, nor the Saviour, nor the Comforter, of the Church." By too severe a sense of personal responsibility, Spurgeon could have turned his concern for the south of London into a detriment as pastor of his flock. "We get tugging away as if the salvation of the world depended upon our straining ourselves to death." Don't cultivate

unconcern, but remember that "you are not God, and you do not stand in God's place; you are not the rulers of providence, and you have not been elected sole managers of the covenant of grace; therefore do not act as if you were."[117] Wise words of advice these, but more intriguing from the mouth of a tired, hurting, and sick Spurgeon that had driven himself to perpetual weakness by his world-saving endeavors in his early ministry and still sought to sustain more than his mind could bear.

As he prepared his return to London from rest late in 1882, he reported that it had been a time of repose of body, mind, and heart, and hopefully, had prepared him for a "good long spell of work." He insisted, however, that his friends not burden him with invitations to extra things as they had done the previous year with the result that his renewed strength was spent in enduring pain instead of public ministry. "Our own work taxes our strength to the utmost," he reminded all his exuberant friends, "and we beg to be pardoned if we cannot accede even to urgent requests."[118]

Spurgeon could not have anticipated the storm of trial that awaited him. He arrived in London on December 19 and on Christmas Eve the wife of his much-esteemed secretary J. W. Harrald died, leaving him a widower with four children. Rheumatism struck Spurgeon with a vengeance, and though he preached on Sunday 24, he could not rise from the couch on Christmas Day. At Harrald's bereavement Spurgeon found himself incapacitated and unable even to attend the traditional Christmas celebration at the orphanage. The beloved and long-time deacon William Higgs died on Christmas also, and at the time of his burial William Mills, another deacon, went into a paralysis never to recover

---

116. S&T, August 1882, 385.

117. S&T, September 1882, 461.
118. S&T, January 1883, 43.

and died on January 12, 1883. Spurgeon hobbled through services, appointments, meetings of societies, and other engagements connected with the Tabernacle for another few weeks, but by April he was so laid aside that for the first time he was unable to attend the conference of the Pastors' College Association.

On Monday afternoon of the Association's conference, he and Mrs. Spurgeon attended tea subsequent to the afternoon prayer meeting but could do nothing else. He could not even deliver his inaugural address or make the report at the subscribers' supper. He wrote on Tuesday morning, "After a night of extreme pain, I find myself unable to leave my bed today." He submitted to divine providence, prayed for the Spirit's blessings on all the proceedings, promised that if he felt able at any moment he would hurry to the conference, but must turn over everything to his brother. He hoped that the intensity of the attack meant that it would not last long but in the mean time, "it is furiously upon me at this moment."[119]

The conference men expressed their deep disappointment at his absence but gave moving assurance of their concern for his recovery and rejoiced that they received a great blessing from God even with the absence of the president. Soon after the conference Spurgeon had to issue his recurring rejection of all invitations to outside labors. "Our own legitimate work has grown so enormously that it is as much as we can possibly accomplish without being laid aside, and we have lately proved once more that it is the extra, outside services that bring about such sad breakdowns as the one we have recently experienced." If any reader, therefore, contemplated a bazaar, tea-meeting, anniversary, debt-removal, school construction, or blue ribbon mission and was

tempted to pose the question, "Shall we invite Mr. Spurgeon?" they immediately should supply their own answer, "Don't." As much as he would like to help, nothing can come of such invitations, for accepting them only would mean a complete cessation of necessary labors at home. "It is a great sorrow to be shut up to this," Spurgeon grimaced, "but what else can we do?"[120] During May, even the meetings held at the Tabernacle Spurgeon was forced to miss. During those festive and joyful gatherings, he was "obliged to tarry at home, suffering pain of body and depression of spirit."[121]

July brought about another bout with inability to preach and for two Sundays he had to have others take his pulpit. The papers reported this as an attack of rheumatic gout. Spurgeon characterized the papers as a flock of sheep following without reason when in fact, Spurgeon replied, "These frequent ailments are incidental to our work, and we must accept them as a part of the price of our service." He illustrated this by referring to a letter from Guiness Rogers, who had preached for Spurgeon on a few hours' notice, in which he came "nearer the cause of our infirmities than most people have been able to do." The letter isolated the difficulty that Spurgeon alone had to bear, and he published it with the hope of gaining a more accurate judgment concerning his case.

Spurgeon was not desperate, but he did feel that Guiness Rogers provided an opportunity for allowing another to help all observers, sympathetic and cynical alike, to have some deeper insight into his constant state of dilemma. Rogers could see clearly that the constant source of Spurgeon's frequent illness and debility was not mere physical weakness and bodily infirmity, but the aggravation of any such tendency by the re-

---

119. S&T, May 1883, 248.

120. S&T, June 1883, 331.
121. Ibid.

lentless mental and emotional strain on his faculties. "Your great congregation is an inspiration," Rogers reported, "but it is also an overwhelming responsibility." He did not find it surprising that continuous labor in this responsibility told on Spurgeon in many ways, in some that even Spurgeon might not suspect. Emotional detachment from all that was at stake in proclamation of the gospel to such a crowd might solve the personal problem but would forecast in the end a failed ministry. "I do not envy the man who can preach there without having his whole nature strained to the utmost, and that means nervous exhaustion, of all others the most difficult to contend against," Rogers observed, with genuine feeling for the dilemma. He could only offer a prayer—"may the Lord spare you many years to do a work to which not one in ten thousand would be equal."[122]

Though he resisted the newspapers in their terminology, by September Spurgeon himself referred to his constant pain as "cruel rheumatism." It hung on to him tenaciously during a visit to Scotland in August. The pain had been violent, he confessed, and made doubly so by the necessity to reply to requests for help with the note, "Too feeble to leave the house."[123] Spiritual strain and concern about infinitely important things intensified the physical strain under which Spurgeon labored, but rheumatism, relentless, sinister, sudden, and severe, made all of his labors a Herculean task and wore away his mind and soul.

Spurgeon's policy of publishing a sermon a week since the beginning of his ministry in London added to the pressure of his weekly work. He had handcuffed himself by the massive distribution of sermon texts making each production unusable for the future. Though he gloried in the expansion of this preaching ministry by the printed

word, he could not come either to the Tabernacle or to other venues and preach sermons in print. "In my own case," Spurgeon wrote in 1884, considering what it meant to be getting old at fifty, "The early strain has been followed by a continuous draft upon the strength through the perpetual printing of all that I have spoken." With twenty-nine years of sermons on the shelves, he still must go on speaking, "plodding on, issuing more, and yet more, which must all be in some measure bright and fresh, or the public will speedily intimate their weariness." The outlook to his own eyes, he confessed, was not cheering, but he had available "other optics" and would use them.[124]

His trip to Mentone in midwinter 1884-85 was delayed as Spurgeon was "smitten" with a painful encounter with his old nemesis. It was so severe that his friends feared that if he did not get an extended period of rest he would soon experience a complete breakdown. He was unable to preach at the annual watch night service on New Year's Eve, so W. Y. Fullerton and J. Manton Smith took the services. On January 5, Spurgeon missed the meeting of the South London branch of the Evangelical Alliance. Seven young men who were going out under the auspices of the China Inland Mission were present and one, C. T. Studd, captain of the "Cambridge eleven," gave the story of his conversion through Moody's preaching and his reason for doing mission work in China. All present, including Anglican, Wesleyan, Primitive Methodist, Congregational, and Baptist ministers, prayed for the recovery of Spurgeon.[125]

At a special called meeting of the church on January 12, the church insisted that Spurgeon take a three-month leave. "Your arduous labours and your incessant anxieties so far exceed the average strength of your constitution, that there

---

122. S&T, August 1883, 461.

123. S&T, September 1883, 514.

124. S&T, March 1884, 103.

125. S&T, February 1885, 91-93.

is an imperative demand for you to take longer and more frequent occasions of retirement." They wanted him to do so at a time when he had energy enough to enjoy it and not when he had used up his last ounce of strength. Spurgeon responded that the coming college conference made it impossible for him to take three months, but he promised that he would rest as much as possible if "we can recover strength enough to travel out of this perpetual fog." For the most rest, he needed to be assured that the ministries would be well supported and that the people would pray for the continued spiritual harvest in the services at the Tabernacle.[126] He went, and from Mentone he attached a letter dated February 16 to a sermon that he had prepared for publication.

DEAR FRIENDS—
May the peace of God abide with you. With great pleasure I perform the weekly duty of preparing the sermon and I pray our Lord to make it a blessing to all my readers. Each day I gather a measure of strength. My walking is measured by steps, few and slow, but then I *can* walk, and this is a great reason for gratitude to one who could not put his foot down without pain. I am recovering in all respects and feel that a fortnight in this place has done more for me than could have been effected by months of medicine. To Him whom I worshipped in pain be grateful praises for restoring mercy.[127]

At the end of March he could write that his rest had "done wonders for the body worn with pain, and almost as much for the mind wearied with labour. If nothing unforeseen should occur, we hope to be in our own pulpit on the second Sabbath of April." He wanted to have a "long stretch of unbroken testimony for the Lord."[128]

The actual reparation of mind and body fell short of what Spurgeon hoped for. He had come close to achieving the common level below which he had fallen both mentally and physically, and while on other occasions he had garnered a storehouse of strength for future use, "on this occasion they have been consumed at once in needful repairs." All he could claim was that "the inner man is somewhat renewed."[129] He relished any indication that someone might understand the great stress under which he labored and which could only intensify as years passed, as expenses grew in each institution, and as Sunday moved forward to Sunday and the need to express something freshly became more and more difficult. A friend made the observation, and Spurgeon quoted his insight as "too true and too good to be lost." The friend found rest necessary for replenishing the mind and allowing its intrinsic creative energies to operate for a while without taxation; he inquired, "I wonder if it is so with sermons. You ought to know, if any one does; for a sermon printed weekly for thirty years must be a great strain on the productive power of a man's mind if he does not merely repeat himself."[130]

Brief moments of restoration of a pain-free day accompanied with a long-absent exuberance, made Spurgeon more confident of his endurance than he had cause for. Previous periods of good feeling had worked to over-exertion and rapid decline. The pattern did not disappoint. In October 1885 Spurgeon reported that he was in vigorous health and working at breakneck speed. He was fulfilling long postponed commitments in preaching and hoped that his own pulpit might have its preacher for many a day. He attributed this surge in good feeling to abstinence from flesh as food. It proved to be "a more effectual preser-

---

126. Ibid..
127. MTP, 1885. 96.
128. S&T, April 1885 194.

129. S&T, May 1885, 244.
130. Ibid.

vative from rheumatism and gout than any of the many systems hitherto tried."[131] By the end of 1885, Spurgeon was in a more distraught condition physically and emotionally than he had been since the Surrey Music Hall disaster. In the December notes, he confessed that he finally must succumb. "Neuralgia has marked us for her own for some time past." His brain was so weary that it refused to perform and it took him an entire day to "produce the thought-fabric which, in better times, was woven in half-an-hour." If the net were not mended it would break. Wretched pain for days on end, and "golden hours lost in miserable incompetence," served to warn him that the greatest efficiency "requires the most willing worker to have his due proportion of Sabbath."[132]

"I am utterly hard up," he explained as he told his readers why they should not expect much that was scintillating from his pen in the preface to the bound volume of *The Sword and the Trowel*, 1885. "Every limb of my body is tormented with pain; there is about as much pain in each limb as any one of them can conveniently bear." Not only so with the body, but the mind-body unit was in a state of "fidgets *malaise*, and depression." Could someone be chained in his place he would gladly yield, but since none is handy "we must tug the oar even if we snap our bones." After two paragraphs, Spurgeon had to put down the pen for he was interrupted by "a hurricane, consisting of rushes of pain, twitches, and all sorts of deadly apprehensions" and only continued later by dictating to an amenuensis.[133] Writing around the same time, but for the notes of the January *Sword*, he reported "Brain weariness has driven the Pastor to take his accustomed rest." The delay in going brought on the painful attack, caused

not so much by the recurrence of his disease as by "general weariness." On December 17 he described a "balmy day of clear sunshine and summer warmth" in Mentone. He could sit outside all day and drink in the healing influences of sun, sea, and air. "There is nothing like it for an invalid, to whom the cold and the damp are killing." He hoped soon to be on his feet with a refreshed brain ready for full work again.[134]

When he addressed the college conference in May 1886 he was in great pain and had had to miss the greater part of the conference. During his inaugural address his pain made it hard to think and "almost impossible to think connectedly." Almost all that he had prepared was forgotten and "no new springs of thought could make channels for themselves while the mind was smothered up in physical suffering." He hesitated to prepare the message for publication in the magazine but friends reminded him that *The Sword and the Trowel* was largely autobiographical and it should certainly appear as the testimony of a man who could "with difficulty keep himself from tears through acute suffering and yet was resolved to take his part in a meeting which he had anticipated with solemn interest for months before." Spurgeon also wanted the reader to know that the revising was accomplished under the same difficulties as its original delivery.[135]

As printed, the message contained slight references to his pain. The message, "What We Would Be," extended a series of tender admonitions to his men for holiness and wisdom and understanding and gentleness with sinners. Their maturity now, after so many years, must qualify them as Fathers in the church, not for the purpose of control and demanding honor, but for service and self-giving, wise counsel. He wanted them to yearn for the

---

131. S&T, October 1885, 558.

132. S&T, December 1885, 645.

133. S&T, 1885, Preface.

134. S&T, January 1886, 42.

135. S&T, June 1886, 253.

growth of their people and to be quick to spot returning sinners that they might deal bountifully with them. About eight minutes before he finished, as it appears, Spurgeon said, "I don't think I can say much more, I am so greatly overcome by pain." He then continued, "I was going to say that as an earthly father stands in the place of God to his children, so do we in a certain measure." He closed with a lament of humble submission to the divine ordering of the individual moments of life; "I wish I could have spoken to you with all my strength, but it may be that my weakness may be used of God to greater purpose. My thoughts are few by reason of pain, which disorders my head, but they are on fire, for my heart remains true to the Lord, to his gospel, and to you. May he use every man of us to the utmost of our capacity for being used, and glorify himself by our health and our sickness, our life and our death! Amen."[136]

He located the cause of this particular setback in his exertion of too much energy in preaching the annual sermon for the Wesleyan Missionary Society. He returned home exhausted and acutely suffering. For three Sabbaths he had to miss preaching at the Tabernacle, and, as mentioned, a major portion of the college conference, as well as all the meetings of the Colportage Society. Many had to suffer because of his illness. "The question continually comes up," Spurgeon revealed, "Is not this too heavy a price to pay for the privilege of rendering occasional service to deserving objects outside our own immediate circle?"[137]

How did Susannah cope with these long and frequent absences of her husband. She had the book fund to occupy her and so had volunteer help coming to the home frequently, to package requested volumes, to aid in correspondence, and to ascertain the fitness of those requesting books to receive them. Especially when the volumes were to be sent to post did the home have intense activity. None of this, however, compensated fully for the absence of the one she loved to call "Tirshatha." When Mrs. Spurgeon wrote her book fund report for the year, she closed with a lamentation of his absence in Mentone, a condition that had prevailed for many years. In her Victorian poetic style, she wrote of "The dim and silent study,—the Pastor's empty chair,—the long, grim rows of unused books,—the closed inkstand, in which the very pens have a forlorn and drooping pose." Adding to the stillness, aloneness, and deep sense of absence were "the lack of scattered papers, and other signs of a busy lifework." She had anxieties, too, that pressed her each day concerning him, "my beloved." Not only was he ill, but was "a thousand miles from wife and home!" Were it not for the given grace to commit all into the Father's loving hand, and the granted faith to believe that "He hath done all things well", she did not think that either of them could bear the separation.[138]

By the middle of 1888, another season of suffering had borne down the sprits and mind of Spurgeon, but had not so debilitated him that he could not unsheathe his *Sword*. "A magazine is in some danger of death when the editor is so completely prostrate that his brain will not think," Spurgeon commented, and noted also a complicating factor, "and his right hand cannot hold a pen." The peculiarly heavy portion of the affliction came on him in between the production of one monthly number and the next, so he found himself, "through restoring mercy, again able to set about our appointed task." Always involved in a conscientious effort to keep the divine good-

---

136. S&T, July 1886, 343.

137. S&T, June 1886, 294.

138. Susannah Spurgeon, *Ten Years After* (London: Passmore & Alabaster, 1895), 26.

ness before him, Spurgeon acknowledged, "There is always some circumstance of grace about the heaviest trial. The thorn-bush bears its rose. The Lord lets us see a bright light in the clouds even when they gather in grimmest fashion."[139] Such was the balance when he wrote to Fullerton from Mentone in January 1889. "I have been very ill but I now feel convalescent. I have had—say four days real holiday: the rest belongs to the head of illness & getting better. No, I had a good week at first."[140] He wanted to remember every blessing. Anything short of hell, was mercy.

The Misapplication of Pain

Spurgeon had suffered so long and in such a variety of ways that it naturally had an effect on his thought processes and his emotional resilience. He freely admitted this, that he was among those that "were most prone to forget the silver lining." Had he not said, "As to mental maladies, is any man altogether sane?"[141] Darkness accompanied him frequently. But that his sickness ever made him paranoid or irrational, thus unable to analyze thought with his normal acuity and frame a response with clarity and punctiliar relevance, there is no evidence, and he resisted the conclusion with vigor. Not his liver or his inflamed joints, but his heart and head assumed his consistently expressed doctrinal position and issued foreboding warnings about the corrosive effects of liberal thought.

Spurgeon resented the feigned kindness by which his critics justified themselves in ignoring his sober alarm as constitutional melancholia aggravated by sickness. These attempts to minimize

Spurgeon's perceptive powers, or attributing his theological alarm merely to a despondent spirit, had surfaced in the middle of 1886. When he published sermon number 1900 of *The Metropolitan Tabernacle Pulpit* he challenged his critics, "Let those who read that sermon see whether gout makes us surly, or even melancholy. Yet that discourse was almost re-written when it was torture to hold a pen."[142]

The sermon was an exposition of the admonition "Rejoice Evermore." The exuberance and exhilaration of the sermon belies any tendency to sourness on account of pain. Many notable passages press relentlessly for the Christian to regard every moment and every situation as an occasion for rejoicing. There is a possible oblique reference to his present state of intense pain in one passage, but it is only at the end of an exhortation to consider how the gospel transforms all earthly experiences into occasions for joy:

> I believe, dear friends, that if we are right-minded every doctrine of the gospel will make us glad, every promise of the gospel will make us glad, every precept of the gospel will make us glad. If you were to go over a list of all the privileges that belong to the people of God, you might pause over each one, and say, I could rejoice evermore in this if I had nothing else. If ever you fail to rejoice, permit me to exhort you to arouse each one of the graces of the Spirit to its most active exercise. Begin with the first of them, faith. Believe, and as you believe this and that out of the ten thousand blessings which God has promised, joy will spring up in your soul. Have you exercised faith? then lead out the sister grace of hope. Begin hoping for the resurrection, hoping for the second coming, hoping for the glory which is then to be revealed. What sources of joy are these! When you have indulged hope, then go on to love, and let this

---

139. S&T, July 1888, 384.

140. Archives of SBTS in the Snell folder, probably mistaken attribution.

141. C. H. Spurgeon, "The Minister's Fainting Fits," *Lectures to My Students*, 4 vols in 1 (Pasadena, TX: Pilgrim Press, 1990), 1:168f.

142. S&T, June 1886, 295.

fairest of the heavenly sisters point you to the way of joy. Go on to love God more and more, and to love his people, and to love poor sinners; and, as you love, you will not fail to rejoice, for joy is born of love! Love has on her left hand sorrow for the griefs of those she loves, but at her right hand a holy joy in the very fact of loving her fellows; for he that loves doeth a joyful thing. If you cannot get joy either out of hope, or faith, or love, then go on to patience. I believe that one of the sweetest joys under heaven comes out of the severest suffering when patience is brought into play. "Sweet," says Toplady, "to lie passive in thy hand, and know no will but thine." And it is so sweet, so inexpressibly sweet, that to my experience the joy that comes of perfect patience is, under certain aspects, the divinest of all the joys that Christians know this side of heaven. The abyss of agony has a pearl in it which is not to be found upon the mountain of delight. Put patience to her perfect work, and she will bring you the power to rejoice evermore.[143]

His detractors resisted him, not with rational argument, but by making him an object of ridicule and pity. When he garnered evidence that the doctrinal decline was indeed real and noticed by other truly sane people, sound in mind and body, scattered throughout the Christian world, he informed his condescending detractors that the illustrations "suffice to show that it is not a solitary dyspeptic who alone judges that there is much evil occurrent."[144]

The Sword and the Trowel in February of 1890 reported that one newspaper attempted to comfort Spurgeon at his "worst stage of depression concerning the doubts of the day" by the assurance that religion can never pass away. Other English Baptists informed some American inquirers that Spurgeon conducted himself in such a manner because "sickness and age had weakened his intellect."[145] A recent historian of English Baptists, A. C. Underwood, has continued that ridicule of Spurgeon by stating, "A sick man, he viewed with deepest concern all departure from the theology of the Puritans." Underwood has added to the insult by implying that Spurgeon was simply intellectually incapable of appreciating the advances of modern thought.[146]

When one critic suggested that Spurgeon's accusations came from his sickness, not his theological acumen, he showed his entire disgust with this dodging of theological issues. "Our opponents," he says, "have set to work to make sneering allusions to our sickness." His solemn observations about theology are suggested by his pain, according to the critic, not his brain. This lack of Christian courtesy showed, in Spurgeon's judgment, that the new theology had introduced a new tone and spirit. Adherence to old-fashioned faith determines that a man must be an idiot and should be treated "with that contemptuous pity which is the quintessence of hate." If a theological watchdog is known also to be ill, "impute their faith to their disease, and pretend that their earnestness is nothing but petulance arising from their pain."[147]

Suffering by Revealed Truth

It was good that Spurgeon had a theology of suffering long before he had the constant experience of it. The severity of it in his own life and the scurrilous way his opponents mined it for useful treasure could have driven a more unstable man to

---

143. MTP, 1886, 350.

144. S&T, October 1887, 513. "The Case Proved."

145. S&T, February 1890, 93.

146. A. C. Underwood, *a History of the English Baptists* (London: The Baptist Union of Great Britain and Ireland, 1947), 231.

147. S&T, September 1887, 462. See also Lewis Drummond, *Spurgeon: Prince of Preachers* (Grand Rapids, MI: Kregel, 1992), 824. Drummond includes several articles on the Downgrade that appeared in Sword and Trowel, March–October, as appendices to his biography of Spurgeon, 802-34.

cynical despair. In 1857 he preached "The Loved Ones Chastened." He explored in detail from scriptural examples why God's people experience so many and such a variety of troubles in this life. Always searching for a biblical foundation, a word from revealed truth, Spurgeon asserted, "Apart from the revelation of God the dealings of Jehovah towards his creatures in this world seem to be utterly inexplicable." Religions say that God gives good to the good; the man that prospers is favored of the gods. He gives bad to the bad; those that suffer and are unsuccessful are obnoxious to the most High. The text of Scripture unravels the mystery; listen and "the riddle is unriddled:" "As many as I love, I rebuke and chasten: be zealous therefore, and repent." The Christian's reward is not in this life and the wicked man's punishment is not here.

He casts the Christian down; he gives the most afflictions to the most pious; perhaps he makes more waves of trouble roll over the breast of the most sanctified Christian than over the heart of any other man living. So, then, we must remember that as this world is not the place of punishment, we are to expect punishment and reward in the world to come; and we must believe that the only reason, then, why God afflicts his people must be this:

> In love I correct thee, thy gold to refine,
> To make thee at length in my likeness to shine.[148]

---

148. SS, 4:333-34. NPSP, 1857, 453.

18

CONDUCT IN THE FACE OF DEATH

The apostle pictures death as a terrible dragon, or monster, which, coming upon all men, must be fought with by each one for himself. He gives us no hopes whatever that any of us can avoid it. He tells us of no bridge across the river Death; he does not give us the faintest hope that it is possible to emerge from this state of existence into another without dying: he describes the monster as being exactly in our path, and with it we must fight, each man personally, separately, and alone; each man must die; we all must cross the black stream; each one of us must go through the iron gate.[1]

In 1889-90, a "world-wide extension of epidemic influenza," began in Russia in October and spread over Europe, into South America and North America, and into the continent of Africa, and resulted in a large number of deaths in London in the four weeks prior to January 25, 1890. Franklin Parsons wrote in the *British Medical Journal* that "the deaths in London from all causes taken together were 2,258 above the average of the corresponding weeks during the previous ten years." Contributing to this great increase was an especially virulent strain of influenza that seemed to bring along with it "whooping cough, phthisis, bronchitis, pneumonia, [and] other diseases of the respiratory organs."[2]

The 1891 epidemic, as in 1890, was "accompanied by an excess of total mortality above that ascribed directly to influenza." In the eight weeks prior to June 20, 1891, "4,584 deaths above the average have been registered in London," Parsons wrote, adding, "Thus the epidemic of the present year has been more protracted and more fatal than that of last year."[3] Sir Peter Eades described the wide variety of manifestations of influenza in 1891 as including "sudden headache, pain of the back and lower limbs, fever, and more or less irritation of the respiratory membranes" and at times "nausea, vomiting, or diarrhea, superadded." Chills and rigors occur at the beginning followed later by "catarrh, tonsillitis, bronchitis, pneumonia, pleurisy, or indeed, irritation or inflammation of almost any or every viscus." Eades also observed, along with other medical colleagues, that "primary disorders of the brain and mind have been exceptionally common, much more so than in 1890. Every degree of mental disturbance has

---

1. SS, 1:275F, "Thoughts on the Last Battle."

2. H. Franklin Parsons "The Influenza Epidemics of 1889-90 and 1891, and their Distribution in England and Wales," *The British Medical Journal*, August 8, 1891, 307.

3. Ibid.

been observed, from simple apathy, drowsiness, or dullness of mind, through various degrees of mental depression or of excitement, up to delirium and absolute mania."[4]

Onset of the Final Struggle

Unlike the outbreak of the plague early in Spurgeon's ministry from which he was spared, providence did not by pass him this time. Whether this outbreak of "influenza" was named properly or not, the ravaging effects of it found a weakened host in Spurgeon. He had just returned from three months in Mentone. While there, struggling with the debilitating illnesses that had tightened their hold on him increasingly for some years, he wrote of his hope that "the afflictions of the Editor" would be not only for his profit but for theirs. He recommended to other sufferers a viewpoint that filled his painful days with confident hope: "Let all the sons and daughters of sorrow know assuredly that the bitters of their portion are weighed and measured by covenant love; and not a drop of wormwood will be wasted if there be grace given to receive it with believing resignation."[5] Suffering happened according to the will of God in accordance with God's specific design for each person. He believed that for others, he accepted it for himself.

When he preached again on February 8 the usual power attended his proclamation. A business meeting, at which he presided, reported a membership in the Tabernacle of 5,328, 23 missions stations capable of seating 3,740, and 27 Sunday Schools with 592 teachers and over 8,000 students in the classes. He continued his steady weekly labors for the next three months. Some

extra services, as usual, pressed the time into more compact and demanding segments.

In the evening service of April 26, Spurgeon was unable to preach. He arrived at the Tabernacle with a sermon in mind and heart, entered the pulpit with the full intention of preaching, when, as he related the event, "an overpowering nervousness oppressed me, and I lost all self-control, and left the pulpit in anguish." He returned the next Sunday morning to preach on that text, Psalm 40:7, "Then said I, Lo, I come." He used the event of the week before to reinforce the intended purpose. It was a classic Spurgeonic evangelistic message with the perfect integration of urgency of need, immediacy of Christ's saving presence, the universal call to embrace gospel promises, and the complete dependence on the purposes of sovereign grace. "Perhaps, also, there are some here this morning who were not here last Lord's-day evening, whom God intends to bless by the sermon," he conjectured. "The people were not here, peradventure, for whom the eternal decree of God had designed the message, and they may be here now." Spurgeon did not submit his sickness the week before to merely fortuitous circumstances. "You that are fresh to this place, should consider the strange circumstance, which never happened to me before in the forty years of my ministry," and thus he pressed the audience to consider "whether my bow was then unstrung that the arrow might find its ordained target in your heart." As he described the utterly desperate condition of despairing sinners weary of all things, including life, and pointed out how to them Christ said, "Lo, I come," Spurgeon remarked, "Should you even lie in all the despair and desolation which I described, I would persuade you to believe in Jesus. Trust him, and you shall find him all that you want." In illustrating how Jesus comes even when unsought, Spurgeon

---

4. Sir Peter Eades, "Influenza in 1891" in *The British Medical Journal* (August 8, 1891), 308, 309.

5. S&T, January 1891, 40.

exclaimed, "Herein is the glorious sovereignty of his love fully exercised, and grace reigns supreme. 'Lo, I come,' is the announcement of majestic grace which waiteth not for man, neither tarrieth for the sons of men." His personal experience, so frequently called upon, provided opportunity for Spurgeon to urge sovereignty as an encouragement to trust: "I know my Lord came to me, or I should never have come to him: why should he not come to you? … Why should he not draw us also? Is he not doing so? Yield to the pressure of his love." At virtually every point Spurgeon punctuated his evangelistic call with the foundation of divine sovereignty. "Because he loved his redeemed from before the foundation of the world, therefore in due time he says, 'Lo, I come.' … There is no good in you; there is no reason in you why the Lord should save you; but because of his free, spontaneous, rich, sovereign, almighty grace, he leaps out of heaven, he descends to earth, he plunges into the grave to pluck his beloved from destruction. … Without asking you, and without your asking him, he puts in an appearance in the sovereignty of his grace."[6]

A Chronicle of Last Things
With a description of this sermon the volume that described the last nine months of Spurgeon's life began. *From the Pulpit to the Palm Branch: A Memorial of C. H., Spurgeon* collected all the articles that had appeared in *The Sword and he Trowel* about Spurgeon's sickness during these months and the events and Spurgeon's activities at Mentone. It included accounts of all the memorial services in Mentone and London, the funeral service, texts of speeches and sermons and telegrams from a variety of persons including those written from Mentone by Susannah Spurgeon.

Texts of sermons by A. T. Pierson preached from Sunday February 7 through Thursday February 25 were included. These sermons highlighted the peculiarly notable gifts of Spurgeon in the context of scriptural examples of those gifts. A list of all persons and organizations that had sent letters of condolence and sympathy up to the time of the book's printing filled the last fourteen pages with an extra page listing fifty-nine religious organizations that sent deputations to the funeral.[7]

The week before May 10 included preaching at the Sunday School Union, a sermon for the benefit of the British and Foreign Sailors' Society on Thursday, and a meeting at Hendon, two hours' distance, with men from the college. He preached on Genesis 24, a sermon about the serious task of the minister in going to claim a bride for his Master. She must indeed be the bride of Christ and none other. Spurgeon had preached on this text in October, 1888, entitled "No Compromise," a sermon to which reference has been made, and would preach the text the next Sunday evening, May 10, 1891, in his own pulpit.[8] After tea, a testimony meeting yielded more work for Spurgeon because two of the three announced speakers were "laid aside by influenza."[9] Not only did the speaking require study, preparation, and energy in the delivery, but required follow-up work for publication of all of them. Spurgeon commented on the week and its labors in *The Sword and Trowel*:

> A drive of two hours there (to Herndon) and two hours back made the engagement a heavy draught upon time. Friends will note that *all*

---

7. *From the Pulpit to the Palm Branch: A Memorial of C. H., Spurgeon* (London: Passmore & Alabaster, 1892), 278-81.

8. SS, 19:345ff.

9. G. Holden Pike, concluding chapters by James C. Fernald, *Charles Haddon Spurgeon* (New York: Funk & Wagnalls Company, 1892), 342.

---

6. MTP, 1891, 253-63.

the above meetings were held in one week, which also included two Sabbath services and the great communion at the Tabernacle, besides all regular home work, correspondence, etc. In addition, the Lord's day morning sermon had to be revised, and published the following Thursday; and the sermons to Sunday-school teachers and sailors were received for revision and duly attended to. Is it any wonder that the worker gets weary, and has to beg friends not to impose further burdens on one who is already terribly overladen?[10]

On May 10, 1891, in the evening, Spurgeon preached on Genesis 24, fresh on his mind, "An Urgent Request for an Immediate Answer." "I believe I am sent," he told his congregation, "to find out some appointed for Christ in the divine purpose and covenant, and I pray my Master that there may be many such."[11] Later, as he increased in expounding the urgency of his mission, he reminded the congregation that late experience had shown how quickly life could be ended. "How many of our friends have been taken away by influenza?" he asked the audience, confirming his statement with, "This congregation has suffered from sickness, in family after family, as I never knew it suffer before."[12] Five days later he reported that during a speaking time in the evening he experienced "peculiar bodily weakness" and "special spiritual strength." Two days after that, consistent with the incubation time for the influenza bacilli as reported by Dr. Eades, Spurgeon "could not preach, and the doctor found him laid aside with congestion of the lungs and other matters, which forbid his quitting his chamber for some little time to come."[13] Spurgeon recorded an event that happened near this time when "we entered

into the pulpit on the Sunday evening, and were obliged to hurry out of it; for a low, nervous condition shut us up."[14] This attack proved to be this strong strain of influenza. As Spurgeon himself recalled, "In the end of May, 1891, I suffered from the virulent influenza then raging."[15]

He recovered well enough in three weeks to preach on June 7 in the morning. He preached on 1 Samuel 30:21-25, "The Statute of David for the Sharing of the Spoil." Spurgeon expressed concern about the "faint ones" in David's army, knowing that he spoke to many of that sort in his congregation. He was one of them and told the listeners, "That was one reason why I took this text. I felt, after my illness, most happy to come forth and meet my Lord in public. I am glad also to meet with you, my comrades. We are still spared for the war. Though laid aside for a while, we are again among our brethren." As he scanned the congregation, though, he felt compelled to notice, "I am sorry to miss so many of our church-members who are laid aside by this sickness."[16]

Deeply conscious of his own recent weakness and his many weeks, even months, of needed convalescence, Spurgeon spoke at times as if he were one of the ones that did not go with David into battle but stayed with the baggage. "I do not know whether you agree with me, but I find that half-an-hour's perplexity takes more out of a man than a month's labor." "This is one reason why certain of our Lord's loyal-hearted ones are on the sick list, and must keep in the trenches for a while." "I will be bound to say it was a great trial to them not to be allowed to march into the fight. ... It is hard to brave men to be convinced to hospital, and have no drive at the foe. The weary one

---

10. Ibid., 342; S&T, June 1891, 350.

11. MTP, 1891, 589.

12. Ibid., 597.

13. Pike, 343.

14. S&T, June 1891, 347.

15. C. H. Spurgeon, *Memories of Stambourne* (London: Passmore & Alabaster, 1891), iii.

16. Pike, 386.

wishes he could be to the front, where his Captain's eye would be upon him. He pants to smite down the enemies, and win back the spoil for his comrades." "I believe the Lord will give to the sick and the suffering an equal reward with the active and energetic, if they are equally concerned for His glory." "Some saints are constitutionally depressed and sad; they are like certain lovely ferns, which grow best under a constant drip." "We are not among those self-praising ones who have wrought such wonders of holiness; but we mourn our shortcomings and transgressions, and yet He hath not cast away the people whom He did foreknow. ... If anybody had told us that we should have been such poor soldiers as we have been, we should not have believed them." As he closed the sermon, he called to mind, "These forty years and more have I served Him, blessed be His name! and I have had nothing but love from Him. I would be glad to continue yet another forty years in the same dear service here below if so it pleased Him. His service is life, peace, joy."[17] He would not have another forty years, nor even another day with his beloved congregation.

The next day, June 8, Spurgeon traveled, even though ill, to Suffolk as a guest of Mr. Gurteen of Haverhill, and brought his photographer, Mr. T. H. Nash, to take shots of scenes in Stambourne.[18] These were used in his volume *Memories of Stambourne*. In the course of the week, "an overpowering headache came on,"[19] he took a chill, had to return quickly to London, relapsed to an immobile state due to the accompaniment of aggravated gout. He was confined to his bed, suffering greatly. He had preached for the last time at the Tabernacle.

Watching, and Waiting, and Looking Above

A report from Westwood made the close followers of Spurgeon's condition aware that many critical moments and days had followed upon one another in wearying succession, hounding him with relentless lapses into weakness and pain, not only in bones and muscles and heart and lungs, but in mind. "For three months," Spurgeon wrote, "I suffered beyond measure, and was often between the jaws of death."[20] Though physicians were ever present, "in such a struggle between life and death, hope and fear alternate with sorrowful frequency."[21] Hopeful mornings followed virtually without exception by frightful evenings gave the watchers alarm and the "most gloomy forebodings." "Delirium," such as had been described as an effect of the current influenza, came and went and was especially intense at times. "Even the sacred hours of the Lord's day were invaded by the dreaded delirium, and day after day, the most trying suspense continued."[22]

Daily reports to the intense watchers in England were supplemented by the first possible report in *The Sword and Trowel* of August 1891. "It was not possible, last month," the writer noted, "to let our readers know how seriously ill Mr. Spurgeon was." As the July issue passed through the press, however, "his symptoms became so alarming" that Dr. Kidd was called in to consult with Dr. Miller, of Upper Norwood, who had been in attendance since May 18. After a brief respite in early July in which they believed that the immediate threats to his health were subdued, on July 4 the delirium returned and it became evident that "a most serious state of affairs had been reached." Dr. Miller stayed at his side every night and Dr. Kidd called each morning to consult. Spurgeon

---

17. Ibid., 382-93.

18. Joseph W. Harrald, "Mr. Spurgeon's Last Drives at Menton," S&T, April 1892, 175.

19. *Stambourne*, iii.

---

20. Ibid.

21. Pike, 344.

22. Ibid., 344f.

hovered at the edge of death and, even with such skilled and constant attention, death seemed certain. At this time, the entire company found hope only in the great confidence expressed in many letters, from a variety of places, stated that they had been impressed "most powerfully that this sickness was 'not unto death,' and that the Lord would raise up his servant even from the very gates of the grave."[23]

Correspondence abounded each day to Mrs. Spurgeon with assurances of prayer and expressions of sincere sympathy with her unremitting task of watching, hoping, despairing, and wondering. William E. Gladstone, who recently had lost a child, wrote Mrs. Spurgeon, and, after conveying his deep admiration of the gifts and character of her husband, expressed his commendation of them both to "the infinite stores of the Divine love and mercy." The chief Rabbi of London, Hermann Adler, wrote Susannah "with earnest prayer to our common Father that his precious life may be spared," and that he would "sustain the patient sufferer on his bed of languishing" and "sustain you and yours during the period of trial."[24] *The Sword and the Trowel* for August 1891 proclaimed that the "The prayers presented for Mr. Spurgeon have been almost, if not wholly, without parallel in the history of the church of Christ." Thousands gathered in the Tabernacle for a day of prayer; special prayer services were held three times daily for weeks during the most severe manifestations of the perfect storm of illness meeting in Spurgeon's body. Those attending insisted that they had never before "witnessed such mighty wrestlings." These public occasions for prayer ran throughout the Christian world in England, throughout the English-speaking world and in many other places where his writings had

been made known. During most of this time Spurgeon was unaware of the great and universal outpouring of concern for him, except for "the occasional intervals between the delirium."[25]

Notes and visits to Westwood arrived in profound numbers and regularity. Assurances of concern and prayer from the Baptist Young People's Convention in Chicago, the Christian Endeavor Society of Minneapolis, the Ontario Home Mission Board, the Northfield Convention signed by D. L. Moody and H. L. Wayland, the Baptist Union of Sydney, New South Wales, the Baptist Union of New Zealand, and the Jamaica Baptist Union. Correspondents and visitors to Westwood included the Prince of Wales, the Earl and Countess of Aberdeen, Earl Fortescue, the Countess of Seafield, Lord Brassey, Lord and Lady Kinnaird, Lord Kilmaine, the Dowager Lady Abercromby, Lady Massy, Lady Peto, Lady Wright, Sir John Burns, Sir Charles Lawson, Sir Wilfrid and Lady Lawson, Sir A. H. Layard, Sir Frederick Perkins, Sir Henry Peto, Sir John and Lady Simon, The Right Hon. W. E. Gladstone, M.P., the Right Hon. Hugh Childers, M.P.; messrs. T. A. Denny, W. J. Evelyn, F. W. N. Lloyd, D. MacLaren, E. Rawlins, J. Herbert Tritton, and George Williams; Dr. Barnardo; a long list of the clergy of the Church of England—High, Low and Broad—headed by the Archbishops of Liverpool, Ripon, Rochester, and Winchester, the Dean of Westminster, the Archdeacons of Llandaff and Liverpool, and several Canons. Representatives of the Reformed Episcopal and Free Churches of England paid their respects as well as Dr. Hermann Adler, the Jewish Chief Rabbi. Letters and telegrams came from Spurgeon's Mentone circle, whom he soon would join, as well as other parts of France. Holland, Germany, Switzerland, Italy, Norway, Russia,

---

23. S&T, August 1891, 465.

24. Pike, 350.

25. S&T, August 1891, 465, 466.

Canada, the United States of America, North Africa, and other places where Spurgeon's influence was noted and they sent their inquiries after his health.

In early August, Spurgeon was able to write a brief note to his congregation thanking them for "so wonderful an outburst of prayer."[26] So many notes had continued to arrive that it has "taxed the powers of all helpers to acknowledge the numerous communications." What also taxed the energies of those attending, as well as Spurgeon himself, was how to communicate the true severity of his condition without discouraging the faith of those who had such confidence that through this sickness God would give irrefutable evidence that his power alone could bring about such a remarkable restoration of health and vigorous ministry. Embedded in this optimistic, overly so, and transcendent vision was the conviction that, through this sickness and in light of the unity of Christians on this one issue, the Tabernacle, and perhaps the world, was on the verge of a massive revival. During the prayer meetings, people searched the Bible for promises that "they might plead before the throne of grace."[27] Spurgeon's sickness would accomplish more for the glory of God than if he "had been enabled to continue preaching all through the summer." Surely, thought his people, "there is, unquestionably, some great purpose of love and mercy in this trying dispensation, although at present it is only apparent to him who seeth the end from the beginning."[28]

In the effort to convey both seriousness about the Pastor's condition as well as respect for the sense of invincible purpose spreading among the people, a note in *The Sword and the Trowel* said,

"It was difficult, last month, to tell what ought to be written about THE EDITOR'S ILLNESS; and it is certainly not easier to know what to say this month." A great change had recently taken place in which the delirium had suddenly ceased; this change made friends "imagine that the dear sufferer was rapidly recovering, whereas, so far as the malady was concerned, there was no material alteration." His actual condition fluctuated from day to day. Efforts at honesty combined with humble gratitude and encouragement tested the ability of the writer, probably James Harrald or Mrs. Spurgeon, to walk lithely:

> At the date when these "Notes" go to the printers, that is, on August 20, the doctors are able to give a more favourable report than they have given for several days. This is a cause for renewed thankfulness; but the need for fervent supplication is as great as in the earlier part of this long and terrible illness; while it ought, in every instance, to be accompanied by hearty thanksgiving that the precious life, so dear to many, has been spared, and that the delirium, which for a while beclouded the over-wrought brain, has been so graciously banished by the Great Physician. Colossians iv.2 is still the watchword for all who desire the Editor's complete restoration to health and strength.[29]

Spurgeon had regained enough strength to work on the final preparations of *Memories of Stambourne*. "I amuse myself," he related, "with arranging what had been previously prepared, and with issuing it from the press."[30] His prefatory note expressed gratitude for prayer that "lengthened the thread of my life," and for such an outpouring of "affectionate sympathy of so many belonging to all parts of the Christian church." During these same days he used the pages of *The Sword and the*

26. *Autobiography*, 2:501; S&T, September 1891, 539.

27. S&T, September 1891, 539.

28. Ibid., 539.

29. Ibid., 538.

30. *Stambourne*, iii.

Trowel to assure readers of his gratitude for prayer and sympathy and "of his firm belief that their petitions had been in part answered in the sparing of his life." He added that through their continued intercession, God "at the right time would fully restore him to his much-loved work." None could tell when such a mercy might ensue, but to all appearances "it must be many months before it will be possible to hold in the Tabernacle the thanksgiving service to which many are already looking forward." Again, the warning must be made that "to those who know how seriously ill he still is, thanksgivings for his 'recovery' appear very premature." The "Thank-offerings" coming in from many were not discouraged, but each must realize that there still was ample time for the "maturing of any plan that may be devised for suitably celebrating the Lord's gracious lovingkindness."[31]

They were sure, however, that steady support of all the works connected with his name would contribute to the Pastor's recovery immensely. The next month, *The Sword and the Trowel* reported, "During the past month, the College and Almshouses have each received a legacy of £250 from a generous friend, who only made his will since Mr. Spurgeon was laid aside." Other large amounts also came in "since the lists were closed," acts of generosity that demonstrated the "lovingkindness of the Lord in preserving his sick servant from any cause for anxiety about funds for the work under his care."[32]

After a "long and wearisome time" of some more weeks of weakness, Spurgeon took a brief carriage ride to Westminster, and supported by two helpers tottered to Westminster Bridge and watched the missions steamer, the "Good Will," move along the Thames. A letter in *The Sword and the Trowel* on October 1 thanked the readers for the massive amount of mail sent to Mrs. Spurgeon during "the dark days of my illness." Particularly did he thank readers for the "unutterable consolation" such concern gave his wife.[33] A visit to Eastbourne for two weeks tested Spurgeon's ability to travel; he passed. Plans for the 1,000- mile trek to Mentone immediately were underway.

In the meantime, Spurgeon, remembering an offer made by A. T. Pierson, began inquiring early in August as to whether the American preacher from Philadelphia could come to fill the pulpit for an indefinite period. Pierson's pan-denominational approach, combined with his attraction for Brethren ideas and dispensationalism, made this choice somewhat puzzling, but his love for simplicity in worship, his emphasis on evangelism to the masses, and his zealous promotion of world missions, plus his growing openness to believers' baptism, give positive rationale for the selection. *The Sword and the Trowel* for October pointed to "his great love for the old truths that are so dear to us, and of his earnest labours on behalf of home and foreign missions." Also important was his work as a pastor and evangelist that "has well qualified him for the double service of feeding the flock of God, and lambs of the Good Shepherd."

Pierson responded almost immediately to Spurgeon's query. "Well now—listen!" Pierson began his reply; "for the first time, I think, since I began to preach at twenty years of age, I am entirely free of all positive engagements from October 1st." Some strange leading, he felt, had kept him clear of all engagements and eliminated "any insuperable barrier to my coming and preaching for you." After a time of fasting and prayer, and sincere hesitation, Pierson consented in the language of Paul's call to Macedonia. He had preached at the Tabernacle in December of 1889 and remembered,

---

31. S&T, September 1891, 538f.

32. S&T, October 1891, 587.

33. Ibid., 586.

"the conscious demand of the congregation for the plain Word of God, with no chaff of science and art and human wisdom, falsely so-called." He felt that such a congregation evoked the best in him and that "such eloquent hearing would make any man mighty to preach." Preachers already had been scheduled for all the services through October 18, so Pierson consented to begin on October 25.[34] Spurgeon was greatly relieved and impressed with the "wonder-working way of God" in giving Pierson for this time. He knew of none "more competent or more suitable," or who could display a "more unselfish desire to serve the cause of God." Pierson, Spurgeon believed, showed great "loving concern to help a brother in his hour of need."[35]

The Last Visit to Mentone

Accordingly, Mr. and Mrs. Charles Spurgeon, J. A. Spurgeon and his wife, accompanied by his secretary Joseph Harrald and some of the Tabernacle deacons left on October 26. While waiting for the train at Herne Hill Station, Spurgeon told one of his friends, "The fight is killing me."[36] In hope of recovery, he arrived with his party at Mentone on October 29. *The Sword and the Trowel* for November 1, began its "notes" with the announcement, "All being well, by the time that the present number of the Magazine is in the hands of our readers, or very shortly afterwards, both Mr. and Mrs. Spurgeon will be in the South of France." Mrs. Spurgeon wanted no correspondence, either contributions or applications, on the Book Fund while she was absent. She could give no attention to it for she must give all to her husband "with whom she is going abroad for the first time for very many years."[37]

Spurgeon's health improved slightly during the first week. On November 7, he wrote readers of his sermons that he was a "sick man physically, but in heart I am strong in the Lord." He could tell that a "great waste of life force still weakens me; but it is not so great as it was, and HE who has spared my life will in his own right time spare me this weakening of my strength by the way." He found some solace for a lost pulpit in his ability to preach through the press. The competence of his helpers in this task convinced him, prophetically so, that sermons "would continue to be forthcoming for several years even if I were taken home to God; for hundreds of manuscripts are in my publishers' stores." By this means he was convinced that "I shall live and speak long after I am dead."[38]

A week later, November 14, he wrote again, recommending the sermon preached on May 10, "An Urgent Request for and Immediate Answer." The short letter proposed with eschatological seriousness that his readers be concerned about their salvation. Spurgeon gave evidence of the severity with which an already-compromised physical condition had been subjected to the whole range of the effects of influenza. "I am a sick man who has narrowly escaped the hand of death, and I feel that the things of eternity ought not to be trifled with. To be saved at the last, our wisdom is to be saved at once." As he had done throughout his life, Spurgeon improved his immediate experience for the serious spiritual reflection of his flock. "If I had left my soul's matters for a sick bed, I could not have attended to them there, for I was delirious, and the mind could not fix itself sensibly upon any subject. Before the cloud lowers over your mind, give your best attention to the Word of the Lord ... for you cannot tell how soon the hour of life may end."[39]

---

34. S&T, November 1891, 436.

35. S&T, February 1892, 81.

36. W. Y. Fullerton, C. H. Spurgeon: Biography (London: Williams & Norgate, 1920), 316.

37. S&T, November 1891, 435.

38. MTP, 1891, 588.

39. Ibid., 600.

When he read the next week in *The Times* that he was "rapidly improving" he sent a note that those "words exactly describe what I am not doing." He let all those concerned know that the reports from the doctor were not at all encouraging, his health had not improved, that "the disease itself was not changed from what it was in Norwood, or if any change was manifest, it was for the worse." So many prayers had been sent forth for his recovery that he felt obliged to say, "I shall recover," but he must emphatically let his friends know, in order to avoid disappointment, that this would be the "slowest of all slow things."[40]

For the December issue of *The Sword and the Trowel*, Spurgeon rallied his strength to write a brief article under the suggestive title of three interrogative signs, ? ? ?. He described the massive deceit that a few pain-free days gave him and applied the contrast between his brief feelings and the hard truth to the necessity of a careful examination of soul. "After a long, wasting sickness, there came a time of gracious improvement to me." A "sense of recovering" impressed him that the warmer climate of southern France had made an immediate impact and that a cure, "which had been granted in answer to the prayers of the universal church, would be carried to perfection with unusual speed." He planned a return to his pulpit "which might surprise my beloved people by its speediness." He praised God for such deliverance, his heart "began to ring out a welcome to returning health and strength," and he wrote with exhilaration and expectation and gave false hope to others through his own vain confidence. When suspicious signs of feebleness reappeared he regarded them as "mere relics of a disease which had fled" until the doctor took a more deliberate and truthful approach. Having received a full account from

the physician in England of the disease and its symptoms and its history, his French attendant determined that the disease not only was not better, rather "if any change was manifest, it was for the worse. The leakage of life-power was not stopped." His resulting severe disappointment fed off of his previous unwarranted confidence. Though his "animal spirits fell below zero," he assured the reader that "my faith in the sure result of prayer in obtaining a full restoration did not waver for a second." But had he continued in his deceived state he would surely have done something—climbing stairs or hills, giving way to excitement, talking too long with friends, extending himself too much in writing or mental labor—that would have effected a "serious catastrophe."[41]

His application of this extended personal anecdote was that each person must take the far more important step of a serious examination for signs of true spiritual life. Every person tends to think of his spiritual condition in more exuberant terms than the evidence warrants. We must put ourselves to this task and ask the Lord to aid us. "He that fears to ring his money on the counter is not a safe man to deal with, neither is he likely to be quite innocent of carrying counterfeit coin about him." Show a man that he is low in the scale and you may stir him to action. Though Satan uses despair to hobble many Christians, "It would be better to go to heaven limping with fear all the way, than to ride proudly to hell on the high-horse of carnal confidence." After a succinct but highly suggestive exhortation in this matter, Spurgeon made the final application of the lesson learned from his vain confidence of physical well-being:

> No one, therefore, may wrap himself about with the foul ferment of self-reliance; there is safety for no one except in the grace of God, and personal

---

40. S&T, December 1891, 677.

41. Ibid., 644f.

reliance upon the Lord Jesus. They are safe who are truly in him, by a living faith, which bears fruit unto holiness; but no others can claim the privilege. To such, the priceless boon of full assurance comes in due time. Their faith is not in frames and feelings, but in the finished work of their Lord and Saviour; and hence they cannot have too much of it, nor can they be too joyful in the infallibility of their foundation. If, indeed, we are dwelling in God, realizing his presence, trusting his promise, united to his Son, and quickened by his Spirit—it is well with our souls. But if these things be not so, the sooner we are aware of our mistake the better.[42]

The Pressure of Prayer

The knowledge that people from many places and out of many denominations and even from outside the Christian faith invoked the help of heaven for Spurgeon's recovery, moved him greatly and perhaps caused him to make misjudgments in his response to this impressive outpouring of intercession. His confidence in "full restoration" and his proclamation, "I shall recover," invested an apparently unwarranted assurance in the purity and clarity of vision of those that claimed they had been given grace to pray "the prayer of faith." There was no doubting their earnestness of desire for his recovery or their faith in the ultimate triumph of God's purpose; but he mistook this impression, and perhaps felt pressured by their faith in it, as a matter of special revelation.

He referred to this outpouring of supplication in the last preface that he wrote for a bound volume of *The Sword and the Trowel*. After pointing to his extremely abbreviated participation in both the magazine and the Tabernacle, when "the customary voice was hushed," Spurgeon mentioned again how deeply impressive and moving was the great concern indicated for his physical renewal. "On no modern occasion known to us," Spurgeon noted, "has more supplication been made to God for the life of a minister of the gospel." In addition to his own people, "it really seemed as if all bodies of Christians, and even others beyond the pale of our holy faith, were at one in crying to God on our behalf." Revisiting themes that had characterized his short letters in recent weeks, Spurgeon took particular notice of the strong confidence some brought to their prayers. "Many children of God wrote," Spurgeon unashamedly told his readers, "that they had received in their own souls an answer to the prayer of faith, and were sure that the sick one would recover." Noting the encouragement Christians have for confidence in the graciousness of God in answering prayer, and the apologetic value this presented, Spurgeon mused, "Had the prayers remained unanswered, great occasion to blaspheme would have been taken by the enemy. As it is, the fact has greatly aided faith in candid minds." If his recovery could not be considered "miraculous," at least one must concede the phenomenon to be "a very remarkable instance of the prevalence of united prayer in a desperate case."[43] He had preached the same idea to a group gathered on December 31: "No case is hopeless when many pray. The deadliest diseases relax their hold before the power of unanimous intercession."[44]

Spurgeon could not have known at the time of the writing, that they, and perhaps he, had misjudged the case. "As long as I live," he acknowledged, "I am a visible embodiment of the fact that, to the prayer of faith, presented by the Church of God, nothing is impossible." Though he believed that "it is worth while to have been sore sick to have learned this truth," he had not seen that the divine purpose for him was distinctly different from what his fervent pray-ers had believed.

---

42. Ibid., 648.

43. S&T, 1891, "Preface."

44. S&T, February 1892, 53.

There was no mistaking, however, the re-markable nature of the world-wide assembly that regularly gathered before God on behalf of their mortally sick brother and friend. His worst days had provided the occasion for "a Pentecost of brotherly love." Should one have predicted twenty years before that "a Dissenting minister would have been lovingly mentioned in St. Paul's Cathedral, and in numerous Episcopal churches" he would have been deemed mad; but such had happened. Spurgeon took this as a hopeful sign of "growing unity among those who are spiritual," when unvarnished brotherly kindness pours out to one "who has been very outspoken concerning religious differences."

Final Lessons from Life at Mentone

In spite, however, of the unpromising vitality of his life, he had one peculiar joy that he had never experienced in Mentone—Wifey was there. Su-sannah reveled in the time they had together dur-ing those days and expressed to the readers of *The Sword and the Trowel* the extent of her joy:

It is that the Lord so tenderly granted to us both three months of perfect earthly happiness here in Menton, before He took him to the "far better" of his own glory and immediate presence! For fifteen years my beloved had longed to bring me here; but it had never been possible. Now, we were both strengthened for the long journey; and the desire of his heart was fully given him. I can never describe the pride and joy with which he introduced me to his favourite haunts, and the eagerness with which he showed me each lovely glimpse of mountain, sea, and landscape. He was hungry for my loving appreciation, and I satisfied him to the full. We took long daily drives, and every place we visited was a triumphal entry for him. His enjoyment was intense, his delight exuberant. He *looked* in perfect health, and rejoiced in the brightest of spirits.

Then, too, with what calm, deep happiness he sat, day after day, in a cosy corner of his sunny room, writing his last labour of love, *The Commentary on Matthew's Gospel*! Not a care burdened him, not a grief weighed upon his heart, not a desire remained unfulfilled, not a wish unsatisfied; he was permitted to enjoy an earthly Eden before his translation to the Paradise above.[45]

Joseph Harrald described these drives that the couple took with each other. Spurgeon often want-ed to put together a book for visitors to Mentone that would lead them into the truly and beauti-fully refreshing vistas, perhaps different from the "usual tourist style." Even with such a weakened body and taxed mind, Spurgeon sought to take advantage of the time for as much refreshment as possible. One drive carried him to the Pont St. Louis that bridges the border between France and Italy. Years earlier he had given theological reflec-tions on the nature of such a bridge that allowed easy passage from one country to another when "a deep gulf frowns beneath." "Is not the Lord Je-sus such a bridge between the state of condemna-tion and the region of salvation?" While our sins and our spiritual inability divided us from God, the Lord Jesus, the "Divine Mediator," makes a way that is safe and unobstructed, at any hour of night or day with no guard to block the path and no toll asked, but only free passage urged.[46]

They passed a cliff with massive rock forma-tions that allowed the imagination to picture sculptures made by nature in the form of many a public figure. A rock quarry nearby provided the building materials for many of the buildings in Mentone, and a mature tree in "Dr. Bennet's garden" allowed Spurgeon to point out to Susan-nah the spot where he sat when he had sketched

---

45. S&T, March 1892, 110, 111.
46. S&T, April 1892, 176.

it for her a decade before when he described the steady growth of the book fund and its maturing influence for the glory of God. "Each outgrowth is nearer heaven, and tends to the perfecting of the tree;" even so, "To you," he wrote "each year's work has less in it whereof you might glory, even as the tree grows less as it climbs higher; but there is to the eye of an onlooker a beauty and a symmetry about the whole of a work which is done for Jesus, and my love may rest assured that her service is beautiful to Him whose approbation is her chief reward."[47]

A particular spectacle that provided special pleasure to Spurgeon was the "Fountain in the sea, "a spring of fresh water that forces its way right through the solid and liquid above it." Spurgeon often went out to its location in a boat. It reminded him of "the divine life within the soul of a believer to overcome all obstacles, and manifest itself to the praise of God's grace." Other places included schools for children and a particularly suggestive location consisting of a cross on a hill just near a turn and a path where one emerged from shadow and cool air into sunshine and warmth. At the particular scene, on January 8, 1892, Harrald instructed the photographer, Mr. Houghton, to take a candid shot of Spurgeon at some point, for when he sought to pose the photograph always was unsatisfactory. After a shot of the cross, Houghton arranged the camera to get a picture of Spurgeon in the carriage. Upon isolating and enlarging Spurgeon's face from the rest of the photograph, it became a classic likeness, Spurgeon decked with his broad brim hat, more white than dark in the beard, and a fur collar on his overcoat. A stop at the Palazzo Orengo allowed Spurgeon to get out of the carriage briefly for a conversation with Mr. Hanbury, owner of the

beautiful residence. On the grounds was an olive tree through which a fountain had been routed so that one could drink water straight from the heart of the olive tree. Obviously, Spurgeon made connections between Christ as the olive tree from whom would flow rivers of living water. In this place Mrs. Spurgeon stayed subsequent to her husband's death in order to gain strength for her return home.

For February 1892, *The Sword and the Trowel* carried two messages by Spurgeon jointly entitled "Breaking the Long Silence." J. W. Harrald wrote, "Few, if any, who read the two addresses, published in *The Sword and Trowel* for February, under the title, "Breaking the Long Silence," expected the startling message that flashed around the globe soon after the last number of the Magazine was issued."[48] These were messages that he had preached on New Year's Eve and New Year's Day respectively. The first took the theme of *Retrospect*, from which he lifted some thoughts for the volume's preface. He reminded the small company that their lives had been preserved by a multitude of providential interventions to preserve in danger and from danger. They should not fail to remember their sins, for Christ has come to save sinners. "Our sinnership is that emptiness into which the Lord pours his mercy."[49] That led to his contemplations on the abundance of mercies that attended every day and every circumstance; "streams of mercy; oceans of mercy, mercy all, and all mercy." He felt these mercies in a very personal way but wanted all to review the record for themselves. "How wonderful is his lovingkindness! How Free! How Tender! How Faithful! How lasting! How everlasting!" He pointed to the lessons of unity of God's people. "We mistake our divergencies of judgment for differences of

---

47. Ibid., 177.

48. S&T, March 1892, 122.

49. S&T February 1892, 51.

heart; but they are far from being the same thing." This did not imply a softening of Spurgeon on the issues of the Downgrade, for he went on to assert, "In these days of infidel criticism, believers of all sorts will be driven into sincere unity." The unity he described was not a fellowship of light with darkness or of belief with unbelief because "between rationalism and faith there is an abyss immeasurable; but where there is faith in the Everlasting Father, faith in the Great Sacrifice, and faith in the Indwelling Spirit, there is a living, loving, lasting union."[50]

Spurgeon's last public address—his last sermon—came on New Year's Day and put his listeners to contemplate *Prospect* for the future. He described the day as "one of the days of heaven upon the earth. Almost cloudless and windless, beneath the bluest of skies, the day was warm and bright with the glorious sun."[51] The sermon overflows with the theological ideas that had governed Spurgeon's ministry for forty-two years. Our finiteness precludes our having precise knowledge of the future. "We know nothing of the events which lie before us—of life or death to ourselves or to our friends, or of changes of position, or of sickness or health."[52] Not only are we incapable of knowing the future, it would be unwise to probe into it if we could. Perhaps as a corrective to himself in putting too much hope in the so-called "prayer of faith" so constantly brought before his mind by his solicitous friends, he resisted the legitimacy of any desire we might have to know specifics about the future as in intrusion into the divine prerogative. Blessings would lose their freshness and troubles would cloud blessings with a foretaste of distress. "Great mercy," he reasoned, "has hung up a veil between us and the future; and there let it hang!"

And yet, all was not hidden in mystery, for the promises and purposes of God still prevailed over history and operated in the lives of his people. Spurgeon taught his listeners what he always had taught his people about God's predestining purpose. "I see a pathway made from this Jan. 1, 1892, to Jan 1, 1893. I see a highway cast up by the foreknowledge and predestination of God." The future in its entirety would bow to the divine purpose and in no instance would chance play a part, including "every stone on the road, and every drop of dew or evening mist that fall upon the grass which grows on the roadside." God's infallible wisdom and infinite love "has ordained our path."[53]

Spurgeon saw also that presence of the Lord to cheer and to guide through his personal counsel. Even if all friends and family receded from view, "there is One who wears our nature, who will never quit our side." His is a felt presence in every situation in the coming year, "whether it be the time of the singing of birds, or the season of ripe fruits, or the dark months when the clods are frozen into iron." His love for Mentone made this idea of divine presence particularly appropriate in his own perception:

> In this Riviera we ought the more readily to realize our Lord's presence, because the country is so like "Thy land, O Immanuel!" Here is the land of oil olive, and of figs, and of the clusters of Eschol. By such a blue sea he walked, and up such rocky hills he climbed. But, whether here or elsewhere, let us look for HIM to abide with us, to make this year truly to be "a year of our Lord."[54]

By the eye of faith, Spurgeon also saw that God would provide strength for the journey. He will

---

50. Ibid., 52.

51. S&T, March 1892, 123.

52. Pike, 394.

53. Pike, 395; S&T, February 1892, 53f.

54. S&T, February 1892, 54.

not provide spare strength, but just what is needed for each moment. We must not wonder if grace will be available for some future crisis, for it is not yet here; "strength will come when it is needed, and not before." What about death? "You do not yet feel," Spurgeon proposed with deep personal investment in his own observation, "that you have grace to die with: what of that?" When you are not dying you need only grace to deal with the immediate demands of life. The time will come, "when life is ebbing out, and your only thought is about landing on the eternal shore," when by gracious instinct you will look to God "for dying grace in dying moments." Only then may the believer "expect an inrush of divine strength when human strength is failing."[55]

Spurgeon also saw "a power overruling all things" for the good of those that are the "called according to his purpose." He told the few gathered together that he saw "a wonder-working hand which turns for us the swords of disease into the ploughshares of correction, and the spears of trial into the pruning-hooks of discipline." By the divine skill "bitters are made sweet, and poisons turned to medicines."[56]

He closed this brief homily with that foundational driving force that had informed his life and ministry for forty years:

One thing more, and this is brightness itself: this year we trust we shall see *God glorified* by us and in us. If we realize our chief end, we reach our highest enjoyment. It is the delight of the renewed heart to think that God can get glory out of such poor creatures as we are. "God is light." We cannot add to his brightness; but we may act as reflectors, which, though they have no light of their own, yet when the sun shines upon them, reflect his beams, and send them where, without such reflection, they might not have come. When the Lord shines upon us, we will cast that light upon dark places, and make those who sit in the shadow of death to rejoice in Jesus our Lord. We hope that God has been in some measure glorified in some of us during the past year, but we trust he will be glorified by us far more in the year which now begins. We will be content to glorify God either actively or passively. We should have it so happen that, when our life's story is written, whoever reads it will not think of us as "self-made men", but as the handiwork of God, in whom his grace is magnified. Not in us may men see the clay, but the Potter's hand. They said of one, "He is a fine preacher"; but of another they said, "We never notice how he preaches, *but we feel that God is great.*" We wish our whole life to be a sacrifice; an altar of incense continually smoking with sweet perfume unto the Most High. Oh, to be borne through the year on the wings of praise to God; to mount from year to year, and raise at each ascent a loftier and yet lowlier song unto the God of our life! The vista of a praiseful life will never close, but continue throughout eternity. From psalm to psalm, from hallelujah to hallelujah, we will ascend the hill of the Lord; until we come into the Holiest of all, where, with veiled faces, we will bow before the Divine Majesty in the bliss of endless adoration.[57]

No Task Left Undone, No Truth left Unsaid
Spurgeon's faithful "armour-bearer," J. W. Harrald, chronicled the day by day events of Spurgeon from early in January until his death. January 8 was the thirty-sixth anniversary of the Spurgeons' wedding day, the day of a memorable drive through Mentone, and the day of his final photograph. On January 9, Spurgeon revised the manuscript on Psalm 105:37, the last one that he would ever produce for *The Metropolitan Tabernacle Pulpit*. On Sunday, January 10, a group

---

55. Ibid., 54.
56. Ibid., 55.

57. Ibid.

of nineteen met in his sitting room in the *Hotel Beau Rivage* for worship where they sang "Come Thou Fount" and Spurgeon read and gave a brief exposition of Psalm 73 and read his sermon on verse 28 entitled "Let Us Pray." On January 13, Mr. Valiant for Truth wrote his note for the February number of *The Sword and the Trowel* entitled "The Bible and Modern Criticism." Harrald noted that this article should serve as a positive corrective to those reporting that Spurgeon had "changed his attitude with regard to the Downgrade controversy." Harrald was convinced, along with Mrs. Spurgeon, that that conflict had contributed in large part to the severity of the illness that eventually took his life. Spurgeon said as much in the article when he wrote, "The position is instructive, as showing that to be free from all ecclesiastical entanglements is to the Christian minister a blessing worth all it has cost, even though an almost fatal illness be reckoned as part of the price."[58]

Ironically, this note appeared in *The Sword and the Trowel* for February 1, the day after the death of Spurgeon, so that one would know that the illness was not "almost" fatal. As Harrald inferred, however, it does show that Spurgeon had no intention of recanting the stance he had taken in the Downgrade. It was on his mind as long as he had conscious mental capacity. He had lost none of his powers of perception or expression on this issue nor any of the intent to ridicule the proponents of modern thought and their supposedly enlightened mental apparatus. He had observed that among Church of England clergy, thirty-eight men had signed a document affirming their adherence to the historic commitment of "the Church" to the "supreme authority and infallibility of Holy Scripture." While he pressed

himself to place the best possible reading on their use of the term "Church," he found great satisfaction in their affirmation and in the witness this bore to his having brought the warning years earlier. "By this time," he wrote, "we shall scarcely again be charged with wantonly raising the cry of 'Wolf' without a cause, when we earnestly warned the churches that infidelity was permeating the ministry." He pointed out that even among Anglican, both high and evangelical, a fierce controversy was raging "over the inspiration of the Holy Scripture; and this is involving the Deity of our Lord, and indeed every other truth of Christianity." Ever hopeful in the midst of distress, Spurgeon believed that love for Scripture would trump ecclesiastical loyalty and party spirit among both groups and bring unity to them over this issue at least, that they would cast over the Bible, they would defend the Scripture, and maintain reverence for the inspired volume.

Spurgeon found the union of diverse clergy on these issues interesting but equally so the way they were treated. They were assailed as bigots, their competency was questioned, and they were sneered at "as if they were a set of imbeciles." Then with his untarnished ability to select the perfect phrases and rhythm for the revelation of irony Spurgeon wrote, "It appears when skeptics vent their idle doubts, this is a brave display of freedom of thought; but if an orthodox man of learning states his belief, it is an insolent imposition of his authority in restraint of the liberty of this progressive age." To Spurgeon it appeared that the bigotry and insolence lay almost exclusively with those whose singular talent was to impute these vices so readily to others.[59]

Other material that appeared in *The Sword and the Trowel* for February shows what Spur-

---

58. Ibid., 93.

59. Ibid.

geon learned about his world-wide concerns as well as his London ministry, and how he continued personal involvement in the spiritual lives of his flock. Book reviews that he had been gathering for sometime but had not had room to publish made their appearance in the February issue. Thirty-five reviews appeared, most of them comparatively substantial with only about four given purely as notices. In these reviews, Spurgeon kept up his relentless attack against unbelief, skepticism, and advanced thought. Commenting on a book about Christian evidences developed from the literature of the second century, Spurgeon noted that "there is among people who have read a little, and fancy that they know much, a widespread feeling that the foundations of the Scripture are insecure." While the peculiar provenance of unbelieving books sends a seductive appeal to young people who cannot bear the possible embarrassment of being old-fashioned, Spurgeon pointed out that the "whole tendency of these lectures is to make those who read them ashamed of any leanings they may have towards the ignorant pretensions of the cheap shilling books of skepticism." He then commented on the method of each author, the relevance of the literature they treated in making their arguments, and the desirability of the book being in "the libraries of young people everywhere."[60]

Another review, *The Word and the Book* by George Hutton, allowed Spurgeon to issue a hearty "Amen" and affirm the author's defense of "the plenary and verbal inspiration of the original Scriptures." In addition, he could not omit the chance to condemn the "ignorance which calls this view 'mechanical'" and urged some rich Presbyterian layman to give a copy to all the ministers of that order, and, while thinking generously, include the Baptists.[61]

Of course, Spurgeon always looked out for Baptists and used his reviews to set forth the distinctives of their ecclesiology. In a review of *The Maze and its Clue*, Spurgeon interacted briefly with James Tyeth Hart's argument that baptism is not "an answer to, or expression of man's faith; but faith is rather an answer to God's baptism." Spurgeon commented that the "elaborate treatise, evidently earnest and devout, omits to deal with the great commission to baptize (only) disciples, and does not even notice the inspired explanation of the ordinance given in Rom. vi. 3-6, and Col. ii.12." Spurgeon commented that if such treatises were necessary to explain the ordinances of the gospel, "simple folk would be in a maze indeed; but verily it is not so."[62]

A book by F. A. Fawkes looked like those of "Professor [Henry] Drummond" and shared his error of "confounding partial analogy with complete identity." The error becomes questionable and unhealthy when the analogy of brotherhood is made to assume the Universal Fatherhood of God despite scriptural teaching that makes it clear that "it is only those who have the Spirit of adoption who belong to the household of faith."[63] Spurgeon had nothing but high marks for the 1891 Yale Lectures in Preaching delivered and published by James Stalker through Hodder and Stoughton. Stalker was a man "with a right to speak to other preachers about their vocation." He set up the prophets and apostles as patterns for ministers today and, in doing so, "set a noble ideal before the Christian preacher." Spurgeon called the book as sound in doctrinal teaching as in wise counsel and devout spirit. "There is not a 'shoddy' paragraph in it."[64]

Begun with great interest and hope, Spurgeon put down *The Sabbath in Puritan New England*

---

60. Ibid., 84.

61. Ibid., 84f.

62. Ibid., 85.

63. Ibid.

64. Ibid., 86.

with disgust. "Where so much that is great, noble, and holy might have been recorded, it is not meet that such a wretched heap of foibles, peculiarities, and bigotries should have been published to the world." It is rather like an artist with opportunity to paint a lovely face and highlights only the freckles.[65] When he perused a review of the Revised Version of the New Testament, he felt that the author had been too harsh and would accomplish little by such "wholesale condemnation;" nevertheless, Spurgeon commented, "let us not forsake the old for the new; for the old is better."[66]

He commended Bishop Alfred Barry's discussion of *Christianity and Socialism.* Barry presented a well-articulated and appropriately nuanced discussion of a variety of plans for social betterment, pointing out strengths and weaknesses, engaging each with a view to their relation to the Christian gospel, and avoided dangling "social Utopias before men's eyes," nor did he "mock the seekers after bread with stones." Spurgeon affirmed the Bishop's "mild commendation of the gospel" as the only balm for broken hearts or cure for social ills. Spurgeon, with a life's ministry to match, commended making the "best of life's conditions for the weak, the helpless, and for all, by all means." His premillennialism, however, reigned in his hopes for anything other than temporary and partial solutions, for "no social plans will make our earth a paradise while sin still curses it, and Satan is abroad." The perfect state exists only in the New Jerusalem and, as for the earth, "the King must come and take to himself his great power and reign ere the glowing promises of the seventy-second Psalm are realized."[67]

Engaging another theme to which he had given much thought in his long and intense ministry, Spurgeon reviewed J. O. Bairdstow's *Sensational Religion.* Bairdstow defined "sensation" and then defended "sensationalism," a totally distinct word, "suggestive of different thoughts and practices." Spurgeon had seen enough of that and would have none of it. "Our strong conviction is, that God's work should be done in God's way. After all, it is the Holy Spirit through and by whom all spiritual work must be accomplished, while his chosen instrument is the Word of God."[68]

A biography of John Allison Macfadyen could have reminded Spurgeon of his own ministry, for Macfadyen was "well known throughout the land as an able preacher of evangelical truth," who built a "large church from which numerous institutions were worked, and other churches sprang." That which can be accomplished by "consecrated energy and sanctified common-sense" found its model in Macfadyen. He was too busy winning souls and spreading the kingdom of Christ to give time to "idle speculations" and had no love for the "vagaries of 'modern thought.'" He was a man of respectable scholarship, held the creed of moderate Calvinism from the inception to the end of his ministry "recognizing to the full the special grace of God as well as the responsibility of man in salvation." The author, Alexander Mackennal, gave a "full and faithful, but not an exaggerated picture of his life-long friend."[69]

Another prolonged battle to which his reviews gave reference was that of the Romanizing of the Anglican church. An analysis and critique by Alfred Burton of Cardinal Newman's *Apologia pro Vita Sua* unveiled the cardinal's "unconscious casuistry," his "amazing self-deception," and that his theological struggle was never between evangelicalism and Romanism but Anglicanism and Romanism, considered, not scripturally, but on

---

65. Ibid.

66. Ibid.

67. Ibid., 87.

68. Ibid.

69. Ibid., 88.

the basis of antiquity. "We are sorry," Spurgeon observed, "that so valuable a criticism should not have been presented in some logical order and that its style should be marred by frequent repetitions and obscure sentences."[70]

About Walter Jerrold's biography of Michael Faraday, Spurgeon wrote that he has come nearer to the heart of the man than a "mere jotter of details" could possible have done. This led Spurgeon to observe, "Certain writers shoot out a mass of incidents which refer to a man, and call the heap a biography: they evidently see no difference between a brickfield and a mansion."[71] While Spurgeon appreciated Jerrold's careful emphasis on Faraday's simple and child-like Christian faith, he felt compelled to remark on the emphasis Jerrold gave to Faraday's reluctance to be more public in his witness. Calling such a sentiment a half-truth, Spurgeon continued, "Our living among men is a circumstance which demands our pleading with them, for God's glory and the good of their souls."

The ethical implications of the treatment of Native Americans was not beyond Spurgeon's willingness to comment. The information contained in a documentary on the American Indian entitled *Redskin and Paleface* promoted Spurgeon's observation, "A thrilling story is the chronicle of the Red Man, and his dealings with the white intruders from across the sea." He believed that the so-called civilized race "has just cause to confess before the Lord its murderous selfishness, which has nearly extirpated one of the families of the earth."[72] Spurgeon's reading was wide, his knowledge grew about all areas of human endeavor until the day he died. His convictions about important issues never wavered and his witness for truth was never far behind his

initial observations on books, men, events, and natural phenomena.

Following his frequent practice, Spurgeon included in his last efforts as editor of *The Sword and the Trowel* an article about one of the faithful officers of the church. W. Payne had worked in the City Chamberlain's office for fifty years and still served as principal clerk. Payne had served as an elder but presently, because of his judicious financial skill, he accepted the office of deacon and regularly conducted audits of the various accounts of the church and its institutions. Spurgeon pointed out that Payne had been an Anglican. Under the influence of the famous minister, Baptist Noel, he left Anglicanism to unite with Baptists for "he shared that good man's views, both as to the Union of Church and State and Believers' Baptism." He was baptized by Noel and became a member of John Street Church. He came to the Tabernacle in May 1861, was installed as elder in 1865 and "his care for the sick and the poor, and his love for the services of the Lord's house, were abundantly known to all associated with that work." In 1876 he became deacon. Spurgeon expressed deep concern over the recent ill-health of Payne but noted, "The Lord has, as in the case of his Pastor, heard the prayer of the Church for him in extreme sickness, and therefore we will pray on." Spurgeon could not afford to lose a friend "so faithful, so earnest, so tried and proved." The Pastor, Spurgeon admitted, "clings to all his old friends with a tenacity only rivaled by the way in which they cling to him."[73]

Spurgeon also wanted to protect A. T. Pierson from the burden of responding unnecessarily to letters. Spurgeon had received many expressing sympathy to him in his illness, but he warned, "Friends may write as much as they please if they

---

70. Ibid.

71. Ibid., 89.

72. Ibid.

---

73. Ibid., 91f.

do not expect replies: but letters requiring answers ought not to be sent except from sheer necessity. It is murderous." Correspondents, he went on to write, "appear to be nearly as unreasonable in writing to Dr. Pierson as they have often been in their communications to the Editor." Pierson and his daughters, it appears, had to work deep into the night to answer letters, "many of which ought not to have been written." One individual had sent Pierson fifteen telegrams. The burden of serving the Tabernacle at this strategic juncture was demanding enough without the useless multiplication of labor. Spurgeon asked his readers to prove their wisdom by "abstaining from asking our friend for service which it is impossible for him to render."[74]

Doubtless he was thrilled to receive words from some of the college men in New Zealand. The defection of valued alumni and the reorganization of the college conference had been soul rending to Spurgeon. For seven of his men, including his son, to report on their work came at a critical time for Spurgeon's spirit. From the meeting of the Baptist Union in New Zealand, they expressed their deep concern about the health of the president, being "pained about the dread thought that you were about to be taken from us to the rest you need, and the reward which by grace awaits you." They prayed that he might be spared longer. Included in the reports of the activities of all seven men, the news of Thomas must have been particularly encouraging. "Your son Thomas has just finished his second year's engagement as Evangelist of the Union, an office in which he has enjoyed singular success." Thomas had held 19 missions, 235 services, delivered 19 lectures, and, according to the letter, "had the enviable privilege of leading over 600 souls to

the Redeemer's feet." Though he had been reappointed evangelist, Thomas would spend part of the year in service of his former charge, the Auckland Tabernacle. Their jointly signed letter closed with an affirmation of truth and practice central to Spurgeon's view of ministry:

> We are all anxious, dear President, according to our varying abilities and opportunities, to spread abroad the gospel of our Lord Jesus in its fullness, purity, and power. We have not swerved aside from the foundation truths of our holy faith, or lost faith in the ultimate triumph of the cause of Christ our King. We are still one with you in our attachment to the truths that cluster around the cross, and in our loving loyalty to the Crucified.[75]

The seven signatures included Thomas Spurgeon at the top, followed by Chas. Dallaston, Harry H. Driver, Jno D. Gilmore, Arthur D. Dewdney, George D. Cox, and Edward Richards.

Labors on the monthly periodical must of necessity be sparse, as his energy waned day by day and some other activities also occupied him. At worship on January 17, Spurgeon read Psalm 103 accompanied by his usual brief expository remarks sprinkled throughout at strategic points. Rather than produce a new exposition, his friends convinced him simply to read his commentary on Matthew 25:21-28. Harrald included Spurgeon's expository text for this in his article in *The Sword and the Trowel* for March. He announced as the last hymn he ever lined out, "The Sands of Time Are Sinking." The hymn bore particularly relevant truth for him. This hymn also was sung by the orphanage choir at Spurgeon's funeral:

> The sands of time are sinking,
> the dawn of Heaven breaks;

---

74. Ibid., 92.

75. Ibid., 94.

The summer morn I've sighed for—
the fair, sweet morn awakes:
Dark, dark hath been the midnight,
but dayspring is at hand,
And glory, glory dwelleth in Immanuel's land.

O Christ, He is the fountain,
the deep, sweet well of love!
The streams of earth I've tasted,
more deep I'll drink above:
There to an ocean fullness
His mercy doth expand,
And glory, glory dwelleth in Immanuel's land.

The King there in His beauty,
without a veil is seen:
It were a well spent journey,
though seven deaths lay between:
The Lamb with His fair army,
doth on Mount Zion stand,
And glory, glory dwelleth in Immanuel's land.

With mercy and with judgment
my web of time He wove,
And aye, the dews of sorrow
were lustred with His love;
I'll bless the hand that guided,
I'll bless the heart that planned
When throned where glory dwelleth in Immanuel's land.

O I am my Beloved's
and my Beloved's mine!
He brings a poor vile sinner
into His "house of wine."
I stand upon His merit,
I know no other stand,
Not even where glory dwelleth in Immanuel's land.

I shall sleep sound in Jesus,
filled with His likeness rise,
To love and to adore Him,
to see Him with these eyes:

'Tween me and resurrection
but Paradise doth stand;
Then, then for glory dwelling in Immanuel's land.

The Bride eyes not her garment,
but her dear Bridegroom's face;
I will not gaze at glory
but on my King of grace.
Not at the crown He giveth
but on His pierced hand;
The Lamb is all the glory of Immanuel's land.

Whether all these verses were sung is not clear from the notes of Spurgeon's last days and, surprisingly, the hymn does not appear in Spurgeon's selection of hymns, *Our Own Hymnbook*. It contains nineteen verses, some of which are clearly autobiographical for the hymn writer Anne Ross Cousin, who adapted words from Samuel Rutherford. Another verse, probably not sung on this worship occasion, Spurgeon might nevertheless have felt was somewhat true of his own situation.

I have borne scorn and hatred,
I have borne wrong and shame,
Earth's proud ones have reproached me
for Christ's thrice blessed Name:
Where God His seal set fairest
they've stamped the foulest brand,
But judgment shines like noonday in Immanuel's land.

Death Comes Quickly

On January 20, after going for his last drive, a short trek to Monti, he had to go to bed because of pain in his hand. He had complained of a difficulty with the hand on many occasions and just recently when he wrote the orphanage children that were he there he could not carve a large joint for them because of the pain in the small joints of his hand. The bed became his home until his death.

The next day, January 21, the pain began again in his head and he was reduced to the necessity of constant nursing, day and night. Spurgeon had been invited to lunch on Saturday, January 23, with Arthur Phelps, a minister whose life had been greatly enriched by Spurgeon's sermons at Mentone, particularly at a crucial time in 1881. Spurgeon fell ill, and instructed Harrald to write to Phelps that "he regrets that he will be unable to meet you and the other brethren at the House of Rest on Saturday as he is suffering from gout in his right hand." He hoped that it would be merely temporary and slight, and that his "visit will not be long delayed, and he sends his kindest Christian regards to you and all the other brethren."[76] On that same day, he told Harrald, "My work is done." By January 26, Dr. Fitzhenry, the attending physician, called the patient's condition "serious."

On the afternoon of January 31, his strength failed so rapidly and his cognitive powers followed suit, that he was unable to recognize friends or even his wife. After 3:30, he slipped into unconsciousness and continually declined until 11:05 when he was pronounced dead. A rumor spread that Spurgeon had quoted the Apostle Paul's words in 2 Timothy beginning with "I have fought the good fight." Harrald emphasized strongly that "He did not utter them." The words were inscribed on his olive-wood casket, but his using them "would have been contrary to the whole spirit of his life." "He had far too humble an opinion of his own work and worth to use the inspired language, which," at the time of Harrald's writing, "by almost universal consent, has been put into his lips." Even G. Holden Pike, in his 1892 volume on Spurgeon, reported the supposed "last quotation from the Scriptures uttered by Mr. Spurgeon to his secretary, Mr. Harrald, before his

death." Fitzhenry the physician did all that was possible in the circumstances, but for the most part Spurgeon remained unconscious, unable to give any parting words to the loved ones gathered around him or any dying testimony.

Spurgeon had envisioned a dramatic scenario in 1890, in which, during the last five minutes of his life he would rise from his bed "to bear witness to the divine sacrifice and the sin-atoning blood" with such force that he would shock his hearers. What a joy that would be, "for how could I regret that, as in heaven my first words would be to ascribe my salvation to my Master's blood, my last act on earth was to shock his enemies by a testimony to the same fact?"[77] He was not surrounded by the Lord's enemies, nor anyone that would be shocked at that testimony; nor was he allowed a testimony of any sort during the last five minutes of life.

Services of Commemoration

Before the body was sent back to England, a memorial service was held in Mentone in the Scotch Presbyterian Church where Spurgeon had preached the year before at the opening of the building. In the context of the remarks of J. E. Somerville, pastor of the Scotch Church, he said, "Only four days ago we prayed that he might be spared to us, and be allowed to labour longer; but Jesus prayed, 'Father, I will that they also whom Thou has given Me be with Me where I am, that they may behold My glory.' We cannot now wish that that prayer had been denied."

Services held at the Metropolitan Tabernacle on January 31 were filled. The people knew from daily correspondence that their pastor's situation was grave indeed. Dr. Pierson conducted the morning service under the knowledge that news could arrive any moment of Spurgeon's death.

---

76. S&T, April 1892, 154.

77. S&T, June 1890, 260.

That evening the service consisted largely of an impressive time of prayer and included an afternoon dispatch from Mentone telling of the unpromising condition of Spurgeon that tended to deepen the gloom. Forty-five minutes after Spurgeon's death, Harrald telegraphed London, "Menton, 11.50. Our beloved pastor entered heaven, 11.5, Sunday night.—Harrald."[78]

February 1 had been set aside as a day of prayer at the Tabernacle for the cessation of the epidemic of influenza. The irony of the moment was not lost that the influenza had been a major aggravating factor in the death of their pastor. They carried on with the planned prayer; within the week the epidemic abated. But they prayed under even a heavier burden. They prayed for their own spiritual strength and the continued blessing of God on all the ministries of the church. Each day persons met for prayer and on Thursday, February 4, A. T. Pierson preached and the church testified to a great time of encouragement. "The little faith of many was rebuked; and new hope born that, though the chief worker was removed, the work of God would be established; and that the beauty of the Lord would yet be given instead of mourning, ay, even in the midst of sorrow."[79]

On the first Sunday after Spurgeon's death, February 7, James Spurgeon and A. T. Pierson officiated during morning worship. Pierson preached on Revelation 14:13, "Blessed are the dead which die in the Lord from henceforth: Yea, saith the Spirit, that they may rest from their labours; and their works do follow them." As he consoled the congregation with the peculiar blessedness of C.H.S. as he entered into the presence of the Lord, Pierson remarked, "Think not that I make light of your grief. God knows I owe too much to Charles Haddon Spurgeon myself for whatever little power there is in my ministry, or strength in my faith, or courage and confidence in my espousal of neglected and despised truths, not to share most keenly this sorrow."[80] He admonished them not to look down but to look up and enjoy something now of the blessedness experienced to the full by their departed pastor.

In the evening, the Tabernacle again was filled for a celebration of the Lord's Supper. At the close of the communion service, Deacon Thomas H. Olney read a statement that came with the unanimous voice of the deacons and elders requesting, as a temporary arrangement, James Spurgeon to remain as "Pastor in Charge," while A. T. Pierson would be retained as "Officiating Minister." The only sentiment concerning this recommendation was one of "deep gratitude." Within a year, however, some internal strife would result leading to the resignations of Pierson and Spurgeon when Thomas Spurgeon returned from New Zealand to assume the role of his father's successor. In the meantime, the church's officers and congregation could do little other than express their great love for these two interim leaders, highlighted all the more by the death of the former pastor:

> We all thanked God that though one brother had been taken, the other was left. As we had never known how much we loved our departed Pastor until he was called away from us, we never knew how much we esteemed and valued his brother until he was left alone. Nobly has he fulfilled his part, and as, between him and Dr. Pierson, for whom we devoutly thank God, there exists a most fraternal union; and between them both and the church, the heartiest sympathy; long may the arrangement last, which has so auspiciously begun![81]

---

78. Pike, 371.

79. S&T., March 1892, 136.

80. A. T. Pierson, "The Blessedness of the Holy Dead," in *From the Pulpit to the Palm Branch*, 74.

81. S&T, March 1892, 137.

Auspiciously begun, but soon turned sour. By January 2, 1893, Thomas Olney wrote James Spurgeon with a note of regret that such a serious disagreement had arisen between them—the first in twenty years—over the idea of Thomas Spurgeon's return to England to assume the pulpit of the Metropolitan Tabernacle.[82] But for the present, the confidence the congregation needed in the continuity of the work was guaranteed by the presence of Pierson and Spurgeon.

With that bit of conflict yet unknown because still future, Pierson again preached a sermon of deep consolation entitled "A Door Opened in Heaven" from Revelation 4:1. Pierson described John's vision of the various scenes in heaven, it inhabitants, its enjoyments and employments, its purity and its beauty, its safety and its joy, and the nature of the faithful Christian's reward, which he likened to the booths built by the Israelites during the feast of booths commemorating their wilderness wanderings. Spurgeon's booth was built on "unselfish ministry to souls," his "triumphs over temptation," his "patient endurance and suffering," and the "manifested life of God in him." "I never knew a man whose personal love for Jesus was more tender and beautiful than his," Pierson remarked, reminding the congregation as to how his "heart beat in response to every such tribute [to the personal majesty and glory of his Redeemer] of personal love to his Lord."[83]

On February 8, the casket, made of beautiful olive wood, which had crossed from Dieppe during the night, arrived at Victoria Station, was loaded on a plain hearse and covered with palm branches sent by Mrs. Spurgeon from southern France. Through a driving rain storm, the hearse made its way to the Pastors' College where it was placed in the common room. Palms and lilies were placed around the room in abundance. Two small services were held, one for church officers and a second for members of the family. Pierson brought a message pointing to God's provision, in the absence of Moses, of Joshua. They were all to hope in the divine provision.

That night at ten o'clock, students bore the casket from the college to its place in the Metropolitan Tabernacle, occupying a place created by the removal of a few of the front pews. The commentary in *The Sword and the Trowel* observed, "The lifeless clay was deposited in the great building where the living voice had so often been in loving persuasion, and in outspoken defence of the truth."[84]

It soon dawned on the officers and others of the congregation that the funeral and all its attendant parts would be a massive undertaking calling for some equally massive and precise plans, cool clear heads and willing, warm hearts and hands. A vast assortment of tickets for various events and venues of services, comfort and safety for those attending, thousands of condolence letters and gifts to be answered promptly, and a variety of other arrangements would be necessary for the days that followed. When all was over, "let it be said, to the praise of the presiding Spirit of God, that not one thing seems to have been forgotten; not a single accident happened; not a jarring note has been heard."[85]

Not only did the planners need to consider the present urgencies and desires of the many involved, but they must take into account the frank outspokenness of the deceased on the issue of funerals. He had written with some fervor against pomp and expense in funerals almost twenty-three years before his death. Spurgeon, under the

---

82. See Craig Skinner, *Lamplighter and Son* (Nashville, Broadman Press, 1984), 111; Fullerton, 156; S&T, 1893, 244, 372.

83. Ibid., 89.

84. S&T, March 1892, 139.

85. Ibid.

pseudonym Nathaniel Plainspeech, spoke about the extravagance and waste involved in funerals. "What can possess some people to spend so much money on putting a poor corpse into the ground?" Mr. Plainspeech spoke of the brass-headed canes, the feathers, the long handled fans that he had seen in funeral processions and lamented the expense of "white satin and black cloth for the worms." He professed, perhaps as an eccentricity, that he would sooner be "eaten by crows than have pride and pomp feeding on my little savings, which are meant for my bereaved wife and children." Nathaniel Plainspeech wanted decency above all with no hired mourners, no pomp, no "lumbering-coach riding," with not a hood worn by the women or more than a plain hatband by the men. "A plain coffin is all the dead can need, and enough help to bear the body to its last bed is all that is required." The grave is "too solemn a place for mimicry and masquerade."[86]

Little did he realize at that time, how extended would be the time between his death and his interment, and how much public notice would need to be given just to show due courtesy to a well-meaning public desiring to express their sympathy and their honest admiration for the good he had done—for the glory of Christ and the kingdom of God as most would acknowledge, or for the well-being of London as many would insist. Keeping it simple, in light of the universal outflow of mourning and sympathy would be difficult indeed, and the planners did not entirely succeed in duplicating what Spurgeon had observed as Nathaniel Plainspeech. A plain coffin indeed! The beautiful olive-wood casket taken from the trees in the vicinity of Mentone made such an impression that all commented on its beauty. Spurgeon's simple views certainly gave

some discipline to this occasion, but could not be implemented with unalloyed faithfulness.

The virtually universal sense of loss may be seen in the wide variety of those that desired to have something judicious and memorable to say on the occasion. A paper that loaded him with severe criticism early in his ministry but found in him much to admire, as his constancy to truth and love refused to fade under such withering sarcasm, summarized this aspect of his ministry in a most appropriate fashion:

> From the Bible, the "Pilgrim's Progress," and the writings of the Puritan Fathers, he derived the simplicity of utterance and nervous energy of phrase which made the common people hear him gladly, and the educated listen with appreciation as to a half-forgotten melody charged with the pathos of the past. To the primitive plainness and directness of English speech the dead preacher united perfect clearness of argument. A hearer might not agree with his opinions, but he could never mistake them. While avoiding the elaborate and formal structure which characterised the early Puritan sermons, Mr. Spurgeon, who knew them better, perhaps, than any man now living, emulated all their higher qualities, and brought to the emotional speech of the nineteenth century the perspicuity of severer and, perhaps, more logical utterances. ... His sterling honesty, fearless outspokenness, and unflinching fidelity to a creed not all the clauses of which are now fashionable, should equally be remembered to his credit.[87]

Spurgeon had never been concerned that his creed be fashionable, only that it be faithful. Such faithfulness obviously had the ring of truth for thousands, for on Tuesday morning, when the Tabernacle was open for public viewing of the body

---

86. S&T, March 1869, 103.

87. G. H. Pike, *The Life and Work of Charles Haddon Spurgeon*, 6 vols (London: Cassell & Co., nd), 6:345-46. See pages 332-52 for a large number of evaluations of Spurgeon from papers and individuals in all walks of life and all religious persuasions.

from seven until seven, 60,000 people streamed through double-file, people of every rank and station. On each end of the casket, plates bearing the following inscription were placed:

In ever-loving memory of
CHARLES HADDON SPURGEON,
Born at Kelvedon. June 19, 1834,
Fell asleep in Jesus at Menton, Jan 31, 1892
"I have fought a good fight, I have finished my course, I have kept the faith."[88]

An abundance of cards in commemoration of the ministry of Spurgeon were placed strategically in the room along with an impressive array of floral wreaths and other arrangements of flowers. The note from Mrs. Spurgeon read, "'With Christ, which is far better.' I will follow thee, my husband. Undying love from 'the wife of thy youth.'" Cards with appropriate scripture verses from James Spurgeon, J. W. Harrald, and twin sons Charles and Tom also were placed around or attached to the casket. Harrald's stated, "In fondest memory of my dearest earthly friend, my beloved Pastor and father in the faith, and 'the good soldier of Jesus Christ', whose armour-bearer desires to be faithful unto death as his captain was." The large number of memorial flowers included a large floral harp formed of lilies sent from Belfast, a sword and trowel made of violets, an anchor composed of lilies and hyacinths, a wreath from the children of the orphanage, and a magnificent wreath sent from pastors and Christians in Paris. The room would not have held all that would have been sent had the family and church officers not requested that memory be made in the form of gifts to the orphanage and the college.[89]

For Wednesday morning, the planners scheduled a service specifically for the members of the Tabernacle Church to which admission was gained only by the communion cards for 1892. James Spurgeon wisely took only a brief part in the introduction of the speakers. Dr. Angus, a former pastor and the head of Regents Park College, gave "reminiscences of fifty years ago," and exhortations for the present. Pike called it "an impressive address" while one of the correspondents reporting to *The Sword and the Trowel* said "he was not clearly heard by everybody," but under the circumstances of the present emergency made remarks "both interesting and edifying." Angus believed Spurgeon's life "gave fresh incentive to completer consecration." His congregation should remember that the mortal remains had nothing to do with Spurgeon now, but he reminded them that "the Christian man is never put into his grave at all, but being absent from the body was immediately present with the Lord." Angus speculated that perhaps Spurgeon missed the orphans, the students, the church, the inquirers, and the converts, but "whatever be the disadvantages of the loss of earthly relationships, to be with Christ is far better." "His sins are behind him; his weakness is behind him; his cares and distractions are behind him; and he is for ever with the Lord."[90]

Pierson, who according to the report "immediately on rising, commanded the sympathetic attention of the meeting," began by reading a letter from Mrs. Spurgeon. She expressed sincere gratitude for Pierson's reliable and devoted leadership during the three months of Spurgeon's final illness, for it gave him assurance of the church's well-being and allowed him thoroughly to enjoy the time with Mrs. Spurgeon. She gave an impassioned expression of how joyful her husband must be in the presence now of his Lord. With

---

88. S&T, March 1892, 140.
89. Ibid., 140ff.

90. *From the Pulpit to the Palm Branch*, 101.

sentiment and emotion overriding theological correctness she wrote, "He is not here; he is risen,' is as true of my beloved as of my beloved's Lord," and assured the reader, "Not for a moment do I wish him back, though he was dearer to me than tongue can tell." She signed the letter, "Your Grateful Friend, Susie Spurgeon."[91] Pierson continued with an evaluation of Spurgeon as an evangelist, pastor, organizer, leader, and Christian. Pierson believed that the key to Spurgeon's power as a believer was his "overwhelming sense of the powers of the world to come." He stressed that Spurgeon's single theme, "Christ and him crucified," rather than being a weakness was the true glory of his ministry. He was a Paganini among preachers, able to do more with that one thematic string than others could with four. Spurgeon took one book, the Bible, "the whole Bible as the inspired book of God; he took Christ, the whole Christ, as the justifier, sanctifier, and redeemer; he believed with all his heart; and every utterance was a speech born of deep conviction."[92]

When Harrald spoke, again he insisted that no one perpetuate the falsehood that Spurgeon had quoted the words of Paul about the close of his ministry. "Let it be known," Harrald emphasized, "as distinctly as possible, *the pastor did not say it at all.* I have taken every opportunity I could get to say that the last message he was able to deliver to the congregation, or to anyone, was that remarkable message telegraphed to you on the very day that you were bringing in thankofferings for his partial recovery." That message had been a simple pledge of contribution of £100 as a "hearty thankoffering towards Tabernacle General Expenses." He closed with "Love to all friends." Harrald was convinced that all this was purposeful. Spurgeon even omitted from the telegram

any word about his physical condition, although Harrald added that himself. As if the simplicity of these final words had not been deemed enough by other friends or members of the congregation, as if some were wanting something more heroic, or prophetic, or canonical in significance, Harrald dwelt a bit longer on this phenomenon:

> This was his last message to you, and it is no use asking for any other. There is no other. We watched day and night with him. Oh what would we not have given if we could have had another word? We hoped against hope that there would have been some other final message, but no other was given. There you have it all: *"Hearty thankoffering. Love to all friends."*[93]

Harrald called Spurgeon "a martyr for the truth's sake." Harrald was convinced that the severity of that last great controversy shortened his life, but Spurgeon "would gladly lay down his life a thousand times for the sake of the gospel."

Six more speakers followed. Vernon Charlesworth, headmaster of the orphanage, read a catena of scripture passages applicable to the ministry and spirituality of Spurgeon. T. W. Medhurst, the first student of the college, prayed and subsequently left "The first Student's Wreath" as a verbal tribute to Spurgeon in *The Sword and the Trowel.* After his expressing his deep love for and indebtedness to Spurgeon, Medhurst wrote, "Thank God, 'the last of the Puritans' is not dead; but the best, the greatest, the noblest of this nineteenth century has gone to his rest and reward." For the nearly 700 who called him "President beloved," Medhurst vowed, "We, by God's grace, have not bowed the knee to the modern Baal, and will not."[94]

---

91. S&T, March 1892, 142.

92. *From the Pulpit to the Palm Branch*, 107.

93. S&T, March 1892, 143.

94. S&T, April 1892, 210.

T. H. Olney, representing the deacons, gave a remarkable testimony about Spurgeon's dealing with men and the power of his enduring impression on them. "He drew out devoted service," Olney testified, and "he always set us to work, and started us in such a happy way that we have kept on at it." He reminded the members present of the number of years that he had been serving and "with regard to the other officers associated with him, how continuous their labors have been." Joseph Passmore had been with him from the beginning also, "The Pastor won our affection and kept it." He often complimented them for their labors and praised them as the best deacons that anyone ever had, but would add, "but do not be proud. You are no better than you ought to be."[95]

J. T. Dunn spoke representing the elders, as did W. Corden Jones of the Colportage Association, and William Olney on behalf of the Missions workers at twenty-three missions stations and twenty-six branch schools. The meeting closed with the reading of a telegram from Mrs. Spurgeon: "My heart bleeds with yours, but our beloved's joy is full. We shall see him again, and our hearts shall rejoice."

Following this meeting, James Spurgeon, as acting-president, convened a brief meeting of the members of the Pastors' College Evangelical Association. His main purpose was to inform those present of the place they would have in the funeral service the next day. They also sang and some shared testimonials concerning the impact of the late president on their lives. Many were thanked including an especially warm word to J. W. Harrald, who "had probably shortened his own life in his desire to spare and save his loved leader."[96]

An afternoon meeting involved around 5,000 ministers of all denominations. Witnesses refer to the singing as "a gloriously elevating experience, and suggested a vision of the power the church of God would have in the world if all sections of it which are loyal to Christ were united to publish his praise." Dr. Alexander MacLaren of Manchester preached briefly before this group and said, "We gather this afternoon united in one sentiment of affectionate reverence for the greatest preacher of his age." He then noted the marvelous phenomenon that "such a gathering as this, of men more or less directly and exclusively engaged in the ministry of the gospel, differing widely from one another in opinion, forms of government, casts of mind, methods of discharging our work, and yet giving one unanimous suffrage as to the supremacy of our departed brother, is an unheard-of thing."[97] MacLaren emphasized that Spurgeon preached the central verities of the Christian faith and preached them in language that could be understood by all. Spurgeon's self-forgetfulness emphasized all the more the beautiful details of his message. In a passage that Spurgeon would not approve, for against its deepest implications he fought with all his might, MacLaren commended his "accent of conviction and the spirit of robust and unfaltering belief." Spurgeon, he said "was little touched by the questions and difficulties which torture some of us." But a man should preach what he knows and "let him keep to himself his doubts." He should set forth the belief that by God's grace he has won; stick to that and "we shall not fail to learn and find more."[98]

Canon Fleming, a Church of England minister, who worked with Spurgeon in the Religious Tract Society, honored him as man who "loved everything that was catholic, good, and evangelical," whose "fruit blossomed in his youth, and

---

95. *From the Pulpit to the Palm Branch*, 120.

96. S&T., March 1892, 145.

97. *From the Pulpit to Palm Branch*, 126.

98. Ibid., 128.

then fell ripe and mellow before the frost of winter had even touched it," a great, homely, rugged teacher who never tampered with truth and never parleyed with error. Monro Gibson, the moderator of the English Presbyterian Synod spoke followed by Herber Evans, chairman of the Congregational Union. Evans portrayed Spurgeon as one "possessed by the gospel," who had "the deepest conviction of its power to save men, because he knew it had saved him." At one point in Evans's presentation the commentator wrote, "Here the speaker almost reached his native Welsh *hwyl*, and hundreds of strong men in the congregation sobbed like little children."[99]

The president of the Wesleyan Conference, T. B. Stephenson, gave a sensitive and deeply insightful evaluation of the true greatness of Spurgeon, recognizing from the start that "People are already asking whether Spurgeon was a great man, and with their Lilliputian measuring-rods they are trying to find the size of his faith, of his work, and of his character." Stephenson pointed to the unprecedented crowd of Christian ministers gathered for the event as remarkable evidence of Spurgeon's universal appeal, a gathering impossible to organize, or even contrive, had he not been "in the noblest sense a great man." He belonged to the Baptists, but he belonged to the holy catholic and apostolic church. He belonged to the Metropolitan Tabernacle but all Christians in England "claim our heritage in his great life and work." Stephenson recognized that Spurgeon had spoken of some aspects of Methodist theology "with some tartness, not to say severity" in his younger days, but through the years had developed relationships with them and "showed that he was not to be divided from those who earnestly and honestly loved the Lord Jesus Christ."

Great central truths mattered much more. For that day differences were not paramount: "We think today only of his exultation of his Master, Christ; only of the passionate fervour with which he besought men to come to Christ and be saved; only of the Spirit of Christ which shone in all his works throughout his noble life." Spurgeon was the embodiment of the majesty of preaching; his manliness combined with his genuine love for his Savior allowed him to speak of the deepest things of God in such a natural and genial way that none ever felt the oppressiveness of sanctimoniousness. "What went ye out to see?" Stephenson posed to the crowd of prophetic men; a man that knew his mind, whose will was his own, and could not be bent "hither and thither by every passing breeze." He repeated, "What went ye out to see?" No comforts, no softness, no special favors did Spurgeon seek, but a man "ready to take the consequence of his deed." "His life was not devoted to having the softest bed, the pleasantest place, the healthiest work, and the largest honour." He was ready to bear the consequences of his faith and duty—ready to suffer and endure, rather than to be false to his convictions, or negligent of his opportunities." For a third time he posed the Lord's question, and answered, "A messenger whom God sent, ... anxious to deliver his message."[100]

The orphanage choir sang, followed by a message from Dr Pierson. The reporter of the meeting, an obvious admirer of Pierson, wrote: "Only a hero would have dared to take the line he adopted before such an audience; but he not only entered upon a cogent argument for the supernatural in the Bible, and in the believer, he triumphantly carried his point."[101] Pierson divided the factors of Spurgeon's greatness, a constant

---

99. Ibid., 136-38.

100. Ibid., 139-43.

101. S&T, March 1892, 147.

theme of the meeting, into two categories, natural and supernatural. Among the natural he pointed most forcefully to his love of truth, and, in an assembly that would have been mixed in their reaction to the Downgrade Controversy, Pierson spoke frankly:

> You may not have agreed with Mr. Spurgeon in the course which he lately pursued with regard to his conviction of doctrine and of duty; but no man is here present who can withhold his hearty admiration from one of the most heroic acts known in the century. There are very few men that make new friends after the age of fifty years. When a man cuts himself loose from the friends of his manhood and his maturer life, and stands virtually isolated and alone because he feels that in some matters, which others consider minor matters, but which he himself thinks are major matters, he is called upon to suffer, for the truth's sake, such heroism would have led a man to the stake in the days of martyrdom.[102]

In speaking of the supernatural factors of Spurgeon's greatness, Pierson dealt with the combination of Spurgeon's belief in the "full infallible inspiration of the Word of God," the operations of the Holy Spirit in inspiration with an intelligent purpose beyond the intelligence of the writers and prophets, so that we seek the meaning of the Spirit in interpretation, and the present, personal indwelling of the Spirit in the believer. The preaching that combines full confidence in an inspired volume, with the presence of its living author operating through the pure life of a preacher, brings about a ministry of "power to convert, power to sanctify, power to edify, and power to redeem."[103] Such was the ministry of Charles Haddon Spurgeon.

A telegram from D. L. Moody was read and, with the time expiring quickly and people waiting at the door for the next service, F. B. Meyer, representing the London Baptist Association, scheduled to close this meeting, "having spoken for a brief space, wisely turned his speaking into a prayer for dedication." The commentator called this "one of the most remarkable meetings of the century."[104]

An evening meeting involved Christian workers of all denominations. The building was crowded as soon as the doors opened. Several speakers from a wide variety of denominational organizations as well as non-denominational Christian benevolences and conferences spoke and told anecdotes. George Williams, president of YMCA, called Spurgeon "the gift of the great Father to the church universal" in that all denominations saw in him "a champion, a holy, mighty man of God, ready to stand in the front, and to maintain those blessed doctrines of the old gospel, which had won his heart, and which he knew would win the hearts of other men." When Sir Arthur Blackwood asked the question of Spurgeon's greatness, he dismissed his intellect, his wit, his use of language, his earnest congeniality and settled on "the unflinching earnestness and faithfulness with which he preached [the gospel], the valour with which he stood in the gap when men fled on all sides, his adherence to the doctrines of grace, and his determination to know nothing among men save Jesus Christ and him crucified."[105]

Ira Sankey was present and, after attributing to Spurgeon an understanding of "how to use the voice that God had given men," sang "Sleep on Beloved, sleep."[106] Canon Palmer, Rector of Newington, the parish in which the Tabernacle was located, made perhaps the longest speech of this

---

102. *From the Pulpit to Palm Branch*, 145.
103. Ibid., 150.

104. S&T, March 1892, 147.
105. *From the Pulpit to Palm Branch*, 158f.
106. Ibid., 162.

meeting. He spoke of the parts of the Anglican catechism upon which he and Spurgeon had affirmed their agreement, called Spurgeon "the greatest preacher of the century," a judgment that recently had been asserted by the Archdeacon of London in St. Paul's Cathedral, and testified that "he was a benefit to every denomination, for he was the great foe to indifference." He related a humorous exchange of correspondence that he had with Spurgeon on the ringing of the parish church bells during the time of worship at the Tabernacle, a clear and friendly stack of letters that gave a good start to their friendship. Other congenialities sealed their beneficent intercourse but, as a final word of testimony, the Canon pointed to a lesson he learned from Spurgeon that "over all that belongs to us, over our orthodoxy, over our eloquence, and over our energy, we must put on that one cloak or dress to which the apostle referred, if we too are to be considered amongst the elect—namely, that charity which the apostle call, 'the bond of perfectness.'"[107]

A Baptist Union representative, Colonel Griffin, spoke of his twenty-five-year friendship with Spurgeon initiated by a visit he paid to the Tabernacle to hear him preach. He recognized the singularity of Spurgeon's focus on Christ and his cross as found prophesied, described, and expounded in the Bible as the true center of Spurgeon's passion and power. Griffin did not avoid the issue of the recent strong and disturbing conflict between Spurgeon and the Baptist Union:

> He and I, although occupying different positions, and sometimes apparently antagonistic, have never had an unfriendly word, nor has he ever breathed aught else than a spirit of Christian love and fervent charity. It is my privilege to stand here, not for my own worth or individual merit, but because of my official position representing the Baptist Union of Great Britain and Ireland. Mr. Spurgeon thought fit to sever his relations with that Union. We honoured him for his sincerity of purpose, although we were sorry he saw it wise to withdraw from us. Amongst the members of that Union today, throughout the length and breadth of this country, there is but one common thought, one common feeling of intense love, and earnest respect for him who was a prince in Israel.[108]

Following such an affirmation of the man, with the caveat of disagreeing with his choice of separation, the atmosphere must have been a bit tense and even surreal when A. G. Barley, representative of the Baptist Union of France, read a letter from their president, R. Saillens, that said, "The same attachment to the divine revelation; the same strong, firm faith in the sovereignty of the all-wise God; the same disdain for mere human theories, traditions, and fashions; the same rock-like fidelity to the truth, however difficult to believe, however hard to practice—these characteristics will make Calvin and Spurgeon appear before the eyes of posterity as men of the same mental and spiritual mould." French Protestants still felt great gratitude to Spurgeon for the multiplication of his sermon translations into French, for they provided spiritual, theological, and biblical instruction during days when the persecuting hand of the empire prohibited dissenting worship, a pastor could not even read the Bible in a private house with friends, and any meetings involving more than twenty persons were prohibited. Whereas Griffin expressed, understandably, regret at Spurgeon's separation from the Baptist Union, the letter from France, though not mentioning that particular event, expressed encouragement. "The recent attitude taken by Mr. Spurgeon," the letter recounted, "with regard to the

---

107. Ibid., 164-70.

108. Ibid., 171.

New Theology has been a wonderful encouragement to those French Protestants who still hold the faith for which their fathers suffered." The struggle between faith and reason even then, so the letter continued, raged in France even more than in England. "The controversy has been long enough to show us where the new doctrines will surely lead their followers." For that reason, they felt special gratitude to Spurgeon for his witness to truth—"so clear, so uncompromising, so full of assurance!" Acknowledging the immediate impact made by Spurgeon's recent production *The Greatest Fight in the World*, the letter expressed the hope that more of Spurgeon's work would soon make their way into French and bless generations to come.[109]

A final message for this meeting used Spurgeon's salvation text, "Look unto Me" combined with another favorite text, "Accepted in the Beloved." C. Russell Hurditch, the preacher of the hour, demonstrated the relevance of the text for evangelism and for Christian service and closed with a strong evangelistic appeal to the congregation.[110]

The last meeting of the day was scheduled to begin at 10:30. Immediately upon the dismissal of the previous service at 9:30, people began to crowd in and by 10:15 no seating was left available. The singers and speakers for the late evening came to the platform by 10:15, including the preacher, W. Y. Fullerton, his evangelistic singer, J. Manton Smith, and Ira Sankey, "the American Songster," and a few others that would have some part in the service. "Many a toiler," so the report surmised, "whose late hours make it difficult to attend ordinary services, had managed to secure his ticket for this, that he might pay his last respects to the world-loved pastor." The singing of the group produced an impressive "massiveness of sound."

Smith and Sankey sang solos and told stories in connection with their songs. Fullerton spoke of the loss that all in the room felt at the passing of Spurgeon and said that he "would willingly have gone instead of Mr. Spurgeon" if he could have secured to him bodily vigour and opportunity for longer service. Again the text for the message was Isaiah 45:22, the "Look unto me" passage "that led to Mr. Spurgeon's conversion when a lad of sixteen." Spurgeon was a man of God, a man of the people, pointed people to God, and pointed to the Christ of God. Fullerton included what the narrator called a "delightful comparison," in pointing to the astronomical curiosity of having discovered a new star in the sky on the night that Spurgeon "was called away." He urged his hearers to "receive Christ, that they might at last meet His honoured servant in glory."[111]

Finally, the Funeral

On the day of the funeral, February 11, a service was held at 11:00 at the Tabernacle. The pastor at Upton, W. Williams, a long-time friend of Spurgeon who said, "It was, in the good providence of God, my singular fortune and unspeakable joy to be honoured with the close and intimate friendship of Mr. Spurgeon for many years," announced the hymn, "Servant of God, well done."[112]

Harrald, present at virtually every service, looked worn but led in a "comprehensive and touching prayer." Archibald Brown, another long-time friend and most ardent supporter of Spurgeon in his life-sapping fight for truth, read a well-selected catena of Scriptures closing with the words at the burial of the body of John the Baptist, "and buried it, and went and told Jesus."

---

109. Ibid., 173-75.

110. S&T, March 1892, 148; *Pulpit to Palm Branch*, 175.

111. S&T, March 1892, 150.

112. W. Williams, *Personal Reminiscenses of Charles Haddon Spurgeon* (London: The Religious Tract Society, 1895), 15; S&T, March 1892, 151.

He then turned back to his chair and said, "That is all we can do." Robert Taylor of Norwood Presbyterian Church announced the next hymn, that one selected by Spurgeon at the last worship in Menton, "The Sands of Time are Sinking." Pierson again spoke, drawing parallels between the brothers Wesley and the brothers Spurgeon. He spoke of Charles Spurgeon's genius in the intellectual, moral and spiritual spheres and ended with an apostrophe: "We bless God for thee, my brother! We are glad that heaven is made richer, though we are made poorer; and, by this bier, we solemnly pledge ourselves that we will undertake, by God's grace, to follow thy blessed footsteps even as thou didst follow the blessed Lord."[113] After a prayer by Newman Hall, the orphan boys choir sang as the coffin was slowly taken down the aisle.

The open hearse had, on both sides, the words, "I have fought a good fight, I have finished my course, I have kept the faith." This silent witness covered the five-mile trek from Newington to Norwood with people crowding both sides of the road. Carriages brought his son Charles and his wife along with Archibald Brown.[114] James Spurgeon rode in the carriage with the Bishop of Rochester. Bells pealed from several churches; shops, including public houses, were closed. Many hung portraits of Spurgeon and flew flags at half mast. While the procession moved toward the cemetery at Norwood, a meeting of the Pastors' College Evangelical Association went forward on the premises awaiting the arrival of their departed president. As the service neared its end and many walkers that accompanied the hearse started arriving, a most impressive mingling of mourners, all dressed in black, formed a curved path for the last yards of the journey. Archibald Brown, called by Fullerton "the most distinguished of Mr. Spurgeon's men," with chosen words and few, committed the body to the ground:

Beloved President, Faithful Pastor, Prince of Preachers, Brother Beloved, Dear Spurgeon,—We bid thee not "farewell," but only for a little while "good-night." Thou shalt rise soon, at the first dawn of the resurrection day of the redeemed. Yet is not the "good-night" ours to bid, but thine; it is we who linger in the darkness; thou art in God's own light. Our night, too, shall soon be past, and with it all our weeping. Then, with thine, our songs shall greet the morning of a day that knows no cloud nor close; for there is no night there.

Hard Worker in the field, thy toil is ended! Straight has been the furrow thou hast ploughed. No looking back has marred thy course. Harvests have followed thy patient sowing, and heaven is already rich with thine ingathered sheaves, and shall be still enriched through years yet lying in eternity.

Champion of God, thy battle long and nobly fought is over! The sword, which clave to thy hand, has dropped at last; the palm-branch takes its place. No longer does the helmet press thy brow, oft weary with its surging thoughts of battle; the victor's wreath from the Great Commander's hand has already proved thy full reward.

Here, for a little while, shall rest thy precious dust. Then shall thy Well-Beloved come, and at His voice thou shalt spring from thy couch of earth, fashioned like unto His glorious body. Then spirit, soul, and body shall magnify thy Lord's redemption. Until then, beloved, sleep! We praise God *for* thee, and by the blood of the everlasting covenant hope and expect to praise God *with* thee. Amen.[115]

---

113. S&T, March 1892, 151.

114. For an excellent biography of Brown, see Iain H. Murray, *Archibald G. Brown: Spurgeon's successor*. Edinburgh: The Banner of Truth Trust, 2011.

115. S&T 1892, 153; See also Fullerton, 335f. Fullerton's biography has "Thou art in God's *holy* light" instead of "God's *own* light." Murray's biography of Brown also has "holy" instead of "own." The *Autobiography* adds "covenant, *we* hope" in the last line instead of just "covenant, hope." Murray omits entirely the next-to-the-last paragraph beginning "Champion of God, thy battle" (Murray, 148).

Scripture Index

SUBJECT INDEX

A

*A Catechism of Geology and Sacred
    History for Young People* (book)... 13
*A Catechism of the Doctrines of the
    Plymouth Brethren* (book) 496
A Caution Against the Darbyites
    (book) 496
A Christian's Delight (book) 445
*A Complete Compend of Revival
    Music* (book) 264
A Critical History of Philosophy
    (book) 437
'A Door Opened in Heaven'
    (sermon) 656
'A Few Questions for Present
    Consideration' (article) 521-2
A Glimpse of the Great Secret Society
    (book) 509
'A Great Gospel for Great Sinners'
    (sermon) 302
A History of British Baptists (book)
    576-7
'A Limited Atonement Not to be
    Preached' (article) 234-5
'A Luther Sermon at Exeter Hall'
    (sermon) 371
A New Basis for Belief in Immortality
    (book) 466
*A Philosophical Treatise on Perpetual
    Peace* (book) 501
'A Picture of Shoreditch'
    (article) 114-15
*A Popular Handbook of Christian
    Evidences* (book) 436
A Review of Mr. Spurgeon's Discourses
    (book) 94
*A Second Friendly Letter to the
    Christians called Brethren, on
    the Subject of Worship and
    Ministry* (pamphlet) 497
'A Shelter in the Time of Storm'
    (hymn) 381
Abbott, Lyman 417-18
Act of Uniformity (1662) 22
Ad Clerum (book) 486, 567

Adam 96, 188-9, 207, 210, 216, 305
'Adelphos' 491-2
Adler, Hermann 638
'Advanced Thinkers' 476-9, 538
Agnew, Rev. D. C. A. 49-50
Agricultural Hall
    (Islington) 133-5, 138
Alabaster, James 397-9, 406
Alexandra, Princess
    (Denmark) 117, 585
Alford, Henry 431
All of Grace (book) 304, 403, 404
'All of Grace' (sermon) 214-15
Allen, J. 94
An All Round Ministry (book) 471
'An Urgent Request for an Immediate
    Answer' (sermon) 299-301,
    .... 636, 641
Andrews, J. R. 426
Angus, Joseph 63, 105, 128
annihilationism 530-2
Annual Butchers' Festival (1881)
    339-40
*Another Word Concerning the
    Downgrade* (article) 544-5
Anselm 232
Antichrist and Her Brood (book) 64
antinomianism 190-2, 200-1,
    .... 210, 222, 294, 296
Anti-Opium Society 434
Apologia pro Vita Sua (book) 650-1
Arnold, Matthew 466
Around the Wicket Gate (book) 304
Artillery Street Primitive Methodist
    Church 36-7
Ashley Down Orphanage (Bristol)
    346
assurance 219-23
Asylums of La Force 347
Augustine 54, 196
Autobiography (of Spurgeon) 9, 34,
    .... 37, 41, 46, 49, 290
'Awakening in the North' (article)
    330

B

Bacon, Ernest W. 360
Bairdstow, J. O. 650
Balfern, W. Pool 349-50
Ball, Edward 126
'Bands of Love: or, Union to Christ'
    (article) 165
Banks, Charles Waters 480
baptism
    and baptismal regeneration
    513-17
    and church membership 127,
    ....252, 253
    and communion 268-70
    of infants 33, 44, 49-50, 128,
    513-17
    and Lord's Supper 268-9
'Baptismal Regeneration' (sermon)
    .... 513-15, 517
Baptist Messenger (magazine) 467
Baptist Reporter (magazine) 397
Baptist Union
    adopts confessional stance ...564-6
    and baptism 127, 272-3
    and Calvinism 567
    Council's response to Spurgeon's
    accusations 554-8, 559-60
    divisions within 365, 533-4
    and evangelism 563-5, 577
    membership of 529
    and memorial services for
    Spurgeon 663-4
    Spurgeon's accusations against
    ... 10, 168, 534-5, 537-8, 542-9
    Spurgeon's resignation from
    ....228, 380, 550-4, 589-90
Barbed Arrows (collection of
    sermons) 150
Barley, A. G. 663-4
Barnes, Albert 234-5
Barry, Bishop Alfred 650
Bartlett, Mrs. 274-5, 311, 373
'Battlements' (sermon) 190
Bayley, Sir Emilius 619-20
Bayne, Peter 20

G

Gadsby, John 480
Gage, Rev. Fredrick Aubert 523
Gambrell, J. B. 587-8
George III, King 116-17
Gibson, Monro 661
Gill, Dr. John 49-50, 105-6,
....120, 452, 581
Gladstone, William 504, 638
'glee singing' 265
Glover, T. R. 577
Goadby, J. J. 492
'God in the Covenant' (sermon) 206-7
'God moves in a Mysterious Way'
    (hymn) 27-8
God With Us; or The Believer's
    Portion (poetry collection) 449
Godet, Frederick 443, 466
'Gone Home' (article) 382
Goode, Rev. W. 515-16
'Gospel Missions' (sermon) 441
Gospel Temperance Movement ..390-1
Grace Abounding (book) 24
Gracey, David 367, 368-9, 370
Graham, Charles 451
Grant, James 444, 484-5, 496-7
Green, Thomas 23
Greenough, J. G. 535
Greenwood, James 109
Gregg, John 147, 423
Grellet, Stephen 427
Griffin, Colonel 663

H

Habershon, Matthew Henry 454-5
Hackney sermon 82
Haddon Hall 354
Hagenbach, K. R. 427, 451-2
Haldane, Robert 347
Hall, Newman 118, 123-4, 527, 665
Hall, Robert 48, 147-8
Hammond, Payson 312-13
Handbook of Revivals (book) 331
Harrald, J. W. 9, 352-3, 595, 623,
.................639, 641, 644-5, 647-8,
.................654-5, 658-60, 664
Hart, James Tyeth 649
Hatcher, William E. ...496, 589-91, 593
Hatton, George 113
Havers, Henry 22-3
Hawker, J. 441

Hawthornes (orphanage) 384-5
'Heaven and Hell' (sermon) 40-1
hell 223-5, 530-2
Hervey, G. N. 154, 202
Hervey, G. W. 148-9
Hezekiah 166
Higgs, William 247, 255, 623
Hill, George 567
Hill, Rowland 368
Hillier, Dr. 266
Hillyard, Mrs. 375, 384
Hinduism 99
Hinton, J. Howard 75-6, 102, 125
'His Name—Wonderful'
    (sermon) 91-2
History of Christian Doctrine
    (book) 451-2
History of the Reformation in Germany
    and Switzerland (book) 427
Hobson, Henry 276-7
Hodge, Charles 194-5
Holt, Emily 424
holy living 256-7
Home Naturalist (book) 420
Home Rule (Ireland) 503, 513
Hood, Paxton 427, 480-1
hop picking 113-14
Hope for Our Race, or God's Government
    Vindicated (book)......................530-1
Hopkins, James 20
Hort, F. J. A. 181
Hosken, C. H. 359
Houghton, Mr. 645
'How to Get at Inquirers' (article) 324
'How to lead the Young to decision
    for Christ' (article) 312-13
'How to Preach so as to convert
    Nobody' (article) 286
'How we get Peace by the Substitute'
    (article) 560-1
Howard, J. E. 496
Howieson, William 122-3
Hoyt, Wayland 24, 50, 153-4,
................................346-7, 391, 617
Hudson, C. H. 579
Hughes, Rev. J. 94
human responsibility 102-3, 217-19
'Human Responsibility'
    (sermon) 102-3
Huntington, William 423, 481, 620
Hurditch, C. Russell 664
Hutchins, W. M. 495
Hutton, George 649

I

Incidents in the Life of Edward Wright
    (book) 426
'Infant Salvation' (sermon) 213
influenza epidemic 633-4, 655
Ingersoll Answered (book) 455-7
Ingersoll, Robert 455-7
Ingle, Edward 64
Ingleside and Wayside Musings
    (poetry collection) 419-20
Inquirers Books 248
Institutes of the Christian Religion
    (book) 129
'Intellectual Calvinism' 95
Irons, Joseph 52, 397
'Is Romanism Christianity?'
    (pamphlet) 360
Isaac 299-300
Isleham 44-7
Israel's Iron Age (book) 461

J

Jackson, John Andrew 504
James I, King 113
James, John Angell 64
Jane Grey's Resolution (novel) 414
Jarvis, Charles 20
Jay, William 64, 139, 445-6
Jerrold, Walter 651
Jesus Christ
    and atonement 229-30, 232-40,
    .... 553-4, 574-5
    authority over church 511
    baptism of 46
    and Christocentric doctrine
    .... 165-70, 227, 229-34, 240-1
    and commission to teach
    the nations 132-3
    and content of sermons 149-50,
    ....227, 229-34
    and covenant theology 186-9
    crucifixion of 227-31, 240-1
    death of 227-41
    deity of 232
    and depression 597, 606
    and evangelism of Spurgeon
    .... 287-8, 298-302
    finished work of 126
    and God's elect 201-2
    grace of 298-9, 301
    and infant baptism 515

OTHER BOOKS OF INTEREST
FROM
CHRISTIAN FOCUS PUBLICATIONS

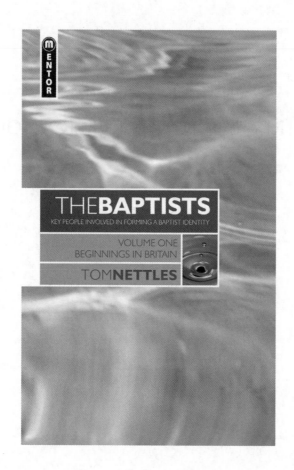

THE**BAPTISTS**

KEY PEOPLE INVOLVED IN FORMING A BAPTIST IDENTITY

VOLUME ONE
BEGINNINGS IN BRITAIN

TOM**NETTLES**

THE BAPTISTS

Volume 1 – Beginning in Britain

Tom Nettles

The nature of Baptist identity has come to a place of critical importance in Baptist studies. What exactly constitutes a Baptist? Tom Nettles seeks to answer this fascinating question through examining the lives of some of the most high profile and influential Baptists in history. The Southern Baptist Theological Seminary in Louisville, Kentucky has an impressive library of Baptist materials including a rich archival collection, which Tom found indispensable for this book.

Nettles establishes a clearly identifiable profile of Baptists. He looks at many influential spokesmen for Baptist lives who embraced the bible as an unerring divine revelation. From John Spilsbury to William Carey we are taken on an enlightening journey through the origin and expansion of the Baptist Church. Tom Nettles has produced a book that is wonderfully informative and, through its profiles of God honouring historical figures, should serve us encouragement to all Christians today.

Tom Nettles has produced a book that is wonderfully informative and, through its profiles of God honouring historical figures, should serve us encouragement to all Christians Today.

ISBN 978-1-85792-995-9

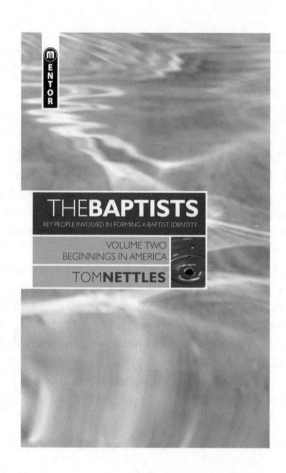

THE**BAPTISTS**

KEY PEOPLE INVOLVED IN FORMING A BAPTIST IDENTITY

VOLUME TWO
BEGINNINGS IN AMERICA

TOM**NETTLES**

M**ENTOR**

THE BAPTISTS

Volume 2 – Beginnings in America

Tom Nettles

Volume 2 tells the story of Baptist beginnings in America, and looks at the inspirational contributions of those such as Lottie Moon and Ann Judson in the growth of the Baptist Church. They shared the views of their English brethren, and were able to be instrumental in the new world in the achievement of separation of church and state.

The pioneer spirit combined with the movement of God's Spirit in the first Great Awakening to produce massive growth of Baptists in New England, the Middle Colonies particularly the South and indeed around the world.

In this delightful second volume Nettles has picked up where he left of, with another hugely informative and authoritative work, which cements his standing as a groundbreaking pioneer in Baptist history.

"In this volume Dr. Nettles moves his readers from Baptists' beginnings in Great Britain to those critical areas of development in Baptist identity: religious liberty, separation between church and state, American Baptist confessional heritage, dynamics of Baptist church government, associational organization, and foreign missions issues. Careful research, clarity of thought, and inspirational quality are evident throughout, and these qualities commend The Baptists as a great blessing to readers in the 21st-century. The wide range Baptist personages, fidelity to historical detail, and warmth of piety, should make this work the definitive choice by readers who seek an accurate and inspiring knowledge of those who contributed so significantly to the Baptist heritage. By the grace of God and for the glory of Christ, may it receive the welcome reception that it deserves among a wide range of readers."

C. Berry Driver Jr., Dean of Libraries,
Southwestern Baptist Theological Seminary, Fort Worth, Texas.

ISBN 978-1-84550-073-3

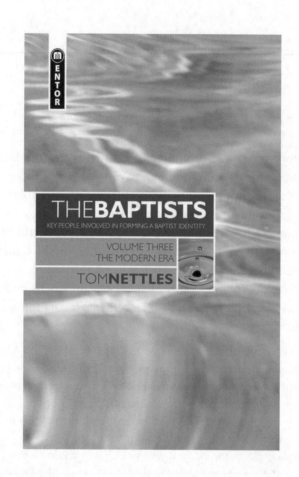

THE**BAPTISTS**

KEY PEOPLE INVOLVED IN FORMING A BAPTIST IDENTITY

VOLUME THREE
THE MODERN ERA

TOM**NETTLES**

THE BAPTISTS

Volume 3 – The Modern Era

Tom Nettles

In the final part of Tom Nettles' Trilogy, he traces some of the modern movements with the Baptist diaspora. Nettles looks at the downgrade in the British Church through the lenses of C.H. Spurgeon and John Clifford and the decline in America looking at the influences of A. H. Strong, E. Y. Mullins and the Baptist Modernists. Key outcomes are explored that inevitably fomulate out of Baptist theology (e.g. separation of church and state).

The 'renewed contours' of the present day Baptist movement are also covered with particular reference to recent changes in the Southern Baptist Convention.

This series is a triumph! It serves as a neccessary addition to the story of the church.

"This volume completes Tom Nettles' magisterial study of Baptist history. Building on his earlier research, Nettles carries the Baptist story into our own times. A work rich in detail and offering a distinctive interpretation of the people of God called Baptists."

Timothy George, Founding Dean,
Beeson Divinity School, Samford University, Birmingham, Alabama

"What has it meant, historically, to be a Baptist? Which modern Baptists would Charles Spurgeon recognize as his theological descendants? What happened between Spurgeon's day and ours? Tom Nettles masterfully explores these and other important questions, setting a new standard for Baptist history. This is a book every Baptist should read. Indeed, anyone interested in the Baptists would do well to start with these three powerful volumes. Nettles has not only given us standard texts on Baptist history, the life stories told here provoke devotional meditation, desire for faithfulness, and careful thought. Praise God for these books, then read them carefully, mark them thoroughly, revisit them through the years, and impart this history to the coming generations."

James M. Hamilton Jr., Associate Professor of Biblical Theology,
The Southern Baptist Theological Seminary, Louisville, Kentucky

ISBN 978-1-84550-211-9

KINDLED FIRE

HOW THE METHODS OF **C. H. SPURGEON**
CAN HELP YOUR PREACHING

ZACK ESWINE

*'Spurgeon comes alive in these pages!
Zack Eswine has done a masterful job. This
book, like Spurgeon's sermons, feeds the
mind and stirs the heart.'*

ALISTAIR BEGG

KINDLED FIRE

How the Methods of CH Spurgeon can help your preaching

Zack Eswine

The preacher today in the West will recognize some profound similarities with Spurgeon and his times. It is true that postmodernism and Enlightenment Rationalism are very different philosophies. But their results are similar in that they promote wide spread scepticism and doubt regarding the authority of the Bible. The debates about the use of art and sermon length at the turn of the twenty-first century are no different in substance than those found in England at the turn of the twentieth. The effect of attention span and the need for story to accompany logic are not new topics of discussion for preachers. In addition, pressures that reduce time for sermon preparation and engender the temptation for shallow or borrowed sermons are nothing essentially new.

> *"Spurgeon comes alive in these pages! Zack Eswine has done a masterful job. This book, like Spurgeon's sermons, feeds the mind and stirs the heart."*

Alistair Begg, Senior Pastor,
Parkside Church, Chagrin Falls, Ohio

> *'Zack Eswine has blessed all who care about preaching by giving us something we need – a down-to-earth theology of preaching made vivid by the exceptional life, ministry, and thought of Charles Haddon Spurgeon. Spurgeon's quest to let the Bible itself shape his preaching and the Holy Spirit give it power supplies a timely paradigm for those of us who preach today. Eswine's well-documented treatment of the subject distills Spurgeon's intentional practice in a way that promises to challenge, convict, instruct, but especially to encourage us to keep preaching in the confident expectation that God will speak when we preach in ways that reflect how he has spoken to us.'*

Greg Scharf, Professor of Practical Theology,
Trinity Evangelical Divinity School, Deerfield, Illinois

ISBN 978-1-84550-117-4

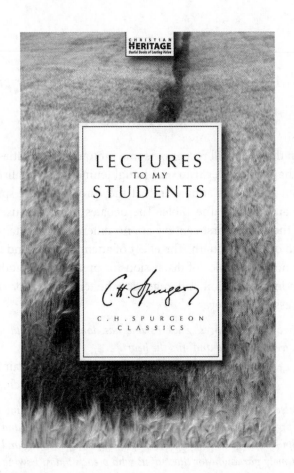

LECTURES
TO MY
STUDENTS

C. H. SPURGEON
CLASSICS

LECTURES TO MY STUDENTS

C. H. Spurgeon

Preachers often quote Spurgeon today because he had an ability to explain Christian truth to ordinary people with pointed, memorable statements. The people who heard and read his words were effectively taught theology and enjoyed it. He was a dogged defender of the Bible as God's truth.

There was another side to Spurgeon's Character, he had a sensitive and loving nature that was the spur to him preaching the gospel, so that as many people as possible could hear the good news about why Jesus Christ came to spend time on earth, building a church for eternity. This also showed through in his warm pasturing of his congregation and the setting up of a college for future ministers of the gospel.

Spurgeon realised that he could influence the church beyond his own lifetime if he could encourage future pastors to trust the Bible, love people and preach the truth fearlessly. To achieve this he collected his lectures to his college students and published this book. It has been a classic of pastoral theology ever since and is still used to train ministers to this day.

ISBN 978-1-85792-417-6

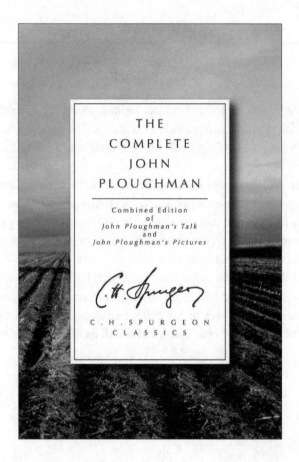

THE
COMPLETE
JOHN
PLOUGHMAN

Combined Edition
of
John Ploughman's Talk
and
John Ploughman's Pictures

C.H.SPURGEON
CLASSICS

THE COMPLETE JOHN PLOUGHMAN

Combined Edition of John Ploughman's Talk and John Ploughman's Pictures

C. H. Spurgeon

C. H. Spurgeon was one of the most widely published ministers of the Victorian era, with sales of his books run into many millions. He had a gift for speaking the language of the man-in-the street and presenting Christian truth in a way that captured the imagination. Two of his publications of this type are here combined into one volume. Both are funny, pointed and profound in their content. They give answers to the common questions of the day on doctrine and behaviour as explained by a ploughman to his wayward audience. The newly typeset edition also contains illustrations included in the original editions of the both books. Spurgeon was a formidable communicator – read him at his best!

ISBN 978-1-84550-278-2

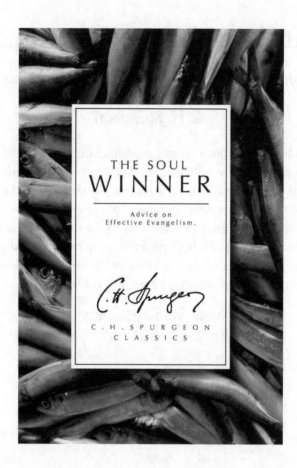

THE SOUL
WINNER

Advice on
Effective Evangelism.

C. H. Spurgeon

C.H.SPURGEON
CLASSICS

The Soul Winner

Advice on Effective Evangelism

C. H. Spurgeon

Spurgeon was one of the most effective evangelists of all time. Under his ministry Victorian London saw revival on a scale never seen since. Yet Spurgeon would be the first to point your finger away from himself to the true author of repentance and reformation– he realised that without God at work, he could do nothing.

Many people sought Spurgeon's advice on evangelism and preaching and so he addressed a wide variety of different groups of people on the subject. Here is a collection of his lectures and talks to take people away from human inspired gimmickry and slavish mimicry to think through for themselves how to enable God to work in their lives and ministry.

Spurgeon was the author of numerous books, his sermons were reprinted and sold in tens of millions. Thousands gathered to hear him preach, but he was not just an eloquent man, he was a man driven to taking the gospel to the people with the utmost urgency.

ISBN 978-1-87167-695-2

Christian Focus Publications

publishes books for all ages

Our mission statement –

STAYING FAITHFUL
In dependence upon God we seek to impact the world through literature faithful to His infallible Word, the Bible. Our aim is to ensure that the Lord Jesus Christ is presented as the only hope to obtain forgiveness of sin, live a useful life and look forward to heaven with Him.

REACHING OUT
Christ's last command requires us to reach out to our world with His gospel. We seek to help fulfil that by publishing books that point people towards Jesus and help them develop a Christ-like maturity. We aim to equip all levels of readers for life, work, ministry and mission.

Books in our adult range are published in three imprints:

Christian Focus contains popular works including biographies, commentaries, basic doctrine and Christian living. Our children's books are also published in this imprint.

Mentor focuses on books written at a level suitable for Bible College and seminary students, pastors, and other serious readers. The imprint includes commentaries, doctrinal studies, examination of current issues and church history.

Christian Heritage contains classic writings from the past.

Christian Focus Publications Ltd,
Geanies House, Fearn, Ross-shire,
IV20 1TW, Scotland, United Kingdom.
www.christianfocus.com